Index to Spanish American Collective Biography
Volume 4 – The River Plate Countries

A
Reference
Publication
in
Latin American
Studies

William V. Jackson
Editor

Index to Spanish American Collective Biography
Volume 4 – The River Plate Countries

SARA DE MUNDO LO

G.K. HALL &CO.
70 LINCOLN STREET, BOSTON, MASS.

Also available:

Index to Spanish American Collective Biography
Volume 1—The Andean Countries
Volume 2—Mexico
Volume 3—The Central American and Caribbean Countries

Library of Congress Cataloging in Publication Data
  (Revised for volume 4)

Mundo Lo, Sara de.
  Index to Spanish American collective biography.

  (A Reference publication in Latin American studies)
  Vol. 3 has series statement: Reference publications
in Latin American studies.
  Includes bibliographies and indexes.
  Contents: v. 1. The Andean countries —v.2. Mexico —
v. 3. The Central American and Caribbean countries —
v. 4. The River Plate countries.
  1. Latin America — Biography — Bibliography — Union
lists. 2. Catalogs, Union — United States. 3. Catalogs,
Union — Canada. I. Series.
Z1609.B6M86CT503   016.92'008   81-4570
ISBN 0-8161-8181-0 (v.1)
ISBN 0-8161-8529-8 (v.2)
ISBN 0-8161-8636-7 (v.3)
ISBN 0-8161-8650-2 (v.4)

This publication is printed on permanent/durable acid-free paper
MANUFACTURED IN THE UNITED STATES OF AMERICA

*To the members of the Seminar on the Acquisition
of Latin American Library Materials (SALALM)*

*A los miembros del Seminario Sobre La Adquisición
de Materiales Latinoamericanos de Biblioteca
(SALALM)*

Contents

THE AUTHOR xi

PREFACE xiii

PREFACIO xvii

ACKNOWLEDGMENTS xxi

BIBLIOGRAPHICAL REFERENCE SOURCES xxiii

LOCATION SYMBOLS xxv

ABBREVIATIONS xxxi

AREA SOURCES 1

ARGENTINA

    Aeronautics 3

    Agriculture 3

    Agriculture--Dictionaries, Encyclopedias, and "Who's Who" 3

    Architecture 3

    Armed Forces 4

    Art 6

    Art--Dictionaries, Encyclopedias, and "Who's Who" 17

    Biography (Miscellaneous) 17

    Biography (Miscellaneous)--Dictionaries, Encyclopedias, and "Who's Who" . . 50

    Economics 52

    Education 52

    Engineering 55

    Freemasonry 56

    Genealogy 57

    History 60

    History--Dictionaries, Encyclopedias, and "Who's Who" 98

    Industry 98

Contents

ARGENTINA (continued)

Journalism 99

Law 99

Library Science 100

Library Science--Dictionaries, Encyclopedias, and "Who's Who" 100

Literature 101

Literature--Dictionaries, Encyclopedias, and "Who's Who" 136

Medicine 137

Medicine--Dictionaries, Encyclopedias, and "Who's Who" 140

Moving Pictures 140

Music 141

Music--Dictionaries, Encyclopedias, and "Who's Who" 146

Natural History 146

Performing Arts 146

Performing Arts--Dictionaries, Encyclopedias, and "Who's Who" 148

Philosophy 148

Postal Communication 149

Printing 149

Pseudonyms 149

Public Health 150

Railroad Transportation 150

Religion 150

Science and Mathematics 154

Sports--Dictionaries, Encyclopedias, and "Who's Who" 154

Welfare 155

Women 155

Women--Dictionaries, Encyclopedias, and "Who's Who" 156

PARAGUAY

Aeronautics 157

Armed Forces 157

Art 157

Biography (Miscellaneous) 158

Biography (Miscellaneous)--Dictionaries, Encyclopedias, and "Who's Who" 162

Education 162

Genealogy 163

Contents

PARAGUAY (continued)

    History 163

    History--Dictionaries, Encyclopedias, and "Who's Who" 170

    Literature 171

    Music 174

    Religion 174

    Women 176

    Women--Dictionaries, Encyclopedias, and "Who's Who" 176

URUGUAY

    Armed Forces 177

    Art 177

    Biography (Miscellaneous) 178

    Biography (Miscellaneous)--Dictionaries, Encyclopedias, and "Who's Who" 185

    Education 186

    Genealogy 186

    History 187

    History--Dictionaries, Encyclopedias, and "Who's Who" 190

    Journalism 190

    Law 191

    Literature 191

    Medicine 201

    Music 202

    Performing Arts 203

    Political Parties 203

    Printing 203

    Pseudonyms 203

    Religion 203

    Science 203

    Sports 204

    Women 204

RIVER PLATE REGION

    Art 205

    Biography (Miscellaneous) 205

    Biography (Miscellaneous)--Dictionaries, Encyclopedias, and "Who's Who" 205

    Genealogy 205

Contents

RIVER PLATE REGION (continued)

History . . . . : 206

Literature 208

Medicine 212

Performing Arts 212

Printing 212

Religion 213

INDEXES

Author Index 217

Short-Title Index 227

Index of Biographees 241

Geographic Index 387

The Author

Sara De Mundo Lo was born in Buenos Aires, Argentina, and is a naturalized U.S. citizen. She earned a Ph.D. in history from the University of Buenos Aires and a M.S. in library science from the University of Illinois. She has taught at the Faculty of Philosophy and Literature of the University of Buenos Aires, Orange Community College, Middletown, New York, and the University of Illinois at Urbana-Champaign, where she is presently the Modern Languages and Linguistics Librarian and Professor of Library Administration.

Dr. Lo's publications include Cruzados en Bizancio, Apolodoro, and, most recently, books and articles in the field of Latin American bibliography. She was awarded a fellowship by the Institute of International Education and grants by the University of Illinois Research Board and the National Endowment for the Humanities.

Preface

Most of those who have a particular interest in Spanish American topics eventually become aware of a common problem. While there is a wealth of information relating to Spanish America stored in our libraries, bibliographic control of these items is very poor and it is often extremely difficult to find certain types of information. It is partly in response to this situation that the Index to Spanish American Collective Biography has been prepared.

The purpose of this work is to provide access to information about the lives of individuals associated with Spanish America, its culture, and its institutions, as recorded in a variety of sources. Although this bibliography is not exhaustive, the compiler hopes that, in a field with few reference tools, it will prove helpful to many people.

The user of this bibliography should bear in mind that the publications it includes are only a selection and do not begin to cover every title ever written containing biographical information relevant to Spanish America. The compiler plans to add to the present work by means of periodical supplements which will include titles published in the future as well as older titles not included in these volumes.

Since this bibliography is selective, and since certain distinctive conventions have been followed in preparing it, the following paragraphs are offered as a guide for the user:

I. SCOPE

A. Sources of collective biography

The area of collective Spanish American biography includes a variety of sources. It is primarily represented by general biographical dictionaries, specialized biographical dictionaries for fields or professions, Who's Who volumes (and their Spanish counterpart Quién es quién), and general and subject encyclopedias. However, collective biography is also likely to be found in the pages of publications whose main intent is not biographical at all. These are literary anthologies, political histories, histories of specialized fields, such as education, art, medicine, etc., commemorative albums, calendars, homenajes, and so on.

The importance of these "secondary material" as potential sources of biographical information cannot be overlooked. In the pages of these publications one finds, along with accounts of the deeds of heroes and academicians, references to more obscure citizens whose lives nevertheless have not gone unrecorded.

B. Works included

The Index to Spanish American Collective Biography includes about 4,500 entries. Each entry represents a work which is available in a library in the United States or Canada and which contains biographical information on three or more persons associated with the development, history, or culture of Spanish America. In all, these works give information on some 100,000 biographees in over 220,000 individual citations.

This bibliography includes primarily monographic titles, issued either separately or as part of a series. An exception has been made for biographical serials such as Who's Who or Quién es quién, which are also cited. Offprints and reprints of articles originally published in journals are included but not journals or other journal articles.

The materials cited were all personally examined by the compiler. They include items written from the 17th century to the present. Although most materials are in Spanish, other languages are also represented. In general only one edition of each title has been included. The edition chosen was the most complete, the latest, or the only one available for examination, in that order of preference.

C. Information contained in cited sources

All the sources found in this bibliography include facts about or events in the lives of people who have contributed to the development of the Spanish American nations. These include pre-Columbian figures, conquistadors, and immigrants, as well as people born in Spanish America since the Conquest. These biographees have been important in a wide variety of fields of endeavor. Although no attempt has been made to cover all areas of activity nor have we discovered books for all of them, some care has been taken to include the major ones, such as art, history, and literature, for most geographic subdivisions.

The amount of biographical information provided by the sources included in this bibliography varies greatly, from lengthy essays to birth dates, death dates, or other single facts. In deciding whether to include a book with minimal biographical data, the period covered and the uniqueness of the information were taken into consideration. For example, a book giving only birth dates of writers active in the last twenty years would be included on the basis that such information is not readily available elsewhere. Another factor considered was the relative fame or anonymity of the biographees.

While books containing information about well-known figures were rarely excluded, an effort has been made to include and analyze books containing information about lesser known individuals who were nevertheless important enough to find their way into a written record.

II. ORGANIZATION

This bibliography consists of five parts. The major grouping is geographical, as follows:

Volume 1 (published 1981):

The Andean Countries: Bolivia, Chile, Colombia, Ecuador, Peru, Venezuela

Volume 2 (published 1982):

Mexico

Volume 3 (published 1984):

Central America and the Caribbean: Costa Rica, Cuba, Dominican Republic, El Salvador, Guatemala, Honduras, Nicaragua, Panama, Puerto Rico

Volume 4:

The River Plate countries: Argentina, Paraguay, Uruguay

Future volumes:

Brazil

General Spanish American Sources

In those parts that include more than one country, the countries are arranged alphabetically. Within each national section there is an alphabetical arrangement by subject according to the field in which the biographees were active. The subjects used are those suggested by the material itself, although an effort has been made to provide broad coverage for all countries. Each source is listed in the section where it would most logically be sought. A general section (Biography--Miscellaneous) appears in the arrangement by subject within each national grouping. The general section includes titles which give equal emphasis to more than one category. The subdivision <u>Dictionaries</u> under specific subjects includes also encyclopedias and <u>Who's Who</u>.

Each subject classification lists entries alphabetically, in accordance with the rules outlined in the following section.

III. ALPHABETIZATION

Alphabetization follows the Spanish alphabet rather than the English. That is, "ch," "ll," and "ñ" are regarded as independent letters. Therefore "<u>Curti</u>" precedes "<u>Chavez</u>," "<u>Valtón</u>" precedes "<u>Valle</u>," etc. Title entries are alphabetized word by word. For example:

Biografía hispanoamericana
Biografía venezolana
Biografías hispánicas

Persons with the same paternal surname are alphabetized by the second surname rather than by the first name. Entries with only one surname precede those with multiple surnames. For example:

González, Victoriano
González Avila, María
González Bustamante, Juan
González, Enrique

IV. ENTRIES

Entries consist of three parts: description, annotation, and location symbols.

A. Description

Entries include the following bibliographic elements, as applicable:

Item number. Author or compiler. <u>Title</u>. Edition. Place of publication: Publisher, Date of publication. Pagination or number of volumes. Portraits. Size. (Series name, volume number)

Each entry, as shown above, begins with an item number. These numbers, which run consecutively in each volume, are the key to locating references in the indexes.

The birth and death dates, when known, of authors and compilers appear in the Author Index. Books without identified authors or compilers are entered under the title. Where a city of publication is given simply as "Santiago," it may be assumed that it indicates the Santiago in the country designated in the chapter heading. Entries note portraits because this information is especially helpful in a biographical work.

B. Annotation

Brief annotations follow the descriptive material in each entry. The scope of the biographies is described with terms such as "extensive," "brief," "limited," etc. These words differentiate lengthy studies from sketchy materials. They should give the user some idea of the type and amount of information to be found in the source.

The most significant portion of most annotations is a detailed analytical listing of the biographees in the work. In general, their names appear in the annotation in the same order as in the work. In many cases, of course, this order is not alphabetical, but it has the advantage of displaying the actual arrangement of each book. The alphabetical Index of Biographees should minimize any problems caused by the arrangement of the annotations.

In the case of some extensive histories of literature, a chronological arrangement of names by century replaces the actual arrangement of the book, in an attempt to make the annotation more helpful to the user. In these cases, biographees are listed in the centuries of their deaths.

It has not been our intent to determine and record all pseudonyms, but they are listed whenever they appear in the title being analyzed. Similarly, family names of nuns and clerics appear along with their religious names wherever they have been found. In addition, the bibliography includes general sources for determining pseudonyms.

If a work includes an alphabetical index of names, this fact is the last element following the analytical list of biographees. No mention of an alphabetical index of names has been made when names are presented in an alphabetical sequence as shown in the contents.

C. Location symbols

The symbols of libraries in the United States and Canada which own the book appear at the end of each entry. At least one location is given for each title. Location symbols used to identify libraries are those of the National Union Catalog. A complete listing of these symbols arranged alphabetically by state is found on p. xxv. Although both upper and lower case letters appear in the symbols, their arrangement in the annotations is strictly alphabetical, letter by letter. Consequently libraries in the same city are not always in sequence.

V. CRITERIA FOR ANALYZING CONTENTS

Deciding whether or not to include a title was much easier than deciding which of the titles included should be analyzed. The following basic guidelines were adopted for analysis:

1. Titles containing biographical information about no more than 300 people were analyzed.

2. Biographical dictionaries, encyclopedias, and works containing information on more than 300 individuals were not analyzed.

Deviations from these guidelines are rare. In a few cases, items with more than 300 entries have been analyzed because of the uniqueness of the material they contain. A few exceptions have also been made for dictionaries.

As we noted before, only one edition of most titles has been listed. However, exceptionally more than one edition of a work has been included. This was done when the contents of the editions differ or are widely available. Reprints are listed when owned by a number of libraries.

VI. INDEXES

Each volume contains the following indexes:

A. Author Index
B. Short Title Index
C. Index of Biographees
D. Geographic Index

References in the indexes are to item number, not to page number. The same rules of alphabetization described in Section III above apply to the indexes.

A. The Author Index includes the names of all authors, compilers, joint authors, illustrators, etc., whose names were found in the bibliographic citations of their books in the body of this work.

B. The Short Title Index provides access by title to all books included in this bibliography.

C. The Index of Biographees is an alphabetical listing of all the individuals whose names appear in the analytical portion of the annotations. Although the annotations list names as they appear in the book described, spelling has been normalized in the index by adopting the fullest or, when known, the most established form of personal names. The task of reconciling under a single entry all references to a particular individual has been monumental. In spite of the effort, regrettably, there are bound to be names that have not been reconciled. The user is therefore advised to look also under alternative forms of a given name for full coverage.

D. The Geographic Index is a listing of geographic locations with which the biographees are associated, as provided in the sources.

There are separate entries in the index of biographees for individuals and families who have identical names. In such cases the name of the country with which they are most closely associated or their profession or trade is given in parentheses following the personal name.

The indexes include cross references for alternative spellings, pseudonyms, and other names. The notation "pseudonym" applies to nicknames, sobriquets, and aliases as well. When a pseudonym clearly indicates a first and last name, it is entered under the last name. Pseudonyms which do not have a first name-surname structure are entered under the first element of the pseudonym (e.g., Juan Sin Ropa). Religious names also appear under the first name (e.g., José Antonio de San Alberto).

In rare cases when an individual is much better known by a pseudonym, it is the primary entry in the index (e.g., Julián Centeya rather than Amleto Vergiati) with the real name following the pseudonym in parentheses.

Prefacio

La mayoría de aquéllos que tienen un interés
especial en temas hispanoamericanos, tarde o tempra-
no se enfrentan con un problema común. A pesar de
que existe una gran cantidad de materiales relativos
a América latina en nuestras bibliotecas, el control
bibliográfico de esos materiales es inadecuado y a
menudo es muy difícil encontrar la información que
se necesita en un momento determinado. El Indice de
Biografía Colectiva Hispanoamericana ha sido preparado con el fin de remediar, en parte, esa situación.

El propósito de esta obra es facilitar el acceso
a información acerca de la vida de individuos asociados con la América hispana, su cultura, y sus instituciones, la cual ha sido registrada en una cantidad
de fuentes diversas. A pesar de que esta bibliografía no es exhaustiva, la compiladora tiene la
esperanza de que en un campo en que escasean las
obras de referencia, ayude a muchos.

Quienes se sirvan de esta bibliografía deben
tener presente que los títulos incluidos son sólo
una selección y no constituyen la totalidad de las
publicaciones en existencia que contiene información biográfica sobre América latina. La compiladora proyecta completar el presente trabajo con
suplementos periódicos que contendrán tanto títulos
a publicarse como títulos publicados y no incluidos
previamente en estos volúmenes.

Teniendo en cuenta que esta bibliografía es
selectiva y como se han seguido ciertas reglas específicas en su preparación, las secciones siguientes
constituyen una guía para su consulta.

I. PLAN

A. Fuentes de biografía colectiva

La biografía colectiva hispanoamericana está
representada en una cantidad de fuentes. Estas
consisten fundamentalmente en diccionarios biográficos generales, diccionarios biográficos por materia, Quién es quién (y su equivalente inglés Who's
Who) y enciclopedias generales y especializadas.
Sin embargo, es posible también hallar biografía colectiva en las páginas de obras cuyo objeto primor-
dial no es biográfico en absoluto. Tales son las
antologías, obras políticas e históricas, historias
de materias como educación, arte, medicina, etc., y
álbumes conmemorativos, calendarios, homenajes, y
otros. La importancia de estos materiales como

posible fuente de información biográfica no debe ser
minorada. Porque es en las páginas de estas publicaciones que a menudo se encuentra junto a las accio-
nes de los héroes y los académicos, referencias a
ciudadanos menos conocidos cuyas vidas, sin embargo,
no han pasado ausentes de documentación.

B. Las publicaciones incluidas

El Indice de Biografía Colectiva Hispanoamericana
incluye aproximadamente 4,500 entradas. Cada entrada
representa una obra que se encuentra en las bibliotecas norteamericanas o canadienses y que contiene
material biográfico acerca de tres o más personas
relacionadas con el desarrollo, la historia, o la
cultura hispanoamericana. En su totalidad estas
obras contienen información biográfica acerca de
aproximadamente 100,000 personas dispersas en alrededor de 220,000 citas individuales.

Esta bibliografía contiene exclusivamente monografías publicadas separadamente o como parte de una
serie. Una excepción se ha hecho con las publicaciones en serie del tipo Quién es quién o Who's
Who, las cuales también han sido incluidas. Tiradas
aparte y reimpresiones de artículos publicados ori-
ginalmente en publicaciones periódicas se han incluido, pero no los periódicos mismos o artículos apare-
cidos en periódicos.

Las obras citadas han sido todas examinadas per-
sonalmente por la compiladora. Se han incluido
materiales publicados desde el siglo 17 hasta el
presente. A pesar de que la mayoría de las obras
están escritas en español, otras lenguas están también representadas. En general, se ha citado sólo
una edición de cada título. La edición elegida es
la más complete, la última, o la única disponible,
en ese orden de preferencia.

C. La información contenida en las fuentes citadas

Todas las fuentes citadas en esta bibliografía
incluyen datos y hechos acerca de la vida de individuos que han contribuido al desarrollo de las na-
ciones hispanoamericanas. Así se hallan personalidades pre-colombinas, conquistadores, inmigrantes,
como también gente nacida en América latina desde
la época de la conquista. Estos biografiados han
hecho contribuciones en una cantidad de disciplinas.
A pesar de que no se ha intentado cubrir todos los
campos de actividad, o no se han encontrado libros
que cubran todos ellos, se ha procurado incluir los

más representativos como arte, historia, literatura, medicina, etc. bajo cada una de las subdivisiones geográficas.

La cantidad de información biográfica contenida en las fuentes registradas en esta bibliografía varía substancialmente desde extensos ensayos hasta sólo fecha de nacimiento, muerte, o hechos aislados. Al considerar si incluir o no una obra conteniendo mínimos datos biográficos se ha tenido en cuenta el período cubierto y la rareza de la información. Por ejemplo, un libro que incluye sólo fechas de nacimiento de escritores destacados durante los últimos veinte años ha sido seleccionado a base de que esa información no es fácil de obtener en fuentes convencionales. Otro factor considerado es la fama o el anonimato de los biografiados. Si bien obras con información acerca de figuras notorias han sido excepcionalmente excluidas, se ha hecho un esfuerzo en incluir y analizar publicaciones que contienen información acerca de individuos poco conocidos, cuyas vidas, sin embargo, fueron suficientemente importantes para merecer una referencia en la obra escrita.

II. ORGANIZACIÓN

Esta bibliografía consiste de cinco partes. La organización es geográfica, como sigue:

Volumen 1 (publicado en 1981):

Países andinos: Bolivia, Chile, Perú, Colombia, Ecuador, Venezuela

Volumen 2 (publicado en 1982):

México

Volumen 3 (publicado en 1984):

América Central y el Caribe: Costa Rica, Cuba, El Salvador, Guatemala, Honduras, Nicaragua, Panamá, Puerto Rico, República Dominicana

Volumen 4:

El Río de la Plata: Argentina, Paraguay, Uruguay

Volúmenes futuros:

Brazil

Fuentes generales hispanoamericanas

En la parte que incluye más de un país, los países están ordenados alfabéticamente. Dentro de cada país el orden es alfabético por materias que representan las disciplinas en que los biografiados has desarrollado sus actividades. Si bien se ha hecho un esfuerzo en incluir un amplio contenido para todos los países, las secciones por materia reflejan específicamente las referencias halladas para cada país en particular. Cada fuente se ha registrado en la sección donde es más probable que se busque. Una sección general (Biografía-- Miscelánea) se ha incorporado a la sección por materias de cada país. Esta sección general incluye títulos que prestan igual atención a más de una categoría. La subdivisión Diccionarios bajo materias específicas, incluye también enciclopedias y Quién es quién.

III. ALFABETIZACIÓN

La alfabetización es de acuerdo al alfabeto español, no al inglés. Esto es, la "ch," "ll,", y "ñ" se consideran letras independientes. Así "Curti" precede "Chavez," "Valtón" precede "Valle," etc. Las entradas bajo título están alfabetizadas palabra por palabra, por ejemplo:

Biografía hispanoamericana
Biografía venezolana
Biografías hispanoamericanas

Las personas con el mismo apellido están alfabetizadas de acuerdo con el segundo apellido en lugar del nombre de pila. Entradas con sólo un apellido preceden aquéllas con apellidos compuestos. Por ejemplo:

Gonzáles, Victoriano
Gonzáles Avila, María
Gonzáles Bustamante, Juan
González, Enrique

IV. ENTRADAS

Las entradas están compuestas de tres partes-- descripción, anotaciones, y siglas de bibliotecas.

A. Descripción

Las entradas consisten de los siguientes elementos bibliográficos:

Número de entrada. Autor o compilador. Título. Edición. Lugar de publicación: Editorial, Fecha de publicación o número de volúmenes. Retratos. Tamaño. (Nombre de la serie, número de la serie)

Cada entrada, como se ve arriba, comienza con el número de entrada. Esta numeración, consecutiva en cada volumen, es la clave para localizar las referencias en los índices.

Las fechas de nacimiento y muerte de los autores y compiladores se han incluido si se conocen en el índice de autores. Libros sin autores o compiladores responsables están catalogados bajo el título. En los casos en que la ciudad en la cual una obra ha sido publicada está designada simplemente como "Santiago" se debe interpretar que es Santiago en el país al que se refiere el capítulo en particular. La existencia de retratos se ha registrado debido a que es pertinente en una obra que trata de biografía.

B. Anotaciones

Anotaciones breves se encuentran a continuación de la entrada descriptiva. Las anotaciones se han escrito con vista a su brevedad. El alcance de los datos biográficos es descrito en términos tales como "extensivos," "breves," "limitados," etc. Estos calificativos se usan para diferenciar descripciones a grandes rasgos, artículos y ensayos, de datos aislados. Ellos deben dar a quienes usen la bibliografía una idea del tipo y cantidad de información que pueden esperar.

La parte más importante de las anotaciones es el registro analítico de los biografiados incluidos en la publicación. En general los nombres están registrados en el orden en que aparecen en la obra analizada. En muchos casos, naturalmente, este orden no es alfabético, pero tiene la ventaja de reproducir el orden real en que los biografiados aparecen en la obra. El Indice Alfabético de Biografiados deberá minorar cualquier problema causado por el orden real en las anotaciones.

En el caso de algunas extensas historias de la literatura, se ha tomado la decisión de substituir el orden real en que aparecen los biografiados en la publicación por el orden cronológico, en un esfuerzo por hacer las anotaciones más útiles a quienes las usen. En estos casos, biografiados cuyas vidas se extienden de un siglo al otro están registrados en el último siglo.

A pesar de que esta bibliografía no ha intentado determinar y registrar seudónimos en gran escala, éstos se han incluido cuando aparecen en las fuentes. Además, esta bibliografía contiene fuentes especializadas en seudónimos.

La presencia de un índice onomástico en orden alfabético en las fuentes, se registra como el elemento final. En los casos en que los biografiados aparecen en orden alfabético en la publicación, no se menciona la existencia de un índice.

C. Siglas de las bibliotecas

Al final de cada entrada se registran las siglas que corresponden a bibliotecas estadounidenses o canadienses que poseen la obra. Por lo menos se incluye una ubicación para cada entrada. Las siglas que se usan para identificar a las bibliotecas son las del National Union Catalog. El catálogo de las siglas, alfabéticamente ordenadas por estados, se encuentra en la p. xxv. Si bien las siglas están compuestas de letras mayúsculas y minúsculas, el orden seguido en su alfabetización es estrictamente letra por letra. Consiguientemente bibliotecas localizadas en la misma ciudad, no siempre están en orden.

V. CRITERIO PARA ANALIZAR EL CONTENIDO

La decisión de incluir o no una publicación fue más fácil que decidir cuáles, entre los títulos citados, deberían ser analizados. Las reglas básicas que siguen se han adoptado con este propósito:

1. Títulos conteniendo información biográfica acerca de 300 personas o menos se han analizado.

2. Diccionarios, enciclopedias y obras conteniendo más de 300 biografiados no se han analizado.

Les desviaciones de estas reglas son raras. En unos pocos casos, publicaciones con más de trescientos biografiados se han analizado debido a la singularidad del material que contienen. Un par de excepciones se han hecho también con referencia a diccionarios.

Como se ha indicado anteriormente, se ha registrado sólo una edición de la mayoría de los títulos. Sin embargo ocasionalmente se ha incluido más de una edición de una obra. Esto se ha hecho cuando el contenido de las ediciones es diferente o cuando varias ediciones se encuentran en bibliotecas. Reimpresiones se han incluido a base de lo mismo.

VI. ÍNDICES

Cada volumen contiene los índices siguientes:

A. Indice de autores
B. Indice de títulos abreviados
C. Indice de biografiados
D. Indice geográfico

Las referencias en los índices corresponden al número de entrada, no al número de página. Las mismas reglas de alfabetización descritas anteriormente en la Sección III se han seguido en la elaboración de los índices.

A. El Indice de Autores incluye todos los autores, compiladores, autores en colaboración, ilustradores, etc. cuyos nombres se han registrado en la entrada bibliográfica de sus obras en el texto de esta bibliografía.

B. El Indice de Títulos Abreviados proporciona acceso, bajo título, a todas las fuentes incluidas en esta bibliografía.

C. El Indice de Biografiados es el índice alfabético de todas las personas que aparecen en la sección analítica de las anotaciones. En tanto que las anotaciones registran nombres en la forma en que se encuentran en las fuentes, la ortografía se ha regularizado en el índice adoptando la más completa, o cuando conocida, la forma más aceptada del nombre. El trabajo de reunir bajo una sola entrada todas las referencias correspondientes a un individuo ha sido monumental. A pesar del esfuerzo, lamentablemente, deben de haber formas del nombre de un mismo individuo que no han sido regularizadas. Quienes usen esta bibliografía deben por lo tanto considerar las formas alternativas de un nombre a fin de cubrir todas las posibilidades.

D. El Indice Geográfico es un registro de lugares con los cuales biografiados están asociados como resulta de las fuentes.

Distintas personas y familias que tienen nombres idénticos se encuentra bajo entradas independientes en el índice de biografiados. En tales casos, el nombre del país con el cual están más estrechamente asociados o sus profesiones y vocaciones se ha incluido en paréntesis a continuación del nombre.

Los índices incluyen referencias correspondientes a cambios de ortografía, seudónimos, y otros

nombres. La notación "seudónimo" corresponde tam-
tián a apodos y alias. Cuando un seudónimo está
claramente compuesto de un nombre de pila y apellido,
se ha registrado bajo el apellido. Seudónimos que
no están compuestos de un nombre y apellido se han
registrado bajo la primera palabra del seudónimo
(e.g., Juan Sin Ropa). Nombres religiosos se han
registrado bajo el primer nombre (e.g., José Antonio
de San Alberto).

En los raros casos en que una persona es más
conocida por el seudónimo, las entradas se han registrado bajo el mismo (e.g., Julián Centeya, no
Amleto Vergiati) seguido del nombre real en
paréntesis.

Acknowledgments

The compiler wants to express her sincere thanks to the National Endowment for the Humanities for financially supporting this research project, and most especially to the staff who provided guidance, undertanding, and cooperation, and display confidence in it.

The compiler is also deeply grateful to

1. Dr. Georgia Portuondo of the Wisconsin University Library. Dr. Portuondo researched the area of Paraguayan collective biography, contributing significantly to the Paraguayan citations and annotations.

2. Ms. Amy Warner, graduate student assistant assigned to the project during the academic year 1980-1981. The project owes much to Ms. Warner's professionalism and consistent striving for excellence.

3. The following student assistants, who performed numerous and various indispensable tasks:

Susan K. Appel   Daniel Gurfinkel
Donna Bruno   Kathleen R. Lynch
Clare Connor   Lisa McDaniel
Helen Davies   Ann M. Mester
Kathleen Fine   Maria On
Margaret Goldsmith   Merle Rosen

Bibliographical Reference Sources

A work of this kind necessarily builds upon previous efforts. We gratefully acknowledge our debt to the many sources that we consulted.

The U.S. Library of Congress National Union Catalog, the Card Catalog and the Library Computerized System (LCS) of the University of Illinois Library at Urbana-Champaign were the primary sources used in the preparation of this work. In addition, a number of general and specialized sources, domestic and foreign, have been invaluable aids. Among them, the following were indispensable in our work:

Bibliographic Guide to Latin American Studies. Boston: G. K. Hall, 1979-83.

Cordeiro, Daniel Raposo. A Bibliography of Latin American Bibliographies: Social Sciences and Humanities. Metuchen: Scarecrow Press, 1979.

Fichero bibliográfico hispano-americano (New York) Oct. 1961-1980.

Geoghegan, Abel Rodolfo. Obras de referencia de América Latina. Buenos Aires: Crisol, 1965.

Gropp, Arthur Eric. A Bibliography of Latin American Bibliographies. Metuchen: Scarecrow Press, 1968. Supplement: 1971.

Hilton, Ronald. A Bibliography of Latin America and the Caribbean: The Hilton Library. Metuchen: Scarecrow Press, 1980.

Knaster, Meri. Women in Spanish America: An Annotated Bibliography from Pre-Conquest to Contemporary Times. Boston: G. K. Hall, 1977.

Libros en venta en Hispanoamérica y España (Buenos Aires) 1964-1981.

Palau y Dulcet, Antonio. Manual del librero hispano-americano. 2. ed. Barcelona: A. Palau, 1948-1977. Indice: A-Carvino. 1981.

Piedracueva, Haydée. A Bibliography of Latin American Bibliographies, 1975-1979. Social Sciences and Humanities. Metuchen: Scarecrow Press, 1982.

Sabor, Josefa Emilia. Manual de fuentes de información. 3. ed. Buenos Aires: Ediciones Marymar, 1979. (Colección bibliotecología y documentación).

Sáinz Rodríguez, Pedro. Biblioteca bibliográfica hispánica. Madrid: Fundación Universitaria Española, 1975-1976.

Sheehy, Eugene P. Guide to Reference Books. Chicago: American Library Association, 1976. Supplements: 1980, 1982.

Slocum, Robert B. Biographical Dictionaries. Detroit: Gale Research Company, 1967. Supplements: 1972, 1978.

Toro, Josefina del. A Bibliography of the Collective Biography of Spanish America. Río Piedras: The University, 1938.

Tulane University of Louisiana. Latin American Library. <u>Catalog of the Latin American Library of the Tulane University Library</u>. Boston: G. K. Hall, 1970. Supplements: 1973, 1975, 1978.

University of California at Berkeley. Bancroft Library. <u>Catalog of Printed Books</u>. Boston: G. K. Hall, 1964. Supplements: 1969, 1974, 1979.

University of Texas. Library. <u>Catalog of the Latin American Collection</u>. Boston: G. K. Hall, 1969. Supplements: 1971, 1973, 1975, 1977.

U.S. Library of Congress. <u>Library of Congress Catalog. Books: Subjects</u>. Washington, D.C., 1950–1982.

Location Symbols

ALABAMA

AAP Auburn University, Auburn.
AU University of Alabama, University.

ALASKA

AkU University of Alaska, Fairbanks.

ARIZONA

AzFu Northern Arizona University, Flagstaff.
AzTeS Arizona State University, Tempe.
AzU University of Arizona, Tucson.

ARKANSAS

ArAO Ouachita Baptist University, Arkadelphia.
ArU University of Arkansas, Fayetteville.

CALIFORNIA

C California State Library, Sacramento.
CBDP Church Divinity School of the Pacific, Berkeley.
CBGTU Graduate Theological Union, Berkeley.
CCC Honnold Library, Claremont.
CCH Obsolete. See CCC.
CCP Obsolete. See CCC.
CFIS California State College at Fullerton.
CFrS Obsolete. See CFS.
CFTS Fresno State College, Fresno.
CL Los Angeles Public Library.
CLCM Los Angeles County Museum.
CLCMar Los Angeles County Museum of Art.
CLgA Alma College, Los Gatos.
CLI Immaculate Heart College, Los Angeles.
CLL Los Angeles County Lair Library.
CLobS California State College at Long Beach (Formerly Long Beach State College, Long Beach).
CLS California State College at Los Angeles.
CLSU University of Southern California, Los Angeles.
CLU University of California, Los Angeles.
CMenSP Saint Patrick's Seminary, Menlo Park.
CMIG Golden Gate Baptist Theological Seminary, Mill Valley.
CNoS San Fernando Valley State College, Northridge.
CSaT San Francisco Theological Seminary, San Anselmo.
CSf San Francisco Public Library.

CSmH Henry E. Huttington Library, San Marino.
CSt Stanford University, Palo Alto.
CSt-H Stanford University, Palo Alto --Hoover Institution on War, Revolution and Peace.
CU University of California, Berkeley.
CU-A University of California, Berkeley --University of California, Davis.
CU-B Obsolete. See CU-BANC.
CU-BANC University of California, Berkeley --Bancroft Library, Berkeley.
CU-I University of California, Berkeley --University of California, Irvine.
CU-M University of California, Berkeley --University of California Medical Center, San Francisco.
CU-S University of California, Berkeley --University of California, San Diego (Includes Scripps Institute of Oceanography).
CU-SB University of California, Berkeley --University of California, Santa Barbara.
CU-SC University of California, Berkeley --University of California, Santa Cruz (Includes Lick Observatory).

COLORADO

CoAIC Adams State College, Alamosa.
CoAT Obsolete. See CoAIC.
CoCA U.S. Air Force Academy, USAF Academy.
CoCC Colorado College, Colorado Springs.
CoD Denver Public Library.
CoDR Regis College, Denver.
CoDU University of Denver.
CoDuF Fort Lewis College, Durango.
CoF Fort Collins Public Library, Fort Collins.
CoFc Obsolete. See CoF.
CoFS Colorado State University, Fort Collins.
CoGrS Colorado State College, Greeley.
CoLH Loretto Heights College, Loretto.
CoU University of Colorado, Boulder.

CONNECTICUT

CtHC Hartford Seminary Foundation, Hartford.
CtU University of Connecticut, Storrs.
CtW Wesleyan University, Middletown.
CtY Yale University, New Haven.
CtY-D Yale University, New Haven ---Divinity School.

CtY-E	Yale University, New Haven --Department of Economics. Economic Growth Center.
CtY-M	Yale University, New Haven --Medical School.
CtY-Mus	Yale University, New Haven --School of Music.

DELAWARE

DeU	University of Delaware, Newark.

DISTRICT OF COLUMBIA

DAU	American University.
DBC	U.S. Bureau of the Census.
DCU	Catholic University of America.
DCU-IA	Catholic University of America --Ibero-American Collection.
DGU	Georgetown University.
DGW	George Washington University.
DHN	Holy Name College.
DHU	Howard University.
DHUD	U.S. Department of Housing and Urban Development.
DI	U.S. Department of the Interior.
DI-GS	U.S. Geological Survey, Reston.
DLC	U.S. Library of Congress.
DLC-P4	U.S. Library of Congress --Priority 4 Collection..
DN	U.S. Department of the Navy.
DNAL	U.S. National Agricultural Library.
DNGA	National Gallery of Art.
DNLM	U.S. National Library of Medicine.
DNR	Obsolete. See DN.
DNW	U.S. National War College, Fort McNair.
DPAHO	Pan American Health Organization, Pan American Sanitary Bureau (Formerly World Health Organization, Pan American Sanitary Bureau).
DPU	Pan American Union.
DS	U.S. Department of State Library (Division of Library and Reference Services).
DSI	Smithsonian Institution.
DWHO-PSB	Obsolete. See DPAHO.

FLORIDA

F	Florida State Library, Tallahassee.
FJUNF	University of North Florida, Jacksonville.
FM	Miami Public Library.
FMFIU	Florida International University, Miami.
FMU	University of Miami, Coral Gables.
FTaSU	Florida State University, Tallahassee.
FTS	University of South Florida, Tampa.
FU	University of Florida, Gainesville.

GEORGIA

GAOC	Oglethorpe College, Atlanta.
GASU	Georgia State University, Atlanta.
GAT	Georgia Institute of Technology, Atlanta.
GAuA	Augusta College, Augusta
GDecA	Obsolete. See GDS.
GDS	Agnes Scott College, Decatur.
GEU	Emory University, Atlanta.
GU	University of Georgia, Athens.

HAWAII

HU	University of Hawaii, Honolulu

IDAHO

IdB	Boise Public Library.
IdPI	Idaho State University, Pocatello.
IdU	University of Idaho, Moscow.

ILLINOIS

I	Illinois State Library, Springfield.
IC	Chicago Public Library.
ICA	Art Institute of Chicago.
ICarbS	Southern Illinois University, Carbondale.
ICIU	University of Illinois at Chicago Circle, Chicago.
ICF	Chicago Natural History Museum, Chicago.
ICJ	John Crerar Library, Chicago.
ICL	Loyola University, Chicago.
ICN	Newberry Library, Chicago.
ICRL	Center for Research Libraries, Chicago (formerly Midwest Inter-Library Center).
ICU	University of Chicago.
IDeKN	Northern Illinois University, DeKalb.
IEdS	Southern Illinois University, Edwardsville Campus.
IEN	Northwestern University, Evanston.
IGK	Knox College, Galesburg.
IMacoW	Western Illinois University, Macomb.
IMunS	Saint Mary of the Lake Seminary, Mundelein.
INS	Illinois State University, Normal.
ITeuS	Saint Joseph Seminary, Teutopolis.
IU	University of Illinois at Urbana- Champaign.

INDIANA

InIL	Eli Lilly and Company, Scientific Library, Indianapolis.
InND	University of Notre Dame, Notre Dame.
InRE	Earlham College, Richmond.
InStme	Saint Meinrad's College and Seminary, Saint Meinrad.
InTi	Indiana State University, Terre Haute.
InU	Indiana University, Bloomington.

IOWA

IaAS	Iowa State University of Science and Technology, Ames.
IaDL	Luther College, Decorah.
IaU	University of Iowa, Iowa City.

KANSAS

K	Kansas State Library, Topeka.
KAS	Benedictine College, North Campus, Atchison.
KEmT	Kansas State Teachers College, Emporia.
KMK	Kansas State University, Manhattan.
KU	University of Kansas, Lawrence.
KU-M	University of Kansas, Lawrence --School of Medicine, Kansas City.

KENTUCKY

Ky	Kentucky State Library and Archives, Frankfort (Library abolished. Books transferred to KyU).
KyLoS	Southern Baptist Theological Seminary, Louisville.
KyLoU	University of Louisville.
KyLx	Lexington Public Library, Lexington.
KyLxCB	Lexington Theological Seminary, Lexington.
KYMoreT	Obsolete. See KyMoreU.
KyMoreU	Morehead State University, Morehead.
KyU	University of Kentucky, Lexington.

LOUISIANA

LLafS	University of Southern Louisiana, Lafayette.
LN	New Orleans Public Library.
LNH	Obsolete. See LNT.
LNHT	Obsolete. See LNT.
LNT	Tulane University, New Orleans.
LNT-MA	Obsolete. See LNT.
LU	Louisiana State University, Baton Rouge.
LU-NO	Louisiana State University, Baton Rouge --Louisiana State University in New Orleans.

MAINE

MeB	Bowdoin College, Brunswick.
MeLB	Bates College, Lewiston.
MeU	University of Maine, Orono.

MARYLAND

MdBE	Enoch Pratt Free Library.
MdBJ	Johns Hopkins University, Baltimore.
MdBP	Peabody Institute, Baltimore.
MdBT	Towson State College, Baltimore.
MdPWA	Walters Art Gallery, Baltimore.
MdSsW	Washington Theological Coalition, Silver Spring.
MdU	University of Maryland, College Park.

MASSACHUSETTS

M	Massachusetts State Library, Boston.
MB	Boston Public Library.
MBAt	Boston Atheneum.
MBBC	Obsolete. See MChB.
MBCo	Countway Library of Medicine, Boston.
MBU	Boston University.
MChB	Boston College, Chestnut Hill.
MCM	Massachusetts Institute of Technology, Cambridge.
MH	Harvard University, Cambridge (Represents Central Collection of College Library and smaller miscellaneous libraries).
MH-A	Harvard University, Cambridge --Arnold Arboretum.
MH-AH	Harvard University, Cambridge --Andover-Harvard Theological Library.
MH-BA	Harvard University, Graduate School of Business Administration, Boston.
MH-Ed	Harvard University, Cambridge --Graduate School of Education.

MH-FA	Harvard University, Cambridge --Fine Arts Library.
MH-G	Harvard University, Cambridge --Gray Herbarium.
MH-L	Harvard University, Cambridge --Law School.
MH-P	Harvard University, Cambridge --Peabody Museum.
MH-PA	Harvard University, Cambridge --Graduate School of Public Administration.
MNS	Smith College, Northampton.
MShM	Mount Holyoke College, South Hadley.
MU	University of Massachusetts, Amherst.
MW	Worcester Public Library and Central Massachusetts Regional Library Headquarters.
MWA	American Antiquarian Society, Worcester.
MWAC	Assumption College, Worcester.
MWelC	Wellesley College, Wellesley.
MWH	College of the Holy Cross, Worcester.
MWiCA	Sterling and Francine Clark Art Institute, Williamstown.
MWiW	Williams College, Williamstown.

MICHIGAN

Mi	Michigan State Library, Lansing.
MiD	Detroit Public LIbrary.
MiDa	Detroit Institute of Arts, Detroit.
MiDU	University of Detroit.
MiDW	Wayne State University, Detroit.
MiDW-M	Wayne State University, Detroit --Medical Library.
MiEa1C	Obsolete. See MiEM.
MiEM	Michigan State University, East Lansing.
MiHM	Michigan Technological University, Houghton.
MiU	University of Michigan, Ann Arbor.
MiU-C	University of Michigan, Ann Arbor --William L. Clements Library.

MINNESOTA

MnCS	Saint John's University, Collegeville.
MnHi	Minnesota Historical Society, Saint Paul.
MnU	University of Minnesota, Minneapolis.
MnU-A	University of Minnesota, Minneapolis --Saint Paul Campus (Formerly Institute of Agriculture).

MISSISSIPPI

MaSM	Mississippi State University, State College.
MsU	University of Mississippi, University.

MISSOURI

MoKL	Linda Hall Library, Kansas City.
MoKU	University of Missouri at Kansas City.
MoSU	Saint Louis University, Saint Louis.
MoSW	Washington University, Saint Louis.
MoU	University of Missouri, Columbia.
MoU-St	University of Missouri at Saint Louis, Saint Louis.

MONTANA

MtBC	Montana State University at Bozeman.
MtU	University of Montana at Missoula.

NEBRASKA

NbU University of Nebraska, Lincoln.

NEVADA

NvU University of Nevada, Reno.

NEW HAMPSHIRE

Nh New Hampshire State Library, Concord.
NhD Dartmouth College, Hanover.
NhU University of New Hampshire, Durham.

NEW JERSEY

NjMD Drew University, Madison.
NjN Newark Public Library, Newark.
NjNbS New Brunswick Tehological Seminary, New Brunswick.
NjP Princeton University, Princeton.
NjPT Princeton Theological Seminary, Princeton.
NjR Rutgers-The State University, New Brunswick.

NEW MEXICO

NmLcU New Mexico State University, Las Cruces.
NmU University of New Mexico, Albuquerque.

NEW YORK

N New York State Library, Albany.
NB Brooklyn Public Library.
NBB Brooklyn Museum.
NBC Brooklyn College, Brooklyn.
NBM Medical Research Library of Brooklyn.
NBrockU State University of New York, College at Brockport.
NBu Buffalo and Erie County Public Library, Buffalo.
NBuC State University of New York, College at Buffalo.
NBuG Grosvenor Reference Division, Buffalo and Erie County Public Library, Buffalo.
NBuU State University of New York at Buffalo.
NFQC Queens College, Flushing.
NFredU State University of New York, College at Fredonia.
NGenoU State University of New York. College at Geneseo.
NHi New York Historical Society, New York.
NIC Cornell University, Ithaca.
NN New York Public Library.
NNAHI Augustinian Historical Institute, New York.
NNBG New York Botanical Garden, Bronx Park.
NNC Columbia University, New York.
NNC-L Columbia University, New York--Law Library.
NNC-M Columbia University, New York --Medical Library.
NNCoCi City College of the City University of New York.
NNCU-G City University of New York --Graduate Center.

NNF Fordham University, New York.
NNG General Theological Seminary of the Protestant Episcopal Church, New York.
NNGr Grolier Club, New York.
NNH Hispanic Society of America, New York.
NNMM Metropolitan Museum of Art, New York.
NNR Russell Sage Foundation Library, City College of New York.
NNU New York University Libraries, New York.
NNU-W New York University Libraries, New York --Washington Square LIbrary.
NNUN United Nations, New York.
NOsU State University of New York, College at Oswego.
NRCR Colgate-Rochester Divinity School, Rochester.
NRU University of Rochester.
NSbSU State University of New York at Stony Brook.
NSchU Union College, Schnectady.
NSyU Syracuse University, Syracuse.
NWM United States Military Academy. West Point.
NYPL Obsolete. See NN.

NORTH CAROLINA

NcCU University of North Carolina at Charlotte, Charlotte.
NcCuW Western Carolina University, Cullowhee.
NcD Duke University, Durham.
NcGU University of Carolina at Greensboro.
NcGuG Guilford College, Guilford.
NcGW Obsolete. See NcGU.
NcRS North Carolina State University at Raleigh.
NcU University of North Carolina, Chapel Hill.
NcWfSB Southeastern Baptist Theological Seminary, Wake Forest.

NORTH DAKOTA

NdU University of North Dakota, Grand Forks.

OHIO

O Ohio State Library, Columbus.
OAk Akron Public Library.
OAkU University of Akron.
OAU Ohio University, Athens.
OCH Hebrew Union College --Jewish Institute of Religion, Cincinnati.
OCl Cleveland Public Library.
OClh Cleveland Heights-University Heights Public Library.
OClJC John Carroll University, Cleveland.
OClJC-U Obsolete. See OClUr.
OClMA Cleveland Museum of Art.
OClND Notre Dame College, Cleveland.
OClStJ Saint John College, Cleveland.
OClStM St. Mary's Seminary, Cleveland.
OClU Cleveland State University, Cleveland. (Formerly Fenn College).
OClUr Ursuline College for Women, Cleveland.
OClW Case Western Reserve University, Cleveland.

OClWHi	Western Reserve Historical Society, Cleveland.
OClW-H	Case Western Reserve University. Cleveland Health Sciences Library, Cleveland.
OCLR	Obsolete. See InIL.
OCU	University of Cincinnati.
OCX	Xavier University, Cincinnati.
ODW	Ohio Wesleyan University, Delaware.
OEac	East Cleveland Public Library.
OKentC	Obsolete. See OKentU.
OKentU	Kent State University, Kent.
OLak	Lakewood Public Library.
OO	Oberlin College, Oberlin.
OOxM	Miami University, Oxford.
OTU	University of Toledo.
OU	Ohio State University, Columbus.
OWicB	Borromeo Seminary of Ohio, Wickliffe.
OWorP	Pontifical College Josephinum, Worthington.
OYesA	Antioch College, Yellow Springs.

OKLAHOMA

OkS	Oklahoma State University, Stillwater.
OkU	University of Oklahoma, Norman.
OkU-M	University of Oklahoma Health Sciences Center, Oklahoma City.

OREGON

Or	Oregon State Library, Salem.
OrAshS	Southern Oregon College, Ashland.
OrCS	Oregon State University, Corvallis.
OrMonO	Oregon College of Education, Monmouth.
OrP	Library Association of Portland.
OrPR	Reed College, Portland.
OrPS	Portland State College, Portland.
OrSaW	Willamette University, Salem.
OrStbM	Mount Angel College, Saint Benedict.
OrU	University of Oregon, Eugene.
OrU-M	University of Oregon, Portland --Medical School.

PENNSYLVANIA

P	Pennsylvania State Library, Harrisburg.
PBa	Academy of the New Church, Bryn Athyn.
PBL	Lehigh University, Bethlehem.
PBm	Bryn Mawr College, Bryn Mawr.
PClvU	Ursinus College, Collegeville.
PHC	Haverford College, Haverford.
PHi	Historical Society of Pennsylvania, Philadelphia.
PIm	Immaculata College, Immaculata.
PJA	Abington Library Society, Jenkintown.
PJB	Beaver College, Jenkintown.
PLF	Franklin and Marshall College, Lancaster.
PLFM	Obsolete. See PLF.
PP	Free Library of Philadelphia.
PPAmP	American Philosophical Society, Philadelphia.
PPAN	Academy of Natural Sciences of Philadelphia, Philadelphia.
PPC	College of Physicians of Philadelphia.
PPCCH	Chestnut Hill College, Philadelphia.
PPComm	Commercial Museum, Philadelphia (Library discontinued).
PPD	Drexel Institute of Technology, Philadelphia.

PPEB	Eastern Baptist Theological Seminary, Philadelphia.
PPF	Franklin Institute, Philadelphia.
PPFr	Friend's Free Library of Germantown, Philadelphia.
PPG	German Society of Pennsylvania, Philadelphia.
PPGi	Girard College, Philadelphia.
PPi	Carnegie Library of Pittsburgh.
PPiPT	Pittsburgh Theological Seminary.
PPiU	University of Pittsburgh.
PPL	Library Company of Philadelphia.
PPL-R	Obsolete. See PPL.
PPLas	La Salle College, Philadelphia.
PPPM	Philadelphia Museum of Art.
PPT	Temple University, Philadelphia.
PPTU	Obsolete. See PPT.
PPULC	Union Library Catalogue of Pennsylvania, Philadelphia.
PRosC	Rosemont College, Rosemont.
PSC	Swarthmore College, Swarthmore.
PSt	Pennsylvania State University, University Park.
PU	University of Pennsylvania, Philadelphia.
PU-FA	University of Penssylvania, Philadelphia --School of Fine Arts.
PU-Mu	University of Pennsylvania, Philadelphia --University Museum.
PU-Mus	University of Pennsylvania, Philadelphia --Obsolete. See PU-Mu
PU-Music	University of Pennsylvania, Philadelphia --School of Music.
PU-Penn	University of Pennsylvania, Philadelphia --Penniman Library of Education.
PV	Villanova University, Villanova.
PWcS	West Chester State College, West Chester.

PUERTO RICO

PrU	University of Puerto Rico, Rio Piedras.

RHODE ISLAND

R	Rhode Island State Library, Providence.
RP	Providence Public Library.
RPB	Brown University, Providence.
RPJCB	John Carter Brown Library, Providence.

SOUTH CAROLINA

ScCleA	Obsolete. See ScCleU.
ScCleU	Clemson University, Clemson.
ScU	University of South Carolina, Columbia.

SOUTH DAKOTA

SdB	South Dakota State University, Brookings.
SdU	University of South Dakota, Vermillion.

TENNESSEE

TCU	University of Tennessee at Chattanooga,
TN	Public Library of Nashville and Davidson County, Nashville.
TNJ	Joint University Libraries, Nashville.
TNJ-P	Joint University Libraries, Nashville --Peabody College.
TU	University of Tennessee, Knoxville.

TEXAS

TxBeaL	Lamar University, Beaumont.
TxCM	Texas A & M University, College Station.
TxCsA	Obsolete. See TxCM.
TxDa	Dallas Public Library.
TxDaDF	DeGolyer Foundation, Dallas.
TxDaM	Southern Methodist University, Dallas.
TxDaM-P	Southern Methodist University, Dallas --Perkins School of Theology.
TxDN	North Texas State University, Denton.
TxFTC	Texas Christian University, Fort Worth.
TxHR	Rice University, Houston.
TxHU	University of Houston.
TxLT	Texas Technological College, Lubbock.
TxSaT	Trinity University, San Antonio.
TxU	University of Texas, Austin.

UTAH

ULA	Utah State University, Logan.
UPB	Brigham Young University, Provo.
UU	University of Utah, Salt Lake City.

VERMONT

VtMiM	Middlebury College, Middlebury.
VtU	University of Vermont and State Agricultural College, Burlington.

VIRGINIA

Vi	Virginia State Library, Richmond.
ViBlbV	Virginia Polytechnic Institute, Blacksburg.
ViU	University of Virginia, Charlottesville.

WASHINGTON

Wa	Washington State Library, Olympia.
WaE	Everett Public Library.
WaMaS	Sno-Isle Regional Library, Marysville.
WaOE	Evergreen State College, Olympia.
WaPS	Washington State University, Pullman.
WaS	Seattle Public Library.
WaSp	Spokane Public Library.
WaSpG	Gonzaga University, Spokane.
WaT	Tacoma Public Library.
WaTC	University of Puget Sound, Tacoma.
WaU	University of Washington, Seattle.
WaWW	Whitman College, Walla Walla.

WEST VIRGINIA

WvU	West Virginia University, Morgantown.

WISCONSIN

WHi	State Historical Society of Wisconsin, Madison.
WMM	Marquette University, Milwaukee.
WMUW	University of Wisconsin, Kenwood Campus, Milwaukee
WU	University of Wisconsin, Madison.
WU-M	University of Wisconsin, Madison --School of Medicine.

CANADA

CaBVa	Vancouver Public Library, Vancouver.
CaBVaU	University of British Columbia, Vancouver.
CaBVIP	Obsolete. See CaBViP.
CaBViP	Legislative Library, Victoria, B.C.
CaBVIPA	Obsolete. See CaBViPA.
CaBViPA	Provincial Archives, Victoria, B.C.
CaOOEC	Economic Council of Canada, Ottawa.
CaOOFF	Canada Department of the Environment, Ottawa.
CaOOU	University of Ottawa, Ottawa.
CaOTP	Toronto Public Library, Metropolitan Bibliographic Centre, Toronto.
CaOTU	University of Toronto, Toronto.
CaOWtU	University of Waterloo, Waterloo.
CaQML	Concordia University. Loyola Campus, Montreal.
CaQMM	McGill University, Montreal.
CaSRL	Legislative Library of Saskatchewan, Regina.

Abbreviations

anot.	anotada	ilus.	ilustraciones, ilustrada
arq.	arquitecto	illmos.	ilustrísimos
asoc.	asociación	illus.	illustrations, illustrated
aum.	aumentada	impr.	imprenta
b.	born	ing.	ingeniero
bros.	brothers	intro.	introduction, introducción
ca.	circa (about)	lic.	licenciado
cía.	compañía	ledo.	licenciado
cm.	centimeters	lito., litogr.	litografía
col.	colección	Ma.	María
comp.	compiler, compilador	n.d.	no date
corr.	corregida	n.p.	no place, no publisher
d.	died	ntra.	nuestra
dept.	department	p.	pages
depto.	departamento	pl.	plates
der.	derecho	pp.	pages
dict.	dictionary	Pres.	Presidente
Dn.	Don	pseud.	pseudonyms, nicknames
Dr.	doctor	rev.	revised, revisada
ed.	editor	s.a.	sociedad anónima
edit.	editorial	ser.	serie
Edo.	Estado	soc.	sociedad
enc.	encyclopaedia	Sr.	Señor
encuad.	encuadernación, encuadernada	Sra.	Señora
enl.	enlarged	St.	Saint
est.	establecimiento	tall.	talleres
et al.	and others	tip.	tipografía
fr.	fray	trans.	translated, translation
hnos.	hermanos	v.	volume, volumen
i.e.	that is	vda.	viuda

Area Sources

Argentina

AERONAUTICS

1 Biedma Recalde, Antonio María. Crónica histórica de la aeronáutica argentina. Buenos Aires: Círculo de Aeronaútica, Dirección de Publicaciones, 1969. 2 v. Portraits. 23 cm. (Colección aeroespacial argentina, v. 1).

A historical account of aeronautics in Argentina, including biographical data throughout on hundreds of individuals who contributed to its development.

MH

AGRICULTURE

2 Hogg, Ricardo. Yerba vieja. Buenos Aires: J. Suárez, Librería Cervantes, 1940. 334 p. (V. 1). Portraits. 19 cm.

An account of British involvement in Argentine agriculture during the 19th century. Scattered biographical information, as well as portraits in many cases, are included for many people associated with this aspect of Argentina's development. The following are particularly featured: James Duff, Patrick Lynch, Jorge Gordon Davis, Domingo Ortiz de Rozas y García de Villasuso, Henry Edwards (Facón Grande, pseud.), John Walker (Facón Chico, pseud.), Ricardo Hogg.

CtY DLC IU NcU

3 Newton, Jorge, and Lily Sosa de Newton. Historia de la Sociedad Rural Argentina, en el centenario de su fundación. Buenos Aires: Editorial y Librería Goncourt, 1966. 381 p. 23 cm.

A history of the Sociedad Rural Argentina covering the 19th and 20th centuries, including brief scattered biographical information for many people who have been affiliated with this organization. Short essays are also provided for the following presidents and their collaborators: José Martínez de Hoz, Eduardo Olivera, José María Jurado, Emilio Duportal, Enrique Sundblad, Leonardo Pereyra, Ricardo Newton, Estanislao S. Zeballos, José Francisco Acosta, Julio Pueyrredón, Ramón Santamarina, Julián Frers, Exequiel Ramos Mexía, Carlos M. Casares, Manuel J. Güiraldes, José de Apellániz, Emilio Frers, José M. Malbrán, Abel Bengolea, Joaquín S. de Anchorena, Pedro T. Pagés, Luis Duhau, Federico L. Martínez de Hoz, Horacio N. Bruzzone, Miguel F. Casares, Cosme Massini Ezcurra, Adolfo Bioy, José María Bustillo, José A. Martínez de Hoz, Enrique Frers, Juan María Mathet, Juan José Blaquier, Faustino Alberto Fano.

CSt CU DcU DPU IaU IEN InU KyLoU
MB MH MiEM MnU MoSW NcD NIC NjR
NmU NN NSyU PPiU TxU WaU WU

4 Pozzo Ardizzi, Luis. Hombres del surco; semblanzas de agricultores. Buenos Aires: Editorial Raigal, 1955. 110 p. Portraits. 19 cm. (Colección Campo argentino, v. 3).

A history of Argentine agriculture, with biographical sketches about the following notable figures from the 18th through the 20th centuries mostly associated with it: Manuel Belgrano, José de San Martín, Bernardino Rivadavia, Domingo Faustino Sarmiento, Almirante Brown, Tomás Grigera, Domingo Olivera, José María Buffé, Richard Arthur Seymour, Juan Leone, Christian Clausen, Aaron Jenkins, Amado Goujand (Bonpland, pseud.), José Guazzone, Enrique Klein.

CtY CU DLC IU MB NN NNC NNR OrU
PSt TxU

AGRICULTURE--DICTIONARIES, ENCYCLOPEDIAS, and "WHO'S WHO"

5 Newton, Jorge. Diccionario biográfico del campo argentino. Buenos Aires: Artes Gráficas Bartolomé U. Chiesino, 1972. 436 p. 23 cm.

Biographical sketches of Argentine agriculturists and farmers of the 19th and 20th centuries.

IU

ARCHITECTURE

6 Buenos Aires. Universidad. Instituto de Arte Americano e Investigaciones Estéticas. La arquitectura en Buenos Aires, 1850-1880.

ARCHITECTURE

Buenos Aires: Instituto de Arte Americano, Facultad de Arquitectura y Urbanismo, 1965. 142 p. 19 cm.

A history of architecture in Buenos Aires with appendix of alphabetically arranged biographical notes about the following architects (1850-1880): Enrique Aberg, Richard Adams, Carlos A. Altgelt, Juan B. Arnaldi, Otto von Arnim, José María Baca, Miguel Barabino, Juan G. Bateman, Pedro Beare, Joaquín M. Belgrano, Pierre Benoit, Pedro Benoit, James Bevans, Blanco Casariego, Pablo Blot, Jacobo Boudier, Próspero Bruyan, Juan Brilli, Ernesto Bunge, Juan A. Buschiazzo, Adolfo F. Buttner, Pedro Cabral, Miguel Cabrera, Pablo Caccianiga, Nicolás Canale, José Canale, Francisco Cañete, Ignacio Casagemas, J. Casanave, Eduardo Castilla, Próspero Catelin, Rafael del Carpio, Juan Coghlan, Teodoro Donati, Julio Dormal, Joseph Dubourdieu, Manuel Eguía, Ignacio Fernández, Santiago Ferrando, Pedro García, Guillermo Goodman, José María Gutiérrez, Enrique Hunt, Agustín Ibáñez de Luca, Carlos Kihnlderg, Germán Kuhr, José María Lagos, Emilio Landois, Jonas Larguía, Robert MacGaw, Antonio Malaver, Fernando Moog, Manuel Moreno, Mariano Moreno, Andrés Olivera, Carlos C. Olivera, Juan León Pallière, Benito Panuzzi, José Parma, José Pedazzi, Carlos Enrique Pellegrini, E. Penot, Anotnio Picarel, Alejandro Pittaluga, Prilidiano Pueyrredón, Virgilio Rabaglio, Manuel Raffo, Agustín Reant, Mathew Reid, Juan Rodríguez, Camilo Romairone, Saturnino Salas, José Santos Sartorio, Pablo Scolpini, Felipe Schwararz, Juan Bautista Segismundo, Saturnino Segurola, Felipe Senillosa, A. Seurot, Daniel Solier, Adolfo Sourdeaux, Francisco Tamburini, Eduardo Taylor, Gabriel Joaquín Tudury, Thomas Weitfield, Diego W. Wilde, Antonio Zelaya, Carlos Zucchi.

CLSU CU CU-SB DPU GU ICA ICarbS
InU IU LNHT MB MH MiEM MiU MoSW
NBuU NIC NjP NN NNC NNMM PPT

7 Fúrlong Cárdiff, Guillermo Juan. Arquitectos argentinos durante la dominación hispánica. Prólogo del Arq. Mario J. Buschiazzo. Buenos Aires: Editorial Huarpes, 1946. 427 p. 23 cm. (His Cultura colonial argentina, v. 4).

An essay about architecture in Argentina during the Hispanic rule including scattered biographical information on the following notable architects (17th through the 19th centuries): Hernando Arias de Saavedra (Hernandarias, pseud.), José Brasanelli, Angel C. Petragrassa, Antonio Sepp, Juan Kraus, Juan Wolff, Pedro Weger, Domingo Petrarca, Andrés Blanqui, Juan Bautista Prímoli, Antonio Masella, Juan Bautista Masella, Juan Narbona, Isidro Lorea, Antonio Forcada, José Grimau, Manuel Alvarez de Rocha, José de Echevarría, José Mateo de Echevarría, Julián Preciado, Francisco Baca, Juan Alberto Cortés, Diego Cardoso, Francisco Rodríguez Cardoso, José Custodio de Sáa y Faría, José García Martínez de Cáceres, Vicente Muñoz, Juan Manuel

López, Juan Bautista Pardo, Esteban Tast, Vicente Troncoso, Francisco Loria, Antonio Viana, José Pujol, Cayetano Ayroldi, Santiago Ayroldi, Tomás Toribio, José Antonio del Pozo y Marquy, Bernardo Lecocq, Miguel Rubín de Celis, Pedro Antonio Cerviño, José M. Cabrer, Antonio Alvarez de Sotomayor, Agustín Conde, Juan de Campos, Santiago Avila, Juan Bartolomé Howel, José Pérez Brito, Juan de la Peña y Zazueta, Julio Ramón de César, Joaquín Antonio Mosquera, Domingo Pallarés, Eustaquio Giannini, Antonio María Durante, Mauricio Rodríguez de Berlanga, Martín de Boneo, Juan Bautista Segismundo, Francisco Cañete.

CtY DAU DLC FU IaU IU LU MH MiU
NIC NSyU OrU OU TxU ViU WaU

ARMED FORCES

8 Argentina Republic. Ejército. Comando en Jefe. El ejército de hoy. Buenos Aires: Círculo Militar, 1976. 142 p. 20 cm.

A collection of short narratives describing the valor and patriotic actions of many modern-day Argentine military men. The following are particularly featured: Pedro Eugenio Aramburu, Juan Duarte Ardoy, Alberto Hugo Vacca, Camilo A. Gay, Héctor Cáceres, Wilfredo N. Méndez, Raúl Cuello, Arturo Horacio Carpani Costa, Argentino del Valle Larrabure.

IU

8a _____. Reseña histórica y orgánica del ejército argentino. Buenos Aires: Círculo Militar, 1972. 4 v. 21 cm. (Biblioteca del oficial, v. 631-632, 635-636, 639-640). (Colección histórico-militar).

A four-volume history of the Argentine army, covering the period from colonial to modern times. Includes very brief, scattered biographical information on many Argentine military men.

CaOTP CaQMM CLU CSt CStH CtY CU-SB
DPU FU IaU InU IU KU MB MH MnU
MoSW MU NcD NcU NN NNC TU WU

9 Burzio, Humberto F. Armada nacional; reseña histórica de su origen y desarrollo orgánico. Buenos Aires: Centro Naval, 1960. 281 p. Portraits. 25 cm. (Historia naval argentina. Serie B, v. 1).

A history of the Argentine national armada, covering the period from the early 19th to the early 20th centuries, and including scattered biographical information and portraits for many men associated with this aspect of Argentina's development. Among those particularly featured are Matías de Irigoyen, José Matías Zapiola, Tomás Espora, Martín Rivadavia, Domingo F. Sarmiento, Joaquín Oytabén, Luis Piedrabuena, Carlos M. Moyano.

CU ICU IU NN NSyU

10 _____. Historia del la Escuela Naval Militar. Buenos Aires: Compañía Impresora Argentina, 1972. 3 v. 1882 p. Portraits. 31 cm.

A three-volume history of the Argentina Naval Academy from the colonial period to the present day. Portraits and scattered biographical information of various amounts are included for many men, mostly personnel, who were in some way affiliated with this organization. Volume 3 has alphabetical index of names.

CaOTP CtY MoSW NjP TxU

10a Caillet-Bois, Teodoro. Ensayo de historia naval argentina. Buenos Aires, 1929. 490 p. Portraits. 25 cm.

Naval history of Argentina from the 16th to the 20th century, with scattered biographical notes on over 300 people.

CU DLC ICU IU

11 _____. Historia naval argentina. Buenos Aires: Emecé editores, 1944. 552 p. Portraits. 24 cm.

Naval history of Argentina with scattered biographical notes on over 300 figures from the 16th to the 20th century. Alphabetical index of names.

CtY CU DLC FMU IU MiU MU NcD NcU NSyU TxU WaU

11a Círculo Militar, Buenos Aires. Reseña histórica de la infantería argentina. Buenos Aires, 1969. 370 p. 20 cm. (Colección histórico militar, v. 601).

A history of the Argentine infantry, covering the period from colonial to modern times. Very brief sketches paying homage to the following military men are included: Nicolás Levalle, Manuel Belgrano, Juan José Viamonte, Pedro Conde.

CSt DLC IU MiU OU

12 Destéfani, Laurio Hedelvio. Manual de historia naval argentina. Buenos Aires: Armada Argentina, 1970. 166 p. Portraits. 23 cm.

A naval history of Argentina, covering the 19th and 20th centuries, and including portraits and biographical information on many naval personnel of this time period. The following are particularly featured: Guillermo Brown, Hipólito Bouchard, Leonardo Rosales, Tomás Espora, Martín Rivadavia, Luis Piedra Buena, Carlos Moyano, Joaquín Oytaben, Cándido de Lasala.

CFS IaU IU NN

13 Gutiérrez, Eduardo. Croquis y siluetas militares: escenas contemporáneas de nuestros campamentos. Estudio preliminar de Alvaro Yunque. Buenos Aires: Hachette, 1956. 254 p. 21 cm.

A series of sketches and profiles on military life and leaders during the 19th century in Argentina. Biographical information is given for the author and also for various military men, whose physical and personal characteristics are emphasized. The following are featured: Eduardo Gutiérrez, José Hederra, Coronel Borges, Hilario Lagos, Luis María Campos, Mamerto Cuenca, Liborio Muzlera, General Rivas, Alejandro Murature, José María Morales, General Racedo, Manuel Rosseti, José Miguel Arrendondo, Capitán Piedrabuena, Joaquín Lora, El tuerto Sarmiento Heredia, Gregorio Carrizo, Comandante Klein, Santiago Borzone.

DLC IaU IU NN TxU

14 Piccirilli, Ricardo, and Leoncio Gianello. Biografías navales (cuarenta y cinco semblanzas de marinos) Buenos Aires: Peuser, 1963. 330 p. Portraits. 25 cm. (Argentine Republic. Departamento de Estudios históricos navales. Serie C, v. 8: Biografías navales argentinas).

A collection of lengthy biographies, accompanied by portraits, of the following Argentine navy men of the 18th and 19th centuries: Guillermo Brown, Santiago J. Albarracín, Alvaro J. Alzogaray, Laureano de Anzoategui, Juan Bautista Azopardo, Guillermo Bathurst, Ricardo Baxter, Hipólito Bouchard, Bartolomé Cordero, Mariano Cordero, Francisco Drummond, Tomás Espora, Guillermo Enrique Granville, Martín Guerrico, Francisco de Gurruchaga, Angel Hubac, Matías de Irigoyen y de la Quintana, Julián Irizar, Constantino Jorge, Nicolás Jorge, Juan King, Juan Larrea, Cándido Lasala, Augusto Lasserre, Carlos María Moyano, Alejandro Murature, José Murature, Erasmo Obligado, Enrique Guillermo Parker, Luis Piedra Buena, Luis Py, Ceferino Ramírez, Martín Rivadavia, Carlos Robinson, Leonardo Rosales, Benjamin Franklin Seaver, Francisco José Seguí, Enrique Sinclair, Antonio Somellera, Miguel Samuel Spiro, Martín Jacobo Thompson, Juan Bautista Thorne, Clodomiro Urtubey, Guillermo Pío White, José Matías Zapiola.

IU NcU NIC TxU

15 Pierrou, Enrique Jorge. 90 [i.e. Noventa] años de labor de la armada argentina en la Antártida. Buenos Aires: Armada Argentina. Servicio de Hidrografía Naval, 1975. 410 p. (V. 1). Portraits. 26 cm.

An account of the history of the exploration of the Antarctic and the participation of the Argentine navy, including biographical data on the following navy men: Luis Piedrabuena, José María Sobral, Eduardo Guerrabut. Also included are listings of crew members of the Uruguay, Guardia Nacional, Austral, Primero de Mayo, and Pampa from 1903 to 1938, and brief biographical sketches of the following personnel who died in Argentine Antarctic stations and in units of the navy stationed in the

ARMED FORCES

Antarctic until 1938: Allan C. Ramsay, Otto Diebel, John Elieson, Heraldo Wiström, Bache Wig, Fortunato Escobar.

IU

16 Ratto, Héctor Raúl. <u>De la marina heroica</u>. Buenos Aires: Talleres Gráficos del Consejo Nacional de Educación, 1936. 238 p. Portraits. 24 cm.
    A collection of biographical sketches, accompanied by portraits, of the following notable Argentine navy men: Hipólito Bouchard, Leonardo Rosales, Tomás Espora, Guillermo Brown, Luis Piedrabuena.

MB TxU

17 _____. <u>Historia de la enseñanza naval en la Argentina</u>; ilus. de Emiliano Celery. Buenos Aires: Fray Mocho, 1944. 148 p. Portraits. 26 cm. (Biblioteca de la Sociedad de Historia Argentina, v. 16).
    A history of naval education in Argentina during the 19th century, including scattered biographical information and portraits for many people associated with this aspect of Argentina's history. The following are emphasized: Antonio Castellini, Roberto Ramsay, Tomás Espora, Antonio Toll, Clodomiro Urtubey, Guillermo Brown, Martín Guerrico.

AAP CtY DLC ICU MB NcU ScU TxU ViU

17a _____. <u>Hombres de mar en la historia argentina</u>. Ed. aumentada. Buenos Aires: Librería y Editorial "El Ateneo," 1938. 368 p. 24 cm.
    Enlarged edition covering the history of the Argentine navy primarily during the 18th and 19th centuries. Includes biographical data on the following people associated with it: Basilio Villarino, Bernardo Taforo, José de la Peña y Zazueta, Alejandro Malaspina, José de Bustamante y Guerra, Juan Gutiérrez de la Concha, José Varela y Ulloa, Juan F. Aguirre, Félix de Azara, Diego de Alvear, Oyarvide, Pablo Zizur, Pedro de Cerviño, José del Pozo, Juan Ravenet, Fernando Brambila, Luis Née, Juan Alzina, Martín Jacobo Thompson, Cándido de Lasala, Pedro de Cerviño, Benito Lynch, Matías Irigoyen, Pascual Ruiz Huidobro, Matías Zapiola, Juan B. Azopardo. Also extensive biographical information about Guillermo Brown and Luis Piedrabuena.

DLC MB NcD TxU

17b Zambra, Eneas. <u>Biografías militares conteniendo hechos históricos y los servicios de los generales del ejército argentino</u>. Buenos Aires: E. Zambra, 1894. 250 p. Portraits. 23 cm.
    A collection of biographical sketches, accompanied by portraits, of the following Argentinean military men of the 19th century: Bartolomé Mitre, Emilio Mitre, Juan Andrés Gelly y Obes, Julio A. Roca, Nicolás Levalle, Luis M. Campos, José M. Bustillo, José M. Arredondo, Joaquín Viejobueno, Eduardo Racedo, Teodoro García, Lucio V. Mansille, Zacarías Supisiche, Francisco B. Bosch, Benjamín Victorica, Manuel Obligado, Manuel J. Campos, Rudecindo Roca, Domingo Viejobueno, Rufino Ortega, Amaro L. Arias, Miguel T. Molina, Félix Benavídez, Daniel Cerri, Sócrates Anaya, Ignacio Garmendia, Juan G. Díaz, Manuel Biedma, Alberto Capdevila. Also biography of Luis Sáenz Peña.

CLU CoU CU ICarbS MH NcU TxU

(See also entries 423, 438, 579, 580, 581.)

ART

18 Acquarone, Ignacio. <u>Pintura argentina, colección Acquarone</u>. Introducción: Córdova Iturburu; compilación: Mario Loza; versión francesa: Monique Sage de Romaña. Buenos Aires: Edición Aleph, 1955. 68 p. Portraits. 26 cm. (Colección Ignacio Acquarone, v. 1).
    Alphabetically arranged catalog of the Acquarone collection of Argentine painting in the 20th century, with biographical notes on the following artists: Horacio Alvarez, Pompeyo Audivert, Aquiles Badi, Héctor Basaldúa, Juan Batlle Planas, Antonio Berni, Horacio Berreta, Alfredo Bigatti, Rodrigo Bonome, Horacio Butler, Carybé, Cerdá Carretero, Juan C. Castagnino, Emilio Centurión, Cleto Ciocchini, Santiago Cogorno, Víctor Cunsolo, Eugenio Daneri, Adolofo De Ferrari, Jorge Luis de la Vega, Walter de Navazio, Juan Del Prato, Miguel Diomede, José Domenichini, Bello E. Estrada, G. Facio Hebecquer, Fernando Fader, Ernesto Farina, Albino Fernández, César Fernández Navarro, Pedro Figari, Raquel Forner, Vicente Forte, Mario Gargatagli, Ramón Gómez Cornet, Mario Darío Grandi, Arturo Gustavino, Alcides Gubellini, Alfredo Guttero, Hugo Hottmann, Primitivo Icardi, Fortunato Lacámera, Jorge Larco, Enrique Larrañaga, Abel Laurens, Luis Lobo de la Vega, César López Claro, Mario Loza, Martín Malharro, Horacio March, Juan Carlos Miraglia, Primaldo Mónaco, Alberto Nicasio, Onofrio Pacenza, H. Panagiatópulos, Emilio Petorruti, Orlando Pierri, Juan Carlos Pinto, Víctor Pissarro, José Planas Casas, Enrique Policastro, Leopoldo Presas, Víctor Rebuffo, Roberto Rosenfeld, Roberto Rossi, Raúl Russo, Ideal Sánchez, Antonio Scordía, Sergio Sergi, Ramón Silva, Oscar Soldati, Raúl Soldi, Mónica Soler Vicens, Lino E. Spilimbergo, Carlos María Squivo, Ricardo Supisiche, V. Thibón de Libián, Marco Tiglio, Demetrio Urruchúa, Bruno Venier, Carlos M. Victorica, Roberto Viola.

DLC DPU InU MB OrU WaS

19 Argentine Republic. Comisión Nacional Ejecutiva del 150 Aniversario de la Revolución de Mayo. <u>150 [i.e. Ciento cincuenta] años de arte argentino</u>. Exposición Catálogo. Buenos Aires, 1961. unpaged 26 cm.

Catalog of Argentine paintings from 1810–1960 with essays covering the major movements and periods. Very brief biographical data are provided for the following artists: José Aguyari, Ignacio Baz, Martín Boneo, Juan L. Camaña, Bernabé Demaría, Cayetano Descalzi, Narcisco E. Desmadryl, Fernando García del Molino, Carlos Morel, Gaspar Palacio, Genaro Pérez, Carlos Enrique Pellegrini, Prilidiano Pueyrredón, Benjamín Franklin Rawson, Augusto Ballerini, José Bouchet, Francisco Cafferata, Lucio Correa Morales, Ernesto de la Cárcova, Angel della Valle, Julio Fernández Villanueva, Reynaldo Giúdice, Martín A. Malharro, Ventura Miguel Marcó del Pont, Graciano Mendiliharzu, Severo Rodríguez Etchart, Eduardo Sívori, Eduardo Schiaffino, Julia Wernicke, Jorge Bermúdez, Faustino Eugenio Brughetti, Mario A. Canale, Emilio Caraffa Brandan, Pío Collivadino, Eliseo Fausto Coppini, Hernán Cullén Ayerza. Cupertino del Campo, Carlos de la Torre, Walter de Navazio, Félix Pardo de Tavera, Carlos Pablo Ripamonte, Ramón Silva, Rogelio Yrurtia, José A. Terry, Pedro Zonza Briano, Antonio Alice, Francisco Bernareggi, Guillermo Butler, Italo Botti, Emilia Bertole, Emilio Centurión, Tito Cittadini, Lía Correa Morales, Arturo Dresco, Fernando Fader, Luis Falcini, José Fioravanti, Juan M. Gavazzo Buchardo, Alfredo Gramajo Gutiérrez, Alfredo Guttero, Alfredo Guido, Alberto Lagos, Nicolás Lamanna, Gregorio López Naguil, José Malanca, Atilio Malinvero, José Antonio Merediz, Americo Panozzi, Adán L. Pedemonte, Antonio Pedone, Emilio Pettoruti, Octavio Pinto, Domingo Pronsato, Martín Benito Quinquela Martín, Cesáreo Bernaldo de Quirós, Agustín Riganelli, Alberto María Rossi, Juan Bautista Tapia, Luis Tessandori, Valentín Thibon de Libián, Ana Weiss de Rossi, Susana Aguirre, Luis Aquino, Aquiles Badi, Juan Antonio Ballester Peña, Héctor Basaldúa, Marina Bengoechea, Antonio Berni, Alfredo Bigatti, Rodrigo Bonome, Norah Borges, Miguel Burgoa Videla, Guillermo Buitrago, Horacio Butler, Domingo Candia, Juan Carlos Castagnino, Gustavo Cochet, Luis Adolfo Cordiviola, Víctor Juan Cunsolo, Pablo Curatella Manes, Adolfo C. de Ferrari, Santiago Eugenio Daneri, Carlos de la Cárcova, Juan Del Prete, Miguel Diomede, Juan Carlos Faggioli, Pedro Domínguez Niera, Lucio Fontana, Raquel Forner, Carlos G. Giambiaggi, Ramón Gómez Cornet, Arturo Gerardo Guastavino, Gastón Jarry, Alberto Güiraldes, Horacio Juárex, Fortunato Lacamera, Jorge Larco, Enrique de Larrañaga, Horacio Gerardo March, Primaldo E. Monaco, Raúl Mazza, Manuel Musto, Julia Peyrou, Víctor Pissarro, Enrique Policastro, Roberto Armando Fidel Rossi, Ideal Sánchez, Ernesto Mariano Scotti, César Sforza, Antonio Sibellino, Raúl Soldi, Jorge Soto Acébal, Mercedes Rodríguez de Soto Acebal, Lino Eneas Spilimbergo, Orlando Stagnaro, Pedro Tenti, Marcos Tiglio, Alejandro Santiago Tomatis, Troiano Troiani, Iván Vasileff, Francisco Vecchioli, Francisco Vidal, Miguel Carlos Victorica, Alejandro Xul Solar, Roberto Aizemberg, Carlos Alonso, José Alonso, Julián Althabe, Manuel Alvarez, Carmelo Ardén Quin, Juan Carlos Badaracco, Libero Badii, Julio Barragán, Luis Barragán, Mane Bernardo, Juan Batlle Planas, Juan Bay, Carlos Cañas, Oscar Capristo, Héctor Bernabé Caribe, Aníbal Carreño, Sergio de Castro, Juan Cerda Carretero, Santiago Cogorno, Víctor Chab, Pedro de Simone, Ernesto Farina, José Antonio Fernández Muro, Manuel Fernández Teijeiro, Vicente Forte, Frank Magda, Leónidas Gambartes, Florencio Garavaglia, Francisco García Carrera, Nicolás García Uriburu, Julio Gero, Noemí Gerstein, Alicia Yadwiga de Giangrande, Claudio Girola, Mario Darío Grandi, Alberto Greco, Juan Grela, Sarah Grilo, Oscar Herrero Miranda, Alfredo Hlito, Arturo Irureta, Hugo Irureta, Enio Iommi, Eduardo Alberto Jonquières, Kenneth Kemble Smith, Gyula Kosice, Rodolfo Krasno, Jorge Abel Krasnopolsky, Abel Laurens, Juan Carlos Labourdette, Julio Le Parc, Jorge E. Lezama, Ezequiel Linares, Mario Loza, Raúl Lozza, Rómulo Maccio, Aurelio Macchi, Eduardo A. Mac Entire, Tomás Maldonado, Víctor Marchese, Horacio Blas Mazza, Febo Martí, Josefina Miguens, Raúl Monsegur, René Morón, José Manuel Moraña, Laura Mulhall Girondo, Luis Felipe Noé, Miguel Ocampo, Rafael Oneto, Hugo Ottman, Homero Panagiotopulos, Blanca Pastor, Anita Payró, Martha Peluffo, Alicia Peñalba, Orlando Pierri, Mario A. Pucciarelli, Rogelio Polesello, Leopoldo Presas, Salvador Presta, Raúl Russo, Luis Seoane, Kasuya Sakai, Osvaldo Svanascini, Juan Manuel Sánchez, Antonio Francisco Scordia, Carlos Torrallardona, Leopoldo Torres Agüuero, Bruno Venier, Leo Vinci, Yente, Roberto Juan Viola, Josefina Zamudio.

CU MiDA VtU

20 Argentine works of art in the John F. Kennedy Center for the Performing Arts. Washington, D.C., 1972. 17 p. 26 cm.
Exhibition catalog of Argentine art with biographical essays on the following notable artists of the 20th century: Líbero Badii and Raquel Forner.

IU NcD NcGU

21 Arias, Abelardo. Ubicación de la escultura argentina en el siglo XX. Buenos Aires: Ediciones Culturales Argentinas, Ministerio de Educación y Justicia, Dirección General de Cultura, 1962. 39 p. 26 cm. (Biblioteca del sesquicentenario. Cuadernos culturales).
An essay about sculpture in Argentina, including brief biographical notes on the following 20th-century artists: Manuel J. Aguirre, Lucio Correa Morales, Francisco Cafferata, Mateo Alonso, Arturo Dresco, Víctor Garino, Hernán Cullén Ayerza, Rogelio Yrurtia, Alberto Lagos, E. Soto Avendaño, Carlos de la Cárcova, Seostris Vitullo, Troiano Troiani, César Sforza, Emilio J. Sarniguet, Pedro Zonza Briano, Agustín Riganelli, Gonzalo Leguizamón Pondal, Luis C. Rovatti, Higinio Puyau, José Fioravanti, Alfredo Bigatti, Nicolás Antonio de San Luis, Horacio Juárez, Lucio Fontana, Libero Badii, Antonio Sibellino, Pablo Cura-

tella Manes, Víctor Marchese, Leo Vinci, José Alonso, Julián Althabe, Enio Iommi, Claudio Girola, Alicia Penalba, Marino DiTeana, Mariano Pagés, Julio Gero.

CtY CU CU-A DPU IaU ICarbS IU MB
MH NBuU NIC NNC PPiU TxU ViU WU

22 Asociación Argentina de Críticos de Arte. *Crítica de arte, Argentina, 1962-63.* Buenos Aires: Impr. Anzilotti, 1963. 51 p. 19 cm.
    Collection of essays about Argentine art with biographical essays on the following notable artists of the 20th century: Emilio Pettoruti, Raquel Forner, Ramón Silva, Líbero Badii, Lorenzo Domínguez, Pompey Audivert.

CLU CtY FU IU MB MoU NbU PPiU TxU

23 Avellaneda, Argentine Republic (City). Museo de Arte. *Diez años a través de treinta pintores argentinos.* Avellaneda, 1957. 30 p. 26 cm.
    A collection of short biographical sketches of the following 20th-century Argentine artists, accompanied by representative samples of their work: Aquiles Badi, Juan Antonio Ballester Peña, Héctor Basaldúa, Juan Batlle Planas, Norah Borges, Horacio Butler, Juan Carlos Castagnino, Emilio Centurión, Santiago Cogorno, Santiago Eugenio Daneri, Juan del Prete, Miguel Diomede, Ernesto Farina, Raquel Forner, Vicente Forte, Ramón Gómez Cornet, Fortunato Lacámera, Onofrio A. Pacenza, Emilio Petorutti, Pierri Orlando, Enrique Policastro, Leopoldo Pedro Presas, Domingo Pronsato, Roberto Armando Rossi, Ideal Sánchez, Raúl Soldi, Lino Eneas Spilimbergo, Alberto J. Trabucco, Marcos Tiglio, Miguel Carlos Victorica.

DLC

24 Banco de la Provincia de Córdoba. *Ochenta años de arte plástico cordobés, 1860-1940: muestra retrospectiva 26 de setiembre al 9 de octubre de 1969. Catálogo.* Córdoba, 1969. 26 p. 22 cm.
    A short work featuring biographical notes on the following artists from Córdoba, Argentina, whose lives spanned the period from 1860 to 1940: José Aguilera, Horacio Alvarez, Fernando Arranz, Carlos Bazzini Barros, Miguel Pablo Borgarello, Miguel Angel Budini, Guillermo Butler, Enrique Borla, Carlos Camilloni, Emilio A. Caraffa, Manuel Cardeñosa, Emilio Casas Ocampo, Luis Gonzaga Cony, Manuel Emilio Coutaret, Gaspar de Miguel, Nicolás Antonio de San Luis, Ernesto Farina, Rosa Ferreyra de Roca, Emiliano Gómez Clara, Primitivo Icardi, Horacio Juárez, Juan Kronfuss, Mauricio Lasansky, Edelmiro Lescano Ceballos, Ricardo López Cabrera, José Malanca, Herminio Malvino, Oscar Meyer, Honorio Mossi, Ricardo Musso, Alberto Nicasio, José María Ortiz, Onofre Palamara, Antonio Pedone, Fidel Pelliza, Genaro Pérez, Juan Carlos Pinto, Octavio Pinto, Andrés Piñero, Vicente R. Puig, Ernesto

Soneira, Héctor Valazza, Francisco Vidal, Roberto Viola, Luis Waysman.

TxU

25 Brughetti, Romualdo. *Historia del arte en Argentina.* México: Editorial Pormaca, 1965. 223 p. Portraits. 20 cm. (Colección Pormaca, v. 17).
    A history of art in Argentina, including biographical sketches on the following 19th- and 20th-centuries artists: Carlos Morel, Prilidiano Pueyrredón, Juan Manuel Blanes, Lucio Correa Morales, Eduardo Sívori, Martín Malharro, Faustino Brughetti, Fernando Fader, Ramón Silva, Walter de Navazio, Valentín Thibón de Libián, Rogelio Yrurtia, Pedro Zonza Briano, Pedro Figari, Ramón Gómez Cornet, Emilio Pettoruti, Miguel Carlos Victorica, Lino Eneas Spilimbergo, Horacio Butler, Aquiles Badi, Héctor Basaldúa, Raquel Forner, Juan del Prete, Eugenio Daneri, Domingo Pronsato, Víctor Pissarro, Emilio Centurión, Domingo Candia, Alfredo Guttero, Norah Borges, Xul Solar, Juan Antonio Ballester Peña, Alberto J. Trabucco, Antonio Berni, Demetrio Urruchúa, Enrique Policastro, Onofrio Pacenza, Jorge Larco, Raúl Soldi, Angeles Ortiz, Zdravco Ducmelic, Luis Falcini, Antonio Sibellino, Alfredo Bigatti, José Fioravanti, Lorenzo Domínguez, Juan Carlos Castagnino, Juan Batlle Planas, Luis Seoane, Gertrudis Chale, Miguel Diómede Orlando Pierri, Luis Barragán, Bruno Venier, Vicente Forte, Leopoldo Presas, José Manuel Moraña, Santiago Cogorno, Antonio Scordia, Raúl Russo, Carlos Torrallardona, Héctor Bernabó (Carybé, pseud.), Marcos Tiglio, Mario Darío Grandi, Leonor Vassena, Primaldo Mónaco, Leónidas Gambartes, Ernesto Farina, Laura Mulhall Girondo, Sergio de Castro, Leopoldo Torres Agüero, Tomás Maldonado, José A. Fernández Muro, Sara Grilo, Miguel Ocampo, Clorindo Testa, Kasuya Sakai, Luis Felipe Noé, Rómulo Macció, Pablo Curatella Manes, Lucio Fontana, Sesostris Vitullo, Líbero Badii, Noemí Gerstein, Gyula Kósica, Ennio Iommi, Aldo Paparella, Martín Blaszko, Gregorio Vardánega, Julián Althabe, Naum Knop, Luis Tomosello, Francesco Marino di Teana, Alicia Pérez Peñalba (Alicia Peñalba, pseud.). Also biographical notes on the following: Antonio Somellera, García del Molino, Benjamín Franklin Rawson, Angel Della Valle, Reinaldo Giudici, Agusto Ballerini, Graciano Mendilaharzu, Severo Rodríguez Etchart, Julio Fernández Villanueva, Cándido López, Ernesto de la Cárcova, Eduardo Schiaffino, Pío Collivadino, Justo Lynch, Hernán Cuyén Ayerza, Agustín Riganelli, Pedro Tenti, Troiano Troiani, Luis Rovatti, Donato Proietto, Nicolás Antonio de San Luis, Eduardo Barnes, Pablo Tosto, Héctor Rocha, Juan Carlos Iramain, Antonio Sassone, Nicolás Lamana, Juan Tapia, Roberto Rossi, Alfredo Guido, Víctor Cúnsolo, Horacio March, Roberto Azzoni, Julio Súarez Marzal, Ernesto Scotti, Enrique de Larrañaga, Adolfo de Ferrari, Pedro Domínguez Neira, Fortunato Lácamara, Alcides Gubellini, Iván Vasileff, César

López Claro, Ricardo Supisiche, Carlos Enrique Uriarte, Juan Grela, Armando Coppola, Eugenia Crenovich, Anito Payró, Mane Bernardo, Francisco Maranca, Roberto Juan Viola, Oscar Herrero Miranda, Oscar Capristo, Osvaldo Svanascini, Víctor Chab, Carlos Alonso, Antonio Seguí, Federico Brook, Claudio Girola, León Ferrari, Julio Gero, Eduardo Sabelli, José Alonso, Aurelio Macchi, Juan Carlos Labourdette, Alberto Carlisky, Antonio Pujía.

AzU CaOTP CLSU CSt CU-S DPU ICA
IEdS InU IU MB MH MiDW MiEM MoSW
MU NbU NBuU NcD NcU NIC NjP NmU
NNC NSyU OU PPiU PPT TxU ViU

26 Buenos Aires. Museo Nacional de Bellas Artes. F. Muro, Grilo, Ocampo, Sakai, Testa; exposición Buenos Aires, julio de 1960. Buenos Aires: Asociación Amigos del Museo Nacional de Bellas Artes, 1960. Unpaged. 23 cm.
    A catalog of an exhibition of the works of F. Muro, Sara Grilo, Miguel Ocampo, Kasuya Sakai, and Clorindo Testa at the Museo Nacional de Bellas Artes in Buenos Aires, including brief biographical sketches.

    FU MH

27 _____. Grabados argentinos, 28 de abril-28 de mayo, 1967; exposición organizada por el Gabinete de Estampas del Museo Nacional de Bellas Artes. Buenos Aires: Asociación Amigos del Museo Nacional de Bellas Artes, 1967. 37 p. 23 cm.
    Exhibition catalog of Argentine prints and engravings with biographical notes about the following notable artists of the 20th century: Eduardo Audivert, Pompeyo Audivert, Américo Balán, Antonio Berni, Aída Carballo, Ernesto Deira, Albino Fernández, Fernando López Anaya, Ana María Moncalvo, Norberto Onofrio, Carlos A. Pacheco, Roberto Páez, Liliana Porter, Osvaldo Romberg, Mabel Rublí, Luis Seoane, Daniel Zelaya.

    CSt DNGA DSI IEN IU KU MH MU NIC
    NN NNC

28 Carril, Bonifacio del. Monumenta iconographica; paisajes, ciudades, tipos, usos y costumbres de la Argentina: 1536-1860. Notas biográficas por Aníbal G. Aguirre y Saravia. Buenos Aires: Emecé, 1964. 2 v. 44 cm.
    A two-volume study of Argentine iconography covering the period from 1536-1860. Biographical information of various amounts is included in volume one for the following artists, whose representative works are found in volume two: Rudolph Ackermann, Albert Adam, Víctor Adam, Richard Adams, Luis Aldao, Andrea Bacle, César Hipólito Bacle, Felipe Bauza, Ignacio Baz, Juan Manuel Besnes e Irigoyen, Luis Philipee Alphonse Bichebois, Auguste Borget, Bartolomé Bossi, Fernando Brambila, Lucien de Brayer, Peircy Brett, Teodoro de Bry, Carlos Germán Conrado Burmeister, Tomás Cabrera, Julio Ramón de César, Augusto Clair-

aux, Julio Daufresne, Cayetano Descalzi, Adlophe D'Hastrel, Justo Doldan, Alcides Dessalines, D'Orbigny, J. D. Dulin, A. Durand, Jean Baptiste Henri Durand-Brager, Robert James Elliot, Augustus Earle, Albin Favier, Silvestre Ferreira da Sylva, Fernando García del Molino, Alphonse Giast, A. Göering, Otto Grashof, Ernest Auguste Coupil, José Cipriano de Herrera, John Frederick Herring, Gregorio Ibarra, Albérico Isola, Eduardo de Kretschmar, Emile Lassalle, Edmond Lebeaud, Raymond Quinsac Monvoisin, Carlos Morel, Hopólito Moulin, P. Mousse, Olivier Van Noort, Arthur Onslow, Hendrik Ottsen, William Gore Ouseley, Juan León Palliere, R. P. Florián Paucke, Julio Pelvilain, Carlos Enrique Pellegrini, A. Pellion, Alejandro Pittaluga, José Del Pozo, Francis Pretty, Prilidano Pueyrredón, Juan Ravenet, Félix Revol, Juan Mauricio Rugendas, Félix Achille Saint-Aulaire, Enrique Sheridan, Ulrich Schmidel, Peter Schmidlmeyer, Carlos Sívori, Nuño da Sylva, Edmond B. de la Touanne, Emeric Essex Vidal, Johannes Vingboons.

    CaOTP DGU ICN InU IU KyU LNHT MB
    MiDW NhD NN OkU RPB WU

29 Colón, Antonio. Artistas del Litoral. Santa Fe: Ediciones Colmegna, 1967. 73 p. 19 cm.
    Bio-bibliographical essays including critical examinations of the works, paintings, and sculptures of the following 20th-century artists from the Litoral region: Juan de Dios Mena, Matías Molina, Pedro Logarzo.

    IaU InU IU NBuU NIC

30 _____. Cuatro artistas del Litoral. Santa Fe: Ediciones Colmegna, 1974. 89 p. 19 cm.
    Critical essays including biographical data of the following 20th-century painters of the Litoral region: Ludovico Paganini, Enrique Estrada Bello, Julio Adriano Lammertyn, Jacinto M. Castillo.

    IU NIC

31 Córdova Iturburu, Cayetano. La pintura argentina del siglo XX. Buenos Aires: Editorial Atlántida, 1958. 272 p. 23 cm. (Colección oro de cultura general, v. 161).
    A historical essay of painting in Argentina in the 20th century, mainly through biographical sketches of the following artists: Augusto Ballerini, Angel Della Valle, Severo Rodríguez Etchart, Ernesto de la Cárcova, Reinaldo Giúdici, Pío Collivadino, Carlos Pablo Ripamonte, Cesáreo Bernaldo de Quirós, Justo Máximo Lynch, José León Pagano, Eduardo Schiaffino, Emilio Caraffa, Eduardo Sívori, Faustino Brughetti, Martín Malharro, Fernando Fader, Antonio Alice, Francisco Vidal, José María Lozano Mouján, Luis A. Codiviola, Raúl Mazza, Jorge Soto Acebal, Alfredo Guido, Jorge Bermúdez, Rodolfo Franco, Gregorio López Naguil, Tito Cittadini, Miguel Carlos Victorica, Ana Weiss de Rossi, Emilia Bertolé, Luis Tessandori, Augusto Marteau, Ramón Silva, Valentín

ART

Thibón de Libián, Walter de Navazio, Eugenio Daneri, Víctor Pissarro, Juan Bautista Tapia, Guillermo Butler, Carlos Gualberto Giambiagi, Alfredo Gramajo Gutiérrez, Benito Quinquela Martín, Ramón Gómez Cornet, Emilio Pettoruti, Aquiles Badi, Lino Enea Spilimbergo, Víctor J. Cúnsolo, Adolfo Tavascio, Norah Borges de Torre, Alejandro Schulz Solari (Xul Solar, pseud.), Raquel Forner, Héctor Basaldúa, Alfredo Guttero, Emilio Centurión, Jorge Larco, Pedro Domínguez Neira, Antonio Berni, Santiago Palazzo, José Arato, Guillermo Facio Hebéquer, Abraham Regino Vigo, José Antonio Merediz, Italo Botti, Angel Domingo Vena, Américo Panozzi, Atilio Malinverno, Octavio Pinto, José Malanca, Antonio Pedone, Enrique de Larrañaga, Vicente Indalecio Pereyra, Juan Antonio Ballester Peña, Francisco Vecchioli, Gastón Jarry, Miguel Burgoa Videla, Luis Barragán, Vicente Forte, Ideal Sánchez, Orlando Pierri, Leopoldo Presas, Bruno Venier, Alberto Altalef, Juan Fuentes, Antonio Miceli, Juan Batlle Planas, Onofrio Pacenza, Horacio March, Susana Aguirre, Oscar Soldatti, Felipe de la Fuente, Luis Borraro, Augusto Ballerini, Ernesto Farina, Horacio Alvarez, Egidio Cerrito, Alejandro Bonome, José Aguilera, Ricardo Supisiche, César López Claro, Enrique Estrada Bello, César Fernández Navarro, Raúl Schurjin, Gustavo Cochet, Carlos de la Torre, Laura Mulhall Girondo, Alberto Güiraldes, Eduardo Timoteo Navarro, Luis Alberto Lobo de la Vega, Rodrigo Bonome, Guillermo Buitrago, Luis Preti, Santos Legname, Luis Lusnich, Blanca R. de Zarlenga, Medardo Pantoja, Roberto Azzoni, Fidel De Lucía, Julio Suárez Marzal, Rosario Moreno, Rosa Stilerman, Osvaldo Juane, Reinaldo Giúdici, Martín L. Boneo, Santiago Palazzo, Juan Carlos Castagnino, Enrique Policastro, Demetrio Urruchúa, Héctor Bernabó (Carybé, pseud.), Carlos Alonso, Ricardo Carpani, Miguel Angel Victorica, Eugenio Daneri, Raúl Soldi, Roberto Rossi, Adolfo De Ferrari, Domingo Pronsato, Mario Darío Grandi, Miguel Diomede, Julio Vanzo, Arturo Gerardo Guastavino, Alberto Trabucco, Antonio Scordia, Primaldo Mónaco, Homero Panagiotópulis, Delia Bucich, Minerva Daltoe, Stella de Pérez Ruiz, Ivan Vasilef, Santiago Tomatis, Marcos Tiglio, Mario Loza, Oscar Capristo, Mónica Soler-Vicenz, Michelle Marx, Alejandro Vainstein, Susana Soro, Elsie Ferrero, Fortunato Lacámera, Juan Cruz Mateo, Domingo Candía, Juan Cerdá Carretero, Carlos Torrallardona, Roberto Juan Viola, Luis Seoane, Julio Barragán, Florencio Juan Garavaglia, Leopoldo Torres Agüero, Clorindo Testa, Raúl Russo, Zdravko Ducmelic, Yadriga Alicia Giangrande, Santiago Cogorno, José Manuel Moraña, René Brusau, Oscar Herrero Miranda, Carlos Enrique Uriarte, Leonor Vasena, Sergio de Castro, Jorge Abel Krasnopolsky, Rodolfo Krasnopolsky (Krasno, pseud.), Osvaldo Svanascini, Ronaldo de Juan, Domingo Bucci, Josefina Miguens, Horacio Berretta, Luis Waisman, Luis Centurión, Alberto Greco, Carlos Sobrino, Pedro De Simone, Miguel Ragonesi, Aurelio Salas, Alfio Grifasi, José de Monte,

Dante Cipulli, Juan Bautista Gatti, José A. Nieto Palacios, Diana Chalikian, Pedro Pont Vergés, Tito Miravet, Hans Aebi, Manuel Alvarez, Néstor Corral, Franco Di Segni, José Antonio Fernández Muro, Sarah Grilo, Nahum Goijman, Eduardo Jonquières, Jorge Edgardo Lezama, Francisco Maranca, Juan Mele, Aldo Paparella, Blanca Pastor, Martha Peluffo, Víctor Magariños D., Miguel Ocampo, Rafael Oneto, Armando Coppola, Ana M. Payró, Fernando Iraolagoitía, Eugenia Crenovich (Yente, pseud.), Abel Laurens, Jorge Luis de la Vega, Kasuya Sakai, Marcelo Bonevardi, Juan Andrés Otano, María Elisa Dearma, Hortensia Tarazi, María Martorell, Tomás Maldonado, Aldredo Hlito, Lidy Prati, Gregorio Vardánega, Gyula Kosice, Juan Bay, Esteban Eitler, Rhod Rothfuss, Aníbal J. Biedma, Guillermo Adolfo Gutiérrez, Abraham Linenberg, Salvador Presta, Alberto Scopelliti, Gina Ionescu, Carmelo Arden Quin, Raúl Lozza. Alphabetical index of names.

ICA IU MH NcD NN

32 <u>Cronología artística</u>; síntesis de lo creado en el campo del arte, en el actual territorio argentino, en los siglos XVI-XVIII. Buenos Aires: Universidad de Buenos Aires, Facultad de Filosofía y Letras, 1963. 120 p. 18 cm. (Biblioteca de historia del arte. Serie argentina, v. 4).

A chronology of artistic activities in the region presently known as the Argentine Republic from the 16th through the end of the 18th century. Includes limited biographical data on the following individuals connected with the arts of the time: Cayetano Marcellano Agramont, Juan Francisco Aguirre, Josef Alexo de Alberro, Pedro Antonio Almeida, Bonifacio Alvarez, Francisco Alvarez, Hernán de Alvarez, Manuel Alvarez, Francisco Alvarez Campana, Manuel Alvarez de Rocha, Félix Arias Rengel y Heredia, Juan de Armasa, Miguel Aucell, Ricardo Aymler, Antonio de Azcona Imberto, Jacinto Bauer, Florián Baucke, Elías Bayala, Ramón Bayeu, Manuel Belgrano, Pedro Benoit, Luis Berger, Francisco Bernal, Miguel de Bidaurre, Acarate de Biscay, Ruperto Blank, Andrés Blanqui, Martín de Boneo, Fernando Brambila, José Brasanelli, Francisco Brecianos, Hernando Brecianos, Francisco de Bustamante, Valentín Cabral, Tomás Cabrera, Francisco Calvo, Isabel de Cámara, Juan de Campos, Francisco Cañete, José Cañete, Bartolomé Cardenosa, José Cardiel, Diego Cardoso, Pedro Carmona, Gonzalo Carvallo, Gregorio de Castañeda, Pedro del Castillo, José Cataldino, Gabriel de Celada, Pedro de Cevallos, José Comte, José Cordero, Manuel de Coyto, Manuel Cueto, Juan Bautista Daniel, Manuel Díaz, Diego Díez Gómez, Zacarías Ditrich, Justo Doldán, Cosme Duarte, Jorge Duarte, José de Echeverría, Alonso de Encinas, Juan Cuaresma Enríquez, Antonio José Escalada, Pedro de Espinosa, Martín Ezcurra, Francisco León Andrés Fernández, Pedro Fernández Castellano, Gregorio Ferreira, Manuel Ferreira, Jacome Ferreira Feo, Roque Ferreira, Antonio de Figueroa, Bacho de Filicaya, Antonio

Forcada, Carlos Franck, José Andrés de la
Fuente, Juan Antonio de la Fuente, Antón de
Fuentes, Dionisio de Fuentes, Antonio Gaete,
Juan de Garay, Francisco García, José García
Martínez de Cáceres, Carlos Gervasoni, Blas
Gómez, Lázaro Gómez de Ledesma, Blas Gómez de
Ledesma, Miguel Gonceras, Francisco González,
Antonio González Balcarce, Tomás González
Flores, José González Merguete, Diego Granero
de Alarcón, José Grimáu, Pedro Juan José Gui-
llelmo, Gabriel Gutiérrez de Escobar, Antonio
Harls, Hernandarias, Juan Antonio Gaspar Her-
nández, Marcos Hernández, Pedro Herrero, Juan
Bartolomé Howel, José Antonio Ibáñez, Andrés
Jiménez de Arce, Juan Kraus, Pablo La Calle,
Bernardo de León, Felipe Lemer, Gerardo Letten,
Juan de Lezica y Alquiz, Juan José de Lezica
y Torrezuri, Juan Manuel López, Juan López
Silba, Isidro Lorea, Adriana Paulina Macaire,
Juan Maciel, Ildefonso Machain, Sebastián
Malvar y Pinto, Ignacio Manzoni, Domingo Mar-
tínez de Irala, José Martínez de Salazar,
Jerónimo Martínez, Martín Martínez, Antonio
Masella, Juan Bautista Masella, Jerónimo Mato-
rras, Pedro de Mendoza, Francisco Salarro de
Montilla, Raimundo Quinsac Monvoisin, Manuel
de Morales, Pedro Morel, José Antonio Mosquera,
Vicente Muñoz, Juan Narbona, Alvar Núñez Cabe-
za de Vaca, Manuel Pablo Núñez de Ibarra, Juan
Ochoa de Zárate, Rodrigo Orgóñez, Juan Orrigón,
Juan Osorio, José Ott, Domingo Pallarés, Sil-
verio Pastor, María Antonia de la Paz y Figue-
roa, Carlos Enrique Pellegrini, Jose de la
Peña y Zarqueta, Domingo Pereira, José Pérez
Brito, Martín de Petris, Angel Camilo Petra-
grassa, Domingo Petrarca, Francisco Pimentel,
Antonio de la Plaza, Manuel del Pozo, Julián
Preciado, Juan Bautista Prímoli, José Antonio
Puig, Lázaro Quintero, Pascual Ramírez, Juan
Ramírez de Velasco, Pedro Ramírez de Velasco,
Andrés Ribera, Elías Ribero Ribas, Manuel Ri-
bero, Juan de Dios Rivera, Antonio de Rocha,
Antonio de Rocha Bautista, Marcos Rodríguez
de Figueroa, Tomás Rosatini, Jacobo Roth,
Antonio Ruiz de Montoya, Francisco Ruiz Galán,
José Custodio Sáa y Faría, Joseph de Salas,
Esteban Salzes, Esteban Samzon, Juan Sánchez
Pompas, José Sánchez Labrador, Antonio Sando-
val, Gaspar de Santa Coloma, Francisco de Paula
Sanz, Marcos Sapaca, Tomás Saravia, Rodrigo
de Sas, Ulrico Schmidel, José Schmidt, Antonio
Sepp, Francisca Silveira de Ibarrola, Diego
de Solís, Juan de Soria, Joseph de Souza,
Melchor Suárez de la Concha, José del Tasso,
Antonio Tomás, Tomás Toribio Domingo Torres,
Lucas Torres, Pedro de Torres, Juan Uriarte,
Esteban de Urízar y Arespacochaga, Diego Val-
dés, Vicente Valverde, Alejandro del Valle,
Manuel de Velasco, Juan José de Vértiz, Emerio
Essex Vidal, Luis de Villegas, Juan Vingboons,
Carlos Vrit, Paul Walthaufer, Pedro Weger,
Juan Wolff, Carlos Wright, Francisco Xarque,
Juan Yapari, Bruno Mauricio de Zabala, Pedro
de Zárate.

IU

33 Chiabra Acosta, Alfredo. Críticas de arte
argentino 1920-1932. Buenos Aires: M. Gleizer,
1934. 399 p. 19 cm.
An essay about Argentine art, including
biographical essays on the following notable
artists from the 18th through the 20th centuries: Martín Malharro, Ramón Silva, Italo
Botti, Gramajo Gutiérrez, Soto Acébal, César
Caggiano, C. P. Ripamonte, Valentín Thibón de
Libián, Guillermo Butler, Octavio Pinto, Ra-
món Gómez Cornet, Emilio Pettoruti, Benito
Quinquela Martín, Alonso, Fernando Fader, Wal-
ter de Navazio, Alberto Lagos, Zonza Briano,
Leonie Matthis, Eduardo Sívori, Santiago Pala-
zzo, Juan Palazzo, Rogelio Irurtia, Américo
Panozzi, José A. Merediz, Gregorio López Naguil,
Antonio Pedone, Luis Falcini, Alfredo Guttero,
Nicolás Lamanna, Agustín Riganelli, Juan Del
Prete, Víctor Pisarro, Pedro Fígari, Camilo
Mauclair, José Arato, Luis Macaya, Angel Vena,
José Fioravanti, Juan B. Tapia, Alfredo Be-
llocq, B. C. Quirós, Elena Cid, Xul Solar,
Antonio Berni, Raquel Forner, Antonio Sibelli-
no, Juan A. Ballester Peña, Carlos Giambiagi,
Rafael Barradas, Héctor Basaldúa, Carlos E.
Pellegrini, Alfredo Bigatti.

CtY DLC IU NcU

34 Fundación Lorenzutti. Obras maestras de la
pintura argentina 1. Buenos Aires: Fundación
Lorenzutti, 1972. 123 p. Portraits. 24 cm.
Exhibition catalog of Argentine painting
with biographical sketches of the following
participating artists of the 20th century:
Juan Batlle Planas, Antonio Berni, Horacio
Butler, Juan Carlos Castagnino, Enilio Centu-
rión, Eugenio Daneri, Juan Del Prete, Miguel
Diomede, Leónidas Gambartes, Ramón Gómez Cor-
net, Emilio Pettoruti, Enrique Policastro,
Raúl Russo, Luis Seoane, Raúl Soldi, Lino Enea
Spilimbergo, Miguel Carlos Victorica, Alejandro
Xul Solar.

IU MB TxU

35 _____. Panorama de la escultura argentina
actual. Buenos Aires, 1971. 79 p. Portraits.
23 cm.
Catalog of an exhibition held at the Museo
Nacional de Bellas Artes, Buenos Aires, Aug.
4-31, 1971. Includes biographical sketches
accompanied by portraits of the following contemporary Argentine sculptors: Julián Althabe,
Libero Badii, Luis Oreste Balduzzi, Esther
Barugel, Martín Blaszko, Ari Brizzi, Ricardo
Martín Daga, Carlos de la Mota, Pablo Edelstein, Rubén Elosegui, Julio Geró, Noemí Gerstein, Silvio Giangrande, Claudio Girola,
María Juana Heras Velasco, Alberto Heredia,
Enio Iommi, Naum Knop, Gyüla Kosice, Juan Car-
los Labourdette, Aurelio Macchi, Víctor Marchese, Moisés Nusimovich, Aldo Paparella,
Ferruccio Polacco, Rogelio Polesello, Antonio
Pujia, Enrique Romano, Osvaldo Romberg, Eduar-

do Sabelli, Dalmiro Sirabo, Antonio Sitro, Miguel Enrique Torroja, Leo Vinci.

CLSU GU NcD NNC TxU WU

36 _____. *Panorama de la pintura argentina.* Buenos Aires, 1969. 1 v. (Unpaged). Portraits. 22 cm.

A collection of biographical essays of the following notable Argentine painters of the 20th century: Aquiles, Badi, Juan Antonio Ballester Peña, Héctor Basaldúa, Antonio Berni, Norah Borges, Horacio Butler, Domingo Candia, Juan Carlos Castagnino, Emilio Centurión, Víctor Cúnsolo, Eugenio Daneri, Adolfo De Ferrari, Juan Del Prete, Miguel Diomede, Pedro Domínguez Neira, Raquel Forner, Carlos Giambiagi, Ramón Gómez Cornet, Luis Gowland Moreno, Alfredo Guttero, Fortunato Lacámera, Jorge Larco, Horacio March, Onofrio Pacenza, Anita Payró, Emilio Pettoruti, Víctor Pissarro, Enrique Policastro, Domingo Pronsato, Roberto Rossi, Raúl Soldi, Lino Enea Spilimbergo, Marcos Tiglio, Demetrio Urruchúa, Julio Vanzo, Miguel Carlos Victorica, Alejandro Xul Solar, Roberto Aizenberg, Carlos Alonso, Julio Barragán, Luis Barragán, Juan Batlle Planas, Oscar Capristo, Ricardo Roque Carpani, Luis Centurión, Santiago Cogorno, Víctor Chab, Gertrudis Chale, Zdravco Ducmelic, Juan Eighler, Ernesto Farina, Vicente Forte, Leónidas Gambartes, Mario Darío Grandi, Juan Grela, César López Claro, Oscar Herrero Miranda, Jorge Abel Krasnopolsky, Horacio Blas Mazza, Primaldo Mónaco, José Manuel Moraña, Laura Mulhall Gironda, Noé Nojechowicz, Hugo L. Ottmann, Orlando Pierri, Pedro Pont Vergés, Leopoldo Presas, Raúl Russo, Ideal Sánchez, Luis Seoane, Ricardo Supisiche, Stefan Strocen, Carlos A. Torrallardona, Leopoldo Torres Agüero, Carlos Enrique Uriarte, Bruno Venier, Manuel Alvarez, Luis Fernando Benedit, Marcelo Bonevardi, Osvaldo Borda, Héctor Borla, Ary Brizzi, Delia Sara Cancela, Carlos Cañas, Miguel Dávila, Ernesto Deira, Jorge De la Vega, Jorge Demirjian, Germaine Derbecq, Juan Carlos Distéfano, Manuel Espinosa, José Antonio Fernández Muro, Nicolás García Uriburu, Alberto Greco, Sarah Grilo, Alfredo Hlito, Kenneth Kemble, César López Osornio, Raúl Lozza, Lea Lublin, Rómulo Macció, Eduardo MacEntyre, Tomás Maldonado, Víctor Mayariños, María Martorell, Fernando Maza, Pablo Mesejean, Gabriel Messil, Luis Felipe Noé, Miguel Ocampo, César Paternosto, Martha Peluffo, Rogelio Polesello, Mario Pucciarelli, Josefina Robirosa, Kasuya Sakai, Antonio Seguí, Carlos Silva, Clorindo Testa, Miguel Angel Vidal, Luis Alberto Wells.

IU NSbSU

37 _____. *Panorama de la pintura argentina joven.* Buenos Aires, 1972. 72 p. Portraits. 24 cm.

Exhibition catalog of 20th-century Argentine painting with biographical notes on the following notable artists: Pedro Leopoldo

Alberti, Artemio Alisio, Federico Víctor Aymá, Nuri Balaguer, Ricardo Sergio Baravalle, Hugo Bastos, Marta Belmes, Miguel Angel Bengochea, Pablo Gustavo Bobbio, Julio César Botta, Mildred Burton, Walter Canevaro, Alicia Carletti, Carmelo Carrá, Graciela Castellano, Américo Juan Castilla, Juan Carlos Castro, Susana Claret, Juan Roberto Cruz, Juan Carlos Chuljak, María Cristina Dartiguelongue, Hugo de Marziani, Diana Dowek, Carlos Falco, Roberto Firpo, Hugo César Font, María Laura Forte Lay, Alcira Fridman, Rosa María Fumagalli, José García Tuñón, Héctor Giuffré, Claudio Gustavo Grynberg, María Helguera, Emilio Fausto Luque y Luque, Martha Magnani, Cristina Manganiello, Eloísa Marticorena, Carlos Alberto Martínez, Beatriz Méndez, Guido Minerbi, Raúl Osvaldo Moneta, Luis Moretti, Carlos Mozo Saravia, Jorge Peirano, Patricia Pereyra Iraola, Felipe Carlos Pino, Angel Oscar Prignano, Roberto Augusto Rojas, Mirta Noemí Rossetti, Domingo Teófilo Sahda, Alberto Sánchez, Hugo A. Sbernini, Eduardo Alberto Serna, Elsa Soibelman, Carlos Tartarini, Raúl Teppa, Ricardo Vanni, Marcelo Evaristo Villafañe.

IaU IU MB TxU WU

38 _____. *Pintura argentina--promoción internacional.* Buenos Aires, 1970. 169 p. Portraits. 24 cm.

Exhibition catalog of 20th-century Argentine painting with biographical sketches on the following notable artists: Antonio Berni, Horacio Butler, Juan Del Prete, Miguel Diomede, Raquel Forner, Emilio Pettoruti, Lino Enea Sp81imbergo, Miguel Carlos Victorica, Alejandro Xul Solar, Roberto Aizenberg, Carlos Alonso, Juan Batlle Planas, Leónidas Gambartes, Raúl Russo, Luis Seoane, Marcelo Bonevardi, Ary Brizzi, Ernesto Deira, Juan Carlos Distéfano, Rómulo Macció, Eduardo MacEntyre, Rogelio Polesello, Antonio Seguí, Miguel Angel Vidal.

GU IaU IU MB MiDW MoSW MU NIC NNC NSbSU TxU ViU WU

39 Fúrlong Cárdiff, Guillermo. *Artesanos argentinos durante la dominación hispánica,* con prólogo de Vicente Nadal Mora. Buenos Aires: Editorial Huarpes, 1946. 454 p. 23 cm. (His Cultura colonial argentina, v. 5).

A history of Argentine industrial art during the 16th through the 18th centuries with scattered biographical information about approximately 1,000 artisans. Alphabetical index of names.

CtY FU ICN IU LU MH MiU NcU NIC NN NNC NSyU TxU ViU WaU

40 Gesualdo, Vicente. *Como fueron las artes en la Argentina.* Buenos Aires: Editorial Plus Ultra, 1973. 111 p. 21 cm. (Colección esquemas históricos, v. 21).

Study of the development of art in Argentina including architecture, painting, sculpture, engraving, and silversmithing. Scattered, limited biographical information is supplied for outstanding individuals in these fields.

CSt   CU   FU   IU   MB   MU   NcD   NIC   NmU
NN   TxU   WU

41   Grabado argentino. Madrid: Gráficas Valeras, 1967.   55 p.   21 cm.

Catalog of an exhibition of Argentine prints held in the Biblioteca Central de la Diputación de Barcelona. Includes biographical sketches of the following exhibitors: Alda María Armagni, Carlos Alberto Aschero, Alberto Juan Borzone, Laico Bou, Rodolfo F. Bracco, Domingo Bucci, Rodolgo Adalberto Bustos, Luis B. Caputo Demarco, Aída Carballo, Juan José Cartasso, Rodolgo Castagna, Antonio G. Console, Armando Jorge Díaz Arduino, Miguel Angel Elgarte, Ana María Erra, Enrique Fernández Chelo, Mario A. Greco, Alfredo Guido, Bernardo Lazansky, Jorge Guillermo Luna Ercilla, Ana María Moncalvo, Eloísa G. Moras, Julio Alberto Leonelo Muñeza, José Murcia, Alicia N. Orlandi, Marcos Paley, María Esther Carmen Ramella, Víctor L. Rebuffo, Juan Carlos Romero, Mabel Rubli, Hemilce M. Saforcada, Antonio Santoro, Enrique Alberto Sorriente, Ricardo Alberto Tau, César Turrillo, Raúl Veroni, Elba Villafañe, Marina Yvorra, Alberto Zienkiewicz.

DLC

42   Lanuza, José Luis.   Pintores del viejo Buenos Aires. Buenos Aires: Ediciones Culturales Argentinas, Ministerio de Educación y Justicia, Dirección General de Cultura, 1961.   59 p. 24 cm. (Biblioteca del sesquicentenerio. Serie Cuadernos culturales).

A collection of biographical essays on the following notable 19th-century painters in Buenos Aires, Argentina: Emeric Essec Vidal, Carlos Enrique Pellegrini, César Hipólito Bacle, Carlos Morel, Raymond Monvoisin, Mauricio Rugendas, Prilidiano Pueyrredón, León Palliére.

CaBVaU   CLSU   CtY   CU   DPU   FU   IaU   ICN
IU   KU   MB   MH   NbU   NBuU   NcD   NIC   NjP
NN   NNC   OU   TxU   ViU   WU

43   Lo Celso, Angel T.   50 [i.e. Cincuenta] años de arte plástico en Córdoba, desde el año 1920 al 1970 con un apéndice por los años 1971 y 1972. Córdoba: Banco de Provincia de Córdoba, 1973.   881 p.   25 cm.

Biographical essays of over 300 artists in Córdoba, Argentina, in the 20th century.

CSt   IU   MB   MU   NmU   TxU   WU

44   López Anaya, Fernando.   El grabado argentino en el siglo XX; principales instituciones promotoras. Buenos Aires: Ediciones Culturales Argentinas, Ministerio de Educación y Justicia,

Dirección General de Cultura, 1963.   51 p. 20 cm. (Biblioteca del sesquicentenario. Serie: Monografías del arte).

Essay on Argentine engraving of the 20th century with biographical notes on the following artists: Pío Collivadino, Lino E. Spilimbergo, Esteban Mira Cató, Catalina Mórtola, Héctor Basaldúa, Adolfo Montero, Lorenzo Gigli, Adolfo Sorzio, Rafael Bertugno, Eduardo Sívori, Mario A. Canale, Ramón Silva, Valentín Thibón de Libián, Raúl Mazza, José León Pagano, Gregorio López Naguil, Guillermo Facio Hebequer, Abraham Vigo, José Arato, Adolfo Bellocq, Víctor Rebuffo, José Mario Cecconi, Enrique Delachaud, Rodolfo Franco, Francisco de Santo, Miguel Angel Elgarte, Carmen Souza Brazuna, Manuel Suero, Margarita Portela Lagos, Raúl Bongiorno, Ernesto Lanziuto, María Esther Leanes, Ofelia Jofré, María Angélica Moreno Kiernan, Ana María Bruno, Hebe Ester Redoano, Juan Carlos Romero, Emiliano Gómez Clara, Octavio Pinto, Antonio Pedone, Alberto Nicasio, Oscar Meyer, Juan Carlos Pinto, Manuel Rueda Mediaville, Laura Bustos Vocos, Ana Bettini, César Tomás Miranda, Manuel Martínez Readigós, Lilián Gómez Molina, José Planas Casas, Gustavo Cochet, Juan Grela, Ricardo A. Supisiche, Juan Berlingieri, Mele Bruniard, Pompeyo Audivert, Juana Briones, Ana Matilde Aybar, Clara Ferrari, Jorge González Mir, Hugo Machado, Pedro Alberto Molina, Brígida Notario, María Kuniko Horie, Myrian Cristina Holgado, Greta Jaime, Elda Victoria Sarmiento, Evelina Mario, Gladis Montaldo, María Estela Mejías, Víctor Delhez, Bernardo Federman, Jaime Alaminos, Sergio Hocevar, Luis Quesada, José María Pineda, Nello Raffo, Santiago Raffo.

CaBVaU   CLSU   CLU   CtY   CU   CU-A   DPU
FTaSU   FU   InU   IU   KU   MB   MH   MU   NcU
NIC   NjP   PPiU   TxU   WU

45   Nessi, Angel Osvaldo.   Situación de la pintura argentina. La Plata: Talleres Gráficos de Angel Domínguez e hijo, 1956.   196 p.   21 cm. (Colección La Reja).

Biographical essays on the following notable Argentine painters in the 19th and 20th centuries: Carlos Morel, Prilidiano Pueyrredón, Juan Manuel Blanes, Martín A. Malharro, Fernando Fader, Cesáreo Barnaldo de Quirós, Alfredo Guttero, Francisco Vecchioli, Emilio Pettoruti. Also biographical notes on the following: Adolphe D'Hastrel, Raymond Monvoisin, Carlos Enrique Pellegrini, Juan León Palliére, Eduardo Sivori, Angel Della Valle, Jorge Bermúdez, Lía Correa Morales de Yrurtia, Lino E. Spilimbergo, Guillermo Martínez Solimán, Raúl Soldi, Guido G. Amicarelli, Antonio Berni.

CU   IaU   ICA   IU   OCU   TxU   WU

46   Nuevas generaciones en la pintura argentina. Buenos Aires: Municipalidad de la Ciudad de Buenos Aires. Secretaría de Cultura y Acción Social, 1959.   1 v. (Unpaged). Portraits. 17 cm.

ART

A collection of biographical sketches, accompanied by portraits, of the following Argentine painters of the 20th century: Carlos Alonso, Manuel Alvarez, Luis Barragán, Judy Bratt de Oliveira Cézar, Domingo Bucci, Oscar Capristo, Cerdá Carretero, Luis Centurión, Víctor Chab, Wilma Dastir, Jaime Davidovich, Jorge de la Vega, Domingo Di Stefano, Elsie Ferrero, Florencio Garavaglia, Martha Gavensky, Naum Goifman, Mario Darío Grandi, Marta Grinberg, Gina Ionescu, Fernando Iraolagoitía, Eduardo Jonquières, Rodolfo Krasno, Jorge Abel Krasnopolsky, Alejandro Lanoël, Marta Lehmann, Julio Le Parc, Eduardo A. MacEntyre, Raúl Víctor Machado, Febo Martí, Federico Augusto Martino, Josefina Miguens, Primaldo Mónaco, José Manuel Moraña, Rodolfo Morelli, Sergio Moyano, Juan Otano, Martha Peluffo, Orlando Pierri, Leopoldo Presas, Francisca Ramos de los Reyes, Kazuya Sakai, Ideal Sánchez, Francisco Sobrino, Stefan Strocen, Osvaldo Svanascini, Elena Tarasido, Clorindo Testa, Leonor Vassena, Bruno Venier, Miguel Angel Vidal, Virgilio Villalba.

DPU   IU   LNHT

47   Pagano Rovissoin, José León.   El arte de los argentinos.   Buenos Aires: Edición del autor, 1937–40.   3 v.   Portraits.   33 cm.
A history of Argentine art.   Includes biographical essays on approximately 500 artists from the colonial era to the 20th century.   Alphabetical index of names in each volume.

CU   DLC   IEN   IU   MiU   NBB   NcD

48   _____.   Historia del arte argentino desde los aborígenes hasta el momento actual, con 334 ilustraciones en negro y 28 citocromías. Buenos Aires: L'Amateur, 1944.   507 p.   Portraits.   30 cm.
A history of Argentine art, covering the period from preconquest to the 20th century, including biographical information as well as portraits in many cases, for many notable artists.   Alphabetical index of names.

CaBViP   CtY   GU   InU   IU   KU   MH   NcRS
NcU   OCl   OClMU   OCU   OOxM   PP   PU-FA   TxU

49   Paris.   Musée National d'Art Moderne.   L'art argentin actuel.   Exposition, décembre 1963–février 1964.   Paris, 1963.   Unpaged.   21 cm.
Catalog of exhibition of Argentine art in the National Museum of Modern Art in Paris with biographical notes on the following notable artists of the 20th century: Carlos Alonso, Luis F. Benedit, Antonio Berni, Horacio Butler, Aníbal Carreño, Juan C. Castagnino, Sergio de Castro, Víctor Chab, Juan Del Prete, Lucio Fontana, Raquel Forner, Vicente Forte, Alicia Y. Giangrande, Eduardo Jonquières, Ronaldo de Juan, Rómulo Maccio, Luis F. Noé, Miguel Ocampo, Martha Peluffo, Mario Pucciarelli, Raúl Russo, Kazuya Sakai, Antonio Sequí, Luis Seoane, Xul Solar, Stefan Strocen,

Sesostris Vitullo, Pablo Curatella Manes, Martha Boto, Leonardo Delfino, León Ferrari, Marino di Teana, Julio Gero, Noemí Gerstein, Silvia Giangrande, Naum Knop, Gyula Kosice, Juan C. Labourdette, Julio Le Parc, Aurelio Macchi, Aldo Paparella, Alicia Peñalba, Enrique Romano, Rubén Santantonin, Osvaldo Stimm, Gregorio Vardanega, Fernando López Anaya, Rodolfo Krasno, Ana M. Moncalvo, Lydia M. Rubli, Juan C. Benítez, Esperillo Bute, Roberto González.

CtY   ICA   ICU   IU   MdBJ   MdU   NcD   NjP
NNC   TxU

50   Payró, Julio E.   Veintidós pintores; facetas del arte argentino.   Buenos Aires: Editorial Poseidón, 1944.   266 p.   38 cm.
An essay about Argentine painting.   Includes biographical essays on the following notable artists of the 19th and 20th centuries: S. Eugenio Daneri, Domingo Pronsato, Miguel C. Victorica, Emilio Pettoruti, Aquiles Badi, Gustavo Cochet, Emilio Centurión, Juan A. Ballester Peña, Héctor Basaldúa, Lino Eneas Spilimbergo, Jorge Larco, Horacio Butler, Juan del Prete, Ramón Gómez Cornet, Horacio G. March, Alberto J. Trabucco, Norah Borges, Raquel Forner, Raúl Soldi, Onofrio A. Pacenza, Juan C. Castagnino, Juan Batlle Planas.

CtY   DLC   IU   MU   NNC   OCl   OClMA   OCU
WaWW

51   _____.   23 [i.e. Veintitrés] pintores de la Argentina, 1810–1900.   Buenos Aires: Editorial Universitaria de Buenos Aires, 1962.   63 p. 25 cm.   (Serie del siglo y medio, v. E2).
An essay about painting in Argentina, including biographical sketches of the following notable artists (1810–1900):   Emeric Essex Vidal, Juan Felipe Goulu, Adolfo d'Hastrel de Rivedoux, Lorenzo Fiorini, Augusto Raimundo Quinsac Monvoisin, Carlos Guillermo Uhl, Ernesto Charton, Juan León Pallière, Ignacio Manzoni, Baltasar Verazzi, Juan Mauricio Rugendas, Carlos Enrique Pellegrini, Prilidiano Pueyrredón, Juan Carlos Morel, Fernando García del Molino, Cándido López, Angel Della Valle, Graciano Mendilaharzu, Eduardo Sívori, José Bouchet, Ernesto de la Cárcova, Eduardo Schiaffino, Martín A. Malharro.

CLSU   ICU   InU   IU   LNHT   MH   MiEM   MoSW
NbU   NcD   NIC   NjP   NNC   NSbSU   NSyU   OCl
PPiU   TxBeaL   TxU

52   Pellegrini, Aldo.   Panorama de la pintura argentina contemporánea.   Buenos Aires: Paidós, 1967.   214 p.   19 cm.   (Biblioteca Mundo moderno, v. 17).
Essay about contemporary Argentine painting with biographical notes on approximately 300 notable artists.   Alphabetical index of names.

CFS   CLSU   CSt   CtY   CU   DeU   DPU   FU   IaU
InU   IU   MB   MiDW   MiEM   MoSW   MU   NbU

NBuU NcU NIC NjP NNC NSyU PPiU
PPULC TxU WU

53 <u>Pintores argentinos</u>. Buenos Aires: Editorial
Pampa, 1950. Unpaged. 37 cm. (Colección
artes plásticas de América).
 An essay about Argentine painters, including biographical essays on the following from
the 20th century: Héctor Basaldúa, Horacio
Butler, Raquel Forner, Raúl Soldi.

DLC IU NN TxU

54 <u>Pintores argentinos</u>. Prólogo de Enrique Azcoaga. Sitges (Spain): Embajada de la República Argentina, etc., 1970. Unpaged. Portraits.
21 cm.
 Catalog of exhibition of Argentine painting in the Palacio de Marciel in Spain with
biographical notes on the following notable
artists of the 20th century: José Antonio
Fernández Muro, Sarah Grilo, Adolfo Estrada.

DLC

55 <u>Pintores argentinos del siglo XX</u>. Buenos
Aires: Centro Editor de América Latina, 1980-
82. 119 v. Portraits. 33 cm.
 A collection of essays on the following
notable Argentine artists (painters, sculptors,
engravers, and photographers) of the 20th cen-
tury, including biographical data:
 Painters: v. 1. Martín Malharro, v. 2.
Ramón Silva, v. 3. Fernando Fader, v. 4. Guillermo Butler, v. 5. Cesáreo Bernaldo de Quirós, v. 6. Ramón Gómez Cornet, v. 7. Miguel
Carlos Victorica, v. 8. Eugenio Daneri, v. 9.
Fortunato Lacamera, v. 10. Emilio Pettoruti,
v. 11. Miguel Diomede, v. 12. Quinquela Martín, v. 13. Emilio Centurión, v. 14. Héctor
Basaldúa, v. 15. Alfredo Guttero, v. 16. Lino
Enea Spilimbergo, v. 17. Juan Del Prete, v. 18.
Demetrio Urruchúa, v. 19. Enrique Policastro,
v. 20. Pedro Domínguez Neira, v. 21. Juan Carlos Castagnino, v. 22. Horacio Butler, v. 23.
Antonio Berni, v. 24. Juan Batlle Planas,
v. 25. Roberto Aizenberg, v. 26. Carlos Alonso,
v. 27. Xul Solar, v. 28. Ricardo Supisiche,
v. 29. Leopoldo Presas, v. 30. Carlos Torra-
llardona, v. 31. Raúl Soldi, v. 32. Luis Seoa-
ne, v. 33. Santiago Cogorno, v. 34. Raúl
Russo, v. 35. Raquel Forner, v. 36. Vicente
Forte, v. 37. Leónidas Gambartes, v. 38. Luis
Barragán, v. 39. Ary Brizzi, v. 40. Eduardo
MacEntyre, v. 41. Kenneth Kemble, v. 42. Jorge
Demirjian, v. 43. Alfredo Hlito, v. 44. Ernes-
to Deira, v. 45. Miguel Angel Vidal, v. 46.
Clorindo Testa, v. 47. Luis Felipe Noé, v. 48.
Antonio Seguí, v. 49. Gabriel Messil, v. 50.
Marcelo Bonevardi, v. 51. Ricardo Roque Car-
pani, v. 52. César Paternosto, v. 53. José
Antonio Fernández Muro, v. 54. Rómulo Maccio,
v. 55. Jorge Luis de la Vega, v. 56. Carlos
Silva, v. 57. Alejandro Puente, v. 58. Enrique
Torroja, v. 59. Sara Grilo, v. 60. Julio Le
Parc, v. 61. Ricardo Garabito, v. 62. Luis
Fernando Benedit, v. 63. Víctor Chab, v. 64.
Guillermo Roux.

 Sculptors: v. 65. Rogelio Yrurtia, v. 66.
Lola Mora, v. 67. Agustín Riganelli, v. 68.
Alberto Lagos, v. 69. José Fioravanti, v. 70.
Antonio Sibellino, v. 71. Alfredo Bigatti,
v. 72. Pablo Curatella Manes, v. 73. Libero
Badii, v. 74. Aldo Paparella, v. 75. Martín
Blaszko, v. 76. Enio Iomni, v. 77. Alberto
Heredia, v. 78. Emilio Renart, v. 79. Lucio
Fontana, v. 80. Juan Carlos Distéfano.
 Engravers: v. 81. Pompeyo Audivert, v. 82.
Fernando López Anaya, v. 83. Aída Carballo,
v. 84. Guillermo Facio Hebequer, v. 85. Víctor
Rebuffo, v. 86. Luis Seoane, v. 87. Sergio
Sergi, v. 88. Mabel Rubli, v. 89. Liliana Por-
ter, v. 90. Daniel Zelaya, v. 91. Carlos File-
vich, v. 92. Antonio Berni, v. 93. Norberto
Onofrio, v. 94. Delia Cugat, v. 95. Eduardo
Audivert, v. 96. José Planas Casas.
 Photographers: v. 97. Juan Disandro,
v. 98. Alicia D'Amico, v. 99. Humberto Rivas,
v. 100. Armando Coppola, v. 101. Grete Stern,
v. 102. Eduardo Comesaña, v. 103. Alfredo Sán-
chez, v. 104. Oscar Pintor, v. 105. Antonio
Legarreta, v. 106. Jorge Aguirre, v. 107.
Anatole Saderman, v. 108. Juan Travnik, v. 109.
Carlos A. Bosch, v. 110. Sara Facio, v. 111.
Annemarie Heinrich, v. 112. Sameer Makarius.
 Sketchers: v. 113. Carlos Gorriarena,
v. 114. Josefina Auslender, v. 115. Ana Tarsia,
v. 116. Artemio Alisio, v. 117. Lino E. Spilimbergo, v. 118. Noé Nojechowicz, v. 119. Juan
Carlos Castagnino.

56 <u>La Pintura argentina</u>. Abraham Haber et al.
Buenos Aires: Centro Editor de América Latina,
1975. 96 p. 29 cm. (Pueblos, hombres y formas en el arte).
 Scattered biographical information on the
following notable Argentine painters of the
19th and 20th centuries: Prilidiano Pueyrredón, Martín A. Malharro, Ramón Gómez Cornet,
Emilio Pettoruti, Alejandro Schulz Solari (Xul
Solar, pseud.), Juan del Prete, Alfredo Guttero, Antonio Berni.

AzU CU IU MU NcU NIC PSt

57 San Martín, María Laura. <u>Pintura argentina</u>
<u>contemporánea</u>. Buenos Aires: Editorial La
Mandrágora, 1961. 265 p. 27 cm. (Colección
panoramas del siglo XX).
 An essay about painting in Argentina including biographical notes on approximately
600 notable artists of the 19th and 20th centuries. Alphabetical index of names.

C CLSU CLU CNoS CtY CU CU-S DeU
DPU FU IaU ICA ICU IEN InU IU LN
LNHT MB MH MiD MiDW N NcD NIC NN
NNC NSyU OCl OU TxHR TxU WaU WU

58 Santa Fe, Argentina Republic (City). Museo
Provincial de Bellas Artes "Rosa Galisteo de
Rodríguez." <u>Exposición de diez pintores rosa-</u>
<u>rinos fallecidos en este siglo</u>. Santa Fe,
1955. Unpaged. Portraits. 20 cm.
 A collection of short biographies of ten
artists from the city of Rosario, Argentina,

who have died in the 20th century. Representative works, many of them self-portraits, are also included. The following are featured: Augusto Juan Olive, Manuel Musto, Salvador Zaino, Augusto Schiavoni, Juan Berlingieri, Enrique Juan Munne, Emilia Bertolé, Domingo J. Garrone, Juan de los Angeles Naranjo, César A. Caggiano.

DLC   MH   TxU

59   Schiaffino, Eduardo.   La pintura y la escultura en Argentina.   Buenos Aires: Edición del Autor, 1933.   413 p.   Portraits.   32 cm.
A history of painting and sculpture in Argentina from the 18th to the 19th centuries, mainly through biographical essays about the following notable artists: Manuel Belgrano, Jean Philippe Goulu, Emeric Essex Vidal, Adolphe d'Hastrel de Rivedoux, Charles Henri Pellegrini, Fernando García del Molino, Carlos Morel, Carlos Lezica, Marcelino San Arromán, Gaetano Descalzi, Raymond Monvoisin, Johan Moritz Rugendas, Jean Marie Chavanne, Prilidiano Paz Pueyrredón, Ernest Charton, L. Noël, Rudolf Julius Carlsen, Edmond Le Beaud, Otto Grashof, Carlos W. Uhl, Ignazio Manzoni, Juan L. Camaña, Baldassare Verazzi, Jean León Pallière, Desmadryl, Enrique Sheridan, Franklin Rawson, Bernabé Demaría, Stutz, Ignacio Baz, Martín L. Boneo, Louis Joseph Daumas, Novarese, Manuel de Santa Coloma, Epaminondas Chiama, Juan M. Blanes, José Aguyari, Eugenia Belin Sarmiento, Genaro Pérez, Alfred Paris, Francesco Romero, Edoardo De Martino, Secundino Salinas, Albert Carrier-Belleuse, Eduardo Sívori, Emilio C. Agrelo, Alfonso Bosco, Ventura R. Lynch, Gustave Doré, Miguel Palleja, Angel Della Valle, Reynaldo Giúdici, Augusto Ballerini, Julio Fernández Villanueva, Eduardo Schiaffino, Adriano E. Rossi, Carlos Guido Spano, Graciano Mendilaharzu, Raymond Monvoisin.

DLC   IaU   IU   KU   MB   MiU   NBB   NcU   OCl   OU   PU

60   Squirru, Rafael Fernando.   Pintura-pintura: siete valores argentinos en el arte actual.   Buenos Aires: Ediciones Arte y Crítica, 1975.   101 p.   20 cm.   (Colección ensayos).
A collection of biographical essays about the following notable Argentine painters of the 20th century: Hugo de Marziani, Héctor Giuffré, Ricardo Laham, Mara Marini, Carlos Alberto Salatino, Pablo Suárez, Juan Lascano.

CLU   CtY   CU-S   ICA   IU   NIC   NmU   OU   TxU   WU

61   Trostiné, Rodolfo.   El grabado en la Argentina durante el período hispánico.   Buenos Aires: Talleres Gráficos San Pablo, 1949.   47 p.   28 cm.
History of engraving in Argentina during the 18th and early 19th centuries, with biographical sketches about the following artists: Juan Antonio Callejas y Sandoval, Pedro Carmona, Manuel Rivera, Juan de Dios Rivera, Manuel P. Núñez de Ibarra.

IU   NIC

62   _____.   La pintura en las provincias argentinas siglo XIX.   Santa Fe: Imprenta de la Universidad, 1950.   53 p.   24 cm.
Essay on 19th century painting in Argentina's provinces.   Varying amounts of biographical data, concentrating on artistic activities, are included for the following: Manuel Pablo Núñez de Ibarra, Félix Revol, Amadeo Gras, Guillermo F. Olivar, José Fonteneau, José Hidalgo, Secundino Salinas, Héctor Facino, Josefa Díaz y Clusellas, Ignacio Baz, Gaspar Palacio y Dolz, Genaro Pérez, Gregorio Torres, Franklin Rawson, Ataliva Lima, Procesa Sarmiento de Lenoir, Manuel Olascoaga.

IU

63   Veinte Pintores y Escultores, Buenos Aires.   20 [i.e. Veinte] pintores y escultores, año 1957.   8. exposición, Van Riel, Galería de Arte.   Buenos Aires, 1957.   Unpaged.   26 cm.
An exhibit of Argentine painting.   Includes biographical sketches on the following painters and sculptors of the 20th century: Julián Pedro Althabe, Luis Orestes Balduzzi, Julio Barragán, Luis Barragán, Oscar Capristo, Florencio Garavaglia, Noemí Gerstein, Naum Goijman, Ideal Sánchez, Fernando Iraolagoitía, Naum Knop, Juan Carlos Labourdette, Fernando López Anaya, Aurelio Macchi, Febo Martí, Primaldo Mónaco, Rodolfo Morelli, Rafael Onetto, Orlando Pierri, Bruno Venier, Josefina Zamudio.

CU   IU   MH

64   Virginia Museum of the Fine Arts, Richmond.   A Comprehensive Exhibition of the Contemporary Art of Argentina.   January 16-February 26, 1940.   Richmond: The Virginia Museum of Fine Arts, 1940.   37 p.   Portraits.   23 cm.
An exhibit of Argentine art, including biographical notes about the following artists of the late 19th and early 20th centuries: Hilda Ainscough, Orestes Assali, Pompeyo Audivert, Aquiles Badi, Laerte Baldini, Juan Antonio Ballester Peña, Jorge de Beristayn, Antonio Berni, Alfredo Bigatti, Alejandro Bonome, Guillermo Butler, Horacio Butler, Rodolfo V. Castagna, Emilio Centurión, Eugenio Daneri, Adolfo De Ferrari, Nicolás Antonio de San Luis, Francisco de Santo, Pedro Domínguez Neira, Juan Carlos Faggioli, Luis Falcini, José Fioravanti, Raquel Forner, Alfredo Gramajo Gutiérrez, Arturo Gerardo Gustavino, Alfredo Guido, Gastón Jarry, Jorge Larco, Gonzalo Leguizamón Pondal, Próspero López Buchardo, Guillermo Martínez Sóliman, W. Melgarejo Muñoz, Adolfo Montero, Ricardo Juan Musso, Emilio Pettourutti, Donato Antonio Proietto, Roberto Ramaugué, Luis C. Rovatti, Helmice Margarita Saforcada, Ernesto M. Scotti, César Sforza, Raúl Soldi, Jorge Soto Acébal, María Mercedes

Rodríguez de Soto Acébal, Ernesto Soto Avendaño, Troiano Troiani, Demetrio Urruchúa, Lía Correa Morales de Yrurtia, Rogelio Yrurtia, Rodrigo Bonome.

DLC   IU   NNC   OC1MA   Or   PPD   TxU   ViU

65   Zabatta, Gioconda de.   16 [i.e. Dieciséis] pintores de Avellaneda.   Avellaneda: Artes Gráficas, 1969.   139 p.   Portraits.   21 cm.
      Alphabetically arranged biographical essays, accompanied by portraits, on the following painters of the Argentine city of Avellaneda: Antonia T. L. Artel, Alberto Castro Couso, José Mario Cecconi, Juan Alberto Danza Elizalde, María D'Avola, Lucía Victoria Farao, Héctor Garmendia, Francisco López Grela, José Luis Menghi, Teresa Mozzón, Rafael Muñoz, José Pérez Sanin, Alfredo Riese, Narciso C. Segato, Carlos Guido Spano, Dante A. Tozzi.

CLU   CSt   CU-SB   FU   IU   MN   MoSW   NIC
NNC   NSyU   TxU   WU

See also entries 154, 768.

ART--DICTIONARIES, ENCYCLOPEDIAS, and "WHO'S WHO"

66   Merlino, Adrián.   Diccionario de artistas plásticos de la Argentina, siglos XVIII-XIX-XX.   Buenos Aires, 1954.   433 p.   23 cm.
      Biographical dictionary of individuals involved in the plastic arts in Argentina from the 18th-mid-20th centuries.

CLU   CtY   CU   DLC   DPU   FU   GU   InU   IU
MB   N   NN   OrU   TxU

BIOGRAPHY (MISCELLANEOUS)

67   Acuña, Angel.   Figuras correntinas.   Buenos Aires: Casa Editora "Coni," 1949.   57 p.   Portraits.   23 cm.
      Detailed biographical information, accompanied by portraits, of the following 20th-century Argentineans from the province of Corrientes: Alfredo Ferreira, Valentín Virasoro, Plácido Martínez.

DLC   IU

68   Album nacional (de la) República Argentina: galería de hombres públicos de actualidad comprendiendo: poder ejecutivo de la Nación, parlamento, ejército y armada.   Basada en documentos oficiales y en hechos históricos de nuestras guerras.   Fundador: Antonio Américo Díaz.   Director: Eduardo González.   Ed. de lujo.   Buenos Aires, 1902-1903.   288 p.   Portraits.   36 x 26 cm.
      Biographical sketches, accompanied by portraits, of Argentine public figures in the early 20th century.   Issued in parts consecutively numbered.   Information includes birth-place, important dates, and contributions to the development of the country.

IEN   IU

69   Album presidencial de la reorganización nacional 1916-1922; síntesis histórica de la vida argentina durante aquel período.   Buenos Aires, 1922.   Unpaged.   Portraits.   27 x 38 cm.
      Album of photographs and essays depicting life in Argentina from 1916-1922.   Biographical sketches, accompanied by portraits, of the following politicians and businessmen of the time: Elpidio González, José Giovane, Leonardo Costas, Héctor Bergalli, Santiago Pertini, Julio E. Neumeyer, Saturnino J. García Anido, Horacio Casco, Pedro Bidegain, Andrés F. Ventre, Honorio Pueyrredón, Pablo Torello, Domingo E. Salaberry, José S. Salinas, Julio Moreno, Gil Ferreyra Sosa, Delfor del Valle, José Luis Cantilo, Juan Quijano, José Néstor Lencinas, Miguel Rodal, Carlos Washington Lencinas, Bautista Gargantini, José Víctor Aldasoro, Antonio Maciel, Camilo Pirosanto, Vicente Mancino, Cecilio Juanto.

NcD   NIC

70   Alfaro, Rogelio E.   Who's Who on the Postage Stamps of Argentina.   Rev. ed. by Albert F. Kunze.   Washington: Pan American Union, 1950.   41 p.   27 cm.   (Pan American Union.   Philatelic series, v. 1).
      Biographical sketches of individuals who played an important part in the national development of Argentina and on whom the government has bestowed the honor of choosing their portraits for the decoration of her postal stamps.

DLC   IU

71   Allende, Andrés R.   Los orígenes del pueblo de Belgrano, 1855-1862.   La Plata: Dirección de Impresiones Oficiales, 1958.   72 p.   27 cm.   (Publicaciones del Archivo Histórico de la Provincia de Buenos Aires.   Contribución a la historia de los pueblos de la Provincia de Buenos Aires, v. 31).
      A history of Belgrano, located in Buenos Aires province, covering the period from 1855 to 1862.   Scattered biographical information is included for many people associated with this town.

CtY   FU   IEdS   InU   IU   MH   NIC   NN   PPT
TxU   ULC   ViU

72   Amadeo, Octavio Ramón.   Doce argentinos; con un prólogo del doctor Angel Acuña.   Buenos Aires: Editorial Cimera, 1945.   238 p.   Portraits.   21 cm.
      Detailed biographical information on the following 19th- and 20th-century Argentineans: Dalmacio Vélez Sársfield, Mamerto Esquiú, Vicente López y Planes, Juan Vucetich, Pedro de

BIOGRAPHY (MISCELLANEOUS)

Mendoza, Justo José de Urquiza, Aristóbulo del Valle, José de San Martín, Domingo French, José Manuel Estrada, Leopoldo Lugones, Lisandro de la Torre.

CoDU CU DLC IU TxU

73 Anadón, Carlos A., and María del Carmen Mura-ture de Badaracco. La colectividad italiana en Victoria E. Ríos. Victoria, 1976. 76 p. Portraits. 21 cm.

A history of the Italian immigrant contri-bution during the 19th century to the develop-ment of the Argentine city of Victoria. Biog-raphical information is given for many people in all fields of endeavor, with the following being particularly emphasized: José Garibaldi, Luis María Gebiedes, Eugenio Albornoz, Vicente Atencio, Antonio Luví (Lubí), Próspero Mar-ciani, Santiago Marciani, Angel Piallo (Pia-ggio), Bartolomé Badín, Joaquín Vivanco, José Copello, Abraham Bartoloni, Pascual Bartoloni, Ciro Placo, Vicente Vela, Miguel Lanieri, Nicholas Elena, Esteban Vaccarezza, Domingo Buzzi, Conrado Maggiorini, Angel B. Balbi.

NmU TxU

74 Angueira, Juan R. El pago de los Lobos; noti-cias y apuntes. La Plata: Taller de Impre-siones Oficiales, 1937. 80 p. Portraits. 27 cm. (Publicaciones del Archivo Histórico de la Provincia de Buenos Aires. Contribu-ción a la historia de los pueblos de la pro-vincia de Buenos Aires, v. 13).

A history of Lobos, located in Buenos Aires province, covering the 18th and 19th centuries, and including brief biographical information for many people associated with this municipality. Among those featured are Manuel Antonio Caminos, Dionisio Urquiola, Domingo Soriano Arévalo, Antonio Cascallares.

CoDU DLC DPU ICN IU MH NcU NN

75 Antonio, Jorge. ¿Y ahora qué? Buenos Aires: Ediciones Militia, 1966. 446 p. 21 cm.

An autobiographical essay focusing on the events that took place in Argentina from 1943 to 1955, and including biographical informa-tion of varying amounts about many individuals with whom the author came into contact. Among those are José María Vila Melo, Marcial V. González, Ernesto Florit, Miguel Araujo, Raúl Matera, Juan Duarte, César Fernández Albariño.

AU CLU CSt DPU FU IaU IU MoU MU
NcD NjR NNC NSyU PPiU ScU TxU

76 Arena, José; Julio H. Cortés; and Alberto Valverde. Ensayo histórico del Partido de Olavarría. Olavarría: Municipalidad de Ola-varría, 1967. 409 p. Portraits. 24 cm.

A history of Olavarría, Argentina, cover-ing the period from the 18th through the 20th centuries, and including scattered biographical information for many people associated with this district.

CLSU CU CU-SB FU IaU ICU InU IU
KU MB MiU MU NIC NmLcU NNC TxU ViU

77 Argentine Republic. Dirección General de Estadística. Censo de los empleados admini-strativos, funcionarios judiciales y personal docente de la República Argentina correspon-diente al 31 de diciembre de 1892. Compila-ción hecha por el Sr. Alejandro Lucadamo, auxiliado por los Sres. Casimiro Prieto Costa y Alfredo Lucadamo. Buenos Aires: Compañía Sud-americana de Billetes de Banco, 1893. 381 p. 27 cm.

Register of over 7,000 Argentine government employees as of December 31, 1892, with infor-mation on age, marital status, nationality, salary, positions held, length of time served, and city of employment.

DLC IU(film)

78 Avellá, José Antonio. Anécdotas de los grandes hombres argentinos, primera serie; contribu-ción a la cultura popular. Buenos Aires: Ar-tes Gráficas Gayo, 1934. 92 p. 18 cm.

A collection of short anecdotes on the following notable Argentines from all walks of life: Domingo Faustino Sarmiento, José de San Martín, Juan Gregorio de Las Heras, Juan La-valle, Gregorio Aráoz de La Madrid, Justo José de Urquiza, Juan Bautista Azopardo, Lucio Man-silla, Dalmacio Vélez Sársfield, Bernardo de Irigoyen, Manuel Augusto Montes de Oca, Nico-lás Avellaneda, Adolfo Alsina, Julio A. Roca, Carlos Pellegrini, Ramón J. Cárcano, Belisario Roldán, Estanislao del Campo, José C. Paz, Pedro B. Palacios (Almafuerte, pseud.), Manuel Láinez, Ignacio Fotheringham, José Manuel Eizaguirre, José Figueroa Alcorta, Martiniano Leguizamón, Rainerio J. Lugones, Diego Fer-nandez Espiro.

DLC

79 Avellaneda, Nicolás, Pres. Argentine Republic, 1837-1885. Escritos y discursos. Edited by Juan M. Garro. Buenos Aires: Compañía Sud-americana de Billetes de Banco, 1910. 12 v. Portraits. 23 cm.

Collection of letters and essays by and about notable Argentines of the 19th century, with biographical notes about the following: Nicolás Avellaneda, Domingo Faustino Sarmiento, Facundo Zuviría, Juan Chassaing, Mateo Luque, Julián S. de Aguero, Pablo Groussac, Mamerto Esquíu, Antonio Gómez, Juan Sala, Mr. Berryer, Bernardino Rivadavia, Arzobispo Escalada, Juan Mariano Larsen, Adolfo Alsina, Amancio Alcorta, Dalmacio Vélez Sársfield.

CtY CU DLC IaU IU MW NcD NcU NN
OCl

80 Avila, Julio P. La ciudad arribena: Tucumán, 1810-1816. Tucumán: Talleres Gráficos de la Gaceta, 1920. 474 p. Portraits. 22 cm.

History of the Argentine province of Tucu-mán from 1810 to 1816 covering such areas as commerce, industry, politics, and economics. In addition, limited biographical material on over 150 families of the time is included.

IU

81 Barreiro Ortiz, Carlos. <u>Provincia de San Luis</u>; diccionario, guía, manual. Buenos Aires: Centro Puntano, 1981. 198 p. 18 cm.

A guide to the Argentine province of San Luis. Includes biographical sketches of the following contemporary figures from all walks of life, associated with it: Ramón Amado Abrahim, Esteban P. Adaro, Julio A. Aguirre Celiz, Carlos Alric, Alberto Arancibia Rodríguez, Alfredo Arancibia Rodríguez, Eugenio Joaquín Arandia, Juan Alejandro Barbeito, Julián Barroso Rodríguez (father), Julián Barroso Rodríguez (son), Guillermo A. Belgrano Rawson, Onofre Betbeder, Adeodato Berrondo, Mauricio P. Daract, Nicolás A. Digennaro, Alberto Domenicone, Víctor W. Endeiza, Teodoro Pablo Fels, Rodolfo S. Follari, Galo Gregorio Funes, Teófilo I. Gatica, León Guillet, Víctor Segundo Guiñazú, Matías Laborda Ibarra, Laureano Landaburu, Roberto Marcelo Levingston, Eleodoro Lobos, Franklin Lucero, José Raúl Lucero, Víctor C. Lucero, Alberto Lucero Funes, Fortunata Funes de Funes, Ricardo Marambio, Eriberto Mendoza, Jerónimo R. Mendoza, Toribio Mendoza, Toribio D. Mendoza, Epifanio Mora Olmedo, Manuel Féliz Origone, Carlos Washington Pastor, Miguel B. Pastor, Reynaldo A. Pastor, Lindor L. Quiroga, Agustín Rodríguez Jurado, Benigno Rodríguez Jurado (father), Benigno Rodríguez Jurado (son), Adolfo Rodríguez Saa, José E. Rodríguez Saa, Ricardo Rodríguez Saa, Umberto Rodríguez Saa, Hipólito Saa, Juan Carlos Saa, Teófilo Saa, Gilberto Sosa Loyola, Carlos Eduardo Sosa Reboyras, Diógenes Taboada, Edmundo Tello Cornejo, Sadoc Vidal Luna, José Rafael Videla, Juan Ovidio Zavala, Juan T. Zavala, Gilberto A. Zavala Ortiz, Miguel Angel Zavala Ortiz, Ricardo Zavala Ortiz, Teobaldo Zavala Ortiz, Carlos Juan Zavala Ortiz.

IU

82 Batolla, Octavio C. <u>Los primeros ingleses en Buenos Aires</u>. Buenos Aires: Editorial Muro, 1928. 178 p. 23 cm.

An account of the actions of prominent British people in Argentina from 1780 to 1830. Biographical information, as well as portraits in many cases, are included for the following: Guillermo Brown, Juan O'Higgins, Guillermo Miller, Guillermo Bathurst, Roberto Gibson, Carlos Bauness, Santiago Jorge Bynon, Isaac Thompson, Juan King, Guillermo Roberto Mason, Oliverio Russell, Enrique Guillermo Parker, Francisco Drummond, Tomás Notter, Elías Smith, Guillermo Enrique Gradville, Roberto Stacy, Carlos Robinson, Juan Parish Robertson, Carlos P. Lumb.

AzU CU DLC IU NcU

83 Bazán, Armando Raúl. <u>Historia de La Rioja</u>. Buenos Aires: Editorial Plus Ultra, 1979. 607 p. 20 cm.

A historical essay about the Argentine province of La Rioja (16th century through the 1930s), including biographical information of varying amounts on the following leading figures: Juan Núñez de Prado, Juan Ramírez de Velasco, Mateo Rozas de Oquendo, Chalimín, Luis de Cabrera, Felipe de Albornoz, Pedro de Bohórquez, Juan Bazán de Cabrera, Pedro Ignacio de Castro Barros, Diego de Barrenechea, Nicolás Dávila, Juan Facundo Quiroga, Manuel Dorrego, Juan Antonio Carmona, Hipólito Tello, Vicente Mota, Manuel Vicente Bustos, Nicanor Molinas, Domingo Antonio Villafañe, Angel Vicente Peñaloza (El Chacho, pseud.), Julio Campos, Felipe Varela, Benjamín de la Vega, Pedro Gordillo, Rubén Ocampo, Vicente Almandos Almonacid, Francisco Vicente Bustos, Baltazar Jaramillo, Jamín Ocampo, Joaquín V. González, Guillermo San Román, Leónidas Carreño, Wenceslao Frías, Guillermo Dávila San Román, Gaspar Gómez, Tomás Vera Barros, Benjamín Rincón, Adolfo Lanús, Juan Zacarías Agüero Vera.

IU

84 Beccar Varela, Adrián. <u>Plazas y calles de Buenos Aires</u>: significación histórica de sus nombres. Buenos Aires: Imprenta Mercatali, 1936. 2 v. 24 cm.

A collection of 1,900 biographical sketches of individuals for whom streets and plazas in Buenos Aires, Argentina, have been named. Alphabetical index of names.

CtY DLC DPU IU NN OCl PPULC PU

85 Berra de Massey, Virginia. <u>Semblanzas argentinas</u> (Bosquejos biográficos). Buenos Aires: J. Perrotti, 1917. 108 p. Portraits. 21 cm.

A collection of biographical sketches alphabetically arranged about the following notable Argentineans: Juan Bautista Alberdi, Manuel Alberti, Juan A. Alvarez de Arenales, Miguel de Azcuénaga, Manuel Belgrano, Luis Beltrán, Antonio Luis Beruti, Guillermo Brown, Juan José Castelli, Feliciano Antonio Chiclana, Manuel Dorrego, Domingo French, Deán Gregorio Funes, Cayetano Grimau y Gálvez, Rufino Guido Juan María Gutiérrez, Juan Larrea, Juan Lavalle, Santiago Liniers, Vicente López, Domingo Matheu, Mariano Moreno, Mariano Necochea, Francisco A. Ortiz de Ocampo, Juan José Paso, José María Paz, Juan Esteban Pedernera, Juan Martín de Pueyrredón, Bernardino Rivadavia, Nicolás Rodríguez Peña, José Rondeau, Cornelio Saavedra, José de San Martín, Justo de Santa María de Oro, Domingo Faustino Sarmiento, Hipólito Vieytes, María de los Remedios Escalada de San Martín, María Sánchez de Thompson, Isabel Calvimontes de Agrelo, Francisca Silveyra de Ibarrola, María Eugenia Escalada de Demaría, Juana Azurduy de Padilla (Bolivian), Manuela Pedraza, Juana Manso.

DLC

BIOGRAPHY (MISCELLANEOUS)

86 Berthelemy, Carlos Jorge. <u>La sombra del cón-</u><u>dor</u>: autobiografía. Buenos Aires: Editorial Stilcograf, 1976. 244 p. 20 cm.

An autobiographical essay with information on Carlos Jorge Berthelemy and his parents, Carlos Raymond Berthelemy and María de las Mercedes Prades Sanz.

OU

87 Bianchi de Terragni, Adelina. <u>Historia de</u> <u>Rafaela</u> (ciudad santafesina), 1881-1940. Santa Fe: Librería y Editorial Colmegna, 1971. 332 p. 22 cm.

A history of Rafaela, Argentina, covering the period from 1881 to 1940, including scattered biographical information, as well as a few portraits, for many people associated with this city. Among those featured are Rafaela Rodríguez de Egusquiza, Bartolomé Podio, Juan Operto, José Buffa, Francisco Lorenzatti, Guillermo Grande, Antonio Chiaraviglio, Guadenico Mainardi, Ataliva Roca, Juan Zanetti, Guillermo Lehmann, José Vaschetto, Juan Soldano, Nicolás Caciolo, Valentín Kaiser, Luis Maggi, Carlos Ercole, Manuel Menchaca, Manuel Giménez, Eduardo Chiarella, Nicolás Gutiérrez.

CFS CLU CtY CU-SB IaU ICU IU KU
MU NcU NjP NmLcU NN NNC TxU WU

88 Birabent, Mauricio. <u>Chivilcoy</u>, la región de las chacras. La Plata: Taller de Impresiones Oficiales, 1941. 136 p. Portraits. 27 cm. (Publicaciones del Archivo Histórico de la Provincia de Buenos Aires. Contribución a la historia de los pueblos de la provincia de Buenos Aires, v. 19).

A history of Chivilcoy, Argentina, located in Buenos Aires province, covering the period from colonial times through the 19th century. Scattered biographical information and portraits are included for many people associated with this city. The following are emphasized: Federico Soares, Manuel Villarino, Adolfo Alsina, Juana Manso.

DLC IU MH NIC NN TxU

89 Bischoff, Efraín U. <u>Historia de Córdoba</u>: cuatro siglos. Buenos Aires: Editorial Plus Ultra, 1977. 720 p. Portraits. 20 cm. (Colección: Historia de nuestras provincias, v. 2).

A history of the Argentine province of Córdoba covering the period from discovery to the present day. Scattered biographical information, as well as a few portraits, are included for many people, particularly political leaders. Among those featured are Francisco de Aguirre, Jerónimo Luis de Cabrera, Fernando de Trejo y Sanabria, Sobre Monte, Nicolás Pérez del Viso, José González de Rivera, Victorino Rodríguez, Juan Gutiérrez de la Concha, Gregorio Funes, Santiago Carrera, Francisco Xavier de Viana, Francisco Ortiz de Ocampo, José Javier Díaz, Ambrosio Funes, Manuel Antonio de Castro, José Miguel Carrera, Francisco

Ramírez, Juan Bautista Bustos, José María Paz, Manuel López, Alejo Carmen Guzmán, Roque Ferreyra, Justiniano Posse, Félix de la Peña, Miguel Juárez Celman, Antonio del Viso, Mamerto Esquiú, Gregorio Ignacio Gavier, Ambrosio Olmos, José Echenique, Marcos N. Juárez, Eleázar Garzón, Julio Astrada, Cleto Peña, Donaciano del Campillo, Manuel Alvarez, José Vicente de Olmos, José A. Ortiz y Herrera, Julio A. Roca, José A. Ceballos, Carlos Ibarguren, Enrique Torino, Pedro J. Frías, Justo Salazar Collado, León S. Scasso, Alberto Guglielmone, Juan Carlos Díaz Cisneros, Argentino S. Auchter, Aristóbulo Vargas Belmonte, Juan Ignacio San Martín, Atilio Antinucci, Raúl F. Lucini, Arturo Orlando Zanichelli, Francisco Antonio de Larrechea, Jorge Bermúdez Emparanza, Justo Páez Molina, Roberto Huerta, Bernardo Bas.

IU

90 Blancas, Alberto. <u>Anécdotas y recuerdos</u>. Buenos Aires: Editorial Tor, 1936. 186 p. 18 cm.

A collection of anecdotes about the following notable Argentineans: Eduardo Wilde, Lucio V. Mansilla, José Ignacio Garmendia, Pedro Goyena, Rufino de Elizalde, Manuel Láinez, Eugenio Garzón, Luis Goyena, Pedro Rivas Acuña, Ignacio Pirovano, Juan Bautista Gil, Federico Errazuriz.

DLC FJUNF NcU

91 _____. <u>Recordando el pasado</u>. Buenos Aires: Editorial Tor, 1934. 186 p. 19 cm.

A collection of sketches, mostly anecdotal, about the following Argentine figures and others associated with the history of Argentina: Nicolás Avellaneda, Domingo Faustino Sarmiento, Juan Bautista Alberdi, Julio A. Roca, Bernardo de Irigoyen, Adolfo Alsina, Roque Sáenz Peña, Carlos Guido Spano, Manuel Augusto Montes de Oca, Manuel Blancas, Mariano Casanova, Rampolla de Tindaro, Nicolás Granada, Guillermo D. Junor, Eduardo Strauss.

CoU DLC NcU TxU

92 Bonastre, Valerio. <u>Figuras legendarias</u> (del pasado correntino). Reseña biográfica por César P. Zoni. Buenos Aires: Imprenta López, 1968. 129 p. 20 cm.

Biographical essays on 19th- and 20th-century Argentineans from the province of Corrientes. Special attention is paid to the following individuals' contributions to life in the province: Valerio Bonastre, Juan Mateo de Arriola, Bernabé Antonio Esquivel (Chiquillo, pseud.), José Félix Leyes, Alberto Villegas, Manuel Antonio Vallejos (El Pájaro, pseud.).

CLSU CLU CSt CtY IU KU MB MoSW
NBuU NcU NIC OU TxU WU

93 _____. <u>Varones correntinos</u>; José Simón García de Cossío, Juan Nepomuceno de Goytía, José Francisco Acosta, Pedro Díaz Colodrero, Joaquín Madariaga, Juan Gregorio Acuña, Desiderio Sosa, Plácido Martínez; prólogo de monseñor Dionisio R. Napal. Buenos Aires: Librería y Editorial "La Facultad," Bernabé y Cía., 1936. 232 p. Portraits. 21 cm.

    Collection of biographical essays on 19th-century citizens of the Argentine province of Corrientes. Dates, birthplace, and career achievements are provided for José S. García de Cossío, Juan Manuel Nepomuceno de Goytía, José Francisco Acosta, Pedro Díaz Colodrero, Joaquín Madariaga, Juan Gregorio Acuña (Mocito, pseud.), Desiderio Sosa, Plácido Martínez.

    CoU DLC IU

94 Borja, J. P. de. <u>Album biográfico</u> en homenaje a los nuevos representantes del pueblo de la capital elevados por la voluntad nacional al H. Congreso de la Nación. Editor: J. P. de Borja. Buenos Aires: J. Tragant y Cía., 1904. 55 p. Portraits. 27 x 38 cm.

    A collection of short biographical essays emphasizing the professional accomplishments of the following notable Argentineans from all fields of endeavor and including members of the Congress: Benito Villanueva, Mariano de Vedia, Eliseo Cantón, Alfredo L. Palacios, Manuel Carlés, Manuel de Iriondo, Pedro M. Cernadas, Francisco J. Oliver, Carlos Delcasse, Rufino Varela Ortiz, Luis Peluffo, Pedro O. Luro, Pedro N. Arata, A. F. Hobet, Carlos Malbrán, Marcial Quiroga, Manuel T. Podestá, Francisco Cobos, Pedro Lagleyze, J. Manuel Irízar, Juan B. Señorans, Cándido González, Manuel Beguerastein, Juan Ferrari, Ambrosio L. Cavo, Cecilio López, Juan Divito, Carlos Seminario, Pascual Luis Oliverio, Téofilo A. Moret, Carlos M. Amaro, Rafael Calzada, Manuel García Fernández, Martín A. Martínez, Gervasio J. Granel, Antonio del Pino, Tomás R. Cullen, Francisco Medina, Zoilo Cantón, Marco M. Avellaneda, Carlos Ibarguren, Carlos M. Coll, Carlos Meyer Pellegrini, Arturo de Gainza, Sylla J. Monsegur, Luis A. Huergo, Carlos del Molino Torres, Miguel P. Malarín, José C. Rodríguez, Conrado Hersfeld, A. Watson Hutton, Cipriano Giménez.

    IU NN

95 Bosch Vinelli, Julia Beatriz. <u>Historia de Entre Ríos</u>. Buenos Aires: Editorial Plus Ultra, 1978. 334 p. Portraits. 20 cm.

    A history of the Argentine province of Entre Ríos, covering the years 1520-1969. Scattered biographical information is included for many people (approximately 1,400 names) from all walks of life, with particular emphasis on the following: Pedro José Agrelo, Apolinario Almada, Dionisio Francisco Alvarez, Carlos de Alvear, Olegario V. Andrade, José Francisco Antelo, José Miguel Carrera, Evaristo Carriego, Salvador M. del Carril, Tomás Cáceres, Gervasio Correa, Antonio Crespo,

Domingo Cullen, Antonio Cuyás y Sampere, José Lino Churruarín, Santiago Derqui, Jose María Domínguez, Alcídes D'Orbigny, Leónidas Echagüe, Pascual Echagüe, Atanasio Eguiguren, Pedro Espino, Ramón Febre, Pedro Ferré, Mariano Fragueiro, José Miguel Galán, Miguel Gerónimo Galarza, José Simón García de Cossio, Mateo García de Zúñiga, Eugenio Garzón, Juan Garrigo, Francisco S. Gigena, Servando Gómez, Pedro M. González, Alfredo M. du Graty, Juan María Gutiérrez, José Hernández, Sabá Z. Hernández, José Eusebio Hereñú, Manuel Hornos, Camilo Idoate, Alberto Larroque, Eduardo Laurencena, Miguel M. Laurencena, Juan Lavalle, Carlos Federico Lecor, Onésimo Leguizamón, Manuel Leiva, Estanislao López, Ricardo López Jordán (father), Ricardo López Jordán (son), Salvador Macía, Joaquín Madariaga, Juan Madariaga, Lucio Mansilla, Juan A. Mantero, Benigno T. Martínez, Blas Martínez, Anacleto Medina, Enrique F. Mihura, Bartolomé Mitre, Nicanor Molinas, Martín de Moussy, Manuel Navarro, Manuel Oribe, Domingo de Oro, Toribio Ortiz, Juan José Paso, José María Paz, César B. Pérez Colman, Luis J. de la Peña, Alejo Peyret, Blas José Pico, Gregorio Piris, Gervasio A. de Posadas, Carlos María Querencio, Mariano Querencio, Eduardo Racedo, Francisco Ramírez, Bernardino Rivadavia, Fructuoso Rivera, Julio A. Roca, Tomás Rocamora, Felipe Rodríguez, José Rondeau, Juan M. de Rosas, Martín Ruiz Moreno, Antonio Sagarna, José Joaquín Sagastume, Gregorio Samaniego, Domingo F. Sarmiento, Pedro Scalabrini, Juan Francisco Seguí, Juan José Antonio Segura, León Solas, Raúl L. Uranga, Manuel A. Urdinarrain, Cipriano J. de Urquiza, Diógenes J. de Urquiza, Josef de Urquiza, Justo José de Urquiza, Crespín Velázquez, José Ignacio Vera, Antonio de Vera Mujica, Juan José Vértiz, Benjamín Victorica, Benjamín Virasoro, Benjamín Yancey, Vicente Zapata. Alphabetical index of names.

    IU

96 _____. <u>Urquiza y su tiempo</u>. Buenos Aires: Editorial Universitaria de Buenos Aires, 1971. 786 p. 23 cm. (Biblioteca de América. Temas).

    An account of the life and times of Justo José de Urquiza, including scattered biographical information for the following people: Juan Bautista Alberti, Valentín Alsina, Evaristo Carriego, Salvador M. del Carril, Juan Coronado, Antonio Crespo, Antonio Cuyás y Sampere, William D. Christie, Santiago Derqui, José María Domínguez, Pascual Echagüe, Angel Elías, Rufino de Elizalde, Pedro Ferré, Venancio Flores, Mariano Fragueiro, José Miguel Galán, Eugenio Garzón, Tomás Guido, Juan María Gutiérrez, Carlos Heras, Manuel Herrera y Obes, Hilario Lagos, José Gregorio Lezama, Carlos Antonio López, Ricardo Lóñez Jordán, Lucio Mansilla, Bartolomé Mitre, Nicanor Molinas, Juan Francisco Monguillot, Vicente Montero, Lucas Moreno, Manuel Navarro, Manuel Oribe, Nicasio Oroño, José María Paz, Marcos Paz, Luis José de la Peña, Juan Pujol, Juan M. de Rosas, Martín Ruiz Moreno, Domingo F. Sarmiento,

BIOGRAPHY (MISCELLANEOUS)

Juan Francisco Seguí, Manuel A. Urdinarrain, Diogénes J. de Urquiza, Justo José de Urquiza, Benjamín Victorica, Benjamín Virasoro. Alphabetical index of names.

AzU CaBVaU CLS CSt CtY CU CU-SC
DGU FMU FU ICU InU IU KyLoU MdU
MH MiDW MnU MoSW NBuU NcD NcU NIC
NmU NN NSyU OKU OrU PPT PSt TNJ
TxU UU WU

97 Botta, Vicente Raúl. <u>Historia de Zárate</u>, 1689-1909. La Plata, 1948. 237 p. 28 cm. Portraits. (Publicaciones del Archivo Histórico de la Provincia de Buenos Aires. Contribución a la historia de los pueblos de la provincia de Buenos Aires, v. 24).

A history of Zárate, located in Buenos Aires province, and covering the period from 1689 to 1909. Biographical information is included for many people associated with this town. The following are particularly featured: Francisco Pérez de Burgas, Francisco de Manzanárez, Hernán Suárez Maldonado, Sebastián de Orduña, José Antonio de Otalora y Larrazábal, Gonzalo de Zárate, Pedro Anta y Cabrera, José Antonio Anta y Cabrera, Manuel José de la Torre y Soler, Gregorio José de Quirno y González Noriega, Ireneo E. Collado.

DLC FU IU TxU ViU

98 Braccialarghe, Comunardo. <u>L'epopea del lavoro italiano nella Repubblica Argentina</u>. Par Folco Testena, pseud. Milano: Fratelli Bocca, 1938. 161 p. 19 cm. (La civiltà ontemporanea, v. 27).

A collection of biographical sketches of Italians associated with the history and cultural development of Argentina during the 19th century and beginning of the 20th. Those particularly featured are Silvino Olivieri, Filippo Caronti, Pietro de Angelis, Pietro Carta, Girolamo Lavagna, Clemente Onelli, Emilio Zuccarini, Basilio Cittadini, Antonio Devoto, Giuseppe Guazzone, Antonio Tomba, Tomaso Ambrosetti.

DLC

99 Braun Menéndez, Armando. <u>Pequeña historia fueguina</u>. Con ilustraciones de Indalecio Pereyra ejecutadas según documentos originales. Buenos Aires: D. Viau y Cía., 1939. 315 p. 19 cm.

A history of Tierra del Fuego, covering the period from preconquest through the 19th century. Brief scattered biographical information is included for many people associated with this region. More substantial information, accompanied by portraits, is given for the following: Allen Francis Gardiner, George Packenham Despard, Waite H. Stirling, Tomás Bridges, José Fagnano, Julio Popper, Luis Piedra Buena, Augusto Lasserre.

CU DLC IU NcU PPULC

100 _____. <u>Pequeña historia patagónica</u>: Orllie Antoine 1er, rey de la Araucanía y Patagonia. Vicisitudes y miserias del primer ensayo de colonización en Santa Cruz. Alrededor de Piedra Buena. Con ilustraciones de Juan Pablo Laverdet ejecutadas según documentos originales. Buenos Aires: Viau y Zona, 1936. 293 p. 19 cm.

A short history of Patagonia covering the period from the mid-1850s through the year 1879. Scattered biographical information, accompanied by portraits in some cases, is included for many people associated with this region. Those particularly featured are Orllie Antoine de Tounens, Ernesto Rouquaud, Luis Piedra Buena.

DLC ICU IU NcU

101 _____. <u>El reino de la Araucania y Patagonia</u>. Buenos Aires: Emecé Editores, 1945. 86 p. Portraits. 18 cm. (Colección Buen Aire, v. 71).

A history of the Patagonian territory during the 19th century, including scattered biographical information, as well as portraits in a few cases, on many people associated with this region. Particular emphasis is given to the following: Orllie-Antoine de Tounens, Cornelio Saavedra, Alberto Blest Gana.

CU DLC ICarbS NcU TxU

102 Bucich, Antonio Juan. <u>Esquema de las generaciones artísticas y literarias boquenses</u>. Buenos Aires: Cuadernos de la Boca del Riachuelo, 1964. 38 p. 21 cm. (Cuadernos de La Boca del Riachuelo, v. 14-15).

A short cultural history of the La Boca neighborhood of Buenos Aires, covering the period from 1860 to 1940. Very brief scattered biographical information is included for many prominent writers, artists, and musicians from this area. The following are among those featured: Pedro Zonza Briano, Santiago Stagnaro, Hernani Mandolini.

CLU CSt CtY CU ICU IEN InU IU MH
MoSW NbU NcD NIC NSyU OU PPiU TxU
WU

103 Bucich Escobar, Ismael. <u>Buenos Aires, ciudad</u>; reseña histórica y descriptiva de la capital argentina desde su primera fundación hasta el presente, 1536-1936. Obra laureada por la Municipalidad de Buenos Aires. Nueva ed. rev. y puesta al día. Buenos Aires: Editorial Tor, 1936. 282 p. 23 cm.

A history of the city of Buenos Aires from its foundation in 1536 to the year 1936. Scattered biographical information is included within the text and in footnotes for many people who made some contribution to the development of this city. The following are particularly emphasized: Pedro de Mendoza, Juan de Garay, Manuel Alvarez, Francisco Victoria, Pedro de Cevallos, Juan José de Vértiz y Salcedo, Bernardino Rivadavia, Juan Manuel de

Rosas, Justo José de Urquiza, Bartolomé Mitre, Domingo F. Sarmiento, Nicolás Avellaneda, Julio A. Roca, Torcuato de Alvear, Antonio F. Crespo, Guillermo A. Cranwell, Francisco Seeber, Francisco P. Bollini, Miguel Cané, Federico Pinedo, Emilio V. Bunge, Francisco Alcobendas, Adolfo J. Bullrich, Alberto Casares, Carlos Roseti, Carlos T. de Alvear, Joaquín S. de Anchorena, Manuel J. Güiraldes, Joaquín Llambías, José Luis Cantilo, Juan B. Barneche, Carlos M. Noel, José Guerrico, Rómulo S. Naón.

CU DLC IU NcU

104 Buenos Aires. Museo Histórico Nacional.
<u>Memorias y autobiografías</u>. Buenos Aires:
Impr. de M. A. Rosas, 1910. 3 v. Portraits.
22 cm.
A collection of biographical essays of the following Argentinean figures from the early 19th century:
V. 1: Tomás Guido, Cornelio Saavedra, Manuel Belgrano, Santiago de Liniers y Bremond, Samuel Auchmuty, John Whitelocke, Pascual Ruiz Huidobro, Juan Martín de Pueyrredón, Bernardo O'Higgins, Juan Ramón Balcarce, Martín Rodríguez, Florencio Terrada, Francisco Antonio Ocampo, Gervasio Antonio Posadas, Miguel de Azcuénaga, Juan José Castelli, Juan Larrea, Ignacio Alvarez, Agustín Donado, Bernardo Monteagudo, Pedro José Agrelo, Hipólito Vieytes, Antonio Alvarez de Jonte, Feliciano A. Chiclana.
V. 2: Mariano Moreno, Manuel Moreno, Rubén de Celis, Ramón de Maya Villa Real, Santiago de Liniers y Bremond, Samuel Achmuty, Baltazar Hidalgo de Cisneros, Pedro José Agrelo, José Moldes, Hipólito Vieytes.
V. 3: Manuel Belgrano, Antonio Martínez, Manuel Artigas, Blas José Pico, Juan Ramón Balcarce, Juan Andrés Pueyrredón, Nicolás Villanueva, Carlos Antonio de Alvear, Miguel Güemes, Rufino Zado, Juan Lavalle, Manuel Dorrego, José de San Martín, Rufino Guido, Martín Rodríguez, Joaquín de la Pezuela, Antonio Quintanilla, Juan G. de las Heras, Bernardo O'Higgins, Antonio González Balcarce, Miguel Brayer, José Melián, José Matías Zapiola, Rudecindo Alvarado, Bernabé Aráoz, Esteban Romero, José de Espinar.

CU CtY DLC IU TxU

105 Busaniche, José Carmelo. <u>Hombres y hechos de Santa Fe</u> (primera serie). Santa Fe: Ediciones Colmegna, 1946. 202 p. 23 cm.
A collection of essays dealing with a variety of topics related to the Argentine province of Santa Fe, including biographical information on many people associated with this region. The following are emphasized: Encarnación Ezcurra de Rosas, Manuel Rodríguez y Sarmiento (physician), Juan Francisco Roldán, Estanislao López, Joaquín Sanguinetti, Juana del Pino y Vera Mujica de Rivadavia, Agustín Sañudo, Justo José de Urquiza, José de Amenábar. Alphabetical index of names.

CLU CSt CU-SB FU ICarbS IU MB MU
NN NNC OU TxU WU

106 _____. <u>Hombres y hechos de Santa Fe</u> (segunda serie). Santa Fe: El Litoral, 1955. 185 p. 24 cm.
A history of the Argentine province of Santa Fe, covering the period from the 17th century to the year 1853. Scattered biographical information of various amounts is included for many people associated with this region. The following are particularly featured: José Crespo, Gregoria Pérez, Francisco Javier de la Rosa, Mariano Vera, Félix de Azara, José López, Juan Manuel Roldán, Juan Basilio Roldán, Estanislao López. Alphabetical index of names.

CLU CoU CSt CU-SB DLC DPU FU
ICarbS IU MB MoSW NN NNC OU WaU
WU

107 _____. <u>Hombres y hechos de Santa Fe</u> (tercera serie). Santa Fe: Colmegna, 1970. 152 p. 20 cm.
A collection of essays dealing with a variety of topics related to Santa Fe, Argentina, including scattered biographical information on many people associated with this region. The following are emphasized: Alvaro José de Alzogaray, José de Amenábar, Pascual Díez de Andino, Estanislao López, Juan Francisco Seguí, Manuel de Toro y Villalobos, Mariano Vera. Alphabetical index of names.

IaU IU MU

108 Cabodi, Juan Jorge. <u>Historia de la ciudad de Rojas hasta 1784</u>. La Plata, 1950. 159 p. 26 cm. (Publicaciones del Archivo Histórico de la Provincia de Buenos Aires. Contribución a la historia de los pueblos de la provincia de Buenos Aires, v. 27).
A history of Rojas, located in Buenos Aires province, covering the period up to 1784. Scattered biographical information is given for many people associated with this city. Among them are Juan José de Vértiz, Diego Trillo, Juan Antonio Hernández, José Borda.

IU

109 Cabrera, Pablo. <u>Misceláneas</u>. Historia, etnografía, datos biobibliográficos y genealógicos, crítica literaria y folklore. Publicación oficial. Córdoba: Talleres Gráficos de la Penitenciaría, 1930-31. 2 v. Portraits. 27 cm.
A two-volume collection of essays dealing with various aspects of Argentina's history, and containing biographical information on many people from all walks of life. The following are particularly featured: Cristóbal de Garay y Saavedra, Bernabé de Garay y Saavedra, Juan de Garay y Saavedra, Isabel de Garay (Isabel Becerra), Mariana de Garay y

BIOGRAPHY (MISCELLANEOUS)

Saavedra, Jerónima de Contreras, María de Garay y Mendoza, Ana de Garay, Domingo Muriel.

CU DLC ICU TxU

110 Caffaro Rossi, José María. <u>Cincuenta semblanzas argentinas</u>. Buenos Aires: G. Kraft, 1954. 218 p. Portraits. 21 cm.
Detailed biographical information of the following 19th- and 20th-century Argentineans: Juan Bautista Alberdi, Valentín Alsina, Juan Antonio Alvarez de Arenales, Florentino Ameghino, Nicolás Avellaneda, Antonio González Balcarce, Manuel Belgrano, Luis Beltrán, Antonio Luis Beruti, Juan José Castelli, Salvador María Del Carril, Manuel Dorrego, Luis María Drago, Esteban Echeverría, Tomás Espora, José Manuel Estrada, Figueroa Alcorta, Gregorio Funes, Joaquín V. González, Martín Güemes, José Hernández, Eduardo Ladislao Kaillitz de Holmberg, José Ingenieros, Bernardo de Irigoyen, Hipólito Yrigoyen, Gregorio Aráoz de Lamadrid, Narcisco de Laprida, Juan Gregorio de Las Heras, Leopoldo Lugones, Bartolomé Mitre, Bernardo Monteagudo, Mariano Moreno, Francisco Javier Muñiz, José María Paz, Carlos Pellegrini, Juan Domigo Perón, Luis Piedrabuena, Juan Martín de Pueyrredón, Ramos Mejía, Guillermo Rawson, Bernardino Rivadavia, Julio A. Roca, Leonardo Rosales, Roque Saénz Peña, Santa María de Oro, José de San Martín, Faustino Sarmiento, Aristóbulo Del Valle, Vélez Sársfield, Estanislao E. Zeballos.

CU DLC DS IU NN TxU

111 Camba, Francisco. <u>Los españoles en el centenario argentino</u>. Buenos Aires: Imprenta Mestres, 1910. 33 p. Portraits. 20 cm.
Scattered biographical information about approximately 300 Spaniards associated with Argentina's development published on the occasion of the centennial.

IU

112 Caminos, Julio A. <u>Páginas de historia</u>. Prólogo del Dr. José Pérez Martín. Santa Fe: Ediciones Colmegna, 1967. 110 p. 19 cm.
An essay about notable people in the history and cultural development of Argentina, including biographical data about them and members of their families. The following are featured: Juan de San Martín, Isidora Gómez, Gregoria Matorras, María Elena San Martín, Rafael González de Menchaca, José de San Martín, Antonio José Escalada, Tomasa de la Quintana de Escalada, Remedios de Escaladas de San Martín, Merceditas San Martín de Balcarce (Chiche, pseud.), Mariano Balcarce, Josefa Dominga Balcarce, Fernando Gutiérrez de Estrada, Manuel Belgrano, Vicente Fidel López, Domingo Faustino Sarmiento, José Clemente Sarmiento, Paula Albarracín de Sarmiento, Domingo Fidel Castro (Dominguito, pseud.), Gregorio Funes, María Josefa Bustos de Lara, Nicolás Avellaneda, Dolores Silva, Marco M. de Avellaneda, Paul Groussac, Carlos A. Aldao.

CLSU CLU CSt CtY FU IaU InU KU MB MoSW MU NBuU NIC NNC NSyU OU TxU ViU WU

113 Caraffa, Pedro Isidro. <u>Contribución italiana al desarrollo intelectual en la República Argentina</u>; ensayo histórico-biográfico. La Plata: Olivieri y Domínguez, 1926. 80 p. Portraits. 19 cm.
An essay about the contribution of Italians to the intellectual development of the Argentine Republic. Includes biographical data about Francisco de Vitoria, Pablo Manuel Beruti, Domingo Belgrano y Peri, Pedro Carta Molina, Octavio Fabricio Massotti, Carlos Ferraris, Pedro de Angelis, Carlos Enrique Pellegrini, Pablo Mantegazza, Pelegrino Strobel, Emilio Rossetti, Bernardino Speluzzi, Juan Ramorino, Camilio M. Giordano.

CU DLC IU

114 Carbia, Rómulo D. <u>Los clérigos Agüero en la historia argentina</u>; un trastrueque bibliográfico aclarado. Buenos Aires: Casa editora "Coni," 1936. 30 p. 28 cm.
A short biographical account of the Agüero family, whose members were 18th- and 19th-century Argentine clerics. They include Juan Cayetano Fernández de Agüero, Juan Manuel Fernández de Agüero, Julián Segundo de Agüero, Eusebio Agüero.

DLC IU

115 Cárcano, Miguel Angel. <u>El estilo de vida argentino en Paz, Mansilla, González, Roca, Figueroa Alcorta y Sáenz Peña</u>. Buenos Aires: Editorial Universitaria de Buenos Aires, 1969. 151 p. 18 cm. (Colección Argentina. Siglo y medio, v. 132).
A collection of biographical sketches of the following notable Argentineans of the 19th century: José María Paz, Lucio Víctor Mansilla, Joaquín Víctor González, Julio A. Roca, José Figueroa Alcorta, Roque Sáenz Peña.

CFS CLSU CNoS CSt CtW CU-SB FMU FTaSU FU InU IU KU LU LU-NO MB MeU MH MiDW MiEM MoSW NbU NcU NhU NIC NjP NNC NSyU OU PPiU PPT PPULC TNJ TU TxLT TxU UU ViU WaU

115a Cárcano, Ramón José. <u>Perfiles contemporáneos</u>. Córdoba: Impr. de "El Interior," 1885. 446 p. (V. 1). 18 cm.
A collection of biographical essays on the following notable Argentineans: Fray Mamerto Esquiú, Rafael García, José Gabriel Brochero, José Javier Díaz.

CU NcU RPB

116 Casal Castel, Alberto. <u>Vidas ejemplares</u>. Ed. ilustrada con 34 grabados. Buenos Aires: Librería Hachette, 1942. 330 p. Portraits. 19 cm.

A collection of biographical sketches, accompanied by portraits, of the following notable Argentineans from all walks of life: Bernardino Rivadavia, Nicolás Avellaneda, Guillermo Rawson, Salvador María del Carril, Santiago Derqui, Bernardo de Irigoyen, Diego Alcorta, Félix Frías, Aristóbulo del Valle, Amancio Alcorta, Adolfo Alsina, José Manuel Estrada, Miguel Cané, Juan María Gutiérrez, Lucio V. Mansilla, Tristán Achával Rodríguez, Luis María Drago, Agustín Alvarez, Amadeo Jacques, Angel de Estrada, Germán Burmeister, Roque Sáenz Peña, Victorino de la Plaza, Paul Groussac, Julio A. Roca, Carlos Pellegrini, Joaquín V. González, César Hipólito Bacle, Dardo Rocha, Angel Gallardo, Juan B. Terán, José María Gutiérrez, Estanislao S. Zeballos, Eduardo Costa.

DLC NN TxU

117 Cestino, Francisco. <u>Apuntes para la historia del partido de la Ensenada</u>, 1821-1882. La Plata: Dirección de Impresiones Oficiales, 1949. 153 p. Portraits. 26 cm. (Publicaciones del Archivo Histórico de la Provincia de Buenos Aires. Contribución a la historia de los pueblos de la Provincia de Buenos Aires, v. 26).

A history of Ensenada, located in Buenos Aires province, covering the period from 1821-1882. Scattered biographical information is given for many people associated with this town.

CtY InU IU NcU

118 Cichero, Félix Esteban. <u>Los Pizzurno</u>, Pablo y sus hermanos Juan y Carlos; ensayos biográficos. Buenos Aires: Editorial Stilcograf, 1965. 244 p. 20 cm.

A series of three lengthy biographies of the Pizzurno brothers, followed by a series of short biographical sketches of many people who influences the work of these three men, particularly Pablo. The following are featured: Pablo Antonio Pizzurno, Juan Tomás Pizzurno, Carlos Higinio Pizzurno, Juan Bautista Alberdi, Próspero G. Alemandri, Nicolás Avellaneda, Julio Ricardo Barcos, Manuel Belgrano, Esteban Echeverría, José Manuel Estrada, José Garibaldi, Bernardo González Arrili, Bartolomé Mitre, Juana Manso, Mariano Moreno, Ernesto Nelson, Clotilde Guillén de Rezzano, Bernardino Rivadavia, Julio Argentino Roca, María Sánchez, Domingo Faustino Sarmiento, Justo José de Urquiza, Félix B. Visillac.

CLSU CLU CSt CtY IU KU MoSU NcU
NIC NSyU TxU

119 Ciria, Alberto, and Horacio Sanguinetti. <u>Los reformistas</u>. Buenos Aires: Editorial J. Alvarez, 1968. 356 p. Portraits. 20 cm. (Los Argentinos, v. 6).

An anthology of representative works of political reformism in Argentina covering the period from 1918-1966. A biographical section is also included for four people who made im-

portant contributions to this movement, giving details on their lives and accomplishments, as well as examples of their work. The following are featured: Deodoro Roca, Saúl Taborda, Julio V. González, Anibal Norberto Ponce.

AzU CFS CLSU CLU CSt CtW CU FU IaU
ICU InU IU MB MdU MH MiU MnU MoSW
MU NBuU NcD NcU NIC NjP NNC NSyU
OU PPiU PPT PPULC RPB TxU ViU
WaU WU

119a Coghian, Eduardo. <u>El aporte de los irlandeses a la formación de la nación argentina</u>. Buenos Aires: Impr. El Vuelo de Fénix, 1982. 670 p. 28 cm.

Alphabetical listings of approximately 30,000 individuals of Irish descent who emigrated to Argentina in the 19th century and contributed to its development.

IU

120 Comandi, Luis Enrique. <u>Capellanía de Santos Lugares</u>; historia de las tierras, pueblos y ferrocarriles. La Plata: Subsecretaría de Cultura, 1969. 219 p. 27 cm. (Publicaciones del Archivo Histórico de la Provincia de Buenos Aires. Contribución a la historia de los pueblos de la Provincia de Buenos Aires, v. 37).

A history of the chaplaincy of Santos Lugares in the General San Martín partido (Buenos Aires), Argentina, covering the 19th and 20th centuries, and including scattered biographical information for many people associated with this area. The following are emphasized: Manuel Lynch, Juan Eduardo Clark, Federico Lacroze, José Cándido Marín, Agustín Nores, Román Heitmann, Antonio Silbermann, Juan Lacabe.

CLU CSt CtY CU-SB IU LNHT MH MnU
NcU NIC NjP NNC OU TxU WU

121 Cora, Luis M. <u>Argentinos ilustres</u>. Corrientes: Editorial Tor, 1941. 361 p. Portraits. 23 cm.

A collection of biographical sketches, accompanied by portraits, about the following notable Argentineans from different walks of life: José de San Martín, Manuel Belgrano, Justo José de Urquiza, Mariano Moreno, Juan Martín de Pueyrredón, Carlos María de Alvear, Manuel Dorrego, Juan Lavalle, Bernardino Rivadavia, Vicente López y Planes, Cayetano José Rodríguez, Adolfo Alsina, Bartolomé Mitre, Carlos Pellegrini, Leandro N. Alem, Luis Sáenz Peña, Bernardo de Irigoyen, Vicente Fidel López, Pastor S. Obligado, Dardo Rocha, Roque Sáenz Peña, Hipólito Irigoyen, José Hernández, Juan María Gutiérrez, Carlos Guido Spano, Calixto Oyuela, Esteban de Luca, Esteban Echeverría, José Mármol, Héctor Florencio Varela, Rafael Obligado, José Ignacio Garmendia, Antonio Dónovan, Pablo A Pizzurno, José Ingenieros, Domingo Cullen, Ignacio Crespo, Estanislao S. Zeballos, Rodolfo Freyre, David Peña, Ovidio Lagos, Francisco Ramírez, Eduardo Race-

BIOGRAPHY (MISCELLANEOUS)

cedo, Miguel M. Laurencena, Herminio J. Quiroz, Osvaldo Magnasco, Onésimo Leguizamón, Martín Ruiz Moreno, Olegario V. Andrade, Juan Miguel Cora, Enrique Berdue, Gervasio Méndez, Ernesto A. Bavio, Antonio E. Berón de Astrada, Leónidas Echagüe, Lorenzo J. Anadón, José S. Alvarez (Fray Mocho, pseud.), Miguel M. Churruarín, Diego Fernández Espiro, Anacleto Bernardi, Juan Bautista Aguirre Silva, Pedro Ferré, Genaro Berón de Astrada, Juan Pujol, José Joaquín Gregorio Madariaga, Cecilio Ignacio Carreras, Manuel Florencio Mantilla, Manuel Derqui, Julio C. Rivero, Mariano Y. Loza, Zacarías Sánchez, Conrado Romero, J. Alfredo Ferreyra, Gregorio Funes, Dalmacio Vélez Sársfield, José María Paz, Manuel Didimo Pizarro, Nicolás Avellaneda, Juan Bautista Alberdi, Uladislao Frías, Juan Martín Güemes, Facundo Zuviría, Domingo Faustino Sarmiento, Salvador María del Carril, Joaquín V. González, Mamerto Esquiú, Juan Pascual Pringles, Juan E. Gez.

DLC

122 Costa, Julio A. <u>Hojas de mi diario</u>; daguerrotipos. Buenos Aires: Cabaut, n.d. 366 p. Portraits. 18 cm.
A collection of biographical sketches of the following notable Argentineans of the 19th century: Luis Acuña, Amancio Alcorta, Santiago Alcorta, Leandro N. Alem, Eduardo Arana, Juan José Atencio, Cosme Béccar, Juan José Biedma, Rodolfo Bilbao la Vieja, Mariano Billinghurst, Adolfo Cambaceres, Adolfo E. Carranza, Alberto Casares, Eduardo Casey, Augusto Coelho, Antonio Devoto, José A. Capdevila, Angel Estrada, Ramón L. Falcón, Luis García, Miguel Goyena, Eduardo Huergo, Juan Bautista de Estrada (Juanón, pseud.), Federico Lacroze, Manuel Láinez, Juan Antonio Víctor Martín de Moussy, Josué Moreno, Clemente Onelli, Juan Ortiz de Rosas, Marcelo Paz, Federico Pinedo, Pascual Roverano, Ramón Santamarina, Guillermo Udaondo.

TxU

123 Craviotto, José A. <u>Historia de Quilmes desde sus orígenes hasta 1941</u>. La Plata, 1967. 221 p. Portraits. 27 cm. (Publicaciones del Archivo Histórico de la Provincia de Buenos Aires. Contribución a la historia de los pueblos de la provincia de Buenos Aires, v. 35).
A history of Quilmes, located in Buenos Aires province, Argentina, covering the period from preconquest to 1941. Scattered biographical information is included for many people associated with this city.

CtY DPU FMU IU MH MU NcD

124 _____. <u>Quilmes a través de los años</u>; extracto de historia de Quilmes. Publicación dispuesta por la municipalidad de Quilmes, en homenaje al tricentenario de la fundación de Santa Cruz de los Quilmes. Quilmes: Secretaría de Gobierno y Cultura, 1966. 340 p. 19 cm.
A history of Quilmes, Argentina, covering the period from approximately 1812 to 1962, including scattered biographical information for many prominent people associated with this city. Among them are José A. Craviotto, Juana Manso, Andrés Baranda, José Antonio Wilde.

AAP CLSU CSt CU CU-SB PPU InU IU KU MB NIC NNC TxU WU

125 Cunietti-Ferrando, Arnaldo J. <u>San José de Flores</u>: el pueblo y el partido (1580-1880). Buenos Aires: Junta de Estudios Históricos de San José de Flores, 1977. 311 p. Portraits. 24 cm.
A history of San José de Flores, Argentina, covering the period from 1580 to 1880 and including biographical information, as well as portraits in a few cases, for many prominent people associated with this region. Among them are Mateo Leal de Ayala, Alonso Pastor, Juan Diego Flores, Nicolás Herrera, Martín Boneo, Carlos Naón, Calixto Silvera, Juan Bautista Gomensoro, José Agustín Ormaechea, Martín Farías, Juan Nepomuceno Terrero, Vicente Zavala, José Eustaquio Martínez, Isidro Silva. Alphabetical index of names.

IU MU

126 Cutolo, Vicente Osvaldo. <u>Argentinos graduados en Chuquisaca</u>. Buenos Aires: Editorial Elche, 1963. 144 p. 21 cm. (Colección histórico-jurídica, v. 5).
A list of Argentineans who graduated at the end of the 18th century and the beginning of the 19th from the University of San Francisco Xavier, in Chuquisaca, Bolivia (now Sucre). Names are organized according to the type of degree granted, and the date of conferral is included for each person. Includes 1,287 names.

AzU CLSU CLU CtY InU IU KU MiEM NjR NN TxU

127 Cuyás y Sampere, Antonio. <u>Apuntes históricos sobre la provincia de Entre Ríos en la República Argentina</u>. Mataró: F. Horts, 1888. 404 p. 25 cm.
A history of the Argentine province of Entre Ríos, covering the period from independence to the death of Urquiza. Scattered biographical information is included for many people associated with this region. Among those particularly featured are the following: Antonio Cuyás y Sampere, Romualdo García, Lucio Mansilla, Mateo García de Zúñiga, León Solas, Pascual Echagüe, Evaristo Carriego, Juan Manuel de Rosas, Justo José de Urquiza, Fructuoso Ribera, Juan Lavalle, José María Paz, Ramón Vilar, Manuel Oribe, José Garibaldi, Manuel Herrera y Obes, Valentín Alsina, Rodrigo

de Sousa de Silva Pontes, Garzón, Juan Coe, Andrés Arguibel, Santiago Derqui, Ricardo López Jordán, José María Domínguez.

MH NcU NjP NN PrU

128 Charras, Julián de. _La patria en marcha_; hombres, glorias, ideales. Buenos Aires: Editorial Minerva, 1926. 217 p. Portraits. 21 cm.

Biographical information on Martín de Alzaga, Martín Miguel de Güemes, Juan José Fernández Campero, Marqués de Yaví, Tomás Guido, José de San Martín, Rufino Guido, Gregorio Aráoz de Lamadrid, Lorenzo Barcala, Martiniano Charras, Carlos Guido y Spano, Osvaldo Magnasco, Joaquín V. González, Pedro B. Palacios, Juan Zorilla de San Martín, José Enrique Rodó, Víctor Pérez Petit.

DLC NcU

129 D'Amico, Carlos. _Buenos Aires, sus hombres, su política (1860-1890)_. Con un extenso índice alfabético de nombres y personas citadas. Buenos Aires: Editorial Americana, 1952. 306 p. 20 cm. (Colección Historia y tradición argentinas).

Collection of biographical essays on leading figures in Argentine politics from 1860-1890. Information on the careers of the following individuals is especially featured: Domingo Faustino Sarmiento, Bernardo de Irigoyen, Bartolomé Mitre, Marcos Paz, Martín Alzaga, Juan Angel Martínez, José Vicente Urdapilleta, Luis M. Drago, Julián Panelo. Alphabetical index of names.

CtY DLC IU NcD NN TxU

130 Dellepiane, Antonio. _Dos patricias ilustres_. Buenos Aires: "Coni," 1923. 272 p. Portraits. 18 cm.

A work featuring lengthy biographies of two notable Argentine women--María Sánchez de Mendeville and Carmen Nóbrega de Avellaneda. Scattered biographical information is also given for many people associated with these women. Among those featured are: María de Todos los Santos Sánchez de Velazco y Trillo, Cecilio Sánchez de Velazco, Magdalena Trillo, Martín Jacobo Thompson, Juan Bautista Washington de Mendeville, Nicolás Avellaneda.

FMU FU TxU

131 Dorcas Berro, Rolando. _Nuestra Señora de los Dolores_. La Plata: Taller de Impresiones Oficiales, 1939. 112 p. Portraits. 27 cm. (Publicaciones del Archivo Histórico de la Provincia de Buenos Aires. Contribución a la historia de los pueblos de la provincia de Buenos Aires, v. 17).

A history of Dolores, located in Buenos Aires province, covering the 19th century,

and including scattered biographical information, as well as a few portraits, for many people associated with this town.

CtY DLC IU NIC

132 Dose de Zemborain, Justa. _Tradiciones del Río de la Plata_. Prólogo de Ricardo Zorraquín Becú. Viñetas de Carlos Alfredo Zemborain. Buenos Aires: Emecé Editores, 1965. 323 p. 26 cm.

A collection of essays, accompanied by letters and documents, dealing with notable people and events in Argentina during the 17th, 18th, and 19th centuries. Those for whom biographical data are most extensive include the following: Francisco de Videla y Aguiar, José de San Martín, Manuel de Olavarrieta, Ana Josefa de Pierreclau, Antonio Martínez de Obligado, José Gómez del Canto, Esteban Villanueva, Bernardino de Ortega, Benancio Ortega, Rufina Ortega Beruti, Rufino Ortega.

CLSU CLU CtY CU ICU InU IU KU MB
MH MiEM Mu NbU NcD NcU NIC NN NNC
OU TxU WU

133 Echagüe, Juan Pablo. _Seis figuras del Plata_. Buenos Aires: Editorial Losada, 1938. 187 p. 18 cm. (Azul y blanco).

A collection of biographical essays on the following notable Argentineans from different walks of life: Domingo Faustino Sarmiento, Leopoldo Lugones, Enrique García Velloso, Martín Gil, Florencio Sánchez, Pedro Chutro.

CU DLC MoSU NcD NcU NIC OO OrU
OU PU TxU

134 Echevarría de Lobato Mulle, Felisa Carmen. _Un conquistador, una dama, una estancia y un decreto_. Prólogo de Ulisis Petit de Murat; ilus. de Eyra Reyes de Holgado. Luján: Librería de Mayo, 1973. 307 p. 24 cm.

History of the city of Luján, Argentina, from its founding to the early 20th century. Scattered biographical data are provided for individuals connected with it. Among those especially featured: Juan de Garay, Marcos de Siqueyra, Ana de Matos, Juan de Arregui, Juan de Lezica y Torrezuri, Francisco de Argerich, Cosme Mariano Argerich, Francisco José Argerich, Bernardino Rivadavia, Bartolomé Cueto.

AzU IU MU NNC TxU

135 _Entre Ríos_. Buenos Aires: Tall. del Instituto Salesiano de Artes Gráficas, 1973. 175 p. Portraits. 31 cm.

History and description of the Argentine province of Entre Ríos with varying amount of biographical information on numerous individuals associated with it.

IU

BIOGRAPHY (MISCELLANEOUS)

136 Escobar, Eduardo. <u>Necochea</u>, ciudad progresis-
ta y poética. Necochea: Talleres Gráficos La
Editorial Lasanta & Cía., 1937. 209 p. Portraits. 22 cm.
     A history of the Argentine city of Neco-
chea, covering the 19th and 20th centuries,
and including scattered biographical information on many people who have contributed to
its development. Among those particularly
featured are Angel Ignacio Murga, Mariano
Necochea, Eustaquio Díaz Vélez, José Rivolta.

          CtY CU DLC DPU ICU IU MiU NcD
          NcU NN NNC PPT PU

137 Estrada, Marcos de. <u>Argentinos de origen
africano</u>. Buenos Aires: Editorial Universitaria de Buenos Aires, 1979. 203 p. 18 cm.
     Collection of essays profiling Argentines
of African descent from the 19th and the 20th
centuries; Information provided includes
birthplace, dates, and activities of Lorenzo
Barcala, José Antonio Viera, Fermín Gayoso,
Joaquín Chaves, Batallón, Antonio Videla,
Andrés Ibáñez, Manuel Macedonio Barbarin,
Antonio Ruiz (Falucho, pseud.), Josefa Teno-
rio, Remigio Navarro, Domingo Sosa, Felipe
Mansilla, Casildo G. Thompson, José María Mo-
rales, Zenón Rolón, José Cipriano Campana,
Carmen Ledesma, Juan Patiño, Federico Espinosa,
Manuel Posadas, Horacio Mendizábal, Froilán P.
Bello, Gabino Ezeiza, Eugenio Sar, Alfredo
Quiroga, Eduardo Magee, Higinio Cazón, Caye-
tano Alberto Silva, Gregorio Badía, Tomás B.
Platero, Juan Blanco de Aguirre.

          IU

138 <u>Los Excéntricos</u>. Buenos Aires: Todo es Historia, 1977. 140 p. 20 cm. (Todo es historia, v. 9).
     Collection of biographical essays on the
following eccentric personalities of 20th-
century Argentina: Fernando Asuero, Omar
Viñole, Enrique Badessich, Juan Baigorri Velar.

139 Favoino, G. M., and A. Bufardeci. <u>Gli italiani nella provincia di Entre Ríos</u>. Paraná:
Artes Gráficas, 1914. 216 p. Portraits.
26 cm.
     An essay about Italians in the Argentine
province of Entre Ríos. Includes biographical
sketches of the following prominent individuals: Michele Raggio, Abelardo Caccialupi,
Tavella (brothers), Dodero (brothers), Giacomo Giacomotti, Giacomo Valli, Giovanni
Antonio Barbagelata, Nicanor Berisso, Michele
Bianchimani, Nazzario Padula, Emanuele Gaggero, Domenico Lambruschini, Giovanni Rossi,
Ignazio Mansueti, Pasquale Grieco, Mosé Battista Ortelli, Orlando Martino Ortelli, Domenico F. Rocco, Enrico P. Trucco, Angelo
Sanguineti, Paolo Natali, Antonio Rossi, Carlos Reggiardo, Giovanni Schiappa-Pietra,

Giorgio Vierci, Angelo Giolitti, Domenico
Nanni.

          IU

140 Fernández, Elbio. <u>Gente de Buenos Aires</u>;
artistas - escritores - poetas; dibujos de
Elbio Fernández. Buenos Aires: F. A. Colom-
bo, 1965. 1 v. (Unpaged). Portraits. 21 cm.
     A collection of biobibliographical ske-
tches, accompanied by portraits, of the fol-
lowing Argentine authors and artists from
Buenos Aires: Alfiero, Ernesto Bianco, Jorge
Luis Borges, Nicolás Cocaro, Osvaldo Francis-
co Colombo, Félix Coluccio, Córdova Iturburu,
Jorge Cruz, Gustavo R. A. Fillol Day, Luis
Franco, Francisco Gil, Alberto Ginastera,
Joaquín Gómez Bas, Beatriz Guido, Fermín
Estrella Gutiérrez, Marta Lynch, Arturo Ma-
rasso, Ricardo E. Molinari, Antonio Pagés
Larraya, Agustín Pérez Pardella, Syria Poletti,
Ernesto Ramallo, Ernesto Sábato, Gustavo Soler,
Juan José de Urquiza, María Elena Walsh,
W. G. Weyland.

          IU NSbSU

141 Fernández, Juan Rómulo. <u>Hombres de acción</u>
(cien biografías sintéticas de personas que
contribuyeron a la independencia, organización y afinzamiento de la República Argentina). Buenos Aires: Librería del Colegio,
1940. 215 p. Portraits. 21 cm.
     A collection of biographical sketches,
accompanied by portraits, of numerous Argentineans from the colonial period to the early
1920s.

          DLC DPU ICU IU MiU NcD NcU

142 Fernández Lalanne, Pedro. <u>Los Alvear</u>. Buenos
Aires: Emecé, 1980. 505 p. Portraits.
23 cm.
     A biographical account, accompanied by
portraits of the following members of the
Alvear family from Argentina: Diego de Alvear, Carlos de Alvear, Emilio de Alvear,
Torcuato de Alvear, Teodelina de Alvear de
Lezica, Elisa de Alvear de Bosch, Marcelo T.
de Alvear. Alphabetical index of names.

          IU

143 Ferns, Henry Stanley. <u>Britain and Argentina
in the Nineteenth Century</u>. Oxford: Claren-
don Press, 1960. 517 p. 23 cm.
     A history of British influence in Argen-
tina during the 19th century, including scattered biographical information on many notable
people, both British and Argentine. Among
them are the following: Home Riggs Popham,
Santiago de Liniers, Julio Roca, Bernardino
de Rivadavia, Manuel Dorrego, Woodbine Parish,
Manuel García, Jose de San Martín, Juan Manuel
Rosas, Fructuoso Rivera, Guillermo Brown,

Lord Ponsonby, Juan Lavalle, Louis Vernet, Justo José de Urquiza, Charles Hotham, Bartolomé Mitre, Carlos Pellegrini, Miguel Juárez Celman.

AAP AU C CaBVaU CaQMM CLSU CLU CoU CSt CtW CtY CU DAU DeU DPU FMU FTaSU FU GI IaU ICU IEdS IEM InU IU KU KyU LU MB MCM MeB MH MiD MiEM MiU MnU MoU MsU MWelC NBC NcD NcU NIC NjP NjR NN NNC NRU OC1 OC1W OCU ODW OKentU OkU OO OOxM OrU OU PBL PPiU RPB ScU TNJ TxDaM TxHR TxU ViU WaU WU

144 Ferrari Rueda, Rodolfo de. <u>Historia de Córdoba</u>. Córdoba: Biffignandi Ediciones, 1964-68. 2 v. 23 cm. (Colección Alma de Córdoba, v. 4-5).

A historical essay about the Argentine province and city of Córdoba (16th-19th centuries). Biographical data are provided for the following individuals associated with it: Diego de Rojas, Francisco de Aguirre, Jerónimo Luis de Cabrera y Toledo, Luisa Martel de los Ríos, Miguel Jerónimo de Cabrera, Gonzalo Martel de Cabrera, Pedro Luis de Cabrera, Petronila de la Cerda, Francisca Martel de Mendoza, Miguel Calixto del Corro, Blas de Rosales, Francisco Solano, Tristán de Tejeda, Luis de Tejeda y Guzmán, Diego de Salguero y Cabrera, Ignacio Duarte y Quirós, Domingo Muriel, Gregorio Funes, Miguel Calixto del Corro, Pedro Bracamonte, María Mercedes Heredia, Pedro de Somellera, Mariano Moreno, María Guadalupe Cuenca.

CLSU CtY ICU IU MoSW NcU NIC NSyU TxU

145 Fregeiro, Clemente L. <u>Vidas de argentinos ilustres</u>. Texto de lectura para las escuelas. Buenos Aires: Igón Hnos., 1883. 122 p. 19 cm.

A collection of biographical sketches of the following notable 19th- century Argentineans: Hipólito Vieytes, Mariano Moreno, Vicente López, Bernardino Rivadavia, Pedro José Agrelo, Esteban de Luca, Julián Segundo de Agüero, Juan Cruz Varela, José Mármol. (<u>See also</u> entry 145a.)

IU

145a _____. <u>Vidas de argentinos ilustres</u>. Nueva ed. corr. aum. e ilustrada. Buenos Aires: P. Igon y Cía., 1899. 206 p. Portraits. 18 cm.

An enlarged edition featuring Manuel Belgrano, Hipólito Vieytes, Mariano Moreno, Vicente López y Planes, José de San Martín, Esteban de Luca, Bernardino Rivadavia, José Segundo de Agüero, Juan Cruz Varela, Pedro José Agrelo, José Mármol, Justo José de Urquiza, Domingo Faustino Sarmiento, Nicolás Avellaneda. (<u>See also</u> entry 145.)

DLC IU (Film)

146 Freije, Eduardo S. <u>Reseña histórica del partido de Mar Chiquita y sus pueblos</u>. La Plata, 1964. 160 p. 28 cm. (Publicaciones del Archivo Histórico de la Provincia de Buenos Aires. Contribución a la historia de los pueblos de la provincia, v. 32).

A history of the towns in the vicinity of Mar Chiquita, Argentina, covering the period from colonial to modern times. Scattered biographical information is included for many people associated with this region.

CSt CtY DLC DPU IU NIC NN PPiU

147 Fumière, Jorge P. <u>Origen y formación del partido y pueblo de Almirante Brown</u> (Adrogué) 1750-1882. La Plata: Subsecretaría de Cultura, 1969. 217 p. Portraits. 27 cm. (Publicaciones del Archivo Histórico de la Provincia de Buenos Aires. Contribución a la historia de los pueblos de la Provincia de Buenos Aires, v. 38).

A history of Almirante Brown (Adrogué), located in Buenos Aires province, Argentina, covering the period from 1750 to 1882. Scattered biographical information, as well as portraits in a few cases, are included for many people associated with this city. The following are emphasized: Roberto Hunt, Esteban Adrogué, Manuel Alejandro Obligado, Pastor Servando Obligado, José Antonio de María, Juan Cayetano Molina, Leandro N. Alem, José María Cruces.

AzU CLU CSt DPU FMU FU InU IU MnU MU NcD NcU NmU NNC TxU WU

148 _____. <u>Los orígines de Campana hasta la creación del partido</u>. Campana: Municipalidad de Campana, 1975. 165 p. 21 cm.

An essay about the history of the Argentine city of Campana, including biographical data on the following people who contributed to its development: Luis del Aguila, Esteban Lomez, Francisco Alvarez Campana, Cayetano Escola, Mariano de Escalada, José Julián Arriola, Ladislao Martínez Castro, Juan María Pueyrredón.

IU NIC

149 Fúrlong Cárdiff, Guillermo. <u>Glorias santafesinas</u>: Buenaventura Suárez, Francisco Javier Iturri, Cristóbal Altamirano; estudios bio-bibliográficos. Buenos Aires: Editorial "Surgo," 1929. 302 p. 23 cm.

An essay about the following notable individuals from the Santa Fe region in Argentina: Buenaventura Suárez, Francisco Javier Iturri, Cristóbal Altamirano.

DLC IU

150 Gandía, Enrique de. <u>Historia de la Boca del Riachuelo</u>. Buenos Aires: Talleres Gráficos "Virtus," 1939. 143 p. 21 cm.

BIOGRAPHY (MISCELLANEOUS)

A history of Boca del Riachuelo, Buenos Aires, covering the period from colonial times to the beginning of the 19th century. Scattered biographical information is included for many people associated with this neighborhood.

DLC NIC

151 _____. Los primeros italianos en el Río de la Plata, y otros estudios históricos. Buenos Aires: A. García Santos, 1932. 173 p. 19 cm.

An essay about the first Italians in Argentina. Includes biographical data on the following individuals: Sebastián Caboto, Nicolás del Benino, Esteban Ferrofino, Miguel Díez de Armendariz, Juan Bautista de Pastene, Francisco Piora, León Pancaldo, Francisco Gambarrota, Leonardo Sasso, Diego Mollano, Juan Calabrés, Juan de Garay, Juan de Salazar, Domingo Martínez de Irala.

CtY DLC IU NcD OrU WU

152 Gandulfo Arce de Ballor, Josefina. Auténticos paladines de la Patagonia en Valcheta. Valcheta, 1977. 19 p. 22 cm.

A collection of biographical sketches of the following individuals associated with Valcheta (Río Negro) and the Patagonia region: Lino Oris de la Roa, Francisco Pascasio Moreno, Ramón Lista, Arturo Casas, Domingo Pronsato.

DLC

152a García, Germán. El inmigrante en la novela argentina. Buenos Aires: Librería Hachette, 1970. 108 p. 20 cm.

An essay about the immigrant in Argentine literature, including scattered biographical information on the following individuals of the 19th and 20th centuries: Eduardo Acevedo Díaz, Luis María Albamonte, Juan Bautista Alberdi, José S. Alvarez (Fray Mocho, pseud.), Enrique Amorím, Juan Antonio Argerich, Nicolás Avellaneda, Elbio Bernárdez Jacques, Miguel Angel Correa (Mateo Booz, pseud.), Jorge Luis Borges, Fausto Burgos, Matías Calandrelli, Silverio Domínguez (Ceferino de la Calle, pseud.), Eugenio Cambaceres, Arturo Cancela, Carlos Carlino, Armando Cascella, Ernesto L. Castro, Emilio P. Corbiere, Juan J. Cornaglia, Martín Coronado, Armando Discépolo, Elsa Durando Mackey, Samuel Glusberg (Enrique Espinoza, pseud.), Francisco Fernández, José Adolfo Gaillardou, Enrique García Velloso, Liborio Justo (Lobodón Garra, pseud.), Alberto Gerchunoff, Joaquín González, Gastón Gori, Juan Goyanarte, Francisco Grandmontagne, Lázaro Grattarola, Alcides Greca, Victoria Gukovsky, Eduardo Gutiérrez, José Hernández, José M. del Hogar, Guillermo Enrique Hudson, Juan B. Justo, Emilio Lestani, Félix Lima, Albert Londres, Lucio Vicente López, Leopoldo Lugones, Eduardo Mallea, José María Miró

(Julián Martel, pseud.), Ezequiel Martínez Estrada, Mariano Moreno, Rafael Obligado, Carlos María Ocantos, Carlos Ortiz, Diego R. Oxley, Carlos Mauricio Pacheco, Luis Pascarella, José Pavlotzky, Roberto J. Payró, José Pedroni, Félix M. Pelayo, José María de Pereda, Benito Pérez Galdós, Manuel T. Podestá, José Prado, Horacio Quiroga, José Rabinovich, Nicolás Rapoport, Bernardino Rivadavia, Adolfo Saldías, Florencio Sánchez, Domingo Faustino Sarmiento, Francisco Sicardi, Eduardo Talero, Nemesio Trejo, Manuel Ugarte, Justo José de Urquiza, Alberto Vacarezza, Enrique de Vedia, Bernardo Verbitsky, Tomás Yañez, Walter Weyland, Emilio Zola.

CFS CLSU CtY CU-S CU-SB GU ICU InU IU MB MiU NBuU NIC NjP NNC OkS PPT TxU ViU WaU

153 García Mansilla, Daniel. Visto, oído y recordado; apuntes de un diplomático argentino. Buenos Aires: G. Kraft, 1950. 443 p. Portraits. 28 cm.

An autobiographical account by the Argentine diplomat Daniel García Mansilla covering the period 1866-1891. Substantial biographical information is not only included for the author but also for his family and others who were involved in their lives and times. Those particularly featured are Daniel García Mansilla, Manuel Rafael García Aguirre, Eduarda Mansilla y Ortiz de Rozas de García, Mariano Balcarce, Isabel II, Lucio Mansilla, Eugenia de Montijo, Eduarda García Mansilla (Eda, pseud.), Rafael García Mansilla, Eduardo García Mansilla, Manuel García Mansilla, General Mansilla (Tata General, pseud.), Charles de Lagatinerie, Isabelle de Lagatinerie, Juan Manuel de Rozas, Martín García Merou, Lucio V. López, Diego Barros Arana, Coronel Czetz, Miguel Cané, Domingo Ortiz de Rozas, Amado Bonpland.

KU NcU NN TxU WU

154 García Salaberry, Adela. Vidas. Buenos Aires: Talleres Gráficos Argentinos L. J. Rosso, 1938-50. 4 v. Portraits. 27 cm.

A collection of sketches, accompanied by portraits, of the following Argentine artists and writers:

V. 1: Margarita Abella Caprile, Ernestina Azlor, Emilia Bertolé, Antonieta Silveyra de Lenhardson, Blanca de la Vega, Quinquela Martín, Lita Rey Posse, Juan Carlos Oliva Navarro, Alfonsina Storni, Mario M. Corretjer, Guillermo Butler, Rosa Bazán de Cámara, María Suásnabar, Josefina Melo, Luis Perlotti, María Antonieta Centrone, Adelia Di Carlo, María Carmen Portela de Aráoz Alfaro, Herminia Brumana, Berta Elena Vidal de Battini, Manuel López Weigel, Olga Praguer-Coelho, Wally Zenner, Ada Negri.

V. 2: J. González Carbalho, Ema Santandreu Morales, Stephan Erzia, Ana Weiss de Rossi, Juan José de Soiza Reilly, Elsa Piaggio-Tarelli, Emilio J. Sarniguet, Berta Singerman,

Ramón Subirats, María Alicia Domínguez, Carlos Vega, María Luisa Anido, César Tiempo, Margarita Portela Lagos, Josué Quesada, Mary Rega Molina, Carlos López Buchardo, Dora Díaz Villafañe, Edgardo Ubaldo Genta, Bibí Zogbe, Fausto Burgos, Clementina Isabel Azlor, Mateo Booz, Esperanza Lothringer, E. Montiel Ballesteros, Ekatherina de Galantha, Gastón Figueira, Carmen Souza Brazuna, Carlos Olivares, Estrella Genta, Julio Díaz Usandivaras, Margarita Arsamasseva, Félix B. Visillac, Delia Sacerdote, Manuel María Oliver, Ida Réboli, Artigas Milans Martínez, Ana S. Cabrera, Oscar Jara Azocar, Ethel Kurlat, Raúl Hugo Espoile, Zulma Núñez, Ataliva Herrera, María Alex Urrutia Artieda, Eugenio Troisi.

V. 3: Enrique Larreta, Ricardo Rojas, Georgina de Uriarte, Antonio Alice, Helena Larrieu, Atilio Chiappori, Emilia Bertolé, Gustavo Martínez Zuviría, Angelita Vélez, Vicente R. Candiano, María Pini de Chrestía, Ricardo Gutiérrez, Leonor Buffo Allende, Luis Cané, Laura Mulhall Girondo, Pastor del Río, Adela García Salaberry.

V. 4: Ceferino M. Namuncurá, Bernardo González Arrili, Alfredo Gramajo Gutiérrez, Lydia Ures Caamaño, Alberto G. Ocampo, María Raquel Adler, Carlos V. Dumont, Benjamín Solari Parravicini, Guido Buffo, María J. S. Barbier, José C. Arcidiácono, Paulina Simoniello, Jorge G. Blanco Villalta, Julia Bustos, María A. Ciordia, Rodolfo M. Ragucci, Santiago E. Cozzolino, Enrique de Larrañaga, Alfonsina Storni.

DLC NcU TxU

155 Garretón, Adolfo. Historia de San Nicolás de los Arroyos desde sus orígenes hasta 1810. La Plata: Taller de Impresiones Oficiales, 1937. 82 p. 27 cm. (Publicaciones del Archivo Histórico de la Provincia de Buenos Aires. Contribución a la historia de los pueblos de la provincia de Buenos Aires, v. 9).

A history of San Nicolás de los Arroyos, located in Buenos Aires province, covering the period from discovery to the year 1810, and including brief scattered biographical information on many people associated with this city.

CPU ICN IU NIC NNC

156 Gascón, Julio César. Orígenes históricos de Mar del Plata. La Plata: Taller de Impresiones Oficiales, 1942. 226 p. 27 cm. (Publicaciones del Archivo Histórico de la Provincia de Buenos Aires. Contribución a la historia de los pueblos de la provincia de Buenos Aires, v. 20).

A history of Mar del Plata, Argentina, covering the period from preconquest through the 19th century, and including scattered biographical information, as well as portraits in some cases, for many people associated with this city. The following are particularly featured: Juan de Samartín, Joseph Cardiel, Tomás Falkner, Martín Rodríguez, Pedro Capdevila, Ladislao Martínez, Marcelino Martínez, José Gregorio Lezama, José Coelho de Meyrelles, Patricio Peralta Ramos, Juan A. Peña, Pedro Luro, Pedro Bouchez, Dardo Rocha.

CtY DLC FU IU MiU NIC NN

157 Gerchunoff, Alberto. Entre Ríos, mi país. Buenos Aires: Editorial Futuro, 1950. 148 p. 20 cm.

A study of various aspects of Entre Ríos, Argentina, including scattered biographical information on many people associated with this region. Among those featured are Alberto Gerchunoff, Osvaldo Magnasco, Cipriano Castro.

DLC IU MH NN WU

158 Gez, Juan Wenceslao. Historia de la provincia de San Luis. Buenos Aires: Talleres Gráficos de J. Weiss y Preusche, 1916. 2 v. Portraits. 27 cm.

A two-volume history of San Luis, Argentina, covering the period from conquest through the 19th century, and including portraits and scattered biographical information for many people associated with this province. The following are among those particularly featured: Martín García Oñez de Loyola, Vicente Dupuy, José Santos Ortiz, José Gregorio Calderón, Pablo Lucero, Mauricio Daract, Justo Daract, Juan Saa, Juan Agustín Ortiz Estrada, Lindor L. Quiroga, Carlos Reichert (Teófilo Iwanoski, pseud.), Rafael Cortez, Zoilo Concha, Eriberto Mendoza.

CU DLC IU

159 _____. La tradición puntana. Bocetos biográficos y recuerdos. Corrientes: Imprenta de T. Heinecke, 1910. 219 p. Portraits. 20 cm.

A collection of biographical essays, accompanied by portraits, of the following notable individuals from the Argentine province of San Luis: Juan Esteban Pedernera, José Santos Ortiz, Pablo Lucero, Justo Daract, Cecilio L. Lucero, Juan Llerena, Paula Domínguez de Bazán.

IU NcU NIC

160 Gianello, Juan María. Hombres de Entre Ríos; ensayos biográficos: Macía, Ambrosetti, Carbó, Magnasco, Solanas. Paraná: Editorial Nueva Impresora, 1966. 33 p. Portraits. 22 cm.

Biographical essays accompanied by portraits on early 20th-century residents of the province of Entre Ríos, Argentina. Dates, birthplace, and career achievements are supplied for Salvador Macía, Juan Bautista Ambrosetti, Enrique Carbó, Osvaldo Magnasco, Fortunato Solanas.

CLSU CSt IaU IU MoSW NBuU NIC NjPT NN NNC WU

BIOGRAPHY (MISCELLANEOUS)

161 Giménez Colodrero, Luis E. Historia de Pergamino hasta 1895. La Plata: Taller de Impresiones Oficiales, 1945. 349 p. 28 cm. (Publicaciones del Archivo Histórico de la Provincia de Buenos Aires. Contribución a la historia de los pueblos de la Provincia de Buenos Aires, v. 23).

A history of Pergamino, located in Buenos Aires province, and covering the period from the 16th century to the year 1895. Scattered biographical information is included for many people associated with this city.

    CtY DLC IU MH NIC ViU

162 Giusti, Roberto Fernando. Visto y vivido; anécdotas, semblanzas, confesiones y batallas. Buenos Aires: Editorial Losada, 1965. 340 p. 20 cm. (Cristal del tiempo).

A series of personal reminiscences of the author, including biographical essays on some eminent acquaintances. The following are featured: Roberto Fernando Giusti, Roberto Payró, Emilio Becher, José Ingenieros, Florencio Sánchez, Charles de Soussens, Evaristo Carriego, Antonio Gellini, Francisco Capello, Alejandro Korn, David Peña, Ricardo Rojas, Francisco Romero, Juan B. Justo, Alfredo Bianchi.

    CaBVaU CFIS CLSU CLU CU CU-S DPU
    FU ICU InU IU KU KyU MB MH MiDW
    MiEM MoSW MU NBuU NcD NcU NnD NIC
    NjP NjR NN NSyU TNJ TxDaM TxU UU
    ViU WaU WU

163 Gómez, Hernán Félix. Historia de la provincia de Corrientes. Corrientes: Imprenta del Estado, 1928. 3 v. 26 cm.

A history of the Argentine province of Corrientes, covering the period from colonial times to the independence movement, and including scattered biographical information for many people associated with this region.

    CtY CU DLC InU IU MH MiU NcU NN
    NSyU ViU

164 _____. Vida pública del Dr. Juan Pujol; historia de la provincia de Corrientes de marzo 1843 a diciembre 1859. Buenos Aires: J. Lajouane & Cía., 1920. 328 p. Portraits. 25 cm.

A history of the Argentine province of Corrientes, covering the period from 1843 to 1956, and including scattered biographical information for many notable people associated with this region. The following are emphasized: Joaquín Madariaga, Juan Pujol, Benjamín Virasoro.

    CSt CU DLC DPU IU MB MiU NcU NN

165 González, Joaquín Víctor. Ideales y caracteres. La Plata: Sesé y Larrañaga, 1903. 269 p. 19 cm.

A work containing biographical essays on the following prominent 19th-century Argen-tines: Manuel Belgrano, Justo José de Urquiza, Vicente Fidel López, Carlos Berg, Nicolás Avellaneda, Amancio Alcorta, Ricardo Gutiérrez, Mamerto Esquiú, Carlos Guido y Spano.

    CoU CtY NN TxU

166 González Arrili, Bernardo. Retratos a pluma. Buenos Aires: J. Menéndez, 1937. 205 p. 20 cm.

A collection of biographical sketches of numerous illustrious individuals associated with the development of the Argentine Republic during the 19th and 20th centuries.

    DLC NcU

167 _____. Tiempo pasado: semblanzas de escritores argentinos. Buenos Aires: Academia Argentina de Letras, 1974. 454 p. 20 cm. (Biblioteca de la Academia Argentina de Letras: Serie Estudios académicos, v. 19).

A collection of biographical essays on the following 19th- and 20th-century Argentine authors: Dalmacio Vélez Sársfield, Francisco de Paula Castañeda, Félix Frías, José Mármol, Juan Llerena, Bartolito Mitre, Federico de la Barra, Carlos Guido y Spano, Estanislao del Campo, Miguel Cané, Lucio Vicente López, José María Ramos Mejía, José Manuel Estrada, Almafuerte, Juan Agustín García, Martín Coronado, Martiniano Leguizamón, Joaquín V. González, Eduardo Ladislao Holmberg, Rodolfo Rivarola, Ernesto Quesada, Estanislao S. Zeballos, Carlos María Urien, Ricardo Monner Sans, Gregorio de Laferrère, Mariano de Vedia (Juan Cancio, pseud.), Juan B. Ambrosetti, Enrique Trejo, Eduardo Talero, Luis García, José Ingenieros, Carlos Octavio Bunge, Angel de Estrada (hijo), Evaristo Carriego, Máximo S. Victoria, Belisario Roldán, Emilio Becher, Clemente Ricci, Juan B. Terán, Alberto Ghiraldo, Rodolfo González Pacheco, Edmundo Montagne, Benito Lynch, Antonio Sagarna, Leopoldo Lugones, Enrique Larreta, Juan Pablo Echagüe, Ernesto Nelson.

    CtY CU CU-S CU-SB FMU IaU ICarbS
    InU IU KU LNT MH MnU MoSW MU NbU
    NBuU NcU NIC NjP NmU NN NNC NSyU
    OrU TxU

168 Gori, Gastón. Colonización suiza en Argentina. Colonizadores de San Carlos hasta 1860. Santa Fe: Librería y Editorial Colmegna, 1947. 148 p. Portraits. 22 cm.

An account of the Swiss presence in Argentina during the 19th century, including biographical information for many prominent families, as well as portraits and scattered data for other notable people. The following are among those featured: Premat, Honorio Buffaz (family), Félix Didier (family), Ramseyer, Groetter, Rey, Plácido Didier (family), Chabrillon, Madoery, Reutemann, Reale, Olivero, Barbero, Taverna, Kappeller, Biedermann, Charles, Houriet, Guinand, Alexandre, Semon, Delachaux, Nicollier, Gossweiler, Hammerly, Jacob, Wyss, Brandenberger, Rua, Bernardi,

Julián Rey (family), Blanche, Place, Voisin, Stettler, Reutlinger, Stelzer, Ineichen, Juan Luis Nicollier (family), Ana María Ayme (family), Juan Bautista Ayme (family), Armando Buffaz (family), Dreyer, Moreillon, Gogniat, Firedrich, Teófilo Romang (family), Chatel, Terretaz, Rossier, Farquet, Pignat, Vogel, Regennass, Jacumin, Pons, Bert. Pablo Tron (family), Marta C. de Tron (family), Schwob, Trombert, Guerin, Tschopp, Antemmatten, Kellerhals, Blank, Schaubli, Moldhahn.

IU NN

169 Grau, Carlos A. El fuerte 25 de mayo en cruz de guerra. Con un estudio sobre las fronteras bonaerenses, y una traducción anotada del Diario redactado por el ingeniero Narciso Parchappe, publicado por Alcides D'Orbigny, sobre el viaje y operaciones de la expedición fundadora del fuerte. La Plata: Dirección de Impresiones Oficiales, 1949. 425 p. 28 cm. (Publicaciones del Archivo Histórico de la Provincia de Buenos Aires. Contribución a la historia de los pueblos de la provincia de Buenos Aires, v. 25).

A history of the fort 25 de mayo, located in Buenos Aires province, and covering the period from colonial times to the mid-19th century. Biographical information is included for the following people: Juan Antonio Hernández Gándara, Manuel de Pinazo, Pablo Zizur, Pedro Andrés García, Francisco Ramos Mexía, Mariano Ibarrola, José María Reyes, Juan Manuel de Rosas, Julián Perdriel, Narciso Parchappe, Juan Bautista Estanislao José Miguel Rafael Izquierdo, Saturnino Salas, Juan José de Olleros, Jorge Pacheco, Miguel Marín, Juan Antonio Garretón, Antonio Espinosa, Pablo Millalicán, Pancho el Ñato, Felipe Julianes, Ramón Maza, Antonio Ramírez, Vicente González, Miguel Casal.

CtY InU IU NIC

170 Greenup, Ruth (Robinson), and Leonard Greenup. Revolution before Breakfast: Argentina: 1941-1946. Chapel Hill: University of North Carolina Press, 1947. 266 p. 24 cm.

A personal history of Ruth and Leonard Greenup's life in Argentina during the period 1941-1946, including brief scattered biographical information on many notable Argentineans from all walks of life. The following are particularly featured: Ruth (Robinson) Greenup, Leonard Greenup, Alberto Baldrich, Juan Sigfrido Becker, Spruille Braden, Molina Campos, Edelmiro J. Farrell, Jordán B. Genta, Quinquela Martín, Alfredo Palacios, Evita Duarte de Perón, Pedro Pablo Ramírez, Arturo Rawson, Manuel de Rosas, Domingo Faustino Sarmiento, Guillermo Otto Siedlitz, Sumner Welles, Gustavo Martínez Zuviría. Alphabetical list of names.

CaBVa CaBVAU CaOTP CU DAU DLC IaU
ICU IdB IdPI MB MH MtBC NBuU NcC

NcD NcU NIC Or OrCS OrP OrU TxU
UU ViU WaE WaS WaSP WaT WaTC

171 Guerrero, César H. Efeméridas sanjuaninas. (San Juan en síntesis histórico-cronológico) 1562-1944. 2a. edición ampliada. San Juan, 1961. 191 p. 24 cm. (Archivo Histórico y Administrativo. Ediciones especiales. Serie C, v. 2).

A calendar, arranged from January to December, of events corresponding to the Argentine province of San Juan (1562-1944), including biographical data throughout about prominent individuals associated with it. Also biographical sketches of the following bishops and archbishops of the region: Justo Santa María de Oro, José Manuel Eufrasio de Quiroga Sarmiento, Nicolás Aldazor, José Wenceslao Achával, Marcolino del Carmelo Benavente, José Américo Orzali, Audino Rodríguez y Olmos.

DLC

172 _____. San Martín y su familia. San Juan: Ediciones Crisol, 1978. 125 p. Portraits. 20 cm.

An essay about José de San Martín and the following members of his family: Juan de San Martín, Gregoria Matorras, María Elena de San Martín y Matorras de González Menchaca, Manuel Tadeo San Martín, Juan Fermín San Martín, Justo Rufino San Martín, José Francisco San Martín, Remedios Escalada de la Quintana, Mercedes de San Martín y Escalada de Balcarce, Mariano Balcarce, María Mercedes Balcarce de San Martín, Josefa Dominga Balcarce de Gutiérrez Estrada, Andrés de San Martín y de la Riguera, Isidora Gómez y Gómez, Domingo Matorras y González, María del Ser y Antón.

IU

173 _____. Sanjuaninos del ochenta. San Juan: Editorial Sanjuanina, 1965. 230 p. Portraits. 23 cm.

Detailed biographical information on the following Argentinean intellectuals from the generation of 1880 who were native to the province of San Juan: Agustín Gómez, Rafael Segundo de Igarzábal, Angel D. Rojas, Juan E. Serú, Vicente C. Mallea, Santiago Lloveras, Cirilo P. Sarmiento, Faustino Espínola, Estanislao L. Tello, Saturnino María de Laspiur, Manuel María Moreno, Santiago S. Cortínez, Hermógenes Ruiz, Nicanor Larraín, Juan Crisóstomo Albarracín, José Pedro Cortínez, Juan Maurín, Ramón Moyano, Alejandro Albarracín, Carlos Doncel, Anacleto Gil, Segundino J. Navarro, Pedro Pascual Ramírez, Benjamín Sánchez, Isidoro Albarracín.

IU MH MU NN OkU

BIOGRAPHY (MISCELLANEOUS)

174 _____. Tres biógrafos de Sarmiento. San
Juan: Municipalidad de San Juan, 1978. 107 p.
19 cm.
Biographical essays on Bienvenida Sarmiento, Secundino J. Navarro, Wherfield A. Salinas.

IU

175 Guía integral argentina (poligrafía urbana de
las capitales argentinas) publicación periódica: definición del nominativo de las calles
y avenidas, pasajes, plazas y parques de las
capitales argentinas, tomando por base la nomenclatura urbana de la ciudad de Buenos Aires.
Topografía, historia, biografía, geografía,
etimología, ciencias naturales, tradiciones,
etc., datos de orden nacional y universal.
C. Parache Cheves, director general. Buenos
Aires, 1932. xxviii, 431 p. 24 cm.
An alphabetical listing of streets and
parks in the city of Buenos Aires, including
biographical data of the people for whom they
are named. Includes approximately 500 names.

DLC

176 Guillén, Horacio Enrique. Los hombres y los
días; calendario escolar. 2. ed. Buenos
Aires: Ediciones La Obra, 1959. 240 p. Portraits. 24 cm.
A calendar of notable people and events,
mostly Argentine, of the 16th to the 20th cen-
tury. Biographical information and portraits
are included for the following people: Mamer-
to Esquiú, Juan Bosco, Guillermo Brown, Mari-
ano Moreno, Juan Martín de Pueyrredón, Roque
Sáenz Peña, Florencio Varela, Pablo Pizzurno,
Cornelio Saavedra, Lucila Godoy Alcayaga
(Gabriela Mistral, pseud.), Vicente Fidel
López, Vicente López y Planes, Blas Parera,
José Martí (Cuban), Manuel Belgrano, Henry
Dunant, Juan de Garay, Leopoldo Lugones, Mar-
tín Güemes, Bartolomé Mitre, Paul Groussac,
Ricardo Rojas, Florentino Ameghino, José de
San Martín, Juan Bautista Alberdi, Bernardino
Rivadavia, Esteban Echeverría, Domingo F.
Sarmiento, José Manuel Estrada, Marcos Sastre,
Julio Argentino Roca, Francisco P. Moreno,
José Hernández, Angel Gallardo, Nicolás Ave-
llaneda, José Eusebio Colombres, Francisco
Javier Muñiz, Juan María Gutiérrez, Joaquín
Víctor González, José María Paz.

DLC

177 Gutiérrez, Juan María. Apuntes biográficos
de escritores, oradores y hombres de estado
de la República Arjentina. Buenos Aires:
Impr. de Mayo, 1860. 294 p. 17 cm. (Bibli-
oteca americana, v. 7).
Collection of biographies of 19th-century
writers, public speakers, and statesmen from
Argentina. Information provided includes
birthplace, dates, educational background,
and achievements for Bernardino Rivadavia,
José Antonio Miralla, Hipólito Vieites, Juan
Ignacio Gorriti, Julián Navarro, Francisco
Javier Iturri, Pantaleón Rivarola, Pantaleón
García, Ramón Díaz, José Rivera Indarte,
Patricio de Basabilbaso, Cayetano José Rodrí-
guez, Bernardo Monteagudo, Manuel José de La-
bardén, Bernardo Vera y Pintado, Julián Leiva,
Antonio Sáenz, Manuel Moreno, Miguel Calisto
del Corro, Estevan Luca y Patrón, Florencio
Balcarce, Francisco Agustín Wright, Juan Cri-
sóstomo Lafinur, Teodoro M. Vilardebó.

CoU DLC IU

177a Hernández, Pablo José. Para que no se vayan.
Buenos Aires: Ditone Hernández Ediciones,
1981. 91 p. Portraits. 20 cm.
A collection of biographical sketches, ac-
companied by portraits, of the following con-
temporary Argentineans from all walks of life:
Julio de Caro, César Tiempo, Vicente Forte,
Jorge Cafrune, Luis Sandrini, Ernesto Palacio,
Leonardo Castellani.

178 Historia de San Justo (1868-1968) por Luis
Avila et al. Santa Fe: Tall. Gráf. de la
Editorial Belgrano, 1968. 219 p. Portraits.
22 cm.
A history of San Justo, in the Argentine
province of Buenos Aires, covering the period
from 1868 to 1968 and including scattered biographical information on many notable people
associated with this city.

AzU CLSU CU-SB IaU IU KI MB NIC
NN NNC OU TxU ViU WU

179 Hudson, Damián. Recuerdos históricos sobre la
provincia de Cuyo. Buenos Aires: Editorial
Revista Mendocina de Ciencias, 1931. 408 p.
28 cm.
An essay about the Argentine region of
Cuyo (1810-1850), including scattered biograph-
ical information about the following notable
individuals associated with it: Domingo de
Torres y Arrieta, Joaquín Pérez de Leaño,
Faustino Anzay, Pascual Ruiz Huidobro, Josefa
María Morales de los Ríos de Ruiz Huidobro,
Rafael Vargas, Tomás Godoy Cruz, Francisco
Cobo, José Ignacio de la Rosa, Facundo Quiro-
ga, José Santos Ortiz, Luis Beltrán, Salvador
María del Carril, Francisco N. de Laprida,
Pablo Lucero, Félix Aldao, Remigio Castellanos,
José Benito Lamas, Francisco Javier Morales,
José Rawson Vera, Guillermo Collisberry, Juan
Guilles, Amán Rawson, Nazario Benavídez, Juan
Cornelio Moyano, Juan E. Pedernera, Toribio
Luzuriaga, Juan Pascual Pringles, Manuel de la
Trinidad Corvalán, Juan Morón, Pedro José Cam-
pos, Juan de Rosas, Pedro Pascual Segura, Cruz,
Cajaravilla, José Miguel Carrera, Francisco
Borja Correas, J. Agustín Moyano, José María
Pérez de Urdininea, Urra, Nicolás Anzorena,
Nolasco Videla, José Ruiz Huidobro, Pedro Mo-
lina, José Albino Gutiérrez, Nicolás Villa-
nueva, Salvador María del Carril, José Aldao,
Juan Moyano, Mariano Acha, José Félix Aldao.
Also listing of the governors of the Argentine
provinces Mendoza and San Juan and biography
of Damián Hudson by Pedro I. Caraffa.

DLC InU IU

180 Hux, P. Meinrado. <u>Coliqueo,</u> el indio amigo
de los toldos. La Plata, 1966. 284 p. Portraits. 28 cm. (Publicaciones del Archivo
Histórico de la Provincia de Buenos Aires.
Contribución a la historia de los pueblos de
la Provincia de Buenos Aires, v. 33.)
　　A history of the Argentine Coliqueo Indian
tribe, including portraits and biographical
information for some of its members, as well
as for others associated with this group.
Among those emphasized are: Ignacio Coliqueo,
Manuel Baigorria, Pablo Emilio Savino, Antonino Coliqueo.

　　CaOTP CLU CtY FMU FU ICU InU IU
　　LNHT MH MiEM MnU MU NBuC NcD NIC
　　NN NSyU NWM PPiU TxU ViU WaU WU

181 Ibáñez Frocham, Manuel. <u>Apuntes para la historia de Saladillo,</u> con advertencia y notas de
Manuel Ibáñez Frocham (hijo). La Plata: Taller de Impresiones Oficiales, 1937. 160 p.
Portraits. 27 cm. (Publicaciones del Archivo
Histórico de la Provincia de Buenos Aires.
Contribución a la historia de los pueblos de
la provincia de Buenos Aires, v. 12.)
　　A history of Saladillo, located in Buenos
Aires province, covering the 18th through the
19th centuries, and including portraits and
biographical information for many people associated with this town, as well as a biographical introduction on the author. The following are featured: Manuel Ibáñez Frocham,
Mariano Acosta, Máximo Cabral, Federico Alvarez de Toledo, Joaquín María Cazón, Máximo
Ledesma.

　　CtY DLC DPU IU NcU NN

182 Ibarguren, Carlos. <u>Estampas de argentinos.</u>
Buenos Aires: Librería y Editorial "La Facul-
tad," Bernabé y Cía., 1935. 221 p. 21 cm.
　　Biographical essays on the following 19th-
century notable Argentineans: Manuel Quintana,
Angel Gallardo, José Manuel Estrada, Vicente
Fidel López, José María Ramos Mejía.

　　CtY CU DLC IU NcU TxU WaU

183 Ingenieros, José. <u>La evolución de las ideas
argentinas.</u> Texto revisado y anotado por
Aníbal Ponce. Buenos Aires: El Ateneo, 1951.
2 v. 20 cm. (Biblioteca "El Ateneo").
　　A 2-volume history of intellectual life
in Argentina, covering the period from conquest to the middle of the 19th century, and
including scattered biographical information
for many notable thinkers. Among those featured are Juan Baltasar Maciel, Mariano Moreno, Gregorio Funes, Juan Crisóstomo Lafinur,
Manuel Fernández de Agüero, Francisco de Paula
Castañeda, Juan Cruz Varela, Juan Ignacio de
Gorriti, Julián Segundo de Agüero, Manuel Mo-

reno, Pedro Ignacio Castro Barros, Esteban
Echeverría, Juan Bautista Alberdi.

　　IU

184 Instituto de Estudios Biográficos, Buenos
Aires. <u>Los directores de la República Argentina.</u> Buenos Aires: Editorial "El Universitario," 1945. 486 p. 20 cm.
　　Biographical sketches of Argentineans
prominent in business, industry, science, and
arts and letters in mid-20th century. Information provided includes educational and family background and professional achievements.

　　CtY DLC IU

185 Irazusta, Julio. <u>Gobernantes, caudillos y
escritores.</u> Buenos Aires: Ediciones Dictio,
1978. 435 p. 20 cm. (Biblioteca Dictio,
v. 31. Sección Historia).
　　Biobibliographical essays about the following 19th- and 20th-century Argentinean political leaders and writers: Pablo Groussac,
Manuel Dorrego, Juan Manuel de Rosas, Charles
Maurras, Bernardino Rivadavia, Juan Bautista
Alberdi, Santiago de Liniers, Pedro de Mendoza, Juan de Garay, Leopoldo Lugones, José
de San Martín, Ricardo Rojas, Pedro de Angelis,
Justo José de Urquiza, Tomás de Anchorena,
Lorenzo Torres, Eduardo Lahitte, Baldomero
García.

　　IU

186 Lafuente Machaín, Ricardo de. <u>Buenos Aires
en el siglo XVII.</u> Buenos Aires: Emecé Editores, 1944. 251 p. Portraits. 24 cm.
　　A history of Buenos Aires during the 17th
century, including biographical notes about
many individuals from all walks of life associated with it.

　　CtY CU DLC IEN IU TxU

187 _____. <u>Los portugueses en Buenos Aires</u>
(siglo XVII). Madrid: Tipografía de Archivos, 1931. 174 p. 21 cm.
　　History of Portuguese people in Buenos
Aires during the 17th century with brief biographical notes about approximately 300 individuals.

　　CoU CtY CU DLC ICU IU MH MiU NcD
　　NcU NIC WaU

188 Larraín, Nicanor. <u>El país de Cuyo;</u> relación
histórica hasta 1872, publicada bajo los auspicios del gobierno de San Juan. Revisada y
anotada por Pedro P. Calderón. Buenos Aires:
Impr. de J. A. Alsina, 1906. 487 p. 25 cm.
　　A history of the Cuyo region in Argentina
from preconquest to 1872. Scattered biographical information of varying lengths is provided for many people who contributed to its

BIOGRAPHY (MISCELLANEOUS)

development. Particular emphasis is given to the following: Luis de Valdivia, Francisco de Villagrán, García Hurtado de Mendoza, Pedro del Castillo, Juan Jufre, Martín García Oñez de Loyola, Juan Pastor, Bartolomé de las Casas, Domingo Ortíz de Rosas, Agustín de Jáuregui, Manuel Amat, Pedro de Ceballos, William Carr Berresford, Santiago Liniers y Bremont, Puey-rredón, José de San Martín, Marcos González Balcarce, Saturnino Zaraza, Francisco Pantaleón de Luna, Manuel Corbalán, José Ignacio de la Roza, Patricio Ceballos, Eugenio Hidalgo, José María de Castro, Santiago Cerreras, Cornelio Saavedra, Francisco Narciso Laprida, Justo de Santa María de Oro, Carrera (brothers), Mariano Mendizábal, Francisco Solano del Corro, Alvarado, Toribio de Luzuriaga, José Miguel Carrera, José Antonio Sánchez, José María Pérez de Urdininea, Salvador M. del Carril, José Aldao, Manuel Olazábal, José de Navarro, Lorenzo Lozada, Manuel Gregorio Quiroga, José María Echegaray, Francisco Ignacio Bustos, Juan Aguilar, José Godoy, José Manuel Eufracio de Quiroga Sarmiento, Nicolás Aldazor, Olegario Correa, Wenceslao Achával, José Martín Yanzón, Lorenzo Barcala, Nazario Benavídes, Tomás Brizuela, Gregorio LaMadrid, Mariano de Acha, José María Oyuela, Angel Vicente Peñaloza, Justo José de Urquiza, Elías Bedoya, Francisco D. Díaz, Timoteo Maradona, Nicanor Molinas, Manuel José Gómez, José Antonio Virasoro, Antonino Aberastain, Juan Saa, Laureano Nazar, Domingo F. Sarmiento, Pablo Irrazábal, Guillermo Rawson, Santiago Lloveras, Saturnino de la Precilla, Camilo Rojo, Cesáreo Domínguez, Julio Campos, Felipe Varela, Manuel José Zavalla, Ruperto Godoy Carril, José María del Carril, Valentín Videla, Bonifacio Vera, Francisco de Sales Pérez, Ignacio Fermín Rodríguez.

CtY CU DLC IU NcU TNJ WU

189 Lascano, Pablo. *Siluetas contemporáneas.* Buenos Aires: Imprenta, Litografía y Encuadernación de J. Peuser, 1889. 342 p. 19 cm.

A collection of biographical sketches about the following citizens of Argentina: Salvador de la Colina, Luis Ponce y Gómez, Alejandro Vieyra, Domingo Faustino Sarmiento, José Posse, Guillermo San Román, Delfín Leguizamón, Julio B. Lezama, Pablo Zubieta, Delletery, Amado J. Ceballos, Sabino O'Donell, José Díaz Rodríguez, Dolores Velasco, Manuel Lucero, Nabor Córdoba, Francisco Lares (Sina-Sina, pseud.), Heredia (general), Javier López, Angel López, Balmaceda, Sauvage, Nicolás Avellaneda, Lisandro Olmos.

CU MH TxU

190 Lazcano Colodrero, Godofredo. *Retablillo de Córdoba: figuras y figurillas lejanas.* Prólogo de Arturo Capdevila. Córdoba: Biffignandi-Ediciones, 1974. 144 p. 17 cm.

Limited biographical information of the following 20th-century individuals from the Argentine city of Córdoba: Rafaela Sánchez, Pedro C. Molina, Alejandro Centeno, Pedro

Vella, Alfonso Aveta, Florindo Tal, Victorio Pinzani, Manuel J. Astrada, Julio Escarguel, Reginaldo Núñez, Rafael García, Manuel Lucero, Leopoldo Lugones, Aníbal Lencinas, Luis J. Ossés, Luis Onetti Lima.

CU CtY FU IU NN

191 López Piacentini, Carlos Primo. *Historia de la Provincia del Chaco.* Ilus. de tapa, Humberto Horianski. Resistencia: Editorial Región, 1979. 5 v. 20 cm. Portraits.

A history of Chaco, Argentina, covering the period from preconquest to the mid-20th century, and including portraits and biographical information for many people associated with this province. They include Carlos Primo López Piacentini, Domingo Martínez de Irala, Alonso de Bárzana, Roque González, Gaspar Osorio, Angel Peredo, Esteban de Urízar, Juan Adrián Fernández Cornejo, Julio de Vedia, Napoleón Uriburu, Pantaleón Gómez, Lucio V. Mansilla, Juan Dillón (son), Francisco Basiliano Bosch, Rudecindo Ibazeta, Juan Samuel MacLean, Luis Jorge Fontana, Félix de Azara, Alcides Dessalines D'Orbigny, Juan Antonio Víctor Martín de Moussy, Eduardo Ladislao Holmberg, Juan de Coinges, Julio M. Crevaux, Enrique de Ibarreta, Ramón Lista, Amadeo Jacques, Guido Boggiani, Gunardo Lange, Juan Queirel, Teodoro Meyer, Augusto Gustavo Schulz, Florentino Ameghino, Carlos Ameghino, Juan Bautista Ambrosetti, Enrique Lynch Arribálzaga, Erland Nordenskiöld, Emilio R. Wagner, Duncan Ladislao Wagner, Styg Ryden, Alfredo Metraux, Enrique Palavecino, Carlos Andrés Merti, José I. Miranda Borelli, José Alumni, Guido Arnoldo Miranda, Seferino Amelio Geraldi, Ernesto Joaquín A. Maeder, Julián Loreto Acosta, Pedro Celestino Luis Denier, Mario Chapo Bortagaray, Rafael Dermidio Galíndez, Alfredo Santiago Pertile, Manuel Sanchis, Yuyo Blanco Silva, José Zali, René Brusau, Lucio Correa Morales, Stephan Erzia, Crisanto Domínguez, Carlos Schenone, Juan de Dios Mena, Carlos Maule, José Mariscal, Héctor Díaz, Víctor Ricardone, Domingo Arenas, María Eloísa Zamudio, Gaspar Lucilo Benavento, Julio Florencio Acosta, José Adán Molfino Venere, Alfredo Veirave, Enrique Gamarra, Adolfo Cristaldo, Víctor Miguel Mercado, Alejo Luis Meloni, Juan Ramón Lestani, José Ricardo Bergallo, José del Carmen Nieto, José Pavlotzky, Ricardo Ríos Ortiz, Oscar Tacca, María Amelia Casco Encinas, Domingo Mancuso, Ricardo A. Zalazar, Lilia Yolanda P. de Elizondo, Juan Govi, Juan Moro, Manuel I. Obligado, Angel Justiniano Carranza, Benjamín Victorica, Ignacio Hamilton Fotheringham, Rosendo María Eduardo Fraga, José María Avalos, Evaristo Ramírez Juárez, Julio José Figueroa, Facundo Solari, Enrique Rostagno, Eliseo Muñiz, Adolfo Cortina, Donato Benítez Torres, Teófila Rodríguez de Martínez, Agustín Andriani, Antonio Brignole, José Ameri, Carlos Corsi, Félix Juan Seitour, Antonio Piccilli, Simeón Borda, Juan Holzer, Miguel Angel Mascaro.

IU

192 Loudet, Osvaldo. <u>Figuras próximas y lejanas</u>; al margen de la historia. Buenos Aires: Academia Argentina de Letras, 1970. 261 p. 21 cm. (Biblioteca de la Academia Argentina de Letras. Serie Estudios académicos, v. 12).

A collection of essays about the following notable Argentineans: Mariquita Sánchez de Thompson, Vicente Fidel López, Saturnino Segurola, Nicanor Albarellos, Pedro Mallo, Baldomero Fernández Moreno, Rafael Alberto Arrieta, Gregorio Aráoz Alfaro, José Ingenieros, Isidro Más de Ayala, Norberto Piñero, Rodolfo Rivarola, Antonio Sagarna, Francisco de Veyga.

FMU   IaU   InU   IU   NNC   OrU

193 Lusarreta, Pilar de. <u>Cinco dandys porteños</u>. Buenos Aires: Editorial Guillermo Kraft, 1943. 241 p. Portraits. 27 cm.

Biographical essays on the following 20th-century Argentinean public figures, with special emphasis on their characteristics of dandyism: Manuel Quintana, Fabián Gómez y Anchorena, Bernardo de Irigoyen, Lucio Victorio Mansilla, Benigno Ocampo. Also biographical data and portrait of Catalina de Henestrosa.

CU   DLC   IU   MB   NcU   PSt

194 Macchi, Manuel E., and Alberto J. Masramón. <u>Entre Ríos, síntesis histórica</u>. 2a. ed., primera en Editorial Sacha. Concepción del Uruguay: Editorial Sacha, 1977. 183 p. 22 cm.

History of the Argentine province of Entre Ríos from 1520 through the first half of the 20th century. Scattered biographical information is supplied for the following individuals who figured prominently in its history: Tomás de Rocamora, Juan León Sola, Evaristo Carriego, Pedro Serrano, José Miguel Carreras, Leónidas Echagüe, Ramón Febre, José Francisco Antelo, Martín Ruiz Moreno, Clemente Basavilbaso, Sabá Z. Hernández, Luis Bilbao, Salvador Macía, Enrique Carbó, Faustino M. Parera, Celestino Marcó, Ramón Mihura, Eduardo Laurencena.

IU

195 Mansilla, Lucio Victorio. <u>Retratos y recuerdos</u>. Buenos Aires, Nueva York: W. M. Jackson, Inc., 1927. 220 p. 18 cm. (Grandes escritores argentinos. Ediciones Jackson, v. 14).

A series of biographical sketches of several notable Argentines, primarily of the 19th century, with emphasis on personality traits and physical characteristics. A short biographical portrait is also provided for the author of this work. The following are featured: Lucio Victorio Mansilla, Nicolás Avellaneda, Domingo Faustino Sarmiento, Salvador María del Carril, Elías Bedoya, Justiniano Posse, Luque, Santiago Derqui, Campillo, Seguí, Lucero, Salustiano Zavalía, Luis Cáceres, Emilio de Alvear, Carlos M. Saravia,

Tomás Guido, Juan Bautista Alberdi, José de Buschenthal (Bouchenthal, pseud.).

CU   IU   MoU   OC1W   OU

196 Mantilla, Manuel Florencio. <u>Crónica histórica de la provincia de Corrientes</u>. Buenos Aires: Espiasse y Cía., 1928-29. 2 v. Portraits. 24 cm.

A 2-volume history of the Argentine province of Corrientes, covering the period from the 16th through the 19th century, and containing biographical information for many people associated with this region. A portrait and a more lengthy essay are included for the author of this work. Among those featured are Juan de Torres de Vera y Aragón, Pedro Bautista José de Casajús, Pedro Bautista de Casajús (son), Sebastián de Casajús, José Francisco de Casajús, Bernardo de Casajús (Bernardino Casajús), José Baltasar de Casajús, Joaquín Legal y Córdoba, Carlos Casal, Toribio Luzuriaga, José León Domínguez, Fermín Félix Pampín, José Fernández Rueda, José López (López Chico), Juan Mexias Sánchez, Francisco Javier Sity, Juan José Fernández Blanco, Agustín Díaz Colodrero, Pedro Ferré, Rafael Atienza, Genaro Berón de Astrada, Manuel Olazábal, Niceto Vega, Antel Salvadores, Pedro Castelli, Juan Estanislao de Elía, José María Paz, Joaquín Madariaga, Juan Pujol.

CSt   CtY   CU   DLC   IU   MB   NcU   WaU

197 Manzi, Francisco. <u>El viejo Taragüy</u>; crónicas, narraciones y leyendas de la tradición y mitología de Corrientes. Buenos Aires: Editorial Claridad, 1946. 254 p. 21 cm. (Colección Claridad, v. 178).

A collection of narratives dealing with various aspects of the Argentine province of Corrientes, covering the period from colonial times through the 19th century, and including scattered biographical information on many people associated with it. Among those featured are Hernandarias de Saavedra, Ambrosio Acosta, Juan Pujol, Juan Torres de Vera y Aragón, Juana Ortiz de Zárate.

CU   DLC   DPU   IU   MB   NcU   TxU

198 Marianetti, Benito. <u>Semblanzas y narraciones</u>. Buenos Aires: Editorial Anteo, 1975. 154 p. 21 cm.

Detailed biographical information on the following 20th-century Argentineans from the province of Mendoza: Agustín Alvarez, Juan B. Justo, José Néstor Lencinas, Ramón Morey, Teodoro Shestakov, Eduardo J. Godoy, Valentín Bonetti, José Peter, Rodolfo Aráoz Alfaro, Florencia Fossati, José Federico García, Gregoria B. Cosarinsky, Juan I. Epósito, Manuel Ruiz, Isaac Kornblihtt, Demetrio, Radomé Canata, Deodoro Roca, David Leibowicz, Leopoldo Suárez, Rosendo Godoy, Juan Aguinaga, Carlos W.

BIOGRAPHY (MISCELLANEOUS)

Lencinas, Lisandro Videla, Filemón Aveiro, Jose E. Leal.

CtY InU IU NIC NN WU

199 Matti, Carlos Horacio. <u>Semblanzas de argentinos</u>. Buenos Aires: Librería Hachette, 1939. 104 p. (V. 1). 19 cm.
   Biographical essays on the following 19th-century notable Argentineans: Mariano Moreno, Domingo F. Sarmiento, Manuel Belgrano, José Hernández, Enrique García Velloso, Gregorio de Laferrère.

   DLC DPU IU MB MnU

200 Melli, Oscar Ricardo. <u>Historia de Carmen de Areco</u>, 1771-1970. La Plata: Archivo Histórico de la Provincia de Buenos Aires "Ricardo Levene," 1974. 295 p. 27 cm. (Publicaciones del Archivo Histórico de la Provincia de Buenos Aires. Contribución a la historia de los pueblos de la Provincia de Buenos Aires, v. 41).
   A history of Carmen de Areco, located in Buenos Aires province, covering the period from 1771 to 1970. Scattered biographical information is given for many people associated with this town.

   CtY DGU FU InU IU LU MH MnU NcD
   NjP NNC TxU

201 Miragaya, Eduardo, and Francisco Solanes. <u>Los españoles en Rosario de Santa Fe</u>; su influencia en el progreso de la ciudad. Prólogo del Dr. Gonzalo Diéguez Redondo. Rosario: Editorial "La Cervantina," 1934. 243 p. 19 cm.
   Study of Spanish influence in the Argentinean city of Rosario de Santa Fe from the 16th to the 20th centuries. Features scattered biographical data of Spaniards involved in its development.

   WU

202 Moldes, José María. <u>La tierra de los Tehuelches</u>, nociones de historia y geografía física, política y económica de la Patagonia. Buenos Aires: Talleres Gráficos "Editorial Lito," de Cavallari y Del Pozo, 1937. 392 p. 28 cm.
   A description of the geography, politics, economy, and history of Patagonia, including portraits for many notable people associated with this region. Among them are Fernando de Magallanes, Basilio Villarino, Alejandro Malaspina, Juan Manuel de Rosas, Roberto Fitz Roy, Jones Perry Madryn, Francisco P. Moreno, Luis Piedra Buena, José Fagnano, Guillermo Greenwood, Julio Argentino Roca, Conrado Villegas, Carlos M. Moyano, Luis Jorge Fontana, Federico Spurr.

   CSt DLC DPU IU NcU NN

203 Moncaut, Carlos Antonio. <u>Biografía del Río Salado de la Provincia de Buenos Aires</u>. 2. ed. aumentada. La Plata: Talleres Gráficos del C.E.I.L.P., 1967. 153 p. illus. map. 23 cm.
   A history of Río Salado, Argentina, covering the period from the 18th to the 20th centuries, and including scattered biographical information for many prominent people associated with this region.

   CLSU CLU CSt CU FU IU MoSW NBuU
   NIC NjR NmLcU NN NSyU OU WU

204 Montes, Alberto. <u>Santiago Montenegro, fundador de la ciudad de Rosario</u>. Rosario: Ediciones IEN, 1977. 164 p. 19 cm.
   A history of Rosario, Argentina, covering the 17th through the 19th centuries, and giving biographical information for the founder, Santiago Montenegro, as well as for other people associated with this city. The following are among those featured: Luis Romero de Pineda, Clemente de Montenegro, Santiago Montenegro, Martín Cardozo, Nicolás Cardozo Vega, Francisco de Lucena.

   AzU IU NIC OU TxU

205 Montes, Aníbal. <u>Historia antigua de la ciudad de Río Cuarto</u>. Córdoba: Dirección General de Publicidad de la Universidad Nacional, 1953. 52 p. 27 cm. (Universidad Nacional de Córdoba. Facultad de Filosofía y Humanidades, Instituto de Estudios Americanistas. Cuaderno de historia, v. 26).
   A short history of Río Cuarto, in the Argentine province of Córdoba, covering the 16th through the 18th centuries, and including scattered biographical information for many people associated with this city. The following are emphasized: Hernandarias de Saavedra, Jerónimo Luis de Cabrera, Tristán de Tejeda.

   DLC IU MB NcU NN TxU

206 Morales, Ernesto. <u>Fisonomías de 1840</u>. Ilustraciones de Indalecio Pereyra, ejecutadas según retratos auténticos. Buenos Aires: El Ateneo, 1940. 206 p. Portraits. 19 cm.
   A collection of biographical essays on the following notable figures in the history of Argentina during the 1840s: Juan Cruz Varela, Domingo Cullen, Diego Alcorta, Pedro de Angelis, Esteban Echeverría, Santiago Viola, Juan Antonio Gutiérrez, Juan Thompson, Pacheco y Obes, Benjamín Villafañe.

   CSt CU DLC IU MB NcU TNJ

207 Morales Guiñazú, Fernando. <u>Historia de la cultura mendocina</u>. Mendoza: Best Hermanos, 1943. 610 p. Portraits. 20 cm.
   A cultural history of the Argentine province of Mendoza covering the period from colonial to modern times. Biographical information, as well as portraits, given for many people representing various professions.

   DLC NcU NN TxU

208 _____. <u>Villavicencio a través de la historia</u>. Mendoza: Peuser lda., impresores, 1943. 139 p. Portraits. 25 cm.

A history of Villavicencio, Argentina, covering the period from colonial to modern times. Scattered biographical information, as well as some portraits, included for many people associated with this region. The following are particularly featured: Joseph de Villavicencio, Ana María Cotapos de Carrera, Martín de Moussy, Carlos Germán Burmeister, Abraham Lemos.

DLC ICU MB

209 Moya, Juan R. Contribución a la historia de Bragado. La Plata: Dirección de Impresiones Oficiales, 1957. 210 p. 27 cm. (Publicaciones del Archivo de la Provincia de Buenos Aires. Contribución a la historia de los pueblos de la provincia de Buenos Aires, v. 30).

A history of Bragado, located in Buenos Aires province, covering the period from the 19th to the early 20th century. Scattered biographical information is given for many people associated with this town. The following are emphasized: Federico Rauch, Eugenio del Busto, Angel Pacheco, Agustín Rodríguez, Francisco Clavero, Laureano José Díaz.

IaU IU NN ViU

210 Mujica Láinez, Manuel. Los porteños. Buenos Aires: Ediciones Librería La Ciudad, 1980. 254 p. 23 cm.

An essay about the city of Buenos Aires and its people, mainly through biographical sketches of the following distinguished citizens from different walks of life: Florencio Varela, Eleuterio Mujica y Covarrubias, Bernabé Láinez Cané, Juan Cruz Varela (art collector), Francisco P. Moreno, Alberto Gerchunoff, Miguel Carlos Victorica, Alberto Lagos, Susana Aguirre, Luis María Carreras Saavedra, Alejandro Schult Solari (Xul Solar, pseud.), Adolfo Mitre, Alberto Greco, Alfredo González Garaño, Héctor Basaldúa, Victoria Ocampo, Augusto Guillermo Adolfo Bullrich, Adolfo J. J. Bullrich, Ricardo E. Molinari, Alejo B. González Garaño.

IU

211 Munzón, Eduardo I. Historia del partido de General Sarmiento. La Plata: Taller de Impresiones Oficiales, 1944. 515 p. Portraits. 28 cm. (Publicaciones del Archivo Histórico de la Provincia de Buenos Aires. Contribución a la historia de los pueblos de la Provincia de Buenos Aires, v. 22).

A history of General Sarmiento located in Buenos Aires province, from conquest to modern times, and including scattered biographical information and portraits for many people associated with this town. The following are emphasized: Salvador Posse, Francisco Planes, Adolfo Sourdeaux, Amancio Alcorta, Blas Pais, Pedro Scala, Pascuala Cueta, Luis María Gonnet, Ventura G. Coll, Carlos de Chapeaurouge, Silvio E. Parodi, Juan Carlos

Vázquez, Juan Luis Hilario Artigue, Eduardo P. Moine, Juan Buzzini, José Altube.

CtY DLC IU KU MH NcU NN TxU ViU

212 Napolitano, Leonardo F. Mendoza; historia de la nomenclatura de sus calles. Buenos Aires: Editorial Buenos Aires, 1943. 124 p. 20 cm.

An essay about the streets in Mendoza, Argentina, including biographical sketches of the individuals after whom they are named. Those featured are Julio Leónidas Aguirre, Juan Bautista Alberdi, Leandro Nicéforo Alem, Agustín Alvarez, Florentino Ameghino, José Francisco Amigorena, Nicolás Avellaneda, Lorenzo Barcala, Juan Manuel Belgrano, Luis Beltrán, Tiburcio Benegas, Eusebio Blanco, José Félix Bogado, Jorge A. Calle, José Videla Castillo, Pedro del Castillo, Juan Clark, Mateo Clark, Emilio Civit, Cristóbal Colón, Agustín Delgado, Pedro I. Díaz, Remedios Escalada de San Martín, Gerónimo Espejo, Esteban Echeverría, José Garibaldi, Vicente Gil, Tomás Godoy Cruz, Joaquín V. González, Gutiérrez, Juan Gregorio de las Heras, Damián Hudson, Emilio Jofre, Gregorio Aráoz de Lamadrid, Juan de Lavalle, Vicente López, Toribio de Luzuriaga, Juan B. Justo, Juan Agustín Maza, General Bartolomé Mitre, José Federico Moreno, Pedro Molina, Mariano Moreno, Bruno Morón, Francisco J. Moyano, Mariano Necochea, Manuel José Olascoaga, Rufino Ortega, José María Paz, Roque Sáenz Peña, Juan Martín de Pueyrredón, José Santos Ramírez, Primitivo de La Reta, Bernardino Rivadavia, Julio Argentino Roca, Juan Esteban Rodríguez, José Rondeau, Martínez de Rosas, José de San Martín, Sobremonte, Miguel Estanislao Soler, Manuel Antonio Sáez, Domingo Faustino Sarmiento, Tropero Sosa, Justo José de Urquiza, Aristóbulo del Valle, Juan de Dios Videla, Arístides Villanueva, Martín Zapata, José Vicente Zapata, Manuel Antonio Zuloaga.

DLC DPU

213 Neustadt, Bernardo. La Argentina y los argentinos. Buenos Aires: Emecé Editores, 1972. 403 p. 19 cm.

Interviews conducted on the Argentine television program "Tiempo Nuevo" from 1975-76. Discussion centers around the political life of the country. The following individuals are featured: Raúl Lastiri, René Favaloro, Ricardo Balbín, Alfredo Gómez Morales, Juan Carlos de Pablo, Alfredo Concepción, Félix Elizalde, Francisco Manrique, Jorge Daniels Paladino, Angel Federico Robledo, Víctor Massuh, María Cristina Guzmán, Alejandro Orfila, Jorge Luis de Imaz, Alcides López Aufranc, Pedro Cossio, Jorge Isaac, Bernardo Neustadt, Mariano Grondona.

CU-S CU-SB ICIU KU MH NcU NIC NN TxU ViU

BIOGRAPHY (MISCELLANEOUS)

214 Newton, Ronald C. German Buenos Aires, 1900-1933. Austin: University of Texas Press, 1977. 225 p. 24 cm. (Texas Pan American series).

An account of the activities of Germans in Buenos Aires from 1900 to 1933, including scattered biographical information on many people associated with this aspect of Argentina's history. Particular emphasis is given to the following: Theodor Alemann, Emil Hayn, Wilhelm Keiper, August Moller, Hipólito Yrigoyen. Alphabetical index of names.

AAP AkU AU AzFU AzU CaBVaU CLSU
CoFS CoU CoU-CS CSt-H CtW CtY CU
CU-S DAU DGU DGW FMU FU GASU GU
IaAS IaU ICarbS IEN InND InU IU
KU LNHT LU MB MdBE MH MiEM MiU
MnU MoSW MoU MShM MsSM MsU MU
NbU NBuU NcCU NcGU NcRS NcU NIC
NjP NjR NmLcU NmU NN NNC NNR NNU
NSbSU NSyU NvU OCl OkU OOxM OrU
OU RPB TNJ TU TxCM TxU ViBlbV ViU
VtU WaU WMUW WU

215 Núñez, Urbano J. Historia de San Luis. Buenos Aires: Editorial Plus Ultra, 1980. 617 p. 20 cm. (Colección: Historia de nuestras provincias, v. 8).

A history of San Luis, Argentina, covering the period from conquest to modern times, and including biographical sketches on the following people: Urbano Joaquín Núñez, Francisco de Villagra, Juan Jufré, Luis Jofré, Marcelino Poblet, Agustín Jorge Donado, José Santos Ortiz, Juan Pascual Pringles, Justo Daract, Juan Crisóstomo Lafinur.

IU

216 Orofino, Alfredo T. Proceridad; retratos histórico-literarios, 1903-1914. Buenos Aires: Editorial G. Kraft, 1943. 125 p. 28 cm.

A collection of biographical essays on the following prominent 19th-century Argentineans: Francisco Pico, Charles Henri Pellegrini, Nicolás Avellaneda, Carlos Pellegrini, Ricardo Gutiérrez, José Mármol, Domingo F. Sarmiento, José Rivera Indarte, Félix Frías, Juan Cruz Varela, Olegario V. Andrade, Domingo Cullen, Juan Chassaing, Julio A. Roca.

CU TxU ViU

217 Ortigosa, Luis. Nuestro folklore y sus nombres ilustres. Buenos Aires: J. Korn, 1954. 67 p. 24 cm. (Selecciones de cultura popular).

A discussion, with examples, of some important aspects of Argentine folklore. Brief biographical notes are also given for the following musicians and authors who have made important contributions to Argentina's culture: Abalos (brothers), Nicolás Alfredo Alessio, María Luisa Anido, Isabel Aretz-Thiele, Ricardo Antonio Barcelo, Oscar Bareilles, Andrés Beltrame, Ana S. de Cabrera, Alberto Carlos Castellán, Andrés Chazarreta, Félix Coluccio, Gabino Coria Peñaloza, Hilario Cuadros, Aurora de Pietro de Torras, Juan de Dios Filiberto, Abel Fleury, Vicente Forte, Ernesto César Galeano, Luis Gianneo, Domingo Vicente Lombardi, Adolfo Luna, José Montero Lacasa, Ismael Moreno, Arturo C. Schianca, Ana Serrano Redonnet, José Vicente Sola, Guillermo Teruel, Carlos Vega, Edmundo P. Zaldívar, Arturo Carranza Casares, Hilario Ascasubi, Atahualpa Yupanqui, Miguel Andrés Camino, Estanislao del Campo, Joaquín V. González, José Hernández, José Ramón Luna, Diego Novillo Quiroga, Rafael Obligado, Amaro Villanueva, Jorge Bermúdez, Cesáreo Bernaldo de Quirós, Fernando Fader, Prilidiano Pueyrredón.

DLC GU NN OCl TxU

218 Paita, Jorge A., comp. Argentina: 1930-1960. Buenos Aires: Sur, 1961. 446 p. Portraits. 22 cm.

A collection of essays dealing with various aspects of Argentine politics and culture during the period from 1930 to 1960, including scattered biographical information and portraits for many notable people and followed by biobibliographical sketches on the contributors: Jorge D'Urbano, Abraham Eidlicz, Carlos S. Fayt, Carlos Alberto Floria, Félix Daniel Frascara, Tulio Halperín Donghi, Ludovico Ivanissevich Machado, Mario Justo López, Sebastián Marotta, José Alfredo A. Martínez de Hoz (son), Carlos A. Méndez Mosquera, José Enrique Carlos Míguens, Joaquín Neyra, Alfredo Orgaz, Hugo Parpagnoli, Enrique Pezzoni, Leandro Pita Romero (son), Leopoldo Portnay, Aníbal Ruiz Moreno, Carlos Sánchez Viamonte, Horacio Jorge Sueldo, Miguel Angel Virasoro, Julia Helena Acuña, Joaquín S. I. Adúriz García, Alberto J. Aguirre, José Babini, Nélida Baigorria, Walter Beveraggi Allende, José A. Blanco, C. A. Burone, Emilio Carreira, Roberto Cortés Conde, Carlos Cossío, Jorge Cruz, Lorenzo Dagnino Pastore.

IU NSyU

219 Palacios, Alfredo Lorenzo. Estadistas y poetas. Buenos Aires: Editorial Claridad, 1951. 250 p. 22 cm. (Biblioteca hombres e ideas, ser 2, v. 3).

Contains biographies of the following Argentine statesmen: Juan B. Justo, Mario Bravo, Joaquín V. González, Aristóbulo del Valle, Roberto M. Ortiz, Marcelo T. de Alvear, Laureano Landaburu, Antonio Sagarna, Nicolás Matienzo. Also the following poets: Pedro B. Palacios, Carlos Guido y Spano, Alfonsina Storni, Arturo Capdevila, and the following artists and scientists: Zonza Briano, Rogelio Yrurtia, Florentino Ameghino, Carlos Spegazzini, Juan Vucetich, Alejandro Korn, Máximo Maldonado. Alphabetical index of names.

CaBVaU CU DLC DPU IaU IU MH MiU
NBuU PSt WaU

220 Palma, Federico. Pago Largo; noticias biográficas sobre los jefes de la batalla. Corrientes: Impr. del Estado, 1939. 94 p. Portraits. 22 cm.
  A collection of biographical essays about
the following leaders in the battle of Pago
Largo (1839) from the Argentine province of
Corrientes: José López, Manuel Vicente Ramírez, Manuel de Olazábal, José Antonio Navarro,
Tiburcio Antonio Rolón, Juan Bautista Ocana,
Santiago Fernando Báez.

  ICarbS TxU

221 Parker, William Belmont, comp. Argentines of
today. Buenos Aires, New York: The Hispanic
Society of America, 1920. 2 v. Portraits.
17 cm.
  Biographical sketches accompanied by portraits of 420 Argentineans from all walks of
life in 1920.

  CaBVaU CU DAU DLC DNW DPU ICJ ICN
  IU MB MeB MtU NBuU NcD NIC NN OC1
  OC1W ODW OO OrSaW OrU OU PBm PHC
  PP PU TxU WaSp

222 Pastor, Reynaldo Alberto. San Luis, su gloriosa y callada gesta, 1810-1967. Buenos
Aires, 1970. 525 p. Portraits. 23 cm.
  A history of the Argentine province of
San Luis covering the 19th and 20th centuries.
Biographical information of varying amounts is
included for many people form all walks of
life who contributed to the development of
this region.

  CtY FU IaU MU NcU

223 Paula, Alberto S. J. de; Ramón Gutiérrez; and
Graciela María Viñuales. Del pago del Ria-
chuelo al partido de Lanús, 1536-1944. La
Plata, 1974. 206 p. Portraits. 27 cm.
(Publicaciones del Archivo Histórico de la
Provincia de Buenos Aires. Contribución a la
historia de los pueblos de la provincia de
Buenos Aires, v. 42).
  A history of Lanús, located in Buenos
Aires province, covering the period from 1534
to 1944. Scattered biographical information,
as well as portraits in a few cases, given for
many people associated with this city. The
following are emphasized: Juan Ruiz de Ocaña,
Melchor Maciel, Pedro de Rojas y Acevedo, Ana-
carsis Lanús, Guillermo F. Gaebeler, José
Marini.

  CtY DGU FMU FU InU IU LU MnU MU
  NcD NIC NjP NNC TxU WU

224 Paula, Alberto S. J. de, and Ramón Gutiérrez.
Lomas de Zamora desde el siglo XVI hasta la
creación del partido, 1861. La Plata, 1969.
228 p. 27 cm. (Publicaciones del Archivo
Histórico de la Provincia de Buenos Aires.
Contribución a la historia de los pueblos de
la Provincia de Buenos Aires, v. 36).

  A history of Lomas de Zamora, Argentina,
covering the period from the 16th century to
the year 1861, and including scattered biographical information on many people associated with this city. Those particularly featured include Juan de Castro, Pedro López de
Tarifa, Francisco García Romero, Inés Romero
de Santa Cruz, Pedro de Espinosa Argüello,
Gaspar de Avellaneda, Juan de Zamora, Tomás
José Grigera, Esteban Adrogué, Juan Parish
Robertson.

  CLU CtY IU MH OU TNJ TxU WU

225 Payró, Roberto Jorge. Evocaciones de un porteño viejo. Buenos Aires: Quetzal-Editorial,
1952. 141 p. 20 cm.
  A collection of fairly lengthy biographies,
which are primarily psychological profiles, of
various notable contemporary Argentines. The
following are featured: Bartolomé Mitre,
Miguel Cané, Fray Mocho, pseud. (José S. Alvarez), Rubén Darío (Nicaraguan), José Ingenieros, Emilio Mitre, Enrique Freixas, Horacio
Quiroga, José Antonio Ojeda, Enrique Hurtado
y Arias.

  DLC FU GEU IaU IEN KU MdBJ MiU
  NcU NmU NN PPiU PSt TxU

226 Peers de Perkins, Carmen. Eramos jóvenes el
siglo y yo. Buenos Aires: Editorial Jorge
Alvarez, 1969. 126 p. Portraits. 20 cm.
  Biographical information about the people
on Ms. Perkins's mother's side of the family:
Gabriel Costa, Pascual Costa, Eduardo Costa,
Angela de Oliveira Cezar, Ernestina Costa y
Oliveira Cézar. Also Gastón Peers, Carlos
Perkins.

  CLSU CLU CSt CU-SB CtY FU IU IaU
  MB MU MoSW NIC NNC NCU OU PPULC
  ViU

227 Pelliza, Mariano A. Críticas y bocetos históricos. Buenos Aires: Impr. de Mayo, 1879.
350 p. 22 cm.
  Biographical accounts, anecdotal in nature,
of the following women associated with the
emancipation period: Mercedes Tapia, Tomasa
Quintana de Escalada, Carmen Quintanilla de
Alvear, María Costa, Petrona Cárdenas, Isabel
Calvimontes, María Sánchez de Thompson, Martina Céspedes, Teresa Lemoine, Juana Azurduy
de Padilla, Gerónima de San Martín. Also the
following men: Mariano Moreno, Camilo Enríquez, Juan Facundo Quiroga, Vicente López y
Planes, José Mármol, Juan Martín Pueyrredón,
Manuel Dorrego, Domingo Acasuso, Juan C. Lafinur, Juan María Gutiérrez, José de San Martín.

  CU DLC ICarbS IU MH NNH TxU

228 _____. Glorias argentinas. Batallas, Para-
lelos, Biografías, Cuadros históricos. Precedidas de un juicio crítico por D. Andrés

BIOGRAPHY (MISCELLANEOUS)

Lamas. Buenos Aires: F. Lajouane, 1885.
228 p. 19 cm.

A collection of essays dealing with various
prominent Argentine people and events of the
19th century. Biographical information is included for the following: José de San Martín,
Carlos María de Alvear, Bernardino Rivadavia,
Manuel Dorrego, Mariano Moreno, Vicente López
y Planes, José Mármol, Juan Martín de Pueyrredón, José María Paz, Martín Rodríguez, Olegario Víctor Andrade, Juan Lavalle.

CtY DLC IU

229 Pérez, Daniel E. Los italianos en Tandil;
centenario de la Sociedad Italiana de Socorros
Mutuos. Prólogo de Enrique de Gandía. Tandil:
Talleres Grafitán, 1977. 176 p. Portraits.
22 cm.

A historical account of the Italian immigration to Argentina in general and the Italian settlers in the city of Tandil in particular mainly through the reviewing of the accomplishments of hundreds of members of the
Sociedad Italiana de Socorros Mutuos in Tandil
from 1877 to the present.

IU

230 Pérez, René. Apuntes para la historia de Junín. La Plata, 1950. 147 p. 29 cm. (Publicaciones del Archivo Histórico de la Provincia
de Buenos Aires. Contribución a la historia
de los pueblos de la provincia de Buenos
Aires, v. 28).

A history of Junín, located in Buenos
Aires province, covering the period from the
late 18th to the late 19th centuries. Scattered biographical information is included for
many people associated with this town. Those
particularly featured include Bernardino Escribano, Mariano García, José Corvalán, José
Seguí.

CtY ICU InU IU NIC NN

231 Petriella, Dionisio. Los italianos en la historia de la cultura argentina. Buenos Aires:
Asociación Dante Alighieri, 1979. 365 p.
23 cm.

An essay about the contribution of Italians to the development of Argentina through
biographical sketches of individuals associated with it. Arrangement by subject covering
all fields of endeavor. Alphabetical index
lists approximately 1,400 names.

MU

232 Piglia, Ricardo, comp. Yo. Buenos Aires:
Editorial Tiempo Contemporáneo, 1968. 114 p.
20 cm.

Selections, autobiographical in nature,
of the following authors: Juan Manuel de
Rosas, José María Paz, Domingo F. Sarmiento,
Lucio V. Mansilla, Leandro N. Alem, Roberto J.
Payró, Horacio Quiroga, Macedonio Fernández,
Hipólito Yrigoyen, Manuel Gálvez, Roberto Arlt,
Ezequiel Martínez Estrada, Juan Domingo Perón,
Jorge Luis Borges, Victoria Ocampo, Julio Cor-
tázar, Ernesto Che Guevara.

FU IU MoSW MU TxU

233 Pinasco, Eduardo H. Hombres de la historia
del puerto de Buenos Aires en el período colonial. Prólogo del capitán de navío contador
(R. S.) Humberto F. Burzio. Buenos Aires:
Tall. Graf. de la DIAB, 1972. 379 p. Portraits. 25 cm. (Commando en Jefe de la Armada. Secretaría General Naval. Departamento
de Estudios Históricos Navales. Publicaciones,
Series B: Historia naval argentina v. 14).

A series of brief biographies of men (approximately 950 names) who directly or indir-
ectly contributed to the development of the
port of Buenos Aires during the colonial era
(16th-18th century). Alphabetical list of
names.

ViU

234 Pineda Yáñez, Rafael. Cómo fue la vida amoro-
sa de Juan Manuel de Rosas. Buenos Aires:
Plus Ultra, 1972. 178 p. 20 cm. (Colección
Esquemas históricos, v. 6).

An account of the involvement of Juan
Manuel de Rosas with women, including scattered
biographical information for the following:
Juan Manuel de Rosas, María Eugenia Castro,
Encarnación Ezcurra y Arguibel, Juanita Sosa,
Nicanora Rosas de Galíndez.

CaQMM CLU CtY CU CU-SB FU GU IaU
IU MB MH MoSW MU NN NNC TxU ViU
WU

235 Pineta, Alberto. Verde memoria, tres décadas
de literatura y periodismo en una autobiografía; los grupos de Boedo y Florida. Buenos
Aires: Ediciones A. Zamora, 1962. 227 p.
23 cm. (Colección Argentoria hombres e ideas
en la cultura argentina de ayer y de hoy,
v. 15).

An autobiography written by a prominent
20th-century Argentina journalist--Alberto
Pineta. Scattered biographical information is
given for many writers who were personal ac-
quaintances of the author. The following are
particularly featured: Alberto Pineta, Rosa
P. Cisterna, Antonio Zamora, Manuel Gleizer,
Samuel Glusberg, Alfonso de Laferrère, Enrique
Méndez Calzada, Eduardo Mallea, Leónidas de
Vedia, Macedonia Fernández, Jorge Luis Borges,
Carlos Mastronardi, Roberto Arlt, Jacobo Fij-
man, José Sebastián Tallón, Lizardo Zía, Ulises
Petit de Murat, Raúl González Tuñón, Enrique
Bernárdez, Manuel Peyrou, Enrique González
Tuñón, Miranda Klix, Ricardo Rojas, Leopoldo
Lugones, Alberto Gerchunoff, Horacio Rega Mo-
lina, Héctor Olivera Lavíe, Carlos Alberto
Leumann, Carlos Muzio Sáenz Peña. Adolfo Ale-
mán, Abelardo González Rillo, Enrique Alemán,
Ricardo Maquieira, Raúl Rubianes, Antonio

Ardizzono, José P. Barreiro, Roberto Ledesma, Manuel Agromayor, José Barcia.

CaBVaU CLSU CLU CtW CtY CU-S DPU FU IaU ICU InU IU MB MH MiEM NcD NcU NhD NIC NNC NSyU TxU VtU WU

236 Ponce, Aníbal. <u>La vejez de Sarmiento</u>. Buenos Aires: Talleres Gráficos Argentinos de L. J. Rosso, 1927. 232 p. 21 cm.
A collection of biographical sketches of the following notable individuals associated with the history of Argentina: Domingo Faustino Sarmiento, Nicolás Avellaneda, Lucio V. Mansilla, Eduardo Wilde, Lucio V. López, Miguel Cané.

DLC IU LNHT

237 Puccia, Enrique Horacio. <u>Barracas</u>, su historia y sus tradiciones, 1536-1936. Buenos Aires: Tall. Graf. de la Compañía General Fabril Financiera, 1968. 416 p. Portraits. 22 cm.
A history of Barracas, Argentina, covering the period from 1536 to 1936, and including scattered biographical information, as well as portraits in many cases, for many of the prominent people associated with this Buenos Airean neighborhood. Among those featured are Enrique Horacio Puccia, Martín de Alzaga, Guillermo Brown, Elija Brown, Francisco Alvarez, Felicitas Guerrero de Alzaga, Manuel A. Montes de Oca, Antero Carrasco, José V. Bosio, Lorenzo Eduardo Arolas, Agustín Bardi.

AzU CLSU CLU CSt CtY CU CU-SB FU IaU ICU IU KU MB MiU MnU MU NcU NIC NjP NmLcU NN NNC NSyU TxU ViU WU

238 Pyzik, Estanislao P. <u>Los polacos en la República argentina, 1812-1900</u>, algunos antecedentes históricos y biográficos, con palabras alusivas del dr. Eduardo Crespo y prólogo del dr. Jorge Castro Nevares. Buenos Aires: Imprenta López, 1944. 370 p. Portraits. 20 cm.
A history of the Polish involvement in Argentina from 1812 to 1900. Portraits and scattered biographical information are included for many Polish people who contributed to various facets of Argentina's development. Those particularly featured are Juan Valerio Bulewski, Ignacio Domeyko, Alejandro Floriano Colonna Walewski, Maximiliano Rymarkiewicz, Enrique Spitczyński (Enrique Spiczchyski, Enrique Spitchski, pseuds.), Teófilo R. Iwanowski, Enrique Spika, Alberto Tomaszewski, Eduardo Tomaszewski, Roberto Adolfo Chodasiewicz, Jordán Czeslaw Wysocki, Eugenio Wysocki, Juan Wysocki, Ricardo Starszy, José Zielinski, (José Ziblsque, pseud.), Carlos Muntawski, Tadeo Sztyrle, Ladislao Czarnecki (Ladislao Czanecki; Ladislao Charnseki; Ladislao Scar-

nesky; Ladislao Ozarnecky; pseuds.), José Anselmo Izarowski, Juan Guzdynowicz, Roberto Skowroński, León Miaskowski, Enrique Ozarowski, Miguel Wyszkowicz, Victorio Woinilowicz, José Bartoszewski, Enrique Sadowski, Julio Jurkowski, Ricardo Sudnik, Carlos Lowenhard, Miguel Gorski, Zdzislaw Celiński, Miguel Szelagowski, Adam Dabrowski, Gustavo Jasiński, José Bialostocki, Casimiro Estanislao Rechniewski, Estanislao Cynalewicz, Ladislao Zakrzewski.

CtY CU DLC ICU MB NcU WU

239 <u>Qué es la Argentina</u>. Con prólogo de Jorge Luis Borges. Buenos Aires: Editorial Columba, 1970. 365 p. Portraits. 20 cm. (Colección Esquemas, v. 100).
A collection of essays dealing with various aspects of Argentine culture, each preceded by a short biobibliographical note and portrait on its author. The following are included: Alfredo J. Grassi, Guillermo Ara, Romualdo Brughetti, Mariano N. Castex, Gustavo F. J. Cirigliano, Augusto Raúl Cortázar, Ismael Quiles, Francisco Valsecchi, Juan Adolfo Vázquez.

CFS CLSU CSt CtY CU-S CU-SB FU GU INS InU IU KU LU MdBJ MdU MoSW MShM MU NbU NBuU NcD NcU NIC NjR NNC OkU OU PPiU RPB TxU ViU VtMiM WaU WU

240 Ramos Mejía, José María. <u>A martillo limpio</u>; estampas y siluetas repujadas. Buenos Aires, 1959. 285 p. Portraits. 21 cm.
A collection of biographical essays, many of them accompanied by portraits, on the following notable Argentines: José María Ramos Mejía, José Tomás Guido, Carlos J. Alvarez, Juan Mariano Larsen, Juan María Gutiérrez, Ricardo Lavalle, Caracciolo Figueroa, Marcelino Ugarte, Rufino Ortega, Dom Frías, Julio A. Roca, Hipólito Yrigoyen, Manuel Vidal Peña, Mariano de Vedia, Juan Manuel de Rosas, Agustina López Osornio de Ortiz de Rosas, Encarnación Ezcurra de Rosas, Oribe, Juan Facundo Quiroga, Juan José Castelli, Mariano Moreno, Santiago de Liniers.

CLU CLSU CtY CU MH MnU NcU NIC NjP NN TxU

241 Reula, Filiberto. <u>Historia de Entre Ríos</u>; política, étnica, económica, social, cultural y moral. Santa Fe: Librería y Editorial Castelví, 1963. 3 v. 20 cm.
A 3-volume history of Entre Ríos, Argentina, covering the period from preconquest to the year 1943, and including scattered biographical information for many prominent people associated with this region. The following are emphasized: Ernesto A. Bavio, Alejandro Carbó, Enrique Carbó, Leónidas Echagüe, Pascual Echagüe, Luis L. Etchevehere, Ramón Febre, José Eusebio Hereñú, Sabá Z. Hernández, Eduardo Laurencena, Miguel M.

BIOGRAPHY (MISCELLANEOUS)

Laurencena, Salvador Maciá, Lucio Mansilla, Celestino Marcó, Enrique Mihura, Ramón Mihura, Faustino M. Parera, Herminio J. Quirós, Eduardo Racedo, Francisco Ramírez, Juan Manuel de Rosas, Martín Ruiz Moreno, Antonio Sagarna, Domingo Faustino Sarmiento, León J. Sola, Eduardo Tibiletti, Cipriano J. de Urquiza, Justo José de Urquiza. Alphabetical index of names.

CFS CLSU CLU CSt CtY CU CU-SB FTaSU FU GU IaU ICarbS ICU InU IU KU MB MH MiEM MnU MoSW MU NbU NBuU NcD NcU NIC NmLcU NN NNC OU PPT TxU ViU WU

242 Reyes, Marcelino. *Bosquejo histórico de la provincia de la Rioja*, 1543-1867. Buenos Aires: H. Cattáneo, 1913. 276 p. Portraits. 27 cm.

A history of the Argentine province of La Rioja, covering the period from 1543 to 1867, and including scattered biographical information, as well as portraits in some cases, for many people associated with this region. Among them are Marcelino Reyes, Francisco Antonio Ortiz de Ocampo, Tomás Brizuela, José Olegario Gordillo, Ramón Gil Navarro, Francisco Alvarez, Ricardo Vera, Domingo Antonio Villafañe.

CSt CU IU LU MH NSyU

243 Rivera, Jorge B. *Los bohemios*. Buenos Aires: Centro Editor de América Latina, 1971. 114 p. Portraits. 18 cm. (La Historia popular, v. 43).

A discussion of Argentinean culture during the years of transition from the past to modern times. The cultural changes of those times are explained as manifestations of the diverse historic, political, and economic changes taking place. Fairly extensive biographical information is given for a number of authors of that period, in particular: Charles de Soussens, Antonio Lamberti, Diego Fernández Espiro, Martín Goycoechea Menédez, Leopoldo Lugones, Alberto Ghiraldo, Antonio Monteavaro, Emilio Becher.

CSt CtY CU-SB FU GU InU IU KU MdBJ MU NcU NIC NmLcU NN NSbSU TxU ViU WU

244 Rodríguez de la Torre, Miguel A. *Significado histórico de las calles de Córdoba*. 2. ed. Buenos Aires: Kraft, 1945. 209 p. 23 cm.

An essay about the names of the streets of the capital city of Córdoba (Argentina), including biographical sketches of the numerous individuals after whom the streets are named.

DLC

245 Rojas, Ricardo. *Los arquetipos*; seis oraciones: Belgrano, Güemes, Sarmiento, Pellegrini,

Amechino [!], Guido Spano. Buenos Aires: J. Roldán y Cía., 1922. 277 p. 20 cm. (Obras, v. 2).

A collection of biographical essays, emphasizing personal characteristics, on the following illustrious 19th-century Argentines: Manuel Belgrano, Martín Güemes, Domingo Faustino Sarmiento, Carlos Pellegrini, Florentino Ameghino, Carlos Guido y Spano.

DLC IU

246 Romero, José Luis. *El desarrollo de las ideas en la sociedad argentina del siglo XX*. México: Fondo de Cultura Económica, 1965. 197 p. Portraits. 21 cm. (Colección Tierra firma: historia de las ideas contemporáneas, v. 8).

A history of the development of ideas in Argentine society spanning the period between the Generation of '98 and the 1940s. Scattered biographical information is included for many who contributed to this era (approximately 400 names). The following are particularly emphasized: Juan Bautista Alberdi, Leandro N. Alem, Agustín Alvarez, Jorge Luis Borges, Carlos Octavio Bunge, Esteban Echeverría, Juan Agustín García, Joaquín V. González, Pedro Goyena, José Ingenieros, Juan B. Justo, Alejandro Korn, Leopoldo Lugones, Bartolomé Mitre, José Ortega y Gasset, Alfredo L. Palacios, Carlos Pellegrini, Juan D. Perón, José María Ramos Mejía, Julio Argentino Roca, Ricardo Rojas, Juan Manuel de Rosas, Domingo Faustino Sarmiento, Lisandro de Torre, Hipólito Yrigoyen. Alphabetical index of names.

AAP CaBVaU CaOTP CFS CLSU CLU CNoS CoU CSt CtY CU CU-B CU-S DAU DPU DS FMU ICU IEdS IEN InS InU IU KU LNHT MB MdU MH MnU MoSW MShM MU MWiW NbU NcU NBuU NIC NjP NN NNC NSyU OrCS OU PPiU TxFTC TxU ViU WaU WU

247 Sáenz Cavia de Morales Torres, Sara. *La Rioja*: Libro de oro, 1939-1943. La Rioja, 1943. 142 p. Portraits. 23 x 32 cm.

Collection of essays about the province of La Rioja, Argentina, covering 1939-1943. Limited biographical information is available for the following prominent residents: Timoteo Gordillo, Gregorio N. Cháves, Lucio Mélendez, Adolfo E. Dávila, Abel Bazán y Bustos, Pelagio B. Luna, Lorenzo Torres, José María Jaramillo, Nicolás Barros, Salvador de la Colina, María Elvira Rojas.

IU

248 Salvadores, Antonino. *Ensayo sobre El Pago de la Magdalena durante el siglo XVIII*. La Plata: Talleres Gráficos Olivieri y Domínguez, 1930. 37 p. 27 cm. (Publicaciones del Archivo Histórico de la Provincia de Buenos Aires. Contribución a la historia de los pueblos de la provincia de Buenos Aires, v. 3).

An essay on El Pago de la Magdalena, located in Buenos Aires province, covering the 18th century, and including brief scattered biographical information on many people associated with this region.

CLU   CtY   InU   IU   NN   NNC   TxU

249   _____. Olavarría y sus colonias. La Plata: Taller de Impresiones Oficiales, 1937. 69 p. 28 cm. (Publicaciones del Archivo Histórico de la Provincia de Buenos Aires. Contribución a la historia de los pueblos de la provincia de Buenos Aires, v. 11).

A short history of Olavarría, located in Buenos Aires province, covering the 19th century, and including scattered biographical information on many people associated with this town. The following are emphasized: Ignacio Rivas, Alvaro Barros, Juan Coquet.

CLU   CtY   DLC   DPU   IU   NcU   NN   TxU

250   Sánchez Ceschi, Eduardo A. Crónica histórica de Carmen de Patagones entre los años 1852-1855; carta-proemio de Enrique Udaondo. Buenos Aires: Editorial Tor, 1938. 230 p. 19 cm.

A history of the Argentine town of Carmen de Patagones, covering the period from 1852-1855. Scattered biographical information is given for many people associated with this town. Those particularly featured include Manuel B. Alvarez, Bernardo Bartruille, Jaime Harris, Marcelino Crespo, Yanguetruz El Grande, José María Yanguetruz, Feliciana Torres.

DLC   MB   TxU   WU

251   Sánchez de Bustamante, Teófilo. Biografías históricas de Jujuy. Tucumán: Universidad Nacional de Tucumán, Facultad de Filosofía y Letras, 1957. 388 p. 28 cm. (Universidad Nacional de Tucumán. Publicación v. 747).

Biographical sketches of citizens of the Argentine province of Jujuy from the colonial period to the early 20th century. Birthplace, important dates, and information on professional activities are provided for over 300 citizens. Alphabetical index of names.

CtY   CU   FU   IU   LU   NN

252   Santos Martínez, Pedro. Historia de Mendoza. Buenos Aires: Plus Ultra, 1979. 358 p. 20 cm. (Colección Historia de nuestras provincias, v. 7).

A history of Mendoza, Argentina, covering the period from the 16th century to the present day, and including biographical information for many people, mostly political leaders, associated with this province, as well as for the contributors to this work. These people include Pedro Santos Martínez, Ramona del Valle Herrera, Ana Edelmira Castro, Aníbal Mario Romano, Pedro del Castillo, Emilio Civit,

José Néstor Lencinas, Carlos Washington Lencinas.

IU

253   Scotto, José Arturo. Notas biográficas publicadas en la sección Efemérides americanas de "La Nación" en los años 1907-1909. Buenos Aires: L. J. Rosso & Cía., 1910. 4 v. 28 cm.

Collection of biographies previously published in the newspaper La Nación from 1907-1909 profiling Argentines from all period of history. Information includes birthplace, dates, and professional achievements for over 800 individuals. Each volume includes an alphabetical index of names. (See also entry 254.)

CLU   CtY   CU   DLC   FU   IaU   InU   IU   MB
MU   NcU   NIC   NSyU   PSt   TxU

254   _____. Notas biográficas publicadas en la sección efemérides americanas de "La Nación" en los años 1907-1912. 2. ser. Buenos Aires: Empresa Administradora y Reimpresora de Obras Americanas, 1912-13. 2 v. 25 cm.

Continuation of the 1910 edition covering biographies in the newspaper La Nación from 1907-1913. (See entry 253.)

CtY   CU   DLC   DPU   FU   IaU   ICarbS   IU
MB   MU   NSyU   TxU

255   Schallman, Lázaro. Los pioneros de la colonización judía en la Argentina. Buenos Aires: Ejecutivo Sudamericano del Congreso Judío Mundial, 1969. 48 p. Portraits. 20 cm. (Biblioteca popular judía. Colección Hechos de la historia judía, v. 25).

A discussion of the Jewish immigration to Argentina in the 19th century. Scattered biographical information is included for many of the pioneers of this movement. The following are particularly featured: Wilhelm Loewenthal, Mauricio de Hirsch, M. Isidore Loeb.

CLU   CtHC   FU   InU   IU   MH   MU   NN   NNJ
TxU   WU

256   Schoo Lastra, Dionisio. La lanza rota; estancias, indios, paz en la Cordillera. Ilus. de Eleodoro Marenco. Buenos Aires: Ediciones Peuser, 1953. 232 p. 28 cm.

A collection of anecdotes about Indian life in Argentina during the 19th century, including biographical information for many notable people. The following are emphasized: Pablo Vargas, Marcelino Vargas, Manuel Payun, Pichi Pincen, Luis Piedra Buena.

DLC   DPU   ICarbS   IU   NN   NSyU   TxU   WU

257   Selva, José Fernando. Dolores, Bs. As.; sus hijos dilectos, sus varones ilustres, sus vecinos destacados. Dolores: Tall. Gráf. de "El Tribuno," 1967. 1 v. (unpaged) 23 cm.

BIOGRAPHY (MISCELLANEOUS)

Biographical sketches of 19th- and 20th-century residents of the city of Dolores in the Argentine province of Buenos Aires, from the fields of business, education, religion, journalism, government, and law. Alphabetical arrangement.

CFIS CLSU CLU CSt IU MB NBuU NcU
NIC NN NNC OU TxU ViU WU

258 Sergi, Jorge F. <u>Historia de los italianos en la Argentina</u>; los italianos y sus descendientes a través del descubrimiento de América y de la historia argentina. Buenos Aires: Editora Italo Argentina, 1940. 536 p. Portraits. 23 cm.
An essay about Italians in Argentina (15th-20th centuries). Includes biographical information on hundreds of native Italians and Argentineans of Italian descent who are associated with the history and cultural development of Argentina.

AzU CaBVaU DLC MB NcD NNC PU
ViU WaU

258a Sigwald Carioli, Susana B. <u>Historia de barbas y caftanes</u>. Buenos Aires: Intendencia Municipal de Carlos Casares, 1976. 17 p. 33 cm. (Serie "Pueblo Maya," v. 4).
A short history of the immigration of Jews, primarily of Russian nationality, which took place in Argentina in 1891. Particular emphasis is given to the colony founded by Mauricio Hirsch, and biographical information is given for those involved in its initial settlement and subsequent development. They are Wilhelm Loewenthal, Mauricio Hirsch, Marcos Alpersohn, Boris Garfunkel, Demetrio Aranovich.

IU

259 Solari, Juan Antonio. <u>Evocaciones políticas y literarias</u>. Buenos Aires: Editorial "La Vanguardia," 1943. 222 p. 24 cm.
A collection of biographical sketches of the following notable individuals associated with the political and literary history of Argentina: Juan B. Justo, José Ingenieros, Enrique del Valle Iberlucea, Esteban Dagnino, Fernando Lanzola, José Guevara, Jean Jaurès, Alejandro Castiñeiras, Adolfo Dickmann, Enzo Bordabehere, Lisandro de la Torre, José María Ramos Mejía, Angel M. Giménez, Mario Antelo, Giacomo Matteotti, Domingo Faustino Sarmiento, Almafuerte, Rafael Barret, Ricardo Gutiérrez.

CSt DLC DPU MB NN TxU

260 _____. <u>Hombres de la República; maestros, amigos, compañeros</u>. Buenos Aires: Editorial Firmación, 1966. 191 p. 21 cm.
A collection of biographical articles on the following 20th-century Argentineans: Mario Bravo, Alejandro Korn, Lucio V. López,

Silvio L. Ruggieri, Octavio R. Amadeo, Indalecio Prieto, Enrique Coira, Luis Ricagno, Agustín de Arrieta, Arturo Storni, Arturo Orgaz, Enrique Dickman, Andrés Beltrame, Julio A. Cruciani, Héctor Rossi, José Belbey, Rufino Inda, David Michel Torino, Manuel V. Besasso, Julio A. Noble, Fernando Peña, Enrique Corona Martínez, Andrés Justo, Emilio López, Ghino Fogli, Alfonso R. Castelao, Alberto Palcos, Juan José Díaz Arana, Nicolás Repetto, Juan Antonio Solari,

CoU CSt CtY CU ICU IU KU MB MiEM
MoSW MoU MU NcD NIC NN NNC NSyU
OU TxU

261 _____. <u>Nuevas evocaciones</u>. Buenos Aires: Editorial Afirmación, 1967. 217 p. 23 cm.
A work featuring biographical essays on the following people, most of them 19th-century Argentineans: José Martí (Cuba), Alberto Ghiraldo, Bartolomé Mitre, Agustín Alvarez, Enrique Martínez, Pedro José Segura, Benjamín José Lavaysse, Juan María Gutiérrez, Emilio Mitre, Nicolás Repetto, Eduardo Wilde, Julio A. Roca, Vicente Fidel López, Mariano Moreno, Esteban Echeverría, Roberto J. Payró, José de San Martín, Florencio Varela, Olegario V. Andrade, Guillermo Rawson, Mamerto Esquiú, Marcos Sastre.

CoU CtY FU IaU InU KU MiEM MoU
MU NSyU TxU

262 Sors de Tricerri, Guillermina. <u>El puerto de la Ensenada de Barragán, 1727-1810</u>. La Plata, 1933. 343 p. 28 cm. (Publicaciones del Archivo Histórico de la Provincia de Buenos Aires. Contribución a la historia de los pueblos de la provincia de Buenos Aires, v. 6).
A history of Ensenada de Barragán, a port located in Buenos Aires province, covering the period from 1727 to 1810, and including very brief scattered biographical information on many people associated with this city.

CtY IU NN NNC

263 _____. <u>Quilmes colonial</u>. La Plata: Taller de Impresiones Oficiales, 1937. 145 p. 27 cm. (Publicaciones del Archivo Histórico de la Provincia de Buenos Aires. Contribución a la historia de los pueblos de la provincia de Buenos Aires, v. 10).
A history of Quilmes, Argentina, located in Buenos Aires province, and covering its colonial period. Brief scattered biographical information is included for many people associated with this city.

CLU CtY DLC DPU FMU IU NcU NN
OrU TxU WU

264 Taboada, Gaspar, comp. <u>Recuerdos históricos</u>; "Los Taboada," luchas de la organización nacional, documentos seleccionados y comentados.

Buenos Aires: Imprenta López, 1929. 5 v.
Portraits. 20 cm.

A five-volume collection of documents deal-
ing with or written by members of the Argen-
tine Taboada family, including portraits and
biographical sketches for the following people:
Manuel Gorostiaga, Antonio María Taboada, Juan
Tomás Taboada, Manuel Taboada, Antonino Taboada,
Eusebio García, José Cueto Taboada, Felipe
Taboada, Gaspar Taboada, Sebastián de Jesús
Gorostiaga, Ana María Taboada, María Antonia
de la Paz y Figueroa, Benjamín H. Lavaysse,
Crisanto Gómez, Aristóbulo E. Mittelbach.

CU DLC IU MnU NcU NN OCl

265 Temas de historia marítima Argentina. Buenos
Aires: Fundación Argentina de Estudios Marítimos, 1970. 320 p. 23 cm.

A collection of essays dealing with Argen-
tine maritime history, accompanied by biogra-
phical sketches on their authors. They are
Laurio H. Destéfani, Enrique González Lonzième,
V. Mario Quartaruolo, Aurelio González Climent,
Ricardo R. Caillet.Bois, Vicente Vázquez Pre-
sedo, Guillermo H. Ferreira, Isidoro Ruis
Moreno.

CLSU CSt CU CU-SB FU GU IaU ICU
InU IU KU MB MoSW MU NIC NNC
NSbSU TxU ViU WU

266 Torassa, Antonio A. El partido de Avellaneda,
1580-1890. La Plata: Taller de Impresiones
Oficiales, 1940. 190 p. Portraits. 27 cm.
(Publicaciones del Archivo Histórico de la
Provincia de Buenos Aires. Contribución a la
historia de los pueblos de la provincia de
Buenos Aires, v. 18).

A history of Avellaneda, located in Buenos
Aires province, covering the period from 1580
to 1890, and including scattered biographical
information, as well as a few portraits, for
many people associated with this city. The
following are emphasized: Mariano Moreno,
Pridiliano Pueyrredón, Guillermo Wheelwright.

CLU CtY DLC IU KU MH NIC NN
TxU WU

267 Torre, José E. de la. Historia de la ciudad
de San Nicolás de los Arroyos. La Plata:
Taller de Impresiones Oficiales, 1938. 134 p.
Portraits. 27 cm. (Publicaciones del Archivo
Histórico de la Provincia de Buenos Aires.
Contribución a la historia de los pueblos de
la provincia de Buenos Aires, v. 16).

A history of San Nicolás de los Arroyos,
located in Buenos Aires province, covering the
period from the 18th to the 20th centuries,
and including scattered biographical information, as well as some portraits, for many
people associated with this city. Biographical footnotes are given for the following:
Antonio Sáenz, Pedro Alurralde, José Francisco
Benítez.

CLU CtY DLC GU ICN IU MH MiU TxU

268 _____. Historia de San Nicolás de los Arroyos: con un prólogo de Marcelino Marcatelli.
Rosario, 1955. 307 p. (V. 1). Portraits.
22 cm.

A collection of biographical sketches,
some accompanied by portraits, of distinguished citizens of the Argentine town of San
Nicolás in the province of Buenos Aires.

CU

269 Troncoso, Oscar A. Los nacionalistas argenti-
nos, antecedentes y trayectoria. Buenos Aires:
Editorial S.A.G.A., 1957. 93 p. 21 cm.
(Coleccion "Tribuna," v. 3).

A study of 20th-century Argentine nation-
ism, giving important dates, events, and scattered biographical information for many notable people associated with that movement.
Those particularly featured are Carlos Ibarguren, Marcelo T. de Alvear, José F. Uriburu,
Leopoldo Lugones, Agustín P. Justo, Manuel A.
Fresco, Federico Ibarguren.

CU CSt DS FU MH MWelC NcD NIC NN

270 Udaondo, Enrique. Apuntes históricos del pueblo de San Fernando. La Plata, 1930. 78 p.
26 cm. (Publicaciones del Archivo Histórico
de la Provincia de Buenos Aires. Contribución
a la historia de los pueblos de la provincia
de Buenos Aires, v. 2).

A history of San Fernando, located in Buenos Aires province, covering the period from
colonial times through the 19th century, and
including scattered biographical information
on many prominent people associated with this
city.

CLU ICN InU IU NN NNC TxU

271 _____. Grandes hombres de nuestra patria.
Buenos Aires: Editorial Pleamar, 1968. 3 v.
Portraits. 27 cm.

Collection of biographical essays on prominent Argentines from various fields of endeavor throughout history. Each volume contains alphabetical list of names.
V. 1: A-E.
V. 2: F-O.
V. 3: P-Z.

CLSU CoU CU ICU InU IU KU MiU NcU
NIC PPULC TxU ViU

272 _____. Reseña histórica de la villa de Luján.
Luján: Talleres Gráficos San Pablo, 1939.
324 p. Portraits. 23 cm.

A history of the town of Luján, Argentina,
covering the period from colonial to modern
times, and including biographical information,
as well as portraits in some cases, for many
prominent people. The following are among
those featured: Juan de Lezica y Torrezuri,
Manuel de Torres, Antonio de Olavarría, Guillermo Carr Beresford, Juan Ramón Balcarce,
Julián de Leiva, Felipe Díaz, José María Paz,
Francisco Javier Muñiz, Esteban Echeverría,

BIOGRAPHY (MISCELLANEOUS)

Fermín Migoya, Bartolomé Mitre, Florentino Ameghino, José Manuel Estrada, Domingo Fernández, Jorge María Salvaire, Antonio Wermter.

DLC   IU   NN   TxU

273   _____. Reseña histórica del partido de Las Conchas. La Plata: Talleres de Impresiones Oficiales, 1942. 136 p. Portraits. 27 cm. (Publicaciones del Archivo Histórico de la Provincia de Buenos Aires. Contribución a la historia de los pueblos de la provincia de Buenos Aires, v. 21).

A history of Las Conchas, located in Buenos Aires province, covering the period from colonial times to the 20th century, and including portraits and biographical information for many prominent people associated with this city. The following are emphasized: Domingo de Acassuso, Sobre Monte, Martín Rodríguez, Francisco de Paula Castañeda y Romero, José María Vilela, Daniel María Cazón.

CLU   CtY   DLC-P4   GU   ICN   InU   MH   NN

274   Ugarteche, Félix de. Hombres del coloniaje, con las biografías de los gobernadores, obispos, oidores, jueces de pesquisa, tenientes generales y tenientes de la gobernación, oficiales de la real hacienda, alcaldes ordinarios y de la hermandad, alféreces reales, regidores, alguaciles, depositarios, almirantes, maestres de campo, capitanes, letrados, médicos, escribanos, maestros, clérigos, comerciantes, etc., de esta ciudad, durante los siglos XVI y XVII. Buenos Aires: Casa Oucinde, 1932. 219 p. (V. 1.) 21 cm.

Collection of biographical essays on outstanding citizens of Buenos Aires, Argentina, from its founding to the end of the 17th century. The following are particularly featured: Francis de Beaumont y Navarra, Enrique Enríquez de Guzmán, Gaspar de Gaete, Francisco Bernardo Jijón.

DLC   ICarbS   IU   NSyU   TxU   ViU

275   Vaccarezza, Jorge Raúl; Oscar L. Vaccarezza; and Roberto A. Vaccarezza. Historia del pueblo Vaccarezza y del partido de Alberti. La Plata, 1972. 210 p. Portraits. 27 cm. (Publicaciones del Archivo Histórico de la Provincia de Buenos Aires. Contribución a la historia de los pueblos de la provincia de Buenos Aires, v. 40).

An essay about Vaccarezza and the Partido Alberti in the Argentine province of Buenos Aires. Includes biographical data about the following citizens from all walks of life: Andrés Vaccarezza, Juan Carlos Cánepa, Manuel Alberti, Vicente Barbieri, Enrique Tornú, Carlos A. Díaz, Roberto A. Vaccarezza. Also listing of the first dwellers of Vaccarezza. Alphabetical index of names.

IU

276   Valle, Aristóbulo del. Oraciones magistrales: oraciones fúnebres (1874-1892) / discursos en el Senado (1877-1884). Compilación y prólogo de Aníbal F. Leguizamón. Buenos Aires: Vaccaro, 1922. 298 p. 22 cm. (La Cultura Argentina).

A collection of speeches, some made in the Argentine senate on political matters, and others made as eulogies to the following notable 19th-century men, most of them Argentines: Miguel Grau (Peru), Juan María Gutiérrez, Domingo F. Sarmiento, Pedro Goyena.

CLSU   IaU   IU   NcU   NjP   NN   NSbSU   TxU

277   Vedia, Joaquín de. Como los vi yo. (Semblanzas de Mitre, Roca, Jaurés, Clemenceau, Alem, Pellegrini, B. de Irigoyen, A. del Valle, A. de Vedia, Herreray Obes, Quintana, P. C. Molina, E. Becher). Buenos Aires: M. Gleizer, 1954. 237 p. 21 cm.

Biographical essays profiling political figures of the late 19th and early 20th centuries in Argentina. Information provided concentrates on the political careers of Joaquín de Vedia, Bartolomé Mitre, Julio Argentino Roca, Leandro Nicéforo Alem, Carlos Pellegrini, Bernardo de Irigoyen, Aristóbulo del Valle, Agustín de Vedia, Manuel Quintana, Pedro C. Molina, Emilio Becher.

DLC   IU   MB   MoSW   NcD   NN   PSt   TxU

278   Velasco Quiroga, Hilario. Perfiles. Mendoza: Best hermanos, 1942. 3 v. 19 cm.

A collection of biographical sketches of the following Argentineans from all walks of life:

V. 1: Juan Bautista Alberdi, Marcelo T. de Alvear, Florentino Ameghino, Manuel Pacífico Antequeda, Nicolás Avellaneda, Pedro Ignacio Anzorena, Julián Barraquero, Manuel Belgrano, Luis Beltrán, Emilio Civit, Adolfo Calle, José Manuel Estrada, Fernando Fader, Tomás Godoy Cruz, Emilio Jofré, Alejandro Mathus, José Federico Moreno, Mariano Moreno, Martín Palero, Carlos Pellegrini, Juan Pascual Pringles, José de San Martín, Domingo Faustino Sarmiento, Manuel Antonio Sáez, Félix Suárez, Arístides Villanueva, Martín Zapata.

V. 2: Julio Leónidas Aguirre, Agustín Alvarez, Juan Francisco Cobo, Gerónimo Espejo, Joaquín V. González, Juan Ignacio Gorriti, Juan Crisóstomo Lafinur, Juan Lavalle, Juan Agustín Maza, Bartolomé Mitre, Manuel José Olascoaga, Justo Santa María de Oro, Rufino Ortega, Angelina Puebla de Day, Manuel Quintana, Casimiro Recuero, José Videla Castillo.

V. 3: Lorenzo Barcala, Tiburcio Benegas, Juan Gualberto Godoy, Leopoldo Herrera, José Ingenieros, Francisco Narciso de Laprida, Avelino B. Maure, Pedro Molina, Juan Esteban Pedernera, Pedro Pascual Segura, Justo José de Urquiza, Leopoldo Zuloaga.

DLC   PSt

279 Vico, Humberto P. Historia de Gualeguay; desde sus orígenes hasta 1910. Santa Fe, Argentina: Colmegna, 1972. 326 p. 22 cm.

A history of Gualeguay, Argentina, covering the period from pre-Columbian times to the year 1910, and including scattered biographical information for many people associated with this region. Among them are Tomás de Rocamora, Sebastián Malvar y Pinto, Fernando Andrés de Quiroga y Taboada, Juan Castares, José María Pagola, Juan Vilar, Miguel Laurencena, Pedro E. Eseyza, Francisco Quintana (son).

CaBVaU CtY IU LNHT MH MU NcU

280 Vidal, Alfredo. Historia de la ciudad de Las Flores; prólogo de Enrique de Gandía. Buenos Aires: García Santos, 1934. 200 p. Portraits. 21 cm.

A history of the city of Las Flores, Argentina, covering the period from the 18th century to 1934, and including biographical information, as well as some portraits, for many notable people associated with this city. The following are emphasized: Pascual Peredo, Mariano Díaz, Isidro Jurado, Máximo Gómez, Higinio Tartabull, Manuel V. Paz.

DLC

281 _____ . Los orígenes de Ranchos (General Paz). La Plata: Taller de Impresiones Oficiales, 1937. 59 p. 28 cm. (Publicaciones del Archivo Histórico de la Provincia de Buenos Aires. Contribución a la historia de los pueblos de la provincia de Buenos Aires, v. 8).

A history of Ranchos (General Paz), located in Buenos Aires province, covering the period from 1771 to 1865, and including brief scattered biographical information for many people associated with this city.

CLU CtY DLC DPU ICN IU NcU NN TxU

282 Vidas de grandes argentinos. Colaboradores: Armando Alonso Piñeiro et al. Buenos Aires: Ediciones A. Fossati, 1960. 3 v. Portraits. 27 cm.

Collection of biographical essays, accompanied by portraits, on outstanding Argentines from various fields of endeavor throughout history.

CLSU CLU CtY CU FTaSU IaU IEN InU
IU NN NNC

283 Videla, Horacio. Historia de San Juan. Buenos Aires: Academia del Plata, 1962. 4 v. 23 cm.

A history of the Argentine province of San Juan, covering the period 1551-1862. Scattered biographical information is included for many people from all walks of life who have contributed to the development of this region. Alphabetical index of names.

CLSU CLU CtY CU ICN InU IU MB
MH NIC NNC TxU

284 Vilanova Rodríguez, Alberto. Los gallegos en la Argentina. Buenos Aires: Ediciones Galicia, 1966. 2 v. 23 cm.

An essay about the Galicians in Argentina, including biographical data on numerous individuals.

IaU IU VtMiM

285 Vita, Buenaventura N. Crónica vecinal de Nueve de Julio, 1863-1870. La Plata: Taller de Impresiones Oficiales, 1938. 113 p. Portraits. 27 cm. (Publicaciones del Archivo Histórico de la Provincia de Buenos Aires. Contribución a la historia de los pueblos de la provincia de Buenos Aires, v. 14).

A history of Nueve de Julio, located in Buenos Aires province, covering the period from 1863 to 1870, and including biographical information and portraits for the following people: Julio de Vedia, Esteban Severo Trejo, Bonifacia Viera de la Plaza, Antonio D'Elia.

CLU CtY DLC ICN IU MiU NcU NN
RPB TxU

286 Williams Alzaga, Enrique. Cinco retratos. Buenos Aires: Emecé Editores, 1980. 66 p. 22 cm.

A collection of biographical essays about the following distinguished Argentineans from different walks of life: Ricardo Rojas, María Antonio de Paz y Figueroa, Cayetano José Rodríguez, Amancio Alcorta, Juan Nielsen.

IU

287 Ygobone, Aquiles D. La epopeya patagónica. Buenos Aires: Editorial "El Ateneo," 1946. 808 p. Portraits. 21 cm.

A history of the Patagonian region, covering the period from the discovery through the 19th century, and including portraits and scattered biographical information for the following people: Hernando de Magallanes, Tomás Cavendish, Basilio Villarino, Alejandro Malaspina, Roberto Fitz-Roy, Valentín Feilberg, Carlos Darwin, Martín Guerrico, Luis Py, Guillermo Rawson, Ernesto Rouquand, Luis Piedra Buena, Francisco P. Moreno, Ramón Lista, Carlos Ameghino, Florentino Ameghino, Nicolás Avellaneda, Conrado E. Villegas, Lorenzo Vintter, Carlos M. Moyano, Jorge Luis Fontana, Manuel J. Olascoaga, Félix Mariano Paz, Juan Cogliero, José Fagnano, Santiago Costamagna, Julio A. Roca.

CtY DLC IU TxU

288 _____ . Figuras señeras de la Patagonia y Tierra del Fuego. Buenos Aires: Ediciones Depalma, 1981. 187 p. Portraits. 23 cm.

An essay about the following prominent individuals from different walks of life associated with the Argentine region of Patagonia and Tierra del Fuego: Luis Piedra Buena, Ramón

BIOGRAPHY (MISCELLANEOUS)

Lista, Carlos María Moyano, Luis Jorge Fontana, Francisco P. Moreno, Estanislao S. Zeballos, Roberto J. Payró.

IU

289 _____. Viajeros científicos en la Patagonia durante los siglos XVIII y XIX. Buenos Aires: Editorial Galerna, 1977. 193 p. 20 cm.
    Study of scientific expeditions in the region of Patagonia, Argentina, in the 18th and 19th centuries. Biographical material includes dates and information on scientific activities for Thomas Falkner, Charles Darwin, George Chaworth Musters, Francisco Pascasio Moreno.

IU MU NIC WU

290 Yribarren, Alfredo A. El origen de la ciudad de Mercedes. Advertencia de Ricardo Levene. La Plata: Taller de Impresiones Oficiales, 1937. 90 p. 29 cm. (Publicaciones del Archivo Histórico de la Provincia de Buenos Aires. Contribución a la historia de los pueblos de la provincia de Buenos Aires, v. 7).
    A discussion of the origin of Mercedes, located in Buenos Aires province, including brief scattered biographical information on many people associated with this city.

CLU DLC-P4 DPU ICN IU LNT NNC TxU

291 Zuberbühler, Ricardo F. Evocaciones criollas. Buenos Aires: Ediciones Librería La Ciudad, 1978. 434 p. 23 cm.
    A biography of Ricardo Zuberbühler, which also includes information for many people, especially gauchos, with whom he was associated. The following are emphasized: Ricardo F. Zuberbühler, Juan Beltrán, Melitón Giles.

DLC IU

292 Zuccarini, Emilio. Il lavoro degli italiani nella Repubblica Argentina dal 1516 al 1910; studi, leggende e ricerche. 2. ed. notevolmente accresciuta. Buenos Aires: Giornale La Patrie degli Italiani, 1910. 592 p. 29 cm.
    A history of the contributions of Italians to the development of Argentina covering the period 1516-1910. Scattered biographical material is included for many people who contributed to all areas of Argentine development.

MH

293 Zuretti, Juan Carlos. Historia de la cultura argentina, arte, ciencia. Buenos Aires: Itinerarium, 1952. 191 p. Portraits. 23 cm.
    An essay about art, science, and the state in the Argentine Republic, including biographical notes about distinguished Argen-

tineans and others associated with the development of Argentina (18th-20th centuries).

IU MnU TxU

BIOGRAPHY (MISCELLANEOUS)--DICTIONARIES, ENCYCLOPEDIAS, and "WHO'S WHO"

294 Abad de Santillán, Diego. Gran enciclopedia de la provincia de Santa Fe. Buenos Aires: Ediar, 1967. 2 v. Portraits. 29 cm.
    Encyclopedia covering the history, economy, and geography of the Argentine province of Santa Fe. Biographical sketches of prominent residents from all periods of history are included.
    V. 1: A-LL.
    V. 2: M-Z.

CLSU CU FU IaU InU IU MB MdU MoSW NBuU NIC NN OU ViU WU

294a Anuario de la aristocracia y alta sociedad. Edición hispano-argentina. Madrid, 1959-71. "Quién es Quién." 14 v. 21 cm.
    A "who's who" of the Hispanic-Argentine aristocracy and high society arranged alphabetically by nobility title and last name.

DLC TxU WU

295 Biedma, José Juan, and José Antonio Pillado. Diccionario biográfico argentino. Buenos Aires: M. Biedma e hijo, 1897. 256 p. 36 x 27 cm.
    Biographical dictionary of prominent Argentineans throughout history. Information provided includes birthplace, dates, and career achievements.
    V. 1: A-Alvarez.

DLC IU

296 Cutolo, Vicente Osvaldo. Nuevo diccionario biográfico argentino (1750-1930). Buenos Aires: Editorial Elche, 1968-78. 5 v. 27 cm.
    A dictionary of Argentinean biography, from 1750 to 1930, alphabetically arranged. Contents:
    V. 1: A-B.
    V. 2: C-E.
    V. 3: F-K.
    V. 4: L-M.
    V. 5: N-Q.
    Lists approximately 10,000 names.

CaBVaU CaQML CaOTP CFS CLS CLSU CLU CoU CSt CtY CU CU-S FTaSU FU IaU ICU IEN InU IU KU LNHT MB MdBJ MdU MH MiDW MiU MoSW MNS MU NcD NcU NhD NIC NjP NN NNC NSyU NRU OU PPULC RPB TNJ TxDaM TxFTC TxU ViU WaU WU

BIOGRAPHY (MISCELLANEOUS)--DICTIONARIES, ENCYCLOPEDIAS, and "WHO'S WHO"

296a Di Lullo, Orestes. <u>Antecedentes biográficos</u>
<u>santiagueños</u>. Santiago del Estero, 1948.
297 p. 28 cm.
    A collection of biographical sketches in
"who's who" format and alphabetically arranged
of approximately 2,000 individuals from all
walks of life associated with the Argentine
province of Santiago del Estero (16th through
18th century).

    DLC TxU

297 Díaz Doin, Guillermo. <u>Diccionario político de</u>
<u>nuestro tiempo</u>: <u>político-biográfico-económico-</u>
<u>sociológico</u>. Buenos Aires: Editorial Mundo
Atlántico, 1943. 557 p. 22 cm.
    A political, biographical, and sociological
dictionary. (<u>See also</u> entry 297a.)

    CU DLC

297a _____. <u>Diccionario político de nuestro tiem-</u>
<u>po</u>: <u>político-biográfico-económico-sociológico</u>.
2. ed., corr. y aumentada. Buenos Aires:
Editorial Mundo Atlántico, 1948. 782 p.
23 cm. (Colección diccionarios en nuestro
tiempo).
    Revised and enlarged version of the 1943
edition. (<u>See</u> entry 297.)

    DLC ICU IU MH NN

297b <u>Diccionario biográfico argentino</u>, 1982-83.
Buenos Aires: Publicaciones Referenciales
Latinoamericanas, 1982. 799 p. 28 cm.
(Quién es quién en América del Sur).
    A biographical dictionary of Argentina for
the years 1982-83.

    IU

298 Echevarrieta, Marcelo. <u>Diccionario biográfico</u>
<u>de la República Argentina</u>. Buenos Aires:
A. M. Echevarrieta, 1940. 401 p. 18 cm.
    Biographical dictionary in a "who's who"
format for Argentina in 1940.

    DLC ICU IU NcU NN OU

299 <u>Guía senior</u>. Buenos Aires: Editorial Servicios Empresarios, 1969. 583 p. 23 cm.
    Directory of Argentinean corporations,
associations, advertising agencies, institutions, and their directors and executives.
Contains approximately 5,000 names and brief
biographical sketches with information such
as birth dates and career background.

    IU KU TxU

299a Hogg, Ricardo. <u>Guía biográfica</u>. Buenos
Aires: Impr. de Peuser, 1904. 250 p. 24 cm.
    A collection of biographical sketches in
"who's who" format of living Argentineans from
all walks of life in the year 1904.

    CLU

300 <u>Hombres de la Argentina</u>; diccionario biográfico contemporáneo. Buenos Aires: Veritas,
1945-47. 3 v. Portraits. 21 cm.
    Biographical dictionary with sketches of
over 1,500 Argentines living at the time of
publication who have distinguished themselves
in some field of endeavor. Biographical data
include important dates, educational background, and achievements. Title varies: 1945,
<u>Diccionario biográfico de hombres de negocios</u>;
<u>biografías contemporaneas</u>.

    IU

301 <u>Hombres del día</u>, 1917. El diccionario biográfico argentino en el cual se ha incorporado
"Who's Who in Argentina, 1917." Buenos Aires:
Sociedad Inteligencia Sud Americana, 1917.
245 p. xcix p. (V. 1). 21 cm.
    A biographical dictionary of Argentina for
1917 presented in "who's who" format. Spanish
text followed by English.

    DLC DNW ICJ MB MiD MiU NN WaS

302 Molina Arrotea, Carlos; Servando García; and
Apolinario C. Casabal. <u>Diccionario biográfico</u>
<u>nacional</u>, que contiene: la vida de todos los
hombres de estado, escritores, poetas, militares, etc. (fallecidos) que han figurado en
el país desde el descubrimiento hasta nuestros
días. T. 1, entrega I-IV: A-Ch. Buenos
Aires: Impr. de M. Sánchez & Cía., 1877-81.
279 p. 27 cm.
    A biographical dictionary of Argentina
covering from the era of the discovery up to
the 19th century presented in "who's who" format. Only deceased individuals included.
Letters A-CH only published.

    CtY DLC ICarbS NN

303 Monte Domecq, F., comp. <u>Quién es quién en</u>
<u>Corrientes</u>. Buenos Aires: Edición Ilustrada,
1949. 430 p. (V. 1). Portraits. 22 cm.
    A "who's who" of Corrientes, Argentina.

    InU

304 Muzzio, Julio A. <u>Diccionario histórico y bio-</u>
<u>gráfico de la República Argentina</u>. Buenos
Aires: J. Roldán, 1920. 2 v. Portraits.
24 cm.
    Historical and biographical dictionary of
Argentina with information on individuals prominent in its history.
    V. 1: A-M.
    V. 2: N-Z.
    Includes approximately 1,700 names.

    CtY DLC IU MB MiU NcD NjP NN OCl
    OU PP TNJ TxU

305 Petriella, Dionisio, and Sara Sosa Miatello.
<u>Diccionario biográfico italo-argentino</u>. Buenos

BIOGRAPHY (MISCELLANEOUS)--DICTIONARIES, ENCYCLOPEDIAS, and "WHO'S WHO"

Aires: Asociación Dante Alighieri, 1976. 771 p. 24 cm.

Biographical dictionary of 19th- and 20th-century native Argentines of Italian ancestry and Italian immigrants in Argentina. Lists approximately 2,500 names.

IU

306 Pinto, Juan. Diccionario de la República Argentina; histórico, geográfico, biográfico, literario. Buenos Aires: Editorial Mundo Atlántico, 1949. 753 p. 24 cm.

Dictionary of Argentina covering history, geography, and literature with biographical sketches of outstanding Argentines throughout history.

CSt DLC ICU IU NcD NN PU TxU

307 Quién es quién en la Argentina; biografías contemporáneas. Buenos Aires: G. Kraft, 1968 (1939). 1083 p. 24 cm.

Biographical dictionary of Argentineans living at the time of publication, in a "who's who" format.

CaBVaU CLSU CSf CU DI-GS DLC DPU ICN IU KU LNHT LU MH-BA NBuU NcD NcU OCl OO OU PPT PU

308 Santillán, Diego A., comp. Gran enciclopedia argentina; todo lo argentino ordenado alfabéticamente; geografía e historia, toponimias, biografías, ciencias, artes, letras, derecho, economía, industria y comercio, instituciones, flora y fauna, folklore, léxico regional. Buenos Aires: Ediar, 1956-64. 9 v. Portraits. 28 x 18 cm.

Encyclopedia of Argentina with over 30,000 biographical sketches of prominent individuals in Argentinean history from the colonial period to the mid-20th century.

V. 1: A-Byn.
V. 2: C-Del.
V. 3: Del-Gw.
V. 4: H-LL.
V. 5: M-Ñ.
V. 6: O-Q.
V. 7: R-S.
V. 8: T-Z.
V. 9: Apéndice.

CaBVaU CU DS ICN IU KU MiDW MiU MnU MoSU NcD NcU NN NNC OkU PU TxU WaU WU

309 Udaondo, Enrique. Diccionario biográfico argentino. Buenos Aires: Casa Editora Coni, 1938. 1151 p. 27 x 18 cm.

Biographical dictionary of Argentina with information on 3,200 individuals from all walks of life from 1800-1920.

CtY CU DLC DPU FMU IaU IU MoU NcD NjR OU PPT PSt

310 _____. Diccionario biográfico colonial argentino. Obra prologada por el dr. Gregorio Aráoz Alfaro. Buenos Aires: Editorial Huarpes, 1945. 980 p. Portraits. 26 x 18 cm.

Biographical dictionary of the colonial period in Argentina covering 1,920 individuals from all walks of life.

CaBVaU CSt CtY DLC InU IU MoU NBuU NcD OCl OClJC PU TU TxU

ECONOMICS

311 Pablo, Juan Carlos de. Los economistas y la la economía argentina. Buenos Aires: Ediciones Macchi, 1977. 250 p. 23 cm.

An assessment of economic conditions in contemporary Argentina, through interviews with the following Argentine economists, including biographical data: Roberto Teodoro Alemann, Alvaro Carlos Alsogaray, Aldo Antonio Arnaudo, Adolfo Martín Prudencio Canitrot, Raúl Ernesto Cuello, Marcelo Diamand, Guido Di Tella, Aldo Ferrer, Rogelio Julio Frigerio, Jorge Miguel Katz, Federico Pinedo.

IU

EDUCATION

312 Bagalio, Alfredo S. Forjadores; personalidad, vida y pasión de maestros inolvidables por Alfredo S. Bagalio (Ceriani del Viurón, pseud.). Prólogos del profesor Roberto E. Alamprese y del autor. Buenos Aires: Confederación de Maestros de la Capital Federal, 1975. 123 p. 20 cm.

A collection of biographical sketches of the following Argentine educators: Italo Américo Foradori, Jacinto Héctor Gandulfo Reyes, Amado Enrique Lamy, José Leanza, Casimiro Aureliano Maciel, Anunciada Mastelli de Miselli, Segundo Pérez, José Polisena, Alfredo Felipe Tonina, José Ucha.

CtY NcU NmU NN TxU

313 Cabrera, Pablo, comp. Universitarios de Córdoba. Córdoba, 1916. 598 p. 28 cm. (Biblioteca del tercer centenario de la Universidad Nacional de Córdoba).

A collection of biographical sketches of the following notable figures from the University of Córdoba in the 18th and 19th centuries: Miguel Calixto del Corro, Gerónimo Salguero de Cabrera y Cabrera, José Antonio Cabrera, Eduardo Pérez Bulnes.

CDU CtY DLC IU TxU WaU

314 Carbia, Rómulo D. Los historiógrafos argentinos menores, su clasificación crítica. Buenos Aires: Talleres Casa Jacobo Peuser, 1923. 22 p. 28 cm. (Buenos Aires. Univer-

sidad Nacional. Publicaciones del Instituto de Investigaciones Históricas, v. 17).

A short discussion of 19th-century Argentine historiographers, including biobibliophical notes on the following: Manuel Ricardo Trelles, Vicente G. Quesada, Angel Justiniano Carranza, Andrés Lamas.

DLC FU IU NcD NN PPULC PU

315 Cordero, Héctor Adolfo. <u>Orígenes de la educación en San Fernando</u>. San Fernando, Argentina: Municipalidad de San Fernando, Dirección de Relaciones Públicas y Cultura, 1969. 16 p. 22 cm.

A short history of the origin of education in the Argentine city of San Fernando during the 19th century, including very brief scattered biographical information on many people associated with this aspect of Argentina's development. Those particularly featured are Manuel de San Ginés, Saturnino Segurola, Marcelina Caudevilla, Juan León de Granada, Marcos Sastre.

IU TxU

316 Fernández, Raúl. <u>Historia de la educación primaria de Córdoba</u>. Córdoba: Dirección General de Publicaciones, Universidad Nacional de Córdoba, 1965. 263 p. 24 cm. (Biblioteca de historia).

A history of primary education in Córdoba, Argentina (18th-19th centuries). Includes scattered biographical information on many individuals associated with its development and in particular the following: Andrés Pajón, Juan Bautista de Mena, Leonor de Tejeda, José Antonio de San Alberto, Francisco Antonio Ortiz, José Javier Díaz, Manuel Antonio de Castro, Juan Bautista Bustos, Miguel Quenón, Mariano Fragueiro, Alejo Carmen Guzmán, José Manuel Solares, Roque Ferreyra, Justiniano Posse, Valentín Mabres.

NbU NBuU NcD NIC

317 Forgione, José D., comp. <u>Antología pedagógica argentina</u>; noticias biobibliográficas y páginas escogidas de maestros y educadores de nuestro país. Buenos Aires: Editorial "El Ateneo," 1949. 548 p. 20 cm.

A collection of essays by the following 18th- to 20th-century educators, for whom biobibliographical essays are also included: Juan Baltasar Maziel, José Antonio de San Alberto, Luis José Chorroarín, Juan Ignacio de Gorriti, Manuel Belgrano, Francisco de Paula Castañeda, Mariano Moreno, Bernardino Rivadavia, Martín Diego Alcorta, José Esteban Antonino Echeverría, Juan María Gutiérrez, Marcos Sastre, Juan Bautista Alberdi, Domingo F. Sarmiento, Juana Paula Manso, Martín Avelino Piñero, Mamerto Esquiú, José María Torres, José Manuel Estrada, Pedro Goyena, Tristán Achával Rodríguez, Francisco Antonio Berra, François-Paul Groussac, Norberto Carlos de

de Corazón de Jesús Vergara, Joaquín V. González, Leopoldo Herrera, Martín A. Malharro, Pablo A. Pizzurno, Víctor Mercante, Rodolfo Senet, Leopoldo Lugones, Carlos Octavio Bunge, José Ingenieros.

DLC IU NcU TxU

318 Fúrlong Cárdiff, Guillermo Juan. <u>Historia del Colegio de la Inmaculada de la ciudad de Santa Fe y de sus irradiaciones culturales, espirituales y sociales</u>, 1610-1962. Buenos Aires: Sociedad de Exalumnos, 1962. 23 cm.

A history of the Colegio de la Inmaculada located in Santa Fe, Argentina, covering the period from 1610 to 1962, and including biographical information for many people, mostly clerics. Among them are Juan Romero, Francisco del Valle, Juan de Sigordia, Pedro de Vega, Cristóbal Altamirano, Gabriel de Ojeda, Francisco Alfano, Juan Darío, Miguel de Sotomayor, Bernardo Rodríguez, Claudio Flores, Pedro de Carranza, Pedro Helgueta, Francisco Velázquez, Juan Ortega, Luis Berger, Francisco de Echagüe y Andia, Bernardo Nusdorffer, Ignacio Oyarzábal, Blanca Godoy, Francisco Burgés, Cosme Agulló, Manuel Arnal, José Brigniel, Jorge Suárez de Macedo, Jerónimo Gama, Juan Francisco Gaete, Pedro Cacho Herrera, Sebastián Garau, Tomás Falkner, Manuel García, Buenaventura Suárez.

IU

319 _____. <u>Historia del Colegio del Salvador y de sus irradiaciones culturales y espirituales en la ciudad de Buenos Aires</u>, 1617-1943. Buenos Aires: El Colegio del Salvador, 1944. 2 v. in 3. Portraits. 24 cm.

A history of the Colegio del Salvador located in Buenos Aires, covering the period from 1617 to 1943. Scattered biographical information, as well as portraits in some cases, included for many people associated with this institution, among them the following: Antonio Rodrígues, Juan Romero, Francisco del Valle, Miguel de Sotomayor, Juan Domínguez, Juan Pastor, Juan Bautista Ferrufino, Francisco Díaz Taño, Diego de Boroa, Juan de la Guardia, Cristóbal Gómez, Juan Francisco de Avila (Juan Francisco Dávila), Ignacio Oyarzábal, José de Peralta Barrionuevo y Rocha Benavides, Cayetano Marsellano y Agremont, Tomás Dombidas, Hernando de Torreblanca, Gregorio Orozco, Ignacio de Frías, José Serrano, Blas de Silva, Diego Ruiz, Jerónimo Herrán, Diego Haze, Angel Camilo Petragrassa, Juan Patricio Fernández, Pedro de Arroyo, Antonio Machoni, Juan José Rico, Ladislao Orosz, Juan Delgado, Domingo Massala, Manuel García, Nicolás Plantich (Nicolás Plantitsch), Lorenzo Ortiz, José de Figueroa, José Cardiel, María Antonia de San José, Pedro de Angelis, Mariano Berdugo, Bernardo Parés, Francisco Ramón Cabré, Juan Coris, Ignacio Gomila, Francisco Majesté. Martín Peñeyro, Mariano Larsen, José J. Guarda, Esteban Salvadó, Mariano Albi, Valentín Francoli, Julián Requena,

EDUCATION

José Sató, José Reverter, Ramón Barrera, Santiago Riva, Félix Del Val, Eduardo Brugier, Vendrell, Camilo Meucci Jordán, Buenaventura Feliú, José Antillach, Francisco Datti, Francisco Ginebra, Juan Castillejo, Pascual Durán, Vicente Gambón, Rafael Fanego, Salvador Barber, Salvador Franco, Martín Gómez, Antonio Binimelis, José López, Pedro Colom, Bernabé Hernández, Pedro Borreguero, Juan José Auweiler, Juan Isern, Joaquín Añón, Enrique Najurieta, Abel Montes Larrain. Alphabetical indices of names.

    CtY DLC ICN IU MH NcD NcU TxU WU

320 Guerra, Juan Néstor. <u>Mar del Plata</u>: sus escuelas y sus maestros. Mar del Plata: Edición Apolo, 1967. 106 p. 23 cm.
    A history of education in Mar del Plata, Argentina, from 1881 to the present day. Short biographical sketches emphasizing numerous professional educators and for the author of this work.

    AzU CLSU CLU CSt CU FU IaU IU KU
    MB MU NcU NIC NSyU TxU WU

321 Gutiérrez, Juan María. <u>Origen y desarrollo de la enseñanza pública superior en Buenos Aires;</u> noticias históricas desde la época de la extinción de la Compañía de Jesús en el año 1767, hasta poco después de fundada la universidad en 1821; con notas biográficas, datos estadísticos curiosos, inéditos o poco conocidos. (2. ed., aum. por su autor). Texto reordenado para la presente reedición, precedida por un estudio de Juan B. Alberdi. Buenos Aires: La Cultura Argentina, 1951. 645 p. 23 cm.
    A history of public higher education in Buenos Aires, covering the period from 1767 to 1821. Biographical essays are included for the following individuals, many of them educators, involved in this aspect of Argentina's development: Juan José de Vertiz y Salcedo, Juan Baltasar Maziel, Vicente Atanasio Juanzaras, Manuel de Basabibaso, Luis José Chorroarín, Miguel O'Gorman, Cosme Argerich, Diego Estanislao Zavaleta, Antonio Sáenz, Domingo Victorio Achega, Juan Crisóstomo Lafinur, Valentín Gómez, Pedro Antonio Someliera, Gregorio José Gómez, Manuel Antonio Castro, Manuel Moreno, Felipe Senillosa, José Lanz, Eusebio Agüero, Avelino Díaz, Juan Francisco Gil, Diego Alcorta, Octavio Fabrizio Mossotti.

    CU DLC ICJ IU MB MiEM NcD NcU

322 Halperín Donghi, Tulio. <u>Historia de la Universidad de Buenos Aires.</u> Buenos Aires: Editorial Universitaria de Buenos Aires, 1962. 227 p. 19 cm. (Biblioteca de América).
    A history of the University of Buenos Aires, covering the period from 1821 to the 1950s. Brief scattered biographical information is included for many people associated with this institution. Among those particularly featured are Juan María Gutiérrez, José Valentín Gómez, Ricardo Rojas, Antonio Sáenz.

    CLSU CLU CtY CU DPU FU GU IaU ICU
    IEdS InU IU LNHT MH MiDW MiEM MiU
    MnU MoSW MoU MU NBuU NcD NcU NIC
    NjP NN NNC NSyU OCl OU TxU ViU
    WaU WU

323 Luiggi, Alice (Houston). <u>65 valiants.</u> Gainesville: University of Florida Press, 1965. 191 p. Portraits. 24 cm.
    An account of 65 teachers from the United States who made contributions to public education in Argentina. Substantial biographical information and portraits are given for these women, for others who were involved with this aspect of Argentina's cultural development, and for the author of this work. These people include Alice Houston Luiggi, Domingo F. Sarmiento, Clara Allyn (Mrs. William Benitz), Franc Allyn (Mrs. Stephen W. Morgan), Clara Jeanette Armstrong, Frances Gertrude Armstrong (Mrs. John A. Besler), Minnie Burrows Armstrong (Mrs. William R. Ridley), Florence Atkinson, Sarah Atkinson, Bernice Avery (Mrs. Richard Agar), Sarah M. Boyd (Mrs. Caleb J. Camp), Antoinette Choate (Mrs. William R. Richardson), Margaret Louise Collord, Mary Elizabeth Conway, Sarah Cook, Elizabeth Boyer Coolidge, Arvilla Cross, Louise Daniels, Rosa Ella Dark, Annette Doolittle, Lucy Doolittle, Anna Dudley (Mrs. Coolidge Roberts), Isabel Dudley, Martha Graham Dudley (Mrs. Charles Dudley), Charles Dudley, Sarah Chamberlin Eccleston, Emily Eccleston (Mrs. Daniel Campbell), Edell Ellis (Mrs. Theodore H. Johnston), Theodora Gay (Mrs. Fernando Schlosser), Clara Gillies (Mrs. George Bischoff), Mary Ann Gillies (Mrs. Walter Grieven), Mary Elizabeth Gorman (Mrs. John H. Sewall), Mary Olstine Graham, Katherine Grant (Mrs. William Hope), Sarah Harrison, Annette Haven, Cora Hill (Mrs. Frank N. Clawson), Ione Hill (Mrs. George L. van Gorder), Laura Haven Hodges (Mrs. William Hodges), Jennie Eliza Howard, Edith Howe, Jane Hunt, Harriet E. Jenness, Myra Kimball (Mrs. Arthur Goldney), Isabel King, Rachel King, Sarah Eleanor Lobb, Mary Gay McMillan (Mrs. Henry S. McMillan), Alcinda Morrow (Mrs. Eli M. Whitson), Mary Olive Morse, Frances A. Nyman, Anna Ackley Rice (Mrs. George L. Roberts), George Lane Roberts, George Albert Stearns, John William Stearns, Julia Adelaide Hope Stearns (Mrs. George), Mary Jeanette Stevens, Sarah Strong, Mrs. Agnes (Inés) Emma Trégent, Susan E. Wade (Mrs. Charles H. Hibbert), Amy or Amelia Wales, Ruth Wales, Frances Angeline Wall (Mrs. John M. Thome), Abigail Nancy Ward (Mrs. James B. T. Marsh), Serena Frances Wood, Mary J. Youmans.

    AU CaBVaU CLSU CLU CU DPU FMU FTaU
    FU GU IaU ICU IEN InU IU KEmT KU
    LNHT LU MB MH MiEM MiU MnU MoSW
    MoU MsU MU N NbU NBuC NBuU NcD NcU
    NdU NIC NjP NjR NN OClW ODW OKentU
    OkU OrU OU PPULC RPB TNJ TU TxU
    UU ViU Wa WaU WU

324 Mercante, Víctor. <u>Maestros y educadores.</u>
Buenos Aires: M. Gleizer, 1927. 3 v. 19 cm.
(Galería de educadores, v. 1).
   A collection of biographical sketches
about the following Argentine educators:
   V. 1: Bartolomé Mitre, Florentino Ame-
ghino, José Ingenieros.
   V. 2: Manuel Belgrano, Juan Manuel Fer-
nández Agüero, Marcos Sastre, Pedro Scalabri-
ni, Joaquín V. González, Juan Vucetich.
   V. 3: Esteban Echeverría, José M. Torres,
Juana Manso, Raúl Legout, Pablo Berutti, José
B. Zubiaur.

   CtY   CU   DLC   NcD   OCl   TxU

325 Murature de Badaracco, María del Carmen. <u>La</u>
<u>educación en La Matanza, Victoria,</u> desde los
orígenes hasta 1900. Victoria: Entre Ríos,
1963. 37 p. 22 cm. (Cuadernos de "Crisol
literario").
   A short history of education in the Argentine city of Victoria in the province of Entre
Ríos, from its origins in the early 19th century to the year 1900. Scattered biographical
information is included for many people associated with this aspect of Argentina's history.
Among them are Justo José de Urquiza, Miguel
Vidal, Abraham Bartoloni.

   CLU   DLC   KU   NIC

326 Newton, Jorge. <u>Historia del Club Universitario</u>
<u>de Buenos Aires.</u> Buenos Aires: Club Univer-
sitario de Buenos Aires, 1968. 307 p. Portraits. 24 cm.
   A history of the Club Universitario of
Buenos Aires, covering the period from 1918
to 1968, and including very brief scattered
biographical information, as well as portraits
in many cases, for many people associated with
this organization.

   CLSU   CLU   FU   InU   IU   KU   MB   MoSW   MU
   NBuU   NcD   NIC   NN   NNC   OU   PPULC   TxU

327 Ortiz Arigós de Montoya, Celia. <u>Momentos cul-</u>
<u>minantes en ciento cincuenta años de educación</u>
<u>pública en Entre Ríos.</u> Con la colaboración
de Inés Montoya de Hirschson. Santa Fe, Argentina: Librería y Editorial Colmegna, 1967.
92 p. 20 cm.
   A history of public education in Entre
Ríos, covering the period from 1816-1966, and
including brief biographical information on
many people associated with this aspect of
Argentina's development. Those particularly
featured are Lucio Mansilla, Justo José Urquiza, Francisco de Paula Castañeda, Pascual
Echagüe.

   CLSU   CLU   FU   IaU   IU   KU   MB   MU   NBuU
   NcU   NIC   NNC   NSyU   PPULC   TxU   ViU   WU

328 Pérez Duprat, Rodolfo. <u>Vidas educadoras.</u> La
Plata: Editora Platense, 1970. 126 p. 20 cm.
   Collection of biographical essays about
the following notable Argentine educators of

the 19th and 20th centuries: María del Carmen
Traverso de Castelli, Leonor B. Destrade de
Leblanc, Angel Acuña, Joaquín J. Barneda, Luis
Alejandro Castelli, Carlos Gómez Iparraguirre,
Juan Néstor Guerra, Evaristo Iglesias, Bernabé
Irazú, Juan Francisco Jáuregui, David Kraisel-
burd, Francisco Legarra, Pascual Lértora, José
D. Méndez, Mariano Molla Villanueva, Antonio
Morello, Luis Morzone, Claudio Ramón Narvarte,
Prudencio C. Soto, José Antonio de la Vega.

   CLU   CU-SB   GU   IU   MiEM   MoSW   NIC   TxU

329 Ramallo, Jorge María. <u>Los rectores de la Uni-</u>
<u>versidad de Buenos Aires en la época de Rosas.</u>
Buenos Aires, 1964. 55 p. 28 cm.
   Biographical essays about presidents of
the "Universidad de Buenos Aires" during the
dictatorship of Juan Manuel de Rosas in the
19th century. Information provided concentrates on the career achievements of the following individuals: Santiago Figueredo, Paulino Gari, Miguel García.

   FU   IaU   IEN   InU   MChB   NbU   NcU   PPT
   TxU

330 Solari, Juan Antonio. <u>Generaciones laicas</u>
<u>argentinas.</u> Hombres de la Ley 1420 y del
liberalismo. Buenos Aires: Bases Editorial,
1964. 217 p. 20 cm.
   A collection of biographical sketches of
the following 19th-century notable individuals
associated with the history of education in
Argentina: Onésimo Leguizamón, Luis Lagos
García, Emilio Civit, Delfín Gallo, Eduardo
Wilde, Eduardo Costa, Nicasio Oroño, Eugenio
Cambaceres, Gregorio F. de la Puente.

   CLU   CNoS   CtY   FU   IaAS   ICU   InU   IU
   MH-L   MiEM   MoSW   MoU   NIC   NjP   NjPT
   NN   NNC   NSyU   PPiU   TxU

331 Tamburini, Juan Isidro. <u>Héroes ignorados;</u>
siembra y dolor en la escuela campesina. Buenos Aires: Plus Ultra. 1967. 100 p. 20 cm.
   A collection of sketches of the following
Argentine educators: Vicente Calderón, Antonio Ramón Fernández, Leoncio Barrios, Brade
(family), Celmira Goncevat de Cabral.

   CLSU   CSt   CtY   IaU   InU   IU   MB   MiEM
   MnU   MoSW   MU   NBuU   NcU   NIC   NNC   OU
   TxU   WU

ENGINEERING

332 <u>Historia de la ingeniería argentina.</u> Buenos
Aires: Centro Argentino de Ingenieros, 1981.
475 p. Portraits. 26 cm.
   A history of Argentine engineering (1700-
1975), including biographical information of
varying amounts and often accompanied by portraits of the following individuals associated
with it:
   1770-1810: José Bermúdez de Castro, Domingo Petrarca, Diego Cardoso del Espino, Juan

ENGINEERING

Francisco Sobrecasas, Antonio Aymerich y Villa Juana, Jean Barthelemy Havelle, José Antonio de Borja, Esteban de O'Brien. Juan Martín Cermeño, Joaquín del Pino, Juan José de Vertiz, Miguel Juárez de Sandoval, Bernardo Lecoco, Ricardo Ayllmer, Santiago José Pérez Brito, José Antonio del Pozo y Marquy, José Custodio de Sá y Faría, Carlos Cabrer y Suñer, José García Martínez de Cáceres, José Antonio de Mosquera, Félix de Azara, Francisco González Carrasco, Félix de Iriarte, José Sourrière de Souvillac, Ramón García de León y Pizarro, Sebastián Undiano y Gastellú, Ramón José Agustín del Pino Rameri, Martín Casimiro de Lasala, José Buzeta de Figueroa, Pedro Antonio Cerviño, Eustaquio Giannini.

1810-1835: Bernardo Lecocq, José María Cabrer, Mauricio Rodríguez de Berlanga, Antonio Arcos, Jacobo Boudier, Eduardo Kaillitz de Holmberg, Antonio Paillardelle, Enrique Paillardelle, Felipe Bertres, Ambrosio Cramer, José Alberto Baclé D'Albé, Felipe Senillosa, Angel de Monasterio, Pedro Andrés García, José María Romero, José Antonio Alvarez Condarco, José Ildefonso Alvarez de Arenales, Esteban de Luca, Luis Beltrán, Martiniano Chilavert, Narciso Parchappe, Octavio Fabrizio Mosotti, Avelino Díaz, José María Romero, Próspero Catelin, Santiago Bevans, Carlos Enrique Pellegrini, Nicolás Descalzi, Feliciano Mariano Chiclana (son), Eduardo Trole, Teodoro Schuster.

1835-1870: Felipe Senillosa, Carlos Enrique Pellegrini, Juan María Gutiérrez, Peregrino Strobel, Bernardino Speluzzi, Emilio Rosetti, Pompeyo Moneta, Camilo Duteil, Mariano Moreno (son), Allan Campbell, Guillermo Wheelwright, Francisco Rave.

1870-1900: Luis Augusto Huergo, Valentín Balbín, Luis Silveyra, Guillermo White, Guillermo Villanueva, Carlos Olivera, Jorge Coquet, Juan Pirovano, Edgardo Moreno, Eduardo Aguirre, Carlos Encina, Santiago Brian, Carlos Echagüue, Emilio Mitre, Carlos Casaffousth, Pedro Benoit, Valentín Virasoro, César Cipolletti, Francisco Lavalle, Matías Sánchez, Luis Luiggi, Alfredo Ebelot, Juan Coghland, Juan Federico Bateman, Knut Lindmark, Carlos Nyströmer, Carlos Malmen, Juan Eduardo Ryberb, Escipión Panizza, Juan Pelleschi, Juan Francisco Czetz, Jordán Czeslaw Wisocki, Nicolás Canale, Juan Bautista Medici, Gustavo Ave-Lallemant, Federico Stavelius, Herman Jungstedt, Arvid Gumlius, Carlos Christiersson, Gustav Folgestrom, Arturo Caspersen, J. A. A. Waldorp, J. A. J. van Haaten, Juan J. Doyer, Augusto Ringuelet, Juan Bateman.

1900-1920: Santiago Esteban Barabino, Otto Krause, Luis Valiente Noailles, José Manuel Saravia, Marcial Rafael Candisti, Luis Monteverde, Belisario Caraffa, Miguel Iturbe, Benjamín Sal, Carlos Bunge, Luis F. Taurel, Carlos Maschwitz, Lorenzo Amespil, Julián Romero, Jerónimo de la Serna, Miguel Tedín, Juan Francisco Sarhy, Eduardo Huergo, Vicente Castro, Rómulo Quartino, Jorge Duclout, Carlos de Urquiza, Conrado Simons, Pedro Ezcurra, Federico Birabén, Carlos María Morales, Enri-

que Lange, Félix Romero, Angel Etcheverri, Alfredo Zimmermann Resta, Domingo Nocetti, Arturo Castaño, Carlos Chapeaurouge, Agustín González, Federico Knoll, Pedro Aguirre, Francisco Roque, H. Magno Tvethe, Alberto Schneidewind, Rufino Varela, Jorge Newbery.

1920-1950: Guillermo Céspedes, Nicolás Besio Moreno, Ferrucio Alberto Soldano, Angel Gallardo, Luis Achával, Félix Aguilar, Luis Dellepiani, Enrique Mosconi, Marcelo Garlot, Claro Cornelio Dassen, Antonio Rebuelto, Enrique de Madrid, Agustín P. Justo, Eduardo Arnaboldi, Martín Félix Langmann, Adriano Borus, Edmundo Piaggio, Vicente Arca, Donato Gerardi, José Laudino Bimbi, Fernando Lizarán, Luis A. Huergo (son), Leónidas Barrancos, Enrique Hermitte, Miguel Simonoff, Rodolfo Ballester, José Luis Delpini, Justo Pascali, Angel Forti, Félix Diego Outes, Manuel Guitarte, Pablo Nogués, Roberto Gorostiaga, Carlos A. Volpi, Julio R. Castineiras, Torcuato Di Tella, Mario Luis Villa, Carlos Della Paolera, Agustín Mercau, Juan Bialet Massé, Elías Senestrari, Daniel Gavier, Marcelo Garlot.

1950-1975: Enrique Butty, Pedro Longhini, Antonio Escudero, Eduardo Baglietto, Luis Lix Klett, Dante Ardigó, Eduardo Arenas, Guido Belzoni, Enrique Pedro Villarreal, Juan Blaquier, Roberto Perazzo, Alberto Devoto, Arturo Sobral, Cortés Pla, Edmundo Parodi, Juan Agustín Valle, Adolfo Antonio Giacobbe, Horacio Montes, Tomás Francisco Lynch, Pedro Petriz, Abel F. Cornejo, Luis A. Herbin, Juan Francisco García Balado, Pedro Mendiondo, Antonio Paitovi, Pascual Palazzo, Gabriel del Mazo, Arturo Acevedo, Enrique Chanourdie, Federico Díaz Lascano, Jorge Dobranich, Ernesto Baldassari, Juan B. Gandolfo, Humberto Meoli, Julio A. Noble, Carlos Revol, Carlos Posadas, Julio de Tezanos Pinto, Ricardo M. Ortiz, Luis María Salazar.

IU

332a Vaquer, Antonio. *Historia de la ingeniería en la Argentina*. Buenos Aires: Editorial Universitaria de Buenos Aires, 1968. 441 p. 22 cm.

A history of engineering in Argentina, covering the period from preconquest to the present and including brief biographical notes on many notable figures from this field of endeavor.

CLSU CLU CSt DPU FU ICU InU IU
KU MnU MoKL MU NBuU NcD NcU NIC
NjP NN NSyU TxDaM TxU WaU

FREEMASONRY

333 Lappas, Alcibíades. *La masonería argentina a través de sus hombres*. Buenos Aires: Belgrano, 1966. 408 p. 23 cm.

A work featuring short biographical sketches on over 2,000 19th- and 20th-century Argentine Freemasons.

IaU ICU InU IU MH MU NcD NcU
NjP TxU ViU

GENEALOGY

334 Azarola Gil, Luis Enrique. Los Maciel en la
historia del Plata, 1604-1814. Buenos Aires:
Librería y Editorial "La Facultad," 1940.
299 p. 21 cm.
Biogenealogical study of the Maciel family
from 1604-1814. The following members are
particularly featured: Melchor Maciel, Luis
Maciel del Aguila, Francisco Maciel del Aguila, Juan Maciel del Aguila, Baltasar Maciel
(general), Manuel Maciel, Juan Baltasar Maciel
(doctor), Joaquín Maciel, Domingo Maciel,
Juan Manuel Maciel, Luis Enrique Maciel,
Francisco Antonio Maciel, Carlos Maciel. Alphabetical index of names.

CU DLC DPU ICN ICU IU NcD TxU

335 _____. Los San Martín en la Banda Oriental.
Buenos Aires: Librería y Editorial "La Facultad," Bernabé y Cía., 1936. 14 p. 22 cm.
Essay on genealogical history of the San
Martín family in 18th-century Argentina featuring biographical information on the following: Juan de San Martín, María Elena de San
Martín, Manuel Tadeo de San Martín, Juan Fermín de San Martín, José de San Martín.

DLC IU

336 Barreiro Ortiz, Carlos. Los Ortiz de San Luis
y otras genealogías. Buenos Aires: Librería
Huemul, 1967. 252 p. Portraits. 24 cm.
Genealogical history of the Ortiz family
in Argentina.

CLSU CSt CtY CU IU KU MB MH MU
NBuU NcU NjP NN NNC NSyU OU TxU
ViU WU

337 Bernard, Tomás Diego. El notariado en la colonia y la emancipación; los Rocha, un linaje
porteño de fundadores. Buenos Aires: Editorial Bibliográfica Argentina, 1960. 123 p.
21 cm.
Genealogical history of the Rocha family
in Argentina.

CLSU CLU CtY CU IaU ICN ICU InU
IU NjP NN TxU

338 Bustillo, José María. Papeles añejos, vidas
ignoradas; relatos íntimos coloniales, de la
independencia y de la tiranía. Buenos Aires:
Ediciones Depalma, 1972. 267 p. 23 cm.
Genealogical history of the Bustillo family of Argentina. José Manuel Bustillo y
Cevallos and José María Bustillo are especially featured.

CaQMM CLU CtY CU CU-S CU-SB FU IaU
IU MB MH MoSW MU NcU OKentU PPiU
TxU WU

339 Carretero, Andrés M. Los Anchorena; política
y negocios en el siglo XIX. Buenos Aires:
Ediciones 8a. Década, 1970. 190 p. 20 cm.
History of the Anchorena family of businessmen in Argentina.

CaBVaU CSt CtY CU-S CU-SB FU ICN
IU MB MH MnU MU NcD NcU NFQC NIC
NjP NmU NN NNC OrU PPiU TxU ViU
WaU WU

340 Castellano Saénz Cavia, Rafael M. Familias
de Traslasierra, jurisdicción de Córdoba.
Prólogo de Alejandro Moyano Aliaga. Buenos
Aires: Talleres Gráficos Dekagraph, 1969.
671 p. 22 cm.
A genealogy of many families who have in-
habited Traslasierra, Córdoba, from the 17th
century to the present. Biographical notes,
including dates and places of birth and death
and important accomplishments, are given for
the more distinguished family members.

CSt CtY CU CU-S CU-SB DGU DPU GU
FU IaU ICU IU MB MnU MoSW MU NcU
NhD NjP NN NNC PPT TNJ TU TxU
ViU WU

341 Cordero, Héctor Adolfo. María de los Santos
Sayas de Bengochea; ascendencia y descendientes. Buenos Aires: Index, 1971. 70 p.
Maps. 35 cm.
A genealogy tracing the family line of the
19th-century Argentine María de los Santos Saya
and consisting mainly of the listing of family
members and their relationships to one another.

CLU CU-SB IU NcU NIC NNC TxU WU

342 Cornejo, Atilio. Genealogías de Salta: los
Fernámdez Cornejo. Editores. Víctor Cornejo
Isasmendi y Miguel Angel Cornejo Costas.
Salta: Instituto de San Felipe y Santiago de
Estudios Históricos de Salta, 1972. 335 p.
Portraits. 28 cm. (Publicaciones del Insti-
tuto de San Felipe y Santiago de Estudios
Históricos de Salta, v. 5).
A genealogy, accompanied by portraits, of
the Fernández Cornejo family of Salta, Argen-
tina.

MU IU

343 Fernández de Burzaco y Barrios, Hugo. Los
antepasados de Alem fueron gallegos. Buenos
Aires, 1955. 9 p. 23 cm.
A genealogical essay of Leandro Nicéforo
Alem and the Alem family.

DLC

344 _____. Fundadores de linajes en el Plata.
Buenos Aires, 1955. 13 p. 23 cm.
A collection of biographical sketches on
the following notable Argentineans (16th
through 18th centuries): Juan Bautista de
Aguirre, Juan Antonio Amigo, Gaspar de Avellaneda, Cristóbal de Barrientos, Domingo del

GENEALOGY

Barrio, Antonio Bermúdez, José Andreas Bethe, Domingo de Burzaco, José Ramón de Burzaco, Juan de Cabezas, Bernabé de la Cal, Ventura Coll, Juan Conde, Francisco Cordero, Manuel Dias, Gabriel Díez Munilla, Nicolás de Echeverría y Galardi, Bartolomé de Esquivel, Casimiro Feijóo, Januario Fernández do Eijo, Antonio de Fresco, Juan Vicente González, Felipe González de Basarra y Guiante, Jerónimo González de Cuenca, Domingo González y Zamudio, Agustín de Labayén, Juan de Lacoizqueta, Antonio de Larrázabal, Juan Lorenzo de Larrerdia, Francisco López Cabezas, Francisco de Paula Mangudo, Francisco Martínez del Monte, José Martínez y Vallejo, Santiago de Meabe, Juan Antonio Navarro de León, Pedro Ochoa, Manuel de Ojeda, Juan Bautista de Olaguibel, Juan Bernardo de Olaguibel, Manuel de Olavarrieta, Francisco Antonio Piñeyro, Nicolás José Llorens Rigi, Gregorio Timoteo Rodríguez de Castro, Diego Rodríguez de Figueroa, Manuel Rodríguez Flores, Juan Rodríguez Vaz, Agustín de la Rosa, Pedro de Salazar, Felipe de Senillosa, Juan Serantes, José Sicardo, Antonio Sebastián de Toledo, Juan Vázquez, Jaime Viamonte, Juan Clemente de Zamora.

DLC

345 Figueroa, Andrés A. _Linajes santiagueños._ Córdoba: Librería Dante, 1927. 140 p. 23 cm.
A collection of genealogies of several prominent families from the Argentine province of Santiago de Estero.

DLC NcU

346 Gammalsson, Hialmar Edmundo. _Los pobladores de Buenos Aires y su descendencia._ Buenos Aires: Municipalidad de la Ciudad de Buenos Aires, 1980. 505 p. 25 cm.
A collection of short genealogies of the first inhabitants of Buenos Aires. Alphabetical index of names.

IU

347 Gandía, Enrique de. _Del origen de los nombres y apellidos y de la ciencia genealógica._ Buenos Aires: Librería y Editorial La Facultad, 1930. 323 p. Portraits. 23 cm.
An essay about personal names and genealogy. Includes extensive biogenealogical information about the Gandía family from 1370 to the 1900s.

CU DLC NcU NhD

348 Lafuente Machain, Ricardo de. _Los de Lafuente._ Buenos Aires: G. Kraft, 1941. 269 p. Portraits. 32 cm.
Genealogical history of the Lafuente family of Argentina, with short genealogies of the following branches of the family: Del Valle, Serna, Tigero, Cuerno de la Riva, Portilla, Sosa, Navarro, Pérez, García, Fernández, Olloqui, González de Santa Cruz, Herrera y Guzmán, Castro, Ramírez de Velasco,

Tapia, Soria Cervantes, Pereira de Matos, Gómez de Camaleño, Ramírez, Galíndez.

DLC IU

349 _____. _Los Machain._ Buenos Aires, 1926. 281 p. 88 cm.
A genealogy of the Machain family of Argentina, including biographical information of varying quantities on many of its members. Alphabetical index of names.

DLC ICarbS

350 _____. _Los parientes del beato padre Roque González de Santa Cruz._ Buenos Aires: Estudios, 1934. 1934. 56 p. 23 cm.
A genealogy of the González de Santa Cruz family, including biographical information for many of its members, particularly the following: Bartolomé González, Francisco González de Santa Cruz, Diego González de Santa Cruz, Pedro González de Santa Cruz, Mateo González de Santa Cruz, María González de Santa Cruz, Mariana González de Santa Cruz.

DLC

351 _____. _Los Sáenz, Valiente, y Aguirre._ Buenos Aires: "La Baskonia," 1931. 215 p. Portraits. 32 cm.
Collection of genealogies about the following families of Argentina: Sáenz, Valiente de Texada, Pueyrredón, Dogan, Soria, Rodrígues Estela, Aguirre, Ursúa, Micheo, Uztariz, Vértiz, Alonso de Lajarrota, Ortiz de Rozas, Quintana, Riglos, Gaete, Díaz, Herrera.

CtY CU DLC IU NSyU TxU WaU

352 Lazcano Colodrero, Arturo Gustavo de. _Linajes de la gobernación del Tucumán,_ los de Córdoba. Córdoba: Establecimientos Gráficos Suc. A. Biffignandi, 1936-69. 3 v. 27 cm.
Alphabetically arranged collection of genealogical histories about the following families of Tucumán (Gobernación): Aliaga, Alfamira, Argüello, Bas, Bengolea, Bustos, Carreño, Casas, Castellano, Centeno, César, Echenique, Escalante, Escuti, Ferreyra, Ferrer, Fuente Rubia, García de Robés, González de Robés, González de Hermida, Herrera y Guzmán, Isasa, Juárez, Liendo, Luján de Medina, Malbrán, Maldonado, Molina, Navarrete, Moral Moyano, Navarro, Nores, Novillo, Obregón, Olmedo, Peña, Pinto, Ramírez de Velasco, Sánchez de Movellán, San Román, Sarría, Suárez, Toledo Pimentel, Torres, Vera, Zamudio. Alphabetical index of families in each volume.

CFIS CtY CU IU NcU

353 Marino Montero, Juan Carlos. _Genealogía de los Tocco._ Buenos Aires, 1965. 15 p. Portraits. 23 cm.
Brief genealogical history of the Tocco family in Argentina.

CLSU CLU IU MoU NIC NN TxU

354 Molina Herrera, Angel José Rafael. <u>Los Herrera y Díaz Herrera de la ciudad de la Santísima Trinidad y Puerto de Santa María del Buen Aire.</u> Buenos Aires: Talleres Gráficos Defensa, 1970. 355 p. Portraits. 24 cm.
Genealogical history of the Herrera y Herrera Díaz families of Argentina.

    CSt CU CU-SB FU ICN IU MB MH MU NIC NjP NN NNC TxU ViU WU

355 Morales Guiñazú, Fernando. <u>Genealogías de Cuyo.</u> Mendoza: Best Hermanos, 1939. 398 p. Portraits. 28 cm.
A collection of genealogies of various prominent families from the Argentine province of Cuyo, including portraits for some notable members.

    DLC ViU

356 Moreno, Iván Carlos. <u>Linaje troncal de los Ruiz de Arellano en el Río de la Plata.</u> Buenos Aires: Impr. López, 1937. 207 p. 24 cm.
A genealogy of the Ruiz de Arellano family of Argentina, including biographical information on the following descendants: José Ruiz de Arellano, Manuel J. Güiraldes, Ricardo Güiraldes, Francisco Florencio de la Serna, Hilarión María Moreno, Enrique B. Moreno, Julia Moreno de Moreno, Rodolfo Moreno, Hilarión Moreno, Enrique Moreno. Alphabetical index of names.

    InU MH TxU

357 Otárola, Alfredo J. <u>Antecedentes históricos y genealógicos:</u> el conquistador don Domingo Martínez Irala, símbolo y espina dorsal de la conquista del Río de la Plata, precursor y fundador de la América del Sur, excepto Chile; su numerosa y distinguida descendencia. Buenos Aires: Casa Pardo, 1967. 185 p. Portraits. 23 cm.
A genealogical essay concerning Domingo Martínez de Irala and his numerous descendants. The following families are also featured: Otarola, Ayala, Ponce de León, Guzmán, Soler, Garay.

    CLSU CLU CSt CtY CU FU InU IU MB MoSW MU NcU NIC NjP NN NNC NSyU PPULC PSt OU TxU WU

358 _____. <u>Cunas de ilustres linajes;</u> descendencia de Domingo Martínez de Irala y otras de la época de la conquista, orígenes de primitivas dinastías medievales. Buenos Aires: Casa Pardo, 1970. 213 p. Portraits. 24 cm.
Collection of Argentine genealogies of the following families from the 16th to the 20th centuries: Domingo Martínez de Irala (family), Garay (family), Rodrigo Ortiz de Zárate (family), Gonzalo Martel de Guzmán (family), Alonso de Escobar (family), Pero Fernández (family), Alonso de Vera y Aragón (El Tupí, pseud.), Cristóbal Altamirano, Juan Basualdo (family), Baltasar Carbajal, Antonio

Higueras (family), Miguel Navarro (family), Antonio Bermúdez (family), Luis Gaytán (family), Diego de Olavarrieta (family), Pedro de Quirós (family), Juan Fernández de Enciso, Pedro de Xerez, Ambrosio de Acosta, Esteban Alegre, Domingo Arcamendía, Pedro Alvarez Gaytán, Sebastián Bello, Francisco Bernal, Juan Carbajal, Miguel del Corro, Ana Díaz, Alonso Gómez (family), Miguel Gómez, Rodrigo Gómez, Lázaro Gribeo, Pedro Hernández, Sebastián Hernández, Pedro Isbraín, Domingo de Irala, Pedro de Izarra, Miguel López Madera, Pedro Luis, Juan Márquez de Ochoa, Juan Martín, Pedro de Medina, Andrés Méndez, Hernando de Mendoza, Pedro Morán, Jerónimo Núñez, Jerónimo Pérez, Antonio de Porras, Antonio Roberto, Juan Rodríguez, Pedro Rodríguez, Juan Ruiz, Pedro Esteban Ruiz, José Sayás, Pedro Sayás Espeluca, Bernabé Veneciano, Pablo Zimbrón, Zárate (family). Also genealogies of medieval families in Spain.

    CLSU CSt CtY CU CU-S CU-SB IU MB MH NoSW NcU NN NNC TxU ViU WU

359 _____. <u>Datos y linajes;</u> nuevos estudios históricos genealógicos milenarios: Domingo Martínez de Irala, Ruy Díaz de Guzmán, el general Miguel Estanislao Soler. Con palabras preliminares por Enrique de Gandía. Buenos Aires: Casa Pardo, 1970. 187 p. Portraits. 24 cm.
A genealogy of many notable names associated with both Spain and Argentina. Biographical information is included for many notable Argentines of the past four centuries. The following are particularly featured: Domingo Martínez de Irala, Ruy Díaz de Guzmán, Miguel Estanislao Soler, Manuel José Soler, Ramón Antonio Peláez de Villa de Moros y Candamo, Carlos Gerónimo de Villademoros Palomeque, Pedro de Villademoros Palomeque, Benjamín de Villademoros Palomeque, Isabelino de Villademoros Palomeque, Carlos Gerónimo de Villademoros, Pedro Cano de Carvajal y Flores, Nicolás Cano de Carvajal y Lucero de Tovar, Nicolás Cano de Carvajal Quiroga Sarmiento, Alberto Cano de Carvajal Lucero de Tovar, Mateo Cano de Carvajal Ramírez de Arellano, Juan Agustín Cano Figueroa, Félix Vicente Cano Figueroa, José Tadeo Cano de Carvajal y Ramírez de Arellano, Fernando Cano Castro, Juan del Monumento Cano Castro, Marciano Nicolás Cano Díaz Vélez, Roberto Cano Díaz Vélez, Roberto Cano Lanús, Néstor Feliciano Cano Lanús, Juan Cano Díaz Vélez, Marciano Juan Cano Hunter, Raúl Cano Hunter.

    CLSU CLU CSt CU-SB FU IU MB MoSW MU NcD NcU NIC NmLcU NNC OU TxU

360 _____. <u>Los Vela, Vera de Aragón, y Vera, y otros linajes;</u> semblanzas y recuerdos. Buenos Aires: Casa Pardo, 1968. 203 p. Portraits. 24 cm.
A work primarily dedicated to the genealogies of several notable Spanish families, but also including short essays dealing with

GENEALOGY

the family lines and contributions of some famous Argentines; a few portraits are also included. Those particularly featured are Domingo Martínez de Irala, Ruy Días de Guzmán, Miguel Estanislao Soler.

CLSU CLU CSt CU CU-SB IU KU MB NBuU NIC NN NNC NSyU OU TxU ViU WU

361 _____. Mar del Plata y genearquía de sus fundadores: los reyes de Asturias y los caudillos de la reconquista hispana; los pipinidas y dinastías medievales. Buenos Aires: Casa Pardo, 1972. 212 p. 23 cm.
Collection of Argentine genealogies of the following families from the 16th to the 20th centuries associated with the Argentine city of Mar del Plata: Peralta Ramos, Martínez de Hoz, Luro, Camet, Coelho de Meyrelles, Pueyrredón, Brown, Julio César Gascón, Gascón, Juan de San Martín, Fruela I, Aurelio, Mauregato, Vermudo I, Ramiro I, Ordoño I, Hunaldo, Vandregisilo, Totilon, Iterio, Berenguer, Wasin, Bernardo del Carpio, Pipino, Saavedra, Ponce de León.

CtY CU CU-SB GU IaU ICarbS IU MU NIC NjP NN NNC NSyU PPT TxU WU

362 _____. Mar del Plata y sus fundadores; antecedentes medievales hispánicos. Mar del Plata: Talleres Rapid-Color, 1971. 14 p. 33 cm.
A genealogy of the following families who were among the founders of Mar del Plata, Argentina: Martínez de Hoz, Luro, Coelho de Meyrelles, Ituarte Pueyrredón, Peralta Ramos, Anchorena.

DLC IU

363 Sebreli, Juan José. Apogeo y ocaso de los Anchorena. Buenos Aires: Ediciones Siglo Veinte, 1972. 348 p. 20 cm.
Genealogical history of the Anchorena family of Argentina.

CaQMM CLU CtY CU CU-SB FU GU IaU IU MB MH MnU MoSW MU NbU NcU NIC NjP NN NNC NSbSU OrU PPiU TxU ViU WU

364 Tisnés Jiménez, Roberto María. Apuntes genealógicos; Los Tisnés en Colombia y Argentina. Félix Tisnés Jaramillo, coordinador y colaborador gráfico. Medellín: Editorial Salesiana, 1971. 112 p. Portraits. 24 cm.
A genealogical essay about the Tisnés family of Colombia and Argentina.

CSt CU-SB FMU FU ICN IU MB MH NIC NN NNC OU ViU WU

365 Urquiza, Eduardo de. La partida de bautismo de don José Narciso de Urquiza y Alzaga, 1762; la villa de Castro Urdiales. Buenos Aires: Talleres Gráficos Julio Kaufman, 1966. 27 p. 23 cm.

Genealogy of the Urquiza family of Argentina.

CLSU CLU CSt IU KU MB NBuU NcU NIC NN NNC OU TxU

366 Videla Morón, Mario Ernesto. Reflexiones sobre el pasado sanjuanino e incursiones en el de Cuyo y Chile. San Juan: Editorial Sanjuanina, 1964. 99 p. Portraits. 22 cm. (Ediciones, v. 5).
Genealogical histories about the following notable families of the Argentine province of San Juan: Sarmiento, Arbestayn, Echegaray, Valdivia, Cepeda.

CSt CtY DLC IU MU NcU NIC TxU

See also entries 172, 383, 556, 628.

HISTORY

367 Abad de Santillán, Diego. Historia argentina. Buenos Aires: Tip. Editora Argentina, 1965. 3 v. Portraits. 3 v. Portraits. 30 cm.
Encyclopedia of Argentine history arranged chronologically from prehistoric times to the first half of the 20th century with biographies of individuals who played a prominent role in the development of the country.

CtY CU DeU DPU ICarbS ICU IEN InU IU MdU MiU MU NcU NjR NN OCl OU

368 Albamonte, Luis María. Con Perón en el exilio. ¡Lo que nadie sabía! Por Américo Barrios, pseud. Buenos Aires: Editorial Treinta Días, 1964. 148 p. Portraits. 25 cm.
An account of Américo Barrios's experiences while in exile with the Argentine dictator, Juan Perón. Scattered biographical information and portraits are given for these two men and for others with whom they were associated. The following are emphasized: Luis María Albamonte (Américo Barrios, pseud.), Juan Perón, Carlos Bastidas, Rafael Trujillo, (Dominican Republic), Joaquín Balaguer, Eustaquio Soler, Benítez.

CLSU CLU CSt-H CtY CU FMU IU MH MoSW NcD NcU NIC NN NSyU OkU TxU

369 Alberdi, Juan Bautista. Bases y puntos de partida para la organización política de la República Argentina. Grandes y pequeños hombres del Plata y Comentarios de la Constitución de la Confederación Argentina por Domingo Faustino Sarmiento. Buenos Aires: Ediciones Depalma, 1964. 569 p. 24 cm.
A discussion of Latin American political thought, concentrating primarily on 19th-century Argentina and including scattered biographical information on many political philosophers. Particular emphasis is given to the following: Juan Bautista Alberdi, Bartolomé Mitre, Manuel Belgrano, José de San

Martín, Domingo Faustino Sarmiento. (See also entry 370.)

DPU FU IU KU NcU NIC NjP NN
NSyU TxU

370 _____. Grandes y pequeños hombres del Plata. 4. ed. Buenos Aires: Plus Ultra, 1974. 297 p. 19 cm. (Colección Los Argentinos, v. 3).
Study of leading figures of Argentina during the Independence era. Biographical data concentrate on the individuals' political and military activities. Among those especially featured are Bartolomé Mitre, Manuel Belgrano, José de San Martín, José Gervasio Artigas (Uruguayan), Martín Güemes.

CSt IU

371 Aldao, Adolfo. Reseña histórica de guerreros de la independencia, Buenos Aires, 25 de mayo de 1910. Buenos Aires: Impr. "La Aurora" de V. Guerra, 1910. 275 p. (V. 1). Portraits. 27 cm.
A collection of biographical articles about the following Argentine patriots during the period from 1806 to 1817: Gerónimo Espejo, Manuel de Olazábal, Indalecio Chenaut, Juan Antonio Casacuberta, Manuel Ramírez, José Ignacio Warnes, Alejandro Danell, Juan A. Michelena. José Arauz, Justo Rufino Guaty, José M. Pinedo, Rudecindo Alvarado, Fernando Abramo, Antonio Latorre, José Roa, Santiago Albarracín, José Segundo Roca, José Félix Correa de Sáa, Ramón Saavedra, Manuel A. Pueyrredón, Román Deheza, Hilarión Plaza, Nicolás M. Fontes, Francisco Acevedo, Juan Medeyros, José María Cortina, José de Obregoso, Juan Argüero, Juan Isidro Quesada, Hipólito Bouchard, Gregorio Murillo, Dámaso Rosales, Luciano Díaz, Angel Rolón, Cayetano Grimau Gálvez, Felipe Pereyra, Juan Méndez, Juan Zevallos, Pedro Nolasco Fonseca, José María López, José María Marmol, Guillermo Zamudio.

CtY DLC DPU ICU

372 Amadeo, Octavio Ramón. Vidas argentinas. 5. ed. Buenos Aires: "La Facultad," 1939. 317 p. 20 cm.
Collection of biographical essays profiling outstanding 19th-century Argentine political figures. Information supplied concentrates on the achievements of Carlos Pellegrini, Julio A. Roca, Adolfo Alsina, Leandro N. Alem, Bernardo de Irigoyen, José Luis Murature, Domingo F. Sarmiento, Roque Sáenz Peña, Indalecio Gómez, Nicolás Avellaneda, David Peña, Dardo Rocha, Eduardo Costa, Bartolomé Mitre, Juan Manuel de Rosas, Bernadino Rivadavia.

CU IU MiU

373 Angelis, Pedro de. Acusación y defensa de Rosas; compilación e introd. biobibliográfica

por Rodolfo Trostiné. Buenos Aires: Editorial "La Facultad," 1945. 536 p. 21 cm. (Biblioteca histórica del pensamiento americano).
An indictment and defense of Juan Manuel José Domingo Ortiz de Rosas. Includes biographical essays about the following notable Argentines of the 18th and 19th centuries: Pedro de Angelis, Estanislao López, Juan Antonio Alvarez de Arenales, Amado Jacobo Alejandro Goujad (Amado Bompland, pseud.). Also essay by Enrique de Gandía entitles Las Ideas políticas de Pedro de Angelis.

AzU CoU CtY CU DLC FMU FU GU IU
MH NcD NcU NN NNC OU PU TxU

374 Los Años de la emancipación política. Rosario: Editorial Biblioteca, 1974. 387 p. Portraits. 23 cm. (Colección Conocimiento de la Argentina: Sección B. V. 1).
A collection of essays including some portraits and biographical information on the following 19th-century Argentines active in the independence movement: Manuel Belgrano, Cornelio Saavedra, Pedro José Agrelo, Gervasio Antonio Posadas, Juan Ignacio Gorriti, Ignacio Alvarez Thomas, Manuel Ignacio Díez de Andino, Juan Manuel Beruti.

CtY CU NmU NSyU TxU

375 Aráoz de la Madrid, Gregorio. Las guerras civiles, el rosismo. Rosario: Editorial Biblioteca, 1974. 424 p. 23 cm. (Colección conocimiento de la Argentina: Seccion B, Escritos testimoniales. V. 2).
Excerpts from their memoirs and biographical sketches of the following 19th-century Argentine military men: Gregorio Aráoz de La Madrid, Tomás de Iriarte, Juan Estanislao de Elías, Miguel Otero, José María Paz, Pedro Ferré.

CtY TxU WaU

376 Arenas Luque, Fermín Vicente. Efemérides argentinas, 1942-1959. Buenos Aires: Concejo Deliberante, 1960. 735 p. 23 cm.
Diurnal record of Argentine history (1492-1959), featuring scattered biographical material on prominent figures of this period.

DPU IU NIC

377 Argentina-Paraguay; homenajes a San Martín por los colaboradores paraguayos, Buenos Aires, 1850-17 de agosto-1950. Buenos Aires, 1950. 32 p. Portraits. 22 cm.
A short work paying homage to San Martín and a few others with whom he was associated. The following are featured: José de San Martín, José Félix Bogado, Ramón Díaz, Patricio Oviedo, Vicente Suárez, Patricio Maciel.

CU-B TxU

HISTORY

378 Argentine Republic. Congreso. El parlamento argentino, 1854-1947. Prólogo del doctor Ricardo C. Guardo. Buenos Aires: Impr. del Congreso de la Nación, 1948. 863 p. Portraits. 28 cm.

A history of Argentina's House of Representatives and the Senate covering the period from 1854 to 1947. Brief scattered biographical information and portraits are included for many people associated with these institutions.

CU DLC DS IaU IU MH PU TxU

379 Astolfi, José Carlos, and Raúl C. Migone. Historia argentina (el siglo XIX en la república). 4. ed. ampliada, corregida y adaptada al programa vigente en la enseñanza secundaria. Buenos Aires: Librería y Editorial "La Facultad," Bernabé y Cía., 1939. 567 p. 20 cm.

A history of Argentina during the 19th century, including scattered biographical information on many people from all walks of life who contributed to this country's development. The following are particularly featured: Baltasar Hidalgo de Cisneros, Mariano Moreno, Manuel Belgrano, Simón Bolivar, José de San Martín, Bernardino Rivadavia, Juan Manuel de Rosas, Esteban Echeverría, Juan Cruz Varela, José Mármol, Francisco de Paula Castañeda, Juan María Gutiérrez, Olegario V. Andrade, Ricardo Gutiérrez, Domingo Faustino Sarmiento, Juan Bautista Alberdi, Vicente Fidel López, Bartolomé Mitre, Luis Domínguez.

DPU NcU

380 Avellaneda, Nicolás, Pres. Argentine Republic, 1837-1885. Escritos literarios. Con una introducción de Alvaro Melián Lafinur. Buenos Aires: La Cultura Argentina, 1915. 266 p. 19 cm.

A collection of biographical sketches about the following Argentine historical figures: Bernardino Rivadavia, Dalmacio Vélez Sársfield, Mamerto Esquiú, Julián Segundo de Agüero, Juan Chassaing.

CU DLC IEN IU MH NcD NcU PSt PPULC PU

381 Bajarlía, Juan Jacobo. Prohombres de la argentinidad. Buenos Aires: Imprenta de la Editorial Araujo, 1941. 118 p. 19 cm.

A collection of biographical sketches about the following Argentine patriots: Mariano Moreno, Bernardo Monteagudo, Manuel Joaquín Corazón de Jesús Belgrano y González Casero, William Brown, José de San Martín, Domingo Faustino Sarmiento, Marco M. de Avellaneda, José Esteban Antonio Echeverría, Juan Bautista Alberdi.

DLC NhD TxU

381a Bazán, Armando Raúl. La Rioja y sus historiadores. Prólogo de A. J. Pérez Amuchastegui. Buenos Aires: Platero, 1982. 227 p. 20 cm.

A collection of sketches including biographical information about the following historiographers of the Argentine province of La Rioja: Domingo Faustino Sarmiento, José Hernández, Antonio Zinny, Marcelino Reyes, Carlos M. Urien, Ramón J. Cárcano, Guillermo Dávila Gordillo, Vicente Almandos Almonacid, Domingo B. Dávila, Carmelo B. Valdés, Salvador de la Colina, Pedro Delheye, Domingo A. de la Colina, Guillermo Dávila San Román, Marcial Catalán, César Reyes, Dardo de la Vega Díaz, Pedro de Paoli, Fermín Chávez, Félix Luna, Juan Alfonso Carrizo, Ricardo R. Caillet Bois.

IU

382 Benavento, Gaspar L. Las sombras tienen luz. Prólogo de Carlos Alberto Erro. Buenos Aires: Instituto Amigos del Libro Argentino, 1967. 139 p. 20 cm.

Detailed biographical information of the following leading Argentine political figures of the 19th century: Manuel Belgrano, José de San Martín, Bernardino Rivadavia, Francisco Ramírez, Francisco Narciso de Laprida, Manuel Dorrego, Juan Galo de Lavalle, Marco Aurelio Avellaneda, Domingo Faustino Sarmiento.

IU MB

383 Bernard, Tomás Diego. Retablo sanmartiniano. Buenos Aires: Instituto Amigos del Libro Argentino, 1967. 170 p. 20 cm.

A work featuring biographical information on José de San Martín and many other people with whom he was associated, particularly members of his family. The following are featured: José de San Martín, Gregoria Matorras, Mercedes San Martín de Balcarce, Juan de San Martín y Gómez, Josefa Balcarce y San Martín de Gutiérrez de Estrada, Mariano Severo Balcarce, Mercedes Tomasa de San Martín y Escalada, María Mercedes Balcarce y San Martín, Fernando María de los Dolores Gutiérrez de Estrada y Gómez de la Cortina, José Balta, Mariano S. Balcarce.

AAP CLSU CLU CSt CU IaU ICU InU IU KU MB McU MiEM MoSW NBuU NcD NcU NIC NN NNC NSyU OU TxU

384 Bianco, José. Orientaciones; prólogo y notas por Pastor de San Martín. Buenos Aires: G. Mendesky é hijo, 1910. 515 p. 24 cm.

Collection of essays and lectures on Argentine history, with biographical sketches about the following notable figures: Pedro R. Leites, Telasco Castellanos, Vélez Sársfield, Juan B. Alberdi, Juan B. Ocampo, Justo José de Urquiza.

CtY CU DLC IU NjP NSyU PPULC PU

385 Bidondo, Jorge A. <u>Notas para la historia de</u>
<u>los gobernadores de Jujuy</u>. Jujuy: Dirección
Provincial de Cultura, 1971. 165 p. 27 cm.
      Chronological list of the governors of
the Argentine province of Jujuy from 1834 to
1967 with biographical sketches about the
following: José María Fascio, Fermín de la
Quintana, Eustaquio Medina, Miguel Puch, Pablo
Alemán, José Mariano de Iturbe, Roque Alvarado,
Pedro Castañeda, Escolástico Zegada, José Ló-
pez del Villar, Mateo José Molina, José Benito
de la Bárcena, Macedonio Graz, Plácido Sánchez
de Bustamente, José de la Quintana, Pedro José
Portal, Daniel Aráoz, Cosme Belaunde, Soriano
Alvarado, Mariano Iriarte, Emilio Quintana,
Teófilo Sánchez de Bustamante, Antonio Más
Oller, José María Alvarez Prado, Cástulo Apa-
ricio, Martín Torino, Fenelón de la Quintana,
Pablo Blas, Eugenio Tello, Pedro José Alvarez
Prado, Jorge Zenarruza, Sergio F. Alvarado,
Julián L. Aguirre, Sergio F. Alvarado, Mariano
Valle, Manuel Bertrés, Daniel Ovejero, Mario
Sáenz, Pedro J. Pérez, Justo P. Luna, Horacio
Carrillo, Mateo C. Córdova, Carlos F. Gómez,
Benjamín Villafañe, Héctor M. González Llama-
zares, Manuel Padilla, Miguel Aníbal Tanco,
Daniel I. Leguiza, Carlos G. Daireaux, José
Lucas Penna, Antonio López Iriarte, Fenelón
Quintana, Daniel González Pérez, Arturo Pérez
Alisedo, Fernando S. Berghnmans, Pedro Buitra-
go, Eliseo Peña, Raúl Bertrés, Nicolás Gon-
zález Iramain, Roberto Repetto, Francisco R.
Galíndez, Argentino Garriz, Fernando R. Nava-
rro, Manuel A. Sueiro, Carlos Kunz, Emilio
Forcher, César Horacio Méndez Chavarría, Al-
berto José Iturbe, Jorge Benjamín Villafañe,
Jorge Roque Teodoro Alvarado, Gastón Carlos
Clement, Andrés Schack, Aníbal Cipriano Vitón,
Horacio G. Guzmán, Oigimer Nereo Silva Ballbé,
Fortunato Daud, Roberto Pomares, Antonio de
la Rúa, Carlos A. Fernández Jensen, Roberto
José Hansen, José Humberto Martiarena, Fer-
nando Aníbal Guillén, Héctor Puente Pistarini,
Darío F. Arias. Also scattered biographical
notes about other minor government officials.

      AzU CtY CU FU GU IaU InU IU KU
      MdU MnU MU NcU NIC NNC TxU WaU
      WU

386 Biedma, José Juan. <u>Iconografía de próceres</u>
<u>argentinos</u>. Buenos Aires: Estab. Gráfico
Cazes, 1932. 181 p. Portraits. 19 cm.
      A collection of biographies, accompanied
by portraits, of the following Argentine
patriots of the 18th and 19th centuries:
Juan Bautista Alberdi, Manuel Alberti, Rude-
cindo Alvarado, Carlos de Alvear y Balvastro,
Juan Antonio Alvarez de Arenales, Nicolás Ave-
llaneda, Miguel de Azcuénaga, Juan Bautista
Azopardo, Juan Ramón Balcarce, Manuel Belgrano,
Antonio Luis Beruti, José Félix Bogado, Carlos
Federico Brandsen, Guillermo Brown, Hipólito
Buchardo, Juan José Castelli, Feliciano Anto-
nio Chiclana, Eustaquio Díaz Velez, Tomás
Espora, Domingo French, Eustaquio Frías, Dean
Gregorio Funes, Martín Miguel Juan de Mata

Güemes, Tomás Guido, Gregorio Aráoz de la
Madrid, Francisco Narciso de Laprida, Juan
Larrea, Juan Galo de Lavalle, Juan Gualberto
Gregorio de las Heras, Vicente López y Planes,
Domingo Matheu, Bartolomé Mitre, Mariano Moreno, Mariano Necochea, José Valentín de Olavarría, Juan José Paso, José María Paz, Antonio de Posadas, Juan Pascual Pringles, Juan
Martín Mariano de Pueyrredón, Bernardino Rivadavia, Martín Rodríguez, Nicolás Rodríguez
Peña, José Rondeau, Leonardo Rosales, Cornelio
de Saavedra, José de San Martín, Domingo Faustino Sarmiento, Manuel de Sarratea, Miguel
Estanislao Soler, Isidoro Suárez, Justo José
de Urquiza, Juan José Viamonte, Hipólito Vieytes, José Matías Zapiola.

      CtY

387 Bonastre, Valerio. <u>Corrientes en la cruzada</u>
<u>de Caseros</u>; prólogo de don José Juan Biedma.
2. ed.--oficial. Corrientes: Impr. del Estado, 1934. 400 p. Portraits. 26 cm.
      A historical essay about the Argentine
province of Corrientes in the 19th century,
mainly through biographical sketches of the
following leading figures: Juan José Pujol,
Benjamín Virasoro, Juan Madariaga, José Domingo Abalos, Manuel Antonio Ocampos, Bernardino López, Félix María Gómez, Cecilio Ignacio
Carreras, Juan Andrés Ricarde, Victoriano
Alemí, Basilio Acuña, Francisco Solano González, Nicanor Cáceres, Simeón Payba, José
Antonio Virasoro, Santiago Acevedo, Salvador
Reyes Bejarano, Wenceslao Martínez, Plácido
López.

      DLC

388 Bortnik, Rubén. <u>Historia elemental de los</u>
<u>argentinos</u>. Buenos Aires: Corregidor, 1973.
386 p. 19 cm.
      History of Argentina with biographical
notes about approximately 300 notable figures
of the 16th through the 20th centuries.

      CLU CSt CtY FU IU MB MU MWelC
      NcU NjP NmU NN NSyU TxU WaU WU

389 Bosch, Mariano Gregorio Gerardo. <u>Historia</u>
<u>del partido radical</u>, la U.C.R. 1891-1930.
Buenos Aires: Talleres Gráficos Argentinos
L. J. Rosso-Sarmiento, 1931. 234 p. 18 cm.
      A history of the Argentine <u>Unión Cívica</u>
<u>Radical</u>, covering the period from 1891 to
1930. Scattered biographical information is
included for many people associated with this
organization. Among those particularly featured are Leandro N. Alem, Carlos Pellegrini,
Bernardo de Irigoyen, Hipólito Irigoyen, Aristóbulo del Valle, Roque Sáenz Peña, Luis
Sáenz Peña.

      CLU CSt CtY CU FU IaU ICU IEN IU
      MU NcD OrU PPULC

HISTORY

390 Brossard, Alfred de. Rosas visto por un diplomático francés; traducción de Alvaro Yunque, pseud., y Pablo T. Palant. Buenos Aires: Editorial Americana, 1942. 372 p. Portraits. 24 cm.

Biography of Juan Manuel José Domingo Ortiz de Rosas, with biographical notes about the following notable figures in his life: Manuel Oribe, Felipe Arana, Alejandro Colonna Walesky, Manuelita Rosas.

DLC GU IU NcU NIC NN OCl PPULC

391 Bucich Escobar, Ismael. Buenos Aires, la gran provincia; cronología de sus gobernantes desde la cesión de la ciudad de Buenos Aires para capital de la nación hasta nuestros días. 1880-1930. Buenos Aires: Tall. Gráf. Ferrari Hnos, 1930. 376 p. 24 cm.

Biographies of the following governors of Buenos Aires (Province) from 1880 to 1930: Carlos Tejedor, José María Moreno, José María Bustillo, Juan José Romero, Dardo Rocha, Carlos D'Amico, Máximo Paz, Julio A. Costa, Juan Carlos Belgrano, Eduardo Olivera, Lucio V. López, Guillermo Udaondo, Bernardo de Irigoyen, Marcelino Ugarte, Ignacio de Irigoyen, José Inocencio Arias, Ezequiel de la Serna, Juan M. Ortiz de Rozas, Luis García, Marcelino Ugarte, José Luis Cantilo, José Camilo Crotto, Luis Monteverde, Valentín Vergara, Nereo Crovetto, Carlos Meyer Pellegrini,

CU DLC PPULC

392 _____. Historia de los presidentes argentinos. Buenos Aires: Roldán, 1934. 623 p. 21 cm.

History of the Argentinean government, with detailed biographical information on the following presidents from 1826-1938: Bernardino Rivadavia, Justo José de Urquiza, Santiago Derquí, Bartolomé Mitre, Domingo Faustino Sarmiento, Nicolás Avellaneda, Julio A. Roca, Miguel Juárez Celman, Carlos Pellegrini, Luis Saénz Peña, José Evaristo Uriburu, Manuel Quintana, José Figueroa Alcorta, Roque Sáenz Peña, Victorino de la Plaza, Hipólito Irigoyen, Marcelo T. de Alvear, José F. Uriburu, Agustín P. Justo.

CtY CU DLC IU MB NBuU NIU NN NNC
OU PPULC PU ViU WU

393 _____. Los presidentes argentinos, 1826-1918; prólogo del doctor Juan G. Beltrán. Buenos Aires: J. A. Herrera, 1918. 272 p. Portraits. 25 cm.

Detailed biographical information, accompanied by portraits, of the following Argentine presidents from 1826-1918: Bernardino Rivadavia, Justo José de Urquiza, Santiago Derqui, Bartolomé Mitre, Domingo Faustino Sarmiento, Nicolás Avellaneda, Julio A. Roca, Miguel Juárez Celman, Carlos Pellegrini, Luis Sáenz Peña, José Evaristo Uriburu, Manuel Quintana, José Figueroa Alcorta, Roque Sáenz

Peña, Victorino de la Plaza, Hipólito Irigoyen. Alphabetical index of names.

CtY CU DLC IU

394 Buenos Aires. Correspondencia de la ciudad de Buenos Aires con los reyes de España; documentos del Archivo de Indias. Cartas del Cabildo; memoriales presentados en la corte por los procuradores, apoderados y enviados especiales de la ciudad. Publicación dirigida por d. Roberto Levillier. Madrid, 1915-18. 3 v. 25 cm. (Colección de publicaciones históricas de la Biblioteca del Congreso argentino).

Collection of letters between the city of Buenos Aires and the kings of Spain from 1588 to 1700, with scattered biographical notes about approximately 500 people. Alphabetical index of names in each volume.

CU DLC InU IU NcD NcU NN PPULC

395 Buenos Aires. Museo Mitre. Documentos del archivo de Belgrano. Buenos Aires: Impr. de Coni hermanos, 1913-17. 7 v. 26 cm.

Collection of documents from Argentina's War of Independence, 1810-1817, with scattered biographical notes about approximately 900 people. Alphabetical index of names in each volume.

CtY CU DLC FU GU IaU InU IU LU
MU NBuU NcU NIC PPULC PU

396 Buenos Aires. Universidad. Facultad de Filosofía y Letras. Documentos para la historia argentina. Buenos Aires: Compañía Sudamericana de Billetes de Banco, 1913. 22 v. Portraits. 38 cm.

Collection of documents about the history of Argentina, with biographical notes on approximately 3,000 people of the 17th to the 20th centuries. Alphabetical index of names in each volume.

CaBVaU CU DLC FTaSU FU GU IaU
ICarbS ICJ ICN IEN IU KU KyU LNHT
MB MiU NcD NIC NN OCl OCU OO
OU PBL

397 Bugatti, Enrique. Breve historia del parlamento argentino: 1813-1974. Buenos Aires: Alzamor Editores, 1974. 220 p. 20 cm. (Colección del alba. V. 2).

A short history of the Argentine parliament during the 19th and 20th centuries, including very brief scattered biographical information on many political leaders. Alphabetical index of names.

FU ICarbS MB MH MiDW MoSW MU NcD
NcU NjR NSyU PPT TxU ViU WU

398 Bunkley, Allison Williams. The Life of Sarmiento. Princeton: Princeton University Press, 1952. 566 p. Portraits. 23 cm.

An account of the life of the 19th-century Argentine Domingo Faustino Sarmiento, which includes scattered biographical data for this man and for many others with whom he was associated. The following are emphasized: Antonio Aberastain, Juan Bautista Alberdi, Félix Aldao, Nicolás de Avellaneda, Nazario Benavídez, Manuel Bulnes, Salvador María del Carril, Santiago Derqui, Ricardo López Jordán, Gregorio Aráoz de Lamadrid, Francisco Solano López, Vidente Fidel López, Mary Mann (Mrs. Horrace Mann), Bartolomé Mitré, Manuel Montt, Domingo de Oro, José María Paz, Juan Facundo Quiroga, Bernardino Rivadavia, Juan Manuel de Rosas, José de San Martín, Domingo Faustino Sarmiento, Domingo Fidel Sarmiento, José Clemente Sarmiento, Paula Albarracín de Sarmiento, Justo José de Urquiza. Alphabetical index of names. (See also entry 399.)

DLC IU MB MiB MiU NcRS NN OC1 ODW OO OOxM OU PP PPULC PV TU TxU UU ViU

399 _____. Vida de Sarmiento. Traducida por Luis Echavárri. Buenos Aires: Eudeba, Editorial Universitaria de Buenos Aires, 1966. 486 p. Portraits. 22 cm. (Biblioteca de América. Temas, historia). Spanish translation of The Life of Sarmiento. (See entry 398.)

AzU CoFS FTaSU IU LU-NO NBuC NBuU PSt TxDaM

400 Busaniche, José Luis. Estampas del pasado; lecturas de historia argentina, ampliadas hasta 1910. Buenos Aires: Librería Hachette, 1959. 896 p. 21 cm. (Colección "El Pasado Argentino").
Collection of essays about the history of Argentina, with scattered biographical notes on over 300 figures from 1527 to 1910.

CLSU CoU CU DPU InU IU KEmT LU MB MiU MnU MoSW NcU NIC NjP NN NNC OC1 OkU TxDaM TxU WU

401 _____. Historia argentina. Buenos Aires: Solar, 1965. 786 p. 20 cm. (Colección "El Pasado argentino").
History of Argentina with scattered biographical notes on over 500 figures of the 15th through the 19th centuries.

CaQMM CLSU CLU CSt CtY CU DeU DPU FTaSU IaAS InU IU KU MdBJ MdU MH MiEM MiU MoSW NbU NBuU NcD NcU NIC NjP NjR NNC NSyU OrPS OrU PPiU PPULC TxU WU

402 _____, comp. Lecturas de historia argentina; relatos de contemporáneos, 1527-1870. Buenos Aires: Ferrari Hnos., 1938. 585 p. 21 cm.
Collection of essays about the history of Argentina, with scattered biographical notes on over 300 figures from 1527 to 1870.

DLC DPU ICN IU NcU NN

403 Caldas Villar, Jorge. Nueva historia argentina. Buenos Aires: J. C. Granda y J. R. Corvalán, 1966. 4 v. Portraits. 26 cm.
History of Argentina from the 16th through the 20th centuries, with scattered biographical notes on over 1,300 people. Alphabetical index of names in volume 4.

CLSU CU FTaSU IaU ICU InU IU KU LNT MB MH MiEM MU NbU NBuU NcU NN NNC NSyU OU PSt RPB TxDaM TxU ViU WU

404 Calderaro, José D. Cien próceres argentinos. Buenos Aires: Editorial Kapelusz y Cía., 1943. 191 p. 20 cm.
A collection of biographical sketches of the following notable individuals in the history of 18th- and 19th-century Argentina: Mariano Acosta, Juan Bautista Alberdi, Manuel Alberti, Leandro N. Alem, Adolfo Alsina, Valentín Alsina, Antonio Alvarez Jonte, Ignacio Alvarez Thomas, Carlos M. de Alvear, Florentino Ameghino, Tomás M. de Anchorena, Olegario V. Andrade, José Antonio Alvarez Arenales, Hilario Ascasubi, Jenaro Berón Astrada, Marco M. Avellaneda, Nicolás Avellaneda, Miguel de Azcuénaga, Juan Bautista Azopardo, Antonio González Balcarce, Juan Ramón González Balcarce, Manuel Belgrano, Luis Beltrán, Antonio Luis Beruti, Federico Brandzen, Guillermo Brown, Juan Bautista Cabral, Estanislao del Campo, Juan José Castelli, Pedro Castelli, Feliciano Antonio de Chiclana, Santiago Derqui, Manuel Dorrego, Pedro Echagüe, José Esteban Echeverría, Manuel Blanco Encalada, Manuel de Escalada, Tomás Espora, José Manuel Estrada, (Antonio Ruiz) Falucho, Domingo French, Gregorio (Deán) Funes, Juan Martín Güemes, Tomás Guido, Carlos Guido Spano, Juan María Gutiérrez, Ricardo Gutiérrez, José Hernández, José Rivera Indarte, Bernardo de Irigoyen, Manuel José de Lavardén, Gregorio A. de Lamadrid, Francisco Narciso Laprida, Juan Larrea, Juan Gregorio Las Heras, Juan Lavalle, Santiago Liniers, Estanislao López, Vicente Fidel López, Vicente López y Planes, Esteban de Luca, José Marmol, Domingo Bartolomé Matheu, Bartolomé Mitre, Bernardo de Monteagudo, Mariano Moreno, Francisco Javier Muñiz, Mariano Necochea, Francisco A. Ortiz de Ocampo, Fray Justo Santa María de Oro, Juan José Paso, José M. Paz, Marcos Paz, Gervasio Antonio Posadas, Pascual Pringles, Juan Martín de Pueyrredón, Juan Facundo Quiroga, Francisco Ramírez, Ildefonso Ramos Mejía, Guillermo Rawson, Bernardino Rivadavia, Julio A. Roca, Fray Cayetano Rodríguez, Martín Rodríguez, Nicolás Rodríguez Peña, José Rondeau, Juan Manuel de Rosas, Cornelio Saavedra, José de San Martín, Domingo Faustino Sarmiento, Manuel de Sarratea, Miguel E. Soler, Carlos Tejedor, Justo José de Urquiza, Florencio Varela, Juan Cruz Varela, Dalmacio Vélez Sársfield, Juan José Viamonte, Hipólito José Vieytes, Facundo Zuviría.

TxU

HISTORY

405 _____. Los presidentes argentinos; de Bernardino Rivadavia a Roberto M. Ortiz. Ilustraciones de R. Mezzadra. Buenos Aires: J. Gil, 1940. 106 p. Portraits. 30 cm.
Biographical sketches accompanied by portraits of the following Argentine presidents (1826-1944): Bernardino Rivadavia, Juan José de Urquiza, Santiago Derqui, Bartolomé Mitre, Domingo Faustino Sarmiento, Nicolás Avellaneda, Julio A. Roca, Miguel Juárez Celman, Carlos Pellegrini, Luis Saénz Peña, José Evaristo Uriburu, Manuel Quintana, José Figueroa Alcorta, Roque Saénz Peña, Victorino de la Plaza, Hipólito Irigoyen, Marcelo T. de Alvear, José F. Uriburu, Agustín P. Justo, Roberto M. Ortiz.

DLC IU NCU TxU

406 Cambón, R. Breves lecciones de historia argentina, arregladas al programa oficial para servir esclusivamente á niños de escuela elemental. Buenos Aires: Impr. de P. E. Coni, 1872. 35 p. 19 cm.
Collection of Argentine history lessons, with biographical notes about the following notable figures from the 16th through the 19th centuries: Cristóbal Colón, Hernando de Magallanes, Sebastián Cabotto, Pedro de Mendoza, Juan de Ayolas, Domingo Martínez de Irala, Alvar Núñez Cabeza de Vaca, Juan de Garay, Hernando Arias de Saavedra (Hernandarias, pseud.), Bruno Mauricio de Zabala, Pedro de Zeballos, Santiago Liniers, Baltasar Hidalgo de Cisneros.

IU

407 Capdevila, Arturo. ¿Quién vive? ¡La libertad! Crónica, evocación e historia de la organización nacional. Buenos Aires: Editorial Losada, 1952. 280 p. 21 cm.
History of Argentina during the period of the national organization in the 19th century with biographical sketches about the following notable figures: Vicente Fidel López, Facundo Zuviría, Ascasubi, José Mármol, Juan Bautista Alberdi.

GEU IU LU MiU MoU NN TxU

408 _____. Los salvajes unitarios . . . y los otros. Rosario: Editorial Rosario, 1949. 180 p. 21 cm.
Military history of Argentina during Juan Manuel de Rosas's era with biographical sketches about the following: Bernardino Rivadavia, José María Paz, Benjamín Villafañe, Juan Chassaing, Manuelita Rosas y Escurra, Juan Manuel Rosas.

CU DLC IU NcD TxU

409 _____. Las vísperas de Caseros. Buenos Aires: Agencia General de Publicaciones, 1922. 156 p. 19 cm.

Discussion of Argentine history during the middle 19th century and especially the battle of Caseros, with biographical essays about the following figures: Juan Manuel Rosas, Manuelita de Rosas y Ezcurra, Manuel López. (See also entry 410.)

CSt IU LU OrCS PPULC PU TxU

410 _____. Las vísperas de Caseros. Buenos Aires: Cabaut & Cía., 1928. 204 p. 19 cm. Same as the 1922 edition, with new introduction. (See entry 409.)

CtY CU DLC IU NcD NcU NIC

411 Caraffa, Pedro Isidro. Celebrità argentine dell'epoca dell'indipendenza nazionale, brevi cenni biografici con ritratti ed annotazioni. Ravenna: E. Lavagna & Figlio, 1921. 256 p. Portraits. 23 cm.
A collection of biographical sketches, accompanied by portraits, about the following Argentine patriots of the period of independence: Manuel Belgrano, Mariano Moreno, Nicolás Rodríguez Paña, Bernardino Rivadavia, Juan Larrea, Justo de Santa María de Oro, José de San Martín, Juan José Castelli, Francisco Narciso Laprida, Tomás Godoy Cruz, Juan Hipólito Vieytes, Antonio Luis Beruti, Manuel M. Alberti, Vicente López y Planes, Juan José Paso, Esteban de Luca. Also portrait of Pedro I. Caraffa.

DLC NN

412 _____. Hombres notables de Cuyo. La Plata: Talleres Sesé, Larrañaga y Cía., 1908-10. 2 v. Portraits. 19 cm.
A collection of biographical sketches of the following outstanding citizens of the Cuyo region in the 18th and 19th century: José Ignacio de la Roza, Tomás Godoy Cruz, Toribio de Luzuriaga, Francisco Narciso de Laprida, Justo de Santa María de Oro, Domingo de Oro, José Bruno Morón, Salvador María del Carril, Juan Agustín Maza, Manuel Corvalán, Vicente Dupuy, Pedro Molina, José de San Martín, Saturnino Lorenzo Saraza, Bonifacio Vera, Eugenio Corvalán, José Manuel Eufrasio de Quiroga Sarmiento, Victorino Corvalán, José María Pérez de Urdininea, Antonio Aberastaín. (See also entre 413.)

CLU CU IEN MiU NN

413 _____. Hombres notables de Cuyo. 2. ed. La Plata: J. Sesé y Cía., 1912. 315 p. 23 cm. Portraits.
Enlarged edition. Contains the same biographies as the first edition, and in addition the following: Damián Hudson, Tristán Echegaray, Saturnino Salas, Juan Gualberto Godoy. (See entry 412.)

DPU IU MH NN

414 Carbia, Rómulo D. Historia crítica de la
historiografía argentina (desde sus orígenes
en siglo XVI). La Plata, Buenos Aires: Imprenta López, 1939. 483 p. 28 cm. (Biblioteca humanidades editada por la Facultad de
Humanidades y Ciencias de la Educación de la
Universidad de La Plata, v. 22).
     Critical history of Argentine historio-
graphy with scattered biographical notes on
approximately 800 figures in the 16th through
the 20th centuries. Alphabetical index of
names. (See also entry 415.)

     DLC DPU ICN ICU IU MH NcD NcU
     NNC PPT PPULC PU

415 _____. Historia crítica de la historiografía
argentina (desde sus orígenes en el siglo
XVI). Ed. definitiva. Buenos Aires: Coni,
1940. 466 p. 22 cm.
     Same as the 1939 edition. (See entry 414.)

     CSt CU DCU DLC IU LU MoU MU NBC
     OCl PPULC PSt ViU

416 _____. Manual de historia de la civilización
argentina; preparado con los materiales de la
Sección de Historia de la Facultad de Filosofía y Letras de la Universidad de Buenos
Aires, y con la cooperación de sus miembros:
Luis María Torres, Rómulo D. Carbia, Emilio
Ravignani y Diego Luis Molinari. Buenos
Aires: Franzetti y Cía., 1917. 509 p. Portraits. 20 cm. (Biblioteca de la Asociación
nacional del profesorado).
     History of Argentine civilization with
scattered biographical notes on approximately
550 figures from the 16th through the 18th
centuries. Alphabetical index of names.

     CU DLC IU

417 Cárcano, Ramón José. Primeras luchas entre
la iglesia y el estado en la gobernación de
Tucumán, siglo XVI. Buenos Aires: "El Ateneo," 1929. 331 p. Portraits. 21 cm. (Junta de historia y numismática. Biblioteca de
historia argentina y americana, v. 4).
     A history of the interaction of church and
state in Tucumán, Argentina, during the 16th
century. Biographical information is included for many officials, particularly the
following: Hernando de Lerma, Gonzalo de
Abreu, Francisco de Victoria, Francisco de
Salcedo, Juan Ramírez de Velasco.

     CoU DLC FU IU NN PPT PPULC TxU ViU

418 _____, comp. Urquiza y Alberdi, intimidades
de una política. Buenos Aires: La Facultad,
1938. 642 p. 22 cm.
     Collection of correspondence between Juan
Bautista Alberdi and Justo José de Urquiza,
19th-century intellectuals and statesmen,
which includes limited biographical material
on the following individuals: Juan Bautista
Alberdi, Justo José de Urquiza, Juan María

Gutiérrez, Francisco Pico, Delfín B. Huergo,
Hilario Ascasubi. Alphabetical index of
names.

     IU

419 Carranza, Adolfo P. Argentinas. Buenos Aires:
G. Mendesky e hijos, 1913. 151 p. 21 cm.
     Collection of essays about various topics,
with biographical essays on the following
figures of the 19th century: Bernardo de
Monteagudo, Nicolás Rodríguez Peña, Juan de
Garay, Juan Hipólito Vieytes.

     DLC IU MH NN

420 _____. Los héroes de la independencia; noticias biográficas. Buenos Aires: J. Lajouane
y Cía., 1910. 47 p. Portraits. 31 cm.
     A collection of biographical sketches of
the following heroes of the Argentine war of
independence (1810-1817): José de San Martín,
Manuel Belgrano, Cornelio Saavedra, Carlos
María de Alvear, Juan Martín de Pueyrredón,
Juan Gregorio de Las Heras, José M. Paz, Juan
Lavalle, Guillermo Brown, Mariano Moreno, Bernardino Rivadavia, Juan José Castelli.

     CU DLC IU NcU

421 _____. La Junta gubernativa de 1810. Buenos
Aires, 1910. 36 p. Portraits. 18 cm.
     A series of biographical essays, emphasiz-
ing major personal and professional accomplishments, on the following members of the revolutionary government of 1810: Cornelio Saavedra, Mariano Moreno, Juan José Paso, Manuel
Belgrano, Juan José Castelli, Juan Larrea,
Manuel Alberti, Domingo Matheu, Miguel de
Azcuénaga.

     CLSU IU

422 _____. Patricias argentinas. Buenos Aires:
Sociedad Patricias Argentinas "Dios y patria,"
1910. 176 p. Portraits. 19 x 11 cm.
     A collection of biographical sketches
about the following women prominent during the
Argentine war for independence: Casilda Igar-
zábal de Rodríguez Peña, Francisca Silveira de
Ibarrola, Bernardina Chavarría de Viamonte,
Dionisia Nazarre de Grandioli, Ana Riglos de
Irigoyen, María Mercedes Coronel de Paso,
María Josefa Lajarrota de Aguirre, Benita
Nazarre de Pico, Mercedes Lasala de Riglos,
Martina Warnes de Unquera, Juana García de
Pinto, Juana Pueyrredón de Sáenz Valiente,
Irene Gutiérrez de Tollo, Micaela Suárez de
Romero, Tiburcia Haedo de Paz, Juana del Signo,
Magdalena Güemes de Tejada, María Tiburcia
Rodríguez de Fernández Blanco, Dolores Vedoya
de Molinas, Tomasa de la Quintana de Escalada,
María Eugenia Escalada de María, María Sánchez
de Thompson, Carmen Quintanilla de Alvear,
Remedios Escalada de San Martín, Rufina Orma
de Rebollo, Isabel Calvimontes de Agrelo, En-
carnación Andonaégui de Valdepares, Angela

HISTORY

Castelli de Igarzábal, Nieves Escalada de Oromí, María de la Quintana, Ramona Esquivel y Aldao, Petrona Cordero, Magdalena Castro, Dolores Prats de Huisi, Mercedes Alvarez de Segura, Jerónima San Martín, Martina Silva de Gurruchaga, Juana Azurduy de Padilla, Gertrudis Medeiros de Cornejo, Laureana Ferrari de Olazábal.

DLC   DCU-IA   MiU   TxU

423   Carranza, Angel Justiniano. Campañas navales de la República Argentina; cuadros históricos. Buenos Aires, 1962. 4 v. Portraits. 25 cm. (Departamento de Estudios Históricos Navales. Serie B: Historia naval argentina. V. 2).
   Naval history of Argentina with scattered biographical notes on approximately 1,600 figures of the 19th and 20th centuries. Alphabetical index of names for each volume.

CLU   CSt   CtY   FU   ICU   IU   MB   MH   MoSW
MU   NN   PSt   WU

424   _____, and Mariano A. Pelliza. Galería biográfica argentina, por A. J. C. y M. A. P. Buenos Aires, 1877. 70 p. Portraits. 26 cm.
   A collection of biographical sketches, accompanied by portraits of the following notable individuals in the history of Argentina during the 19th century: Juan Martín Pueyrredón, Rudecindo Alvarado, Juan Felipe Ibarra, José Mármol, Vicente López y Planes.

CU   DLC

425   Carranza, Arturo Bartolomé. La cuestión capital de la República. 1826 a 1887 (antecedentes, debates parlamentarios, iniciativas, proyectos de leyes) . . . (con ilustraciones, biografías y retratos). Buenos Aires: Talleres Gráficos Argentinos de L. J. Rosso, 1926. 5 v. Portraits. 25 cm.
   A five-volume history of the politics and government of Argentina covering the period 1826-1887. Biographical sketches and portraits are included in each volume (Section Retratos y biografías), for many notable Argentine leaders of that period (approximately 550 names). Alphabetical index of names for the five volumes in vol. 5.

CU   DLC   FU   GU   IU   InU   MiU   NcD   NcU
NSyU

426   Carretero, Andrés. Anarquía y caudillismo; la crisis institucional en febrero de 1820. Buenos Aires: Ediciones Pennedille, 1971. 217 p. 21 cm. (Colección estudios históricos y sociales. V. 7).
   History of Argentina in 1820 with scattered biographical notes on approximately 300 notable figures.

CLSU   CLU   CSt   CtY   CU   CU-SB   FU   IaU
ICU   IU   KU   MH   MU   NcD   NcU   NIC   NjP
NmU   NN   OU   TxU   ViU   WU

427   Carriegos, Ramón C. La Revolución de Mayo i el general i caudillo don José Gervasio Artigas; Corrientes, 1946. 301 p. Portraits. 24 cm.
   History of the Argentine War of Independence, 1810 to 1817, with biographical essays about José Gervasio Artigas, and biographical notes about the following: Juan Antonio Artigas, Francisco Miranda, Home Popham, Pascual Ruiz Huidobro, Santiago Liniers, Juan Bazo Berry, Saturnino Rodríguez Peña, Carlota Joaquina, José Manuel Goyeneche, Juan Martín Pueyrredón, Martín de Alzaga, Baltasar Cisneros, Benito Lué i Riega, Mariano Moreno, Juan José Passo, Matías Irigoyen, Antonio Alvarez Jonte, Atanasio Duarte, Juan Bautista Azopardo, Manuel Belgrano, José Rondeau, Javier de Elío, Juan Rademaker, Elías Galván, José de San Martín, Carlos Antonio José de Alvear, Diego de Alvear, Bernardo de Monteagudo, Manuel de Sarratea.

CtY   DLC   IU   NcU   NN   TxU

428   Carril, Bonifacio del. Crónica interna de la revolución libertadora. Buenos Aires, 1959. 277 p. Portraits. 21 cm.
   Collection of chronicles about some of the events of the "revolución libertadora" in Argentina with biographical notes about notable contemporary figures, particularly Eduardo Lonardi and General Aramburu.

AzU   CaBVaU   CSt-H   CtY   CU   DeU   DHU
FU   IaU   ICU   IEN   InU   MH   MoU   MU   NcU
NhD   NjP   NjR   NN   NNC   OrPS   PPiU   TxU
WaU

429   Los Caudillos de este siglo. Buenos Aires: Todo es historia, 1976. 143 p. Portraits. 20 cm. (Todo es historia. V. 4).
   Biographical essay on the following 20th-century Argentinean political leaders: José Néstor Lencinas, Carlos Washington Lencinas, Juan Ramón Vidal, Aldo Cantoni, Federico Cantoni.

IU

430   Ciria, Alberto. Partidos y poder en la Argentina moderna (1930-1946). 3a. edición corregida, ampliada y actualizada. Buenos Aires: Ediciones de la Flor, 1975. 414 p. 21 cm.
   A political history of Argentina covering the years 1930-46 providing information on political parties and economic systems, and including brief, scattered biographical information on over 300 Argentines who were associated with the government and politics during this period.

CLU   CSt   CU-SB   DGU   FU   IU   MH   MoSW
MnU   MU   NcU   NIC   NjR   NNU   OU   TxU

431   Con Rosas o contra Rosas. Buenos Aires: Editorial Freeland, 1968. 212 p. 20 cm. (Colección "Escritores de América Latina").

A collection of essays dealing with the life and work of Juan Manuel de Rosas. Bio-bibliographical sketches are also included for the authors of the essays. The following are featured: Juan Manuel de Rosas, Félix Luna, Jauretche, Benjamín Villegas Basavilbaso, Jaime Gálvez, León Rebollo Paz, Fermín Chávez, José Antonio Ginzo (Tristán, pseud.), Luis Soler Cañas, Arturo Capdevila, Julio Irazusta, Enrique de Gandía, Ernesto Palacio, Bernardo González Arrili, Emilio Ravignani, José Antonio Saldías, Arturo Orgaz, Manuel Gálvez, Diego Luis Molinari, Ricardo Font Ezcurra, Héctor Pedro Blomberg, Ramón Doll, Adolfo Mitre, Rafael Padilla Borbón, Alberto Gerchunoff, Mariano G. Bosch, Ramón de Castro Ortega, Carlos Steffens Soler, Julio E. Donato Alvarez, Roberto de Laferrère, Justiniano de la Fuente, Federico Barbará, Ricardo Caballero.

CLSU CoU CSt CtW CtY CU CU-S DPU
FU IaU ICarbU ICU IEN InU IU KU
MB MiU MnU MU NBuU NIC NjP NjR
NN NNC NSyU OU PPT PPULC TU TxU
UU ViU WU

432 Cornejo, Atilio. *San Martín y Salta.* Buenos Aires: Talleres Gráficos Pedro Goyena, 1951. 221 p. Portraits. 20 cm.
A discussion of the actions of San Martín in the Argentine province of Salta, including portraits and biographical information for this leader and others with whom he was associated. The following are featured: José de San Martín, Gerónimo Matorras, Martín Güemes, José M. Pérez de Urdininea.

InU IU PU TxHU TxU

433 Correa Luna, Carlos. *La campaña del Brasil y la batalla de Ituzaingó.* Documentos oficiales. Notas biográficas, por Enrique Udaondo. Buenos Aires: Talleres Gráficos del Instituto Geográfico Militar, 1927. 144 p. Portraits. 22 cm.
An essay about the Battle of Ituzaingó of 1827 published on occasion of its centennial, including biographical sketches of the following members of the Republican Army: Bernardino Rivadavia, Carlos de Alvear, José María Paz, Miguel Estanislao Soler, Juan Antonio Lavalleja, Federico de Brandsen, Lucio Mansilla, Julián Laguna, Juan Lavalle, Félix Olazábal, José de Olavarría, Tomás de Iriarte, Manuel Oribe, Manuel Besares, Juan Zufriátegui, Angel Pacheco, José María Aguirre, Román Antonio Deheza, Nicolás Medina, Paulino Rojas, Eugenio Garzón, Manuel Correa, Domingo Eduardo Trolé, Benito Martínez, José María Vilela.

CU DLC NN PU

434 Cowles, Fleur. *Bloody precedent.* New York: Random House, 1952. 270 p. 21 cm.
A biographical account of the Argentine dictators: Juan Manuel de Rosas and Juan Domingo de Perón.

CoU CU DLC FTaSU IU KMK MB NBuC
NBuU NcU NIC NN TxU ViU

435 Chávez, Fermín. *Historia del país de los argentinos.* Buenos Aires: Ediciones Theoria, 1967. 343 p. 20 cm.
History of Argentina with scattered biographical notes on approximately 300 figures from the 16th through the early 20th centuries.

CFS CLSU CLU CSt CtY CU FU IaU
InU IU KU MB MH MiD MnU MoSW MU
NBuU NcU NIC NjR NmU NN NNC NSyU
OU TU TxU ViU WU

436 D'Amico, Carlos. *Buenos Aires, su naturaleza, sus costumbres, sus hombres;* observaciones de un viajero desocupado, por Carlos Martínez, pseud. México: Tip. de Aguilar, 1890. 310 p. 19 cm.
A work dealing with Argentine geography and culture, which also includes substantial biographical information on the following 19th-century statesmen: Domingo Faustino Sarmiento, Bernardo de Irigoyen, Bartolomé Mitre, Máximo Paz.

Cu NN TxU

437 Damonte Taborda, Raúl. *Ayer fué san Perón,* 12 años de humiliación argentina. 1. ed. en la república liberada. Buenos Aires: Ediciones Gure, 1955. 271 p. 20 cm.
An account of the Perón dictatorship, including scattered biographical information for this man and for many others with whom he was associated. The following are emphasized: Juan Domingo Perón, Fritz Mandl, Ludwig Freude.

CU DLC IaU IEN IU MB MH MoU NN
NNC ScU

438 Destéfani, Laurio Hedelvio. *Famosos veleros argentinos.* Ilus. de Emilio Biggeri. Buenos Aires: Centro Naval, Instituto de Publicaciones Navales, 1968. 208 p. Portraits. 28 cm. (Colección Historia, 2. libro).
A history of famous Argentine sailing vessels, covering the period from colonial to modern times, and including portraits and scattered biographical information on many people, mostly explorers, pirates, and naval officers, associated with this aspect of Argentina's history. The following are particularly featured: Guillermo Brown, Hipólito Bouchard, César Fournier, Jorge de Kay, Luis Piedra Buena.

CLSU CSt CU FU IaU ICU InU IU MB
MH MoSW MU NBuU NIC NmLcU NNC
PPULC TxU ViU WU

HISTORY

439 Díaz de Raed, Sara. Signatarios de la independencia argentina en unión y libertad, en el sesquicentenario de su independencia. Santiago del Estero, 1966. 163 p. Portraits. 22 cm.

Collection of biographical sketches of the following signers of the Argentinean Declaration of Independence in 1816: Tomás Manuel de Anchorena, José Darragueira, Esteban Agustín Gascón, Pedro Medrano, Juan José Paso, Cayetano José Rodríguez, Antonio Sáenz, Pedro José Miguel Aráoz, José Ignacio Thames, Pedro León Díaz Gallo, Pedro Francisco de Uriarte, Manuel Antonio Acevedo, José Eusebio Colombres, Francisco Narciso de Laprida, Justo Santa María de Oro, Tomás Godoy Cruz, Juan Agustín Maza, José Severo Feliciano Malabia, Mariano Sánchez de Loria, José Mariano Serrano, José Andrés Pacheco de Melo, Pedro Ignacio de Rivera, José Antonio Cabrera, Manuel Eduardo Pérez de Bulnes, Luis Gerónimo Salguero de Cabrera y Cabrera, Pedro Ignacio Castro Barros, Mariano Boedo, José Ignacio Gorriti, Teodoro Sánchez de Bustamante. Also biography of Juan Martín de Pueyrredón, "Director Supremo" of Buenos Aires.

CLSU CSt CU MB MoSW N NBuU NIC NNC

440 Dorrego, Alejandro, and Victoria Azurduy. El caso argentino: hablan sus protagonistas. México: Editorial Prisma, 1977. 313 p. 21 cm. (América Latina: los actores. V. 1).

A collection of interviews with the following contemporary Argentineans prominent in the national scene: Rodolfo Puiggrós, Manuel Sadosky, Héctor Sandler, Adolfo Gass, Raimundo Ongaro, Ricardo Obregón Cano, Alberto Cárdenas, Pedro Orgambide, Héctor Bruno, Eduardo Luis Duhalde, Julio Santucho.

AzU CU-S IU MH WU

441 Dufourq, Esteban. El país de los argentinos. Buenos Aires: Ediciones Pleamar, 1966. 370 p. 20 cm. (Colección itinerario americano).

A social and political history of Argentina, covering the period from the conquest through the 20th century, and including scattered biographical information on many Argentine leaders.

AzU CLSU CLU CSt CtW CU DPU IaU ICU InU IU KyU MB MH MiEM MoSW MoU MU NbU NBuU NcU NIC NmU NN NNC NSyU OkU OU PPiU TxU VtU WU

442 Echagüe, Juan Pablo. Hombres y episodios de nuestras guerras. Buenos Aires: Editorial Sopena Argentina, 1941. 156 p. 20 cm. (Colección "Ayer y hoy").

A collection of biographical essays on the following 19th-century Argentine military men: José María Paz, Mariano de Acha, Juan Lavalle, Juan Ramón Estomba, Santos Pérez, Gregorio Aráoz de Lamadrid.

DLC IU

443 Eizaguirre, José Manuel. ¿Cómo se formó el país argentino? 2. ed. corr. Buenos Aires: Talleres Gráficos Argentinos de L. J. Rosso, 1928. 241 p. 19 cm.

A history of Argentina covering the period from its discovery through the independence movement. Scattered biographical information is given for many people associated with this period in Argentina's history. Those particularly featured include Hernando de Magallanes, Pedro de Mendoza, Domingo Martínez de Irala, Juan de Garay, Pedro de Cevallos Cortés y Calderón, Sobremonte, Santiago Liniers, Diego Mendieta, Baltasar Hidalgo de Cisneros, Manuel Belgrano, Justo José de Urquiza.

DLC IaU IU MB NcD NcU TxU

444 _____. ¿Donde está el pueblo? Buenos Aires: Talleres Gráficos Argentinos de L. J. Rosso, 1929. 254 p. 19 cm.

A collection of essays on Argentine history and culture, including biographical information on the following notable 19th-century Argentines: Bernardo Monteagudo, Domingo Faustino Sarmiento, Bartolomé Mitre, Justo José de Urquiza, José C. Paz.

DLC IaU IU MH TxU

445 _____. El Senado de 1890. Buenos Aires: J. Escary, 1891. 252 p. Portraits. 19 cm.

A discussion of the Argentine Senate of 1890, including biographical sketches and portraits of the following senators: Manuel Derqui, Toribio Mendoza, Benjamín Paz, Manuel D. Pizarro, Absalón Rojas, Miguel M. Nouguéz, Máximo Paz, Sofanor de la Silva, Rufino Ortega, Domingo T. Pérez, Carlos J. Rodríguez, Antonio del Pino, Gerónimo Cortés, Martín G. Güemes, Dardo Rocha, Anacleto Gil, José V. Zapata, Francisco V. Bustos, José Gálvez, Carlos Doncel, Benjamín Figueroa, Sabá Z. Hernández, Maximino de la Fuente, Antonio F. Crespo, Juan R. Vidal, Carlos F. Rodríguez, Carlos Tagle, Eugenio Tello, Alem del Valle.

NcU TxU

446 Encuesta sobre el caudillo. La Plata: Departamento de Filosofía, Instituto de Historia de la Filosofía y el Pensamiento Argentino, 1965. 201 p. 22 cm. (Universidad Nacional de La Plata. Facultad de Humanidades y Ciencias de la Educación. Cuaderno de sociología. V. 4).

An essay about the politics and government of Argentina, including biographical sketches about the following leading figures of the 19th century: Nazario Benavídes, Justo José de Urquiza, Martín Güemes, Juan Manuel de Rosas, Bernabé Aráoz, Gregorio Aráoz de la Madrid, Alejandro Heredia, Estanislao López.

LU NcD NIC TxHR

447 Equipos de Investigación Histórica. Pavón y la crisis de la Confederación. Buenos Aires,

1965. 634 p. Portraits. 22 cm. (Serie Investigaciones. V. 1).

A military and political history of Argentina, covering the period from 1852 to 1870, and including scattered biographical information on many notable Argentine leaders. The following, for whom portraits are also featured, are particularly emphasized: Santiago Derqui, Bartolomé Mitre, Manuel Ocampo, Justo José de Urquiza, Benjamín Victorica. Alphabetical index of names.

CLSU   CLU   CSt   CtY   FTaSU   IEN   KU   MH
MiU   MoSU   NbU   NBuU   NcU   NIC   NjP   NjR
NNC   NSyU   OU   PPT   TxU

448   Estrada, Santiago. <u>Catecismo de historia argentina desde el descubrimiento de América hasta nuestros días</u>. 2. ed. corregida y aumentada con rasgos biográficos. Buenos Aires: Igon Hermanos Editores, 1884. 138 p. 18 cm.

A short history of Argentina, covering the period from preconquest through the 19th century, and including biographical information, as well as portraits in most cases, for many notable people, mostly political leaders. The following are particularly featured: Cristóbal Colón, Américo Vespucio, Santiago de Liniers, Mariano Moreno, Manuel Belgrano, José de San Martín, Guillermo Brown, Bernardo Rivadavia, Juan Manuel Rosas, Juan Lavalle, Manuel Dorrego.

IU

449   _____. <u>Estudios biográficos</u>. Con prólogo de D. Valentín Gómez. Barcelona: Impr. Henrich, 1889. 276 p. 24 cm.

A collection of biographical sketches of the following 19th-century Argentinean patriots: Félix Frías, Santiago de Liniers y Bremond, Juan Esteban Pedernera, Domingo Sarmiento, Juan B. Estrada, Juan Lavalle.

DPU   IU   TxU

450   Farina Núñez, Porfirio. <u>Los amores de Sarmiento</u>. Buenos Aires: Editorial Tor, 1935. 248 p. 18 cm. (Ediciones argentinas "Condor." Las grandes biografías contemporáneas. V. 12).

A biography of Domingo Faustino Sarmiento, focusing on his relationships with the many people in his life and including substantial amounts of biographical information for the following: Dalmacio Vélez Sársfield, Domingo Faustino Sarmiento, Aurelia Vélez Sársfield, Domingo Fidel Sarmiento, Benita Martínez Pastoriza (Benita Martínez de Sarmiento, Benita Martínez de Castro y Calvo).

DLC   MH   MoU

451   Ferla, Salvador. <u>Historia argentina con drama y humor</u>. Buenos Aires: Granica, 1974. 333 p. 21 cm. (Colección Nuestra América).

A history of Argentina that deals mainly with the revolutionary movement of 1810.

Scattered biographical information is given for many notable Argentines, mostly military and political leaders, of this era and after. The following are particularly featured: Santiago de Liniers, Mariano Moreno, Saavedra, José Artigas, Manuel Belgrano, Manuel Dorrego, Juan Manuel Rosas, Hipólito Yrigoyen.

AzU   CLU   CSt   CtY   CU   IU   MB   MH   NN
NNC   ViU

452   Fitzgibbon, Russell Humke, comp. <u>Argentina: A Chronology and Fact Book</u>, 1516-1973. Dobbs Ferry: Oceana Publications, 1974. 148 p. 24 cm. (World chronology series).

A short chronology, accompanied by historical documents and lists of eminent people, covering the period from 1516 to 1973 in Argentina. Scattered biographical information is included for many famous Argentines, most of them political leaders. Among those particularly featured are José de San Martín, Bernardino Rivadavia, Juan Manuel de Rosas, Justo José de Urquiza, Domingo Faustino Sarmiento, Bartolomé Mitre, Hipólito Irigoyen, Roque Sáenz Peña, Ramón S. Castillo, Juan Domingo Perón, Eva Duarte (Eva Perón). Alphabetical index of names.

AzU   CaOTP   CLSU   CStH   DGU   DS   FU   GAT
GU   IaAS   IaU   ICU   InND   IU   KU   LN
LNHT   LU   MB   MiDW   MoSW   MoU   NbU   NcD
NcGU   NcRS   NcU   NIC   NjP   NjR   NmU   NN
NNC   NNR   NNU   NSyU   NyU   OkU   OOxM   OrPS
OU   RPB   TNJ   WU

453   Florit, Ernesto. <u>San Martín y la causa de América</u>. Buenos Aires: Círculo Militar, 1967. 637 p. Portraits. 20 cm. (Círculo Militar. Biblioteca del oficial. V. 577/79. Colección histórico-militar).

A biography of the 19th-century Argentine liberator, José de San Martín, including substantial information for this man, as well as less extensive, scattered information for others with whom he was associated. The following are emphasized: José de San Martín, Juan Antonio Alvarez de Arenales, Manuel Belgrano, Simón Bolívar, José Canterac, Thomas Cochrane, Andrés García Camba, Tomás Guido, José de La Serra, Juan Gerónimo de Las Heras, Bartolomé Mitre, Bernardo Monteagudo, Bernardo O'Higgins, José P. Otero, Mariano Felipe Paz Soldán, Joaquín de Pezuela, Juan Martín de Pueyrredón, Antonio José de Sucre. Alphabetical index of names.

CLSU   CSt   CtY   DPU   FU   IaU   ICU   IEdS
InU   IU   KU   MH   MoSW   MU   NbU   NcD   NcU
NIC   NmLcU   OU   TxU   WU

454   Franco, Luis Leopoldo. <u>Los grandes caciques de la Pampa</u>. Buenos Aires: Ediciones del Candil, 1967. 131 p. 17 cm. (Colección historia. V. 2).

A collection of essays featuring biographical information on the following great 19th-century Indian leaders of the Argentine pam-

HISTORY

pas: Yanguetruz, Painé Guor (Zorro Celeste), Baigorria, Calfucurá (Piedra Azul), Cipriano Catriel, Paguitruz (Mariano Rosas), Pincén, Saihuegue, Namuncurá.

CLSU CoU CSt CtY FU IaU InU IU KU MB MnU MU NbU NBuU NcU NIC NjP NNC OU PPiU PPULC ScU TU TxU ViU WU

455 Fregeiro, Clemente Leoncio. Lecciones de historia argentina; profesadas en el Colegio Nacional de la capital y arregladas al nuevo programa. Buenos Aires: G. Mendesky e Hijo, 1910. 2 v. Portraits. 20 cm.
A history of Argentina, covering the period from 1842 to 1905, and including scattered biographical information, as well as portraits in some cases, for many prominent people. Among those featured are Cristóbal Colón, Juan Díaz de Solís, Hernando de Magallanes, Pedro de Mendoza, Alvar Núñez Cabeza de Vaca, Domingo Martínez de Irala, Juan de Garay, Nicolás de Arredondo, Manuel Belgrano, Gregorio Funes, José de San Martín, Gervasio Antonio Posadas, José Artigas, Bernardino Rivadavia.

CU-B DCU-IA ICU IU NN

456 Frías, Bernardo. Tradiciones históricas (República Argentina). Buenos Aires: J. Menéndez e Hijo, 1923. 2 v. 19 cm.
A 2-volume collection of historical essays dealing with the Argentine province of Salta, including scattered biographical information for many people associated with this region. The following are emphasized: Hernando de Lerma, Manuela Tineo, Cayetano González, Isidoro Fernández, Lorenza de la Cámara.

DLC ICN ICU InU IU MH MiU NcU NIC NN TxU

457 Fúrlong Cárdiff, Guillermo. El Congreso de Tucumán. Buenos Aires: Ediciones Theoría, 1966. 412 p. 21 cm. (Biblioteca de estudios históricos).
An essay about the Argentine Congress (1816-1820), including biographical sketches of the following participants: Manuel Antonio Acevedo, Manuel de Anchorena, Pedro Miguel Aráoz, Mariano Boedo, José Antonio Cabrera, Pedro Buenaventura Carrasco, Pedro Ignacio de Castros Barros, José Eusebio Colombres, Miguel Calixto de Corro, José Darregueira, Pedro León Gallo, José Ignacio de Gorriti, Esteban Agustín Gascón, Tomás Godoy Cruz, Felipe Antonio de Iriarte, Francisco Narciso Laprida, José Severo Feliciano Malabia, Juan Agustín de la Maza, Pedro Medrano, Justo de Santa María de Oro, José Andrés Pacheco de Melo, Juan José Esteban de Paso, Eduardo Pérez Bulnes, Juan Martín de Pueyrredón, Pedro Ignacio de Rivera, Cayetano José Rodríguez, Antonio Sáenz, Jerónimo Salguero de Cabrera y Cabrera, Teodoro Sánchez de Bustamante, Mariano Sánchez de

Loria, José Mariano Serrano, José Ignacio Thames, Pedro Francisco de Uriarte.

CSt FU GU IU LU MdU MH MiEM MiU MnU NbU NcD

458 _____. La revolución de Mayo; los sucesos, los hombres, las ideas. 3. ed. Buenos Aires: Club de Lectores, 1960. 189 p. 20 cm.
A discussion of the prominent people and events of the Argentine war for independence. Scattered biographical information is included for many people, with particular emphasis on the following: Francisco Suárez, Juan Pablo Vizcardo, Juan José Godoy, José Gabriel Condorcanqui (Tupac Amarú), Cornelio Saavedra, Belgrano, Manuel Moreno, Benito Lué, José Zambrana, Julián Navarro.

CLSU CLU CtY CU DPU ICU InU IU KU LNHT MH MiU NcD NIC NjP NN TxU UU WU

459 Galería de celebridades argentinas; biografías de los personages más notables del Río de la Plata, por los señores Bartolomé Mitre, Domingo F. Sarmiento, Juan M. Gutiérrez, Félix Frías, Luis Domínguez, general Ignacio Alvarez y Thomas, y otros más. Con retratos litografiados por Narciso Desmadryl. Buenos Aires: Ledoux y Vignal, 1857. 253 p.
Collection of biographical essays on the following notable figures in 19th-century Argentina: Juan de San Martín, Bernardo Rivadavia, Manuel Belgrano, Gregorio Funes, Guillermo Brown, Manuel José García, Mariano Moreno, Florencio Varela, Juan Lavalle.

DLC IU (Film)

460 Gálvez, Manuel. Biografías completas. Prólogo de Carmelo Bonet. Buenos Aires: Emecé, 1962. 2 v. Portraits. 22 cm.
A collection of biographical sketches on the following notable individuals associated with the history of Argentina:
V. 1: Hipólito Yrigoyen, Mamerto Esquiú, Gabriel García Moreno, Francisco de Miranda.
V. 2: Juan Manuel de Rosas, Domingo Faustino Sarmiento, Aparicio Saravia.

CLSU CSt CtY FU IaU IEN IU MdU MH MoU NIC NjP NN NSyU TxU

461 Gambini, Hugo. El 17 [i.e., diecisiete] de octubre de 1945. Buenos Aires: Editorial Brújula, 1969. 140 p. Portraits. 17 cm. (Biblioteca de las cuestiones. V. 2).
An account of selected aspects of the Perón dictatorship, including scattered biographical information and portraits for many prominent politicians of that period. Particular emphasis is given to the following: Juan Domingo Perón, Edelmiro J. Farrell,

Eduardo J. Avalos, Héctor Vernengo Lima, Juan Alvarez, Juan Fentanes.

CLSU CLU CoU CSt CtY CU CU-S CU-SB IaU InU IU KU MB MH MnU MoSW MU NbU NcD NcU NIC NjP NmU NN NNC NSyU OU TU TxU ViU WU

462 Gambón, Vicente. <u>Lecciones de historia argentina</u>. Buenos Aires: A. Estrada y Cía., 1907. 2 v. 20 cm.

A two-volume history of Argentina, covering the period from discovery to the early 20th century. Scattered biographical information is included for many people, mostly political leaders. Among those featured are Cristóbal Colón, Juan Díaz de Solís, Hernando de Magallanes, Sebastián Gaboto, Pedro de Mendoza, Domingo Martínez de Irala, Alvar Núñez Cabeza de Vaca, Juan de Garay, Hernandarias, Pedro de Ceballos, Baltasar Hidalgo de Cisneros, José de San Martín, Carlos M. de Alvear, Belgrano, Rondeau, Juan Martín de Pueyrredón, Juan Gregorio de Las Heras, Bernardino Rivadavia, Juan Manuel de Rosas, Justo José de Urquiza, Valentín Alsina, Bartolomé Mitre, Domingo Faustino Sarmiento, Nicolás Avellaneda.

CSt DLC IU NcU NN

463 Gandía, Enrique de. <u>Buenos Aires colonial</u>. Buenos Aires: Editorial Claridad, 1957. 205 p. 21 cm. (Biblioteca de historia. V. 2).

A colonial history of Buenos Aires, including scattered biographical information on many notable Argentines associated with this period. The following are particularly featured: Gaspar de Santa Coloma, Martín de Alzaga, Santiago Liniers.

CtY CU DPU FU ICarbS ICN ICU IEN InU IU LNT LU MB MH MiU MoSW NBuU NcD NIC NjP NN NNC OkU OU PPULC ScU TNJ TxDaM TxFTC TxU ViU WaU WU

464 _____. <u>La ciudad encantada de los Césares</u>. Buenos Aires: A. García Santos, 1933. 174 p. 19 cm.

A collection of essays on various aspects of the discovery and settlement of Argentina, including scattered biographical information on many eminent people of that period. The following are emphasized: Andrés Manso, Pedro de Mendoza, Juan de Ayolas.

DLC IaU IU NcD NcU NN

465 _____. <u>Fisonomías de conquistadores</u>. Rosario, 1941. 48 p. 19 cm.

A collection of biographical sketches of the following conquistadors associated with the history of Argentina: Pedro Mendoza, Juan de Ayolas, Francisco Ruiz Galán, Domingo de Irala, Juan de Salazar de Espinosa, Hernando de Ribera, Diego González Baitos.

TxU

466 _____. <u>Historia de la República Argentina en el siglo XIX</u>. Buenos Aires: A. Estrada y Cía., 1940. 1018 p. Portraits. 23 cm.

A history of Argentina during the 19th century, including biographical information and portraits for many people, most of them political leaders. The following are emphasized: Santiago Liniers, Guillermo Brown, José de San Martín, Juan Manuel de Rosas, Esteban Echeverría, Domingo Cullen, Florencio Varela, Juan Bautista Alberdi, Bartolomé Mitre, Francisco Solano López, Elisa Alicia Lynch, Julio A. Roca, Domingo Faustino Sarmiento, Aarón Castellanos, Carlos Pellegrini, Luis Sáenz Peña, José Evaristo Uriburu, Manuel Quintana, José Figueroa Alcorta, Roque Sáenz Peña, Victorino de la Plaza, Hipólito Irigoyen, Marcelo T. de Alvear, José F. Uriburu, Agustín P. Justo, Roberto M. Ortiz.

DLC IU NcD NcU OCl TU

467 _____. <u>Historia de los piratas en el Río de la Plata</u>. Buenos Aires: Librería y Editorial Cervantes de J. Suárez, 1936. 362 p. 20 cm.

A history of the activities of pirates in Argentina, concentrating on the period from 1580 to 1660 and including biographical information on many people associated with that aspect of Argentina's history. The following are particularly featured: Juan de Rivadeneira, Juan Pinto, Juan Drake, Hernando de Vargas.

CU DLC IU NBuU NcU OU

468 _____. <u>San Martín</u>; su pensamiento político. Buenos Aires: Ediciones Pleamar, 1964. 466 p. 20 cm. (Colección Arquetipos).

An account of the political thinking of José de San Martín, including biographical information for this leader and for others with whom he was associated. The following are emphasized: José de San Martín, John Miers, Alejandro María Aguado.

CLSU CLU CSt CtY CU-S DAU DPU FU GU IaU ICU InU IU KU LNT MH MiEM NB NbU NcU NjP NN NNC NSyU OU PPiU PPT TU TxU UU WU

469 Gandolfi Herrero, Arístides. <u>Historia de los argentinos</u>, por Alvaro Yunque, pseud. Buenos Aires: Ediciones Anfora, 1968-70. 5 v. 27 cm.

A five-volume history of Argentina, covering the period from preconquest to modern times and including scattered biographical information and portraits for many people. The following are emphasized: Manuel Belgrano, Mariano Moreno, Juan Martín de Pueyrredón, José de San Martín, Bernardino Rivadavia, Manuel Dorrego, Esteban Echeverría, Justo José de Urquiza, Bartolomé Mitre, Domingo F. Sarmiento, Nicolás Avellaneda, Julio A. Roca, Leandro Alem, Aristóbulo del Valle, Roque

HISTORY

Sáenz Peña, Juan B. Justo, Enrique Mosconi, Hipólito Yrigoyen, Lisandro de la Torre, Juan Perón, Eva Perón.

CaBVaU CLSU CoU CSt CtY CU FU IaU
ICN ICU IEN IU KU MB MiU MoSW MU
NBuU NcU NIC NN NNC NSyU PSt TxU
ViU

470 _____. Hombres en las guerras de las pampas: héroes, mártires, aventureros, apóstoles, 1536–1886, por Alvaro Yunque, pseud. Buenos Aires: Ediciones Sílaba, 1969. 156 p. Portraits. 20 cm.

A history of the battles fought on the Argentine pampas, covering the period from 1536 to 1886. Scattered biographical information, as well as portraits in some cases, included for many people associated with this region. The following are particularly featured: Julio Argentino Roca, Aurelio Antonio Tounens, Francisco Bibolini, Félix de Azara, Luis de la Cruz, Francisco Ramos Mejía, Alvaro Barros.

CLSU CLU CoU CSt CtY CU FU IaU
ICU InU IU KU MB MiEM MiU MoSW
NbU NcU NIC NjP NN NNC NSyU PPiU
PSt TxU ViU VtU WU

471 García Al-Deguer, Juan. Historia de la Argentina. Madrid: La España Editorial, 1902–3. 2 v. 19 cm.

A 2-volume history of Argentina, covering the period from discovery through the 19th century, and including scattered biographical information on many notable people, particularly the following: Juan Díaz de Solís, Fernando de Magallanes, Sebastián Gaboto, Pedro de Mendoza, Juan de Ayolas, Domingo Martíndez de Irala, Alvar Núñez Cabeza de Vaca, Juan Ortiz de Zárate, Juan de Garay, Bruno de Zavala, Pedro de Cevallos, José de Antequera, Juan José de Vértiz, Manuel Belgrano, Santiago Liniers, Alzaga, Baltasar Hidalgo de Cisneros, Mariano Moreno, José Artigas, Pedro Somellera, José Gaspar Rodríguez de Francia, José de San Martín, Joaquín de la Pezuela, Carlos Alvear, Güemes, Rondeau, Manuel Dorrego, Pueyrredón, José Miguel Carrera.

CtY CU DLC IU MH NcD NN NNH OU

472 García Merou, Martín. Historia de la República Argentina. Obra escrita de acuerdo con el programa de los colegios nacionales de la República. Buenos Aires: A. Estrada, 1905. 2 v. 20 cm.

A 2-volume history of Argentina, covering the period from discovery through the 19th century. Scattered biographical information is given for many people, including the following: Cristóbal Colón, Juan Díaz de Solís, Hernando de Magallanes, Sebastián Caboto, Diego García, Pedro de Mendoza, Juan de Ayolas, Domingo Martínez de Irala, Alonso de Cabrera, Alvar Núñez Cabeza de Vaca, Felipe

Gutiérrez, Diego de Rojas, Francisco de Villagra, Juan Núñez de Prado, Francisco de Aguirre, Pedro del Castillo, Francisco Solano, Nuflo de Chaves, Juan Ortiz de Zárate, Juan de Garay, Hernando Arias de Saavedra (Hernandarias, pseud.), Francisco de Alfaro, Alonso Pérez de Salazar, Francisco de Céspedes, Pedro Esteban Dávila, Mendo de la Cueva y Benavides, Ventura Mujica, Jerónimo Luis de Cabrera, Jacinto de Láriz, Manuel de Frías, Bernardino de Cárdenas, José de Antequera y Castro, Miguel de Salcedo, José de Andonciegui, Pedro de Cevallos, Francisco de Paula Bucarelli, Juan José de Vértiz, Tupac Amarú, Santiago Liniers y Bremond, Home Popham, Martín de Alzaga, José de San Martín, Manuel Belgrano, José Artigas, Juan Manuel de Rosas, Beresford, Sobremonte, Baltasar Hidalgo de Cisneros, Mariano Moreno, Martín de Alzaga, Bernardino Rivadavia, Carlos Alvear, José Miguel Carrera, José Rondeau, Juan Martín de Pueyrredón, Güemes, Manuel de Sarratea, Bernardo Monteagudo, Manuel José García, Manuel Dorrego, Lavalle, Justo José de Urquiza.

CU IU

473 García y Mellid, Atilio. Proceso al liberalismo argentino. 2. ed. Buenos Aires: Ediciones Theoría, 1964. 585 p. (Biblioteca de estudios históricos).

A political history of Argentina, concentrating on the 19th century, and including scattered biographical information on many notable leaders.

CSt CtY DGU IaAS IaU ICU IEN IU
LU MB MdU MH MU NIC NjPT NmU NSyU
PPT

474 Garmendia, José Ignacio. La cartera de un soldado (bocetos sobre la marcha). 4. ed. Buenos Aires: Casa Editora Imprenta, Litografía y Encuadernación de J. Peuser, 1890. 411 p. Portraits. 25 cm.

A collection of biographical sketches on the following Argentine military men associated with the Paraguayan war (1865–1870): Juan Bautista Charlone, Miguel Martínez de Hoz, Alejandro Díaz, Manuel Rosetti, Luis María Campos, Mariano Paunero.

CU DLC-P4 DPU IU NcU

475 Gauna Vélez, Eduardo. Argentinos ilustres. Biografías. Buenos Aires: Cabaut y Cía., 1925. 306 p. Portraits. 19 cm.

A collection of biographies accompanied by portraits of the following heroes of the Argentine independence: Gregorio Funes, Miguel Azcuénaga, Juan José Paso, Cornelio Saavedra, Hipólito Vieytes, Manuel Alberti, Domingo Matheu, Juan José Castelli, Juan Alvarez de Arenales, Manuel Belgrano, Juan Martín Pueyrredon, Guillermo Brown, Mariano Moreno, José de San Martín, Juan Gregorio de las Heras, Bernardino Rivadavia, Martín Ròdríguez, Juan Larrea, Tomás Guido, Vicente López Planes, Bernardo Monteagudo, Martín Güemes, Esteban de Luca, Manuel Dorrego, Carlos M. de Alvear, José M. Paz, Manuel P. Rojas, Rudecindo Alvarado, Manuel de Escalada, Juan Lavalle.

NN

476 Gianello, Leoncio. *Historia argentina*, instituciones políticas y sociales; cuarto año del ciclo del magisterio. Buenos Aires: A. Estrada, 1964. 157 p. Portraits. 22 cm.

A history of Argentine political and social institutions, covering the period from colonial to modern times, and including brief scattered biographical information, as well as portraits in some cases, for many notable people. The following are particularly featured: Bernardino Rivadavia, Esteban Echeverría, Justo José de Urquiza.

IU LU MU

477 _____. *Historia de Santa Fe*. 3. ed., ampliada y actualizada. Buenos Aires: Plus Ultra, 1978. 475 p. Portraits. 20 cm. (Colección Historia de nuestras provincias. V. 5).

A history of the Argentine province of Santa Fe, covering the period from preconquest to the present. Scattered biographical information is included for many people associated with this region. Particular emphasis is given to the following: Juan Díaz de Solís, Sebastián Gaboto, Pedro de Mendoza, Alvar Núñez Cabeza de Vaca, Juan de Garay, Hernando Arias de Saavedra (Hernandarias, pseud.), Francisco de Sierra, Antonio de Vera y Mujica, Hernando de Rivera y Mondragón, Alonso de Herrera y Velazco, Francisco Pascual de Echagüe y Andía, Francisco Javier de Echagüe y Andía, Francisco Antonio de Vera y Mujica, Mariano Vera, Estanislao López, Pascual Echagüe, Simón de Iriondo, Luciano Leiva, Rodolfo Freyre, Pedro Antonio Echagüe, Rodolfo B. Lehmann, Pedro Gómez Cello, Joaquín Argonz.

IU

478 González Arrili, Bernardo. *Historia de la Argentina*, según las biografías de sus hombres y mujeres. Buenos Aires: Editorial Nobis, 1966. 10 v. in 5. 3881 p. Portraits. 23 cm.

History of Argentina as told through biographies of its most distinguished citizens. Information provided concentrates on the following individuals' contributions to Argentina's development.

V. 1-2: Manuel Belgrano, Manuela Pedraza, Gregoria Pérez, Cornelio Saavedra, Juana Pueyrredón, Mariano Moreno, Juan José Paso, Miguel de Azcuénaga, Juan José Castelli, Nicolás Rodríguez Peña, Hipólito Vieytes, Juan Larrea, Manuel Alberti, Domingo Matheu, Martín José de Altolaguirre, Gregorio Funes, Feliciano Antonio Chiclana, Francisco A. Ortiz de Ocampo, Agustín José Donado, Juan Florencio Terrada, Martín Rodríguez, Antonio José de Escalada,

Manuel Hermenegildo de Aguirre, Gervasio Antonio de Posadas, Vicente López y Planes, Andrés Arguibel, Francisco de Gurruchaga, José I. Fernández Maradona, Juan Francisco Tarragona, Antonio Sáenz, Antonio Luis Beruti, Elías Galván, Leonardo Domingo de la Gándara, José Darregueira, Julián Alvarez, Francisco Planes, Matías de Irigoyen, Miguel de Irigoyen, Manuel Artigas, Vicente Dupuy, Miguel Cajaravilla, Martín Thompson, Juan Andrés Gelly, Juan de Alagón, Joaquín Campana, Antonio Antonini, Martín de Alzaga, Juan José Viamonte, Fray Cayetano Rodríguez, Victoriano Rodríguez, Manuel José de Godoy, Tomás Manuel de Anchorena, Juan José de Lezica, José de San Martín, Remedios de Escalada, Lorenzo Barcala, Mercedes San Martín, Pedro Bargas.

V. 3-4: Jerónima San Martín, Pascuala Meneses, Laureana Ferrari, Toribio de Luzuriaga, Guillermo Brown, Juan Bautista Azopardo, Carlos de Alvear, José Gervasio de Artigas, José Rondeau, Juan Ignacio de Gorriti, Juan Martín de Pueyrredón, Tomás Guido, José Miguel Carrera, Francisco Narciso de Laprida, Teodoro Sánchez de Bustamante, Manuel Antonio Acevedo, Justo Santa María de Oro, Pedro Francisco de Uriarte, José Ignacio de Thames, Tomás Godoy Cruz, Lucía Aráoz, Enrique Martínez, Juan Ramón Balcarce, Antonio Balcarce, Marcos Balcarce, Diego Balcarce, Cosme Argerich, Bernardo de Monteagudo, Bernardino Rivadavia, Juana del Pino de Rivadavia, Joaquina Izquierdo, José Moldes, Candelaria Somellera, Martín Güemes, Carmen Puch, Macacha Güemes, Antonio Alvarez Jonte, Juana Mora, Pedro Antonio Cerviño, Loreto Sánchez Peón, Manuel Eduardo Arias, Domingo French, Julián Navarro, Ignacio Núñez, Manuel Dorrego, Juan Lavalle, Dolores Correas, Juan Manuel de Rozas, Encarnación Ezcurra, Manuelita Rozas, Mercedes Rozas de Rivera, Mariquita Sánchez, Crisóstomo Alvarez, Agustina Palacio de Libarona, José María Paz, Margarita Weild.

V. 5-6: Gregorio Aráoz de La Madrid, Luisa Díaz Vélez de La Madrid, Marco Manuel de Avellaneda, Crescencia Sánchez Boado, Pedro Feliciano de Cavia, Juan Crisóstomo Lafinur, Manuela Gómez de Calzadilla, Manuel Bonifacio Gallardo, Esteban Echeverría, Estanislada Tartás, Francisco Ramírez, Delfina (la portuguesa), Florencio Varela, Félix Aldao, Petrona Rosende, Juan Facundo Quiroga, Severa Villafañe, Domingo Faustino Sarmiento, Paula Albarracín, Procesa Sarmiento, Dalmacio Vélez Sarsfield, Tomasa Vélez Sarsfield, Domingo Victorio de Achega, Juana Manso, José Mármol, Camila O'Gorman, Justo José de Urquiza, Salvador María del Carril, Ricardo López Jordán, Juan Bautista Alberdi, Eduarda Mansilla, Marcos Sastre, Rosa Guerra, Juan María Gutiérrez, Facundo de Zuviría, Juan Francisco Seguí, Manuel Guillermo Pinto, Vicente Fidel López, Juan Nepomuceno Madero, Bartolomé Mitre, Delfina de Vedia, María Antonia de la Paz, Rufino de Elizalde.

V. 7-8: Rufino de Elizalde, Angel Vicente Peñaloza, Marcos Paz, Juan Bautista Charlone,

HISTORY

José Murature, Petrona Beláustegui, Adolfo Alsina, Toribia de los Santos, Lucio V. Mansilla, Nicolás Avellaneda, El rey Orllie, Bernardo de Irigoyen, Juana Manuela Gorriti, Hilario Ascasubi, Julio A. Roca, Luis María Drago, Manuel Prado, Leandro Alem.

V. 9-10: Conrado E. Villegas, José Hernández, Miguel Juárez Celman, Ida Edelvira Rodríguez, José Manuel Estrada, Aristóbulo del Valle, Francisca Jacques, Juan B. Justo, Carlos Encina, Carlos Pellegrini, Lucio V. López, Luis Sáenz Peña, Miguel Cané, Jose Evaristo Uriburu, Manuel Quintana, Bartolomé Mitre y Vedia, Juan Pedro Esnaola, Pastor Servando Obligado, José Figueroa Alcorta, Joaquín Castellanos, Roque Sáenz Peña, J. Alfredo Ferreira, Victorino de la Plaza, Julia Wernicke, Carlos Vega Belgrano, Joaquín V. González, Agustín Alvarez, Ignacio L. Albarracín, Hipólito Yrigoyen, Ernesto Nelson, Lisandro de la Torre, William C. Morris, Marcelo T. de Alvear, Antonio Sagarna, Raquel Camaña, Victorina Malharro, Vicenta Castro Cambón, Lola Mora, Pedro B. Palacios (Almafuerte, pseud.), Alfonsina Storni, César Duayen, Cecilia Grierson, José Ingenieros, Alejandro Korn, Elvira Aldao de Díaz, Florentino Ameghino.

CaOTP CLSU CoU CU DAU FU ICU InU
IU MB MiEM NBuU NIC NNC TxU WU

479 _____. Hombres de Mayo. Buenos Aires: Editorial Crespillo, 1960. 188 p. Portraits. 23 cm.

Collection of biographical sketches, many accompanied by portraits, of individuals involved in the Argentine independence movement of May 1810. Biographical material supplied concentrates on the following individuals' political activities: Manuel Belgrano, Mariano Moreno, Juan José Castelli, Cornelio Saavedra, Juan José Paso, Miguel de Azcuénaga, Domingo Matheu, Manuel Alberti, Juan Larrea, Feliciano Antonio Chiclana, Juan Martín de Pueyrredón, Francisco A. Ortiz de Ocampo, Agustín José Donado, Juan Florencio Terrada, Juan José Viamonte, Cayetano Rodríguez, Hipólito Vieytes, Nicolás Rodríguez Peña, Martín Rodríguez, Antonio José de Escalada, Manuel Hermenegildo de Aguirre, Gervasio Antonio de Posadas, Vicente López y Planes, José Moldes, Juan Ramón Balcarce, Antonio Balcarce, Marcos Balcarce, Diego Balcarce, Andrés Arguibel, Gregorio Funes, Francisco de Gurruchaga, José I. Fernández Maradona, Juan José de Gorriti, Pedro Francisco de Uriarte, Bernardino Rivadavia, Juan Francisco Tarragona, Cosme Argerich, Bernardo de Monteagudo, Enrique Martínez, Antonio Sáenz, Antonio Alvarez Jonte, Martín José de Altolaguirre, Pedro Antonio Cerviño, Domingo French, Antonio Luis Beruti, Elías Galván, Leonardo Domingo de la Gándara, José Darregueira, Tomás Guido, Julián Alvarez, Francisco Planes, Vicente Dupuy, Miguel Cajaravilla, Martín Thompson, Juan Andrés Gelly, Juan de Alagón, Joaquín Campana, Antonio Antonini.

CLSU CLU CU FTaSU NcU NIC NN TxU

480 _____, comp. La tiranía y la libertad; jucio histórico sobre Juan Manuel de Rozas. Buenos Aires: Ediciones Líbera, 1970. 776 p. 21 cm.

A collection of essays dealing with many aspects of the life of the Argentine dictator Juan Manuel de Rosas. Biographical information is given for this man and for others with whom he was associated. Among those featured are Juan Manuel de Rosas, Gervasio Rosas, Encarnación Ezcurra, Manuelita Rosas, Domingo Cullen, Videla (brothers), Florencio Varela, Carlos Morel, Camila O'Gorman, Juan José Hernández.

CFS CLSU CLU CSt CtY CU-S CU-SB
ICU INS IU KU MB MH MiEM MiU MnU
MoSW NcD NcU NIC NmLcU NN NNC OU
PPT TxU ViU WaU WU

481 González Ruiz, Felipe. Argentina. Madrid: Studium, 1947. 228 p. 22 cm.

A description of the history and geography of Argentina, including scattered biographical information on many prominent people, many of them political leaders. Among those particularly featured are Juan Díaz de Solís, Juan de Ayolas, Domingo Martínez de Irala, Juan de Garay, Bernardino Rivadavia.

CtY DLC IU NN

482 Groussac, Paul. Anales de la Biblioteca; publicación de documentos relativos al Río de la Plata. Buenos Aires: Coni hermanos, 1900. 10 v.

Collection of essays and documents in the National Library of Buenos Aires, with biographical essays about the following notable figures in the history of the River Plate: Tadeo Haenka, Diego de Alvear, Diego Alcorta, Santiago Liniers, Juan Francisco de Aguirre, José Guevara, Ruy Díaz de Guzmán, Juan de Garay.

DLC IU

483 _____. Estudios de historia argentina. Buenos Aires: J. Menéndez, 1918. 371 p. Portraits. 23 cm.

A collection of essays about the following notable Argentine figures of the 19th century, including biographical data: José Guevara, Diego de Alvear y Ponce de León, Martín Diego Alcorta.

CtY CU DLC DCU-IA ICU IU MB NcU
NN TxU WU

484 _____. Los que pasaban. José Manuel Estrada. - Pedro Goyena. - Nicolás Avellaneda. - Carlos Pellegrini. - Roque Sáenz Peña. Buenos Aires: J. Menéndez, 1919. 355 p. 23 cm. Same as the 1939 edition. (See entry 485.)

CtY DLC IaU MB NcU NN OkU OU PP
TxU

485 _____. Los que pasaban. 2. ed. Buenos Aires: Editorial Sudamericana, 1939. 445 p. 21 cm.

A collection of essays including biographical information on the following 19th-century Argentineans: José Manuel Estrada, Pedro Goyena, Nicolás Avellaneda, Carlos Pellegrini, Roque Sáenz Peña. (See also entry 484.)

CU DLC IU MB NcD NSyU OKentU OU
PU TxU ViU

486 _____. Mendoza y Garay. Prólogo de Carlos Ibarguren. Buenos Aires: Academia Argentina de Letras, 1949. 2 v. Portraits. 21 cm. (Biblioteca de la Academia Argentina de Letras. Serie: Clásicos argentinos. V. 9).

A 2-volume collection featuring lengthy biographies for Pedro de Mendoza y Juan de Garay as well as a biographical preface and portrait for the author of this work. The following are included: Paul Groussac, Pedro de Mendoza, Juan de Garay.

CLobS CtY DLC IaU ICU IU MH MiU
NN TxU WaU

487 Guerrero, César H. El aporte de la mujer sanjuanina a la gesta libertadora del Gral. San Martín. San Juan, 1960. 49 p. Portraits. 20 cm.

A short essay on the contributions made by women of San Juan, Argentina, to the independence movement of San Martín. Brief scattered biographical information, as well as portraits in many cases, given for many people, mostly women, associated with this aspect of Argentina's history. The following are particularly featured: José de San Martín, José Ignacio de la Roza, Félix de la Roza.

CU FU PSt

488 Gutiérrez, Juan María. A través de una correspondencia; don Juan María Gutiérrez, por Luis Barros Borgoño. Santiago: Prensas de la Universidad de Chile, 1934. 320 p. 23 cm.

A study about Argentina history (1817-1860), mainly through biographical essays about Juan María Gutiérrez, Juan Manuel de Rosas, Justo José Urquiza. Also biographical sketch of Gregorio Beeche.

CtY CU DLC DSI IU MH NBuU NcU PU
ViU WaU WU

489 Halperin Donghi, Tulio, comp. Historia argentina. Buenos Aires: Editorial Paidós, 1972. 7 v. Portraits. 23 cm.

A history of Argentina, covering the period from preconquest to the present, and including scattered biographical information, as well as some portraits, for many notable people. The following are emphasized: Juan José de Vértiz, Carlos María de Alvear, José Gervasio Artigas, Manuel Belgrano, Juan Bau-

tista Bustos, Manuel Dorrego, Manuel José García, Tomás Guido, Estanislao López, José María Paz, Juan Martín de Pueyrredón, Facundo Quiroga, Bernardino Rivadavia, Fructuoso Rivera, Juan Manuel de Rosas, José de San Martín, Justo José de Urquiza, Bartolomé Mitre, Miguel Angel Juárez Celman, Carlos Pellegrini, Julio A. Roca, Marcelo T. de Alvear, Ramón S. Castillo, Agustín P. Justo, Roberto M. Ortiz, Federico Pinedo, Hipólito Yrigoyen, Pedro E. Aramburu, Arturo Frondizi, Juan Domingo Perón. Alphabetical index of names.

CaQMM CSt CU FTaSU GU IEN InU IU
LNHT LU MdU MH MiEM MnU MoSW MU
NjP NmU NNC OrU PPiU PPT PSt TxU
ViU WaU WU

490 Hidalgo, Alberto E. Sarmiento y la cuestión de la Patagonia. Rosario: Librería y Editorial Ruiz, 1945. 73 p. 24 cm.

A short account of the involvement of Domingo Faustino Sarmiento in the Patagonian question, including biographical information for the following: Domingo Faustino Sarmiento, Félix Frías, Luis Piedrabuena.

CU DLC IU OU TxU

490a Historia de las Malvinas argentinas; desde 1520 hasta nuestros días. Buenos Aires: Gam Ediciones, 1982. 385 p. (24 V.) Portraits. 28 cm.

A history of the Falkland/Malvinas Islands (1520-1982), including scattered biographical information, often accompanied by portraits, on numerous individuals associated with them.

IU

491 Historia integral argentina. Buenos Aires: Centro Editor de América Latina, 1970. 7 v. Portraits. 29 cm.

A seven-volume collection exploring many aspects of Argentina's history from colonial to modern times, and including portraits and biographical information for many notable people. The following are emphasized: Manuel José de Lavardén, Juan Hipólito Vieytes, Mariano Moreno, Bernardo de Monteagudo, José de Artigas, Bernardino González de Rivadavia, Juan Facundo Quiroga, Juan Manuel de Rosas, Justo José de Urquiza, Bartolomé Mitre, Dalmacio Vélez Sársfield, Hipólito Yrigoyen.

CLSU CLU CSt CtY CU-SB DcU IaU IU
KU MB MoSW NcU NIC NN NNC OU TxU
ViU WU

492 Ibarguren, Carlos. En la penumbra de la historia argentina. 2. ed. corregida y aumentada. Buenos Aires: Unión de Editores Latinos, 1956. 239 p. 21 cm. (Colección histórica americana. V. 2).

A collection of essays on various aspects of Argentine history, including biographical information on many people, mostly of the 19th

HISTORY

century. The following are particularly featured: María Remedios del Valle, José de San
Martín, Alejandro Danel, Manuel Hermenegildo
de Aguirre, Juan José Paso, Bartolomé Mitre.

AzU CtW CU IaU IU MdU MH MiU NcU
NIC NN NNC OrU OU PPT TxFTC TxU
WaU

493 _____. La historia que he vivido. Buenos
Aires: Ediciones Peuser, 1955. 504 p. 24 cm.
The memoirs of the author Carlos Ibarguren,
including scattered biographical information
for this man, as well as for many people,
mostly political leaders, with whom he was
associated. The following are particularly
featured: Julio A. Roca, Carlos Ibarguren,
Miguel Juárez Celman, José Evaristo Uriburu,
Manuel Quintana, Roque Sáenz Peña, Hipólito
Yrigoyen, Marcelo T. de Alvear.

AU CLU CU DLC FU IU NcD NcU NNC
OU PU WaU

494 _____. Manuelita Rosas. 3. ed. Buenos
Aires: C. y R. Nalé, 1953. 157 p. 20 cm.
A biography of Manuelita Rosas, the
daughter of the 19th-century Argentine dictator, Juan Manuel de Rosas, which also includes information for many people with whom
she was associated. The following are emphasized: Manuelita Rosas de Terrero, Encarnación Ezcurra, Juan Manuel de Rosas.

InU IU TxU WaU

495 Ibarra Pedernera, Augusto. Reconquista y defensa de Buenos Aires, 12 de agosto de 1806-5
de julio de 1807; el elemento nativo en las
invasiones inglesas; gran triunfo del pueblo
argentino. Buenos Aires: Impr. de A. Perrone,
1927. 64 p. 20 cm.
An essay about the English invasions of
Buenos Aires in 1806-7, including brief biographical notes on the natives who participated in its defense and liberation.

InU NcU TxU

496 Instituto argentino de ciencias genealógicas.
Hombres de Mayo; biografías de cada uno de
los asistentes al memorable Cabildo abierto
del 22 de mayo de 1810. Buenos Aires, 1961.
ciii, 383 p. Portraits. 23 cm.
A collection of biographical sketches of
notable Argentineans associated with the 1810
War of Independence. Includes approximately
300 names.

TxU

497 Instituto Sarmiento de sociología e historia,
Buenos Aires. Creación y actividades en su
primer quinquenio, 14-VII-1945-14-VII-1950.
Buenos Aires, 1953. 188 p. 24 cm.
A work featuring biographical information
for the 19th-century Argentine president Do-

mingo Faustino Sarmiento and for many others
with whom he was associated. The following
are emphasized: Domingo Faustino Sarmiento,
Paula Albarracín de Sarmiento, Domingo Fidel
Sarmiento.

ICarbS ICU IU

498 Irazusta, Julio. Ensayos históricos. Buenos
Aires: Editorial Universitaria de Buenos
Aires, 1968. 230 p. 23 cm. (Colección Ar-
gentina).
An essay about Argentine history, includ-
ing biographical data on Estanislao López,
Juan Bautista Alberdi, José María Paz, Carlos
Guido y Spano, Adolfo Saldías.

CLU CNoS CtW IaU IU MiDW MoSW MU
NBuU NcU NIC OrU OU TU

499 Iriarte, Tomás de. Memorias del general
Iriarte; textos fundamentales. Selección y
commentarios por Enrique de Gandía. Buenos
Aires: Fabril Editora, 1962. 2 v. Portraits.
23 cm.
The memoirs of the 19th-century Argentine
general Tomás de Iriarte, including scattered
biographical information and portraits for
this man and for many with who he was associa-
ted. The following are included: Tomás de
Iriarte, Cornelio Saavedra, Manuel Belgrano,
José de San Martín, Juan Martín de Pueyrredón,
Feliciano Chiclana, Manuel de Sarratea, José
Miguel de Carrera, Francisco Ramírez, Juan
Facundo Quiroga, Fructuoso Rivera, Manuel
Dorrego, Tomás Guido, Gregorio Aráoz de La
Madrid, Bartolomé Mitre, José María Paz, Juan
Lavalle, Carlos María de Alvear, Federico de
Brandsen, Juan Manuel de Rosas, Esteban Eche-
verría, Bernardino Rivadavia, Estanislao López,
José Garibaldi, Guillermo Brown.

CtY ICU InU IU MH NcU NN NSyU

500 Jaimes Freyre, Ricardo. Historia del descubrimiento de Tucumán, seguida de investigaciones históricas. Publicación de la Universidad de Tucumán. Buenos Aires: Impr. de
Coni Hnos, 1916. 312 p. 19 cm.
An account of the discovery of the Argentine province of Tucumán, including scattered
biographical information on many people involved with this aspect of Argentina's history.
The following are particularly featured:
Diego de Rojas, Felipe Gutiérrez, Nicolás de
Heredia, Francisco de Mendoza.

CtY CU DCU-IA DLC ICN ICU IU LNHT
LU NcD NIC OCl PU WU

501 _____, comp. El Tucumán colonial (documentos
y mapas del Archivo de Indias). Buenos Aires:
Coni hermanos, 1915. 193 p. (V. 1). 27 cm.
A collection of letters and documents
dealing with the Argentine province of Tucumán
during the colonial period, each preceded by a
short biographical sketch of its author.

These people include Alonso Díaz Caballero, Juan de Matienzo, Diego Pacheco, Pedro Sotelo Narváez, Juan Ramírez de Velasco, Francisco de Barranza y Cárdenas, Alonso de Ribera, Julián Cortazár, Felipe de Albornoz, Angelo de Peredo, Juan Díez de Andino, Nicolás de Ulloa.

CtY CU DCU-IA DLC IU LU MdBJ MH-P
NcU NjP PU

502 Kirkpatrick, Frederick Alexander. <u>A History of the Argentine Republic</u>, with an introduction by Harold Temperley. Cambridge, Eng.: The University Press, 1931. 255 p. Portraits. 24 cm.
A history of Argentina, covering the period from the conquest to the early 20th century. Scattered biographical information is given for many notable people, particularly the following: Carlos María de Alvear, José Artigas, Nicolás Avellaneda, Manuel Belgrano, Manuel Dorrego, Hipólito Irigoyen, Santiago Liniers, Francisco Solano López, Bartolomé Mitre, Mariano Moreno, Carlos Pellegrini, Juan Martín de Pueyrredón, Bernardino Rivadavia, Julio Roca, Juan Manuel Rosas, Cornelio Saavedra, Domingo Faustino Sarmiento, Justo José Urquiza. Alphabetical index of names.

CaBVaU CoU CtY CU DLC DN DS ICU
IdU IU MB MdU MH MiU MtU NbU NBuC
NcU NN NNR OC1 OO OrCS OrP OrPR
OrU PBa PLF PPT PV TU ViU WaS WaT
WaTC WaWW

503 Korn, Guillermo. <u>La palabra y el hombre</u>. Buenos Aires: Editorial La Vanguardia, 1943. 159 p. 19 cm.
A collection of biographical essays about the following Argentine political figures: Alfredo L. Palacios, Juan B. Justo, Enrique del Valle Iberlucea, Nicolás Repetto, Enrique Dickmann, Mario Bravo, Lisandro de la Torre.

CU DLC

504 Laconich, Marco Antonio. <u>Caudillos de la conquista</u>; romance de una cédula real. 2. ed. [n.p.]: Ediciones Nizza, 1961. 136 p. 20 cm. (Obras paraguayas).
A discussion of the activities of the leaders of the conquest of Argentina, including scattered biographical information for the following people: Francisco Ruiz Galán, Domingo Martínez de Irala, Alonso Cabrera, Alvar Núñez Cabeza de Vaca, Diego de Abreu, Nuflo de Chaves, Francisco Ortiz de Vergara, Felipe de Cáceres.

CLU CSt CtY CU FU ICN InU IU
KyLoU MH MnU MoSW NIC NSyU PPT
TxU WU

505 Lafuente Machain, Ricardo de. <u>El gobernador Domingo Martínez de Irala</u>. Buenos Aires: Librería y Editorial "La Facultad," Bernabé y Cía., 1939. 568 p. 29 cm. (Biblioteca de la Sociedad de historia argentina. V. 10).

A study of the activities of the colonial Argentine governor Domingo Martínez de Irala, including scattered biographical information for this man and for many with whom he was associated. The following are emphasized: Domingo Martínez de Irala, Francisco Ruiz Galán, Alvar Núñez Cabeza de Vaca, Juan Salazar de Espinosa.

CU DLC DPU ICN IU MB MH NcD NcU
NN NNC OC1 PPT PU ViU

506 Lanuza, José Luis. <u>Un inglés en San Lorenzo</u>, y otros relatos. Buenos Aires: Editorial Universitaria de Buenos Aires, 1964. 93 p. Portraits. 16 cm. (Libros del caminante. V. 2).
A collection of stories on various aspects of Argentine history, including scattered biographical information and some portraits for many prominent people. The following are emphasized: Juan Parish Robertson, Juan de Dios Rivera, Manuelita Rosas, Bartolito Mitre, Dominguito Sarmiento.

CLSU CtY DPU ICN IU KU MB MH NbU
NcU NIC NjR NmLcU NN NSyU OU PSt
TxBeal TxU UU ViU WU

507 _____. <u>Instantáneas de historia</u>. Buenos Aires: Emecé Editores, 1943. 72 p. 18 cm. (Colección buen aire. V. 21).
Biographical data about Martín del Barco Centenera, Luis José de Tejeda y Guzmán, Manuel Belgrano, Mariano Moreno, Esteban Echeverría, Juan Manuel de Rosas, Juan Bautista Alberdi, Juan María Gutiérrez, Domingo Faustino Sarmiento, Carlos Enrique Pellegrini, Lucio V. Mansilla.

DLC IU MB NcU

508 _____. <u>La pequeña historia de la Revolución de Mayo</u>. Buenos Aires: Editorial Perrot, 1957. 76 p. 19 cm. (Colección Nuevo Mundo. V. 6).
A work featuring biographical essays on the following 19th-century Argentine patriots: Francisco Planes, Cornelio Saavedra, Bernardo de Monteagudo, Manuel Belgrano.

CSt CU FU IU MH MnU TxU

509 Lapuente, Ernesto. <u>Símbolos y próceres</u>. Buenos Aires: Ediciones "La Obra," 1945. 284 p. 21 cm.
An essay about Argentine history in the 19th century, mainly through biographical sketches of the following prominent individuals: Antonio Berutti, Mariano Moreno, Juan José Paso, Bernardo de Monteagudo, Vicente López, Blas Parera, Juan Pedro Esnaola, Juan Martín de Pueyrredón, Gregorio Funes, Manuel Belgrano, José de San Martín, Martín Güemes, Guillermo Brown, Martín Rodríguez, Bernardino Rivadavia, Esteban Echeverría, Juan María Gutiérrez, Juan Bautista Alberdi, Justo José

HISTORY

de Urquiza, Bartolomé Mitre, Domingo Faustino
Sarmiento, Nicolás Avellaneda.

DPU

510 Larreta, Enrique Rodríguez. Las dos fundaciones de Buenos Aires, estudio preliminar de
Enrique de Gandía. Buenos Aires: Editorial
Sopena Argentina, 1940. 133 p. 19 cm. (Colección Orbe).
    A collection of brief essays dealing with
various aspects of Buenos Aires, including
biographical information on Pedro de Mendoza,
Rodrigo de Cepeda, Juan de Garay.

DLC FMU IU LU MH OCl OU

511 Leguizamón, Martiniano. La cinta colorada;
notas y perfiles. Buenos Aires: Compañía
Sud-americana de Billetes de Banco, 1916.
341 p. Portraits. 21 cm.
    A collection of essays dealing with vari-
ous aspects of Argentina's history, including
biographical information, as well as some
portraits, for the following prominent people:
Angel Vicente Peñaloza (el Chacho, pseud.),
Manuela Pedraza, Marcos Sastre, Martín Ruiz
Moreno, Hilario Ascasubi, Diego Fernández
Espiro, José Inocencio Arias, César Caggiano.

DLC IU LU MH MWiCA NcU PPT TxU

512 _____. Hombres y cosas que pasaron. Buenos
Aires: J. Lajouane, 1926. 440 p. Portraits.
24 cm.
    A collection of essays dealing with vari-
ous aspects of Argentina's history, including
biographical information, as well as portraits
in a few cases, for the following people of
the 19th century: Pancho Ramírez, Domingo F.
Sarmiento, Antonio Zinny, Juan Francisco Seguí, Eduardo Wilde, Joaquín V. González, Justo
José de Urquiza, Aime Bonpland, Olegario Andrade, Lucio V. Mansilla, Juan Manuel de
Rosas.

CU DLC DPU IU LU MB NcU NN PU

513 Levene, Gustavo Gabriel. La Argentina se hizo
así. Buenos Aires: Librería Hachette, 1960.
298 p. 23 cm.
    A history of Argentina covering the peri-
od from preconquest to modern times, including
scattered biographical information on many
notable people. The following are particularly featured: Francisco Miranda, Juan Manuel
de Rosas, Arturo Frondizi.

CLSU CLU CSt CU FU InU IU KU LNHT
MH MiD MiDW MnU NcU NIC NjP NN
NRU OrPS PPiU ScU TU TxU WU

514 _____. Historia argentina; panorama costum-
brista y social desde la conquista hasta
nuestros días. Buenos Aires: Editorial Cam-
pano, 1964. 3 v. Portraits. 23 cm.

A social history of Argentina, covering
the period from the conquest to modern times,
and including scattered biographical information, as well as portraits in some cases, for
many prominent people. Emphasis is placed on
the following: Manuel Belgrano, Francisco
Miranda, Guillermo Carr Beresford, Cornelio
de Saavedra, Mariano Moreno, Gregorio Funes,
Strangford, José María Paz, Bernardino Rivadavia, José Francisco de San Martín, José
Gervasio Artigas, Juan Martín de Pueyrredón,
Guillermo Brown, Juan Manuel de Rosas, Esteban Echeverría, Juan Bautista Alberdi, Domingo
Faustino Sarmiento, Justo José de Urquiza,
Nicolás Avellaneda, Miguel Juárez Celman,
Aristóbulo del Valle.

CLSU CU FU ICarbS ICU INS InU IU
KU LU MB MH MiU MnU NbU NBuU NcU
NIC OOxM PPiU TxDaM UU WU

515 _____. Historia de los presidentes argentinos. Buenos Aires: O. R. Sánchez Teruelo,
1973. 2 v. Portraits. 27 cm.
    A history of Argentine presidents with
chronologically arranged biographical essays
about the following (1826 to 1973): Bernardino Rivadavia, Justo José de Urquiza, Santiago Derqui, Bartolomé Mitre, Domingo Faustino Sarmiento, Nicolás Avellaneda, Julio
Argentino Roca, Miguel Juárez Celman, Carlos
Pellegrini, Luis Sáenz Peña, José Evaristo
Uriburu, Manuel Quintana, José Figueroa Alcorta, Roque Sáenz Peña, Victorino de la Plaza, Hipólito Yrigoyen, Marcelo T. de Alvear,
José Félix Uriburu, Agustín P. Justo, Roberto
M. Ortiz, Ramón S. Castillo, Pedro Pablo
Ramírez, Edelmiro J. Farrell, Juan Domingo
Perón, Eduardo Lonardi, Pedro Eugenio Aram-
buru, Arturo Frondizi, José María Guido, Ar-
turo U. Illía, Juan Carlos Onganía, Roberto
Marcelo Levingston, Alejandro Agustín Lanusse.

CU InU IU MU

516 _____. Presidentes argentinos; contó con la
dirección y coordinación de Gustavo Gabriel
Levene y la colaboración de Alberto Palcos.
Buenos Aires: Fabril Editora, 1961. 299 p.
Portraits. 27 cm.
    Chronologically arranged collection of
biographical essays about the following Ar-
gentine presidents (1826-1964): Bernardino
Rivadavia, Justo José de Urquiza, Santiago
Derqui, Bartolomé Mitre, Domingo Faustino Sar-
miento, Nicolás Avellaneda, Julio Argentino
Roca, Miguel Juárez Celman, Carlos Pellegrini,
Luis Sáenz Peña, José Evaristo Uriburu, Manuel
Quintana, José Figueroa Alcorta, Roque Sáenz
Peña, Victorino de la Plaza, Hipólito Irigoyen,
Marcelo T. de Alvear, José Félix Uriburu,
Agustín Edelmiro J. Farrell, Juan Domingo
Perón, Eduardo Lonardi, Pedro Eugenio Aram-
buru, Arturo Frondizi.

DLC IU NN NSyU

517 Levene, Ricardo. Ensayo histórico sobre la Revolución de Mayo y Mariano Moreno. Contribución al estudio de los aspectos político, jurídico y económico de la revolución de 1810. 3. ed., corregida y ampliada. Buenos Aires: "El Ateneo," 1949. 3 v. 24 cm.

A history of the Argentine war for independence and the involvement of one its leaders, Mariano Moreno. Scattered biographical information is included for this man and for others associated with this period in Argentina's history. Those particularly featured include José de Abascal, Martín de Alzaga, Manuel Belgrano, Carr Berresford, Carlos José Bloud, Pedro Vicente Cañete, Antonio Caspe, Juan José Castelli, Feliciano Chiclana, Baltazar Hidalgo de Cisneros, Javier de Elío, Gregorio Funes, Julián de Leiva, Santiago Liniers, Bartolomé Mitre, Manuel Moreno, Mariano Moreno, Francisco de Paula Sanz, Juan Martín de Pueyrredón, Nicolás Rodríguez Peña, Saturnino Rodríguez Peña, Cornelio de Saavedra, Felipe Sentenach, Sobremonte, Victorián de Villava, Manuel Genaro de Villota. Alphabetical index of names.

CLL   IU   MH   NcU   OrU   TxU

518 _____. A History of Argentina. Translated and edited by William Spence Robertson. New York: Russell & Russell, 1963. 565 p. Portraits. 25 cm. (The Inter-American historical series).

A history of Argentina, covering the period from preconquest through the early 20th century, and including scattered biographical information, as well as portraits in some cases, for many prominent people. Among those particularly featured are Carlos M. de Alvear, Hernando Arias de Saavedra, José G. Artigas, Manuel Belgrano, Alvar Núñez Cabeza de Vaca, Pedro de Cevallos, Baltasar Hidalgo de Cisneros, Manuel Dorrego, Gregorio Funes, Juan de Garay, Hipólito Irigoyen, Bartolomé de Las Casas, Santiago Liniers, Domingo Martínez de Irala, Pedro de Mendoza, Bartolomé Mitre, Mariano Moreno, Juan Martín de Pueyrredón, Juan Facundo Quiroga, Bernardino Rivadavia, Juan Manuel de Rosas, Cornelio Saavedra, José de San Martín, Domingo F. Sarmiento, Justo J. Urquiza. Alphabetical index of names.

DLC   IU   OkU

519 _____. Lecciones de historia argentina. Con una introducción del Dr. Joaquín V. González, 5. ed., corregida. Buenos Aires: J. Lajouane & Cía., 1920. 2 v. Portraits. 19 cm.

A 2-volume history of Argentina, covering the period from preconquest to the early 20th century. Scattered biographical information and portraits are included for many notable people, among them the following: Cristóbal Colón, Sebastián Caboto, Pedro de Mendoza, Alvar Núñez Cabeza de Vaca, Juan de Garay, Hernando Arias de Saavedra, Pedro de Cevallos,

Francisco Miranda, Santiago Liniers, Baltasar Hidalgo de Cisneros, José Artigas, Matías de Irigoyen, Mariano Moreno, Cornelio Saavedra, Gregorio Funes, Manuel Belgrano, José de San Martín, Carlos M. de Alvear, Gervasio A. Posadas, Martín Güemes, Juan Martín de Pueyrredón, Francisco Ramírez, Martín Rodríguez, Bernardino Rivadavia, Manuel Dorrego, Juan Manuel de Rosas, José María Paz, Gregorio Aráoz de La Madrid, Juan Facundo Quiroga, Esteban Echeverría, José Mármol, Juan María Gutiérrez, Justo José de Urquiza, Bartolomé Mitre, Nicolás Avellaneda, Domingo F. Sarmiento.

IU   MH

520 Levillier, Roberto. Biografías de conquistadores de la Argentina en el siglo XVI; Tucumán. Madrid: Impr. de J. Pueyo, 1933. 250 p. 24 cm.

Collection of essays profiling the "conquistadores" of the Argentine province of Tucumán in the 16th century. Biographical data provided includes dates, family background, and activities of Alonso Abad, Hernando de Aguirre, Miguel de Ardiles, Francisco de Argañarás, Juan Gregorio Bazán, Santos Blázquez, Alonso de la Cámara, Juan Cano, Nicolás Carrizo, Francisco de Carvajal, Alonso de Cepeda, Alonso de Contreras, Alonso Días Caballero, Nicolás de Garnica, Pedro González de Prado, Luis de Luna, Lorenzo Maldonado, Bartolomé de Mansilla, Gaspar de Medina, Hernán Mejía Miraval, Diego Pacheco, Juan Pedrero de Trejo, Juan Pérez Moreno, Juan Pérez de Zorita, Blas Ponce, Martín de Rentería, Hernando de Retamoso, Juan Rodríguez Juárez, Blas de Rosales, García Sánchez, Gonzalo Sánchez Garzón, Julián Sedeño, Pedro Sotelo Narváez, Lorenzo Suárez de Figueroa, Tristán de Tejeda, Fernando de Toledo Pimentel, Alonso de Tulacerbin, Bartolomé Valero, Diego de Villarroel, Pedro de Zárate.

AU   DLC   FU   ICU   IU   MN-P   NcD   NcU   OU

521 _____, comp. Historia argentina. Buenos Aires: Plaza y Janés, 1968. 5 v. Portraits. 24 cm. (Colección historia de los pueblos de América).

A history of Argentina covering the period from preconquest to the modern times, and giving scattered biographical information, as well as portraits in some cases, for many prominent people, including the contributors to this work.

CaBVaU   CoU   CtY   FU   IaU   InU   IU   MH
MiU   MU   NjP   NSyU   OOxM   PPiU   PSt   WU

522 _____. Nueva crónica de la conquista del Tucumán, documentada en los archivos de Sevilla y de Lima y en los XXIV volúmenes de publicaciones históricas de la Biblioteca del Congreso Argentino editadas o en vía de editarse bajo la dirección del autor.

HISTORY

Precedida de un ensayo sobre los tiempos pre-hispánicos. Buenos Aires: "Editorial Nosotros," 1926. 3 v. Portraits. 27 cm.

A three-volume history of Tucumán, Argentina, covering the period from 1542 to 1600, and including scattered biographical information, as well as portraits in a few cases, for many people associated with this province. The following are emphasized: Lope García de Castro, Juan de Matienzo, Francisco de Aguirre, Gerónimo Luis de Cabrera, Juan de Abreu, Hernando de Lerma, Alonso de Sotomayor, Ramírez de Velasco, Pedro de Mercado de Peñalosa.

CaBVaU CtY CU DLC IU LU MB MnU
NcU NN OCl OrU PSt PU ViU

523 _____. Orígenes argentinos; la formación de un gran pueblo; contiene 12 grabados y 3 planos fuera del texto. Paris: E. Fasquelle, 1912. 324 p. Portraits. 19 cm.

A history of Argentina covering the period from the 16th to the 19th century. Biographical information and portraits are included for the following: Bernardino Rivadavia, Juan Manuel de Rosas, Bartolomé Mitre, Domingo F. Sarmiento.

CLU CoU CtY CU DCU-IA DLC GU IU
MH MH-P MiU-C NcD NN OCl PSt TxU
WaSp WaU

524 Lezama, Hugo Ezequiel. Balcarce 50 [i.e. cinquenta]; los presidentes argentinos y la guerra psicológica. Interpretó las caras de los presidentes Hermenegildo Sabat. Buenos Aires: Ediciones La Bastilla, distribuidor exclusivo: Editorial Astrea de R. Depalma, 1972. Portraits. 20 cm. (Serie Las Riendas del poder).

A volume collection dealing with Argentine politics and government from 1860 to 1910 and featuring caricatures and biographical information on the presidents of that period. The following are particularly featured: Julio Argentino Roca, Leandro Nicéforo Alem, Manuel Quintana, Roque Sáenz Peña, Hipólito Yrigoyen, José Félix Uriburu, Agustín Pedro Justo, Roberto Mario Ortiz, Ramón Santiago Castillo, Juan Domingo Perón.

CSt CtY CU FU IaU MH MU NcU PPT
TxU WU

525 Livacich, Serafín. Recordando el pasado; historia argentina - tradiciones americanas - biografías - notas bibliográficas y literarias. Buenos Aires: J. Peuser, 1909. 172 p. 21 cm.

An essay about Argentine history, including biographical sketches about Martín Barco Centenera, Cornelio Saavedra, Juan José Castelli, Manuel Belgrano, Manuel Alberti, Juan Larrea, Juan José Paso, Mariano Moreno, Bernardo Monteagudo, Bartolomé Mitre. Also biographical sketches of Isabel Flores de Oliva (Saint Rosa de Lima).

DLC TxU

526 Lizondo Borda, Manuel. Guía ilustrativa de la casa histórica de la independencia argentina. Tucumán: Universidad Nacional de Tucumán, 1969. 105 p. Portraits. 26 cm. (Colección del sesquicentenario de la independencia argentina. V. 5).

An essay about the "Casa de la Independencia" in Tucumán, Argentina, mainly through biographical sketches, accompanied by portraits, of the following delegates to the Congress of July 9, 1816:

Buenos Aires: Tomás Manuel de Anchorena, José Darregueyra, Esteban Agustín Gazcón, Pedro Medrano, Juan José Paso, Cayetano José Rodríguez, Antonio Sáenz.

Catamarca: Manuel Antonio Acevedo, José Eusebio Colombres.

Cordoba: José Antonio Cabrera, Eduardo Pérez Bulnes, Jerónimo Salguero Cabrera y Cabrera. Cabrera.

Charcas: José Severo Feliciano Malabia, Mariano Sánchez de Loria, José Mariano Serrano.

Chichas: José Andrés Pacheco de Melo.

Jujuy: Teodoro Sánchez de Bustamante.

La Rioja: Pedro Ignacio de Castro Barros.

Mendoza: Tomás Godoy Cruz, José Agustín Maza.

Mizque: Pedro Ignacio de Rivera.

Salta: Mariano Boedo, José Ignacio Gorriti.

Tucumán: Pedro Miguel Aráoz, José Ignacio Thomas.

San Juan: Francisco Narciso de Laprida, Justo de Santa María de Oro.

Santiago del Estero: Pedro León Gallo, Pedro Francisco Uriarte.

CLSU CSt CU CU-SB FU IaU IU MB MU
NcU NIC NmLcU NNC TxU ViU WU

527 _____. Historia de la gobernación del Tucumán (siglo XVI). Publicación de la Universidad de Tucumán. Buenos Aires: "Coni," 1928. 292p. 19 cm.

A political history of the "gobernación" of Tucumán, Argentina, during the 16th century, including scattered biographical information on many people associated with this region. The following political leaders are particularly featured: Francisco de Aguirre, Juan Pérez de Zurita, Georgio de Castaneda, Diego Pacheco, Nicolás Carrizo, Gerónimo Luis de Cabrera, Gonzalo de Abreu, Hernando de Lerma, Juan Ramírez de Valasco.

CtY CU DLC DSI IU LNHT MB MH-A
MiU MU NcU NN OU PU TxU WU

528 López, Vicente Fidel. Manual de la historia argentina. Buenos Aires: Librería "La Facultad" de J. Roldán, 1920. 2 v. 20 cm.

A 2-volume history of Argentina, covering the period from colonial times through the 19th century, and including scattered biographical information on many prominent people most of them political leaders. Among those featured are Cristóbal Colón, Sebastián Gabotto, Pedro de Mendoza, Juan de Ayolas, Alvar Núñez Cabeza de Vaca, Domingo Martínez de Irala, Juan Hortiz de Zárate, Juan de Garay, Hernandarias de Saavedra, Santiago Liniers, José de Artigas, Cornelio Saavedra, Mariano Moreno, Gregorio Funes, José de San Martín, Carlos de Alvear, Vicente López y Planes, José

María Paz, José Miguel Carrera, Bernardo Monteagudo, Francisco Ramírez, Juan Facundo Quiroga, Félix Aldao, Juan Ramón Balcarce, Alejandro Heredia, Andrés de Santa Cruz, Hipólito Bacle, Juan Lavalle, Justo José de Urquiza, Domingo Faustino Sarmiento.

CU   FU   IU   NN   NNC   OC1   OU

529   _____. Panoramas y retratos históricos. Prólogo de Joaquín V. González. Buenos Aires: W. M. Jackson, 1938. 278 p. 19 cm. (Grandes escritores argentinos. 2. ser. Director: Alberto Palcos. V. 16).

A work featuring biographical information on the following prominent 19th-century Argentines: Vicente Fidel López, Santiago Liniers, Juan Gregorio de Las Heras, Mariano Moreno, Gastelli, Gregorio Funes, Tomás Grigera, Joaquín Campana, Bernardo Monteagudo, Bernardino Rivadavia, José de San Martín, Carlos María de Alvear, José de Alcaraz, Manuel Belgrano, Juan Martín de Pueyrredón, Martín Güemes, Javiera Carrera, José Valentín Gómez, Pancho Ramírez, Martín Rodríguez, Juan Manuel de Rosas, Manuel Dorrego, Manuel José García, Julián Segundo de Agüero, Manuel Moreno, Paso, Gorriti, Lavalleja, Juan Lavalle, Paz, Brandzen, Olavarría, Juan Facundo Quiroga.

DLC   IU   MB   MH   MoU   OC1W   OU   TxU

529a   Lozano, Pedro. Historia de la conquista del Paraguay, Río de la Plata y Tucumán. Ilustrada con noticias del autor y con notas y suplementos por Andrés Lamas. Buenos Aires: Casa Editora "Impr. Popular," 1873-75. 5 v. 23 cm. (Biblioteca del Río de la Plata. V. 1-5).

A historical account of Paraguay (to 1811), Argentina (to 1810), and the Gobernación of Tucumán. Scattered biographical data throughout. Volume five features essays including biographical information about the following gobernadores of Tucumán: Estevan de Urizar y Arespacochaga, Isidro Ortiz de Haro, Baltasar de Abarca, Manuel Félix de Arache, Juan de Armasa y Arregui, Matías Anglés. Also biographical data about the following bishops of Tucumán: Francisco Victoria, Fernando Trejo de Sanabria, Julián de Cortázar, Tomás de Torres, Melchor Maldonado de Saavedra, Francisco de Borja, Nicolás de Ulloa, Juan Bravo Dávila y Cartagena, Manuel Mercadillo, Manuel Virtus, Alonso de Pozo y Silva, Juan de Sarricolea y Olea, Jose Antonio de Gutiérrez y Ceballos.

CaOTP   DLC   FTaSU   FU   IU   MdBP   MH   MH-P   MU   NIC   NjR   NN   NNH   ViU   WU

530   Luca de Tena, Torcuato. Yo, Juan Domingo Perón: relato autobiográfico. Torcuato Luca de Tena, Luis Calvo, Esteban Peicovich. Barcelona: Editorial Planeta, 1976. 285 p. Portraits. 25 cm. (Espejo del mundo. V. 2).

A biography of Argentine dictator, Juan Domingo Perón, which contains scattered information, as well as portraits in some cases, for this man, for others with whom he was associated, and for the authors of this work. The following are among those featured: Torcuato Luca de Tena, Luis Calvo, Esteban Peicovich, Juan Domingo Perón, José María de Areilza, Spruille Braden, Alberto Dodero, Eva Duarte, Edelmiro J. Farell, José Figuerola, María Estela Martínez, Miguel Miranda, Marcos Pérez Jiménez, Rafael Leónidas Trujillo. Alphabetical index of names.

AzU   CLU   CSt-H   CU   CU-SB   DGU   FMU   FTaSU   InU   IU   LN   MH   MoSW   MU   NBuU   NcU   NFQC   NIC   NmU   NN   NSbSU   PPIU   PPT   PSt   ViU   TxU   WU

531   Lugones, Leopoldo. Los argentinos y su historia interna. Actuación de sus presidentes. 2. ed. Buenos Aires: Ediciones Centurión, 1962. 264 p. 21 cm. (Colección Centuria).

A 19th-century political history of Argentina, including scattered biographical information for many prominent leaders. The following are emphasized: Gregorio Aráoz de La Madrid, Nicolás Avellaneda, Santiago Derqui, Hipólito Irigoyen, Miguel Juárez Celman, Juan Lavalle, Estanislao López, Bartolomé Mitre, José María Paz, Carlos Pellegrini, Manuel Quintana, Juan Facundo Quiroga, Julio A. Roca, Juan Manuel Rosas, Roque Sáenz Peña, Domingo Faustino Sarmiento, Justo José de Urquiza. Alphabetical index of names.

CLSU   CLU   CtY   IaU   IU   KU   LNHT   MB   MH   MiEM   MiU   MoSW   NbU   NcU   NhD   NIC   NN   NNC   NSyU   OrPS   TxU   ViU   WaU   WU

532   Luna, Félix. Los caudillos. Buenos Aires: Editorial J. Alvarez, 1966. 285 p. Portraits. 20 cm. (Los Argentinos. V. 1).

Biographical sketches of the following "caudillos" associated with the history of Argentina: José Artigas, Francisco Ramírez, Juan Facundo Quiroga, Angel Vicente Peñaloza, Felipe Varela.

CtY   ICU   InU   IU   NcU   ViU

533   Macchi, Manuel E. Urquiza última etapa. 3. ed. corr. y aumentada con los hechos que ocurrierón de inmediato al asesinato de Urquiza. Santa Fe: Librería y Editorial Castellvi, 1971. 257 p. 21 cm.

A biography of the 19th-century Argentine statesman Justo José de Urquiza, including scattered information for this man as well as for others with whom he was associated. Among those featured are Ricardo López Jordán, José Mosqueira, Ramón Gil Navarro. Alphabetical index of names.

CaBVaU   CLU   CtY   CU   CU-SB   IaU   IU   KU   MdU   MH   MU   NIC   NN   NSbSU   NSyU   OU   PPT   TxU   ViU   WU

HISTORY

534 _____. Urquiza y el catolicismo. Santa Fe: Librería y Editorial Castellví, 1969. 152 p. 21 cm. (Palacio San José, Museo Monumento Nacional Justo José de Urquiza. Publicaciones. Serie 3: Monografías, traducciones y disertaciones históricas relacionadas con el período de actuación del general Urquiza. V. 8).

A discussion of Urquiza's influence on catholicism including biographical information for this man as well as for many clerics with whom he was associated. The following are emphasized: Justo José de Urquiza, Leonardo Acevedo, Francisco Dionisio Alvarez, Lorenzo Cot, Juan José Alvarez, Domingo Ereño.

CLSU CSt CtY CtY-D CU CU-SB DLC
FMU FU IEdS IU KU MB NcD NcU TxU

535 Madero, Eduardo. Historia del puerto de Buenos Aires; descubrimiento del Río de la Plata y de sus principales afluentes, y fundación de las más antiguas ciudades en sus márgenes. 3. ed. Buenos Aires: Ediciones Buenos Aires, 1939. 432 p. Portraits. 24 cm.

A history of Buenos Aires, from the discovery of the River Plate region to the end of the 16th century. Scattered biographical information is included for many people associated with this city, particularly political leaders. More lengthy biographies are given for the following: Juan Díaz de Solís, Pedro de Mendoza, Diego García, Sebastián Caboto, Juan de Garay, Hernando Arias de Saavedra.

DLC IaU IU MH NcD

536 Madero, Guillermo. Capítulos de historia. Buenos Aires: Emecé Editores, 1967. 244 p. 21 cm. (Colección Emecé de obras contemporáneas).

A collection of essays dealing with various aspects of Argentina's history. Biographical information is included for the following: Domingo F. Sarmiento, Bernabé y Madero (family), Bernardino Rivadavia, Justo Santa María de Oro.

CLSU CLU CSt FU IaU InU IU MB
MiEM MU N NbU NBuU NIC NmU NN NNC
NSyU OU TxU

537 Maeder, Ernesto J. Nómina de gobernantes civiles y eclesiásticos de la Argentina durante la época española (1500-1810). Resistencia: UNNE (i.e. Universidad Nacional del Nordeste) Instituto de Historia, Facultad de Humanidades, 1972. 173 p. 28 cm.

A book containing 31 lists of Argentine civil authorities and 19 of ecclesiastical authorities (1500-1810), with each name being accompanied by a short biographical note. Alphabetical index of names.

CtY CU CU-SB FU GU IaU IU MB MU
NcD NIC NN NNC PPT TxU ViU WU

538 Mansilla, Lucio Victorio. Rozas; ensayo histórico-psicológico. Con una introducción de Aníbal Ponce. 2. ed. Buenos Aires, 1925. 233 p. ("La cultura argentina").

A biography of Juan Manuel de Rosas that also includes biographical data for many people with whom he was associated, as well as a sketch on the author of this work. The following are emphasized: Lucio V. Mansilla, Juan Manuel de Rozas, León Ortiz de Rozas, Agustina López de Osornio.

IU PP PSt

539 Mantilla, Manuel Florencio. Estudios biográficos sobre patriotas correntinos. Buenos Aires: C. Casavalle, 1884. 315 p. 21 cm.

A collection of lengthy biographies of the following 19th-century patriots from the Argentine province of Corrientes: Genaro Perugorría, Angel Fernández Blanco, Genaro Berón de Astrada, Pedro Ferré, Nicolás M. Tedesqui, Joaquín Madariaga.

CaBVaU CU DLC MB TxU

540 _____. Páginas históricas. Buenos Aires: Impr. de P. E. Coni, 1890. 420 p. 18 cm.

A collection of biographical essays about José Nicolás Arriola, Juan José Quesada, Elías Galván, Diego de Velaustegui, Gertrudis Medeiros, Bartolomé Mitre, Pedro J. Quijano, Valentín Virasoro, Raymundo J. Reguera.

DLC IU MB MH TxU

541 Marcó del Pont, Augusto. Roca y su tiempo (cincuenta años de historia argentina). Buenos Aires: Talleres Gráficos Argentinos L. J. Rosso, 1931. 481 p. Portraits. 19 cm.

An account of the life of Julio A. Roca and of events during his presidency. Scattered biographical information is included for this man and for many people with whom he was associated. Among those featured are María Antonia Tejerina y Medina, José Roca, Julio Argentino Roca, Isaac M. Chavarría.

CSt CtY DLC GU IEN IU MH NcD NcU
NIC NSyU OrU OU PSt TNJ

542 Martínez, Benigno Tejeiro, comp. Antología argentina; colección de trozos históricos crítico-literarios; discursos y poesías patrióticas de escritores argentinos en prosa y verso, precedidas de breves rasgos biográficos y bibliográficos desde la época colonial hasta nuestros días. Buenos Aires: J. Peuser, 1890-91. 2 v. 19 cm.

An anthology of Argentine historical, literarary and political writings, including biobibliographical sketches of the following authors featured in the text: Julián Leiva, José Valentín Gómez, Mariano Moreno, Manuel Moreno, Bernardino Rivadavia, Julián Segundo de Agüero, Vicente López y Planes, Bernardo Monteagudo, Tomás Guido, Dalmacio Vélez Sarsfield, Juan Alvarez de Arenales, Facundo Zuviría, Esteban Echeverría.

CLSU DLC MB NcU OU

543 Martínez, Benjamín Demetrio. <u>Los generales de Urquiza</u>; desfile de valientes. Buenos Aires: Editorial Tor, 1932. 126 p. 19 cm.
A collection of biographical sketches about the following Argentine generals of Urquiza's army: Apolinario Almada, Manuel Basavilbaso, Pascual Echagüe, José María Francia, Miguel Galán, Miguel Gerónimo Galarza, Ricardo López Jordán, Manuel A. Palavecino, José Luis Piris, Wenceslao Taborda, Crispín Velásquez, Manuel Antonio Urdinarrain.

CU DLC MN TxU

544 Martínez, Teófilo. <u>Contemporáneos ilustres</u> (argentinos). Primera serie. Paris: Garnier Hermanos, 1910. 330 p. 22 cm.
A collection of biographical articles on the following distinguished Argentineans of the 19th century: Bartolomé Mitre, Domingo F. Sarmiento, Dalmacio Vélez-Sarsfield, Juan María Gutiérrez, Carlos Tejedor, Manuel Quintana, José María Moreno, Antonio E. Malaver.

DPU KU MB NcU PU

545 Martínez Estrada, Ezequiel. <u>X-ray of the pampa</u>. Translated by Alain Swietlicki. Introd. by Thomas F. McGann. Austin: University of Texas Press, 1971. 415 p. 24 cm. (The Texas Pan American series).
An analysis of the history and culture of Argentina, including brief scattered biographical information for many prominent people. The following are emphasized: Marcelo Torcuato de Alvear, José Gervasio Artigas, Manuel Belgrano, Manuel Dorrego, Martín Güemes, Hipólito Irigoyen, Juan Lavalle, Estanislao López, Bartolomé Mitre, José María Paz, Carlos Pellegrini, Bernardino Rivadavia, Juan Manuel de Rosas, José Francisco de San Martín, Domingo Faustino Sarmiento, Justo José de Urquiza. Alphabetical index of names.

AAP AU CaOTP CaOTU CLSU CLU CoU
CtY CU DAU DPU FTaSU FU GU IaAS
IaU ICU IEN InU IU KU LNHT LU MB
MH MiEM MiU MnU MoSW MoU MU NbU
NBuU NcD NcGU NcU NIC NjP NjR NN
NNC NSyU NWM OC1U OCU OKentU OkU
OO OrPS OrU OU PSt RPB TNJ TU
TxU UU ViU WaU WU

545a Martínez Paz, Enrique. <u>La formación histórica de la provincia de Córdoba</u>. Córdoba: Imprenta de la Universidad, 1941. 292 p. Portraits. 29 cm. (Córdoba. Universidad Nacional. Instituto de Estudios Americanistas. V. 5).

A historical essay about the Argentinean province of Córdoba (1810-1862), including biographical data, mostly accompanied by portraits, of the following notable individuals associated with it: Francisco Antonio Ortiz de Ocampo, Juan Martín de Pueyrredón, José Esteban Bustos, Mariano Boedo, Diego José de Pueyrredón, Gregorio Funes, Santiago Carrera, Gervasio Posadas, Francisco Javier de Viana, Miguel Calixto del Corro, José Javier Díaz, Juan Pablo Bulnes, Ambrosio Funes, Juan Andrés Pueyrredón, Manuel Antonio de Castro, Juan Bautista Bustos, Felipe Alvarez, José Gregorio Baigorrí, José Norberto de Allende, José María Paz, Pedro Feliciano Cavia, Juan José Cernadas, José Julián Martínez, Mariano Fragueiro, José Roque Funes, José Vicente Reynafé, José Antonio Reynafé, Calixto María González, Domingo Aguirre, Benito Lazcano, Pedro Nolasco Rodríguez, Manuel López, José Francisco Alvarez, Fermín Manrique, José Victorio López, Alejo Carmen Guzmán, Félix de la Peña, José Severo de Olmos, Tristán de Achával, José Alejo Román, Marcos Paz, Wenceslao Paunero, Justiniano Posse, Rodrigo Antonio de Orellana, José Vicente Ramírez de Arellano, Eduardo Ramírez de Arellano, Olegario Correa. Alphabetical index lists approximately 1,100 names.

CaBVaU CU DLC ICU IU MH NcU NN PU

546 Maurín Navarro, Emilio B. <u>Adalides sanjuaninos de la emancipación americana</u>. San Juan: Editorial Sanjuanina, 1967. 169 p. 22 cm. (Obras publicadas por la Editorial Sanjuanina. V. 14).
Detailed biographical information of the following 19th-century political figures from the Argentine province of San Juan: Francisco Narciso de Laprida, José Ignacio de la Roza, José Ignacio Fernández Maradona, José Luis Marcelo Beltrán, Tadeo Rojo, Mariano Sánchez de Loria, Lorenzo Maurín, José María de Lahora.

CLSU CSt CU FU IaU InU IU KU MB
MU NcU NiC NN NNC NSyU OU TxU
ViU WU

547 _____. <u>Forjadores de la república</u>. San Juan: Editorial Sanjuanina, 1967. 196 p. 22 cm.
An essay about the Argentine province of San Juan in the late 18th century and the beginning of the 19th, mainly through biographical studies of the following friars: Justo Santa María de Oro, José Fermín Sarmiento, Bonifacio Vera.

CLSU IaU InU IU NBuU OU WU

548 _____. <u>Liderazgo de Cuyo en la emancipación continental</u>. San Juan: Editorial Sanjuanina, 1969. 44 p. Portraits. 27 cm.

HISTORY

Biographical data about the following leading figures from the Cuyo region of Argentina in the 19th century: Bonifacio Vera, Justo Santa María de Oro, José Fermín Sarmiento, Juan José Godoy y del Pozo, José Ignacio de la Roza, José Clemente Sarmiento, Francisco Narciso de Laprida, Pedro Regalado Cortínez, José Teodoro Sánchez de Loria.

MU   TxU   WU

549   _____. Precursos cuyanos de la independencia de América y patriotas sanjuaninos de la hora inicial. San Juan: Editorial Sanjuanina, 1968. 430 p. Portraits. 22 cm.

Biographical essays of individuals from the area of Argentina called Cuyo who were involved in the early stages of the struggle for Independence. Special attention is paid to the residents of the present day province of San Juan. Information provided concentrates on the political activities of Juan José Godoy y del Pozo, Juan Martínez de Rozas, José de Oro, José Ignacio de la Roza, Francisco Narciso de Laprida, José Fermín Sarmiento, Bonifacio Vera, José Ignacio Fernández Maradona, Justo de Santa María de Oro, Tadeo Rojo, Mariano Sánchez de Loria, José Luis Marcelo Beltrán, Lorenzo Maurín, José M. de Lahora.

CLSU CLU CoU CSt CtY CU FU IaU
ICarbS ICU IU KU MB MoSW MU NbU
NBuU NIC NN NNC NSyU OU PPULC TxU
ViU WU

550   Mazo, Gabriel del. Recordando a Yrigoyen. Buenos Aires: Artes Gráficas Bartolomé U. Chiesino, 1965. 132 p. Portraits. 18 cm.

A short biography, accompanied by portraits, of Hipólito Yrigoyen, which also includes brief scattered information on many people associated with this leader. Among those featured are Hipólito Yrigoyen, Aristóbulo del Valle, Adolfo Güemes.

IU   MU   NjP   PSt

551   Mendoza, Edelmiro A. Desde la colonia hasta 1961; reseña histórica financiera, económica y política de la Argentina. Buenos Aires: Librería Perlado, 1962. 159 p. 18 cm.

A political, financial, and economic history of Argentina, covering the period from colonial times to the year 1961, and including scattered biographical information for many prominent people. The following are emphasized: Martín Güemes, Roque Sáenz Peña, Hipólito Yrigoyen.

CLSU CLU CtY IaU ICU InU IU MB
MH NhD NIC NjP NN NNC WU

551a Misiones, Argentine Republic (Province). Governors. Crónica de los gobernantes de Misiones. Posadas: Centro de Investigación y Promoción Científico-Cultural. Instituto

Superior del Profesorado Antonio Ruiz de Montoya, 1979. 156 p. (V. 1). 24 cm. (Serie historia. V. 3).

A collection of essays about the following governors of the Argentine province of Misiones including biographical sketches:

V. 1 (1882-1922): Rudecindo Roca, Benjamín Moritán, Juan Balestra, Juan José Lanusse, Manuel Bermúdez, Justino Solari, Gregorio López, Héctor Barreyro, Guillermo J. Doll.

ViU

552   Mitre, Bartolomé, Pres. Argentine Republic, 1821-1906. Historia de Belgrano y de la independencia argentina. Buenos Aires: 1903-13. 4 v. in 2. 17 cm. (Biblioteca de la Nación. V. 28, 30, 32, 34).

A history of the Argentine struggle for independence, including scattered biographical information for many people involved in this movement. Alphabetical index of names.

IU   TxU

553   _____. Obras completas. Ed. ordenada por el H. Congreso de la Nación Argentina. Ley no. 12,328. Buenos Aires, 1938-49. 12 v. Portraits. 24 cm.

A 12-volume complete works of the 19th-century Argentine president Bartolomé Mitre, including scattered biographical information, as well as a few portraits, for this leader and for others with whom he was associated. Alphabetical index of names.

DLC   IU

554   Molinari, Diego Luis. "¡Viva Ramírez!" El despotismo en las Provincias de la Unión del Sur (1816-1820). La batalla de un minuto: Cepeda (1 de febrero de 1820). La definición de un siglo: El tratado del Pilar (23 de febrero de 1820). Buenos Aires: "Coni," 1938. 360 p. 28 cm.

A work dealing with the political events in Argentina from 1816 to 1820, including scattered biographical information for a number of notable people, many of them political and military leaders of that period. The following are emphasized: Juan Pedro Aguirre, José Gervasio Artigas, Juan Ramón Balcarce, Juan Bautista Bustos, José Miguel Carrera, Vicente Anastasio Echeverría, Antonio José de Escalada, Domingo French, Estanislao López, Juan José Paso, Juan Martín de Pueyrredón, Hilarión de la Quintana, Francisco Ramírez, Martín Rodríguez, José Rondeau, José de San Martín, Manuel Sarratea, Miguel Estanislao Soler, Gregorio Tagle. Alphabetical index of names.

CoU   CU   DLC   IU   NN   TxU

555   Morales Guiñazú, Fernando. Los corregidores y subdelegados de Cuyo, 1561-1810. Buenos Aires: Coni, 1936. 120 p. Portraits. 28 cm. (Buenos Aires. Universidad Nacional. Publi-

caciones del Instituto de Investigaciones Históricas. V. 70).

A collection of short biographical essays, some accompanied by portraits, on 152 corregidores and subdelegates who held office in Argentina's Cuyo region during the period from 1561 to 1810.

DLC FU InU IU NjP NN OCU OrU PU
TxU WU

556 _____. Genealogía de los conquistadores de Cuyo y fundadores de Mendoza. Buenos Aires: Talleres Casa Jacobo Peuser, 1932. 58 p. 28 cm. (Buenos Aires. Universidad Nacional. Publicaciones del Instituto de Investigaciones Históricas. V. 59).

A collection of short biographical essays on the conquerors of the Cuyo region of Argentina and founders of the city of Mendoza.

DLC FU InU IU NN OCU PU TxU

557 Muertos por la patria. Buenos Aires: Angel Estrada y Cía., 1908. 104 p. 20 cm.

A collection of brief biographical sketches, alphabetically arranged, of approximately 1,000 Argentine heroes who died in the service of their country during the 19th century.

DLC

558 Navarro Gerassi, Marysa. Los nacionalistas. Traducción: Alberto Ciria. Buenos Aires: Editorial J. Alvarez, 1969. 251 p. Portraits. 21 cm. (Los Argentinos. V. 7).

An account of 20th century Argentine politics, including scattered biographical information, as well as some portraits, for many prominent leaders. The following are among those particularly featured: Marysa Navarro Gerassi, Juan Manuel de Rosas, Hipólito Yrigoyen, Leopoldo Lugones, José Félix Uriburu, Carlos Ibarguren, Manuel Gálvez, Marcelo Sánchez Sorondo, Ernesto Palacio, Juan Perón.

CoU CtY CU FU IaU ICU InU IU KU
MH MiU MnU MU NcD NcU NIC NjP
NjR NmU NN NSyU PPiU TNJ TU TxU
UU ViU WaU WU

559 Newton, Jorge. Facundo Quiroga; aventura y leyenda. Buenos Aires: Plus Ultra, 1965. 221 p. 23 cm. (Colección Los Caudillos argentinos).

A biography of the 19th-century Argentine leader Juan Facundo Quiroga, including scattered information for this man and for others with whom he was associated: Juan Facundo Quiroga, Reinafé (brothers), José Ruiz Huidobro, Santos Pérez.

CaBVaU CLU CSt CtW CtY CU DPU FU
IaU InU IU KU MH MiEM MoSW MU
NcD NcU NIC NN NSyU OU PSt RPB
TxU

560 Nudelman, Santiago I. El régimen totalitario: la antidemocracia en acción, la educación antiargentina, la era del terror, las torturas, los presos políticos, los negociados y el enriquecimiento ilícito, en defensa de la libertad de prensa, el fraude electoral, etc., etc. Buenos Aires, 1960. 767 p. 20 cm.

An account of the totalitarianism of the Perón administration, including biographical information for the following people who were arrested and tortured during that period: Aldo Lombardero, Otto Carlos Franchi, César Mancedo, Horacio Lombardero, Jorge Alfredo González, O. Berueta, Alfredo Bernardo Estrabou, Cipriano Reyes, Adolfo Pedro Tasso, Luis A. Vila Ayres, Rafael Mensch, Abel Gioia, Ernesto Mario Bravo, Jorge R. Fauzón Sarmiento, Vicente Centurión, Carlos Alberto González Dogliotti, Roque Guillermo Carranza, Héctor Hadrowa, Miguel Angel de la Serna, Rafael Douek, Patricio Cullen, Emilio de Vedia y Mitre, José Luis Bustamante, Eduardo Ocantos, Julio Enrique Morón, Alberto da Rosa, César Macedo, David Michel Torino, Miguel Lanz Daret, Luis Eugenio García Villoso, Leopoldo Suárez, Manuel Ordóñez, Emilio E. Carreira, Emilio A. Ibarra, Alberto Attias.

AzU CLSU CLU CStH CtY CU IaU ICU
IEN InU IU MB MH MU NhD NIC NN
TxU ViU

561 Otero, José Pacífico. Historia del libertador don José de San Martín. Buenos Aires: Cabaut y Cía., 1932. 4 v. Portraits. 25 cm.

A 4-volume biography of José de San Martín, including portraits and substantial information for this leader and for others with whom he was associated. The following are among those featured: José de San Martín, Juan de San Martín, Gregoria Matorras, Martín de Pueyrredón, Bernardo O'Higgins, Guillermo Bowles, Antonio Bellina, Tomás Cochrane, Alejandro Aguado y Ramírez.

CaBVaU DLC FMU FU GU IU MiU NcU
OCl OU PPT TxU WU

562 Pajuelo Mejía, Abdón Max. El general José de San Martín en su centenario. Prólogo del Dr. Ricardo Cavero Egusquiza. Lima: Ediciones Pajuelo-Mejía, 1965. 221 p. Portraits. 22 cm.

A biography of José de San Martín, including portraits and information for this leader and for many others with whom he was associated. Among those featured are José de San Martín, Manuel Lorenzo de Vidaurre, Francisco de Miranda, Bernardo de Monteagudo, Manuel Belgrano, Juan Martín de Pueyrredón, Tomás Alejandro Cochrane, Andrés de Santa Cruz, Francisco Vidal, Agustín Gamarra, Felipe Santiago Salaverry, Toribio de Luzuriaga, José de La Mar.

CLSU CSt CtY CU ICU InU IU MB MH
MoSW NBuU NcU NIC PSt TxU WU

HISTORY

563 Palcos Sulques, Alberto. <u>La visión de Riva-
davia</u>; ensayo sobre Rivadavia y su época hasta la caída del Triunvirato. Buenos Aires: Librería y Editorial "El Ateneo," 1936. 296 p. Portraits. 20 cm.

A biography of Bernardino Rivadavia, including scattered information on this man and many others with whom he was associated. The following are emphasized: Bernardino Rivadavia, Martín de Alzaga, Manuel Belgrano, Feliciano Antonio de Chiclana, Santiago Liniers, Bernardo Monteagudo, Mariano Moreno, Juan Martín de Pueyrredón, Benito González Rivadavia, Gabriela Rivadavia, Santiago Rivadavia, Manuela Julia Rivadavia, Cornelio Saavedra, Francisco Javier de Viana, Guillermo White. Alphabetical index of names.

CaBVaU CtY CU DLC IaU ICarbS IU
NcD NcU PSt TxU ViU

564 Paoli, Pedro de. <u>Sarmiento</u>; su gravitación en el desarollo nacional. Buenos Aires: Ediciones Theoria, 1964. 327 p. 20 cm. (Biblioteca de estudios históricos).

A biography of 19th-century Argentine president Domingo Faustino Sarmiento, concentrating on his political activities, Biographical data also included for many people with whom he was associated. Among those featured are José Clemente Sarmiento, Domingo Faustino Sarmiento, Aurelia Vélez Sársfield de Ortiz.

AzU CLSU CoU CSt CtY CU-SB DPU FU
IaU ICU IEN INS IU LU MH MiU NbU
NcD NcU NjP NN NNC NSyU PPiU PSt
TxFTC TxHR TxU WU

565 <u>Los parlamentarios radicales</u>; senadores y diputados al Congreso Nacional, 1919 (biografías y retratos). Buenos Aires: J. A. Herrera y Cía., 1919. 31 p. Portraits. 22 cm.

A collection of biographical sketches and portraits of the following early 20th-century Argentine congressmen: Pelagio B. Luna, Juan B. Aramburu, Miguel A. Aráoz, Juan V. Atencio, Ricardo Aldao, Ireneo de Anquín, Rogelio Araya, Carlos A. Becú, Valentín Berrondo, Benjamín Bonifacio, Francisco Beiro, Enrique Cabrera, Pedro Caracoche, Wenceslao C. Carranza, José O. Casas, Octavio Cordero, Aníbal Cabrera, Ricardo Caballero, Santiago E. Corvalán, Alberto H. Carosini, Manuel C. Cáceres, Delfor del Valle, Ricardo J. Davel, Andrés Ferreira, Juan Luis Ferraroti, Jacinto Fernández, José Antonio González, Arturo Goyeneche, Teófilo I. Gatica, Vicente C. Gallo, Carlos Gallegos Moyano, Pedro Francisco Gibert, Diógenes Hernández, Néstor de Iriondo, A. Arturo Isnardi, Miguel Laurencena, Guillermo Lehmann, Lauro Lagos, Pedro Larlus, Carlos F. Melo, Víctor M. Molina, Leopoldo Melo, José Antonio Montes, Enrique Martínez, José María Martínez, Enrique Mosca, Eduardo Mouesca, Juan O'Farrell, José E. Páez, Carlos M. Pradere, Eduardo Padilla, Marcial V. Quiroga, Carlos J. Rodríguez, Jorge Raúl Rodríguez, F. Remonda Mingrand, Francisco Rubilar, Napoleón Robín Castro, Francisco Aníbal Riu, Fernando Saguier, Teófilo Sánchez de Bustamante, Pedro Solanet, Pedro Numa Soto, Martín M. Torino, José P. Tamborini, Jesús Vaca-Narvaja, Octaviano S. Vera, Valentín Vergara, Agustín J. Villarroel, Lauro Yolde, José María Zalazar.

DLC

566 Pastor, Reynaldo Alberto. <u>La guerra con el indio en la jurisdicción de San Luis.</u> Prólogo de Héctor R. Ratto. Buenos Aires: Talleres Gráficos de G. Kraft ltda., 1942. 569 p. 24 cm. (Biblioteca de la Sociedad de Historia Argentina. V. 13).

An account of the 19th war with the Indians in the Argentine province of San Luis, including scattered biographical information for many notable people, both Indians and Argentine military leaders, engaged in this conflict. Emphasis is placed on the following: Yanquetruz, Painé, Mariano Rosas, Baigorrita, Ramón Cabral (Ramón Platero, pseud.), Epugner Rosas, Pincén, Huenchuil, Ñancuman, Pichi Pincén, Carripilun, Manuel Baigorria, Justo Daract, Juan Esteban Pedernera, V. Martín de Moussy, José Iscas, Juan A. Ortiz de Estrada, Juan Pascual Pringles.

CtY CU DLC ICU InU IU MB MH NcU
NjP TxU ViU

567 Pavón Pereyra, Enrique. <u>Vida de Perón</u>; única biografía de Juan Domingo Perón; preparación de una vida para el mando, 1895-1945. Edición "Regreso de Perón," actualizada por Roberto Gasparini. Buenos Aires: Editorial Justicialista, 1965. 255 p. (V. 1). Portraits. 20 cm.

A volume biography of Juan Domingo Perón, featuring scattered biographical information and portraits for this man and for others with whom he was associated. The following are emphasized: Juan Domingo Perón, Mario Tomás Perón, Cornelio Gutiérrez, Tomás L. Perón.

CtY DS ICU IU MH MnU NIC NjP NjR
NNC NSyU OU PSt WU

568 Paz, José María. <u>Memorias póshumas.</u> Reedición precedida por una arenga del General Bartolomé Mitre. Buenos Aires: La Cultura Argentina, 1917. 3 v. 23 cm.

A three-volume collection of the memoirs of the 19th-century Argentine José María Paz, including scattered biographical information for this man and for many with whom he was associated. Among those featured are José María Paz, Eduardo Holmberg, Juan R. Balcarce, Juan Escobar, Manuel Belgrano, Martín Miguel de Güemes, Saturnino Castro, Juan Rondeau, Martín Rodríguez, José Miguel Carrera, Román Deheza, Luna, Estanislao López, Juan Lavalle, Fructuoso Rivera, Ferré, Juan Andrés Ferrera, Justo José de Urquiza, Juan Madariaga.

CLU IU MB MH MU NN UU ViU

569 _____. <u>Varones de su tiempo</u>. Ordenamiento, introducción, y notas de León Rebollo Paz. Buenos Aires: Talleres Gráficos Lombardi y Cía., 1969. 111 p. 23 cm.
Collection of essays about the following notable Argentine military figures of the 19th century: José de San Martín, Manuel Belgrano, Pedro Ignacio Castro Barros, Román Deheza, Ignacio Oribe, Estanislao López, Gregorio Aráoz de la Madrid, José María Pirán, Pedro Ferré, Pascual Echagüe, Juan Lavalle, José Manuel Salas, Julián Segundo de Agüero, Juan Pablo López, Fructuoso Rivera, Juan Gregorio Acuña, Juan Andrés Ferrera, Francisco Cruz, Martín Rodríguez, Diego Balcarce, Eduardo Kailitz, Juan Ramón Balcarce, José Rondeau, José Manuel de Goyeneche, José María Paz.

    CLSU CLU CoU CSt CtY CU CU-SB IaU
    ICU IU KU MB MoSW NcU NIC NN NNC
    NSyU OU TxU ViU WU

570 Pelliza, Mariano A. <u>Historia argentina desde su origen hasta la organización nacional</u>. Nueva ed., ilustrada [!]. Buenos Aires: J. Lajouane y Cía., 1910. 2 v. Portraits. 25 cm.
A history of Argentina covering the period from preconquest to the year 1863, including scattered biographical information and portraits for many notable people. Volume 1 contains brief biographical sketches for the following leaders: Pedro de Mendoza, Alvar Núñez Cabeza de Vaca, Juan Ortiz de Zarate, Juan Torres de Vera y Aragón, Hernandarias de Saavedra, Fernando de Zárate, Juan Ramírez de Velazco, Diego Martín Negrón, Diego de Góngora, Alonso Pérez de Salazar, Francisco de Céspedes, Mendo de la Cueva de Benavídes, Pedro Esteban de Avila, Ventura Moxica, Jerónimo Luis de Cabrera, Jacinto de Lariz, Pedro Ruiz Baygorri, Alonso de Mercado y Villacorta, José Martínez de Salazar, Andrés de Robles, José de Garro, José de Herrera, Agustín de Robles, Manuel de Prado Maldonado, Alonso Juan de Valdez Indán, Manuel Velazco, Alonso de Arce y Soria, Baltazar García Ros, Bruno Mauricio Zavala, Miguel de Salcedo, Domingo Ortiz de Rozas, José de Andonaegui, Pedro de Ceballos Cortés y Calderón, Francisco de Paula Bucarelli y Ursúa, Juan José de Vertiz y Salcedo, Nicolás del Campo, Nicolás de Arredondo, Pedro Melo de Portugal y Villena, Gabriel de Avilés y del Fierro, Joaquín del Pino, Rafael de Sobremonte, Santiago Liniers y Bremont, Baltasar Hidalgo de Cisneros y la Torre.

    CtY DCU-IA DLC DPU IU MiU NcU OCl
    OrPS TxU ViU VtU WU

571 Pérez de Costilla, Perla Lydia. <u>Gobernadores de La Pampa</u>, 1886-1975. Prólogo, Héctor Walter Cazenave. Santa Rosa: Consejo Provincial de Difusión, Dirección de Prensa, 1976. 29 p. 22 cm. (Biblioteca pampeana: Serie de folletos. V. 22).

A listing of the governors of the Argentine province of La Pampa.

    IU

572 Piccirilli, Ricardo. <u>Los López</u>; una dinastía intelectual; ensayo histórico literario, 1810-1852. Buenos Aires: Editorial Universitaria de Buenos Aires, 1972. 196 p. Portraits. 23 cm. (Biblioteca cultural). (Colección Argentina).
A biographical account, accompanied by portraits, of the following members of the López family: Vicente López y Planes, Vicente Fidel López, Lucio Vicente López.

    AzU CaBVaU CaQMM CLS CSt CtY CU
    CU-SB CU-SC FU GU IaU ICU InU IU
    KyLoU LNHT MB MH MiDW MiEM MnU
    MoSW NBuU NcD NIC NjP NmU NN NSyU
    OkU OU PPiU PPT PSt TNJ TU TxU
    UU WU

573 _____. <u>San Martín y la política de los pueblos</u>. Buenos Aires: Ediciones Gure, 1957. 494 p. Portraits. 28 cm.
A biography of 19th-century Argentine José de San Martín, containing portraits and scattered information for this man and for many others with whom he was associated. The following are emphasized: Carlos de Alvear, José Gervasio Artigas, Manuel Belgrano, William Bowles, José Miguel Carrera, Enrique Roberto Castlereagh, J. W. Croker, Juan García del Río, José Valentín Gómez, Tomás Guido, Antonio José de Irisarri, Francisco Miranda, Bartolomé Mitre, Bernardo de O'Higgins, Manuel Aniceto Padilla, James Paroissien, Joaquín de la Pezuela, Juan Martín de Pueyrredón, Bernardino Rivadavia, José de San Martín, Manuel Sarratea, Roberto P. Staples, José Matías Zapiola. Alphabetical index of names.

    CU ICU IU MH MiDW NIC NjP NN NNC
    OkU TxU VtMiM WaU

574 Piñeiro, Armando Alonso. <u>Cronología histórica argentina</u>. Buenos Aires: Ediciones Depalma, 1981. 531 p. 20 cm.
A diary of important Argentine events of the 16th through the 20th centuries, including biographical information for the following people: Marcos Paz, Guillermo White, César Hipólito Bacle, Gregorio Funes, Bartolomé Mitre, Juan Cruz Varela, Malvina Vernet, Juan Gregorio de las Heras, Juan José Viamonte, José Eusebio Colombres, Juan Pascual Pringles, Florencio Varela, José Matías Zapiola, Mariano Necochea, Francisco Javier Muñiz, Mariano Boedo, Miguel Juárez Celman, Luis María Drago, Amado Bonpland, Manuel Belgrano, Juan Pedro Esnaola, Francisco de Miranda, Carlos Pellegrini, José Ignacio Alvarez Thomas, Pedro Ignacio Castro Barros, Luis Piedra Buena, José de San Martín, Juan Bautista Alberdi, Juan Bautista Bustos, Tomás Guido, Santiago Derqui, José María Paz, Domingo Faustino Sarmiento, Carlos Morel,

HISTORY

Cornelio de Saavedra, Feliciano Antonio Chiclana, Tomás Espora, Manuel de Sarratea, Tomás de Iriarte, Victorino de la Plaza, Hipólito Vieytes, Julio A. Roca, Carlos Antonio José Gabino del Angel de la Guardia de Alvear, José Hernández, Antonio Luis Beruti, Remedios Escalada, Domingo French, Nicolás Avellaneda, Roberto Billinghurst, Juan Martín de Pueyrredón, Joaquín V. González, Pedro de Cevallos Cortés Hoyos y Calderón, Adolfo Alsina.

IU

575 _____. Dramas y esplendores de la historia argentina. Buenos Aires: Librería Editorial Platero, 1974. 207 p. (V. 1). 22 cm. (Colección Ensayos e investigaciones históricas).
Collection of essays on various aspects of Argentine history featuring limited biographical material about the following individuals:
V. 1: Manuel Belgrano, Facundo Quiroga, José de San Martín, Juan Manuel de Rosas, Domingo Fidel Castro Martínez, Antonio Saturnino Sánchez, Ricardo Walter Oscar Darré, Santiago de Liniers y Bremond. Alphabetical index of names.

CLU CSt CtY IU MH MU NmU TxU WU

576 Los Radicales. Buenos Aires: Todo es Historia, 1976. 2 v. Portraits. 20 cm. (Todo es Historia. V. 1).
A two-volume history of the Yrigoyen era, including biographical information on this man and many people with whom he was acquainted. Particular emphasis is given to the following: Hipólito Yrigoyen, Leandro N. Alem, Alvear.

TxU

577 Ramos Mejía, José María. Las neurosis de los hombres célebres en la historia argentina. Precedido de una introducción por Vicente Fidel López. 2. ed. (completa en 1 volumen) con un prólogo de José Ingenieros. Buenos Aires: La Cultura Argentina, 1915. 455 p. 23 cm.
An essay about neurosis as it relates to the following famous men in the history of Argentina: José Manuel de Rosas, José Gaspar de Francia, Francisco Aldao, Bernardo Monteagudo, Guillermo Brown. Also biographical essay about José María Ramos Mejía.

CSt DLC IU MiU TxU ViU

578 _____. Rosas y su tiempo. 2. ed. corr. Buenos Aires: F. Lajouane, 1907. 3 v. 19 cm.
A 3-volume biography of Argentine dictator Juan Manuel de Rosas, including information for this man and for many others with whom he was associated. Emphasis is placed on the following: Juan Manuel de Rosas, Francisco de Paula Castañeda, Vicente González, Encarnación Ezcurra de Rosas.

CoU CU DLC IU OKentU PU

579 Ratto, Héctor Raúl. Actividades marítimas en la Patagonia durante los siglos XVII y XVIII. Buenos Aires: Guillermo Kraft, ltda., 1930. 194 p. 27 cm.
An account of maritime activities in the Patagonian region during the 17th and 18th centuries, including scattered biographical information for many notable naval officers. Among those featured are Domingo Perler, Francisco Gil y Lemos, José Goicoechea, Antonio Viedma, Basilio Villarino, Antonio de Córdoba, Alejandro Malaspina, Juan Gutierre de la Concha.

CSt DLC IaU ICU IU LU MB MH NcU NN NNC PSt TxU

580 _____. Los comodoros británicos de estación en el Plata (1810-1852). Buenos Aires: Sociedad de Historia Argentina, 1945. 231 p. 21 cm. (Biblioteca de la Sociedad de Historia Argentina. V. 17).
An account of the activities of British commodores from 1810 to 1852, including scattered biographical information for many officers. The following are emphasized: Pedro Heywood, Guillermo Bowles, Carlos Montagú Fabián, J. M. Hardy, D. H. O'Brien, Archibaldo Maclean, Roberto Ramsay, Brett Purvis, Tomás S. Pasley, Samuel H. Inglefield, Carlos Hotham, Sullivan, Thomas Herbert, Colonna Walewsky, Juan Hobert Howden, Barrington Reynolds.

CtY CU DLC FTaSU FU ICU IU LNHT MB MH MiU NcD NcU NNC NSyU TxU ViU

581 _____. Jefes navales de la intervención francesa en el Plata, 1829-1852. Prólogo de Eros Nicola Siri. Buenos Aires, 1947. 184 p. 21 cm. (Biblioteca de la sociedad de historia argentina. V. 18).
A history of the activities of French naval officers in Argentina, covering the period from 1829 to 1852. Scattered biographical information is included for many people associated with this aspect of Argentina's history. The following are particularly featured: José Darieux de Grivel, Luis Francisco Juan Leblanc, Juan Enrique José Dupotet, Armand René de Mackau, Pedro Eduardo Halley, Massie de Clerval, Page, Lainé, José Le Predour.

CU MB TxU

582 Repetto, Nicolás. Hombres y problemas argentinos. Buenos Aires: Editorial La Vanguardia, 1944. 271 p. 24 cm.
A collection of essays some of which pay homage to the following notable 19th-century Argentine political leaders: Domingo Faustino Sarmiento, Julio Argentino Roca, Roque Sáenz Peña, Hipólito Irigoyen, Juan Bautista Justo, Lisandro de la Torre.

CSt-H CtY DLC IU MB MH NcD NN TxU

583 Rimondi, Rómulo Juan. <u>Humanizando los próceres</u>. Buenos Aires: Editorial Plus Ultra, 1978. 99 p. 20 cm.

An essay about the following Argentine patriots, including biographical data: José de San Martín, Manuel Belgrano, Bernardino Rivadavia, José María Paz, Domingo Faustino Sarmiento, Carlos Luis Federico Brandsen, Luis Beltrán, Mamerto Esquiú, Joaquín Víctor González.

IU

583a Rivanera Carles, Raúl. <u>Nuestros próceres</u>. (Biografías sintéticas). Contribución a la verdad histórica. Buenos Aires: Liding, 1979. 266 p. (V. 1). 26 cm. (Serie historia argentina).

A collection of biographical sketches, alphabetically arranged, of leading figures in the history of Argentina. V. 1 covers A-D.

IU

584 Rivera Indarte, José. <u>Rosas y sus opositores</u>. Prólogo de Bartolomé Mitre. Londres: W. M. Jackson, Inc., 1936. 3 v. 18 cm. (Grandes escritores argentinos. V. 19-21).

A historical account of Juan Manuel de Rosas and his opponents, including biographical data about the following:

V. 1: Manuel Dorrego, Francisco Aldao, Villafañe (Colonel), Gregorio Aráoz Alfaro de La Madrid, José María Paz, Fructuoso Rivera, Melchor Pacheco, Juan Pablo López, José Rivera Indarte, Pedro Angelis.

V. 2: Nicolás Mariño, Bernardino Rivadavia, Juan Manuel de Rosas, Luis Dorrego, Juan Ramón Balcarce, Martín Rodríguez, Manuel Vicente Maza, Francisco Reinafé, Manuel Vicente Reinafé.

V. 3: List of hundreds of people who died during the Rosas era (1829-1943). Alphabetical arrangement by name with limited biographical information.

ViU

585 Rivero Astengo, Agustín P. <u>Hombres de la organización nacional</u>; retratos literarios. Primera serie. Buenos Aires: "Coni," 1936. 170 p. 23 cm.

Brief biographical essays on the following 19th- and 20th-century Argentinean presidents and statesmen: Justo José de Urquiza, Bartolomé Mitre, Domingo Faustino Sarmiento, Nicolás Avellaneda, Juan Bautista Alberdi, Esteban Echeverría, Adolfo Alsina, Dalmacio Vélez Sársfield, Julio A. Roca, Leandro N. Alem, José María Moreno, Carlos Tejedor, José Manuel Estrada, Aristóbulo del Valle, Emilio Mitre, Miguel Cané.

CLU CU DLC IU MH NcD TxU

586 _____. <u>Hombres de la organización nacional</u>; retratos literarios. Segunda serie. Buenos Aires: Edición del Jockey Club de Buenos Aires, 1937. 336 p. 23 cm.

A collection of biographical sketches of the following Argentine statesmen: Carlos Pellegrini, Florencio Varela, Salvador María del Carril, Valentín Alsina, Santiago Derqui, Marcos Paz, Guillermo Rawson, Félix Frías, Bernardo de Irigoyen, Justo Santa María de Oro, Juan María Gutiérrez, Rufino de Elizalde, Eduardo Wilde, Roque Sáenz Peña, Manuel Quintana, Antonio E. Malaver, Juan Manuel de Rosas.

CLU CU DLC DPU MH NcD

587 Roberts, Carlos. <u>Las invasiones inglesas del Río de la Plata</u> (1806-1807), y la influencia inglesa en la independencia y organización de las provincias del Río de la Plata (con 13 planos y 57 ilustraciones). Buenos Aires: Talleres Gráficos Jacobo Peuser, 1938. 458 p. Portraits. 27 cm.

An account of British military activities in the River Plate region during the early 19th century, including biographical information as well as portraits in some cases, for the following, most of them military officers: Francisco Miranda, Santiago Luis Enrique Liniers, Guillermo Pío White, Perichon (family), Tomás O'Gorman, Duclos Guyot, Santiago Antonini, James Florence Burke, Home Riggs Popham, William Carr Beresford, Samuel Auchmuty, John Whitelocke, Denis Pack, Thomas Arbuthnot, Alexander Gordon, Roberto Patrick, John Levison Gower, Robert Craufurd, William Lumley, Henry Cadogan, Henry Torrens, Richard Bourke, John Squire, Augustus Fraser, Alexander Dixon, Philip Roche, William Carrol, Samford Whittingham. Alphabetical index of names.

CaBVaU CtY CU DLC GU ICU IU NN OC1 PP

588 Rodó, José Enrique, and José Salgado. <u>Ensayos históricos rioplatenses</u>. Montevideo: Imprenta Nacional, 1935. 117 p. 24 cm.

A collection of biographical sketches of the following 18th- and 19th-century notable Argentine patriots: Manuel Belgrano, Juan Hipólito Vieytes, Manuel José de Lavardén, Cayetano José Rodríguez, José Joaquín Araujo, Julián Leiva.

DLC IU TxU

589 Rodríguez Bustamante, Norberto, comp. <u>Hombres de la Argentina</u>. Buenos Aires: Editorial Universitaria de Buenos Aires, 1962-63. 2 v. 18 cm. (Serie del siglo y medio. V. 42, 47).

A collection of biographical sketches of the following illustrious Argentineans of the 18th through 20th centuries:

V. 1: (De Mayo a Caseros). Mariano Moreno by Gustavo Gabriel Levene, Manuel Belgrano by Gregorio Weinberg, Bernardino Rivadavia by Alberto Palcos, José de San Martín by Germán O. Tjarks, José María Paz by Luis Franco, Facundo Quiroga by Angel Héctor Azeves,

HISTORY

Juan Manuel de Rosas by Enrique M. Barba, Esteban Echeverría by Félix Weinberg, Justo José de Urquiza by Beatriz Bosch.

V. 2: (De la organización a la crisis del 30). Juan Bautista Alberdi by Bernardo Canal Feijóo, Bartolomé Mitre by Juan Angel Farini, Domingo Faustino Sarmiento by Javier Fernández, Julio A. Roca by Alfredo Galletti, Leandro N. Alem by Samuel Amaral, Juan B. Justo by Marcos Merchensky, Hipólito Yrigoyen by Roberto Etchepareborda, Lisandro de la Torre by Raúl Larra.

CLSU CLU CtY CU DPU GU IaU FU
FTaSU MH MiEM MoSW NIC NNC NSyU
PPiU TxU

590 Rodríguez Sánchez, Margarita. _Gravitación política de Perón_. México: Editorial Extemporáneos, 1979. 148 p. 19 cm. (Colección Latino-america. V. 10).

A critical account of the Perón dictatorship, covering the period from 1955-1973, and which includes scattered biographical information for many people, mostly political leaders. Among them are Juan Domingo Perón, Arturo Frondizi, Juan Carlos Onganía, Roberto M. Levingston, Héctor Campora.

IU

591 Rodríguez Tarditi, José. _Semblanza de tres líderes_. Buenos Aires: Editorial Bases, 1960. 75 p. 18 cm.

A collection of lengthy biographies, emphasizing personal and professional accomplishments, dealing with the following great Argentine leaders: Hipólito Yrigoyen, Lisandro de la Torre, Juan B. Justo.

CLSU CLU CU IU MH NIC

592 Roldán, Belisario. _Discursos_. Buenos Aires: J. M. Míguez, 1910. 373 p. 23 cm.

A collection of speeches on various aspects of Argentina's history and society, including tributes to the lives and works of the following: Bartolomé Mitre, Manuel José de Labardén, José Garibaldi, Estevan Echeverría, Carlos Pellegrini, Manuel Quintana, Emilio Mitre, Juan María Gutiérrez.

CU DLC DPU IU MB NbU NcU PU ViU

593 Romero, José Luis. _Breve historia de la Argentina_. Buenos Aires: Editorial Huemul, 1978. 226 p. 17 cm. (Colección Temas del Hombre).

A short history of Argentina, covering the period from preconquest to 1958. Many people who have contributed to Argentine development during this time are mentioned. Particular emphasis is given to the following: Hernando Arias de Saavedra (pseud. Hernandarias), Bruno Mauricio de Zabala, Pedro de Cevallos, Juan José de Vértiz, Santiago de Liniers, Mariano Moreno, Carlos María de Alvear, José Gervasio Artigas, Bernardino Rivadavia, Juan Facundo Quiroga, Juan Manuel de Rosas,

Juan Lavalle, Justo José de Urquiza, Bartolomé Mitre, Domingo Faustino Sarmiento, Nicolás Avellaneda, Julio A. Roca, Carlos Pellegrini, Roque Sáenz Peña, Hipólito Yrigoyen, Manuel Quintana, Agustín P. Justo, Ramón S. Castillo, Juan D. Perón, Pedro Eugenio Aramburu, Arturo Frondizi, Alvaro Alsogaray, Arturo Illia, Juan Carlos Onganía.

IU

594 _____. _La experiencia argentina y otros ensayos_. Compilados por Luis Alberto Romero; diseño de tapa, Pablo Barragán. Buenos Aires: Editorial de Belgrano, 1980. 522 p. 23 cm.

An account of the history, politics, and culture of Argentina, including biographical essays, emphasizing personal characteristics, for the following notable people: Mariano Moreno, José María Paz, Domingo Faustino Sarmiento, Vicente Fidel López, Bartolomé Mitre, Emilio Mitre, José Ingenieros, Pablo Groussac, Alejandro Korn, Pedro Henríquez Ureña (Dominican Republic), Ezequiel Martínez Estrada, Alfredo Palacios, Julio E. Payró, Victoria Ocampo.

IU

595 Roque, Benjamín. _La República Argentina_: 1906-1907. Buenos Aires: Talleres Gráficos de L. J. Rosso, 1907. Unpaged. Portraits. 27 x 37 cm.

Album of photographs of various regions in Argentina in 1906-1907. Included are portraits of prominent individuals of the time with biographical sketches of the following: José Figueroa Alcorta, Benito Villanueva, Manuel Quintana, Bernardo de Irigoyen, Bartolomé Mitre, Carlos Pellegrini, Carlos Calvo.

IU

596 Rosa, José María. _La caída de Rosas_: El Imperio de Brasil y la Confederación Argentina, 1843-1851. Guerra argentino-brasileña de 1851. Gestión del pronunciamiento de Urquiza. Caseros. Los tratados de Río de Janeiro. Madrid: Instituto de Estudios Políticos, 1958. 628 p. 22 cm.

An account of the 19th-century war between Argentina and Brazil, including scattered biographical information on many people involved in this struggle. The following are emphasized: Honorio Hermeto Carneiro Leão, Paulino José Soares de Souza, Bernardo de Vasconcellos, Juan Manuel de Rosas, Fructuoso Rivera, Ireneo Evangelista de Souza, Justo José de Urquiza, Antonio Cuyás y Sampere.

CoU CU GU ICU IU LU MH MiU MnU
NBuU NcD NcU NhD NIC NjP NN NNC
OkU PPT ScU TNJ TxU WaU WU

597 Ruiz-Guiñazú, Enrique. _Lord Strangford y la revolución de mayo_, 1937. Buenos Aires: Librería y Editorial "La Facultad," Bernabé y Cía., 1937. 304 p. Portraits. 29 cm.

A biography of Lord Strangford, emphasizing his involvement in the Argentine independence movement, which also includes information and a few portraits for others with whom he was associated. The following are emphasized: Percy Clinton Sydney Smythe Strangford, 6th Viscount, Saturnino Rodríguez Peña, Manuel Aniceto Padilla.

CtY DLC FU GU IaU IU MB NcD NcU NN OCl PU TxU ViU

598 Sabsay, Fernando Leónidas. La Sociedad argentina. Buenos Aires: La Ley, 1973-74. 4 v. 23 cm. Issued by Fedye (Fondo Editorial de Derecho y Economía).

A discussion in four volumes of various aspects of Argentina's history and society, including scattered biographical information for many notable people, as well as longer biographical essays in volume 4 for the following 19th-century presidents: Bartolomé Mitre, Domingo Faustino Sarmiento, Nicolás Avellaneda, Julio Argentino Roca, Miguel Juárez Celman, Carlos Pellegrini, Luis Sáenz Peña, José Evaristo Uriburu, Manuel Quintana, José Figueroa Alcorta, Roque Sáenz Peña.

AzU CtY DGU FU IU NbU NcU NIC NmU PSt VtMiM WU

599 Saldaña Retamar, Reginaldo de la Cruz. Los domínicos en la independencia argentina; monografía documentada. Buenos Aires, 1920. 192 p. Portraits. 21 cm.

A work featuring biographical sketches, as well as a few portraits, for the following Dominican friars who were active in the 19th-century Argentine independence movement: Ignacio Grela, Julián Perdriel, José Zambrana, Isidoro Celestino Guerra, José Marcelino Pelliza, Mariano Suárez, Justo Ponce de León, José Rizo, Manuel Albariño, Gregorio Pizarro Grimau, Román Grela, Juan Antonio Cruz Valle, Francisco Sosa, Mariano Amaro, Pedro Pablo Gómez, Isidoro González, Benito Lucio Lucero, Francisco Alvarez, Baltasar Ponce de León, Domingo Pedernera, José Matías del Castillo, Pedro Fernández, José Domingo Carballo, José Manuel Pérez, Ignacio Maestre.

CtY CU-B DLC IU MB MiU NcD WU

600 Saldías, Adolfo. Páginas históricas de la historia de la Confederación Argentina. Montevideo: Impr. de "España Moderna," 1894. 309 p. 18 cm.

A collection of essays on various 19th-century Argentine events and people, with particular biographical emphasis on the following: Manuel Dorrego, Juan Manuel de Rosas, Juan Facundo Quiroga, Juan Lavalle, Rivera Indarte, Manuel de Egúa, Martiniano Chilavert, Florencio Varela, José de San Martín.

MnU TxU

601 Sánchez Sorondo, Matías Guillermo. Cinco esbozos: el espíritu de Sarmiento, Mitre, Estrada, González, Uriburu. Buenos Aires: Librería El Ateneo, 1944. 81 p. 22 cm.

Brief biographical essays on the following 19th- and 20th-century Argentinean presidents and statesmen: Domingo Faustino Sarmiento, Bartolomé Mitre, José Félix Uriburu, José Manuel Estrada, Joaquín Víctor González.

IU MiU TxU

602 Santander, Silvano. Técnica de una traición; Juan D. Perón y Eva Duarte, agentes del nazismo en la Argentina. Ed. argentina. Buenos Aires: Editorial Antygua, 1955. 127 p. Portraits. 22 cm.

An account of the activities of the Nazi party in Argentina including biographical information, as well as portraits in a few cases, for many people associated with this aspect of Argentina's history. The following are emphasized: H. Theiss, Willy Tank, Hans Ulrich Rudel, Adolf Galland, Ludwig Freude (Lucovico Freude), Juan Domingo Perón, Eva Duarte, Wilhelm Faupel. Alphabetical index of names.

CSt-H CtY CU GU IaU IU MH NNC ScU ViU

603 Sarmiento, Domingo Faustino, Pres. Argentine Republic, 1811-1888. El Civilizador; síntesis del pensamiento vivo de Sarmiento. Presentación, selección y notas por Julio R. Barcos. Buenos Aires: Ediciones A. Zamora, 1961. 429 p. 23 cm. (Colección los genios. V. 12).

A synthesis of the works of Domingo Faustino Sarmiento, including biographical information for this man and for others with whom he was associated. The following are emphasized: Domingo Faustino Sarmiento, Justo de Santa María de Oro, Domingo de Oro, Manuel Montt, Juan Facundo Quiroga, Francisco J. Muñiz, Domingo Fidel Castro (Dominguito, pseud.).

CLSU CLU CSt CtY CU CU-S DPU FMU IaAS ICU InU IU LU-NO MH MiU MoSW MoU MU MWelC NhD NIC NN NSyU OkU OrCS OU ScU TxDaM TxHR TxLT TxU WU

604 _____. Domingo Faustino Sarmiento, selección, notas biográficas y comentario de Pedro de Alba; advertencia preliminar de Julio Jiménez Rueda. México: Imprenta Universitaria, 1944. 255 p. 22 cm.

An anthology of writings by the 19th-century Argentine president. Substantial biographical data included for the following: Domingo Faustino Sarmiento, Paula Albarracín, Juan Facundo Quiroga.

IU

605 _____. Life in the Argentine Republic in the Days of the Tyrants; or, Civilization and Barbarism. From the Spanish with a biographical

sketch of the author by Mrs. Horace Mann. 1st American from the 3d Spanish ed. New York: Hafner Pub. Co., 1960. 400 p. 21 cm. (The Hafner library of classics. V. 21).

A political history of 19th-century Argentina, which includes extensive biographical information for the following people: Juan Facundo Quiroga, José Félix Aldao, Domingo Faustino Sarmiento.

IU

606 _____. *Sarmiento selecto*; homenaje de la Comisión popular en su centenario, 1811-1911. Buenos Aires: Otero & Cía., Impresores, 1911. 254 p. 16 cm.

A collection of essays by 19th-century Argentine Domingo Faustino Sarmiento, including biographical information for the following people: Paula Alberracín, José de San Martín, Juan Facundo Quiroga, Gauna, Baigorria, Dominguito, Rosario Vélez Sársfield.

CSt CtY CU DLC IU LU NcU NN

607 _____. *Sarmiento-Mitre*; correspondencia, 1846-1868. Buenos Aires: Impr. de Coni Hermanos, 1911. 382 p. 26 cm.

Collection of letters between Domingo Faustino Sarmiento and Bartolomé Mitre from 1846 to 1868, with biographical information about both.

CaBVaU CU DLC ICU IU NcD NcU PU WU

608 _____. *Textos fundamentales*. Selección de Luis Franco y Ovidio Omar Amaya. Buenos Aires: Compañía General Fabril, 1959. 2 v. 23 cm. Portraits.

A 2-volume collection of essays by the 19th-century Argentine president, including biographical essays, as well as portraits in many cases, for the following:

V. 1: Camila O'Gorman, Navarro, José Fructuoso Rivera, Domingo de Oro, Manuel Hornos, Aquino, Gauna, Baigorria, Ambrosio Sandes, Antonio Aberastain, Juan Chipaco.

V. 2: Juan Facundo Quiroga, Juan Manuel de Rosas, Félix Alzaga, José de San Martín, Simón Bolívar, Justo José de Urquiza, Dominguito Sarmiento. Also autobiography of Domingo Faustino Sarmiento.

CLSU IaAS IaU IEdS IU KU MH MoU MsU NBuC NBuU NN NNC TxFTC TxU WaU WU

609 Scenna, Miguel Angel. *Los que escribieron nuestra historia*. Buenos Aires: Ediciones La Bastilla, Editorial Astrea, 1976. 430 p. 20 cm.

An essay about Argentine historiography (16th century through 20th), including bio-bibliographical information about the following historians: Ulrico Schmidel, Ruy Díaz de Guzmán, Reginaldo de Lizárraga, Saturnino Se-gurola, José Joaquín de Araujo, Gregorio Funes, Ignacio Núñez, Pedro de Angelis, Bartolomé Mitre, Luis L. Domínguez, Antonio Zinny, Manuel Ricardo Trelles, Vicente G. Quesada, Angel Justiniano Carranza, Vicente Fidel López, José Manuel Estrada, Mariano Pelliza, Clemente Fregeiro, Adolfo Saldías, Ernesto Quesada, Paul Groussac, Ramón J. Cárcano, David Peña, Ricardo Rojas, Juan Alvarez, José Ingenieros, Miguel Angel Cárcano, Emilio Ravignani, Diego Luis Molinari, Rómulo D. Carbia, Guillermo Furlong, Ricardo Levene, Enrique Ruiz Guiñazú, Roberto Levillier, Carlos Ibarguren, José Torre Revello, Alberto Palcos, Juan Canter, Raúl Alejandro Molina, Armando Braun Menéndez, Ricardo Piccirilli, León Rebollo Paz, Ricardo Caillet-Bois, Carlos Heras, Andrés Roberto Allende, Joaquín Pérez, José Luis Busaniche, Julio Irazusta, Raúl Scalabrini Ortiz, Manuel Gálvez, Ernesto Palacio, Vicente D. Sierra, Enrique de Gandía, Enrique J. Fitte, Enrique M. Barba, Enrique Williams Alzaga, Leoncio Gianello, Ricardo Zorraquín Becú, José María Rosa, Rodolfo Puiggrós, Juan Pablo Oliver, Roberto H. Marfany, Gabriel A. Puente, Boleslao Lewin, Jorge Abelardo Ramos, Roberto Etchepareborda, Félix César Luna, Tulio Halperín Donghi, Andrés Carretero, Fermín Chávez, Enrique Díaz Araujo, Armando Alonso Piñeiro, Norberto Galasso, Miguel Angel de Marco, Beatriz Bosch, Cristina V. Minutolo, Hebe Clementi, Trinidad Delia Chianelli, María Sáenz Quesada.

AzU CU-S CU-SB InU IU LNT MH MoSW NcU NIC NjP NN PPT TNJ TxU

610 Seminario de estudios de historia argentina. *Gobernantes de Mayo*. Buenos Aires: Ediciones Humanismo, 1960. 361 p. 21 cm.

An account of the Argentinean May Revolution in the early 1800s, with detailed biographical information of the following prominent leaders: Cornelio de Saavedra, Mariano Moreno, Juan José Paso, Manuel Alberti, Miguel de Azcuénaga, Domingo Matheu, Manuel Belgrano, Juan José Castelli,

CLU IaU InU IU NjR NN PPT

611 *Servidores beneméritos de la patria*. Buenos Aires, 1909. 91 p. 20 cm.

A collection of brief biographical sketches, alphabetically arranged, on approximately 300 Argentinean patriots of the 19th century.

DLC

612 Solari, Juan Antonio. *Bajo el signo de mayo*; temas históricos. Buenos Aires, 1955. 70 p. 19 cm.

A short history of Argentine government and politics from 1817-1860. Scattered biographical information is given for many people associated with this period of Argentine development, with particular emphasis on the following: Enrique LaFuente, Ramón Maza, Juan B. Alberdi, Esteban Echeverría, Roque Sáenz Peña, Justo José de Urquiza, Juan B. Justo.

DLC NN TxU

613 _____. Días y obras de Sarmiento. Buenos Aires: Plus Ultra, 1968. 123 p. 20 cm.
An a collection of essays dealing with various aspects of the life of 19th-century Argentine Domingo Faustino Sarmiento, which includes biographical information for this leader and for others with whom he was associated. The following are emphasized: Domingo Faustino Sarmiento, Domingo Fidel Castro (Domingo Fidel Sarmiento), Eduardo Wilde.

CLU CoU CSt CtY DPU FU IaU ICU INS
InU IU KU MB MiEM MiU MoSW MoU MU
NbU NBuU NIC NN NNC NSyU OU TxDaM
TxU ViU VtU WU

614 _____. Perfiles parlamentarios argentinos. Buenos Aires: Bases Editorial, 1965. 194 p. 19 cm.
A collection of biographical sketches by the following Argentine parliamentary figures of the 19th century: Vicente Fidel López, Domingo Faustino Sarmiento, Juan Bautista Alberdi, David Peña, Luis María Drago, Joaquín V. González, Nicolás Repetto.

CLSU CtY DLC IaU ICU IU MiEM NcU
NIC NNC OU PPIU TU TxU

615 _____. Sacerdotes liberales: Gorriti, Oro, Beltrán, Lavaysse y Esquiú. Prólogo del Dr. Octavio R. Amadeo. Buenos Aires: Editorial Claridad, 1946. 172 p. Portraits. 20 cm. (Biblioteca Hombres e ideas. V. 24).
Biographical essays profiling Argentine priests who participated in the Revolution. Special attention is paid to the political activities of the following: Juan Ignacio de Gorriti, Justo de Santa María de Oro, Luis Beltrán, Benjamín José Lavaysse, Mamerto Esquiú.

DLC IU

616 Speroni, Miguel Angel. San Martín: la grandeza del Libertador en un enfoque nuevo y original. Buenos Aires: Plus Ultra, 1975. 253 p. 21 cm. (Colección Los Argentinos. V. 4).
A biography of José de San Martín, which also contains information for many others with whom he was associated. The following are among those featured: José de San Martín, José Miguel Carrera, Rosita Campusano, Manuela Sáenz, Micaela Villegas (Miquita; Perricholi, pseuds.), María de los Remedios Escalada de San Martín, Juan Lavalle.

AzU CU-SB ICU InU IU KU MB MH MU
NIC NN ViU

617 Stieben, Enrique. De Garay a Roca; la guerra con el indio de las pampas. Buenos Aires: Imprenta de R. P. Marinelli, 1941. 890 p. Portraits. 20 cm.
An account of the 19th-century war with the Indians of the Pampa, including portraits and scattered biographical information for the following: Pedro Andrés García, Angel Pacheco, Manuel Baigorria, Lucio V. Mansilla, Hilario Lagos, Adolfo Alsina, Manuel Namuncurá, Julio Argentino Roca, Conrado E. Villegas, Eduardo Racedo, Napoleón Uriburu, Enrique Godoy, Nicolás Levalle, Estanislao Zeballos, Lorenzo Vinttner.

CU DLC IU

618 Suárez Danero, Eduardo María. Monteagudo; la servidumbre del poder. Buenos Aires: Editorial Universitaria de Buenos Aires, 1968. 239 p. 18 cm. (Colección Argentina).
A biography of 19th-century Argentine statesman Bernardo Monteagudo, which also includes biographical information for others with whom he was associated. Among those featured are Bernardo Monteagudo, Miguel Monteagudo, José Antonio Medina.

ICU IU NcU NSyU PPiU

619 Tagliaferro, M. Miguel. Presidentes constitucionales de la nación argentina, 1854-1954. Buenos Aires: Distribuidora y Editora Argentina, 1954. 141 p. Portraits. 23 cm.
Biographical sketches, accompanied by portraits, of the following Argentinean presidents (1854 to 1954): Justo José de Urquiza, Santiago Derqui, Bartolomé Mitre, Domingo Faustino Sarmiento, Nicolás Avellaneda, Julio Argentino Roca, Miguel Juárez Celman, Carlos Pellegrini, Luis Sáenz Peña, José Evaristo Uriburu, Manuel Quintana, José Figueroa Alcorta, Roque Sáenz Peña, Victorino de la Plaza, Hipólito Irigoyen, Marcelo Torcuato de Alvear, José Félix Uriburu, Agustín P. Justo, Roberto M. Ortiz, Ramón S. Castillo, Arturo Rawson, Pedro Pablo Ramírez, Edelmiro J. Farrell, Juan D. Perón.

DLC IU MH NN

620 Tucumán. Gobernación. Gobernación del Tucumán. Probanzas de méritos y servicios de los conquistadores; documentos del Archivo de Indias. Publicación dirigida por D. Roberto Levillier. Prólogo de D. Rufino Blanco-Fombona. Madrid: Sucesores de Rivadeneyra, 1919-1920. 2 v. 26 cm. (Colección de publicaciones históricas de la Biblioteca del Congreso argentino).
A collection of documents dealing with the merits and accomplishments of the conquerors of Tucumán Province, Argentina.
V. 1: Pedro González de Prado, Juan Núñez de Prado, Gonzalo de Bardales, Nicolás de Heredia, Francisco de Aguirre, Alonso Domínguez, García de Mendoza y Manrique, Bartolomé Díaz,

HISTORY

Juan Bautista de Alcántara, Rodrigo de Cantos, Lorenzo Suárez de Figueroa, Hernando de Retamoso, Juan Pérez de Zorita.

V. 2: Francisco Rengifo, Hernán Mexía Miraval, Juan Gregorio de Bazán, Nicolás de Garnica, Alonso de la Cámara, Juan Ramírez de Velasco, Francisco de Argañarás, Juan Pedrero de Trejo.

CaDTP DLC InU IU NcD NIC PU WaU

621 Udaondo, Enrique. <u>Congresales de 1816, apuntes biográficos</u>. Buenos Aires, 1916. 321 p. 23 cm.
Biographical essays on the following Argentineans who took part in the "Congreso de Tucumán" of 1816: Francisco Narciso de Laprida, Manuel Antonio Acevedo, Tomás Manuel de Anchorena, Pedro Miguel Aráoz, Mariano Boedo, José Antonio Cabrera, Pedro Ignacio de Castro Barros, José Eusebio Colombres, Miguel Calixto del Corro, José Darregueyra, Pedro León Gallo, Esteban Agustín Gascón, Tomás Godoy Cruz, José Ignacio de Gorriti, José Severo Feliciano Malavia, Juan Agustín Maza, Pedro Medrano, Justo de Santa María de Oro, José Andrés Pacheco de Melo, Juan José Paso, Eduardo Pérez Bulnes, Pedro Ignacio de Rivera, Cayetano José Rodríguez, Antonio Sáenz, Luis Jerónimo Salguero de Cabrera, Teodoro Sánchez de Bustamante, Mariano Sánchez de Loría, José Mariano Serrano, José Ignacio Thamés, Pedro Francisco de Uriarte.

IU MH TxU

622 Uzal, Francisco Hipólito. <u>Los enemigos de San Martín</u>: Alvear, Rivadavia, Carrera, Cochrane y el Partido Unitario. Buenos Aires: Corregidor, 1975. 156 p. 19 cm. (Serie popular).
A work featuring biographical information on the 19th-century Argentine liberator José de San Martín, and four of his adversaries. The following are featured: José de San Martín, Carlos María de Alvear, Bernardino Rivadavia, José Miguel Carrera, Tomás Alejandro Cochrane.

AU AzU CtY CU CU-S CU-SB FU InU
IU MB MH MU NcD NIC NmU NN OU
TxU WU

623 Vásquez, Aníbal S. <u>Caudillos entrerrianos</u>. 2. ed. Paraná: Casa Predassi, 1937-40. 2 v. Portraits. 19 cm.
An essay about the following leaders from the Argentine province of Entre Ríos.
V. 1: Francisco Ramírez.
V. 2: José Ricardo López Jordán.

DLC KMK PPT TxU

624 Vita-Finzi, Paolo. <u>Perón: mito e realtà</u>. Milano: Pan, 1973. 222 p. 19 cm. (Il Timone. V. 17).
An account of the Perón dictatorship, including scattered biographical information for this man as well as for others with whom he was associated. Among those featured are Juan Domingo Perón, Pedro Eugenio Aramburu, Arturo Frondizi, Juan Carlos Onganía, Eva Duarte de Perón. Alphabetical index of names.

CU InU IU MB MH NBuU NIC NN TxU
WU

625 Yaben, Jacinto R. <u>Los capitanes de Güemes</u>. Salta: Comité Ejecutivo del Sesquicentenario de la muerte del general Martín Miguel de Güemes, 1971. 132 p. 23 cm.
Biographical article on the following Argentinean military and navy figures who served under general Martín Miguel Güemes in the early 1800s: Manuel Eduardo Arias, Alejandro Burela, Luis Burela y Saavedra, Francisco de Gurruchaga, Eusebio Martínez de Mollinedo, Eustaquio Méndez, José Moldes, Mariano Morales ("El Costeño", pseud.), Santiago Morales, Sinforoso Morales, Bernardino Olivera, Pastor Padilla, Francisco Pérez de Uriondo, Dionisio Puch, Domingo Puch, Manuel Puch, Mateo Ríos, Juan Antonio Rojas, Gregorio Victoriano Romero y González, Bonifacio Ruiz de loa Llanos, Pedro José de Saravia, José Domingo Saravia, José Gabino Sardina, José Toribio Tedín.

IU

626 Yani, José Ignacio, comp. <u>La independencia</u>. Buenos Aires, 1916. 127 p. 23 cm.
Biographical sketches about the following Argentineans who participated in the Congress of Tucumán (1816): Francisco Narciso de Laprida, Isidro Sáinz de la Maza, Pedro Francisco de Uriarte, José de Darregueira, José Severo Malavia, Jerónimo Salguero de Cabrera y Cabrera, Mariano Boedo, Andrés Pacheco de Melo, Tomás Manuel de Anchorena, Pedro Medrano, José Moldes, José Teodoro Sánchez Bustamante, Esteban Agustín Gascón, Antonio Sáenz, José Ignacio Gorriti, Tomás Godoy Cruz, Eduardo Pérez Bulnes, José Mariano Serrano, Miguel Calixto del Corro, José Ignacio Thames, Pedro Ignacio de Castro Barros, Pedro Ignacio de Rivera, Cayetano Rodríguez, Pedro León Gallo, Justo de Santa María de Oro, Pedro Miguel Aráoz, Juan José Paso, Mariano Sánchez de Loria, José Antonio Cabrera, José Colombres, Manuel Antonio Acevedo. Also biographical data about the following women: Rosa Robín de Plá, Elena Alurralde de Muñecas, Jerónima de San Martín y Ceballos, Juana Montenegro, Martina Silva de Gurruchaga, Magdalena Güemes de Tejada, Loreto Peón de Frías, Francisca Silveira de Ibarrola, Ana Riglos de Irigoyen, María Sánchez de Thompson, Paula Jaraquemada de Martínez.

ICarbS IU

627 Zapata Gollán, Agustín. <u>El Paraná y los primeros cronistas</u>. Santa Fe: Ministerio de Gobierno e Instrucción Pública, 1942. 40 p. 28 cm.

A discussion of the impressions of the first chroniclers concerning the Paraná River, including brief, scattered biographical information on the following men: Diego García, Luis Ramírez, Alonso de Santa Cruz, Pero Lopes de Sousa.

CU   DLC

628 Zavalía Matienzo, Roberto. La Casa de Tucumán; historia de la Casa de la Independencia. Tucumán: Archivo Histórico de Tucumán, 1971. 277 p. 28 cm. (Serie independencia. Publicación 19. V. 1).

An essay about the Argentinean "Casa de la Independencia" in the province of Tucumán. Includes genealogical data about the Bazán family and the Zavalía family. Alphabetical index lists approximately 1,200 names.

CtY CU InU KU IU NcU WU

629 Zinny, Antonio. Estudios biográficos. Estudio preliminar de Narciso Binayán. Buenos Aires: Librería Hachette, 1958. 344 p. 21 cm. Portraits. (Colección "El Pasado argentino").

Biographical sketches about the following notable Argentineans from the colonial period, plus biographical information on the author: Miguel de Azcuénaga, Fernando López Aldana, Andrés Pazos, José Camilo Henríquez, Dámaso Antonio de Larrañaga, César Augusto Rodney, Juan Ramón Balcarce, Francisco de Paula Castañeda, Pedro José Agrelo, Pedro Ignacio de Castro Barros, Pedro Feliciano Sáenz de Cavia, Victorio García de Zúñiga, Juan Martín de Pueyrredón, José Matías Deogracias Zapiola, Julián de Gregorio Espinosa, Felipe Senillosa, Antonio José de Irisarri, Juan Manuel Cabot, Pedro de Angelis, Bernardo Monteagudo, José Miguel Carrera, Manuel Dorrego, Ignacio Alvarez y Thomas, José Tomás Guido, Mariano Benítez, Juan Gualberto Godoy, Tomás de Iriarte, Salvador María del Carril, Justo Pastor Donoso, Domingo de Oro, Antonio de Fahy, Juan María Gutiérrez, Domingo Faustino Sarmiento, Andrés Lamas, Bartolomé Pizarro.

CU IaU IU NcD NcU TxU

630 _____. Historia de los gobernadores de las provincias argentinas. Edición reordenada, con un prólogo de Pedro Bonastre. Buenos Aires: Administración General, "Vaccaro," 1920-21. 5 v. 23 cm. ("La cultura argentina").

Chronology of the rulers of the Argentine provinces up to the end of the 19th century. Biographical material provided is limited to the individual's activities while in office.

V. 1: Río de la Plata.
V. 2: Buenos Aires, Santa Fe, Entre Ríos, Corrientes.
V. 3: Córdoba, Tucumán, Santiago del Estero, San Luis.

V. 4: Mendoza, San Juan, La Rioja, Catamarca.
V. 5: Salta, Jujuy.

DLC IU

631 Zorrilla, Manuel Marcos. Al lado de Sarmiento y de Avellaneda (Recuerdos de un secretario). 2. ed. Buenos Aires: Editorial Ayacucho, 1943. 332 p. 21 cm. (Colección épocas, costumbres, recuerdos. V. 1).

An account of various episodes in the political lives of Argentine presidents Domingo Faustino Sarmiento and Nicolás Avellaneda, as well as biographical essays on several ministers during their terms of office. The following are featured: Domingo Faustino Sarmiento, Nicolás Avellaneda, Dalmacio Vélez Sársfield, Eduardo Olivera, Carlos Tejedor, Uladislao Frías, José B. Gorostiaga, Luis L. Domínguez, Martín de Gainza, Bernardo de Irigoyen, Adolfo Alsina, Simón de Iriondo, Norberto de la Riestra, Rufino de Elizalde, Carlos Pellegrini, Benjamín Paz, Manuel D. Pizarro, Vicente F. López, Santiago J. Cortínez, José V. Zapata, Amancio Alcorta.

CoU CU IU MH MiU MnU NNC OCU TxU

632 Zorrilla, Rubén H. Extracción social de los caudillos, 1810-1870. Buenos Aires: Editorial La Pléyade, 1972. 190 p. 21 cm.

A sociological study including biographical information on the following 19th-century Argentine political leaders and others associated with Argentina: José Gervasio de Artigas, Bernabé Aráoz, Martín Güemes, Estanislao López, Francisco Ramírez, Juan Bautista Bustos, Juan Felipe Ibarra, Facundo Quiroga, Juan Manuel de Rosas, Fructuoso Rivera, Alejandro Heredia, Pedro Ferré, Félix Aldao, Nazario Benavídez, Justo José de Urquiza, A. Vicente Peñaloza, Felipe Varela, Antonio Taboada.

AzU CSt CU CU-SB DGU FU ICN KU MH
MnU MoU NBuU NbU NcD NcU NjP NN
OrU PPT TxU ViU WU

633 Zuviría, José María. Anales contemporáneos. Sarmiento, 1868-1874; estudios sobre política argentina. Buenos Aires: J. Peuser, 1889. 416 p. 28 cm.

An account of the activities of Domingo Faustino Sarmiento during the period from 1868 to 1874, including biographical information for this leader and for others with whom he was associated. Among those featured are Domingo Faustino Sarmiento, Adolfo Alsina, Luis L. Domínguez, Carlos Tejedor, Uladislao Frías.

AzU CtY CU DLC FTaSU ICU IU MB
NcD NSyU TxU WU

HISTORY

634 _____. Los constituyentes de 1853. Buenos Aires: F. Lajouane, 1889. 400 p. 24 cm.
A history of the signing of the Argentine constitution of 1853 through biographical sketches of the following participants: Facundo de Zuviría, Salvador María del Carril, Juan Manuel Pérez, José Benjamín Gorostiaga, Juan del Campillo, Juan María Gutiérrez, Juan Llerena, Pedro Ferré, Santiago Derqui, Martín Zapata, Pedro Díaz Colodrero, Luciano Torrent, Benjamín J. Lavaisse, Pedro Zenteno, Manuel Leiva, Ruperto Godoy, Salustiano Zavalía, Delfín Huergo, Ruperto Pérez, Juan Francisco Seguí, Domingo Faustino Sarmiento, José de la Quintana, Manuel Padilla, Regis Martínez, Agustín Delgado.

CU DPU IU MB MH NcD NcU NjP NNC
NSyU RPB

See also entries 78, 79, 85, 91, 94, 96, 103, 104, 110, 112, 115, 116, 121, 127, 129, 141, 142, 143, 145, 145a, 153, 165, 172, 176, 177, 183, 185, 195, 212, 216, 227, 228, 234, 236, 245, 246, 277, 278, 927.

HISTORY--DICTIONARIES, ENCYCLOPEDIAS, and "WHO'S WHO"

635 Marrazzo, Javier. Nuevo diccionario geográfico histórico de la República Argentina. Buenos Aires: R. Radaelli, 1921. 550 p. 27 cm.
Geographical and historical dictionary of Argentina featuring brief biographies of prominent citizens throughout history.

DLC IaU ICU IU LNHT MB MH-G MoU
NcU NcD NN OC1

636 Monte Domecq, F., comp. Quién es quién en el Río de la Plata; histórico. Buenos Aires, 1958. 392 p. (V. 1). Portraits. 24 cm.
A "who's who" of Argentina including business and commerce and industrial information as well as biographical data of prominent individuals of the time.

TxU

637 Piccirilli, Ricardo; Francisco L. Romay; and Leoncio Gianello, comps. Diccionario histórico argentino. Buenos Aires: Ediciones Históricas Argentinas, 1953-54. 6 v. 24 cm.
Historical dictionary of Argentina with biographical material of outstanding individuals primarily from the period 1810-1910.

CaBVaU CaOTP CSt CU DLC FMU FU ICU
IU LU NcD NcU NN OU TxU ViU WaU

638 Sánchez Gacio, Héctor E. Diccionario de historia argentina. Buenos Aires: Instituto Rioplatense de Ciencias, Letras, y Artes (IRCLA), 1972. 143 p. 18 cm. (Colección La patria toda. V. 7).

A dictionary of Argentine history, including biographical information for approximately 200 prominent Argentines representing all time periods and walks of life.

CU IU MU TxU

639 Sanguaio, Osvaldo. Diccionario político. (Ministros). Buenos Aires: Editorial Platero, 1980. 96 p. 18 cm.
A dictionary of 19th- and 20th-century Argentine men of history, government, and politics (approximately 450 names). Sketches include brief biographical information, such as dates and places of birth and death and professional positions held. Alphabetical arrangement.

IU

640 Trelles, Manuel Ricardo. Revista patriótica del pasado argentino. Buenos Aires: Imp. Europea, 1888-1892. 5 v. 26 cm.
A work featuring a "Diccionario de Apuntamientos," A-S, giving biographical data on many people associated with the River Plate republics, most of them Argentines, covering the 16th to the 19th centuries. More extensive biographies are included for the following: Juan Cayetano Fernández de Agüero, Nuño Fernández Lobo, Ignacio Fernández de Agüero, Amador Fernández de Agüero, Tomás Faulkner, Pedro Andrés García, Juan de Garay, Pedro Montenegro, Juan Díaz de Solís, Juan Ortiz de Zárate, Juan de Torres de Vera y Aragón, Francisco Trelles, Antonio de Alurralde.

InU IU MH MiU NmLcU TxU

641 Wright, Ione Stuessy, and Lisa M. Nekhom. Historical Dictionary of Argentina. By Ione Wright and Lisa M. Nekhom. Metuchen: Scarecrow Press, 1978. 1113 p. 23 cm. (Latin American historical dictionaries. V. 17).
Historical dictionary of Argentina with biographical sketches of prominent individuals from all time periods.

IU

See also entry 900.

INDUSTRY

642 Nicolau, Juan Carlos. Antecedentes para la historia de la industria argentina. Buenos Aires: Talleres Gráficos Lumen, 1968. 192 p. 20 cm.
A history of Argentine industry, covering the period from colonial times through the 19th century. Scattered biographical information is given for many prominent people associated with this aspect of Argentina's history.

AzU CLSU CLU CoU CSt CtY CU FU
IaU ICU IEN IU KU MB MH MiU MoSW
MU NBuU NcD NcU NIC NjP NN NNC
NSyU OU PPiU PPULC TxU WU

JOURNALISM

643 Fernández, Juan Rómulo. <u>Historia del perio-</u>
<u>dismo argentino</u>. (Dibujos de Busquets y de
otros). Buenos Aires: Librería Perlado, 1943.
405 p. Portraits. 28 cm.

A historical account of journalism in Argentina. Includes scattered biographical information throughout, mostly accompanied by
portraits. The following journalists are particularly featured: Juan María Gutiérrez,
Ricardo Gutiérrez, Eduardo Gutiérrez, Juan
Cruz Varela, Florencio Varela, Héctor Florencio Varela, Mariano Varela, Luis V. Varela,
José C. Paz, Justo S. López de Gomara, José
R. Lence.

    CSt ICU IU MiU NcD NcU NN OCU OU
    PSt PU ViU

644 Galván Moreno, C. <u>El periodismo argentino</u>.
Buenos Aires: Editorial Claridad, 1944.
520 p. Portraits. 21 cm. (Biblioteca de
escritores argentinos, obras de autores clásicos y contemporáneos).

A history of Argentine newspaper journalism, covering the period from its origins in
the 16th century to the 1940s. Biographical
information, as well as portraits in a few
cases, given for many notable journalists.
The following are particularly featured: Antonio Cabello y Mesa, Juan Hipólito Vieytes,
Pedro Antonio Cerviño, Manuel Belgrano, Mariano Moreno, Francisco de Paula Castañeda,
Pedro de Angelis, Pedro Feliciano Cavia, Juan
Cruz Varela, Florencio Varela, Salvador María
del Carril, Manuel Antonio Castro, Julián Segundo Agüero, Domingo Faustino Sarmiento,
Bartolomé Mitre, Juan María Gutiérrez, Antonio
Zinny, Manuel Láinez, José Manuel Estrada,
Manuel Ricardo Trelles, Paul Groussac, Manuel
de Eyzaguirre, Estanislao S. Zeballos, Eleodoro Lobos, Juan B. Justo, Juan Crisóstomo
Lafinur, Juan Gualberto Godoy. Alphabetical
index of names.

    CSt DLC DPU FU MH NcD NcU NIC OcU
    PSt PU TxU ViU

644a Llano, Francisco Luis. <u>La aventura del perio-</u>
<u>dismo</u>. Buenos Aires: A. Peña Lillo Editor,
1978. 201 p. Portraits. 20 cm.

An essay about journalism in Argentina including biographical data on many individuals
associated with it. The following are emphasized: Roberto Talice, Helvio Botana (Poroto,
pseud.), Carlos de la Púa, Edmundo Guibourg,
Natalio Botana, José W. Agusti, José Barcia,
Luis Batlle Berres, Roberto Noble. Also biographical data about the author.

    IU

645 Talice, Roberto A. <u>100,000 [i.e. Cien mil]</u>
<u>ejemplares por hora</u>: memorias de un redactor
de Crítica, el diario de Botana. Buenos Aires:
Corregidor, 1977. 544 p. 20 cm. (Biblioteca
de Buenos Aires).

A collection of reminiscences and memoirs
by Roberto A. Talice, a journalist associated
with the newspaper <u>Crítica</u> of Buenos Aires.
Includes biographical data on its director
Natalicio Félix Botana and contains references
of many other people who were active in the
journalistic and political life of Buenos
Aires in the last decades. The following are
particularly featured: Santiago Lareu, Juan
B. A. Reyes, Luis Diéguez, Cipriano Arrué,
Alberto Cordone, Aniceto Martínez, Enrique
Gustavino, Gustavo Germán González (Gegegé,
pseud.), Poroto Botana, Tito Botana, Pablo
Suero, Memé Botana.

    AzTeS

<u>See also</u> entry 235.

LAW

646 Cutolo, Vicente Osvaldo. <u>Abogados criollos</u>
<u>en el Buenos Aires del 1600</u>. Santa Fe, 1950.
58 p. 24 cm.

An essay about native lawyers in Buenos
Aires in 1600, with biographical notes on the
following: Francisco Bermúdez de Pedraza,
Gerónimo Castillo de Bovadilla, Fernando de la
Horta, Gabriel Sánchez de Ojeda, Antonio Ro-
sillo, Pedro de Ovando y Zárate, Diego Fernán-
dez de Andrada, José de Fuensalida Meneses,
Diego Molina de Lasarte, Francisco Pérez, Lá-
zaro de Zuleta y Xirón, Luis de Azpeitía,
Juan de Escobar y Carrillo, Diego de Ribera y
Maldonado, Luis Alemán de Avilés, Juan Bernardo
de la Cueva y Benavidez, Salvador Agreda de
Vergara, Antonio Rodríguez de León Pinelo.

    DLC IU MH-L NN

647 Lanfranco, Héctor Pedro. <u>Glosadores eminentes</u>
<u>de la Constitución</u> (conferencia pronunciada en
el Instituto Popular de Conferencias de <u>La</u>
<u>Prensa</u>, el 15 de setiembre de 1941). Buenos
Aires, 1945. 37 p. 24 cm.

A collection of biographical sketches of
the following notable Argentineans associated
with constitutional law: Guillermo Rawson,
Félix Frías, José Manuel Estrada, Joaquín V.
González, José Nicolás Matienzo.

    DLC

648 Marcó, Miguel Angel de. <u>Abogados del antiguo</u>
<u>Rosario</u>. Rosario: Ediciones Facultad Cató-
lica de Humanidades, 1966. 31 p. Portraits.
23 cm. (Ediciones de la Facultad Católica de
Humanidades de Rosario. V. 1).

Collection of biographical sketches about
the following notable 19th-century lawyers
from the Argentine city of Rosario: Severo
González, Avelino Ferreira, Melquíades Selva,
Eugenio Pérez, Evaristo Carriego, Agustín
Matienzo, Emeterio C. Regunaga, Juan Francisco
Monguillot, Pedro Rueda, Antonio Tarnassi,
Desiderio Rosas, José Severo Olmos, Lucas Gon-
zalez, Manuel Lucero.

    IU MH-L

LAW

649 _____. Abogados, escribanos, y obras de derecho en el Rosario del siglo XIX. Rosario: Facultad de Derecho y Ciencias Sociales, 1973. 180 p. 21 cm.

History of jurisprudence in Rosario, Argentina, with biographical information including dates, educational background, and legal careers of the following individuals from the 19th and 20th centuries: Severo González, Avelino Ferreira, Melquíades Selva, Eugenia Pérez, Evaristo Carriego, Agustín Matienzo, Emeteris C. Regunaga, Juan Francisco Monguillot, Pedro Rueda, Antonio Tarnassi, Desiderio Rosas, José Severo Olmos, Lucas González, Manuel Lucero, Luis María Arzac, Manuel Rogelio Tristany, José Olegario Machado, Pablo Julio Rodríguez, José Benito Graña, Juan del Campillo, Gerónimo del Barco.

IU

649a Oddo, Vicente. Abogados de Santiago del Estero durante el primer siglo de existencia de la ciudad (1553-1653). Santiago del Estero: Editorial Herca, 1981. 253 p. 23 cm.

Biographical essays of the following licenciados who lived in the Argentine city of Santiago del Estero during its first century (1553-1653): Juan de Herrera, Jerónimo de Bustamante, Juan Matienzo de Peralta, Hernando de Lerma y Valladares, Juan Bautista de Mena, Diego Fernández de Andrada, Antonio Rosillo, Gabriel Sánchez de Ojeda, José de Fuensalida y Meneses, Luis de Azpeitia, Luis del Peso Morales, Francisco de Alfaro, Juan Darío. Biographical sketches of varying amounts of Hernando Gomar, Hernando Díaz, Francisco Pérez de Herrera, Martín del Barco Centenera, Francisco de Salcedo, Diego Pedrero de Trejo, Juan Romero, Pedro Farfán, Manuel de Acosta, Juan de Ocampo, Jaramillo, Pedro de Oñate, Julián T. de Cortázar, Pedro Chávez del Sueldo, Fernando Francisco de Rivadeneira, Matías Delgado Flores, Juan Ruiz de Longa, Francisco Rodríguez Guido, Pedro de Carranza, Francisco Vaz de Rosende, Gregorio Martínez Ternero, Juan Martínez Baz, Isidro Juárez Babiano, Pedro de Gastanaza, Antonio Pérez de Salazar, Tomás de Torres, Sebastián Rodríguez de Ruescas, Juan Estevez Galindo, Diego Fernández Frías, Diego de Herrera, Gaspar de Villarroel, Andrés de Guzmán, Antonio de Ulloa, Melchor Maldonado de Saavedra, Adrián Cornejo, Juan Carrizo Mercadillo, Pedro Carmenatiz Jover, Luis de Molina, Parraguez, Cosme del Campo, Gaspar Alvarez de Monroy, Gregorio Suárez Cordero, Damián Carrillo, Pedro Benegas de Toledo, Miguel Gaona y Carrizo.

IU

650 Silva Riestra, Juan. Académicos de derecho y hombres de gobierno. Prólogo por Jorge M. Mayer. Buenos Aires: Distribuidor Abeledo-Perrot, 1969. 462 p. 23 cm. (Biblioteca de la Academia Nacional de Derecho y Ciencias Sociales de Buenos Aires. Serie 2: obras. V. 5).

Collection of biographical essays on the following notable Argentine lawyers: Roque Sáenz Peña, Osvaldo Magnasco, Luis María Drago, Manuel Quintana, Victorino de la Plaza, Carlos Octavio Bunge, Vicente C. Gallo, Adolfo Bioy, Clodomiro Zavalía, Bartolomé Mitre, Domingo Faustino Sarmiento, Mariano Moreno, Juan José Castelli, Manuel Belgrano, Juan José Paso, Guillermo Brown, Genaro Berón de Astrada, Lucio V. Mansilla, Juan Madariaga, Julio A. Roca, Mamerto Esquiú, Miguel de Andrea. Alphabetical index of names.

CLSU CSt FU IU MH NcD NcU NN TxU

LIBRARY SCIENCE

651 Fúrlong Cárdiff, Guillermo Juan. Bibliotecas argentinas durante la dominación hispánica. Discurso, a guisa de introducción, por José Torre Revello. Buenos Aires: Editorial Huarpes, 1944. 180 p. 23 cm. (Cultura colonial argentina. V. 1).

A history of libraries in Argentina during the colonial period, including very brief scattered biographical information for many people associated with this aspect of Argentina's history.

DLC FU IaU ICN ICU IU LU MH MiU-C
MnU MU NIC NNC OU TxU ViU

LIBRARY SCIENCE--DICTIONARIES, ENCYCLOPEDIAS, and "WHO'S WHO"

652 Matijevic, Nicolás. Quién es quién en la bibliotecología argentina. Bahía Blanca: Centro de Documentación Bibliotecológica, Universidad Nacional del Sur, 1965. 157 p. 26 cm.

A "who's who" for librarians in Argentina in 1965. Information provided includes dates, educational background, and professional achievements for María I. Ader, Raúl G. Aguirre, Jorge A. Alcorta, Dora E. Alende, Sara J. Ali Jafella, Martha E. Andueza de Benítez, Catalina R. Antelo de Husson, María del Carmen Aravena López de Granillo F., Argentina Armatti de Bove, Ofelia Avancini de Potenza, Carlos A. Ayarragaray, Ruth S. Baili de Murphy, Graciela T. Barbeito, Alicia M. Barreiro, Abilio Bassets, Horacio J. Becco, Omar L. Benítez, Guillermo M. Berazategui, Luisa E. Berretta, Jorge L. Borges, Eva Borkowska de Mikusinski, Domingo J. Buonocore, Josefa Cacciolo, Rogelio Calabrese, Mario N. Caramia, Raúl L. Cardon, Miguel P. Carrol, Julieta M. J. Casañas de Peyrano, Hildegard R. Cejka, Ercilia F. Chana de Navarro, Edith R. Chazarreta, Elisabeth Cigankova, Raúl C. Cisneros Malbrán, José E. Clemente, Alfredo Console, Augusto R. Cortazar, Juan Cortés del Pino, Roberto J. C. Couture de Troismonts, María del Carmen Crespi, Lilia E. Degiovanni, María Delfino, Renato De Luca, María J. Devecchi Cordoba, Manuel L. Díaz Etchevehere,

Demetrio Dimitroff, Laudelina Domínguez de Sampayo, Olga Dreyer Zunino, Isaac Efron, Rubi A. Escende de Vujacich, Helena del Carmen Espinosa Centeno, Alfredo Estévez, Angel Fernández, María J. Fernández de Loureiro, Stella Maris Fernández de Vidal, José F. Fino, Susana Franchini, Emilia Gagarin, Elsa M. Galeotti, Antonio S. Gallardo Valdez, Héctor Ganduglia, Germán García, Araceli M. García Acosta, Laureano García Elorrio, Araceli García Ugaldevere, Abel R. Geoghegan, Ernesto G. Gietz, Ricardo A. Gietz, Carlos Alberto Giuffra, Guillermo R. Gordónez, Hans G. Gravenhorst, Horacio H. Hernández, Luis A. Hourcade, Roberto David Juarroz, Nélida Kahan, María J. Klein de Villamayor, Carnetta Kramer, Enrique Kreibohm, Guillermo J. Kreibohm, Emma Linares de Los Santos, Norma E. Link, Ricardo J. Lois, Raúl O. López, Amalia R. Lore, Eduardo Lozano, Miguel A. Lucero G., Silvia E. N. Lucero, Nodier Lucero, Carlos G. Maier, Alice Manini, Nydia E. Margenat, Betty B. Margulis, Isidoro C. Martínez, José M. Martínez, Laura Martínez, María I. Martínez de Dimitroff, María C. Marzano de Pérez Baratcabal, José M. Massini Ezcurra, Nicolás Matijevic, Ricardo J. Miliano, Flora Miller, Marta Molteni, María E. Montero, Marta I. Montes de Oca, María E. Morales Torres, María A. Morra Ferrer, Ana E. Mühsam, Elda T. Nocetti de Maggipinto, Julio Novillo Corvalán, Agustín A. Olmedo, Elena J. Orden, María L. A. Ordóñez Carasa, Raúl A. Palacios, Evanthea C. Paraskeva de Curti, Pablo D. Parodi, Martha S. Parra de Pérez Alen, Carlos V. Penna, Juan C. Pena, Atilio Peralta, Juan M. Peralta Pino, Luciano C. Pesacq, Alicia Peycere de Couture de Troismonts, Atanasio C. Pimenides, Ana M. Platero Prola, Alberto S. Querejeta, Pascual M. Racca, Raúl Ramella, Ernesto Reguera Sierra, Lydia H. Revello, Helvia N. Rigamonti de Funes, Julia L. Ríos, Nicolás A. Rivero, Matilde Robino de Garaggioli, Carlos M. Rodríguez Ibáñez, Amira H. Romero, Nicolás Rosa Laubenheimer, Estela E. Rossi, Iris Rossi, Nelly Y. Rossi Etchelouz, J. Enrique Rothe, Ana Rouce de Coudannes, Jorge L. Rouges, Rubén I. Ruarte, Emilio R. Ruiz, J. Eleonor Ruiz de Lois, Josefa E. Sabor, Graciela B. Salas, Nazareth Salibian, Nilda R. Sandes, Susana E. Santos Gómez, Raquel E. Scala de Viniegra, Silia Schujman de Kovarasky, Francisco Scibona, Edgardo A. Scotti, Nilo Sidero, Iván G. Simko, Apolinario Sosa, Enrique Sparn, Reinaldo J. Suárez, Rodolfo A. Tannchen, Aurelio Tanodi, Beatriz E. Tavano, Miguel L. Toman, Ilse Trein de Maubach, Natividad C. Trigueros, Nilda Urrutia, Enrique Ricardo del Valle, Elena O. Vega, Elvira Vergara, Juan Vernazza, Olga E. Veronelli, Edelmira R. Vigil Howe, Angel Vilanova, Tycho D. A. Weber, José S. Wiernes, Sada J. Zalba, Alcira Zavala de Beney, Enrique Zuleta Alvarez, Clara R. Zwanck de Villegas.

CaBVaU   CU   DLC   DPU   FTaSU   ICU   IU
OClW   TxU

653   Adet, Walter, comp. <u>Cuatro siglos de literatura salteña</u>, desde la fundación a nuestros días, 1582-1981. Salta: Ediciones Tobogán, 1981. 291 p. 22 cm.

An enlarged edition of the work published in 1973 under the title <u>Poetas y prosistas salteños</u>. (<u>See</u> entry 654.) In addition to the writers included in the 1973 edition, it features the following: Carlos F. Agüero, Fernando R. Figueroa, Luiz Azán Arteaga, Andrés Rodolfo Villalva, Celso Molina, César Díaz Peralta, Ramiro A. Peñalva, Francisco Zamora, César Antonio Alurralde, Mario Ernesto Villada, Teresa Leonardi Herrán, Ricardo "Serenata" Saavedra, Alberto Díez Gómez, Elva Rosa Arredondo, Juan Manuel Ovalle, Edmundo A. del Cerro, Luis Antonio Escribas, Víctor Hugo Escandell, Juan Ahuerna, Nelson Francisco Muloni, Marcelo Eduardo López Arias, Silvia Juárez, Isabel Ibarra, Juan A. Saavedra, Juan Carlos Ruiz, Gabriel Castilla, Héctor Aníbal Aguirre, Baltazar Dávalos, Rosa Machado, José Arnaldo Lobo, Graciela Gonta, Sergio Antonio Teseyra, Ana María Fernández, María Inés Dávalos, Luis Alvarez, Juan Marcos Cejas, David Antonio Sorich, Liliana del Carmen Bellone, Norberto Bonini, Gerardo Rosenstrauj, Raquel Adet, Jesús Ramón Vera, Marcelo Rafael Sutti, Estela Raquel Escudero, Gustavo Rubén Agüero.

IU

654   _____. <u>Poetas y prosistas salteños</u>, 1582-1973. Salta: Dirección de Cultura de la Provincia, 1973. 315 p. 19 cm.

An anthology of contemporary prose and poetry by authors from the Argentine province of Salta, including brief biobibliographical sketches of the following writers: Francisco Sánchez Solano, Felipe Fernández de Córdoba y Espinosa, Francisco Javier Fernández, Arcediano Juan Ignacio de Gorriti, Juan Ramón Múñoz Cabrera, Facundo Zuviría, Juana Manuela Gorriti, Micaela Calvimonte de Fowlis, José María Zuviría, Mariano Zorreguieta, José Arturo L. Dávalos, Juana Fowlis, José María Todd, Juan Güemes, José Francisco López, Joaquín Castellanos, Juan López, Moisés Numa Castellanos, Tomás Zapata, Bernardo Frías, María Torres Frías, Nicolás López Isasmendi, Carlos Ibarguren, Juan Carlos Dávalos, Francisco Centeno, Ernesto M. Aráoz, Miguel Solá, Carlos S. Cornejo, David Saravia Castro, Víctor Zambrano, Elena Avellaneda de González de Ayala, Emma Solá de Solá, Atilio Cornejo, Sara Solá de Castellanos, Carlos Serrey, Lola García de Cornejo, Calixto Linares Fowlis, José Hernán Figueroa Aráoz, Guillermo Usandivaras, Clara Saravia Linares de Arias, Armando Castillo, José María Gallo Mendoza, Juan Carlos García Santillán, Ciro Torres López, Miguel Angel Vergara, Tomás Yáñez, José Cirilo Sosa, Amadeo Rodolfo Sirolli, Arturo Peñalva, Julio Campero y Aráoz, Federico Gauffín, Ernesto Rodríguez

LITERATURE

Pérez, Hilda Emilia Postiglione, Moisés Zevi, Gerónimo Delgado Pérez, José María Mirau, José Palermo Riviello, Carlos M. Barbarán Alvarado, Ernesto Díaz Villalba, Aristóbulo Wayar, Carlos Gregorio Romero Sosa, Roberto García Pinto, Guillermo Villegas, José Solís Pizarro, Julio César Luzzatto, Julio Díaz Villalba, Néstor Saavedra, Augusto Raúl Cortazar, Carlos Cortez Ruiz de los Llanos, José Mohnblatt, Francisco Alvarez Leguizamón, Delia Mirtha Blanco, Elsa Castellanos Solá, Alberto Cajal, Gladys Lucero de Poma, Gustavo Leguizamón, José Fernández Molina, Manuel J. Castilla, Antonio Nella Castro, Jaime Dávalos, Raúl Aráoz Anzoátegui, María Angélica de la Paz Lezcano, Luis D'Jallad, Farat Sire Salim, Julio Ovejero Paz, Mercedes Clelia Sandoval, José Edmundo Clemente, Juana Yarad, Sara San Martín, Arturo L. Dávalos, Juan José Coll, Hernán Arancibia, Raica Dávalos, César Perdiguero, Julio César Ranea, Roberto Albeza, Carlos Matorras Cornejo, José Juan Botelli, Joaquín Morillo, Abel Mónico Saravia, Rosa G. de Gonorazky, José Ríos, Ervar Gallo Mendoza, Carlos Di Leandro, Antonio Vilariño, Julio Espinoza, Holver Martínez Borelli, Miguel Angel Pérez, Walter Adet, Jacobo Regen, Carlos Michaelsen Aráoz, Víctor Abán, Martín Adolfo Borelli, Carlos Hugo Aparicio, Benjamín Toro, Luis Andolfi, Ariel Petrocelli, Jorge Díaz Bavio, Sergio Rodríguez, Santiago E. Sylvester, José Brizzi, Miguel A. Carreras, Hugo Roberto Ovalle, José Gallardo, Carlos Edmundo Adet, Hugo Alarcón, Angel Zapata, Gregorio A. Caro, Leopoldo Castilla.

CtY NmU NN TxU ViU

655 Agon 20 [i.e. Veinte] en clave de magia. Buenos Aires: Ediciones Galea, 1978. 118 p. 20 cm.
A collection of short stories with a magico-fantastic theme in various degrees, by the following contemporary authors, including limited biographical data: Miguel Andrade, María de los Angeles Campos, Haydée Lili Canaletti, Miguel R. Canegalli, Juan Tomás Cánepa, Armando Díaz Colodrero, María Elena Dubecq, Teresa Carmen Freda, Alicia de la Fuente, Lisandro Gayoso, Alberto Gilardoni, José Guelerman, David Daniel Jovtis, Félix Alberto Lázaro, Magdalén Liddle, Julio Linares, Luis Mercandante, Alicia Régoli de Mullen, Elena Torres, Matilde Zimerman.

IU

656 Agon 22 [i.e. Veintidós] en clave de enigma. Buenos Aires: Ediciones Agón, 1981. 104 p. 19 cm.
An anthology of contemporary Argentine short stories, including biobibliographical sketches of the following authors featured in the text: María del Carmen Casco de Aguer, María de los Angeles Campos, Zaida de Castelán, Aída J. Nebbia de Codega, Armando Díaz Colodrero, María Elena Dubecq, Alicia de la Fuente,

Mónica Aída Furman, Alberto Gilardoni, Miguel A. Guelerman, Ismael Marcos Jiam, David Daniel Jovtis, Magdalen Liddle, Alicia Regoli de Mullen, Elsie Osorio, María Emilia Pérez, Lila Duffau de Rabaudi, Ana María Torres, Elena Torres, María Inés Ure, Alejandro von der Heyde Garrigós, Matilde Zimerman.

MU

657 Aguirre, Raúl Gustavo, comp. Antología de la poesía argentina. Buenos Aires: Ediciones Librerías Fausto, 1979. 3 v. 20 cm.
Anthology of Argentine poetry from 1604 to 1979 featuring biographical sketches of over 300 poets. Contents:
V. 1: 1604-1918.
V. 2: 1919-1930.
V. 3: 1931-present day. Alphabetical index of names.

IU

658 _____. Literatura argentina de vanguardia: el movimiento poesía Buenos Aires (1950-1960). Buenos Aires: Editorial Fraterna, 1979. 489 p. 23 cm.
A discussion, with examples, of various aspects of poetic avantguardism (1950-1960), with primary emphasis on Buenos Aires and from the point of view of various prominent authors of that period. Biobibliographical sketches are also given for the following Latin American poets (principally Argentine) of that era: Raúl Gustavo Aguirre, Rodolfo Alonso, Omar Rubén Aracama, Juan Carlos Aráoz, Carmelo Ardén Quin, Braulio Arenas, Elizabeth Azcona Cranwell, Juan-Jacobo Bajarlía, Edgar Bayley, Osmar Luis Bondoni, Miguel A. Brascó, Santiago Bullrich, Jorge Carrol, Emma de Cartosio, Ramiro de Casasbellas, Juan José Ceselli, Alfonso Cortés, Carlos Drummond de Andrade, Nicolás Espiro, Macedonio Fernández, Baldomero Fernández Moreno, Daniel Giribaldi, Oliverio Girondo, Hugo Gola, Ricardo Güiraldes, Alfredo Hlito, Natalio Hocsman, Vicente Huidobro, Leónidas C. Lamborghini, Carlos Latorre, Julio Antonio Llinás, Francisco José Madariaga, Jorge Enrique Móbili, Franco Mogni, Enrique Molina, Pablo Neruda, Juan L. Ortiz, Aldo Pellegrini, Flora Alejandra Pizarnik, Alberto Polat, Wolf Roitman, Jorge Souza, Osvaldo Svanascini, Mario Trejo, César Vallejo, Alberto Vanasco, Juan Antonio Vasco, Rubén Vela, Luis Yadarola, Emilio Zolezzi.

IU

659 Alba sonora. Buenos Aires: Plus Ultra, 1976. 108 p. 20 cm.
An anthology of contemporary Argentine poetry, including biobibliographical sketches of the following authors featured in the text: Jorge Antolini, José E. Peire, Ferdinando Ricci, Mario Strubbia, Beatriz Vallejos, Felipe Zeinstejer.

TxU

660 Alposta, Luis, comp. <u>Antología del soneto lunfardo</u>. Buenos Aires: Ediciones Corregidor, 1978. 222 p. 18 cm.

An anthology of Argentine poetry including biobibliographical sketches of the following writers featured in the text: Felipe H. Fernández (Yacaré, pseud.), Ricardo M. Llanes, Jorge Luis Borges, Alvaro Yunque, Nicolás Olivari, Enrique Dizeo, Enrique Cadícamo, Carlos De La Púa, Dante A. Linyera, Celedonio E. Flores, Iván Diez, Alberto Vacarezza, Bartolomé Rodolfo Aprile, Joaquín Gómez Bas, Amaro Villanueva, Santiago Ganduglia, Julián Centeya, León Benarós, Nyda Cuniberti, Jorge Melazza Muttoni, Federico Guillermo Pedrido, Fernando Guibert, Luis Ricardo Furlán, Alcídes Gandolfi Herrero, José Pagano, Juan Bautista Devoto, Héctor Negro, Juan Carlos La Madrid, Lily Franco, Daniel Giribaldi, José Alonso Delgado, Horacio Ferrer, Juan Carlos Andrade, Saramaría Duhart, Carlos A. Alberti, Darwin Sánchez, Héctor Chaponick, Enrique Otero Pizarro, Natalio Schmucler, Orlando Mario Punzi, Luis Alposta.

IU

661 <u>Antología consultada de la joven poesía argentina</u>. Prólogo de Héctor Yanover. Bibliografía de Horacio Jorge Becco. Buenos Aires: Fabril Editora, 1968. 238 p. 21 cm.

Anthology of Argentine poetry from the last half of the 20th century. Biobibliographical sketches of the following individuals contain dates, outstanding achievements, and a personal statement by the poet on his art: Rodolfo Alonso, Juan Gelman, Alejandra Pizarnik, Antonio Requeni, Horacio Salas, Alfredo Veirave, Oscar Hermes Villordo, María Elena Walsh.

CLU   FU   IaU   IU   KU   MH   NIC   OU   PPULC
WU

662 <u>Antología generacional</u>: poemas de Liliana Báez et al. La Plata: Ediciones "La Fábula de Piedra," 1965. 39 p. 20 cm.

An anthology of poetry of 20th-century Argentine authors. Short biobibliographical notes are also included for each poet. The following are featured: Liliana Báez, Osvaldo Ballina, José María Calderón Pando, Pablo Cantier, Enrique Dillon, Osvaldo Elliff, Omar Gancedo, Oscar Godoy, Jorge de Luján Gutiérrez, Néstor Mux, Rafael Felipe Oteriño, Horacio Ponce de León, Ernesto Solari.

CLSU   IU   KU   MB   NBuU   NcU   TxU

663 <u>Antología poética bonaerense</u>. La Plata: Fondo Editorial Bonaerense, 1977. 410 p. 19 cm.

An anthology of poetry by the following contemporary authors from the Province of Buenos Aires (Argentina) including brief biographical notes: Thelma de Aguirre, Nelly Alfonso, Raúl Amaral, Norberto Antonio, Julio Arístides, Pablo Atanasiu, Osvaldo Ballina,

Vicente Barbieri, Josefina de Barilari, Susana Boechat, César Bustos, María Celia Cailliait, César Emilio Cantoni, Horacio Castillo, Enrique Catani, Manuel Cazalla, Leonor Centeno, Francisco Mario Cintora, Néstor Amílcar Cipriano, Nicolás Cócaro, César Corte Carrillo, Patricia Herminia Coto, J. Ramón Couchet, Rafael Henzo D'Alessio, Enrique Alfredo Dillon, Ismael Dozo, Osvaldo Elliff, Myrta Nydia Escariz, Martha Faure Blum, María Cecilia Font, Lysandro Z. D. Galtier, Gustavo García Saravi, Blanca de Garibaldi, Delia González de Rapp, María Granata, Clara E. Grosso, Osvaldo Guglielmino, Susana Iturralde, Ricardo Juan Klala Domian, Cristina Angela Knoll de Ferenc, Angélica Beatriz Lacunza, Ana Emilia Lahitte, Abel Osvaldo Lema, Oscar Abel Ligaluppi, Francisco López Merino, Oscar Luciani, Néstor D. Malbrán, Pedro César Malvigne, Deidamia Martín, Ernesto D. Marrone, Juan Carlos Mena, María Imelda Micucci, Fulvio Milano, Atilio Milanta, Néstor Mux, Héctor Negri, Horacio Núñez West, Rafael Felipe Oteriño, Federico Peltzer, Nélida Pessagno, Alberto Ponce de León, Horacio Ponce de León, Mario Porro, Narciso Pousa, Edna Pozzi, Héctor Prado, Horacio Preler, Juan Octavio Prenz, Horacio Esteban Ratti, Elba Ricciardi de Cerrudo, Héctor Rico, Gregorio Robertazzi, Abel Robino, Raquel Sajón de Cuello, Azucena Rosa Salpeter, Ana Sampol de Herrero, Silvia Nora Sciommarella, Marta Schofs de Maggi, Lucrecia Amelia Silva Noseda, Norberto Silvetti Paz, Ismael Marcelo Siri, Roberto Themis Speroni, Matilde Alba Swann, Horacio Urbanski, Amelia Urrutibeheity, Luis Horacio Velázquez, Aurora Venturini, Mario Verandi, Alfredo Villata, Antonio Viviano Hidalgo. (<u>See also</u> entry 781.)

IU

664 Aragón, Roque Raúl. <u>La poesía religiosa argentina</u>. Buenos Aires: Ediciones Culturales Argentinas, 1967. 142 p. 20 cm.

An anthology of Argentine religious poetry, including brief biobibliographical data on the following poets: Luis José de Tejeda y Guzmán, Pantaleón Rivarola, Juan Gualberto Godoy, Esteban Echeverría, José Agustín Molina, Ventura de la Vega, Florencio Balcarce, José Rivera Indarte, José Mármol, Carlos Guido y Spano, Estanislao del Campo, Ricardo Gutiérrez, Martín Coronado, Jorge Mitre, Martín García Merou, Daniel García Mantilla, Angel de Estrada, Gervasio Méndez, Luis Nicolás Palma, Moisés Numa Castellanos, José Hernández, Leopoldo Lugones, Enrique Banchs, Baldomero Fernández Moreno, Ricardo Güiraldes, Juan Carlos Dávalos, Tobías Garzón, Manuel Lizondo Borda, Sara Solá de Castellanos, Delfina Bunge de Gálvez, Sara Montes de Oca de Cárdenas, Pedro Miguel Obligado, Carlos Obligado, Alfredo R. Bufano, Horacio Caillet Bois, Susana Calandrelli, Dimas Antuña, Eduardo Keller Sarmiento, Jacobo Fijman, Antonio Vallejo, Leonardo Castellani, Francisco Luis Bernárdez, Leopoldo Marechal, Juan Oscar Ponferrada, Alberto Franco, Rafael Jijena Sánchez,

LITERATURE

José Ramón Luna, Isabel Farías Gómez, Emma Solá de Solá, Salvador Santore, Enrique Viana, Raúl Artieda, Ricardo E. Molinari, Eduardo González Lanuza, Ignacio Braulio Anzoategui, Osvaldo Horacio Dondo, Lisardo Zia, Julio Pablo Fingerit, Margarita Abella Caprile, Enrique Lavie, Lysandro Z. O. Galtier, Luis Gorosito Heredia, Ulyses Petit de Murat, Mario José Petit de Murat, Nydia Lamarque, Miguel Angel Etcheverrigaray, Vicente Barbieri, Omar Viñole, Raúl Entraigas, José Soler Darás, Marcos Fingerit, Luis de Paola, Carlos Marfani, Bruno Jacovella, José María de Estrada, Miguel Angel Gómez, Alfonso Solá González, Carlos Alberto Disandro, José María Castineiras de Dios, Helvio C. Botana, Clemente Ruppel, Domingo Renaudière de Paulis, Rodolfo Juan Charchaflié, Miguel D. Etchebarne, Augusto Falciola, Raúl Galán, César Corte Carrillo, Jorge Calvetti, María Elena Walsh, Alberto Girri, Emilio Sosa López, Carlos Greiben, Oscar Hermes Villordo, Carlos Luis Wagenfhürer, Héctor Pedro Soulé Tonelli, Bernardo Ranalletti.

CaQmm CSt CtHC CtY CU FU IU IaU
MH MdU NcU NSyU OU

665 Arrieta, Rafael Alberto. Historia de la literatura argentina. Buenos Aires: Ediciones Peuser, 1958-60. 6 v. Portraits. 24 cm.
A history and criticism of Argentine literature (16th century-1950) including many portraits and biobibliographical information on hundreds of writers. Alphabetical index of names in V. 6.

CaBVaU CLSU ICU IU KU MH MiU MoSW
MoU NcD NcU NIC OU TxHR TxU ViU

666 Así escriben los argentinos. Abelardo Arias et al. Prólogo y notas, Haydée M. Jofre Barroso. Buenos Aires: Ediciones Orión, 1975. 279 p. 20 cm. (Colección Así escriben).
A collection of short stories including brief biographical sketches of the following Argentine prose writers of the 20th century: Abelardo Arias, José Blanco, Adolfo Bioy Casares, Poldy Bird, Jorge Luis Borges, Haroldo Conti, Marco Denevi, Antonio Di Benedetto, Marta Lynch, Manuel Mujica Laínez, Silvina Ocampo, María Rosa Oliver, Elvira Orphée, Ernesto Sábato.

FMU IU NmU TU TxHR WU

667 Badano, Alcira. Los prosistas del 80; antología. Buenos Aires: Colihue/Hachette, 1980. 138 p. 18 cm.
A collection of prose selections written in the 1880s by the following Argentinean authors, including biographical sketches: Lucio V. Mansilla, Eduardo Wilde, Lucio V. López, José S. Alvarez (Fray Mocho, pseud.), Joaquín V. González, José M. Estrada.

IU

668 Bajarlía, Juan Jacobo, comp. Cuentos de crimen y misterio. Buenos Aires: J. Alvarez, 1964. 287 p. 18 cm.
A collection of Argentine mystery short stories preceded by brief biobibliographical sketches of the authors. They are Enrique Anderson Imbert, Adolfo Bioy Casares, Jorge Luis Borges, María Angélica Bosco, Bustos Domecq, Leonardo Castellani, César Dabove, Marco Denevi, Max Duplán, Alfonso Ferrari Amores, Abel Mateo, Adolfo L. Pérez Zelaschi, Manuel Peyrou, Syria Poletti, Rodolfo J. Walsh, Donald A. Yates, Juan Jacobo Bajarlía.

CLSU CLU CSt CtY GEU ICU InU IU
KU LNHT MdBJ MH MiU MoSW NbU NcU
NIC NjR NN NNC NSyU OkU OU PSt
TNJ TxU UU WU

669 Barreda, Ernesto Mario. Nuestro parnaso, colección de poesías argentinas. Buenos Aires: J. L. Dasso & Cía., 1914. 4 v. 22 cm.
An anthology of Argentine poetry including biographical sketches of the poets featured. Those included:
V. 1: Juan Baltasar Maziel, Manuel José de Labardén, Pantaleón Rivarola, Cayetano Rodríguez, Vicente López y Planes, Domingo de Azcuénaga, Esteban de Luca y Patrón, José Agustín Molina, Juan de la Cruz Varela, Florencio Balcarce, Ventura de la Vega, Juan Crisóstomo Lafinur, Juan María Gutiérrez, Florencio Varela, Juan Gualberto Godoy, Luis L. Domínguez, Claudio Mamerto Cuenca, José Mármol, Esteban Echeverría.
V. 2: Carlos Guido Spano, Hilario Ascasubi, José Rivera Indarte, Bartolomé Mitre, Juan Chassaing, Ricardo Gutiérrez, Estanislao del Campo, José Hernández, Carlos Encina, Gervasio Méndez, Martín Coronado, Calixto Oyuela, Rafael Obligado, Olegario Víctor Andrade.
V. 3: Pedro Bonifacio Palacios (Almafuerte), Leopoldo Díaz, Joaquín Castellanos, Martín García Mérou, Domingo Martinto, Moisés Numa Castellanos, Diego Fernández Espiro, Belisario Roldán, Guillermo Stock, Manuel Ugarte, Alberto Ghiraldo, Angel de Estrada, Pedro J. Naón, Carlos Ortiz, Francisco Aníbal Riú, Eugenio Díaz Romero, José María Quevedo, Oscar Tiberio, Leopoldo Lugones.
V. 4: Mario Bravo, Ricardo Rojas, Federico A. Gutiérrez, Arturo Giménez Pastor, Manuel Gálvez, Evar Méndez, Juan Aymerich, José de Maturana, Tomás Allende Iragorri, Carlos Alberto Leumann, Doelia Miguez, Alfredo Arteaga, Gustavo Caraballo, Delfina Mitre y Vedia de Bastianini, Rafael Alberto Arrieta, Luis González Calderón, Luis María Jordán, Domingo Robatto, Arturo Capdevila, Luis Fernández de la Puente, Enrique Banchs, Ernesto Mario Barreda, Evaristo Carriego.

AU CU CtY DLC LU NIC IU NSyU NcD
ODW

670 Becco, Horacio Jorge, comp. Cuentistas argentinos. Buenos Aires: Ediciones Culturales

Argentinas, Ministerio de Educación y Justicia, Dirección General de Cultura, 1961. 381 p. 20 cm. (Biblioteca del sesquicentinario. Colección antologías).

An anthology of Argentine short stories, including biobibliographical sketches about the following writers featured in the text: Roberto J. Payró, Juan Pablo Echagüe, Horacio Quiroga, Atilio Chiáppori, Mateo Booz, Alberto Gerchunoff, Benito Lynch, Ricardo Güiraldes, Juan Carlos Dávalos, Guillermo Guerrero Estrella, Arturo Cancela, Roberto Mariani, Justo P. Sáenz, Héctor Eandi, Ezequiel Martínez Estrada, Pablo Rojas Paz, Luis Gudiño Kramer, Enrique Méndez Calzada, Conrado Nalé Roxlo, Jorge Luis Borges, Roberto Arlt, Nicolás Olivari, Enrique González Tuñón, Leónidas Barletta, Lobodón Garra, Manuel Peyrou, Carmen Gándara, Eduardo Mallea, Silvina Ocampo, Augusto Mario Delfino, Enrique Anderson Imbert, Adolfo Bioy Casares.

DLC   IU   NN

671 _____, and Osvaldo Svanascini, comps. Diez poetas jóvenes: ensayo sobre moderna poética, antología, y ubicación objetiva de la poesía joven desde 1937 a 1947. Prólogo de Guillermo de Torre. Buenos Aires: Editorial Ollantay, 1948. 195 p. Portraits. 21 cm. (Colección "Raíz de sueño." V. 2).

An anthology of contemporary Argentine poetry (1937-1947), including brief biobibliographical sketches of the following writers: Horacio Jorge Becco, Fernando Birri, Alberto Claudio Blasetti, Miguel A. Brascó, Mario Briglia, Tomás Enrique Briglia, Alberto Girri, Ernesto B. Rodríguez, Marcelino R. Sussini, Osvaldo Svanascini.

AzU   DLC   FMU   MoU   PPULC   PU   ScU   TU   TxU

672 _____, comp. Poetas argentinos contemporáneos. Buenos Aires: Extensión Cultural Dos Muñecos, 1974. 123 p. 20 cm.

An anthology of contemporary Argentine poetry, including biobibliographical sketches of the following authors featured in the text: Raúl Gustavo Aguirre, Rodolfo Alonso, Edgar Bayley, Alberto Claudio Blasetti, Juan José Ceselli, César Fernández Moreno, Luisa Futoransky, Juan Gelman, Alberto Girri, Roberto Juarroz, Carlos Latorre, Francisco Madariaga, Enrique Molina, Olga Orozco, Aldo Pellegrini, Alejandra Pizarnik, Osvaldo Svanascini, Mario Trejo, Basilio Uribe, Francisco Urondo, Alberto Vanasco.

CFS   CoFS   CtY   CU-S   FMU   FTaSU   FU   IaU   InU   KMK   KU   LNHT   MH   MnU   NBuU   NcD   NcU   NIC   NJP   NmU   NN   NNC   NNU   NSbSU   OU   PPT   PSt   TU   WU

673 Beltrán, Oscar Rafael. Los orígenes del teatro argentino. Portada en colores e ilustraciones a pluma de Juan Hohmann. Buenos Aires:

Editorial Luján, 1934. 158 p. Portraits. 19 cm.

A history of Argentine theater, covering the period from colonial times through the 19th century, and including scattered biographical information for many prominent authors of this genre. The following are particularly featured: Francisco de Paula Castañeda, Juan Bautista Alberdi, Eduardo Gutiérrez.

AzU   CU   DLC   FU   MiD   NBC   NBuU   NcD   NcU   OCU   OO   OOxM   PPULC   ViU   WaU

674 Berenguer Carisomo, Arturo, comp. Antología argentina contemporánea. Buenos Aires: Librería Huemul, 1970. 350 p. 19 cm.

Anthology of poetry and prose by Argentine writers belonging to the postmodernists and the generations of 1922 and 1940. Features biobibliographical sketches outlining the important dates and achievements of Enrique Banchs, Rafael Alberto Arrieta, Baldomero Fernández Moreno, Pedro Miguel Obligado, Alfonsina Storni, Ricardo Güiraldes, Luis Cané, Jorge Luis Borges, Horacio Rega Molina, José Pedroni, Francisco Luis Bernárdez, Ricardo E. Molinari, Vicente Barbieri, Mario Binetti, César Fernández Moreno, Enrique Larreta, Benito Lynch, Arturo Cancela, Juan Carlos Dávalos, Alberto Gerchunoff, Macedonio Fernández, Conrado Nalé Roxlo, Leopoldo Marechal, Eduardo Mallea, Marco Denevi, Silvina Bullrich, Julio Cortázar. Alphabetical index of names.

AzU   CLSU   CU-SB   GU   InU   IU   MB   MoSW   NIC   NSyU   OU   PPT   TxU   ViU   WU

675 _____. Teatro argentino contemporáneo. Madrid: Aguilar, 1960. 478 p. Portraits. 20 cm. (Teatro contemporáneo).

An anthology of contemporary Argentine theater, including portraits and short biobibliographical sketches for the authors whose works are included. They are Nicolás de las Llanderas, Arnaldo Malfatti, Conrado Naxlé Roxlo (Chamico, Alguien, pseuds.), Juan Oscar Ponferrada, José León Pagano, Pedro E. Pico, Samuel Eichelbaum. (See also entry 676.)

CoU   CU   IaU   InU   IU   LNHT   MoSW   NNC   NRU   OkU   OOxM   OU   PPULC   ScU   TU   TxU   WU

676 _____. Teatro argentino contemporáneo. 2. ed. Madrid: Aguilar, 1972. 480 p. Portraits. 20 cm. (Teatro contemporáneo).

Same as the 1960 ed. (See entry 675.)

CU   IU   NNC

677 Blanco Amores de Pagella, Angela, comp. Iniciadores del teatro argentino. Buenos Aires: Ediciones Culturales Argentinas: Ministerio de Cultura y Educación, 1972. 322 p. 19 cm. (Los Fundadores de la literatura argentina).

LITERATURE

An anthology of the works of several notable playwrights of the 18th and 19th centuries and accompanied by short biobibliographical sketches on each author. They include Manuel José de Lavardén, Juan Francisco Martínez, Manuel Belgrano (writer), Juan de la Cruz Varela, Luis Ambrosio Morante, José Manuel Sánchez, Bartolomé Hidalgo, Francisco de Paula Castañeda, José Mármol, Bartolomé Mitre, Juan Bautista Alberdi, Claudio Cuenca, Bernabé Demaría, Rosa Guerra, Pedro Echagüe, Ataliva Herrera, Miguel Ortega, Francisco Fernández. Also brief biographical data of the following 19th-century actors: Aurelio Casacuberta and Trinidad Guevara.

AzU CLSU CLU CSt CtY CU CU-S CU-SB
FU GU IaU InU IU LU MB MH MnU
MoSW MoU MU NbU NBuU NcD NcU NIC
NjR NmU NN NNC NSyU OO OU PPiU
PSt TxHR TxU ViU WU

678 Borges, Jorge Luis; Silvina Ocampo; and Adolfo Bioy Casares. Antología poética argentina. Buenos Aires: Editorial Sudamericana, 1941. 808 p. 21 cm. (Colección Laberinto).
An anthology of Argentine poetry (1900-1941), including brief biobibliographical sketches. Dates, places of birth and death, and publication dates are provided for the following poets and poetesses: Almafuerte (pseud.), Pedro B. Palacios, Leopoldo Lugones, Enrique Larreta, Ricardo Rojas, Enrique Banchs, Arturo Vázquez Cey, Rafael Alberto Arrieta, Marcelina del Mazo, Evaristo Carriego, Arturo Capdevila, Arturo Marasso, Alfonsina Storni, Fernández Moreno, Ricardo Güiraldes, Juan Carlos Dávalos, Juan Pedro Calou, Ezequiel Martínez Estrada, Amado Villar, Alvaro Melián Lafinur, Horacio Rega Molina, Margarita Abella Caprile, Pedro Miguel Obligado, Luis L. Franco, Brandán Caraffa, Miguel A. Camino, Enrique Méndez Calzada, Oliverio Girondo, Francisco Luis Bernárdez, González Carbalho, Carlos M. Grünberg, Conrado Nalé Roxlo, José Pedroni, Córdova Iturburu, Francisco López Merino, Adán C. Diehl, Fermín Estrella Gutiérrez, Nicolás Olivari, Eduardo González Lanuza, Roberto Ledesma, María Alicia Domínguez, Norah Lange, Carlos Vega, Carlos Mastronardi, Leopoldo Marechal, Raúl González Tuñón, Marcos Fingerit, César Tiempo, Ricardo E. Molinari, Horacio Schiavo, Emilia Bertolé, Augusto González Castro, Eduardo Keller, Ulyses Petit de Murat, María de Villarino, E. González Trillo, L. Ortiz Behety, Wally Zenner, Juan L. Ortiz, Roberto Godel, Ignacio B. Anzoátegui, Hortensia Margarita Raffo, Carlos Carlino, Elvira de Alvear, Gloria Alcorta, Silvina Ocampo, Juan G. Ferreyra Basso, César Fernández Moreno, Mario Binetti, Alejo González Garaño, Juan Bautista Bioy, Juan Rodolfo Wilcock.

AzU DLC FTaSU IEN IU MH NcU OClJC
OClW OCU OrCS OrU OU PPULC TU TxU
UPB

679 Bravo Figueroa, Gustavo, comp. Poetas de Tucumán, siglo XX. Tucumán: Ediciones Atenas, 1965. 153 p. 23 cm.
An anthology of Argentine poetry of the 20th century from the Argentine province of Tucumán, including biobibliographical sketches. Those featured:
1901-1940: Ricardo Jaimes Freyre, Mario Bravo, Luis Eulogio Castro, Ricardo Chirre Danós, Rafael Jijena Sánchez, Manuel Lizondo Borda, Juan Eduardo Piatelli, Teresa Ramos Carrión, Víctor Toledo Pimentel, Antonio Torres.
1941-1955: Raúl Galán, Manuel Aldonate, Julio Ardiles Gray, Omar Estrella, Eduardo Joubin Colombres, María Elvira Juárez, Guillermo Orce Remis, Nicandro Pereyra, Leda Valladores.
1956-present: Arturo Alvarez Sosa, Ariadna Chávez, Dora Fornaciari, Juan González, Juan José Hernández, David Lagmanovich, Tiburcio López Guzmán, Néstor Silva.

IU MU

680 _____. 27 [i.e. Veintisiete] cuentos del Norte Argentino. Tucumán: Editorial Atenas, 1972. 224 p. 18 cm.
An anthology of short stories by the following contemporary writers from the northern region of Argentina, including biobibliographical sketches: Jorge W. Abalos, Julio Aramburu, Julio Ardiles Gray, Juan J. Botelli, Carola Briones, Fausto Burgos, Bernardo Canal Feijoo, Manuel J. Castilla, Juan Carlos Dávalos, Francisco Ramón Díaz, Hugo R. Foguet, Luis Franco, Juan José Hernández, Alberto Córdoba, Daniel Ovejero, Miguel A. Pereyra, Alberto Pérez, Carlos B. Quiroga, Ricardo Rojas, Pablo Rojas Paz.

CaQMM CU-SB IU MB MoSW NNC OU WU

681 Bucich, Antonio Juan, and Fulvio Milano, comps. Indice poético boquense. Grabado de Víctor L. Rebuffo. Buenos Aires, 1963. 39 p. 20 cm. (Cuadernos de la Boca del Riachuelo. V. 8-9).
An anthology of 19th- and 20th-century poetry emanating from the Boca del Riachuelo area of Buenos Aires, and preceded by short biobibliographical notes on the authors whose works are represented. They are Juan L. Alemany Villa, Bartolomé Botto, Francisco Isernia, Roberto Mariani, Hernani Mandolini, Santiago Stagnero, Rafael Amato, Héctor Miguel Angeli, Clara I. Caffarena de Balestra, Antonio J. Bucich, Germán Candau Carrizo, Adolfo Casagrande, Roberto Cupido, Blanca de Garibaldi, Francisco Ghigliaza, Adolfo Likerman, Clemente Sancho Lozano, Ricardo M. Llanes, Fulvio Milano, Marcelo Olivari, Nene Padro, Francisco Juan Poliza, José Pugliese, José Rodríguez Itoiz, Santiago G. Sturla, Pedro Juan Vignale.

CLSU CLU CNoS CtY CU IU MH NIC
NN NSyU TxU WU

682 Capdevila, Arturo. Tiempos y poetas; cinco próceres del verso: Guido y Spano, Andrade, Obligado, Castellanos, Almafuerte, y un poeta de la acción: Alfredo L. Palacios. Buenos Aires: Editorial Clydoc, 1944. 292 p. 20 cm.
Collection of critical and biographical essays on the following notable Argentinean poets of the 19th and early 20th centuries: Carlos Guido y Spano, Olegario Víctor Andrade, Rafael Obligado, Joaquín Castellanos, Pedro Bonifacio Palacios (Almafuerte, pseud.), Alfredo Lorenzo Palacios.

DLC FMU FTaSU IaU IU LU NcU NjP TxU

683 Carilla, Emilio. Literatura argentina; palabra e imagen. Buenos Aires: Editorial Universitaria de Buenos Aires, 1969. 149 p. (V. 1). Portraits. 23 cm. (Colección Argentina).
A short anthology of colonial Argentine literature, accompanied by biographical essays, as well as some portraits, on the authors whose works are represented. They are Luis de Miranda de Villafaña, Rosas de Oquendo, Ruy Díaz de Guzmán, Reginaldo de Lizárraga, Luis de Tejeda, Alonso Carrió de la Vandera (Concolorcorvo, pseud.), Francisco Javier Iturri, Manuel José de Lavardén.

AAP AU CFIS CFS CLSU CLU CNoS CoFS CSt CtY CU-SB FMU FTaSU FU GU IaAS IaU ICU IEN IU KU LNHT MeU MH MiDW MiEM MNS MnU MWelC NBuU NbU NcD NcU NhU NIC NjP NjR NN NNC NSyU OkU OrU OU PPiU PPT RPB ScCleU TNJ TU TxDaM TxHR TxLT TxU UU ViU VtU WaU WU

683a Cattarossi Arana, Nelly. Literatura de Mendoza (Historia documentada desde sus orígenes a la actualidad) 1820-1980. Mendoza: Inca Editorial, 1982. 2 v. 26 cm.
A history of Argentine literature from the province of Mendoza (1820-1980) including biobibliographical sketches of the following authors:
V. 1: Emilio Antonio Abril, Darío Hugo Acevedo, J. Enrique Acevedo, Hortensia Acevedo de Grenci, Ibis Aguirre, Julio Leónidas Aguirre, Agustín Alvarez, Adela Alvarez Faur, Luis Alfonso Anmella, Rosa Antonietti Filippini, José Miguel Aranda Suárez, José Santiago Arango, Estela Beatriz Arenas, Abelardo Arias, Catalina Arias de Ronchietto, Carlos Alberto Arroyo, María B. Badui de Zogbi, José Baidal, Mario Ballario, Fernando Jorge Barcia Gigena, Juan Antonio Barrera, Julio Barrera Oro, Hilda Basulto, Marta Bertolini, Humberto Bertoni, Susana Bombal, Rodolfo A. Borello, Rodolfo E. Braceli, Roberto Brillaud, Alfredo R. Bufano, Aurelio Bujaldón, Fausto Burgos, Andrés Cáceres, Américo Calí, Graciela Calí de Molinelli, Jorge A. Calle, Isabel E. Cardullo, Luis Ricardo Casnati, Rosa Ana Casteller, Juana Castellino de Estupiñán, María

Sara L. de Castorino, J. Alberto Castro, Eliseo Castro, Nelly Cattarossi Arana, Rino Cattarossi, Vicente Carubin, Emilio Ceriotto, Vicente Cicchitti, Alberto C. F. Cirigliano, Iverna Codina de Giannoni, Filomena Codorniú Almazán, Luis Codorniú Almazán, Juan Coletti, Méneca de Conselmo, pseud., Celia Correas de Zapata, Edmundo Correas, Pedro C. Corvetto, Humberto Crimi, Manuel E. Cuadra Zúñiga, Víctor Hugo Cúneo, Elena Chiapasco, Gildo D'Accurzio, Blanca Dalla Torre Vicuña, Luis José Dalla Torre Vicuña, Angel Delpodio, Matilde Delpodio, Raúl Marcó Del Pont, Santos De Paula, Rafael Díaz Guzmán, Nilda Díaz Pessina, Antonio Di Benedetto, Juan Draghi Lucero, Jerónimo Espejo, Isabel Estrella de Suárez, Raimundo Farés, Julio Fernández Peláez, Lucrecia María Filippini, Florencia Fossatti, Justo Pedro Franco, Lucio Funes.
V. 2: Jorge García de Luca, Zelmira, Garrigós de Von Der Heyde, María Tindara Gatani, María de las Mercedes Gobbi, Juan Gualberto Godoy, Alfredo Goldsack Guiñazú, Sara Goldstein de Tapiola, María Rosa Gómez, Teresa Gómez Saá, Marta Gómez de Rodríguez Brito, José González Muñoz, Luis Gorosito Heredia, Luis A. Grandin, Ignacio Granero, Juan Ramón Guevara, Julio P. Guevara, Carlos Guevara Laval, Armando Herrera, Ricardo Ciro Higginson, Elena Jancarik, Guillermo Kaul Grünwald, Francisco Alberto López, Fernando Lorenzo, Dolly María Lucero, Juan Carlos Lucero, Manuel A. Lugones, Celia E. Lúquez, Benito Marianetti, Sixto Martelli, Alejandro C. Marti, Ana Selva Marti, Miguel Martos, Rafael Mauleón Castillo, Elvira Maure de Segovia, Joaquín Méndez Calzada, Guillermo Evaristo González Méndez, Beatriz Menges François, Angélica Mendoza, Juan Jorge Molinelli, Esther Monasterio, Fernando Morales Guiñazú, Manuela Mur, Vicente Nacarato, Carlos Orlando Nallim, Leonardo S. Napolitano, Alfredo Nomi, Iris Núñez de Bossut, Manuel Núñez Calleja, María Florencia Oderigo, José Manuel Olascoaga, Mónica Oliva Serpez, Serafín Ortega, Aurelia Oton de Oña Sola, Jorge Enrique Oviedo, Antonio Pagés Larraya, Juan Carlos Palavecino, Ernesto Mario Panero, José E. Peire, Efraín Peralta Andrade, Susana Pérez Diez, Guillermo Petra Sierralta, Pieter Pessina, pseud., Carlos Ponce, María Angélica Pouget, Ilia Ada Porta, Diego F. Pro, Rosario Puebla de Godoy, Angel Puente Guerra, Juan Bautista Ramos, Jorge Enrique Ramponi, Alberto Rodríguez (h), Arturo Andrés Roig, Ricardo Romagnoli, Eduardo B. Ruiz, Adolfo Ruiz Díaz, Teresita Saguí, Nélida Salvador, Samuel Sánchez de Bustamante, Alejandro Santa María Conill, Mario Guillermo Saraví, Samuel Sedero, Alicia Serú de Leal, Ricardo Setaro, Alfonso Sola González, Graciela Maturo de Sola González, Claudio Soria, Amilcar Urbano Sosa, Juan José Sota, Susana Tampieri de Estrella, Armando Tejada Gómez, Mafalda Tinelli, Odino Tomei, Esther Trozzo, Ricardo Tudela, Abelardo Vázquez, Antonio Vázquez, Néstor W. Vega, Vilma Vega, Hilario Velasco Quiroga, Gloria Videla de Riveros, Ana F. de Villalba, Delia Villa-

LITERATURE

lobos de Piccone, Alejandro Von Der Heyde, Yago Zalazar, René Zapata Quesada, Martín Zubiría, Emilia de Zuleta, Enrique Zuleta Alvarez, Leopoldo Zuloaga.

IU

684 Cien poesías. Córdoba: Ediciones Grossi, 196-. 1 v. (Unpaged). 22 cm.
An anthology of Argentine poetry, including brief biographical notes of the following writers featured in the text: Ana María Servera, José Domingo Amaya, Daniel Salzano, Jesús Panero de Miguel, Hugo Remedi, Martha Alamo, Enrique Rabal, Guillermina Tognazzi, Humberto Lescano, Ambrosio Agustoni, Lucía Alinari, Domingo A. Allasino, Marcelo A. Allasino, Hernán Diego Alvarez, María Esther Otero de Amelio Ortiz, Blanca Estela Barrionuevo Soria, Fabián Blazquez, Efraín Abel Barbosa, Juan Carlos Berhend, Ricardo Bogetti, Martha Caballero, Reyna Carranza, Carlos Raúl Ceballos, María Susana Ciceri, Raúl Andrés Cortez, José Pedro David, Martha Dorgan, Irma Droz, Juan Carlos Durilen, Graciela Elías, José Luis Ferreyra, Jorge Alberto Farías, Ramiro Alejandro Figueroa, Antonia Teresa Gallardo, Isabel Leonor García, Eva Lida Gioino, Plácido Mario Iudicello, Eloisa Jeandrevin, Inés Kaplun, Carlos Alberto Maggi, Elvira Marcía, Carlos Isaac Meirovich, Nora Elena Montes, Olinda Teresita Moreno, María Angélica Bertea de Moroni, José Enrique Muñoz Salcedo, Martha Nascher, Ricardo Navarro, Marcelino José Peláez, Alan Gálvez Parodi, Blanca Pérez, Elda Priotti, Susana Penenory, Myriam Elizabeth Ponce, Ana María del Pozo, Ana Carolina E. Pugliese, Raquel de Reyes, Inés Ricci Hidalgo, Susana Clara Rodríguez, María Esther Rodríguez de la Torre, Julia Isabel Rossi, Mercedes Beatriz Madoery de Moreno, Amelia Saieg, María Josefa Sarmiento, Angel Bernardo Schiavetta, José Rodolfo Sorribes, Nilda Norma Sosa, Juan Carlos Testori, Adolfo Tuviansky, Adoración Valdarenas, Antonio Vlajovich, Moisés Zak.

CLSU CLU CSt MB NBuU NIC NN NNC NSyU OU TxU WU

685 Cócaro, Nicolás, comp. Cuentos fantásticos argentinos. Buenos Aires: Emecé Editores, 1970. 226 p. 19 cm.
A collection of short stories by the following fantastic fiction writers, including biobibliographical sketches: Vicente Barbieri, Santiago Dabove, Leopoldo Lugones, Horacio Quiroga, Enrique Anderson Imbert, Adolfo Bioy Casares, Jorge Luis Borges, Leonardo Castellani, Guillermo Enrique Hudson, Julio Cortázar, Augusto Mario Delfino, Manuel Mujica Láinez, Alberto Girri, H. A. Murena, Conrado Nalé Roxlo, Silvina Ocampo, Manuel Peyrou.

CaQMM CLSU CSt CtY FU GU IaU IEN InU IU MB MH MoSW MU NNC TxU ViU

686 Cócaro, Nicolás. Las letras y el destino argentino: Lugones, Borges, Sábato, Cortázar y otros. Buenos Aires: Editorial Sopena Argentina, 1969. 125 p. 18 cm.
Collection of essays dealing with the 20th century featuring stylistic analyses and information on birthplace, dates, and educational background for Martín García Mérou, Benito Lynch, Enrique Banchs.

CaQMM CFS CLSU CLU CSt CtY CU CU-SB DPU GU IaU ICIU ICU InU IU MB MoSW NBuU NbU NcD NcU NIC NjP OCl OkU OU PPT TxU ViU VtU WU

687 Corbacho, Oscar; Fernando Sánchez Sorondo; and Héctor G. Solanas. Poetas juntos. Buenos Aires: Editorial Rodolfo Alonso, 1979. 78 p. 19 cm.
An anthology of the works of three contemporary Argentine poets, accompanied by very brief biobibliographical notes. The following are included: Oscar Corbacho, Fernando Sánchez Sorondo, Héctor G. Solanas.

IU

688 Cortázar, Augusto Raúl, comp. Poesía gauchesca. Buenos Aires: Ministerio de Cultura y Educación, 1970. 146 p. Portraits. 20 cm. (Los fundadores de la literatura argentina).
An anthology of gaucho poetry including brief bibliographical sketches of the following 19th- and 20th-century writers: Horacio Jorge Becco, Agusto Raúl Cortázar, José Carlos Maubé, Ricardo Emilio Rodríguez Molas, Jorge Luis Borges, Femín Chávez, E. M. S. Danero, Rafael Alberto Arrieta, Ricardo Rojas, Juan Alfonso Carrizo, Olga Elena Fernández Latour, Jorge M. Furt, Carlos Ibarguren, Ventura Robustiano Lynch, Ramón Menéndez Pidal, Ismael Moya, Julio César Caillet-Bois, Carlos Alberto Leumann, Leopoldo Lugones, Antonio J. Pérez Amuchástegui, Miguel de Unamuno, Juan Gualberto Godoy, Juan Draghi Lucero, Arturo Andrés Roig, Bartolomé Hidalgo, Lauro Ayestarán, Mario Falcao Espalter, Juan María Gutiérrez, Martiniano Leguizamón, Luis Soler Cañas, Hilario Ascasubi, Eduardo Jorge Bosco, Robert Lehmann Nietsche, Manuel Mujica Láinez, Estanislao del Campo, Enrique Anderson Imbert, Rafael Alberto Arrieta, Angel José Battistessa, Rubén Angel Benítez, Arturo Berenguer Carisomo, Elías Carpena, Roberto Ferrando Giusti, Rafael José Hernández, José Hernández, Angel Héctor Azeves, Rafael Jijena Sánchez, Alejandro Losada Guido, Julio Mafud, Ezequiel Martínez Estrada, Federico de Onís, Antonio Pagés Larraya, Pedro de Paoli, Luis C. Pinto, José Roberto del Río, Rodolfo Senet, Eleuterio Felipe Tiscornia, Amaro Villanueva.

CSt GU IaU ICarbS InU IU KMK MB MoSU MoU MWH MU OU TxBeal TxSat TxU

689 Corvalán, Octavio, comp. Cuentos del NOA.
Buenos Aires: Editorial Andes, 1975. 152 p.
18 cm.
    A collection of contemporary Argentine
short stories, each preceded by a short bio-
bibliographical sketch on its author. The
following are featured: Juan Carlos Dávalos,
Daniel Ovejero, Luis Leopoldo Franco, Carlos
Domingo Yáñez, Angel María Vargas, Tito Maggi,
Jorge W. Avalos, Ramón Alberto Pérez, Manuel
J. Castilla, Julio Ardiles Gray, Guido Orlan-
do Avila, Octavio Cejas, Héctor Tizón, Juan
José Hernández, Carlos Hugo Aparicio, Jorge
Estrella.

    IU MU NN WU

690 Cossa, Roberto M. La ñata contra el libro
por Roberto M. Cossa. No hay función por
Néstor Kraly. La bolsa de agua caliente por
Carlos Somigliana. Sainete con variaciones
por Francisco Urondo. Buenos Aires: Talía,
1967. 87 p. Portraits. 19 cm. (Colección
argentina de teatro. V. 55/56).
    A collection of four contemporary plays
by the following 20th-century Argentine writers, for whom short biobibliographical
sketches and portraits are also included:
Roberto M. Cossa, Néstor Kraly, Carlos Somigliana, Francisco Urondo.

    AU CLSU CLU CSt DPU FU IaU INS
    IU KU MB MH MoSW MU NBuU NcU NIC
    NN NNC NSyU OU ScU TNJ TxU ViU WU

691 Creadores literarios argentinos. Poesía '82.
Buenos Aires: Editorial Libros de América,
1981. 158 p. 20 cm.
    An anthology of contemporary Argentine
poets, including biographical sketches. The
following are featured: Carmen Aguinaga de
Ricci, Osvaldo R. Aguirre, Cristián Alberto
Aliaga, José Rafael Aluz, Emil Alva, pseud.,
(Emilio Andrés Alvarez), Esther Mafalda Anzo-
átegui de Braun, Clara Inés Argibay, Raúl
Arué, Marcos Barrionuevo, Olivio Sergio Bení-
tez, María Isabel Berardi de Loaiza, Oscar
Luis Bernasconi, Araceli Dameglio de Borsani,
Nelly Borroni MacDonald, María Lidia Brunori
de Civilotti, Luis Antonio Caraballo, Carlos
Alberto Casellas, Jorge Castañeda, Vilma Cas-
tro, Guillermo Omar Cortese, Susana Virginia
Cunqueiro, María Cristina Charro, H. Daniel
Dei, Rosina Depaolis de Varizat, Carmen B.
De Simón de Sánchez, Liliana Susana Doyle,
René E. Duturel, Luis Primo Farías, Marta Ali-
cia Femenía, Alfredo Julio Ferrarassi, Amelia
Fraigne, Norberto Daniel Frazzetta, Pablo A.
Freinkel, Ricardo E. Fuchs, Adolfo Cecilio
Fulquet, Luis Alberto Galassi, Julio César
Gallardo, Irma A. Galletti de Mastrángelo,
Tomás García Giménez, Germán Gargano, Oscar S.
Gavotti, Norma González Falderini, Clotilde
Grané, Juan Carlos Gruski, Mirtha Harenchisin,
Eva Susana Hernández, Mirta Graciela Itchart,
Odila Jacobs, pseud. (Odila Haydée Girotti de
Jacob), Juana Haydée Kossman, Mabel López,

Oscar Miguel López Zenaruzza, Jesús Daniel
Los Arcos Vidaurreta, Roberto César Lucero,
Elba Alicia Machado, Alejandra Marta Mailhe,
Enrique Martínez, Martha Julia Merlo, Barto-
lomé Mezquida, Michèle, pseud. (Olga Lidia
Madorno), Nelly de Miras, Rodolfo Misiti,
Luis Moselli Erut, Irene M. de Nieto Blanc,
Ana María Nocita, Hugo Olmos, Carmen Otero de
Carbone, Federico Paitoux, pseud. (Federico
Esteban), Alfredo C. Palacio, Sara Papini de
Rodríguez Nally, María Laura Pardo, María
Gabriela Patiño, Norma Pereyra de Mora, Gladys
Liliana Piccolini de Marín, Nora Pietroboni
de Jourdan, Jorge A. Piñero García, María
Isabel Plorutti, Nelly A. Posas de Merani,
Oscar H. Pralong, Irma Matilde Ramos, Eduardo
Ranea, Carlos Alberto Redondo Berasategui,
Daniel Ríos, Osvaldo Risso Perondi, Deisde
Rocni, pseud. (Delia Isabel D'Ambrosio de
Ronconi), Héctor Pedro Rodríguez, María Inés
Rodríguez de Loustanunau, Adriana Noemí Rodrí-
guez Sibuet, Segundo Alberto Rodríguez Toran-
zos, Lidia Rodríguez Torres, Julia Romero,
Inmaculada Ruiz y Santana de Laborde, Osvaldo
Sacco Capalbo, Iris Saldaña, María Elsa Sán-
chez Linari, Adriana A. Sappia, Nelba C. Sa-
racho, Clelia Paleo de Silvero, Beatriz M.
Sollazzo de Lew, Eugenio A. Somadossi, Noemí
Stiefel de Orías, Norberto Suárez, Raúl Walter
Tajes, Beatriz Toncovich de Barassi, Marcela
Rosa Toso, Ana Tripi De Márquez, Waldemar Ye
Urunday de los Exocetos, pseud. (Rodolfo Vi-
cente Robertson Stoof), Milca María Vargas,
Ramón Horacio Vespa, Nilda Visentín de Robert,
Martín Visuara, Claudia Roxana Volpin, Sergio
J. Winocur.

    IU

692 Criado, Emilio Alonso. Literatura argentina.
4. ed. Buenos Aires: Librería de A. García
Santos, 1916. 166 p. 19 cm.
    A history of Argentine literature, cover-
ing the period from colonial times through the
19th century, and including biographical in-
formation on many writers. The following are
particularly featured: Manuel José de Labar-
dén, Cayetano Rodríguez, Gregorio Funes, Flo-
rencio Varela, José Esteban Echeverría, José
Mármol, Juan María Gutiérrez, Olegario Andrade,
José Hernández, Domingo F. Sarmiento, Juan
Bautista Alberdi, Bartolomé Mitre, Vicente
Fidel López, Nicolás Avellaneda, José Manuel
Estrada, Pedro Goyena, Mariano Moreno, Manuel
Antonio Castro, Antonio Sáenz, Bernardino
Rivadavia, Bernardino Monteagudo, Mamerto
Esquiú, Félix Frías, Dalmacio Vélez Sársfield,
Guillermo Rawson, Aristóbulo del Valle.

    CU IU LU MU TxU

693 Cruz, Jorge, comp. Teatro argentino romántico,
1972. Buenos Aires: ECA [i.e. Ediciones Culturales Argentinas], 1972. 396 p. 19 cm.
    A collection of 3 romantic Argentine plays,
preceded by a brief prologue outlining the
history and characteristics of Argentine ro-

LITERATURE

manticism. Very brief, scattered biographical information is given for many authors of this genre, with particular emphasis on the following: Esteban Echeverría, José Mármol, Bartolomé Mitre, Pedro Echagüe.

AAP CaBVaU CLSU CLU CNoS CtY CU
CU-SB FU GU IaAS IaU InU IU KU LU
MB MnU MoSW MU NB NBuU NcD NcU NIC
NjP NjR NmU NN NNC NSbSU NSyU OU
PPiU PPT PSC PSt TU TxDaM TxHR TxU
ViU WaU WU

694 Cuentistas premiados. Buenos Aires: G. Dávalos, D. C. Hernández, 1954. 102 p. 20 cm. (Biblioteca El escarabajo de oro).
An anthology of contemporary Argentine short stories by the following authors, including biobibliographical sketches: Miguel Briante, Ricardo Piglia, Romeo B. A. Medina, Octavio Getino, Juan Carlos Villegas Vidal.

CLSU CoFS CSt CtY DPU FU ICU IU
MB MH MiU MoU NbU NcU NIC NN
NSbSU NSyU OU ViU TxFTC TxU

695 Cuento. Mar del Plata: Municipalidad del Partido de General Pueyrredón, Subsecretaría de Cultura y Educación, 1972. 66 p. 20 cm.
An anthology of contemporary Argentine short stories by the following writers, including biobibliographical notes: Enrique David Borthiry, Susana Beltrán, Rodolfo Oscar Noodt, Raquel Iglesias de Pérez Speranza, Graciela Tarantino.

CtY CU-SB IU MB MU NIC

696 El cuento argentino, 1959-1970; antología. Buenos Aires: CEDAL, 1981. 155 p. 18 cm. (Capítulo; biblioteca argentina fundamental. V. 107).
An anthology of short stories by the following Argentine writers (1959-1970), including biographical sketches: Dalmiro Sáenz, David Viñas, Beatriz Guido, Martha Lynch, Abelardo Castillo, Humberto Costantini, Andrés Rivera, Pedro Orgambide, Jorge Riestra, Germán Rozenmacher, Haroldo Conti, Jorge Asís.

IU

697 El cuento argentino contemporáneo. Buenos Aires: Centro Editor de América Latina, 1976. 154 p. 19 cm. (Biblioteca total. Panorama de la literatura).
An anthology of contemporary Argentine short-story writers, including biobibliographical information. Those featured are Jorge Luis Borges, Julio Cortázar, Silvina Ocampo, Bernardo Kordon, Daniel Moyano, Humberto Costantini, Haroldo Conti, Rodolfo Walsh, Juan José Saer, Juan José Hernández, Germán Rozenmacher, Abelardo Castillo.

IU

698 Cuentos de periodistas. Buenos Aires: Ediciones Noé, 1973. 102 p. 21 cm.
An anthology of 20th-century short stories written by Argentine journalists, each preceded by a short biographical sketch on its author. These people include Juan Carlos Cerro, Voltaire José Cosentino, Daniel Garibaldi, Hernando Kleimans, Elena Lunghi, Lázaro Ottonello, Tiburcio Padilla, Jorge Ernesto Siga, Roberto Traini, Daniel Vic.

AzTeS CLU CSt CtY CU-SB FU IU MB
MH MU NcU NmU NN NNC NSbSU OKentU
TxU

699 Los cuentos inéditos premiados en Salta. 1975. Salta: Ediciones de la Dirección General de Cultura, 1977. 56 p. 22 cm.
A collection of short stories by the following writers from the Argentine province of Salta who won distinctions in the 1975 literary contest, including brief biobibliographical notes: Néstor Saavedra, Oscar Pérez, Andrés Rodolfo Villalba, Jacobo Regen, Rodolfo I. Bravo.

IU

700 Cuentos 70. Buenos Aires: Editorial Cono Sur, 1970. 126 p. 20 cm.
A collection of contemporary Argentine short stories, each preceded by a short biobibliographical note on its author. These people include Alicia de la Fuente, Anamaría Brodersen, Olga Margarita Daglietto, Betty Pancelli, Eduardo Leunda Moya, Leónidas Cristián Ziehl, Elisabeth Davio, Delchis Girotti, Hercilia H. Tommasi.

CLSU CLU CSt CU-S CU-SB FU GU IaU
IU MB MoSW MU NcU NSbSU OU TU TxU
ViU WU

701 De orilla a orilla; cuentos. Santa Fe: Librería y Editorial Colmegna, 1972. 139 p. 18 cm.
An anthology of Argentine short stories by the following contemporary writers, including biobibliographical sketches: Sofía Acosta, César Actis Brú, Ricardo H. Alcolea, Lermo Rafael Balbi, Angel Domingo Balzarino, Arnaldo H. Cruz, Susana Etcharrán, Adolfo Argentino Golz, Edgardo A. Pesante, Marta Elena Samatán.

CU-S IaU IU MU

702 16 [i.e. Dieciséis] poetas en Mar del Plata. Mar del Plata: Sociedad de Escritores de la Provincia de Buenos Aires, 1964. 164 p. 23 cm.
An anthology of 20th-century Argentine poetry from the city of Mar del Plata, including brief biobibliographical information. Those featured are Julio César Ranca, Graciela Tarantino, Gladys C. A. Smith, Leonardo Eloy Riesgo, Antonieta de Treviño, Ñusta de Piorno,

Félix Coluccio, Concepción Ventura Lleti, Marta Beatriz Souto, Leonor G. de Butti, Ismael Manuel López Merino, Lidia de Iure, Celina de Ithusarri, Armando Chulack, Raquel Guidi de Elordi, Indalecio Tizón Covello.

CLSU CLU CoFS LNHT MnU MoSW MU
NIC TxHU TxU

703 10 [i.e. Diez] de nosotros; poemas. Buenos Aires: Ediciones Eleo, 1971. 170 p. 20 cm.
An anthology of Argentine poetry of the 20th century including brief biobibliographical sketches of the following authors featured in the text: Norberto Corti, Rubén Derlis, Ricardo Egles, C. Alberto Polat, Fernando Sánchez Zinny, Jorge Sichero.

CU-SB IU MoSW WU

704 10 [i.e. Diez] poetas, primera muestra, Córdoba, 1965. Ilus.: Luis Saavedra; diagramó y cuidó la edición: Juan Croce. Córdoba: Ediciones El Taller del Escritor, 1965. 20 p. 27 cm. (Serie de poesía: Calicanto).
An anthology of contemporary Argentine poetry, accompanied by very brief biobibliographical notes on the authors who live in Córdoba. They include María Teresa Carrara, Blanca Ofelia Castillo, Francisco Colombo, Alberto Espejo, Osvaldo Guevara, Miguel Angel Piccato, Roberto Sánchez.

CLSU CU-SB InU IU MB MoSW MU NBuU
NIC PPiU TxU

705 10 [i.e. Diez] poetas, segunda muestra. Córdoba, 1967. Cordoba: Ediciones El Taller del Escritor, 1967. 20 p. 27 cm. (Serie de poesía: Calicanto).
An anthology of contemporary Argentinean poetry, accompanied by very brief biobibliographical notes on the authors who now live in Córdoba. They include Luis Ammann, José B. Caribaux, Julio Castellano, Myrta Christiansen, Graciela Ferrari, Ricardo Martín-Crosa, Alejandro Nicotra, Rafael David Sucari, Daniel Vera, Carolina Vocos Caturelli.

CLSU IU KU NcU NIC OU TxU

706 XX [i.e. Doce] cuentistas argentinos. Cuidado de ed.: Hugo Acevedo y Luis Vera. Buenos Aires: Cooperativa Editorial Hoy en la Cultura, 1965. 117 p. 18 cm. (Colección Cuentos. V. 1).
An anthology of Argentine short stories by the following contemporary authors, including brief biobibliographical sketches: Isidoro Blaistein, Lubrano Zas, Estela Dos Santos, Laura Devetach, Octavio Getino, Jorge Carnevale, Jorge Carlos Caballero, Julio Guillermo Martínez, Gustavo Roldán, Amílcar G. Romero, Eduardo Goligorski, Alvaro Abós.

CtY IU TxU

707 Domínguez, Mignon, comp. 16 [Diez y seis] cuentos argentinos; selección prólogo y notas. Buenos Aires: Lajouane, 1955. 194 p. 18 cm.
A collection of 16 contemporary Argentine short stories, each accompanied by a short biobibliographical sketch on its author. A brief essay on the editor of this work is also given. The following are featured: Fausto Burgos, Juan Carlos Dávalos, Pablo Rojas Paz, Luis L. Franco, Angel María Vargas, Clementina Rosa Quenel, Horacio C. Rodríguez, Juan Pablo Echagüe, Lobodón Garra, Agustín Guillermo Casá (Guillermo House, pseud.), Ricardo Güiraldes, Susana Calandrelli, Miguel Angel Correa (Mateo Booz, pseud.), Justo P. Sáenz (son), Ernesto E. Ezquer Zelaya, Horacio Quiroga, Mignon Domínguez.

CU DLC DPU IU MH TNJ TxU

708 Donghi Halperín, Renata. Cuentistas argentinos del siglo XIX. Buenos Aires: A. Estrada, 1950. 288 p. 18 cm.
An anthology of 19th-century Argentine short stories, each preceded by a brief biobibliographical sketch on its author. These people include Esteban Echeverría, José Tomás Guido, Juana Manuela Gorriti, Vicente G. Quesada, Santiago Estrada, José María Cantilo, Eduardo Wilde, Lucio V. López, Bartolomé Mitre y Vedia, Miguel Cané, José S. Alvarez (Fray Mocho, pseud.), Martín García Mérou, Joaquín V. González.

CaBVaU CU-S DLC IU MH MiU
MU NBuU NN TNJ TxU WU

709 Echagüe, Juan Pablo. Escritores de la Argentina. Buenos Aires: Emecé Editores, 1945. 149 p. 19 cm.
A collection of essays featuring critical analyses of the works of six 19th- and 20th-century Argentinean writers, as well as scattered biographical information on these men. They are Paul Groussac, Roberto J. Payró, Manuel Láinez, Gregorio Laferrère, Eduardo Wilde, Leopoldo Lugones.

CtY CU-S DLC ICU INS IU LU MU
NcD NcU OkU OrU TxU ViU WaU

710 Elliff, Osvaldo. Introducción a la poesía rantifusa. Buenos Aires: Ediciones Aga Taura, 1967. 79 p. 19 cm.
An essay about contemporary poetry from the "arrabales" of Buenos Aires, including biographical information on the following representative writers: Bartolomé Rodolfo Aprille, Enrique D. Cadicamo, Carlos de la Púa, Iván Díez, Felipe H. Fernández (Yacaré, pseud.), Celedonio Esteban Flores, Dante A. Linyera, pseud. (Francisco Bautista Rímoli), Félix Lima, Augusto Gandolfi Herrero (Juan Guijarro, pseud.), Juan Carlos Lamadrid.

CLU CSt FU IaU InU IU KU MB MH
MnU NcC NcU NIC NN NNC OU TU TxU
ViU WU

LITERATURE

711 Esquiú Barroetaveña, Eloísa, comp. <u>Parnaso femenino</u>. Buenos Aires: Editora Argentinidad, 1936. 61 p. 21 cm.

An anthology of poetry by the following contemporary Argentine women, including brief biobibliographical notes: Margarita Abella Caprile, Emilia Bertolé, Alcira Nobazzola, Lola S. B. de Bourguet, Susana Calandrelli, Sara Solá de Castellanos, Sara Montes de Oca de Cárdenas, María Alicia Domínguez, Beatriz Eguía Muñoz, Rosa García Costa, Adela Garáa Salaberry, Margot Guezúraga, Nydia Lamarque, Norah Lange, Amalia Prebisch de Piossek, Teresa Ramos Carrión, Mary Rega Molina, María del Carmen Vázquez de Montiel (Concepción Ríos, pseud.), Paulina Simoniello, Emma Solá de Solá, Alfonsina Storni.

DLC FMU NN NNC

712 Etchenique, Nira, and Mario Jorge de Lelis, comps. <u>Veinte cuentos de Buenos Aires</u>. Buenos Aires: Compañía General Fabril Editora, 1961. 181 p. 18 cm. (Los libros del mirasol. V. 43).

An anthology of contemporary Argentine short stories, each accompanied by a short biobibliographical sketch on the author. Those included are Roberto Arlt, Leónidas Barletta, Andrés Cinqugrana, Humberto Constantini, Augusto Mario Delfino, Julio Ellena de la Sota, José S. Alvarez (Fray Mocho, pseud.), Enrique González Tuñón, David José Kohon, Norah Lange, Eduardo Mallea, Roberto Mariani, Manuel Mujica Láinez, Nicolás Olivera, Adolfo Pérez Zelaschi, Dalmiro A. Sáenz, Javier Villafañe, David Viñas, Enrique Wernicke, Alvaro Yunque.

CSt CU-S PPU ICarbS ICIU IU LNHT
MB MnU MoSW NcU NIC NP NSyU OU
PPiU PSt TNJ TxLT ViU WaU

713 Fidalgo, Andrés. <u>Panorama de la literatura jujeña</u>. Buenos Aires: Ediciones La Rosa Blindada, 1975. 191 p. 21 cm. (Colección de ensayos Los tiempos nuevos).

Biobibliographical sketches and stylistic analyses of writers resident in the Argentine province of Jujuy throughout history. Birthplace, dates, and data on the literary activities of the following individuals are provided: Reginaldo de Lizarraga, Juan de Matienzo, Garcilaso de la Vega (El Inca, pseud.), Martín del Barco Centenera, Acarette du Biscay (Acarette, pseud.), Pedro Lozano, Alonso Carrio de la Vandera (Concolorcorvo, pseud.), José Andrews, Woodbine Parish, J. Antonio King, Edmundo Temple, Alcide D'Orbigny, Martín de Moussy, Eric von Rosen, Eric Boman, Juan Ignacio de Gorriti, Benjamín Villafañe, Escolástico Zegada, Macedonio Graz, Guillermo Enrique Hudson, Joaquín Carrillo, Alberto Coutoune, Benjamín Villafañe, José de la Iglesia, Aníbal E. A. Villafañe, Normando Baca Cau, Domingo Bonifai, Gaspar Medrano Rosso (Catón, pseud.), Horacio Carrillo (Ignotus,

pseud.), Fausto Burgos, Carlos Hansen, Alberto Córdoba, Bernardo González Arrilli, Daniel Ovejero, Julio Aramburu, Teófilo Sánchez de Bustamante, Miguel Angel Vergara, David Salmón Cadenau, Jorge Villafañe, Guillermo Zalazar Altamira (Dinty Moore, pseud.), José Pichetti (Piquio Palino, pseud.), Gaspar L. Benavento, José Armanini, Fausto de Tezanos Pinto, Félix Infante, Oscar Rebaudi Basavilbaso, Atahualpa Yupanqui, Mario Busignani, M. Elda Noro, Domingo Zerpa, Manuel Puch Blas, Joaquín Burgos, Alcira Cazón, Raúl Galán, María Laura Oyuela de Pemberton, Tito U. Maggi, Jorge Calvetti, Rubén Alejo Barros, Víctor Aban, Ernestina Acosta, Libertad Demitropulos, Marcos Paz, Rafael H. Reyes, Sara San Martín, José Murillo, César Corte Carrillo, Luis D'Jallad, Francisco Ramón Díaz, Carlos E. Figueroa, Miguel Angel Pereira, Néstor Groppa, Antonio Alvarado, Héctor Tizón, Federico Undiano, Carlos Hugo Aparicio, Benito Carlos Garzón, Juan Carlos Palavecino, Raúl Dorra, María del Carmen Mendiola de Quiroga, Leonor Picchetti, Pedro Deolindo Reyna (Rusiñol, pseud.), Cecilio Garzón, Eduardo Morera (Duplán, Max, pseud.), Enrique Lafuente, Rodolfo Alvarez, Leopoldo Aban, Amalia Prebisch Linares de Piossek, Elvira Palacios de Zorroaquín, Aristóbulo Wayar, Manuel Corte Carrillo, Oscar Manuel Oliveira, Julio Antonio Sánchez, Andrés Fidalgo.

AzU CtY IU KU MoSW MU NcU NmU NN
OU TxU WU

714 Flesca, Haydée, comp. <u>Antología de literatura fantástica argentina</u>. Edición dirigida por María Hortensia Lacau. Buenos Aires: Editorial Kapelusz, 1970. 261 p. 17 cm. (Grandes obras de la literatura universal).

An anthology of 19th-century Argentine fantastic literature, accompanied by short biobibliographical sketches on the authors whose works are represented. They include Juana Manuela Gorriti, Lucio V. Mansilla, Eduardo Wilde, Miguel Cané, Eduardo L. Holmberg, Carlos Olivera, Carlos Monsalve, Martín García Mérou, Carlos Octavio Bunge.

CNoS CtY InU IU MdU MH MiU MU NcD
NNC TxHU TxU

715 Foster, David William. <u>Currents in the contemporary Argentine novel</u>: Arlt, Mallea, Sábato, and Cortázar. Columbia: University of Missouri Press, 1975. 155 p. 24 cm.

A literary criticism of the 20th century Argentine novel, accompanied by biobibliographical sketches on four authors of this genre. They are Roberto Arlt, Eduardo Mallea, Ernesto Sábato, Julio Cortázar.

AAP AkU AzU CaBVaU CLSU CLU CoFS
CoLH CoU CSt CtW CtY CU DAU DHU
DPU DSI F FMU FU GASU GU IaAS IaU
ICarbS ICU IEN InNd InU IU KEmT KU
LN LU MB MH MiEM MiU MnU MoSW MoU

MShM NBC NbU NBuU NcCU NcD NcGU
NcRS NcU NdU NIC NjP NjR NmLcU
NmU NN NNC NNCoCi NNU NRU NSbSU
NSyU NvU NWM OC1 OCU OKentU OkU
OOxM OrPS OrU OU OWorP PPCCH PSt
R SdB TNJ TU TxU UU ViBlbV ViU
VtU WaU WU

716 Fundación Argentina para la Poesía. <u>Poesía
argentina contemporánea</u>. Buenos Aires: Fundación Argentina Para La Poesía, 1978. 6 V.
Portraits. 20 cm.

Anthology of Argentinean poets from the
second half of the 20th century. Includes
biobibliographical information, photos, crit-
icisms, and personal statements by the writers
on their own poetry. The following are featured:

V. 1, part 1: Horacio Armani, Edgar
Bayley, Amelia Biagioni, Manuel Castilla,
Juan José Cesselli, Carlos Alberto Débole.

V. 1, part 2: Alberto Girri, Roberto
Juárroz, Enrique Molina, Olga Orozco, Alfredo
Veiravé, Rubén Vela.

V. 1, part 3: Romualdo Brughetti, Atilio
Jorge Castelpoggi, Joaquín O. Giannuzzi, Magdalena Harriague, José Isaacson, Carlos Latorre, Francisco Madariaga, David Martínez,
Osvaldo Rossler.

V. 1, part 4: Rodolfo Alonso, Raul Aráoz
Anzoátegui, Emma de Cartosio, Gustavo García
Saraví, Orlando Mario Punzi, Sigfrido Radae-
lli, Antonio Requeni, Manuel Serrano Pérez,
Alfonso Solá González.

V. 1, part 5: Raúl Gustavo Aguirre, León
Benarós, Ariel Canzani D., Nicolás Cócaro,
María Granata, Néstor Groppa, Norberto Sil-
vetti Paz, Armando Tejada Gómez, María Elena
Walsh.

V. 1, part 6: Héctor Miguel Angeli, Elizabeth Azcona Cranwell, Jorge Calvetti, Alfredo De Cicco, Fernando Guibert, Alejandro
Nicotra, Nicandro Pereyra, Alejandra Pizarnik, Héctor Villanueva, Emilio Zolezzi.

IU

717 Furlan, Luis Ricardo. <u>Generación poética del
cincuenta</u>. Buenos Aires: Ediciones Culturales Argentinas, 1974. 150 p. 21 cm.

An anthology of Argentine poetry featuring the generation of 1950, 1950-1975, including place, date of birth with bibliographical
information for the following poets and poetesses: Raúl Gustavo Aguirre, Rodolfo Alonso,
Héctor Miguel Angeli, Julio Arístides, Horacio Armani, Elizabeth Azcona Cranwell, Némer
Barud, Rubén Benítez, Amelia Biogioni, Alberto Claudio Blasetti, Alberto Oscar Blasi,
Alberto Blasi Brambilla, Martín Campos, Ariel
Canzani D., Emma de Cartosio, Atilo Jorge
Castelpoggi, Juan José Ceselli, Adriana Chaves, Fermín Chávez, Osiris U. Chiérico, Ra-
fael Henzo D'Alessio, Jaime Dávalos, Libertad
Demitrópulos, Julio Carlos Díaz Usandivaras,
Betina Edelberg, Nira Etchenique, Ana Teresa
Fabani, Manrique Fernández Moreno, Ariel

Ferraro, Lily Franco, Alma García, Gustavo
García Saravi, Juan Gelman, Joaquín O. Gian-
nuzzi, María Giménez Pastor, Daniel Giribaldi,
Magdalena Harriague, Juan José Hernández,
Roberto Hurtado de Mendoza, José Isaacson,
Ana Emilia Lahitte, Carlos Latorre, Elva de
Lóizaga, Fernando Lorenzo, Francisco José
Madariaga, Inés Malinow, Ana Selva Martí,
Juan Carlos Martínez, Ricardo Massa, Jorge
Melazza Muttoni, Enrique Menoyo, Fulvio Mila-
no, María Mombrú, Edgar Morisoli, Héctor A.
Murena, Héctor Negro, Alejandro Nicotra,
Luisa Pasamanik, Jorge Perrone, Antonio Re-
queni, Osvaldo Rossler, Nélida Salvador, Lu-
cía de Sampietro, Flor Schapira Fridman,
Julio César Silvain, Susana Esther Soba, Gra-
ciela de Sola, Apolinario Héctor Sosa, Emilio
Sosa López, Rafael Squirru, Matilde Alba Swan,
Adela Tarraf, Mario Trejo, Carlos Enrique Ur-
quía, Leda Valladares, Alberto Vanasco, Al-
fredo Veiravé, Rubén Vela, Enrique Vidal Mo-
lina, María Angélica Villar, Oscar Hermes
Villordo, Miguel Angel Viola, Jorge Vocos
Lescano, María Elena Walsh, Héctor Yánover.
Alphabetical index of names.

CtY InU IU MH MiDW MoSW MU NcU
NIC NmU NN OU PPiU PPT TxU ViU
WU

718 Fustinoni, Osvaldo, and Federico Pérgola.
<u>Médicos en las letras argentinas</u>. Buenos
Aires: La Prensa Médica, 1981. 108 p.
23 cm. (Biblioteca de humanismo médico).

An essay about the following Argentine
physicians who are also writers, including
biographical data: Gregorio Aráoz Alfaro,
Eduardo Wilde, Guillermo Rawson, Manuel T.
Podestá, Francisco A. Sicardi, Gonzalo Bosch,
Pedro Benjamín Aquino, José Eneas Riú, Fau-
stino Juan Trongé, Arturo Lorusso, Enrique T.
Susini, Pedro Mallo, Eliseo Cantón, Baldomero
Eugenio Fernández Moreno, Claudio Mamerto
Cuenca, José Belbey, Nicolás Repetto, Juan B.
Justo, Alejandro Korn, José Ingenieros.

IU

719 Gallo, Blas Raúl. <u>Historia del sainete na-
cional</u>. Buenos Aires: Editorial Quetzal,
1959. 236 p. 20 cm.

A history of the one-act farce in Argentina, covering the period from 1868-1930.
Although emphasis is given to analyses of
representative works of this genre, brief
scattered biographical information is also
provided for several authors whose works are
discussed. Among them are Ezequiel Soria,
Enrique de María, Enrique Buttaro, Agustín
Fontanella, Pablo Podestá, Alberto Novión,
Carlos Mauricio Pacheco, Raúl Esteban Caravallo, José Antonio Saldías, Antonio Reynoso,
José Carrilero, Francisco Payá, Eduardo García Lalanne, Arturo de Bassi.

CLSU CLU CSt CU DeU IaU IU NIC
NN TxHR TxU

LITERATURE

720 García Velloso, Enrique. Historia de la literatura argentina. Buenos Aires: A. Estrada y Cía., 1914. 474 p. 20 cm.
    A literary history of Argentina covering
the period from colonial times to the end of
the 19th century, and including biographical
information on many authors. The following
are emphasized: Juan Baltazar Maziel, Manuel
José de Labardén, José Joaquín Araujo, Pedro
Antonio Cerviño, Manuel Belgrano, Pantaleón
Rivarola, Mariano Moreno, Vicente López y
Planes, Gregorio Funes, Cayetano Rodríguez,
José Casacuberta, Juan Crisóstomo Lafinur,
Esteban de Luca y Patrón, Francisco Javier
Iturri, Bernardo Vera y Pintado, Juan Cruz
Varela, Florencio Balcarce, Antonio Sáenz,
Miguel Calixto del Corro, Tomás Guido, José
Esteban Antonio Echeverría, Florencio Varela,
Rivera Indarte, José Mármol, Juan María Gutié-
rrez, Pedro de Angelis, Claudio Mamerto Cuenca,
Luis L. Domínguez, Domingo Faustino Sarmiento,
Juan Gualberto Godoy, Bartolomé Hidalgo, Hila-
rio Ascasubi, Vicente Fidel López, Santiago
Estrada, Nicolás Avellaneda, Olegario V. An-
drade, Ricardo Gutiérrez, Jorge Mitre, Adolfo
Mitre, Bartolomé Mitre.

    CtY CU DLC DPU MB MiU NcU NIC NN
    OU PU

721 Ghiano, Juan Carlos. Constantes de la literatura argentina; Echeverría, Cané, Güiraldes,
Mallea, el teatro, literatura siglo XX. Buenos Aires: Editorial Raigal, 1953. 178 p.
21 cm. (Biblioteca Juan María Gutiérrez.
V. 3).
    A critical analysis of 19th- and 20th-
century Argentine literature. Brief scattered biographical information is included
for the following authors: Esteban Echeverría,
Miguel Cané, Ricardo Güiraldes.

    CoU CSt CU DPU GEU GU IaU ICarb
    InU IU MiU MoSU MtU MU NBuU NcD
    NcGU NjR OU RPB TU TxHU TxU UU
    ViU WaU WU

722 _____. Poesía argentina del siglo XX. México: Fondo de Cultura Económica, 1957.
285 p. 22 cm. (Colección tierra firme.
V. 65).
    A chronology of 20th-century Argentine
poetry (1896-1950). Biographical information
such as dates of birth and death and analyses
of works is included for several authors in
each of the modern schools of poetry. The
following are featured: Leopoldo Lugones,
Enrique Banchs, Arturo Marasso, Rafael Alberto Arrieta, Enrique Larreta, Arturo Capdevila,
Alfonsina Storni, Baldomero Fernández Moreno,
Ezequiel Martínez Estrada, Alvaro Melián Lafinur, Angel de Estrada, Leopoldo Díaz, Pedro
Miguel Obligado, Ricardo Rojas, Pedro B. Palacios (Almafuerte), Evaristo Carriego, Miguel A. Camino, Juan Carlos Dávalos, Antonio
de la Torre, Bernardo Canal Feijóo, Ricardo
Güiraldes, Macedonio Fernández, Oliverio

Girondo, Jorge Luis Borges, Eduardo González
Lanuza, Carlos Mastronardi, Francisco Luis
Bernárdez, Leopoldo Marechal, Ricardo E. Mo-
linari, Conrado Nalé Roxlo, José González
Carbalho, Roberto Ledesma, Fermín Estrella
Gutiérrez, Ulyses Petit de Murat, Juan L.
Ortiz, Norah Lange, Jacobo Fijman, Brandán
Caraffa, Amado Villar, Nicolás Olivari, Is-
rael Zeitlin (César Tiempo), Pedro Juan Vigna-
le, José Sebastián Tallón, Lysandro Z. D. Gal-
tier, Francisco López Merino, Alfredo R.
Burano, Enrique Méndez Calzada, Horacio Rega
Molina, José Pedroni, Luis L. Franco, Raúl
González Tuñón, Cayetano Córdova Iturburu,
Carlos M. Grünberg, Aristóbulo Echegaray,
José Ananía (José Portogalo), María de Villa-
rino, Ignacio B. Anzoátegui, Mario Binetti,
Osvaldo Horacio Dondo, Fryda Schultz de Man-
tovani, Vicente Barbieri, Silvina Ocampo,
Enrique Molina, Olga Orozco, Juan Rodolfo
Wilcock, Roberto Paine, Daniel J. Devoto,
César Fernández Moreno, Eduardo A. Jonquières,
Alfonso Solá González, Alberto Ponce de León,
César Rosales, Guillermo Orce Remis, Mario
Busignani, Raúl Galán, Horacio Esteban Ratti,
Jorge Vocos Lescano, León Benarós, Héctor E.
Ciocchini, Miguel D. Etchebarne, Eduardo Jorge
Bosco, Juan G. Ferreyra Basso, Jorge Calvetti,
Manuel J. Castilla, Antonio Esteban Agüero,
Nicandro Pereyra, Osvaldo Svanascini, Jorge
Enrique Ramponi, Ernesto B. Rodríguez, Hora-
cio Jorge Becco, Alberto Girri, Emilio Sosa
López, Fernando Guibert.

    IU

723 _____. 26 [i.e. Veintiséis] poetas argen-
tinos (1810-1920). Buenos Aires: Editorial
Universitaria, 1960. 165 p. 19 cm. (Serie
del siglo y medio. V. 4).
    An anthology of Argentine poetry, cover-
ing the period between 1810 and 1920. Short
biobibliographical sketches are included for
each author whose works are represented.
They are Vicente López y Planes, Esteban de
Luca, Bartolomé Hidalgo, Juan Cruz Varela,
Esteban Echeverría, Juan María Gutiérrez,
José Mármol, Hilario Ascasubi, Estanislao del
Campo, José Hernández, Carlos Guido y Spano,
Ricardo Gutiérrez, Olegario Víctor Andrade,
Rafael Obligado, Pedro Bonifacio Palacios
(Almafuerte, pseud.), Leopoldo Díaz, Leopoldo
Lugones, Evaristo Carriego, Enrique Banchs,
Ricardo Rojas, Rafael Alberto Arrieta, Arturo
Capdevila, Arturo Marasso, Baldomero Fernán-
dez Moreno, Alfonsina Storni, Ricardo Güiral-
des.

    CSt CU FU IU LNHT MH MiU NIC

724 Giménez Pastor, Arturo. Historia de la li-
teratura argentina. Buenos Aires, Montevideo:
Editorial Labor, 1945. 2 v. Portraits.
19 cm. (Colección Labor. Sección III:
Ciencias literarias. V. 420-423).
    A two-volume history and criticism of
Argentine literature, covering the period from

preconquest to the 20th century, and including scattered biographical material, as well as portraits in most cases, on the authors whose works are discussed. The following are particularly featured: Vicente López y Planes, Esteban de Luca, Juan Cruz Varela, Esteban Echeverría, Claudio Mamerto Cuenca, José Rivera Indarte, José Mármol, Juan Bautista Alberdi, Juan María Gutiérrez, Domingo Faustino Sarmiento, Hilario Ascasubi, Estanislao del Campo (Anastasio el Pollo, pseud.), Olegario Víctor Andrade, Carlos Guido Spano, Rafael Obligado, Pedro B. Palacios (Almafuerte, pseud.), Calixto Oyuela, Eugenio Cambaceres, Lucio Vicente López, José Miró (Julián Martel, pseud.), Miguel Cané, Eduardo Wilde, Lucio V. Mansilla, Enrique García Velloso, Nicolás Granada, Florencio Sánchez, Alberto Novión, José S. Alvarez, Ema de la Barra de Llanos (César Duayen, pseud.), Roberto J. Payró, Horacio Quiroga. Alphabetical index of names.

CaBVaU DLC DPU IU MB MoSU MtU NcD OCl OClJC OrU OU PU ViU

725 Giménez Pastor, Marta, and José Daniel Viacava. <u>Selección poética femenina, 1940-1960</u>. Buenos Aires: Ediciones Culturales Argentinas, 1965. 307 p. Portraits. 20 cm. (Colección antologías).

An anthology of poetry written by Argentine women between 1940 and 1960. Portraits and bibliographical information are given for the following whose works are included: María Adela Agudo, Elvira Amado, Elizabeth Azcona Cranwell, Amelia Biagioni, Carmen Blanco Amores, Carola Briones, Emma de Cartosio, Iverna Codina, Ana María Chouhy Aguirre, Libertad Demitropulos, Magdalena D'Onofrio, Betina Edelberg, María del Mar Estrella, Nira Etchenique, Ana Gándara, Marta Elena Groussac, Magdalena Harriague, Ana Emilia Lahitte, Elva de Lóizaga, Inés Malinow, Dora Martínez Díaz de Vivar, Dora Melella, María Mombrú, Helena Muñoz Larreta, Manuela Mur, Olga Orozco, Luisa Pasamanik, Irma Peirano, Diana Piazzolla, Alejandra Pizarnik, Perla Rotzait, María Luisa Rubertino, Flor Schapira Fridman, Susana Esther Soba, Adela Tarraf, Susana Thenon, María Dhialma Tiberti, Celina Haydée Uralde, Leda Valladares, Beatris Vallejos, Aurora Venturini, María Angélica Villar, María Elena Walsh, Laura Yusem, Ofelia Zuccoli Fidanza.

IU KU MU NIC

726 Giusti, Roberto Fernando, comp. <u>13 [i.e. Trece] poetas</u>. Buenos Aires: Stilcograf, 1958. 80 p. 20 cm.

An anthology of contemporary Argentine poetry by the following people, for whom short biobibliographical sketches are also included: Martha Di Matteo, Juan Enrique Acuña, Rogelio L. Ameri, Germán Candau Carrizo, Margot Gelabert, Pedro Lieʰbe, Clemente López Passarón, Horacio Peroncini, Orlando

Mario Punzi, Romilio Ribero, Margot de Segovia, Julio César Silvaín, Lía Esther Rossi de Torres.

IU LNHT MH MnU MoSW TxU

727 Gobello, José. <u>Nueva antología lunfarda</u> (autores argentinos). Buenos Aires: Plus Ultra, 1972. 238 p. 20 cm.

An anthology of Argentine prose and poetry in colloquial language, including bio-bibliographical data of the following authors: Benigno B. Lugones, Miguel Ocampo, José S. Alvarez (Fray Mocho, pseud.), Angel Villoldo, Nemesio Trejo, Roberto Lino Cayol, Josué Quesada, José González Castillo, Félix Lima, Silverio Manco, Alberto Vacarezza, José Antonio Saldías, Luis C. Villamayor, Juan Francisco Palermo, Felipe Fernández (Yacaré, pseud.), Pascual Contursi, Juan Manuel Pintos, Máximo Teodoro Sáenz (Last Reason, pseud.), Francisco Alfredo Marino, Enrique González Tuñón, Dante A. Linyera, Carlos de la Púa, Luciano Payet, Celedonio Esteban Flores, Irán Díez, Roberto Arlt, Bartolomé Rodolfo Aprile, Enrique Candícamo, Amaro Villanueva, Juan Mondiola, Julián Centeya, Alcides Gandolfi Herrero, José Pagano, Alvaro Yunque, Osvaldo Elliff, Roberto Jorge Santoro, Jorge Melazza Muttoni, Luis Alfredo Sciutto, Juan Bautista Devoto, Joaquín Gómez Bas, Luis Ricardo Furlán, Luis Alposta, Daniel Garibaldi.

DLC NIC NNU

728 Goligorsky, Eduardo, comp. <u>Los argentinos en la luna</u>. Buenos Aires: Ediciones de la Flor, 1968. 215 p. 20 cm.

An anthology of Argentine science fiction, including biobibliographical sketches of the following authors featured in the text: Eduardo Ladislao Holmberg, Angela Gododischer, Juan Jacobo Bajarlía, Marie Langer, Héctor Yanover, Héctor G. Oesterheld, Alfredo Julio Grassi, Pablo Capanna, Alberto Lagunas, Jorge Iegor, Carlos María Caron, Eduardo Stilman.

AzU Fu IU MiDW NBuU NjR NvU PPiU

729 Grondona, Adela. <u>¿Por qué escribimos?</u> Buenos Aires: Emecé Editores, 1969. 239 p. 20 cm. (Selección Emecé de obras contemporáneas).

A collection of interviews, including biographical information, with the following contemporary Argentine authors: Margarita Abella Caprile, Adolfo Bioy Casares, Susana Bombal, Jorge Luis Borges, Silvina Bullrich, Nicolás Cócaro, Rosa Chacel, Celia de Diego, Osvaldo Horacio Dondo, Sara Gallardo, Carmen Gándara, Gustavo García Saraví, Alberto Girri, Juan Carlos Ghiano, Juan Goyanarte, Magdalena Harriague, Alicia Jurado, Mario A. Lancelotti, José Luis Lanuza, Roberto Ledesma, Luisa Mercedes Levinson, Salvador de Madariaga, Eduardo Mallea, Carlos Mastronardi, Ricardo E. Molinari, Manuel Mujica Láinez, Helena Muñoz

LITERATURE

Larreta, Héctor A. Murena, Martín Alberto Noel, Pedro Miguel Obligado, Silvina Ocampo, Victoria Ocampo, Miguel Alfredo Olivera, Dalmiro A. Sáenz, Guillermo de Torre, Oscar Hermes Villordo, Jorge Vocos Lescano, Guillermo Whitelow, Enrique Williams Alzaga, Adela Grondona.

IEN   IU   KyU   LNHT   MH   NSyU   OkU

730   Groppa, Néstor; Héctor Tizón; Miguel Angel Pereira; and Andrés Fidalgo, comps. <u>Poesía y prosa en Jujuy</u>; selección a cargo de Groppa, Tizón, Pereira y Fidalgo. Prólogo y notas de estos dos últimos. Tapa de Ofelia Bertolotto. Compilación, selección y notas de la Sociedad Argentina de Escritores (SADE), Filial Jujuy. Jujuy: Dirección Provincial de Cultura, 1969. 200 p. 26 cm.
    An anthology of prose and poetry from the Argentine province of Jujuy, including bio-bibliographical sketches of the following 20th-century writers: Benjamín Villafañe, Augusto Villafañe, Gaspar Medrano Rosso, Horacio Carrillo, Daniel Ovejero, Julio Aramburu, Jorge Villafañe, José Armanini, Félix Infante, Enrique Lafuente, Mario Busignani, Domingo Zerpa, Guillermo Benito Meyer Cicarelli, Raúl Galán, María Laura Oyuela de Pémberton, Tito Maggi, Marcos Paz, Jorge Calvetti, Andrés Fidalgo, Libertad Demitropulos, José Murillo, Ernestina Acosta, Sara San Martín, Luis D'Jallad, César Corte Carrillo, Francisco Ramón Díaz, Carlos E. Figueroa, Miguel Angel Pereira, Néstor Groppa, Héctor Tizón, Carlos Hugo Aparicio, Benito Carlos Garzón, María del Carmen Mendiola de Quiroga, Leonor Pichetti, Pedro Raúl Noro, Ricardo Martínez, Luis A. Wayar, Alberto Espejo, María Inés Andrada, María Celina Pedilla de Mengual. Chronological arrangement. Alphabetical index of names.

CLSU   CSt   CtY   CU-S   CU-SB   IaU   InU
IU   MoSW   MU   NIC   TxU   WaU

731   Guerra, Hidalgo. <u>Clava frío</u>. Buenos Aires: Casa de don Domingo E. Taladriz, 1975. 169 p. 20 cm.
    An anthology of Argentinean poets active during the last 30 years, including biographical sketches. Those featured are Pablo Organiz, Alfonso Cibrián, León Sicardi, Carlos Hostal, Fermín de Zapater, Alarico Bolson, Manuel Castaño, Pedro Alcabuz, Tierno Cortegoso, Alberto Obregón, Jaime Frain, Aníbal Barrionuevo.

IU

732   Guglielmini, Homero M. <u>Fronteras de la literatura argentina</u>. Buenos Aires: Editorial Universitaria de Buenos Aires, 1972. 115 p. 23 cm. (Biblioteca cultural). (Colección Argentina).
    A collection of essays dealing with various aspects of Argentine literature. Biographical information of various amounts is included for the following 19th- and 20th-century authors: Guillermo Hudson, Carlos de la Púa, Fernández Moreno, Esteban Echeverría, Homero M. Guglielmini.

AzU   CaQMM   CLS   CLU   CoFS   CSt   CtY   CU
CU-S   CU-SB   CU-SC   FMU   FTaSU   FU   GU
IaU   ICarbS   IU   KyLoU   KyU   LNU   MB   MH
MiDW   MiEM   MoSW   NBuU   NcD   NcU   NIC
NmU   NN   NSyU   OCl   OKentU   OkU   OU   PPiU
PPT   PSt   TNJ   TU   TxHR   TxU   UU   ViU   WU

733   Gutiérrez, Juan María. <u>Los poetas de la revolución</u>. Buenos Aires: Academia Argentina de Letras, 1941. 511 p. 20 cm. (Biblioteca de la Academia Argentina de Letras. Serie clásicos argentinos. V. 1).
    A collection of essays including biographical data and criticism of the following Argentine poets from the period of the May revolution of 1810: Esteban de Luca y Patrón, Juan Ramón Rojas, Juan de la Cruz Varela. Also biographical essay about Juan María Gutiérrez by Juan P. Ramos.

CSt   CU-S   DLC   FMU   ICU   IU   MiU   MU
NBuU   NcU   OkU   OO   OrU   OU   PU   WU

734   Henríquez Ureña, Pedro, and Jorge Luis Borges, comps. <u>Antología clásica de la literatura argentina</u>. Buenos Aires: A. Kapelusz y Cía., 1937. 445 p. 20 cm.
    An anthology of Argentine literature, covering the period form the 16th to the 20th centuries, accompanied by short biobibliographical sketches, as well as portraits in some cases, on the authors. The following are included: Ruy Díaz de Guzmán, Luis de Tejeda, Francisco Javier Iturri, Gregorio Funes, Manuel José de Lavardén, María Sánchez, Bernardo de Monteagudo, Bartolomé Hidalgo, José Antonio Miralla, José María Paz, Juan Cruz Varela, Esteban Echeverría, Hilario Ascasubi, Juan María Gutiérrez, Juan Bautista Alberdi, Domingo Faustino Sarmiento, Vicente Fidel López, José Mármol, Juana Manuela Gorriti, Bartolomé Mitre, Carlos Guido Spano, Lucio Victorio Mansilla, Estanislao del Campo, José Hernández, Ricardo Gutiérrez, Nicolás Avellaneda, Olegario Víctor Andrade, William Henry Hudson, José Manuel Estrada, Eduardo Wilde, Paul Groussac, José María Ramos Mejía, Martín Coronado, Rafael Obligado, Miguel Cané.

CaBVaU   CtY   CU   CU-I   DLC   IU   MoSU   MU
NcD   PBm   OO   OOxM   OrU   OU

735   Hernández, Jorge Alberto. <u>Seis poetas de Santa Fe de principios de siglo</u>. Santa Fe: Colmegna, 1971. 50 p. 18 cm.
    An anthology of poetry by the following writers from the Argentine province of Santa Fe, including biobibliographical sketches: José Cibils, Angela Geneyro, Horacio F. Rodríguez, Gastón H. Lestard, Juan Julián Lastra, Alfonsina Storni.

CaQMM CLU CNoS CtY CU CU-S CU-SB
FU GU ICU InU IU MoSW MU NBuU NN
NNC TxU

736 Hidalgo, Bartolomé José. <u>Poetas gauchescos</u>:
Hidalgo, Ascasubi, del Campo. Buenos Aires:
Editorial Losada, 1940. 366 p. 20 cm.
(Colección de textos literarios, dirigida por
Amado Alonso).
An anthology of the poetry of the follow-
ing 19th-century Argentines for whom biogra-
phical essays are also featured: Bartolomé
José Hidalgo, Hilario Ascasubi, Estanislao
del Campo.

CaBVaU DLC FU ICU IdU IU NcD NcU
NFQC NIC NN OClJC OrU OU PU PV

737 <u>Historia de la literatura argentina</u>. Buenos
Aires: Centro Editor de América Latina, 1980.
4 v. Portraits. 26 cm.
A history of Argentine literature (16th-
20th centuries) including biobibliographical
essays, notes, and portraits on many writers.
The following are particularly featured:
V. 1: Ruy Díaz de Guzmán, Luis de Tejeda,
Juan Baltasar Maciel, Manuel José de Lavardén,
Vicente López y Planes, Pantaleón Rivarola,
Juan Cruz Varela, Bartolomé José Hidalgo,
Francisco de Paula Castañeda, Marcos Sastre,
Pedro de Angelis, Vicente Fidel López, Marco
M. de Avellaneda, Claudio M. Cuenca, Esteban
Echeverría, José Mármol, Juan María Gutiérrez,
Juan B. Alberdi, Domingo F. Sarmiento, Hilario
Ascasubi, Estanislao del Campo, Ricardo Gu-
tiérrez, Olegario Víctor Andrade, Vicente Fi-
del López, Bartolomé Mitre.
V. 2: José Hernández, Lucio V. Mansilla,
Miguel Cané, Eduardo Wilde, Eugenio Cambaceres,
José J. Podestá, Carlos Guido y Spano, Rafael
Obligado, Eduardo Gutiérrez, Almafuerte,
pseud. (Pedro B. Palacios), Fray Mocho, pseud.
(José S. Alvarez), Florencio Sánchez, Gregorio
de Laferrère.
V. 3: Leopoldo Lugones, Enrique Larreta,
Roberto J. Payró, Evaristo Carriego, Enrique
Banchs, Horacio Quiroga, Manuel Gálvez, Ri-
cardo Rojas, Baldomero Eugenio Otto Fernández
Moreno, Ricardo Güiraldes, Alfonsina Storni,
Juan Carlos Dávalos, Samuel Eichelbaum.
V. 4: Macedonia Fernández, Oliverio Gi-
rondo, Raúl González Tuñón, Roberto Arlt,
Bernardo Canal Feijóo, Jorge Luis Borges,
Silvina Ocampo, Eduardo Mallea, Ezequiel Mar-
tínez Estrada, Ricardo Molinari.

IU

738 Huberman, Silvio E., comp. <u>Otros trece cuen-
tos</u>. Buenos Aires: Instituto Amigos del
Libro Argentino, 1967. 105 p. 20 cm.
A collection of 13 contemporary Argentine
short stories, all preceded by short biobibliographical notes on their authors, most of
whom were born in the 1940s. They include
Roberto Adolfo Nicoli, Daniel Nelson Salzano,

Jorge Bernardino Mosqueira, Eduardo Tomás
Godoy, Alma de Amézola, Guillermo Féliz Orsi,
Osvaldo Roberto Soriano, Susana Mercedes Max-
well, Jorge Vicente Penna Regueiro, Elena
Mayte, Juan José Vilche, Luisa Peluffo, Luis
Wainerman.

CLSU CLU CSt IaU INS IU KU MiU
MoSW MN N NBuU NcU NIC NNC NSyU
OU PPULC TxU WU

739 Isaacson, José and Carlos Enrique Urquía,
comps. <u>40 [i.e. Cuarenta] años de poesía ar-
gentina</u>, 1920-1960. Buenos Aires: Editorial
Aldaba, 1962-64. 3 v. 20 cm.
An anthology of forty years of Argentine
poetry (1920-1960). Includes biobibliographi-
cal sketches of the following authors featured
in the text:
V. 1 (1920-1930): Leopoldo Lugones, Mace-
donio Fernández, Enrique Larreta, Miguel Andrés
Camino, Ricardo Rojas, Ricardo Güiraldes, Bal-
domero Fernández Moreno, Juan Carlos Dávalos,
Pedro Miguel Obligado, Rafael Alberto Arrieta,
Arturo Capdevila, Juan Pedro Calou, Arturo
Marasso, Alvaro Yunque, Oliverio Girondo, Al-
fonsina Storni, Alfredo R. Bufano, Ezequiel
Martínez Estrada, Francisco Isernia, Luis
Cané, Bernardo Canal Feijóo, Carlos de la Púa,
Enrique Méndez Calzada, Alfredo Brandán Cara-
ffa, Luis Leopoldo Franco, Ricardo Molinari,
Conrado Nalé Roxlo, Jorge Luis Borges, José
Pedroni, Horacio Rega Molina, Amado Villar,
Francisco Luis Bernárdez, José González Car-
balho, Fermín Estrella Gutiérrez, Jacobo Fij-
man, Eduardo González Lanuza, Leopoldo Mare-
chal, Carlos Mastronardi, Nicolás Olivari,
Gustavo Angel Riccio, Margarita Abella Caprile,
Roberto Ledesma, Cayetano Córdoba Iturburu,
Lysandro Z. D. Galtier, Carlos M. Grunberg,
Pedro Juan Vignale, Antonio de la Torre,
Aristóbulo Echegaray, Rafael Jijena Sánchez,
Francisco López Merino, José Sebastián Tallón,
Ulises Petit de Murat, Raúl González Tuñón,
Nydia Lamarque, Norah Lange, César Tiempo,
Jorge Enrique Ramponi, María Alicia Domínguez.
V. 2 (1930-1950): Antonio Porchia, Juan
L. Ortiz, Augusto González Castro, Germán Ber-
diales, Miguel Alfredo D'Elia, Elías Carpena,
Mario Luis Descotte, Gaspar L. Benavento, Os-
valdo Horacio Dondo, Ilka Krupkin, Juan Pinto,
Vicente Barbieri, Salvador Merlino, Silvina
Ocampo, Aldo Pellegrini, Horacio Esteban
Ratti, Marcos Victoria, Amaro Villanueva, Víc-
tor Luis Molinari, José Portogalo, Andrés del
Pozo, María de Villarino, Juan Burghi, Lázaro
Liacho, Joaquín Gómez Bas, Arturo Cambours
Ocampo, Juan Carlos Aráoz de la Madrid, Carlos
Carlino, Juan G. Ferreyra Basso, Alfredo Mar-
tínez Howard, Enrique Molina, Antonio Puga
Sabaté, Javier Villafañe, Miguel Angel Gómez,
Romualdo Brughetti, Victorino de Carolis, Raúl
Galán, Fernando Guibert, Adolfo de Obieta,
Fryda Schultz de Mantovani, Eduardo Jorge
Bosco, María Adela Agudo, Ernesto B. Rodríguez,
Juan Enrique Acuña, Mario Busignani, León Be-

LITERATURE

narós, Martín Alberto Boneo, Miguel D. Etchebarne, José Rodríguez Itoiz, César Rosales, Alfonso Solá González, Julia Prilutzky Farny, Mario Binetti, Jorge Calvetti, Daniel J. Devoto, Roberto Paine, Basilio Uribe, Antonio Esteban Agüero, Guillermo Etchebehere, Guillermo Orce Remis, Nicandro Pereyra, Raúl Amaral, Manuel J. Castilla, Ana María Chohuy Aguirre, Alberto Girri, Eduardo A. Jonquières, Edgar Bayley, César Fernández Moreno, Alberto Ponce de León, Juan Rodolfo Wilcock, Clara Lifsichtz, Aurora Venturini, Juan Jacobo Bajarlía, Américo Calí, José María Castiñeira de Dios, Angel Mazzei, Olga Orozco, Oswaldo Svanascini, María Granata, David Martínez, Miguel Alfredo Olivera, María Luisa Rubertino, Gregorio Santos Hernando, Mario Jorge de Lellis, Francisco Tomat-Guido, Horacio Jorge Becco, Miguel Brascó, Raúl Gustavo Aguirre.

V. 3 (1950-1960): Domingo Zerpa, Bernardo Verbitsky, Horacio Ponce de León, Emilio Carilla, Juan José Ceselli, Carlos Alberto Debole, Elva de Loizaga, Carlos Latorre, Jorge de Obieta, Carlos Alberto Alvarez, Néstor Groppa, Damián Carlos Bayón, Jaime Dávalos, Andrés Fidalgo, Horacio Núñez West, Alfredo A. Roggiano, Gustavo García Saraví, Juan Carlos Ghiano, Bernardo Horrach, Eduardo Joubín Colombres, Emilio Sosa López, Celina H. Uralde, Abelardo Vázquez, Julio Arístides, Carlos F. Grieben, Norberto Silvetti Paz, Amelia Biagioni, Rafael Henzo D'Alessio, Carlos Alberto Lanzillotto, Inés Malinow, Carlos Viola Soto, Héctor Yanover, Raúl Aráoz Anzoátegui, Héctor E. Ciocchini, Fernando Lorenzo, H. A. Murena, Atilio Jorge Castelpoggi, Fermín Chávez, Joaquín O. Giannuzzi, Gyula Kosice, José Martinano Paredes, Jorge Vocos Lezcano, Hugo Acevedo, Horacio Armani, Nemer Barud, Roberto E. Corvalán Posse, Ariel Ferraro, Roberto Juarroz, Luis Alberto Murray, Alberto Luis Ponzo, Alberto Vanasco, Nicolás Cócaro, Simón Kargieman, Agustín Pérez Pardella, Osvaldo Rossler, Julio César Silvain, Mario Trejo, Emma de Cartosio, Francisco José Madariaga, Jorge Enrique Móbili, Máximo Simpson, Miguel Angel Viola, Osiris U. Chierico, Luis Ricardo Furlan, Juan Carlos Pellegrini, Graciela de Sola, Adela Tarraf, Alfredo Veiravé, Rubén Vela, Oscar Hermes Villordo, Martín Campos, Fulvio Milano, Mario Norberto Silva, Matilde Alba Swan, Héctor Miguel Angeli, Alberto Oscar Blasi, Betina Edelberg, Nira Etchenique, Juan Gelman, Marta Elena Groussac, Juan José Hernández, Magdalena Harriague, Ester de Izaguirre, Ana Emilia Lahitte, Edgar Morisoli, Luisa Pasamanik, Esteban Peicovich, Antonio Requeni, Nélida Salvador, Flor Schapira Fridman, Francisco Urondo, María Angélica Villar, María Elena Walsh, Rogelio Bazán, Osvaldo Guevara, Roberto Hurtado de Mendoza, Gustavo Soler, Elizabeth Azcona Cranwell, Alberto Blasi Brambilla, Jorge Carrol, Rodolfo Alonso, Arnoldo Liberman, César Magrini, Carlos Alberto Merlino, Julio Huasi, Alejandra Pizarnik, Ramón Plaza,

Carlos A. Velazco. Alphabetical index of names in V. 3 for V. 1-3.

CU DPU ICarbS ICU InU IU LNHT MH
MiDW NcU NIC NjP NjR NN NSyU SdU

740 Isaacson, José, comp. <u>Poesía de la Argentina, de Tejeda a Lugones</u>. Buenos Aires: Editorial Universitaria de Buenos Aires, 1964. 126 p. 18 cm. (Serie del Nuevo Mundo).

An anthology of Argentine poetry (17th-20th centuries), including biobibliographical notes on the following authors: Luis de Tejeda, Manuel José de Labardén, Vicente López y Planes, Bartolomé Hidalgo, Juan Cruz Varela, Esteban Echeverría, Hilario Ascasubi, Juan María Gutiérrez, Luis L. Domínguez, José Mármol, Bartolomé Mitre, Carlos Guido y Spano, Estanislao del Campo, José Hernández, Ricardo Gutiérrez, Olegario Víctor Andrade, Rafael Obligado, Almafuerte, Belisario Roldán, Macedonio Fernández, Leopoldo Lugones, Ricardo Rojas, Evaristo Carriego, Ricardo Güiraldes, Baldomero Fernández Moreno, Juan Carlos Dávalos, Enrique Banchs, Rafael Alberto Arrieta, Arturo Capdevila, Arturo Marasso, Alfonsina Storni.

AAP CLSU CLU CoFS CSt CtY CU-S
FMU ICU InU IU KU MB MdBJ MH MiU
MU MWelC NbU NBuU NcU NhD NIC NjP
NN NSyU OOxM PSt TxDaM TxU UU

741 Jitrik, Noé. <u>Los viajeros</u>. Buenos Aires: J. Alvarez, 1969. 223 p. Portraits. 20 cm. (Los Argentinos. V. 9).

An anthology of Argentine prose and poetry reflecting description and travel in Europe. Includes biographical sketches, accompanied by portraits, of the following writers: Domingo Faustino Sarmiento, Miguel Cané (father), Miguel Cané (son), Lucio V. Mansilla, José Ingenieros, Florencio Sánchez, María R. Oliver, Rodolfo Aráoz Alfaro, Ricardo Güiraldes, Jorge Luis Borges, Vicente Rossi, Leopoldo Marechal, Roberto Arlt, Raúl González Tuñón, Miguel A. Cárcano, Victoria Ocampo, César Fernández Moreno, Julio Cortázar.

CFS CLSU CSt CU-S CU-B FU IaU ICU
InU IU MB MH MnU MoSW MWelC NIC
NjP NN NNC OU PPULC WaU ViU VtU
TxU

742 Justo, Liborio. <u>Literatura argentina y expresión americana</u> por Lobodon Garra, pseud. Buenos Aires: Editorial Rescate, 1977. 190 p. 20 cm.

An essay about Argentine literature, including biobibliographical data on the following writers: Leopoldo Lugones, Horacio Quiroga, Manuel Gálvez, Eduardo Mallea, Ezequiel Martínez Estrada, Ernesto Sábato, Elías Castelnuovo, Roberto Arlt.

IU

743 Koremblit, Bernardo Ezequiel. El ensayo en la Argentina. Buenos Aires: Ministerio de Relaciones Exteriores y Culto, Dirección General de Relaciones Culturales, 1968. 29 p. 22 cm.

An essay about the development of the essay in Argentine literature, mainly through biobibliographical sketches about the following notable Argentine essayists of the late 18th to the early 20th centuries: Mariano Moreno, Esteban Echeverría, Domingo Faustino Sarmiento, Juan Bautista Alberdi, Juan María Gutiérrez, Bartolomé Mitre, José Hernández, Pedro Goyena, Eduardo Wilde, Paul Groussac, Miguel Cané, Calixto Oyuela, Alejandro Korn, Martín García Mérou, Juan Agustín García, Agustín Alvarez, Joaquín V. González, Leopoldo Lugones, José León Pagano, José Ingenieros, Juan Pablo Echagüe, Manuel Ugarte, Ricardo Rojas, Manuel Gálvez, Alberto Gerchunoff, Carmelo Bonet, Roberto F. Giusti, Ricardo Sáenz Hayes, Rafael Alberto Arrieta, Arturo Marasso, Francisco Romero, Jorge Max Rohde, Ricardo Tudela, Ezequiel Martínez Estrada, Juan Mantovani, Pablo Rojas Paz, Luis Reissig, Bernardo Canal Feijóo, Luis Franco, Emilio De Matteis, Raúl Scalabrini Ortiz, Leónidas de Vedia, Marcos Victoria, Victoria Ocampo, Jorge Luis Borges, Guillermo de Torre, Carlos Mastronardi, Angel Battistessa, Luis Emilio Soto, Carlos Alberto Erro, Vicente Fatone, Eduardo Mallea, Enrique Anderson Imbert, Armando Tagle, Ernesto Sábato, Romualdo Brughetti, José Edmundo Clemente, Antonio Pagés Larraya, Juan Carlos Ghiano, Pedro Larralde, H. A. Murena, Víctor Massuh, Julio Mafud, José Luis Ríos Patrón.

CU-S DPU FMU MiU TxHR

744 Lagh, Domingo, comp. Cuentos argentinos. Buenos Aires: Ediciones Paulinas, 1962. 148 p. 19 cm. (Biblioteca Selva de cuentos modernos. V. 3).

A collection of 20th-century Argentine short stories, each accompanied by a short biobibliographical sketch on its author. These people include Pedro Inchauspe, Miguel Angel Correa (Mateo Booz, pseud.), María Alicia Domínguez, Leonardo Castellani, Ricardo E. Posse, Gustavo Martínez Zubiría (Hugo Wast, pseud.), Ada María Elflein, Arturo Cerretani, Germán Berdiales, Luis Garosito Heredia, Celia Reguera de Diego (Celia de Diego), Bonifacio Lastra.

CLSU CLU CtY CU IaU IU KU NbU NIC
NjR NN NSyU TNJ TU ViU WU

745 _____. Cuentos del folklore argentino. Buenos Aires: Ediciones Paulinas, 1962. 151 p. 19 cm. (Biblioteca Selva de cuentos modernos. V. 4).

A collection of Argentine short stories, including biobibliographical sketches of the following contemporary authors featured in the text: Leonardo Castellani, Velmiro Ayala Gauna, Santiago Ellena Gola, Martín del Pospós, Lily Franco, Eduardo A. Dughera, Juan Carlos Dávalos, Luis Gorosito Heredia, Horacio Quiroga, María Cañete de Rivas Jordán, Hugo Wast, Juan Draghi Lucero.

CLSU CtY IaU InU IU KU LNHT NbU
NIC NN NSyU OkU TxU ViU WU

745a Lancelotti, Mario A., comp. El cuento argentino, 1840-1940. Buenos Aires: Editorial Universitaria de Buenos Aires, 1965. 135 p. 18 cm. (Serie del Nuevo Mundo).

An anthology of Argentine short stories from the period 1840-1940, each preceded by a brief biobibliographical sketch on its author. They include Esteban Echeverría, Eduardo Wilde, Miguel Cané, Roberto J. Payró, Ricardo Güiraldes, Horacio Quiroga, Benito Lynch, Roberto Arlt, Macedonio Fernández, Santiago Dabove, Eduardo Mallea, Conrado Nalé Roxlo, Jorge Luis Borges, Ezequiel Martínez Estrada.

AU CLU CLSU CoFS CSt CtY DPU FMU
GU INS InU IU KU MB MH MiDW MiU
MnU MoSW MU NBuU NIC NjP NjR NN
NNC NSyU OCl OkU TxDaM TxU UU WaU

746 Lewkowicz, Lidia F. Generación poética del treinta. Buenos Aires: Ediciones Culturales Argentinas, Ministerio de Cultura y Educación, Secretaría de Estado de Cultura, 1974. 291 p. 21 cm. (Coleccción movimientos literarios argentinos).

An anthology of Argentine poetry from the "Generation of 1930," 1928-1940, including limited biobibliographical information and critical essays on the following poets and poetesses: Elvira de Alvear, Ignacio B. Anzoátegui, Carlos A. Barry, Gaspar L. Benavento, Romualdo Brughetti, Arturo Cambours Ocampo, Carlos Carlino, Luis de Paola, José R. Destéfano, Manuel Francioni, Alberto Franco, Haydée M. Ghio, María Julia Gigena, Enrique González Trillo, Luis Ortiz Behety, Teófilo Hiroux Funes, José Luis Lanuza, Homero Manzi, Alfredo Martínez Howard, Víctor Luis Molinari, Juan L. Ortiz, Antonio Miguel Podestá, Juan Oscar Ponferrada, José Portogalo, Andrés del Pozo, Sigfrido Radaelli, Jorge Enrique Ramponi, Marcelino M. Román, Luis Horacio Velásquez, Marcos Victoria, Javier Villafañe, María de Villarino, Roberto Zavalía Matienzo.

CSt CtY CU-S DGU GU InU MH MoSW
MU NBuU NcU NIC NN PPiU PPT TxU
ViU WU

747 Lichtblau, Myron I. The Argentine Novel in the Nineteenth Century. New York: Hispanic Institute in the United States, 1959. 225 p. 21 cm.

A study of the origin and development of the Argentine novel during the 19th century.

LITERATURE

Biographical information is included for many famous authors of that period, among them the following: Juana Manso de Noronha, José Mármol, Vicente Fidel López, Miguel Cané, Juana Manuela Gorriti, Pedro Echagüe, Eduardo Ladislao Holmberg, Luis Vicente Varela, Eduardo Gutiérrez, Eugenio Cambaceres, Carlos María Ocantos.

AU CaBVaU CLU CtY CU CU-I DHU FMU
FTaSU FU IaAS ICarbS ICU InU IU
KyU MH MiEM MiU MnU MoSW MoU MtU
MU NBC NbU NBuU NcD NcU NhD NIC
NjP NjR NN NNC OCU OKentU OkU OO
OrU OU PPULC TNJ TU TxU UU ViU
WU

748 Lóizaga, Elva de, comp. Poesía argentina para los niños. Buenos Aires: Ediciones Culturales Argentinas, 1961. 141 p. 23 cm.
An anthology of 20th-century children's poetry by Argentine authors followed by a short biobibliographical note on each writer whose work is represented. The following are included: Rafael Alberto Arrieta, Enrique Banchs, Ernesto Mario Barreda, Germán Berdiales, Francisco Luis Bernárdez, Amelia Biagioni, Alfredo Bufano, Luis Cané, Rodolfo Cárdenas Behety, Carlos Carlino, Emma de Cartosio, Córdova Iturburu, Ana María Chouy Aguirre, Fermín Estrella Gutiérrez, Baldomero Fernández Moreno, Juan G. Ferreyra Basso, Luis Franco, Raúl Galán, María Julia Gigena, José González Carbalho, Augusto González Castro, Eduardo González Lanuza, Rafael Jijena Sánchez, Leopoldo Lugones, Inés Malinow, Fryda Schultz de Mantovani, Angel Mazzei, Ricardo E. Molinari, Conrado Nalé Roxlo, Silvina Ocampo, José Pedroni, Ricardo Pose, Alfonsina Storni, José Sebastián Tallón, Pedro Juan Vignale, Javier Villafañe, María Elena Walsh.

CLSU IU

749 Loprete, Carlos Alberto. Poesía romántica argentina. Buenos Aires: Plus Ultra, 1965. 198 p. 20 cm.
A study of 19th-century romanticism in Argentina through the works of various famous poets of the period. Biographical material, including important events and analyses of works, is given for the following: Florencio Balcarce, Bartolomé Mitre, Juan María Gutiérrez, Esteban Echeverría, José Mármol, Olegario Víctor Andrade, Ricardo Gutiérrez, Rafael Obligado, Carlos Guido y Spano, Martín Coronado, Domingo D. Martinto.

CFS CLSU CoFS CSt CU-S De-U GU ICU
INS InU IU KyU MB MH MiDW MiU MnU
MoSW MoU NbU NBuU NcU NIC NjP
NjR NNC NSyU OU TNJ TxDaM TxHR
TxU UU WaU

750 Los que siguen. Buenos Aires: Ediciones Noé, 1972. 78 p. 19 cm. (Colección de poesía papeles para el arca).

A collection of Argentine poetry including limited biobibliographical information on the following poets of the second half of the 20th century (1945-1971): Lucina Alvarez, Guillermo Boido, Daniel Freidemberg, Guillermo Martínez Yantorno, Armando Najmanovich, Rubén Reches, Jorge Ricardo, Manuel Ruano.

AzTeS CtY IU NN

751 Loudet, Enrique. Letras argentinas en las Antillas; poetisas, poetas y prosistas argentinos. Labor diplomática. Ciudad Trujillo: Imprenta de la Marina de Guerra, 1957. 498 p. 24 cm.
An anthology of Argentine prose and poetry including biobibliographical sketches of the following men and women writers of the 19th and 20th centuries:
Poeteses: Margarita Abella Caprile, María Raquel Adler, Elvira de Alvear, Clementina Isabel Azlor, Emilia Bertolé, María Enriqueta Betnaza, Delia Mirtha Blanco, Alcira Bonazzola, Cecilia Borja, Lola S. B. de Borguet, Delfina Bunge de Gálvez, Julia Bustos, Herminia C. Brumana, Luisa Buren de Sanguinetti, Avelina Bustos de Quiroga, Susana Calandrelli, Isabel Cascallares Gutiérrez, Vicenta Castro Cambón, Mercedes Dantas Lacombe, Adelia Di Carlo, María Alicia Domínguez, Beatriz Eguía Muñoz, Ada M. Elflein, María Elena Fernández Madero, Eloísa Ferraría Acosta, Rosa García Costa, María Julia Gigena, Julieta Gómez Paz, Haydée Graciela Gerlero, Juana Manuela Gorriti, Beatriz Guido, Laura Holmberg de Bracht, Gisberta S. de Kurth, Nydia Lamarque, Norah Lange, Lili Loudet, Juana Manso, S. Medina Onrubia, Delfina Molina y Vedia de Bastianini, Sara Montes de Oca de Cárdenas, Zulma Núñez, Silvina Ocampo, Victoria Ocampo, Nené Padró, Nelda Palermo, Clotilde Pascua Lozzia, Laura Piccinini de la Cárcova, Malvina Rosa Quiroga, Hortensia Margarita Raffo, Ida Réboli, Mary Rega Molina, Frida Schultz C. de Mantovani, Gladys Smith, Aurora Suárez, Alfonsina Storni, Bertha L. de Tabbush, María Torres Frías, Sara del Carmen Ugazzi, María de Villarino, Maruja de Vidal Fernández, María Amalia Zamora, Ofelia Zúccoli Fidanza.
Poets: Gregorio Alvarez, Tomás Allende Irragorri, Olegario V. Andrade, Ignacio B. Anzoátegui, Rafael Alberto Arrieta, Hilario Ascasubi, Domingo de Azcuénaga, Florencio Balcarce, Enrique Banchs, Mario Ernesto Barreda, Francisco Luis Bernárdez, Germán Berdiales, Héctor Pedro Blomberg, Mario Bravo, Mario Binetti, Juan Bautista Bioy, Jorge Luis Borges, Alfredo R. Bufano, Vicente Bove, Juan Burghi, Estanislao del Campo, Ricardo del Campo, Bernardo Canal Feijóo, Luis Cané, José María Cantilo, Arturo Capdevila, Gustavo Caraballo, Brandán Caraffa, Evaristo Carriego, Joaquín Castellanos, Martín Coronado, J. C. Clemente, Córdova Iturburu, Julián de Charras, Pedro Mario Delheye, Leopoldo Díaz, Julio Díaz Usandivaras, Héctor Díaz Leguizamón, Eugenio Díaz Romero, Rafael de Diego, Luis L. Domínguez,

Andrés Chabrillón, Esteban Echeverría, Fermín Estrella Gutiérrez, Raúl T. de Ezeiza Monasterio, Fernán Félix de Amador, Baldomero Fernández Moreno, César Fernández Moreno, Diego Fernández Espiro, Ricardo Figueroa, Luis L. Franco, Juan G. Ferreyra Basso, Bartolomé Galíndez, Domingo V. Gallardo, Juan Carlos García Santillán, Alberto Ghiraldo, Oliverio Girondo, J. González Carvalho, Roberto Godel, Joaquín Gómez Bas, Raúl González Tuñón, Alejo González Garano, Augusto González Castro, Eduardo González Lanuza, Juan Bautista Grosso, Ricardo Gutiérrez, Federico A. Gutiérrez, Juan María Gutiérrez, Carlos Guido y Spano, José Hernández, Ataliva Herrera, Pedro Herreros, Eugenio Julio Iglesias, Francisco Isernia, Ricardo Jaimes Freyre, Rafael Jigena Sánchez, Luis María Jordán, Carlos Jovellanos y Paseyro, Eduardo Keller, Manuel José de Labardén, Juan Crisóstomo Lafinur, Honorio Lartigau Lespada, Visconde Emilio Lascano Tegui, Carlos Alberto Leumann, Roberto Ledesma, Vicente López y Planes, Manuel López de Mingorande, Enrique Loudet, Francisco López Meriño, Esteban de Luca, Leopoldo Lugones, Arturo Marasso, Juan Baltasar Maciel, Roberto Mariani, Vicente Martínez Cuitiño, Ezequiel Martínez Estrada, José Mármol, Carlos Mastronardi Negri, Luis Matharán, José de Maturana, Carlos F. Melo, Enrique Méndez Calzada, Salvador Merlino, Héctor F. Miri, José Antonio Miralla, Evar Méndez, Gervacio Méndez, Ricardo E. Molinari, Edmundo Montagne, José María Monner Sans, Antonio Monti, Artemio Moreno, Ismael Moya, Ernesto Morales, Conrado Nalé Roxlo, Pedro J. Naón, Ismael Navarro Puentes, Rafael Obligado, Carlos Obligado, Jorge Obligado, Pedro Miguel Obligado, Julio Ortiz, Juan L. Ortiz, Carlos Ortiz, Calixto Oyuela, Pedro B. Palacios (Almafuerte), Delio Panizza, José Pedroni, Félix M. Pelayo, Adolfo L. Pérez Zelaschi, Juan Pinto, Juan Oscar Ponferrada, Carlos de la Púa, Horacio Rega Molina, Ricardo Riccio, Francisco Aníbal Riú, Pantaleón Rivarola, Enrique Rivarola, Rodolfo Fausto Rodríguez, Fray Cayetano Rodríguez, Jorge Max Rodhe, Ricardo Rojas, Belisario Roldán, Carlos Gregorio Romero Sosa, Carlos C. Sanguinetti, José María Samperio, Horacio Schiavo, Alejandro Sux, José Sebastián Tallón, Antonio de la Torre, C. Tubio Torrecillas, César Tiempo, Manuel Ugarte, Florencio Varela, Juan Cruz Varela, Natalio Abel Vadell, Arturo Vázquez Cey, Carlos Vega, Ricardo Victorica, Amado Villar, Victoria Manso, Pedro Juan Vignale, Félix B. Visillac, Juan Rodolfo Wilcock, Alvaro Yunque, Lizardo Zía, Carlos de Zavalía.

Prose writers: Juan Bautista Alberdi, Agustín Alvarez, Octavio R. Amadeo, Florentino Ameghino, Vicente Arias, Nicolás Avellaneda, Lucas Ayarragaray, José J. Berrutti, Jorge G. Blanco Villalta, Carmelo M. Bonet, Antonio J. Bucich, Carlos Octavio Bunge, Miguel Cané, José Luis Cantilo, Ramón J. Cárcano, Félix Esteban Cichero, Nicolás Coronado, Juan Carlos Dávalos, Juan Pablo Echagüe, Angel de Estrada, José Manuel Estrada, Pedro B. Franco, Gustavo

J. Franceschi, Félix Frías, Juan Ignacio de Gorriti, Germán de Laferrere, Gregorio de Laferrere, José Sixto Alvarez (Fray Mocho, pseud.), Manuel Gálvez, Enrique García Velloso, Juan Agustín García, Alberto Gerchunoff, Roberto F. Giusti, Bernardo González Arrili, Joaquín V. González, Pedro Goyena, Paul Groussac, Ricardo Güiraldes, Carlos Ibarguren, José Ingenieros, Enrique Larreta, Lucio V. López, E. López Serrot, Benito Lynch, Eduardo Mallea, Lucio V. Mansilla, Fernando Márquez, Alvaro Melián Lafinur, Víctor Mercante, Bartolomé Mitre, W. Jaime Molins, Ernesto Nelson, Santiago I. Núdelman, Clemente Onelli, Alfredo L. Palacios, Roberto J. Payró, Juan Manuel Pintos, Pablo A. Pizzurno, Aníbal Ponce, David Peña, Juan Manuel Prat, Vicente G. Quesada, Carlos B. Quiroga, Cesáreo Rodríguez, Ricardo Rojas, Carlos Gregorio Romero Sosa, Domingo F. Sarmiento, Rodolfo Senet, Juan José de Soiza Reilly, Eduardo Schiaffino, José León Suárez, Juan B. Terán, Juan S. Valmaggia, Alberto Viñas, Constancio C. Vigil, Hugo Wast, Eduardo Wilde, Rómulo Zabala, Facundo de Zuviría.

DLC-P4 DPU IU WU

752 Lugones, Piri. *Memorias de infancia.* Buenos Aires: Editorial J. Alvarez, 1968. 92 p. 18 cm.
A collection of childhood reminiscences of the following Argentine writers: Beatriz Guido, Juan José Hernández, Leopoldo Marechal, Manuel Mujica Láinez, Victoria Ocampo, Augusto Roa Bastos, Rodolfo Walsh, José Donoso, Manuel Puig.

CaBVaU CLSU CSt CtY FMU FU IaU ICIU
IU MB MiDW MoSW MU NcGU NIC NSyU
NN OU PPULC TU TxDaM TxU ViU

753 Maggio de Taboada, María, comp. *Cuentos del interior.* Buenos Aires: Ediciones Coluihue, 1981. 156 p. 18 cm.
An anthology of short stories by the following Argentine writers, including biobibliographical sketches. Those featured are Daniel Ovejero, Pablo Rojas Paz, Luis Leopoldo Franco, Juan Draghi Lucero, Asencio Abeijón, Juan Carlos Neyra, Velmiro Ayala Gauna, Mateo Booz, Horacio Quiroga, Jorge W. Abalos.

TU

754 Magis, Carlos Horacio. *La literatura argentina.* México: Editorial Pormaca, 1965. 307 p. 21 cm. (Colección Pormaca. V. 20).
A history and criticism of Argentine literature, covering the period from conquest to the present day. Biographical information is included for many authors, particularly the following: Luis de Miranda, Ulrich Schmidl, Baltasar de Ovando (Reginaldo de Lizárraga, pseud.), Ruy Díaz de Guzmán, Luis José de Tejeda y Guzmán, Félix de Azara, Manuel José de Lavardén, Esteban de Luca, Vicente López y Planes, Juan Crisóstomo Lafinur, Cayetano

LITERATURE

Rodríguez, Juan Cruz Varela, Esteban Echeverría, José Mármol, Juan María Gutiérrez, Bartolomé Mitre, Vicente Fidel López, Domingo Faustino Sarmiento, Juan Bautista Alberdi, Hilario Ascasubi, Estanislao del Campo, José Hernández, Miguel Cané, Eduardo Wilde, Lucio Vicente López, Eugenio Cambaceres, Francisco Sicardi, José María Miró (Julián Martel, pseud.), Carlos María Ocantos, Olegario Víctor Andrade, Pedro Bonifacio Palacios, Rafael Obligado, Carlos Guido y Spano, Roberto J. Payró, Florencio Sánchez, Leopoldo Lugones, Jorge Luis Borges.

AAP CaQMM CLSU CLU CoFS CSt CtY
CU-S DPU FTaSU GASU IaDL ICU InU
IU KU MdU MH MiEM MoSW MU MWUC
NbU NBuU NcRS NIC NjP NjR NN NNC
OU PPT RPB TxDaM TxFTC TxU ViU WU

755 Malvigne, Pedro César. <u>Pedro Miguel Obligado y el dolor de los grandes</u>. Buenos Aires: Falbo, 1967. 132 p. 21 cm.
Collection of biobibliographical essays about the following notable Argentine poets of the 20th century: Pedro Miguel Obligado, Evaristo Carriego, Alfonsina Storni, Carlos Guido Spano, Baldomero Fernández Moreno, Pío Collivadino, Arturo Marasso, Gabriela Mistral (Chilean).

AzU CLSU CLU CSt CtY CU IaU InU
IU KU MB MH MiDW MIU MoSW MU
NBuU NcU NIC NjP NN NNC OU ScU
TNJ TxU WU

756 Manguel, Alberto, comp. <u>Antología de literatura fantástica argentina</u>; narradores del siglo XX por Adolfo Bioy Casares et al. Buenos Aires: Editorial Kapelusz, 1973. 203 p. 18 cm. (Grandes obras de la literatura universal. V. 99).
An anthology of Argentine 20th-century fantastic fiction, accompanied by short biobibliographical sketches on the authors, who include Adolfo Bioy Casares, Angel Bonomini, Jorge Luis Borges, Julio Cortázar, Marco Denevi, Manuel Mujica Láinez, Héctor A. Murena, Silvina Ocampo, Bernardo Schiavetta.

CaBVaU CLU CSt CtY CU CU-S FU GASU
InU IU MB MU NIC NNC OOxM PPiU
TxU WU

757 _____. <u>Variaciones sobre un tema policial</u>. Buenos Aires: Editorial Galerna, 1968. 126 p. 20 cm. (Serie mayor. Letras. V. 1).
An anthology of contemporary short-story writers, including biobibliographical sketches. Those featured are Abelardo Díaz, Leónidas Barletta, Estela Canto, Marta Lynch, Manuel Mujica Láinez, Roger Plá, Eduardo Quiroga, Dalmiro Sáenz.

IU

758 Martínez, David. <u>Poesía argentina actual</u>, 1930-1960. Buenos Aires: Ediciones Culturales Argentinas, Ministerio de Educación y Justicia, Dirección General de Cultura, 1961. 262 p. 20 cm. (Biblioteca del sesquicentenario. Colección: Movimientos literarios).
An anthology of Argentine poetry (1930-1960), including biobibliographical sketches of the following writers featured in the text: Ignacio Anzoátegui, Vicente Barbieri, Osvaldo Horacio Dondo, Silvina Ocampo, Juan L. Ortiz, Jorge Enrique Ramponi, Horacio Esteban Ratti, Javier Villafañe, María de Villarino, León Benarós, Eduardo Jorge Bosco, Jorge Calvetti, José María Castiñeira de Dios, Ana María Chouhy Aguirre, Miguel D. Etchebarne, César Fernández Moreno, Juan G. Ferreyra Basso, Miguel Angel Gómez, María Granata, Enrique Molina, Olga Orozco, Roberto Paine, César Rosales, Gregorio Santos Hernando, Alfonso Solá González, Juan Rodolfo Wilcock, Raúl Aráoz Anzoátegui, Horacio Armani, Horacio Jorge Becco, Mario Busignani, Atilio Jorge Castelpoggi, Manuel J. Castilla, Emma de Cartosio, Nicolás Cócaro, Julio Carlos Díaz Usandivaras, Guillermo Orce Remis, Nicandro Pereyra, Norberto Silvetti Paz, Jorge Vocos Lescano, María Elena Walsh, Rodolfo Alonso, Juan José Ceselli, Héctor Eduardo Ciocchini, Juan Carlos Ghiano, Joaquín O. Giannuzzi, Alberto Girri, Fernando Guibert, Eduardo A. Jonquières, Francisco José Madariaga, Héctor A. Murena, Osvaldo Rossler, Emilio Sosa López, Mario Trejo, Alberto Vanasco, Hugo Acevedo, Héctor Miguel Angeli, Amelia Biagioni, Magdalena Harriague, Juan José Hernández, Roberto Juarroz, Fernando Lorenzo, Antonio Requeni, Adela Tarraf, Héctor Viel Temperley, Enrique Vidal Molina, Oscar Hernes Villordo.

CU ICU IU NIC NN

759 Martini Real, Juan Carlos, comp. <u>Los mejores poemas de la poesía argentina</u>. 3. ed. aum. y corr. Buenos Aires: Ediciones Corregidor, 1977. 384 p. 20 cm. (Biblioteca de poesía).
An anthology of Argentine poetry from the 19th century to contemporary times including biobibliographical sketches of the following writers featured in the text: Raúl Gustavo Aguirre, Almafuerte, Rodolfo Alonso, Martín Alvarenga, Américo Alvarez, Carlos Alberto Alvarez, Pablo Anania, Olegario Víctor Andrade, Héctor Miguel Angeli, Raúl Aráoz Anzoategui, Horacio Armani, Rafael Alberto Arrieta, Azcona Cranwell, Juan Jacobo Bajarlía, Enrique Banchs, Vicente Barbieri, Leopoldo José Bartolomé, Edgar Bayley, León Benaros, Francisco Luis Bernárdez, José Betinoti, Amalia Biagioni, Juana Bignozzi, Alberto Claudio Blasetti, Héctor Pedro Blomberg, Jorge Luis Borges, Eduardo Jorge Bosco, Alfredo Brandán Caraffa, Miguel Brasco, Mario Bravo, Alfredo R. Bufano, Mario Busignani, Miguel Angel Bustos, Enrique Caricamo, Juan Pedro Calou, Jorge Calvetti,

Arturo Cambours Ocampo, Luis Cané, Arturo Cap-
devila, Elías Carpena, Evaristo Carriego,
Manuel J. Castilla, Horacio Castillo, José
María Castiñeira de Dios, Juan José Ceselli,
Jorge Conti, Pascual Contursi, Ana María
Chouhy Aguirre, Eduardo D'Anna, Jaime Dávalos,
Juan Carlos Dávalos, Ramiro de Casasbellas,
Carlos de la Púa, Mario Jorge de Lellis, Leo-
poldo Díaz, Hugo Diz, Alicia Dujovne Ortiz,
Fermín Estrella Gutiérrez, Miguel D. Etche-
barne, Homero Expósito, Gabino Ezeiza, Mace-
donio Fernández, Baldomero Fernández Moreno,
César Fernández Moreno, Ariel Ferraro, Juan
G. Ferreyra Basso, Andrés Fidalgo, Jacobo
Fijman, Celedonio Esteban Flores, Luis Franco,
Héctor Gagliardi, Raúl Galán, Gustavo García
Saravi, Juan Gelman, Alberto Ghiraldo, Joa-
quín O. Giannuzzi, Antonio Alejandro Gil,
Oliverio Girondo, Alberto Girri, Pedro Godoy,
Hugo Gola, José González Carbalho, Eduardo
González Lanuza, Raúl González Tuñón, Federico
Gorbea, María Granata, Néstor Groppa, Carlos
M. Grunberg, Carlos Guido y Spano, Ricardo
Güiraldes, José Isaacson, Noé Jitrik, Roberto
Juarroz, Leónidas Lamborghini, Enrique Larreta,
Carlos Latorre, Roberto Ledesma, Francisco
López Merino, Luis Luchi, Leopoldo Lugones,
Julio Llinas, Francisco Madariaga, Homero
Manzi, Arturo Marasso, Leopoldo Marechal,
Ezequiel Martínez Estrada, Alfredo Martínez
Howard, Carlos Mastronardi, Angel Mazzei,
Martín Micharvegas, Jorge Enrique Mobili, En-
rique Molina, Ricardo Molinari, Mario Morales,
H. A. Murena, Conrado Nalé Roxlo, Pedro Miguel
Obligado, Rafael Obligado, Silvina Ocampo,
Nicolás Olivari, Olga Orozco, Juan L. Ortiz,
Roberto Paine, José Pedroni, Aldo Pellegrini,
José Peroni, Marcelo Pichón Riviere, Alejandra
Pizarnik, Antonio Porchia, José Portogalo,
Jorge Ramponi, Horacio Rega Molina, Antonio
Requeni, Gustavo Riccio, Ricardo Rojas, Beli-
sario Roldán, Eduardo Romano, Osvaldo Rossler,
Roberto Sánchez, Enrique Santos Discépolo,
Mario Satz, Norberto Silvetti Paz, Gianni
Siccardi, Francisco Squeo Acuña, Alfonsina
Storni, María del Carmen Suárez, Alberto
Szpunberg, José Sebastián Tallón, Luis O.
Tedesco, Armando Tejada Gómez, Roberto Themis
Speroni, César Tiempo, Mario Trejo, Ricardo
Tudela, Manuel Ugarte, Francisco Urondo, Car-
los Enrique Urquía, Alberto Vanasco, Alfredo
Veirave, Jorge Vocos Lescano, María Elena
Walsh, Juan Rodolfo Wilcock, Atahualpa Yupan-
qui, Domingo Zerpa.

IU

760 Mastrángelo, Carlos, comp. <u>Diez cuentistas
de urumpta</u>. Buenos Aires: Plus Ultra, 1973.
174 p. 18 cm.
An anthology of stories written by ten
contemporary authors living in the Argentine
city of Río Cuarto in the province of Córdoba,
and each preceded by a short biobibliographical sketch. The following are featured:
Juan Filloy, Juan A. Floriani, Joaquín T.

Bustamante (Chañi Lao, pseud.), Oscar Maldonado Carulla, José Martorelli, Carlos Mastrángelo, Cecilio Pérez de la Rosa, Miguel Angel
Solivellas, Antonio Stoll, Sara Zimerman.

CLU CSt CtY CU FU IU KU MB MH MU
NcU NIC NmU NN TxU WU

761 Matteis, Emilio de. <u>Storia della civiltà
argentina nelle fonti letterarie</u>; introduzione
e traduzione dall'originale spagnolo inedito,
di Sandro Cassone. Torino: Fratelli Bocca,
1932. 290 p. 25 cm. (Biblioteca de scienze
moderne. V. 111).
A literary history of Argentina, covering
the period from colonial to modern times, and
including biobibliographical information on
many authors representing all time periods
and genres. The following are particularly
featured: Luis de Tejeda, Baltasar de Obando
(Reginaldo de Lizárraga, pseud.), Garcilaso
de la Vega, Ruy Díaz de Guzmán, Nicolás del
Techo, Pedro Lozano, José Guevara, Gaspar
Juárez, Juan Baltazar Maziel, Manuel de Labardén, Bartolomé Hidalgo, Juan Gualberto Go-
doy, Mariano Moreno, José Martí (Cuba), Simón
Bolívar, Benito Juárez (Mexico), Gregorio
Funes (Decano Funes), Ventura de la Vega,
Luis Roque Gondra, Bernardo Monteagudo, Este-
ban de Luca, Juan Ramón Rojas, Cayetano Rodrí-
guez, Juan Cruz Varela, José Antonio Miralla,
Bernardo Vera y Pintado, Florencio Balcarce,
Esteban Echeverría, Domingo Faustino Sarmiento,
José Mármol, Juan Ignacio Gorriti, Benjamín
Villafañe, Félix Frías, Pedro Echague, Flo-
rencio Varela, José Rivera Indarte, Claudio
Mamerto Cuenca, Pedro de Angelis, Facundo de
Zuviría, Mariano Fragueiro, Valentín Alsina,
Francisco Agustín Wright, Juan Bautista Al-
berdi, Bartolomé Mitre, Juan María Gutiérrez,
Vicente Fidel López, Hilario Ascasubi, José
Hernández, Juan B. Ambrosetti.

DLC IaU IU NcU

762 Maubé, José Carlos, and Adolfo Capdevielle,
comps. <u>Antología de la poesía femenina ar-
gentina</u>, con referencias biográficas y bibliográficas; seleccionada y ordenada por José
Carlos Maubé y Adolfo Capdevielle. Prólogo de
Rosa Bazán de Cámara. Carátula y ex-libris
de Sara Capdevielle. Buenos Aires: Impresores Ferrari hnos, 1930. 509 p. 20 cm.
An anthology of poetry including biobibliographical sketches of the following Argentine
women poets of the 20th century: Margarita
Abella Caprile, Raquel Adler, Amalia Alcoba
Martínez, María Aliaga Rueda, Emilia Altomare
de Pereyra (Cleta Masa, pseud.), Agustina Andrade, María Henriqueta Argüello, Elena Ave-
llaneda, Clementina Isabel Azlor, Irene Barthalot (Amarilis, pseud.), Juana María Begino,
Emilia Bertolé, María Enriqueta Bourguet,
Delfina Bunge de Gálvez, Julia Bustos, Susana
Calandrelli, María Tránsito Cañete de Rivas
Jordán, Blanca C. E. Colt de Hume, Blana C.

LITERATURE

de Hume, María Luisa Carnelli, Isabel Cascalleres Gutiérrez, Vicenta Castro Cambón, Lucrecia Centeno del Campillo, Josefina Crosa, Mercedes Dantas Lacombe, Matilde Delpodio, María Alicia Domínguez, Josefina Durbec de Routín (Vero, pseud.), Beatriz Eguía Muñoz, Sofía Espíndola, Silvia Fernández, María Elena Fernández Madero, Léonie Julieta Fournier (Nirene Jofre Oliú, pseud.), Hebe Foussats, Angélica Fuselli, Justa B. Gallardo de Zalazar Pringles, Rosa García Costa, Julia García Games, Sarah Felisa García y Onrubia (Chérie García y Onrubia, pseud.), Adela García Salaberry, Haydée M. Ghio, Irasema Gómez Gersbach, Pastora González de Nicolai, Rosa Guerra, Margot Guezúraga, Elina Herrera (Eros, pseud.), María A. Hevia, Laura Holmberg de Bracht, Nydia Lamarque, Norah Lange, Chita de Leonardo, Juana Paula Manso de Noronha, Salvadora Medina Onrubia, Doelia S. Míguez, María Esther Milesi (Stella Maris, pseud.), Delfina Molina y Vedia de Bastianini, Esther Monasterio, Sara Montes de Oca de Cardénas, Anita Nieva de Muñoz, María Hortensia Palisa Mujica, Josefina Pelliza de Sagasta, Tilde Pérez Pieroni, Laura Piccinini de la Cárcova, Amalia Prebisch de Piossek, Mercedes Pujato Crespo de Camelino Vedoya, Malvina Rosa Quiroga, Teresa Ramos Carrión, Ida L. Réboli, Mary Rega Molina, Estela Riganelli Celini, María Elina Rodríguez Bustamante de Demaría, Angela Rousset de San Martín, María Helena Saavedra Basavilbaso, Mercedes Saavedra Zelaya (M. de Saavedra Z., pseud.), Isolina Sáenz de Centeno, Cándida Santamaría, Clara Saravia Linares, Ana Rosa Serrano Redonnet, Paulina Simoniello, Sara Solá de Castellanos, Emma Solá de Solá, Edelina Soto y Calvo, Alfonsina Storni, Aurora Suárez, María Torres Frías, María del Carmen Vázquez de Montiel (Concepción Ríos, pseud.), Matilde A. Vera, Berta Elena Vidal de Battini, Carmen Villalba de Lentati, María de Villarino, María Amalia Zamora. Alphabetical index of names.

DLC   IU   NcU   PSt

763   Menéndez y Pelayo, Marcelino. <u>Historia de la poesía argentina</u>. Buenos Aires: Institución Cultural Española, 1943. 203 p. 16 cm.
An essay about Argentine poetry of the 19th century, including biographical data, of varying amounts, of the following writers associated with it: Juan Bautista Maciel, Gregorio Funes, Manuel José de Labardén, Prego de Oliver, José Vicente Alonso, José Fernández Guerra, Juan Cruz Varela, Florencio Varela, Ventura de la Vega, Esteban Echeverría, Juan María Gutiérrez, José Rivera Indarte, José Mármol. Also biographical essay of Marcelino Menéndez y Pelayo.

IU   PSt   ViU   TxU

764   <u>Mi mejor cuento</u>. Buenos Aires: Ediciones Orión, 1973. 227 p. 19 cm. (Colección alfa de Orión).

An anthology of Argentine short stories by the following contemporary writers, including brief biobibliographical sketches: Abelardo Arias, Adolfo Bioy Casares, Poldy Bird, Jorge Luis Borges, Antonio Di Benedetto, Eduardo Gudino Kieffer, Beatriz Guido, Manuel Mujica Láinez, Silvina Ocampo, Syria Poletti.

IU   MU   NcD   PSt   WU

765   Miranda Klix, José Guillermo. <u>Cuentistas argentinos de hoy</u>. Buenos Aires: Ed. Claridad, 1929. 241 p. Portraits. 18 cm.
A collection of contemporary Argentine short stories, each preceded by a portrait and a short biobibliographical essay on its author. The following are included: Roberto Arlt, Leónidas Barletta, Rolando Cartasegna, Armando Cascella, Elías Castelnuovo, Juan I. Cendoya, Héctor I. Eandi, Samuel Eichelbaum, Guillermo Estrella, José Hernán Figueroa, E. González Lanuza, Samuel Glusberg, Victoria Gukovski, Juan Guijarro, Manuel Kirs, Ilka Krupkin, Eduardo Mallea, Roberto Mariani, Enrique Méndez Calzada, Salvadora Medina Onrubia, Miranda Klix, Arturo S. Mom, José C. Picnoe, Alberto Pinetta, Abel Rodríguez, José Salas Subirat, Raúl Scalambrini Ortiz, Alvaro Yunque.

CLU   DPU   IU   MH   MiU   MWelC   NcD   NcU   PSt

766   Monti, Antonio, comp. <u>Antología poética de la revolución justicialista</u>. Buenos Aires: Librería Perlado, 1954. 174 p. 24 cm.
An anthology of Argentine poetry dedicated to the movement for justice that took place in Argentina during the leadership of Juan and Eva Perón, including brief biobibliographical sketches of the following authors: Oscar Aguirre, Alberto Oscar Blasi, Raúl Bustos Fierro, José María Castiñeiras De Dios, Juan Carlos Clemente, Fermín Chávez, Alfonso Depascale, Francisco Dibella, Rolando Dorcas Berro, Julio Ellena de la Sota, Raúl Ezeiza Monasterio, J. M. Fernández Unsain, Alfonso Ferrari Amores, Zulema Foassa, Alberto Franco, Juan Fuscaldo, Santiago Ganduglia, Juan Francisco Giacobbe, Miguel Angel Gómez, Luis Gorosito Heredia, María Granata, Rafael Gigena Sánchez, Pedro M. Larroca, López Ruiz, A. López Torres, Ofelia Magariños Pinto, Teófilo Marín, Leopoldo Marechal, Claudio Martínez Paiva, Raúl A. Mende, Antonio Monti, Antonio Nella Castro, E. A. Olmedo, Maruca Ortega de Carrasco, Luis Ortiz Behety, Juan Oscar Ponferrada, Julia Prilutzky Farny, Gregorio Santos Hernando, Alfonso Solá González, J. Soler Daras, Rodolfo I. Turdera, Alberto Vacarezza, Luis Horacio Velázquez, Héctor V. Villanueva, Omar Viñole, Beatriz Yane de Scillatto, Lisardo Zía, Ofelia Zuccoli Fidanza.

CSt-H   CtY   DLC   IU   NN   TxU

767   Morales, Ernesto. <u>Lírica popular rioplatense</u>; antología gaucha. Buenos Aires: El Ateneo, 1927. 244 p. 19 cm.

A collection of extracts of 19th-century gaucho poetry, accompanied by short biobibliographical sketches on their authors. They include Bartolomé Hidalgo, Hilario Ascasubi, Estanislao del Campo, José Hernández, Rafael Obligado, José Alonso Trelles (Viejo Pancho, pseud.), Fernán Silva Valdes, Pedro Leandro Ipuche, Epifanio Orozco Zárate.

CtY DLC IU MH OClW OO PHC TU
TxU ViU

768 Morán, Rosa Blanca de. <u>Plumas y pinceles de la pampa</u>. Buenos Aires: Editorial Dinámica Gráfica, 1955. 163 p. Portraits. 27 cm.
Selections of prose, poetry, and paintings whose subject matter is the Argentine pampas, including biobibliographical sketches, accompanied by portraits, of the following Argentine authors and painters of the 20th century:
Poets: Advíncula Rubio de Garrido, Julio Nery Rubio, Manuel Ignacio Segovia (Atahualpa, pseud.), Carlos Alberto Torres, Juan Alberto Torres, Juan Alberto Videla, Armando C. Forteza, Francisco Morales, Tomás Niceto de Pablos, Alina Esther Pico de Negrotto, Juan Ricardo Nervi, Miguel Iribarne, Coca Amanda Coronel, José Adolfo Gaillardou, José Alejandro Lucero, Olga Orozco, Miguel Angel Gómez, Martha Sara Giménez Pastor.
Prose writers: Alberto J. Grassi, Enrique Stieben, Carlos Sfondrini, Ramón T. Elizando, Arturo Veliz Díaz, José Prado Escol, Mariano Vélez, Miguel de Fougéres.
Artists: Nicolás Toscano, Juan Carlos Durán, Victorio Pesce, Electra Haydée Vázquez, Elba Valdez Leiva, Emilio González Moreno, Juan Ricardo Nervi.

DLC IU TxU

769 Murray, Luis Alberto, comp. <u>Humorismo argentino</u>. Buenos Aires: Ediciones Culturales Argentinas, 1961. 202 p. 19 cm. (Biblioteca del sesquicentenario; colección antologías.)
A collection of numerous works by the following 19th- and 20th-century Argentine writers for whom short biobibliographical sketches are also included: Juan Cruz Varela, Domingo Faustino Sarmiento, Estanislao del Campo, Lucio V. Mansilla, Eduardo Wilde, Lucio V. López, Godofredo Daireaux, José S. Alvarez (Fray Mocho, pseud.), Roberto J. Payró, Gregorio de Laferrère, Macedonio Fernández, Pedro E. Pico, Alberto Gerchunoff, Baldomero Fernández Moreno, Oliverio Girondo, Arturo Cancela, Luis Cané, Raúl Scalabrini Ortiz, Enrique Méndez Calzada, Luis Franco, Conrado Nalé Roxlo (Chamico, pseud.), Horacio Rega Molina, Jorge Luis Borges, Nicolás Olivari, Enrique González Tuñón, Florencio Escardó (Piolín de Macramé, pseud.), Ignacio B. Anzoátegui, Raúl González Tuñón, Carlos H. Warnes (César Bruto, pseud.), Arturo Núñez García (Wimpi, pseud.), Ernesto Sábato, Arturo Horacio Guida, Helvio I. Botana (Poroto, pseud.), Jaime A. Botana (Jaimote Botanilla, pseud.), Pedro Pernías (Jordán de la Cazuela,

pseud.), Carlos Peralta (Carlos del Peral, pseud.), Miguel Brascó, Julio Gil (Pericles, pseud.).

CaBVaU CtY CU DPU ICarbS IEN InU
IU LNHT MB MH MoSW NBuU NcU NIC
NjP NN NNC NSyU OOxM OU PPT PSt
TxU ViU

770 <u>Narradores argentinos contemporáneos</u>. Buenos Aires: Editorial Sapientia, 1958. 124 p. (Colección narradores).
A two-volume anthology of short stories by Argentine writers of the 20th century, preceded by a biobibliographical sketch of the author. Those included:
V. 1: Roberto Hosne, Juan José Manuata, Jorge Onetti, Víctor Pronzato, Enrique Wernicke.
V. 2: Leónidas Barletta, Andrés Cinquagrama, Luis Pico Estrada, Gerardo Pisarello, Andrés Rivera.

CLSU ICarbS IU MoU NBuU NcU NSyU
PPiU PPULC

771 <u>Narrativa argentina del Litoral</u>, por Rosa Boldori, Inés Santa Cruz, Roberto Schiro, Edelweis Serra. Rosario: Grupo de Estudios Semánticos, 1981. 226 p. 22 cm. (Cuadernos Aletheia).
An essay about the following contemporary writers from the Litoral region of Argentina, including biographical data: Alcídes Greca, Leonardo Castellani, Gerardo Pisarello, Juan José Saer, Jorge Riestra, Angélica Gorodischer. Also biobibliographical sketches of the authors: Rosa Boldori de Baldussi, Inés Santa Cruz, Roberto Schiro, Edelweis Serra.

IU

772 <u>Narrativa argentina '75</u>. Buenos Aires: Lumen Latinoamericana, 1975. 248 p. 18 cm.
An anthology of Argentine short stories, including brief biographical data about the following contemporary writers: Alberto Alba, Enrique Anderson Imbert, Alfredo Andrés, Julio Ardiles Gray, Roberto Arlt, Jorge Luis Borges, Guillermo Cantore, Julio Cortázar, Marco Denevi, Carlos Joaquín Durán, Jorge García Alonso, Joaquín Gómez Bas, Alberto Gurbanov, Bernardo Kordon, Leopoldo Marechal, Horacio Martínez, Gustavo Martínez Zuviría, Silvina Ocampo, Pedro Orgambide, Syria Poletti, Fernando Sorrentino, Osvaldo Svanascini, Noemí Ulla, Enrique Wernicke.

IU

773 Noé, Julio, comp. <u>Antología de la poesía argentina moderna</u> (1896-1930) con notas biográficas y bibliográficas. 2. ed. Buenos Aires: El Ateneo, 1931. 685 p. 21 cm.
An anthology of Argentine poetry (1900-1925), including biobibliographical sketches of the following authors featured in the text: Leopoldo Lugones, Ernesto Mario Barreda, Leopoldo Díaz, Eugenio Díaz Romero, Angel de Estrada, Alberto Ghiraldo, Federico A. Guti-

LITERATURE

érrez, Edmundo Montagne, Carlos Ortiz, Ricardo Rojas, Manuel Ugarte, Tomás Allende Iragorri, Fernán Félix de Amador, Rafael Alberto Arrieta, Evaristo Carriego, Andrés Chabrillón, Juan Carlos Dávalos, Pablo Della Costa, Rafael De Diego, Bernabé de la Orga, Pedro Mario Delheye, Héctor Díaz Leguizamón, Baldomero Fernández Moreno, Manuel Gálvez, Rosa García Costa, Ricardo Gutiérrez, Ataliva Herrera, Pedro Herreros, Luis María Jordán, Emilio Lascano Tegui (Vizconde de Lascano Tegui, pseud.), Carlos Alberto Leumann, Arturo Marasso, Roberto Mariani, Ezequiel Martínez Estrada, Alvaro Melián Lafinur, Evar Méndez, Alberto Mendioroz, Ernesto Morales, Carlos Obligado, Pedro Miguel Obligado, Octavio Pinto, Héctor Ripa Alberdi, Jorge Max Rohde, Alfonsina Storni, Benjamín Taborga, Arturo Vázquez Cey, René Zapata Quesada, Margarita Abella Caprile, Francisco Luis Bernárdez, Emilia Bertolé, Jorge Luis Borges, Alfredo Brandán Caraffa, Susana Calandrelli, Luis Cané, Cayetano Córdoba Iturburu, María Alicia Domínguez, Fermín Estrella Gutiérrez, Jacobo Fijman, Luis L. Franco, Oliverio Girondo, José González Carvalho, Augusto González Castro, Eduardo González Lanuza, Raúl González Tuñón, Ricardo Güiraldes, Eugenio Julio Iglesias, Héctor M. Irusta, Rafael Jijena Sánchez, Nydia Lamarque, Nora Lange, Roberto Ledesma, Francisco López Merino, Leopoldo Marechal, Enrique Méndez Calzada, Ricardo E. Molinari, Conrado Nalé Roxlo, Jorge Obligado, José Pedroni, Horacio Rega Molina, José S. Tallón, César Tiempo, Marcos Victoria, Pedro Juan Vignale, Amado Villar.

CtY DLC FU IU KU LU MsU MtU NcD
NIC NN OCl OU ViU

774 Noel, Martín Alberto. Novelistas post-románticos. Buenos Aires: Ediciones Culturales Argentinas, Ministerio de Cultura y Educación, 1972. 138 p. 20 cm. (Los fundadores de la literatura argentina).
An essay about postromantic fiction in Argentina, including biobibliographical sketches of the following authors featured in the text: Francisco Sicardi, Angel de Estrada, Eugenio Cambaceres, José María Miró (Julián Martel, pseud.), Manuel T. Podestá, Francisco Grandmontagne, Carlos María Ocantos, Lucio V. López, Martín García Merou, Adolfo Saldías.

GU IaU MoSW NBuU

774a Nosotros siete. Prólogo de Ulyses Petit de Murat. Buenos Aires: Botella al Mar, 1981. 107 p. 19 cm.
An anthology of contemporary Argentinean poetry, including biobibliographical sketches of the following authors featured in the text: Nelly Borroni Mac Donald, Beatriz Iacoviello, Julio Iglesias Rey, Jorge Rafael Otegui, Martha Pella, Luis María Salvaneschi, Beatriz Schaefer Peña.

IU

775 Nosotros también; 10 cuentos esperanzados y un poema de amor, por Lina Salim et al. San Martín: Ediciones Quijote, 1967. 83 p. 21 cm.
An anthology of prose and poetry including biobibliographical sketches of the following 20th-century Argentine writers: Lina Salim, Armando Buenaventura Dattoli, Elido U. Di Serio, Alberto Gurbanov, Mario Sterman, Domingo J. Martos, Reynaldo H. Rondón, Santiago E. Ledesma.

CLSU CSt IaU ICarbS IU MU NBuU
NIC NN NSyU OU PPULC TxU ViU

776 9 [i.e. nueve] cuentos laureados. Buenos Aires: Instituto Amigos del Libro Argentino, 1964. 216 p. 19 cm. (Colección Cuadernos del Instituto. V. 10).
A collection of contemporary Argentine laureate short stories. Includes brief biobibliographical sketches of the following authors: Angel María Vargas, Abelardo Castillo, Jorge Di Paola Levin, Ricardo Piglia, Miguel Angel Solivellas, Lina Giacobone, Héctor Libertella Riesco, Alberto Rodríguez Muñoz.

IU NSyU

777 Onega, Gladys S. La inmigración en la literatura argentina, 1880–1910. Santa Fe: Facultad de Filosofía y Letras, Universidad Nacional del Litoral, 1965. 134 p. 23 cm. (Cuadernos del Instituto de Letras).
A work which primarily deals with the theme of immigrants in Argentine literature of 1880 to 1910, but which also contains brief biographical information on the following authors: José Ingenieros, Fray Mocho, Francisco F. Fernández.

AAP CtW CtY FMU GU ICU IEN InU
MH MiU MnU MoSW MoU MU NbU NcD
NhD NIC NjR NN NNC NSyU PPT TU
TxU ViU VtU WaU WU

778 Ordaz, Luis, comp. El drama rural. Buenos Aires: Librería Hachette, 1959. 349 p. Portraits. 21 cm. (Colección El Pasado argentino).
A collection of Argentine rural dramas of the 19th and 20th centuries accompanied by portraits and biobibliographical sketches of their authors. They are Florencio Sánchez, José de Maturana, Rodolfo González Pacheco, Alberto T. Weisbach, Alejandro Berruti, Bernardo González Arrili, Enzo Aloisi.

CLSU CLU CNoS CoU CSt CtY CU ICU
InU IU MH MiU MNS MnU MoSW MU
NBuU NhD NIC NjR NN NNC OrU PPiU
TNJ TxU ViU WU

779 Pagés Larraya, Antonio, comp. Cuentos de nuestra tierra. Buenos Aires: Editorial Raigal, 1952. 447 p. 21 cm.

A collection of short stories by the following 19th- and 20th-century Argentines, for whom bibliographical sketches are also included: Esteban Echeverría, Domingo F. Sarmiento, Joaquín V. González, Manuel F. Mantilla, Martiniano Leguizamón, José S. Alvarez (Fray Mocho, pseud.), Roberto J. Payró, Horacio Quiroga, Ricardo Güiraldes, Benito Lynch, Guillermo E. Hudson, Ricardo Rojas, Carlos B. Quiroga, Juan Carlos Dávalos, Miguel Angel Correa (Mateo Booz, pseud.), Juan Pablo Echagüe, Fausto Burgos, Julio Aramburu, Armando Cascella, Justo P. Sáenz, Liborio Justo (Lobodón García, pseud.), Héctor Eandi, Juan Cornaglia, Alberto Córdoba, Antonio Stoll, Luis Gudiño Kramer, Juan Manuel Prieto, Angel María Vargas, Daniel Ovejero, Adolfo Pérez Zelaschi.

> CtY CU-S DLC GU IU MH MiU MU
> NBuU NcD NcU NIC NN NSyU OkU OrU
> OU PSt TU TxU WU

780   _____. 20 [i.e. Veinte] relatos argentinos, 1838-1887. Buenos Aires: Editorial Universitaria, 1961. 182 p. 19 cm. (Serie del siglo y medio. V. 25).
      An anthology of Argentinean short stories including information about the following writers: Esteban Echeverría, Juan Bautista Alberdi, Juan María Gutiérrez, Domingo Faustino Sarmiento, José Tomás Guido, Juana Manuela Gorriti, Lucio V. Mansilla, Eduardo L. Holmberg, Carlos Guido Spano, Lucio V. López, Carlos Monsalve, Miguel Cané, Carlos Olivera.

> CaBVaU CLSU CtY CtW CU CU-S ICarbS
> InU IU KU MH MoSW NjR NN NNC
> NSyU OOxM TU TxU

781   Panorama poético bonaerense. La Plata: Fondo Editorial Bonaerense, 1977. 2 v. 19 cm.
      An anthology of poetry by the following contemporary authors from the Province of Buenos Aires (Argentina) including brief biographical notes:
      V. 1: Alicia Margarita Agnese de Ripa, Alberto J. Altopiedi, Berta Barcia, María Rosa Bautista, Roberto Oscar Becherini, Marcos Bianchini, Efraím Burgos Márquez, Domingo Cioppi, Efraín Isaac Chaves, Beatriz D'Amico de Rebossio, Gonzalo Delfino, Hebe Episcopo, Nisa Forti, Haydée Galimberti de Guacci, Rubén Oscar Giusso, Lola Guzmán Reyes, Lylia Hernández, Oscar Eduardo Hoffmann, Carlos A. Linares Quintana, Gloria Merlo de Alba, Violeta R. Mutti Ward de Smith, Marta Peralta, Yatay Ramírez Abella, Horacio Félix Reynaldi, Julio Anselmo Rica, Miguel Scioscia.
      V. 2: María Isabel Arredondo, Jorge Artola Florenzano, María Esther Becker, María Belén, Roque Bonafina, María L. Brunori de Civilotti, Diana Felicitas Calvo, Angel R. Canegalli, Mario Julio Eguía, María Victoria Espinel, Carlos Facci, Elvira Fontana, José Gerola, Cristina Claudia Gómez, Domingo Marchetti, Celia Teresa Maure, Víctor Mesas Miranda, Paula Mustapic, Carlos H. Pacheco,

Juan Pereyra Mont, María C. Ponce de Massara, Felipe Protzucov, Angela R. Scalella de Parisi, Pura G. Serradilla de Naranjo, Paula Toledo, Domingo Vallarino. (See also entry 663).

> AzU CtY FU IU MiDW MnU NcU NIC
> WU

782   Pedro, Valentín de. Nuevo parnaso argentino. Barcelona: Maucci, 1927. 304 p. 18 cm.
      An anthology of the works of the following 19th- and 20th-century Argentine poets, for whom short biobibliographical notes are also included: Pedro B. Palacios (Almafuerte, pseud.), Carlos Ortiz, Ricardo Rojas, Manuel Ugarte, Mario Bravo, Manuel Gálvez, Evaristo Carriego, Ernesto Mario Barreda, Enrique Banchs, Arturo Capdevila, Rafael Alberto Arrieta, Evar Méndez, Fernández Moreno, Luis María Jordán, Héctor Pedro Blomberg, Alfonsina Storni, Pablo Della Costa, Pedro Miguel Obligado, Miguel A. Camino, Alfredo R. Bufano, Juan Carlos Dávalos, Luis L. Franco, Margarita Abella Caprile, González Carbalho, Ricardo Gutiérrez, Enrique Méndez Calzada, Horacio Rega Molina, Francisco Luis Bernárdez, Ricardo Güiraldes, Oliverio Girondo, Jorge Luis Borges, Francisco M. Piñero, Leopoldo Marechal, José Sebastián Tallón, Brandán Caraffa, Norah Lange, Mayorino Ferraría, Conrado Nalé Roxlo, Carlos Mastronardi, Leopoldo Lugones.

> CaBVaU DLC IaU IU LU NBuU WU

783   Percas, Helena. La poesía femenina argentina, 1810-1950. Madrid: Ediciones Cultura Hispánica, 1958. 738 p. 21 cm.
      A critical analysis of poetry written by Argentine women between 1810 and 1950. Biobibliographical information is given for many of these women. Among them are Edelina Soto y Calvo, Alfonsina Storni, Rosa García Costa, Mary Rega Molina, Margarita Abella Caprile, Mercedes de Saavedra Zelaya, María Raquel Adler, María Alicia Domínguez, Amalia Prebisch de Piossek (Amalia Previsch de Piossek), Emma Solá de Solá, Clementina Isabel Azlor, Emilia Bertolé, María Alex Urrutia Artieda, Susana Calandrelli, Norah Lange, Nydia Lamarque, María de Villarino, Ana María Chouhy Aguirre, María Granata, Fryda Schult Cazenueve de Mantovani, Silvina Ocampo. Alphabetical index of names.

> AAP AU CLSU CLU CNoS CSt CtY CU
> CU-S DPU FMU FTaSU FU GU IaU ICU
> IEN INS InU IU KY LNHT LU MH
> MiDW MiU MnU MoSU MoSW MoU MtU
> NbU NBuU NcD NcU NhD NIC NjP NjR
> NN NNC NSyU OCl OClW OCU OkU OrU
> OU OWicB PSt ScU TNJ TxDaM TxFTC
> TxLT TxU ViU WU

784   Pinto, Juan. Panorama de la literatura argentina contemporánea. Buenos Aires: Editorial Mundi, 1941. 385 p. 20 cm. (Autores argentinos. V. 1).

LITERATURE

A collection of brief biobibliographical sketches on over 300 contemporary Argentine authors. Alphabetical index of names.

CaBVaU DLC FU LU MoSU MtU MU NcD
NcU PPT PSt PU OCU OO OrU OU TxU

785   Poemario '72 [i.e. setenta y dos].   Buenos Aires: Ediciones del Alto Sol, 1972. 94 p. 20 cm.
A collection of 20th-century Argentine poetry, followed by very brief biobibliographical notes on the authors. They include Sofía Acosta, Norma Amato, Gladys Barretta, Nelly Borroni, Eduardo Carballo, Lucía Carmona, Alicia Carreño, José Antonio Cedrón, Angela Colombo, Rubén Derlis, Nilda Díaz Pessina, Rafael Farfán Arosemena, Pedro Giacaglia, Virginia Hansen, Guillermo Ibáñez, María Luz Maggi, Peñarol Méndez, Pancho Muñoz, Carlos Penelas, Alberto Polat, Susy Quinteros, Rogelio Ramos Signes, Ruth Repetto, Any Segal, Jorge Sichero, Marcos Silber, Enrique Suárez, Victoria Sus, Marta Toiberman.

IU

786   Poemas. Buenos Aires: Ministerio de Educación, Subsecretaría de Cultura, Dirección de Coordinación, Promoción y Difusión, Departamento Editorial, 1968. 5 sheets. 37 x 55 cm. fold. to 19 x 14 cm.
An anthology of poetry by the following 20th-century Argentineans for whom short biobibliographical sketches are included: Norberto Silvetti Paz, Manuel Cazalla, Enrique Catani, Catalina Lerange Albamonte, Carlos Ringuelet.

CLSU CSt CU-SB FU IU MB MU NIC
OU TxU

787   Poemas taller de SADE. Buenos Aires: Ediciones Fígaro, 1975. 118 p. 18 cm.
A collection of poems of contemporary Argentine writers, including brief biobibliographical notes about the following writers: Leopoldo Argañarás, Daniel Altamiranda Minahk, Magdalena Iglesias, Josefina Arroyo, Jorge Bonfiglio, Rubén Lombardo, Patricia Buengiorno, Elena Cabrejas, María Alicia Cavagnaro, Alicia Masú, Elida Galego, Marcelo Luna, María Vallejos, Alicia Pedro, Beatriz Schaefer Peña.

IU

788   Poesía viva de Rosario. Rosario: Ediciones del Instituto Estudios Nacionales, 1976. 233 p. Portraits. 18 cm.
An anthology of Argentinean poetry by contemporary writers from the city of Rosario, including brief biobibliographical notes accompanied by portraits. Those featured are Francisco Gandolfo, Hugo Padeletti, Willy Harvey, Rubén Sevlever, Armando Raúl Santillán, Alberto C. Vila Ortiz, Orlando Florencio Calgaro, Rafael Oscar Ielpi, Hugo Diz,

Jorge Isaías, Rubén Plaza, Elvio Gandolfo, Alejandro Pidello, Eduardo D'Anna, Guillermo Ibáñez, Guillermo Colussi, Guillermo Thomas, Hugo Ojeda, Juan José Vitiello, Sergio Kern.

IU

789   Poetas al sur de Buenos Aires. Buenos Aires: Editorial Suburbio, 1975. 54 p. 19 cm.
An anthology of contemporary Argentinean poetry by authors native of or living in the suburbs and region south of the city of Buenos Aires, including biobibliographical sketches. The following are featured: Jorge Alejandro Boccanera, Oscar Raúl Fernando García, Jorge Horacio Paredes, Alberto Rubén Villagra, Susana Isac, Graciela Arambarri, Graciela Da Luz, Angela Novoa, Gioconda De Zabatta.

IU

790   Los poetas que cantan. Dibujos y grabados de Jorge A. Mattalia. Cosquín: A.I.B.D.E.A., 1972. 83 p. 35 cm.
A collection of representative works accompanied by very short biobibliographical notes of the following 20th-century Argentine poets: Manuel J. Castilla, Ariel Ferraro, Hamlet Lima Quintana, José Augusto Moreno, Ariel Petrocelli, Armando Tejada Gómez.

CLU CU-SB GU IaU IU MB MU NBuU
NIC NN TxU WU

791   Portogalo, José. 16 [i.e. Diez y seis] poetas inéditos. Buenos Aires: Cooperativa Editorial Hoy en la Cultura, 1965. 94 p. 18 cm. (Colección Poesía. V. 2).
A collection of 20th-century Argentine poetry, accompanied by biographical information of various amounts on their authors. They are Julio Calvo Encinar, Sandra Filippi, Lidia Geldstein, Gerardo Mario Goloboff, Carlos Jmelnitzky, Lucy Larra, Angel Leiva, Mariano Manutara, Hugo David Otero, Irene Parnisari, Ariel Peña, Raúl Edgardo Press, Rodolfo Oscar Habanal, Luis Roberto Sassi, Ernesto Vázquez Rivera.

IU KU

792   Prieto, Adolfo. La literatura autobiográfica argentina. Buenos Aires: Editorial J. Alvarez, 1966. 198 p. 20 cm.
A discussion, including examples, of Argentine autobiographical literature during the 19th and 20th centuries. Particular emphasis is given to the following: Domingo Faustino Sarmiento, Calzadilla, Carlos Guido Spano, Lucio Victorio Mansilla, Joaquín V. González, Alberto Delac.

CaBVaU CFS CLSU CLU CNoS CSt CU
CU-S FTaSU FU GU ICU InU IU KU
MB MiU MnU MoSW NBuU NcU NhD NIC
NjP NjR NSyU OOxM OrU ScU TNJ
TxHR TxU ViU WU

793 Primera muestra de poetas. Buenos Aires: Editorial Caro, 1964. 43 p. 18 cm. (Colección Altazor. V. 1).

An anthology of contemporary Argentinean poetry, including biobibliographical notes on the following authors featured in the text: Raúl Castro, Angélica Manero, Diego Jorge Mare, Eduardo París, Rodolfo Ramírez, Vicente Zito Lema.

IU

794 Prostibulario por Enrique Amorim et al. y un ensayo de Cátulo Castillo. Buenos Aires: Editorial Merlín, 1967. 108 p. 18 cm. (Colección espejo de Buenos Aires).

An anthology of contemporary Argentine short-story writers dealing with the theme of prostitution, including biobibliographical sketches. Those featured are Cátulo Castillo, Enrique Amorim, Julián Centeya, pseud. (Amleto Vergiati), Nira Etchenique, Joaquín Gómez Bas, Juan José Hernández, Bernardo Kordón, Pedro Orgambide.

CLSU CSt CtY CU-S IaU IU KU MB MU
NbU NBuU NcD NcU NIC NjP NjR NSyU
OU PPULC TNJ TxU WU

795 Ríos Ortiz, Ricardo. Cuentan para usted. Santa Fe: Ediciones Colmegna, 1979. 102 p. 18 cm.

Anthology of Argentinean short stories with dates, bibliographical information, and achievements of the following contributors, all members of the generation of 1955: Ricardo Ríos Ortiz, Adolfo Argentino Golz, Edgardo A. Pesante, Inés Fornaso.

IU

796 Romano, Eduardo, comp. Narradores argentinos de hoy. Ed. dirigida por María Hortensia Lacau. Buenos Aires: Editorial Kapelusz, 1971. 163 p. 16 cm. (Grandes obras de la literatura universal. V. 73).

An anthology of contemporary Argentine prose writers, including biobibliographical sketches of the following authors featured in the text: Juan José Hernández, Haroldo Conti, Syria Poletti, Jorge Riestra, Daniel Moyano.

InU IU MH MU TxU UU

797 Ronda de poetas jóvenes pampeanos. Santa Rosa: Comisión Municipal de Cultura, 1971. 71 p. 21 cm.

A collection of contemporary poetry emanating from the Argentine province of La Pampa, accompanied by short biographical notes and sketches on the authors whose works are represented. They are Anita López Urcola, Lía Susana Montero, Eduardo Di Nardo, Irma Zanardi de Rivera, Susana Estela Rodríguez, Dora Battiston.

CaQMM CSt GU IaU MoSW NIC TxU ViU
WU

798 Rosales, César, comp. Antología de la poesía argentina contemporánea. Prólogo de Guillermo de Torre. Buenos Aires: Ministerio de Relaciones y Culto. Dirección General de Relaciones Culturales, 1964. 284 p. 22 cm.

An anthology of contemporary Argentine poetry, accompanied by a short biobibliographical sketch on each author whose work is represented. The following are those included: Francisco Luis Bernárdez, Jorge Luis Borges, Oliverio Girondo, Leopoldo Marechal, Carlos Mastronardi, Ricardo E. Molinari, Juan L. Ortiz, Jorge Enrique Ramponi, Vicente Barbieri, León Benarós, Romualdo Brughetti, Manuel J. Castilla, Alberto Girri, Enrique Molina, Olga Orozco, Alberto Ponce de León, César Rosales, Alfonso Solá González, Emilio Sosa López, Raúl Gustavo Aguirre, José Isaacson, Julio Llinás, Francisco Madariaga, Alejandra Pizarnik, Osvaldo Rossler, Rubén Vela.

CFS CLSU CLU CSt DGU IaU IU KU MH
MiEM MoSW MU NIC PPT TNJ TxU WU

799 Rovere, Susan Inés. Cuentos argentinos del siglo XX. Buenos Aires: Editorial Huemul, 1977. 352 p. 18 cm.

An anthology of Argentine short stories of the 20th century including biobibliographical sketches of the following authors featured in the text: Leopoldo Marechal, Leonardo Castellani (Rey, Jerónimo del, pseud.), Angel Bonomini, Silvina Ocampo, Augusto Mario Delfino, Ana María Seoane, Enrique Banchs, Roberto Payró, Juan Carlos Ghiano, Horacio Quiroga, Roberto Mariani, Juan Carlos Dávalos, Jorge Luis Borges (Bustos Domecq, Honorio; Suárez Lynch, B., pseuds.), Conrado Nalé Roxlo (Chamico, pseud.), Julio Cortázar (Denís, Julio, pseud.), Enrique Anderson Imbert, Joaquín Gómez Bas, Marco Denevi, Lila Padilla, Manuel Mujica Láinez, Ricardo Güiraldes, Pablo Rojas Paz.

IU

800 Ruiz, Luis Alberto, comp. Entre Ríos cantada; primera antología iconográfica de poetas entrerrianos. Buenos Aires: A. Zamora, 1955. 218 p. Portraits. 24 cm. (Colección Argentoria. V. 7).

An anthology of the works of various poets from the province of Entre Ríos. Short biobibliographical sketches are included for each author whose works are represented. They are Diego Fernández Espiro, Olegario V. Andrade, Gervasio Méndez, Luis N. Palma, Damián P. Garat, Emilio Berisso, Andrés Chabrillón, Juan L. Ortiz, Daniel Elías, Delio Panizza, Guillermo Saraví, Luis María Grané, Manuel Portela, Carlos Mastronardi, Amaro Villanueva, Mateo Dumón Quesada, Galo Zaragoza, Gaspar L. Benavento, P. Jacinto Zaragoza, Luis Gudiño Krámer, Ernesto Bourband, Reynaldo Ros, Marcelino M. Román, Alfredo Martínez Howard, José Eduardo Seri, Carlos María Dardán, José María Fernández Unsain, Carlos Alberto Alvarez, Poldy de Bird, José María Díaz, Rubén A. Turi,

LITERATURE

Alfonso Sola González, Ana Teresa Fabani, Luis Sadi Groso, Emma de Cartosio, Rosa Isabel Lucero, Luis Alberto Ruiz, Clara Luz Zaragoza.

DLC DPU IU MU NBuU NcU NN NSyU
TxU ViU

801 Salas, Horacio. La poesía de Buenos Aires; ensayo y antología. Buenos Aires: Editorial Pleamar, 1968. 263 p. 20 cm. (Colección Mar abierto).

An anthology of 20th-century poetry from Buenos Aires, with essays and biobibliographical sketches of the following Argentineans: Vicente Barbieri, Daniel Barros, Jorge Luis Borges, Enrique Cadícamo, Arturo Cambours Ocampo, Martín Campos, Evaristo Carriego, Atilio Jorge Castelpoggi, Córdova Iturburu, Carlos de la Púa, Mario Jorge de Lellis, Enrique Santos Discépolo, Baldomero Fernández Moreno, César Fernández Moreno, Celedonio Flores, Juan Gelman, Oliverio Girondo, Raúl González Tuñón, Fernando Guibert, Homero Manzi, Ricardo Molinari, Manuel Mujica Láinez, Nicolás Olivari, José Portogalo, Horacio Rega Molina, Gustavo Riccio, Osvaldo Rossler, Roberto Jorge Santoro, César Tiempo, Francisco Urondo, Rafael Alberto Vásquez, Alfredo Veiravé. Alphabetical index of names.

CLSU FU InU IU

802 Salvador, Nélida. La nueva poesía argentina (estudio y antología). Buenos Aires: Editorial Columba, 1969. 280 p. Portraits. 18 cm. (Nuevos esquemas. V. 21).

A study of present-day Argentine poetry, followed by representative works and short biobibliographical sketches on their authors. They include Rodolfo Alonso, Héctor Miguel Angeli, Julio Arístides, Horacio Armani, Elizabeth Azcona Cranwell, Amelia Biagioni, Emma de Cartosio, Atilio Jorge Castelpoggi, Nicolás Cócaro, Betina Edelberg, Nira Etchenique, Ariel Ferraro, Luis Ricardo Furlan, Joaquín O. Giannuzzi, Marta Giménez Pastor, Magdalena Harriague, José Isaacson, Roberto Juarroz, Simón Kargieman, Fulvio Milano, Héctor A. Murena, Alejandra Pizarnik, Alberto Luis Ponzo, Antonio Requeni, Osvaldo Rossler, Flor Schapira Fridman, Máximo Simpson, Graciela de Solá, Abelardo Vázquez, Alfredo Veiravé, Rubén Vela, Carlos Velazco, Oscar Hermes Villordo, María Elena Walsh, Héctor Yánover.

AAP CaBVaU CLSU CNoS CoFS CSt CtY
CU CU-SB DPU FMU FTaSU IEN INS IU
LNHT MB MdBJ MH MiDW MiU MnU MoSW
MoU MU NBuU NcD NcU NIC NjMD NjP
NjR NNC NSyU OCl OrU OU PPiU PPULC
TU TxU ViU WaU WU

803 Santiago, José Alberto, comp. Antología de la poesía argentina. Madrid: Editora Nacionla, 1973. 466 p. 21 cm. (Escalada).

Anthology of Argentine poetry covering from 1515 to the generation of 1940 with brief historical and critical overviews of significant literary periods. Features biobibliographical sketches of the following contributors: Luis de Tejeda y Guzmán, Manuel José de Lavardén, Vicente López y Planes, Bartolomé Hidalgo, Juan Cruz Varela, Esteban Echeverría, Hilario Ascasubi, Juan María Gutiérrez, José Mármol, Estanislao del Campo, Ricardo Gutiérrez, Olegario Víctor Andrade, José Hernández, Rafael Obligado, Carlos Guido y Spano, Pedro B. Palacios (Almafuerte, pseud.), Leopoldo Díaz, Leopoldo Lugones, Evaristo Carriego, Ricardo Güiraldes, Baldomero Fernández Moreno, Enrique Banchs, Alfonsina Storni, Macedonio Fernández, Oliverio Girondo, Ezequiel Martínez Estrada, Juan L. Ortiz, Carlos de la Púa, pseud. (Carlos Raúl Muñoz del Solar), Ricardo Molinari, Conrado Nalé Roxlo, Jorge Luis Borges, Francisco Luis Bernárdez, Nicolás Olivari, Leopoldo Marechal, Enrique Santos Discépolo, José Portogalo (José Ananía, pseud.), Francisco López Merino, Raúl González Tuñón, Homero Manzi (Homero Nicolás Manzione), César Tiempo (Israel Zetlin), Jorge Enrique Ramponi, Vicente Barbieri, Enrique Molina, Julio Cortázar, Miguel D. Etchebarne, Manuel J. Castilla, Alberto Girri, César Fernández Moreno, Edgar Bayley, Jaime Dávalos, Roberto Juárroz.

CLU CNoS CSf CtY CU-S FU GU IaAS
ICIU InU IU KyU LNHT MdBJ MH MoU
NB NcU OU PPiU PPT TxDaM TxHR TxU

804 Santiago: 7 [i.e. siete] poetas. Santiago del Estero: Sociedad Argentina de Escritores, Filial Santiago del Estero, 1972. 53 p. 24 cm.

An anthology of contemporary Argentine poetry emanating from the province of Santiago del Estero. Biobibliographical sketches are also included for each poet whose works are represented. They are Carlos Alberto Artayer, Jorge Andrés Antón, Miguel A. Brevetta Rodríguez, Carlos Eduardo Figueroa, Alfonso Nussif, Felipe Rojas, Ricardo Dino Taralli.

CtY CU-SB GU IaU IU MB NIC NN
TxU WU

805 Saravi Cisneros, Roberto, comp. Primera antología poética platense. Buenos Aires: Ediciones A. Zamora, 1956. 191 p. Portraits. 24 cm. (Colección Argentoria. V. 10).

Anthology of contemporary poetry emanating from the Argentine city of La Plata, accompanied by portraits and biobibliographical sketches on the authors whose works are represented. They include Pedro B. Palacios (Almafuerte, pseud.), Rafael Alberto Arrieta, Arturo Marasso, Alfredo Fernández García, Pedro Mario Delheye, Alberto Mendioroz, Héctor Ripa Alberdi, Juan Carlos Mena, Francisco López Merino, Marcos Fingerit, Arturo Horacio Ghida, María de Villarino, Elena Duncan, Carlos Ringuelet, Alejandro de Isusi, Enriqueta A. de Dougherty, Horacio Ponce de León, Aurora Venturini, Raúl Amaral, Carlos A. Disandro,

Horacio Núñez West, Gustavo A. García Saraví, Narciso Pousa, Mario Porro, Vicente Silvetti Paz, María Mombrú, Héctor Eduardo Ciocchini, Roberto Themis Speroni, Ana Emilia Lahitte, Carlos Albarracín Sarmiento, Apolinario Héctor Sosa, María Dhialma Tiberti, Enrique Mario Rafaelli.

CU DGW DPU FU IEN IU KU LNHT LU
MH MoU NBuU NcD NcU NjP NN NSyU
PPiU TxHR TxU ViU WU

806 Sarlo Sabajanes, Beatriz, comp. <u>Cuentos de dos orillas</u>. Notas preliminares: Luis Gregorich. Buenos Aires: Centro Editor de América Latina, 1971. 150 p. 18 cm. (Biblioteca fundamental del hombre moderno. V. 4).

An anthology of Argentine short story writers, including biobibliographical sketches. Those featured are Roberto Arlt, Mario Benedetti, Adolfo Bioy Casares, Jorge Luis Borges, Julio Cortázar, Felisberto Hernández, Carlos Martínez Moreno, Silvina Ocampo, Juan Carlos Onetti, Horacio Quiroga.

DLC IU

807 Saz Sánchez, Agustín del. <u>Antología de poesía argentina</u> (Desde el siglo XV hasta nuestros días). Barcelona: Bruguera, 1969. 779 p. 18 cm. (Libro clásico. V. 62).

An anthology of Argentine poetry (15th century to the present), including biobibliographical sketches of the following writers featured in the texg: Luis de Tejeda y Guzmán, Manuel de Lavardén, Vicente López y Planes, Esteban de Luca, Juan Cruz Varela, Esteban Echeverría, Luis L. Domínguez, José Mármol, José Rivera Indarte, Claudio Mamerto Cuenca, Bartolomé Mitre, Juan María Gutiérrez, Ventura de la Vega, Olegario Andrade, Leopoldo Lugones, Enrique Banchs, Pedro B. Palacios (Almafuerte, pseud.), Baldomero Fernández Moreno, Carlos Guido y Spano, Calixto Oyuela, Leopoldo Díaz, Alfonsina Storni, Rafael Alberto Arrieta, Ezequiel Martínez Estrada, Pedro Miguel Obligado, Ricardo Gutiérrez, Estanislao del Campo, José Hernández, Hilario Ascasubi, Rafael Obligado, Miguel A. Camino, Pedro C. de María, Enrique Santos Discépolo, Evaristo Carriego, Arturo Marasso, Arturo Capdevila, Loepoldo Marechal, Oliverio Girondo, Evar Méndez, Jorge Luis Borges, Norah Lange, Horacio Rega Molina, Francisco Luis Bernárdez, Macedonio Fernández, Eduardo González Lanuza, Ricardo Güiraldes, Silvina Ocampo, Ricardo E. Molinari, César Tiempo (Israel Zeitlin), Luis L. Franco, Raúl González Tuñón, José Pedroni, Ignacio G. Anzoátegui, Alfredo R. Bufano, Juan L. Ortiz, Conrado Nalé Roxlo, Enrique Méndez Calzada, Héctor Pedro Blomberg, Benjamín Taborga, Ernesto Mario Barreda, Carlos Obligado, Luis Cané, Cayetano Córdova Iturburu, Nicolás Olivari, José González Carbalho, Francisco López Merino, Miguel Angel Gómez, Ana María Chouhy Aguirre, Juan Rodolfo Wilcock, Juan G. Ferrey-

ra Basso, Enrique Molina, Eduardo Jorge Bosco, Alberto Ponce de León, Horacio Jorge Becco, César Fernández Moreno, Jorge Vocos Lescano, León Benaros, Alberto Girri, Osvaldo Svanascini, Jorge Enrique Ramponi, Edgar Bayley, Juan Jacobo Bajarlía, Raúl Gustavo Aguirre, Alejandro Pizarnik, Emma de Cartosio, Rodolfo Alonso, Marcos Ricardo Barnatan, David Martínez, Horacio Armani, Roy Bartolomew, Miguel Brasco, Amelia Biagioni, Julio Cortázar, Gustavo García Saraví, Rafael Jijena Sánchez, Noé Jitrik, César Magrini, Federico Peltzer, Adela Tarraf, Mario Trejo, Alberto Vanasco, Ulises Torres, Héctor M. Rivera, Bernardo Horrach, Santos Ersen.

AzU CaBVaU CaQMM CFS CSt CtY CU-S
CU-SB GU InU KU MB MdU MH MiDW
MShM MU NB NbU NcD NcU NjR NSyU
OrU OU PPULC WU

808 <u>Selección de cuentos</u>. Buenos Aires: Cooperativa Editorial Hoy en la Cultura, 1966. 181 p. 18 cm. (Colección Cuentos. V. 4).

A collection of 20th-century Argentine short stories, accompanied by biobibliographical notes on their authors. Those particularly featured are Ariel Bignami, Bernardo Jobson, César Dimant.

CLSU CSt CtY IU InU KU MB NBuU
NIC NN NSbSU NSyU OU PPiU TNJ TU
TxU ViU WU

809 Signo. <u>Antología poética de Signo</u>. Selección, prólogo y notas de Serafín José Aguirre. Tucumán: Ediciones de "Signo," 1966. 60 p. 18 cm. (Colección "Espartaco").

An anthology of 20th-century poetry which has appeared in the Argentine publication <u>Signo</u>, accompanied by short biobibliographical sketches on each author represented. They include Luis Franco, Raúl Aráoz Anzoátegui, Armando Tejada Gómez, Néstor Groppa, Andrés Fidalgo, Pedro A. Herrera, Eugenia Elbein.

CSt IU MB MoSW MU NIC OU TxU

810 Sociedad argentina de escritores. Filial Neuquén. <u>Expresiones literarias del Neuquén</u>. Buenos Aires: Ediciones Crisol, 1980. 174 p. 20 cm.

An anthology of poetry and prose by the following writers from the Neuquén region of Argentina, including biobibliographical notes:

Poetry: Milton Aguilar, María Cristina Peralta de Alvarez Yofré, Laura Suyai Aguilar, Alejandro Benjamín Baier, Leonel Damián Bellucci, Rosalba Montejano de Catella, Reumay, pseud. (Alvaro Cayol), Aurora Alba de Coronel, Alicia A. Corsini, Néstor Cuello, Elena Soto de Cuenca, Angel Mario de Gerardi Escudero, Paula Bustos de Emma, Rodrigo Fernández, Oscar Raúl Ferro, Elidia Beatriz Rodríguez de Gallegos, Lidia Muñoz Obeid de Gercek, Andrés Guevara, Adán Guzmán, Valentina Castillo de Guzmán, Gladis Edith Igle-

LITERATURE

sias, Soledad Nancy S. de Iriarte, Esmeralda
Salomé Lastra, María Elena T. de Lastra, Sil-
via A. Montoto de Lazzeri, Ercilia Leva, Dora
Alanis de López, Herbert Raúl López, Agustín
A. Orejas, Norma Pavia de Otero, Eduardo Pal-
ma, Clelia Espinosa Pascale, Hortensia Zambo-
ni de Pecini, Haydée Polidoro, Juan Mario
Raone, Mario Eduardo Suárez, Margarita de Su-
rán, Adolfo Turrín, Carlos Alberto Vaccaro,
Dévora Liliana Werchowsky.

Prose: Gregorio Alvarez, Fernando Albero,
José Antonio Alcaraz, Osvaldo O. Arabarco,
Valentín José Barrios, Rosalba Montejano de
Catella, Prima Aide Erickson, Graciela Fanti,
Silvia A. Gallo, Lili Muñoz Obeid de Gercek,
Iliana Lascaray, Basilio Marquina, Alicia
Pekarek, Carlos Agustín Ríos, María Elena
Romero Cuevas L., Tito del Vo.

IU MU

811 Soler Cañas, Luis. <u>Cuentos y diálogos lun-
fardos, 1885-1964</u>. Buenos Aires: Ediciones
Theoria, 1965. 242 p. 21 cm. (Biblioteca
argentina de letras).

An anthology of Argentine prose and poetry
(1885-1964) featuring literature based on
street language of Buenos Aires, including
biobibliographical essays of the following
20th-century writers: Juan A. Piaggo, Florencio Iriarte, Juan Manuel Pintos, Nemesio Trejo, Federico S. Mertens, Roberto L. Cayol,
Edmundo Montagne (Pancho Mingo, pseud.), Javier de Viana, Enrique Gunguito, Josué A.
Quesada, Jorge J. M., pseud., Agapito Sánchez,
pseud., Agustín Fontanella, Germán M. Méndez,
Aniceto Juan Francisco Benavente (F. Bena-
vente y Oyarzún, pseud.), Santiago Dallegri,
Ramón Aymerich, J. Víctor Tomey, Angel G.
Villoldo, Felipe H. Fernández (Yacaré, pseud.),
Alejandro C. del Conte, Grafófono, pseud.,
Julio Cruz Ghío (Cruz Orellana, pseud.), José
Antonio Saldías (Rubén Fastrás, pseud.), Numa
P. Córdoba (Numa Criollo, pseud.), Juan Fran-
cisco Palermo, Félix Lima, Máximo Teodoro
Sáenz (Last Reason; A Rienda Suelta; Bala
Perdida, pseuds.), Natalio Scunio Ferreyra,
Silverio Manco, Silvia Guerrico, Bartolomé
Rodolfo Aprile, Jerónimo Gradito, Vicente
Trípoli, José Gobello, Luis Alfredo Sciutto
(Diego Lucero, pseud.), Israel Chas de Cruz.

CaBVaU CLSU CSt CtY DPU FTaSU IaU
IcU InU IU LNHT MiDW MoSW NBuU NcD
NcU NhD NjP NN NNC NSyU OU PPiU
TU TxHR TxU ViU WU

812 _____. <u>La generación poética del 40</u>. Buenos
Aires: Ediciones Culturales Argentinas, 1981.
474 p. (V. 1). 22 cm.

An anthology of Argentine poetry by the
following writers from the 40s generation including biobibliographical sketches:
V. 1: Vicente Barbieri, Julio Ellena de
la Sota, Marcos Fingerit, Arturo Horacio Ghida,
Joaquín Gómez Bas, Alfredo Martínez Howard,
Silvina Ocampo, Antonio Porchia, Amaro Villa-

nueva, Atahualpa Yupanqui, Juan Enrique Acuña.
María Adela Agudo, Antonio Esteban Agüero,
Carlos Alberto Alvarez, Raúl Amaral, Raúl
Aráoz Anzoátegui, Alberto F. Arbonés, José
Oscar Arverás, Julio César Avanza, Angel Héc-
tor Azeves, Edgar Bayley, Damián Carlos Bayón,
León Benarós, Mario Binetti, Alberto Claudio
Blasetti, Martín Alberto Boneo, Eduardo Jorge
Bosco, Mario Briglia, Tomás Enrique Briglia,
Eduardo S. Calamaro, Jorge Calvetti, Andrés
C. Caraballo, Tulio Carella, Carlos Carlino,
Manuel J. Castilla, José María Castiñeira de
Dios, Julián Centeya, Juan Carlos Clemente,
José Manuel Conde, Julio Cortázar, Ana María
Chouhy Aguirre, Jaime Dávalos, Victorino De
Carolis, Mario Jorge De Lellis, Félix Della
Paolera, Daniel J. Devoto, Juan B. Devoto,
Francisco Dibella, Elena Duncan, Miguel D.
Etchebarne, Guillermo Etchebehere, Raúl de
Ezeyza Monasterio, César Fernández Moreno,
José María Fernández Unsain.

IU

813 _____. <u>Orígenes de la literatura lunfarda</u>.
Prólogo de José Gobello. Buenos Aires: Ediciones Siglo Veinte, 1965. 268 p. 21 cm.

An essay about the following 20th-century
Argentine authors who represent the use of
slang language in literature, including biobibliographical sketches and excerpts of their
work:
Prose: Benigno B. Lugones, Silverio Domínguez (Ceferino de la Calle, pseud.), Juan A.
Piaggio, Vital Montes, Antonio B. Massioti,
José S. Alvarez (Fray Mocho; Fabio Carrizo,
pseuds.), Nemesio Trejo, Agustín Fontanella,
Javier de Viana, Juan Francisco Palermo, Ed-
mundo Montagne, Federico Mertens, Josué Que-
sada, Santiago Dallegri, Félix Lima, Félix
Alberto de Zabalía (FAZ, pseud.), Luis C.
Villamayor, José Antonio Saldías (Rubén Fas-
trás, pseud.).
Poetry: José J. Podestá, Florencio Iriar-
te, Gabino Ezeiza, Higinio Cazón, Antonio A.
Caggiano, José Betinoti, Angel Villoldo, Juan
Manuel Pintos, Roberto L. Cayol, Francisco
Benavente, Silverio Manco, Felipe H. Fernán-
dez (Yacaré, pseud.).
Theater: Miguelito Ocampo, Pedro E. Pico,
Carlos Mauricio Pacheco, José González Cas-
tillo, Alberto Vacarezza, Juan Francisco Pa-
lermo.

CaBVaU CLU CLSU CNoS CSt CU CU-S
IaU ICU InU IU LNHT LU MB MiEM
MiU MoSW MoU MU NBuU NcU NhD NIC
NjP NNG NSyU TxU ViU WaU WU

814 Sorrentino, Fernando, comp. <u>40 [i.e. cuarenta]
cuentos breves argentinos: siglo XX</u>. Buenos
Aires: Plus Ultra, 1977. 234 p. 20 cm.

A collection of short stories by the following contemporary writers, including biobibliographical sketches: Jorge W. Abalos,
José Baidal, Angel Balzarino, Andrés Balla,
Enrique Barbieri, Leónidas Barletta, Isidoro

Blaistein, Angel Bonomini, Eugenia Calny, Emma de Cartosio, Felipe Justo Cervera, Nicolás Cócaro, Aarón Cupit, Aristóbulo Echegaray, Ricardo Feierstein, Cayetano Ferrari, Alfonso Ferrari Amores, Juan A. Floriani, Luis Gasulla, Gastón Gori, Ana María Junquet, María Hortensia Lacau, Benito Lynch, Maximiliano Mariotti, Ivo Marrochi, Carlos Mastrángelo, Carlos Alberto Merlino, Rodolfo E. Modern, Fortunato E. Nari, Federico Peltzer, Agustín Pérez Pardella, Edgardo A. Pesante, Alicia Régoli de Mullen, Guillermo Rodríguez, Osvaldo Rossler, Fernando Sánchez Sorondo, Jaime Julio Vieyra, Oscar Hermes Villordo, Fina Warschaver, Enrique Wernicke.

IU

815 _____. 17 [i.e. diecisiete] cuentos argentinos: siglo XX. Buenos Aires: Plus Ultra, 1978. 188 p. 20 cm.
A collection of short stories by the following contemporary Argentine authors including biographical sketches: Godofredo Daireaux, Ricardo Güiraldes, Santiago Dabove, Vicente Barbieri, Silvina Ocampo, Pilar Lusarreta, Enrique Anderson Imbert, Manuel Mujica Láinez, Adolfo Bioy Casares, Horacio Peroncini, Juan Carlos Ghiano, Antonio Di Benedetto, Eugenia Calny, Edgardo A. Pesante, Fernando Sorrentino, Enrique Barbieri.

IU

816 _____. 35 [i.e. Treinta y cinco] cuentos breves argentinos: siglo XX. Buenos Aires: Plus Ultra, 1973. 181 p. 21 cm.
A collection of 20th-century Argentine short stories, accompanied by brief biobibliographical essays on their authors. They include Enrique Anderson Imbert, Julio Ardiles Gray, Roberto Arlt, Juan-Jacobo Bajarlía, Enrique Banchs, Adolfo Bioy Casares, Jorge Luis Borges (H. Bustos Domecq, pseud.), Juan Burghi, Julio Cortázar, Santiago Dabove, Marco Denevi, Antonio Di Benedetto, Guillermo Estrella, Macedonio Fernández, Juan Carlos Ghiano, Martín Gil, Oliverio Girondo, Joaquín Gómez Bas, Eduardo Gudiño Kieffer, Luis Gudiño Kramer, Ricardo Güiraldes, Arturo Jauretche, Liborio Justo, Leopoldo Marechal, Gustavo Martínez Zuviría, Manuel Mujica Láinez, Héctor A. Murena, Conrado Nalé Roxlo, Silvina Ocampo, Roberto J. Payró, Horacio Quiroga, Pablo Rojas Paz, Fernando Sorrentino, Osvaldo Svanascini.

CLU CSt CtY CU DGU FU IU KU MB MH NcU NIC NN NNC TxU UU WU

817 _____. 38 [i.e. Treinta y ocho] cuentos breves argentinos: siglo XX. Buenos Aires: Editorial Plus Ultra, 1980. 279 p. 20 cm.
An anthology of 20th-century Argentine short stories accompanied by brief biobibliographical sketches on their authors. They include Antonio Alberti, Carlos Arcidiácono, Luis Alberto Ballester, Vicente Barbieri,

Ariel Bignami, Mario Bravo, Teresa Caballero, Elías Carpena, Carlos Alberto Crespo, Juan José Delaney, Juan Draghi Lucero, María Elena Dubecq, Fernando Elizalde, Lily Franco, Juan Luis Gallardo, Beatriz Gallardo de Ordóñez, Antonio J. González, Santiago Grimani, Julio Imbert, Ester de Izaguirre, Ricardo Juan, Godofredo Lazcano Colodrero, Leopoldo Lugones, Pilar de Lusarreta, Martha Mercador, María Esther de Miguel, Nilda Rosa Nicolini, José Luis Pagés, Luisa Peluffo, Horacio Peroncini, Luis Portalet, Ana María Ramb, Marcela Righini, María Luisa Rubertino, Zita Solari, Jorge Tidone, Bernardo Verbitsky, Juan Bautista Zalazar.

IU

818 Stilman, Eduardo, comp. Antología del verso lunfardo. Buenos Aires: Editorial Brújula, 1965. 108 p. 20 cm.
An anthology of Argentine poetry written in slangy language. Includes biographical sketches of the following poets featured in the text: Vicente Barbieri, José Bettinoti, Antonio Caggiano, Carlos de la Púa, Evaristo Carriego, Roberto Cayol, Higinio Cazón, Dante Linyera, Florencio Iriarte, Iván Díez, Hugo Pedemonte, Alberto Vacarezza, Angel Villoldo, Felipe H. Fernández (Yacaré, pseud.),

CLSU CLU CtY CU IaU InU IU KU LNHT MB MH MiEM MnU MoSW NbU NIC NSyU PPiU TxU VtU WU

819 El tango; antología. Montevideo: Centro Editor de América Latina, 1969. 129 p. 18 cm. (Capítulo oriental: biblioteca uruguaya fundamental. V. 43).
An anthology of Argentine short stories, each preceded by a brief biobibliographical sketch of the author. Those included are Bernardo Kordon, José Luis Lanuza, María Rosa Oliver, José Antonio Saldías, Francisco García Jiménez, Pedro Larralde, Julio César Puppo (El Hachero, pseud.), César Tiempo, Carlos Gardel, Amaro Villanueva, Jorge Koremblit, Alicia Dujovne Ortiz, Edmundo E. Eichelbaum, Norberto Folino.

CtY IU MH MiEM NjP VtMiM

820 Tijeras, Eduardo. Relato breve en Argentina. Madrid: Cultura Hispánica, 1973. 168 p. 22 cm.
A discussion of many well-known Argentinean short-story writers (approximately 320 names), including biographical data and critical analyses of their most important works. Alphabetical index of names.

CaBVaU CoFS CSt CtW CtY CU CU-S CU-SB DGU FMU GU IaAS IU KU MH MiDW MiU MoU MU NcU NFQC NjP NN NNC OKentU OU PPiU PSC TxCM TxU ViMiU ViU VtU WU

LITERATURE

821 Tinker, Edward Larocque. <u>Life and literature of the Pampas</u>. Gainesville: University of Florida Press, 1961. 51 p. 23 cm. (The Latin American monograph series. V. 13).

Essay on gauchesque literature profiling a number of writers who have contributed to the genre. Among those especially featured with information on their literary activities are Bartolomé Hidalgo, Hilario Ascasubi, Esteban Echeverría, Eduardo Gutiérrez, Florencio Sánchez, Javier de Viana, Carlos Reyles, Justino Zavala Muñiz, Ricardo Güiraldes.

AAP CLSU CLU CtY FMU FTaSU GU ICU LNT-MA MH MiU MnU NcD NIC NjP OOxM OrU OU ScU TxU ViU

822 Togno, María Elena, comp. <u>Así escriben las mujeres</u>. Buenos Aires: Ediciones Orión, 1975. 187 p. 19 cm. (Colección Así escriben).

An anthology of short stories by the following contemporary Argentine women writers, including brief biobibliographical notes: Poldy Bird, María A. Bosco, Sylvina Bullrich, Lilian Goligorsky, Liliana Hecker, Luisa Mercedes Levinson, Marta Lynch, María Ester de Miguel, Silvina Ocampo, María Rosa Oliver, Olga Orozco, Syria Poletti, Hebe Uhart.

CSt CU-S InU IU MU NBuU NcU NIC NmU NN TxU VtMiM

823 13 [i.e. Trece] cuentos argentinos. Buenos Aires: Instituto Amigos del Libro Argentino, 1965. 152 p. 20 cm.

A collection of 20th-century Argentine short stories, each preceded by a brief biobibliographical sketch on its author. These people include Ana Arauco, Pedro Buchignani, Eugenia Calny, Luján Carranza, Ezequiel Díaz, Fernando Moreno, Dora Ochoa de Masramón, José Prado, Ismael Enrique Ricci, Osvalda Rovelli de Riccio, Fernando Rosemberg, Andrés Sila Mercer, J. R. Sparrow.

CLSU CLU CtU CU InU MiEM MiU MoSW MU NcU NIC NjP NNC NSyU OkU OU TxU ViU

824 13-19 [i.e. Trece-Diecinueve]: cuentos. Santa Fe: Colmegna, 1967. 160 p. 19 cm.

A collection of 20th-century Argentine short stories, accompanied by brief biobibliographical sketches on their authors. They include Isaac Aizenberg (Guiche Aizenberg, pseud.), Lermo Rafael Balbi, Nelly Borroni MacDonald, Ricardo Frete, Carlos María Gómez, Arturo Lomello, Hugo Mandón, Fortunato E. Nari, Luis Fernando Gudiño (L. F. Oribe, pseud.), Edgardo A. Pesante, Eduardo Raúl Storni, Jorge Vázquez Rossi, José Luis Vittori.

CLSU CLU CSt CtY FU IaU IU MB MiU MoSW MU NBuU NN NNC NSbSU NSyU OU TNJ TxLT TxU

825 <u>Treinta cuentos argentinos</u>, 1880-1940. Prólogo y notas de Angel Mazzei. Buenos Aires: Editorial Guadalupe, 1968. 319 p. 20 cm. (Biblioteca pedagógica. Extensión de la Sección 3: Literatura argentina).

A collection of 30 Argentine short stories, written between 1880 and 1940, and accompanied by brief biobibliographical sketches on their authors. They are Joaquín V. González, Roberto J. Payró, Macedonio Fernández, Leopoldo Lugones, Horacio Quiroga, Miguel Angel Correa (Mateo Booz, pseud.), Alberto Gerchunoff, Ricardo Güiraldes, Guillermo Guerrero Estrella, Arturo Cancela, Roberto Mariani, Daniel Ovejero, Héctor Eandi, Ezequiel Martínez Estrada, Pablo Rojas Paz, Elías Cárpena, Juan Draghi Lucero, Jorge Luis Borges, Leonardo Castellani, Roberto Arlt, Leónidas Barletta, Lobodón Garra, Manuel Peyrou, Carmen Gándara, Eduardo Mallea, Augusto Mario Delfino, Manuel Mujica Láinez, Angel María Vargas, Adolfo Bioy Casares, Julio Cortázar.

CLSU CSt DPU FU IaU ICIU IEN INS InU IU KU MB MH MiU MnU MoSW NbU NIC NN NSyU OU TU TxHR TxU ViU Wa

826 <u>Tres clásicos argentinos</u>: Miguel Cané, Joaquín V. González, Paul Groussac. Prólogo de Julio Molina Aguirre. Buenos Aires: Aguilar, 1953. 683 p. Ports. 13 cm. (Colección Crisol. V. 360).

An anthology, including biobibliographical essays accompanied by portraits, of the following 20th-century Argentine prose writers: Miguel Cané, Joaquín V. González, Paul Groussac,

IU

827 3 [i.e. Tres] de Buenos Aires: Guibert, Isaacson, Rossler. Prólogo de Bernardo Canal Feijóo. Buenos Aires: Pleamar, 1969. 91 p. 20 cm.

An anthology of poetry of 3 contemporary Argentineans, accompanied by short biobibliographical sketches on these men. They are Fernando Guibert, José Isaacson, Osvaldo Rossler.

CLSU CLU CSt CtY CU-SB FU IaU MB MoSW MU NIC OU PPULC TxU

828 Vadell, Natalio Abel. <u>Estudio histórico crítico de la literatura argentina</u> (rasgos gráficos y antología de sus poetas y escritores más notables). Primera serie. Buenos Aires: Talleres Gráficos de Spinelli, 1937. 205 p. Portraits. 26 cm.

An essay about 19th-century Argentine literature. Includes biobibliographical sketches of the following representative writers: Manuel José de Lavardén, Vicente López y Planes, José Antonio Miralla, Cayetano José Rodríguez, Esteban de Luca, Juan Ramón Rojas, Juan Crisóstomo Lafinur, Esteban Echeverría, Florencio Balcarce, José Mármol, Juan Cruz

Varela, Florencio Varela, Ventura de la Vega, José Hernández, Hilario Ascasubi, Estanislao del Campo.

DLC IU

829 25 [i.e. Veinticinco] cuentos argentinos magistrales: historia y evolución comentada del cuento argentino/repertorio. Prólogo, estudios, notas bibliográficas y comentarios de Carlos Mastrángelo. Buenos Aires: Plus Ultra, 1975. 334 p. 21 cm.
A collection of 20th-century Argentine short stories, accompanied by brief biobibliographical sketches on their authors. They include Esteban Echeverría, Horacio Quiroga, José María Cantilo, José Sixto Alvarez (Fray Mocho, pseud.), Joaquín V. González, Roberto J. Payró, Juan Draghi Lucero, Juan Carlos Dávalos, Alberto Gerchunoff, Guillermo Estrella, Leónidas Barletta, Silvina Ocampo, Alvaro Yunque (Arístides Gandolfi Herrero, pseud.), Bernardo Verbitsky, Abelardo Castillo, Angel María Vargas, Luis Gudiño Kramer, Adolfo Bioy Casares, Ricardo Juan, Haroldo Conti, Jorge Luis Borges, Dalmiro A. Sáenz, Héctor Lastra, Alberto Rodríguez Muñoz, Humberto Costantini, Augusto Mario Delfino, Julio Cortázar.

CSt CU-S CU-SB IU MH MoSW MU NBuU
NcU NhD NIC NjP NmU OU PPT TxU WU

830 27 [i.e. Veintisiete] cuentos del norte argentino. Prólogo de G. A. Bravo Figueroa. 3. ed. Tucumán: Editorial Atenas, 1970. 224 p. 18 cm.
An anthology of contemporary Argentine short stories, each preceded by a brief biobibliographical sketch on its author. They include: Jorge W. Abalos, Julio Aramburu, Julio Ardiles Gray, Juan J. Botelli, Carola Briones, Fausto Burgos, Bernardo Canal Feijóo, Manuel J. Castilla, Juan Carlos Dávalos, Francisco Ramón Díaz, Hugo R. Foguet, Luis Franco, Juan José Hernández, Alberto Córdoba, Daniel Ovejero, Miguel A. Pereyra, Alberto Pérez, Carlos B. Quiroga, Ricardo Rojas, Pablo Rojas Paz.

IU PPT

831 Veiravé, Alfredo, comp. . . . Y argentino en todas partes; 50 poetas del país presentados por Alfredo Veiravé. Buenos Aires: Ediciones S.A.D.E., 1971. 228 p. 24 cm.
An anthology of poetry by contemporary writers from the provinces of Argentina, including brief biobibliographical notes. The following are featured: Juan L. Ortiz, José Pedroni, Antonio de la Torre, Horacio G. Rava, Jorge Enrique Ramponi, Marcelino Román, Alfredo Martínez Howard, Américo Cali, Alejo Luis Meloni, Raúl Martín Galán, Franklin Ruveda, Mario Busignani, Alfonso Solá González, Juan José Coll, Antonio Esteban Agüero, Carlos Alberto Alvarez, Manuel J. Castilla, Andrés F. Fidalgo, Horacio Núñez West, Clementina Rosa

Quenel, Jaime Dávalos, Emilio Sosa López, Francisco Gandolfo, Roberto Themis Speroni, Raúl Aráoz Anzoátegui, Héctor Eduardo Ciocchini, Carlos Mario Lanzillotto, Ariel Ferraro, Hugo Gola, Néstor Groppa, Enrique Menoyo, Ariadna Chávez, Holver Martínez Borelli, Myrta Nydia Escariz, Osvaldo Guevara, Juan Luis Morabes, Alejandro Nicotra, Julio Requena, Guillermo Rodríguez, Irma Cuña, Abel Julio Cuenca, Enrique Gamarra, Juan E. González, Arturo Alvarez Sosa, Dora Fornaciari, Héctor David Gatica, Alberto Vila Ortiz, Jorge Vázquez Rossi, Aldo Cristanchi, Leopoldo Castilla.

AzTeS CLU CNoS CtY CU-S CU-SB FU
GU IaU IU MB MdU MU NcU NIC PPT
TxU WU

832 Verhesen, Fernand. Poésie vivante en Argentine. Le Cormier: 1962. 59 p. 19 cm.
A collection of representative works of 23 contemporary poets living and working in Argentina, followed by very brief biobibliographical notes. The following are featured: Raúl Gustavo Aguirre, Rodolfo Alonso, Edgar Bayley, Néstor Casazza, Osvaldo Elliff, Ariel Ferraro, Federico Gorbea, Eduardo Jonquières, Roberto Juarroz, Dieter Kasparek, Julio Llinás, Luis Edgardo Massa, Enrique Molina, Mario Morales, Aldo Pellegrini, Halma Cristiana Perry, Alejandro Pizarnik, Antonio Porchia, Jorge Sergio, Mario Trejo, Francisco Urondo, Rubén Vela, Laura Yusem.

IU NNC PPiU WaU WU

833 Vignale, Pedro Juan, and César Tiempo, pseud. Exposición de la actual poesía argentina (1922-1927), organizada por Pedro Juan Vignale y César Tiempo, pseud. Buenos Aires: Editorial Minerva, 1927. 256 p. Portraits. 19 cm.
An anthology of Argentine poetry (1922-1927), including biobibliographical sketches about the following poets: Alvaro Yunque, pseud. (Arístides Gandolfi Herrero), Oliverio Girondo, Angel Guido, Luis Cané (Luis Malmierca Cané), Conrado Nalé Roxlo, Carlos Vega, Luis Leopoldo Franco, Alfredo Brandán Caraffa, Cándido Delgado Fito, Amado Villar, Cayetano Córdova Iturburu, Horacio Angel Rega Molina, José B. Pedroni, Gustavo Angel Riccio, Eduardo González Lanuza, Leopoldo Marechal, Enrique M. Amorim, Jorge Luis Borges, Nicolás Olivari, Francisco Luis Bernárdez, Carlos Mastronardi Negri, Roberto Ledesma, Jacobo Fijman, Pedro Juan Vignale, Antonio Vallejo, Francisco López Merino, José Sebastián Tallón, Mateo Aristóbulo Echegaray, Raúl González Tuñón, Norah Lange, Andrés Luis Caro, Santiago A. Ganduglia, Juan Guijarro, Antonio Gullo, Guillermo Juan, Eduardo Keller Sarmiento, Ricardo E. Molinari, Leopoldo Pondal Ríos, Horacio Angel Schiavo, José Soler Darás, César Tiempo, pseud. (Israel Zeitlín), Carlos Raúl Muñoz (Carlos de la Púa, pseud.), Antonio A. Gil, Francisco Isernia, Lizando Z. D. Galtier.

CU CtY DLC IaU ICarbS ICU IU MoU
NBuU NcU NN NNC OU PBm TxU

LITERATURE

834 Williams Alzaga, Enrique. La pampa en la novela argentina. Buenos Aires: A. Estrada,
1955. 382 p. Portraits. 24 cm. (Ediciones
argentinas de cultura).

   An essay about the theme of "La Pampa" in
Argentine literature including biobibliogra-
phical sketches about the following writers
of the 18th through the 20th centuries: Car-
los Gervasoni, Tomás Falkner, Florián Paucke,
Pedro José de Parras, Calixto Bustamante
(Concolorcorvo, pseud.), Félix de Azara, José
de Espinosa y Tello, Alejandro Gillespie, Juan
Parish Robertson, Guillermo Parish Robertson,
Samuel Haigh, Francisco Bond Head, José An-
drews, Carlos Darwin, Guillermo Mac Cann,
Esteban Echeverría, Lina Beck-Bernard, San-
tiago Estrada, Eduarda Mansilla de García,
José Mármol, Miguel Cané, Juan María Gutiérrez,
Juana Manso de Noronha, José Joaquín de Vedia,
Manuel Olascoaga, Eduardo Gutiérrez, Eugenio
Cambaceres, Segundo Villafañe, Carlos María
Ocantos, Francisco Grandmontagne, José Luis
Cantilo, Lucio V. Mansilla, Estanislao S.
Zeballos, Roberto J. Payró, Benito Lynch,
Ricardo Güiraldes, Max Daireaux, Enrique La-
rreta, Eduardo Acevedo Díaz (hijo), Agustín
Guillermo Casa (Guillermo House, pseud.),
Delfor Méndez, Juan Manuel Prieto, Juan Goya-
narte, Carmen R. L. de Gándara, Juan Cornaglia,
Roberto J. Payró, Paul Groussac, Gustavo Mar-
tínez Zuviría, Fernando Gilardi, Eduardo
Mallea, Alcides Greca, Luis María Albamonte,
Guillermo Enrique Hudson, José Sixto Alvarez
(Fray Mocho, pseud.), Javier de Viana, San-
tiago Maciel, Godofredo Daireaux, Francisco
Soto y Calvo, Jorge Lavalle Cobo, Manuel
Ugarte, Vicente Rossi, Carlos Pío Sagastume,
Juan Cruz Ghío, Ernesto Mario Barreda, Ber-
nardo González Arrili, Julio Díaz Usandivaras,
Victoria Gucovsky, Juan Manuel Cotta, Carlos
Molina Massey, Diego Novillo Quiroga, Adolfo
Pérez Zelschi, Roberto Cunningham Graham,
Justo P. Sáenz.

   IU

835 Yahni, Roberto, comp. 70 [i.e. Setenta] años
de narrativa argentina: 1900-1970. Madrid:
Alianza Editorial, 1970. 212 p. 19 cm.
(El Libro de bolsillo. V. 267. Sección:
Literatura).

   An anthology of 20th-century Argentine
short stories, preceded by a collection of
brief biobibliographical sketches on their
authors. They include José Sixto Alvarez,
Leopoldo Lugones, Ricardo Güiraldes, Horacio
Quiroga, Ezequiel Martínez Estrada, Jorge
Luis Borges, Roberto Arlt, Eduardo Mallea,
Manuel Mujica Láinez, Adolfo Bioy Casares,
Silvina Ocampo, Julio Cortázar, Marco Denevi,
Beatriz Guido, Haroldo Conti, Rodolfo Walsh,
Pedro Orgambide, Juan José Hernández.

   AzU CaQMM CFS CLSU CoFS CtY CU
   CU-S CU-SB DeU FMU FU GASU IaU
   ICIU InU IU KMK KU KyLoU LU MdU
   MH MiDW MiU MoSW MU NBuU NjP

   NjR NN NNC NNCU-G NSyU OCU OkS OU
   PPiU PPT PSC ScCleU ScU TxBeaL
   TxDaM TxFTC TxHR TxSaT ViU VtMiM
   WaU WU

836 Zas, Lubrano, comp. Cuentistas argentinos
contemporáneos. Buenos Aires: Ediciones
"El Matadero," 1960. 61 p. 20 cm.
   A two-volume collection of contemporary
Argentine short stories, including biobiblio-
graphical sketches of the authors:
   V. 1: Juan Palazzo, Leónidas Barletta,
Pedro G. Orgambide, Abelardo Castillo, A. A.
Balán, Oscar A. Castelo, Rodolfo Cuenca, Juan
Carlos Trigo, Lubrano Zas.
   V. 2: Roberto Mariani, Andrés Cinqugrana,
Mario Lesing, Arminda Ralesky.

   IU NIC

837 Zeinstejer, Felipe, comp. Primera antología
de poetas del Litoral. Santa Fe: Castellví,
1957. 114 p. 19 cm.
   An anthology of the works of 27 contem-
porary poets from the Argentine province of
Santa Fe, accompanied by short biobibliogra-
phical essays for each author. They include
Jorge A. Antolini, Velmiro Ayala Gauna, Ho-
racio Correas, Leoncia Gianello, Enriqueta
González Svetko, Gastón Gori, Fausto Hernán-
dez, J. Bernardo Iturraspe, Horacio José
Lencina, José Rafael López Rosas, Julio Migno,
Roque Nosetto, Irma Peirano, José E. Peire,
Andrés del Pozo, Robger, Ecio Rossi, Arsenio
V. Salces, Osvaldo Salvañá, Domingo Santoro
Villarruel, José Eduardo Seri, Rosaura Schwei-
zer, Paulina Simoniello, Elena Siró, J. M.
Taverna Irigoyen, Mario R. Vecchioli, Felipe
Zeinstejer.

   CU InU IU MH PPiU PPULC TxU

See also entries 154, 167.

LITERATURE--DICTIONARIES, ENCYCLOPEDIAS,
and "WHO'S WHO"

838 Bertodatti, Juan Domingo. Diccionario de
poetas argentinos, por Vanber, pseud. Rosario: Editorial Lira, 1972. 110 p. 21 cm.
   A dictionary of Argentine poets. Very
short biobibliographical notes, including
dates of birth and death, and titles and
dates of important works, are given for each.
Contains approximately 1,500 names.

   CNoS CSt CtY CU FTaSU IaU InU IU
   MH MnU NcU NN NNC OO OU

839 Orgambide, Pedro G., and Roberto Yahni, comps.
Enciclopedia de la literatura argentina.
Dirigida por Pedro Orgambide y Roberto Yahni.
Buenos Aires: Editorial Sudamericana, 1970.
639 p. 20 cm.
   An encyclopedia of titles, concepts,
and people associated with Argentine litera-

ture, past and present. Biobibliographical information is included for several hundred men and women Argentine writers.

AU CaQMM CLSU CLU CNoS CSt CtW CtY
CU CU-SB DPU FU GASU GU IaU ICarbS
ICU InS InU IU KU KyU LU MB MdBJ
MdU MH MiEM MnU MoSW MoU MU NbU
NBuC NBuU NcD NcU NFQC NhD NIC
NjP NjR NN NNC OkU OrU OU PPiU
PPt PSt TxU ViU WaU WU

840 Prieto, Adolfo. *Diccionario básico de lite-*
ratura argentina. Buenos Aires: Centro Editor de América Latina, 1968. 159 p. (Capítulo: Biblioteca fundamental argentina.
V. 59).
   Dictionary of Argentine literature featuring brief biobibliographical sketches of prominent writers born before 1930.

CSt CU-SB DeU ICarbS IU MH MnU NIC
NSyU OkS

841 *Quiénes son los escritores argentinos.* Buenos
Aires: Ediciones CRISOL, 1980. 206 p. 19 cm.
   A dictionary containing brief biobibliographical sketches on over 1,200 Argentine
writers.

IU

MEDICINE

842 Aráoz Alfaro, Gregorio. *Crónicas y estampas*
del pasado. Buenos Aires: Librería "El
Ateneo," 1938. 363 p. 23 cm.
   A collection of essays paying homage to
the following, many of them physicians, who
were friends or acquaintances of the author:
Guillermo Rawson, Ignacio Pirovano, Osvaldo
Loudet, Tiburcio Padilla, Antonino Ibarguren,
Leopoldo Montes de Oca, Rafael Herrera Vegas,
Jaime R. Costa, Horacio G. Piñero, Máximo
Castro, Alfredo Lanari, Maximiliano Aberas-
tury, Rómulo H. Chiappori, Julio Iribarne,
Juan Carlos Navarro, José Mariano Astigueta,
Roberto Wernicke, Eufemio Uballes, Gregorio
N. Chaves, Abel Ayerza, Enrique E. del Arca,
Luis Güemes, José Penna, Pedro N. Arata,
Telemaco Susini, Samuel Gache, Emilio R. Coni,
Elmina Paz de Gallo, Helena Larroque de Roffo,
Elisa Funes de Juárez Celman, Pedro Lacavera,
José A. Frías, Herminio J. Quirós, Marco M.
Avellaneda.

DLC IU NN

843 Beltrán, Juan Ramón. *Historia del protomedi-*
cato de Buenos Aires: estado de los conoci-
mientos sobre medicina en el Río de la Plata,
durante la época colonial. Los galenos españoles y los magos o curanderos indígenas.
Antecedentes históricos y legales de la fundación del protomedicato y de la Escuela Mé-

dica de Buenos Aires; Buenos Aires: El Ateneo, 1937. 316 p. 19 cm.
   A history of medicine and the organization
of medical services in Buenos Aires during
the colonial period. Brief scattered biographical information is included for many
people in this aspect of Argentina's history.
Longer biographical essays, emphasizing professional accomplishments, are given for the
following physicians: Miguel Gorman, Agustín
Eusebio Fabre and Cosme Argerich.

DLC ICJ NcD NIC NjP NN OClWHi OU
PPC PPULC PU

844 Cantón, Eliseo. *Historia de la Facultad de*
Medicina y sus escuelas. Buenos Aires: Coni,
1921. 4 v. Portraits. 25 cm.
   A history of the Faculty of Medicine in
Buenos Aires, Argentina, 16th century to the
early 20th century, including biographical
data of varying amounts about many people
associated with it. The following are par-
ticularly featured:
   V. 1: Manuel Alvarez, Francisco Bernardo
Xixón, Juan Escalera, Blas Gutiérrez, Nicolás
Xaques, Cristóbal Gómez Polanco, Andrés Ge-
deón, Alonso Garro de Aréchaga, Atanasio de
la Piedad, Pedro Montenegro, Segismundo As-
perger, José González, Roberto Joun, Francisco
Argerich, Matías Grimau, José Alberto Capde-
vila y Pallarés, Ramón Gómez, José Plá, José
Giró, Diego Garrido, Juan Cayetano Molina,
Francisco Antonio Maciel, Saturnino Segurola,
Francisco Javier Muñiz, Miguel Gorman, Agustín
Eusebio Fabre, Adeodato Olivera, Cosme Mariano
Argerich, Baltasar Tejerina, Salvio Gaffarot,
José Reedhead, Diego Paroissien.
   V. 2: Francisco Cosme Argerich, Carlos
Durand, Aime Bonpland, Cristóbal Martín de
Montúfar, Juan Antonio Fernández, Francisco
de Paula del Rivero, Pedro Carta, Juan Madera,
José Fuentes Arguivel, Juan José Montes de
Oca, Francisco Javier Muñiz, Pedro Rojas,
Remigio Díaz, Ireneo Portela, Diego Alcorta,
Claudio Mamerto Cuenca, Salustiano Cuenca,
Francisco Pico, Leopoldo Montes de Oca, Pedro
Mallo, Santiago Larrosa, Luis Gómez, Adolfo
Peralta, Carlos Furst, Martín García, Manuel
Aránz, Joaquín Díaz de Bedoya, José P. Lucena,
Manuel Blancas, Guillermo Rawson, Nicanor
Albarellos, Manuel Augusto Montes de Oca,
Eduardo Wilde, Manuel Porcel de Peralta, Mar-
tín Spuch, Teodoro Alvarez, Juan A. Argerich.
   V. 3: Miguel Puiggari, Manuel Blancas,
Jacob de Tezanos Pinto, Antonio Crespo, José
María Gómez de Fonseca, Pedro Antonio Pardo,
José María Bosch, Bartolomé Novaro, Roberto
Wernicke, Lucio Meléndez, Cleto Aguirre,
Domingo Parodi, Juan José Naón, José M. Asti-
gueta, Pedro N. Arata, Pedro Lagleyze, Mauri-
cio González Catán, Eufemio Uballes, Marcial
Quiroga, Juan A. Boeri, Pedro Mattos, Juan
Ramón Fernández, Enrique E. del Arca, Teodoro
Baca, Adalberto Ramaugé, Eduardo Wilde, Eduar-
do Pérez, Antonio Crespo, Melitón González

MEDICINE

del Solar, Ignacio Pirovano, Manuel Blancas, Juan B. Señorans, Juan Ramón Fernández, Eliseo Cantón, Nicasio Etchepareborda, Francisco Barraza, Baldomero Sommer, Ricardo Gutiérrez, Jaime R. Costa, Leopoldo Montes de Oca, Domingo Cabred, Atanasio Quiroga, José Penna, Manuel Araúz, Pascual Palma, Alejandro Posadas, Eduardo Obejero, Manuel Irízar, Juvencio Z. Arce, Luis Güemes, Adolfo Mugica, Obdulio Hernández, Enrique Bazterrica, Andrés Llobet, Rodolfo de Gainza, Carlos Malbrán, Abel Ayerza, Pedro Coronado, Federico Texo, Francisco Sicardi, Alejandro Castro, León Pereira, Edmundo Nocard, Emilio R. Coni, Eduardo Pérez, Francisco de Veiga, Gregorio N. Chaves, Olinto Magalhaes, Marcial V. Quiroga, Cristian Jakob, Pedro Lacavera, Pablo Marengo, Enrique Revilla, Julio Méndez, Julián Aguilar, Juan B. Justo, Diógenes Decoud, Juan D. Piñero, Ignacio Allende, José María Ramos Mejía, Antonio Gandolfo, Pascual Palma.

    V. 4: Pedro Lagleyze, Eliseo Cantón, Roberto Wernicke, Pedro N. Arata, Luis Güemes, José María Ramos Mejía, Ignacio Pirovano, Eduardo Wilde, Enrique Bazterrica, Telémaco Susini, Miguel Puiggari, Carlos Murray, Juan A. Boeri, Francisco C. Barraza, Nicasio Etchepareborda, Domingo Cabred, Luis Agote, Pedro Rojas.

    DCU-IA IaU InU NcD OU

845 Cervera, Federico Guillermo. <u>Historia de la medicina en Santa Fe</u>. Santa Fe: Talleres Gráficos de la Librería y Editorial Colmegna, 1973. 386 p. Portraits. 23 cm.

    A history of medicine in the Argentine province of Santa Fe, covering the period from colonial times through the 19th century. Biographical information of various amounts, as well as portraits in a few cases, are included for the following: Hernando de Alcázar, Hernando de Molina, Maestre Juan, Pedro de Mesa, Diego Núñez, Hernando de Zamora, Sebastián de León, Blas de Testanova, Ablas, Juan de Arca, Martín de Armencia, Domingo Martínez, Pedro de Gualdas, Pedro de Hernández, Francisco de Pastrana, Barsio, Galiano Mérida, Diego Barba, Esteban Bocería, Antonio Fernández, López Fernández, Juan Herrador, Maestre Jaques, Pedro Portugués, Vasco Rodríguez, Diego Verguero, Maese Bernal, Pedro de Sayas, Pedro Soleto, Juan de Porras, Diego Hernández de Bozmediano, Diego Núñez, Pedro de Castro, Nicolás Florentín, Miguel Herrero, Leonardo Jaso, Juan Rodríguez de Escobar, Luis Beltrán, Juan de Córdoba, Andrés de Arteaga, Lorenzo de Menagliotto, Cristóbal Gómez Polaino, Luis Carvallo (Luis Carballo), Díaz Taño, José Cataldino, Cristóbal Altamirano, Juan Fernández, José Casarena, Pedro de Piña Cervantes, Francisco de la Concepción, Diego Jofre de Bareda Estrada, Manuel Días Correa, Luis de las Cuebas, José de Abalos, Juan de Alvarado, Andrés de la Bastida, Francisco Caraballo Suárez, Carlos Antonio de los Angeles, Bernardo Lajus, Juan de Coll, José Gómez, Francisco de la Palma, Tomás Falkner, Segismundo Asper-

ger, Miguel Benavídez, Marciano Xambó, Juan de Silva, Esteban Huguet, Esteban Rayón, Juan de los Reyes, Atanasio de la Piedad, Agustín Domínguez, Carlos de la Rosa, Buenaventura Suárez, Vicente Morales, Juan José Leite, Manuel Rodríguez y Sarmiento, Ramón del Fresno, José Ramón Tarragona, Andrés Quiñones, Domingo Benjamín Aixten, Bernabé Vargas, Pedro García Romero, Felipe Reynoso, Manuel Rodríguez y Sarmiento, Manuela Michaela Rodríguez del Fresno, Bonifacio Rodríguez del Fresno, Bernardino Rodríguez del Fresno, Antonio Rodríguez del Fresno, María Joaquina Rodríguez del Fresno, María Josefa del Pilar Rodríguez del Fresno, Fortunata Rodríguez del Fresno, Pedro José Celestino Rodríguez del Fresno, Luciano Torrent, Mauricio Garrido, Alejandro García, Manuel D. García, Francisco Rodríguez Amoedo, Eugenio Pérez, Juan Bautista Arengo, Mauricio Hertz, Francisco Riva, Mauricio Hertz, Francisco Riva, José Olguin, Cándido Pujato.

    CLU CtY IU MB MU NN WU

845a Cranwell, Daniel J. <u>Nuestros grandes médicos</u>. Buenos Aires: El Ateneo, 1937. 179 p. 23 cm.

    A collection of biographical sketches of the following notable Argentinean physicians: Rafael Herrera Vegas, Pedro N. Arata, Toribio de Ayerza, José A. Ayerza, Abel Ayerza, Roberto Wernicke, Luis Güemes, Pedro Lagleyze, Angel M. Centeno.

    CSt NN

846 Fúrlong Cárdiff, Guillermo Juan. <u>Médicos argentinos durante la dominación hispánica</u>. Prólogo del Dr. Aníbal Ruiz Moreno. Buenos Aires: Editorial Huarpes, 1947. 311 p. Portraits. 28 cm. (His. Cultura colonial argentina. V. 6).

    A history of medicine in Argentina during the colonial period, including scattered biographical information on many prominent physicians. The following are particularly featured: Ascensio Telles de Rojas, Gaspar Cardozo Pereyra, Pedro Montenegro, Buenaventura Suárez, Segismundo Aperger, Tomás Falkner, Miguel Gorman, José Alberto Capdevila y Pallarés, Agustín Eusebio Fabre, Manuel Rodríguez y Sarmiento. Alphabetical index of names.

    CtY CU DLC FU IEN IU MH MiU MnU
    NcU NIC OU TxU ViU WaU

847 Loudet, Osvaldo. <u>Médicos argentinos</u>. Buenos Aires: Editorial Huemul, 1966. 238 p. 21 cm.

    A collection of lengthy biographies on the following Argentine physicians whose lives spanned the 19th and 20th centuries: Luis Güemes, Abel Ayerza, José María Ramos Mejía, Marcelino Herrera Vegas, Pedro Mallo, Juan B. Señorans, Domingo Cabred, Juan M. Obarrio, Lucio V. López (son), Juan A. Sánchez.

CLSU   CLU   CU   ICU   InU   IU   MB   MiU
MoSW   MU   NbU   NBuU   NcD   NIC   NjR   NN
NNC-M   OU   PPLC   TxU

848   Maurín Navarro, Emilio.   Tres maestros de la
medicina argentina: Rawson, Quiroga y Navarro.   San Juan: Academia Provincial de la
Historia, 1972.   220 p.   Portraits.   22 cm.
(Academia Provincial de la Historia.   Ediciones extras.   V. 8).
     A collection of portraits and biographi-
cal essays on the following notable 19th- and
20th-century Argentine teachers of medicine:
Guillermo Rawson, Marcial V. Quiroga, Juan
C. Navarro.

     GU   IaU   IU   MB   MU   NIC   OU   TxU

849   Molina, Raúl A.   Primeros médicos de la ciudad de la Santísima Trinidad; prólogo del dr.
José Luis Molinari.   Buenos Aires en el siglo
XVII.   Buenos Aires: Editorial Lancestremere,
1948.   187 p.   Portraits.   24 cm.   (Publicaciones del Instituto Argentino de Ciencias
Genealógicas).
     A history of medicine in Buenos Aires,
covering the period before and during the
conquest.   Biographical information and a few
portraits are given for some physicians, as
well as for the author of this work.   The following are particularly featured: Raúl A.
Molina, Pedro Díaz, Francisco Bernardo Xijón,
Luis Caraballo, Pablo Francisco de Luca,
Baltasar de Grasaum.

     OU   TxU

850   Molinari, José Luis.   Historia de la medicina
argentina; tres conferencias.   Buenos Aires:
Imprenta López, 1937.   147 p.   24 cm.
     A history of medicine in Argentina, con-
centrating almost exclusively on the colonial
era.   Biographical information of various
amounts is included for many physicians, most
of them missionaries.   The following are particularly featured: Cristóbal Gomes Polaino,
Atanasio de la Piedad (Atanasio de la Soledad,
pseud.), Roque González, Claudio Royer, Antonio Ruiz de Montoya, Diego Bassauri, Cristóbal Altamirano, Blas Gutiérrez, Pedro Añasco,
Juan Saloni, Tomás Fields, Manuel Ortega,
Vicente Griffi, José Cataldino, Simón Massetta, Francisco Díaz Taño, Padre Pakman, En-
rique Peschke, Marcos Villodas, Juan Icart,
Juan Escobar, Enrique Adami, Tomás Heyrle,
José Jenig, Ruperto Dahlhammer, Pedro Korn-
mayer, Wenceslao Horski, Cristian Maier,
Norberto Zuilak, Carlos Kramer, Esteban Font,
Juan de la Cruz Montealegre, Juan Bautista
Zea, Segismundo Aperger, Buenaventura Suárez,
Tomás Falkner, Pedro Montenegro, Manuel Alva-
rez, Jerónimo de Miranda, Francisco Bernardo
Xixow (Francisco Bernardo Gijón, pseud.),
Juan Escalera, Andrés Navarro, Nicolás Xaques,
Francisco de Argerich, José Alberto Capdevila
y Pallarés.

     CU   DLC   DNLM   OU   TxU

850a   Oddo, Vicente.   Primeros médicos de la ciudad
de Santiago del Estero; siglo XVI.   Santiago
del Estero: Editorial Herca, 1981.   213 p.
23 cm.
     An essay about 16th-century physicians in
the Argentine province of Santiago del Estero.
The following are featured: Alonso de Villadiego, Juan Muñoz, Andrés de Arteaga, Orlando
Faya.

     IU

851   Pelosio, Anselmo.   El médico y la cultura.
Buenos Aires: Editorial Plus Ultra, 1971.
165 p.   19 cm.
     A collection of biographical sketches of
the following Argentine physicians: Alejandro
Korn, Luis Güemes, Christofredo Jakob, Ricardo
Gutiérrez, José María Ramos Mejía, Guillermo
Rawson, Juan B. Justo, Ricardo Finochietto,
Francisco Anselmo Sicardi, José Ingenieros,
Eduardo Wilde, Julio Méndez, Francisco Javier
Muñiz, Eduardo Ladislao Holmberg, Pablo Luis
Mirizzi.

     TxU

852   Torres, Antonio.   Historia médica del Tucumán.
Tucumán: Urueña, 1969.   142 p.   23 cm.
     A history of medicine in the Argentine
province of Tucumán, covering the period from
colonial to modern times, and including short
biographies for the following 19th- and 20th-
century physicians: Víctor Bruland, Manuel
Esteves, Francisco Mendioroz, Benigno Vallejo,
Joaquín Corbalán, Gerardo Palacio.

     CLSU   CLU   CU   CU-SB   IU   MB   NmU   NN   OU
PSt   TxU   ViU   WU

853   Túmburus, Juan.   Síntesis histórica de la
medicina argentina.   Buenos Aires: El Ateneo,
1926.   126 p.   18 cm.
     A short history of medicine in Argentina,
covering the period from preconquest to modern
times.   Very brief scattered biographical information is included for many people, mostly
physicians, associated with this aspect of
Argentina's development.

     CtY   CU-M   DNLM   ICJ   ICU   MB   MBCo
MiDW-M   OrU-M   PPC   PPJ   ViU

853a   Vaccarezza, Oscar Andrés.   El santo del bis-
turí y otras biografías.   Buenos Aires: La
Prensa Médica Argentina, 1982.   274 p.   23 cm.
(Colección humanismo médico).
     A collection of biographical essays about
contemporary leading Argentine physicians and
surgeons and others associated with them.
The following are featured: Enrique Fino-
chietto, David F. Pando, Rodolfo E. Pasman,
Bernardo A. Houssay, James Lepper, Nicolás
Repetto, Benjamín Dupont, Juan H. Scrivener,
Pablo Emilio Coni, Avelino Gutiérrez, Adolfo
Noceti, Juan Mateo Franceschi.

     IU

MEDICINE

854 Vaccarezza, Raúl F. <u>Vida de médicos ilustres</u>.
Buenos Aires: Editorial Troquel, 1980. 167 p.
Portraits. 19 cm.
A collection of biographical essays, ac-
companied by portraits of the following no-
table Argentine physicians: Emile Sergent,
Francisco Javier Muñiz, Juan José Montes de
Oca, Enrique Tornú, Luis Agote, Gregorio
Aráoz Alfaro, Alejandro Raimondi.

  IU

855 Zapata Gollán, Agustín. <u>Médicos y medicinas</u>
<u>en la época colonial de Santa Fe</u>. Santa Fe:
Editorial Castellví, 1949. 157 p. Portraits.
24 cm.
A history of medicine in the Argentine
province of Santa Fe during the colonial era.
Brief scattered biographical notes are included for many notable medical practitioners
of that era and place. Alphabetical index of
names.

  DLC DNLM MoU TxU

See also entry 718.

MEDICINE--DICTIONARIES, ENCYCLOPEDIAS, and "WHO'S WHO"

856 Gajardo Cruzat, Enrique, comp. <u>Diccionario</u>
<u>médico argentino</u>. Buenos Aires: Talleres
Gráficos Argentinos L. J. Rosso, 1932. 240 p.
Portraits. 27 x 18 cm.
Biographical dictionary of practicing
physicians in Argentina in 1932. Limited biographical data are supplied for a number of
individuals. Contains also an essay on the
history of the medical profession in the
River Plate area with biographies of outstanding individuals.

  DNLM

MOVING PICTURES

857 Abel Martín, Jorge. <u>Cine argentino '76 [i.e.</u>
<u>setenta y seis]</u>. Buenos Aires: Ediciones
Metrocop, 1977. 83 p. 22 cm.
Record of film production in Argentina in
1976. Included are biographical sketches
profiling the professional careers of the
following individuals connected with films
and their production: Fernando Ayala, Ar-
mando Bó, Carlos Borcosque, Enrique Cahen
Salaberry, Enrique Carreras, Rafael Cohen,
Raúl de la Torre, Leonardo Favio, Simón Feld-
man, Domingo Carlos Galettini, Juan José
Jusid, Bebe Kamín, David José Kohon, José
Antonio Martínez Suárez, Hugo Moser, Héctor
Olivera, Palito Ortega, Juan Carlos Pelliza,
Sergio Renán, Sandro, Julio Saraceni, Gerar-
do Sofovich, Hugo Sofovich, Leopoldo Torre
Nilsson, Orestes A. Trucco, Ricardo Wülicher.

Alphabetical index of names. (<u>See also</u>
entries 857a, 857b, 857c, 857d.)

  IU

857a _____. <u>Cine argentino '77 [i.e. setenta y</u>
<u>siete]</u>. Buenos Aires: Ediciones Metrocop,
1978. 99 p. Portraits. 22 cm.
Biographical sketches of the following
individuals connected with the Argentine
moving-pictures industry who made headlines
in 1977: Angel Acciaresi, Manuel Antin, Fernando Ayala, Enrique Dawi, Ricardo Alberto
Defilippi, Jorge Zuhair Jury, Eva Landeck,
Martín Maisler, Sergio L. Mottola, Daniel
Pires Mateus, Mario Sábato, Fernando Siro.
Alphabetical index of names. (<u>See also</u> entries 857, 857b, 857c, 857d.)

  OU

857b _____. <u>Cine argentino '78 [i.e. setenta y</u>
<u>ocho]</u>. Buenos Aires: Ediciones Cero Seis,
1979. 137 p. Portraits. 22 cm.
Biographical sketches of the following
individuals connected with the Argentine
moving-pictures industry who made headlines
in 1978: Adolfo Aristarain, Oscar Barney
Finn, Waldo Belloso, Abel Rubén Beltrami,
Mario David, Julio De Grazia, Alejandro Doria,
Juan Schroeder, Aníbal Uset. Includes also
obituaries of Jorge Cafrune, Conrado Diana,
Roberto Bensaya, Mario Danesi, Alberto An-
chart, Antonio Herrero, Augusto Codeca,
Esteban Serrador, Atilio Marinelli, Ramón
Martínez, Mariano Bauza, Blanca Lagrotta,
Gregorio Barrios, María del Río, Alfonso Paso,
Catalina Bárcena, Florence Marly, Leopoldo
Torre Nilsson. Alphabetical index of names.
(<u>See also</u> entries 857, 857a, 857c, 957d.)

  OU

857c _____. <u>Cine argentino '79 [i.e. setenta y</u>
<u>nueve]</u>. Buenos Aires: Corregidor, 1980.
131 p. Portraits. 22 cm.
Biographical sketches of the following
individuals connected with the Argentine
moving-pictures industry who made headlines
in 1979: Massimo Giuseppe Alviani, Rodolfo
Corral, Guillermo Fernández Jurado, Hugo Fili,
Néstor Lescovich, Miguel Angel Lumaldo, Carlos Orgambide, Julio Porter, Carlos Rinaldi,
Luis Saslavsky, Emilio Vieyra, Clara Zappettini. Includes also obituaries of Angel
Eleta, Juan Bono, Lalo Hartich, George Andreani, Tito Alonso, Narciso Machinandiarena,
Gloria Guzmán, Jorge W. Abalos, María Luisa
Santes, Marcos Caplan, Martín Rodríguez Mentasti, Amedeo Nazzari, Augusto César Vatteone,
Yago Blass, Olga Casares Pearson. Alphabeti-
cal index of names. (<u>See also</u> entries 857,
857a, 857b, 857d.)

  OU

857d _____. Cine argentino 80. Buenos Aires: Ediciones Corregidor, 1981. 141 p. 23 cm.

Analysis of the Argentine moving-pictures industry in 1980. Includes obituaries of the following individuals associated with the performing arts that died in 1980: Carlos Latorre, Clemente Lococo, Dorita Davis, Mario Vanadia, Claudio Levrino, Raúl Alejandro Apold, Eloísa Vigo, Orlando Viloni, Dringue Farías, Héctor Méndez, Fernando Soto ("Mantequilla," pseud.), José Cedrón, Juan Carlos Pelliza, Pepe Calvo, Luis Politti, Carlos López Moctezuma, Rodolfo Crespi, Jesús Gómez, Adolfo Stray, Oscar Alemán, César Tiempo, Adolfo Z. Wilson, Milagros de la Vega, Luis Sandrini. Also biographical essays about María Herminia Avellaneda, María Luisa Bemberg, Máximo Berrondo, Rubén W. Cavallotti, Gino Landi, Carlos Otaduy, Eliseo Subiela. Alphabetical index of names. (See also entries 857, 857a, 857b, 857c.)

IU OU

858 Di Núbila, Domingo. Historia del cine argentino. Buenos Aires: Edición Cruz de Malta; distribuidores: Editorial Schapire, 1960. 2 v. 24 cm. Portraits.

A two-volume history of the Argentine film industry, including scattered biographical information on many people associated with this field of endeavor, with particular emphasis on film makers. Among those included are Elías Alippi, Luis César Amadori, Pepe Arias, Carlos Borcosque, Hugo del Carril, Lucas Demare, Alberto de Zavalía, José A. Ferreyra, José Gola, Libertad Lamarque, Angel Magaña, José L. Moglia Barth, Enrique Muiño, Francisco Mugica, Carlos Olivari, Manuel Peña Rodríguez, Sixto Pondal Ríos, Manuel Romero, Luis Sandrini, Luis Saslavsky, Enrique Serrano, Mario Soffici, Ernesto Arancibia, Fernando Ayala, Cahen Salaberry, Alberto Closas, Carlos H. Christensen, Tulio Demicheli, Mirthce Legrand, Gori Muñoz, Julio Saraceni, Carlos Schliepper, Daniel Tinayre, Leopoldo Torre Nilsson, Leopoldo Torres Ríos. Alphabetical index of names.

DPU CLSU

MUSIC

859 Bosch, Mariano Gregorio Gerardo. Historia de la ópera en Buenos Aires. Buenos Aires: Impr. El Comercio, 1905. 256 p. Portraits. 21 cm.

A history of opera in Buenos Aires, primarily during the 19th century. Scattered biographical information is included for many musicians, among them the following: Juan A. Picazzarri, Esteban Massini, Massoni, Pablo Rosquellas, Miguel Vaccani, Angelita Tanni, María Tanni, Pascual Tanni, Marcelo Tanni, Nina Barbieri, Ida Edelvira, Tamberlick, Arturo Beruti, Pablo María Beruti.

CtY DLC IU MB NcD NcU

860 Bozzarelli, Oscar. Ochenta años de tango platense. La Plata: Editorial Osboz, 1972. 244 p. 23 cm.

Essay on the history of the tango in Argentina from 1890-1970 featuring biographical sketches of the following individuals connected with it: Carlos Aimar, Antonio Albanese, Oscar Allevato, Raúl Oscar Bach (Coco, pseud.), José María Bagnati, Tito Balbi, Tulio Bartolini, Raquel C. de Belmonte, Antonio Blasi (El Gaucho, pseud.), Miguel Bosch, Domingo Bozzarelli, José Capella, Gabriel Eduardo Cativa, Juan Carlos Cobos (El Quique, pseud.), Genaro Chimenti, Víctor D'Amario, Edelmiro D'Amario, Eulogio Dávila, Jorge de la Fuente, Germán de la O., Horacio Delbueno, Juan Bautista Devoto, Pablo Luis Elía, Fermín Valentín Favero, José Fiore, Alberto Forte (Chiche, pseud.), Juan Furia, Hugo Galli, Ponciano García, Atilio Gariboto (Polenta, pseud.), Dante Garófalo, Rafael Gaskín Vucetich, Oscar González, Casimiro Labat, Antonio Lamardo (Pinín, pseud.), Jorge Lavaller, Rafael Lavecchia, Gregorio Levchuk, Raúl Licastro, Emilio Lodi, Pedro Lofeudo (Toto, pseud.), Angel Lombardi, Aquiles Lombardi, Chino Lombardi, Horacio Lombardi, Oscar Lombardi (Piruncho, pseud.), Pedro Lopérfido, Robert López Osorio, Angel Hermenegildo Lovisuto, Mario Lovisuto, Victorio Lovisuto, Jacinto Lozzi, Chila Luna (Alcira Camen Luna), Omar Rufino Lupi, César Malnatti (Cholo, pseud.), Juan Carlos Marambio Catán, Mario Luis (María Luisa Carnelli), José Marmonti, Hugo Alberto Marozzi, Juan Cruz Mateo, Osvaldo Molino, Bartolomé Domingo Montero (Monterito; Bartolito, pseuds.), Polo Orlando (Leopoldo Soria Orlando), Roberto Parietti (Cacho, pseud.), Néstor Parodi, José Pendón, Ricardo Pérsico, Baltasar Piñero, Natalio Porcellana, Carlitos Porcellana, Luisita Porcellana, Fernando Potenza, Angel Eladio Ramos (Ramito, pseud.), Angel Resiga, Ricardo Rómulo, Dardo Ernesto Saborido (Tantín, pseud.), Angel Saldías, Luis Scalón, Lideano Silvestrini, Mercedes Simone, Horacio Omar Valente, Oscar César Veghetti (Cholo, pseud.), Celestino Vidal, Ernesto Wolcán, Juan Wolcán, Martín Yuspa, Severo Zingoni.

IU

861 Cavadini, Rubén. ¿Tango o nueva expresión de Buenos Aires? En busca de una letra y una música que interpreten al porteño de hoy. Buenos Aires: Colombo, 1969. 103 p. 18 cm.

History of the tango in Buenos Aires with biographical essays about the following artists: Osmar Maderna, Carlos Gardel, Homero Manzi, Enrique Santos Discépolo, Astor Piazolla, Mariano Mores.

CLSU CSt CtY FU IaU IU KU MB MoSW MU NIC NN PSt TxU

MUSIC

862 D'Alessandro, Néstor. <u>Poemas populares</u>.
Buenos Aires: Aconcagua, 1973. 53 p. 22 cm.
    A collection of biographical poems honor-
ing the following artists associated with
Buenos Aires, Argentina, popular music:
Mercedes Sosa, Aníbal Troilo, Atahualpa Yu-
panqui, Astor Piazzolla, Enrique Santos Dis-
cépolo, Tita Merrello, Cátulo Castillo, En-
rique Mario Francici, Félix Ramírez Luna,
Lucio Demare, Julián Centeya, Anselmo Aieta,
Francisco García Jiménez, Alfredo Gobbi,
Julio De Caro, Francisco De Caro, Edmundo
Rivero, José Asunción Flores, Horacio Salgán,
Enrique Delfino, Homero Expósito, Virgilio
Expósito, Tania, Enrique Maciel, José Damés,
Benito Bianquet (El Cachafaz, pseud.).

        NmU TxU

863 Ferrer, Horacio Arturo. <u>El libro del tango</u>:
crónica y diccionario, 1850-1977. Buenos
Aires: Editorial Galerna, 1977. 769 p.
25 cm.
    A history of the tango, including bio-
graphical sketches of individuals associated
with it.

        IU

864 Flury, Lázaro. <u>Breve historia de la música
argentina y folklore</u>; adaptado a los progra-
mas de las Escuelas Superiores de música e
institutos afines. Santa Fe: Ediciones
"Colmegna," 1959. 132 p. 19 cm.
    History of Argentine music with biogra-
phical notes about the following figures:
José Antonio Picazarri, Francisco A. Har-
greaves, Dalmiro Costa, Telésforo Cabero,
Luis Moreau Gottschalk, Nicanor Albarellos,
Mariquita Sánchez de Velasco, Alberto Williams,
Arturo Berutti, Pablo Berutti, Julián Aguirre,
Carlos López Buchardo, Pascual de Rogatis,
Constantino Gaito, Ricardo Rodríguez, Felipe
Boero, Juan Bautista Massa, Floro Ugarte,
Juan José Castro, José María Castro, Luis
Gianneo, Gilardo Gilardi, Nicolás Alfredo
Alesio, José André, Ernesto Drangosh, Arnaldo
D'Esposito, Martín Fierro.

        IaU ICarbS ICU InU IU LNHT MiD
        MoSW NcD NIC NjR NN OU

865 _____. <u>Historia de la música argentina</u>.
Santa Fe: Ediciones Colmegna, 1967. 101 p.
18 cm.
    History of Argentine music with biogra-
phical notes about the following representa-
tive figures: Francisco Solano, Jean Valseau,
Antón Von Sepp Seppenbur zu Reinegg, Florián
Baucke, Martín Schmid, Martín Dobrizhoffer,
Johan Mesner, Julianus Knosler, Cristóbal
Pirioby, Juan Crisóstomo Lafinur, María Sán-
chez de Velasco, Nicanor Albarellos, Juan
Bautista Alberdi, Amancio Alcorta, Arturo
Berutti, Pablo Berutti, Alberto Williams,
Julián Aguirre, Cayetano Troiani, León Fon-
tova, Carlos Pedrell, Arturo Luzatti, Carlos
López Buchardo, Pascual de Rogatis, Constan-
tino Gaito, Ricardo Rodríguez, Felipe Boero,
Juan Bautista Massa, Floro Ugarte, Ernesto
Drangosch, Celestino Raggio, José Andre,
Gilardo Gilardi, Enrique Mario Casella, Athos
Palma, Pedro Valenti Costa, Washington Castro,
Juan José Castro, José María Castro, Luis
Gianneo, Jacobo Fischer, Honorio Sicardi,
Roberto García Morillo, Juan Carlos Paz,
Mauricio Kagel, César Mario Francisena, Carlos
Vega, Alberto Ginastera, Héctor Iglesia Vi-
lloud, Carlos Gustavino, Angel Lasala, Nicolás
Alfredo Alesio, Julio Viggiano Esain, Luis
Milici, Oscar S. Bareilles, Ernesto César
Galeano, Jorge Fontenla, Virtú Maragno,
Roberto Caamaño, Jorge Martínez Zázate, María
Luisa Anido.

        CaBVaU CLSU CLU CSt DAU DPU GU IaU
        InU IU KU MB MH MiU MnU MoSW MU
        NbU NcD NcU NhD NN NSyU OU PPiU
        PPULC TxU WU

866 Fúrlong Cárdiff, Guillermo Juan. <u>Músicos
argentinos durante la dominación hispánica</u>;
exposición sintética precedida de una introd.
por Lauro Ayestarán. Buenos Aires: Editorial "Huarpes," 1945. 203 p. 23 cm. (Cultura colonial argentina. V. 2).
    An essay about the history of music in
Argentina during the Spanish rule, including
biographical data of the following people associated with it: José Dadey, Alonso Barzana,
Roque González, Pedro Comental, Juan Vaisseau
(or Vaseo), Luis Berger, Claudio Ruyer, Antonio Sepp, Domenico Zípoli, Florián Baucke,
Martín Schmid, Juan Mesner, Juan Fecha, Víctor de la Prada, Luis Joben (or Oben). Alphabetical index of names.

        CU DLC FU IU LU MiU MU NBuC NcU
        NSyU PSt TxU

867 García Acevedo, Mario. <u>La música argentina
durante el período de la organización nacio-
nal</u>. Buenos Aires: Ediciones Culturales
Argentinas, Ministerio de Educación y Justicia, Dirección General de Cultura, 1962.
115 p. Portraits. 20 cm. (Biblioteca del
sesquicentenario. Colección Textos).
    History of Argentine music (1852-1910)
with biographical data about figures of the
time: Salustiano Zavalía, Amancio Alcorta,
Alberto Williams, Juan Bautista Alberdi, Juan
Alais, Ignacio Alvarez, Dalmiro Costa, Francisco Hargreaves, Miguel Moreno, Miguel Rojas,
Juan Gutiérrez, Justino Clerice, Hilarión Moreno, Eduardo García Mansilla, Arturo Beruti,
Julián Aguirre, Constantino Vicente Gaito,
Héctor Panizza, José André, Pascual de Rogatis,
Ernesto Drangosch, Carlos López Buchardo.

        AU CLU CU CU-S DPU FU IaU IEN IU
        KU MB MH MnU NBuC NcU NIC NjP NmU
        NN OU TxU ViU

868 García Jiménez, Francisco. <u>El tango</u>; historia
de medio siglo, 1880-1930. Buenos Aires:
Editorial Universitaria de Buenos Aires, 1964.

77 p. Portraits. 25 cm. (Serie del siglo y medio, E5).

History of the tango from 1880 to 1930 with biographical essays about Angel Villoldo and Carlos Gardel. Also, with biographical notes about the following: José Betinotti, Agustín Bardi, Evaristo Carriego, Eduardo Arolas, Juan Maglio (Pacho, pseud.), Paquita Bernardo, Vicente Greco, Ermelinda Spinelli (Linda Thelma, pseud.), Azucena Maizani, Alfredo Gobbi, Enrique Muiño, Pascual Contursi, Gerardo Matos Rodríguez, Enrique Santos Discépolo, Astor Piazzollo, Carlos Di Sarli.

CLSU CLU CSt CtW CU CU-I IaU ICU
IU LNHT MdU MH MnU NcGU NcU NIC
NjP NSyU TxBeaL TxU UU ViU

869 Gesualdo, Vicente. <u>Historia de la música en la Argentina</u>. Buenos Aires: Editorial Beta, 1961. 3 v. (1081 p.) Portraits. 23 cm.

A history of music in Argentina (1536-1961), including biographical information throughout. Alphabetical index of names for each volume.

CLSU DPU IaU IU MiDW NcU NSyU OU
ViU

870 _____. <u>Pablo Rosquellas y los orígenes de la ópera en Buenos Aires</u>. Buenos Aires: Editorial Artes en América, 1962. 53 p. Portraits. 23 cm. (Colección hechos y figuras de América. V. 1).

An essay about Mariano Pablo Rosquellas and the origin of the opera in Buenos Aires, Argentina. Includes biography of Luis Pablo Rosquellas and scattered biographical references to Esteban Massini and Amadeo Gras.

IU NIC

871 Gobello, José, and Jorge Alberto Bossio. <u>Tangos, letras y letristas</u>. Buenos Aires: Plus Ultra, 1975. 21 cm.

Anthology of tango lyrics with brief bio-bibliographies consisting of birth and death dates and information on their contributions to the genre for the following: Luis Alfredo Alposta, Ricardo Luis Brignolo, Enrique Domingo Cadícamo, Eduardo Calvo, María Luisa Carnelli, Juan Andrés Caruso, Cátulo Castillo, Roberto L. Cayol, Pascual Contursi, Gabino Coria Peñaloza, Dante A. Linyers, pseud. (Francisco Bautista Rimoli), Enrique Santos Discépolo, Eduardo Escaris Méndez, Homero Expósito, Horacio Arturo Ferrer, Celedonio Esteban Flores, Emilio Fresedo, Francisco García Jiménez, Eduardo Giorlandini, Froilán Francisco Gorrindo, José González Castillo, Ivo Pelay, pseud. (Guillermo Juan Robustino Pichot), Julián Centeya, pseud. (Amleto Vergiati), Carlos César Lenzi, Alfredo Le Pera, Samuel Linnig, Francisco J. Lomuto, Homero Manzi, pseud. (Homero Nicolás Manzione), Francisco Alfredo Marino, Enrique P. Maroni, Alfredo Navarrine, Julio P. Navarrine, Héctor Negro, pseud. (Ismael Héctor Varela), Nicolás

Olivari, José Eneas Riú, Manuel Romero, Osvaldo Rossler, Víctor Soliño, Armando José Tagini, Benjamín Tagle Lara, Lorenzo Juan Traverso, Eduardo Trongé, Alberto Vacarezza, Antonio Martínez Viergol, Angel G. Villoldo.

AzU CtY CU IU MnU NjP NmU NN
NSyU TxU WU

872 <u>La historia del tango</u>. Buenos Aires: Corregidor, 1976. 16 v. Portraits. 20 cm. (Serie mayor).

A history of the tango with biographical notes and essays on approximately 400 figures of the 19th and 20th centuries associated with it.

IU

873 Maurín Navarro, Emilio. <u>San Juan en la historia de la música: los hermanos Arturo y Pablo Beruti; María Isabel Curubeto Godoy</u>. 2. ed. aumentada. San Juan: Editorial Sanjuanina, 1965. 196 p. Portraits. 22 cm. (Edición de la Editorial Sanjuanina. V. 7).

A study of the role played by San Juan in the history of Argentine music, including biographical information of illustrious musicians from San Juan and others associated with them. The following are particularly featured: Antonio Luis Beruti, Domingo Faustino Sarmiento, Arturo Beruti Quiroga, Pablo Manuel Beruti, María Isabel Curubeto Godoy.

CLSU CLU CU DLC IU NcU TxU WU

874 Otero, Higinio. <u>Música y músicos de Mendoza</u>; desde sus orígenes hasta nuestros días. Buenos Aires: Ministerio de Cultura y Educación, 1970. 197 p. Portraits. 25 cm.

A history of Argentine music from the province of Mendoza, mainly through biographical sketches (some in notes), often accompanied by portraits, of people associated with it. The following are especially featured: Rafael Vargas, Tomás Godoy Gruz, Pedro Bebelaqua, Fernando Guzmán, Cayetano Guzmán, Juan Crisóstomo Lafinur, Eustaquio Guzmán, Francisco Guzmán, Segundo P. Cabrera, Víctor Guzmán, Paulino Pizarro, Antonio Luis Beruti, Telésforo Cabero, Federico Guzmán, Fernando Segundo Guzmán, Ignacio Alvarez, Paulino Segundo Pizarro, Avelino Aguirre, Enrique George Varalla, Juan Augusto Bosshardt, Arturo Beruti, Pablo Beruti, Mariano Cortijo Vidal, Franco Fazio, Fidel María Blanco, Ernesto Fluxá, Giuseppe Resta, Modesto Alvarez, Aggeo Ascolese, Attilio Pelaia, Salvador Petronio, Adela Sciesa de Couto, Gaetanina Ciancio, Fermín Hita, Alexis Vladimir Abutov, Adela Ponce Aguirre de Bosshardt Zapata, Ernesto Domingo Casciani, Herminia Máxima Casciani de Castro, Fedora Cappelli de Mantovani, Ernesto Domingo Casciani, Ramón Gutiérrez del Barrio, Concepción Requena de del Barrio, Eduardo Gutiérrez del Barrio, Carlos Washington Barraquero, Alfredo Dono, Víctor Volpe, José

MUSIC

Felipe Vallesi, Nilda Pallucchini de Rodrí-
guez, Juan Gualberto Godoy, Juan Antonio
Carreras, Félix González, Javier Molina, Ole-
gario Méndez, Ulderico Ibáñez, Angel Vidadel
Olivera, Rubén Videla, Heriberto Videla, Luis
E. Nieto, Federico Vargas Videla, Secundino
Gómez, Rodolfo Vargas Videla, Pedro Gil Yan-
zón, Carlos María Tascheret, Miguel Bustos
Cáceres, Carlos A. Tascheret, Julio Quinta-
nilla, Ismael Moreno, Carlos Mombrunt Ocampo,
Alberto Rodríguez, Hilario Cuadros, Esteban
Morales Sancán, Fioravante (Tito) Francia,
Manuel (Nolo) R. Tejón, Juan Carlos Sedero,
Julio Perceval, Vicente Mazzoco, Felipe Cole-
cchia, Cayetano Alberto Silva, Antonio Mar-
ranti, José Cosentino, Julio Guillermo Paul-
sen, Valentín Bidaola, Agustín Roig, Emilia
Icart de Rodríguez, Aquiles Pedrolini, Carlos
Ponce, José Aguirre, Julio Corona, Juan B.
Crocco, Mario Vitetta, Fidel Roig Matons,
Astor Bolognini, Juan José de Gallastegui,
Alfredo Nicolás Otero, Narciso Benacot, Hor-
tensia Godoy Videla de Colomer, Elina Molina
Estrella, Dolores Jesús Vera Arenas, Isolde
Kleitman, Nina Verchinina, Alfredo M. Pelaia,
Antonio Tormo, Ezequiel Daniel Ortiz, Pedro
Francisco Alcaraz, Domingo Antonio Morales,
Hilda Rufino, Genaro Scafatti, José Ruta,
Andrés Mannucia, Bernardo Castillo, Antonio
Marranti, Carmelo Duci, Salvador Terranova,
Conrado Carbone, Luis Clemente Carrillo, Luis
Ambrosio Morante, Edith Cardozo Avendaño,
Lucrecia Gómez de Dublanc, Ruth Leal, Marta
Riba, Haydée Di Giacomo, Angela Carola de
Priore, Elena D'Almeida de Correa Alvarez,
Cirilo Rosales, María del Rosario Cicchitti
de Aranda, Ida Sierra, Romo Casetti, Lubila
Tamisier de Bowlin, Fanny Gallegos de Rosas,
Raquel Howard, Noemi Spivacoff de Yagupsky,
Angela Olivier, Carmen Rodero de Di Leo, Juan
Florentino Salomone, Filarmida Alejandrina
Suárez de Perceval, Ada Vicenta Adela Sen-
zacqua, Enrique Diego Gelusini, Aldo Teló,
Luis Mario Pontino, Salvador Amato, Carlos
Félix Cilario, Emilio Dublanc, Eduardo Grau,
Elifio Rosáenz, Miguel B. Francese.

    IU NmU NN

875   Priore, Oscar del. El tango de Villoldo a
      Piazzolla. Buenos Aires: Crisis; distribui-
      dor en capital, Troisi y Vaccaro, 1975. 80 p.
      Portraits. 25 cm. (Cuadernos de Crisis.
      V. 13).
        History of the tango with biographical
      essays about the following notable figures
      of the 19th and 20th century: Angel Villoldo,
      Pancho Alsina, Eduardo Arolas, Roberto Firpo,
      Pascual Contursi, Carlos Gardel, Enrique
      Delfino, Julio De Caro, Pedro Maffia, Astor
      Piazzolla.

    CtY CU-S IU NIC NmU NNC TxU WU

876   Revista de derecho, historia y letras. Can-
      cionero popular de la Revista de derecho,
      historia y letras, compilado y reimpreso por

Estanislao S. Zeballos. Buenos Aires: Impr.
de J. Peuser, 1905. 416 p. (V. 1). 23 cm.
   A collection of 19th century Argentine
ballads and songs, accompanied by biographical footnotes on many people, most of them
the authors of these works. Those particularly featured include Juan Baltazar Maziel,
Eusebio Valdenegro, Vicente López y Planes,
Manuel de Araucho, Francisco de Araucho, José
Prego de Oliver, Bartolomé Hidalgo, María de
los Remedios Escalada de San Martín, José
Agustín Molina y Villafañe, Rosa Justiniana
Josefa Ugarte.

    DLC GEU ICU IaU IU MoU NcD OkU
    TxU

877   Rossler, Osvaldo. Protagonistas del tango.
      Buenos Aires: Emecé Editores, 1974. 157 p.
      20 cm.
        Collection of essays with some biographi-
      cal information about the following notable
      figures in the history of the tango: Evaris-
      to Carriego, Enrique Santos Discépolo, Pascual
      Contursi, Carlos de la Púa, Celedonio Flores,
      Gavino Coria Peñaloza, Homero Manzi, Francisco
      García Jiménez, Cátulo Castillo, Enrique Ca-
      dícamo, Rosita Quiroga, Azucena Maizani, Mer-
      cedes Simone, Libertad Lamarque, Sofía Bozán,
      Agustín Magaldi, Ignacio Corsini, Francisco
      Fiorentino, Julio Sosa, Roberto Goyeneche,
      Roberto Firpo, Osvaldo Fresedo, Julio de Caro,
      Aníbal Troilo, Astor Piazzolla, Osvaldo
      Pugliese.

    IU MB MU NN

878   Sánchez Sívori, Amalia. Diccionario de paya-
      dores: selección de payadas y composiciones
      de payadores. Buenos Aires: Editorial Plus
      Ultra, 1979. (Temas argentinos. V. 2).
      163 p. Portraits. 19 cm.
        Dictionary of Argentine "payadores" from
      all periods of history featuring brief bio-
      graphical sketches of the following musicians:
      Luis Acosta García, Agapito, Gregorio Aguilar,
      Andrés Alfaro, Cornelio Amarito, José Amaya,
      Alberto Anchart, Antonio Anselmi, Constantino
      Arias, Alejandro Baigorria, Ramón Barrera,
      Evaristo Barrios, Marcelo Beatriz, Sebastián
      Celestino Berón, José Betinoti, Francisco N.
      Bianco, Rodolfo Enrique Boris, Juan Antonio
      Bourdieu, Alfredo Santos Bustamante, Miguel
      Bustos Cáceres, Vicente Bustos Zenteno, An-
      tonio Anastasio Caggiano, Juan Antonio Carre-
      ras, Casimiro, Martín Castro, Higinio Cazón,
      Andrés Cepeda, Manuel Cientofante, Angel
      Colovini, Cirilo Isabel Cotrofe, Federico
      Curlando, Cayetano Daglio (Pachequito, pseud.),
      Generoso D'Amato, Juan Damilano, Tomás María
      Davantés, José Domingo Díaz, Mamerto Díaz,
      Julio Díaz Usandivaras, José Agustín Dillón,
      Celestino Dorrego (Juan Poca Ropa, pseud.),
      Juan de la Cruz Dular Cabello, Carlos Echa-
      zarreta, Juan Etchepare, Gabino Ezeiza,
      Constantino Ferreti (Cielito, pseud.), Valen-
      tín Ferreyra, Rosendo Flores, Juan B. Fulgi-

niti, Vicente Funes, Víctor Galieri, Nicodemo Galíndez, Facundo Galván, Pedro Garay, Luis García, Giovanelli, Juan Gualberto Godoy, Rosauro Gómez, Teodoro Gómez, Lorenzo Gorosito, Máximo Herrera, César Hidalgo, Félix Hidalgo, Eugenio de Igarzábal, Pablo Jerez, Felipe Juárez, Valentín Ledesma, Jorge Leguía, Alejandro López, Ignacio López, Pancho Luna, A. Mac Carthy, Silverio Manco, Martín (Matilimbimbe, pseud.), Juan A. Martínez, Juan Mas, Olegario Méndez, Simón Méndez (Guasquita, pseud.), Angel Montoto, Pedro Moyano, Jorge Enrique Ordóñez, Liberato Orqueda, Pajarito, Pedro F. Ponce de León, L. Prieto, Domingo Puleio (Domingo de la Torre, pseud.), Ramírez, Esteban Ramos, Reyes (El Ciego Reyes, pseud.), José Rico, Ambrosio del Río, Felipe Rueda, Maximiliano Santillán, Martín Santos, Avelino Sarmiento, Donato Sierra Gorosito, Pancho Sierra, José María Silva, Domingo Spíndola, Rudecindo Suárez, Felipe Suárez, Rafael Tabanera, Carlos María Tascheret, Manuel Terán, Nemesio Trejo, Ramón Rosa Ureña, Pablo J. Vázquez, Félix Vega, Angel Vilael Olivera, Ramón P. Vieytes, Angel Villoldo, Domingo Zenteno. The following Uruguayan "payadores" performed in Argentina: Ignacio Aguiar, Juan Carlos Bares, Cayetano Daglio, Sócrates Figoli, Juan Pedro López, José Madariaga, Alcides De María (Calixto el Ñato, pseud.), Pedro Medina, Edmundo Montagne, Arturo de Nava, Juan de Nava, Eduardo Sagredo, Eugenio Sallot, Arturo Santos, Pelegrino Torres.

IU

879 Santos, Estela dos. *Las mujeres del tango.* Buenos Aires: Centro Editor de América Latina, 1972. 109 p. Portraits. 18 cm. (La Historia popular. V. 97; vida y milagros de nuestro pueblo).

History of the tango with scattered biographical information about the following women artists associated with it: Azucena Maizani, Rosita Quiroga, Ada Falcón, Anita Palermo, Celia Gómez, Amanda Ledesma, Dora Davis, Nelly Omar, Mercedes Carné, Fany Loy, Juanita Laurrauri, María Teresa Greco, Zulema Ucelli, Aída Luz, Sabina Olmos, Chola Luna, Sofía Bozán, Tita Merello, Mercedes Simone, Virginia Luque, Paquita Bernardo, Aída Denis, Alba Solís, Elsa Rivas, Ranko Fujisawa, Silvia del Río, Fany Navarro, Elba Berón, Susana Rinaldi, Amelita Baltar, Maruja Pacheco Huergo.

AzTeS CtY IU MH MU NcU NjP OU

880 Schiuma, Oreste. *Cien años de música argentina:* precursores, fundadores, contemporáneos directores, concertistas, escritores. Buenos Aires: Asociación Cristiana de Jóvenes, 1956. 379 p. 23 cm.

Biographical dictionary of outstanding Argentineans in the field of music. Information supplied concentrates on musical achievements and studies of various individuals from all periods of history.

IaU ICN MH NN

881 _____. *Música y músicos argentinos.* 2. ed. Buenos Aires: M. Lorenzo Rañó, 1943. 237 p. 21 cm.

A collection of biographical sketches on the following Argentine musicians: Blas Parera, Alberto Williams, Julián Aguirre, Alfredo L. Schiuma, Gilardo Gilardi, Felipe Boero, Juan B. Massa, Pascual de Rogatis, Floro M. Ugarte, Carlos López Buchardo, Athos Palma, Constantino Gaito, Raúl H. Espoile, Ana Carrigue, Pascual Quarantino, Pedro Sofía, José Gil, Luis Sammartino, Luis Gianneo, Celestino Piaggio, José André, Celia Torrá, Héctor Panizza, Alejandro Inzaurraga, Alberto Inzaurraga, Ernesto Drangosch, Armando Chimenti, Castro (family).

DLC MB

882 _____. *Músicos argentinos contemporáneos.* Buenos Aires, 1948. 208 p. 24 cm.

A collection of biographical sketches on the following Argentine musicians: María Luisa Anido, Salvador Axenfeld, Rodolfo Barbacci, Roberto Caamaño, Ana S. Cabrera, Domingo S. Calabró, Elsa Calcagno, Enrique M. Casella, Lía Cimaglia Espinosa, Angel Victorino Colabella, Joaquín Cortez López, María Isabel Curubeto Godoy, Andrés A. Chazarreta, Francisco de Medina, José de Nito, Humberto de Nito, Arnaldo D'Esposito, Clementino del Ponte, Emilio Dublanc, Evaristo E. Escobio, Jacobo Fischer, Florencio Fossati, Héctor I. Gallac, José León Gallardo, Juan Agustín García Estrada, Roberto García Morillo, Magdalena García Robson, Pascual Grisolía, Segundo Gennero, Juan Francisco Giacobbe, Alberto E. Ginasterra, Lucio Goldberg, Manuel Gómez Carrillo, Jorge Grippa, Carlos Guastavino, Alejandro Gutiérrez del Barrio, Héctor Iglesias Villoud, Abraham Jurafsky, Nicolás Lamuraglia, Angel E. Lasala, Adolfo V. Luna, Arturo Luzzatti, Alberto José Machado, Isidro B. Maiztegui, Luis María Martínez, Antonino Miceli, Emilio Angel Napolitano, Francisco Paolantonio, María E. Pascual Navas, Víctor Antonio Pasqués, Graciela Patiño Andrade, Juan Carlos Paz, Carlos Pedrell, Aquiles Pedrolines, Emilio Pelaia, Julio Perceval, Alfredo Pinto, Laureano Rodríguez, Ricardo Rodríguez, Pedro A. Sáenz, Pía Sebastiani, Ana Serrano Redonnet, Armando Schiuma, Honorio M. Siccardi, Lita Spena, Juan Carlos Spreafico, César Alberto Stiattesi, Carlos Suffern, José Torre Bertucci, Cayetano Troiani, Alberto O. Toscano, Pedro Valenti Costa, Josué Teófilo Wilkes, Irma Williams, Carlos Vega, Isabel Aretz-Thiele, Sylvia Eisenstein.

IU (film) NN

MUSIC

883 Senillosa, Mabel. <u>Compositores argentinos</u>.
2. ed. aumentada. Buenos Aires: Casa Lotter-
moser, 1956. 451 p. Portraits. 16 cm.
   Collection of biographical essays accom-
panied by portraits of 20th-century Argentine
composers. Information supplied includes
dates, birthplace, educational background,
and career achievements for Julián Aguirre,
José André, Alfredo Andrés, María Luisa Ani-
do, Rodolfo Arizaga, Bruno Bandini, Felipe
Boero, Roberto Caamaño, Elsa Calcaño, Enrique
Casalla, José María Castro, Juan José Castro,
Washington Castro, Lía Espinosa de Cimaglia,
Gilda Citro, María Isabel Trucco de Curubeto
Godoy, Arnaldo D'Espósito, Humberto De Nito,
José De Nito, Pascual De Rogatis, Ernesto
Drangosch, Raúl H. Espoile, Jacobo Fischer,
Jorge Fontenla, Constantino Gaito, Roberto
García Motillo, Carmen García Muñoz, Magda
Moreira de García Robson, Juan Francisco
Giacobbe, Luis Gianneo, José Gil, Gilardo
Gilardi, Alberto Ginastera, Manuel Gómez
Carrillo, Pascual Grisolía, Carlos Guasta-
vino, Héctor Iglesias Villud, Alejandro Inza-
urraga, Abraham Jurafsky, Marcelo Koc, Nico-
lás Lamuraglia, Angel Lasala, Pedro Santiago
Lichius, Carlos López Buchardo, Adolfo Luna,
Arturo Luzzatti, Isidro Maiztegui, Virtu
Maragno, Luis Milici, Emilio A. Napolitano,
Tirso de Olazábal, Athos Palma, Héctor Pa-
nizza, Juan Carlos Paz, Rafael Peacan del
Sar, Julio Perceval, Carlos Percuoco, Celes-
tino Piaggio, Astor Piazzola, Alfredo Pinto,
Pascual Quaratino, Ricardo Rodríguez, Elifio
Eduardo Rosáenz, Pedro Sáenz, Luis R. Sammar-
tino, Pía Sebastiani, Valdo Sciammarella,
Alfredo Schiuma, Honorio Siccardi, Jose Sici-
liani, Antonio Tauriello, Celia Torrá, José
Torre Bertucci, Cayetano Troiani, Carlos
Tuxen Bang, Floro M. Ugarte, Pedro Valenti
Costa, Silvia Eisenstein de Vega, Alberto
Williams.

   CU

<u>See also</u> entry 217.

MUSIC--DICTIONARIES, ENCYCLOPEDIAS, and "WHO'S WHO"

884 Sobrino, Constantino. <u>Diccionario del tango</u>.
Buenos Aires: Instituto Docente y Editor
Las Llaves, 1971. 191 p. Portraits. (Colección La patria toda. V. 1).
   Dictionary of the tango with biographical
notes on approximately 500 notable figures
of the 19th and 20th centuries.

   AzTeS IU MU NSbSU TxU

NATURAL HISTORY

885 Fúrlong Cárdiff, Guillermo Juan. <u>Naturalis-
tas argentinos durante la dominación hispá-
nica</u>. Prólogo de Gregorio Williner. Buenos

Aires: Editorial "Huarpes," 1948. 438 p.
Portraits. 23 cm. (His Cultura colonial
argentina. V. 7).
   An essay about the development of natural
history in the River Plate region with empha-
sis on Argentina during the Hispanic rule,
mainly through biobibliographical accounts of
hundreds of individuals associated with it.
The following are particularly featured:
José de Acosta, Bernabé Cobo, Diego de Torres,
Nicolás Mastrilli, Antonio Ruiz de Montoya,
Antonio de León Pinelo, Antonio Sepp, Pedro
Lozano, José Guevara, Buenaventura Suárez,
Luis Feuillée, José Eusebio Llano Zapata,
Alvaro Alonso Barba, José Sánchez Labrador,
Florián Baucke, Gaspar Juárez, Ramón Termeyer,
Tomás Falkner, Martín Dobrizhoffer, Juan
Ignacio Molina, Joaquín Camaño, Bartolomé
Francisco de Maguna, Francisco de Ibarra,
Miguel Rubín de Celis, Esteban de Luca, Manuel
de Torres, Tadeo H. Haenke, Antonio de Pineda
y Ramírez, Luis Née, Antonio José Pernetty,
José de Jussieu, Félix de Azara, Cristián
Heuland, Conrado Heuland, Andrés de Oyarvide,
Bartolomé Muñoz, Dámaso Antonio Larrañaga,
José Manuel Pérez Castellano, Saturnino Segu-
rola, Benito María de Moxó y Francoli, Martín
José de Altolaguirre, Felipe Haedo, Pedro
Antonio Cerviño (Cipriano Orden Vedoño,
pseud.), Hipólito Vieytes, Antonio de Hevia
y Pando, Manuel José de Labardén, Pedro
Truella, Gervasio Algarate, Aimé Jacques
Alexandre Goujaud (Bonpland). Alphabetical
index of names.

   DLC IU

PERFORMING ARTS

886 Castagnino, Raúl Héctor. <u>El circo criollo;</u>
datos y documentos para su historia, 1757-
1924. Buenos Aires: Lajouane, 1953. 143 p.
Portraits. 18 cm. (Colección Lajouane de
folklore argentino. V. 4).
   A history of the Argentine circus, covering the period from colonial times to the
20th century, and including scattered biographical information, as well as a few portraits, for many prominent figures in this
field. The following are emphasized: Pablo
Raffetto, José Podestá, Frank Brown.

   CtY DLC FU IaU IU MH MoU MU NBuU
   NcU NN TxU ViU WaU

887 _____. <u>Contribución documental a la historia
de el teatro en Buenos Aires durante la época
de Rosas (1830-1852)</u>. Buenos Aires: Comisión
Nacional de Cultura, Instituto Nacional de
Estudios de Teatro, 1944. 728 p. Portraits.
26 cm. (Biblioteca teatral. Sección Ensayos
y crítica. V. 1).
   A history of the theater in Buenos Aires
during the Rosas dictatorship (1830-1852),
including biographical sketches on the following actors and actresses: Trinidad Ladrón de

Guevara, Francisco Cáceres, Felipe David, Joaquín Culebras, Antonina Montes de Oca, Dominga Montes de Oca, Juan Antonio Viera, Manuel Martínez, Juan Villarino, Francisca Briones, Francisco Ramírez, Bernardino Hernández, Santiago González, Antonio González, Juan Aurelio Cascuberta, Fernando Quijano, Alejandra Pacheco, Manuel Cossío, Antonio Castañera (Antonino Castañera), Francisca Peñaloza, Felipe Catón, Carolina Catón, Salvador Figueroa, Julio Pasquier, Manuela Funes, Matilde Díez, Ana Rodríguez de Campomanes, Alvara García de Rossi, Pascual Ruiz, Máximo Jiménez (Máximo Giménez, Máximo Ximénez), Eulogio Zemborán, Juan Cordero, Benito Jiménez (Benito Giménez, Benito Ximénez), Modesto Vázquez, Guillermina Priggioni, Vicente Molina, Telémaco González, Emilia González, Ignacia González, Alberto Larroque.

DLC FTaSU IU MoU NBuU NcU OCU

888 _____. Crónicas del pasado teatral argentino, siglo XIX. Buenos Aires: Editorial Huemel, 1977. 265 p. 18 cm. (Colección temas del hombre. V. 9).

Study of Argentina's theater in the 19th century featuring limited biographical material on the following individuals connected with it: Julio Pasquier, Juan José de los Santos Casacuberta, Francisco Cáceres, Pedro Bonifacio Palacios (Almafuerte, pseud.), Ventura de la Vega, Nicanor Albarellos, Luis Bernasconi, Juan Gutiérrez, Francisco Hargreaves.

IU

889 Naios Janchaus, Teresa. Conversaciones con el teatro argentino de hoy, 1970-1980. Buenos Aires: Editorial Agon, 1981. 166 p. 20 cm.

A collection of interviews with the following individuals who are significant in the Argentine theater (1970-80):

Actors: Inda Ledesma, Eduardo Prous, Walter Soubrié, Horacio Dener, Cipe Lincovsky, Zelmar Guenol, Alberto Bussaid, Hugo Caprera, Alberto Fernández de Rosa, Esteban Peláez, Santiago Doria, Carlos Marchi, María Rosa Gallo, Golde Flami, Virginia Lago, José María Gutiérrez, Walter Santa Ana, Perla Santaya, Adela Gleijer, María Luisa Robledo, Leonor Galindo, Martín Webb, Jorge Rivera López, Onofre Lovero.

Directors: Marcela Solá, Augusto Boal, Raúl Serrano, Alejandro Oster, Villanueva Cosse, José Bove, Inda Ledesma, Héctor Tealdi, Agustín Alezzo, Enrique Laportilla, Hugo Gregorini, Manuel Iedvabni, Rubens Correa, Julio Ordano.

Authors: Walter Operto, Ricardo Monti, Carlos Gorostiza, María Rosa Gallo, Diana Raznovich, Mario Rolla, Roma Mahieu, Roberto Cossa, Roberto A. Tálice.

Scenographers: Saulo Benavente.

Musicians: Norberto Califano. Also Jordana Fain, Francisco Petrone.

IU

890 Ordaz, Luis. Breve historia del teatro argentino. Buenos Aires: Editorial Universitaria de Buenos Aires, 1962-66. 8 v. Portraits. 19 cm.

A seven-volume history of Argentine theater, including representative works of several notable playwrights from various genres and covering the period from the 18th century to the present day. Brief scattered biobibliographical information and some portraits are given for many authors and others associated with them. Particular emphasis is placed on the following: Juan José de Vértiz y Salcedo, Manuel José de Lavardén, Juan Cruz Varela, Juan Bautista Alberdi, Martiniano Leguizamón, Florencio Sánchez, Gregorio de Laferrère, Roberto J. Payró, Angelina Pagano, David Peña, José León Pagano, Enrique García Velloso, Nemesio Trejo, Carlos Mauricio Pacheco, José González Castillo, Alberto Vacarezza, Armando Discépolo, Francisco Defelippis Novoa, Alberto Novión, Julio Sánchez Gardel, Arturo Lorusso, Rafael José de Rosa.

CLSU CLU CoFS CSt CtW CtY CU DcU DPU FU GU IEA IEdS INS InU IU KU LNHT LU MB MdU MH MiDW MiEM MiU MNS MnU NbU NBuU NcD NGenoU NhD NIC NjP NjR NN NNC NNCU-G NSyU OCl OCLU OKU OOxM PPiU TU TxHR TxU UU ViU VtU WaU

891 Quién fue en el teatro nacional. Buenos Aires: Secretaría de Estado de Cultura y Educación, 1969. 284 p. Portraits. 25 cm.

Collection of biographical essays on the following notable Argentine actors of the late 19th century and the 20th: Guillermo Battaglia, Francisco Ducasse, Orfilia Rico, Florencio Parravicini, Elías Alippi, Antonio Podestá, Juan Podestá, José Podestá, Pablo Podestá, Elsa O'Connor, Enrique de Rosas, Camila Quiroga, Enrique Muiño, Miguel Faust Rocha, Angelina Pagano, Blanca Podestá, Luis Arata.

CtU CtY DLC IaU InU IU MH MU NBuU NcU PPT PSt TU

891a Sierra, Luis Adolfo. Tango. Buenos Aires: Todo es Historia, 1976. 126 p. Portraits. 20 cm. (Todo es historia. V. 3).

An essay about the tango, mainly through biographies, accompanied by portraits, of the following musicians and performers: Pedro Maffia, Osvaldo Fresedo, Francisco De Caro, Elvino Vardaro, Cayetano Pugliesi.

IU

PERFORMING ARTS

892 Sosa Cordero, Osvaldo. <u>Historia de las vari-
etas en Buenos Aires</u>. Buenos Aires: Corregidor, 1978. 433 p. Portraits. 20 cm.

A history of the variety theater in Buenos
Aires from 1900 to 1925, including biographi-
cal data about hundreds of people associated
with it and in particular the following:
José Luis Bettinoti, Florencio Parravicini
(Flo, pseud.), José Razzano, René Ruiz, Cris-
tino Tapia, Ignacio Corsini, Carlos Gardel,
Rosa Rodríguez Quiroga, Azucena Maizani,
Rafael Buonavoglia, Leopoldo Frégoli, Fátima
Miris, Enrique Delfino, Bernardino Terés,
Antonia Mercé (La Argentina, pseud.), Carmen
Tórtola Valencia, Esperanza Alonso (La Mara-
villa, pseud.), Encarnación Hurtado (La Mala-
gueñita, pseud.), María Teresa Jauffret,
María Antonia Vallejo Fernández, Juan Martínez
Abades, Lola Membrives, Carolina Otero (La
Bella Otero, pseud.), Amalia Molina, Encarna-
ción López (La Argentinita, pseud.), Pastora
Imperio, Teresa Maraval (La Zazá, pseud.),
Iris Pauri (Iris Marga, pseud.), Inés Berutti,
Aurora Mañanós Jauffrett de Borrás (La Goya,
pseud.), Raquel Meller.

IU

893 Zeitlin, Israel (Tiempo, César, pseud.).
<u>Máscaras y caras</u> por César Tiempo, pseud.
Buenos Aires: Editorial Arrayán, 1943. 502 p.
22 cm. (Colección argentina).

A collection of biographical sketches of
the following Argentine people, most of whom
are associated with the theater: Elías Alippi,
Francisco Alvarez, Enrique Amorím, Eduardo
Aparicio, Luis Arata, Ana Arneodo, Nelly
Ayllón, José Roger Balet, Alberto Ballerini,
Amelia Bence, Alejandro E. Berruti, Félix
Blanco, Olinda Bozán, Ana S. de Cabrera,
Alfredo Camiña, Tulia Ciámpoli, Miguel Coiro,
Baby Correa, Carlos Hugo Christensen, Pierina
Dealessi, Santiago H. del Castillo, Rafael
José de Rosa, Armando Discépolo, Lina Esteves,
Agustín Fontanella, Tito Livio Foppa, Evita
Franco, Arturo García Buhr, Enrique García
Velloso, Mony Hermelo, Ricardo Levene, Pedro
López Lagar, Juan Mangiante, Herminia Mancini,
Arturo Mario, Salvador Merico, Enrique Muiño,
Manuel Zolezzi (Odronoffs, pseud.), José León
Pagano, Florencio Parravicini, Pedro E. Pico,
Teodoro Prieto, Carlos Alberto Pueyrredón,
Camila Quiroga, Héctor G. Quiroga, Enrique
de Rosas, Raúl Savarese, Anita Lassalle,
Julio Scarzella, Carlos Serrey, Leopoldo
Simari, Tomás Simari, Berta Singerman, Julio
C. Traversa, Blanca Vidal, Alicia Vignoli,
León Zárate, Félix Alberto de Zavalía.

MH NcD NIC

<u>See also</u> entries 677, 861, 862, 868, 877, 878, 879.

PERFORMING ARTS--DICTIONARIES,
ENCYCLOPEDIAS, and "WHO'S WHO"

894 Foppa, Tito Livio. <u>Diccionario teatral del
Río de la Plata</u>. Buenos Aires: Argentores,
Ediciones del Carro de Tespis, 1961. 1046 p.
25 cm.

Historical dictionary with biographical
sketches of Argentineans connected with the
performing arts: Orlando Aldama, Luis Ansel-
mi, Pedro Benjamín Aquino, Manuel Arostegui,
Abdón Arosteguy, Alberto T. Ballesteros, José
Pedro Bellán, Juan León Bengoa, Edmundo
Bianchi, Samuel Blixen, José Pedro Blixen
Ramírez, Carlos Brussa, José Américo Bugliot,
Miguel Buranelli, Paco Bustos, Enrique Buttaro,
Francisco Canaro, Alberto Candeau, Arturo
Carril, Enrique Mario Casella, Elías Castel-
nuovo, Estela Castro, Telémaco Contestabile,
César Cortinas, Ismael Cortinas, Dalmiro
Costa, Enrique Crosa, Héctor Cuore, Angel
Curotto, Celia Daneri, Enrique De María,
Carlos Denis Molura, Joaquín De Vedia, Javier
De Viana, Alfredo Duhau, Cyro Escosería,
Miguel Héctor Escuder, Eduardo Facio Hebecquer,
Carlos H. Faig, Uliseo Favaro, Mario Lirio
Fernández, Jorge Freire Tabare, Roberto
Fugazot, Domingo Gallicchio, Santiago Gómez
Cou, Enrique Guarnero, Ernesto Herrera, Juan
Ilaria, Francisco Imhof, Wilfredo Jiménez,
Carlos César Lenzi, Ramón Marán, Juan Carlos
Mareco (Pinocho, pseud.), Vicente Martínez
Cuitiño, Carmen Méndez, Julia Méndez, Edmundo
Montagne, Orosmán Moratorio, Arturo B. Navas,
Carlos Mauricio Pacheco, Ricardo Passano,
Juan Carlos Patrón, Carlos Pedrell, Alejandro
Peñasco, Víctor Pérez Petit, Ernesto Pinto,
Amadea Podestá, Antonio Domingo Podestá, José
Francisco Podestá, José J. Podestá (Don Pepe,
pseud.), Juan Vicente Podestá, Luis Podestá,
Pablo Podestá, María de Podestá Fontanilla,
Carlos María Princivalle, Aída Queirola
(Tita, pseud.), Enrique Queirola, Horacio
Quiroga, José Razzano, Carlos Claudio Reyles,
Orfilia Rico, Yamandú Rodríguez, Enrique
Saborido, Isidoro Sagües, Alberto Sánchez,
Florencio Sánchez, Domingo Sapelli, Heraclio
Sena, Fernán Silva Valdés, Jules Supervielle,
Atilio Supparo, Roberto A. Talice, Lola Tapia
de Lesquerre, Angela Tesada, Celia Torrá,
Luis V. Varela, Abraham Regino Vigo, Manlio
Vitale D'Amico, Luis Vittone, Alberto Weis-
bach, Justino Zavala Muñiz, Concepción
Zorrilla.

CLSU CLU IU LNHT NcU NIC NjR NN
NNC NSyU PSt TU

PHILOSOPHY

895 Fúrlong Cárdiff, Guillermo Juan. <u>Nacimiento
y desarrollo de la filosofía en el Río de la
Plata, 1536-1810</u>. Buenos Aires: G. Kraft,
1952. 758 p. 28 cm. (Publicaciones de la
Fundación Vitoria y Suárez. V. 2).

A history of philosophy in the River Plate region, with emphasis on Argentina, covering the period from 1536 to 1810, and including biobibliographical information on many eminent philosophers. Among those featured are: Antonio Rubio, Juan de Albiz, Cristóbal Gómez, Cristóbal Grijalba, Lauro Núñez, Ignacio de Frías, Diego Ruiz, Ignacio de Arteaga, José de Aguirre, Jaime Tejedor, Agustín de Aragón, Antonio de León Pinelo, Diego de León Pinelo, Garcilaso de la Vega, Bartolomé Navarro, Juan de Alzola, Juan de León, Juan Rico, Manuel Querini, Ignacio Leiva, Ladislao Orosz, Benito Riva, José Rufo, Ramon Rospigliosi, Francisco Suárez, José Cayetano Rodríguez, José Elías del Carmen, Isidoro Celestino Guerra, Antonio Cruz del Valle, Melchor Fernández, Mariano Medrano, Diego Estanislao Zavaleta, Valentín Gómez, Gregorio José Gómez, Mariano Chambo, Pantaleón Rivarola, Luis Chorroarín, Antonio de Herrera, Carlos José Montero, Vicente A. Jaunzaras, Francisco Sebastiani, Juan Baltasar Maciel, Domingo Neyra, Francisco Javier Miranda, José Eusebio de Llano Zapata, Benito María de Moxó, Juan José Mariano Barón del Pozo, Juan José Paso, Manuel Gervasio Gil, José Godoy, Manuel Morales, Cosme de la Cueva, Miguel Rubín de Celis, Joaquín Millás, Francisco José Planes, Juan Crisóstomo Lafinur, Manuel Belgrano, Cornelio Saavedra, Juan Hipólito Vieytes, Juan José Castelli, Mariano Moreno, Gregorio Funes, Juan Ignacio de Gorriti, Pedro Ignacio de Castro Barros, Bernardo Monteagudo, Pedro José Agrelo, José Moldes, Bernardo de Vera y Pintado, Miguel Calixto del Corro, Julián Perdriel, Vicente López y Planes. Alphabetical index of names.

CaBVaU CU CU-S CU-SB DLC DPU FU
ICU IU KU MU NcU NN NSyU OrU TxU
WaTC

896 Lértora Mendoza, Celina Ana. <u>La enseñanza de la filosofía en tiempos de la colonia.</u> Buenos Aires: Fundación para la Educación, la Ciencia y la Cultura, 1979. 381 p. 23 cm.
    A collection of short biographies and analyses of the works of several philosophers from the colonial period in Argentina. The following are featured: Manuel Gregorio Alvarez, Fernando Braco, Mariano Medrano, Elías del Carmen Pereyra, Nicolás Plantich, Benito Riva, Cayetano José Rodríguez, Francisco Sebastiani, Manuel Suárez, Diego Estanislao de Zavaleta.

    IU

897 Lipp, Solomon. <u>Three Argentine Thinkers.</u> New York: Philosophical Library, 1969. 177 p. 23 cm.
    A collection of essays discussing the lives and ideas of the following three Argentine philosophers: José Ingenieros, Alejandro Korn, Francisco Romero.

AU AzU CLU CSt CtY CU FMU FU GAT
GAuA IaU ICU IEN InU IU KU LNHT
MH MiEM MnU MShM MsU N NBuC NBuU
NcD NcRS NcU NIC NjP NjR NmU NN
OCU OrCS RPB TNJ TxFTC TxU ViU
WaU WU

POSTAL COMMUNICATION

898 Galván Moreno, C. <u>Los directores del correo argentino.</u> Buenos Aires: Talleres Gráficos de Correos y Telecommunicaciones, 1944-46. 2 v. Portraits. 27 cm.
    A historical essay about the postal service in Argentina (16th century through the beginning of the 19th). Includes biographical data about numerous individuals associated with it, and in particular biographical sketches about the following:
    V. 1: Juan Vicente de Vetolaza y Luna, Juan Manuel de Vetolaza y Luna, Juan Martín de Mena y Mascarua, Francisco Antonio Domínguez Maneiro, Mateo Ramón de Alzaga y Sobrado, Domingo de Basavilbaso, Manuel de Basavilbaso, Félix de la Roza Queipo del Llano, Lorenzo Galíndez de Carvajal, Diego Vargas de Carvajal. Also extensive biographical data about Antonio Romero de Texada.
    V. 2: Melchor de Albin y Cañedo.
    Alphabetical index lists approximately 1,200 names.

    DLC NN TxU

PRINTING

899 Fúrlong Cárdiff, Guillermo Juan. <u>Orígenes del arte tipográfico en América, especialmente en la República Argentina.</u> Buenos Aires: Editorial Huarpes, 1947. 225 p. 29 cm.
    A history of typographic art in Latin America, with emphasis on Argentina, covering the period through the 19th century, and including very brief scattered biographical information on many eminent people.

    CLSU CoU CSt CtY CU-S DLC FU IEN
    IU LU MH MiU MoSW NcU NNC NNGr
    NSyU PV TxU ViU

PSEUDONYMS

900 Cutolo, Vicente Osvaldo. <u>Apodos y denominativos en la historia argentina.</u> Vicente O. Cutolo, Carlos Ibarguren. Buenos Aires: Editorial Elche, 1974. 437 p. 21 cm.
    A dictionary of pseudonyms corresponding to individuals prominent in the history of Argentina. Biographical sketches give real name and date of birth and death. Lists approximately 800 names. Alphabetical index of real names.

    CLU CSt CU ICarbS ICU IU MB MH
    MoSW MU NcU PPT WU

PSEUDONYMS

901 _____. Diccionario de alfónimos y seudónimos de la Argentina, 1800-1930. Buenos Aires:
Editorial Elche, 1962. 160 p. 27 cm.
    Dictionary of 1,100 pseudonyms and sigla
pertaining to Argentina from 1800-1930. Alphabetical index of names.

    CLSU CLU CtY ICU IU NIC NN NSyU
    WU

902 Durán, Leopoldo. Contribución a un diccionario de seudónimos en la Argentina. Noticia
preliminar de León Benarós. Buenos Aires:
Librería Huemul, 1961. 60 p. 27 cm.
    Alphabetical list of pseudonyms used by
Argentineans.

    CtY ICU IU NcU NN

PUBLIC HEALTH

903 Grau, Carlos A. La sanidad en las ciudades
y pueblos de la Provincia de Buenos Aires.
Eva Perón: Dirección de Impresiones Oficiales, 1954. 174 p. Portraits. 18 cm. (Publicaciones del Archivo Histórico de la Provincia de Buenos Aires. Contribución a la
historia de los pueblos de la Provincia de
Buenos Aires. V. 29).
    A history of health services in Buenos
Aires province, covering the period from
colonial times to the early 20th century.
Biographical notes and portraits are given
for the following people associated with this
aspect of Argentina's history: Tomás L.
Perón, Guillermo Salom, Pablo E. Baudín,
Vicente Gallastegui, Pedro J. Pando, Carlos
Berri, Miguel A. Mercader, Luis Demarco,
Alejandro Korn.

    CtY CtY-M DLC DPAHO IU NcU NN WU

RAILROAD TRANSPORTATION

904 Rögind, William. Historia del Ferrocarril
Sud. Buenos Aires: Establecimiento Gráfico
Argentino (antes Turtl y Compiani), 1937.
692 p. Portraits. 29 cm.
    A history of the Argentine Southern Rail-
road, covering the period from 1861 to 1936,
and including biographical information and
portraits for many people associated with
this industry. Among them are Eduardo Lumb,
Dardo Rocha, José de Olavarría, Patricio
Peralta Ramos, Luis A. Huergo, Esteban Adro-
gué, Henry Charles Allen, Guillermo White,
Juan B. Wanklyn, Guillermo Wheelwright, Jorge
Drabble, Jason Rigby, Juan Fair, Henry Bell,
Santiago Brian, S. Nield, Percy Clarke, Carlos
Maschwitz, David Simson, Guillermo Domínico,
Carlos A. B. Myströmer, Víctor José Martín
Rivadavia y Villagrán, Juan María Gutiérrez,
Sam Fay, J. M. Eddy, Robin Stuart, Albert
Bowen, Follett Holt, Gaspar E. Ferrer, Fer-
nando D. Guerrico, Herbert Gibson, Guillermo

Leguizamón, Gilberto Ramsay Darbyshire, Frank
P. Oliver, Arturo H. Coleman, Reginald Harris,
Oscar Loewenthal, Tomás B. Stewart, Henry
Norman Anderson, Juan F. Glennon, Dante Ar-
digó, William Rogind, Ezequiel Ramos Mexía.

    CtY CU DLC ICJ IU LU MB NcD NcU
    NmU NN OU

905 Scalabrini Ortiz, Raúl. Historia de los
ferrocarriles argentinos. 2. ed. Buenos
Aires: Editorial Devenir, 1958. 360 p.
20 cm.
    A history of the Argentine railroad in-
dustry during the 19th century. Very brief
scattered biographical information is included
for many people associated with this aspect of
Argentina's development.

    CtY CU IU MU NjP OkU OrU TxDaM
    TxU

RELIGION

906 Arancibia, José M., and Nelson Dellaferrera.
Los sínodos del antiguo Tucumán celebrados
por Fray Fernando de Trejo y Sanabria, 1597,
1606, 1607. Buenos Aires: Teología, 1979.
334 p. 23 cm. (Estudios y documentos. V. 3).
    History of the Catholic Church in Tucumán,
Argentina, from 1534-1614, especially the
synods of 1597, 1606, and 1607. Features
biographical data and information about the
contributions of the following individuals
to the development of the Church: Francisco
de Victoria, Hernando de Lerma, Francisco
Solano, Fernando de Trejo y Sanabria.

    IU

907 Biografías de obispos y arzobispos de Buenos
Aires (1622-1917). Buenos Aires: L. Mirau,
1917. 138 p. Portraits. 19 cm.
    Biographical sketches accompanied by por-
traits of the following bishops and archbishops of Buenos Aires from 1622-1917: Pedro
de Carranza, Cristóbal de Aresti, Cristóbal de
la Mancha y Velazco, Antonio Azcona Imberto,
Gabriel de Arregui, Pedro de Fajardo, Juan de
Arregui, José Peralta, Cayetano de Marcellano
y Agramont, José Antonio Bazurco, Manuel Antonio de la Torre, Sebastián de Malvar y
Pinto, Manuel Agamor y Ramírez, Benito de Lué
y Riega, Mariano Medrano y Cabrera, Mariano
José de Escalada, Federico Aneiros, Uladislao
Castellano, Mariano A. Espinosa.

    IU NN

907a Bruno, Cayetano. Los salesianos y las hijas
de María Auxiliadora en la Argentina. Buenos
Aires: Instituto Salesiano de Artes Gráficas,
1981. 524 p. (V. 1). Portraits. 27 cm.
    A history of the Salesians and the daugh-
ters of María Auxiliadora in Argentina. Biographical information throughout concerning

hundreds of people associated with them. The following are particularly featured:

V. 1 (1875-1894): Federico Aneiros, José María Beauvoir, Francisco Bodratto, Juan Bosco, Juan Cagliero, Santiago Costamagna, Raúl A. Entraigas, Antonio Espinosa, José Fagnano, Domingo Milanesio, Pío IX, Julio A. Roca, Miguel Rúa, José Vespignani. Alphabetical index of names.

IU

908 Carranza, Adolfo P. <u>El clero argentino de 1810 á 1830</u>. Buenos Aires: Impr. de M. A. Rosas, 1907. 2 v. Portraits. 21 cm.

A collection of patriotic and funeral orations by members of the Argentine clergy from 1810 to 1830. Includes "Apuntes biográficos" by Pedro I. Caraffa, a series of biographical sketches of the following members of the clergy featured in the text: Diego Estanislao Zavaleta, Juan Antonio Neirot, José Agustín Molina, Domingo Victorio de Achega, Gregorio Funes, Pantaleón García, Pedro Ignacio de Castro Barros, Francisco de Paula Castañeda, Juan Esteban Soto, Julián Segundo de Agüero, Felipe Antonio de Iriarte, Pedro Luis Pacheco, Julián Navarro, Miguel Calixto del Corro, Cayetano González, José Zambrana, Juan Ignacio de Gorriti, José Valentín Gómez, Cayetano Rodríguez, José Ignacio Grela, Santiago Figueredo, Ramón Olavarrieta, Bartolomé D. Muñoz.

CU   DLC   ICarbS   MH   NcU   NIC   NN   PPULC
PU   TxU

909 <u>100 [i.e. Cien] años, iglesia danesa de Tandil</u>: 28 de octubre, 1877-1977. Tandil: Congregación Protestante del Tandil, 1977. 92 p. Portraits. 23 cm.

An essay commemorating the centennial of the Danish church in Tandil (Buenos Aires Province, Argentina), including scattered biographical information, as well as some portraits, for many of its members.

IU

910 Fúrlong Cárdiff, Guillermo Juan. <u>Diócesis y obispos de la iglesia argentina, 1570-1942</u>. Buenos Aires, 1942. 58 p. Portraits. 20 cm.

A series of short discussions of important dioceses and bishops of the Argentine church from 1570-1942. Brief biographical notes, including places of birth and death and religious appointments held, are given for the following: Juan de Barrios Toledo, Pedro Fernández de la Torre, Luis López de Solís, Juan Almaraz, Alonso de Guerra, Luis López, Juan de Andrade, Tomás Vázquez de Liaño, Martín Ignacio de Loyola, Reginaldo Lizárraga, Diego de Borja, Lorenzo Pérez de Grado, Tomás de Torres, Francisco Beaumant, Jerónimo de Villa Carrillo, Jerónimo Albornoz, Francisco de Victoria, Fernando Trejo y Sanabria, Alonso Pacheco, Julián de Cortázar,

Tomás de Torres, Melchor Maldonado y Saavedra, Nicolás de Ulloa y Hurtado de Mendoza, Julián Bravo Dávida y Cartagena, Manuel Mercadillo, Manuel González Virtus, Juan Laisega Alvarado, Alonso del Pozo y Silva, Juan Manuel de Sarricolea y Olea, José Antonio Gutiérrez y Ceballos, Felicianos Palomares, Fernando de la Sota, Pedro Miguel de Argendoña, Manuel de Abad e Illana, Juan Manuel Moscoso y Peralta, José Antonio de San Alberto, Mariano Calvo y Llatequera, Angel Mariano Moscoso Pérez y Oblitas, Rodrigo Antonio de Orellana, Benito Lascano y Castillo, José Gregorio Baigorri, José Vicente Ramírez de Orellano, Eduardo Alvarez, Mamerto Esquiú, Juan Capistrano Tissera, Reginaldo Toro, Zenón Bustos y Ferreyra, Fermín LaFitte, Pedro Carranza, Cristóbal de Aresti, Cristóbal de Mancha y Velasco, Antonio de Azcona Imberto, Juan Bautista Sicardo, Pedro Fajardo, Gabriel de Arregui, Juan de Arregui, José de Peralta Barrionuevo y Rocha Benavides, Felipe Manrique de Lara, José Cayetano Pacheco y Cárdenas, Cayetano Marsellano y Agramont, José Antonio Bazurco y Herrera, Manuel Antonio de la Torre, Sebastián de Malbar y Pinto, Manuel Azamor y Ramírez, Pedro Inocencio Bejarano, Benito Lué y Riega, Mariano Medrano y Cabrera, Mariano José Escalada Bustillo y Ceballos, Federico Aneiros, Uladislao Castellano, Mariano Antonio Espinosa, José María Bottaro, Santiago Luis Copello, Justo José Colombres, Buenaventura Rizo Patrón, Pablo Padilla y Bárcena, Matías Linares y Zanzetenea, José Gregorio Romero, Julio Campero y Aráoz, Roberto José Tavella, Rodrigo González Marmolejo, Fernando de Barrionuevo, Diego de Medellín, Pedro de Azuaga, Juan Pérez de Espinosa, Francisco Salcedo, Gaspar de Villaroel, Diego Zambrano y Villalobos, Fernando de Avendaño, Diego Humanzoro, Bernardo Carrasco, Francisco de la Puebla González, Luis Francisco Romero, Alejo Fernando de Rojas, Alonso de Pozo y Silva, Juan de Sarricolea y Olea, Juan Braco de Rivero y Borrea, Juan González Melgarejo, Manuel de Alday y Aspée, Blas Sobrino y Minayo, Francisco de Borja, José de Morán y Geles, Justo Santa María de Oro, José Eufrasio Quiroga y Sarmiento, Nicolás Aldazor, Olegario Correa, José Wenceslao Achával y Medina, Marcolino del Carmelo Benavente, José Américo Orzali, Audino Rodríguez y Olmos, Leonardo de Acevedo, Luis Gabriel Segura y Cubas, José María Gelabert y Crespo, Rosendo de la Lastra y Gordillo, Abel Bazán y Bustos, Julián P. Martínez, Zenobio Guilland, Mariano Antonio Espinosa, Juan Nepomuceno Terrero, Francisco Alberti, Juan Pascual Unimento, Juan Agustín Boneo, Nicolás Fasolino, Pablo Padilla y Bárcena, Bernabé Piedrabuena, Agustín Barrére, Juan Martín Yániz y Paz, Audino Rodríguez y Olmos, José Weimann, Inocencio Dávila y Matos, Vicente Peira, Carlos Hanlón, Luis María Niella, Francisco Vicentín, César Cáneva, Leandro B. Astellarra, Enrique Mühn, Froilán Ferreira Reinate, José Aníbal Verdaguer y Corominas, Alfonso Buteler, Anunciado Serafini,

RELIGION

Leopoldo Buteler, Antonio Caggiano, Dionisio
P. Tibiletti, Nicolás Esandi, Nicolás de
Carlo.

DLC IU

911 Galería biográfica: obispos y arzobispos de
Buenos Aires (1622-1897). Buenos Aires:
J. A. Berra, 1897. 126 p. Portraits. 18 cm.
Collection of biographical sketches accom-
panied by portraits of the bishops and arch-
bishops of Buenos Aires from 1622-1897.
Dates, birthplace, and information on the
religious activities of the following individ-
uals are provided: Pedro de Carranza, Cris-
tóbal de Aresti, Cristóbal de la Mancha y
Velazco, Antonio Azcona Imberto, Gabriel de
Arregui, Pedro de Fajardo, Juan de Arregui,
José Peralta, Cayetano de Marcellano y Agra-
mont, Antonio Bazurco, Manuel Antonio de la
Torre, Sebastián de Malvar y Pinto, Manuel
Agamor y Ramírez, Benito de Lué y Riega,
Mariano Medrano y Cabrera, Mariano José de
Escalada, Federico Aneiros, Uladislao Cas-
tellano.

CU NNH

912 Isérn, Juan. La formación del clero secular
de Buenos Aires y la Compañía de Jesús; reseña histórica. Buenos Aires: Editorial
"San Miguel," 1936. 519 p. Portraits.
24 cm.
A history of the Jesuits in Buenos Aires,
covering the period from colonial times to
the present, and featuring scattered biographical information, as well as portraits in
some cases, for many notable clerics. The
following are emphasized: Pedro de Carranza,
Mariano Medrano, Mariano Berdugo, Mariano
José de Escalada, Martín Boneo, León Federico
Aneiros, José Sató, Mariano Antonio Espinosa,
José Claret, Luis Duprat, Vicente Peira.

CLU CU InU MH NcU NNC WU

913 Levillier, Roberto. Papeles eclesiásticos
del Tucumán; documentos originales del Archivo de Indias. Madrid: Impr. de J. Pueyo,
1926. 2 v. 25 cm. (Colección de publicaciones históricas de la Biblioteca del Congreso argentino).
A two-volume collection of religious documents dealing with 16th- and 17th-century
Tucumán, including scattered biographical information on many notable clerics. Among
them are Fernando de Trejo y Sanabria, Francisco de Salcedo, Julián de Cortázar, Tomás
de Torres, Melchor Maldonado de Saavedra,
Francisco de Vitoria, Leonor de Tejeda y
Mejía, Sebastián de Tejeda, Fernando de Tejeda, Tristán de Tejeda, María de Tejeda,
Clara de Tejeda, Juan de Tejeda Mirabal.
Alphabetical indices of names.

CLSU CSt CU CU-S DLC InU IU LU
MiU NcD NcU TNJ

914 Palacio, Eudoxio de Jesús. Los mercedarios
en la Argentina; documentos para su historia
(1535-1754). Con pref. y anotaciones de José
Brunet. Buenos Aires: Ministerio de Cultura
y Educación, 1971. 548 p. Portraits.
25 cm. (Ediciones culturales argentinas).
A history of the Mercedarian religious
order in Argentina, covering the period from
1535 to 1754. Scattered biographical information is given for many people (approximately
2,000 names), mostly clerics, in both the
text and in documents from that era. The following are particularly featured: Miguel de
Aguirre, Cristóbal de Albarrán, Diego de Almagro, Juan Alvarez, Francisco Aredes, Felipe
de Avila (Felipe de Dávila), Gonzalo Ballesteros, Víctor Manuel Barriga, Juan Bravo de
Zamora, José Brunet, Vicente Calvo de Laya,
Juan Cano de la Cerda, Alonso Cantador, Fer-
nando Carvajal y Rivera, Melchor Casco de
Mendoza, Ignacio del Castillo, Juan de Castro,
Buenaventura Díaz (Ventura Díaz, pseud.),
Alonso Enríquez de Armendáriz, Pablo Enriques
Nuño del Aguila, Antonio de Escobar, Antonio
Fernando Ferreyra Abad, Baltasar Flores,
Policarpo Gazulla, Bernardino Godoy, Andrés
Gómez, Nicolás Gómez, Pedro Guerra, Hernanda-
rias de Saavedra, Juan de Iturrios, Antonio
Juárez Mejía, Juan de Leguizamo, Gregorio
Leguizamo, Nicolás de Leiva, Ignacio Lescano,
Pedro López Valero, José López de Salazar,
Ambrosio Maldonado de la Cerda, Antonio Mar-
chena, Francisco Martel, Juan Martínez, Juan
Nieto, Eudoxio de Palacio, Juan Silveiro Pabón,
Antonio Pereyra, Pedro Nolasco Pérez, Juan
Pérez de Arce, Diego de Porres, Jeronimo de
Póveda, Alonso Puertas y Valverde, Juan Puga,
Gonzalo Quintero, Lázaro Quintero, Juan Ramí-
rez de Velasco, Antonio Rendón Sarmiento,
Francisco de Rivas Gavilán, Lorenzo de Rivera,
Antonio Rodríguez Flores, Francisco Rodríguez
de la Torre, Juan de Salazar, Juan de Salazar
de Espinosa, Pedro Nolasco de Santa María,
Antonio Tobar y Osorio Baldés, Bernardino
Toledo, Fernando de Trejo y Sanabria, Juan
Miguel de Valdivia y Alderete, Alejo Valdivia
y Brizuela, Andrés de Valdivia y Brizuela,
Bartolomé de Valenzuela, Tomás Vallejo y
Villasanti, Bernardo de Vargas, Juan de Vargas,
Francisco Velázquez, Félix Ventura, Francisco
de Vera, Francisco Antonio de Vetolaza y
Meléndez, Ramón de Villanueva, Pedro de Villa-
vicencio, José de Villegas, José de Villoldo,
Francisco Zarza. Alphabetical index of names.

CaBVaU CFS CtY CU CU-SB GU IaU MB
MH MnU MoSW MU NIC NjP OU PPT PSt
TxU WU

915 Piaggio, Agustín. Influencia del clero en la
independencia argentina (1810-1820). 2. ed.
Buenos Aires: Tip. del Colegio Pío IX, 1934.
436 p. 21 cm.
An account of the influence of the Argentine clergy in the struggle for independence,
including biographical essays of varying
lengths on the following religious leaders:

Juan Nepomuceno de Solá, Julián Segundo de Agüero, Nicolás Calvo, Domingo Estanislao Belgrano, Melchor Fernández, Andrés Florencio Ramírez, Antonio Sáenz, Pascual Silva Braga, Domingo Viola, Bernardo José Antonio de la Colina, Juan Dámaso Fonseca, Pantaleón Rivarola, Manuel Maximiliano Alberti, Juan León Ferragut, Vicente Montes Carballo, Diego Estanislao Zavaleta, Gregorio Funes, Julián Navarro, Felipe Antonio de Iriarte, Francisco Javier Iturri Patiño, Bartolomé Doroteo Muñoz.

    CaBVaU CLU CST CU DLC OCl ViU TxU

916 Ramayón, Eduardo E. <u>Capellanes militares en los territorios argentinos</u>. Buenos Aires: Tall. Gráf. J. Calloni, 1946. 277 p. Portraits. 21 cm.

    A study of the activities of military chaplains in Argentina during the 19th century, including brief scattered biographical information on many people associated with this aspect of Argentina's history.

    MB NN TxU

917 Segura, Juan José Antonio. <u>Historia eclesiástica de Entre Ríos</u>. Nogoyá: Impr. Nogoyá, 1964. 402 p. Portraits. 25 cm.

    A historical essay about the Catholic Church in the Argentine province of Entre Ríos including biographical data about people associated with it. The following are particularly featured: José Leonardo Acevedo, Francisco Dionisio Alvarez, Francisco Antonio Alvarez, Manuel Azamor y Ramírez, Domingo Ereño, Pantaleón Galloso, José Sixto García Isasa, José María Gelabert y Crespo, Antolín Gil Obligado, Benito Lué y Riega, Marino Martini, Sebastián Malvar y Pinto, Luis José Segura, Manuel de la Torre, Miguel Vidal. Alphabetical index of names.

    CLU CLSU CSt CtY-D IU NIC WU

918 Toledo, Bernadino. <u>Estudios históricos</u>. Provincia mercedaria de Santa Bárbara del Tucumán, 1594-1918. Córdoba: Est. Gráfico Los Principios, 1919-21. 3 v. 26 cm.

    A historical essay about the Mercedarian province of Santa Bárbara del Tucumán (1594-1918) including biographical data throughout about the friars associated with it. The following are particularly featured:

    V. 2: Juan Salazar, Cristóbal Albarrán, Juan de los Barrios y Toledo, Luis de Valderrama, Diego de Porres, Nicolás Gómez, Antonio Marchena, Pedro Guerra, Antonio Torino, Juan Lozano, Melchor Prieto, Faustino de las Casas, Feliciano Palomares, José Bernardo Sena, Bartolomé Poggio, Inocencio Cañete, Juan Antonio Oliva, Saturnino Villalón, José Aravena, Lorenzo Morales, Benjamín Rencoret.

    CU ICU NN NNC

919 Verdaguer, José Aníbal. <u>Historia eclesiástica de Cuyo</u>. Milano: Premiata Scuola Tipográfica Salesiana, 1931-32. 2 v. in 3. 23 cm.

    History of the Catholic Church in the Cuyo region of Argentina from the 16th to the early 20th century with biographical data on approximately 1,000 individuals connected with it.

    DLC IU MB MH NcU NNC

920 Vivero, Domingo de. <u>Obispos y arzobispos de Buenos Aires</u> (1622-1897). Buenos Aires: Impr. de Obras de J. A. Berra, 1897. 126 p. Portraits. 18 cm.

    A collection of biographical sketches, accompanied by portraits, of the following bishops and archbishops of Buenos Aires (1622-1897): Pedro de Carranza, Cristóbal de Aresti, Cristóbal de la Mancha y Velasco, Antonio Azcona Imberto, Gabriel de Arregui, Pedro de Fajardo, Juan de Arregui, José Peralta, Cayetano de Marcellano y Agramont, José Antonio Bazurco, Manuel Antonio de la Torre, Sebastián de Malvar y Pinto, Manuel Agamor y Ramírez, Benito de Lué y Riega, Mariano Medrano y Cabrera, Mariano José de Escalada, Federico Aneiros, Uladislao Castellano.

    CU DLC FMU NcD NcU NNH

921 Zuretti, Juan Carlos. <u>Historia eclesiástica argentina</u>. Buenos Aires: Editorial "Huarpes," 1945. 339 p. Portraits. 24 cm.

    An essay about the Catholic Church in Argentina. Includes biographical data about hundreds of people associated with it, in particular the following: Juan de Rivadeneyra, Luis de Bolaños, Francisco Solano, Luis de Tejeda, Alonso Bárzana, Roque González de Santa Cruz, Francisco de Vitoria, Fernando de Trejo y Sanabria, Pedro Ortiz de Zárate, Juan Grande, Antonio de San Alberto, Francisco Castañeda, Juan José Archeberroa, María Antonia de la Paz y Figueroa, María Taboada, Gregorio Funes, Juan Baltasar Maciel, Saturnino Segurola Lezica, Luis José Chorroarín, Blas Gutiérrez, Pedro Montenegro, Atanasio de la Piedad, Diego Rosales, Nicolás Mascardi, Rodrigo de Orellana, Cayetano Rodríguez, Julián Navarro, Pedro Miguel Aráoz, Justo Santa María de Oro, Juan Ignacio Gorriti, Pedro Andrés Pacheco de Melo, Manuel Antonio Acavedo, Pedro Francisco Uriarte, Mariano Sánchez de Loria, Nicolás Videla del Pino, Ignacio de Castro Barros, Antonio Sáenz, José Eufrasio de Quiroga, Olegario Correa, Benjamín Lavaisse, Juan Manuel Pérez, Pedro A. Centeno, Facundo Zuviría, Escolástico Zegada, Mamerto Esquiú, Mariano José Escalada Bustillo y Ceballos, Federico Aneiros, Jerónimo Emiliano Clara, Francisco Bibolini, Félix Frías, José Manuel Estrada, Pedro Goyena, Tristán Achával Rodríguez, Federico Grote, Gregorio Romero, Pablo Padilla, Mariano A. Espinosa, Juan Nepomuceno Alegre, Juan José Alvarez, José Saturnino Allende, José de Amenábar, Ramón Eduardo Anchoris, Miguel

RELIGION

Moisés Aráoz, Abraham Argarañaz, Francisco
Javier Argerich, Juan Antonio Argerich, José
Gregorio Baigorri, Serafín Balestra, José
León Benegas, Eusebio Bedoya, Domingo Esta-
nislao Belgrano, Martín Boneo, Francisco
Brizuela, José Gabriel Brochero, José María
Bustamante, Filemón Cabanillas, Francisco
Solano Carrera, Pablo Cabrera, Tomás Canaveri,
Lino Carvajal, Genaro Carranza, Juan José
Castañer, Hipólito Castañar, Mariano Chambo,
Manuel Antonio Delgado, Milcíades Echagüe,
José Fagnano, Antonio Fahy, Julián Faramiñán,
Aquilino Ferreyra, Santiago Figueredo, José
Manuel Figueroa, Ignacio Garay, Miguel García,
José Gabriel García de Zúñiga, Paulino Gari,
Eusebio Garrone, Tomás Javier Gomensoro,
Gregorio José Gómez, Roque Illescas, Camilo
Jordán, José Benito de Lamas, Francisco Lap-
hiz, Pedro Larrouy, Jerónimo Lavagna, Ray-
nerio J. Lugones, David Luque, Francisco
Majesté, Fortunato Marchi, Juan Antonio Medina,
Manuel Vicente Mena, Vicente Monte Carballo,
Miguel Angel Mossi, Idelfonso Escolástico de
las Muñecas, Bartolomé Doroteo Muñoz, Juan
Antonio Neirot, Bernardo Ocampo, Eduardo
O'Gorman, Eugenio Olavarrieta Lamas, José
de Oro, Diego Palma, Luis Palma, Mariano
Pedriel, Martín Avelino Piñero, Bartolomé
Poggio, Feliciano Pueyrredón, Andrés Floren-
cio Ramírez, José Rafael Reyna, Domingo de la
Riestra, Pantaleón Rivarola, Gregorio Romero,
José Joaquín Ruiz, Pablo Salas, Cornelio San-
tillán, Polidoro Segger, Facundo Segura, José
de Sevilla Vázquez, Antonio María Taboada,
Victoriano Tolosa, Luis de la Torre y Zúñiga,
Bonifacio Vera, Pedro Pablo Vidal, Manuel
Zevallo. Alphabetical index of names.

CoU CtY DLC FU IU LNHT MB OU PV
TxU

See also entries 114, 171, 318, 319, 529a, 534,
537, 547, 599, 850.

SCIENCE and MATHEMATICS

921a Dassen, Claro Cornelio. Las matemáticas en
la Argentina. Buenos Aires: Coni, 1924.
140 p. 26 cm. (Evolución de las ciencias
en la República Argentina. V. 4).
An essay about the history of mathemetics
in Argentina (18th century through the 1920s),
including biographical information of varying
amounts, about the following people who contributed to its development: Pedro Antonio
Cerviño, José de Lanz, Felipe Senillosa,
Avelino Díaz y Salgado, Amadeo Jacques, Juan
María Gutiérrez, Bernardino Speluzzi, Emilio
Rosetti, Luis A. Viglione, Juan Pirovano,
Valentín Balbín, Jorge Duclout, Marcial R.
Candioti, Francisco Beuf.

NjP PPAN PPWI

922 Fúrlong Cárdiff, Guillermo. Matemáticos argentinos durante la dominación hispánica.

Buenos Aires: Editorial Huarpes, 1945.
255 p. Portraits. 23 cm. (His Cultura
colonial argentina. V. 3).
An essay about the history of mathematics
and physical sciences in Argentina during the
Spanish rule. Biographical data throughout
about many individuals associated with them.
The following are particularly featured:
Pedro Comental, Luis de la Cruz, Mario Falcón,
Felipe Lemer, Buenaventura Suárez, José Ber-
múdez, Domingo Petrarca, Diego Cardoso,
Blanqui, José Brassanelli, Tomás Falkner,
Domingo Muriel, José Quiroga, José Custodio
de Sáa y Faría, Bartolomé Panigay, Ignacio
Martín Schmid, Juan Mesner, José Eusebio de
Llano Zapata, Cosme Agulló, José Sánchez
Labrador, Antonio Harl, Pero Azara, José
María Cabrer, Bernardo Lecocq, Jose de Eche-
varría, Juan A. López, Manuel Antonio de
Flores, Eustaquio Gianini, Pablo Zizur, Andrés
de Oyarvide, Joaquín Antonio Mosquera, Juan
Manuel Ozores, Joaquín del Pino, Basilio
Villarino, Miguel Rubén de Celis, Alejandro
Malaspina, Juan Gutiérrez de la Concha, José
de la Peña y Zazueta, Bernardo Talaforo,
Luis Flores, Antonio Frías y Alfaro, Juan
Alsina, Pedro Cerviño, Luis Feuillée, Juan B.
Enrique Guinoyseau, José Bernardo Jussieu,
José Sourrière Souillac, Luis Antonio de
Bougainville, Martín José de Altolaguirre,
Carlos O'Donnell, Cayetano Rodríguez. Alpha-
betical index of names.

CtY CU DLC FU ICN IEN IU NcD NcU
NIC NN NNC NSyU OU RPB TxU

923 United Nations Educational, Scientific and
Cultural Organization. Science Cooperation
Office for Latin America. Argentina. Montevideo, 1950. 5 v. 35 cm. (UNESCO's
Scientific Institutions and Scientists in
Latin America).
A listing of contemporary Argentinean
scientists and scientific institutions. Biographical information, such as academic degrees earned, professional positions held,
and memberships in scientific societies, is
included for approximately 1,500 individuals.

DLC IU

SPORTS--DICTIONARIES, ENCYCLOPEDIAS, and "WHO'S WHO"

923a Cutter, Robert. The Encyclopedia of Auto
Racing Greats, by Robert Cutter and Bob Fen-
dell. Englewood Cliffs: Prentice-Hall,
1973. 675 p. Portraits. 29 cm.
Includes biographical sketches, accompanied by portrait, of Juan Manuel Fangio.

AAP AkU GU InU IU LN NmU RP RPB
TU VtU

923b Georgano, G. N., comp. The Encyclopedia of Motor Sport. Advisory editor: Albert R. Bochroch. Foreword by Stirling Moss. New York: Viking Press, 1971. 656 p. Portraits. 29 cm. (A Studio book).

Includes biographical sketch, accompanied by portrait, of Juan Manuel Fangio.

IU

923c Pritchard, Anthony, comp. The Encyclopedia of Motor Racing, compiled by Anthony Pritchard and Keith Davey. New York: D. McKay, 1969. 304 p. Portraits. 24 cm.

Includes biographical sketch of Juan Manuel Fangio.

FTaSU IU MB NbU OkU OU UU WaU

WELFARE

924 Correa Luna, Carlos. Historia de la Sociedad de Beneficencia, obra escrita por encargo de la sociedad en celebración de su primer centenario, con un prefacio del doctor Antonio Dellepiane, 1823-1923. Buenos Aires: Sociedad de Beneficencia de la Capital, 1923-55. 2 v. 24 cm.

A history of the Argentine Socieded de Beneficencia, covering the period from 1823 to 1923. Scattered biographical information of various amounts is included for over 1,200 people associated with this organization. The following are particularly featured: María del Rosario de Azcuénaga, María de las Carreras, Crescencia Boado de Garrigós, Estanislao Cossio de Gutiérrez, Mercedes de Lasala y Riglos, Dolores Lavalle de Lavalle, Isabel Casamayor de Luca, María Sánchez de Mendeville, Bartolomé Mitre, Josefa Gabriela Ramos Mexía, Bernardino Rivadavia, Juan Manuel de Rosas, Justa Foguet de Sánchez, Domingo Faustino Sarmiento, Justo José de Urquiza, Dalmacio Vélez Sarsfield.

CU DPU InU IU NcD NcU TxU

925 Sociedad de Beneficencia de la capital, Buenos Aires. Origen y desenvolvimiento de la Sociedad de Beneficencia de la capital 1823-1912. Buenos Aires: Estab. Tip. M. R. Giles, 1913. 521 p. Portraits. 29 cm.

A history of the Sociedad de Beneficencia of Buenos Aires from 1823 to 1913, including very brief biographical information, as well as portraits in some cases, on many people associated with this institution.

DCU-IA DLC NN

WOMEN

926 Abeijón, Carlos, and Jorge Santos Lafauci. La mujer argentina antes y después de Eva Perón. Buenos Aires: Editorial Cuarto Mundo, 1975. 280 p. 21 cm.

An account of the status of Argentine women before and after the influence of Eva Perón. Scattered biographical information is given for many women from all time periods and walks of life. The following are emphasized: Victoria Ocampo, Alfonsina Storni, Herminia Brumana, Alicia Moreau de Justo, Eva Duarte de Perón, Isabel Martínez de Perón.

AzU CFS CSt CSt-H CtY CU CU-S DCU DGU FU ICarbS InU IU MB MH MiEM MnU MoSW MU NBuU NcD NcU NIC NjP NjR NmU NN NNC NSyU OrU OU PPT PSt TxDaM TxU ViU VtMiM WaU WU

927 Bernard, Tomás Diego. Mujeres en la epopeya sanmartiniana. Buenos Aires: Editorial Sopena Argentina, 1941. 153 p. 23 cm. (Colección Ayer y Hoy).

A collection of biographical essays on four women who played important roles in the life of José de San Martín. Biographical information is included for the following: Gregoria Matorras, María Elena de San Martín, Remedios de Escalada, Mercedes Tomasa de San Martín. Also biographical data of José de San Martín.

DLC NBC NcU

928 Bertolé de Cané, Cora María. El amor. Buenos Aires: Ministerio de Cultura y Educación, 1970. 56 p. Portraits. 20 cm. (Almario de Buenos Aires).

Essay about love in Argentina from the 16th to the 20th century, with biographical notes about the following women: María Dávila, Mariquita Sánchez de Thompson, María de la Quintana, Isabel Calvimontes de Agrelo, Remedios Escalada de San Martín, Manuelita Rosas, Camila O'Gorman, Elisa Brown, Raquel Meller, Alfonsina Storni.

CLU CSt CU-SB FU IU KU MB NIC NNC OU TU TxLT WU

929 González Arrili, Bernardo. Mujeres de nuestra tierra. Ilus. de M. Martínez Parma. Buenos Aires: Ediciones La Obra, 1950. 143 p. Portraits. 20 cm.

A collection of biographical sketches about the following Argentine women from all walks of life: Manuela Pedraza, Juana Pueyrredón de Sáenz Valiente, Jerónima San Martín, Gregoria Pérez, Laureana Ferrari de Olazábal, María de los Remedios de Escalada de San Martín, Pascuala Meneses, Joaquina Izquierdo, Juana del Pino, Margarita Weild de Paz, Carmen Puch, Macacha Güemes, Dolores Correas de Lavalle, Mercedes de San Martín de Balcarce, Paula Albarracín de Sarmiento, María Sánchez de Thompson, Procesa Sarmiento de Lenoir, Petrona Rosende, Rosa Guerra, Delfina de Vedia de Mitre, Tomasa Vélez Sársfield,

WOMEN

Agustina Palacio de Libarona, Manuela de Rosas de Terrero, Eduarda Mansilla, Toribia de los Santos, Juana Manuela Gorriti de Belzú, Juana Manso de Noronha, Francisca Jacques, Ida Edelvira Rodríguez, Julia Wernicke, Victorina Malharro, Raquel Camaña, Vicenta Castro Cambón, Lola Mora de Hernández, Cecilia Grierson, Emma de la Barra de Llanos (César Duayen, pseud.), Alfonsina Storni. Alphabetical index of names.

DLC DPU

930 Guerrero, César H. _Mujeres de Sarmiento_. Buenos Aires: Artes Gráficas, 1960. 332 p. Illus. 21 cm.
Collection of biographical essays on the following women who influenced the life of 19th-century Argentinean president Domingo Faustino Sarmiento: Paula Albarracín de Sarmiento, Paula de Oro de Sarmiento, Angela Salcedo de Sarmiento, Mary Mann, Juana Manso, Aurelia Vélez Sársfield, Faustina Sarmiento de Belín, Benita Martínez Pastoriza, Tránsito de Oro de Rodríguez, Clara Rosa Cortínez, Procesa Sarmiento de Lenoir, Bienvenida Sarmiento, Paula Sarmiento de Gómez, María del Rosario Sarmiento, Eugenia Belín Sarmiento, Sofía Lenoir de Klappenbach, Victorina Lenoir de Navarro, Rosa Suárez de Gómez, Magdalena Brihuega de Aberastáin, Emilia Herrera de Toro, Elizabet Peabody, Mary O. Graham, Ida Wickersham, Emilia Belín Sarmiento, Luisa Belín Sarmiento, Helena Belín Sarmiento, Kate N. Dogget, Lucy L. Smith, Eduarda Mansilla de García, Josefina Pelliza de Sagasta, Adelaida Ristori, Jennie E. Howard, Jeanette Stevens.

CLSU CSt IU MH NIC NN

931 _____. _Patricias sanjuaninas_. Buenos Aires: Tall. Gráf. de L. López, 1943. 259 p. Portraits. 28 cm.
A historical account of the contribution of women from the Argentine province of San Juan. Includes biographical sketches about the following: Theresa de Ascencio de Mallea, Micaela de Vega Sarmiento, Magdalena Ladrón de Guevara, Ana María Sánchez de Loria, Juliana Pastoriza, Paula Albarracín de Sarmiento, Tránsito de Oro de Rodríguez, Mercedes Sarmiento de Mallea, Tránsito de Oro de la Roza, Gertrudis Funes, Bienvenida Sarmiento, Borja Toranzo de Zavalla, Telésfora Borrego de Benavides, Benita Martínez Pastoriza, Serafina Durán de Rojo, Paula Sarmiento de Gómez, Rosario Sarmiento, Juana García de Labal, Procesa Sarmiento de Lenoir, Clara Rosa Cortínez, Magdalena Brihuega de Aberastáin, Juana Godoy de Brandes, Antonio Villascusa, Lucila Antepara de Godoy, Candelaria Albarracín de Godoy, Rosa Suárez de Gómez, Cenobia Bustos, Juana Cardoso Aberastain, Magdalena Bilbao, Francisca Ríos de Páez, Lucía Bosque Moreno, Clara de la Precilla de Jameson.

IU MiU

932 Marín, Rufino. _Perfiles de mujer_; 21 temperamentos femeninos, vistos a través de la compresión rápida, certera y elegante de un croniqueur de jerarquía. Buenos Aires: Editorial "Amistad," 1941. 168 p. 18 cm.
A collection of biographical essays, emphasizing the personality traits of 21 contemporary women, mostly Argentines. Those featured include Lola Nucífora, Olga Bettino, Thelma Carló, Libertad Lamarque, Tita Vidal, Rocío Romero Pinzón de Cuenca Muñoz, Josefina Rubiales (Amanda Ledesma, pseud.), Leonor Fernández, Josefina Aguilar (Chacha Aguilar, pseud.), Delly Dumas, Irene Clavier, Lita Morales, Angelita Vélez, Elsa Buck, Celia Gómez, Yolanda Rifano (Yola Yoli, pseud.), Elena Segovia.

TxU

See also entries 19, 31, 36, 37, 41, 44, 46, 49, 85, 112, 130, 154, 172, 227, 234, 323, 422, 487, 494, 652, 655, 656, 678, 691, 711, 717, 725, 729, 730, 739, 746, 748, 751, 762, 773, 781, 783, 785, 787, 789, 797, 800, 802, 805, 810, 814, 817, 822, 874, 879, 883, 889, 892, 893, 924.

WOMEN--DICTIONARIES, ENCYCLOPEDIAS, and "WHO'S WHO"

933 Sosa de Newton, Lily. _Diccionario biográfico de mujeres argentinas_. Buenos Aires, 1972. 414 p. 23 cm. (Colección diccionarios biográficos argentinos).
Biographical dictionary of Argentine women from all walks of life and all periods of history. (See also entry 934.)

CSt CtY CU CU-S FU ICU InU LU MH MiEM MnU MoU MU NcU NjP NjR NmU NSyU OU PSt ViU WU

934 _____. _Diccionario biográfico de mujeres argentinas_. Aumentado y actualizado. 2. ed. Buenos Aires: Editorial Plus Ultra, 1980. 533 p. 23 cm.
An enlarged edition. (See entry 933.)

IU

Paraguay

AERONAUTICS

935 Aponte Benítez, Leandro. Cincuenta años de aeronáutica en el Paraguay. Asunción: El Arte, 1957. 355 p. 24 cm.

A history of aeronautics in Paraguay, covering the period from the beginning to the middle of the 20th century, including scattered biographical information for many people associated with this aspect of Paraguayan history. Longer essays are given for the following: Alfredo Stroessner, Marcial Samaniego, Epifanio Ovando.

IU

ARMED FORCES

936 Vittone, Luis. Las fuerzas armadas paraguayas en sus distintas épocas; la infantería paraguaya y su patrono. Asunción: Editorial El Gráfico, 1969. 323 p. Portraits. 20 cm.

A history of the armed forces in Paraguay, covering the period from colonial times to the present day. Scattered biographical information is included for many people involved in this aspect of Paraguay's development. More substantial information and portraits are included for the author of this work and some notable men who contributed to the military movement. These people include Luis Vittone, José Gaspar Rodríguez de Francia, Carlos Antonio López, Francisco Solano López, José Félix Estigarribia, Eugenio Alejandrino Garay.

CLSU CLU CSt CU IaU ICU IU KU MB
MoSW MU NcU NIC NN NNC TxU WaU

ART

937 Báez, Jorge. Artes y artistas paraguayos. Período renacentista. Asunción: Editorial "El Liberal," 1941. 88 p. 20 cm.

A discussion of art and music in Paraguay during the late 19th and early 20th centuries, with biographical essays about the following artists: Remberto Giménez, José Asunción Flores, Fernando Centurión, Juan A. Samudio, Andrés Campos Cervera (Julián de la Herrería, pseud.), Héctor Da Ponte, Santiago Alborno, Modesto Delgado Rodas, Jaime Bestard, Roberto Holdenjara. Also, biographical sketches about the following: Francisco Almeida, Vicente Pollarolo, E. May, Amadeo Peña y Lorenzo Orsini.

NN TxU

938 Fernández, Miguel Angel. Paraguay. English translation by Ralph E. Dimmick. Washington, D.C.: General Secretariat of the Organization of American States, 1969. 18 p. 19 cm. (Art in Latin America today).

An essay on Paraguayan art, including scattered biographical information about the following artists in the late 19th and 20th centuries: Andrés Campos Cervera, Andrés Guevara, Pole Wolf Bandurek, João Rossi, Ofelia Echagüe Vera, Olga Blinder, Lili del Mónico, Edith Jiménez, Joel Filártiga, Aldo Delphino, Carlos Colombino, Laura Márquez, Michael Burt, Pedro de Lascio, Guillermo Ketterer, José Antonio Pratt, Enrique Careaga, Fernando Orillón, William Riquelme, Ricardo Yustman, Alberto Miltos, Julián de la Herrería, José L. Parodi, Josefina Plá, Hermann Guggiara, Leonor González Cecotto.

CLSU CLU CNoS CtY CtW CU-SB DI
DPU GU ICarbS IEdS IU KU KyU MH
MoU MWelC NbU NcD NcGU NcRS NcU
NhD NIC NN OrPS PSt TNJ TxU UU
WU

939 Plá, Josefina. Treinta y tres nombres en las artes plásticas paraguayas. Asunción: Editorial Cultura, 1973. 59 p. 20 cm.

A collection of biographical sketches of the following Paraguayan plastic artists of the 19th and 20th centuries: Livio Abramo, Pablo Alborno, Wolf Bandurek, Jaime Bestard, Olga Blinder, Enrique Careaga, Carlos Santiago Colombino, Carlos Colombo, Héctor Da Ponte, Andrés Campos Cervera (Julián de la Herrería, pseud.), Modesto Delgado Rodas, Lilí del Mónico, Pedro Di Lascio, Aurelio García, Genaro Espinola, Leonor González Ceccotto, Andrés Guevara, Herman Guggiari, Roberto Holdenjara, Edith Jiménez, Laura Márquez Moscarda, Serafín Marsal, José L. Parodi, Josefina Plá, Vicente Pollarolo, Saturio

ART

Ríos, João Rossi, Juan Samudio, Carlota
Schulz, Miguela Vera, Yaparí.

CLU CtY CU CU-S CU-SB FU IU MB
NbU NIC NmU NN NSyU OU PSt

BIOGRAPHY (MISCELLANEOUS)

940 Almada, Zenón. Reminiscencias de Itacurubí
de la Cordillera. Asunción: El Arte, 1952.
22 p. 20 cm.
A very brief collection of reminiscences
about Itacurubí, Paraguay, covering the period from 1862 to 1949, and featuring scattered biographical information for many
people associated with this town. They include Zenón Almada, Daniel García, Francisco
Solano López, Pedro Aguilera (Chantelo,
pseud.).

IU

941 Ayala Aquino, Gumersindo, and Eladio Martínez.
Libro de oro: IV [Cuarto] centenario de
Villarrica por Gumersindo Ayala Aquino y Eladio Martínez. Asunción, 1970. 114 p. Portraits. 26 cm.
A work dealing with various aspects of
the culture, history, and politics of Villarrica, Paraguay including biographical essays
and portraits for the following notable people
who have been associated with this city:
Delfín Chamorro, Zoilo Trebe, Ramón I. Cardozo, Simeón Carisimo, Ernesto Pérez Acosta
(Paí Pérez), Carlos Barciela, Fernán Elizardo
Benítez, Cirilo Cáceres Zorrilla, Gloria Ermelinda, Marcelo De Bleecker, Luis Recalde.

CtY

942 Báez, Cecilio. Cuadros históricos y descrip-
tivos. Asunción: Talleres Nacionales de H.
Kraus, 1906. 334 p. Portraits. 27 cm.
An essay about the history of Paraguay,
including biographical data on José Gaspar
Rodríguez de Francia, Carlos Antonio López,
Francisco Solano López, Cirilo Antonio Riva-
rola, Benjamín Aceval, Clara Queirolo de
Bajac, Serafina Dávalos.

DLC IU

943 Benítez, Luis G. Historia cultural; reseña
de su evolución en el Paraguay. Asunción:
El Arte, 1966. 307 p. 20 cm.
A cultural history of Paraguay covering
the period from preconquest to modern times
and including biographical information on
distinguished individuals from all walks of
life associated with it.

CLSU CLU CoFS CSt CSt-H CU FTaSU
FU IaU ICU INS InU IU KU MB MoSW
MU NBuU NcU NIC NN NNC OCU OrU
OU TxU WaU WU

943a Cáceres de Thomas, Carmen. Aportes al desarrollo de la ciudad de Asunción. Asunción,
1977. 195 p. 21 cm.
A collection of writings by Carmen Cáceres
de Thomas, who served on the city council of
Asunción from 1975 to 1977. Biographical information is included for this woman and
others from all time periods and walks of
life who are discussed in the context of her
writings. Particular emphasis is given to
the following: Carmen Cáceres de Thomas,
Pastora Concepción Céspedes, Mauricio Baranda,
Carlos Eduardo Abdala, Ezequiel Dolores González, Domingo Robledo, Ramona Dolores Fanego
de Miño (Lola de Miño), Serafina Dávalos,
Eligia Mora de Stroessner, Francisco Solano
López, Alfredo Stroessner, Fulgencio R.
Moreno, Remberto Giménez, Elisa Alicia Lynch,
Bernardino Caballero.

MnU

944 Cáceres Zorrilla, Cirilo. Cronología histó-
tica de la antigua Provincia del Guairá.
Asunción: Edit. "El Gráfico," 1962. 85 p.
23 cm.
A chronology of events in the province
of Guairá, covering the period from 1453 to
1701. Brief scattered biographical notes
are included for many people who contributed
in some way to the development of this region.

CtY ICarbS KU LNHT NbU NcU NIC
NmLcU NN TxU

945 Cardozo, Ramón Indalecio. La antigua provincia de Guairá y la Villa Rica del Espíritu
Santo. Buenos Aires: J. Menéndez, 1938.
195 p. 21 cm.
A history of the Paraguayan province of
Guairá and the city of Villa Rica del Espíritu Santo, covering the period from 1554 to
1676, and including scattered biographical
information for many notable people associated
with this region.

CtY DLC DPU MBU NBuG NcU TxU

946 Centurión, Carlos R. Historia de la cultura
paraguaya. Asunción: Biblioteca Ortiz
Guerrero, 1961. 2 v. 20 cm.
A history of Paraguayan civilization.
Biographical information throughout about
hundreds of people associated with it (16th-
20th centuries). Alphabetical index of names
lists approximately 1,200 names.

CLSU CLU DPU ICU InU IU LNHT MH
MiU NIC NN NNC NSyU OkU TNJ TxU

947 Franco Preda, Artemio. El Guairá y su aporte
a la cultura paraguaya; historia cultural del
Guairá. Prólogo del Dr. Hermógenes Rojas
Silva. Asunción, 1972. 460 p. 20 cm.
History of the Paraguayan province of
Guairá from the 16th to the 20th century as

told through biographies of its leading citizens. Information supplied includes dates, educational background, and professional activities.

CaQMM CtY CU-S CU-SB GU IaU ICU IU MH NBuU NcD NcU NIC NmLcU PPT TxU ViU

948 Galería de paraguayos ilustres. Asunción: Editorial Don Bosco, 1968-70. 14 v. Portraits. 18 cm.
A collection of essays on the following notable Paraguayans:
V. 1: Félix Paiva.
V. 2: Silvio Pettirossi.
V. 3: Emilio Sosa Gaona.
V. 4: José Félix Estigarribia.
V. 5: Sebastián Pinto Correa Doria.
V. 6: Francisco Solano López.
V. 7: José Eduvigis Días.
V. 8: Bernardino Caballero.
V. 9: Domingo Martínez de Irala.
V. 10: Hernando Arias de Saavedra.
V. 11: Juan de Ayolas.
V. 12: Aurelio García.
V. 13: Juan de Garay.
V. 14: Arsenio Erico.

CLSU DLC IU

949 González Torres, Dionisio M. Boticas de la colonia y cosecha de hojas dispersas. Asunción: Instituto Colorado de Cultura, 1978. (Biblioteca colorados contemporáneos. V. 4). 503 p. 20 cm.
Collection of essays on various aspects of Paraguayan culture and history with scattered biographical data on individuals from all periods of history.

IU

950 Kallsen, Osvaldo. Asunción y sus calles. Asunción: Imprenta Comuneros, 1974. 354 p. 22 cm.
Alphabetical listing of the streets in Asunción, Paraguay, including brief biographical sketches of the individuals after whom they are named (mostly Paraguayans).

IU

951 López Decoud, Arsenio. Album gráfico de la República del Paraguay, 1811-1911. Buenos Aires: Talleres Gráficos de la Compañía General de Fósforos, 1911. CXXXVI p. Portraits. 37 cm.
An album describing in pictures and words the history, economics, politics, geography, and culture of Paraguay during the period from 1811 to 1911. Portraits and biographical information are included for many prominent people.

DLC IU MB NcU NN TxU

952 Majavacca, José, and Juan F. Pérez Acosta. El aporte italiano al progreso del Paraguay (1527-1930). Buenos Aires: Tall. Gráf. Lucania, 1951. 219 p. Portraits. 28 cm.

(Biblioteca de la Sociedad Científica del Paraguay. V. 12).
A discussion of the Italian participation in the religious, political, social, economic, and cultural development of Paraguay from 1527 to 1930. Biographical information is included for approximately 850 individuals.

DLC ICU InU NcU

953 Martínez, Sindulfo. Hombres y pasiones. Asunción: Editorial El Gráfico, 1966. 184 p. Portraits. 19 cm.
Collection of essays profiling 19th- and 20th-century Paraguayans with special attention paid to their contributions to the Paraguayan culture. The following individuals from all walks of life are featured: Sindulfo Martínez, José Félix Estigarribia, José Gil, Justo Pastor Benítez, Juan Martincich, Juan Francisco Recalde, Andrés Barbero, Domingo Montanaro, Luis A. Riart, César Vasconcellos, Enrique L. Pinho, Felipe Molas López, Vicente Lamas, Antonia Espínola, Agustina Cáceres de Zayas, Joel Estigarribia, Walter Bauer, Francisco Brizuela.

CLSU CU IaU InU IU MB MoSW N NBuU NcU NIC NN NNC OU WU

954 Monte Domecq, Raúl. La República del Paraguay en su sesquicentenario, 1811-1961, 1813-1963. Asunción: Album Gráfico del Paraguay, Editorial F. Monte Domecq, 1964. 303 p. Portraits. 37 cm.
A review of 150 years of Paraguay's history, ending with the year 1963. Scattered biographical information is given for hundreds of people from all walks of life. Alphabetical index of names.

CLSU CU DLC FU IU NcU NIC NNC

955 Mosqueira, Silvano. Nuevas semblanzas. Civilización arábiga. Asunción: La Colmena, 1937. 160 p. Portraits. 24 cm.
A series of articles--some biographical, others historical--dealing with Paraguayan people and events along with one lengthy discourse on Arabic civilization. Biographical information, such as detailes on lives, accomplishments and characters, is included for many 19th- and 20th-century Paraguayans. The following are particularly featured: Juan Silvano Godoi, Manuel Gondra, Manuel Domínguez, José P. Montero, Manuel J. Duarte, Gonzalo Bulnes, José Eduvigis Días, Francisco Solano López, Vicente Mongelós, Dionisio de Mosqueira, José Antonio González Lanuza, Luis Mariani, Cándida Aseretto de Mariani, Juan Escolástico Rojas, Chelita Cuevas, Adalita Ayala Cabeda, María Estela Beascoechea, Esther Cándida Mariani, Mima Palermo, María Antonio Duarte Galli.

DLC DPU FU NmLcU NSyU TxU WU

956 _____. Siluetas femeninas; Los españoles en el Paraguay; El ocaso de los grandes hombres. Asumción: La Colmena, 1930. 142 p. Portraits. 25 cm.

BIOGRAPHY (MISCELLANEOUS)

A collection of articles, consisting mostly of biographical tributes to many contemporary Paraguayan women, but also featuring biographical material on some notable men. The following are particularly featured: Josefina Sapena Pastor, Isabel Llamosas, Rubí Gutiérrez, Josefa Bourdette, Rosa Cándida Acosta, Joaquím Nabuco, Francesca de Nozières, Aparicia Mosqueira de Benítez, Adalita Ayala Cabeda, Juan Carlos Aceval Palmerola, Mariano Luis de Galeano Lara Castro, Juan Silvano Godoi, Adelina González Navero, Eduvigis Doldán, María Elena González Navero, Aquiles Casali, Carmen Ambrosio Guerin, Susanita Elizeche Benítez, Lidia Frutos, Beatriz Pirovano, Patricio Isasi, Tutula Herken, Ruben Darío (Nicaragua), José Enrique Rodó (Uruguay), Silvano Mosqueira, Max Grillo.

InU   NN   NNC   TxU

957   O'Leary y Urdapilleta, Juan Emiliano. <u>Los legionarios</u>. Asunción: Editorial de Indias, 1930. 235 p. 19 cm.
An account of the activities of 19th-century Paraguayan legionaries. Scattered biographical information is given for many people associated with this aspect of Paraguay's history. Among those featured are Carlos Antonio López, Juan José Decoud, Manuel Pedro de Pena, Adolfo Decoud, Juan Francisco Decoud.

CtY   DLC   FU   ICarbS   IU

958   Olmedo, Natalicio. <u>Album gráfico de Concepción</u>. Asunción: Talleres Gráficos La Colmena, 1927. 191 p. Portraits. 35 cm.
A commemorative album of the department and town of Concepción, Paraguay, including scattered biographical data on prominent citizens from all walks of life, and among them Agustín Fernando de Pinedo. Also featured are the towns of Bella Vista, Horqueta, Belén, and Loreto.

DLC

959   Parker, William Belmont, comp. <u>Paraguayans of Today</u>. London, New York: The Hispanic Society of America, 1921. 317 p. Portraits. 17 cm. (Hispanic notes & monographs; essays, studies, and brief biographies, issued by the Hispanic Society of America. V. 6).
Collection of biographies of prominent Paraguayans in 1921 from all walks of life. Information provided includes birthplace, dates, and career achievements for Manuel Gondra, Juan Sinforiano Bogarín, Cecilio Báez, Juansilvano Godoi, María F. González, Venancio Víctor López, Teodosio González, Eloy Fariña Núñez, Juan Monte, Alfonso Belisario Campos, Gómes Freire Esteves, Federico García, Juan B. Nacimiento, Pedro Bruno Guggiari, Fermín Casco Espinosa, Ernesto Velásquez, J. Alfredo Aponte, Manuel W. Chaves, Manuel J. Duarte, Eulojio Jiménez, Evaristo Acosta, Juan L.

Mallorquín, Daniel Codas, J. Benigno Escobar, Teresa L. C. de Rodríguez Alcalá, Luis de Gásperi, Gustavo M. Crovatto, Enrique Ayala, Rogelio Ibarra, Juan Stefanich, José Tomás Legal, Fernando Centurión, Francisco Antonio Brizuela, Pablo M. Ynsfrán, Pedro Saguier, Juan B. Benza, Félix Paiva, Eliseo Zavala, Federico Codas, Juan Bautista Gaona, Adolfo Francisco Antúnez, Juan Francisco Recalde, Juan Emiliano O'Leary, Andrés Barbero, Carlos Rodríguez Santos, Juan Vicente Ramírez, Emilio Acebal, Víctor Abente Haedo, Manuel Riquelme, Marcial Sosa Escalada, Juan A. Samudio, Ovidio Rebaudi, Manlio Schenoni Lugo, Antonio Sosa, José Antonio Ortiz, José P. Montero, Eusebio A. Lugo, Teodoro Rojas, Cristóbal Duarte, Eduardo Schaerer, Fulgencio R. Moreno, Enrique Bordenave, Hermenegildo Roa, Héctor Velázquez, Pedro Bobadilla, Ramón Indalecio Cardozo, Juan Francisco Pérez, Enrique L. Pinho, Delfín Chamorro, Serafina Dávalos, Francisco C. Chaves, Justo Pastor Vera, Guillermo Tell Bertoni, Juan Manuel Sosa Escalada, José P. Guggiari, Pedro L. Barbosa, Eliseo Da Rosa, José Irala, Arsenio López Decoud, Narciso R. Colman, Benigno Ferreira, José Antonio Pérez, Adolfo Aponte, Leo Centurión, Eusebio Ayala, Justo Pastor Duarte, Alejandro Arce, Pablo Alborno, Juan José Soler, Adolfo Chirife, M. Eliseo Sisa, Juan R. Dahlquist, Atilio A. Peña, Carlos Calcena, Ramón Lastra Castro, Emiliano González Navero, Eladio Velázquez, Patricio Alejandrino Escobar, Arturo Rebaudi, Liberato Marcial Rojas, Manuel Peña, Raimundo D. Obelar, Luis E. Migone, Mario Usher, Ricardo Odriosola, Rómulo Goiburú, Genaro Romero, Concepción Silva de Airaldi, Pedro A. Mendoza, Gualberto Cardús Huerta, Pedro Peña, Carlos Luis Isasi, Estanislao Pereira, Emilia Recalde de Recalde, José Natalicio Rojas, Jerónimo Zubizarreta, Luis Alberto Riart, Manuel Gamarra, Manuel Domínguez, Eligio Ayala, Héctor F. Decoud, J. Isidro Ramírez, Manuel Rojas A., Silvano Mosqueira. Alphabetical index of names.

CU   DLC   LNHT   MB   MiU   NcGU   NjP   OCl
OO   TxU   ViU   WaSpG

960   Pitaud, Henri. <u>Les français au Paraguay</u>. Préf. de Daniel Halévy. Bordeaux: Editions Bière, 1955. 217 p. 22 cm.
A history of the French involvement in the history of Paraguay, from the 15th to the 20th century. Scattered biographical information is included for many men and women of French descent who made some contribution to the development of Paraguay. Separate biographical sections are included for the author of this work and for 25 French Jesuits involved in various aspects of Paraguay's history. The following names represent those who are emphasized in the text or who are featured in the separate sections: Henri Pitaud, Ignace de Loyola, Aimé Corjaud dit Bonpland, Madame Bonpland, Escoffier, Alice Lynch, Le docteur Crevaux, Benjamin Balansa, Gilbert Lejeune,

La Soeur Cabane, Michel Garicoïts, Mademoiselle de Villeneuve, Silvio Petirossi, François Sauvageot de Dupuis, Casimir Seux, Madame Jeantou, Fabre (family), Roberto Petit, Manuel González Ligier, Jacques de Liniers, Jean Vaisseau, Louis Berger, Noël Berthot, Ignace Chomé, Barthélemy de Blende, Nicolas Hénard, Jacques Ransonnier, Philippe Lemaire, Jacques Lolieu, François Ricquart, Nicolas du Toit, Flores, Pierre de Boschère, Claude Royer, Louis la Croix, Jacques Claret, Jacques de Haze, André Gillis, Henri Matthys, Jean Conti, Louis Charlet, Joseph Guinet, Salvador (Sauveur) Colon, Félix Blanic.

CU CU–S DLC LU MsU NIO NjP NN TxU WaU

961 Plá, Josefina. The British in Paraguay 1850–1870. Translated from the Spanish by Brian Charles MacDermot. Richmond (Eng.): Richmond Pub. Co., 1976. 277 p. 23 cm.
    Study of British residents in Paraguay and their influence on life there from 1850–1870. Scattered biographical data provided on a number of individuals, with the following especially featured: Carlos Antonio López, William Keld Whytehead, John Johnston, George Piggott Barton, William Stewart, Eliza Alicia Lynch. Alphabetical index of names.

AzU CNoS CtY CU–S DGU GU IEN IU MB MH MoU–St NcU NIC NjP NNU PPiU TxU WU

962 Roa Bastos, Augusto Antonio, comp. Las culturas condenadas. México: Siglo Veintiuno Editores, 1978. 349 p. 21 cm. (Colección América nuestra. América colonizada. V. 18).
    An essay about the Indians of Paraguay. Includes biographical sketches of the following contributors: León Cadogan, Juan Balaieff, Branislava Susnik, Bartomeu Meliá, Mark Münzel, Miguel Chase-Sardi, Pierre Clastres, Helene Clastres, Georg Grünberg, Augusto Roa Bastos.

WU

963 Sánchez Quell, Hipólito. Comentarios: actualidad asunceña; cosas del tiempo ido; al vibrar del cable; ¿quién es quién?; horizontes lejanos; lo que debe hacerse. Asunción: El Arte, 1953. 207 p. 20 cm.
    A collection of short articles which appeared in the Paraguayan newspaper La Unión during 1950 and 1951. Scattered biographical information is included for many people, mostly Paraguayans, from all time periods and walks of life. The following are particularly featured: Federico Chaves, Juan E. O'Leary, Pedro DeFelice, Benjamín Aceval, Marcelino Noutz, Juan de Salazar, Hernando de Trejo y Sanabria, Bernardino de Cárdenas, José Gaspar de Francia, Carlos Antonio López, Francisco Acuña de Figueroa, Francisco Sauvageot de Dupuis, Francisco Solano López, Bernardino

Caballero, Spruille Braden (Argentina), Juan Perón (Argentina), Alfredo R. Bufano, José de San Martín (Argentina), José Félix Bogado, Hernando Arias de Saavedra (Hernandarias, pseud.), José Garibaldi, Juan Bautista Alberdi, Fulgencio Yegros, Juan Caballero, José de Antequera y Castro, Natalicio Talavera, Juan Andrés Gelly, Domingo de Irala, Guido Boggiani, José Batlle y Ordóñez (Uruguay).

FU TxU

963a United Nations Educational Scientific and Cultural Organization. Science Cooperation Office for Latin America. Paraguay. Montevideo, 1959. 93 p. 22 cm.
    A collection of biographical sketches of the following contemporary Paraguayans prominent in different fields: Carlos Alvarez, Salvador Amodei, Telmo Manuel Aquino, Enrique Barrail, Guillermo Tell Bertoni, Blas Antonio Bestard, Eduardo Antonio Bestard, Juan Max Boettner, Ricardo Boettner, Juan Boggino, Juan B. Britez Caballero, Juan Camerón (hijo), Honorio Campuzano, Arquímedes Canese, Carlos G. Castillo, Ramón Codas, Quirno Codas Thompson, Armin Z. Cuevas, Vicente Chase Sosa, Luis Daumas Ladouce, Pablo Daumas Ladouce, Rodolfo Antonio Duarte Troche, José Esculies, César F. B. Franco, Miguel Angel Fresco, Carlos Gatti, M. Vicente González Oddone, Dionisio M. González Torres, Jaime Grau Chover, Andrés Gubetich, Jorge Hamuy D., Crispín Insaurralde, Carlos Iribas, Juan Carlos Lebrón Boettner, Silvio Lofruscio, Luis Carlos Maas, Antonio G. Masi, Domingo A. Masi, Francisco Migliore, Enrique Migone, Alberto Miquel, Jerónimo Molas, Julio Manuel Morales, Angel Morassi, Miguel Angel Morra, Fernando Oca del Valle, Roberto F. Olmedo, Mauricio Tomás Osuna, Luis A. Paleari, José Danilo Pecci, Carlos M. Ramírez Boettner, Manuel Riveros, Eduardo Rodríguez, Héctor Blas Ruiz, Francisco Schade, Isaac Schvartzman, Francisco Solano F., Branislava J. Susnik, Víctor M. Vera, Rodolfo Vera Gruhn, Stephan Vysokolan, José Vicente Ynsfrán, Pierpont Ynsfran, Roque F. Zaldívar.

DLC

964 Velázquez, Rafael Eladio. Breve historia de la cultura en el Paraguay. Asunción, 1965. 328 p. 18 cm.
    A cultural history of Paraguay, covering the period from preconquest to the present day. Brief scattered biographical information is included for many people who contributed to Paraguay's cultural development. The following are particularly featured: Francisco de Zaldívar, Francisca de Bocanegra, José Bernardino Servín, José Dávalos y Peralta, Juan de Salazar de Espinoza, Alvar Núñez Cabeza de Vaca, Ruy Díaz de Guzmán, Bernardino de Cárdenas, Juan de Arregui, Gabriel de la Anunciación, Luis Bolaños, Roque González de Santa Cruz, Miguel de Vargas Machuca, Iñigo López de Recalde, Antonio Ruiz de Montoya, Nicolás

BIOGRAPHY (MISCELLANEOUS)

Yapuguay, Nicolás del Techo, Pedro Lozano, José Guevara, José Sánchez Labrador, Carlos Penayos de Castro, José de Antequera y Castro, José de Avalos y Mendoza, Fernando de Mompó (Fernando de Mompás, pseud.), Miguel de Vargas Machuca, Sebastián Fernández Montiel, Ramón de las Llanas, Félix de Azara, Juan Francisco Aguirre, José Gaspar Rodríguez de Francia, Fernando de la Mora, Mariano Antonio Molas, José Agustín Molas, Manuel Antonio Corvalán, Fulgencio Yegros, Amancio González y Escobar, Pedro Alcántara de Somellera, Carlos Antonio López, Juan Bautista Rivarola, José Domingo Campos, Juan Andrés Gelly, Benito Martínez Varela, José María Martínez Varela, Juan Vicente Estigarribia, Francisco Acuña de Figueroa, Francisco Solano López, Natalicio de María Talavera, Ildefonso Antonio Bermejo, Juan José Decoud, José Segundo Decoud, Facundo Machaín, Gregorio Benítez, Juan Silvano Godoi, Benjamín Aceval, Ramón Zubizarreta, Victorino Abente Lago, Diógenes Decoud, Juan Crisóstomo Centurión, Alejandro Audibert, Blas Garay, José de la Cruz Ayala (Alón, pseud.), Emeterio González, Guido Boggiani, Manuel Amarilla, Adela Speratti, Ramón I. Cardozo, Manuel Riquelme, María Felicidad González, Centurión Miranda, Cecilio Báez, Manuel Domínguez, Manuel Gondra, Fulgencio R. Moreno, Agustín Barrios, Juan Samudio, Pablo Aborno, Jaime Bestard, Andrés Campos Cervera, Reinaldo Decoud Larrosa, Justo Prieto, Viriato Díaz Pérez, Rafael Barret, Justo Pastor Benítez, J. Natalicio González, Efraím Cardozo, Julio César Chaves, Hipólito Sánchez Quell, R. Antonio Ramos, Manuel Domínguez, Félix Paiva, Teodosio González, Juan José Soler, Teodoro Rojas.

AU CLSU CLU CNoS CoU CSt CSt-H CtY
CU IaU InU IU KU LNHT LU-NO MoSW
MU NBrockU NBuU NcD NcGU NcU NIC NN
NNC TxU ViU WaU

965 Verón de Astrada, Manuel. Hombres en la vida y en la muerte. Asunción: Impr. Zamphiropolos, 1975. 112 p. 21 cm.
A collection of biographical sketches of the following distinguished Paraguayans associated with the development of the country: Juan E. O'Leary, José Asunción Flores, Hérib Campos Cervera, Carlos Gatti, Gustavo González, Francisco Alejo Alvarenga (Menin, pseud.), Adolfo Yegros, Guillermo Tell Bertoni, Juan Sorazábal (Chuchín, pseud.), Anselmo Jóver Peralta, Andrés Guevara, Facundo Recalde, Carlos A. Centurión (physician), Juan C. Díaz (writer), Emiliana Escalada, Rosendo Rodríguez Gavilán, Leandro Aponte, Guido Rodríguez Alcalá, Petronio Muñoz Portillo, Juan Maldonado, Carlos Daniel Peña, Raúl Galindo (Nito, pseud.), Reinaldo Decoud Larrosa, Eduardo B. Gómez, Manuel Bernardes, Julio César Tiempo (Chonchón, pseud.), Angela Deivalle, Félix Pérez Cardozo, Ramón Jiménez Gaona, Manuel Riveros, Quirno Codas Thompson, Juan F. Bazán, Juan Emigdio Samaniego, José Muñoz Cota.

IU NIC NmU

966 Viola, Alfredo. Reseña del desarrollo cultural del Paraguay. Asunción: Ediciones Comuneros, 1979. 194 p. 21 cm.
Study of cultural development in Paraguay from the conquest to the present day, featuring brief biographical notes on artists, scientists, historians, chroniclers, clergymen, and members of other professions.

IU

BIOGRAPHY (MISCELLANEOUS)--DICTIONARIES, ENCYCLOPEDIAS, and "WHO'S WHO"

967 ¿Quién es quién en al Paraguay? Buenos Aires: F. Monte Domecq, 1941-58. 6 v. Portraits. 21-23 cm.
A "who's who" for Paraguay for the years 1941-1958.

DLC FMU FU IU InU NN NNUN TxU

EDUCATION

968 Massare de Kostianovsky, Olinda. La instrucción en la época colonial. 2. ed. aumentada y corr. Prólogo de R. Antonio Ramos. Asunción: Talleres Gráficos de la Escuela Técnica Salesiana, 1975. 396 p. 21 cm.
History of public education in Paraguay during the colonial era. Varying amounts of biographical data are provided in the form of dates, education, and religious affiliation for various individuals. Among those especially featured are Francisco de Alfaro, Francisca Jesusa de Bocanegra, José Antonio de San Alberto, Francisco Saldívar, Diego de Torres, Diego de Borda, Maciel de Lorenzana, Pedro Lozano, Nicolás del Techo, Domingo Muriel, José Manuel Peramas, Antonio Ruiz de Montoya, Roque González de Santa Cruz, Lázaro de Ribera y Espinosa.

CLU CtY CU-S InNd IU KU KyLoU MB
MU NcU NmU NN

969 Speratti, Juan. Historia de la educación pública en el Paraguay, 1812-1932. San Lorenzo: Escuela Técnica Salesiana, 1979. 210 p. Portraits. 20 cm.
A history of public education in Paraguay (1812-1932) and the origin and evolution of the school "España de San Lorenzo" (1869-1975), including biographical data. The following are particularly featured: José Gaspar Rodríguez de Francia, Carlos Antonio López, Clotilde Emilia Paredes.

IU

970 Velázquez, Rafael Eladio. La educación paraguaya en el siglo XVIII. Asunción: Academia Paraguaya de la Historia, 1968. 28 p. 20 cm.
Essay dealing with education in 17th-century Paraguay. Brief biographical data are

supplied for the following individuals involved in the field: Andrés Garavito de León, José Bernardino Servín, José Servín, Manuel Servín, José Dávalos y Peralta.

IaU IU NbU

GENEALOGY

971 Ortellado Rojas de Fossati, María Antonia. Buscando a los que fueron. Asunción: Artes Gráficas Zamphiropolos, 1970. 147 p. Portraits. 22 cm.

A collection of biographical sketches, some accompanied by portraits, of the following members of the García family and the Viana family of Paraguay: Roque González de Santa Cruz, José Antonio García, Angel Fernández García, Adelaida Escalada Fernández de Rojas de Aranda, Juan Pedro Escalada, Víctor Rojas de Aranda Escalada Fernández, Mariano Antonio Molas, María de la Oliva Corvalán de García, Francisca Carlota Viana de la Mora de Rodríguez, Fernando de la Mora, María Fulvia Carreras Saguier (Condesa Bobbio), Oscar Fernando Carreras Saguier, Manuel Quintana Sáenz.

CU–SB GU IaU IU MU NNC TxU ViU WU

972 _____. Líneas vinculadas a Cavallero Bazán. Asunción: Tall. Gráf. de la Escuela Técnica Salesiana, 1977. Portraits. 23 cm.

Genealogical history of the Cavallero Bazán family of Paraguay from its origins in Spain to the 20th century. Included are the following families and individuals: Bazán, Juana María de la Oliva Corvalán Montiel de García, Víctor Augusto Natalicio Vasconcellos Ortúzar, Martínez Sáenz, Cavallero Bazán, Juan Antonio Montiel, Juan Manuel Gamarra.

IU

973 Recalde A., Sergio. Crónica de una estirpe prócer. Asunción: Talleres Gráficos de Orbis, 1976. 298 p. 20 cm.

A genealogy of the Recalde family, including biographical information of various amounts on many of its members. Particular emphasis is given to the following: Juan Francisco Recalde Valdez, Manuel Gondra, Juan Francisco Recalde Mongelós, Rafael Antonio Recalde Mongelós, Rafaela Antonio Recalde, Mercedes Valdez, Manuel José Duarte Valdez, Juan Francisco Recalde Sosa, Victoriano Recalde Arévalo, Rufino Recalde Milesi, Herminia Recalde Milesi, Sergio A. T. Recalde Ammiri, Juan Francisco Recalde Ammiri, Pedro Plutarco Recalde Valdez, Manuel Antonio Sosa, Dámaso Antonio Sosa, Ignacio Antonio Sosa, Pedro Antonio Sosa (Ño Pelo, pseud.), Daniel Sosa Valdez, Ignacio Sosa Valdez, Juan Manuel Sosa Escalada, Manuel Antonio Amarilla, María Isabel Sosa, Juana Sosa Valdez, Dámaso Sosa Valdez, Vicente Ignacio Sosa, Tomasa Valdez,

Pedro Luis Valdez, Atanasia de la Cruz Valdez, Giulio Ammiri, Bruna Ammiri.

CtY IU MH MU NmU NIC TxU

HISTORY

974 Aponte Benítez, Leandro. Hombres ... armas ... y batallas de la epopeya de los siglos. Asunción: Imprenta Comuneros, 1971. 242 p. Portraits. 19 cm.

A work featuring short biographical essays, as well as portraits in most cases, for the following 19th-century Paraguayans, most of them military men: Francisco Solano López, Bernardino Caballero, José Eduvigis Díaz, Patricio Escobar, Vicente Barrios, José María Bruguez, José María Delgado, Francisco Isidoro Resquín, Elizardo Aquino, Germán Serrano, Florentino Oviedo, José Vicente Mongelós, Valois Rivarola, Crisóstomo Centurión M., Silvestre Aveiro, Pedro Victoriano Gill, Pedro Ignacio Meza, Remigio Cabral, José de la Cruz Estigarribia, José de Jesús Martínez, Sebastián Bullo, Eduardo Vera, José Matías Bado, Fidel Maíz, Francisco Roa, Francisco Solano Espinosa, Pedro Duarte, Elisa Alicia Lynch.

CFS CLSU CLU CSt CtY CU CU-S CU-SB
IaU ICU IU MB MH MoSW MU NcD NcU
NIC NjR NN NNC OU PPT ViU WaU WU

975 Argaña, Luis María. Perfiles políticos: perfiles doctrinarios e ideológicos de los partidos y de los movimientos políticos en el Paraguay. Asunción: Departamento de Prensa e Información de la Junta de Gobierno del Partido Colorado, 1977. 234 p. 26 cm.

A discussion of Paraguayan political movements and ideologies during the 19th and 20th centuries. Scattered biographical information is given for many political leaders who are discussed within the chronology of Paraguayan governments. The following are particularly featured: José Gaspar Rodríguez de Francia, Francisco Solano López, Carlos Antonio López, Benigno Ferreira, Bernardino Caballero, José Félix Estigarribia, Higinio Morinigo, Gral. Machuca, Alfredo Stroessner.

WU

976 Barrett, William Edmund. Woman on Horseback, the biography of Francisco López and Eliza Lynch. New York: Frederick A. Stokes, 1938. 360 p. 21 cm.

A biography of 19th-century Paraguayan president Francisco Solano López and his wife, Elisa Alicia Lynch, which also includes some information for Francisco's father, Carlos López.

CoD CoDR CoGrS CU DLC DPU IdB KMK
KyLx NN OCl OEac OLak Or OrP OrU
OU PP PPL PPULC ULA WaS WaSp WaSpG

HISTORY

977 Bejarano, Ramón César. <u>Caciques guaraníes de la época colonial</u>. Paraguay: Editorial Toledo, 1979. 16 p. 22 cm.

Alphabetical index of approximately 100 names of Guarani caciques from the colonial era, who appear in <u>Historia de la provincia del Paraguay de la Compañía de Jesús</u> by Nicolás del Techo, 1897. Also 25 names, some non-Guaraní, gathered from other sources. Very brief biographical data on the following: Abacatí, Ignacio Abiaru, Aniangara, Apemondi, Aperará, Apicabiyá, Araguirá, Arapizandú, Arará, Ararepa, Ararera, Araria, Ararundi, Arazay, Areguati, Miguel Artiguaye, Aticai, Caabure, Caarupe, Candirá, Caraichure, Caruay, Cohé, Alonso Cuanará, Juan Cuará, Cuarabay, Cuaracipú, Cuaracipucú, Cuararé, Cuaray, Cuniambí, Cuniaracúa, Cunumipita, Cuñambo, Curiti, Curuba, Curupay, Cheacabi, Chemombé, González, Guabairi, Guaimica, Guairamina, Roderigo Guambairo, Juan Guaray, Guarobay, Guiraqueray, Guiraverá, Ibapiri, Itapay, Marcelo Maendi, Mangoré, Maracaná, Marangoa, María, Mbacaba, Mbocarata, Mboipe, Mboroseni, Mburúa, Nantabagua, Nambahay, Diego Niezá, Ñanduabusú, Diego Nienguiri, Paraverá, Pataguiruzú, Pindó, Pipirí, Piracúa, Piracuatí, Piraví, Potirava, Sandapila, Siripo, Tabaca, Tabacambi, Taitetú, Tambabé, Tambatay, Tamboy, Tataendi, Tataguazú, Tataurana, Taupa, Tayaoba, Tayaoy, Tayubay, Tuca, Tucudán, Tucambi, Tupamini, Yaguacaporu, Yaguapini, Vicente Yapuy, Yaviey, Abacoté, Alabos, Aracaré, Caracará, Carayá, Cuatí, Francisco (el indio), Guarambaré, Pyta Guaraní, Ñandasuvi, Neenguirú (Nicola Languirú), Tabaré, Tamatía, Taparí, Tavor, José Tiarayú, Tilcara, Yaparí, Angel María Zaya.

IU

978 Benítez, Justo Pastor. <u>Los comuneros del Paraguay, 1640-1735</u>. Prólogo del dr. Enrique Bordenave. Asunción: Imprenta Nacional, 1938. 55 p. 23 cm.

A history of the Paraguayan revolution of the <u>comuneros</u>, which lasted from 1640 to 1735. Scattered biographical information is given for many people in some way connected with this uprising, with emphasis on the following: Bernardino de Cárdenas, Diego de los Reyes Balmaceda, José de Antequera y Castro, Fernando Mompox de Zayas.

CU DPU MnU NN OU TxU

979 _____. <u>Mancebos de la tierra</u>. Buenos Aires: Talleres Gráficos Lucania, 1961. 109 p. Portraits. 20 cm.

An essay on Paraguayan history of the period of the War of Independence (1810-1811). Includes biographical data about the following patriots: Fulgencio Yegros, Antonio Tomás Yegros, Pedro Juan Caballero, José Gaspar Rodríguez de Francia, Fernando de la Mora, Mariano Antonio Molas, Vicente Ignacio Iturbe, Juan Bautista Rivarola, Juan Manuel Grance, Ventura Díaz de Bedoya, Manuel José Báez,

Mariano Larios Galván, Pedro Pablo Martínez Sáenz, Sebastián Martínez Sáenz, José Matías Isasi, Juan Bautista Acosta, Andrés Acosta, Fortunato Acosta, Francisco Antonio González, Mariano Careaga, Narciso Echagüe y Andía, Mauricio José Troche, José Fernández Montiel. Also biographical essays on José Díaz and Juan Sinforiano Bogarín.

CLU CtY CU FU ICU InU IU MH NbU
NcU NSyU TxU ViU

980 _____. <u>La ruta</u>. Asunción: Imprenta Nacional, 1939. 115 p. 22 cm.

An essay about Paraguayan history, including biographical sketches of the following individuals associated with it: Domingo de Irala, Hernando Arias de Saavedra, Pedro Vicente Cañete, José Félix Bogado, Fulgencio Yegros, Pedro Juan Caballero, Vicente Ignacio Iturbe, Mariano Antonio Molas, José Gaspar de Francia, Carlos Antonio López, José Eduvigis Díaz, Bernardino Caballero, Juan Silvano Godoi, Blas Garay, Manuel Domínguez, Fulgencio R. Moreno, Manuel Gondra, Eloy Fariña Núñez, Eligio Ayala.

CU DLC TxU WaU

981 Benítez Flores, Juan G. <u>Album paraguayo</u>. Asunción: Editorial Guaraní, 1955. 242 p. Portraits. 36 cm.

Biographical notes and sketches on approximately 300 notable Paraguayans associated with the Chaco war. Alphabetical index of names.

IU TxU

982 Bordón, F. Arturo. <u>Liberales ilustres</u>. Asunción: Editado por la Sociedad 18 de Octubre, 1966. 89 p. 19 cm.

Biographical sketches of individuals involved in the founding and development of the "Partido Liberal" in Paraguay. Birthplace, dates, and information on the political activities of the following 19th- and 20th-century individuals are provided: Esteban Gorostiaga, Antonio Taboada, Marcelino Rodas, Florentín Oviedo, Bernardino Bordón, Rómulo Decamilli, Antonio Medina, Antonio Peralta, Antonio Fernández, Evaristo Fernández, Marcelino Arias, Fabio Queirolo, José de la Cruz Ayala (Alón, pseud.), Pedro Victoriano Gill, Cirilo Solalinde, José Mateo Collar, Ignacio Ibarra, Felipe Torrens, Manuel Avila, Juan Ascencio Aponte, Francisco Fernández, José Guillermo González, Eduardo Vera, Pedro P. Caballero.

CSt-H DLC IU NcU NIC NN

983 Bray, Arturo. <u>Hombres y épocas del Paraguay</u>. 3. ed. Prólogo de Higinio Arbo. Buenos Aires: Ediciones Nizza, 1957. 2 v. Portraits. 21 cm.

A collection of biographical essays, mostly accompanied by portraits, on the following notable historical figures of Paraguay:

V. 1: José Gaspar Rodríguez de Francia, Carlos Antonio López, Francisco Solano López, Bernardino Caballero, Patricio Escobar, Juan B. Egusquiza, Manuel Gondra, Eligio Ayala.
V. 2: Hernando Arias de Saavedra, Fulgencio Yegros, José Berges, Elisa Lynch, Benigno Ferreira, Juan Sinforiano Bogarín.

CLU DPU FU InU IU KU MH NIC NN TxU

984   Capdevielle, Bernardo. <u>Historia del Paraguay desde los orígenes hasta nuestros días</u>. Asunción: Talleres Nacionales H. Kraus, 1927. 463 p. 18 cm.

A history of Paraguay, covering the period from preconquest to the 20th century. Scattered biographical information of varying lengths is included for many people, particularly military and political leaders, who contributed to the development of this country. The following are particularly featured: Cristóbal Colón, Juan Díaz de Solís, Alejo García, Sebastián Gaboto, Diego García, Juan de Osorio, Pedro de Mendoza, Juan de Ayolas, Juan de Salazar de Espinosa, Francisco Ruiz Galán, Alonso de Cabrera, Domingo Martínez de Irala, Alvar Núñez Cabeza de Vaca, Diego Centeno, Juan de Sanabria, Gonzalo de Mendoza, Francisco Ortiz de Vergara, Juan Ortiz de Zárate, Felipe de Cáceres, Martín Suárez de Toledo, Diego Ortiz de Mendieta, Juan de Garay, Juan Torres Navarrete, Hernandarias, Diego Marín de Negrón, Manuel de Frías, Luis Céspedes y Jeria, Martín de Ledesma Valderrama, Pedro Lugo y Navarra, Gregoria de Hinestrosa, Diego de Escobar y Osorio, Bernardino de Cárdenas, Sebastián de León y Zárate, Andrés de León y Garabito, Cristóbal de Garay y Saavedra, Juan Antonio Blásquez de Valverde, Alfonso Sarmiento de Sotomayor y Figueroa, Juan Díez de Andino, Felipe Rege Corvalán, Francisco de Monforte, Sebastián Félix de Mendiola, Gregorio Bazán de Pedraza, Diego de los Reyes Balmaceda, José de Antequera Enríquez y Castro, Baltasar García Ros, Bruno Mauricio de Zavala, Martín de Barúa, Fernando Mompo y Zayas, José L. Barreyro, Manuel Agustín de Ruiloba, Rafael de la Moneda, Marcos José de Larrazábal, Jaime Sanjust, José Martínez Fontes, Agustín Fernando de Pinedo, Pedro Ceballos, Pedro Melo de Portugal, Joaquín de Alós y Brú, Lázaro de Rivera y Espinosa de los Monteros, Bernardo de Velasco y Huidobro, José Espínola y Peña, Bernardo Velasco, Manuel Belgrano, Nicolás de Herrera, García Rodríguez de Francia, Policarpo Patiño, Carlos A. López, Manuel Rosas, Justo José Urquiza, Bartolomé Mitre, Francisco Solano López, Juan Antonio Saravia, Venancio Flores, General Robles, Vicente Barrios, Juan de la Cruz Estigarribia, José Eduwigis Díaz, Caxías, Salvador Jovellanos, Juan B. Gill.

ICarbS

984a   Cardozo, Efraím. <u>Efemérides de la historia del Paraguay</u>. "Hoy en nuestra historia." Asunción: Ediciones Nizza, 1967. 517 p. 23 cm.

A historical calendar of Paraguay (1524-1949). Biographical data included in essays featuring José Gaspar Rodríguez de Francia, José Eduvigis Díaz, Roque González de Santa Cruz, Juan Ortiz de Zárate, José Félix Estigarribia, Juan Sinforiano Bogarín, Bernardino Caballero, Bernardino de Cárdenas, Manuel Gondra, Alvar Núñez Cabeza de Vaca, Domingo Martínez de Irala, Adolfo Riquelme, Pedro Fernández de la Torre, Lázaro de Ribera, Juana de Zárate, Juan Bautista Gill, Pedro de Mendoza, Eusebio Ayala, Manuel Franco, Ruy Díaz de Guzmán, José de Antequera, Juan de Mena, Hernando Arias de Saavedra, Elizardo Aquino, Fulgencio Yegros, Juan José Montiel, Pedro Juan Caballero, Juan de Sanabria, Francisco Solano López, Francisco Ortiz de Vergara, Eduardo Schaerer, Pedro Bobadilla, Carlos Antonio López, Moisés S. Bertoni, José Gervasio Artigas, Saturio Ríos, Luis de Bolaños, Silvio Pettirossi, Eligio Ayala, Facundo Machaín, José Dolores Molas, José de Antequera y Castro, Juan de Osorio, Blas Garay, Cirilo Antonio Rivarola.

CLSU CtY CU CU-S FU GU IaU ICU IU MB MoSW MU NcD NcU NjR NN NNC OU TxU ViU WU

985   _____. <u>Historiografía paraguaya</u>. México: 1959- . 610 p. 24 cm. (Instituto Panamericano de Geografía e Historia. Comisión de Historia. Publicaciones. V. 83. Historiografías. V. 5).

An account of Paraguayan historiography, covering the period from preconquest to the 19th century. Biobibliographical information is given for many famous historiographers, including the following: Emilio Hassler, Guido Baggiani, Domingo Martínez de Irala, Pedro Dorantes (Pedro de Orantes, pseud.), Jaime Rasquín, Hans Staden, Juan Sánchez de Vizcaya, Francisco Ortiz de Vergara, Gregorio de Acosta, Hernandarias de Saavedra, Reginaldo de Lizárraga, Diego Marín de Nagróu, Alvar Núñez Cabeza de Vaca, Pero Hernández, Ulrico Schmidl, Luis de Miranda de Villafaña, Marín Barco de Centenera, Ruy Díaz de Guzmán, Antonio Ruiz de Montoya, Francisco Xarque, Antonio Sepp, Nicolás del Techo, Pedro Lozano, José Guevara, Ludovico Antonio Muratori, Pierre-François-Xavier Charlevoix, José Cardiel, José Manuel Peramas, Martín Dobrizhoffer, José Jolís, Florián Baucke, José Sánchez Labrador, Bernardo Ibáñez de Echávarri, Félix de Azara, Juan Francisco Aguirre, Diego de Alvear. Alphabetical index of names.

CaOOFF CaOOU CLU CoU CtU DCU DS FMU ICN IEN IGK LNHT MB MdBT MH MiU MnU MoSU NcD NcU NjR NN NNC PPAmP RPB ViU TxU WU

HISTORY

986 Centurión, Carlos R. <u>Los hombres de la Convención de 70</u>. Asunción: Talleres gráficos "El Arte," 1938. 31 p. 20 cm.

A collection of biographical sketches of the following outstanding members of the Paraguayan national convention of 1870: Facundo Machain, José Segundo Decoud, Juan Silvano Godoy, Miguel Palacios, Juan José Decoud, José del Rosario Miranda, Jaime Sosa Escalada, Sotero Cayo Miltos.

   CU ICarbS MiU-L NcU

987 _____. <u>Precursores y actores de la independencia del Paraguay</u>. Asunción: Editorial Alas, 1962. 63 p. 20 cm.

A historical essay about the Paraguayan War of Independence (1810-1811), including biographical sketches of the following individuals associated with it: Fulgencio Yegros, Pedro Juan Cavallero, Juan Bautista Rivarola, Vicente Ignacio Iturbe, Mariano Antonio Molas, Fernando de la Mora, Fernando Cavallero, Francisco Xavier Bogarín, José Gaspar de Francia, Juan Bautista Acosta, Blas José Roxas de Aranda, Mauricio José Troche, Mariano Recalde, Facunda Speratti, Juan Baleriano de Zeballos, Carlos Argüello, José Martín Iturbe, Juan María Iturbe, José Agustín Molas, Mariano Larios Galván, Sebastián Antonio Martínez Sáenz, Manuel Cumá, Vicente Morales. Also Pedro Manuel Domecq, Narciso de Echagüe, José Fermín Sarmiento, Nicolás Ibarbalz, Santiago Aráoz, Marcelino Rodríguez, Manuel Hidalgo, José María Aguirre, Julián de la Villa, Juan Manuel de la Villa, Manuel José Báez, Juan Manuel Grance, Francisco Baca, Martín José de Orué, José de María, José Fortunato Roa, Dionisio Cañiza, José Antonio Zelada, Gregorio Tadeo de la Cerda.

   CLU CLSU CtY ICN InU IU KU NIC NN NSyU TxU WU

988 Centurión, Juan Crisóstomo. <u>Mocedades</u>: Los sucesos de "Puerto Pacheco." Asunción: Instituto Colorado de Cultura, 1975. 169 p. 20 cm. (Biblioteca Clásicos Colorados. V. 1).

The memoirs of the 19th-century soldier Juan Crisóstomo Centurión, including biographical information for this man and for others with whom he was associated. Among those featured are Juan Crisóstomo Centurión, M. N. Dupuy, Ildefonso Antonio Bermejo, Natalicio Talavera, Carlos Antonio López.

   KU TxU

989 Charlevoix, Pierre François Xavier de. <u>Historia del Paraguay</u>, escrita en francés por el p. Pedro Francisco Javier de Charlevoix. Con las anotaciones correcciones latinas del p. Muriel; tr. al castellano por el p. Pablo Hernández. Madrid: V. Suárez, 1910-16. 6 v. 20 cm. (Colección de libros y documentos referentes a la historia de América. V. 11-13, 15-16, 18).

A six-volume history of Paraguay, covering the period from its discovery to the early 1800s. Scattered biographical information is included for many people from all walks of life who contributed to the development of this region. Those particularly featured: Juan de Solís, Sebastián Gaboto, Pedro de Mendoza, Maldonada, Ruiz Mosquera, Juan de Ayolas, Domingo Martínez de Irala, Alvar Núñez Cabeza de Vaca, Hernando de Ribera, Francisco de Mendoza, Diego de Abrego, Diego Centeno, Nuflo de Chaves, Juan Ortiz de Vergara, Alonso de Riquelme, Felipe de Cáceres, Manuel de Ortega, Alfonso Bársena, Juan Romero, José Cataldino, Diego de Torres, Simón Maceta, Bernardino de Cárdenas, Roque González de Santa Cruz, Diego de Borra, Antonio Ruiz de Montoya, Cristóbal de Mendoza, Francisco Díaz Taño, Diego de Alfaro, Justo Mansilla, Gregorio Hinestrosa, Pedro de Cárdenas, Laureano Sobrino, Sebastián de León, Andrés Garavito de León, Andrés de Rada, José Agustín Arce, Juan Bautista Zea, Lucas Cavallero, Esteban de Urizar, Antonio Machoni, Jaime de Aguilar, Diego de los Reyes, José de Avalos, Antonio Ruiz de Arellano, José de Antequera y Castro, Ramón de Llanas, Juan Cavallero y Añasco, Baltasar García Ros, Bruno Mauricio de Zavala, José de Palos, Juan de Mena, José de Armendáriz, Sebastián Fernández de Montiel, Martín de Barúa, Fernando Mompo, Ignacio de Soroeta, Juan de Arregui, Julián de Lizardi, Agustín de Castañares, Matías Strobel, José Quiroga. Alphabetical index of names.

   CtY-D CU DCU DCL GU NBuU NcD NcU OCl OU PPULC PU TxU ViU

990 Chaves, Julio César. <u>Paraguayos con San Martín</u>. Conferencia pronunciada bajo los auspicios de la Casa Argentina en su local social el 7 de julio de 1955, en el acto de homenaje a la Argentina con motivo de la fiesta de julio. Asunción, 1957. 28 p. 20 cm.

A short account of the part played by Paraguayans in the 19th-century struggle for independence led by San Martín. Scattered biographical information, emphasizing important accomplishments is given for some Paraguayan leaders of the colonial era, for those military men who were part of the emancipatory movement, and for the author of this work. The following are particularly featured: Julio César Chaves, Agustín Fernando de Pinedo, Pedro Melo de Portugal, Joaquín de Alós y Bru, Lázaro de Rivera y Espinosa de los Monteros, Eusebio Mariña, José María Rivera, Bonifacio Ramos, Patricio Oviedo, Ramón Díaz, Patricio Maciel, Félix Bogado.

   CU NmLcU TxU

991 Decoud, Héctor Francisco. <u>Los emigrados paraguayos en la guerra de la Triple Alianza</u>, 1930. Buenos Aires: Talleres Gráficos Argentinos L. J. Rosso, 1930. 156 p. Portraits. 21 cm.

A discussion of the part played by Paraguayans in the 19th-century war of the Triple Alliance. Portraits and very brief biographical captions are included for many people who were involved in this movement, with particular emphasis on the following: Serapio Machain, Juan Francisco Decoud, Pedro Nolazco Decoud, Benigno Ferreira, Fernando Iturburu, Carlos Loizaga, Juan Bautista Eguzquiza, Federico Guillermo Báez, Pío Otoniel Peña, Pedro Recalde, Federico Alonso, Juan José Decoud, José Segundo Decoud, Juan G. González, Jaime Sosa, Rufino Taboada, Pablo Recalde, Antonio Taboada, Dolores Recalde, Juliano Insfrán, Manuel Antonio, Juana Pabla Carrillo, José María Bruguez, José Berges, Facundo Machain.

CU DLC ICU NcU NSyU TxU

992   Domínguez, Manuel. El alma de la raza. Prólogo de Juan E. O'Leary. Buenos Aires: Editorial Ayacucho, 1946. 278 p. Porttaits. 21 cm.

An essay about Paraguayan history. Includes biographical data on the following people associated with the "founding" of the city of Asunción: Juan de Ayolas, Juan de Salazar de Espinosa, Gonzalo de Mendoza, Garci Venegas, Felipe de Cáceras, Hernando de Ribera, Pedro Genovés, Andrés de Arzamendia, Gonzalo Pérez de Morán, Juan Pérez, Richarte Limón, Juan de Rute, Nicolás Corma o Colina, Hernando de Laguardia, Juan Ruiz, Antonio Tomás, Amador de Montoya, Esteban Gómez. Also features Juan de Osorio and the author, Manuel Domínguez.

DLC IU

993   Duarte Prado, Bacón. 5 [i.e. Cinco] semblanzas republicanas. Asunción, 1976. 123 p. Portraits. 20 cm.

A collection of biographical sketches about the following Paraguayan leaders associated with the Partido Colorado: Bernardino Caballero, Blas Garay, Ignacio A. Pane, Pedro P. Peña, Manuel Talavera.

TxU

994   Franco, Víctor Ignacio. Un hispano y un italiano en la guerra contra la Triple Alianza. Asunción: Academia Paraguaya de la Historia, 1979. 72 p. Portraits. 19 cm.

Text of a lecture given at the "Instituto Paraguayo de Cultura Hispánica" on the lives of Dionisio Lirio and Sebastián Bullo, European immigrants who fought for Paraguay in the war against the "Triple Alianza" (1864-1870). Also a biobibliographical sketch of Víctor Ignacio Franco.

IU

995   Gaona, Silvio. Capellanes de la Guerra de del Chaco (1932-1935). Asunción, 1964. 161 p. Portraits. 23 cm.

A discussion of the role played by military chaplains in Paraguay's Chaco War of 1932-1935. Scattered biographical information, as well as some portraits, are included for many of these men. The following are particularly featured: Joaquín Fariña Ferreira, Vicente Musa, Domingo Queirolo, Sixto Zenón Ferreira, José D. Molas, Jovino Bogado, Egidio Cardozo, Pedro J. Fariña Arce, José León Mercado, Juan Benítez Balmaceda, Benito Filemón Bogado, Florencio Fernández, Ricardo Müsth, Roberto Pérez Gaona, Vicente Arzamendia, Julio Duarte Ortellado, Carlos García, José Domingo Samudio, Felipe Barrios, Heliodoro Valenzuela, Arnaldo Lévera, Juan Bautista Ovelar, José Gabriel Escobar.

CtY FU NcU NIC NN

995a   _____. El clero en la guerra del 70. 2. ed. enriquecida con nuevos documentos. Asunción: El Arte, 1961. 168 p. 20 cm.

A work featuring biographical sketches for the following clerics who were active during the Paraguayan war: Juan Manuel Idoyaga, José del Carmen Moreno, Bonifacio Moreno, Francisco Hermógenes Flores, Elías Aguiar, Francisco Ignacio Maíz, Juan Galiano, Eustaquio Estigarribia, José Félix González, Francisco Solano Espinoza, José del Rosario Medina, Manuel Antonio Adorno, José Ramón González, Justo Carmelo Román, Francisco Hermosilla, Ramón Yahari, Juan de la Cruz Ortigoza, Manuel Antonio Palacios, Eugenio Bogado, Faustino Rodríguez, Vicente Antonio Bazán, Eliseo Patiño, Policarpo Valdovinos, José Joaquín Talavera, Juan Nepomuceno Arza, Martín Serapio Servín, Juan Evangelista Barrios, Jaime Antonio Corvalán, Santiago Esteban Narváez, José León Gavilán, Pedro León Caballero, Carlos Antonio Vázquez, Juan de Mata Ortellado, José Ramón Ferriol, Basiliano Landini, Antonio Medina, Gaspar Jacquet, Pedro José Acosta, Juan Vicente Benítez, José Aniceto Benítez, Angel Maramico, Juan Bautista Zalduondo, Olegario Borja, José María Velázquez, Justo David Bueno, Adonais Aurelio Urbieta, Rufino Insfrán, Domingo Tomás Candía, Angel Torres, Angel María Céspedes, Juan Bautista Villasboa, Roque A. Campos, Juan Bautista Céspedes, Blas Antonio Núñez, José Teodoro Escobar, Nicolás de Isasi, Felipe Santiago León, José Gaspar Téllez, Juan Manuel Aquino, Pedro Nolasco Aquino, José Donato Avahay, Sebastián Ramón Benegas, José Inocencio Gauts, José Domingo Guairare, Hilario Haedo, Leonardo Molinas, Pedro Baltazar Ortigoza, Martín José Román, Fermín Valdovinos, Francisco del Rosario Chuchi, Juan Francisco Vázquez, Francisco Javier Velastiqui, José Antonio Ortiz, José Gregorio Moreno, Santiago Cariay, Nazario de Jesús Sánchez, Juan Francisco Zayas, Rafael Ríos, Pedro P. Azuaga, Andrés Aranda, Gabriel Nazario Sánchez, Donato Gamarra, Manuel Vicente Moreno, Fidel Maíz, Claudio Arrúa, Dionisio Riveros, Pedro Juan Aponte, Blas Ignacio Duarte, Daniel Sosa, Mariano del Rosario Aguiar, Juan Carlos Casco, Tomás Antonio

HISTORY

Castelvi, Gerónimo Becchis, Bernardino Sandoval, Juan Facundo Gill, José Ignacio Acosta, Cecilio Román, José del Pilar Giménez, Pedro Pablo Benítez, José del Carmen Arzamendia, Miguel de Dios Pintos, Pedro Félix Cazal, Eliseo Díaz Cantero, Policarpo Páez, Gerónimo Dolores Ortiz, Juan Isidro Insaurralde, Claudio Astigarraga, Eleuterio Benítez, Francisco Pablo Aguilera, Bartolomé Aguirre, Feliciano Elizeche, Rufino Jara, José María Núñez, Alejandro Sosa, Manuel Antonio Corvalán.

CLU CtY CU FU ICU InU MU NBuU
NcU NIC NN NSyU PPT TxU WaU WU

996 <u>Historia edilicia de la ciudad de Asunción</u>. Asunción: Artes Gráficas Zamphiropolos, 1967. 397 p. Portraits. 24 cm.
A history of the city of Asunción, Paraguay, with special emphasis on the development of its architecture. Includes biographical sketches of Juan Salazar de Espinoza and Domingo Martínez de Irala. Also listing of the mayors of Asunción (1891-1960).

CU IU MH

997 Koebel, William Henry. <u>Paraguay</u>. London: T. F. Unwin, 1919. 348 p. Portraits. 23 cm.
A discussion of Paraguay's culture, geography, and history through 1870, including scattered biographical information for many people, mostly political leaders, involved in the development of this region. The following are particularly featured: Alvar Nuñez Cabeza de Vaca, Domingo Martínez de Irala, Juan de Garay, Hernando Arias de Saavedra (Hernandarias, pseud.), José Gaspar Rodríguez de Francia, Carlos Antonio López, Francisco Solano López. Alphabetical index of names.

DLC DN DS TxU

998 Llorens Mora, Alcides. <u>Héroes y mártires de la epopeya del Chaco</u>. Asunción: Editorial El Gráfico, 1969. Unpaged. (V. 1). Portraits. 32 cm.
Biographical sketches, accompanied by portraits, of Paraguayans who lost their lives in the Chaco War (1932-35).

CLSU CSt CtY CU-SB IaU IU KU MB
MH NbU NIC NNC TxU ViU

999 Marcet, José Carlos. <u>Datos para una reseña cronológica sobre los antecedentes, desarrollo y resultado de la guerra del Chaco</u>. Asunción: Ediciones Comuneros, 1974. 113 p. 19 cm.
Chronology of the principal events of the Chaco War (1932-1935) with a register of army officers' names.

CLU CtY CU NcU ViU

1000 Massare de Kostianovsky, Olinda. <u>La mujer paraguaya</u>: su participación en la Guerra Grande. Prólogo de R. Antonio Ramos. Asunción: Talleres Gráficos de la Escuela Técnica Salesiana, 1970. 125 p. Portraits. 20 cm.
An account of the role played by women in the 19th-century Paraguayan war against the Triple Alliance. Biographical information is given for many of these women and for the author of this work. They include Olinda Massare de Kostianovsky, Francisca Cabrera, Encarnación de Alviso, Ramona Martínez, Silveria Benítez de Yegros.

CFS CLSU CSt CSt-H CtY CU CU-S
CU-SB CU-SC IaU ICU IU KU LNHT MB
MH MnU MoSW MU NbU NcD NcU NIC
NmLcU NN NNC NSbSU NSyU OU TxU
ViU VtU WaU WU

1001 Micó, Tomás L. <u>Antecedentes históricos de Encarnación de Itapúa</u>. Asunción: Imprenta Nacional, 1975. 127 p. 24 cm.
A short history of Encarnación in the Itapúa department, Paraguay, covering the period from the 17th century to the beginning of the 19th century, and including biographical information and portraits for the following: Roque González de Santa Cruz, Fulgencio Yegros, Manuel Belgrano.

CLU CtY FU IU KyLoU MU NIC NmU
NN TxU

1002 Mosqueira, Silvano. <u>Semblanzas paraguayas</u>. Asunción: Talleres Nacionales de H. Kraus, 1908. 209 p. (V. 1). 24 cm.
Biographical essays on Manuel Domínguez, Cecilio Báez, Blas Garay, Héctor Velásquez, Manuel Gondra, Juan Silvano Godoy.

CtY CU DLC DPU IaU PPComm TxU

1003 O'Leary y Urdapilleta, Juan Emiliano. <u>El libro de los héroes</u>: páginas históricas de la guerra del Paraguay (Edición especial). Asunción: Librería La Mundial, 1970. 511 p. 17 cm.
A description of the people and events surrounding the Paraguayan war, including biographical information on the following heroes and patriots: José María Fariña, José Díaz, Caballero, Patricio Escobar, Natalicio Talavera, Silvestre Aveiro, José Matías Bado, Valois Rivarola, Florentín Oviedo, Sebastián Bullo, José Sebastián Ortigoza (Sargento Cuatí, pseud.), López Yacaré, José González (Real Peró, pseud.), Ezequiel Román, Romero, Saturio Ríos.

CSt CtY CU-SB ICarbS IU PPT

1004 Oxilia, Héctor. <u>Oratorio de Nuestra Señora de la Asunción y Panteón Nacional de los Héroes</u>. Asunción, 1969. 83 p. Portraits. 20 cm.

An essay about the Oratorio de Nuestra Señora de la Asunción y Panteón Nacional de los Héroes in Asunción, Paraguay, mainly through biographical sketches of the following heroes: Roque González de Santa Cruz, Fulgencio Yegros, Pedro Juan Caballero, Vicente Ignacio Iturbe, Antonio Tomás Yegros, José Gaspar Rodríguez de Francia, Carlos Antonio López, Francisco Solano López, Bernardino Caballero, José Eduvigis Díaz, Juan Sinforiano Bogarín, José Félix Estigarribia, Julia Miranda Cueto de Estigarribia.

    CLSU CLU CU-SB IaU ICarbS IU MoSW
    NIC NN NNC PSt TxU ViU

1005 Peña Villamil, Manuel. La fundación del Cabildo de la Asunción; antecedentes históricos y jurídicos. Asunción: Editorial El Gráfico, 1969. 183 p. 20 cm.
    A history of the cabildo of Asunción in the 16th century, including scattered biographical information on many people associated with it. The following are emphasized: Carlos Dubrín, Alonso Cabrera, Domingo Martínez de Irala.

    CFS CLSU CLU CSt CU CU-S CU-SB GU
    IaU ICU IU KU MB MH MiU MoSW MU
    NcD NcU NIC NN NNC OU PPT PPULC
    TxU ViU WaU

1006 Rodríguez Alcalá de González Oddone, Beatriz. Testimonios veteranos; evocando la guerra del Chaco. Asunción: Talleres Gráficos de Casa América, 1977. 608 p. Portraits. 20 cm.
    A collection of biographical sketches, many accompanied by portraits, of the following Paraguayan military men associated with the Chaco war between Paraguay and Bolivia (1929-1935): Edmundo Tombeur Ferraro, Manuel Domecq García, José Félix Estigarribia, Raimundo Rolón, Amancio Rufino Pampliega, Juan Bautista Ayala, Carlos J. Fernández, Alfredo Ramos, Andrés Ayala, Eugenio Ayala Velázquez, Juan N. Barrios, Dámaso Sosa Valdez, Rafael Franco, Feliciano Morales, Eugenio Alejandrino Garay, Atilio J. Benítez, Manlio Schenoni L., Félix Cabrera, Camilo Recalde, Federico W. Smith, Francisco Brizuela, Ramón L. Paredes, Carlos J. Fernández, José A. Ortiz, Francisco Andino, José Alfredo Bozzano, Basiliano Caballero Irala, Felipe Velilla, Virgilio Larrosa, Basilio Peralta, Isabelino Díaz Chaves, José de Jesús Cáceres, Carlos Domaniczky, Fructuoso Flores, Antonio E. González, Eugenio A. Garay, Sampson Harrison, Abdón Palacios, Carlos José Fernández, José A. Ortiz, Enrique Vázquez Ortellado, Clodomiro Morel, Augusto Guggiari, Enrique Páez, Gorgonio González Colman, Nicolás Delgado, Luis Irrazábal, Luis Santiviago, Camilo Recalde, Basiliano Caballero Irala, Antonio E. González, Atilio Benítez, Ramón L. Paredes, Félix Cabrera, Ramón Avalos Sánchez, Arturo Bray, José

Julián Sánchez, Juan Martincich, José Infante Rivarola, Pablo Lagerenza, Hermán Velilla, Víctor Cordobés, Florentino Ocampo, Alfredo Plá, Marcial Samaniego, Lorenzo Medina, Julio P. Saldívar, Atilio José Migone, Rodolfo Dávalos, Julio César Chaves, Juan E. Melgarejo, José María Cazal. Also portrait of Eusebio Ayala, president of Paraguay.

    DLC IU ViU

1007 Rolón Medina, Anastasio. Arquetipos de la raza: Hernando Arias de Saavedra; Roque González de Santa Cruz; José Félix Bogado. Asunción, 1961. 70 p. 19 cm.
    A collection of fairly lengthy biographies of the following three notable Paraguayans: Hernando Arias de Saavedra, Roque González de Santa Cruz, José Félix Bogado.

    CtY DLC ICN NN NSyU TxU

1008 Ruiz Fernández, Antonio. Los gobernantes del Paraguay; transmisión del poder público 25 de noviembre de 1886. Asunción: Imprenta de Obras, 1886. 36 p. 23 cm.
    A collection of biographical essays on the following 19th-century Paraguayan leaders: Bernardino Caballero, Patricio Escobar, Juan Antonio Jara, José del Rosario Miranda, José Segundo Decoud, Agustín Cañete, Juan G. González, Juan A. Meza, Pedro Duarte.

    MH TxU

1009 Vittone, Luis. Tres guerras, dos mariscales, doce batallas. Asunción: Editorial El Gráfico, 1967. 457 p. Portraits. 22 cm.
    A military history of Paraguay, giving details on three wars and twelve battles, beginning with the war for independence and ending with the 20th-century Chaco War. Brief scattered biographical information, concentrating on their involvements in these conflicts, is included for many Paraguayan military men. Portraits and longer essays are provided for Francisco Solano López and José Félix Estigarribia.

    CLS CLSU CSt CU IaU ICU InU IU
    KU MB MH MU NBuU NcU NIC NmLcU
    NN OU TxU

1010 Warren, Harris Gaylord. Paraguay, an Informal History. Norman: University of Oklahoma Press, 1949. 393 p. Portraits. 24 cm.
    An essay on Paraguayan history including biographical data on many people associated with it. The following are particularly featured: Alvar Núñez Cabeza de Vaca, Domingo Martínez de Irala, Bernardino de Cárdenas, José de Antequera y Castro, José Gaspar Rodríguez de Francia, María Josefa de Velasco, Carlos Antonio López, Francisco Solano López, Charles Ames Washburn, Fulgencio Yegros, José Félix Estigarribia, Higinio Morínigo.

CaBVa CaBViP CaBVaU CoU CSt-H CoU
DLC FU IdB IdU IU MiU MtU NBuU
NmLcU NN OO OrCS OrP OrU PHC PPAN
PPL PPT PSt Wa WaE WaS WaSp WaSpG
WaT

1011 Zinny, Antonio. Historia de los gobernantes
del Paraguay, 1535-1887. Buenos Aires: Impr.
y Librería de Mayo, 1887. 515 p. 23 cm.
    History of political leaders in Paraguay
from 1535-1887. Biographical data concentrating on activities while in office are included
for Pedro de Mendoza, Juan de Ayolas, Domingo
Martínez de Irala, Alvar Núñez Cabeza de
Vaca, Juan de Salazar Espinosa, Francisco
Ortiz de Vergara, Juan de Ortega, Juan Ortiz
de Zárate, Martín Suárez de Toledo, Diego
Ortiz de Zárate y Mendieta, Juan de Garay,
Alonso de Vera y Aragón, Juan Torres de Vera
y Aragón, Hernandarias de Saavedra, Fernando
de Zárate, Bartolomé Sandoval Ocampo, Juan
Caballero Bazán, Juan Ramírez de Velazco,
Diego Ramírez Valdez y de la Banda, García de
Mendoza, Diego Marín Negrón, Francisco de
Alfaro, Francisco González de Santa Cruz,
Manuel de Frías, Diego de Rego y Mendoza,
Luis de Céspedes García Xaría, Martín de Le-
desma Valderrama, Pedro de Lugo y Navarra,
Gregorio de Hinestrosa, Diego de Escobar Oso-
rio, Bernardino de Cárdenas, Sebastián León
y Zárate, Cristóbal de Garay y Saavedra, Juan
Blásquez de Valverde, Alonso Sarmiento Soto-
mayor y Figueroa, Juan Díez de Andino, Felipe
Rege Corvalán, Diego Ibáñez de Faría, Antonio
de Vera Mugica, Alonso Fernández Marcial,
Francisco de Monforte, Sebastián Félix de
Mendiola, Juan Rodríguez Cota, Antonio de
Escobar y Gutiérrez, Baltasar García Ros,
Manuel de Robles Lorenzana, Juan Gregorio
Bazán de Pedraza, Antonio Victoria, Diego de
los Reyes Balmaceda, José de Antequera y
Castro, Martín de Barúa, Bartolomé de Aldu-
nate, Ignacio de Soroeta, Antonio Ruiz de
Arellano, Cristóbal Rodríguez de Obelar,
Isidoro Mirones Benavente, Manuel Agustín de
Ruiloba y Calderón, Juan Caballero de Añasco,
Juan de Arregui, Bruno Mauricio de Zavala,
Martín José de Echauri, Rafael de la Moneda,
Marcos José de Larrazábal, Jaime Sanjust,
José Martínez Fontes, Fulgencio Yegros y Le-
desma, Carlos Morphi, Agustín Fernando de
Pinedo, Pedro Melo de Portugal, Joaquín de
Alós y Bru, Lázaro de Rivera, Bernardo de
Velazco, Manuel Gutiérrez, Eustaquio Gianini,
Pedro García, José Gaspar R. de Francia,
Juan Valeriano de Zevallos, Fulgencio Yegros,
Policarpo Patiño, Ramón Duré, José Domingo
Campos, Mariano Roque Alonzo, Carlos Antonio
López, Francisco Solano López, Cirilo Antonio
Rivarola, Salvador Jovellanos, Juan Bautista
Gill, Higinio Uriarte, Cándido Bareiro, Ber-
nardino Caballero, Patricio Escobar.

    IU

1012 Zubizarreta, Carlos. Cien vidas paraguayas.
Buenos Aires: Ediciones Nizza, 1961. 201 p.
20 cm.

    A collection of biographical sketches of
the following notable people associated with
the history of Paraguay who are no longer
living: Victorino Abente, Alejo García,
Sebastián Caboto, Pedro de Mendoza, Juan de
Ayolas, Juan de Salazar y Espinosa, Alvar
Núñez Cabeza de Vaca, Domingo Martínez de
Irala, Ruiz Díaz Melgarejo, Pedro Dorantes,
Nufrio de Chaves, Juan de Garay, Ruy Díaz de
Guzmán, Luis de Bolaños, Hernando Arias de
Saavedra (Hernandarias, pseud.), Hernando de
Trejo y Sanabria, Roque González de Santa
Cruz, Antonio Ruiz de Montoya, Bernardino de
Cárdenas, José de Antequera y Castro, Fernan-
do Mompox de Zayas, Rafael de la Moneda,
Pedro Lozano, Félix de Azara, Juan Francisco
de Aguirre, Amancio González, Pedro Vicente
Cañete, Fulgencio Yegros, Pedro Juan Cavalle-
ro, Vicente Ignacio Iturbe, Mauricio José
Troche, Manuel Atanasio Cabañas, José Félix
Bogado, José Gaspar de Francia, Fernando de
la Mora, Mariano Antonio Molas, Aimé Bonpland,
Carlos Antonio López, Juan Bautista Rivarola,
Juan Andrés Gelly, Andrés Gill, José Berges,
Francisco Solano López, Elisa Alicia Lynch,
José Díaz, José María Fariña, Fidel Maíz,
Pancha Garmendia, Natalicio Talavera, Fran-
cisco Wirner de Morgenstern, Bernardino Caba-
llero, Cirilo Antonio Rivarola, Juan Bautista
Gill, José Segundo Decoud, Facundo Machain,
Facundo Ynsfrán, Patricio Escobar, José de la
Cruz Ayala (Alón, pseud.), Ramón Zubizarreta,
Benigno Ferreira, Juan B. Egusquiza, Benjamín
Aceval, Juan Silvano Godoy, Blas Garay, Manuel
Domínguez, Fulgencio R. Moreno, Cecilio Báez,
Manuel Gondra, Viriato Díaz Pérez, Andrés
Barbero, Victoriano Abente, Guido Boggiani,
Adela Speratti, Celsa Speratti, Rafael Barret,
Ignacio A. Pane, Ramón Indalecio Cardozo,
Alejandro Guanes, Moisés Bertoni, Juan Sin-
foriano Bogarín, Arsenio López Decoud, Silvio
Pettirossi, Delfín Chamorro, Eloy Fariña
Núñez, Antolín Irala, Eligio Ayala, Adriano
Irala, Juan Belaieff, Eugenio Garay, Julián
de la Herrería, Manuel Ortiz Guerrero, Agus-
tín Barrios, Eusebio Ayala, José Félix Esti-
garribia, Gerónimo Zubizarreta, Francisco
Brizuela, Julio Correa, Félix Cabrera, Teo-
doro Rojas, Luis Irrazábal, Herib Campos
Cervera. Alphabetical index of names.

    CLSU CLU CSt CU DPU FU GU InU IU
MiU NcU NIC NN NSyU OCl OOxM RPB
ScU TxU

See also entry 474.

HISTORY--DICTIONARIES, ENCYCLOPEDIAS, and "WHO'S WHO"

1013 Kolinski, Charles J. Historical Dictionary
of Paraguay. Metuchen: Scarecrow Press,
1973. 282 p. 22 cm. (Latin American historical dictionaries. V. 8).

A historical dictionary of Paraguay, including biographical sketches of prominent Paraguayans.

AzU CaBVaŪ CaOTP CLSU CLU CoU CtY
CU DS FMU InU IU LU MnU NBuU
NSyU OKentU OOxM OU RPB Wa

LITERATURE

1014 Buzo Gómez, Sinforiano, comp. Indice de la poesía paraguaya. 3. ed. Asunción: Ediciones Nizza, 1959. 343 p. 20 cm.
      An anthology of Paraguayan poetry covering the period from preconquest to the 20th century. Brief biobibliographical sketches, emphaizing dates and places of birth and death, important accomplishments, and title of works, are included for the following people: Natalicio de María Talavera, Juan José Decoud, Próspero Pereira Gamba, Enrique D. Parodi, Adriano M. Aguiar, Venancio López, Delfín Chamorro, Liberato Rojas, José Cándido Diana, Fulgencio R. Moreno, Alejandro Guanes, Héctor L. Barrios, Ignacio A. Pane, Juan E. O'Leary, Francisco Luis Bareiro, Heriberto Campos Cervera, Daniel Jiménez Espinosa, Juan R. Dahlquist, Ricardo Marrero Marengo, Marcelino Pérez Martínez, Gomes Freire Esteves, Angel I. González, Fortunato Toranzos Bardel, Manuel Gamarra, Cecilio Báez, Victorino Abente, Rafael Barrett, Juan Pablo Casabianca, Eloy Fariña Núñez, Narciso R. Colman, Leopoldo A. Benítez, Doroteo Melgarejo, Fermín Domíngez, Adriano Irala, Néstor Eduardo Rivero, Pedro Pérez, Pablo Max Ynsfrán, Guillermo Molinas Rolón, Serviliana Guanes M. de Brugada, Leopoldo Ramos Giménez, Manuel Ortiz Guerrero, Francisco Martín Barrios, Facundo Recalde, Enriqueta Gómez Sánchez de Jiménez Espinoza, Anastasio Rolón Medina, J. Natalicio González, José Arturo Alsina, Fernando Rivarola, Carlos A. Jara, Jorge Báez, Francisco Ortiz Méndez, Aníbal Codas, Mariano A. Molas, José Concepción Ortiz, Vicente Lamas, Emilio Prats Gill, Heriberto Fernández, Raúl Battilana de Gásperi, Pedro Herrero Céspedes, María Josefina Plá Guerra Galvany, Luis Resquín Huerta, Ida Talavera de Fracchia, José Luis Nicora, Dora Gómez Bueno de Acuña, Néstar Rosa Mazó de Pérez, Alcira Veia de García Kinen, Basiliano Caballero Irala, Nathalie Bruel Perés, Julián Villamayor, Julio Correa, Eladio Battilana de Gásperi, Ricardo Hug de Belmont, Hipólito Sánchez Quell, Antonio Ortiz Mayans, Arístides Díaz Peña, Arnaldo Valdovinos, Mariano Celso Pedroso, Pedro P. Domínguez, Darío Gómez Serrato, Félix Fernández, Hérib Campos Cervera, Manuel Verón de Astrada, Renée Checa, Carlos Miguel Jiménez, Alba Luz Benítez Capurro (Alba Luz, pseud.), Hugo Rodríguez Alcalá, Optaciano Franco Vera, Augusto Roa Bastos, Alfredo Andrés Jacquet, Juan Silvano Díaz Pérez, Néstor Romero Valdovinos, Leopoldo Céspedes, Jesús Amado Recalde (Papotín, pseud.), Ezequiel González Alsina (Gastón Chevallier Paris, pseud.), Oscar Ferreiro, Elvio Romero, José Antonio Bilbao, Lola Gómez

Figueredo, Azucena Zelaya, Elsa Wiezell de Espínola, Rodrigo Díaz Pérez, José Luis Appleyard Urdapilleta, José Ricardo Mazó Ugarriza, Rubén Bareiro Saguier, José María Gómez Sanjurjo, María Luisa Artecona de Thompson, Ramiro Domínguez, Hugo Ríos Castillo, Carlos Villagra Marsal, Santiago Dimas Aranda.

  CSt DLC FU IU NIC NN

1015 Carlisle, Charles Richard, comp. Beyond the Rivers; an anthology of twentieth century Paraguayan poetry. Berkeley: Thorp Springs Press, 1977. 72 p. 23 cm.
      An anthology of Paraguayan poetry, including brief biobibliographical data on the following poets featured in the text: Alejandro Guanes, Juan E. O'Leary, Eloy Fariña Núñez, Guillermo Molinas, Rolón Heriberto Fernández, Herib Campos Cervera, Josefina Plá, Hugo Rodríguez-Alcalá, Augusto Roa Bastos, José Antonio Bilbao, Oscar Ferreiro, Elvio Romero, Elsa Weizell, José-Luis Appleyard, Ramiro Domínguez, Rubén Bareiro Saguier, Francisco Pérez-Maricevich, Esteban Cabanas, Miguel Angel Fernández, J. A. Rauskin, René Dávalos, Guido Rodríguez-Alcalá, Adolfo Ferreiro, Emilio Pérez-Chaves, Juan Manuel Marcos, Lourdes Espínola. Also biographical notes about the following translators: Bruce Cutler, Willis Knapp Jones, Edward James Schuster, Charles R. Carlisle.

  IU

1016 Centurión, Carlos R. Historia de las letras paraguayas. Buenos Aires: Editorial Ayacucho, 1947-51. 3 v. 20 cm.
      An anthology of Paraguayan literature (16th-20th centuries). Includes biobibliographical information throughout. Alphabetical index lists approximately 2,500 names.

  CtY DLC IEN IU LU MU NcU NIC NN
  OCl TxU ViU

1017 Concepción en las artes: la región norteña en la cultura de la nación paraguaya: exponentes de su narrativa: cuentos, relatos y páginas literarias de los escritores norteños del siglo XX. Concepción: Ediciones Futuro, 1973. 382 p. 21 cm.
      A colldction of stories by the following 20th-century northern Paraguayans, primarily from the city of Concepción, including biographical data: Pedro Alvarenga Caballero, Héctor Anzoátegui, Miguel Angel Aponte Albertini, Emilio Armele, Emilio Armele Jara, Nayib Armele, Eusebio Aveiro Lugo, Antonio Bonzi Penayo, Esteban Cabañas, Vicente Cabrera Carduz, Feliciano Cal, Carmelo Castiglioni Pérez, Leopoldo Centurión, Julián Milcíades Concha Miranda, Teodosio Cueto, Sergio Enrique Dacak Frutos, Leónidas Diana, Angélica Domínguez, Teófilo Domínguez, Martín de Goicoechea y Menéndez, Justa Pastora González Rivas, Carlos Grosso Sosa, Lucianao Gutiérrez, Juan Bautista Ibáñez, Alejandro Islas, Carmen Petrona

LITERATURE

López González de Guggiari, Laureano López Giménez, Thelma Virginia Mariño Calvi de Arestivo, Aurelia Martínez de Morillo, Reinaldo Martínez, Lorenzo Medina, Jorge Sebastián Miranda, José D. Molas, Cándido Núñez, Cecilio Ocariz, Juan Bernardo Otaño, Marcelino Pérez Martínez, José Domingo Portillo Benítez, Sergia Ramos Ferreira, Luis Resquín Huerta, Jorge Rodolfo Ritter, Marcial Suárez Ayala, Fortunato Toranzos Bardell, Carlos Zacarías Torres, Cáesar Torres Antúnez, Benigno Villa, Carlos Colombino.

CLU CSt CtY CU-S FU IU KU MU
NBuU NcD NmU NN NNC TxU ViU

1018 Marcos, Juan Manuel. El ciclo romántico modernista en el Paraguay. Asunción: Ediciones Criterio, 1977. 147 p. 21 cm.
An anthology of Paraguayan lyric poetry by writers representative of the "modernismo" in literature. Includes brief biobibliographical sketches of the following authors: José de Antequera y Castro, Natalicio Talavera, Enrique D. Parodi, Venancio Víctor López, Cecilio Báez, Juan Emiliano O'Leary, Ignacio Alberto Pane, Alejandro Guanes, Eloy Fariña Núñez, Leopoldo Ramos Giménez, Juan Natalicio González, Manuel Ortiz Guerrero, Julio Correa, Heliberto Fernández.

IU

1018a Pecci, Antonio. Teatro breve del Paraguay. Asunción: Ediciones Napa, 1981. 138 p. 23 cm. (Libro paraguayo del mes, año 1, no. 6, marzo de 1981).
An anthology of Paraguayan drama corresponding to the last 50 years, including biobibliographical sketches of the following authors featured in the text: Julio Correa, Josefina Plá, José Luis Appleyard, Ramiro Domínguez, Alcibíades González Delvalle, Pedro Molinier, Ovidio Benítez Pereira, Tadeo Zarratea, Carlos Colombino.

IU

1019 Pérez-Maricevich, Francisco, comp. Breve antología del cuento paraguayo. Asunción: Ediciones Comuneros, 1969. 199 p. 19 cm.
An anthology of Paraguayan short stories, including brief biographical data on the following writers: Rafael Barrett, Eloy Fariña Núñez, José Santiago Villarejo, Gabriel Casaccia, Augusto Roa Bastos, Josefina Plá, Hugo Rodríguez Alcalá.

CLSU CU-SB GU KU IU MB MoSW MU
NcU PPULC TxU ViU WaU WU

1020 _____. La poesía y la narrativa en el Paraguay. Asunción: Editorial del Centenario, 1969. 72 p. 22 cm. (Colección ensayos. V. 1).
A history and critical analysis of the literary movements of both prose and poetry in Paraguay, 1850-present, including brief biobibliographical information on the following Paraguayan writers: Alejandro Guanes, Juan E. O'Leary, Ignacio A. Pane, Victorino Abente, Pablo Max Insfrán, Guillermo Molinas Rolón, Fortunato Toranzos Bardel, Manuel Ortiz Guerrero, Natalicio González, Leopoldo Ramos Giménez, Facundo Recalde, Heriberto Fernández, Vicente Lamas, José Concepción Ortiz, H. Sánchez Quell, Eloy Fariña Núñez, Elvio Romero, Ramiro Domínguez, Miguel Angel Guillén-Roa, Luis María Martínez, Herib Campos Cervera, Julio Correa, Josefina Plá, Hugo Rodríguez-Alcalá, Arnaldo Valdovinos, Augusto Roa Bastos, Elvio Romero, Oscar Ferreiro, Ezequiel González Alsina, José Antonio Bilbao, Manuel Verón de Astrada, Ramiro Domínguez, José-Luis Appleyard, Rubén Bareiro Saguier, Gustavo Gatti, José María Gómez Sanjurjo, Ricardo Mazó, Carlos Villagra Marsal, Miguel Angel Fernández, Esteban Cabañas, Roque Vallejos, Carlos Antonio López, Gabriel Cassaccia, Ildefonso Antonio Bermajo, Eugenio Bogado, Rafael Barrett, Martín de Goycoechea Menéndez, José Rodríguez-Alcalá, Juan Stefanich, Juan Natalicio González, Leopoldo Centurión, Roque Capece Faraone, María Teresa Lamas de Rodríguez-Alcalá, María Concepción Leyes de Chaves, José Santiago Villarejo, Augusto Roa Bastos, Carlos Zubizarreta, Juan F. Bazán, José María Rivarola Matto, Reinaldo Martínez, Jorge Ritter, Carlos Garcete, Mario Halley Mora, Anairis Chaves de Ferreiro, María Talavera, Diógenes Decoud, Francisco F. Fernández, Juan Crisóstomo Centurión, José de la Cruz Ayala, Adriano M. Aguiar, Z. Albornoz y Montoya, Miguel González Medina, Charles Frutos, Luis Alvarez, David de Valladares, Eudoro Acosta Flores.

CLSU CoFS CSt CtY CU-SB CU FU IaU
ICU InU IU KU LU MB MH MoSW MU
NcU NjR NN NNC ViU WaU WU

1021 Rodríguez Alcalá, Hugo. Historia de la literatura paraguaya. México: Ediciones De Andrea, 1970. 196 p. 20 cm. (Colección Studium. V. 63).
Basically the same as the Asunción 1971. ed. (See entry 1022.)

AAP CaBVaU CaQMM CFS CLSU CoFS CSt
CtY CU CU-SB DeU FMU FU GU IaAS
IaU InU IU KU KyU LNHT MB MdBJ
MH MiDW MiU MoSW MU MWiW NbU
NBuC NBuU NcD NIC NjP NjR NN NNC
NNCU-G OCU PPiU PSt TNJ TU TxDaM
TxHR ViU WaU WiU WU

1022 _____. Historia de la literatura paraguaya. Asunción: Colegio de San José, 1971. 202 p. Portraits. 22 cm.
A history of Paraguayan literature covering from the early 16th to 20th century. Includes biographical sketches of many writers and personalities of the period as well as portraits. Those featured:

16th-18th centuries: Luis de Miranda de Villafaña, Martín Barco de Centenera, Ruy Díaz de Guzmán, José de Antequera y Castro, Pedro Lozano.

19th century: Fulgencio Yegros, José Gaspar de Francia, Juan Andrés Gelly, Carlos Antonio López, Francisco Solano López, Fidel Maíz, Natalicio Talavera, Juan José Decoud, José Segundo Decoud, Juan Crisóstomo Centurión, Juan Silvano Godoi, Victoriano Abente, Diógenes Decoud, Héctor Francisco Decoud.

20th century: Cecilio Báez, Juan E. O'Leary, Blas Garay, Manuel Gondra, Manuel Domínguez, Fulgencio R. Moreno, Arsenio López Decoud, Alejandro Guanes, Eloy Fariña Núñez, Pablo Max Ynsfrán, Justo Pastor Benítez, J. Natalicio González, Justo Prieto, Arturo Bray, Luis de Gasperi, Carlos Zubizarreta, Efraín Cardozo, Julio César Chaves, Hipólito Sánchez Quell, Carlos R. Centurión, Manuel Ortiz Guerrero, Leopoldo Centurión, Guillermo Molinas Rolón, Leopoldo Ramos Giménez, Facundo Recalde, Heriberto Fernández, Vicente Lamas, José Concepción Ortiz, Francisco Ortiz Méndez, Dora Gómez Bueno de Acuña, Julio Correa, Herib Campos, Josefina Plá, Augusto Roa Bastos, Elvio Romero, José Antonio Bilbao, César Alonso, Rubén Bareiro Saguier, José Luis Appleyard, Ramiro Domínguez, Elsa Wiezell de Espínola, Miguel Angel Fernández, Francisco Pérez-Maricevich, Roque Vallejos Pérez Garay, Concepción Leyes de Chaves, José María Rivarola Matto, B. Gabriel Cassaccia, José Arturo Alsina, Roque Centurión Miranda, Luis Ruffinelli.

Contemporary poets after 1940: Ezequiel González Alsina, Oscar Ferreiro, Rodrigo Díaz-Pérez, Carlos Villagra Marsal, Ricardo Mazo, María Luisa Artecona de Thompson, José María Gómez Sanjurjo, Esteban Cabañas, Luis María Martínez, Teresa Lamas de Rodríguez Alcalá. Birth dates only for Rigoberto Rontao Meza and Félix Fernández. Alphabetical index of names.

CNoS CtY CU-S FU GU IaU InU IU KU MiEM MoSW MU NcD NcU NIC NmLcU NSyU OCl OrU PPT TxU VtU

1023 _____. La literatura paraguaya. Buenos Aires: Centro Editor de América Latina, 1968. 64 p. 20 cm. (Enciclopedia literaria. V. 39. España e Hispanoamérica).

An anthology of Paraguayan literature from 16th to 20th centuries. Includes brief bio-bibliographical sketches of the following writers:

19th century: Fulgencio Yegros, José Gaspar de Francia, Carlos Antonio López, Francisco Solano López, Fidel Maíz, Juan Silvano Godoy.

20th century: Cecilio Báez, Blas Garay, Manuel Gondra, Fulgencio R. Moreno, Juan E. O'Leary, Alejandro Guanes, Eloy Fariña, José Rodríguez-Alcalá, Manuel Ortiz Guerrero, Efraím Cardozo, Justo Prieto, Augusto Roa

Bastos, Josefina Plá, Elvio Romero, Rubén Bareiro Saguier, Arturo Alsina.

AU CFS CLSU CNoS CoFS CSt CtW CU FU GU IaAS ICIU ICU INS InU IU KU KyU LNHT MB MdU MH MiU MoSW MWelC NBuU NcD NIC NjR NmU NNC NSyU OkU PPiU PPT RPB TU TxDaM TxLT TxU ViU VtU WU

1024 Rodríguez Alcalá, José. Antolojía paraguaya. Asunción: Casa editora: Talleres Nacionales de H. Kraus, 1910. 163 p. 22 cm.

An anthology of Paraguayan poetry of the 19th-20th century. Includes biobibliographical sketches of Natalicio Talavera, Venancio V. López, Juan Francisco Pérez.

CSt DLC FU IU NcU TxU WaU

1025 Vallejos Pérez Garay, Roque, comp. Antología crítica de la poesía paraguaya contemporánea. Asunción: Editorial Don Bosco, 1968. 195 p. 19 cm. (Colección ñandutí literario. V. 4).

An anthology of contemporary Paraguayan poetry including biobibliographical information on the following authors: José Antonio Bilbao, Herib Campos Cervera, Oscar Ferreiro, Josefina Plá, Augusto Roa Bastos, Hugo Rodríguez Alcalá, José Luis Appleyard, Manuel E. B. Arguello, Rubén Barreiro Saguier, Ramiro Domínguez, José María Gómez Sanjurjo, Mario Halley Mora, Elvio Romero, Marialuisa Artecona de Thompson, Carlos Villagra Marsal, Esteban Cabañas, Miguel Angel Fernández, Luis María Martínez, Francisco Pérez Maricevich, J. A. Rauskin, Mauricio Schvartzman, Roque Vallejos, René Dávalos, Adolfo Ferreiro, Osvaldo González Real, José Carlos Rodríguez, Guido Rodríguez Alcalá, Lincoln Silva.

CaBVaU CLSU CSt DPU IaU ICU INS IU KU MaU MB MH MiDW MU NbU NBuU NIC NjR PSt TNJ TU TxU ViU VtMiM WU

1026 Wey, Walter. La poesía paraguaya; historia de una incógnita. Traducción del portugués por Haydée Lagomarsino y Gladys Torres. Montevideo: Biblioteca Alfar, 1951. 109 p. 20 cm.

A history of Paraguayan literature from the 16th century to the 1940s. Includes bio-bibliographical information throughout. The following are particularly featured: Eloy Fariña Núñez, Alejandro Guanes, Julio Correa, Hugo Rodríguez Alcalá, Augusto Roa Bastos, Helvio Romero, Enrique Parodi, Juan O'Leary, Delfín Chamorro, Fulgencio R. Moreno, Ignacio Alberto Pane, Pablo Max Insfrán, Manuel Ortiz Guerrero.

CSt DLC IaU IU MH MU NBuU NcD NcU NN OCL PU WaU TxU

MUSIC

1027 Agrupación Folklórica Guaraní, Buenos Aires.
<u>Concierto de la Agrupación Folklórica Guaraní</u>,
Institución Cultural Paraguaya, domingo, 15
de setiembre, a los 10 horas de la mañana.
José Asunción Flores, Ariel Ramírez y Emilio
Vaesken. Programa. Buenos Aires: n.d.
12 p. Portraits. 23 cm.
   A concert program featuring short biographical sketches and portraits for the performers. They include the following 20th-
century Paraguayan musicians: José Asunción
Flores, Emilio Vaesken, Ariel Ramírez, Jacinto Herrera.

   IU TxU

1028 <u>Biografía de nuestros artistas</u>. Asunción:
Tall. Gráf. de la Impr. Trujillo, 1959. 49 p.
Portraits. 20 cm. (Colección Ocara poty cué
mi. V. 1).
   Brief biographical essays accompanied by
portraits on 20th-century Paraguayan musicians.
Birthplace, dates, and achievements in the
field of music are supplied for Manuel Ortiz
Guerrero, Quirino Báez Allende, Remberto Gi-
ménez, Juan Max Boettner, Agustín Barrios,
Luis Alberto del Paraná, Sila Godoy, Emiliano
R. Fernández, Juan Carlos Moreno González.

   IU NIC TxU

1029 Boettner, Juan Max. <u>Música y músicos del
Paraguay</u>. Asunción: Edición de Autores Aso-
ciados, 1956. 294 p. 26 cm.
   A history of Paraguayan music including
biographical data, in varying amounts, on the
following people associated with it: Quintana,
Francisco Sauvageot de Dupuis, Ana Monnier de
Dupuy, Indalecio Odrisola, Tomás Amavet,
Francisco Acuña de Figueroa, José Giuffra,
Francisco José Debali, Agustín Pío Barrios,
Remberto Giménez, José Asunción Flores, Juan
Carlos Moreno, Gustavo Sosa Escalada, Quirino
Báez Allende, Cayo Sila Godoy. Alphabetical
index of Paraguayan musicians with brief bio-
graphical notes ound in p. 258-286.

   CU DPU FTaSU IaU InU IU MH NIC
   NN OCl TxU ViU WU

See also entry 937.

RELIGION

1030 Anglés y Gortari, Matías de. <u>Los jesuítas en
el Paraguay</u>. Copia del informe que hizo el
general d. Mathías de Anglés y Gortari, corregidor del Potosí, sobre los puntos que han
sido causa de las discordias sucedidas en la
ciudad de la Asunción, de la provincia del
Paraguay, y motivaron la persecución de d.
Josef de Antequera, de parte de los regulares
de la Compañía. Reimpresa según la edición
de 1769, hecha en Madrid en la Imprenta real

de la "Gaceta." Asunción del Paraguay: A.
de Uribe y Cía., 1896. 215 p. 17 cm.
(Biblioteca paraguaya).
   An account of the discords which developed
in the city of Asunción during the 18th century and which resulted in the persecution of
José de Antequera by the Jesuits. Brief scattered biographical information is given for
many people, mostly clerics, involved in this
aspect of Paraguay's history. The following
are particularly featured: Diego de los
Reyes, Matheo Sánchez, Bartolomé de Niebla,
Hilario Vázquez, Balthasar García Ros, Roque
de Herrera, Martín de Chavarri y Vallejo,
Juan Caballero de Añasco, Dionysio de Otazu,
Andrés Benítez, Joseph de Urunaga.

   DLC ICU MH NIC PAU PBm PPULC

1031 Baucke, Florián. <u>Memorias del P. Florián
Paucke</u>, 1748-1767, por A. V. Buenos Aires:
Impr. Encuad. y Esterrotipia de L. Mirau,
1900. 161 p. 18 cm.
   The memoirs of the 18th-century Jesuit
Florián Baucke, including biographical information for this man and for others with
whom he was associated. The following are
emphasized: Florián Paucke, Aletín, Nevedag-
nack, Cathaalín, Francisco Javier de Echagüe,
Francisco Burgés, Pedro de Zeballos.

   CU NcU WU

1032 Blanco, José María. <u>Historia documentada de
la vida y gloriosa muerte de los padres Roque
González de Santa Cruz, Alonso Rodríguez y
Juan del Castillo</u> de la Compañía de Jesús
mártires del Caaro e Yjuhi, con un prólogo de
Rómulo D. Carbia. Buenos Aires: S. de Amo-
rrortu, 1929. 742 p. Portraits.
   Biographical essay about Roque González
de Santa Cruz, Alonso Rodríguez, and Juan del
Castillo, Jesuits in Paraguay. (See also
entry 1032a.)

   CU WU

1032a _____. <u>Los mártires de Caaró e Yjuhí</u>; com-
pendio de la historia de los padres Roque
González de Santa Cruz, Alonso Rodríguez y
Juan del Castillo, primeros mártires de las
misiones guaraníticas. Ilustraciones de
Mastrojanni. Buenos Aires: Editorial Surgo,
1931. 161 p. Portraits. 23 cm.
   An abbreviated version of the 1929 edition. (See entry 1032.)

   CU DLC FU IU TxU

1033 Capdevielle, Bernardo. <u>Misiones jesuíticas
en el Paraguay</u>. 2. ed. ampliada. Asunción:
Impr. y Librería "La Mundial," 1934. 262 p.
Portraits. 19 cm.
   A history of Jesuit missions in Paraguay,
covering the period from the 17th to the 19th
centuries. Brief scattered biographical information, along with some portraits, included

for many people involved with this aspect of Paraguay's history, as well as longer sections on Antonio Ruiz de Montoya and Bernardino de Cárdenas.

AzU DLC ICN MH MiU

1034 Córdoba, Antonio Santa Clara. Los franciscanos en el Paraguay. Buenos Aires, 1937. 226 p. Portraits. 21 cm.

A history of the involvement of the Franciscan religious order in Paraguay, covering the period from 1537 to 1937. Scattered biographical information is included for many people, mostly clerics, who were involved in this aspect of Paraguay's development. Two sections containing biographical essays of various lengths are also provided, one accompanied by a portrait of Luis de Bolaños. The following are particularly featured: Juan de Salazar de Espinosa, Bernardo de Armenta, Alonso Lebrón, Alonso de San Buenaventura, Luis de Bolaños, Juan de San Bernardo, Gabriel de la Anunciación, Alonso de la Torre, Juan de Escobar, Juan de Córdoba, Gregorio de Osuna, Luis Gámez, Antonio Arredondo, Juan de Barrios y Toledo, Pedro Fernández de la Torre, Juan del Campo, Martín Ignacio de Loyola, Bernardino de Cárdenas, Gabriel de Guilestegui, José de Palos, José Cayetano Palavicino, Luis de Velazco y Maeda, Pedro García de Panés, Basilio Antonio López.

CtY CU CU-I DLC ICN NcD NN

1035 La evangelización en el Paraguay: cuatro siglo de historia. Asunción: Ediciones Loyola, 1979. 217 p. 22 cm.

A collection of essays discussing various aspects of the evangelization of Paraguay from colonial times to the present day. Scattered biographical information is included for many people, mostly clerics, associated with this movement. The following are particularly featured: Bernardo de Armenta, Alonso de San Buenaventura, Luis de Bolaños, Juan de San Bernardo, Martín Ignacio de Loyola, Antonio Ruiz de Montoya, Nichole du Toict, Antonio Sepp, Juan de Escandón, Gaspar Astete, Simón Bandini, Cristóbal Altamirano, Nicolás Yapuguay, Gabriel de Peralta, José Bernardino Servín, Carlos Penayos de Castro, Antonio Fernández de Valenzuela, José Francisco Armancio González y Escobar, José Gaspar Rodríguez de Francia, Carlos Antonio López, Basilio Antonio López, Marco Antonio Maíz, Juan Gregorio Urbieta, Manuel Vicente Moreno, Fidel Maíz, Pedro Juan Aponte, Juan Sinforiano Bogarín, Juan José Aníbal Mena Porta.

IU

1035a Lozano, Pedro. Historia de la Compañía de Jesús en la provincia del Paraguay. Madrid: Viuda de M. Fernández, 1754-55. 2 v. 28 cm.

A history of the Jesuits in Paraguay province, including biographical information on the following:

V. 1: Juan de Atienza, Balthasar de Piñas, Diego López de Salazar, Alonso de Barzana, Juan Saloni, Pedro de Aññasco, Diego de Torres Bollo.

V. 2: Martín de Aranda Valdivia, Horacio Vechi, Diego de Montalván, Francisco Salzedo, Juan Romero, Hernando de León Garavito, Martín Urtafun Xavier, Balthasar Seña.

CtY DLC InU MB NN NNH OCX RPJCB TxU WU

1035b _____. Historia de la Compañía de Jesús en la provincia del Paraguay. Madrid: Impr. de la Viuda de M. Fernández, 1754-55. Farnborough, Eng.: Gregg International Publishers, 1970. 2 v. 31 cm.

Same as the 1754-55 edition. (See entry 1035a.)

CSt CU IU MoU NhD

1036 Peramas, José Manuel. Josephi Emmanuelis Peramas, De vita et moribus sex sacerdotum paraguaycorum. Faventiae: Ex typ. Archii, 1791. 299 p. 22 cm.

A collection of biographical sketches of the following 18th-century Jesuits associated with the history of Paraguay: Emmanuel de Vergara, Emmanuel Querini, Petrus Joannes Andreu, Joannes Escandon, Vicentius Sans, Segismundus Griera. (See also entry 1038.)

CtY-D DLC InU NN RPJCB

1037 _____. Josephi Emmanuelis Peramas, De vita et moribus tredecim virorum paraguaycorum. Faventiae: Ex typ. Archii, 1793. 462 p. 21 cm.

A collection of biographical sketches of the following 18th-century Jesuits associated with the history of Paraguay: Ignatius Morro, Joannes Mesner, Joannes Suarez, Ignatius Chome, Franciscus Ruiz de Villegas, Joannes Angelus Amilaga, Antonius del Castillo, Stephanus Pallozius, Clemens Baigorri, Franciscus Urrejola, Joachimus Iribarren, Cosmas Agullo, Martinus Schmid. Also biography of Jose Manuel Peramas.

DLC InU

1038 _____. Vida y obra de seis humanistas. Traducción de Antonio Ballus. Prólogo de Guillermo Furlong. Buenos Aires: Editorial Huarpes, 1946. 300 p. 23 cm. (Biblioteca americana de escritores coloniales. V. 1).

Translation of De vita et moribus sex sacerdotum paraguaycorum. (See entry 1036.)

IU TxU

1039 Los salesianos en el Paraguay; reseña histórica, 1895-1960; homenaje filial al Rvmo. P. Renato Ziggiotti. Asunción: 1960. 115 p. 22 cm. Portraits.

RELIGION

A history of the Salesians in Paraguay from 1896 to 1960. Many people, mostly clerics, are mentioned in connection with the work of this religious order. Additional biographical information, as well as some photographs, included for the following: Juan Bosco, Luis Lasagna, Juan Sinforiano Bogarín, Domingo Queirolo, Emilio Sosa Gaona, Vicente Gastavino, Ernesto Pérez Acosta, Pedro Foglia, Benito Conte Grand, Pablo Rojas, Juan M. Cassenallo, Pedro Garnero, Salvador de Bonis, Livio Farina, Justo Bottignoli, Celestino Soba, Augusto García, Sebastián Pinto Correa, Ricardo Richter, Valentín Gottardi, Carlos Dungani, Gregorio Acosta, Jorge Bongiovanni.

CLU

1039a Storni, Hugo. Catálogo de los jesuitas de la Provincia del Paraguay (Cuenca del Plata) 1585-1768. Roma: Institutum Historicum S. I., 1980. 350 p. 20 cm. (Subsidia ad historiam S. I. Bibliothecae Instituti Historici S. I. Series minor. V. 9).
An alphabetical listing of the Jesuits associated with the Province of Paraguay (1585-1786), including brief biographical data. Contains the following indexes: first name, country of origin, Jesuit province of origin.

ICL

1040 Xarque, Francisco. Insignes missioneros de la Compañía de Jesús en la provincia del Paraguay. Estado presente de sus missiones en Tucumán, Paraguay, y Río de la Plata, que comprehende su distrito. Que remite, y consagra á los religiosos operarios, y apostólicos missioneros, que al presente prosiguen sus heroycas empressas, por mano del padre Thirso Gonçalez de Santalla. En Pamplona: J. Micón, impressor, 1687. 432 p. 21 cm.
A work dealing with the activities of the Jesuit order in Paraguay during the colonial period, featuring biographical information on the following clerics: Simón Mazeta, Francisco Díaz Taño, Juan Antonio Solinas, Pedro Ortiz de Zárate.

IU

1041 Zinny, Antonio. Cronología de los obispos del Paraguay. Buenos Aires: Imprenta Europea, 1887. 29 p. 26 cm.
A chronology of the bishops of Paraguay (1584-1879) in the form of sketches. The following bishops are featured: Juan de Barros y Toledo, Pedro Fernández de la Torre, Fernán González de la Cuesta, Juan del Campo, Luis López de Solís, Juan de Almaraz, Alonso de Guerra, Tomás Vázques de Liaño, Baltasar de Covarrubia, Martín Ignacio de Loyola, Reginaldo de Lizárraga, Lorenzo Pérez del Grado, Tomás de Torres, Agustín de Vega, Leandro de Garfias, Melchor Prieto, Cristó-

bal de Aresti, Francisco de la Serna, Bernardino de Cárdenas, Francisco Godoy, Gabriel de Guilléstegui, Fernando de Balcázar, Faustino de las Casas, Sebastián de Pastrana, Pedro de Durana, Martín de Sarricolea y Olea, José de Palós, José Cayetano Palavecino, Fernando Pérez de Oblitas, Manuel López de Espinosa, Manuel Antonio de la Torre, Luis de Velazco, José Priego y Caro, Lorenzo Suárez de Cantillana, Francisco Arquellada, Nicolás Videla del Pino, Pedro Ignacio García de Panés, José Vicente de Orué, Basilio López, Marco Antonio Maíz, Juan Gregorio Urbieta, Manuel Antonio Palacios, Fidelis de Avola, Manuel Vicente Moreno, Fidel Maíz, Claudio Arrúa, Dionisio Riveros, Juan Aponte.

MH

See also entries 995, 995a.

WOMEN

1042 Urbieta Rojas, Pastor. La mujer paraguaya; esquema historiográfico. Prólogo de Juan Boggino; xilografías de Lotte Schulz. Asunción, 1962. 81 p. 18 cm. (Colección Paraguay).
A short tribute to the accomplishments of past and present-day Paraguayan women, citing in particular their contributions to education and the arts. Scattered biographical information is given for many of these women. Among those particularly featured are Mencía de Calderón de Sanabria, María de Sanabria, Juana de Lara, Josefa Facunda Speratti de Yegros, Margarita Quiñones y Osorio, Luisa Balet, Asunción Escalada, Rosa Peña de González, Joaquina Machaín, Manuela González Filisbert de Domínguez.

CtY   CU   FU   ICarbS   InU   IU   KyLoU
LNHT   MU   NcU   NIC   NN   NSyU   TxU

See also entries 956, 1000.

WOMEN--DICTIONARIES, ENCYCLOPEDIAS, and "WHO'S WHO"

1043 Ríos Velazco de Caldi, Ramona Luisa. Diccionario de la mujer guaraní. Asunción: Editorial Siglo Veintiuno, 1977. 327 p. 21 cm.
Biographical dictionary containing information on approximately 1,000 Paraguayan women from all periods of history.

CU-S   IU   KU

Uruguay

ARMED FORCES

See entry 1122.

ART

1044 Dieste, Eduardo. Teseo: los problemas del
arte: clasicismo, academicismo, impresionis-
mo, cubismo, futurismo, expresionismo, crónicas. Prólogo de Esther de Cáceres. Montevideo: Ministerio de Instrucción Pública y
Previsión Social, 1964. 227 p. 20 cm.
(Biblioteca Artigas. Colección de clásicos
uruguayos. V. 43).
     An essay on the philosophy of art, in-
cluding biographico-critical studies about
the following notable Uruguayan artists of
the 20th century: Bernabé Michelena, Adolfo
Pastor, José Cúneo, Carmelo de Arzadum,
Andrés Etchebarne Bidarte, Humberto Causa,
Pedro Figari.

     CLU CtY CU DPU FTaSU FU IaU ICU
     IU KMK KyU LU LU-NO MdBJ MH MiEM
     MnU MoSW MoU MU N NBuU NcD NcU
     NIC NNC NSyU OU PPiU TNJ TU TxU
     WU WvU

1045 Imágenes 1980; trece pintores uruguayos.
Montevideo: Ministerio de Educación y Cul-
tura, 1977. Unpaged. Portraits. 22 cm.
     Stylistic analyses of Uruguayan artists
of the last half of the 20th century. In-
cluded are dates, birthplace, major exhibi-
tions, and awards won for the following in-
dividuals: Mario Arroyo, Norman Botrill,
Jorge Damiani, Tulio Carbone, Atilio Buriano,
Miguel A. Guerra, Osvaldo Paz, Jorge Páez
Vilaro, Leonel Pérez Molinari, Miguel Angel
Pareja, Sara Pérez, Angel Tejera, Rodolfo
Kliche.

     IU

1046 Laroche, Ernesto. Algunos pintores y escultores. Montevideo: Morales Hermanos, Impresores, 1938. 215 p. Portraits. 25 cm.
     Collection of biographical essays on the
following notable Uruguayan artists of the
19th and 20th centuries: Juan Manuel Blanes,
Eduardo Carbajal, Diógenes Héquet, Juan Manuel
Ferrari, Domingo Laporte, Carlos María Herrera,
Pedro Blanes Viale, Carlos Federico Sáez,
Manuel Larravide, Carlos Grethe, Carlos Cas-
tells, Juan Luis Blanes, Federico Renóm, José
Felipe Parra, Domingo Mora, José María Rodrí-
guez Lozada, Antonio Cabral Bejarano, Luis
Graner, Jan Peeter Van Bredael, Siene de
Maline, Pieter Momper, Thomas Van Apshoven,
Jan Van Goyen, Francisco Octavio Tassaert.

     DLC DPU NN

1047 _____. Algunos pintores y escultores. 3.
ed. Montevideo: Ministerio de Instrucción
Pública y Previsión Social, República Oriental del Uruguay, 1939. 214 p. Portraits.
25 cm.
     Biographical essays on the following not-
able native Uruguayan painters and sculptors
and foreign artists associated with the fine
arts in Uruguay during the 19th century and
who are represented in the "Museo Nacional de
Bellas Artes": Juan Manuel Blanes, Eduardo
Carbajal, Diógenes Héquet, Juan M. Ferrari,
Domingo Laporte, Carlos María Herrera, Pedro
Blanes Viale, Carlos Federico Sáez, Manuel
Larravide, Carlos Grethe, Carlos Castells,
Juan Luis Blanes, Federico Renóm, José Felipe
Parra, Domingo Mora, José María Rodríguez
Lozada, Antonio Cabral Bejarano, Luis Graner,
Jan van Goyen.

     CSmH CtY DLC DPU IU NBB NcU NSyU
     OClMA PPPM

1048 Montevideo. Biblioteca del Poder Legislativo.
Plásticos uruguayos; compilado hasta el año
1970 por la Biblioteca del Poder Legislativo.
Montevideo: La Biblioteca, 1975. 2 v.
24 cm.
     Biographies of over 600 20th-century
Uruguayan artists with illustrations and
examples of artists' signatures.

     IU

1049 Torrens Fontán, María Luisa. 12 [i.e. Doce]
pintores nacionales por María Luisa Torrens.
Montevideo: Ediciones de la Plaza, 1979.
78 p. Portraits. 22 cm.
     Collection of critical essays on 20th-
century Uruguayan artists. Included is a

portrait, a chronology of important events, a
list of awards and exhibitions for the follow-
ing artists: Oscar García Reins, Vicente
Martín, Jorge Damiani, Hugo Longa, Manuel
Pailos, Luis Solari, José Pedro Castigliolo,
María Freire, Miguel Angel Guerra, Enrique
Medina Ramela, Hermenegildo Sabat, Gustavo
Vázquez.

IU

BIOGRAPHY (MISCELLANEOUS)

1050   Alava, César de. Cien años de vida: historia
completa de Villa Colón: Colón y Melilla,
1872-1972. Montevideo: Impr. García, 1973.
156 p. 20 cm.
History of Colón, Uruguay, from 1872-1972
featuring biographical material and dates and
achievements of the following individuals in-
fluential in the development of the city:
Cornelio Guerra Botet, Perfecto Giot, Román
Freire, Arturo Mossman Gros, Delia Castellanos de Etchepare, Juan Carlos Fioroni, César
Máximo Rapalini.

CSt CtY Iu MB MU NcU NN WU

1051   Apolant, Juan Alejandro. Operativo Patagonia;
historia de la mayor aportación demográfica
masiva a la Banda Oriental, con la nómina
completa, filaciones y destino de las familias
pobladoras. Montevideo: Impr. Letras, 1970.
429 p. 24 cm.
A history of the largest emigration of
people to Montevideo, occurring between 1778
and 1784. Biographical sketches of the families who came by ship at that time are featured. Information, including names, relationships and some physical descriptions of
important members, is given for approximately
400 families who were part of this settlement.

CFS CLSU CSt CtY CU CU-SB FU GU
ICU InU IU MB MH MoSW MU NcU NIC
NjP NN NNC PPT TxU ViU

1052   Araújo, Orestes. Perfiles biográficos, tra-
zados para la niñez; con un preámbulo de Don
José H. Figueira. Montevideo: Dornaleche y
Reyes, 1892. 206 p. Portraits. 17 cm.
Biographical sketches, written for chil-
dren of the following 19th-century individuals:
José Gervasio Artigas, Manuel Pérez Castella-
nos, Francisco Antonio Maciel, Dámaso Antonio
Larrañaga, Joaquín Suárez, Juan Antonio La-
valleja, Fructuoso Rivera, Santiago Vázquez,
Francisco Acuña de Figueroa, Luis Eduardo
Pérez, Alejandro Chúcarro, Lucas José Obes,
Eugenio Garzón, Teodoro Vilardebó, Jacinto
Vera, Adolfo Berro, Eduardo Acevedo, José
Pedro Varela, Teófilo Daniel Gil. (See also
entry 1953.)

CtY DLC

1053   _____. Perfiles biográficos, trazados para
la niñez; con un preámbulo de Don José H.
Figueira y un juicio crítico del professor D.
José A. Fontela. 8. ed. Montevideo: Dorna-
leche Hnos., 1925. 268 p. Portraits. 18 cm.
Biographical sketches, written for chil-
dren, of the following Uruguayans from all
periods of history. Continues and supersedes
Perfiles biográficos, 1892. (See entry 1052.)
Juan Díaz de Solís, Bruno Mauricio de Zabala,
Manuel Pérez Castellanos, Félix de Azara,
Francisco Antonio Maciel, José Gervasio Arti-
gas, Dámaso Antonio Larrañaga, José Rondeau,
Joaquín Suárez, Juan Antonio Lavalleja, Fruc-
tuoso Rivera, Santiago Vázquez, Francisco
Acuña de Figueroa, Luis Eduardo Pérez, Lucas
José Obes, José María Reyes, Eugenio Garzón,
Teodoro Vilardebó, Jacinto Vera, Eduardo Ace-
vedo, José Pedro Varela, Teófilo Daniel Gil,
Pascual Harriague.

CU

1053a   Araujo Villagrán, Horacio. Los italianos en
el Uruguay (diccionario biográfico). Versión
italiana de Andrés Isetta. Barcelona:
Escardó y Araujo, 1920. 561 p. Portraits.
27 cm.
A collection of biographical sketches
accompanied by portraits of approximately
1,200 Italians who lived in Uruguay and contributed to its development.

IU

1054   Auria, Lorenzo F. d'. Entre la historia y la
leyenda. Montevideo: Editorial Mosco Hnos.,
1966. 93 p. 19 cm.
Collection of biographical essays on prominent 19th- and 20th-century Uruguayans from
various fields of endeavor. The following
individuals are featured: Francisco de los
Santos, Dionisio Díaz, Leonardo Olivera, Cayetano Silva, Juan Carlos Gómez, Francisco Soca,
Fausto Aguilar, José Pedro Varela, Melchor
Pacheco y Obes, Joaquín Suárez, Elías Regules,
Florencio Sánchez, José Enrique Rodó, Gustavo
A. Volpe.

DLC NmU

1055   Azarola Gil, Luis Enrique. Aportación al
padrón histórico de Montevideo, época fundacional. Madrid: Tip. de la Revista de Archivos, Bibliotecas y Museos, 1932. 91 p.
25 cm.
Alphabetically arranged biographical notes
on approximately 300 notable figures in the
history of Montevideo in the 18th century.

CU DLC IU NcU NN PU

1056   _____. Contribución al estudio de la nomenclatura histórica de Montevideo. Montevideo:
Casa A. Barreiro y Ramos, 1942. 24 p. 22 cm.

An essay about Uruguayan geographical names, including brief biographical data on Juan Antonio Artigas, Juan de Achucarro, Bernardo Gaytán, Francisco Antonio de Lemos, José González de Melo, Francisco de Céspedes, Sosa Mascareñas, Ignacia Javiera Carrasco, Francisca Javiera Carrasco, Freitas de Fonseca, José Nicolás Barrales, Domingo Santos de Uriarte, Hernandarias de Saavedra, Francisco de Céspedes, Pascual de Chena, Francisco Javier de Viana, José Francisco de Sostoa, Cristóbal Cayetano de Herrera, Juan de Ellauri, Eusebio Vidal. Also biographical data on Luis Enrique Azarola Gil.

DLC IU

1057 Bauzá, Francisco. _Estudios literarios_. Montevideo: A. Barreiro y Ramos, 1885. 291 p. 19 cm. (Biblioteca de autores uruguayos).
A collection of essays containing biobibliographical material on the following 19th-century Uruguayans from different walks of life: Francisco Acuña de Figueroa, Juan Francisco Martínez, Eusebio Valdenegro, Francisco Araúcho, Bartolomé Hidalgo, César Díaz, Juan Carlos Gómez.

IU

1058 _Biblioteca básica de cultura uruguaya_. Montevideo: Editores Reunidos/Arca, 1968. 5 v. 27 cm.
A 5-volume collection of essays, poems, and stories which deal with various aspects of Uruguayan culture and history. Brief biographical information is included for the following:
V. 1: Silvestre González, Raymundo Larrobla, Martín Sánchez de la Rozuela.
V. 2: José Artigas, Lavalle, Rivera.
V. 3: Latorre, Marta Rivière.
V. 4: Rafael Barret.
V. 5: Luis Alberto de Herrera.

CtW DPU ICU IU NbU NmU PSt TxHR WaU

1059 Bonavita, Luis. _Hombres de mi tierra_; por Luis Bonavita (M. Ferdinand Pontac, pseud.). Montevideo, 1959. 135 p. 20 cm.
A collection of essays dealing with many prominent Uruguayans of the 19th and 20th century. Biographical information ranges from very brief notes to lengthy descriptions of the personality traits and important events in the lives of the protagonists. The following are particularly featured: José Artigas, José Batlle y Carreó, José Batlle y Ordóñez (Don Pepe, pseud.), Brum, Melchor, Pacheco y Obes, Eduardo Acevedo Díaz, Pedro Visca, José Irrueta Goyena, Féliz Lacuesta, El indio Recoba, Ignacio Núñez, Manuel Meléndez, José Leguizamón, Norberto Ortiz, Pantaleón Artigas, Andrés Cheveste, Pablo Zufriateguy, Andrés Spíkerman, Simón del Pino, Juan

Ortiz Santiago Gadea, Jacinto Trápani, Manuel Lavalleja, Joaquín Artigas, Celedonio Rojas, Dionisio Oribe, Manuel Oribe, Manuel Freire, Atanasio Sierra, Juan Spíkerman, Ramón Ortiz, Carmelo Colman, Tiburcio Gómez, Juan Rosas.

CLU CU DPU MH

1060 _____. _Sombras heroicas_. Montevideo: Editorial Ceibo, 1945. 212 p. 20 cm. Portraits.
A collection of lengthy essays including portraits and biographical information on 3 notable leaders and some of the people, particularly women, who influenced their lives. They include José Gervasio Artigas, Isabel Sánchez, Rafaela Rosalía Villagrán, Melchora Cuenca, Juan Antonio Lavalleja, José Fructuoso Rivera, Sinforosa Camila de Navarreta, Ana Monterroso, Manuel Oribe.

DLC DPU NbU

1061 Castellanos, Alfredo Raúl. _Nomenclatura de Montevideo_. Montevideo: Intendencia Municipal de Montevideo, 1977. 547 p. 24 cm.
Dictionary of the nomenclature of Montevideo, Uruguay, with biographical sketches of individuals for whom streets, plazas, and parks have been named.

IU

1062 Comisión de Actos Conmemorativos de los 250 Años de la Fundación de Montevideo. _Cronología de Montevideo en los 250 años de su proceso fundacional_. Montevideo: Biblioteca del Palacio Legislativo, 1976. 2 v. 25 cm.
A chronology of Montevideo for the last 250 years published to commemorate the city's 250th anniversary. Includes limited biographical information.
V. 1: Contains an alphabetical index of approximately 3,000 names.
V. 2: Includes a listing of rulers of Montevideo from 1724 to 1976.

IU

1063 De-María, Isidoro. _Rasgos biográficos de hombres notables de la República Oriental de Uruguay_ (con una biografía y notas bibliográficas de J. E. Pivel Devoto). Montevideo: C. García, 1939. 4 v. in 1. 25 cm. V. 4 has title: _Rasgos biográficos de hombres notables de la República Oriental del Uruguay aumentados con algunos de la Argentina_.
First published in 1879-86. Contents:
V. 1: Gervasio Artigas, Antonio Larrañaga, Fructuoso Rivera.
V. 2: Francisco Antonio Maciel, Juan Antonio Lavalleja, Juan Francisco Giró, José Benito Lamas, Teodoro Vilardebó, José Manuel Pérez y Castellano, Julián Laguna, Francisco Joaquín Muñoz, Luis Eduardo Pérez, Julián Alvarez, Francisco Araucho, Francisco Remigio Castellanos, Nicolás de Herrera, Pablo Zufriátegui, Eduardo Acevedo, Miguel Barreiro,

BIOGRAPHY (MISCELLANEOUS)

Francisco Magariños, Francisco Acuña de Figueroa, Juan María Pérez, Eugenio Garzón, Juan Manuel Besnes Irigoyen.

    V. 3: Joaquín Suárez del Rondelo, Carlos Anaya, Francisco Aguilar, Santiago Vázquez, Ignacio Oribe, Andrés Durán, Ambrosio Mitre, Juan Casacuberta, Rufino Bauzá, Manuel Vicente Pagola, Joaquín Campana, Ventura Vázquez, Lucas José Obes, Julián Gregorio de Espinosa, José Ellauri.

    V. 4: Francisco Javier de Viana, José Viera, Venancio Flores, Ramón Masini, Miguel Antonio Vilardebó, José María Reyes, Pablo Pérez, Florentino Castellanos, Jacinto Vera, Félix Eduardo Aguiar.

    CLU CU DLC DPU GU ICarbS IU NcD
NcU NN ViU

1064   Ellis Ximénez, Roberto Jorge G. <u>Anecdotario uruguayo</u>, por Roberto J. G. Ellis. Montevideo: Imprenta Mercur, 1978. 99 p. 20 cm.
    Collection of anecdotes about various Uruguayans of the 19th and 20th centuries from all walks of life. Among those featured: Daniel García Acevedo, Juan Zorrilla de San Martín, César Cortinas, José Salgado, Vicente Pablo, Francisco Imhof, Juan Fitz Patrick, Oscar D. Gestido, Juan Pedro Eduardo Etchevers Lemoine, Angel Falco, Amador Sánchez, Pilar Cabrera, César Miranda, Duvimioso Terra, Julio Herrera y Obes, Alejandro Zorrilla de San Martín, Ernesto Ruete, Juan Carlos Sabat Pebet, Juan J. Chiappara, Germán Roosen Regalía, Diego Noboa Courrás, Dardo Regules, Julio Lerena Juanicó, Osvaldo Crispo Acosta, Pedro Piñeyrúa, Cristóbal de Salvañach, Adriana Bereciartua de Borderre, Juan Pedro Borderre, Diego Serpa, Luis T. de Azevedo, Alejandro Magariños, Cendra, Gorrechateguy.

    IU

1065   _____. <u>Bocetos biográficos</u>; segunda parte de <u>Rescatándolos del olvido</u>, por Roberto J. G. Ellis. Montevideo: 1978. 167 p. 20 cm.
    Collection of biographical essays of prominent Uruguayans of the 19th and 20th centuries from various fields of endeavor. (<u>See also</u> entry 1067.) Biographical information provided includes dates, educational background and professional achievements. Those featured include Dámaso Antonio Larrañaga, Carlos A. Arocena, Eduardo N. Calcagno, Clara Camino, Francisco Aguilar y Leal, Mauricio Demolin, Luis Pedro Lenguas, María Francisca de Viana y Alzáibar, Petrona Cibils, Juana de Ibarbourou, María García Lagos de Hughes, Guillermo M. Pérez Butler, Augusto Turenne, Arturo E. Xalambri, Miguel Ximénez, Pedro Ximénez Pozzolo, José Luis Zorrilla de San Martín.

    IU NmU

1066   _____. <u>Evocaciones montevideanas</u>: su pasado; nombres dignos de recordar; la casa de

Don Manuel Ximénez y Gómez, futura sede de una sección del Museo Histórico Nacional. Montevideo: Barreiro y Ramos, 1969. 107 p. 20 cm.
    A historical essay about Montevideo, Uruguay, including biographical sketches of the following people associated with it: Stephen Robert Koek-Koek, Salvador Ximénez, Enrique Badaraco, Pedro Campbell, Raúl Montero Bustamante, Francisco J. Ros, Francisca de Viana y Alzáibar de Oribe, José Abiaré, La China María, Gregoria Pérez.

    CLSU CLU CSt CtY CU-SB DPU FU IaU
IU MB MU NcD NIC OU PPULC TxU
ViU WU

1067   _____. <u>Rescatándolos del olvido</u> (Bocetos biográficos), por Roberto J. G. Ellis. Prólogo del Prof. Alonso Llambías de Azevedo. Montevideo: A. Monteverde, 1972. 181 p. 19 cm.
    Collection of biographical essays featuring information on 19th- and 20th-century Uruguayans from all walks of life. Dates, educational background, and professional achievements are provided for:
    V. 1: Alberto Boerger, Félix Buxareo Oribe, Luis Cluzeau Mortet, Carlos E. Druillet, Horacio Ellis, Eduardo Fabini, Alejandro Gallinal, Claudio García, Doroteo García, Julio García Otero, Juan D. Jackson, Miguel Jaureguiberry, Ernesto Laroche, Pedro Menéndez Lees, Domingo Ordañana, Luis Piñeyro del Campo, Guillermo C. Rodríguez, Francisco J. Ros, Joaquín de Salterain, Javier de Viana, Claudio Williman. (<u>See also</u> entry 1065.)

    IU NcU

1068   Falcao Espalter, Mario. <u>Interpretaciones</u>; lira - cincel - color y forma. Montevideo: A. Monteverde & Cía., 1929. 389 p. 19 cm.
    Collection of critical essays and personal reminiscences about Uruguayans involved in the arts and letters in the first half of the 20th century. Features limited biobibliographical data on Carlos Sábat Ercasty, Roberto Sienra, Guzmán Papini y Zas, Emilio Frugoni, Julio Raúl Mendilaharsu, Luis Torres Ginart, Fernán Silva Valdés, Osvaldo Crispo Acosta (Lauxar, pseud.), Eduardo Dualde, Bernabé Michelena, Emilio Oribe, Juan D'Aniello, Gustavo Gallinal, José Enrique Rodó, Justino Zavala Muñiz, Adolfo Montiel Ballesteros.

    DLC IaU IU LU NBuU NcD NcU NIC
NjP TxU

1069   Filartigas, Juan M. <u>Arandu</u>: inteligencia, pueblo, creación: Baltasar Brum, J. Zavala Muñiz, Carlos Vaz Ferreira. Montevideo, 1936. 109 p. 21 cm.
    A collection of biographical essays on the following notable Uruguayans: Baltasar Brum, Justino Muñiz Zavala, Carlos Vaz Ferreira.

    ICarbS TxU WU

1070 Frick Davie, Carlos. ¿Actividades nazis en el Uruguay? Montevideo: Impr. Germ. Urug., 1941. 194 p. 20 cm.

A discussion of the possible Nazi movement in Uruguay, seen mostly through the correspondence of some of its members, and including biographical information on the following people: Arnulf Fuhrmann, Rolf Meissner, Federico Schönfeld Gordon.

AzU DLC MH NcD

1071 Fusco Sansone, Nicolás. Figuras y paisajes del Uruguay. Montevideo: Editorial Selección, 1942. 124 p. Portraits. 20 cm.

A profile of Uruguayan landscape and figures. Includes biographical essays on Ernesto Herrera, Bartolomé Hidalgo, Adolfo Berro, Juan Carlos Gómez, José Pedro Varela, Horacio Quiroga.

CLU DLC MB MoU NcU TxU

1072 Gomensoro, Javier. Figuras y estampas de Montevideo. Montevideo: 1943. 170 p. 20 cm. (Biblioteca de cultura uruguaya. Colección moderna. V. 5).

A collection of essays on various notable Uruguayan events and 19th-century people. The following are featured: Jacinto Acuña de Figueroa, Roque Antonio Gómez, Melchor Pacheco y Obes, Andrés Lamas, Francisco Juanicó, Juan Carlos Blanco, Manuel B. Otero, José Enrique Rodó.

DLC MoU NN TxU

1073 Grandes figuras de la República Oriental del Uruguay y homenaje a los Estados Unidos de Norte América. Montevideo: Ediciones de la Biblioteca Americana, 1953. Unpaged. Portraits. 24 cm.

A book which, in addition to paying homage to the United States of America, contains biographical essays of varying length on numerous notable Uruguayans.

NNF

1074 Hirst, Lloyd. Britons at Maldonado. Montevideo: Ediciones Géminis, 1975. 149 p. 20 cm. (Colección Novus orbis).

History of British activity in the city of Maldonado, Uruguay, from the 16th–20th centuries featuring scattered biographical material on the exploits of various explorers, scientists, and businessmen.

FU InU IU MU NIC

1075 Jalabert, Ricardo M. Album biográfico ilustrado y descripción histórico-geográfica de la República Oriental del Uruguay, año 1904; directores propietarios: Ricardo M. Jalabert y Rodolfo Cabal. Buenos Aires: Ortega y Radaelli, 1903. 254 p. Portraits. 36 cm.

Biographical data with photos of approximately 150 prominent individuals in early 20th-century Uruguay. Photographs only of many others.

CtY DLC IU MiU TxU

1076 Maeso, Carlos M. El Oriental; descripción general de la República Oriental del Uruguay, su comercio, industrias, rentas y riquezas, narraciones históricas, rasgos biográficos de uruguayos célebres, etc. Montevideo: Impr. y Encuadernación de Ríus y Becchi, 1884. 206 p. 23 cm.

History and description of Uruguay featuring biographical data on the following 19th-century Uruguayans: José G. Artigas, Fructuoso Rivera, Juan Antonio Lavalleja, Eugenio Garzón, Pablo Zufriátegui, Santiago Vázquez, José Pedro Varela, Teodoro Vilardebó, Miguel Barreiro, Luis Eduardo Pérez, José Manuel Pérez y Castellanos, Manuel Vicente Pagola, Dámaso Antonio Larrañaga, Francisco Antonio Maciel, Francisco Acuña de Figueroa, Joaquín Suárez, Jacinto Vera. Later editions have title Tierra de promisión. (See entry 1118.)

DLC

1077 Mancebo, Noel A. Hombres representativos. Montevideo, 1960. 344 p. 19 cm.

A collection of biographical sketches of the following notable Uruguayans: José Artigas, Juan Zorrilla de San Martín, Juan Manuel Blanes, José Enrique Rodó, José Batlle y Ordoñez, José Alonso y Trelles, Raúl Montero Bustamante, Alfredo Baldomir.

CLSU CLU CU DPU IaU IaAS NIC NN
NNC RPB TxU

1078 Martínez, José Luciano. Laderas y cumbres (estudios, juicios, episodios). Montevideo: Impr. Dornaleche Hnos, 1935. 274 p. Portraits. 20 cm.

Collection of essays on various periods of Uruguayan history featuring brief biographies with dates and career achievements of the following 19th- and 20th-century individuals: Santiago Vázquez, José María Muñoz, Hipólito Gallinal, Duvimioso Terra, Daniel Martínez Vigil, José Enrique Rodó, Víctor Pérez Petit, Carlos Martínez Vigil, Guzmán Papini y Zas. Alphabetical index of names.

DLC IU MoU NcU

1079 Nin y Silva, Celedonio. La República del Uruguay en su primer centenario (1830-1930). 2. ed. corr. y aum. Montevideo: J. Sureda, 1930. 232 p. 20 cm.

A book commemorating Uruguay's first 100 years of independence, containing sections on geography, history, culture, government, industry, commerce, and education. Scattered biographical information is included for many people who have made contributions to all as-

BIOGRAPHY (MISCELLANEOUS)

pects of Uruguayan life and development. Alphabetical index of names.

DLC IaU IU MnU MU NcU NN OU PSt

1080 Otaegui, Tomás. *Los vascos en el Uruguay*; fundación de Montevideo. Buenos Aires: Editorial Vasca Ekin, 1943. 168 p. Portraits. 18 cm. (Biblioteca de cultura vasca. V. 13).

Historical essay dealing with Basques in Uruguay, particularly their importance in the founding of Montevideo. Mention is made of many Uruguayans of the 19th and 20th centuries of Basque origin. The following are particularly featured: Bruno Mauricio de Zabala, Francisco de Alzaibar Padura y Arteta, Antonio Dámaso Larrañaga, Francisco Araucho, Juan de Laguna, Juan José de Ortiz, Juan de Larrobla, José Benito Lamas, Francisco Bruno de Rivarola, Juan Ascarza, José Ignacio Otazu, Tomás de Gomensoro, Marcelino Pelliza, Enrique Peña, Lázaro Gadea, Esteban Méndez.

CtY CU DLC FU ICN ICRL ICU IdU
IU MiD MnU NcU NN TxU WaU

1081 *Panteón nacional.* Montevideo: República Oriental del Uruguay, Palacio Legislativo. Biblioteca, 1979. 148 p. Portraits. 24 cm. (Serie de temas nacionales. V. 8).

Biographical sketches of prominent Uruguayans whose remains lie in the "Panteón Nacional." Dates, birthplace, and major achievements of the following individuals are supplied: Eduardo Acevedo, Francisco Acuña de Figueroa, Félix Eduardo Aguiar, Fausto Aguilar, Juan Manuel Blanes, Clemente César, Carmelo Colman, Dionisio Coronel, Pedro Figari, Eugenio Garzón, Juan Carlos Gómez, Julio Herrera y Obes, Manuel Herrera y Obes, Julio Herrera y Reissig, Juan Idiarte Borda, Andrés Latorre, Lorenzo Latorre, Manuel Antonio Ledesma, Melchor Pacheco y Obes, León de Palleja, Pablo Pérez, Emeterio Regúnaga, Carlos Reyles, Américo Ricaldoni, José Enrique Rodó, José Rondeau, Florencio Sánchez, Francisco Soca, Juan Zorrilla de San Martín.

IU

1082 Parallada, Huáscar. *Coronel Andrés Latorre* (una reliquia artiguista en el Durazno). Florida: Tall. Gráf. GADI, 1970. 260 p. Portraits. 25 cm.

A biography of the Uruguayan colonel Andrés Latorre. Biographical information is given for this man and also for many of his relatives and friends. The following are particularly featured: Antonio de la Torre, José Abalos y Mendoza, Pedro José Borda, María Matilde Borda, Bonifacio Figueredo, Melchor Mendoza, Micaela Medina, Gregoria Tomasa Mendoza Medina, Simón del Pino, Buenaventura de la Torre, Josefa Arias y Palacios, Andrés Morlote, Juan Antonio de Haedo, Lorenzo de Larrauri, Fernando Martínez, Andrés Latorre, Juan Antonio Lavalleja,

Demetrio Latorre Alzogaray, Gabino Latorre Alzogaray, Diógenes Floro Latorre Alzogaray, Rosaura Carolina Latorre Alzogaray, Reinaldo Latorre Alzogaray, Eloisa Adelina Latorre Alzogaray, Leopoldo Latorre Mansilla, Eugenia Servanda Latorre Mansilla, María Josefa Latorre Mansilla, Nicolasa Tolentina Latorre Mansilla, Maura Latorre Mansilla, Andrea Isibonia Latorre Mansilla, Gregoria Juliana Pietas, Alcira Latorre de Navajas, Miguel Antonio Navajas, Andrés Latorre Pietas, Claudio Gregorio Latorre Pietas, Eustaquia Amelia Latorre Ojeda, Asunción Ojeda, Antonio Guerrero, Marcelo Imaz, Rafael Rodríguez, Antonio Galó, Domingo Cullen.

CtY CU DLC IaU ICU MU NcU NSyU

1083 Parker, William Belmont, comp. *Uruguayans of Today.* London, New York: The Hispanic Society of America, 1921. 575 p. Portraits. 17 cm. (Hispanic notes and monographs: essays, studies, and brief biographies issued by the Hispanic Society of America. V. 7).

Biographies, some with photos, of numerous prominent 20th-century Uruguayans.

CaBVaU CU DLC ICJ IU LNHT MB MeB
MiU MtU NcD NN NNBG NSyU OCl OClW
ODW OO OrSaW PPm PHC PP PU TxU
ViU

1084 Pedemonte, Juan Carlos. *Montevideo: hombres, bronce, mármol.* Montevideo: Barreiro y Ramos, 1971. 111 p. 25 cm.

Collection of biographical essays on outstanding citizens of Montevideo throughout history featuring information on their contributions to the development of the city: Francisco Acuña de Figueroa, Víctor Constante, Emilio García Wich, Uladislao Montes, José María Azarola, Emilio Reus, Tomás Thomkinson, Alejo Rosell y Rius, Francisco Piria, Atilio Pelossi. Biographical sketches of the following individuals who are the subjects of monuments in Montevideo and also the sculptors who designed them: José Livi, Rosa Pittaluga, Joaquín Suárez, José Pedro Varela, José Zorrilla de San Martín, José María Gutiérrez, José Belloni, Javier Amarillo, Nereo Sosa, Ciriaco Burgos, Julián Rolón, Gregorio Suárez, Antonio Floricio Saravia (Chiquito, pseud.).

CLU CSt CtY CU CU-SB IaU IU MB
MU NcU NIC NNC TxU ViU WU

1085 Pereda, Setembrino Ezequiel. *Miscelánea.* Paysandú: Establecimiento Tipográfico de El Paysandú, 1891. 104, 104, 55 p. 21 cm.

Collection of writings featuring biographical information on the following 19th- and 20th-century Uruguayans: Santiago Alberti, Pedro Bayce, Félix Fernández, Castro Rodríguez, Ricardo Tajes, Pablo De María, José Gervasio Artigas, Teófilo D. Gil, Vicente Mongrell, Juan C. Brunet.

DLC ICarbS

1086   Pivel Devoto, Juan E., and Alcira Ranieri de
Pivel Devoto. Uruguay a fines del siglo XIX.
Montevideo: Editorial Medena, 1972. 92 p.
18 cm. (Colección cientemas básicos. V. 20).
   Study of Uruguay at the end of the 19th
century in the areas of population, politics,
arts, and letters. Brief biographies are in-
cluded with information on educational back-
ground and the professional careers of the
following individuals: Juan Manuel Blanes,
Eduardo D. Carbajal, Diógenes Héquet, José
Livi, Carlos María Herrera, Alejandro Maga-
riños Cervantes, Eduardo Acevedo Díaz, Juan
Zorrilla de San Martín, Francisco Bauzá,
Carlos Vaz Ferreira, José Enrique Rodó,
Carlos Reyles, Julio Herrera y Reissig,
María Eugenia Vaz Ferreira, Delmira Agustini,
Florencio Sánchez, Javier de Viana, José
Pedro Varela. Alphabetical index of names.

   IU

1087   Ramírez, Juan Vicente. Visiones uruguayas
(impresiones de un viaje). Prólogo de J.
Natalicio González. Asunción: Imp. "Ariel,"
1920. 132 p. Portraits. 18 cm. (Biblio-
teca paraguaya del Centro e. de derecho.
V. 6).
   Memoirs of a trip to Uruguay for the
funeral of José Enrique Rodó in 1917 with
biographical sketches of the following: Bal-
tazar Brum, Rufino T. Domínguez, Rodolfo
Mezzera, Luis Alberto de Herrera, José M.
Fernández Saldaña, Julio Raúl Mendilaharsu,
José María Delgado, Fernán Silva Valdés,
Eduardo de Salterain Herrera, Emilio Frugoni,
José Enrique Rodó.

   DLC DUP IU TxU

1088   Ríos, José. Breve biografía de intelectuales
uruguayos. Montevideo: Tall. Gráficos de
Shera's, 1978. 125 p. 19 cm.
   A collection of biographical sketches,
alphabetically arranged, of numerous contemporary intellectual figures of Uruguay.

   IU

1089   Rodríguez Vigoy, J. España en el Uruguay.
Prólogo de Julio de la Cuesta. Biografías,
ilustraciones, comercio, industria, artes,
ciencias, centros, sociedades, etc. Buenos
Aires: La Iberia, 1924. 207 p. Portraits.
30 cm.
   A collection of biographical sketches,
most of them accompanied by portraits, of
numerous Spaniards living in Uruguay.

   IU NN

1090   Salterain Herrera, Eduardo de. Perspectivas;
meditaciones ambiguas, cuadros, ideas y sen-
saciones, figuras, libros. Montevideo:
Agencia General de Librería y Publicaciones,
1926. 156 p. 19 cm.

   Collection of literary essays with biographical data on José Enrique Rodó, Guillermo C. Rodríguez, Eduardo Acevedo Díaz.

   MoU

1091   Scarone, Arturo. Efemérides uruguayas. Prólogo de Raúl Montero Bustamante. Montevideo,
1956. 3 v. Portraits. 26 cm. 417 p.
25 cm.
   A diary of important events in the history of Uruguay, covering the period from the
17th to the 20th century. Scattered biographical information, such as dates of birth
and death and important accomplishments, is
included for many people from all fields of
endeavor. The following are especially featured: Francisco Acuña de Figueroa, Atanasio
Cruz Aguirre, Carlos de Alvear, Timoteo Apa-
ricio, Andrés Artigas (Andresito, pseud.),
José Artigas, Miguel M. F. Barreiro, Lorenzo
Batlle, José Batlle y Ordóñez, Bernardo P.
Berro, Juan Manuel Blanes, Guillermo Brown,
Pedro de Ceballos, Juan L. Cuestas, César
Díaz, Manuel Dorrego, Francisco Xavier de
Elío, José E. Ellauri, Fernando VII, Fermín
Ferreira, Venancio Flores, Tomás García de
Zúñiga, José Garibaldi, Eugenio Garzón, Juan
Francisco Giró, Ariosto D. González, Nicolás
Herrera, Julio Herrera y Obes, Juan Idiarte
Borda, Andrés Lamas, Dámaso Antonio Larrañaga,
Lorenzo Latorre, Juan Antonio Lavalleja,
Carlos Federico de Lecor, Santiago de Liniers,
Anacleto Medina, Francisco Joaquín Muñoz,
Manuel Oribe, Fernando Otorgués, Melchor Pa-
checo y Obes, Gabriel Antonio Pereira, Juan
María Pérez, Luis Eduardo Pérez, Gervasio
Antonio Posadas, Juan Martín de Pueyrredón,
José Pedro Ramírez, Bernardino Rivadavia,
Fructuoso Rivera, José Enrique Rodó, José
Rondeau, Juan Manuel de Rosas, Pascual Ruiz
Huidobro, Florencio Sánchez, Máximo Santos,
Aparicio Saravia, Manuel Sarratea, Marqués
de Sobremonte, Mariano Soler, Miguel E. Soler,
Joaquín Suárez, Máximo Tajes, Justo José de
Urquiza, José Pedro Varela, Pedro Varela,
Santiago Vázquez, Jacinto Vera, Francisco A.
Vidal, Gaspar de Vigodet, Inocencio María
Yéregui, Bruno de Zabala, Juan Zorilla de
San Martín. Alphabetical index of names for
each volume. A cumulative index as well as
indices for births, deaths, and baptisms are
also included in volume 4.

   CLU DPU IaU IU MH NN TxU

1092   Taborda, Eduardo S. Salto de ayer y de hoy
(Selección de charlas radiales). Salto:
Intendencia Municipal, 1955. 329 p. 20 cm.
   Collection of historical essays dealing
with institutions and people connected with
the city of Salto, Uruguay, throughout its
history. Varying amounts of biographical
information included about the following individuals' participation in the history of
the city: Agustín Maimus, José Antonio Garbarini, José Verdemiró, Antonio Invernizzi,

BIOGRAPHY (MISCELLANEOUS)

Miguel Pacot, María Delfina Barbosa, Rufina Otorgués, Luis Dasllagas Antúnez Maciel, Ernesto Larré, Beltrán Larré, Eulogio Melitón Alfonso, Pablo Aguirrezábal, Manuel Estevez Dos Santos, Estelvina Migliaro, Marciano Díez Plaza, José Lino Amorim, Augusto Gonzalbo, Francisco Esteban Acuña de Figueroa, Bartolomé Hidalgo, Saturnino Ribes, Pascual Harriague, Anastasio Albisu.

IU

1093 Ureña González, Camilo, comp. Reseña histórica de Cerro Largo. Montevideo: Estudio Ideas, 1945. 191 p. 23 cm. (Ediciones de Estudio ideas. V. 1).
Study of the Uruguayan department of Cerro Largo concentrating on various aspects of life there, in the first half of the 20th century. Biographical material in varying amounts is included for the following 19th- and 20th-century residents: Juan Díaz, José Mariano Muñoz, José Apolinario Pérez, Isidoro Noblia, Saviniano Pérez, Pedro Martins Marins, Angélica Ferrari de Plaza, Lola Noblia de Plaza, Angélica Plaza, Elida Mestre de Villalba, Nazareth Perdomo Coronel, Simón López Aspiroz, Abner Collazo, Gervasio Piro, Antenor Estavillo, Genaro Zavala Fontaine, Pedro Marín Sánchez, Angelina Silveira Aguiar, Federico Acosta y Larra, María Esther Espínola de Acosta y Lara, Paulina Medeiros, Gumersindo Saravia, Aparicio Saravia, Basilisio Saravia, José Rogelio Fontela, Agustín Muñoz, Pedro Aguiar Elizalde, Alfredo Alvarez Preve, José M. Alvarez Sasiain, Juan Alvez Antúnez, Antonio Amestoy, Aníbal Artigas, Ceibal Artigas, Rincón Artigas, Gonzalo Arrarte, Néstor Collazo, Ulises Collazo, Nicanor Dos Santos, Giordano Eccher, Ulises Escobar, Silvestre Echeverría, Antonio Gianola, Oscar D. Gestido, Enrique F. Gamio, Juan Ganzo Fernández, Manuel B. García, Juan José Gari, Manuel López Benítez, Manuel F. Mazziotta, Héctor Mattos, Angel Muñiz Silva, Ulises Morales Zavala, Héctor Víctor Miralles, Julián Murguía, Osvaldo Noblia, Rufino Noblia, Gerardo Noblia, Germán Núñez, Juan Muñoz Olmos, Enrique Oribe Coronel, Carlos M. Paravis, Omar Porciuncula, Edmundo Pica, Joaquín P. Rebollo, Elisa Fagundez de Ramos, Carlos A. Ros, Juan Darío Silva, José Francisco Saravia, Antonio F. Saravia, Exequiel Silveira, Euclides Sosa Aguiar, Antonio María Ubilla, Saúl Urbina, José V. Urrutia, Emilio Vila, Franco P. Vázquez, Omar Viera, Jacinto Cipriano Viera, José Ganzo Fernández, Juan María Ramasso, Miguel Jaume Torres, Pedro M. de Freitas, Manuel Francisco Lucas, Enrique Saravia, Augusto de Giuli, Doroteo R. Navarrete, Francisco Mata, Juan Collazo, Cándido Monegal, Juan Ramasso, Luis G. Murguía, José de la Cruz Guerrero, Fernando E. Guerrero, José Nicasio Guerrero, Ramón E. Silveira, Febrino L. Vianna.

IU TxU

1093a Uruguay. Comisión Nacional de Bellas Artes. Exposición Cayetano Gallino, 1804-1884; catálogo, Salón Nacional de Bellas Artes. Montevideo, Uruguay: Impresora Uruguaya, 1944. 21 p. 59 portraits.
An exhibition of Cayetano Gallino's works. Contains portraits of the following people: Prudencia Castro de Capurro, Manuel Villagrán Artigas, Plácida Buxareo de Cibils, José Augusto Possolo, Francisca Rondeau de Maines, Luis Baena, Paz de Vargas Viana de García Wich, Juan García Wich, Juana Santuario de Montero, José María Montero, Jaime Illa, Valentina Viamonte de Illa, Agustina Zufriategui de Periz, Josefa Periz, Florencio Varela, Silvestre Blanco, María Juana del Río de Ocampo, Juan C. Acosta Menéndez, Jacinta Menéndez Larriera de Acosta, Rosa Acosta, Cristóbal Bertrán, Felicia Peña de Bertrán, José Luis Bertrán, Francisco Luna, Anacleta Balbín y Vallejo de Luna, José G. Monterroso, Manuel Herrera y Obes, Pedro Pablo de la Sierra, Mónica de la Sierra, Antonia Viana de Vargas, José Garibaldi, Melchor Pacheco y Obes, Carmen Alagón de Fernández, Enrique Martínez, Natividad Echeverriarza de Blanco, Cristóbal Bertrán y Peña, Francisca Reyes de Llambi, Juan María Pérez, Rosario Maguna, Pedro Maguna, Bernarda Castilla de Arrien, Enriqueta Pereyra de Jones, Juan Pedro Ramírez, María de la Encarnación Sáenz de la Maza de García de Zúñiga, Francisco Llambi, María Wich de García, Manuela Arancibia, Domingo González, Juan Bautista Capurro, María Elizondo de Gestal, Félix Eduardo Aguiar, Juan Fernández, Antonia Avellaneda de Garzón, Josefa Muñoz de Pérez, Servando Gómez, Julián Alvarez, Jacinto Estivao, Manuel García Tejedor, Juan Susviela, Melchora Possolo, Augusto Possolo, Carlos Possolo, Orfilia Possolo. Also biography of Cayetano Gallino.

DLC IU

1094 Valls, Luis, and Jaime Moragues. Los españoles del Uruguay. Montevideo: Tipografía Moderna, 1918. 276 p. 28 x 20 cm.
Collection of biographies with portraits of Spaniards who have emigrated to Uruguay. Biographical material includes dates and professional activities for individuals active in the early 20th century. Among those especially featured: José R. García y Fraga, Felipe Arrospide, Salvador García, Mariano Suárez, Luis Valls y Valls, Federico de Velazco, José Moirón y Paz, Lorenzo Torres Caldera, Pedro Ferres y Carrau, Francisco Vilaró, José Ordeig Figueras, José Ferrés y Carrau, Pedro L. Ramos, Juan Imaz, Arturo Grau, Juan Roldós y Pons, Francisco Vázquez Cores, Orestes Araiyo, José Luis Ugartemendia, Leoncio Gandos, José García Conde, Francisco B. Helguera, José Elorza, Manuel Piñera, José María Serrano, Narciso Lladó, Cosme Fernández, Angel Gelpi, Segundo Fernández, Matías Alonso Criado, José María Turienzo, Constancio Castells Cumella, Fernando García,

Domingo Fernández, Miguel Jaume y Bosch, José Jaume y Bosch, Alejandro Fiol y Perera, Vicente Pita, Francisco González, Manuel Martínez, Francisco Suñer y Capdevila, Antonio Serratosa, Antonio Barreiro y Ramos, Bartolomé Triay, Ramón Villarnobo, José López Martínez, Emilio A. Castells, Joaquín Carbonell y Vila, Joaquín Fernando Carbonell, Antonio Helguera Ortega, Víctor J. Arcelus, Alejandro Fiol Solé, Juan B. Estévez, Francisco Vidiella, Manuel Rodríguez Castromán, Juan Abal, Ramón S. Vázquez, Pedro Compte, Félix M. Martínez Castro, Marcial Yáñez, Laura Carreras de Bastos, Carmelo Calvo, Vicente Cabrera Pérez, Manuel Amado y Moreira.

IU

1095 Zubillaga Barrera, Carlos A. Los gallegos en el Uruguay; apuntes para una historia de la inmigración gallega hasta fines del siglo XIX. Montevideo: Ediciones del Banco de Galicia, 1966. 232 p. 23 cm.
Historical essay dealing with Galicians in Uruguay up to the end of the 19th century with biographical information on the following: Antonio Díaz, Joaquín de la Sagra y Periz, Francisco Antonio de Lemos, Bernardo Lecocq, Benito Chain, Pedro Manuel García, Francisco Javier Díaz, José Neira, Benito Rivadeneyra, Manuel de Amenedo Montenegro, Pedro Montenegro, Manuel Verdía, Ramón S. Vázquez, Manuel Rodríguez Castromán, Manuel Cacheiro, Manuel Albo, Pablo Fontaina, Francisco Vázquez Cores, Manuel G. Alvarez, Juan B. Estévez, Manuel Riguera Montero, José A. Fontela, José María Campos, Manuel Sánchez Caballero, Manuel Magariños, José Alonso y Trelles, Manuel Senra, José García Conde, Benigno Salgado y Vázquez, Juan Vicente Arcos, Francisco San Román, Nicolás Martínez, Iglesias, Avalos, Francisco Rodríguez (Farruco, pseud.), Jacinto Acuña de Figueroa, Vicente Fernández, Manuel Francisco Bermúdez, Manuel Barreiro y Camba, Marcos José da Porta Monterroso, Juan Rodríguez Vaz, Blas Vidal, Pascuala Josende, Gregorio Durán, Domingo Infesta, Juan Núñez, Luisa Graña, José Pérez Brito, Manuel Balao, Alberto Camino, Juan Antonio Presa, Antonio Agraña, Juan de Castro, José Ignacio Seide, Roque Antonio Gómez, Francisco A. Calvo, José Ramón Mariño, Pedro Fragoso y Muñoz, Juan Fernández, Dionisio Fernández, Juan Bautista Ruiz de Salinas, Bernardo Pampillo Teijeiro, José García y Fraga, Antonio Luis Pereyra, Félix Ortiz de Taranco, Antonio Baltasar Pérez, Juan Antonio Porrúa, Antonio Montero, José Díaz Armesto, Ulpiano Bulrigas y Prat, Félix Martínez Castro, Antonio Barreiro y Ramos, Ramón Villarnobo, José Alonso y Trelles (El Viejo Pancho, pseud.).

IU KU

1096 Fernández Saldaña, José María. Diccionario uruguayo de biografías, 1810-1940. Montevideo: Editorial Amerindia, 1945. 1366 p. 25 cm.
Biographical material on approximately 800 important figures in Uruguayan history between 1810-1940. Continues and supersedes Fichas para un diccionario uruguayo de biografías. (See entry 1097.)

1097 _____. Fichas para un diccionario uruguayo de biografías. Montevideo: Talleres Gráficos "33" Sociedad Anónima, 1945. 2 v. 23 cm.
Biographical data on approximately 500 prominent figures in 19th and 20th century Uruguayan history. Continued and superseded by Diccionario uruguayo de biografías, 1810-1940. (See entry 1096.)

DLC IaU ICU IU NcU

1098 Guerra, María Amelia Díaz de. Diccionario biográfico de la ciudad de Maldonado (1755-1900). Montevideo: IMCO (Imprenta Cooperativa), 1974. 506 p. Portraits. 20 cm.
Biographical dictionary of the Uruguayan city of Maldonado from 1755 to 1900 with the names of approximately 1,000 citizens. Alphabetical arrangement.

CtY CU FU IU TxU ViU

1099 Montevideo. Biblioteca del Poder Legislativo. Sección Identificación de Autores. Uruguayos contemporáneos; noticias biográficas. Montevideo, 1965. 4 v. 25 cm.
Biographical sketches of approximately 1,000 contemporary Uruguayans from all walks of life. Contents:
V. 1: A-CH.
V. 2: D-K.
V. 3: L-Q.
V. 4: R-Z.

AAP CSt CtY CU DPU FTaSU FU IaU
ICU InNd InU IU LU MH-L MiU MoSW
MoU NcD

1100 Quién es quién. Montevideo: Editorial 33, 1941. 256 p.
A "who's who" for Uruguay featuring brief biographies of over 350 individuals prominent in 1941.

CSt-H DLC NSyU

1101 Quién es quién en el Uruguay. Montevideo: Central de Publicaciones, Panamérica Uruguaya, 1980. 688 p. Portraits. 24 cm.
A "who's who" for Uruguay in 1979-80 featuring biographies of notable individuals from the arts, commerce, science, industry, and other professions.

IU

BIOGRAPHY (MISCELLANEOUS)--DICTIONARIES, ENCYCLOPEDIAS, and "WHO'S WHO"

1102   Scarone, Arturo. Uruguayos contemporáneos.
Diccionario de datos referentes a compatrio-
tas y de algunos extranjeros desde largo
tiempo incorporados y descollantes en nuestra
vida pública; prólogo del doctor Juan Antonio
Buero. 1. ed., con un apéndice. Montevideo:
"Renacimiento," 1918. 676 p. Portraits.
19 cm.
   Dictionary containing biobibliographical
sketches, some with photographs, of approximately 1,000 individuals prominent in 19th-
and 20th-century Uruguay. Superseded by
Uruguayos contemporáneos, 1937. (See entry
1103.)

   CU DLC DNW FU IU LNT NcD NcU OCl
   OKentU TxU UU WaU

1103   _____. Uruguayos contemporáneos; nuevo
diccionario de datos biográficos y bibliográficos. Montevideo: "Casa A. Barreiro y
Ramos," s.a., 1937. 610 p. 26 cm.
   Dictionary with biobibliographical data
on more than 1,300 important individuals in
19th- and 20th-century Uruguay. Continues
and supersedes Uruguayos contemporáneos,
1918. (See entry 1102.)

   CI CSt CSt-H DLC FMU GU IEdS LNT
   MH MoU MU NBuU NcD NcU NIC NN
   NSyU OkU OO OU PPT UU

EDUCATION

1104   Otero y Roca, Solis. Hombres y surcos.
Montevideo: Editorial Libertad, 1938. 162 p.
Portraits. 20 cm.
   Biographical essays on Domingo Faustino
Sarmiento (with particular emphasis on his
impact on education in Uruguay), Américo
Ricaldoni, and Benigno S. Paiva. Featured
also are Pedro Ricaldoni and Pedro Visca.

   DLC NcU TxU

GENEALOGY

1105   Apolant, Juan Alejandro. Génesis de la familia uruguaya; los habitantes de Montevideo
en sus primeros 40 años, filiaciones, ascen-
dencias, entronques, decedencias. Prólogo
de Flavio A. García. Montevideo: Instituto
Histórico y Geográfico del Uruguay, 1966.
972 p. 25 cm.
   Genealogical history of Montevideo from
1726-1767 based on the marriage records on
file at the Cathedral of Montevideo. Included are biographical data on over 500 key
families. Also baptismal records for the
same time period. Alphabetical index of
names.

   CLSU CLU CSt CtY CU DLC IaU ICN
   InU IU LNHT MH MiU MoSW NBuU McU
   NIC NjP NSyU TxHU TxU WU

1106   Azarola Gil, Luis Enrique. Contribución a la
historia de Montevideo. Veinte linajes del
siglo XVIII. Paris: Casa Editorial Franco-
ibero-americana, 1926. 190 p. Portraits.
23 cm.
   Genealogical history of the following
18th-century families of Montevideo: Zabala,
Alzaybar, Achucarro, Camejo Soto, Sostoa,
Maciel, Viana, Soria, Vargas, Artigas, Herrera, Haedo, Oribe, Mitre, Urquiza, Rozas.

   CSt CU DLC IU LNHT NN TxU

1107   Ferreira, Mariano. Apuntes biográficos de
la familia Artigas y Ferreira, seguidos de
una corona fúnebre. Montevideo: Renacimiento, 1919. 400 p.
   Biogenealogical history and portraits of
members of the Artigas and Ferreira families
of 19th-century Uruguay featuring data on the
following: Manuel A. Artigas, Fermín Ferreira,
Rosalía Artigas de Ferreira, Fermín Ferreira
y Artigas, Teodoro Ferreira, Carolina Muñoz
de Ferreira, Rosa Ferreira de Ordóñez.

   ICarbS NcU NSyU

1108   Goldaracena, Ricardo. El libro de los linajes: familias históricas uruguayas del
siglo XIX . Montevideo: Arca, 1976. 3 v.
20 cm.
   Genealogical history of distinguished
19th-century Uruguayan families. Biographi-
cal information consisting of dates, activi-
ties, and descendants of the following fami-
lies is provided:
   V. 1: Aguiar, Aguirre, Algorta, Alvarez,
Blanco, Brito del Pino, Buxareo, Camusso,
Caravia, Carrasco Melo-Coutinho, de las
Carreras, Castellanos, Castro, Errazquin,
Estrázulas, García, Guerra, Lavalleja, Llambí,
Marqués, Márquez, Martínez, Obes, Oribe,
Pérez, Pérez Castellano, Piñeyrúa, Real de
Azúa, Roo, Rücker, Saavedra, Salvañach, Sus-
viela, Varela, Zufriategui.
   V. 2: Acevedo, Acosta y Lara, Aguilar,
Balparda, Batlle, Carve, Casaravilla, Conde,
Chopitea, Gallinal, García de Zúñiga, Garzón,
Gómez, Jiménez de Aréchaga, Larravide, Mac-
Eachen, Margarinos, De María, Ponce de León,
Ramírez de Arellano, Regules, Reyes, Rivera,
Sienra, De La Sierra, Solsona, Urtubey, Viana,
Zas, Zubillaga.
   V. 3: Anaya, Arrue (Arrien), Díaz, Durán,
Estrada, Flores, Gomensoro, Gonzalez Vallejo,
Gowland, Illa, Maturana, Méndez Caldeira,
Montero, Muñoz, Navia, Pagola, Pereira,
Rodríguez, Toledo, Tomkinson, Vaeza, Vásquez,
Vidal. Alphabetical index of names in each
volume.

   IU

HISTORY

1109 Acevedo, Eduardo. Manual de historia uruguaya, desde los tiempos heroicos de la fundación del pueblo uruguayo por Artigas, a base de grandes ideales, los más grandes ideales de la democracia y de la libertad, hasta 1935. 2. ed. Montevideo: "Imprenta Nacional Colorada," 1936. 416 p. 23 cm.

A manual of the policy actions of the governments of Uruguay from the time of Artigas to the year 1935. Scattered biographical information is included for the following political leaders: José Artigas, José Fructuoso Rivera, Juan Antonio Lavalleja, Juan Francisco Giró, Venancio Flores, Gabriel Antonio Pereyra, Bernardo P. Berro, Atanasio C. Aguirre, Lorenzo Batlle, Timoteo Aparicio, José E. Ellauri, Pedro Varela, Lorenzo Latorre, Francisco Antonino Vidal, Máximo Santos, Máximo Tajes, Julio Herrera y Obes, Juan Idiarte Borda, Juan Lindolfo Cuestas, José Batlle y Ordóñez, Aparicio Saravia, Claudio Williman, Feliciano Viera, Baltasar Brum, José Serrato, Juan Campisteguy.

DLC MB MiU MU NcU PPULC PU ViU TxU

1110 Araújo, Orestes. Gobernantes del Uruguay. Montevideo: Impr. de Dornaleche y Reyes, 1903. 2 v. Portraits. 18 cm.

Essay on Uruguayan history between 1825-1856 including scattered biographies of the following political leaders and military men:

V. 1: Juan Antonio Lavalleja, Manuel Oribe, Pablo Zufriátegui, Manuel Lavalleja, Fructuoso Rivera, José Rondeau.

V. 2: Joaquín Suárez, Bernabé Rivera, Eugenio Garzón, Luis Baena, Marceleiro Sosa, Antonio Crespo, Santiago Vásquez, Florencio Varela, Giuseppe Garibaldi, Melchor Pacheco y Obes, Bernardo P. Berro, Juan Francisco Giró, César Díaz, Venancio Flores, Manuel Basilio Bustamante.

CU DLC ICJ MiU MsSM NcU PPULC PU TNJ TxU

1111 Barrios Pintos, Aníbal. Los libertadores de 1825. Montevideo: Ediciones de la Banda Oriental, 1976. 95 p. Portraits. 19 cm.

Biographical sketches of individuals involved in the Uruguayan Independence movement of 1825. Data include family background, dates, and political activities of Manuel Durán, Pedro Trápani, Juan Antonio Lavalleja, Manuel Ceferino Oribe, Pablo José Zufriátegui, Basilio Antonio Araujo, Manuel Pantaleón Artigas, Manuel Florentino Freyre, Santiago Cristóbal Gadea, Juan Joaquín Manuel Eustaquio Pérez de Lavalleja, Manuel Meléndez, Atanasio Domingo Sierra, Jacinto Trápani, Juan Nicomedes Spikerman, Nicolás Celedonio Rojas, Andrés Cheveste, Juan Acosta, José del Carmen Colman, Avelino Miranda, Juan José Ortiz, Dámaso Ramón Giquiau Ortiz, Juan Rosas, Andrés

Spikerman, Tiburcio Gómez, Simón del Pino, Gregorio Sanabria, Pedro Antonio Areguati, Felipe Patiño, Francisco Romero (Manuel Lavalleja, pseud.), Luciano Romero, Joaquín Artigas, Dionisio Oribe, Matías Alvarez, Juan Arteaga, José Leguizamón, Miguel Martínez, Ignacio Medina, Santiago Nievas, José Ignacio Núñez, Norberto Ortiz, Agustín Velázquez, José Yaguarete.

InU IU

1112 Bermúdez, Washington Pedro. Los oradores de la Cámara; retratos, bocetos y caricaturas de algunos diputados de 1873. Por un aficionado. Primera serie. Montevideo: Impr. el Obrero español, 1876. 134 p. 19 cm.

A collection of biographical sketches of the following members of the Cámara de Representantes in the 1876 Uruguayan Asamblea General: Pedro Bustamante, José P. Ramírez, Julio Herrera y Obes, José Vázquez Sagastume, Agustín de Vedia, Carlos A. Lerena, Isaac de Tezanos, José C. Bustamante, Ambrosio Velazco, Juan José Soto, Narciso del Castillo.

DLC TxU

1113 Bonavita, Luis. Escenario y actores de la revolución oriental de 1811. Montevideo, 1954. 48 p. Portraits.

A short discussion of the Uruguayan revolution of 1811, including scattered biographical information, of varying amounts, about many notable figures of that movement. The following are particularly featured: José de Salazar, Francisco Javier de Elío, Manuel Francisco Artigas.

DLC

1114 Craviotto Casas, Wilson. Orientales ilustres; los tenientes de Artigas: Rivera y Lavalleja. Montevideo: Ministerio de Educación y Cultura, 1981. 109 p. (V. 1). Portraits. 24 cm.

An essay on Fructuoso Rivera and Juan Antonio Lavalleja. Includes also biographical data about Pablo Hilarión Perafán de la Rivera, Andrea Toscano de la Rivera, Bernardina Fragoso de Rivera, Ana Monterroso de Lavalleja.

IU

1115 Fernández Cabrelli, Alfonso. Artigas y los curas rebeldes. Montevideo: Ediciones Grito de Ascencio, 1968. 165 p. 19 cm.

A short account of the activities of the radical Uruguayan clergy, covering the period from 1810 to the present independence movement. Very brief scattered biographical information is given for many people, mostly clerics. Particular emphasis on the following: José Artigas, Larrañaga, José Benito Monterroso, Carlos Partelli.

CLSU CLU CSt CtY-D CU DS FU InU IU KU MB MoSW NcU NIC NjP NN NNC NSyU PPiU TxU ViU

HISTORY

1116 Herrera, Luis Alberto de. <u>Por la patria</u>; la revolución de 1897 y sus antecedentes. Montevideo: Barreiro Y Ramos, 1953. 2 v. 22 cm.
 Study of the revolution of 1897 in Uruguay covering the period of 1830-1904. Varying amounts of biographical material included for the participants concentrating mainly on their actions during the struggle. Among those mentioned are
 V. 1: Aparicio Saravia, José Núñez, Diego Lamas, Duvimioso Terra, José F. González, José Villar, Ricardo Flores, Rafael A. Pons, Francisco Solano Alvarez, Eduardo Montautti, Juan C. González, Jaime Coll, Albín Pereyra, Manuel Durante.
 V. 2: Justino Muñiz, Melitón Muñoz, Rufino Domínguez, Julio Barrios, Carmelo Cabrera, Arturo Ramos Suárez, Alberto Maldonado, Ramón Orique, Nicolás Imas.

 CtY CU IU MiU NcD NcU NIC NNC
 NSyU

1117 <u>La independencia nacional</u>. Montevideo: Ministerio de Educación y Cultura, Biblioteca Artigas, 1975. 2 v. 20 cm. (Biblioteca Artigas: Colección de clásicos uruguayos. V. 145-146).
 Study of Uruguayan independence featuring writings of prominent 19th- and 20th-century Uruguayans. Biographical notes include birthplace, dates, and professional activities for the following contributors:
 V. 1: Francisco Bauzá, José Pedro Ramírez, Agustín de Vedia, José Espalter, Gustavo Gallinal, Juan Zorrilla de San Martín, Felipe Ferreiro.

 IU TxLT

1118 Maeso, Carlos M. <u>Tierra de promisión</u>: descripción general de la república o. del Uruguay: su comercio, industrias, rentas, riquezas, educación y progresos. Situación de los extranjeros en ella. Narraciones históricas. Rasgos biográficos de próceres de la independencia, etc. Montevideo: Impr. á Vapor de la Nación, 1900. 211 p. 25 cm.
 An earlier edition has title: <u>El Oriental: descripción general de la república</u>. 1884. (<u>See</u> entry 1076.) Biographical sketches of the following 19th-century Uruguayan military men and politicians who contributed to the Independence: José G. Artigas, Fructuoso Rivera, Juan Antonio Lavalleja, Joaquín Suárez, Eugenio Garzón, Pablo Zufriátegui, Santiago Vázquez, Miguel Barreiro, Luis Eduardo Pérez, Manuel Vicente Pagola.

 DLC DNW IU NcU NNH

1119 Montero Bustamante, Raúl. <u>Estampas</u>: Fructuoso Rivera, Melchor Pacheco y Obes, Juan Carlos Gómez, Julio Herrera y Obes. Montevideo: Ediciones Ceibo, 1942. 188 p. Portraits. 20 cm.
 Collection of biographical essays on the following Uruguayan political figures of the 19th century: José Fructuoso Rivera, Melchor Pacheco y Obes, Juan Carlos Gómez, Julio Herrera y Obes.

 DLC ICarbS ICRL IU NcD NcU NN PU
 TxU

1120 _____. <u>Estampas del Montevideo romántico</u>. Montevideo: Ediciones de la Banda Oriental, 1968. 93 p. 17 cm. (Colección del bolsillo. V. 11).
 Collection of essays profiling the following 19th- and 20th-century Uruguayans including information on their early lives and later achievements: Julio Herrera y Obes, José de Buschental, Carlos María Ramírez, Juan Carlos Gómez.

 CLSU CSt CU-SB FU IaU ICU IU MoSW
 NbU NBuU NIC NSyU OU TxU

1121 _____. <u>Políticos y románticos</u>: Andrés Lamas, Melchor Pacheco y Obes, Cándido Juanicó y el ocaso de Julio Herrera. Montevideo: Centro Editor de América Latina, 1969. 96 p. 18 cm. (Capítulo oriental: biblioteca uruguaya fundamental. V. 40).
 Collection of biographical essays on the following notable political figures of Uruguay in the 19th century: Andrés Lamas, Melchor Pacheco y Obes, Cándido Juanicó, Julio Herrera y Obes.

 CtY IU MH MiEM NjP NSyU OU

1122 Montes, Eudaldo G. <u>Estampas heroicas</u>. Montevideo: Impresora Adroher, 1950. 111 p. Portraits. 23 cm.
 A military history of Uruguay, consisting mainly of biographical information of varying amounts, as well as portraits in many cases, on many 19th- and 20th-century military men. Among them are Aparicio Saravia, Eduardo Acevedo Díaz, Luis Alberto de Herrera, Arturo Berro, José Luis Baena, Juan B. Morelli, Francisco Trotta, Modesto Morales, Andrés Ceverio, Bernardo Rospide, Arturo Lussich, Basilio Muñoz (son), Javier de Viana, Carlos Roxlo, José Peña, Gabino Coronel, Orlando Landívar, Luis Santiago Bottana, Clodomiro Enrique Olivera, Diego Lamas, Antonio Floricio Saravia (Chiquito, pseud.), Cayetano Gutiérrez, Nepomuceno H. Saravia, Dionisio Coronel, Antonio María Fernández, Pedro J. Berro, Sergio Santiago Muñoz, Dalmiro Coronel, Juan Escayola, Manuel E. Nieto, Luis Seguí, Froilán Pereira Carrasco, Alfredo Hafliger, Antonio Medero.

 DLC

1123 Montevideo. Intendencia municipal. <u>Gobernantes municipales de Montevideo</u>; datos biográficos - fotografías. Montevideo: Intendencia Municipal de Montevideo. Dirección de Publicaciones y Prensa, 1972. 72 p. Portraits. 25 cm.

Biographical sketches accompanied by portraits of mayors of the city of Montevideo, Uruguay, from the early 20th century to 1972. Important dates, birthplace, and information on political activities are provided for Daniel Muñoz, Ramón V. Benzano, Santiago Rivas, Francisco Acchinelli, Eugenio Martínez Thedy, Juan P. Fabini, Luis P. Ponce, León Peyrou, José P. Astigarraga, Félix Polleri, César Batlle Pacheco, Alberto Dagnino, Juan B. Maglia, Luis A. Zanzi, Horacio Acosta y Lara, Benigno Paiva Irisarri, Pedro Onetti, Andrés Martínez Trueba, Germán Barbato, Alvaro Correa Moreno, Armando Malet, José Acquistapace, Daniel Fernández Crespo, Luis A. Fígoli, Ledo Arroyo Torres, Fermín Sorhueta, Glauco Segovia, Carlos B. Herrera, Oscar V. Rachetti, E. Mario Peyrot.

IU

1124 Muñoz, Juan José. *Apuntes históricos.* Con una biografía, por Bernardino E. Orique. Montevideo: Barreiro y Ramos, 1952. 80 p. Portraits. 20 cm.

A collection of the historical notes kept by the Uruguayan general Juan José Muñoz. A lengthy biographical essay and portrait are included for this man, as well as less biographical information for Bernardino E. Orique, author of Muñoz's biography, and Guillermo Muñoz, for whom a portrait is also provided.

DLC TxU

1125 Palomeque, Alberto. *La dinastía Santos-Vidal.* Buenos Aires: Impr. del Porvenir, 1886. 130 p. Portraits. 23 cm.

An essay on the politics and government of Uruguay during the 19th century. Includes biographical essays, accompanied by portraits, of the following patriots associated with the events of El Quebracho: Julián Urán, Segundo Posada, Teófilo Gil, Juan Pedro Sampere, Juan A. Magariños Veyra, Alfredo M. Giménez. Also biographical data of Francisco A. Vidal and Máximo Santos.

IU MH

1126 _____. *Mis derrotas.* Montevideo: "El Siglo ilustrado," 1899. 607 p. Portraits. 27 cm.

A constitutional history of Uruguay, covering the last quarter of the 19th century, and including biographical information and portraits for many representatives. The following are particularly featured: Aureliano Rodríguez Larreta, Martín C. Martínez, José P. Espalter, Alvaro Guillot, Juan P. Castro, Pedro Echeverría, Anacleto Dufort y Alvarez, José Román Mendoza, Evaristo G. Ciganda, José Serrato, Juan B. Schiaffino, Eduardo Moreno, Alfredo Vidal y Fuentes, Elías Regules, Joaquín de Salterain, Agustín de Vedia, Eduardo Acevedo Díaz, Pereda, Diego M. Martínez,

Laudelino Vázquez, Domingo González, Ramón Montero y Paullier, Pedro E. Garzón, Jacinto D. Real.

CLU NcU TxU

1127 _____. *¡Triunfos!* Montevideo: Impr. El Siglo Ilustrado, 1900. 367 p. (V. 1). 20 cm.

A collection of essays, many of them dealing with Uruguayan 19th-century politics, with portraits and biographical information on many Uruguayan statesmen. The following are particularly featured: Samuel Blixén, Juan Carlos Blanco, Emilio Avegno, Carlos María de Pena, Alfredo Vásquez Acevedo, Eugenio Madalena, Martín Berinduague, José G. Palomeque, José A. Ferreira, José Arrieta, Dionisio Ramos Montero, Arturo Santa Anna, Juan Zorrilla de San Martín, Carlos A. Berro, Ramón Pampillo Novas.

MB MiU NSyU TxU

1128 Patiño, Enrique. *Los tenientes de Artigas.* Montevideo: Impresores A. Monteverde & Cía., 1936. 270 p. Portraits. 21 cm.

A collection of biographical sketches, accompanied by portraits, of the following deputies of José Gervasio Artigas: Andrés Guacurarí, Blas Basualdo, Fernando Otorgués, Manuel Vicente Pagola, Pedro Campbell.

CtY CU DLC DPU NcD NN NSyU OrU TxU ViU

1129 Pedemonte, Juan Carlos. *El año terrible;* Latorre, Santos, Tajes: hombres y hechos de su tiempo. Montevideo: Barreiro y Ramos, 1956. 210 p. 19 cm.

Study of politics and government from 1875 to 1904 featuring biographical information centering on the political careers of the following presidents of Uruguay: Lorenzo Latorre, Máximo Santos, Máximo Tajes.

CtY IU NN ViU

1130 Pereda, Setembrino Ezequiel. *Paysandú patrió-tico.* Montevideo: Imprenta "El Siglo Ilustrado," 1926. 2 v. 19 cm.

An essay on the seizure of the Uruguayan town of Paysandú by the Portuguese in 1811. Includes biographical sketches on the following figures associated with it: Francisco Bicudo, Silverio Antonio Martínez, Ignacio Maestre, Jorge Pacheco, José Ambrosio Carranza, Miguel del Cerro.

CtY CU DLC WU

1131 Quesada, Efraín. *La emancipación oriental:* antología gráfica y literaria. Montevideo: Ediciones de La Plaza, 1980. 375 p. Portraits. 23 cm.

A history of the Uruguayan independence movement, including biographical information. as well as portraits in a few cases for the

HISTORY

following: José Artigas, Dámaso Larrañaga, Eduardo Acevedo Díaz, Héctor Miranda, Manuel Oribe, Fructuoso Rivera, Juan Antonio Lavalleja.

IU

1132 Revuelta, Luis. La gloriosa cruzada de los treinte y tres patriotas orientales, 19 de abril de 1825. Montevideo: Impr. de La Reforma, 1879. 39 p. 24 cm.
    A short account of the military activities of a group of 32 19th-century Uruguayan patriots. Brief scattered biographical information is included for many of them and for others involved in this period of Uruguay's history. The following are particularly featured: Juan Lavalleja, Fructuoso Rivera, Manuel Oribe, Pablo Zufriategui.

IU TxU

1133 Salterain Herrera, Eduardo de. Hombres y faenas; estudios uruguayos. Montevideo: Palacio del Libro, 1960. 493 p. 24 cm.
    A collection of biographical sketches of the following notable figures in Uruguayan history: Marcos José da Porta Monterroso, José Gervasio Artigas, Fructuoso Rivera, Bernardina Fragoso de Rivera, Ana Monterosso de Lavalleja.

DLC DPU NIC NN

1134 Stewart Vargas, Guillermo. Veinte perfiles significativos de la historia nacional; ensayos. Montevideo, 1962. 359 p. 20 cm.
    Collection of biographical essays on 19th- and 20th-century Uruguayans with concentration on their political activities: Manuel Oribe, Eduardo Acevedo, Francisco Lavandeira, Jaime Estrázulas, Gonzalo Ramírez, Pedro Bustamante, José María Muñoz, Alfredo Vázquez Acevedo, José Pedro Ramírez, Luis Alberto de Herrera, Aureliano Rodríguez Larreta, José A. Otamendi, Juan Antonio Lavalleja, Leandro Gómez, Diego Lamas, Basilio Muñoz, Aparicio Saravia.

CLSU CLU CtY GU InU IU KU NcU NIC
NN NSyU TNJ

1135 Torterolo, Leogardo Miguel. Semblanzas históricas. Montevideo: J. S. Serrano, Librería Cervantes, 1912. 166 p. 19 cm.
    Historical essays dealing with the Uruguayan Independence movement in the 19th century featuring varying amounts of biographical data on the following: José Gervasio Artigas, Santiago Vázquez, José Ellauri, Juan Bautista Brie de Loustán, Pedro de Cevallos, Ansina.

DLC

1136 Uruguay. Ejército. Estado mayor. Departamento de estudios históricos. División historia. Los escudos de armas de los gobernadores de Montevideo. Montevideo, 1977. 14 p. 23 cm.

Description of the coats of arms of the following political leaders of Montevideo: Joaquín de Viana, Agustín de la Rosa, Joaquín del Pino, Antonio Olaguer y Feliú, José de Bustamante y Guerra, Pascual Ruiz Huidobro, Joaquín de Soria, Francisco Javier de Elío, Gaspar de Vigodet.

IU

HISTORY--DICTIONARIES, ENCYCLOPEDIAS, and "WHO'S WHO"

1137 Araújo, Orestes. Diccionario popular de historia de la República Oriental del Uruguay, desde la época del descubrimiento de su territorio, hasta la de su independencia. Montevideo: Impr. Artística de Dornaleche y Reyes, 1901-08. 3 v. Portraits. 24 cm.
    Biographical sketches of more than 300 important individuals in Uruguayan history from discovery to Independence. Contents:
    V. 1: A-B.
    V. 2: C-Ll.
    V. 3: M-Z.

CtY CU DLC IaU IU NcD NIC OCl WU

1138 Schulkin, Augusto I. Historia de Paysandú, diccionario biográfico. Buenos Aires: Van Roosen, 1958. 3 v. 23 cm.
    Biographies of approximately 450 19th- and 20th-century residents of Paysandú, Uruguay. With photos. Contents:
    V. 1: A-Frag.
    V. 2: Frag-O.
    V. 3: P-Z.

CU IU

1139 Willis, Jean L. Historical Dictionary of Uruguay. Metuchen: Scarecrow Press, 1974. 275 p. 22 cm. (Latin American historical dictionaries. V. 11).
    Historical dictionary with over 350 biographical sketches of prominent individuals in Uruguayan history.

CaBVaU CoU FMU IEN InU IU LU MB
MoSW MShM MU N NbU NcD NcGU NcRS
NjR NmLcU NNC NNU NSyU OKentU OrPS
OU PSt RPB ScU TU TxU ViU

JOURNALISM

1140 Urueña González, Camilo. Crónicas de Treinta y Tres; siete lustros de periodismo bravio. Montevideo: Estudio "Ideas," 1948. 83 p. 20 cm.
    History of journalism in Uruguay featuring biographical sketches of journalists (first half of the 20th century) from the Uruguayan province of Treinta y Tres. Biographical information concentrates on the following individuals' professional activities: Ricardo Hierro, Julio Ramón de la Cerda, Javier de

Viana, Manuel Cacheiro, Hilario Percibal, Isidoro J. Amorín, Manuel Coronel, Luis Hierro, Juan Paseyro y Monegal, Eduardo Juanicó Otorgués, Olavo Amaro Macedo, Mariano Berro Antuña, Lucas Urrutia, Aureliano G. Berro, Anselmo E. Balsaldúa, José Remigio Gómez, Valentín González Castro, Tomás B. Muñiz.

CU

1141 Villa, Oscar Jorge, and Gerardo Mendive. La prensa y los constituyentes en el Uruguay de 1830: fundamentos técnicos, económicos y sociales. Montevideo: Biblioteca Nacional, 1980. 258 p. 24 cm.

A history of the Uruguayan press during the period of independence, including biographical information on many prominent journalists. Among them are Carlos Eduardo Bladh, José Pedro Varela, Francisco Bauzá, Carlos María Ramírez, Martín C. Martínez, Justino Jiménez de Aréchaga, Juan Andrés Ramírez.

IU

1142 Zinny, Antonio. Historia de la prensa periódica de la República Oriental del Uruguay, 1807-1852. Buenos Aires: C. Casavalle, 1883. 504 p. 24 cm.

History of journalism in Uruguay from 1807 to 1852 with scattered biographical information on notable individuals connected with it. Alphabetical index of names.

DLC IU

LAW

1143 Pastorino, Víctor A. Inventario honorífico; capital intelectual de graduados, con el que, la Facultad de Derecho y Ciencias Sociales, enriqueció el aservo intelectual del país, en cuarenta años de docencia. Montevideo: Pap. e Impr. Cervantes, 1951. 145 p. 29 cm.

Biographical dictionary containing the names of the graduates of the "Facultad de Derecho y Ciencias Sociales" in Montevideo up to 1951. Information provided includes profession, nationality, date of graduation, and frequently professional activities and achievements for over 2,000 individuals.

DLC IU(film) MH-L

LITERATURE

1144 Andrade Coello, Alejandro. Cultura femenina uruguaya. Juana de Ibarbourou. Quito: Tall. Gráf. del Ministerio de Educación, 1943. 63 p. 22 cm.

Essay dealing with 20th-century Uruguayan poetesses with biobibliographical material in varying amounts and critical comment. Those especially featured are María Eugenia Vaz

Ferreira, Luisa Luisi, Delmira Agustini, Juana de Ibarbourou.

DPU IEN IU MnU NcD NN WaU

1145 Artucio Ferreira, Antonio, comp. Parnaso uruguayo, 1905-1922. Barcelona: Casa Editorial Maucci, 1922. 336 p. 19 cm.

Anthology of Uruguayan poetry between 1905 and 1922 with brief biographical sketches of the following: Delmira Agustini, José G. Antuña, Antonio Artucio Ferreira, Segundo Barreiro, R. Bas y Pi, Manuel Benavente, Enrique Bianchi, Ernesto de los Campos, Enrique Casaravilla Lemos, Buenaventura Caviglia, Bernabé Cosme, Julio J. Casal, Manuel de Castro, José María Delgado, Angel Falco, Ovidio Fernández Ríos, Alfredo C. Franchi, Carlos T. Gamba, Julio Garet y Mas, Edgardo Ubaldo Genta, Ernesto Herrera, Juana de Ibarbourou, María Carmen Izcua Barbat de Muñoz Ximénez, Alberto Lasplaces, Carlos César Lenzi, Andrés Héctor Lerena Acevedo, Luisa Luisi, Alfredo E. Martínez, Julio Raúl Mendilaharsu, Mario Menéndez, Casiano Monegal, Adolfo Montiel Ballesteros, Orosmán Moratorio, Miguel Nébel Alvarez, Luis Onetti Lima, Juan María Oliver, Emilio Oribe, Héctor Parra y Freire, Manuel Peris y Curis, Víctor Pérez Petit, José Enrique Rodó, Yamandú Rodríguez, Enrique Rodríguez Fabregat, Armando Víctor Roxlo, Jules Supervielle, Carlos Sabat Ercasty, Francisco Alberto Schinca, Arturo S. Silva, Melitón J. Simois, Fernán Silva Valdés, Luis Torres Guinart, José Trelles, Natalio Abel Vadell, Carlos María del Vallejo, Lorenzo Vicens Thievent, Alberto Zum Felde.

AzU CtY CU DLC IaU MiU MU NBuU NN PBm

1146 Barbagelata, Hugo David. Una centuria literaria (poetas y prosistas uruguayos) 1800-1900. Paris: Biblioteca Latino-Americana, 1924. 486 p. Portraits. 26 cm.

Anthology of 19th-century Uruguayan literature arranged chronologically with bio-bibliographical data on the following: Francisco Acuña de Figueroa, Bartolomé Hidalgo, Dámaso Antonio Larrañaga, José Manuel Pérez Castellano, Pedro P. Bermúdez, Adolfo Berro, Pedro Bustamante, Isidoro De María, Juan Carlos Gómez, Andrés Lamas, Alejandro Magariños Cervantes, Melchor Pacheco y Obes, Marcos Sastre, Aurelio Berro, Angel Floro Costa, Heraclio C. Fajardo, Fermín Ferreira y Artigas, Julio Herrera y Obes, José Pedro Ramírez, Ramón de Santiago, José Sienra Carranza, Eduardo Acevedo Díaz, Francisco Bauzá, Matías Behety, Wáshington P. Bermúdez, Juan Carlos Blanco, Teófilo E. Díaz, Anacleto Dufort y Alvarez, Antonio Lamberti, Luis Melián Lafinur, Victoriano E. Montes, Daniel Muñoz, Gonzalo Ramírez, Carlos María Ramírez, Ricardo Sánchez, Mariano Soler, José Pedro Varela, Prudencio Vázquez y Vega, Agustín de Vedia, Juan Zorrilla de San Martín, Víctor Arreguine,

LITERATURE

Antonio Bachini, Manuel Bernández, Samuel Blixen, José G. del Busto, Rafael Fragueiro, Enrique Kubly y Arteaga, Santiago Maciel, Carlos M. Maeso, Abel J. Pérez, Elías Regules, Carlos Roxlo, Joaquín de Salterain, Francisco Sora, Roberto de las Carreras, Benjamín Fernández y Medina, Eduardo Ferreira, Luis Alberto de Herrera, Daniel Martínez Vigil, Carlos Martínez Vigil, Guzmán Papini, Víctor Pérez Petit, Carlos Reyles, José Enrique Rodó, Carlos Vaz Ferreira, María Eugenia Vaz Ferreira, Javier de Viana, Juan Antonio Zubillaga.

AzU CtY DLC FTaSU IU NcD NcU OClW

1147 Bartholomew, Roy, comp. Cien poesías rioplatenses, 1800-1950. Antología, ordenación, prólogo, notas sobre la poesía en el Río de la Plata y bio-bibliográficas de los poetas. Apéndice con los poemas de William Henry Hudson. Buenos Aires: Editorial Raigal, 1954. 398 p. 24 cm.
    Anthology of Uruguayan poetry between 1800 and 1950 arranged by period with biobibliographical material on the following: Bartolomé Hidalgo, Olegario Víctor Andrade (Argentinean), Juan Zorrilla de San Martín, Julio Herrera y Reissig, Emilio Frugoni, Alvaro Armando Vasseur, Delmira Agustini, María Eugenia Vaz Ferreira, Julio J. Casal, Emilio Oribe, Fernán Silva Valdés, Carlos Sabat Ercasty, Juana de Ibarbourou.

CU DLC IaU IU MiU NBuU NSyU NN OrU TxU WaU

1148 Benedetti, Mario. Literatura uruguaya siglo XX; ensayos. Montevideo: Alfa, 1963. 174 p. 18 cm. (Colección Carabela. V. 19).
    A collection of essays containing biobibliographical material on the following 20th-century Uruguayan writers: Emilio Oribe, Juan José Morosoli, Enrique Amorim, Francisco Espínola, Felisberto Hernández, Líber Falco, Juan Carlos Onetti, Carlos Martínez Moreno, Domingo Luis Bordoli (Luis Castelli, pseud.), Idea Vilariño, Julio C. Da Rosa, Humberto Megget, Milton Schinca, Mario César Fernández, Juan Carlos Somma. (See also entry 1149.)

IU

1149 _____. Literatura uruguaya siglo XX; ensayo. 2. ed. ampliada. Montevideo: Editorial Alfa, 1969. 364 p. 18 cm. (Colección Carabela).
    Enlarged 2. edition. (See entry 1148.) Collection of critical essays including varying amounts of biobibliographical information on the following: Carlos Reyles, Emilio Oribe, Juan José Morosoli, Enrique Amorim, Francisco Espínola, Felisberto Hernández, Clara Silva, Líber Falco, Juan Carlos Onetti, L. S. Garini, Roberto Fabregat Cúneo, Arturo Sergio Visca, Carlos Martínez Moreno, Domingo Luis Bordoli (Luis Castelli, pseud.), Mario Arregui, Armonía Somers, Idea Vilariño, Julio C. da Rosa, José Pedro Díaz, Carlos Maggi,

Amanda Berenguer, Ida Vitale, Humberto Megget, Milton Schinca, Mario César Fernández, María Inés Silva Vila, Juan Carlos Somma, Circe Maia, Eduardo Galeano, Cristina Peri Rossi.

AU CtY FMU GU IaU IU MdBJ MH MU NBuU NcD NjP PSt TU TxHR

1150 Bollo, Sarah. Literatura uruguaya, 1807-1965. Montevideo: Orfeo, 1965. 2 v. 17 cm.
    Literary history containing biobibliographical information on more than 300 Uruguayan writers arranged chronologically within each period (1807-1965).

CLSU CoU CtY DeU DPU KU LNHT MH MiDW MiU MoU NcU NhD NIC NjP NjR OU PPULC PrU TU ViU

1151 Bordoli, Domingo Luis, comp. Antología de la poesía uruguaya contemporánea. Montevideo: Departamento de Publicaciones, Universidad de la República, 1966. 2 v. 20 cm. (Letras nacionales. V. 9).
    Anthology of 20th-century Uruguayan poets featuring birth and death dates, limited biobibliographical data, and stylistic analyses of the following contributors:
    V. 1: José Alonso y Trelles, Alvaro Armando Vasseur, Emilio Frugoni, Romildo Risso, Guillermo Cuadri, Carlos Sabat Ercasty, Fernán Silva Valdés, Vicente Basso Maglio, Enrique Casaravilla Lemos, Julio J. Casal, Pedro Leandro Ipuche, Yamandú Rodríguez, Juan Carlos Abellá, Emilio Oribe, Juan Parra del Riego, Agustín R. Bisio, Juana de Ibarbourou, Carlos Rodríguez Pintos, Manuel de Castro, Humberto Zarrilli, Ildefonso Pereda Valdés, María A. Bonavita, Alfredo M. Ferreiro, Esther de Cáceres, Selva Márquez, Sarah Bollo, Nicolás Fusco Sansone, Clara Silva, Líber Falco, Roberto Ibáñez, Juvenal Ortiz Saralegui.
    V. 2: Susana Soca, Cipriano S. Vitureira, Fernando Pereda, Alvaro Figueredo, Serafín García, Pedro Piccatto, Juan Cunha, Sara de Ibáñez, Mario Benedetti, Idea Vilariño, Amanda Berenger, Dora Isella Russell, Osiris Rodríguez Castillos, Ricardo Paseyro, Humberto Megget, Ida Vitale, Washington Benavídez, Jorge Medina Vidal, Circe Maia, Ramón Montero y Brown, Juan E. Fagetti, Leandro Vilariño, Dimas Antuña, Junio Aguirre, Federico Morador, Blanca Luz Brum, María Elena Muñoz, César M. Rappalini, Juan de Gregorio, Luis Alberto Varela, Pedro Montero López, Walter González Penelas, Uruguay González Poggi, Beltrán Martínez, Alejandro Peñasco, Luis Alberto Caputti, Carlos Denis Molina, Ariel Badano, Mirtha Gandolfo, Orfila Bardesio, Silvia Herrera, Sarandy Cabrera, Hugo Emilio Pedemonte, Generoso Medina, Juan Carlos Legido, Umberto T. Pereira, Carlos Brandy, Luis Víctor Anastasía, Cecilio Peña, Pablo Aurelio Chiarelli, Milton Schinca, Octavio Larriera, Saúl Pérez Gadea, Walter Ortiz y Ayala, Carlos Flores Mora, Saúl Ibargoyen Islas, Iván Kmaid, Nancy Bacelo, María Ester Cantonnet.

CaOOEC CLSU DPU FTaSU GU ICIU IU
LNHT MiU MU NcU NIC NN NNC PPiU

1152 Brena Bellotti, Tomás Germán. Exploración
estética, por Tomás G. Brena. Montevideo:
Impresora Record, 1974. 2 v. 20 cm.
  Critical study and brief biobibliographi-
cal sketches of the following 20th-century
Uruguayan poets:
  V. 1: Juana de Ibarbourou, Carlos Sabat
Ercasty, Emilio Oribe, Fernán Silva Valdés,
Sara de Ibáñez, Amanda Berenguer, Alvaro
Figueredo, Roberto Ibáñez.
  V. 2: Esther de Cáceres, Idea Vilariño,
Clara Silva, Líber Falco, Guillermo Chaparro,
Saúl Ibargoyen, Circe Maia, Juan Cunha, Selva
Márquez, Milton Schinca, Ida Vitale, Cristina
Peri Rossi.

CLU CoU ICarbS IU LU MH MiU MoSW
MU NcU NIC NN NSbSU OU PPiU TxLT
ViU WU

1153 Brughetti, Romualdo. 18 [i.e. Dieciocho]
poetas del Uruguay. Buenos Aires: Montevideo, 1937. 163 p. Portraits. 21 cm. (Ediciones de la Sociedad amigos del libro rioplatense. V. 40).
  Anthology containing biobibliographical
material about the following Uruguayan poets
of the twentieth century: Jules Supervielle,
Delmira Agustini, Angel Aller, Sofía Arzarello,
Vicente Basso Maglio, Blanca Luz Brum, Esther
de Cáceres, Julio J. Casal, Enrique Casaravilla Lemos, Juan Cunha Dotti, Julio Herrera
y Reissig, Juana de Ibarbourou, Pedro Leandro
Ipuche, Carlos Maeso Tognochi, Juan Parra del
Riego, Fernando Pereda, Alvaro Armando Vasseur,
María Eugenia Vaz Ferreira.

DLC IU

1154 Caillava, Domingo A. La literatura gauchesca
en el Uruguay. Sinópsis histórica. Proemio
de Don Mario Falcao Espalter. Montevideo:
C. García, 1921. 71 p. 19 cm.
  Essay dealing with the development of
gauchesque literature in 19th and 20th century featuring biobibliographical material on
the following: Bartolomé Hidalgo, Alejandro
Magariños Cervantes, Benjamín Fernández y
Medina, Eduardo Acevedo Díaz, Orosmán Moratorio, Javier de Viana, Yamandú Rodríguez,
José A. Trelles (El Viejo Pancho, pseud.).

CU DLC IU NcU ViU

1155 Cardoso, Heber. El cuento uruguayo contemporáneo. Buenos Aires: Centro Editor de América Latina, 1978. 173 p. 19 cm. (Biblioteca total. Panoramas de la literatura.
V. 59).
  An anthology of contemporary Uruguayan
short stories, including biobibliographical
notes about the following writers featured in
the text: Francisco Espínola, Juan José Morosoli, Enrique Amorim, Felisberto Hernández,

Juan Carlos Onetti, Mario Benedetti, Carlos
Martínez Moreno, Armonía Somers, Julio C. da
Rosa, Mario Arregui, Sylvia Lago, Mario César
Fernández, Cristina Peri Rossi, Eduardo Gale-
ano, Gley Ehyerabide, Mercedes Rein, Teresa
Porzecanski.

IU

1156 Casal, Julio J. Exposición de la poesía uruguaya, desde sus orígenes hasta 1940. Montevideo: Editorial Claridad, 1940. 767 p.
21 cm.
  An anthology of poetry with varying
amounts of biobibliographical material on
more than 300 Uruguayan authors of the early
19th century up to 1940.

IU

1157 Cavallaro Cadeillac, Víctor. Lluvias de primavera; cuentos gauchescos y regionales.
Montevideo: Editorial Popular Republicana,
1961. 77 p. Portraits. 20 cm. (Colección
patria y tradición. C. 1. V. 3).
  Anthology of gauchesque short stories by
20th-century Uruguayan writers, including
biobibliographical sketches with dates and
works of the following contributors: Yamandú
Rodríguez, Juan José Morosoli, Julio C. da
Rosa, Javier de Viana, Horacio Quiroga.

CLSU IU NIC TU TxU

1158 Cotelo, Rubén, comp. Narradores uruguayos;
antología. Caracas: Monte Avila, 1969.
289 p. 18 cm. (Colección Continente).
  Anthology of short stories by Uruguayan
authors primarily from the last half of the
20th century. Brief biobibliographical
sketches include dates, information on literary careers, and stylistic analyses of the
following writers: Felisberto Hernández,
Juan Carlos Onetti, L. S. Garini, pseud.
Héctor Urdangarín), María de Monserrat, Armonía Somers, Mario Arregui, Carlos Martínez
Moreno, Mario Benedetti, Mario César Fernández, María Inés Silva, Jorge Onetti, Silvia
Lago.

AzU CSt CtY GU ICU INS IU KU MoU
NBuU NcU OU PPiU PPT PSt TNJ TU
TxU VtMiM WMM

1159 Da Rosa Caetano, Julio César. Antología del
cuento criollo del Uruguay, por Julio C. Da
Rosa. Montevideo: Ediciones de la Plaza,
1979. 247 p. 19 cm.
  Anthology of 20th-century Uruguayan
criollo short stories featuring brief bio-
bibliographical sketches of the following con-
tributors: Eduardo Acevedo Díaz, Pedro Figari,
Javier de Viana, Benjamín Fernández y Medina,
Vicente A. Salaverri, Fernán Silva Valdés,
Adolfo Montiel Ballesteros, Pedro Leandro
Ipuche, Yamandú Rodríguez, José Monegal, Juan
Mario Magallanes, Valentín García Sáiz, Celes-
tino M. Fernández, Juan José Morosoli, Enrique

LITERATURE

Amorín, Francisco Espínola, Santiago Dossetti, Serafín J. García, Angel María Luna, Víctor M. Dotti, Wenceslao Varela, Eliseo Salvador Porta, Mario Serafín Fernández, Alfredo Dante Gravina, Adolfo González González, Mario Arregui, Ricardo Leonel Figueredo, Milton Stelardo, Julio C. da Rosa, Rolina Ipuche Riva, Domingo Luis Pastorino, José María Obaldía, Elbio Pérez Tellechea, Alberto C. Bocage, Juan Capagorry.

IU

1160 Dodera, Julio W. 12 [i.e. Doce] autores. Montevideo: Fundación Editorial "Unión del Magisterio," 1969. 54 p. 20 cm.

Essay containing brief biobibliographical sketches of the following 20th-century Uruguayan writers: Eduardo Acevedo Díaz, José Enrique Rodó, Juan Zorrilla de San Martín, Florencio Sánchez, José Pedro Bellán, Juana de Ibarbourou, Montiel Ballesteros, Fernán Silva Valdés.

CSt   IU   MB   ViU   WU

1161 Falcao Espalter, Mario, comp. Antología de poetas uruguayos, 1807-1921. Montevideo, 1921. 342 p. 20 cm.

Anthology of Uruguayan poetry written between 1807 and 1921 with an introductory essay containing scattered biobibliographical data on poets of this period.

IU

1162 Filartigas, Juan M., comp. Antología de narradores del Uruguay. Montevideo: Editorial Albatros, 1930. 144 p. 20 cm.

Anthology of writings by the following 20th-century Uruguayans with biobibliographical data in varying amounts: Carlos Reyles, Justino Zavala Muñiz, Francisco Espínola, Manuel Acosta y Larra, Javier de Viana, Eduardo Acevedo Díaz, Valentín García Saíz, Manuel de Castro, Luis Giordano.

DLC   IU

1163 _____. Artistas del Uruguay; impresiones literarias (primera serie). Montevideo: Editorial Renacimiento, 1923. 65 p. 17 cm.

A collection of biographical sketches of the following Uruguayan authors: José Enrique Rodó, Julio Herrera y Reissig, Delmira Agustini, Emilio Frugoni, Juana de Ibarbourou.

CU   DLC   FU   MoU   TxU

1164 Fusco Sansone, Nicolás, comp. Antología y crítica de literatura uruguaya. Prólogo de Raúl Montero Bustamante. Montevideo: C. García, 1940. 495 p. 25 cm. (Colección Cultura).

Literary anthology with biobibliographical sketches and critical opinion of the fol-

lowing 20th-century Uruguayans: Juan Zorrilla de San Martín, Eduardo Acevedo Díaz, Javier de Viana, Carlos Reyles, Horacio Quiroga, Florencio Sánchez, José Enrique Rodó, Julio Herrera y Reissig, Delmira Agustini, María Eugenia Vaz Ferreira.

DLC   IU

1165 Gallinal, Gustavo. Letras uruguayas. Prólogo de Carlos Real de Azúa. Montevideo: Biblioteca Artigas, 1967. 402 p. 20 cm.

Collection of essays dealing with many facets of Uruguayan literature of the 19th and 20th centuries, featuring biobibliographical material on the following: Dámaso Antonio Larrañaga, Alejandro Magariños Cervantes, José Alonso y Trelles (El Viejo Pancho, pseud.), Delmira Agustini, María Eugenia Vaz Ferreira, Juana de Ibarbourou, Juan Zorrilla de San Martín, Juan Carlos Gómez, Julio Raúl Mendilaharsu, Emilio Frugoni, Andrés Héctor Lerena Acevedo, Emilio Oribe, Antonio Soto (Boy, pseud.), Osvaldo Crispo Acosta (Lauxar, pseud.), Adolfo Agorio, Pedro Leandro Ipuche, Francisco Acuña de Figueroa, José Prego de Oliver, Juan Francisco Martínez, Jacinto Acuña de Figueroa, Agustín Acuña de Figueroa, Claudio Acuña de Figueroa, Manuel Acuña de Figueroa, José Enrique Rodó.

DPU   IaU   ICU   IU   MH   NBuU   OU

1166 García, Serafín J. Diez poetas gauchescos del Uruguay. Montevideo: Librería Blundi, 1963. 121 p. 20 cm.

Anthology of gauchesque poetry of Uruguay featuring biobibliographical sketches of the following 19th- and 20th-century poets: Bartolomé Hidalgo, Manuel Araúcho, Antonio D. Lussich, Elías Regules, José Alonso y Trelles (El Viejo Pancho, pseud.), Juan Escayola (Juan Torora, pseud.), Juan María Oliver (Juan Solito, pseud.), Romildo Risso, Guillermo Cuadri (Santos Garrido, pseud.), Yamandú Rodríguez.

CtY   IU   LU   NIC   NjP   NSyU

1167 _____, comp. Panorama de la poesía gauchesca y nativista del Uruguay, desde Bartolomé Hidalgo hasta nuestros días; selección, prólogo y notas de Serafín J. García. Montevideo: Editorial Claridad, 1941. 312 p. 22 cm. (Biblioteca de escritores uruguayos. Dirección general: Antonio Zamora. V. 9).

Anthology of gauchesque and nativist Uruguayan writers of the 19th and 20th centuries with biobibliographical material in varying amounts on the following: Bartolomé Hidalgo, Manuel Araúcho, Antonio D. Lussich (Luciano Santos, pseud.), José Alonso y Trelles (El viejo Pancho, pseud.), Juan Escayola (Juan Torora, pseud.), Julio Alberto Lista, Ricardo Eguía Puentes, Juan María Oliver (Juan Solitos, pseud.), Niceto S. Loizaga, Atilio Supparo, Bartolomé Firpo y Firpo, Francisco

Alvarez Alonso, Guillermo Cuadri (Santos Garrido, pseud.), Rafael J. Abella, Romildo Risso, Raúl E. Baethgen, Ernesto V. Silveira, Juan Carlos Sabat Pebet (Rosales, el Arriador, pseud.), Juan Rodríguez Can, Víctor V. Bergalli, Serafín J. García, Juan Carlos Guarnieri, Mario Roldán, Valentín R. Macedo, Omar Odriozola, José Gorosito Tanco, Alejandro Magariños Cervantes, Ramón de Santiago, Luis Piñeyro del Campo, Orosmán Moratorio (Julián Perujo, pseud.), Alcides de María (Calisto, el Ñato, pseud.), Elías Regules, Carlos Roxlo, Víctor Pérez Petit, Benjamín Fernández y Medina, Santiago Maciel, Buenaventura Caviglia, Pedro Erasmo Callorda, Emilio Frugoni, Julián Silva Serrano, Fernán Silva Valdés, Enrique Noguera, Pedro Leandro Ipuche, Yamandú Rodríguez, Manuel Benavente, José Pedro Bastitta, Valeriano Magri, Elbio Prunell Alzaibar, Ildefonso Pereda Valdés, Juan José Morosoli, Julio Estavillo, Dardo E. Clare, Julio Casas Araújo, Enrique Amorim, Julio Silva, Diego Larriera Varela, Juan Burghi, Angel Aller, José M. González Larriera, Ramón Melo, Alvaro Figueredo, José Monegal, Justo Olarans Chans, Celestino M. Fernández, Alfredo Morosoli, Artigas Milans Martínez, José María Candela, Eliseo Porta.

DLC ICU IU MH MoU MU NBuU NcU TU TxU WU

1168 _____. Panorama del cuento nativista del Uruguay. Ilustraciones de Julio E. Suárez. Montevideo: Editorial Claridad, 1943. 319 p. Portraits. 21 cm. (Biblioteca de escritores uruguayos. V. 11).
Anthology of Uruguayan short stories containing biobibliographical material on the following 20th-century writers: Eduardo Acevedo Díaz, Manuel Bernárdez, Carlos Reyles, Domingo Arenas, Benjamín Fernández y Medina, Víctor Pérez Petit, Javier de Viana, Otto Miguel Cione, Constancio C. Vigil, Pedro Leandro Ipuche, Adolfo Montiel Ballesteros, Vicente A. Salaverri, Agustín M. Smith, Yamandú Rodríguez, Enrique Amorím, Valentín García Sáiz, Juan José Morosoli, Francisco Espínola, Julio Estavillo, Víctor M. Dotti, Juan Mario Magallanes, Alfredo Lepro, Santiago Dossetti, Serafín J. García, Alfredo D. Gravina, José E. Ormaechea.

IU MH

1169 Garet Más, Julio. Letras uruguayas. Montevideo: Ediciones del Numen, 1966. 62 p. 19 cm.
Collection of essays dealing with 20th-century Uruguayan letters. Biobibliographical data, stylistic analyses, and achievements of the following individuals are featured: Juan Zorrilla de San Martín, Adolfo Montiel Ballesteros, Sarah Bollo, Melitón I. Sunois, José María Fernández Saldaña.

CSt INS IU NBuU NNC OkU OU

1170 Lasplaces, Alberto, comp. Antología del cuento uruguayo. Montevideo: C. García, 1943. 2 v. Portraits. 20 cm. (Biblioteca "Rodó." V. 106-109).
Anthology of 20th-century Uruguayan short stories with biobibliographical sketches of the following writers:
V. 1: Eduardo Acevedo Díaz, Enrique Amorim, Domingo Arenas, Víctor Arreguine, José P. Bellán, Manuel Bernárdez, Otto Miguel Cione, Roberto de las Carreras, Santiago Dossetti, Víctor Dotti, Francisco Espínola, Benjamín Fernández y Medina, Serafín J. García.
V. 2: Julio Herreira y Reissig, Alberto Lasplaces, Carlos María Maeso, Juan Mario Magallanes, Francisco R. Mazzoni, Manuel Medina Betancourt, Montiel Ballesteros, Juan J. Morosoli, Daniel Muñoz, Ildefonso Pereda Valdés, Víctor Pérez Petit, Horacio Quiroga, Carlos Reyles, Yamandú Rodríguez, Fernán Silva Valdés, Agustín M. Smith, Javier de Viana.

CU DLC DPU FU GU ICU IU MH MoU NBuU NcD NcU OCU OrU OU PJB TxU ViU WaU

1171 _____. Nuevas opiniones literarias. Ovidio Fernández Ríos, director. Montevideo: C. García y Cía., 1939. 179 p. Portraits. 20 cm. (Biblioteca Rodó. V. 33).
Collection of critical essays on 20th-century Uruguayan literature with varying amounts of biobibliographical information on the following writers: Alberto Lasplaces, Eduardo Acevedo Díaz, Montiel Ballesteros, Emilio Oribe, Horacio Quiroga.

CtY CU-S DLC FTaSU IaU IU LU MoU NBuU NcD NcU NIC OkU TxU

1172 Legido, Juan Carlos. El teatro uruguayo; de Juan Moreira a los independientes, 1886-1967. Montevideo: Ediciones Tauro, 1968. 159 p. 20 cm. (Colección "El Baldío." V. 5).
History of Uruguayan theater from 1886-1967 with scattered biobibliographical information on individuals involved with it. Those especially featured: Francisco Imhof, Carlos María Princivalle, Yamandú Rodríguez, José Pedro Bellán, Carlos Salvaño Campos, Angel Curotto, Carlos César Lenzi, Orlando Aldama, Arturo Despouey, Carlos Denis Molina, Ernesto Pinto, Armengol P. Font, Juan León Bengoa, Antonio Larreta, Héctor Plaza Noblía, Andrés Castillo, Jacobo Langsner, Elzear de Camilli, Juan Carlos Patrón, Carlos Maggi, Angel Rama, Luis Novas Terra, Enrique Guarnero, Hiber Conteris, Rubén Deugenio, Mauricio Rosencof, Juan Carlos Legido. Alphabetical index of names.

CLU IaU IU MH MoSW MU NBuU

1173 Los más jovenes cuentan. Prólogo, Arturo S. Visca. Montevideo: Arca, 1976. 149 p. 17 cm.

LITERATURE

An anthology of short stories written by the following contemporary Uruguayan writers, including brief biobibliographical sketches: Hugo Burel Guerra, Mario Delgado Aparaín, Tomás de Mattos, Milton Fornaro, Hugo Giovanetti Viola, Ramiro Núñez y Malacoda (Malacoda, pseud.), Adriana Mendizábal Cabral, César Murillo, Carlos Pellegrino, Teresa Porzecanski Cohen, Antonio Carlos Pádova, Gabriela Revel.

IU

1174 Montero Bustamante, Raúl, comp. El Parnaso oriental; antología de poetas uruguayos con un prólogo y notas crítico-biográficas. Ed. ilustrada con varios medallones foto-grabados de poetas uruguayos. Montevideo: Maucci Hnos e Hijos, 1905. 383 p. 21 cm.
Anthology of Uruguayan poetry from the 18th to early 20th centuries with biobibliographical sketches of the following: Francisco Acuña de Figueroa, Bartolomé Hidalgo, Manuel de Araúcho, Adolfo Berro, Juan Carlos Gómez, Bernardo P. Berro, Melchor Pacheco y Obes, Alejandro Magariños Cervantes, Pedro P. Bermúdez, Francisco Xavier de Acha, Enrique de Arrascaeta, Fermín Ferreira y Artigas, Heraclio C. Fajardo, Carlos A. Fajardo, Ramón de Santiago, Rafael Ximénez, Antonino Lamberti, Laurindo Lapuente, Eduardo G. Gordon, José Pedro Varela, Victoriano E. Montes, Aurelio Berro, José M. Sienra Carranza, Carlos María Ramírez, Gonzalo Ramírez, Matías Behety, Luis Piñeyro Del Campo, Luis Melián Lafinur, José Román Mendoza, Anacleto Dufort y Alvarez, Juan Zorrilla de San Martín, Rafael Fragueiro, Joaquín de Salterain, Manuel Herrero y Espinosa, Alcides De María, Alberto Flangini, Constantino Becchi, Orosmán Moratorio, Elías Regules, Pedro Ximénez Pozzolo, Washington P. Bermúdez, Carlos Roxlo, Santiago Maciel, José G. del Busto, Ricardo Sánchez, Enrique Kubly y Arteaga, Víctor Arreguine, Benjamín Fernández y Medina, Manuel Bernárdez, Ricardo Passano, Guillermo P. Rodríguez, Adela Castell, Daniel Martínez Vigil, Alfredo Zuviría, Enrique Rivera, Guzmán Papini y Zas, Ubaldo Ramón Guerra, José Salgado, Emilio Frugoni, Julio Herrera y Reissig, Raúl Montero Bustamante, María Eugenia Vaz Ferreira, Toribio Vidal Belo, Armando Vasseur, María H. Sabbia y Oribe, Ernestina Méndez Reissig, Joaquín Sacco Illa, Pedro Erasmo Callorda, Asdrúbal E. Delgado, Horacio Quiroga, Justino Jiménez de Aréchaga, Julio Lerena Juanicó, Ramón Montero Brown, Pablo Minelli González.

CU DLC FU IaU IU MB MiU MU NBuU
NcU NIC NSyU

1175 Montevideo. Universidad de la República. 5 [i.e. Cinco] cuentos uruguayos. Montevideo, 1965. 88 p. 24 cm.
Anthology of short stories by Uruguayan authors from the first half of the 20th century, including brief biobibliographical

sketches with important dates and achievements of Eduardo Acevedo Díaz, José Pedro Bellán, Horacio Quiroga, Carlos Reyles, Javier de Viana.

IU

1176 Narradores '72 [i.e. setenta y dos]. Montevideo: Biblioteca de Marcha, 1972. 164 p. 20 cm. (Colección Los premios. V. 7).
Anthology of writings by the winners of the 1972 "Concurso Marcha" in Montevideo. Brief interviews and limited biobibliographical data of the following writers are included: Cástor, Anderssen Banchero, Alvaro Castillo, Manuel Márquez, Hugo Giovanetti Viola.

CaQMM CtY CU-SB FU IaU InU IU
LNHT MH MiDW MoSW MU NcU NNC OO
OOxM PPiU PPT

1177 Paganini Buquet, Alberto. Cien autores del Uruguay, por Alberto Paganini. Montevideo: Centro Editor de América Latina, 1969. 92 p.
Biobibliographical sketches of the following Uruguayan writers covering all periods of literary history to the generation of 1945: Eduardo Acevedo Díaz, Francisco Acuña de Figueroa, Delmira Agustini, José Alonso y Trelles (El Viego Pancho, pseud.), Enrique Amorim, Arturo Ardao, Mario Arregui, Lauro Ayestarán, Orfilia Bardesio, Rafael Barrett, Vicente Basso Maglio, Francisco Bauzá, José Pedro Bellán, Mario Benedetti, Amanda Berenguer, Bernardo Prudencio Berro, Domingo Luis Bordoli, Carlos Brandy, Sarandy Cabrera, Julio J. Casal, Enrique Casaravilla Lemos, Juan Cunha, Julio C. Da Rosa, Esther de Cáceres, Sara de Ibáñez, Juana de Ibarbourou, Roberto de las Carreras, Isidoro De María, Carlos Denis Molina, José Pedro Díaz, Santiago Dossetti, Francisco Espínola, Líber Falco, Pedro Figari, Alvaro Figueredo, Emilio Frugoni, Serafín J. García, Alfredo Gravina, Gervasio Guillot Muñoz, Felisberto Hernández, Ernesto Herrera, Julio Herrera y Reissig, Bartolomé Hidalgo, Roberto Ibáñez, Pedro Leandro Ipuche, Jules Laforgue, Jacobs Langsner, Dámaso Antonio Larrañaga, Lautréamont (Isidore Lucien Ducasse), Wáshington Lockhart, Antonio Dionisio Lussich, Mateo Magariños Solsona, Carlos Maggi, Selva Márquez, Carlos Martínez Moreno, Humberto Megget, José Monegal, Raúl Montero Bustamante, Adolfo Montiel Ballesteros, Juan José Morosoli, Daniel Muñoz, Juan Carlos Onetti, Emilio Oribe, Juan Parra del Riego, Ricardo Paseyro, Fernando Pereda, José Manuel Pérez Castellano, Víctor Pérez Petit, Pedro Piccatto, Juan E. Pivel Devoto, Eliseo Salvador Porta, Horacio Quiroga, Angel Rama, Carlos María Ramírez, Carlos Real de Azúa, Carlos Reyles, José Enrique Rodó, Emir Rodríguez Monegal, Carlos Rodríguez Pintos, Yamandú Rodríguez, Carlos Sabat Ercasty, Florencio Sánchez, Clara Silva, Fernán Silva Valdés, María Inés Silva Vila, Susana Soca,

Armonía Somers, Jesualdo Sosa, Jules Supervielle, José Pedro Varela, Alvaro Armando Vasseur, Carlos Vaz Ferreira, María Eugenia Vaz Ferreira, Javier de Viana, Idea Vilariño, Arturo Sergio Visca, Ida Vitale, Giselda Zani, Justino Zavala Muñiz, Juan Zorrilla de San Martín, Alberto Zum Felde.

IU   KMK   MH

1178 Paternain, Alejandro, comp. <u>Treinta y seis años de poesía uruguaya</u>; antología. Montevideo: Editorial Alfa, 1967. 190 p. 17 cm.
    Anthology of Uruguayan poetry between 1930 and 1966 with brief biobibliographical sketches of the following poets: Fernando Pereda, Esther de Cáceres, Roberto Ibáñez, Selva Márquez, Alvaro Figueredo, Juan Cunha, Beltrán Martínez, Líber Falco, Pedro Piccatto, Sara de Ibáñez, Susana Soca, Clara Silva, Idea Vilariño, Humberto Megget, Sarandy Cabrera, Carlos Brandy, Mario Benedetti, Ida Vitale, Zelmar Riccetto, Emilio Ucar, Amanda Berenguer, Ricardo Paseyro, Jorge Medina Vidal, Carlos Flores, Saúl Ibargoyen Islas, Marosa Di Giorgio Medicis, Washington Benavides, Nancy Bacelo, Cecilio Peña, Circe Maia, Walter Ortiz y Ayala, Milton Schinca.

    CLU CLSU CSt CtY FU IaU InU IU KU
    MH MiU MnU MU NBuU NcD NIC NjP
    NjR NN NNC NSyU OU PPiU PPULC TU
    WU

1179 Pedemonte, Hugo Emilio, comp. <u>Nueva poesía uruguaya</u>. Madrid: Ediciones Cultura Hispánica, 1958. 323 p. 20 cm. (Colección de veintiuna antologías de poesía nueva).
    Anthology and critical study of all periods of Uruguayan poetry, particularly the 20th century, with biobibliographical sketches of varying lengths. Those especially featured: Bartolomé Hidalgo, Francisco Acuña de Figueroa, Cándido Juanicó, Esteban Echeverría, Adolfo Berro, Juan Carlos Gómez, Alejandro Magariños Cervantes, Ramón de Santiago, Orosmán Moratorio, Elías Regules, Juan Zorrilla de San Martín, Carlos Roxlo, Julio Herrera y Reissig, Armando Vasseur, Ovidio Fernández Ríos, Angel Falco, Pablo Minelli González, Julio Raúl Mendilaharzu, José Alonso y Trelles (El viejo Pancho, pseud.), Delmira Agustini, María Eugenia Vaz Ferreira, Juana de Ibarbourou, Andrés Héctor Lerena Acevedo, José María Delgado, Emilio Frugoni, Fernán Silva Valdés, Romildo Risso, Guillermo Cuadri, Emilio Carlos Tacconi, Edgardo Ubaldo Genta, Ildefonso Pereda Valdés, Pedro Leandro Ipuche, Emilio Oribe, Carlos Sábat Ercasty, Vicente Basso Maglio, Maeso Tognochi, Enrique Casaravilla Lemos, Julio J. Casal, Manuel de Castro, Carlos Rodríguez Pintos, Federico Morador, Nicolás Fusco Sansone, Cipriano Vitureira, Enrique Amorim, Alvaro Figueredo, Serafín J. García, Concepción Silva Bélinzon, Selva Márquez, Sofía Arzarello, Esther de Cáceres, Clara Silva, Sarah Bollo, Sara de Ibáñez, Roberto Ibáñez,

Juvenal Ortiz Saralegui, Ernesto Pinto, Líber Falco, Juan Cunha, Walter González Penelas, Luis Alberto Caputi, Daniel D. Vidart, Sarandy Cabrera, Ariel Badano, Carlos Brandy, Generoso Medina, Ricardo Paseyro, Orfila Bardesio, Idea Vilariño, Mirtha Gandolfo, Dora Isella Russell, Luis Alberto Varela, Hugo Emilio Pedemonte, Silvia Herrera, Ida Vitali. Alphabetical index of names.

    IU

1180 Penco, Wilfredo, comp. <u>Breve antología del cuento campero</u>. Montevideo: ACALI Editorial, 1980. 255 p. 17 cm. (Colección ABC del lector. V. 22).
    A short anthology of 19th- and 20th-century Uruguayan short stories dealing with rural life. Short biobibliographical sketches on their authors are also included. They are Eduardo Acevedo Díaz, Serafín J. García, Santiago Dossetti, Domingo Arenas, Enrique Amorim, Víctor Dotti, Benjamín Fernández y Medina, Fernán Silva Valdés, Juan José Morosoli, Manuel Bernárdez, Carlos Reyles, Javier de Viana, Francisco Espínola, Yamandú Rodríguez, Adolfo Montiel Ballesteros.

    IU

1181 Pereda Valdés, Ildefonso. <u>Antología de la moderna poesía uruguaya, 1900-1927</u>. Palabras finales por Jorge Luis Borges. Buenos Aires: El Ateneo, 1927. 224 p. 21 cm.
    Anthology of Uruguayan poetry between 1900 and 1927 containing biobibliographical material on the following: Julio Herrera y Reissig, Delmira Agustini, Julio Supervielle, Juana de Ibarbourou, Emilio Frugoni, Fernán Silva Valdés, Pedro Leandro Ipuche, Julio Raúl Mendilaharsu, Emilio Oribe, Vicente Basso Maglio, Carlos Sabat Ercasty, Enrique Casaravilla Lemos, Juan Parra del Riego, Julián J. Casal, Federico Morador, Ildefonso Pereda Valdés, Alvaro Guillot Muñoz, Gervasio Guillot Muñoz, Nicolás Fusco Sansone, María Elena Muñoz.

    CU DLC IaU IU MU NcD NN OCl PBm

1182 Rama, Angel, comp. <u>Aquí Montevideo</u>; gentes y lugares. Montevideo: Arca, 1965. 106 p. 18 cm.
    Anthology of short stories set in Montevideo by Uruguayan writers born between 1926 and 1940. Information on birth dates, educational background, and achievements of the following individuals is featured: Hiber Conteris, Mario C. Fernández, Eduardo H. Galeano, Jorge Musto, Jorge Onetti, Jorge Sclavo.

    CLSU CLU CtY IU KU MdU MU NBuU NIC
    NN NNC TU

1183 Raviolo, Heber, comp. <u>Trece narradores uruguayos contemporáneos</u>. Montevideo: Cámara Uruguaya del Libro, 1981. 116 p. 16 cm.

LITERATURE

An anthology of short stories by the following contemporary Uruguayan authors (1945 through the present), including brief bio-bibliographical sketches: Julio C. Da Rosa, Mario Arregui, Milton Stelardo, Anderssen Banchero, Alberto C. Bocage, Diego Pérez Pintos, Enrique Estrazulas, Rubén Loza Aguerrebere, Milton Fornaro, Hugo Giovanetti Viola, Tarik Carson, Antonio María Dabezies, Víctor Cunha.

IU

1184 Real de Azúa, Carlos, comp. Antología del ensayo uruguayo contemporáneo. Montevideo: Universidad de la República, Departamento de Publicaciones, 1964. 2 v. (645 p.) 20 cm. (Letras nacionales. V. 5).

Anthology of 20th-century Uruguayan essayists with brief biobibliographical sketches of the following:

V. 1: Julio Martínez Lamas, José Irureta Goyena, Joaquín Torres García, Emilio Frugoni, Eduardo Dieste, Dardo Regules, Gustavo Gallinal, Alberto Zum Felde, Antonio M. Grompone, Emilio Oribe, Clemente Estable, Servando Cuadro, Carlos Benvenuto, Luis Gil Salguero.

V. 2: Carlos Quijano, Luis Pedro Bonavita, Esther de Cáceres, Roberto Fabregat Cúneo, Susana Soca, Juan Llambías de Azevedo, Arturo R. Despouey, Arturo Ardao, Rodney Arismendi, Washington Lockhart, Baltasar Mezzera, Carlos Martínez Moreno, Arturo Sergio Visca, Domingo Luis Bordoli, Mario Benedetti, Daniel Vidart, Roberto Ares Pons, Emir Rodríguez Monegal, Guido Castillo, Carlos Maggi, Aldo Solari, Vivian Trías, Gustavo Beyhaut, Juan Segundo, S. J., Angel Rama, Luis H. Vignolo, Alberto Method Ferré.

IU MH NN NSyU

1185 Rela, Walter. Historia del teatro uruguayo, 1808-1968. Montevideo: Ediciones de la Banda Oriental, 1969. 187 p. 20 cm. (Colección Reconquista. V. 36).

Brief biobibliographical information on the following individuals connected with Uruguayan theater from 1808-1968: Bartolomé Hidalgo, Manuel Araucho, Carlos Villademoros, Francisco Xavier de Archa, Heraclio Fajardo, Eduardo Gordon, Antonio Díaz, Gregorio Pérez Gomar, José Tavolara, Pedro Pablo Bermúdez, José Pedro Ramírez, Estanislao Pérez Nieto, Guillermo Kubly y Arteaga, Rafael Fraguiero, Washington Bermúdez, Samuel Blixen, Orosmán Moratorio, Benjamín Fernández y Medina, Alfred Duhau, José Podestá, Abdón Arósteguy, Elías Regules, Enrique de María, Víctor Pérez Petit, Florencio Sánchez, Carlos Brussa, Ernesto Herrera, Otto Miguel Cione, Alberto Weisbach, Ismael Cortinas, Edmundo Bianchi, Enrique Crosa, Ulises Favaro, Francisco Imhof, Juan León Bengoa, Carlos Salvagno Campos, Carlos María Princivalle, José Pedro Bellán, Angel Curotto, Yamandú Rodríguez, Justino Zavala Muñiz, Orlando Aldama, Julián García,

Agustín Minelli, Carlos César Lenzi, Ernesto Pinto, Juan Carlos Patrón, Fernán Silva Valdés, Armengol P. Font, Andrés Castillo, Angel Rama, Juan Carlos Legido, Héctor Plaza Noblía, Antonio Larreta, Carlos Denis Molina, Carlos Maggi, Luis Novas Terra, Hiber Conteris, Rubén Deugenio, Mauricio Rosencof. Alphabetical index of names.

DLC IU

1186 _____. 20 [i.e. Veinte] cuentos uruguayos magistrales. Montevideo: Editorial Plus Ultra, 1980. 237 p. (V. 1). 19 cm.

Anthology of Uruguayan short stories from the period 1892-1979. Biobibliographical notes include dates, birthplace, professional activities, and a brief stylistic analysis for the following contributors: Eduardo Acevedo Díaz, Manuel P. Bernárdez, Carlos Reyles, Javier de Viana, Horacio Quiroga, Adolfo Montiel Ballesteros, Víctor Dotti, Yamandú Rodríguez, Juan José Morosoli, Felisberto Hernández, Giselda Zani, Julio C. Da Rosa, Luis Castelli, Armonía Somers, Santiago Dosetti, Milton Stelardo, José Monegal, María de Monserrat, L. S. Garini, Alberto C. Bocage.

IU

1187 Reyles, Carlos, comp. Historia sintética de la literatura uruguaya. Montevideo: A. Vila, 1931. 3 v. 20 cm.

Collection of critical essays on 19th- and 20th-century Uruguayan literature with varying amounts of biobibliographical data on the following writers:

V. 1: Francisco Acuña de Figueroa, Jacinto Acuña, Agustín Acuña de Figueroa, Claudio Acuña de Figueroa, Manuel Acuña de Figueroa, Francisco Esteban Acuña de Figueroa, Bartolomé Hidalgo, Antonio D. Lussich, Elías Regules, Julio Herrera y Reissig, Daniel Muñoz (Sansón Carrasco; Fígaro, pseuds.), Carlos M. Maeso (Máximo Torres, pseud.), Teófilo Eugenio Díaz (Tax, pseud.), Eugenio Garzón, Samuel Blixen, Eduardo Acevedo Díaz, Carlos Reyles, José Enrique Rodó.

V. 2: Carlos Roxlo, Julio Raúl Mendilaharsu, Fernando Nebel, Carlos Zum Felde, Armando Vasseur, Emilio Frugoni, Delmira Agustini, Florencio Sánchez, Juana de Ibarbourou, Enrique Amorim, Luis Giordano, Manuel de Castro, Germán Roosen Regalia, Manuel Acosta y Lara, Alberto Nin Frías, Salterain Herrera, Mercedes Pinto, Laura Cortínes, Ofelia Machado, Sarah Bollo, Luisa Luisi, María Eugenia Vaz Ferreira, María Carmen Izcua Barbat de Muñoz Ximénes, Esther Parodi Uriarte, Sofía Arzarello de Fontana, Alicia Porro Freire, Ofelia Calo Berro, Layly Daverio de Bonavita, Ana María de Foronda, María Adela Bonavita, Esther de Cáceres, Edgarda Cadenazzi, Clotilde Luisi de Podestá, Juan Parra del Riego, Ildefonso Pereda Valdés, Julio J. Casal, Carlos Rodríguez Pintos.

V. 3: Fernán Silva Valdés, Francisco Espínola, Víctor Dotti, Ernesto Herrera, José

Pedro Bellán, Andrés Lamas, Miguel Cané, Alejandro Magariños Cervantes, Francisco Bauza, Eduardo Ferreira, Víctor Pérez Petit, Carlos Vaz Ferreira, Raúl Montero Bustamante, Gustavo Gallinal, Mario Falcao Espalter, Adolfo Agorio, Francisco A. Schinca, Julio Supervielle, Andrés H. Lerena Acevedo, Alvaro Guillot Muñoz, Gervasio Guillot Muñoz, Jesualdo Sosa (Jesualdo, pseud.), Carlos Alberto Garibaldi, Manuel Ruiz Díaz, Fernando Pereda, Ramón M. Díaz, Homero Martínez Albin, Juan M. Filartigas, Juan Carlos Welker, Giselda Zanni (Giselda Welker, pseud.), Francisco Espínola, Julio Silva, Juan Cunha Dotti, Carlos Alberto Cluhow, María Elena Muñoz, Roberto Ibáñez, Juan C. Abella, Elbio Prunell Alzáibar, Carlos Scaffo.

CLSU CtY CU DLC FU InU IU MoSU
MoU MU NBuU NcD NcU NIC OCU OO OU
PU TU TxU ViU

1188 Roxlo, Carlos. Historia crítica de la literatura uruguaya. Montevideo: A. Barreiro y Ramos, 1912-1916. 7 v. 23 cm.
   Contents:
   V. 1-2: 1810-1885. El romanticismo.
   V. 3-5: 1885-1898.
   V. 3: El arte de la forma.
   V. 4-5: La influencia realista.
   V. 6: 1885-1898. El cuento nativo y el teatro nacional.
   V. 7: 1900-1916. La edad ecléctica.
   Critical history of Uruguayan literature from 1810-1916 with varying amounts of biographical data and stylistic analyses of the following writers:
   V. 1: Dámaso Antonio Larrañaga, Manuel Araucho, Francisco Acuña de Figueroa, Andrés Lamas, Adolfo Berro, Juan Carlos Gómez, Bernardo Prudencio Berro, Enrique de Arrascaeta, Rafael Ximénez, Francisco Xavier de Acha, Heraclio C. Fajardo, Carlos A. Fajardo, Fermín Ferreira y Artigas, Eduardo Acevedo, José Gabriel Palomeque, José Vázquez Sagastume, Cándido Juanicó, Juan Carlos Gómez.
   V. 2: Eduardo G. Gordon, Laurindo Lapuente, Antonino Lamberti, Isidoro De María, Alejandro Magariños Cervantes, Agustín de Vedia, Eduardo Acevedo Díaz, Alberto Palomeque, Aurelio Berro, Washington P. Bermúdez, Orosmán Moratorio, Matías Behety, Joaquín de Salterain, Mariano Soler, Angel Floro Costa, José Sienra y Carranza, Carlos María Ramírez, Francisco Bauzá, Lozano, Marcos Sastre, Juan Zorrilla de San Martín.
   V. 3: José Pedro Varela.
   V. 4: Luis de Piñeyro del Campo, Justino Jiménez de Aréchaga, Rafael Fragueiro, Víctor Arreguine, Santiago Maciel, Manuel Bernárdez, Ricardo Passano, Carlos M. Maeso, Samuel Blixen, Carlos Rayles, Víctor Pérez Petit.
   V. 5: Daniel Martínez Vigil, Carlos Martínez Vigil.
   V. 6: Julio Herrera y Reissig, Bartolomé Mitre, Eugenio Garzón, Julio Piquet, Julián Julián Quintana, Constancio C. Vigil, José

María de Souza Reilly, Tomás Estruch, Carlos María Morales, Emilio Frugoni, Armando Vasseur, Angel Falco, Dardo E. Clare, Julio Raúl Mendilaharzu, Carlos Vaz Ferreira, Luis Alberto de Herrera, Lorenzo Batlle.
   V. 7: Julio Herrera y Reissig, Bartolomé Mitre (Argentinean), Eugenio Garzón, Julio Piquet, Julián Quintana, Constancio C. Vigil, José María de Souza Reilly, Tomás Estruch.

CaBVaU CU DLC IU MB MoSU MoU NBuU
NcU OCU OKentU OkU OOxM OrU TNJ
ViU

1189 Ruffinelli, Jorge. Palabras en orden. Buenos Aires: Ediciones de Crisis, 1974. 218 p. 20 cm. (Colección Esta América).
   Collection of interviews with prominent 20th-century Uruguayan writers. Each interview is preceded by a biobibliographical sketch containing dates, educational background, and achievements of Alberto Zum Felde, Paco Espínola, Juan Carlos Onetti, Carlos Martínez Moreno, Mario Arregui, Julio C. da Rosa, Mario Benedetti, José Pedro Díaz, Jorge Onetti, Eduardo Galeano.

CLU CtY CU FTaSU InU IU MB MdU
MH MnU MoSW MU NIC NjR NmU NN
NNC PPiU TxU ViU WU

1190 Salaverri, Vicente A. Florilegio de prosistas uruguayos: los ensayistas, los articulistas, los cuentistas, los novelistas, los periodistas. Buenos Aires: Editorial Cervantes, 1918. 264 p. 19 cm.
   Anthology of 20th-century Uruguayan writers arranged by genre with brief biobibliographical data on the following: José Enrique Rodó, Carlos Vaz Ferreira, Héctor Miranda, Alberto Nin Frías, Samuel Blixen, Constancio C. Vigil, Adolfo Agorio, Guillermo Kubly Arteaga, Horacio Maldonado, Francisco Alberto Schinca, Raúl Montero Bustamante, Juan Antonio Buero, Wilfredo Pi, Mario Falcao Espalter, Horacio Quiroga, Javier de Viana, Manuel Bernárdez, Benjamín Fernández y Medina, Juan José de Soiza Reilly, Víctor Arreguine, Rodolfo Romero, Manuel Medina Betancourt, Santiago Dallegri, Vicente A. Salaverri, Carlos Reyles, Eduardo Acevedo Díaz, Mateo Magariños Solsona, José Batlle y Ordóñez, Antonio Bachini, Juan Andrés Ramírez, Domingo Arenas, Julio María Sosa, Pedro Manini Ríos, Hugo Antuña.

CtY CU DLC DPU FMU FU IEN IU LU
MiU NBuU NcD NcU NjP NN NWM OkU

1191 Semana de la Juventud, 2d, Minas, Uruguay, 1964. IR: cuento, ensayo, poesía. Minas: Ediciones Hoy, 1965. 60 p. 22 cm.
   Anthology of prize-winning writings from a 1964 literary contest in Minas, Uruguay. Very brief biographical sketches of the following Uruguayans from the second half of the 20th century: Zulma Sosa, Argimiro Ramón

LITERATURE

Beovide, Rubén Loza Aguerrebere, Ariel Muñiz, Beatriz Echavarría, Domingo Guillén Garín, Néstor Plada, Edgar Martínez Lucero.

IU

1192   7 [i.e. Siete] escritores de hoy. Montevideo: Sandino, 1968. 64 p. 24 cm.
    Anthology of short stories dealing with the theme of rebellion. Biobibliographical sketches with dates and achievements of the following Uruguayan writers from the second half of the 20th century: Jorge Onetti, Mario Benedetti, Fernando Ainsa Amigues, Carlos María Gutiérrez, Mario Arregui, Jesús Guiral, Alberto Cid.

    CSt   CU-SB   IU   NmLcU   OrU

1193   Sociedad de hombres de letras del Uruguay. Biblioteca. Montevideo, 1944-55. 11 v. 21 cm.
    Collection of writings of 19th- and 20th-century Uruguayan authors with varying amounts of biographical information:
    V. 1-3: Carlos Martínez Vigil, Francisco Acuña de Figueroa, Daniel Muñoz (Sansón Carrasco, pseud.).
    V. 4-7: Carlos Roxlo, Julio Herrera y Obes, Carlos María Ramírez.
    V. 8-11: Juan Carlos Gómez, Julio Eugenio Santiago Piquet García.

    IU   NNC

1194   Teatro uruguayo contemporáneo. Prólogo de Fernán Silva Valdés. Madrid: Aguilar, 1960. 556 p. Portraits. 20 cm. (Teatro contemporáneo).
    Anthology of 20th-century Uruguayan dramatists with biobibliographical sketches and portraits of the following: Florencio Sánchez, Ernesto Herrera, Vicente Martínez Cuitiño, José Pedro Bellán, Yamandú Rodríguez, Fernán Silva Valdés.

    IU

1195   Villagrán Bustamante, Héctor. Autores y libros. Montevideo: A. Monteverde & Cía., 1940. 112 p. 22 cm.
    Critical essays of the works of the following 20th-century Uruguayan authors, including limited biographical information. Carlos Reyles, Samuel Blixén, Domingo F. Sarmiento (Argentinean), Eugenio Garzón, Daniel Muñoz, José Enrique Rodó, María Eugenia Vaz Ferreira, Delmira Agustini, Julio Raúl Mendilaharsu.

    DLC   IEN

1196   Visca, Arturo Sergio, comp. Aspectos de la narrativa criollista. Montevideo: Biblioteca Nacional, 1972. 356 p. 17 cm.
    Collection of critical essays concerning Uruguayan criollo literature with varying amounts of biobibliographical material on the following: Benjamín Fernández y Medina, Manuel Bernárdez, Domingo Arenas, Juan Carlos Blanco Acevedo, Santiago Maciel, Javier de Viana, Eduardo Acevedo Díaz, Carlos Reyles, Montiel Ballesteros, Enrique Amorim, Francisco Espínola, Yamandú Rodríguez, Víctor Dotti, Juan José Morosoli, Pedro Leandro Ipuche, Santiago Dossetti, Juan Mario Magallanes, José Monegal, Serafín J. García, Alfredo Gravina, Eliseo Salvador Porta, Mario Arregui, Luis Castelli, Julio C. Da Rosa, Milton Stelardo.

    CtY   CU-SB   GU   IaU   IU   MoSW   NBuU   PPiU   PPT   ViU   WU

1197   Visca, Arturo Sergio. Ensayos sobre literatura uruguaya. Montevideo: Comisión Nacional de Homenaje del Sesquicentenario de los hechos históricos de 1825, 1975. 232 p. 25 cm. (Ediciones del sesquicentenario).
    Collection of critical essays on Uruguayan literature featuring varying amounts of biographical data on 19th- and 20th-century writers. Among those especially featured: Horacio Quiroga, Mateo Magariños Solsona, Ramón Píriz Coelho, Javier de Viana, Roberto Sienra, Carlos Reyles, Fernán Silva Valdés, Delmira Agustini.

    CtY   CU-S   CU-SB   FU   InU   IU   KU   LNT   MH   MU   NBuU   NcU   NIC   NjP   NmU   OU   PPiU   PPT   TxU   ViU   WU

1198   Zum Felde, Alberto. Crítica de la literatura uruguaya. Montevideo: M. García, 1921. 356 p. 20 cm. (Colección Estudio).
    Critical survey of all periods of Uruguayan literature featuring limited biobibliographical data on the following writers: Francisco Acuña de Figueroa, Juan Zorrilla de San Martín, Eduardo Acevedo Díaz, Carlos Roxlo, José Enrique Rodó, Carlos Reyles, Julio Herrera y Reissig, Florencio Sánchez, Armando Vasseur, Javier de Viana, Horacio Quiroga, Delmira Agustini, Juana de Ibarbourou, Emilio Oribe, Enrique Casaravilla Lemos.

    IU

1199   _____. Proceso intelectual del Uruguay; crítica de su literatura. 3. ed. Montevideo: Ediciones del Nuevo Mundo, 1967. 3 v. 18 cm. (Biblioteca uruguaya. V. 1-3).
    History of Uruguayan literature from all periods and genres with biobibliographical sketches of the following:
    V. 1: José Manuel Pérez Castellano, Dámaso Antonio Larrañaga, Benito Lamas, Juan Francisco Martínez, José Prego de Oliver, Bartolomé Hidalgo, Eusebio Valdenegro, Manuel Araúcho, Carlos Villademoros, Bernardo Berro, Petrona Rosende de la Sierra, Francisco Acuña de Figueroa, Andrés Lamas, Juan Carlos Gómez, Alejandro Magariños Cervantes, Eduardo M. Gordon, Heraclio Fajardo, Ramón de Santiago, Fermín Ferreira y Artigas, José Pedro Varela,

Julio Herrera y Obes, Carlos María Ramírez, Prudencio Vázquez y Vega, Juan Carlos Blanco, Luis Melián Lafinur, Daniel Muñoz, Teófilo Díaz, Orosmán Moratorio, Elías Regules, Washington Bermúdez, José G. del Busto, Sienra Carranza, Joaquín de Salterain, Francisco Bauza, Juan Zorrilla de San Martín, Eduardo Acevedo Díaz.

V. 2: Benjamín Fernárdez y Medina, Manuel Bernárdez, Samuel Blixen, Eduardo Ferreira, José Enrique Rodó, Carlos Vaz Ferreira, Carlos Reyles, Javier de Viana, Florencio Sánchez, Julio Herreira y Reissig, Delmira Agustini, María Eugenia Vaz Ferreira, Horacio Quiroga, José Alonso y Trelles (El viejo Pancho, pseud.), Alvaro Armando Vasseur, Roberto de las Carreras, Carlos Roxlo, Víctor Pérez Petit, Mateo Magariños Solsona, Pablo Minelli y González, César Miranda, Otto Miguel Cione, Angel Falco, Emilio Frugoni, Raúl Montero Bustamante, Vicente Carrera.

V. 3: Juana de Ibarbourou, Emilio Oribe, Fernán Silva Valdés, Carlos Sabat Ercasty, Jules Supervielle, Enrique Casaravilla Lemos, Vicente Basso Maglio, Esther de Cáceres, Juan Cunha, Fernando Pereda, Alfredo Mario Ferreiro, Roberto Ibáñez, Carlos Rodríguez Pintos, Julio J. Casal, Pedro Leandro Ipuche, Carlos Maeso Tognochi, Humberto Zarrilli, Ildefonso Pereda Valdés, Nicolás Fusco Sansonne, Sarah Bollo, Jesualdo Sosa, Juvenal Ortiz Saralegui, Juan Carlos Abellá, Santiago Vitrueira, Ernesto Pinto, José María Delgado, Carlos Scaffo, Serafín J. García, Ernesto Herrera, Francisco Espínola, Felisberto Hernández, Justino Zavala Muñiz, Adolfo Montiel Ballesteros, José Pedro Bellán, Juan José Morosoli, Enrique Amorim, Manuel de Castro, Eduardo Dieste, Roberto Sienra, Adolfo Agorio, Francisco Imhof, Carlos Princivalle, Gustavo Gallinal, Alberto Lasplaces, José G. Antuña, Mario Falcao Espalter, Vicente Salaverri, Víctor Dotti, Giselda Zani. Alphabetical index of names.

FU   IaU   IU   LU   MdU   MU   NjP   NSyU   TxU
UU   WU

MEDICINE

1200   Eirale, Alberto. Memorias de un médico; biografía ampliada con seis apartados; Milésimo; aeronáutica; misión sanitaria; vapor griego "Polyktor"; cruzada por niños desamparados; justicia en vida; el ejército del sur durante toda la guerra civil de 1904; sanidad militar móvil. 3. ed. Montevideo, 1957. 304 p. Portraits. 24 cm.

The memoirs of 20th-century Uruguayan doctor Juan Alberti Eirale. Biographical information is given for this man and others associated with him. The following, for whom portraits are also included, are particularly featured: Juan Alberto Eirale, Justino Muñiz, Pablo Galarza, Aparicio Saravia.

CtY   DNLM   MU   TxU

1201   Martínez Montero, Alcides A. Los cruzados del Uruguay; historia de la Cruz Roja Uruguaya. Montevideo: Centro Militar, República Oriental del Uruguay, 1959. 143 p. Portraits. 19 cm. (Obras de la Biblioteca General Artigas. V. 43).

A history of the Uruguayan Red Cross, covering the period from the mid 1800s to the mid 1900s. Brief scattered biographical information, as well as a few portraits, given for many people associated with this organization.

FU   MB   NIC   NmLcU   NN   TxU

1202   Martínez Munua, Ricardo. El presidente Santos y la Facultad de Medicine de la República. Montevideo: Impr. Latina, 1942. 44 p. Portraits. 20 cm.

A short discussion of the involvement of President Santos in Uruguay's medical school, including brief scattered biographical information and portraits for this man and for three of those physicians he influenced. The following are featured: Máximo Santos, Francisco Soca, Joaquín de Salterain, Enrique Pouey.

DLC-P4   IU   TxU

1203   Pérez Fontana, Velarde. Historia de la medicina en el Uruguay, con especial referencia a las comarcas del Río de la Plata. Montevideo, 1967. 4 v. Portraits. 29 cm.

History of medicine in the River Plate region with special attention paid to Uruguay. Features scattered information on individuals from all periods of history. Among those especially featured:

V. 1: Juan María Gutiérrez, Rafael Schiaffino, Juan Díaz de Solís, Sebastián Gaboto, Diego García, Gonzalo Fernández de Oviedo y Valdez, Juan Gaboto, Francisco del Puerto, Antón de Grajeda, Luis Ramírez, Juan de Junco, Pedro de Mendoza, Juan de Ayolas, Hernando de Zamora, Alvar Núñez Cabeza de Vaca, Pedro de Zayas, Rodrigo Ortiz de Zárate, Maese Andrés, Hernando de Molina, Juan de Sanabria, Diego de Sanabria, Domingo Martínez de Irala, Mencia Calderón de Sanabria, María de Sanabria, Hernandarias de Saavedra, Ruiz Díaz de Melgarejo, Juan de Garay, Hernando de Alcázar, Bernardo Vargas Machuca, Alonso de Espinar, Diego de Góngora, Juan de Vergara, Roque González de Santa Cruz, Domingo Ordoñana, Lambert Picard.

V. 2: Juan de Lara, José Giró, Juan Cayetano de Molina, Segismundo Asperger, Tomás Falkner.

V. 3: Francisco Antonio Maciel, José Manuel Pérez Castellano, Dámaso Antonio Larrañaga, Saturnino Segurola.

V. 4: Ramón Escarza.

CLSU   CtY-M   CU   FU   ICU   InU   IU   KU   MB
MBCo   MU   NcD   NcU   NIC   NN   NNC-M   OU
TxU   WaU

MEDICINE

1204 Ríos, Barsabás. <u>Unos médicos nuestros</u>. Prólogo de Carlos Martínez Moreno. Montevideo:
Biblioteca de Marcha, 1973. 111 p. 18 cm.
     A collection of speeches which discuss
medicine in modern Uruguay, including scattered biographical information on many Uruguayan doctors and surgeons. Those particularly featured are 10 men to whom the author
pays homage in essays, dealing with their
work and personalities. They are Emilio Penza, Domingo Prat, Alberto Barrague, Fernando
Abente Haedo, Juan Carlos del Campo, Francisco
Fernández Lascano, Pedro Larghero, Eduardo
Calleri, Victorino Pereira, Ivo Ferreira.

     CLU IU NIC NN TxU WU

MUSIC

1205 Ayestarán, Lauro. <u>La música en el Uruguay</u>.
Prólogo de Juan E. Pivel Devoto. Montevideo:
Servicio Oficial de Difusión Radio Eléctrica,
1953. 818 p. (V. 1). Portraits. 30 cm.
V. 1 first published under title: <u>Los orí-
genes de la música escénica en el Uruguay</u>.
     A history of Uruguayan music (18th-20th
centuries) including biographical sketches of
the following people associated with it:
     V. 1: (18th century through 1860).
Manuel Ubeda, Juan José de Sostoa, Juan Caye-
tano Barros, Antonio Barros, Antonio Sáenz,
Mariano Pablo Rosquellas, Luis Smolzi, José
María de Arzac, Jacinta Furriol, Francisco
Cassale, Roque Rivero, Carmen Luna, Francisco
José Debali, Pelegrin Baltasar, Antonio Aulés,
Amelong, Demetrio Rivero, Nicanor Albarellos,
Fernando Quijano, Orfilia Pozzolo, Dolorcita
Rentería, Ignacio Pensel, Alejandro Marotta,
José Amat, Luis Petri, César Dominicetti,
Santiago Ramos, Clemente Castagneri, Oscar
Pfeiffer, Luis Cavedagni. Alphabetical index
of names.

     DLC IU LNHT MH NcD NNG NSyU TxU
     WaU

1206 <u>150 [i.e. Ciento cincuenta] años de música
uruguaya</u>: ciclo de 22 conciertos a realizar-
se en el paraninfo de la Universidad, los
días miércoles a las 18 y 30 horas, desde el
7 de mayo hasta el 8 de octubre, organizado
por el Conservatorio Universitario de Música,
Facultad de Humanidades y Ciencias, auspicia-
do por la Comisión Nacional de Homenaje del
Sesquicentenario de los Hechos Históricos de
1825. Montevideo: Conservatorio Universitario de Música, 1975. 56 p. 31 cm. (Ediciones del sesquicentenario).
     Collection of programs of concerts held
at the "Conservatorio Universitario de Música"
(Montevideo), in 1975, to commemorate the
150th anniversary of Uruguayan Independence.
Included are biographies of the following
musicians from 1825-1975 with information on
their educational background and musical
achievements: Manuel Ubeda, Francisco José

Debali, Oscar Pfeiffer, Dalmiro Costa, Carmelo
Calvo, Tomás Giribaldi, León Ribeiro, Luis
Sambucetti, Juan José Sambucetti, Gerardo
Grasso, Alfonso Broqua, Eduardo Fabini, José
Tomás Mujica, Benone Calcavecchia, Ramón
Rodríguez Socas, José Pierri Sapare, Carmen
Barradas, Luis Cluzeau Mortet, César Cortinas,
Vicente Ascone, Julio Martínez Oyanguren,
Guido Santórsola, Carlos Giucci, Gregorio del
Puerto, Carlos Estrada, Mario Sagradini, San-
tiago Baranda Reyes, Roberto Lagarmilla,
Atilio Frigerio, Jaurés Lamarque Pons, Abel
Carlevaro, Nydia Pereyra Lizaso, Héctor Tosar
Errecart, Pedro Ipuche Riva, Daniel Conte,
León Biriotti, Ricardo Storm, Luis Ricardo
Campodónico, Yolanda Rizzardini, Eduardo
Gilardoni, René Marino Rivero, José Serebrier,
Antonio Mastrogiovanni, Sergio Cervetti,
Beatriz Lockhart, María Angélica Piola, Amelia
Repetto.

     FU GU IU MnU MU NcU NIC NmU TxU
     WU

1207 Lagarmilla, Roberto. <u>Músicos uruguayos</u>.
Montevideo: Editorial Medina, 1970. 91 p.
18 cm. (Colección cien temas básicos. V. 5).
     A collection of biobibliographical
sketches of the following Uruguayan composers
chronologically arranged (1760-1940s):
Manuel Ubeda, Oscar Pfeiffer, Francisco José
Debali, Jacinta Furriol, Carmen Luna, Dalmiro
Costa, Carmelo Calvo, Tomás Giribaldi, León
Ribeiro, Luis Sambucetti, Gerardo Grasso,
Miguel Almada, Alfonso Broqua, Eduardo Fabini,
José Tomás Mujica, Benone Calcavecchia, Ramón
Rodríguez Socas, Carmen Barradas, Luis Clu-
zeau Mortel, César Cortinas, Vicente Ascone,
Guido Santórsola, Carlos Giucci, Antonio Már-
quez, Carlos Estrada, Santiago Baranda Reyes,
Alberto Soriano, Jaurés Lamarque Pons, Héctor
Tosar Errecart, Pedro Ipuche Riva, Diego
Legrand, León Biriotti, Ricardo Storm, Eduar-
do Gilardoni, José Serebrier, Daniel Viglietti,
Antonio Mastrogiovanni, René Marino Rivero,
Ariel Martínez, Corium Aharonian, Conrado
Silva. Also the following women musicians:
María Galli, Socarrito Morales de Villegas,
Celia Correa Luna, Zulema Morua, Estela San-
germano, Nydia Pereira Lizaso, Amalia Repetto,
Susana Etchepare Castellanos, Beatriz Lock-
hart Genta. Alphabetical index of names.

     IaU IU

1208 Salgado, Susana. <u>Los músicos uruguayos desde
1830 al nacionalismo</u>. Montevideo: Editorial
Instituto Estudios Superiores de Montevideo,
1960. 54 p. 22 cm.
     Collection of essays on Uruguayan musi-
cians from 1830 to the early 20th century.
Biographical information concentrates on the
musical achievements of the following: Dalmiro Costa, Tomás Giribaldi, León Ribeiro,
Luis Sambucetti, Alfonso Broqua, Eduardo Fabini, César Cortinas, Luis Cluzeau Mortet.

     IU

PERFORMING ARTS

1209 Candeau, Alberto. <u>Cada noche es un estreno</u>.
Montevideo: ACALI Editorial, 1980. 2 v.
Portraits. 18 cm.
A 2-volume biography of the contemporary
Uruguayan actor Alberto Candeau, including
information and portraits for this man and
for many others with whom he was associated.
The following are emphasized: Alberto Can-
deau, Carlos Brussa, Margarita Xirgú.

IU

POLITICAL PARTIES

1210 Cano, Diógenes. <u>Cabezas rojas en el Uruguay</u>.
Montevideo, 1963. 225 p. Portraits. 23 cm.
Biographical sketches of numerous Uruguayans who are active in the Communist movement.

IU NcD

1211 Gómez, Eugenio. <u>Los intelectuales en el Partido Comunista</u>. Montevideo: Comisión de
Cultura y Propaganda del Partido Comunista,
1945. 75 p. 20 cm.
Essay on communism followed by limited
biographical sketches of leading members of
the Communist party in Uruguay. Information
supplied includes career information, party
positions held, and a personal statement of
political philosophy for Eugenio Gómez, Juan
Francisco Pazos, Gisleno Aguirre, Guillermo
García Moyano, Atahualpa del Cioppo, Bernabé
Michelena, Julio Dutrenit, Amalia Polleri de
Viana, Jesús Gimeno, Juan Lorenzo Pons, Felipe
Seade, Rosa Baffico, Indalecio Buño, María
Cristina Zerpa, Sonia Bialous, Alberto Savio,
Celia Mieres de Centrón, Angel Rodríguez,
Diógenes de Giorgi, Ofelia Naveira de del
Cioppo, Lía Mainero, Merced Massera de Galea-
no, Olivio Albini, Martín Oronz Lucho.

DLC IU NmU NN ViU

PRINTING

1212 Pivel Devoto, Juan E. <u>Las imprentas históricas que estuvieron al servicio de la causa
de la independencia, 1826-1828</u>. Montevideo:
Sección de Artes Gráficas, Universidad del
Trabajo del Uruguay, 1945. 30 p.
Essay dealing with the role of the printing press in Uruguay during the struggle for
independence (1826-1828). Features information on contributions made to the cause by
the following printers: Pedro Trapani, José
de la Puente, José A. Caldas, Lázaro Almada.

IU MH

PSEUDONYMS

1213 Scarone, Arturo. <u>Apuntes para un diccionario
de seudónimos y de publicaciones anónimas</u>.
2. ed. (notablemente aumentada y corregida).
Prólogo de Ariosto D. González. Montevideo:
Imprenta Nacional, 1934. 351 p. 24 cm.
(Publicaciones de la Biblioteca nacional de
Montevideo).
Dictionary of approximately 500 pseudonyms and initials used by Uruguayans in the
19th and 20th centuries with biographies.
Section of anonymous works and their probable
authors. Continued and superseded by <u>Diccio-
nario de seudónimos del Uruguay</u>, 1941. (See
entry 1214.)

IU

1214 _____. <u>Diccionario de seudónimos del Uru-
guay</u>. 3d. ed. Prólogo de Ariosto D. González. Montevideo: C. García & Cía., 1941.
582 p. 25 cm.
Dictionary of approximately 1,100 pseudonyms and initials used by Uruguayans in the
19th and 20th centuries with biographical
data. Section on anonymous works and their
probable authors. Supersedes <u>Apuntes para
un diccionario de seudónimos y de publicaciones anónimas</u>. (See entry 1213.)

DLC FU IU KU TxU

RELIGION

1215 <u>La iglesia en el Uruguay</u>. Libro conmemorativo
en el primer centenario de la erección del
obispado de Montevideo. Primero en el Uruguay, 1878-1978. Montevideo: Instituto Teo-
lógico del Uruguay, 1978. 356 p. 22 cm.
(Cuadernos. V. 4).
A historical account of the Catholic
Church in Uruguay. Scattered biographical
information throughout. Includes listing,
with limited biographical data, of the pastors
of the cathedral in the capital city of Mon-
tecideo from 1724 to 1978.

IU

See also entry 1115.

SCIENCE

1216 United Nations, Educational Scientific and
Cultural Organization. Science Cooperation
Office for Latin America. <u>Uruguay</u>. Montevideo, 1949-53. 2 v. 35 cm. (UNESCO's
scientific institutions and scientists in
Latin America).
A list of contemporary Uruguayan scientific institutions and scientists. Biographical
information, including names of important

SCIENCE

> publications, professional positions held and
> academic degrees earned, is given for appro-
> ximately 320 members of the Uruguayan scien-
> tific community.

> IU

SPORTS

1216a Buzzetti, José Luis, and Eduardo Gutiérrez
Cortinas. Historia del deporte en el Uruguay,
1830-1900, por José L. Buzzetti y Eduardo
Gutiérrez Cortinas. Montevideo: Tall. Gráf.
Castro, 1965. 97 p. 20 cm.
A historical account of sports in Uruguay
(1830-1988), including scattered biographical
information on individuals associated with
it. The following are particularly featured:
William L. Poole, Paul Lebet, Enrique C.
Lichtenberger, Horacio Quiroga.

> IU KU MU TxBeaL

WOMEN

1217 Moratorio, Arsinoe. Mujeres del Uruguay.
Montevideo: Editorial Independencia, 1946.
123 p. 20 cm.
Collection of brief biobibliographical
essays on 20th-century Uruguayan women from
all walks of life. Includes dates and out-
standing achievements of Delmira Agustini,
Paulina Luisi, Juana de Ibarbourou, María
Stagnero de Munar, María Eugenia Vaz Ferreira,
Aureliz Viera, Luisa Luisi, Clotilde Luisi
de Podestá, Raquel Sáenz, María Orticochea,
Esther de Cáceres, Sofía Alvarez Vignoli de
Demicheli, Sarah Bollo, María L. Saldún de
Rodríguez, Sara de Ibáñez, Socorrito Morales
de Villegas, Socorrito Villegas Morales,
Ofelia Machado de Benvenuto, Bettina Rivero,
Laura de Arce, María Rosa de Ferrari, Alicia
Porro Freire de Maciel, Enriqueta Comte y
Riquet, Marisa Lusiardo de De León, Adela
Barbitta Colombo, Elizabeth Durand, Ema San-
tandreu Morales, Débora Vitale D'Amico, Sara
Orlandi de Larramendy, Concepción Antonelli
de Requessens, Carmen Guastavino.

> DLC IU LU NcU NN NSyU TU WU

See also entries 1060, 1066, 1088, 1093, 1093a,
1107, 1114, 1133, 1144, 1147, 1149, 1151, 1152,
1153, 1155, 1158, 1163, 1164, 1165, 1174, 1177,
1178, 1179, 1181, 1186, 1187, 1199, 1205, 1206,
1207, 1211.

River Plate Region

ART

1218 Romero Brest, Jorge. Pintores y grabadores rioplatenses. Buenos Aires: Argos, 1951. 300 p. 21 cm. (El arte y los artistas).

Biographical essays on 19th- and 20th-century artists working in the River Plate region concentrating on achievements in their professional careers: Juan Manuel Blanes, Martín Malharro, Ramón Silva, Valentín Thibon de Libián, Fernando Fader, Miguel Carlos Victorica, Emilio Pettoruti, Lino Spilimbergo, Ramón Gómez Cornet, Horacio I. Butler, Jorge Larco, Raúl Soldi, Juan del Prete, Manuel Angeles Ortiz, Manuel Colmeiro, Rafael Barradas, Pedro Figari, Joaquín Torres-García, Víctor Rebuffo, Adolfo Pastor, Clément Moreau.

CtY DLC IU MiU NjP NmU NN

BIOGRAPHY (MISCELLANEOUS)

1219 Lewin, Boleslao. El judío en la época colonial; un aspecto de la historia rioplatense. Buenos Aires: Colegio Libre de Estudios Superiores, 1939. 158 p. 24 cm.

Study of Jews during the colonial period in Argentina and Uruguay with special attention paid to their part in the economy and their treatment during the Inquisition. Brief biographical information on Francisco Maldonado de Silva, Diego de León Pinelo.

CaBVaU CtY DLC IaU ICN ICU IU MB MiU MsSM NcU OCH OU PU TxU ViU

1220 Poucel, Benjamín. Les otages de Durazno; souvenirs du Rio de la Plata pendant l'intervention anglo-française de 1845 à 1851. Paris: A. Faure; Marseille, Camoin, 1864. 351 p. 25 cm.

A description of the geography, culture, and history of the River Plate region, including biographical essays on the following people: Félix Frías, Manuel Herrera y Obes, Florentino Castellanos.

CtY CU DLC IU MiU TxU

BIOGRAPHY (MISCELLANEOUS)--DICTIONARIES, ENCYCLOPEDIAS and "WHO'S WHO"

1221 Lamb, Wilfred John, comp. River Plate Personalites; a biographical dictionary. Buenos Aires: Sociedad Anónima Imprenta Lamb & Cía. Ltda., 1937. 246 p. 19 cm.

Collection of biographical sketches of over 350 distinguished individuals living in the River Plate area in the early 20th century. Alphabetical index of names. (See also entry 1222.)

DPU IU MiD NN

1222 _____. River Plate personalities. Buenos Aires: Sociedad Anónima Imprenta Lamb, 1939. 351 p. Portraits. 19 cm.

A revised and enlarged version of the 1937 edition. (See entry 1221.)

DLC IU NcD

GENEALOGY

1223 Azarola Gil, Luis Enrique. Apellidos de la patria vieja. Buenos Aires: Librería y Editorial "La Facultad," 1942. 233 p. 23 cm.

Biogenealogical study of some of the earliest families to settle in the River Plate. Biographical data include dates, marriages, and offspring of family members. Those especially featured: Rafael de Sobremonte, Perafán de Ribera, Leonor de Morales, Cristóbal de Castro y Calhorda, Pedro de Castro y Callorda, Bartolomé de Castro y Callorda, Domingo de Sostoa, José Francisco de Sostoa, José María Guillermo de Sostoa y Achucarro, Tomás de Sostoa y Achucarro, Rafael de Sostoa y Ordóñez, Fernando de Sostoa y Ordóñez, Tomás de Sostoa y Ordóñez, Joaquín de Sostoa y Ordóñez, Enrique de Sostoa y Ordóñez, Tomás de Sostoa y Martínez, María Manuela de Viana, Miguel Ordóñez de Villaquirán, Dolores Ordóñez y Viana, Antonio Ordóñez y Viana, José Ordóñez de Villaquirán y Viana, Victoria Ordóñez y Viana, Melchor Ordóñez y Viana, Melchor Ordóñez y Ortega, Juan de Ellauri, María Eustaquia Ellauri, José Ellauri, Plácido

Ellauri, Expectación Ellauri, Prudencio León
Ellauri, José Eugenio Ellauri, Pascual de
Araucho, Manuel Araucho, Francisco Araucho,
Antonio Luis Pereyra, Enriqueta Leriget, José
Valentín Gómez, Francisco Zorrilla de San
Martín, Pedro Zorilla de San Martín, José
Zorilla de San Martín, Bernabé Antonio Zori-
lla de San Martín, Juan Manuel Zorilla de San
Martín, Jose de Silva, Juana Policarpa Silva
y Lazcano, Juan Francisco Silva y Lazcano,
Luciano de las Casas, Juan Bautista de Lasala,
Cándido de Lasala, Indalecia de Lasala, María
Mercedes de Lasala, Martín de Lasala, Fran-
cisco Lasala, Miguel de Fortaleza, Andrés
Gómez de la Quintana, Pedro de la Quintana,
Andrés Nazario de la Quintana, Teodosio de
la Quintana, Pablo de la Quintana, Jaime
Badell, Josefa Villarreal de Badell, Juan de
la Cruz Badell, Mónico Badell, Prudencia
Badell, Miguel Badell, Ruperto Badell, Eusta-
quio Estevan, Francisco de Paula Estevan,
Vicente Sáenz, José Díaz Armesto, Antonio
Díaz Armesto, Manuel Barrero y Bustillo, Cor-
nelio Donovan, Daniel Donovan, Samuel Donovan,
Frutos Pagalday, Nicolás Pagalday, Eugenio
Pagalday, Francisco de Andújar, Ramón (Román)
Carro, Juan José Carro.

    DLC IU NN

1224 _____. *Crónicas y linajes de la gobernación
del Plata*: documentos inéditos de los siglos
XVII y XVIII. Buenos Aires: J. Lajouane &
Cía., 1927. 142 p. Portraits. 23 cm.
    Biogenealogical history of 18th-century
leaders in the River Plate area featuring
biographical data on the following families:
Zabala, Ortiz de Zárate, Garay, Carrasca,
Melo y Cuitiño, Izaguirre, Basavilbaso,
Camejo Soto, Gil, Acucharro, Ruiz de Ocaña,
Mitre, Chucarro, Castellanos, Maciel, Maciel
del Aguila.

    DLC ICU IU MH MiU NcU NN PPULC
    PU TxU

1225 Calvo, Carlos. *Nobiliario del antiguo virreynato del Río de la Plata*. Buenos Aires:
Librería y Editorial "La Facultad," Bernabé
y Cía., 1936-43. 6 v. 27 cm.
    A collection of genealogies of over 300
families of the River Plate region. Alphabetical index of families in each volume.

    CU DPU IU MH NcD

1226 Campos, Ricardo D. *Los García de Zúñiga y
los Warnes*. Montevideo, 1948. 99 p. Portraits. 25 cm.
    Genealogy of the García de Zúñiga and
the Warnes families of the River Plate area
in the 18th and 19th centuries. Biographical
information includes important dates and professions of family members.

    CU DLC IU NN ViU

1226a Castells Montero, Carlos A. *Familia Castells*.
n.p., 1978. 15 p. 21 cm.
    An essay about the Castells family of
Uruguay and Argentina. The following members
are particularly featured: Jaime Castells y
Comas, Enrique Castells y Montestruch, Laura
Carafí de Castells, Enrique Martín Castells
y Montestruch, Alberto Castells y Montestruch,
Enrique Castells Capurro.

    IU TxU

1227 Otárola, Alfredo J. *Estudios genealógicos
sobre antiguos apellidos del Río de La Plata
y remotos orígenes del patriarcado argentino*.
Buenos Aires: Casa Pardo, 1969. 211 p.
Portraits. 24 cm.
    A genealogical study of several River
Plate families dating from the colonial period and accompanied by portraits of many of
their more illustrious members.

    CLSU CLU CSt CU CU-SB FU IaU InU
    IU KU MB MH MoSW NcU NIC NN NNC
    OU TxU ViU WU

1228 Valle Lersundi, Fernando del, and Ricardo
Lafuente Machain. *Irala*; algunos documentos
inéditos relativos al gobernador Domingo
Martínez de Irala, a sus padres y hermanas
por Fernando del Valle Lersundi y R. Lafuente
Machain. Madrid: Tip. de Archivos, 1932.
228 p. 23 cm.
    A discussion accompanied by unedited
documents, giving biographical information of
various amounts on the predecessors and im-
mediate family of the famous conqueror and
colonizer, Domingo Martínez de Irala.

    CaBVaU CtY DLC MB NcU TxU

HISTORY

1229 Angelis, Pedro de, comp. *Colección de obras
y documentos relativos a la historia antigua
y moderna de las provincias del Río de la
Plata*. Con prólogos y notas de Andrés M.
Carretero. Buenos Aires: Plus Ultra, 1969.
8 v. 20 cm.
    Collection of documents dealing with the
history of the River Plate region up to the
early 19th century. Scattered information is
provided for notable individuals including
the following:
    V. 1: Rui Díaz de Guzmán, Alvar Núñez
Cabeza de Vaca, Domingo de Irala, Francisco
Aguirre, Nuflo Chaves, Juan Garay, José Guevara.
    V. 2: Luis de la Cruz.
    V. 3: Martín del Barco Centenera, Fran-
cisco de Viedma.
    V. 4: Pedro Andrés García.
    V. 5: Félix de Azara, Diego de Alvear y
Ponce de León, Buenaventura Sánchez.
    V. 6: José María Cabrer, Félix de Azara.

V. 7: Juan del Pino Manrique, José Gabriel Tupac Amaru.

V. 8 (pt. 1): Jerónimo Matorras, Juan Adrián Fernández Cornejo, Francisco Morillo, Pablo de Zizúr.

V. 8 (pt. 2): Francisco Gabino Arias.

CaOTP CFS CLSU CLU CSt CtY CU-SB
GU IU KU MdU MnU MU NcD NIC NNC
OU PSt TxU ViU WaU WU

1230 Cruz, Josefina, comp. Cronistas de Indias.
Buenos Aires: Ministerio de Cultura y Educación, 1970. 132 p. 20 cm. (Colección Los fundadores de la literatura argentina).

A collection of writings by various chroniclers of the conquest of the River Plate region. Biobibliographical information is also given for these people, who include Luis Ramírez, Ulrich Schmidl, Isabel de Guevara, Luis de Miranda, Ruiz Díaz de Guzmán, Domingo Martínez de Irala, Pedro González de Prado, Alvar Núñez Cabeza de Vaca, Juan de Garay, Martín del Barco Centenera, Hernando de Montalvo, Jerónimo Luis de Cabrera, Reginaldo de Lizárraga, Pedro Lozano, Calixto Bustamante Carlos Inca (Concolorcorvo, pseud.).

IaU ICN InU IU MH TU

1231 Fitte, Ernesto J. Hambre y desnudeces en la conquista del Río de la Plata. Buenos Aires: Emecé Editores, 1963. 322 p. 21 cm.

An essay on the history of the River Plate region during the period of the conquest, mainly through essays about Sebastián Caboto, Pedro de Mendoza, Alvar Núñez Cabeza de Vaca, Juan Ortiz de Zárate, Juan de Garay.

CLU CoU CtY DLC ICarbS ICU MH NIC
NjP NN NSyU TxU

1232 Graham, Robert Bontine Cunninghame. The Conquest of the River Plate. London: W. Heinemann, 1924. 313 p. Portraits. 23 cm.

An account of the conquest of the River Plate region, including scattered biographical information on many notable people, with emphasis on the following: Juan de Ayolas, Felipe Cáceres, Nuflo de Chaves, Sebastián Gaboto, Juan de Garay, Domingo de Irala, Ruy Díaz de Melgarejo, Pedro de Mendoza, Hulderico Schmidel, Alvar Núñez Cabeza de Vaca, Juan Ortiz de Zárate. Alphabetical index of names.

CaBVaU CaBViP CSt DLC ICU IU MH-P
MiU MiU-C MU NcD NIC NN ODW OOxM
OrU PPL PPT ViU

1233 Greenbie, Sydney. Republics of the Pampas; Argentina, Uruguay, Paraguay. Illustrated by Fiore Mastri. Evanston, Ill., New York: Row, Peterson, 1943. 84 p. Portraits. 23 x 18 cm. (His good neighbor series).

A short description of the history, geography, and people of Argentina, Paraguay, and Uruguay, including biographical information and portraits for many prominent people. Particular emphasis is given to the following: José Artigas, Carlos Alvear, José de San Martín, Manuel Rosas, Francisco Solano López.

CU DLC OCl OCU OLak OO Or OrP OrU
P PP TxU WaS WaSp WaT

1234 Lafuente Machain, Ricardo de. Conquistadores del Río de la Plata; prólogo de Juan B. Terán. Buenos Aires: Talleres Gráficos de S. de Amorrotu e hijos, 1937. 696 p. Portraits. 25 cm.

Alphabetically arranged collection of biographical sketches of approximately 3,300 conquerors of the River Plate between 1535 and 1617.

DLC IaU ICarbS NcD TxU

1235 Marco, Miguel Angel de. La armada española en el Plata. Rosario: Talleres Gráficos Raúl Fernández, 1981. 477 p. Portraits. 23 cm.

An account of the activities of the Spanish navy in the River Plate region, covering the period from 1845 to 1900, and containing scattered biographical information, as well as a few portraits, for many prominent people, most of them naval officers. A biographical sketch on the author is also included. The following are emphasized: Miguel Angel de Marco, Jacinto Albistur, Ramón Auñón y Villalón, Carlos Creus, Luis Hernández Pinzón, Miguel Lobo y Malagamba, Casto Méndez Núñez, José Polo de Bernabé. Alphabetical index of names.

IU

1236 Mariluz Urquijo, José María. Los proyectos españoles para reconquistar el Río de la Plata, 1820-1833. Buenos Aires: Editorial Perrot, 1958. 211 p. Portraits. 19 cm. (La Torre de Babel. V. 5).

An account of the Spanish attempt to reconquer the River Plate region from the year 1820 to 1833, including biographical information for the following key people involved in this movement: Vicente de Echeverría, Rafael Gravier del Valle, José Antonio del Pozo y Marquy, Francisco de Borja Magariños, Francisco Agustini, Félix D'Olhaberriague y Blanco, Valentín Ortigosa, Antonio Carrasco, Gabriel Julián Ouvrard, El Marqués del Guarany, Cecilio de Alzaga, Francisco Viola, Mariano Javier de la Torre y Vera, El caballero de Fonvielle, Miguel Lastarria, Francisco de P. Alcón, Gerónimo Valdés, Francisco de Paula del Villar, José Gastero Serrano, El Vizconde de Venancourt.

CLSU CoU CSt CtY CU FMU GU ICU InU
IU LNHT MH MiU MnU NcU NIC NjP NNC
PSt TxLT TxU ViU

HISTORY

1237 <u>Memorias de los virreyes del Río de la Plata</u>. Buenos Aires: Editorial Bajel, 1945. 588 p. Portraits. 24 cm. (Biblioteca histórica colonial, dirigida por el profesor Julio César González. V. 4).

A collection of memoirs, accompanied by portraits, of the following colonial River Plate viceroys: Pedro de Cevallos, Juan José de Vértiz y Salcedo, Nicolás del Campo, Nicolás de Arredondo, Pedro Melo de Portugal y Villena, Antonio Olaguer Feliú y Heredia, G. de Avilés y del Fierro, Joaquín del Pino y Rosas, Rafael de Sobremonte, Santiago Liniers y Bremond, Baltasar Hidalgo de Cisneros.

CBVaU CoU CSt CtY CU DLC FU IU
LNHT MiEM MU NcD NIC NNC OCl OrU
OU PSt ScU TxU ViU WaU

1238 Piñero, Tulia. <u>Navegantes y maestres de bergantines en el Río de la Plata</u>, siglo XVI. Buenos Aires, 1962. 264 p. 25 cm. (Departamento de estudios históricos navales, Serie B: Historia naval argentina. V. 3).

A work featuring biographical information of various amounts on the following 16th-century explorers of the River Plate region: Fernando de Magallanes, Juan Rodríguez de Mafra, Gaspar de Quesada, Miguel de Rodas, Andrés de San Martín, Juan López Carvalho, Jerónimo Guerra, Vasco Gallego, Juan Sebastián del Cano, Sebastián Caboto, Martín Vizcaíno, Diego García, Martín Alfonso de Sousa, Pedro Lopez de Sousa, Pedro de Mendoza, Gonzalo de Acosta, Luis Jacome, Pedro Quintero, Hernán Báez, Antonio Thomas, Hernando de Ribera, Juan Cano, Francisco de Sobrecianos, Hernando de Sobrecianos, Luis Simón, Alfonso Bastián, Miguel Maese, Alvaro Suárez de Carvajal, Alonso Herrero, Juan Portugués, Andrés Ximenes, Vasco Rodríguez, Maestre Miguel, Juan de Salamanca, León Pancaldo, Alonso Cabrera, Martín de Orue, Maestre Axa, Maestre Pedro, Maestre Antonio, Maestre Luis, Maestre Pedro, Maestre Daxa, Maestre Blas, Miguel de Candia, Cristóbal de Arévalo, Juan de Orona, Luis Beneciano, Juan de Sanabria, Diego de Sanabria, Francisco de Victoria, Pedro Sarmiento de Gamboa.

FU ICN ICU IU MH MoSW NIC NmU
NNC WU

1239 Radaelli, Sigfrido Augusto. <u>Blasones de los virreyes del Río de la Plata</u>. Buenos Aires: Institución Cultural Española, 1945. 137 p. 31 cm.

An essay about the viceroyalty of the River Plate, mainly through biographical sketches by Pedro Massa and Sigfrido Radaelli of leading figures (1776-1810). Information includes dates and places of birth and death, important contributions, portraits, and coats of arms. The following are featured: Pedro Antonio de Cevallos, Juan José de Vértiz y Salcedo, Nicolás Francisco Christoval del Campo (Marqués de Loreto), Nicolás Antonio de Arredondo, Pedro Melo de Portugal y Villena, Antonio Olaguer Feliú y Heredia, Gabriel de Avilés y del Fierro, Joaquín del Pino y Rozas, Rafael de Sobremonte, Santiago Liniers y Bremond, Baltasar Hidalgo de Cisneros y La Torre. (See also entries 1240, 1241).

CU DLC NcD TxHU TxU

1240 _____. <u>Blasones de los virreyes del Río de la Plata</u>. Madrid: Ediciones Cultura Hispánica, 1954. 174 p. 22 cm.

Same as the 1945 and 1959 editions. (See entries 1239, 1241.)

DLC ICU MU NN NcD NNC TxU WU

1241 _____. <u>Los virreyes del Plata</u>. Buenos Aires: Editorial Perrot, 1959. 120 p. Portraits. 19 cm. (Colección nuevo mundo. V. 25).

Same as the 1945 and 1954 editions. (See entries 1239, 1940.)

CLSU CLU CU FU IU MH MnU NIC NN
OkU TxU WaU

LITERATURE

1242 Becco, Horacio Jorge. <u>Antología de la poesía gauchesca</u>. Ed. española. Bilbao: Aguilar, 1972. 1778 p. 19 cm. (Colección Obras eternas).

Gauchesque poetry anthology with biobibliographical sketches of the following 18th- and 19th-century poets primarily Argentinians: Juan Baltasar Maziel, Bartolomé Hidalgo, Juan Gualberto Godoy, Hilario Ascasubi, Manuel Araúcho, Estanislao del Campo, Antonio D. Lussich, José Hernández, Esteban Echeverría, Juan María Gutiérrez, Bartolomé Mitre, Rafael Obligado.

CaBVaU CNoS CU-SB InU IU MoSW PPT
TxFTC TxHR TxU VaU ViU WU

1243 Blanco, Floreal P., comp. <u>Antología poético-gauchesca de ambas márgenes del Plata</u>. Notas biográfico-didácticas: Carlos Alberto Moyano. Buenos Aires: Ediciones Almafuerte, 1969. 610 p. 23 cm. (Biblioteca poemática del decir criollo).

Anthology of poetry featuring brief bio-bibliographical sketches of the following 19th- and 20th-century River Plate poets: Bartolomé Hidalgo, Juan Gualberto Godoy, Esteban Echeverría, Hilario Ascasubi, Juan María Gutiérrez, Claudio Mamerto Cuenca, Florencio Balcarce, Luis L. Domínguez, Bartolomé Mitre, Carlos Guido Spano, Estanislao del Campo, Nicolás Granada, Olegario Víctor Andrade, Antonio D. Lussich, Antonino Lamberti, José Hernández, Martín Coronado, Rafael Obligado, Ventura R. Lynch, Martiniano Leguizamón, Elías Regules, Carlos Roxlo, Javier de Viana, Atilio Supparo, Belisario Roldán, S. I. Villafañe,

Diego Novillo Quiroga, Pedro Bonifacio Palacios (Almafuerte, pseud.), Joaquín Castella-
nos, Alberto Ghiraldo, Serafín J. García,
Atahualpa Yupanqui, Evaristo Carriego, Amaro
Villanueva, Armando Tejada Gómez, Leopoldo
Lugones, Edmundo Montagne, Baldomero Fernán-
dez Moreno, Ricardo Güiraldes, Juan Carlos
Dávalos, Claudio Martínez Payva, Martín Goy-
cochea Menéndez, Fernán Silva Valdés, Yamandú
Rodríguez, Alfredo R. Bufano, Florencio Iriar-
te, Jaime Dávalos, A. Poleró Escamilla, Alci-
des De María, Héctor Pedro Blomberg, Boris
Elkin, Miguel A. Camino, José de Maturana,
Romildo Risso, Julio Díaz Usandivaras, Alber-
to Vacarezza, Roberto Mariani, Ivo Pelay,
José Ramón Luna, Miguel H. Bustingorri, Luis
Acosta, Julio Alberto Lista, Juan María Oli-
ver, Francisco Martino, Domingo Rémoli, José
Alonso y Trelles (El Viejo Pancho, pseud.),
Andrés Cepeda, Salvador Riesi, Arsenio Cavi-
lla Sinclair, Valentín Cavilla Sinclair,
Bartolomé R. Aprile, Enrique Uzal, Francisco
Aníbal Riu, Enrique P. Maroni, Fernando Ochoa
(Goyo Godoy, pseud.), Mario César Arrieta,
J. Ernesto Brasseco, Pedro Boloqui, Mario
Raffo, Emilio Germán Andrich, H. E. Calderón
Ferreyra, Guillermo Cuadri, Isidoro Juan Dá-
vila, C. Damián Galván, Enrique Guadino,
Gualberto Márquez (Charrúa, pseud.), Julio
Migno, Nicolás Zinni, Santos Vega, José María
Silva, Sebastián Celestino Berón, Gabino
Ezeiza, Nemesio Trejo, Pablo J. Vázquez, Hi-
ginio D. Cazón, José Betinotti, Federico Cur-
lando, Pedro Garay, Martín Castro, Juan Pedro
López, Generoso D'Amato, Evaristo Barrios,
Luis Acosta García, Ramón Vieytes, Juan A.
Martínez, Juan B. Fulginiti, Juan Antonio
Bourdieu, Francisco N. Bianco, Francisco
Sciscente.

    IU MB PPULC

1244 Borges, Jorge Luis, and Adolfo Bioy Casares,
comps. Poesía gauchesca. Edición, prólogo,
notas y glosario de Jorge Luis Borges y Adolfo
Bioy Casares. México: Fondo de Cultura Económica, 1955. 2 v. 22 cm. (Biblioteca americana. V. 29-30. Serie de literatura
moderna).
    Anthology of River Plate gauchesque poetry
featuring brief biobibliographical sketches
of the following 18th- and 19th-century
writers:
    V. 1: Bartolomé Hidalgo, Hilario Asca-
subi.
    V. 2: Estanislao del Campo, Antonio Dio-
nisio Lussich, José Hernández, Ventura R.
Lynch.

    AU AzTeS CaBVaU CoDU CoU CSt CtY
    CU DCU DLC DPU FTaSU FU GU ICU
    InU IU LU MH MiU MnU NcD NcU NjR
    NmU NN OC1 OC1W OO OrCS OU PPULC
    ScU TU TxLT TxU ULA

1245 Cuentistas rioplatenses de hoy. Buenos Aires:
Vértice, 1939. 425 p. 19 cm.
    Anthology containing brief biobibliogra-
phical sketches of the following 20th-century
short-story writers of the River Plate area:
Enrique Amorim, Ignacio B. Anzoátegui, Rober-
to Arlt, Leónidas Barletta, Héctor Pedro Blom-
berg, Mateo Booz, Fausto Burgos, Arturo Can-
cela, César Carrizo, Armando Cascella, Elías
Castelnuovo, Arturo Cerretani, Juan Carlos
Dávalos, Augusto Mario Delfino, Héctor I.
Eandi, Juan Pablo Echagüe (Jean Paul, pseud.),
Samuel Eichelbaum, Enrique Espinoza, Alberto
Gerchunoff, Enrique González Tuñón, Guillermo
Guerrero Estrella, Eugenio Julio Iglesias,
Bruno Jacovella, José Luis Lanuza, Enrique
Loncán (Américus, pseud.), Benito Lynch,
Eduardo Mallea, Alvaro Melián Lafinur, En-
rique Méndez Calzada, Nicolás Olivari, Justo
P. Sáenz, Lorenzo Stanchina, Alvaro Yunque,
Guillermo Zalazar Altamira.

    DLC DPU IaU IU NcD OU PU TxU

1246 Danero, Eduardo M. S., comp. Antología
gaucha, cuentos. Santa Fe: Librería y Edi-
torial Castellví, 1956. 236 p. 25 cm.
    An anthology of gauchesque short stories
including short biobibliographical sketches
of the following 19th- and 20th-century River
Plate writers: Eduardo Acevedo Díaz, Agustín
Alvarez, José S. Alvarez (Fray Mocho, pseud.),
Juan B. Ambrosetti, Sócrates Anaya, Pedro N.
Arata, Víctor Arreguine, Santiago Avendaño,
Félix de Azara, Rafael Barreda, Manuel Ber-
nárdez, Mariano Bosch, Mario Bravo, Carlos
Octavio Bunge, Fausto Burgos, Miguel Cané,
Ramón J. Cárcano, Evaristo Carriego, Otto
Miguel Cione, Emilio A. Coni, Mateo Booz
(pseud.), Miguel Angel Correa, Roberto B.
Cunningham-Graham, Atilo M. Chiaporri, Godo-
fredo Daireaux, Enrique Demaría, Alfredo Ebe-
lot, Juan Pablo Echagüe (Jean Paul, pseud.),
Pedro Echagüe, Esteban Echevarría, Santiago
Estrada, Alberto I. Gache, Enrique García
Velloso, Alberto Gerchunoff, Julio Cruz Ghío
(Cruz Orellana, pseud.), Alberto Ghiraldo,
Arturo Giménez Pastor, Joaquín V. González,
Pedro Goyena, Nicolás Granada, Francisco
Grandmontagne, Paul Groussac, Ricardo Güiral-
des, Eduardo Gutiérrez, Juan María Gutiérrez,
José Hernández, Ricardo Hogg, Guillermo En-
rique Hudson, Martiniano Leguizamón, Lucio
Vicente López, Mario A. López Osornio, Seve-
riano Lorente, Benito Lynch, Ventura R. Lynch,
Benito Llanos, Santiago Maciel, Lucio V. Man-
silla, José Mármol, Diego Novillo Quiroga,
Filisberto de Oliveira Cézar, Roberto J. Payró,
Horacio Quiroga, Carlos Reyles, Arturo Reynal
O'Connor, Florencio Sánchez, Domingo Faustino
Sarmiento, Marcos Sastre, Charles de Soussens,
Eduardo Talero, Nemesio Trejo, Carlos M.
Urien, Javier de Viana, Alberto T. Weisbach,
Estanislao S. Zeballos. Alphabetical index
of names.

    DPU IaU IU MH MoU

LITERATURE

1247 _____. Antología gaucha (poesía). 2. ed. aumentada. Santa Fe: Editorial Castellvi, 1956. 382 p. 23 cm. (Clásicos argentinos Castellví. Fuera de serie).

An anthology of gaucho poetry, including biobibliographical sketches of the following 18th- to 20th-century River Plate authors: Pedro Bautista Palacios (Almafuerte, pseud.), José Alonso y Trelles (El Viejo Pancho, pseud.), Olegario Víctor Andrade, Hilario Ascasubi, Florencio Balcarce, Adolfo Berro, José Betinoti, Héctor Pedro Blomberg, Mario Bravo, Alfredo R. Bufano, Miguel A. Camino, Estanislao del Campo, Evaristo Carriego, Joaquín Castellanos, Higinio D. Cazón, Alejandro Cervantes Magariños, Martín Coronado, Claudio Mamerto Cuenca, Juan Chassaing, Luis L. Domínguez, Esteban Echeverría, Gontrán Ellauri y Obligado, Gabino Ezeiza, B. Fernández Moreno, Benjamín Fernández y Medina, Alberto Ghiraldo, Ricardo Güiraldes, Juan Gualberto Godoy, Juan Carlos Gómez, Carlos Guido y Spano, Juan María Gutiérrez, Ricardo Gutiérrez, José Hernández, Bartolomé Hidalgo, Félix Santiago Hidalgo, Florencio Iriarte, Adolfo Lamarque, Antonio Lamberti, Manuel José de Lavardén, Martiniano Leguizamón, Juan Pablo López, Leopoldo Lugones, Antonio D. Lussich, Ventura R. Lynch, Alcides de María, Roberto Mariani, José de Maturana, Baltasar Juan Maziel, Bartolomé Mitre, Martín Menéndez Goycoechea, Edmundo Montagne, Diego Novillo Quiroga, Carlos Obligado, Rafael Obligado, Carlos Ortiz, Carlos M. Pacheco, Teodoro Palacios, A. Poleró Escamilla, Luis Pérez, José J. Podestá, Elías Regules, Romildo Risso, Pantaleón Rivarola, Cayetano Rodríguez, Belisario Roldán, Carlos Roxlo, Ramón de Santiago, Nemesio Trejo, Manuel Ugarte, Pablo J. Vázquez, Javier de Viana, S. I. Villafañe.

CtY DPU GEU IaU IU MH MoU

1248 Gandolfi Herrero, Arístides (Yunque, Alvaro, pseud.), comp. Poesía gauchesca y nativista rioplatense. Selección anotada y organizada por Alvaro Yunque, pseud. Buenos Aires: Editorial Periplo, 1952. 143 p. 23 cm.

Anthology of gauchesque and nativist poetry from the River Plate area. Brief biobibliographical sketches of the following 19th- and 20th-century poets from Uruguay or Argentina: Bartolomé Hidalgo, Hilario Ascasubi, Estanislao del Campo, José Hernández, Rafael Obligado, José Alonso Trelles, Miguel Andrés Camino, Fernán Silva Valdés, Pedro Leandro Ipuche, Diego Novillo Quiroga, Serafín García, José Ramón Luna, Amaro Villanueva, Guillermo Cuadri, Atahualpa Yupanqui. Alphabetical index of names.

CSt DLC ICU IU MiU MoU MtU NBuU NN NSyU OC1W OkU PSt TNJ TxU WaU

1249 Garganigo, John Frank, and Walter Rela. Antología de la literatura gauchesca y criollista. Montevideo: Delta Editorial, 1967. 521 p. 25 cm.

Anthology of 19th- and 20th-century gauchesque and criollo literature of Argentina and Uruguay with brief biobibliographical information on the following: Bartolomé Hidalgo, Hilario Ascasubi, Estanislao del Campo, José Hernández, Rafael Obligado, Domingo Faustino Sarmiento, Eduardo Acevedo Díaz, José Sixto Alvarez (Fray Mocho, pseud.), Martiniano Leguizamón, Roberto J. Payró, Javier de Viana, Carlos Reyles, Benito Lynch, Ricardo Güiraldes, Enrique Amorim, Eduardo Gutiérrez, Florencio Sánchez, Ernesto Herrera.

IU MH MU NcU

1250 Garganigo, John Frank. The Gaucho in Some Novels of Argentina and Uruguay. Ann Arbor: University Microfilms, 1965. 181 p. 29 cm.

Same as the Spanish edition entitled El perfil del gaucho en algunas novelas de Argentina y Uruguay. (See entry 1251.)

IU

1251 _____. El perfil del gaucho en algunas novelas de Argentina y Uruguay. Montevideo: Editorial Síntesis, 1966. 126 p. 25 cm.

Doctoral dissertation on gauchesque literature featuring varying amounts of biobibliographical material on the following 20th-century writers: Eduardo Acevedo Díaz, Javier de Viana, Roberto Payró, Carlos Reyles, Ricardo Güiraldes, Enrique Larreta, Benito Lynch, Enrique Amorim, Carlos Alberto Leumann, Agustín Guillermo Casa (Guillermo House, pseud.), Adolfo Montiel Ballesteros.

AU CSt CtY FU IaU InU IU MH MU NcU NIC NjR NSyU PPiU TNJ TxU UU WU

1252 Hayden, Rose Lee. An Existential Focus on Some Novels of the River Plate. East Lansing: Latin American Studies Center, Michigan State University, 1973. 84 p. 28 cm. (Michigan State University. Latin American Studies Center. Monograph series. V. 10).

Study of the existential theme in the works of 20th-century authors from the River Plate region. Limited biobibliographical data on Eduardo Mallea, Carlos Mazzanti, Juan Carlos Onetti, Ernesto Sábato.

AzU CaBVaU CSt CtY ICU InU IU MiEM NcU OrU WaU

1253 Montero Bustamante, Raúl. Ensayos; período romántico. Montevideo: Arduine Hnos., Impresores, 1928. 308 p. 21 cm.

Biographical essays on the following 19th-century River Plate writers: Andrés Lamas, Carlos María Ramírez, Melchor Pacheco y Obes, Alejandro Magariños Cervantes, José de Buschental, Cándido Juanicó, Esteban Echeverría, Juan Carlos Gomez.

CU DLC IU LU M MoSI NSyU OU ViU WU

1254 Murguía, Theodore Infante. <u>The Evolution of</u> <u>the Gaucho in Literature</u>. Ann Arbor: University Microfilms, 1961. 346 p.

Historical and literary study of the gaucho in the River Plate area from the colonial era to 1926 with stylistic and limited biobibliographical material on the following writers who portrayed him in literature: José Marmol, Hilario Ascasubi, Estanislao del Campo, José Hernández, Rafael Obligado, Eduardo Gutiérrez, Florencio Sánchez, Martiniano P. Leguizamón, Roberto Payró, Eduardo Acevedo Díaz, Javier de Viana, Justino Zavala Muñiz, Carlos Reyles, Benito Lynch, Ricardo Güiraldes.

IU(film) WaU

1255 Ordaz, Luis. <u>El teatro en el Río de la Plata</u>; desde sus orígenes hasta nuestros días. 2. ed. corr. y aumentada. Buenos Aires: Ediciones Leviatán, 1957. 347 p. 20 cm.

A critical history of the theater of the River Plate region, covering the period from colonial times to the present day. Scattered biographical information is given for many authors of this genre, with particular emphasis on the following: Florencio Sánchez, Pablo Podestá, Francisco DeFilippis Novoa, Samuel Eichelbaum. Alphabetical index of names.

AU CaBVaU CFS CLSU CLU CNoS CoU
CSt CtW CtY CU CU-I CU-S FMU IaU
INS InU IU KU LNHT LU MB MdU MH
MiDS MiEM MiU MNS MnU MoSW MoU
MtU NbU NBuU NcD NcU NnD NIC NjP
NjR NN NNC NSyU OC1W OkU OOxM
OrCS OrU OU PPULC ScCleU TNJ TxFTC
TxHR TU UU ViU VtMiM VtU WaU WU

1256 Pi, Wilfredo Francisco. <u>Antología gauchesca</u>: los clásicos. Montevideo: M. García, 1917. 204 p. 18 cm.

Anthology of gauchesque poetry with biographical data on the following poets from the River Plate area: Bartolomé Hidalgo, Esteban Echeverría, Juan María Gutiérrez, Eusebio Valdenegro.

AU DLC FU IU MoU NcU NSyU OC1
OKentU OU TU ViU WU

1257 Rela, Walter. <u>El mito Santos Vega en el</u> <u>teatro del Río de la Plata</u>. 3. ed. corregida y aumentada. Montevideo: Editorial Ciudad Vieja, 1966. 57 p. 20 cm.

An analysis of the ways in which the theater of the River Plate region has dealt with the myth of Santos Vega. Scattered biographical information is included for many authors from the 17th to the 20th century who have written about the myth. Particular emphasis is given to the following: Luis de Tejeda, Manuel de Lavardén, Vicente López y Planes, Pantaleón Rivarola, Juan Gualberto Godoy, Celestino Dorrego (Juan Sin Ropa;

Juan Poca Ropa, pseuds.), Bartolomé Mitre, Luis Bayón Herrera, Fernán Silva Valdés, Antonio Pagés Larraya, Antonio D. Lussich.

AzU CLU CoU CSf CSt ICU INS IU
KU MB MH MnU MoSW MoU MtU N
NBuU NcU NNC NSyU OU TxDaM TxU

1258 Rivera, Jorge, comp. <u>La primitiva literatura</u> <u>gauchesca</u>. Buenos Aires: Editorial J. Alvarez, 1968. 221 p. 20 cm.

Study of the early works of gauchesque poetry from the River Plate area. Features biobibliographical sketches of the following 18th- and 19th-century writers: Manuel de Araucho, Francisco de Paula Castañeda, Pedro Feliciano Sáenz de Cavia, Juan Gualberto Godoy, Juan Baltazar Maciel, José Prego de Oliver, Luis Pérez.

AAP CaQMM CFS CLSU CLU CoU CSt
CU FU GU IaU ICN ICU INS InU IU
KU MB MH MiDW MiU MoSW MU NbU
NBuU NcU NhD NIC NjP NN NNC NSyU
OkU OrPS OU PPiU TU TxDaM TxHR
TxU ViU VtU WU

1259 Seluja Cecín, Antonio. <u>El modernismo litera-</u> <u>rio en el Río de la Plata</u>; ensayo premiado por la Academia Nacional de Letras concurso "Raúl Montero Bustamante," 1960. Montevideo: Imprenta Sales, 1965. 166 p. 25 cm.

Study of modernism in 20th-century Latin American literature with special emphasis on the River Plate region. Features brief biobibliographical sketches of the following writers: José Martí, Julián del Casal, Manuel Gutiérrez Nájera, Salvador Díaz Mirón, José A. Silva, Rubén Darío, Leopoldo Lugones, Ricardo Jaime Freyre, Luis Berisso, Carlos Ortiz, Diego Fernández Espiro, Angel de Estrada, Eugenio Díaz Romero, Darío Herrera, Horacio Quiroga, Roberto de las Carreras, Toribio Vidal Belo, Julio Herrera y Reissig, María Eugenia Vaz Ferreira, Delmira Agustini, Alvaro Armando Vasseur, Pablo Minelli González, Raúl Montero Bustamante, Juan José Illa Moreno, Julio Lerena Juanicó.

AU CLSU CtY DPU ICarbS IU KU MH
MU NcU TxU

1260 Tinker, Edward Laroque. <u>The Cult of the</u> <u>Gaucho and the Creation of a Literature</u>. Worcester, Mass.: American Antiquarian Society, 1947. 42 p. 25 cm.

Discussion of the gaucho figure in the literature of the River Plate with biographical data consisting of dates, publications, and experiences with the gauchos, by the following 19th- and 20th-century writers: Bartolomé Hidalgo, Hilario Ascasubi, Esteban Echeverría, Rafael Obligado, José Hernández, Estanislao del Campo, Eduardo Gutiérrez, José J. Podestá, Florencio Sánchez, Javier de Viana, Carlos Reyles, Justino Zavala Muñiz, Benito Lynch, Ricardo Güiraldes.

DLC IU PU

MEDICINE

MEDICINE

1261 Cantón, Eliseo. Historia de la medicina en el Río de la Plata desde su descubrimiento hasta nuestros días, 1512 à 1925. Madrid: Sociedad de Historia Hispano-Americana, 1928. 6 v. Portraits. 25 cm. (Biblioteca de historia hispanoamericana).

A six-volume history of medicine in the River Plate region, covering the period from the discovery to modern times. Biographical information, as well as portraits in many cases, are included for many notable people, most of them physicians. The following are particularly featured: Pedro de Mesa, Maestre Juan, Pedro de Mendoza, Martín del Barco Centenera, Juan de Garay, Atanasio de la Piedad, Pedro Montenegro, Segismundo Asperger, Tomás Falkner, Bruno Mauricio de Zavala, Francisco de Argerich, José Alberto Capdevila y Pallarés, Ramón Gómez, José Plá, José Giró, Diego Garrido, Saturnino Segurola, Cosme Mariano Argerich, Miguel Gorman, Agustín Eusebio Fabre, Baltasar Tejerina, Salvio Gaffarot, José Reedhead, Diego Paroissien, Amadeo Jacques Alexandre Goujaud (Amado Bonpland), Cristóbal Martín de Montúfar, Francisco Cosme Argerich, Juan Antonio Fernández, Francisco de Paula Rivero, José Pedro Oliveira, Teodoro Vilardebó, Martín de Moussy, Manuel Herrera y Obes, Lorenzo Antonio Fernández, Fermín Ferreira, Francisco Javier Muñiz, Juan José Montes de Oca, Diego Alcorta, José María Gómez de Fonseca, Claudio Mamerto Cuenca, Vicente Fidel López, Angel Gallardo y Esnaola, Martín García, Manuel Porcel de Peralta, Teodoro Alvarez, Rafael Herrera Vegas, Santiago Larrosa, Tristán Narvaja, Francisco Suñer y Capdevila, Julio Jurkowski, José María Carafí, Pedro Vizca, Elías Regules, José Scosería, Francisco Soca, Alfredo Navarro, Augusto Turenne, Manuel Quintela, Américo Ricaldoni, Gerardo Arrizabalaga, Luis Morquio, Pedro Antonio Pardo, José María Bosch, Cleto Aguirre, Juan José Naón, Mauricio González Catán, Leopoldo Montes de Oca, Enrique del Arca, Abel Ayerza, José María Astigueta, Pedro Mallo, Juan Ramón Fernández, Guillermo Rawson, Eufemio Uballes, Pedro Lagleyze, Eliseo Cantón, Manuel Blancas, Roberto Wernicke, Pedro N. Arata, Luis Güemes, José María Ramos Mejía, Francisco A. Sicardi, Ignacio Pirovano, Eduardo Wilde, Telémaco Susini, José Penna, Miguel Puiggari, Carlos Murray, Juan A. Boeri, Francisco C. Barraza, Nicasio Etchepareborda, Domingo Cabred, Luis Agote, Emilio R. Coni, Pedro Rojas, Marcelino Herrera Vegas.

CU DLC NcD NN TxU WU

1262 Mallo, Pedro. Páginas de la historia de la medicina en el Río de la Plata. Buenos Aires: Imprenta Industrial, 1897-99. 3 v. in 1. 25 cm. (Buenos Aires. Universidad Nacional. Facultad de Ciencias Médicas. Anales. V. 1-3)

A history of medicine in the River Plate region, covering the period from colonial times through the 19th century, including biographical information for many notable people, most of them phsyicians. Among those featured are Miguel de Gorman, Francisco Argerich, José Alberto Capdevila y Pallarés, Ramón Gómez, Cosme Mariano Argerich, Baltasar Tejerina, Eduardo Jenner, Pedro Feliciano Cavia, Joseph de Garro, Antonio de Vera y Mujica, José de Herrera Sotomayor, Alonso Juan de Valdés Inclán, Baltazar García Ros, Marqués de Valdelirios, Pedro de Cevallos, Sebastián Delgado, Juan de San Martín, Martín José de Echauri, Alonso de la Vega, Gonzalo de Villoldo y Minaya, Lucas Manuel Belorado, Antonio Gallegos, Miguel Rodríguez de Lossa, Juan Gutiérrez de Paz, Bruno de Zavala, Pedro Millán, Juan José Almirón, Pedro Gronardo, José Gonzáles de Melo, Jorge Burgues, Bernardo Gaitán, Sebastián Carrasco, Juan Antonio Artigas, Juan Bautista Callo, Gerónimo Pistolete, Alonso Alvares, Francisco Rodríguez Cardoso, José Nicolás Barrales, Juan José Ortiz, Luis de Sosa Mascareno, Juan José de Vértiz y Salcedo, Joaquín del Pino y Rozas, Diego Garrido, Félix de Azara, Pedro Antonio Cerviño, Vicente Gregorio Mariano Buenaventura Verdú, Nicolás Antonio de Arredondo, Francisco de Paula Sáenz Caballero, Pedro Melo de Portugal y Villena, Antonio Olaguer Feliú, Nicolás Francisco Christóbal del Campo, José Moreno, Diego Antonio Miguel de Alcalá y Serrano, Manuel Ruiz, Lucas Antonio García, Samuel Auchmuty, Salvio Gafarot, Agustín Eusebio Fabre.

CtY-M CU NcD NN OU

PERFORMING ARTS

1263 Rossi, Vicente. Teatro nacional rioplatense. Contribución a su análisis y a su historia. Córdoba: Impr. Argentina, 1910. 198 p. 26 cm.

History of the theater in the River Plate region in the 19th century with biographical information on individuals connected with it. Those especially featured: Ricardo Passano, Orosmán Moratorio, Eduardo Gutiérrez, José J. Podestá, Elías Regules, Alfredo Duhau, Samuel Blixen, Nicolás Granada, Martín Coronado, Jerónimo Podestá, Pablo Podestá, Antonio Podestá, Juan Podestá.

DLC DPU IU NcU NIC NN PSt WaU WU

PRINTING

1264 Fúrlong Cárdiff, Guillermo. Historia y bibliografía de las primeras imprentas rioplatenses, 1799-1850; misiones del Paraguay, Argentina, Uruguay. Buenos Aires: Editorial Guaranía, 1953-1975. 4 v. 28 cm.

History and bibliography of printing in the River Plate region from 1700-1850. Biographical material pertaining to their contributions to the art of printing is given for:

V. 1: Antonio Ricardo, Juan Bautista Neumann, José Serrano, Fernando de Trejo y Sanabria, Carlos Gervasoni, Manuel Querini, Ladislao Orosz, Pablo Karrer, Manuel Ignacio Fernández, José Silva y Aguiar, Juan José de Vértiz y Salcedo, Pedro José de Parras, Antonio Ortiz, Alfonso Sánchez Sotoca, Antonio José Dantás, Francisco Antonio Marradas, Agustín Garrigós, Juan José Pérez, Agustín Donado, José Rolland, Jaime Mora, Juan N. Alvarez, Bernardo Vélez.

V. 4: Antonio Zinny. Alphabetical index of names.

ICN   IU

RELIGION

1265   Antonio María de Montevideo. Los capuchinos genoveses en el Río de la Plata; apuntes históricos. Montevideo, 1933. 246 p. 19 cm.

History of the Capuchin Franciscsn order in the River Plate region from the 17th to 19th centuries. Biographical data on the religious activities of members are provided. Those especially featured are Hernando Arias de Saavedra (Hernandarias), Emilio de Strevi (Juan de Mantelli), Nicolás de Castiglione, Pablo de Camerino, Nicolás Migone, Vita Angel de Gioia, Luis Toribio, Benito de Moano.

DLC   MiEM

1266   Córdoba, Antonio Santa Clara. La orden franciscana en las repúblicas del Plata (síntesis histórica) 1536-1934. Buenos Aires: Imprenta López, 1934. 379 p. Portraits. 20 cm.

A history of the activities of the Franciscan order in the River Plate region, covering the period from 1536 to 1934. Biographical information and portraits are given for many people, mostly clerics, associated with this period. The following are particularly featured: Bernardo de Armenta, Juan Pascual de Rivadeneira, Juan de Garay, Luis de Bolaños, Francisco Solano, Juan de Vergara, Ramón de la Quintana, Juan José Archeverroa, Mamerto Esquiú y Medina, José de San Martín, Luis Beltrán, Francisco Altolaguirre, Bernardino de Guzmán, Alonso del Pozo, Marcos Donati, Quírico Porreca, José de la Quintana, Benito Duro.

CU   DLC   MH   NcD

1267   Eguía Ruiz, Constancio. España y sus misioneros en los países del Plata. Madrid: Ediciones Cultura Hispánica, 1953. 634 p. 23 cm.

History of Spanish missions in the River Plate region featuring scattered biographical material pertaining to the church-related activities of the following individuals: Diego de Torres Bollo, Nicolás Durán Mastrilli, Francisco Vázquez Trujillo, Francisco Lupercio Zurbano, Cristóbal Gómez, Agustín Aragón, Tomás de Baeza, Gregorio Orozco, Juan Bautista Zea, Lauro Núñez, Diego Francisco Altamirano, Luis de la Roca, Lorenzo Rillo, Jerónimo Herrán, Jaime de Aguilar, Antonio Machoni, Manuel Querini, Pedro Juan Andreu, Manuel Vergara, Domingo Muriel, Juan de Avila, Francisco Burgés, Domingo Bandeira, José Manuel Peramas, Jerónimo Núñez, José Eugenio de Uriarte, Pedro Juan Andreu, Domingo Muriel, Diego González, Juan Escandón, Antonio Sepp, Martín Schmidt, Esteban Font, Benito Pan, Juan Sánchez, Pedro Sanna, Lorenzo Balda, Antonio Rivera, Lucas Pizarro, José de Arce, Julián de Lizardi. Alphabetical index of names.

CtY-D   DLC   IaU   ICU   IU   MH   NcD   NN   PU   TxU

1268   Fúrlong Cardiff, Guillermo. Los jesuitas y la cultura rioplatense. 1946. Nueva edición (Corregida y aumentada). Buenos Aires: Editorial Huarpes, 1946. 281 p. Portraits. 18 cm. (Biblioteca enciclopédica. V. 9).

An essay on the work of the Jesuits in the River Plate area (17th century through 18th). Limited biographical data throughout about Jesuit explorers, geographers, ethnographers, linguists, historians, botanists, geologists, mathematicians, astronomers, pharmacists, physicians, poets, architects, painters, etc.

CU   DLC   FU   IaU   IU   MH   MiEM   NcD   NcU   NIC   NNC   OCl   OrU   OU   TxU   WaU   WU

1269   Hernández, Pablo. El extrañamiento de los jesuítas del Río de la Plata, y de las misiones del Paraguay por decreto de Carlos III. Madrid: V. Suárez, 1908. 420 p. 20 cm. (Colección de libros y documentos referentes a la historia de América. V. 7).

An essay on the Jesuits in the River Plate region including biographical data about Francisco Bucarelli y Ursúa, María Antonio de la Paz, Martín Dobrizhoffer, Florián Pauke, Tomás Falkner, Ladislao Orosz, Domingo Muriel, José Cardiel, José Quiroga, José Jolís, José Manuel Peramas, José Sánchez Labrador, Gaspar Juárez (Xuarez), José Guevara, Juan Francisco Ocampo, Francisco Iturri, Joaquín Camaño, Joaquín Millas, Pedro Arduz, José Rivadavia, Diego León de Villafañe. Alphabetical index of names.

CaBVaU   CtY-D   CU   DCU   DCL   FU   ICU   MU   NcD   NcU   NIC   NNC   PU   OU   ViU   WaPS   TxU

1270   Medina, José Toribio. El tribunal del Santo Oficio de la Inquisición en las provincias del

RELIGION

Plata. Santiago de Chile: Imprenta Elzeviriana, 1890. 424 p. 25 cm.

A discussion of the activities of the Inquisition in the River Plate region, including brief biographical information for the following: Juan de Abreo, Gonzalo Abreu de Figueroa, Juan Acuña de Noronha, Francisco de Aguirre, Hernando de Aguirre, Jerónimo de Aguirre, Marco Antonio de Aguirre, Antonio de Alfaro, Manuel de Almeida Pereira, Rodrigo Alonso, Mateo de Alvarado, Juan de Arregui, Pedro de Avis Lobo, Francisco de Benavente, Gregorio de Bibaldo, Alberto Cáceres, Felipe de Cáceres, Alonso de Carvajal, María de la Cerda, Ana de Córdoba, Manuel de Coyto, Bartolomé de la Cruz, Diego de Chávez, Alonso Díaz, Diego Díaz Moreira, Alonso Díaz Vizoso, Alonso Díez, Juan Domínguez, Juan Drac, Roque Espilcueta y Roda, Richarte Ferrue, Gaspar de Frías Miranda, Blas Galván, Rodrigo Gómez de Ojeda, Pedro Gómez Pardo, Francisco Guillén Chaparro, Alvaro Hernández, Félix de Insaurralde, Juan Jufré, Pedro de León, Hernando de Lerma, Rodrigo López, Diego López de Lisboa, Francisco Maldonado de Silva, Maldonado el Zamorano, Juan de Mansilla, Diego Manuel, Andrés Martínez de Zavala, Francisco de Matienzo, Martín de Medina, Miguel Melo, Duarte Méndez, Francisco Mexia Mirabel, Antonio de Mirabal, Juan Muñoz, Alonso Nizoso, Alvaro Núñez, Diego Núñez de Silva, Manuel Núñez Magro, Juan de Ocampo, Antonio de la Oliva, Juan de Oliva, Cristóbal de Oña, Manuel de Ortega, Rodrigo Ortiz Melgarejo, Diego de Padilla, Andrés Pajón, Jorge de Paz, Carlos Pedroso Catalán, Juan de Pendones, Diego Pérez de Acosta, Miguel Jerónimo de Porras, Francisco de Riofrío, Cristóbal Rodríguez Colmenero, Alvaro Rodríguez de Acevedo, Juan Rodríguez Estela, Manuel Rodrí-Guerrero, Francisco Romano, José del Rosario, Francisco Sáez de Mena, Diego de Sanabria, Agustín de San Bernardo, Gabriel Sánchez de Ojeda, Gonzalo Sánchez Garzón, Mateo Sánchez Rendón, Luis de San Román, Gonzalo Santos, Rafael Sedano, Diego de Silva, García de Torres, Juan de Ullós, Andrés de Valenzuela, Bartolomé Valero, Francisco Vásquez, Félix Andrés Vellerche de Aguirre, Francisco de Victoria, Alonso de Videla, Pedro de Villalba, Francisco Zapata, Gaspar Zapata de Mendoza.

CtY DLC FU IaU InU IU NcD NcU
NIC NN NNH OCH PU TxU

Indexes

Author Index

A.J.C., pseud.
  see Carranza, Ángel Justiniano
A.V., pseud.
  see BAUCKE, Florián
ABAD DE SANTILLÁN, Diego, 294, 367
ABEIJÓN, Carlos, 926
ÁBEL MARTÍN, Jorge, 857, 857a, 857b, 857c, 857d
ACEVEDO, Eduardo (1858-1918), 1109
ACEVEDO, Hugo, 706
ACQUARONE, Ignacio (b. 1910), 18
ACUÑA, Angel (b. 1882), 67, 72
ADET, Walter (b. 1930), 653, 654
AFICIONADO, Un, pseud.
  see BERMUDEZ, Washington Pedro
AGEVES, Angel Héctor, 589
AGRUPACIÓN FOLKLÓRICA GUARANÍ, 1027
AGUIRRE, Raúl Gustavo, 657, 658
AGUIRRE, Serafín José, 809
AGUIRRE Y SARAVIA, Aníbal G., 28
ALAMPRESSE, Roberto Enrique, 312
ALAVA, César de, 1050
ALBA, Pedro de, 604
ALBAMONTE, Luis María (BARRIOS, Américo, pseud.)
  (b. 1911), 368
ALBERDI, Juan Bautista (1810-1884), 321, 369,
  370, 418
ALDAO, Adolfo, 371
ALEMÁN, Bernardo, 178
ALFARO, Rogelio E. (b. 1915), 70
ALMADA, Zenón (b. 1868), 940
ALONSO CRIADO, Emilio
  see CRIADO, Emilio Alonso
ALONSO PIÑEIRO, Armando
  see PIÑEIRO, Armando Alonso
ALPOSTA, Luis (b. 1937), 660
ÁLVAREZ Y THOMAS, Ignacio, 459
ALLENDE, Andrés R. (b. 1911), 71
AMADEO, Octavio Ramón (1878-1955), 72, 372
AMARAL, Samuel, 589
AMAYA OVIDO, Omar, 608
AMORIM, Enrique (1900-1960), 794
ANADÓN, Carlos A., 73
ÁNGELIS, Pedro de (1784-1859), 373, 1229
ANGLÉS Y GORTARI, Matías de, 1030
ANGUEIRA, Juan R., 74
ANTONIO, Jorge (b. 1917), 75
ANTONIO MARÍA DE MONTEVIDEO, 1265
APOLANT, Juan Alejandro (b. 1903), 1051, 1105
APONTE, Leandro
  see APONTE BENÍTEZ, Leandro
APONTE BENÍTEZ, Leandro (b. 1904), 935, 974

ARAGÓN, Roque Raúl, 664
ARANCIBIA, José M., 906
ARÁOZ ALFARO, Gregorio (1870-1955), 310, 842
ARÁOZ DE LA MADRID, Gregorio (1795-1857), 375
ARAUJO, Orestes (1853-1916), 1052, 1053, 1110,
  1137
ARAUJO VILLAGRÁN, Horacio, 1053a
ARBO, Higinio, 983
ARENA, José, 76
ARENAS LUQUE, Fermín Vicente (b. 1909), 376
ARGAÑA, Luis María, 975
ARGENTINE REPUBLIC.
    COMISIÓN NACIONAL EJECUTIVA DEL 150
    ANIVERSARIO DE LA REVOLUCIÓN DEL MAYO, 19
ARGENTINE REPUBLIC. CONGRESO, 378
ARGENTINE REPUBLIC. DIRECCIÓN GENERAL DE
    ESTADÍSTICA, 77
ARGENTINE REPUBLIC. EJÉRCITO. COMANDO EN
    JEFE, 8, 8a
ARIAS, Abelardo (b. 1908), 21
ARRIETA, Rafael Alberto (1889-1968), 665
ARTUCIO FERREIRA, Antonia, 1145
ASOCIACIÓN ARGENTINA DE CRÍTICOS DE ARTE, 22
ASTOLFI, José Carlos, 379
ATALAYA, pseud.
  see CHIABRA ACOSTA, Alfredo
AURIA, Lorenzo F. d', 1054
AVELLÁ, José Antonio (1887-1958), 78
AVELLANEDA. ARGENTINE REPUBLIC (CITY). MUSEO
    DE ARTE, 23
AVELLANEDA, Nicolás, Pres. Argentine Republic
    (1837-1885), 79, 380
ÁVILA, José Luis, 178
ÁVILA, Julio P., 80
AYALA AQUINO, Gumersindo (d. 1972), 941
AYESTARÁN, Lauro (b. 1913), 866, 1205
AZAROLA GIL, Luis Enrique (b. 1882), 334, 335,
  1055, 1056, 1106, 1223, 1224
AZCOAGA, Enrique, 54
AZEVES, Angel Héctor, 589
AZURDUY, Victoria, 440

BADANO, Alcira (b. 1922), 667
BÁEZ, Cecilio (1862-1941), 942
BÁEZ, Jorge (1897-1959), 937
BAGALIO, Alfredo S. (CERIANI DEL VIURÓN, pseud.),
  312
BAJARLÍA, Juan Jacobo (b. 1913), 381, 668
BALLUS, Antonio, 1038
BANCO DE LA PROVINCIA DE CÓRDOBA, 24
BARBA, Enrique M., 589
BARBAGELATA, Hugo David (b. 1886), 1146

BARCOS, Julio R., 603
BARRAGAN, Pablo, 594
BARREDA, Ernesto Mario, 669
BARREIRO ORTIZ, Carlos, 81, 336
BARRETT, William Edmund (b. 1900), 976
BARRIOS, Américo, pseud.
    see ALBOMONTE, Luis María
BARRIOS PINTOS, Aníbal (b. 1918), 1111
BARROS BORGOÑO, Luis, 488
BARTHOLOMEW, Roy, 1147
BATTOLLA, Octavio C., 82
BAUCKE, Florián (A. V., pseud.) (1719-1780), 1031
BAUZÁ, Francisco (1849-1894), 1057
BAZÁN, Armando Raúl, 83, 381a
BAZÁN, DE CÁMARA, Rosa, 762
BECCAR VARELA, Adrián (1880-1929), 84
BECCO, Horacio Jorge (b. 1924), 661, 670, 671, 672, 1242
BEJARANO, Ramón César, 977
BELTRÁN, Juan G., 393
BELTRÁN, Juan Ramón (1894-1947), 843
BELTRÁN, Oscar Rafael (1895-1951), 673
BENARÓS, León, 902
BENAVENTO, Gaspar L. (b. 1902), 382
BENEDETTI, Mario (b. 1920), 1148, 1149
BENÍTEZ, Justo Pastor (1896-1962), 978, 979, 980
BENÍTEZ, Luis G. (b. 1925), 943
BENÍTEZ FLORES, Juan G., 981
BERENGUER CARISOMO, Arturo (b. 1905), 674, 675, 676
BERMÚDEZ, Washington Pedro (Un AFICIONADO, pseud.) (1847-1913), 1112
BERNARD, Tomás Diege (b. 1919), 337, 383, 927
BERRA DE MASSEY, Virginia, 85
BERTHELEMY, Carlos Jorge, 86
BERTODATTI, Juan Domingo (VANBER, pseud.), 838
BERTOLÉ DE CANÉ, Cora María, 928
BERTOLOTO, Ofelia, 730
BIANCO, José (1870-1935), 384
BIANCHI DE TERRAGNI, Adelina, 87
BIDONDO, Jorge A., 385
BIEDMA, Antonio María
    see BIEDMA RECALDE, Antonio María
BIEDMA, José Juan (1864-1933), 291, 386, 991
BIEDMA RECALDE, Antonio María (b. 1897), 1
BIGGERI, Emilio, 438
BINAYÁN, Narciso, 629
BIOY CASARES, Adolfo (BUSTOS DOMECQ, H.; SUÁREZ LYNCH, B., pseuds.) (b. 1914), 678, 756, 1244
BÍRABENT, Mauricio, 88
BISHOFF, Efraín U. (b. 1912), 89
BLANCA DE MORÁN, Rosa
    see MORÁN, Rosa Blanca de
BLANCAS, Alberto (1859-1937), 90, 91
BLANCO, Floreal P., 1243
BLANCO, José María, 1032, 1032a
BLANCO AMORES DE PAGELLA, Angela, 677
BLANCO-FOMBONA, Rufino, 620
BOETTNER, Juan Max (1899-1958), 1029
BOGGINO, Juan, 1042
BOLDORI DE BALDUSSI, Rosa, 771
BOLLO, Sarah (b. 1904), 1150
BONASTRE, Pedro, 630
BONASTRE, Valerio (1881-1949), 92, 93, 387
BONAVITA, Luis (PONTAC, M. FERDINAND, pseud.), 1059, 1060, 1113
BONET, Carmelo, 460
BORDENAVE, Enrique, 978
BORDOLI, Domingo Luis (b. 1919), 1151
BORDÓN, F. Arturo, 982
BORGES, Jorge Luis (b. 1899), 239, 678, 734,

1181, 1244
BORJA, J.P. de, 94
BORTNIK, Rubén, 388
BOSCH, Beatriz
    see BOSCH VINELLI, Julia Beatriz
BOSCH, Mariano Gregorio Gerardo (1865-1948), 389, 859
BOSCH VINELLI, Julia Beatriz, 95, 96, 589
BOSSIO, Jorge Alberto, 871
BOTTA, Vincente Raúl, 97
BOZZARELLI, Óscar, 860
BRACCIALARGHE, Comunardo (TESTENA, Folco, pseud.) (1875-1951), 98
BRAUN MENÉNDEZ, Armando (b. 1898), 99, 100, 101
BRAVO FIGUEROA, Gustavo A., 679, 680, 830
BRAY, Arturo (b. 1898), 983
BRENA, Tomás G.
    see BRENA BELLOTTI, Tomás Germán
BRENA BELLOTTI, Tomás Germán (b. 1900), 1152
BROSSARD, Alfred de, 390
BRUGHETTI, Romualdo (b. 1912), 25, 1153
BRUNET, José, 914
BRUNO, Cayetano, 907a
BUCICH, Antonio Juan (b. 1904), 102, 681
BUCICH ESCOBAR, Ismael (1888-1945), 103, 391, 392, 393
BUENOS AIRES, 394
BUENOS AIRES. MUSEO HISTÓRICA NACIONAL, 104
BUENOS AIRES. MUSEO MITRE, 395
BUENOS AIRES. MUSEO NACIONAL DE BELLAS ARTES, 26, 27
BUENOS AIRES. UNIVERSIDAD. FACULTAD DE FILOSOFÍA Y LETRAS, 396
BUENOS AIRES. UNIVERSIDAD. INSTITUTO DE ARTE AMERICANO E INVESTIGACIONES ESTÉTICAS, 6
BUERO, Juan Antonio, 1102
BUFARDECI, A., 139
BUGATTI, Enrique, 397
BUNKLEY, Allison Williams, 398, 399
BURZIO, Humberto F., (b. 1902), 9, 10, 233
BUSANICHE, José Carmelo (b. 1910), 105, 106, 107
BUSANICHE, José Luis (1892-1959), 400, 401, 402
BUSQUETS, 643
BUSTILLO, José María (b. 1884), 338
BUZO GÓMEZ, Sinforiano (b. 1906), 1014
BUZZETTI, José Luis, 1216a

CABAL, Rodolfo, 1075
CABODI, Juan Jorge, 108
CABRERA, Pablo (1857-1936), 109, 313
CÁCERES, Esther de, 1044
CÁCERES DE THOMAS, Carmen (b. 1925), 943a
CACERES ZORRILLA, Cirilo, 944
CAFFARO ROSSI, José María, 110
CAILLAVA, Domingo A. (b. 1890), 1154
CAILLET-BOIS, Teodoro (1879-1949), 10a, 11
CALDAS VILLAR, Jorge (b. 1931), 403
CALDERARO, José D., 404, 405
CALDERÓN, Pedro P., 188
CALVO, Carlos (1822-1902), 1225
CALVO, Luis, 530
CAMBA, Francisco, 111
CAMBÓN, R., 406
CAMINOS, Julio A., 112
CAMPOS, Ricardo D., 1226
CANAL FEIJÓO, Bernardo, 589, 827
CANDEAU, Alberto, 1209
CANO, Diógenes, 1210
CANTÓN, Eliseo (1861-1931), 844, 1261
CAPDEVIELLE, Adolfo, 762
CAPDEVIELLE, Bernardo, 984, 1033
CAPDEVIELLE, Sara, 762
CAPDEVILA, Arturo (1889-1967), 190, 407, 408, 409,

410, 682

CARAFFA, Pedro Isidro (b. 1868), 113, 179, 411, 412, 413, 908

CARBIA, Rómulo D. (1885-1944), 114, 314, 414, 415, 416, 1032

CÁRCANO, Miguel Ángel (1889-1978), 115

CÁRCANO, Ramón José (1860-1946), 115a, 417, 418

CARDOSO, Heber, 1155

CARDOZO, Efraím (1906-1973), 984a, 985

CARDOZO, Ramón Indalecio (1876-1943), 945

CARILLA, Emilio (b. 1914), 683

CARLISLE, Charles Richard, 1015

CARBANZA, Adolfo P. (1857-1914), 419, 420, 421, 422, 908

CARRANZA, Angel Justiniano (1834-1899), 423, 424

CARRANZA, Arturo Bartolomé (1868-1946), 425

CARRETERO, Andrés M., 339, 426, 1229

CARRIEGOS, Ramón C., 427

CARRIL, Bonifacio del (b. 1911), 28, 428

CASABAL, Apolinario C. (1855-1920), 302

CASAL, Julio J. (b. 1889), 1156

CASAL CASTEL, Alberto (1904-1948), 116

CASSONE, Sandro, 761

CASTAGNINO, Raúl Héctor (b. 1914), 886, 887, 888

CASTELLANO SÁENZ CARIA, Rafael M., 340

CASTELLANOS, Alfredo Raúl, 1061

CASTELLS MONTERO, Carlos A., 1226a

CASTILLO, Cátulo (b. 1906), 794

CASTRO NEVARES, Jorge, 238

CATTAROSSI ARANA, Nelly (b. 1926), 683a

CAVADINI, Rubén, 862

CAVALLARO CADEILLAC, Víctor, 1157

CAVERNO EGUSQUIZA, Ricardo, 562

CAZENAVE, Héctor Walter, 571

CELERY, Emiliano, 17

CENTURIÓN, Carlos R. (1902-1969), 946, 986, 987, 1016

CENTURIÓN, Juan Crisóstomo (1840-1903), 988

CERIANI DEL VIURÓN, pseud.
    see BAGALIO, Alfredo S.

CERVERA, Federico Guillermo, 845

CESTINO, Francisco (1838-1899), 117

CICHERO, Félix Esteban (b. 1889), 118

CÍRCULO MILITAR, BUENOS AIRES, 11a

CIRIA, Alberto (b. 1934), 119, 430, 558

CÓCARO, Nicolás (b. 1926), 685, 686

COGHIAN, Eduardo, 119a

COLÓN, Antonio, 29, 30

COMANDI, Luis Enrique, 120

COMISIÓN DE ACTOS CONMEMORATIVOS DE LOS 250 AÑOS DE LA FUNDACIÓN DE MONTEVIDEO, 1062

CORA, Luis M., 121

CORBACHO, Oscar, 687

CORDERO, Héctor Adolfo (b. 1915), 315, 341

CORDOBA. ARGENTINE REPUBLIC. UNIVERSIDAD NACIONAL.
    see CABRERA, Pablo

CÓRDOBA, Antonio Santa Clara, 1034, 1266

CÓRDOVA ITURBURU, Cayetano (b. 1899), 31

CORNEJO, Atilio (b. 1899), 342, 432

CORNEJO COSTAS, Miguel Angel, 342

CORNEJO ISASMENDI, Víctor, 342

CORREA LUNA, Carlos (1874-1936), 433, 924

CORTÁZAR, Augusto Raúl (1910-1974), 688

CORTÉS, Julio H., 76

CORVALÁN, Octavio (b. 1923), 689

COSSA, Roberto M. (b. 1934), 690

COSTA, Julio A. (1854-1939), 122

COTELO, Rubén (b. 1930), 1158

COWLES, Fleur, 434

CRANWELL, Daniel J. (1870-1953), 845a

CRAVIOTTO, José A. (1900-1965), 123, 124

CRAVIOTTO CASAS, Wilson, 1114

CREADORES LITERARIOS ARGENTINOS, 691

CRESPO, Eduardo, 238

CRIADO, Emilio Alonso (b. 1883), 692

CROCE, Juan, 704

CRUZ, Jorge (b. 1930), 693

CRUZ, Josefina, 1230

CUESTA, Julio de la, 1090

CUNIETTI-FERRANDO, Arnaldo J., 125

CUTOLO, Vincente Osvaldo (b. 1922), 126, 296, 646, 900, 901

CUTTER, Robert (b. 1930), 923a

CUYÁS Y SAMPERE, Antonio (b. 1802?), 127

CHARLEVOIX, Pierre François Xavier de (1682-1761), 989

CHARRAS, Julián de (1889-1945), 128

CHÁVES, Julio César (b. 1907), 990

CHÁVEZ, Fermín (b. 1925), 435

CHIABRA ACOSTA, Alfredo (ATALAYA, pseud.) (1889-1932), 33

DA ROSA, Juan Justino, 1159

DA ROSA, Julio C.
    see DA ROSA CAETANO, Julio César

DA ROSA CAETANO, Julio César (b. 1920), 1159

D'ALESSANDRO, Néstor, 862

D'AMICO, CARLOS (MARTÍNEZ, Carlos, pseud.) (1839-1917), 129, 436

DAMONTE TABORDA, Raúl (b. 1909), 437

DANERO, Eduardo M., 1246, 1247

DASSEN, Claro Cornelio (1873-1941), 921a

D'AURIA, Lorenzo F.
    see AURIA, Lorenzo d'

DE MARÍA, Isidoro (1815-1906), 1063

DECOUD, Héctor Francisco (1855-1934), 991

DELLAFERRERA, Nelson, 906

DELLEPIANE, Antonio (1864-1939), 130, 924

DESMADRYL, Narciso, 459

DESTEFANI, Laurio Hedelvio, 12, 438

DI LULLO, Orestes (b. 1898), 296a

DI NUBILA, Domingo, 858

DÍAZ, Antonio Américo, 68

DÍAZ DE GUERRA, María Amelia
    see GUERRA, María Amelia Díaz de

DÍAZ DE RAED, Sara, 439

DÍAZ DOIN, Guillermo (b. 1904), 297, 297a

DIÉGUEZ REDONDO, Gonzalo, 201

DIESTE, Eduardo (1893-1954), 1044

DIMICK, Ralph E., 938

DODERA, Julio W., 1160

DOMÍNGUEZ, Luis, 459

DOMÍNGUEZ, Manuel (1869-1935), 992

DOMÍNGUEZ, Mignon, 707

DONGHI HALPERÍN, Renata (b. 1905), 708

D'ORBIGNI, Alcides
    see ORBIGNI, Alcides d'

DORCAS BERRO, Rolando, 131

DORREGO, Alejandro, 440

DOS SANTOS, Estela
    see SANTOS, Estela dos

DOSE DE ZEMBORAIN, Justa, 132

DUARTE PRADO, Bacón (b. 1915), 993

DUFOURQ, Esteban, 441

DURÁN, Leopoldo (b. 1881), 902

ECHAGÜE, Juan Pablo (1877-1950), 133, 442, 709

ECHAVARRI, Luis, 399

ECHEVARRÍA DE LOBATO MULLE, Felisa Carmen, 134
ECHEVARRIETA, Marcelo, 298
EGUÍA RUIZ, Constancio (b. 1871), 1267
EIRALE, Alberto (b. 1870), 1200
EIZAGUIRRE, José Manuel (1862-1930), 443, 444, 445
ELÍAS, Juan Estanislao de, 375
ELLIFF, Osvaldo (b. 1904), 710
ELLIS, Roberto J.G.
    see ELLIS XIMÉNEZ, Roberto Jorge G.
ELLIS XIMÉNEZ, Roberto Jorge G. (b. 1890), 1064, 1065, 1066, 1067
EQUIPOS DE INVESTIGACIÓN HISTÓRICA, 447
ERRO, Carlos Alberto, 382
ESCOBAR, Eduardo, 136
ESQUIÚ BARROETAVEÑA, Eloísa, 711
ESTRADA, Marcos de (b. 1913), 137
ESTRADA, Santiago (1841-1891), 448, 449
ETCHENIQUE, Nira, 712
ETCHEPAREBORDA, Roberto, 589

FALCAO ESPALTER, Mario (b. 1892), 1068, 1154, 1161
FARINI, Juan Angel, 589
FARIÑA NÚÑEZ, Porfirio (d. 1937), 450
FAVOINO, G.M., 139
FERLA, Salvador, 451
FERNÁNDEZ, Elbio, 140
FERNÁNDEZ, Javier, 589
FERNÁNDEZ, Juan Rómulo (b. 1884), 141, 643
FERNÁNDEZ, Miguel Angel (b. 1938), 938
FERNÁNDEZ, Raúl, 316
FERNÁNDEZ CABRELLI, Alfonso, 1115
FERNÁNDEZ DE BURZACO Y BARRIOS, Hugo, 343, 344
FERNÁNDEZ LALANNE, Pedro, 142
FERNÁNDEZ RÍOS, Ovidio, 1171
FERNÁNDEZ SALDAÑA, José María (1879-1961), 1096, 1097
FERNS, Henry Stanley (b. 1913), 143
FERRARI RUEDA, Rodolfo de, 144
FERRÉ, Pedro, 375
FERREIRA, Mariano (b. 1834), 1107
FERRER, Horacio Arturo (b. 1933), 863
FIDALGO, Andrés Francisco (b. 1919), 713, 730
FIGUEIRA, José H., 1052, 1053
FIGUEROA, Andrés A. (1867-1930), 345
FILARTIGAS, Juan M. (b. 1901), 1069, 1162, 1163
FITTE, Ernesto J. (b. 1905), 1231
FITZGIBBON, Russell H. (b. 1902), 452
FLESCA, Haydée, 714
FLORIT, Ernesto (b. 1889), 453
FLURY, Lázaro (b. 1909), 864, 865
FONTELA, José A., 1053
FOPPA, Tito Livio (1884-1960), 894
FORGIONE, José D. (b. 1898), 317
FOSTER, David William, 715
FRANCO, Luis, 608
FRANCO, Luis Leopoldo (b. 1898), 454, 608
FRANCO, Víctor Ignacio, 994
FRANCO PREDA, Artemio, 947
FREGEIRO, Clemente Leoncio (1853-1933), 145, 145a, 455
FREIJE, Eduardo S., 146
FRÍAS, Bernardo (1866-1930), 456
FRÍAS, Félix, 459
FRICK DAVIE, Carlos, 1070
FUMIÈRE, Jorge P., 147, 148
FUNDACIÓN ARGENTINA PARA LA POESÍA, 716
FUNDACIÓN LORENZUTTI, 34, 35, 36, 37, 38
FURLAN, Luis Ricardo (b. 1928), 717
FURLONG, Guillermo
    see FURLONG CÁRDIFF, Guillermo Juan

FURLONG CÁRDIFF, Guillermo Juan (1889-1974), 7, 39, 149, 318, 457, 458, 651, 846, 866, 885, 895, 899, 910, 922, 1038, 1264, 1268
FUSCO SANSONE, Nicolás (b. 1904), 1071, 1164
FUSTINONI, Osvaldo (b. 1909), 718

GACHE, Alberto I., 459
GAJARDO CRUZAT, Enrique, 856
GALVÁN MORENO, C. (b. 1896), 644, 898
GÁLVEZ, Manuel (1882-1962), 460
GALLETTI, Alfredo, 589
GALLINAL, Gustavo (1889-1951), 1165
GALLO, Blas Raúl, 719
GAMBINI, Hugo, 461
GAMBÓN, Vincente (1857-1925), 462
GAMMALSSON, Hialmar Edmundo, 346
GANDÍA, Enrique de (b. 1906), 150, 151, 229, 280, 347, 359, 373, 463, 464, 465, 466, 467, 468, 499, 510
GANDOLFI HERRERO, Arístides (YUNQUE, Alvaro, pseud.) (b. 1890), 13, 390, 469, 470, 1248
GANDULFO ARCE DE BALLOR, Josefina, 152
GAONA, Silvio (b. 1912), 995, 995a
GARCÍA, Flavio A., 1105
GARCÍA, Germán (b. 1903), 152a
GARCÍA, Serafín J., 1166, 1167, 1168
GARCÍA, Servando (1841-1883), 302
GARCÍA ACEVEDO, Mario, 867
GARCÍA AL-DEGUER, Juan (b. 1855), 471
GARCÍA DE GÓMEZ, Raquel, 178
GARCÍA JIMÉNEZ, Francisco, 868
GARCÍA MANSILLA, Daniel (1869-1957), 153
GARCÍA MÉROU, Martin (1862-1905), 472
GARCÍA SALABERRY, Adela, 154
GARCÍA VELLOSO, Enrique (1880-1938), 720
GARCÍA Y MELLID, Atilio (b. 1901), 473
GARET MÁS, Julio, 1169
GARGANIGO, John Frank (b. 1937), 1249, 1250, 1251
GARMENDIA, José Ignacio (1841-1925), 474
GARRA, Lobodón, pseud.
    see JUSTO, Liborio
GARRETÓN, Adolfo (b. 1891), 155
GARRO, Juan M., 79
GASCÓN, Julio César (b. 1877), 156
GASPARINI, Roberto, 567
GAUNA VÉLEZ, Eduardo, 475
GEORGANO, G.N., 923b
GERCHUNOFF, Alberto (1883-1950), 157
GESUALDO, Vincente (b. 1922), 40, 869, 870
GEZ, Juan Wenceslao (1865-1932), 158, 159
GHIANO, Juan Carlos (b. 1920), 721, 722, 723
GIANELLO, Juan María, 160
GIANELLO, Leoncio (b. 1908), 14, 476, 477, 637
GIMÉNEZ COLODRERO, Luis E. (1900-1956), 161
GIMÉNEZ PASTOR, Arturo (1872-1949), 724
GIMÉNEZ PASTOR, Marta, 725
GIUSTI, Roberto Fernando (1887-1978), 162, 726
GOBELLO, José (b. 1919), 727, 813, 871
GOLDARACENA, Ricardo (b. 1936), 1108
GOLIGORSKY, Eduardo, 728
GOMENSORO, Javier, 1072
GÓMEZ, Eugenio, 1211
GÓMEZ, Hernán Félix (1888-1945), 163, 164
GÓMEZ, Valentín, 449
GONÇALEZ DE SANTALLA, Thirso, 1040
GONZÁLEZ, Ariosto D., 1213, 1214
GONZÁLEZ, Eduardo, 68
GONZÁLEZ, Joaquín Víctor (1863-1923), 165, 519, 529
GONZÁLEZ, Julio César, 1237
GONZÁLEZ ARRILI, Bernardo (b. 1892), 166, 167, 478,

479, 480, 929
GONZÁLEZ RUIZ, Felipe (b. 1904), 481
GONZÁLEZ TORRES, Dionisio M., 949
GORI, Gastón (b. 1915), 168
GRAHAM, Robert Bontine Cunninghame (1852-1936), 1232
GRAU, Carlos A. (b. 1893), 169, 903
GREENBIE, Sydney (b. 1889), 1233
GREENUP, Leonard, 170
GREENUP, Ruth, 170
GREGORICH, Luis, 806
GRONDONA, Adela (b. 1912), 729
GROPPA, Néstor (b. 1928), 730
GROUSSAC, Paul (1848-1929), 482, 483, 484, 485, 486
GUARDO, Ricardo C., 378
GUERRA, Hidalgo, 731
GUERRA, Juan Néstor (b. 1904), 320
GUERRA, María Amelia Díaz de (b. 1924), 1098
GUERRERO, César H. (b. 1901), 171, 172, 173, 174, 487, 930, 931
GUGLIELMINI, Homero M. (1903-1968), 732
GUILLÉN, Horacio Enrique, 176
GUTIÉRREZ, Eduardo (1851-1889), 13
GUTIÉRREZ, Juan María (1809-1878), 177, 321, 459, 488, 733
GUTIÉRREZ, Ramón, 223, 224
GUTIÉRREZ CORTINAS, Eduardo, 1216a

HABER, Abraham, 56
HALÉVY, Daniel, 960
HALPERÍN DONGHI, Tulio, 322, 489
HAYDEN, Rose Lee, 1252
HENRÍQUEZ UREÑA, Pedro (b. 1884), 734
HERNÁNDEZ, Jorge Alberto, 735
HERNÁNDEZ, Pablo (1852-1921), 989, 1269
HERNÁNDEZ, Pablo José, 177a
HERRERA, Luis Alberto de (1873-1959), 1116
HIDALGO, Alberto E. (1893-1954), 490
HIDALGO, Bartolomé José (1788-1822), 736
HIRST, Lloyd (1887-1974), 1074
HOGG, Ricardo (1879-1963), 2, 299a
HORIANSKI, Humberto, 191
HUBERMAN, Silvio E., 738
HUDSON, Damián (1808-1875), 179
HUX, P. Meinrado, 180

IBÁÑEZ FROCHAM, Manuel (1871-1927), 181
IBÁÑEZ FROCHAM, Manuel (son), 181
IBARGUREN, Carlos (1877-1956), 182, 486, 492, 493, 494, 900
IBARRA PEDERNERA, Augusto, 495
INGENIEROS, José (1877-1925), 183, 577
INSTITUTO ARGENTINO DE CIENCIAS GENEALÓGICAS, 496
INSTITUTO DE ESTUDIOS BIOGRÁFICOS, BUENOS AIRES, 184
INSTITUTO SARMIENTO DE SOCIOLOGÍA E HISTORIA, BUENOS AIRES, 497
IRAZUSTA, Julio (b. 1899), 185, 498
IRIARTE, Tomás de (1794-1876), 375, 499
ISAACSON, José (b. 1922), 739, 740
ISÉRN, Juan (1860-1941), 912

JAIMES FREYRE, Ricardo (1868-1933), 500, 501
JALABERT, Ricardo M., 1075
JIMÉNEZ RUEDA, Julio, 604
JITRIK, Noé (b. 1928), 741
JOFRE BARROSO, Haydée M., 666
JUSTO, Liborio (GARRA LOBODÓN, pseud.), 742

KALLSEN, Osvaldo, 950

KIRKPATRICK, Frederick Alexander (b. 1861), 502
KOEBEL, William Henry (1872-1923), 997
KOLINSKI, Charles J., 1013
KOREMBLIT, Bernardo Ezequiel (b. 1916), 743
KORN, Guillermo (b. 1906), 503
KRALY, Néstor, 690
KUNZE, Albert F., 70

LACAU, María Hortensia, 714, 796
LACONICH, Marco Antonio, 504
LAFAUCI, Jorge Santos, 926
LAFUENTE MACHAIN, Ricardo de (1882-1960), 186, 187, 348, 349, 350, 351, 505, 1228, 1234
LAGARMILLA, Roberto, 1207
LAGH, DOMINGO, 744, 745
LAGOMARSINO, Haydée, 1026
LAMAS, Andrés, 228, 529a
LAMB, Wilfred John (1879-1939), 1221, 1222
LANCELOTTI, Mario A., 745a
LANFRANCO, Héctor Pedro (b. 1900), 647
LANUZA, José Luis (b. 1903), 42, 506, 507, 508
LAPPAS, Alcibíades (b. 1919), 333
LAPUENTE, Ernesto, 509
LAROCHE, Ernesto (1879-1940), 1046, 1047
LARRA, Raúl, 589
LARRAIN, Nicanor (b. 1902), 188
LARRETA, Enrique Rodríguez (1875-1961), 510
LASCANO, Pablo (1854-1925), 189
LASPLACES, Alberto (b. 1887), 1170, 1171
LAVERDET, Juan Pablo, 100
LAZCANO COLODRERO, Arturo Gustavo de (b. 1894), 352
LAZCANO COLODRERO, Godofredo, 190
LEGIDO, Juan Carlos, 1172
LEGUIZAMÓN, Aníbal F., 276
LEGUIZAMÓN, Martiniano (1858-1935), 511, 512
LELLIS, Mario Jorge de, 712
LÉRTORA MENDOZA, Celina Ana, 896
LEVENE, Gustavo Gabriel (b. 1910), 513, 514, 515, 516, 589
LEVENE, Ricardo (1885-1959), 290, 517, 518, 519
LEVILLIER, Roberto (b. 1881), 394, 520, 521, 522, 523, 620, 913
LEWIN, Boleslao (b. 1908), 1219
LEWKOWICZ, Lidia F., 746
LEZAMA, Hugo Ezequiel, 524
LICHTBLAU, Myron I. (b. 1925), 747
LIPP, Solomon, 897
LIVACICH, Serafín, 525
LIZONDO BORDA, Manuel (b. 1889), 526, 527
LO CELSO, Angel T. (b. 1900), 43
LOBODÓN, Garra
    see JUSTO, Liborio
LÓIZAGA, Elva de (1915-1963), 748
LÓPEZ, Vicente Fidel (1815-1903), 528, 529, 577
LÓPEZ ANAYA, Fernando (b. 1905), 44
LÓPEZ DECOUD, Arsenio (1868-1945), 951
LÓPEZ PIACENTINI, Carlos Primo, 191
LOPRETE, Carlos Alberto (b. 1923), 749
LOUDET, Enrique (b. 1890), 751
LOUDET, Osvaldo (b. 1889), 192, 847
LOZANO, Pedro (1697-1752), 529a, 1035a, 1035b
LUCA DE TENA, Torcuato, 530
LUCADAMO, Alejandro, 77
LUCADAMO, Alfredo, 77
LUGONES, Leopoldo (1874-1938), 531
LUGONES, Piri, 752
LUIGGI, Alice (Houston) (1886-1963), 323
LULLO, Orestes di
    see DI LULLO, Orestes
LUNA, Félix (b. 1925), 532

LUSARRETA, Pilar de, 193

LLAMBÍAS DE AZEVEDO, Alonso, 1067
LLANO, Francisco Luis, 644a
LLORENS MORA, Alcides, 998

M.A.P., pseud.
     see PELLIZA, Mariano A.
MacDERMOT, Brian Charles, 961
MACCHI, Manuel E., 194, 533, 534
MADERO, Eduardo (1833-1894), 535
MADERO, Guillermo, 536
MAEDER, Ernesto J., 537
MAESO, Carlos M., 1076, 1118
MAGGIO DE TABOADA, Maria, 753
MAGIS, Carlos Horacio, 754
MAJAVACCA, José (1890-1948), 952
MALVIGNE, Pedro César (b. 1916), 755
MALLO, Pedro (1838-1899), 1262
MANCEBO, Noel A., 1077
MANGUEL, Alberto, 756, 757
MANN, Horace, 605
MANSILLA, Lucio Victorio (1831-1913), 195, 538
MANTILLA, Manuel Florencio (1853-1909), 196,
     539, 540
MANZI, Francisco (1883-1954), 197
MARCATELLI, Marcelino, 268
MARCET, José Carlos, 999
MARCÓ, Miguel Angel de, 648, 649, 1235
MARCÓ DEL PONT, Augusto (1870-1933), 541
MARCOS, Jual Manuel (b. 1950), 1018
MARENCO, Eleodoro, 256
MARIANETTI, Benito (b. 1903), 198
MARILUZ URQUIJO, José María (b. 1921), 1236
MARÍN, Rufino (1895-1961), 932
MARINO MONTERO, Juan Carlos, 353
MARRAZZO, Javier, 635
MARTIN, Jorge Abel
     see ABEL MARTIN, Jorge
MARTÍNEZ, Benigno Tejeiro (1846-1925), 542
MARTÍNEZ, Benjamín Demetrio (1864-1939), 543
MARTÍNEZ, Carlos, pseud.
     see D'AMICO, Carlos
MARTÍNEZ, David (b. 1921), 758
MARTÍNEZ, Eladio, 941
MARTÍNEZ, José Luciano (b. 1870), 1078
MARTÍNEZ, Pedro Santos
     see SANTOS MARTÍNEZ, Pedro
MARTÍNEZ, Sindulfo (1919-1967), 953
MARTÍNEZ, Teófilo, 544
MARTÍNEZ ESTRADA, Ezequiel (1895-1964), 545
MARTÍNEZ MONTERO, Alcides A., 1201
MARTÍNEZ MORENO, Carlos, 1204
MARTÍNEZ MUNUA, Ricardo, 1202
MARTÍNEZ PARMA, M., 929
MARTÍNEZ PAZ, Enrique (1882-1952), 545a
MARTINI REAL, Juan Carlos (b. 1940), 759
MASRAMÓN, Alberto J., 194
MASSA, Pedro, 1239
MASSARE DE KOSTIANOVSKY, Olinda, 968, 1000
MASTRÁNGELO, Carlos (b. 1911), 760, 829
MASTRI, Fiore, 1233
MASTROJANNI, 1032a
MATIJEVIC, Nicolás (b. 1910), 652
MATTALIA, Jorge A., 790
MATTEIS, Emilio de, 761
MATTI, Carlos Horacio, 199
MAUBÉ, José Carlos (1894-1964), 762
MAURÍN NAVARRO, Emilio B. (b. 1911), 546, 547, 548,
     549, 848, 873
MAYER, Jorge M., 650
MAZO, Gabriel del (b. 1898), 550

MAZZEI, Angel, 825
MCGANN, Thomas F., 545
MEDINA, José Toribio (1852-1930), 1270
MELIÁN LAFINUR, Alvaro, 380
MELLI, Oscar Ricardo, 200
MENDIVE, Gerardo, 1141
MENDOZA, Edelmiro A., 551
MENÉNDEZ Y PELAYO, Marcelino (1856-1912), 763
MERCANTE, Víctor (1870-1934), 324
MERCHENSKY, Marcos, 589
MERLINI, Adrián (b. 1911), 66
MEZZADRA, R., 405
MICO, Tomás L., 1001
MIGONE, Raúl C. (b. 1898), 379
MILANO, Fulvio, 681
MIRAGAYA, Eduardo, 201
MIRANDA KLIX, José Guillermo (1907-1931), 765
MISIONES, ARGENTINE REPUBLIC (PROVINCE). GOVERNORS,
     551a
MITRE, Bartolomé (1821-1906), 459, 552, 553, 568,
     584
MOLDES, José María, 202
MOLINA, Raúl A. (b. 1897), 849
MOLINA AGUIRRE, Julio, 826
MOLINA ARROTEA, Carlos (1849-1908), 302
MOLINA HERRERA, Angel José Rafael (1895-1970),
     354
MOLINARI, Diego Luis (b. 1889), 416, 554
MOLINARI, José Luis (b. 1898), 849, 850
MONCAUT, Carlos Antonio, 203
MONTE DOMECQ, F., 303, 636
MONTE DOMECQ, Raúl, 954
MONTERO BUSTAMANTE, Raúl (1881-1958), 1091, 1119,
     1120, 1121, 1164, 1174, 1253
MONTES, Alberto, 204
MONTES, Aníbal (1886-1959), 205
MONTES, Eudaldo G., 1122
MONTEVIDEO. BIBLIOTECA DEL PODER LEGISLATIVO,
     1048, 1099
MONTEVIDEO. INTENDENCIA MUNICIPAL, 1123
MONTEVIDEO. Universidad, 1175
MONTI, Antonio (b. 1900), 766
MONTOYA DE HIRSCHSON, Inés, 327
MORAGUES, Jaime, 1095
MORALES, Ernesto (1890-1949), 206, 767
MORALES GUIÑAZÚ, Fernando (1885-1948), 207, 208,
     355, 555, 556
MORÁN, Rosa Blanca de, 768
MORATORIO, Arsinoe, 1217
MORENO, Iván Carlos, 356
MOSQUEIRA, Silvano (1875-1955), 955, 956, 1002
MOYA, Juan R., 209
MOYANO, Carlos Alberto, 1243
MOYANO ALIAGA, Alejandro, 340
MUJICA LAÍNEZ, Manuel (b. 1910), 210
MUÑOZ, Juan José (1853-1934), 1124
MUNZÓN, Eduardo I., 211
MURATURE DE BADARACCO, María del Carmen, 73, 325
MURGUÍA, Theodore Infante (b. 1925), 1254
MURIEL, 989
MURRAY, Luis Alberto, 769
MUZZIO, Julio A., 304

NAIOS JANCHAUS, Teresa, 889
NAPAL, Dionisio R., 93
NAPOLITANO, Leonardo F., 212
NAVARRO GERASSI, Marysa, 558
NEKHOM, Lisa M., 641
NESSI, Ángel Osvaldo (b. 1915), 45
NEUSTADT, Bernardo (b. 1925), 213
NEWTON, Jorge, 3, 5, 326, 559

NEWTON, Ronald C. (b. 1933), 214
NICOLAU, Juan Carlos, 642
NIN Y SILVA, Celedonio (b. 1875), 1079
NOÉ, Julio (b. 1893), 773
NOEL, Martín Alberto (b. 1919), 774
NUBILA, Domingo di
   see DI NUBILA, Domingo
NUDELMAN, Santiago I. (1904-1961), 560
NÚÑEZ, Urbano J., 215

OCAMPO, Silvina, 678
ODDO, Vincente (b. 1932), 649a, 850a
O'LEARY, Juan Emiliano
   see O'LEARY Y URDAPILLETA, Juan Emiliano
O'LEARY Y URDAPILLETA, Juan Emiliano (1880-1968),
   957, 992, 1003
OLMEDO, Natalicio, 958
ONEGA, Gladys S., 777
ORBIGNI, Alcides d', 169
ORDAZ, Luis (b. 1912), 778, 890, 1255
ORGAMBIDE, Pedro, 839
ORIQUE, Bernardino E., 1124
OROFINO, Alfredo T., 216
ORTELLANO ROJAS DE FOSSATI, María Antonia, 971,
   972
ORTIGOSA, Luis (b. 1901), 217
ORTIZ ARIGOS DE MONTOYA, Celia, 327
ORTIZ MUÑOZ, Antonio, 481
OTAEGUI, Tomás (b. 1870), 1080
OTÁROLA, Alfredo J., 357, 358, 359, 360, 361, 362,
   1227
OTERO, Higínio (b. 1901), 874
OTERO, José Pacífico (1874-1937), 561
OTERO, Miguel, 375
OTERO Y ROCA, Solís, 1104
OXILIA, Héctor, 1004

PABLO, Juan Carlos de, 311
PAGANINI, Alberto
   see PAGANINI BUQUET, Alberto
PAGANINI BUQUET, Alberto (b. 1932), 1177
PAGANO, José León
   see PAGANO ROVISSOIN, José León
PAGANO ROVISSOIN, José León (1875-1964), 47, 48
PAGÉS LARRAYA, Antonio (b. 1918), 779, 780
PAITA, Jorge A., 218
PAJUELO MEJÍA, Abdón Max, 562
PALACIO, Eudoxio de Jesús (1883-1961), 914
PALACIOS, Alfredo Lorenzo (1879-1965), 219
PALANT, Pablo T., 390
PALCOS, Alberto
   see PALCOS SULQUES, Alberto
PALCOS SULQUES, Alberto (b. 1894), 516, 563, 589
PALMA, Federico (b. 1912), 220
PALOMEQUE, Alberto (1852-1937), 1125, 1126, 1127
PAOLI, Pedro de, 564
PARACHE CHAVES, C., 175
PARALLADA, Huáscar, 1082
PARCHAPPE, Narciso, 169
PARIS. MUSÉE NATIONAL D'ART MODERNE, 49
PARKER, William Belmont (1871-1934), 221, 959,
   1083
PASTOR, Reynaldo Alberto (b. 1898), 222, 566
PASTORINO, Víctor A., 1143
PATERNAIN, Alejandro (b. 1923), 1178
PATIÑO, Enrique, 1128
PAULA, Alberto S. J. de, 223, 224
PAVÓN PEREYRA, Enrique, 567
PAYRÓ, Julio E. (b. 1899), 50, 51
PAYRÓ, Roberto Jorge (1867-1928), 225
PAZ, José María (1791-1854), 375, 568, 569

PECCI, Antonio, 1018a
PEDEMONTE, Hugo Emilio (b. 1923), 1179
PEDEMONTE, Juan Carlos (b. 1911), 1084, 1129
PEDRO, Valentín de (b. 1896), 782
PEERS DE PERKINS, Carmen, 226
PEICOVICH, Esteban, 530
PELOSIO, Anselmo, 851
PELLEGRINI, Aldo, 52
PELLIZA, Mariano A. (M.A.P., pseud.) (1837-1902),
   227, 228, 424, 570
PENCO, Wilfredo, 1180
PEÑA VILLAMIL, Manuel, 1005
PERAMAS, José Manuel (1732-1793), 1036, 1037, 1038
PERCAS, Helena, 783, 1130
PEREDA, Setembrino Ezequiel (1859-1940), 1085
PEREDA VALDÉS, Ildefonso (b. 1899), 1181
PEREIRA, Miguel Angel (b. 1926), 730
PEREYRA, Indalecio, 99, 206
PÉREZ, Daniel E., 229
PÉREZ, René, 230
PÉREZ ACOSTA, Juan F., 952
PÉREZ AMUCHASTEGUI, A. J., 381a
PÉREZ DE COSTILLA, Perla Lydia, 571
PÉREZ DUPRAT, Rodolfo, 328
PÉREZ FONTANA, Velarde (b. 1897), 1203
PÉREZ-MARICEVICH, Francisco (b. 1937), 1019, 1020
PÉREZ MARTÍN, José, 112
PÉRGOLA, Federico, 718
PETIT DE MURAT, Ulyses, 774a
PETRIELLA, Dionisio (b. 1904), 231, 305
PI, Wilfredo Francisco (b. 1893), 1256
PIAGGIO, Agustín (1860-1922), 915
PICCIRILLI, Ricardo (b. 1900), 14, 572, 573, 637
PIERROU, Enrique Jorge, 15
PIGLIA, Ricardo, 232
PILLADO, José Antonio (1845-1914), 295
PINASCO, Eduardo H., 233
PINEDA YÁÑEZ, Rafael (b. 1898), 234
PINETA, Alberto (b. 1906), 235
PINTO, Juan (b. 1902), 306, 784
PIÑEIRO, Armando Alonso, 282, 574, 575
PIÑERO, Tulia, 1238
PITAUD, Henri, 960
PIVEL DEVOTO, Juan E., 1063, 1086, 1205, 1212
PLÁ, Josefina (b. 1909), 939, 961
PONCE, Aníbal (1898-1938), 183, 236, 538
PONTAC, M. Ferdinand, pseud.
   see BONAVITA, Luis
PORTOGALO, José (1904-1973), 791
POUCEL, Benjamín (1807-1872), 1220
POZZO ARDIZZI, Luis, 4
PRIETO, Adolfo, 792, 840
PRIETO COSTA, Casimiro, 77
PRIORE, Oscar del, 875
PRITCHARD, Anthony, 923c
PUCCIA, Enrique Horacio (b. 1910), 237
PYZIK, Estanislao, 238

QUESADA, Efraín, 1131

RADAELLI, Sigfrido Augusto (b. 1909), 1239, 1240,
   1241
RAED, Sara D. de
   see DÍAZ DE RAED, SARA
RAMA, Ángel, 1182
RAMALLO, Jorge María, 329
RAMAYÓN, Eduardo E. (1865-1963), 916
RAMÍREZ, Juan Vicente (b. 1877), 1087
RAMOS, Juan P., 733
RAMOS, R. Antonio, 968, 1000
RAMOS MEJÍA, José María (1849-1914), 240, 577, 578

RANIERI DE PIVEL DEVOTO, Alcira, 1086
RATTO, Héctor Raúl (1892-1948), 16, 17, 17a, 566, 579, 580, 581
RAVIGNANI, Emilia, 416
RAVIOLO, Heber, 1183
REAL DE AZÚA, Carlos (b. 1916), 1165, 1184
REBOLLO PAZ, José María, 569
REBUFFO, Víctor L., 681
RECALDE A., Sergio (b. 1917), 973
RELA, Walter (b. 1922), 1185, 1186, 1249, 1257
REPETTO, Nicolás (1871-1965), 582
REULA, Filiberto, 241
REVISTA DE DERECHO, HISTORIA, Y LETRAS, 876
REVUELTA, Luis, 1132
REYES, Marcelino (1845-1905), 242
REYES de HOLGADO, Eyra, 134
REYLES, Carlos (1868-1938), 1187
RIMONDI, Rómulo Juan, 583
RÍOS, Barsabas, 1204
RÍOS, José, 1088
RÍOS ORTIZ, Ricardo, 795
RÍOS VELAZCO DE CALDI, Ramona Luisa (b. 1902), 1043
RIVANERA CARLES, Raúl (d. 1949), 583a
RIVERA, Jorge, 1258
RIVERA, Jorge B., 243
RIVERA INDARTE, José (1814-1845), 584
RIVERO ASTENGO, Agustín P. (1896-1951), 585, 586
ROA BASTOS, Agusto Antonio (b. 1917), 962
ROBERTS, Carlos (1865-1942), 587
ROBERTSON, William Spence, 518
RODÓ, José Enrique (1872-1917), 588
RODRÍGUEZ ALCALÁ, Hugo, 1021, 1022, 1023
RODRÍGUEZ ALCALÁ, José (1884-1959), 1024
RODRÍGUEZ ALCALÁ DE GONZÁLEZ ODDONE, Beatriz, 1006
RODRÍGUEZ BUSTAMANTE, Norberto, 589
RODRÍGUEZ DE LA TORRE, Miguel A., 244
RODRÍGUEZ LARRETA, Enrique
    see LARRETA, Enrique Rodríguez
RODRÍGUEZ SÁNCHEZ, Margarita, 590
RODRÍGUEZ TARDITI, José (b. 1902), 591
RODRÍGUEZ VIGOY, J., 1089
RÖGIND, William, 904
ROJAS, Ricardo (1882-1957), 245
ROJAS SILVA, Hermógenes, 947
ROLDÁN, Belisario (1873-1922), 592
ROLÓN MEDINA, Anastasio, 1007
ROMANO, Eduardo (b. 1938), 796
ROMAY, Francisco L., 637
ROMERO, José Luis (1909-1977), 246, 593, 594
ROMERO, Luis Alberto, 594
ROMERO BREST, Jorge, 1218
ROQUE, Benjamín, 595
ROSA, José María (b. 1906), 596
ROSALES, César, 798
ROSENWASSER, Mauricio, 332
ROSSI, Vincente, 1263
ROSSLER, Osvaldo (b. 1927), 877
ROVERE, Susan Inés, 799
ROXLO, Carlos (1860-1926), 1188
RUFFINELLI, Jorge, 1189
RUIZ, Luis Alberto (b. 1923), 800
RUIZ FERNÁNDEZ, Antonio, 1008
RUIZ-GUIÑAZÚ, Enrique (1882-1967), 597
RUIZ MORENO, Aníbal, 846

SAAVEDRA, Luis, 704
SABAT, Hermenengildo, 524
SABSAY, Fernando, 598
SÁENZ CAVIA DE MORALES TORRES, Sara, 247
SALAS, Horacio (b. 1938), 801
SALAVERRI, Vicente A. (b. 1887), 1190

SALDAÑA RETAMAR, Reginaldo de la Cruz, 599
SALDÍAS, Adolfo (1850-1914), 600
SALGADO, José, 588
SALGADO, Susana, 1208
SALIM, Lina, 775
SALTERAIN HERRERA, Eduardo de (b. 1892), 1090, 1133
SALVADOR, Nélida, 802
SALVADORES, Antonino (1898-1953), 248, 249
SAN MARTÍN, María Laura, 57
SAN MARTÍN, Pastor de, 384
SÁNCHEZ CESCHI, Eduardo A., 250
SÁNCHEZ DE BUSTAMANTE, Teófilo (1868-1930), 251
SÁNCHEZ GACIO, Héctor E., 638
SÁNCHEZ QUELL, Hipólito (b. 1907), 963
SÁNCHEZ SÍVORI, Amalia, 878
SANCHEZ SORONDO, Matías Guillermo (1880-1959), 601
SANGUIAO, Osvaldo J., 639
SANGUINETTI, Horacio, 119
SANTA CRUZ, Inés, 771
SANTA FE, ARGENTINE REPUBLIC (City). MUSEO PROVINCIAL DE BELLAS ARTES "ROSA GALISTEO DE RODRIGUEZ," 58
SANTANDER, Silvano (b. 1895), 602
SANTIAGO, José Alberto (b. 1934), 803
SANTILLÁN, Diego A. de, 308
SANTOS, Estela dos, 879
SANTOS MARTÍNEZ, Pedro, 252
SARAVÍ CISNEROS, Roberto (b. 1906), 805
SARLO SABAJANES, Beatriz, 806
SARMIENTO, Domingo Faustino, President Argentine Republic (1811-1888), 369, 459, 603, 604, 605, 606, 607, 608
SAZ SÁNCHEZ, Agustín, 807
SCALABRINI ORTIZ, Raúl (1898-1959), 905
SCARONE, Arturo (1885-1958), 1091, 1102, 1103, 1213, 1214
SCENNA, Miguel Ángel, 609
SCOTTO, José Arturo, 253, 254
SCHALLMAN, Lázaro (b. 1905), 255
SCHIAFFINO, Eduardo (1858-1935), 59
SCHIRO, Roberto, 771
SCHIUMA, Oreste (1881-1957), 880, 881, 882
SCHOO LASTRA, Dionisio (b. 1889), 256
SCHULKIN, Augusto I., 1138
SCHULZ, Lotte, 1042
SEBRELI, Juan José, 363
SEGURA, Juan José Antonio, 917
SELUJA CECÍN, Antonio, 1259
SELVA, José Fernando, 257
SEMANA DE LA JUVENTUD, 2d, MINAS, URUGUAY, 1964, 1191
SEMINARIO DE ESTUDIOS DE HISTORIA ARGENTINA, 610
SENILLOSA, Mabel, 883
SERGI, Jorge F. (1890-1961), 258
SERRA, Edelweis, 771
SIERRA, Luis Adolfo, 891a
SIGNO, 809
SIGWALD CARIOLI, Susana B., 258a
SILVA RIESTRA, Juan, 650
SILVA VALDÉS, Fernan, 1194
SIRI, Eros Nicola, 581
SOBRINO, Constantino, 884
SOCIEDAD ARGENTINA DE ESCRITORES. FILIAL NEUQUÉN, 810
SOCIEDAD DE BENEFICENCIA DE LA CAPITAL, BUENOS AIRES, 925
SOCIEDAD DE HOMBRES DE LETRAS DEL URUGUAY, 1193
SOLANES, Francisco, 201
SOLARI, Juan Antonio (b. 1899), 259, 260, 261, 330, 612, 613, 614, 615
SOLER CAÑAS, Luis (b. 1918), 811, 812, 813

SOMIGLIANA, Carlos, 690
SONZOGNI, Marina Celia, 178
SORRENTINO, Fernando (b. 1942), 814, 815, 816, 817
SORS DE TRICERRI, Guillermina (1904-1958), 262, 263
SOSA CORDERO, Osvaldo, 892
SOSA DE NEWTON, Lily, 933, 934
SOSA MIATELLO, Sara, 305
SPERATTI, Juan, 969
SPERONI, Miguel Ángel (b. 1911), 616
SPIKA, Alfredo, 332
SQUIRRU, Rafael Fernando (b. 1925), 60
STEWART VARGAS, Guillermo, 1134
STIEBEN, Enrique (1893-1958), 617
STILMAN, Eduardo, 818
STORNI, Hugo, 1039a
SUÁREZ, Julio E., 1168
SUÁREZ DANERO, Eduardo María (b. 1897), 618
SVANASCINI, Osvaldo, 671
SWIETLICKI, Alain, 545

TABOADA, Gaspar (1861-1957), 264
TABORDA, Eduardo S., 1092
TAGLIAFERRO, M. Miguel (b. 1894), 619
TALICE, Roberto A. (b. 1902), 645
TAMBURINI, Juan Isidro, 331
TEMPERLEY, Harold, 502
TERÁN, Juan B. 1234
TESTENA, FOLCO, pseud.
    see BRACCIALARGHE, Comunardo
TIEMPO, César, pseud.
    see ZEITLIN, Israel
TIJERAS, Eduardo, 820
TINKER, Edward Larocque (b. 1881), 821, 1260
TISNÉS JIMÉNEZ, Roberto María (b. 1926), 364
TIZÓN, Héctor (b. 1929), 730
TJARKS, Germán O. E., 589
TOGNO, María Elena, 822
TOLEDO, Bernadino, 918
TORASSA, Antonio A., 266
TORRE, Guillermo de la, 671, 798
TORRE, José E. de la (b. 1905), 267, 268
TORRE REVELLO, José, 651
TORRENS, María Luisa
    see TORRENS FONTÁN, María Luisa
TORRENS FONTÁN, María Luisa (b. 1929), 1049
TORRES, Antonio, 852
TORRES, Gladys, 1026
TORRES, Luis María, 416
TORTEROLO, Leogardo Miguel, 1135
TRELLES, Manuel Ricardo (1821-1893), 640
TRONCOSO, Oscar A., 269
TROSTINÉ, Rodolfo, 61, 62, 373
TUCUMÁN. GOBERNACIÓN, 620
TÚMBURUS, Juan (1861-1928), 853

UDAONDO, Enrique (1880-1962), 250, 270, 271, 272,
    273, 309, 310, 433, 621
UGARTECHE, Félix de, 274
UN AFICIONADO, pseud.
    see BERMÚDEZ, Washington Pedro
UNITED NATIONS EDUCATIONAL, SCIENTIFIC AND
    CULTURAL ORGANIZATION. SCIENCE COOPERATION
    OFFICE FOR LATIN AMERICA, 963a
UNITED NATIONS EDUCATIONAL, SCIENTIFIC AND
    CULTURAL ORGANIZATION. SCIENCE COOPERATION
    OFFICE FOR LATIN AMERICA, 923, 1216
URBIETA ROJAS, Pastor, 1042
URONDO, Francisco, 690
URQUÍA, Carlos Enrique, 739
URQUIZA, Eduardo de, 365
URQUIZA, Justo José, 418

URUEÑA GONZÁLEZ, Camilo, 1093, 1140
URUGUAY. COMISIÓN NACIONAL DE BELLAS ARTES, 1093a
URUGUAY. EJÉRCITO. ESTADO MAYOR. DEPARTAMENTO
    DE ESTUDIOS HISTÓRICOS. "DIVISIÓN HISTORIA,"
    1136
UZAL, Francisco Hipólito (b. 1913), 622

VACCAREZZA, Jorge Raúl (b. 1929), 275
VACCAREZZA, Oscar Andrés, 853a
VACCAREZZA, Oscar L., 275
VACCAREZZA, Raúl F., 854
VACCAREZZA, Roberto A., 275
VADELL, Natalio Abel (1884-1961), 828
VALVERDE, Alberto, 76
VALLE, Aristóbulo del (1847-1896), 276
VALLE LERSUNDI, F. del, 1228
VALLEJOS PÉREZ GARAY, Roque (b. 1943), 1025
VALLS, Luis, 1094
VANBER, pseud.
    see BERTODATTI, Juan Domingo
VAQUER, Antonio (b. 1900), 332a
VÁSQUEZ, Aníbal S. (1892-1961), 623
VEDIA, Joaquín de (1877-1936), 277
VEIRAVÉ, Alfredo (b. 1928), 831
VELASCO QUIROGA, Hilario, 278
VELÁZQUEZ, Rafael Eladio (b. 1926), 964, 970
VERA, Luis, 706
VERDAGUER, José Aníbal (1877-1940), 919
VERHESSEN, Fernand, 832
VERÓN DE ASTRADA, Manuel (b. 1903), 965
VIACAVA, José Daniel, 725
VICO, Humberto, 279
VIDAL, Alfredo (1905-1950), 280, 281
VIDELA, Horacio (b. 1905), 283
VIDELA MORÓN, Mario Ernesto (b. 1902), 366
VIGNALE, Pedro Juan (b. 1903), 833
VILANOVA RODRÍGUEZ, Alberto, 284
VILLA, Oscar Jorge, 1141
VILLAGRÁN BUSTAMANTE, Héctor (1887-1941), 1195
VIÑUALES, Graciela María, 223
VIOLA, Alfredo, 966
VIRGINIA. MUSEUM OF FINE ARTS, RICHMOND, 64
VISCA, Arturo Sergio (b. 1917), 1173, 1196, 1197
VITA, Buenaventura N., 285
VITA-FINZI, Paolo, 624
VITTONE, Luis, 936, 1009
VIURÓN, Ceriani del, pseud.
    see BAGALIO, Alfredo S.
VIVERO, Domingo de, 920

WARREN, Harris Gaylord (b. 1906), 1010
WEINBERG, Gregorio, 589
WEY, Walter, 1026
WILLIAMS ALZAGA, Enrique (b. 1905), 286, 834
WILLINER, Gregorio, 885
WILLIS, Jean L., 1139
WRIGHT, Ione Stuessy, 641

XARQUE, Francisco (1609-1691), 1040

YABEN, Jacinto R. (b. 1887), 625
YAHNI, Roberto, 835, 839
YANI, José Ignacio, 626
YANOVER, Héctor, 661
YGOBONE, Aquiles D. (b. 1901), 287, 288, 289
YRIBARREN, Alfredo A., 290
YUNQUE, Alvaro, pseud.
    see GANDOLFI HERRERO, Arístides

ZABATTA, Gioconda de, 65
ZAMBRA, Eneas, 17b

ZAMORA, Antonio, 1167

ZAPATA GOLLÁN, Agustín (b. 1895), 627, 855

ZAS, Lubrano, 836

ZAVALÍA MATIENZO, Roberto, 628

ZEBALLOS, Estanislao S., 876

ZEINSTEJER, Felipe, 837

ZEITLIN, Israel (TIEMPO, César, pseud.) (b. 1906), 833, 893

ZEMBORAIN, Carlos Alfredo, 132

ZINNY, Antonio (1821-1890), 629, 630, 1011, 1041, 1142

ZONI, César P., 92

ZORRAQUÍN BECÚ, Ricardo, 132

ZORRILLA, Manuel Marcos (d. 1915), 631

ZORRILLA, Rubén H., 632

ZUBERBÜHLER, Ricardo F., 291

ZUBILLAGA BARRERA, Carlos A., 1095

ZUBIZARRETA, Carlos (1904-1972), 1012

ZUCCARINI, Emilio, 292

ZUM FELDE, Alberto (b. 1888), 1198, 1199

ZURETTI, Juan Carlos (b. 1907), 293, 921

ZUVIRÍA, José María (1830-1891), 633, 634

Short-Title Index

A martillo limpio, 240 (Ramos Mejía)
A través de una correspondencia, 488 (Gutiérrez)
Abogados criollos en el Buenos Aires de 1600,
    646 (Cutolo)
Abogados de Santiago del Estero, 649a (Oddo)
Abogados del antiguo Rosario, 648 (Marco)
Abogados, escribanos, y obras de derecho en el
    Rosario del siglo XIX, 649 (Marco)
Académicos de derecho, 650 (Silva Riestra)
Actividades marítimos en la Patagonia, 579 (Ratto)
¿Actividades nazis en el Uruguay?, 1070 (Frick
    Davie)
Acusación y defensa de Rosas, 373 (Ángelis)
Adalides sanjuaninos de la emancipación americana,
    546 (Maurín Navarro)
Agon 20 [i.e. Veinte] en clave de magia, 655
Agon 22 [i.e. Veintidós] en clave de enigma, 656
Al lado de Sarmiento y de Avellaneda, 631
    (Zorrilla)
Alba sonora, 659
Album biográfico, 94 (Borja)
Album biográfico ilustrado y descripción histórico
    geográfica de la República Oriental del
    Uruguay, 1075 (Jalabert)
Album gráfico de Concepción, 958 (Olmedo)
Album gráfico de la República del Paraguay, 951
    (López Decoud)
Album nacional (de la) República Argentina, 68
    (Díaz)
Album paraguayo, 981 (Benitez Flores)
Album presidencial de la reorganización nacional
    1916-1922, 69
Algunos pintores y escultores, 1046, 1047 (Laroche)
El alma de la raza, 992 (Domínguez)
Los Alvear, 142 (Fernández Lalanne)
El amor, 928 (Bertolé de Cané)
Los amores de Sarmiento, 450 (Fariña Núñez)
Anales contemporáneos, 633 (Zuviría)
Anales de la Biblioteca, 482 (Groussac)
Anarquía y caudillismo, 426 (Carretero)
Los Anchorena, 339 (Carretero)
Anecdotario uruguayo, 1064 (Ellis)
Anécdotas de los grandes hombres argentinos, 78
    (Avellá)
Anécdotas y recuerdos, 90 (Blancas)
Antecedentes biográficos santiagueños, 296a
    (DiLullo)
Antecedentes históricos de Encarnación de Itapúa,
    1001 (Micó)
Antecedentes históricos y genealógicos, 357
    (Otárola)
Antecedentes para la historia de la industria

argentina, 642 (Nicolau)
La antigua provincia de Guairá y la Villa Rica
    del Espíritu Santo, 945 (Cardozo)
Los antepasados de Alem fueron gallegos, 343
    (Fernández de Burzaco y Barrios)
Antología argentina, 542 (Martínez)
Antología argentina contemporánea, 674 (Berenguer
    Carisomo)
Antología clásica de la literatura argentina,
    734 (Henríquez Ureña)
Antología consultada de la joven poesía argentina,
    661
Antología crítica de la poesía paraguaya, 1025
    (Vallejos Pérez Garay)
Antología de la literatura gauchesca y criollista,
    1249 (Garganigo)
Antología de la moderna poesía uruguaya, 1181
    (Pereda Valdés)
Antología de la poesía argentina, 657 (Aguirre)
Antología de la poesía argentina, 803 (Santiago)
Antología de la poesía argentina contemporánea,
    798 (Rosales)
Antología de la poesía argentina moderna, 773
    (Noé)
Antología de la poesía femenina argentina, 762
    (Maubé)
Antología de la poesía gauchesca, 1242 (Becco)
Antología de la poesía uruguaya contemporánea,
    1151 (Bordoli)
Antología de literatura fantástica argentina,
    714 (Flesca)
Antología de literatura fantástica argentina,
    756 (Manguel)
Antología de narradores del Uruguay, 1162
    (Filartigas)
Antología de poesía argentina, 807 (Saz Sánchez)
Antología de poetas uruguayos, 1161 (Falcao
    Espalter)
Antología del cuento criollo del Uruguay, 1159
    (Da Rosa)
Antología del cuento uruguayo, 1170 (Lasplaces)
Antología del ensayo uruguayo contemporáneo, 1184
    (Real de Azúa)
Antología del soneto lunfardo, 660 (Alposta)
Antología del verso lunfardo, 818 (Stilman)
Antología gaucha, cuentos, 1246 (Danero)
Antología gaucha (poesía), 1247 (Danero)
Antología gauchesca, 1256 (Pi)
Antología generacional, 662
Antología pedagógica argentina, 317 (Forgione)
Antología poética argentina, 678 (Borges)
Antología poética bonaerense, 663

Antología poética de la Revolución Justicialista, 766 (Monti)

Antología poética de Signo, 809 (Signo)

Antología poético-gauchesca de ambas márgenes del Plata, 1243 (Blanco)

Antología y crítica de literatura uruguaya, 1164 (Fusco Sansone)

Antolojía paraguaya, 1024 (Rodríguez Alcalá)

Anuario de la aristocracia y alta sociedad, 294a

El año terrible, 1129 (Pedemonte)

Los años de la emancipación política, 374

Apellidos de la patria vieja, 1223 (Azarola Gil)

Apodos y denominativos en la historia argentina, 900 (Cutolo)

Apogeo y ocaso de los Anchorena, 363 (Sebreli)

Aportación al padrón histórico de Montevideo, 1055 (Azarola Gil)

El aporte de la mujer sanjuanina a la gesta libertadora del Gral. San Martín, 487 (Guerrero)

El aporte de los irlandeses a la formación de la nación, 119a (Coghlan)

El aporte italiano al progreso del Paraguay, 952 (Majavacca)

Aportes al desarrollo de la ciudad de Asunción, 943a (Cáceres de Thomas)

Apuntes biográficos, 177 (Gutiérrez)

Apuntes biográficos de la familia Artigas y Ferreira, 1107 (Ferreira)

Apuntes genealógicos: los Tisnés en Colombia y Argentina, 364 (Tisnés Jiménez)

Apuntes históricos, 1124 (Muñoz)

Apuntes históricos del pueblo de San Fernando, 270 (Udaondo)

Apuntes históricos sobre la provincia de Entre Ríos, 127 (Cuyás y Sampere)

Apuntes para la historia de Junín, 230 (Pérez)

Apuntes para la historia de Saladillo, 181 (Ibáñez Frocham)

Apuntes para la historia del partido de la Ensenada, 117 (Cestino)

Apuntes para un diccionario de seudónimos y de publicaciones anónimas, 1213 (Scarone)

Aquí Montevideo, 1182 (Rama)

Arandú, 1069 (Filartigas)

Argentina, 481 (González Ruiz)

Argentina, 923 (United Nations Educational, Scientific and Cultural Organization. Science Cooperation Office for Latin America)

Argentina: A chronology and fact book, 452 (Fitzgibbon)

Argentina: 1930-1960, 218 (Paita)

Argentina-Paraguay, 377

La Argentina se hizo así, 513 (Levene)

Argentina Works of Art in the John F. Kennedy Center for the Performing Arts, 20

La Argentina y los argentinos, 213 (Neustadt)

Argentinas, 419 (Carranza)

The Argentine Novel in the Nineteenth Century, 747 (Lichtblau)

Argentines of Today, 221 (Parker)

Argentinos de origen africano, 137 (Estrada)

Los Argentinos en la luna, 728 (Goligorsky)

Argentinos graduados en Chuquisaca, 126 (Cutolo)

Argentinos ilustres, 121 (Cora)

Argentinos ilustres, 475 (Gauna Vélez)

Los argentinos y su historia interna, 531 (Lugones)

La armada española en el Plata, 1235 (Marco)

Armada nacional, 9 (Burzio)

Los arquetipos, 245 (Rojas)

Arquetipos de la raza, 1007 (Rolón Medina)

Arquitectos argentinos durante la dominación hispánica, 7 (Fúrlong Cárdiff)

La arquitectura en Buenos Aires, 6 (Buenos Aires. Universidad. Instituto de Arte Americano e Investigaciones Estéticas.)

L'art argentin actuel, 49 (Paris. Musée national d'art moderne)

El arte de los argentinos, 47 (Pagano)

Artes y artistas paraguayos, 937 (Báez)

Artesanos argentinos durante la dominación hispánica, 39 (Fúrlong Cárdiff)

Artigas y los curas rebeldes, 1115 (Fernández Cabrelli)

Artistas del Litoral, 29 (Colon)

Artistas del Uruguay, 1163 (Filartigas)

Así escriben las mujeres, 822 (Togno)

Así escriben los argentinos, 666

Aspectos de la narrativa criollista, 1196 (Visca)

Asunción y sus calles, 950 (Kallsen)

Auténticos paladines, 152 (Gandulfo Arce de Ballor)

Autores y libros, 1195 (Villagrán Bustamente)

La aventura del periodismo, 644a (Llano)

Ayer fué san Perón, 437 (Damonte Taborda)

Bajo el signo de mayo, 612 (Solari)

Balcarce 50, 524 (Lezama)

Barracas, 237 (Puccia)

Bases y puntos de partida para la organización política de la República Argentina, 369 (Alberdi)

Beyond the Rivers, 1015 (Carlisle)

Biblioteca, 1193 (Sociedad de Hombres de Letras del Uruguay)

Biblioteca básica de cultura uruguaya, 1058

Bibliotecas argentinas durante la dominación hispánica, 651 (Fúrlong Cárdiff)

Biografía de nuestros artistas, 1028

Biografía del Río Salado de la Provincia de Buenos Aires, 203 (Moncaut)

Biografías completas, 460 (Gálvez)

Biografías de conquistadores de la Argentina en el siglo XVI, 520 (Levillier)

Biografías de obispos y arzobispos de Buenos Aires, 907

Biografías históricas de Jujuy, 251 (Sánchez de Bustamante)

Biografías militares, 17b (Zambra)

Biografías navales argentinas, 14 (Piccirilli)

Blasones de los virreyes del Río de la Plata, 1239, 1240 (Radaelli)

Bloody Precedent, 434 (Cowles)

Bocetos biográficos, 1065 (Ellis)

Los bohemios, 243 (Rivera)

La bolsa de agua caliente, 690 (Somigliana)

Bosquejo histórico de la provincia de la Rioja, 242 (Reyes)

Boticas de la colonia y cosecha de hojas dispersas, 949 (González Torres)

Breve antología del cuento campero, 1180 (Penco)

Breve antología del cuento paraguayo, 1019 (Pérez Maricevich)

Breve biografía de intelectuales uruguayos, 1088 (Ríos)

Breve historia de la Argentina, 593 (Romero)

Breve historia de la cultura en el Paraguay, 964 (Velázquez)

Breve historia de la música argentina y folklore, 864 (Flury)

Breve historia del Parlamento argentino, 397 (Bugatti)

Breve historia del teatro argentino, 890 (Ordaz)
Breves lecciones de historia argentina, 406 (Cambon)
Britain and Argentine in the Nineteenth Century, 143 (Ferns)
The British in Paraguay 1850–1870, 961 (Pla)
Britons at Maldonado, 1074 (Hirst)
Buenos Aires, ciudad, 103 (Bucich Escobar)
Buenos Aires colonial, 463 (Gandía)
Buenos Aires en el siglo XVII, 186 (Lafuente Machain)
Buenos Aires, la gran provincia, 391 (Bucich Escobar)
Buenos Aires, su naturaleza, sus costumbres, sus hombres, 436 (D'Amico)
Buenos Aires, sus hombres, su política, 129 (D'Amico)
Buscando a los que fueron, 971 (Ortellano Rojas de Fossati)

Cabezas rojas en el Uruguay, 1210 (Cano)
Caciques guaraníes de la época colonial, 977 (Bejerano)
Cada noche es un estreno, 1209 (Candeau)
La caída de Rosas, 596 (Rosa)
La campaña del Brasil y la batalla de Ituzaingó, 433 (Correa Luna)
Campañas navales de la República Argentina, 423 (Carranza)
Cancionero popular de la Revista de derecho, historia y letras, 876 (Revista de derecho, historia y letras)
Capellanes de la Guerra del Chaco, 995 (Gaona)
Capellanes militares en los territorios argentinos, 916 (Ramayón)
Capellanía de Santos Lugares, 120 (Comandi)
Los capitanes de Güemes, 625 (Yaben)
Capítulos de historia, 536 (Madero)
Los capuchinos genoveses en el Río de la Plata, 1265 (Antonio María de Montevideo)
La cartera de un soldado, 474 (Garmendia)
La casa de Tucumán, 628 (Zavalía Matienzo)
El caso argentino, 440 (Dorrego)
Catálogo de los jesuitas de la Provincia del Paraguay, 1039a (Storni)
Catecismo de historia argentina, 448 (Estrada)
Los caudillos, 532 (Luna)
Los caudillos de este siglo, 429
Caudillos de la conquista, 504 (Laconich)
Caudillos entrerrianos, 623 (Vásquez)
Celebrità argentine dell'epoca dell'indipendenza nazionale, 411 (Caraffa)
Censo de los empleados administrativos, funcionarios judiciales y personal docente de la República Argentina correspondiente al 31 de diciembre de 1892, 77 (Argentine Republic. Dirección general de estadística)
Una centuria literaria (poetas y prosistas uruguayos), 1146 (Barbagelata)
El ciclo romántico modernista en el Paraguay, 1018 (Marcos)
Cien años de música argentina, 880 (Schiuma)
Cien años de vida, 1050 (Alava)
100 [i.e. Cien] años, iglesia danesa Tandil, 909
Cien autores del Uruguay, 1177 (Paganini)
100.000 [i.e. Cien mil] ejemplares por hora, 645 (Talice)
Cien poesías, 684
Cien poesías rioplatenses, 1147 (Bartholomew)
Cien próceres argentinos, 404 (Calderarc)
Cien vidas paraguayas, 1012 (Zubiz reta)

150 [i.e. Ciento cincuenta] años de arte argentino, 19 (Argentine Republic. Comisión Nacional Ejecutiva del 150 Aniversario de la Revolución de Mayo)
150 [i.e. Ciento cincuenta] años de música uruguaya, 1206
5 [i.e. Cinco] cuentos uruguayos, 1175 (Montevideo. Universidad de la República)
Cinco dandys porteños, 193 (Lusarreta)
Cinco esbozos, 601 (Sánchez Sorondo)
Cinco retratos, 286 (Williams Alzaga)
5 [i.e. Cinco] semblanzas republicanas, 993 (Duarte Prado)
Cincuenta años de aeronáutica en el Paraguay, 935 (Aponte)
50 [i.e. Cincuenta] años de arte plástico en Córdoba, 43 (Lo Celso)
Cincuenta semblanzas argentinas, 110 (Caffaro Rossi)
Cine argentino '76–80, 857, 857a, 857b, 857c, 857d (Abel Martín)
La cinta colorada, 511 (Leguizamón)
El circo criollo, 886 (Castagnino)
La ciudad arribeña, 80 (Ávila)
La ciudad encantada de los Césares, 464 (Gandía)
El civilizador, 603 (Sarmiento)
Clavafrío, 731 (Guerra)
Los clérigos Agüero en la historia argentina, 114 (Carbia)
El clero argentino de 1810 á 1830, 908 (Carranza)
El clero en la guerra del 70, 995a (Gaona)
Colección de obras y documentos relativos a la historia antigua y moderna de las provincias del Río de la Plata, 1229 (Angelis)
La colectividad italiana en Victoria E. Ríos, 73 (Anadón)
Coliqueo, 180 (Hux)
Colonización suiza en Argentina, 168 (Gori)
Comentarios: actualidad asunceña, 963 (Sánchez Quell)
Cómo fue la vida amorosa de Rosas, 234 (Pineda Yáñez)
Cómo fueron las artes en la Argentina, 40 (Gesualdo)
Cómo los vi yo, 277 (Vedia)
Cómo se formó el país argentino, 443 (Eizaguirre)
Los comodores británicos de estación en la Plata, 580 (Ratto)
Compositores argentinos, 883 (Senillosa)
A Comprehensive Exhibition of the Contemporary Art of Argentina, 64 (Virginia Museum of Fine Arts, Richmond)
Los comuneros del Paraguay, 978 (Benítez)
Con Perón en el exilio, 368 (Albamonte)
Con Rosas contra Rosas, 431
Concepción en las artes, 1017
Concierto de la Agrupación Folklórica Guaraní, 1027 (Agrupación Folklórica Guaraní)
Congresales de 1816, apuntes biográficos, 621 (Udaondo)
El Congreso de Tucumán, 457 (Fúrlong Cárdiff)
The Conquest of the River Plate, 1232 (Graham)
Un conquistador, 134 (Echevarría de Lobato Mulle)
Conquistadores del Río de la Plata, 1234 (Lafuente Machain)
Constantes de la literatura argentina, 721 (Ghiano)
Los constituyentes de 1853, 634 (Zuviría)
Contemporáneos ilustres, 544 (Martínez)
Contribución a la historia de Bragado, 209 (Moya)
Contribución a la historia de Montevideo, 1106 (Azarola Gil)
Contribución a un diccionario de seudónimos en la Argentina, 902 (Durán)

Contribución al estudio de la nomenclatura histórica
de Montevideo, 1056 (Azarola Gil)
Contribución documental a la historis de el teatro
en Buenos Aires, 887 (Castagnino)
Contribución italiana al desarrollo intelectual
en la República Argentina, 113 (Caraffa)
Conversaciones con el teatro argentino de hoy,
889 (Naios Janchaus)
Coronel Andrés Latorre, 1082 (Parallada)
Los corregidores y subdelegados de Cuyo, 555
(Morales Guiñazú)
Correspondencia de la ciudad de Buenos Ayres con
los reyes de España, 394 (Buenos Aires)
Creación y actividades en su primer quinquenio,
497 (Instituto Sarmiento de Sociología e
Historia)
Corrientes en la cruzada de Caseros, 387
(Bonastre)
Crítica de arte, Argentina, 22 (Associación
Argentina de Críticos de Arte)
Crítica de la literatura uruguaya, 1198 (Zum
Felde)
Críticas de arte argentino, 33 (Chiabra Acosta)
Críticas y bocetos históricos, 227 (Pelliza)
Crónica de los gobernantes de Misiones, 551a
(Misiones)
Crónica de una estirpe prócer, 973 (Recalde A.)
Crónica histórica de Carmen de Patagones entre
los años 1852-1855, 250 (Sánchez Ceschi)
Crónica histórica de la aeronáutica argentina, 1
(Biedma Recalde)
Crónica histórica de la provincia de Corrientes,
196 (Mantilla)
Crónica interna de la Revolución Libertadora,
428 (Carril)
Crónica vecinal de Nueve de Julio, 285 (Vita)
Crónicas de Treinta y Tres, 1140 (Urueña González)
Crónicas del pasado teatral argentino, 888
(Castagino)
Crónicas y estampas del pasado, 842 (Aráoz Alfaro)
Crónicas y linajes de la gobernación del Plata,
1224 (Azarola Gil)
Cronistas de Indias, 1230 (Cruz)
Cronología artística, 32
Cronología de los obispos del Paraguay, 1041
(Zinny)
Cronología de Montevideo en los 250 años de su
proceso fundacional, 1062 (Comisión de Actos
Commemorativos de los 250 años de la
Fundación de Montevideo)
Cronología histórica argentina, 574 (Piñeiro)
Cronología histórica de la antigua Provincia del
Guairá, 944 (Cáceres Zorilla)
Croquis y siluetas militares, 13 (Gutiérrez)
Los cruzados del Uruguay, 1201 (Martínez Montero)
Cuadros históricos y descriptivos, 942 (Báez)
40 [i.e. Cuarenta] años de poesía argentina,
739 (Isaacson)
40 [i.e. Cuarenta] cuentos breves argentinos,
814 (Sorrentino)
Cuatro artistas del Litoral, 30 (Colón)
Cuatro siglos de literatura salteña, 653 (Adet)
Cuentan para usted, 795 (Ríos Ortiz)
Cuentistas argentinos, 670 (Becco)
Cuentistas argentinos contemporáneos, 836 (Zas)
Cuentistas argentinos de hoy, 765 (Miranda Klix)
Cuentistas argentinos del siglo XIX, 708 (Donghi
Halperín)
Cuentistas premiados, 694
Cuentistas rioplatenses de hoy, 1245
Cuento, 695

El cuento argentino, 696
El cuento argentino, 745a (Lancelotti)
El cuento argentino contemporáneo, 697
El cuento uruguayo contemporaneo, 1155 (Cardoso)
Cuentos argentinos, 744 (Lagh)
Cuentos argentinos del siglo XX, 799 (Rovere)
Cuentos de crimen y misterio, 668 (Bajarlía)
Cuentos de dos orillas, 806 (Sarlo Sabajanes)
Cuentos de nuestra tierra, 779 (Pagés Larraya)
Cuentos de periodistas, 698
Cuentos del folklore argentino, 745 (Lagh)
Cuentos del interior, 753 (Maggio de Taboada)
Cuentos del NOA, 689 (Corvalán)
Cuentos fantásticos argentinos, 685 (Cócaro)
Los cuentos inéditos premiados en Salta, 699
Cuentos 70 [i.e. Setenta], 700
Cuentos y diálogos, 811 (Soler Cañas)
La cuestión capital de la República, 425 (Carranza)
The Cult of the Gaucho and the Creation of a
Literature, 1260 (Tinker)
Cultura femenina uruguaya, 1144 (Andrade Coello)
Las culturas condenadas, 962 (Roa Bastoa)
Cunas de ilustres linajes, 358 (Otárola)
Currents in the Contemporary Argentine Novel,
715 (Foster)

Chivilcoy, 88 (Bírabent)

Datos para una reseña cronológica sobre los
antecedentes, desarrollo y resultado de la
Guerra del Chaco, 999 (Marcet)
Datos y linajes, 359 (Otarola)
De Garay a Roca, 617 (Stieben)
De la marina heroica, 16 (Ratto)
De orilla a orilla, 701
De vita et moribus sex sacerdotum paraguaycorum,
1036, 1037 (Peramas)
Del origen de los numbres y apellidos y de la
ciencia genealógica, 347 (Gandía)
Del pago del Riachuelo al partido de Lanús,
223 (Paula)
El desarrollo de las ideas en la sociedad argentina
del siglo XX, 246 (Romero)
Desde la colonia hasta 1961, 551 (Mendoza)
Días y obras de Sarmiento, 613 (Solari)
Diccionario básico de literatura argentina, 840
(Prieto)
Diccionario biográfico argentino, 297b
Diccionario biográfico argentino, 295 (Biedma)
Diccionario biográfico argentino, 309 (Udaondo)
Diccionario biográfico colonial argentino, 310
(Udaondo)
Diccionario biográfico contemporáneo
see Hombres de la Argentina
Diccionario biográfico de hombres de negocios
see Hombres de la Argentina
Diccionario biográfico de la ciudad de Maldonado,
1098 (Guerra)
Diccionario biográfico de la República Argentina,
298 (Echevarrieta)
Diccionario biográfico de mujeres argentinas,
933, 934 (Sosa de Newton)
Diccionario biográfico del campo argentino, 5
(Newton)
Diccionario biográfico italo-argentino, 305
(Petriella)
Diccionario biográfico nacional, 302 (Molina Arrotea)
Diccionario de alfónimos y seudónimos de la
Argentina, 901 (Cutolo)
Diccionario de artistas plásticos de la Argentina,
66 (Merlino)

Diccionario de historia argentina, 638 (Sánchez Gacio)

Diccionario de la mujer guaraní, 1043 (Ríos Velazco de Caldi)

Diccionario de la República Argentina, 306 (Pinto)

Diccionario de payadores, 878 (Sánchez Sívori)

Diccionario de poetas argentinos, 838 (Bertodatti)

Diccionario de seudónimos del Uruguay, 1214 (Scarone)

Diccionario del tango, 884 (Sobrino)

Diccionario histórico argentino, 637 (Piccirill)

Diccionario histórico y biográfico de la República Argentina, 304 (Muzzio)

Diccionario médico argentino, 856 (Gajardo Cruzat)

Diccionario político, 639 (Sanguaio)

Diccionario político de nuestro tiempo, 297, 297a (Díaz Doin)

Diccionario popular de historia de la República Oriental del Uruguay, 1137 (Araújo)

Diccionario teatral del Río de la Plata, 894 (Foppa)

Diccionario uruguayo de biografías, 1096 (Fernández Saldaña)

18 [i.e. Dieciocho] poetas del Uruguay, 1153 (Brughetti)

16 [i.e. Dieciséis] pintores de Avellaneda, 65 (Zabatta)

16 [i.e. Dieciséis] poetas en Mar del Plata, 702

16 [i.e. Dieciséis] poetas inéditos, 791 (Portogalo)

17 [i.e. Diecisiete] cuentos argentinos, 815 (Sorrentino)

El 17 [i.e. Diecisiete] de Octubre de 1945, 461 (Gambini)

Diez años a través de treinta pintores argentinos, 23 (Avellaneda, Argentine Republic. (City) Museo de Arte)

Diez cuentistas de urumpta, 760 (Mastrángelo)

10 [i.e. Diez] de nosotros, 703

Diez poetas gauchescos del Uruguay, 1166 (García)

Diez poetas jóvenes, 671 (Becco)

10 [i.e. Diez] poetas, primera muestra, 704

10 [i.e. Diez] poetas, segunda muestra, 705

16 [i.e. Diez y seis] cuentos argentinos, 707 (Domínguez)

La dinastía Santos-Vidal, 1125 (Palomeque)

Diócesis y obispos de la iglesia argentina, 910 (Fúrlong Cárdiff)

Los directores de la República Argentina, 184 (Instituto de Estudios Biográficos)

Los directores del correo argentino, 898 (Galván Moreno)

Discursos, 592 (Roldán)

Doce argentinos, 72 (Amadeo)

12 [i.e. Doce] autores, 1160 (Dodera)

XII [i.e. Doce] cuentistas argentinos, 706

Doce pintores nacionales, 1049 (Torrens)

Documentos del archivo de Belgrano, 395 (Buenos Aires. Museo Mitre)

Documentos para la historia argentina, 396 (Buenos Aires. Facultad de Filosofía y Letras)

Dolores, Bs. As., 257 (Selva)

Domingo Faustino Sarmiento, 604 (Sarmiento)

Los domínicos en la independencia argentina, 599 (Saldaña Retamar)

¿Dónde está el pueblo?, 444 (Eizaguirre)

Las dos fundaciones de Buenos Aires, 510 (Larreta)

Dos patricias ilustres, 130 (Dellepiane)

El drama rural, 778 (Ordaz)

Dramas y esplendores de la historia argentina, 575 (Piñeiro)

Los economistas y la economía argentina, 311 (Pablo)

La educación en La Matanza, Victoria, 325 (Murature de Badaracco)

La educación paraguaya, 970 (Velázquez)

Efemérides argentinas, 376 (Arenas Luque)

Efemérides de la historia del Paraguay, 984a (Cardozo)

Efemérides sanjuaninas, 171 (Guerrero)

Efemérides uruguayas, 1091 (Scarone)

El ejército de hoy, 8 (Argentine Republic. Ejército. Comando en Jefe)

La emancipación oriental, 1131 (Quesada)

Los emigrados paraguayos en la guerra de la Triple Alianza, 991 (Decoud)

En la penumbra de la historia argentina, 492 (Ibarguren)

Enciclopedia de la literatura argentina, 839 (Orgambide)

Encuesta sobre el caudillo, 446

Encyclopaedia of Motor Racing, 923c (Pritchard)

Encyclopaedia of Motor Sport, 923b (Georgano)

Encyclopaedia of Auto Racing Greats, 923a (Cutter)

Los enemigos de San Martín, 622 (Uzal)

Ensayo de historia naval argentina, 10a (Caillet-Bois)

El ensayo en la Argentina, 743 (Koremblit)

Ensayo histórico del partido de Olavarría, 76 (Arena)

Ensayo histórico sobre la revolución de mayo y Mariano Moreno, 517 (Levene)

Ensayo sobre El Pago de la Magdalena, 248 (Salvadores)

Ensayos, 1253 (Montero Bustamante)

Ensayos históricos, 498 (Irazusta)

Ensayos históricos rioplatenses, 588 (Rodó)

Ensayos sobre literatura uruguaya, 1197 (Visca)

La enseñanza de la filosofía en tiempos de la colonia, 896 (Lértora Mendoza)

Entre la historia y la leyenda, 1054 (Auria)

Entre Ríos, 135

Entre Ríos cantada, 800 (Ruiz)

Entre Ríos, mi país, 157 (Gerchunoff)

Entre Ríos síntesis histórica, 194 (Macchi)

L'epopea del lavoro italiano nella Republica Argentina, 98 (Braccialarghe)

La epopeya patagónica, 287 (Ygobone)

Eramos jóvenes el siglo y yo, 226 (Peers de Perkins)

Escenario y actores de la revolución oriental de 1811, 1113 (Bonavita)

Escritores de la Argentina, 709 (Echagüe)

Escritos literarios, 380 (Avellaneda)

Escritos y discursos, 79 (Avellaneda)

Los escudos de armas de los governadores, 1136 (Uruguay. Ejército. Estado Mayor. Departamento de Estudios Históricos)

España en el Uruguay, 1089 (Rodríguez Vigoy)

España y sus misioneros en los países del Plata, 1267 (Eguía Ruiz)

Los españoles del Uruguay, 1094 (Valls)

Los españoles en el centenario argentino, 111 (Camba)

Los españoles en Rosario de Santa Fe, 201 (Miragaya)

Esquema de las generaciones artísticas y literarias boquenses, 102 (Bucich)

Estadistas y poetas, 219 (Palacios)

Estampas, 1119 (Montero Bustamante)

Estampas de argentinos, 182 (Ibarguren)

Estampas del Montevideo romántico, 1120 (Montero Bustamante)

Estampas del pasado, 400 (Busaniche)

Estampas heroicas, 1122 (Montes)

El estilo de vida argentino en Paz, Mansilla, González, Roca, Figueroa Alcorta y Sáenz Peña, 115 (Cárcano)
Estudio histórico crítico de la literatura argentina, 828 (Vadell)
Estudios biográficos, 449 (Estrada)
Estudios biográficos, 629 (Zinny)
Estudios biográficos sobre patriotas correntinos, 539 (Mantilla)
Estudios de historia argentina, 483 (Groussac)
Estudios genealógicos sobre antiguos apellidos del Río de La Plata y remotos orígenes del patriarcado argentino, 1227 (Otárola)
Estudios históricos, 918 (Toledo)
Estudios literarios, 1057 (Bauzá)
La evangelización en el Paraguay, 1035
Evocaciones criollas, 291 (Zuberbühler)
Evocaciones de un porteño viejo, 225 (Payró)
Evocaciones montevideanas, 1066 (Ellis)
Evocaciones políticas y literarias, 259 (Solari)
La evolución de las ideas Argentinas, 183 (Ingenieros)
The Evolution of the Gaucho in Literature, 1254 (Murguía)
Los excéntricos, 138
An Existential Focus on Some Novels of the River Plate, 1252 (Hayden)
La experiencia argentina y otros ensayos, 594 (Romero)
Exploración estética, 1152 (Brena)
Exposición Cayetano Gallino, 1093a (Uruguay. Comisión Nacional de Bellas Artes)
Exposición de diez pintores rosarinos fallecidos en este siglo, 58 (Santa Fe. Argentine Republic (City). Museo provincial de Bellas Artes "Rosa Galisteo de Rodríguez")
Exposición de la actual poesía argentina, 833 (Vignale)
Exposición de la poesía uruguaya, 1156 (Casal)
Expresiones literarias del Neuquén, 810 (Sociedad Argentina de Escritores. Filial Neuquén)
Extracción social de los caudillos, 632 (Zorilla)
El extrañamiento de los Jesuitas del Río de la Plata, 1269 (Hernández)

F. Muro, Grilo, Ocampo, Sakai, Testa, 26 (Buenos Aires. Museo Nacional de Bellas Artes)
Facundo Quiroga, 559 (Newton)
Familia Castells, 1226a (Castells Montero)
Familias de Traslasierra, jurisdicción de Córdoba, 340 (Castellano Sáenz Caria)
Famosos veleros argentinos, 438 (Destéfani)
Fichas para un diccionario uruguayo de biografías, 1097 (Fernández Saldaña)
Figuras correntinas, 67 (Acuña)
Figuras legendarias, 92 (Bonastre)
Figuras próximas y lejanas, 192 (Loudet)
Figuras señeras de la Patagonia y Tierra del Fuego, 288 (Ygobone)
Figuras y estampas de Montevideo, 1072 (Gomensoro)
Figuras y paisajes del Uruguay, 1071 (Fusco Sansone)
Fisonomías de conquistadores, 465 (Gandía)
Fisonomías de 1840, 206 (Morales)
Florilegio de prosistas uruguayos, 1190 (Salaverri)
Forjadores, 312 (Bagalio)
Forjadores de la República, 547 (Maurín Navarro)
La formación del clero secular de Buenos Aires y la Compañía de Jesús, 912 (Isern)
La formación histórica de la provincia de Córdoba, 545a (Martínez Paz)

Les français au Paraguay, 960 (Pitaud)
Los franciscanos en el Paraguay, 1034 (Córdoba)
Fronteras de la literatura argentina, 732 (Guglielmini)
El fuerte 25 de mayo en cruz de guerra, 169 (Grau)
Las fuerzas armadas paraguayas, 936 (Vittone)
La fundación del Cabildo de la Asunción, 1005 (Peña Villamil)
Fundadores de linajes en el Plata, 344 (Fernández de Burzaco y Barrios)

Galería biográfica, 911
Galería biográfica argentina, 424 (Carranza)
Galería de celebridades argentinas, 459 (Gache)
Galería de paraguayos ilustres, 948
Los gallegos en el Uruguay, 1095 (Zubillaga Barrera)
Los gallegos en la Argentina, 284 (Vilanova Rodríguez)
Los García de Zúñiga y los Warnes, 1226 (Campos)
The Gaucho in Some Novels of Argentina and Uruguay, 1250 (Garganigo)
Genealogía de los conquistadores de Cuyo y fundadores de Mendoza, 556 (Morales Guiñazú)
Genealogía de los Tocco, 353 (Marino Montero)
Genealogías de Cuyo, 355 (Morales Guiñazú)
Genealogías de Salta: los Fernández Cornejo, 342 (Cornejo)
Generación poética del cincuenta, 717 (Furlan)
La generación poética del cuarenta, 812 (Soler Cañas)
Generación poética del treinta, 746 (Lewkowicz)
Generaciones laicas argentinas, 330 (Solari)
El general José de San Martín en su centenario, 562 (Pajuelo Mejía)
Los generales de Urquiza, 543 (Martínez)
Génesis de la familia uruguaya, 1105 (Apolant)
Gente de Buenos Aires, 140 (Fernández)
German Buenos Aires, 214 (Newton)
Clorias argentinas, 228 (Pelliza)
Glorias santafesinas, 149 (Furlong Cárdiff)
La gloriosa cruzada de los treinta y tres patriotas orientales, 1132 (Revuelta)
Glosadores eminentes de la Constitución, 647 (Lafranco)
Gobernación del Tucumán, 620
El gobernador Domingo Martínez de Irala, 505 (Lafuente Machain)
Gobernadores de La Pampa, 571 (Pérez de Costilla)
Gobernantes, caudillos y escritores, 185 (Irazusta)
Gobernantes de Mayo, 610 (Seminario de Estudios de Historia Argentina)
Los gobernantes del Paraguay, 1008 (Ruiz Fernández)
Gobernantes del Uruguay, 1110 (Araujo)
Gobernantes municipales de Montevideo, 1123 (Montevideo. Intendencia Municipal)
Grabado argentino, 41
El grabado argentino en el siglo XX, 44 (López Anaya)
El grabado en la Argentina durante el período hispánico, 61 (Trostine)
Grabados argentinos, 27 (Buenos Aires. Museo Nacional de Bellas Artes)
Gran enciclopedia argentina, 308 (Santillán)
Gran enciclopedia de la provincia de Santa Fe, 294 (Abad de Santillán)
Los grandes caciques de la Pampa, 454 (Franco)
Grandes caciques de la Pampa, 454 (Franco)
Grandes figuras de la República Oriental del Uruguay y homenaje a los Estados Unidos de Norte América, 1073
Grandes hombres de nuestra patria, 271 (Udaondo)

Grandes y pequeños hombres del Plata, 369 (Alberdi)
Gravitación política de Perón, 590 (Rodríguez Sánchez)
El Guairá y su aporte a la cultura paraguaya, 947 (Franco Preda)
La guerra con el indio en la jurisdicción de San Luis, 566 (Pastor)
Las guerras civiles, 375 (Aráoz de La Madrid)
Guía biográfica, 299a (Hogg)
Guía ilustrativa de la Casa Histórica de la Independencia Argentina, 526 (Lizondo Borda)
Guía integral argentina, 175
Guía Senior, 299

Hambre y desnudeces en la conquista del Río de la Plata, 1231 (Fitte)
Los héroes de la independencia, 420 (Carranza)
Héroes ignorados, 331 (Tamburini)
Héroes y mártires de la epopeya del Chaco, 998 (Llorens Mora)
Los Herrera y Díaz Herrera, 354 (Molina Herrera)
Un hispano y un italiano en la guerra contra la triple alianza, 994 (Franco)
Historia antigua de la ciudad del Río Cuarto, 205 (Montes)
Historia argentina, 367 (Abad de Santillán)
Historia argentina, 379 (Astolfi)
Historia argentina, 401 (Busaniche)
Historia argentina, 476 (Gianello)
Historia argentina, 489 (Halperin Donghi)
Historia argentina, 514 (Levene)
Historia argentina, 521 (Levillier)
Historia argentina con drama y humor, 451 (Ferla)
Historia argentina desde su origen hasta la organización nacional, 570 (Pelliza)
Historia crítica de la historiografía argentina, 414, 415 (Carbia)
Historia crítica de la literatura uruguaya, 1188 (Roxlo)
Historia cultural, 943 (Benítez)
Historia de barbas y caftanes, 258a (Sigwald Carioli)
Historia de Belgrano y de la independencia argentina, 552 (Mitre)
Historia de Carmen de Areco, 200 (Melli)
Historia de Córdoba, 89 (Bischoff)
Historia de Córdoba, 144 (Ferrari Rueda)
Historia de Entre Ríos, 95 (Bosch Vinelli)
Historia de Entre Ríos, 241 (Reula)
Historia de Gualequay, 279 (Vico)
Historia de la Argentina, 471 (García Al-Deguer)
Historia de la Argentina, 478 (González Arrili)
Historia de la Boca del Riachuelo, 150 (Gandía)
Historia de la ciudad de Las Flores, 280 (Vidal)
Historia de la ciudad de Rojas hasta 1784, 108 (Cabodi)
Historia de la ciudad de San Nicolás de los Arroyos, 267 (Torre)
Historia de la Compañía de Jesús, 1035a, 1035b
Historia de la conquista del Paraguay, Río de la Plata y Tucumán, 529a (Lozano)
Historia de la cultura argentina, 293 (Zuretti)
Historia de la cultura mendocina, 207 (Morales Guiñazú)
Historia de la cultura paraguaya, 946 (Centurión)
Historia de la educación primaria de Córdoba, 316 (Fernández)
Historia de la educación pública en el Paraguay, 969 (Speratti)
Historia de la enseñanza naval en la Argentina, 17 (Ratto)

Historia de la Escuela Naval Militar, 10 (Burzio)
Historia de la Facultad de Medicina, 844 (Cantón)
Historia de la gobernación del Tucumán, 527 (Lizondo Borda)
Historia de la ingeniería argentina, 332
Historia de la ingeniería en la Argentina, 332a (Vaquer)
Historia de la literatura argentina, 737
Historia de la literatura argentina, 665 (Arrieta)
Historia de la literatura argentina, 720 (García Velloso)
Historia de la literatura argentina, 724 (Giménez Pastor)
Historia de la literatura paraguaya, 1021, 1022 (Rodríguez Alcalá)
Historia de la medicina argentina, 850 (Molinari)
Historia de la medicina en el Río de la Plata, 1261 (Cantón)
Historia de la medicina en el Uruguay, 1203 (Pérez Fontana)
Historia de la medicina en Santa Fe, 845 (Cervera)
Historia de la música argentina, 865 (Flury)
Historia de la música en la Argentina, 869 (Gesualdo)
Historia de la ópera en Buenos Aires, 859 (Bosch)
Historia de la poesía argentina, 763 (Menéndez y Pelayo)
Historia de la prensa periódica de la República Oriental del Uruguay, 1142 (Zinny)
Historia de la provincia de Corrientes, 163 (Gómez)
Historia de la provincia de San Luis, 158 (Gez)
Historia de la provincia del Chaco, 191 (López Piacentini)
Historia de la República Argentina, 466 (Gandía)
Historia de la República Argentina, 472 (García Mérou)
Historia de La Rioja, 83 (Bazán)
Historia de la Sociedad de Beneficencia, 924 (Correa Luna)
Historia de la Sociedad Rural Argentina, 3 (Newton)
Historia de la Universidad de Buenos Aires, 322 (Halperín Donghi)
Historia de las letras paraguayas, 1016 (Centurión)
Historia de las Malvinas argentinas, 490a
Historia de las varietés en Buenos Aires, 892 (Sosa Cordero)
Historia de los argentinos, 469 (Gandolfi Herrero)
Historia de los ferrocarriles argentinos, 905 (Scalabrini Ortiz)
Historia de los gobernadores de las provincias argentinas, 630 (Zinny)
Historia de los gobernantes del Paraguay, 1011 (Zinny)
Historia de los italianos en la Argentina, 258 (Sergi)
Historia de los piratas en el Río de la Plata, 467 (Gandía)
Historia de los presidentes argentinos, 392 (Bucich Escobar)
Historia de los presidentes argentinos, 515 (Levene)
Historia de Mendoza, 252 (Martínez)
Historia de Paysandú, 1138 (Schulkin)
Historia de Pergamino, 161 (Giménez Colodrero)
Historia de Quilmes, 123 (Craviotto)
Historia de Rafaela, 87 (Bianchi de Terragni)
Historia de San Juan, 283 (Videla)
Historia de San Justo, 178 (Avila)
Historia de San Luis, 215 (Núñez)
Historia de San Nicolás de los Arroyos, 155 (Garretón)
Historia de San Nicolás de los Arroyos, 268 (Torre)
Historia de Santa Fe, 477 (Gianello)

Historia de Zárate, 97 (Botta)
Historia del arte argentino, 48 (Pagano)
Historia del arte en Argentina, 25 (Romualdo)
Historia del cine argentino, 858 (Di Núbila)
Historia del Club Universitario de Buenos Aires, 326 (Newton)
Historia del Colegio de la Immaculada de la ciudad de Santa Fe, 318 (Fúrlong Cárdiff)
Historia del Colegio del Salvador, 319 (Fúrlong Cárdiff)
Historia del deporte en el Uruguay, 1216 (Buzzetti)
Historia del descubrimiento de Tucumán, 500 (Jaimes Freyre)
Historia del Ferrocarril Sud, 904 (Rögind)
Historia del libertador don José de San Martín, 561 (Otero)
Historia del país de los argentinos, 435 (Chávez)
Historia del Paraguay, 984 (Capdevielle)
Historia del Paraguay, 989 (Charlevoix)
Historia del partido de General Sarmiento, 211 (Munzón)
Historia del partido radical, 389 (Bosch)
Historia del periodismo argentino, 643 (Fernández)
Historia del protomedicato de Buenos Aires, 843 (Beltrán)
Historia del pueblo Vaccarezza y del partido de Alberti, 275 (Vaccarezza)
Historia del puerto de Buenos Aires, 535 (Madero)
Historia del sainete nacional, 719 (Gallo)
La historia del tango, 872
Historia del teatro uruguayo, 1185 (Rela)
Historia documentada de la vida y gloriosa muerte, 1032 (Blanco)
Historia eclesiástica argentina, 921 (Zuretti)
Historia eclesiástica de Cuyo, 919 (Verdaguer)
Historia eclesiástica de Entre Ríos, 917 (Segura)
Historia edilicia de la ciudad de Asunción, 996
Historia elemental de los argentinos, 388 (Bortnik)
Historia integral argentina, 491
Historia médica del Tucumán, 852 (Torres)
Historia naval argentina, 11 (Caillet-Bois)
La historia que he vivido, 493 (Ibarguren)
Historia sintética de la literatura uruguaya, 1187 (Reyles)
Historia y bibliografía de las primeras imprentas rioplatenses, 1264 (Fúrlong Cárdiff)
Historical Dictionary of Argentina, 641 (Wright)
Historical Dictionary of Paraguay, 1013 (Kolinski)
Historical Dictionary of Uruguay, 1139 (Willis)
Historiografía paraguaya, 985 (Cardozo)
Los historiógrafos argentinos menores, 314 (Carbia)
A History of Argentina, 518 (Levene)
A History of the Argentine Republic, 502 (Kirkpatrick)
Hojas de mi diario, 122 (Costa)
Hombres, armas y batallas de la epopeya de los siglos, 974 (Aponte Benítez)
Hombres de acción, 141 (Fernández)
Hombres de Entre Ríos, 160 (Gianello)
Hombres de la Argentina, 300
Hombres de la Argentina, 589 (Rodríguez Bustamante)
Los hombres de la Convención del 70, 986 (Centurión)
Hombres de la historia del puerto de Buenos Aires, 233 (Pinasco)
Hombres de la organización nacional, 585, 586 (Rivero Astengo)
Hombres de la República, 260 (Solari)

Hombres de mar en la historia argentina, 17a (Ratto)
Hombres de Mayo, 479 (González Arrili)
Hombres de Mayo, 496 (Instituto Argentino de Ciencias Genealógicas)
Hombres de mi tierra, 1059 (Bonavita)
Hombres del coloniaje, 274 (Ugarteche)
Hombres del día, 301
Hombres del surco, 4 (Pozzo Ardizzi)
Hombres en la vida y en la muerte, 965 (Verón de Astrada)
Hombres en las guerras de las pampas, 470 (Gandolfi Herrero)
Hombres notables de Cuyo, 412, 413 (Caraffa)
Hombres representativos, 1077 (Mancebo)
Hombres y cosas que pasaron, 512 (Leguizamón)
Hombres y episodios de nuestras guerras, 442 (Echagüe)
Hombres y épocas del Paraguay, 983 (Bray)
Hombres y faenas, 1133 (Salterain Herrera)
Hombres y hechos de Santa Fe, 105, 106, 107 (Busaniche)
Los hombres y los días, 176 (Guillén)
Hombres y pasiones, 953 (Martínez)
Hombres y problemas argentinos, 582 (Repetto)
Hombres y surcos, 1104 (Otero y Roca)
Humanizando los próceres, 583 (Rimondi)
Humorismo argentino, 769 (Murray)

Iconografía de próceres argentinos, 386 (Biedma)
Ideales y caracteres, 165 (González)
Las ideas políticas de Petro de Angelis, 373 (Gandía)
La iglesia en el Uruguay, 1215
Imágenes 1980, 1045
Las imprentas históricas que estuvieron al servicio de la causa de la independencia, 1212 (Pivel Devoto)
La independencia, 626 (Yani)
La independencia nacional, 1117
Índice de la poesía paraguaya, 1014 (Buzó Gómez)
Indice poético boquense, 681 (Bucich)
Influencia del clero en la independencia argentina, 915 (Piaggio)
Un inglés en San Lorenzo, 506 (Lanuza)
Iniciadores del teatro, 677 (Blanco Amores de Pagella)
La inmigración en la literatura argentina, 777 (Onega)
El inmigrante en la novela argentina, 152a (García)
Insignes misioneros de la Compañía de Jesús en la provincia de Paraguay, 1040 (Xarque)
Instántaneas de historia, 507 (Lanuza)
La instrucción pública en la época colonial, 968 (Massare de Kostianovsky)
Los intelectuales en el Partido Comunista, 1211 (Gómez)
Interpretaciones, 1068 (Falcao Espalter)
Introducción a la poesía rantifusa, 710 (Elliff)
Las invasiones inglesas del Río de la Plata, 587 (Roberts)
Inventario honorífico, 1143 (Pastorino)
IR: cuento, ensayo, poesía, 1191 (Semana de la Juventud, 2d, Minas, Uruguay)
Irala, 1228 (Valle Lersundi)
Gli italiani nella provincia di Entre Ríos, 139 (Faviono)
Los italianos en el Uruguay, 1053a (Araujo Villagrán)
Los italianos en la historia de la cultura argentina, 231 (Petriella)
Los italianos en Tandil, 229 (Pérez)

Jefes navales de la intervención francesa en el
    Plata, 581 (Ratto)
Los jesuítas en el Paraguay, 1030 (Anglés y
    Gortari)
Los jesuítas y la cultura rioplatense, 1268
    (Fúrlong Cárdiff)
Josephi Emmanuelis Peramas De vita et moribus
    tredecim virorum paraguaycorum, 1036, 1037
    (Peramas)
El judío en la época colonial, 1219 (Lewin)
La junta gubernativa de 1810, 421 (Carranza)

La Rioja, 247 (Sáenz Cavia de Morales Torres)
La Rioja y sus historiadores, 381a (Bazán)
Laderas y cumbres, 1078 (Martínez)
La lanza rota, 256 (Schoo Lastra)
Il lavoro degli Italiani nella Repubblica
    Argentina, 292 (Zuccarini)
Lecciones de historia argentina, 455 (Fregeiro)
Lecciones de historia argentina, 462 (Gambón)
Lecciones de historia argentina, 519 (Levene)
Lecturas de historia argentina, 402 (Busaniche)
Los legionarios, 957 (O'Leary y Urdapilleta)
Letras argentinas en las Antillas, 751 (Loudet)
Letras uruguayas, 1165 (Gallinal)
Letras uruguayas, 1169 (Garet Mas)
Las letras y el destino argentino, 686 (Cócaro)
Liberales ilustres, 982 (Bordón)
Los libertadores de 1825, 1111 (Barrios Pintos)
El libro de los héroes, 1003 (O'Leary y
    Urdapilleta)
El libro de los linajes, 1108 (Goldaracena)
Libro de oro, 941 (Ayala Aquino)
El libro del tango, 863 (Ferrer)
Liderazgo de Cuyo en la emancipación continental,
    548 (Maurín Navarro)
Life and literature of the Pampas, 821 (Tinker)
Life in the Argentine Republic in the Days of
    the Tyrants, 605 (Sarmiento)
The Life of Sarmiento, 398 (Bunkley)
Linaje troncal de los Ruiz de Arellano, 356
    (Moreno)
Linajes de la gobernación del Tucumán, 352
    (Lazcano Colodrero)
Linajes santiagueños, 345 (Figueroa)
Líneas vinculadas a Cavallero Bazán, 972 (Ortellano
    Rojas de Fossati)
Lírica popular rioplatense, 767 (Morales)
Literatura argentina, 683 (Carilla)
Literatura argentina, 692 (Criado)
La literatura argentina, 754 (Magis)
Literatura argentina de vanguardia, 658
    (Aguirre)
Literatura argentina y expresión americana, 742
    (Justo)
La literatura autobiográfica argentina, 792
    (Prieto)
Literatura de Mendoza, 683a (Cattarossi)
La literatura gauchesca en el Uruguay, 1154
    (Caillava)
La literatura paraguaya, 1023 (Rodríguez Alcalá)
Literatura uruguaya, 1150 (Bollo)
Literatura uruguaya siglo XX, 1148, 1149 (Benedetti)
Lomas de Zamora desde el siglo XVI, 224 (Paula)
Lord Strangford y la revolución de Mayo, 597
    (Ruiz Guiñazú)
Los de Lafuente, 348 (Lafuente Machain)
Los López, 572 (Piccirilli)
Los más jóvenes cuentan, 1173
Los que escribieron nuestra historia, 609 (Scenna)
Los que pasaban, 484, 485 (Groussac)

Los que siguen, 750

Lluvias de primavera, 1157 (Cavallaro Cadeillac)

Los Maciel en la historia de Plata, 334 (Azarola
    Gil)
Los Machain, 349 (Lafuente Machain)
Maestros y educadores, 324 (Mercante)
Mancebos de la tierra, 979 (Benítez)
Manual de historia argentina, 528 (López)
Manual de historia de la civilización argentina,
    416 (Carbia)
Manual de historia naval argentina, 12 (Destefani)
Manual de historia uruguaya, 1109 (Acevedo)
Manuelita Rosas, 494 (Ibarguren)
Mar del Plata: sus escuelas y sus maestros, 320
    (Guerra)
Mar del Plata y genearquía de sus fundadores, 361
    (Otárola)
Mar del Plata y sus fundadores, 362 (Otárola)
María de los Santos Sayas de Bengochea, 341
    (Cordero)
Los mártires de Caaro e Yjuhi, 1032a (Blanco)
Máscaras y caras, 893 (Zeitlin)
La masonería argentina a través de sus hombres,
    333 (Lappas)
Las matemáticas en la Argentina, 921a (Dassen)
Matemáticos argentinos durante la dominación
    hispánica, 922 (Fúrlong Cárdiff)
El médico y la cultura, 851 (Pelosio)
Médicos argentinos, 847 (Loudet)
Médicos argentinos durante la dominación hispánica,
    846 (Fúrlong Cárdiff)
Médicos en las letras argentinas, 718 (Fustinoni)
Médicos y medicinas en la época colonial de Santa
    Fe, 855 (Zapata Gollán)
Los mejores poemas de la poesía argentina, 759
    (Martini Real)
Memorias de infancia, 752 (Lugones)
Memorias de los virreyes del Río de la Plata, 1237
Memorias de un médico, 1200 (Eirale)
Memorias del general Iriarte, 499 (Iriarte)
Memorias del P. Florián Paucke, 1031 (Baucke)
Memorias pósthumas, 568 (Paz)
Memorias y autobiografías, 104 (Buenos Aires.
    Museo Histórico Nacional)
Mendoza, 212 (Napolitano)
Mendoza y Garay, 486 (Groussac)
Los mercedarios en la Argentina, 914 (Palacio)
Mi mejor cuento, 764
Mis derrotas, 1126 (Palomeque)
Miscelánea, 1085 (Pereda)
Misceláneas, 109 (Cabrera)
Misiones jesuíticas en el Paraguay, 1033
    (Capdevielle)
El mito Santos Vega en el teatro del Río de la
    Plata, 1257 (Rela)
Mocedades, 988 (Centurión)
El modernismo literario en el Río de la Plata, 1259
    (Seluja Cecín)
Momentos culminantes en ciento cincuenta años de
    educación pública en Entre Ríos, 327 (Ortiz
    Arigos de Montoya)
Monteagudo, 618 (Suárez Danero)
Montevideo, 1084 (Pedemonte)
Monumenta iconographica, 28 (Carril)
El movimiento poesía Buenos Aires, 658 (Aguirre)
Muertos por la patria, 557
La mujer argentina antes y después de Eva Perón,
    926 (Abeijón)
La mujer paraguaya, 1000 (Massare de Kostianovsky)

La mujer paraguaya, 1042 (Urbieta Rojas)
Mujeres de nuestra tierra, 929 (González Arrili)
Mujeres de Sarmiento, 930 (Guerrero)
Las mujeres del tango, 879 (Santos)
Mujeres del Uruguay, 1217 (Moratorio)
Mujeres en la epopeya sanmartiniana, 927
    (Bernard)
La música argentina durante el período de la
    organización nacional, 867 (García Acevedo)
La música en el Uruguay, 1205 (Ayestarán)
Música y músicos argentinos, 881 (Schiuma)
Música y músicos de Mendoza, 874 (Otero)
Música y músicos del Paraguay, 1029 (Boettner)
Músicos argentinos contemporáneos, 882 (Schiuma)
Músicos argentinos durante la dominación hispánica,
    866 (Fúrlong Cárdiff)
Músicos uruguayos, 1207 (Lagarmilla)
Los músicos uruguayos desde 1830 al nacionalismo,
    1208 (Salgado)

Nacimiento y desarrollo de la filosofía, 895
    (Fúrlong Cárdiff)
Los nacionalistas, 558 (Navarro Gerassi)
Los nacionalistas argentinos, 269 (Troncoso)
Narradores argentinos contemporáneos, 770
Narradores argentinos de hoy, 796 (Romano)
Narradores '72, 1176
Narradores uruguayos, 1158 (Cotelo)
Narrativa argentina del Litoral, 771
Narrativa argentina '75, 772
Naturalistas argentinos durante la dominación
    hispánica, 885 (Fúrlong Cárdiff)
Navegantes y maestres de bergantines en el Río de
    la Plata, 1238 (Pinero)
Necochea, 136 (Escobar)
Las neurosis de los hombres célebres en la
    historia argentina, 577 (Ramos Mejía)
No hay función, 690 (Kraly)
Nobilario del antiguo virreynato del Río de la
    Plata, 1225 (Calvo)
Nomenclatura de Montevideo, 1061 (Castellanos)
Nómina de gobernantes civiles y eclesiásticos de
    la Argentina durante la época española, 537
    (Maeder)
Nosotros siete, 774a
Nosotros también, 775
El notariado en la colonia y la emancipación, 337
    (Bernard)
Notas biográficas publicadas en la sección
    efemérides americanas de "La Nación", 253, 254
    (Scotto)
Notas para la historia de los gobernadores de
    Jujuy, 385 (Bidondo)
Novelistas post-románticos, 774 (Noel)
90 [i.e. Noventa] años de labor de la armada
    Argentina en la Antártida, 15 (Pierrou)
Nuestra Señora de los Dolores, 131 (Dorcas
    Berro)
Nuestro folklore y sus nombres ilustres, 217
    (Ortigosa)
Nuestro parnaso, 669 (Barreda)
Nuestros grandes médicos, 845a (Cranwell)
Nuestros próceres, 583a (Rivanera Carles)
Nueva antología lunfarda, 727 (Gobello)
Nueva crónica de la conquista del Tucumán, 522
    (Levillier)
Nueva historia argentina, 403 (Caldas Villar)
La nueva poesía argentina, 802 (Salvador)
Nueva poesía uruguaya, 1179 (Pedemonte)
Nuevas evocaciones, 261 (Solari)
Nuevas generaciones en la pintura argentina, 46

Nuevas opiniones literarias, 1171 (Lasplaces)
Nuevas semblanzas, 955 (Mosqueira)
9 [i.e. Nueve] cuentos laureados, 776
Nuevo diccionario biográfico argentino, 296 (Cutolo)
Nuevo diccionario geográfico histórico de la
    República Argentina, 635 (Marrazzo)
Nuevo parnaso argentino, 782 (Pedro)

La ñata contra el libro, 690 (Cossa)

Obispos y arzobispos de Buenos Aires, 920 (Vivero)
Obras completas, 553 (Mitre)
Obras maestras de la pintura argentina, 34
    (Fundación Lorenzutti)
Ochenta años de arte plástico cordobés, 24 (Banco
    de la Provincia de Córdoba)
Ochenta años de tango platense, 860 (Bozzarelli)
Olavarría y sus colonias, 249 (Salvadores)
Operativo Patagonia, 1051 (Apolant)
Oraciones magistrales, 276 (Valle)
Los oradores de la Cámara, 1112 (Bermúdez)
Oratorio de Nuestra Señora de la Asunción y
    Panteón Nacional de los Héroes, 1004 (Oxilia)
La Orden franciscana en las repúblicas del Plata,
    1266 (Córdoba)
Orientaciones, 384 (Bianco)
El Oriental, 1076 (Maeso)
Orientales ilustres, 1114 (Craviotto)
El origen de la ciudad de Mercedes, 290 (Yribarren)
Origen y desarrollo de la enseñanza pública
    superior en Buenos Aires, 321 (Gutiérrez)
Origen y desenvolvimiento de la Sociedad de
    Beneficencia de la capital 1823-1912, 925
    (Sociedad de Beneficencia de la capital,
    Buenos Aires)
Origen y formación del partido y pueblo de
    Almirante Brown (Adrogué), 147 (Fumière)
Orígenes argentinos, 523 (Levillier)
Los orígenes de Campana, 148 (Fumière)

Orígenes de la educación en San Fernando, 315
    (Cordero)
Orígenes de la literatura lunfarda, 813 (Soler
    Cañas)
Los orígenes de la música escénica en el Uruguay,
    1205 (Ayestarán)
Los orígines de Ranchos (General Paz), 281 (Vidal)
Orígenes del arte tipigráfico en América,
    especialmente en la República Argentina, 899
    (Fúrlong Cárdiff)
Orígenes del pueblo de Belgrano, 71 (Allende)
Los orígenes del teatro argentino, 673 (Beltrán)
Orígenes históricos de Mar del Plata, 156 (Gascón)
Los Ortiz de San Luis y otras genealogías, 336
    (Barreiro Ortiz)
Les otages de Duranzo, 1220 (Poucel)
Otros trece cuentos, 738 (Huberman)

Pablo Rosquellas y los orígenes de la ópera en
    Buenos Aires, 870 (Gesualdo)
Páginas de história, 112 (Caminos)
Páginas de la historia de la medicina en el Río de
    la Plata, 1262 (Mallo)
Páginas históricas, 540 (Mantilla)
Páginas históricas de la historia de la
    Confederación Argentina, 600 (Saldías)
El pago de los Lobos, 74 (Angueira)
Pago Largo, 220 (Palma)
El país de Cuyo, 188 (Larrain)
El país de los argentinos, 441 (Dufourq)
La palabra y el hombre, 503 (Korn)

Palabras en orden, 1189 (Ruffinelli)

La pampa en la novela argentina, 834 (Williams Alzaga)

Panorama de la escultura argentina actual, 35 (Fundación Lorenzutti)

Panorama de la literatura argentina contemporánea, 784 (Pinto)

Panorama de la literatura jujeña, 713 (Fidalgo)

Panorama de la pintura argentina, 36 (Fundación Lorenzutti)

Panorama de la pintura argentina contemporánea, 52 (Pellegrini)

Panorama de la pintura argentina joven, 37 (Fundación Lorenzutti)

Panorama de la poesía gauchesca y nativista del Uruguay, 1167 (García)

Panorama del cuento nativista del Uruguay, 1168 (García)

Panorama poético bonaerense, 781

Panorama y retratos históricos, 529 (López)

Panteón nacional, 1081

Papeles añejos, vidas ignoradas, 338 (Bustillo)

Papeles eclesiásticos del Tucumán, 913 (Levillier)

Para que no se vayan, 177a (Hernández)

Paraguay, 938 (Fernández)

Paraguay, 997 (Koebel)

Paraguay, 963a (United Nations Educational, Scientific and Cultural Organization)

Paraguay, 1010 (Warren)

Paraguayans of Today, 959 (Parker)

Paraguayos con San Martín, 990 (Chaves)

El Paraná y los primeros cronistas, 627 (Zapata Gollán)

Los parientes del beato padre Roque González de Santa Cruz, 350 (Lafuente Machain)

Los parlamentarios radicales, 565

El parlamento argentino, 1854-1947, 378 (Argentine Republic. Congreso. Cámara de Diputados)

Parnaso femenino, 711 (Esquiú Barroetaveña)

El parnaso oriental, 1174 (Montero Bustamante)

Parnaso uruguayo, 1145 (Artucio Ferreira)

La partida de bautismo de don José Narciso de Urquiza y Alzaga, 365 (Urquiza)

El partido de Avellaneda, 266 (Torassa)

Partidos y poder en la Argentina moderna, 430 (Ciria)

La patria en marcha, 128 (Charras)

Patricias argentinas, 422 (Carranza)

Patricias sanjuaninas, 931 (Guerrero)

Pavón y la crisis de la confederación, 447 (Equipos de Investigación Histórica)

Paysandú patriótico, 1130 (Pereda)

Pedro Miguel Obligado y el dolor de los grandes, 755 (Malvigne)

La pequeña historia de la Revolución de Mayo, 508 (Lanuza)

Pequeña historia fueguina, 99 (Braun Menéndez)

Pequeña historia patagónica, 100 (Braun Menéndez)

El perfil del gaucho, en algunas novelas de Argentina y Uruguay, 1251 (Garganigo)

Perfiles, 278 (Velasco Quiroga)

Perfiles biográficos trazados para la niñez, 1052, 1053 (Araújo)

Perfiles contemporáneos, 115a (Cárcano)

Perfiles de mujer, 932 (Marín)

Perfiles parlamentarios argentinos, 614 (Solari)

Perfiles políticos, 975 (Argaña)

El periodismo argentino, 644 (Galván Moreno)

Perón: mito e realtà, 624 (Vita-Finzi)

Personalidades de la Argentina
    see Hombres de la Argentina

Perspetivas, 1090 (Salterain Herrera)

Pintores argentinos, 53, 54

Pintores argentinos del siglo XX, 55

Pintores del viejo Buenos Aires, 42 (Lanuza)

Pintores y grabadores rioplatenses, 1218 (Romero Brest)

La pintura argentina, 56

Pintura argentina, 38 (Fundación Lorenzutti)

Pintura argentina, colección Acquarone, 18 (Acquarone)

Pintura argentina contemporánea, 57 (San Martín)

La pintura argentina del siglo XX, 31 (Córdoba Iturburu)

La pintura en las provincias argentinas siglo XIX, 62 (Trostiné)

Pintura-Pintura, 60 (Squirru)

La pintura y la escultura en Argentina, 59 (Schiaffino)

Los pioneros de la colonización judía en la Argentina, 255 (Schallman)

Los Pizzurno, 118 (Cichero)

Plásticos uruguayos, 1048 (Montevideo. Biblioteca del Poder Legislativo)

Plazas y calles de Buenos Aires, 84 (Beccar Varela)

Plumas y pinceles de la pampa, 768 (Morán)

Los probladores de Buenos Aires y su descendencia, 346 (Gammalsson)

Poemario '72, 785

Poemas, 786

Poemas populares, 862 (D'Alessandro)

Poemas taller de SADE, 787

Poesía argentina actual, 758 (Martínez)

Poesía argentina contemporánea, 716 (Fundación argentina para la poesía)

Poesía argentina del siglo XX, 722 (Ghiano)

Poesía argentina para los ninos, 748 (Lóizaga)

La poesía de Buenos Aires, 801 (Salas)

Poesía de la Argentina, 740 (Isaacson)

La poesía femenina argentina, 783 (Percas)

Poesía gauchesca, 1244 (Borges)

Poesía gauchesca, 688 (Cortázar)

Poesía gauchesca, 1248 (Gandolfi Herrero)

Poesía, 82, 691 (Creadores Literarios Argentinos)

La poesía paraguaya, 1026 (Wey)

La poesía religiosa argentina, 664 (Aragón)

Poesía romántica argentina, 749 (Loprete)

Poesía viva de Rosario, 788

La poesía y la narrativa en el Paraguay, 1020 (Pérez-Maricevich)

Poesía y prosa en Jujuy, 730 (Groppa)

Poésie vivante en Argentine, 832 (Verhesen)

Poetas al sur de Buenos Aires, 789

Poetas argentinos contemporáneos, 672 (Becco)

Los poetas de la revolución, 733 (Gutiérrez)

Poetas de Tucumán, soglo XX, 679 (Bravo Figueroa)

Poetas gauchescos, 736 (Hidalgo)

Poetas juntos, 687 (Corbacho)

Los poetas que cantan, 790

Poetas y prosistas salteños, 653, 654 (Adet)

Los polacos en la República Argentina, 238 (Pyzik)

Políticos y románticos, 1121 (Montero Bustamante)

Por la patria, 1116 (Herrera)

Por qué escribimos, 729 (Grondona)

Los porteños, 210 (Mujica Laínez)

Los portugueses en Buenos Aires (siglo XVII), 187 (Lafuente Machain)

Precursores cuyanos de la independencia de América y patriotas sanjuaninos de la hora inicial, 549, (Maurín Navarro)

Precursores y actores de la independencia del Paraguay, 987 (Centurión)

La prensa y los constituyentes en el Paraguay, 1141 (Villa)

El presidente Santos y la Facultad de Medicina de la República, 1202 (Martínez Munua)
Los presidentes argentinos, 393 (Bucich Escobar)
Los presidentes argentinos, 405 (Calderaro)
Presidentes argentinos, 516 (Levene)
Presidentes constitucionales de la nación argentina, 1854-1954, 619 (Tagliaferro)
Primera antología de poetas del Litoral, 837 (Zeinstejer)
Primera antología poética platense, 805 (Saraví Cisneros)
Primera muestra de poetas, 793
Primeras luchas entre la iglesia y el estado en la gobernación de Tucumán, 417 (Cárcano)
Los primeros ingleses en Buenos Aires, 82 (Battolla)
Los primeros italianos en el Río de la Plata, 151 (Gandía)
Primeros médicos de la ciudad de la Santísima Trinidad, 849 (Molina)
Primeros médicos de la ciudad de Santiago del Estero, 850a (Oddo)
La primitiva literatura gauchesca, 1258 (Rivera)
Proceridad; retratos histórico-literarios, 216 (Orofino)
Proceso al liberalismo argentino, 473 (García y Mellid)
Proceso intelectual del Uruguay, 1199 (Zum Felde)
Prohombres de la argentinidad, 381 (Bajarlía)
Los prosistas del 80, 667 (Badano)
Prostibulario, 794
Protagonistas del tango, 877 (Rossler)
Provincia de San Luis, 81 (Barreiro Ortiz)
Los proyectos españoles para reconquistar el Río de la Plata, 1236 (Mariluz Urquijo)
El puerto de la Ensenada de Barragán, 262 (Sors de Tricerri)

Qué es la Argentina, 239
Quién es quién, 1100
Quién es quién en Corrientes, 303 (Monte Domecq)
Quién es quién en el Paraguay, 967
Quién es quién en el Río de la Plata, 636 (Monte Domecq)
Quién es quién en el Uruguay, 1101
Quién es quién en la Argentina, 307
Quién es quién en la bibliotecología argentina, 652 (Matijevic)
Quién fue en el teatro nacional, 891
¿Quién vive? ¡La libertad! 407 (Capdevila)
Quienes son los escritores argentinos, 841
Quilmes a través de los años, 124 (Craviotto)
Quilmes colonial, 263 (Sors de Tricerri)

Los radicales, 576
Rasgos biográficos de hombres notables, 1063 (De-María)
Reconquista y defensa de Buenos Aires, 495 (Ibarra Pedernera)
Recordando a Yrigoyen, 550 (Mazo)
Recordando el pasado, 91 (Blancas)
Recordando el pasado, 525 (Livacich)
Los rectores de la Universidad de Buenos Aires en la época de Rosas, 329 (Ramallo)
Recuerdos históricos, 264
Recuerdos históricos sobre la provincia de Cuyo, 179 (Hudson)
Reflexiones sobre el pasado sanjuanino, 366 (Videla Morón)
Los reformistas, 119 (Ciria)
El regimen totalitario, 560 (Nudelman)
El reino de la Araucania y Patagonia, 101 (Braun Menéndez)

Relato breve en Argentina, 820 (Tijeras)
Reminiscencias de Itacurubí de la Cordillera, 940 (Almada)
La República Argentina, 595 (Roque)
La república del Paraguay en su sesquicentenario, 954 (Monte Domecq)
La república del Uruguay en su primer centenario, 1079 (Nin y Silva)
Republics of the Pampas, 1233 (Greenbie)
Rescatándolos del olvido, 1067 (Ellis)
Reseña del desarrollo cultural del Paraguay, 966 (Viola)
Reseña histórica de Cerro Largo, 1093 (Ureña González)
Reseña histórica de guerreros de la independencia, 371 (Aldao)
Reseña histórica de la infantería argentina, 11a (Círculo Militar, Buenos Aires)
Reseña histórica de la villa de Luján, 272 (Udaondo)
Reseña histórica del partido de Las Conchas, 273 (Udaondo)
Reseña histórica del partido de Mar Chiquita y sus pueblos, 146 (Freije)
Reseña histórica y orgánica del Ejército Argentino, 8a (Argentine Republic. Ejército. Comando en Jefe)
Retablillo de Córdoba, 190 (Lazcano Colodrero)
Retablo sanmartiniano, 383 (Bernard)
Retratos a pluma, 166 (González Arrili)
Retratos y recuerdos, 195 (Mansilla)
Revista patriótica del pasado argentino, 640 (Trelles)
La Revolución de Mayo, 458 (Fúrlong Cárdiff)
La Revolución de Mayo i el general i caudillo don José Gervasio Artigas, 427 (Carriegos)
Revolution Before Breakfast, 170 (Greenup)
River Plate Personalities, 1221, 1222 (Lamb)
Roca y su tiempo, 541 (Marcó del Pont)
Ronda de poetas jóvenes pampeanos, 797
Rosas visto por un diplomático francés, 390 (Brossard)
Rosas y su tiempo, 578 (Ramos Mejía)
Rosas y sus opositores, 584 (Rivera Indarte)
Rozas, 538 (Mansilla)
La ruta, 980 (Benítez)

Sacerdotes liberales, 615 (Solari)
Los Sáenz Valiente y Aguirre, 351 (Lafuente Machain)
Sainete con variaciones, 690 (Urondo)
Los salesianos en el Paraguay, 1039
Los salesianos y las hijas de María Auxiliadora, 907a (Bruno)
Salto de ayer y de hoy, 1092 (Taborda)
Los salvajes unitarios, 408 (Capdevila)
San José de Flores, 125 (Cunietti-Ferrando)
San Juan en la historia de la música, 873 (Maurín Navarro)
San Luis, 222 (Pastor)
San Martín, 468 (Gandía)
San Martín, 616 (Speroni)
San Martín en la Banda Oriental, 335 (Azarola Gil)
San Martín y la causa de América, 453 (Florit)
San Martín y la política de los pueblos, 573 (Piccirilli)
San Martín y Salta, 432 (Cornejo)
San Martín y su familia, 172 (Guerrero)
La sanidad en las ciudades y pueblos de la provincia de Buenos Aires, 903 (Grau)
Sanjuaninos del ochenta, 173 (Guerrero)
Santiago Montenegro, 204 (Montes)
Santiago: 7 poetas, 804

El santo del bisturí, 853a (Vaccarezza)
Sarmiento, 564 (Paoli)
Sarmiento-Mitre, 607 (Sarmiento)
Sarmiento selecto, 606 (Sarmiento)
Sarmiento y la cuestión de la Patagonia, 490 (Hidalgo)
Seis figuras del Plata, 133 (Echagüe)
Seis poetas del Santa Fe de principios de siglo, 735 (Hernández)
Selección de cuentos, 808
Selección poética femenina, 725 (Giménez Pastor)
Semblanza de tres líderes, 591 (Rodríguez Tarditi)
Semblanzas argentinas, 85 (Berra de Massey)
Semblanzas de argentinos, 199 (Matti)
Semblanzas históricas, 1135 (Torterolo)
Semblanzas paraguayas, 1002 (Mosqueira)
Semblanzas y narraciones, 198 (Marianetti)
El Senado de 1890, 445 (Eizaguirre)
Servidores beneméritos de la patria, 611
70 [i.e. Setenta] años de narrativa argentina, 835 (Yahni)
7 [i.e. Siete] escritores de hoy, 1192
Signatarios de la independencia argentina, 439 (Díaz de Raed)
65 [i.e. Sixty-five] Valiants, 323 (Luiggi)
Significado histórico de las calles de Córdoba, 244 (Rodríguez de la Torre)
Siluetas contemporáneas, 189 (Lascano)
Siluetas femeninas, 956 (Mosqueira)
Símbolos y próceres, 509 (Lapuente)
Los sínodos del antiguo Tucumán, 906 (Arancibia)
Síntesis histórica de la medicina argentina, 853 (Túmburus)
Situación de la pintura argentina, 45 (Nessi)
La sociedad argentina, 598 (Sabsay)
La sombra del cóndor, 86 (Berthelemy)
Sombras heroicas, 1060 (Bonavita)
Las sombras tienen luz, 382 (Benavento)
Storia della civiltà argentina nelle fonti letterarie, 761 (Matteis)

El tango, 819
El tango, 868 (García Jiménez)
Tango, 891a (Sierra)
El tango de Villoldo a Piazzolla, 875 (Priore)
¿Tango o nueva expresión de Buenos Aires?, 861 (Cavadini)
Tangos, letras y letristas, 871 (Gobello)
Teatro argentino contemporáneo, 675, 676 (Berenguer Carisomo)
Teatro argentino romántico, 693 (Cruz)
Teatro breve del Paraguay, 1018a (Pecci)
El teatro en el Río de la Plata, 1255 (Ordaz)
Teatro nacional rioplatense, 1263 (Rossi)
Teatro uruguayo contemporáneo, 1194
El teatro uruguayo; de Juan Moreira a los independientes, 1172 (Legido)
Técnica de una traición, 602 (Santander)
Temas de historia marítima argentina, 265
Los tenientes de Artigas, 1128 (Patiño)
Teseo, 1044 (Dieste)
Testimonios veteranos, 1006 (Rodríguez Alcalá de González Oddone)
Textos fundamentales, 608 (Sarmiento)
Three Argentine Thinkers, 897 (Lipp)
Tiempo pasado, 167 (González Arrili)
Tiempos y poetas, 682 (Capdevila)
La tierra de los Tehuelches, 202 (Moldes)
Tierra de promisión, 1118 (Maeso)
La tiranía y la libertad, 480 (González Arrili)
La tradición puntana, 159 (Gez)

Tradiciones del Río de la Plata, 132 (Dose de Zemborain)
Tradiciones históricas, 456 (Frías)
13 [i.e. Trece] cuentos argentinos, 823
13-19 [i.e. Trece-diecinueve] cuentos, 824
Trece narradores uruguayos contemporáneos, 1183 (Raviolo)
13 [i.e. Trece] poetas, 726 (Giusti)
Treinta cuentos argentinos, 825 (Mazzei)
35 [i.e. Treinta y cinco] cuentos breves argentinos, 816 (Sorrentino)
38 [i.e. Treinta y ocho] cuentos breves argentinos, 817 (Sorrentino)
Trienta y seis años de poesía uruguaya, 1178 (Paternain)
Treinta y tres nombres en las artes plásticas paraguayas, 939 (Plá)
Tres biógrafos de Sarmiento, 174 (Guerrero)
Tres clásicos argentinos, 826
3 [i.e. Tres] de Buenos Aires, 827
Tres guerras, dos mariscales, doce batallas, 1009 (Vittone)
Tres maestros de la medicina argentina, 848 (Maurín Navarro)
El tribunal del Santo Oficio de la Inquisición en las provincias del Plata, 1270 (Medina)
Triunfos, 1127 (Palomeque)
El Tucumán colonial, 501 (Jaimes Freyre)

Ubicación de la escultura argentina en el siglo XX, 21 (Arias)
Universitarios de Córdoba, 313 (Cabrera)
Unos médicos nuestros, 1204 (Ríos)
Urquiza última etapa, 533 (Macchi)
Urquiza y Alberdi, intimidades de una política, 418 (Cárcano)
Urquiza y el catolicismo, 534 (Macchi)
Urquiza y su tiempo, 96 (Bosch Vinelli)
Uruguay, 1216 (United Nations Educational Scientific and Cultural Organization. Science Cooperation Office for Latin America)
Uruguay a fines del siglo XIX, 1086 (Pivel Devoto)
Uruguayans of Today, 1083 (Parker)
Uruguayos contemporáneos, 1099 (Montevideo. Biblioteca del Poder Legislativo)
Uruguayos contemporáneos, 1102, 1103 (Scarone)

Variaciones sobre un tema policial, 757 (Manguel)
Varones correntinos, 93 (Bonastre)
Varones de su tiempo, 569 (Paz)
Los vascos en el Uruguay, 1080 (Otaegui)
Veinte cuentos de Buenos Aires, 712 (Etchenique)
20 [i.e. Veinte] cuentos uruguayos magistrales, 1186 (Rela)
Veinte perfiles significativos de la historia nacional, 1134 (Stewart Vargas)
20 [i.e. Veinte] pintores y escultores, 63
20 [i.e. Veinte] relatos argentinos, 780 (Pagés Larraya)
25 [i.e. Veinticinco] cuentos argentinos magistrales, 829
Veintidós pintores, 50 (Payró)
26 [i.e. Veintiseis] poetas argentinos, 723 (Ghiano)
27 [i.e. Veintisiete] cuentos del norte argentino, 830
27 [i.e. Veintisiete] cuentos del norte argentino, 680 (Bravo Figueroa)
23 [i.e. Veintitrés] pintores de la Argentina, 51 (Payró)
La vejez de Sarmiento, 236 (Ponce)
Los Vela, 360 (Otárola)

Verde memoria, 235 (Pineta)
Los viajeros, 741 (Jitrik)
Viajeros científicos en la Patagonia durante los
    siglos XVIII y XIX, 289 (Ygobone)
Vida de médicos ilustres, 854 (Vaccarezza)
Vida de Perón, 567 (Pavón Pereyra)
Vida de Sarmiento, 399 (Bunkley)
Vida pública del Dr. Juan Pujol, 164 (Gómez)
Vida y obra de seis humanistas, 1038 (Peramas)
Vidas, 154 (García Salaberry)
Vidas argentinas, 372 (Amadeo)
Vidas de argentinos ilustres, 145, 145a (Fregeiro)
Vidas de grandes argentinos, 282 (Piñeiro)
Vidas educadoras, 328 (Pérez Duprat)
Vidas ejemplares, 116 (Casal Castel)
El viejo Taragüy, 197 (Manzi)
Villavicencio a través de la historia, 208
    (Morales Guiñazú)
Los virreyes del Plata, 1241 (Radaelli)
La visión de Rivadavia, 563 (Palcos Sulques)
Visiones uruguayas, 1087 (Ramírez)
Las vísperas de Caseros, 409, 410 (Capdevila)
Visto, oído y recordado, 153 (García Mansilla)
Visto y vivido, 162 (Giusti)
¡Viva Ramírez!, 554 (Molinari)

Who's Who on the Postage Stamps of Argentina,
    70 (Alfaro)
Woman on Horseback, 976 (Barrett)

X-Ray of the Pampa, 545 (Martínez Estrada)

¿Y ahora qué? 75 (Antonio)
Y argentino en todas partes, 831 (Veiravé)
Yerba vieja, 2 (Hogg)
Yo, 232 (Piglia)
Yo, Juan Domingo Perón, 530 (Luca de Tena)

Index of Biographees

A RIENDA SUELTA, pseud.
  see SÁENZ, Máximo Teodoro
ABACA, Francisco R., 268
ABACATÍ, 977
ABACOTÉ, 977
ABAD, Alonso, 520
ABAD, Andrés J. 923
ABAD E ILLANA, Manuel de, 910
ABAD REYES, Juan Bautista, 135
ABADI, Mauricio, 923
ABAL, Juan, 1094
ABALOS (brothers), 217
ABALOS, Jorge Washington, 680, 689, 753, 814, 830, 857c, 923
ABALOS, José de
  see AVALOS, José de
ABALOS, José Domingo, 387
ABALOS Y MENDOZA, José, 1082
ABAN, Leopoldo, 713
ABAN, Víctor, 653, 654, 713
ABARCA, Baltasar de, 529a
ABASCAL, José de, 517
ABASOLO, Horacio Julián, 320
ABASOLO DE ATKINSON, María Felina, 320
ABASOLO DE RODRÍGUEZ, Etelvina, 320
ABDALA, Carlos Eduardo, 943a
ABDALA GUARILLA, Alberto, 1210
ABECASIS, Sara Mabel, 923
ABEIJÓN, Asencio, 753
ABELEDO, Carlos Arturo, 923
ABELEDO OTERO, Valerio, 284
ABELLA, Juan Carlos, 1151, 1187, 1199
ABELLA, Rafael J., 1167
ABELLA CAPRILE, Margarita, 154, 664, 678, 711, 729, 739, 751, 762, 773, 782, 783
ABENTE, Victoriano
  see ABENTE LAGO, Victoriano
ABENTE HAEDO, Fernando, 1204
ABENTE HAEDO, Víctor, 959
ABENTE LAGO, Victoriano, 964, 1012, 1014, 1020, 1021, 1022
ABERASTAIN, Antonio, 141, 188, 283, 398, 412, 608, 611
ABERASTAIN, Remigio, 254
ABERASTURY, Maximiliano, 842
ABERG, Enrique, 6
ABIARE, José, 1066
ABIARU, Ignacio, 977
ABIUSSO, Noemí Graciana, 923
ABLAS, 845
ABORNO, Pablo, 964
ABOS, Alvaro, 706

ABRAHIM, Ramón Amado, 81
ABRAMO, Fernando, 258, 371
ABRAMO, Livio, 939
ABREGO, Diego de, 989
ABREO, Juan de, 1270
ABREU, Diego de, 504, 1011
ABREU, Gonzalo de, 417, 521
ABREU, Juan de, 522
ABREU, Manuel, 521
ABREU DE FIGUEROA, Gonzalo, 1270
ABRIL, Eduardo R., 923
ABRIL, Emilio Antonio, 683a
ABULAFIA ALGRANATI, Isaac, 1210
ABUTCOV, Alexis Vladimir, 874
ACARETE DU BISCAY, 32, 713
ACASUSO, Domingo de, 227, 273
ACASUSO LATORRE, Rubén, 1210
ACCIARESI, Angel, 857a
ACCINELLI, Felipe, 258
ACCINELLI, Francisco, 1123
ACEBAL, Emilio, 959
ACEVAL, Benjamín, 942, 943, 963, 964
ACEVAL PALMEROLA, Juan Carlos, 956
ACEVEDO (family), 1108
ACEVEDO, Arturo, 332
ACEVEDO, Bruno, 254
ACEVEDO, Darío Hugo, 683a
ACEVEDO, Edberto O., 521
ACEVEDO, Eduardo, 1034, 1052, 1053, 1063, 1073, 1079, 1081, 1083, 1188
ACEVEDO, Eliseo, 268
ACEVEDO, Francisco, 371
ACEVEDO, Hugo, 739, 758
ACEVEDO, J. Enrique, 683a
ACEVEDO, José Leonardo, 917
ACEVEDO, Leonardo de, 534, 910
ACEVEDO, Manuel Antonio, 439, 457, 478, 526, 611, 621, 626, 921
ACEVEDO, Miguel, 943, 966
ACEVEDO, Paulino, 254
ACEVEDO, Santiago, 387
ACEVEDO ALVAREZ, Eduardo, 1073
ACEVEDO DE BOTET, Justina, 268
ACEVEDO DE GRENCI, Hortensia, 683a
ACEVEDO DÍAZ, Eduardo (father), 1059, 1075, 1079, 1083, 1086, 1090, 1122, 1126, 1131, 1146, 1154, 1159, 1160, 1162, 1164, 1168, 1170, 1171, 1175, 1177, 1180, 1186, 1187, 1188, 1190, 1196, 1198, 1199, 1246, 1249, 1251, 1254
ACEVEDO DÍAZ, Eduardo (son), 152a, 834, 1251
ACKERMANN, Rudolph, 28
ACOSTA, Ambrosio de, 197, 358
ACOSTA, Andrés, 979

ACOSTA, Bernardino de, 186
ACOSTA, César Romeo, 954
ACOSTA, Claudio, 998
ACOSTA, Ernestina, 713, 730
ACOSTA, Evaristo, 959
ACOSTA, Fortunato, 979
ACOSTA, Gonzalo de, 1238
ACOSTA, Gregorio, 985, 1039
ACOSTA, Ignacio, 126
ACOSTA, José D., 951
ACOSTA, José de, 885
ACOSTA, José Francisco, 3, 93
ACOSTA, José Ignacio, 995a
ACOSTA, Juan, 1111
ACOSTA, Juan Bautista, 979, 987
ACOSTA, Juan Hilarión, 998
ACOSTA, Julio Florencio, 191
ACOSTA, Luis, 1243
ACOSTA, Manuel de, 649a
ACOSTA, Mariano, 166, 181, 404
ACOSTA, Pedro de, 186
ACOSTA, Pedro José, 995a
ACOSTA, Rosa, 1093a
ACOSTA, Rosa Cándida, 956
ACOSTA, Sofía, 701, 785
ACOSTA ALBEGUERIA, Francisco de, 186
ACOSTA BALADÓN, Ricardo Mario, 1210
ACOSTA FLORES, Eudoro, 1020
ACOSTA GARCÍA, Luis, 878, 1243
ACOSTA MENÉNDEZ, Juan C., 1093a
ACOSTA MORENO, Juan M., 954
ACOSTA Y LARA (family), 1108
ACOSTA Y LARA, Federico E., 1083, 1093
ACOSTA Y LARA, Horacio, 1123
ACOSTA Y LARA, Manuel, 1162, 1187
ACQUEVIRA, Claudio, 952
ACQUISTAPACE, José, 1123
ACTIS BRÚ, César, 701
ACUCHARRO (family), 1224
ACUÑA, Angel, 328
ACUÑA, Basilio, 387
ACUÑA, Jacinto, 1187
ACUÑA, Juan Enrique, 726, 739, 812
ACUÑA, Juan Gregorio (Mocito, pseud.), 93, 569
ACUÑA, Julia Helena, 218
ACUÑA, Luis, 122
ACUÑA CARNEIRO, Juan Pablo, 1210
ACUÑA DE ALOMÓN, Francisco, 1095
ACUÑA DE FIGUEROA, Agustín, 1165, 1187
ACUÑA DE FIGUEROA, Claudio, 1165, 1187
ACUÑA DE FIGUEROA, Francisco Esteban, 963, 964,
    1029, 1052, 1053, 1057, 1063, 1076, 1079, 1081,
    1084, 1091, 1092, 1146, 1165, 1174, 1177, 1179,
    1187, 1188, 1193, 1198, 1199
ACUÑA DE FIGUEROA, Jacinto, 1072, 1095, 1165
ACUÑA DE FIGUEROA, Manuel, 1165, 1187
ACUÑA DE NORONHA, Juan, 1270
ACZEL, Martín Ladislao, 923
ACHA, Francisco Xavier de, 1174, 1185, 1188
ACHA, Mariano de, 166, 179, 188, 283, 442
ACHÁVAL, José Wenceslao, 171, 188
ACHÁVAL, Luis, 332
ACHÁVAL RODRÍGUEZ, Tristán, 116, 244, 317, 545a,
    921
ACHÁVAL Y MEDINA, José Wenceslao, 910
ACHÁVAL Y SASTURRI, Domingo Antonio de, 496
ACHEGA, Domingo Victorio de, 321, 478, 611, 908
ACHMUTY, Samuel, 104
ACHUCARRO (family), 1106
ACHUCARRO, Juan de, 1056

ACHUCARRO E., José Maximiliano, 954
ADAM, Alberto, 28
ADAM, Víctor, 28
ADAMI, Enrique, 850
ADAMO, Luis, 952
ADAMS, Richard, 6, 28
ADARO, Carmen, 222
ADARO, Dalmiro S., 222
ADARO, Esteban P., 81, 222
ADARO Y ARROSOLA, Juan de, 555
ADER, María I., 652
ADET, Carlos Edmundo, 653, 654
ADET, Raquel, 653
ADET, Walter, 653, 654
ADLER, María Raquel, 154, 751, 762, 783
ADORNI, Orestes E., 923
ADORNO, Manuel Antonio, 995a
ADROGUÉ, Esteban, 147, 224, 904, 923
ADURIZ GARCÍA, Joaquín S. I., 218
AEBI, Hans, 31
AFARA, Roque Yamil, 954
AFFANNI, Garibaldi, 258
AGAMOR Y RAMÍREZ, Manuel, 907, 911, 920
AGAPITO, 878
AGAR, Richard (Mrs.)
    see AVERY, Bernice
AGEITOS DE CASTELLANOS, Z. Judith, 923
AGNESE DE RIPA, Alicia Margarita, 781
AGORIO, Adolfo, 1079, 1083, 1165, 1187, 1190, 1199
AGOSTI CERISOLA, Héctor Pablo, 1210
AGOTE, Luis, 282, 293, 844, 854, 1261
AGRAMONT, Cayetano Marcellano, 32
AGRAÑA, Antonio, 1095
AGREDA, Pedro José de, 126
AGREDA DE VERGARA, Salvador, 646
AGRELO, Emilio C., 59
AGRELO, Pedro José, 95, 104, 145, 145a, 374, 552,
    611, 629, 895
AGRELO SOTELO, Inocencio Antonio, 1095
AGROMAYOR, Manuel, 235
AGUADO, Alejandro María, 468
AGUADO Y RAMÍREZ, Alejandro, 561
AGUDO, María Adela, 725, 739, 812
AGUER, Carmen
    see CASCO DE AGUER, Carmen
AGÜERO, Antonio Esteban, 222, 722, 739, 812, 831
AGÜERO, Carlos F., 653
AGÜERO, Eusebio
    see AGÜERO, José Eusebio
AGÜERO, Gustavo Rubén, 653
AGÜERO, José Eusebio, 114, 321, 611
AGÜERO, Julián Segundo de, 79, 114, 145, 166, 183,
    380, 529, 542, 569, 611, 644, 908, 915
AGÜERO, Manuel de, 254
AGÜERO VERA, Juan Zacarías, 83
AGUIAR (family), 1108
AGUIAR, Adriano M., 1014, 1029, 1075
AGUIAR, Elías, 995a
AGUIAR, Félix Eduardo, 1063, 1081, 1093a
AGUIAR, Ignacio, 878
AGUIAR, Mariano del Rosario, 995a
AGUIAR, Rafael de, 268
AGUIAR ELIZALDE, Pedro, 1093
AGUIARI, José, 258
AGUILA, Luis de, 148
AGUILAR (family), 1108
AGUILAR, Adolfo, 954
AGUILAR, Fausto, 1054, 1081
AGUILAR, Félix, 332
AGUILAR, Francisco, 1063

AGUILAR, Gregorio, 878
AGUILAR, Jaime de, 989, 1267
AGUILAR, Josefina, 932
AGUILAR, Juan, 188
AGUILAR, Julián, 844
AGUILAR, Marcelino, 254
AGUILAR, Milton, 810
AGUILAR, Oscar Pedro, 923
AGUILAR, Victoriano, 611
AGUILAR Y LEAL, Francisco, 1065
AGUILERA, Amancio, 954
AGUILERA, Francisco, 954, 995a
AGUILERA, Javier, 552
AGUILERA, José, 24, 31
AGUILERA, Pedro (CHANTELO, pseud.), 940
AGUINAGA, Juan, 198
AGUINAGA DE RICCI, Carmen, 691
AGUIRRE (family), 351, 1108
AGUIRRE, Alberto J., 218
AGUIRRE, Atanasio C., 1109
AGUIRRE, Avelino, 874
AGUIRRE, Bartolomé, 995a
AGUIRRE, Cicerón, 207
AGUIRRE, Cleto, 844, 1261
AGUIRRE, Cristóbal de, 254, 496
AGUIRRE, Domingo, 545a
AGUIRRE, Eduardo, 332
AGUIRRE, Francisco de, 89, 144, 283, 472, 521, 522,
    527, 620, 1229, 1270
AGUIRRE, Gisleno, 1211
AGUIRRE, Héctor Aníbal, 653
AGUIRRE, Hernando de, 520, 1270
AGUIRRE, Ibis, 683a
AGUIRRE, Jerónimo de, 1270
AGUIRRE, Jorge, 55
AGUIRRE, José (musician), 874
AGUIRRE, José de, 895
AGUIRRE, José María, 433, 611, 987
AGUIRRE, José Norberto, 923
AGUIRRE, Juan Andrés de, 126
AGUIRRE, Juan Bautista de, 186, 344
AGUIRRE, Juan de, 186
AGUIRRE, Juan Francisco, 17a, 32, 482, 943, 964,
    966, 985, 1012
AGUIRRE, Juan Pedro de, 496, 552, 554, 611
AGUIRRE, Julián, 282, 293, 864, 867, 881, 883
AGUIRRE, Julián L., 385
AGUIRRE, Julio Leónidas, 207, 212, 278, 683a
AGUIRRE, Junio, 1151
AGUIRRE, Manuel Hermenegildo de, 478, 479, 492, 611
AGUIRRE, Manuel J., 21
AGUIRRE, Marco Antonio de, 1270
AGUIRRE, Martín, 1075
AGUIRRE, Miguel de, 914
AGUIRRE, Osvaldo R., 691
AGUIRRE, Pantaleón, 998
AGUIRRE, Pedro, 332
AGUIRRE, Raúl, 652
AGUIRRE, Raúl Gustavo, 658, 672, 716, 717, 739, 759,
    798, 807, 832
AGUIRRE, Susana, 19, 31, 210
AGUIRRE, Thelma de, 663
AGUIRRE CELIZ, Julio A., 81, 222
AGUIRRE DE ORTIZ, Juana Lydia, 320
AGUIRRE MOLINA, Raúl, 207
AGUIRRE SILVA, Juan Bautista, 121
AGUIRRE Y GONZÁLEZ, Juan, 1083
AGUIRRE Y TEJADA, Juan Luis de, 126
AGUIRREZÁBAL, Pablo, 1092
AGULLÓ, Cosme, 922, 1036
AGUSTI, José W., 644a

AGUSTINI, Delmira, 1075, 1079, 1086, 1144, 1145,
    1147, 1153, 1163, 1164, 1165, 1177, 1179, 1181,
    1187, 1195, 1197, 1198, 1199, 1217, 1259
AGUSTINI, Francisco, 1236
AGUSTONI, Ambrosio, 684
AGUYARI, José, 19, 59
AHARONIAN, Corium, 1207
AHUERNA, Juan, 653
AHUMADA, Cristóbal de, 555
AHUMADA, Juan Carlos, 923
AIELLO, Carmelo, 320
AIETA, Anselmo, 862
AIMAR, Carlos, 860
AINSA AMIGUES, Fernando, 1192
AINSCOUCH, Hilda, 64
AIQUEL, Federico, 923
AIRALDI, Concepción Silva de
    see SILVA DE AIRALDI, Concepción de
AIXTEN, Domingo Benjamín, 845
AIZENBERG, Guiche
    see AIZENBERG, Isaac
AIZENBERG, Isaac, 824
AIZENBERG, Roberto, 19, 36, 38, 55
AIZPURÚA, Benito, 611
ALABOS, 977
ALAGÓN, Juan de, 478, 479
ALAGÓN DE FERNÁNDEZ, Carmen, 1093a
ALAIS, Carlos F., 268
ALAIS, Juan 867
ALAIS, Pedro de, 254
ALAMINOS, Jaime, 44
ALAMO, Martha, 684
ALAMO VILABOA, Juan Domingo, 1240
ALANIS DE LÓPEZ, Dora, 810
ALANIZ, Anesimo, 222
ALARA PAVÍA, Julio, 954
ALARCÓN, Hugo, 653, 654
ALARCÓN, José de, 254
ALBA, Alberto, 772
ALBA, Enrique de, 923
ALBA DE CORONEL, Aurora, 810
ALBA LUZ, pseud.
    see BENÍTEZ CAPURRO, Alba Luz
ALBA SWAN, Matilde, 717, 739
ALBAMONTE, Luis María (BARRIOS, Américo, pseud.),
    152a, 368, 834
ALBANELL MACCOLL, Eduardo, 954
ALBANESE, Antonio, 860
ALBANI, Félix, 923
ALBANO, Julio, 299
ALBANO, Pedro Valerio, 479
ALBANO, Vicente, 923
ALBARELLOS, Nicanor, 192, 844, 864, 865, 888, 1205
ALBARELLOS, Ruperto, 254, 496
ALBARIÑO, Domingo, 611
ALBARIÑO, Manuel, 284, 599
ALBARIÑO, Ramón Amancio, 135
ALBARIÑOS, José María, 254
ALBARRACÍN, Alejandro, 173
ALBARRACÍN, Ignacio L., 478
ALBARRACÍN, Isidoro, 173
ALBARRACÍN, Juan Antonio, 254
ALBARRACÍN, Juan Crisóstomo, 173
ALBARRACÍN, Paula
    see ALBARRACÍN DE SARMIENTO, Paula
ALBARRACÍN, Santiago, 371, 611
ALBARRACÍN, Santiago J., 14
ALBARRACÍN, Santiago Rufino, 611
ALBARRACÍN DE GODOY, Candelaria, 931
ALBARRACÍN DE SARMIENTO, Paula, 112, 398, 478, 497,
    604, 606, 929, 930, 931

ALBARRACÍN SARMIENTO, Carlos, 805

ALBARRÁN, Cristóbal de, 914, 918

ALBERDI, Juan Bautista (FIGARILLO, pseud.), 70, 85, 91, 96, 110, 118, 121, 141, 152a, 166, 176, 183, 185, 195, 212, 246, 278, 282, 283, 293, 317, 369, 379, 381, 384, 386, 398, 404, 407, 418, 466, 478, 498, 507, 509, 514, 521, 574, 585, 589, 612, 614, 673, 677, 692, 724, 734, 737, 743, 751, 754, 761, 780, 865, 867, 890, 963

ALBERO, Fernando, 810

ALBERRO, Josef Alexo de, 32

ALBERTI, Carlos A., 660

ALBERTI, Francisco, 910

ALBERTI, Manuel Maximiliano, 70, 85, 244, 258, 275, 282, 386, 404, 411, 421, 475, 478, 479, 496, 525, 610, 611, 915

ALBERTI, Pedro Leopoldo, 37

ALBERTI, Santiago, 1085

ALBEZA, Roberto, 653, 654

ALBÍ, Mariano, 319

ALBÍN Y CAÑEDO, Melchor, 898

ALBINI, Olivio, 1211

ALBISTUR, Jacinto, 1235

ALBISU, Anastasio, 1092

ALBIZ, Juan de, 895

ALBIZZATI, Carlos Miguel Jesús, 923

ALBO, Manuel, 1095

ALBORNO, Pablo, 939, 959, 966

ALBORNO, Santiago, 937

ALBORNO WEYER, Miguel Angel, 954

ALBORNOZ, Eugenio, 73

ALBORNOZ, Felipe de, 83, 501

ALBORNOZ, Jerónimo, 910

ALBORNOZ Y MONTOZA, Z., 1020

ALCABUZ, Pedro, 731

ALCAIRE HERNÁNDEZ, Plácido, 1210

ALCALÁ Y SERRANO, Diego Antonio Miguel de, 1262

ALCÁNTARA, Juan Bautista de, 620

ALCÁNTARA DE SOMELLERA, Pedro, 964

ALCARAZ, Eugenio, 923

ALCARAZ, José Antonio, 810

ALCARAZ, José de, 529

ALCARAZ, Pedro Francisco, 874

ALCARAZ, Ramón A., 923

ALCARAZ, Saúl J., 954

ALCARRAZ FERNÁNDEZ, Edemar Eduardo, 1210

ALCÁZAR, Hernando de, 845, 1203

ALCOBA MARTÍNEZ, Amalia, 762

ALCOBENDAS, Francisco, 103

ALCOLEA, Ricardo H., 701

ALCÓN, Francisco de P., 1236

ALCORTA (family), 122

ALCORTA, Amancio, 68, 79, 116, 165, 211, 286, 293, 631, 865, 867

ALCORTA, Diego, 116, 206, 293, 321, 482, 611, 844, 1261

ALCORTA, Gloria, 678

ALCORTA, Jorge A., 652

ALCORTA, Martín Diego, 317, 483

ALCORTA FLEYTAS, Juan M., 998

ALDAMA, José, 951

ALDAMA, Orlando, 894, 1172, 1185

ALDAO, Andrés de, 496

ALDAO, Camilo, 254

ALDAO, Carlos A., 112

ALDAO, Fabián de, 126

ALDAO, Félix, 179, 398, 478, 528, 632

ALDAO, Francisco, 577, 584

ALDAO, José, 179, 188

ALDAO, José Félix, 179, 283, 605

ALDAO, Luis, 28

ALDAO, Pedro, 126

ALDAO, Ricardo, 565

ALDAO DE DÍAZ, Elvira, 478

ALDASORO, José Víctor, 69

ALDAY, Manuel de, 283

ALDAY Y ASPÉE, Manuel de, 910

ALDAZOR, Nicolás, 171, 188

ALDONATE, Manuel, 679

ALDREY Y SALVADO, Cayetano Antonio, 284

ALDROVANDI CASTILLO, Severino Pedro, 1210

ALDUNATE, Bartolomé de, 1011

ALEGRE, Efraín, 998

ALEGRE, Esteban, 358

ALEGRE, Juan Nepomuceno, 921

ALEGRE, Ventura, 611

ALEM (family), 343

ALEM, Leandro Nicéforo, 121, 122, 141, 147, 166, 212, 232, 246, 277, 282, 343, 372, 389, 404, 469, 478, 524, 576, 585, 589

ALEMÁN, Adolfo, 235

ALEMÁN, Enrique, 235

ALEMÁN, Oscar, 857d

ALEMÁN, Pablo, 222, 385

ALEMÁN DE AVILÉS, Luis, 646

ALEMÁN DE GALLARDO, Modesto, 320

ALEMANDRI, Próspero G., 118, 135

ALEMANN, Theodor, 214, 311

ALEMANY VILLA, Juan L., 681

ALEMI, Victoriano, 387

ALENDE, Dora E., 652

ALESIO, Nicolás Alfredro, 217, 864, 865

ALETÍN, 1031

ALEXANDER, Juan Francisco, 954

ALEXANDRE (family), 168

ALEZZO, Agustín, 889

ALFAMIRA (family), 352

ALFANO, Francisco, 318

ALFARO, Andrés, 878

ALFARO, Antonio de, 1270

ALFARO, Diego de, 989

ALFARO, Francisco de, 472, 521, 649a, 968, 1011

ALFARO, José, 254

ALFIERO, 140

ALFONSO, Eulogio Melitón, 1092

ALFONSO, Joaquín Luis, 923

ALFONSO, Nelly, 663

ALGARATE, Gervasio, 885

ALGHISI, Angel, 258

ALGORTA (family), 1108

ALGUIEN, pseud.
    see NALÉ ROXLO, Conrado

ALI JAFELLA, Sara J., 652

ALIAGA (family), 352

ALIAGA, Cristián Alberto, 691

ALIAGA RUEDA, María, 762

ALIBERTI, Antonio, 817

ALICE, Antonio, 19, 31, 154

ALICO, José Alejandro, 254, 611

ALICU, José Alejandro
    see ALICO, José Alejandro

ALINARI, Lucía, 684

ALIO, Enrique, 320

ALIO DE FRANCHERI, Isabel, 320

ALIPPI, Elías, 858, 891, 893

ALISIO, Artemio, 37, 55

ALMADA, Amadeo, 1073

ALMADA, Apolinario, 95, 543

ALMADA, Facundo, 998

ALMADA, Lázaro, 1212

ALMADA, Miguel, 1207

ALMADA, Tristán M., 68, 244
ALMADA, Zenón, 940
ALMAFUERTE, pseud.
    see PALACIOS, Pedro Bonifacio
ALMAGRO, Diego de, 521, 914
ALMAGRO DE LA TORRE, Juan María de, 496
ALMANDOS ALMONACID, Vicente, 83, 381a
ALMARAZ, Juan de, 910, 1041
ALMEIDA, Francisco, 937
ALMEIDA, Pedro Antonio, 32
ALMEIDA PEREIRA, Manuel de, 1270
ALMEIRA, Hilario de, 611
ALMEYDA, Agustín, 254
ALMIRÓN, Juan José, 1262
ALOISI, Enzo, 778
ALÓN, pseud.
    see AYALA, José de la Cruz
ALONSO, 33
ALONSO, Carlos, 19, 25, 31, 36, 38, 46, 49, 55
ALONSO, César, 1021, 1022
ALONSO, Esperanza (Maravilla, La, pseud.), 892
ALONSO, Federico, 991
ALONSO, Jesús Vicente, 1089
ALONSO, José, 19, 21, 25
ALONSO, José A., 284
ALONSO, José Vicente, 763
ALONSO, Juan Carlos, 284
ALONSO, Justo M., 1073
ALONSO, Manuel R., 1075
ALONSO, Mariano Alonso, 254
ALONSO, Mariano Roque, 1011
ALANSO, Mateo, 21
ALONSO, Ramón, 1089
ALONSO, Raúl R. (Kali, pseud.), 299
ALONSO, Rodolfo, 658, 661, 672, 716, 717, 739, 758,
    759, 802, 807, 832
ALONSO, Rodrigo, 1270
ALONSO, Tito, 857c
ALONSO DE LAJARROTA (family), 351
ALONSO DE SAN BUENAVENTURA, 1034, 1035
ALONSO DELGADO, José, 660
ALONSO LEMA, Mario, 1210
ALONSO PIÑEIRO, Armando
    see PIÑEIRO, Armando Alonso
ALONSO QUINTANA, Antonio, 954
ALONSO Y TRELLES, José (Viejo Pancho, El, pseud.),
    767, 1077, 1095, 1151, 1154, 1165, 1166, 1167,
    1177, 1179, 1199, 1243, 1247
ALONZO MARTÍNEZ, Severino, 1210
ALOS Y BRU, Joaquín de, 984, 990, 1011
ALPERSOHN, Marcos, 258a
ALPOSTA, Luis Alfredo, 660, 727, 871
ALRIC, Carlos, 81, 222
ALSINA, Adolfo, 78, 79, 88, 91, 116, 121, 166, 244,
    282, 372, 404, 478, 574, 617, 631, 633
ALSINA, Fidel R., 923
ALSINA, José Arturo, 1014, 1021, 1022, 1023
ALSINA, Juan, 922
ALSINA, Pancho, 875
ALSINA, Valentín, 96, 110, 127, 166, 244, 282, 404,
    462, 586, 611, 761
ALSINA FUERTES, Fidel Antonio, 923
ALSINA GASSA, Juan, 284
ALSINA THEVENET, Homero, 1088
ALSOGARAY, Alvaro Carlos, 311, 593
ALTALEF, Alberto, 31
ALTAMIRA, Angel, 268
ALTAMIRANDA MINAHK, Daniel, 787
ALTAMIRANO, Cristóbal, 149, 318, 358, 845, 850,
    1035

ALTAMIRANO, Diego Francisco, 1267
ALTAVISTA, Carlos Alberto, 923
ALTESOR BAFLIGER, Vladimir Iván, 1210
ALTESOR MEZQUITA, Alberto, 1210
ALTGELT, Carlos A., 6
ALTHABE, Julián Pedro, 19, 21, 25, 35, 63
ALTOLAGUIRRE, Francisco, 1266
ALTOLAGUIRRE, Martín José de, 478, 479, 885, 922
ALTOMARE DE PEREYRA, Emilia (MASA CLETA, pseud.),
    762
ALTOPIEDI, Alberto J., 781
ALTUBE, José, 211
ALUMNI, José, 191
ALURRALDE, Antonio de, 640
ALURRALDE, César Antonio, 653
ALURRALDE, Pedro, 267, 268
ALURRALDE, Pedro Eugenio, 923
ALURRALDE DE GARMENDIA, Elena María de, 611
ALURRALDE DE MUÑECAS, Elena, 626
ALURRALDE HELGUERA, Pedro, 268
ALVARADO, 188
ALUZ, José Rafael, 691
ALVA, Emil, pseud.
    see ALVAREZ, Emilio Andrés
ALVARADO, Antonio, 713
ALVARADO, Carlos Alberto, 923
ALVARADO, Jorge Roque Teodoro, 385
ALVARADO, José León, 283
ALVARADO, Juan de, 845
ALVARADO, Mateo de, 1270
ALVARADO, Roque, 385
ALVARADO, Rudecindo, 104, 283, 371, 386, 424, 475,
    553, 611
ALVARADO, Sergio F., 385
ALVARADO, Soriano, 385
ALVARENGA, Alejo (MENIN, pseud.), 965
ALVARENGA, Martín, 759
ALVARENGA, Néstor, 998
ALVARENGA CABALLERO, Pedro, 1017
ALVAREZ (family), 1108
ALVAREZ, Agustín, 116, 141, 198, 207, 212, 246, 261,
    278, 478, 683a, 743, 751, 1246
ALVAREZ, Alonso, 1262
ALVAREZ, Américo, 759
ALVAREZ, Bonifacio, 32
ALVAREZ, Carlos, 963a
ALVAREZ, Carlos Alberto, 135, 739, 759, 800, 812,
    831
ALVAREZ, Carlos J., 240
ALVAREZ, Crisóstomo, 478
ALVAREZ, Dionisio Francisco, 95
ALVAREZ, Eduardo, 910
ALVAREZ, Emilio Andrés (ALVA, Emil, pseud.), 691
ALVAREZ, Felipe, 545a
ALVAREZ, Francisco, 32, 237, 242, 599, 893
ALVAREZ, Francisco Antonio, 917
ALVAREZ, Francisco Dionisio, 534, 917
ALVAREZ, Gregorio, 751, 810
ALVAREZ, Hernán de, 32
ALVAREZ, Hernán Diego, 684
ALVAREZ, Horacio, 18, 24, 31
ALVAREZ, Ignacio, 104, 207, 867, 874
ALVAREZ, José Francisco, 545a
ALVAREZ, José Sixto (FRAY MOCHO; CARRIZO, Fabio,
    pseuds.), 121, 135, 152a, 225, 282, 667, 708,
    712, 724, 727, 737, 751, 769, 777, 779, 813,
    829, 834, 835, 1246, 1249
ALVAREZ, Juan, 135, 461, 609, 914
ALVAREZ, Juan José, 534, 921
ALVAREZ, Juan N., 1264

ALVAREZ, Julián, 478, 479, 1063, 1093a
ALVAREZ, Lucina, 750
ALVAREZ, Luis, 653, 1020
ALVAREZ, Manuel, 19, 31, 32, 36, 46, 89, 103
ALVAREZ, Manuel (physician), 844, 850
ALVAREZ, Manuel B., 250
ALVAREZ, Manuel G., 1095
ALVAREZ, Manuel Gregorio, 896
ALVAREZ, Matías, 1111
ALVAREZ, Modesto, 874
ALVAREZ, Pedro A., 954
ALVAREZ, Ramón, 496
ALVAREZ, Rodolfo, 713
ALVAREZ, Romualdo, 254
ALVAREZ, Saturnino José, 496
ALVAREZ, Saturnino M., 1075
ALVAREZ, Teodoro, 844, 1261
ALVAREZ ALONSO, Francisco, 1167
ALVAREZ ARENALES, José Antonio, 404
ALVAREZ CAMPANA, Francisco, 32, 148
ALVAREZ CINA, Héctor, 1073
ALVAREZ CONDARCO, José Antonio, 332, 553, 611
ALVAREZ COVARRUBIAS, Miguel, 186
ALVAREZ DE ACOSTA, Francisco, 186
ALVAREZ DE ARENALES, José Antonio, 166, 244, 453, 542, 553
ALVAREZ DE ARENALES, José Ildefonso, 332
ALVAREZ DE ARENALES, Juan Antonio, 85, 110, 373, 386, 475, 552, 611
ALVAREZ DE BALSATEGUI, Concepción, 320
ALVAREZ DE BURGOS, Francisco, 186
ALVAREZ DE JONTE, Antonio, 104
ALVAREZ DE MAYORCA, Ursula, 1088
ALVAREZ DE MONROY, Gaspar, 649a
ALVAREZ DE ROCHA, Manuel, 7, 32
ALVAREZ DE SEGURA, Mercedes, 422, 611
ALVAREZ DE SOTOMAYOR, Antonio, 7
ALVAREZ DE TOLEDO, Federico, 181
ALVAREZ DE TOLEDO Y VENEGAS, Pedro, 555
ALVAREZ ERMIDA, Angel Nazario, 1210
ALVAREZ FAUR, Adela, 683a
ALVAREZ GAYTÁN, Pedro, 358
ALVAREZ JONTE, Antonio, 282, 404, 427, 478, 479
ALVAREZ LEGUIZAMÓN, Francisco, 653, 654
ALVAREZ PEDRIEL, Julián Baltazar, 126
ALVAREZ PRADO, José María, 385
ALVAREZ PRADO, Pedro José, 385
ALVAREZ PREVE, Alfredo, 1093
ALVAREZ REY, Perfecto, 1089
ALVAREZ RODRÍGUEZ, Basilio, 284
ALVAREZ SASIAIN, José M., 1093
ALVAREZ SOSA, Arturo, 679, 831
ALVAREZ THOMAS, Ignacio
    see ALVAREZ THOMAS, José Ignacio
ALVAREZ THOMAS, José Ignacio, 282, 283, 374, 404, 552, 574, 611, 629
ALVAREZ VARELA, Antonio, 1088
ALVAREZ VIGNOLI DE DEMICHELI, Sofía, 1217
ALVARIÑO, Manuel, 496
ALVARIZA SANCHEZ, Roque, 1210
ALVEAR, Angel T. de, 68
ALVEAR, Carlos Antonio José Gabino del Angel de la
    Guardia de
    see ALVEAR Y BALVASTRO, Carlos María de
ALVEAR, Carlos de
    see ALVEAR Y BALVASTRO, Carlos María de
ALVEAR, Carlos María de
    see ALVEAR Y BALVASTRO, Carlos María de
ALVEAR, Carlos Torcuato de, 103
ALVEAR, Diego de, 17a, 142, 427, 482, 985

ALVEAR, Elvira de
    see PACHECO DE ALVEAR, Elvira
ALVEAR, Emilio de, 142, 195
ALVEAR, Marcelo Torcuato de, 142, 219, 269, 278, 392, 405, 466, 478, 489, 493, 515, 516, 521, 545, 619
ALVEAR, Torcuato de, 103, 142
ALVEAR DE BOSCH, Elisa de, 142
ALVEAR DE LEZICA, Teodelina de, 142
ALVEAR Y BALVASTRO, Carlos María de, 70, 95, 104, 121, 141, 142, 166, 228, 244, 282, 283, 386, 404, 420, 427, 433, 462, 471, 472, 475, 478, 489, 499, 502, 518, 519, 528, 529, 553, 573, 574, 576, 593, 611, 622, 1063, 1079, 1091, 1233
ALVEAR Y PONCE DE LEÓN, Diego de, 483, 1229
ALVES DA SILVA, Carlos, 923
ALVEZ ANTÚNEZ, Juan, 1093
ALVIANI, Massimo Giuseppe, 857c
ALVISO, Encarnación.de, 1000
ALZAGA, Cecilio de, 1236
ALZAGA, Félix, 608
ALZAGA, Martín de, 128, 129, 166, 237, 254, 427, 463, 471, 472, 478, 517, 553, 563
ALZAGA Y SOBRADO, Mateo Ramón de, 898
ALZAIBAR PADURA Y ARTETA, Francisco de, 1080
ALZAYBAR (family), 1106
ALZINA, Juan, 17a
ALZOGARAY, Alvaro José de, 14, 107
ALZOLA, Juan de, 895
ALLARD, Claudio P., 299
ALLASINO, Domingo A., 684
ALLASINO, Marcelo A., 684
ALLEN, Henry Charles, 904
ALLEN GÓMEZ, Felipe, 998
ALLENDE, Andrés Roberto, 609
ALLENDE, Carlos Ignacio, 923
ALLENDE, Eduardo M., 320
ALLENDE, Faustino, 244, 611
ALLENDE, Ignacio, 844
ALLENDE, José Norberto de, 545a
ALLENDE, José Saturnino, 921
ALLENDE, Juan de, 186
ALLENDE, Lucas, 254
ALLENDE, Matheo de, 186
ALLENDE, Tomás, 611
ALLENDE, Tránsito C. de, 244
ALLENDE IRAGORRI, Tomás, 669, 751, 773
ALLENDE LEZAMA, L. Pedro, 923
ALLER, Angel, 1153, 1167
ALLER, Dictinio, 320
ALLEVATO, Oscar, 860
ALLYN, Clara (Mrs. William Benitz), 323
ALLYN, Franc (Mrs. Stephen W. Morgan), 323
AMADEO, Octavio R., 260, 751
AMADEO, Víctor, 954
AMADO, Elvira, 725
AMADO, Ramón, 1089
AMADO Y MOREIRA, Manuel, 1094
AMADOR, Fernán Félix de, 751, 773
AMADORI, Luis César, 858
AMARAL, Raúl, 663, 739, 805, 812
AMARILIS, pseud.
    see BARTHALOT, Irene
AMARILLA, Manuel Antonio, 943, 964
AMRILLA GONZÁLEZ, Carlos S., 954
AMARILLO, Javier, 1084
AMARITO, Cornelio, 878
AMARO, Carlos M., 94
AMARO, Mariano, 599
AMARO MACEDO, Olavo, 1140
AMAT, José, 496, 1205

AMAT, Manuel, 188
AMATO, Jorge Enrique, 299
AMATO, Norma, 785
AMATO, Rafael, 681
AMATO, Salvador, 874
AMAVET, Thomas, 949, 1029
AMAYA, José, 878
AMAYA, José Domingo, 684
AMAYA, Manuel, 254
AMBROSETTI, Giovanni Battista, 135, 141, 160, 167,
    191, 258, 292, 293, 761, 1246
AMBROSETTI, Juan Bautista
    see AMBROSETTI, Giovanni Battista
AMBROSETTI, Tomaso, 98, 258
AMEGHINO, Antonio, 258
AMEGHINO, Carlos, 191, 287
AMEGHINO, Florentino, 110, 141, 166, 176, 191, 212,
    245, 258, 272, 278, 282, 287, 293, 324, 404,
    478, 751
AMELONG, 1205
AMENÁBAR, José de, 105, 107, 611, 921
AMENEDO MONTENEGRO, Manuel de, 1095
AMERI, José, 191
AMERI, Rogelio L., 726
AMERICUS, pseud.
    see LONCAN, Enrique
AMÉSAGA, José, 126
AMESPIL, Lorenzo, 332
AMESTOY, Antonio, 1093
AMÉZAGA, Juan José de, 1083
AMÉZOLA, Alma de, 738
AMICARELLI, Guido G., 45
AMIEVA, Juan Adolfo, 222
AMIGO, Juan Antonio, 344
AMIGORENA, José Francisco, 212
AMILAGA, Joannes Angelus, 1037
AMMANN, Luis, 705
AMMIRI, Bruna, 973
AMMIRI, Giulio, 973
AMODEI, Salvador, 963a
AMORETTI, Giovanni Battista, 258, 292
AMORIM, Enrique, 152a, 794, 833, 893, 1148, 1149,
    1155, 1159, 1167, 1168, 1170, 1177, 1179, 1180,
    1187, 1196, 1199, 1245, 1249, 1251
AMORIM, José Lino, 1089, 1092
AMORIN, Isidoro J., 1140
AMOS, Arturo Jorge, 923
ANADÓN, Lorenzo J., 121
ANANIA, José, pseud.
    see PORTOGALO, José
ANANIA, Pablo, 759
ANASTASIA, Luis Víctor, 1151
ANASTASIO EL POLLO, pseud.
    see CAMPO, Estanislao del
ANAYA (family), 1108
ANAYA, Carlos, 1063
ANAYA, Enrique, 1075
ANAYA, Sócrates, 17b, 1246
ANCHART, Alberto, 857b, 878
ANCHORENA (family), 362, 363
ANCHORENA, Joaquín S. de, 3, 103
ANCHORENA, Juan de, 141
ANCHORENA, Manuel de, 457
ANCHORENA, Nicolás, 126
ANCHORENA, Tomás Manuel de, 126, 185, 283, 404, 439,
    478, 526, 611, 621, 626
AHCORIS, Ramón Eduardo de, 126, 254, 611, 921
ANDENA, Mario, 952
ANDERSON, Henry Norman, 904
ANDERSON IMBERT, Enrique, 668, 670, 685, 688, 743,
    772, 799, 815, 816

ANDINO, Francisco, 1006
ANDINO, Manuel, 998
ANDOLFI, Luis, 653, 654
ANDONAEGUI, José de, 472, 521, 570
ANDONAEGUI, María de la Encarnación
    see ANDONAEGUI DE VALDEPARES, María de la
    Encarnación
ANDONAEGUI DE VALDEPARES, María de la Encarnación,
    422, 611
ANDRADA, Carlos F., 299
ANDRADA, María Inés, 730
ANDRADE, Agustina, 762
ANDRADE, Bartolomé, 126
ANDRADE, Eliseo, 1089
ANDRADE, Fernando de, 284
ANDRADE, Juan Carlos, 660
ANDRADE, Juan de, 910
ANDRADE, Juan José, 126
ANDRADE, Mariano de, 126
ANDRADE, Miguel, 655
ANDRADE, Olegario Víctor, 95, 121, 135, 141, 166,
    216, 228, 261, 282, 379, 404, 512, 669, 682,
    692, 720, 723, 724, 734, 737, 740, 749, 751,
    754, 759, 800, 803, 807, 1147, 1243, 1247
ANDRADE, Oriol, 1210
ANDRADE, Valentín, 1089
ANDRÉ, José, 293, 864, 865, 867, 881, 883
ANDREA, Miguel de, 650
ANDREANI, George, 857c
ANDREOLI, L. Enrique, 1083
ANDREONI, L., 1079
ANDRÉS, Alfredo, 772, 883
ANDRÉS, José María, 923
ANDRÉS Y ARROYO, Juan de, 496
ANDRESITO
    see ARTIGAS, Andrés
ANDREU, Pedro Juan, 1036, 1267
ANDREU, Peter Joannez
    see ANDREU, Pedro Juan
ANDREUZZI, Silvio, 952
ANDREWS, José, 713, 834
ANDRIANI, Agustín, 191
ANDRICH, Emilio Germán, 1243
ANDRIS, Víctor, 299
ANDUEZA DE BENÍTEZ, Martha E., 652
ANDÚJAR, Francisco de, 1223
ANEIROS, León Federico, 907, 907a, 910, 911, 912,
    920, 921
ANGELELLI, Victorio, 923
ANGELES, Carlos Antonio de los, 845
ANGELI, Héctor Miguel, 681, 716, 717, 739, 758,
    759, 802
ANGELIS, Pedro de
    see ANGELIS, Pietro de
ANGELIS, Pietro de, 98, 113, 185, 206, 258, 292,
    293, 319, 373, 521, 584, 609, 629, 644, 720,
    737, 761
ANGHILERI, Leopoldo José, 923
ANGLÉS, Matías, 529a
ANGLI, Jerónimo, 923
ANIANGARA, 977
ANIDO, Angel, 284
ANIDO, María Luisa, 154, 217, 865, 882, 883
ANMELLA, Luis Alfonso, 683a
ANQUIN, Ireneo de, 565
ANSAY, Faustino, 283
ANSELMI, Antonio, 878
ANSELMI, Luis, 894
ANSELMI VALDENEGRO, Enrique, 1210
ANSINA, 1135

ANTA Y CABRERA, José Antonio, 97
ANTA Y CABRERA, Pedro, 97
ANTEGUERA Y CASTRO, José de, 472, 964
ANTELO, José Francisco, 95, 135, 194
ANTELO, Mario, 259
ANTELO CARÓU, Ramón, 1089
ANTELO DE HUSSON, Catalina R., 652
ANTELO RIAL, Ramón, 1089
ANTELO ROMERO, Francisco, 1089
ANTELO ROMERO, Ramón, 1089
ANTEMMATTEN (family), 168
ANTEPARA DE GODOY, Lucila, 931
ANTEQUEDA, Manuel Pacífico, 207, 278
ANTEQUERA, José de
    see ANTEQUERA ENRÍQUEZ Y CASTRO, José de
ANTEQUERA ENRÍQUEZ Y CASTRO, José de, 471, 963,
    978, 984, 984a, 989, 1010, 1011, 1012, 1018,
    1021, 1022
ANTEQUERA Y CASTRO, José de
    see ANTEQUERA ENRÍQUEZ Y CASTRO, José de
ANTEZANA, Atanasio, 126
ANTIER, Wanda, 299
ANTILLACH, José, 319
ANTÍN, Manuel, 857a
ANTÍN, Ricardo, 299
ANTINUCCIO, Atilio, 89
ANTOLINI, Jorge A., 659, 837
ANTÓN, Jorge Andrés, 804
ANTONELLI, Enrique F., 923
ANTONELLI DE REQUESSENS, Concepción, 1217
ANTONIETTI FILIPPINI, Rosa, 683a
ANTONINI, Antonio, 478, 479
ANTONINI, Santiago, 587
ANTONIO, 1238
ANTONIO, Jorge, 75
ANTONIO, Manuel, 991
ANTONIO, Norberto, 663
ANTONIO DE SAN ALBERTO, 921
ANTUÑA, Dimas, 664, 1151
ANTUÑA, Hugo, 1079, 1190
ANTUÑA, José G., 1145, 1199
ANTÚÑEZ, Adolfo Francisco, 959
ANZAY, Faustino, 179, 555
ANZOÁTEGUI, Francisco Tomás de, 496
ANZOÁTEGUI, Héctor, 1017
ANZOÁTEGUI, Ignacio Braulio, 664, 678, 722, 746,
    751, 758, 769, 807, 1245
ANZOÁTEGUI, Laureano de, 14
ANZOÁTEGUI DE BRAUN, Esther Mafalda, 691
ANZORENA, Jacinto de, 207, 555
ANZORENA, Nicolás, 179
ANZORENA, Pedro Ignacio, 278
AÑASCO, Pedro, 850, 1035a, 1035b
AÑÓN, Joaquín, 319
AÑÓN, José, 1089
AÑÓN, Plácido, 1089
APARICIO, Carlos Hugo, 653, 654, 689, 713, 730
APARICIO, Castulo, 385
APARICIO, Eduardo, 893
APARICIO, Emiliano Pedro, 923
APARICIO, Francisco de, 923
APARICIO, Hipólito, 254
APARICIO, Juan Manuel, 496
APARICIO, Timoteo, 1091, 1109
APELLANÍZ, José de, 3
APEMONDI, 977
APERERÁ, 977
APERGER, Segismundo, 846, 850
APICABIYÁ, 977
APOLD, Raúl Alejandro, 857d
APOLLONIO, Giovanni, 292

APONTE, Adolfo, 947, 959
APONTE, J. Alfredo, 959
APONTE, Juan, 1041
APONTE, Juan Ascencio, 982
APONTE, Leandro, 965
APONTE, Pedro Juan, 943, 995a, 1035
APONTE ALBERTINI, Miguel Angel, 1017
APPLEYARD, Bartolomé Rodolfo, 660, 710, 727, 811,
    1243
APPLEYARD, José Luis
    see APPLEYARD URDAPILLETA, José Luis
APPLEYARD URDAPILLETA, José Luis, 943, 1014, 1015,
    1018a, 1020, 1021, 1022, 1025
APRILE, Humberto, 923
APRILLE, Bartolomé Rodolfo, 710
APSHOVEN, Thomas Van, 1046
AQUINO, 608
AQUINO, Elizardo, 974, 984a
AQUINO, Juan Manuel, 995a
AQUINO, Luis, 19
AQUINO, Pedro Benjamín, 135, 718, 894
AQUINO, Pedro León, 258
AQUINO, Telmo Manuel, 963a
AQUINO ARRIETA, José Raúl, 1210
ARA, Guillermo, 239
ARABARCO, Osvaldo O., 810
ARACAMA, Omar Rubén, 658
ARACARÉ, 977
ARACE, Manuel Félix de, 258
ARACHE, Félix, 529a
ARAGÓN, Agustín de, 895, 1267
ARAGÓN, Alfonso de, 952
ARAGÓN Y ETCHART, Florencio, 1083
ARAGONE, Juan Francisco, 1083
ARAGUIRÁ, 977
ARAMAYO, José Agustín, 126
ARAMBARRI, Graciela, 789
ARAMBURU, Héctor Guillermo, 923
ARAMBURU, Juan Bautista, 268, 565
ARAMBURU, Julio, 680, 713, 730, 779, 830
ARAMBURU, Pedro Eugenio, 8, 428, 489, 515, 516,
    593, 624
ARAN, Jesús, 1089
ARANA, Eduardo, 122
ARANA, Felipe de, 390, 496
ARANCIBIA, Ernesto, 858
ARANCIBIA, Manuela, 1093a
ARANCIBIA RODRÍGUEZ, Alberto, 81, 222
ARANCIBIA RODRÍGUEZ, Alfredo, 81, 222
ARANDA, Andrés, 995a
ARANDA SUÁREZ, José Miguel, 683a
ARANDA VALDIVIA, Martín de, 1035a, 1035b
ARANDIA, Eugenio Joaquín, 81
ARANGO, José María, 923
ARANGO, José Santiago, 683a
ARANÍBAR, Tomás de, 126
ARANOVICH, Demetrio, 258a
ARÁNZ, Manuel, 844
ARÁOZ, Bartolomé, 126
ARÁOZ, Bernabé, 104, 446, 611, 632
ARÁOZ, Daniel, 385
ARÁOZ, Ernesto M., 653, 654
ARÁOZ, Juan Carlos, 658
ARÁOZ, Lucía, 478
ARÁOZ, Miguel A., 565
ARÁOZ, Miguel Moisés, 921
ARÁOZ, Pedro José Miguel, 126, 439, 457, 526, 611,
    621, 626, 921
ARÁOZ, Santiago, 987
ARÁOZ ALFARO, Gregorio
    see ARÁOZ ALFARO DE LA MADRID, Gregorio

ARÁOZ ALFARO, Rodolfo, 198, 741
ARÁOZ ALFARO DE LA MADRID, Gregorio, 70, 78, 110,
    128, 166, 188, 192, 212, 244, 283, 375, 386,
    398, 404, 442, 446, 478, 499, 519, 521, 531,
    552, 553, 569, 584, 611, 718, 854, 923
ARÁOZ ANZOÁTEGUI, Raúl, 653, 654, 716, 739, 758,
    759, 809, 812, 831
ARÁOZ DE LA MADRID, Gregorio
    see ARÁOZ ALFARO DE LA MADRID, Gregorio
ARÁOZ DE LA MADRID, Juan Carlos, 739
ARÁOZ DE LAMADRID, Ciriaco, 283
ARANCIBIA, Hernán, 653, 654
ARAPIZANDÚ, 977
ARARÁ, 977
ARAREPA, 977
ARARERA, 977
ARARIA, 977
ARARUNDI, 977
ARATA, Luis, 891, 893
ARATA, Nicolás, 258
ARATA, Pedro N., 94, 842, 844, 845a, 1246, 1261
ARATA, Pietro, 292
ARATO, José, 31, 33, 44
ARAUCO, Ana, 823
ARAUCHO, Francisco de, 876, 1057, 1063, 1080, 1223
ARAUCHO, Manuel de, 876, 1166, 1167, 1174, 1185,
    1188, 1199, 1223, 1242, 1258
ARAUCHO, Pascual de, 1223
ARAUJO, Basilio Antonio, 1111
ARAUJO, José Joaquín, 588, 609, 720
ARAUJO, Miguel, 75
ARAUJO, Orestes, 1079, 1094
ARÁUZ, José, 371
ARÁUZ, Manuel, 844
ARAVENA, José, 918
ARAVENA LÓPEZ DE GRANILLO F., María del Carmen, 652
ARAYA, Emilio, 923
ARAYA, Rogelio, 565
ARAYA, Ursula de (La menor de Araya, pseud.), 556
ARAZAY, 977
ARBELECHE CORTÉS, Jorge, 1088
ARBESTAYN (family), 366
ARBO, Antonio H., 947
ARBONÉS, Alberto F., 812
ARBUTHNOT, Thomas, 587
ARCA, Enrique E. del, 842, 844, 1261
ARCA, Juan de, 845
ARCA, Vicente, 332
ARCAMENDÍA, Domingo, 358
ARCE, Alejandro, 959
ARCE, Esteban, 611
ARCE, José Agustín de, 126, 989
ARCE, José de, 1267
ARCE, Juvencio Z., 844
ARCE, Laura de, 1217
ARCE CABEZA DE VACA, Felipe de, 555
ARCE PEIRANO, Julmer, 1210
ARCE ROJAS, Juan, 998
ARCE Y SORIA, Alonso de, 570
ARCELUS, Víctor J., 1094
ARCIDIÁCONO, Carlos, 817
ARCIDIÁCONO, José C., 154
ARCOS, Antonio, 332, 611
ARCOS, Juan Vicente, 1095
ARCOS PÉREZ, Ignacio, 1083
ARCHANGELSKY, Sergio, 923
ARCHEVERROA, Juan José, 921, 1266
ARDAO, Arturo, 1177, 1184
ARDEN QUIN, Carmelo, 19, 31, 658
ARDIGÓ, Dante, 332, 904

ARDILES, Miguel de, 520
ARDILES GRAY, Julio, 679, 680, 689, 772, 816, 830
ARDISSONE, Romualdo, 923
ARDIZZONO, Antonio, 235
ARDOY, Héctor Eugenio, 135
ARDUINO, Juan, 258
ARDUZ, Pedro, 1269
AREAL ALONSO, Prudencio, 284
ARECO, Isaac P., 68
ARECO, Ricardo Julio, 1083
ARECHAVALETA NORIK, Arturo, 1210
AREDES, Francisco, 914
AREGUATI, 977
AREGUATI, Pedro Antonio, 1111
AREILZA, José María de, 530
ARENA, Andrés Ricardo, 923
ARENAL, Concepción, 244
ARENAS, Braulio, 658
ARENAS, Domingo, 191, 254, 1083, 1168, 1170, 1180,
    1190, 1196
ARENAS, Eduardo, 332
ARENAS, Estela Beatriz, 683a
ARENAS, Luis, 126
ARENAS, Normando, 923
ARENAS LUQUE, Fermín V., 521
ARENGO, Juan Bautista, 845
ARES DE PARGA, Ignacio, 284
ARES OTERO, José, 1089
ARES PONS, Roberto, 1184
ARESTI, Cristóbal de, 907, 910, 911, 920, 1041
ARESTI, Luis de, 186
ARETZ-THIELE, Isabel, 217, 882
ARÉVALO, Cristóbal de, 1238
ARÉVALO, José, 135
ARÉVALO, Roberto, 299
ARÉVALO PARÍS, Rufino, 947
ARÉVALO SUÁREZ DE ROCHE, Julia Deanora, 1210
ARGANDOÑA, Pedro Miguel de, 910
ARGANDOÑA, Tomás Félix de, 244
ARGAÑARÁS, Francisco de, 520, 620
ARGAÑARÁS, Leopoldo, 787
ARGAÑARÁS, Manuel, 68
ARGAÑARÁZ, Raúl, 923
ARGARAÑÁZ, Abraham, 921
ARGENTINA, LA, pseud.
    see MERCÉ, Antonia
ARGENTO, Felipe, 258
ARGERICH, Cosme Mariano, 134, 282, 321, 478, 479,
    496, 611, 843, 844, 1261, 1262
ARGERICH, Francisco Cosme, 844, 1261
ARGERICH, Francisco de, 134, 844, 850, 1261, 1262
ARGERICH, Francisco Javier, 921
ARGERICH, Juan Antonio, 152a, 844, 921
ARGIBAY, Clara Inés, 691
ARGONZ, Joaquín, 477
ARGÜELLO (family), 352
ARGÜELLO, Carlos, 987
ARGÜELLO, Eladio, 947
ARGÜELLO, Manuel, 1025
ARGÜELLO, María Henriqueta, 762
ARGÜELLO, Nicolás, 998
ARGÜERO, Juan, 371
ARGUIBEL, Andrés, 127, 478, 479, 611
ARGULLÓ, Cosme, 318
ARIAS, Abelardo, 666, 757, 764, 683a
ARIAS, Amaro L., 17b
ARIAS, Constantino, 878
ARIAS, Darío F., 385
ARIAS, Eduardo, 299
ARIAS, Francisco Gabino, 1229

ARIAS, Guillermo, 998
ARIAS, Héctor D., 283
ARIAS, José Apolinario, 254
ARIAS, José Inocencio, 391, 511
ARIAS, Manuel Eduardo, 478, 611, 625
ARIAS, Marcelino, 982
ARIAS, Pepe, 858
ARIAS, Vicente, 751
ARIAS DE MANCILLA, Francisco, 186
ARIAS DE MOLINA, Luis, 555
ARIAS DE RENGEL, José Antonio, 126
ARIAS DE RONCHIETTO, Catalina, 683a
ARIAS DE SAAVEDRA, Hernando (HERNANDARIAS, pseud.),
   7, 32, 197, 205, 406, 462, 472, 477, 518, 519,
   521, 528, 535, 555, 556, 570, 593, 914, 943,
   948, 963, 980, 983, 984, 984a, 985, 997, 1007,
   1011, 1012, 1056, 1079, 1203
ARIAS DE SAAVEDRA, Juan, 186
ARIAS HIDALGO, José Antonio, 126
ARIAS RENGEL Y HEREDIA, Félix, 32
ARIAS Y PALACIOS, Josefa, 1082
ARIÑO, Emilio, 299
ARISMENDI, Rodney
   see ARISMENDI MATTOS CARRASCO, Tibaldo Rodney
ARISMENDI MATTOS CARRASCO, Tibaldo Rodney, 1184
   1210
ARISTARAIN, Adolfo, 857b
ARÍSTIDES, Julio, 663, 717, 739
ARISTIQUETA, Rodolfo, 998
ARIZAGA, Rodolfo, 883
ARLECONA de THOMPSON, María Luisa, 1021, 1022
ARLETTI, Carlos, 258
ARLT, Roberto, 232, 235, 670, 712, 715, 727, 737,
   741, 742, 745a, 765, 772, 806, 816, 825, 835,
   1245
ARMADA, Benito, 284
ARMAGNI, Alda María, 41
ARMAND UGON, Rubén, 1073
ARMANI, Horacio, 716, 717, 739, 758, 759, 802, 807
ARMANINI, José, 713, 730
ARMASA, Juan de
   see ARMASA Y ARREGUI, Juan de
ARMASA Y ARREGUI, Juan de, 32, 529a
ARMATTI de BOVE, Argentina, 652
ARMEDARIZ, José de, 989
ARMELE, Emilio, 1017
ARMELE, Nayib, 1017
ARMELE JARA, Emilio, 1017
ARMELL, Juan, 1089
ARMENCIA, Martín de, 845
ARMENTA, Bernardo de, 1034, 1035, 1266
ARMESTO, Indalecio, 284
ARMSTRONG, Clara I., 268
ARMSTRONG, Clara Jeanette, 323
ARMSTRONG, Francis Gertrude (Mrs. John A. Besler),
   323
ARMSTRONG, Minnie Burrows (Mrs. William R. Ridley),
   323
ARMSTRONG de BESLER, Francisca G., 268
ARNABOLDI, Eduardo, 332
ARNAL, Manuel, 318
ARNALDI, Juan B., 6
ARNAUDO, Aldo Antonio, 311
ARNEODO, Ana, 893
ARNIM, Otto Von, 6
ARNOLD, Prudencio, 268
AROCENA, Alfredo, 1083
AROCENA, Carlos A., 1065
AROLAS, Eduardo, 868, 875
AROLAS, Lorenzo Eduardo, 237

ARÓN MÁRQUEZ, Juan Angel, 1210
ARÓSTEGUI, Antonio, 68
ARÓSTEGUI, Manuel, 894
ARÓSTEGUY, Abdón, 894, 1075, 1083, 1185
ARPIDE, Juan Miguel de, 186
ARQUELLADA, Francisco, 1041
ARQUEZ, José León, 254
ARRANZ, Fernando, 24
ARRARTE, Gonzalo, 1093
ARRASCAETA, Enrique de, 1174, 1188
ARRECHAVALETA, José, 1075
ARREDONDO, Antonio, 1034
ARREDONDO, Elva Rosa, 653
ARREDONDO, José Miguel, 13, 17b
ARREDONDO, María Isabel, 781
ARREDONDO, Nicolás Antonio de, 455, 521, 570, 1237,
   1239, 1240, 1241, 1262
ARREGUI, Gabriel de, 907, 910, 911, 920
ARREGUI, Juan Antonio de, 186
ARREGUI, Juan de, 134, 907, 910, 911, 920, 964,
   989, 1011, 1270
ARREGUI, Mario, 1149, 1155, 1158, 1159, 1177, 1183,
   1189, 1192, 1196
ARREGUINE, Víctor, 923, 1146, 1170, 1174, 1188,
   1190, 1247
ARRIBIO, Santos, 1075
ARRIETA, Agustín de, 260
ARRIETA, José, 1127
ARRIETA, Mario César, 1243
ARRIETA, Rafael Alberto, 192, 521, 669, 674, 678,
   688, 722, 723, 739, 740, 743, 748, 751, 759,
   773, 782, 805, 807
ARRILLAGA, Francisco C., 923
ARRIOLA, José Julián, 148
ARRIOLA, José Nicolás, 540
ARRIOLA, José Tomás, 954
ARRIOLA, Juan Mateo de, 92
ARRIZABALGA, Gerardo, 1261
ARROSPIDE, Felipe, 1094
ARROYO, Carlos Alberto, 683a
ARROYO, Josefina, 787
ARROYO, Juan Andrés de, 254
ARROYO, Mario, 1045
ARROYO, Pedro de, 319
ARROYO TORRES, Ledo, 1073, 1123
ARROYO Y ARTEAGA, Francisco, 186
ARRÚA, Claudio, 995a, 1041
ARRUE (Arrien) (family), 1108
ARRUÉ, Cipriano, 645
ARRUS, Martín de, 186
ARSAMASSEVA, Margarita, 154
ARTAGAVEYTIA, Adolfo, 1075
ARTAYER, Carlos Alberto, 804
ARTAYETA, Enrique Amadeo, 923
ARTEAGA, Alfredo, 669
ARTEAGA, Andrés de, 845, 850a, 949
ARTEAGA, Ignacio de, 895
ARTEAGA, Juan, 1111
ARTEAGA, Pedro Francisco de, 496
ARTECONA DE THOMPSON, María Luisa, 943, 1014, 1025
ARTEL, Antonia T. L., 65
ARTENSAC, Germaine d', 949
ARTIACH, Leonardo, 268
ARTIEDA, Raúl, 664
ARTIGAS (family), 1106
ARTIGAS, Andrés (ANDRESITO, pseud.), 1091, 1128
ARTIGAS, Aníbal, 1093
ARTIGAS, Ceibal, 1093
ARTIGAS, Joaquín, 1059, 1111

ARTIGAS, José Gervasio de, 166, 244, 282, 283, 370, 451, 455, 471, 472, 478, 489, 491, 502, 514, 518, 519, 528, 532, 545, 552, 553, 573, 593, 632, 984a, 1052, 1053, 1058, 1059, 1060, 1063, 1076, 1077, 1079, 1085, 1091, 1109, 1115, 1118, 1131, 1133, 1135, 1233, 1262
ARTIGAS, Juan Antonio, 427, 1056
ARTIGAS, Manuel, 104, 254, 478
ARTIGAS, Manuel A., 1107
ARTIGAS, Manuel Francisco, 1113
ARTIGAS, Manuel Pantaleón, 1059, 1111
ARTIGAS, Rincón, 1093
ARTIGAS DE FERREIRA, Rosalía, 1107
ARTIGUAYE, Miguel, 977
ARTIGUE, Juan Luis Hilario, 211
ARTOLA FLORENZANO, Jorge, 781
ARTUCIO FERREIRA, Antonia, 1145
ARTUSI, Pietro, 139
ARUÉ, Raúl, 691
ARVERÁS, José Oscar, 812
ARVIA, Alejandro Jorge, 923
ARZA, Juan Nepomuceno, 995a
ARZAC, Buenaventura de, 496
ARZAC, José María de, 1205
ARZAC, Luis María, 68, 649
ARZADUM, Carmelo de, 1044
ARZAMENDIA, Andrés de, 992
ARZAMENDIA, José del Carmen, 995a
ARZAMENDIA, Vicente, 995
ARZARELLO, Sofía
    see ARZARELLO DE FONTANA, Sofía
ARZARELLO DE FONTANA, Sofía, 1153, 1179, 1187
ASCARZA, Juan, 1080
ASCASUBI, Hilario, 217, 244, 404, 407, 418, 478, 511, 611, 669, 688, 720, 723, 724, 734, 736, 737, 740, 751, 754, 761, 767, 803, 807, 821, 828, 1242, 1243, 1244, 1247, 1248, 1249, 1254, 1260
ASCENSIO DE MALLEA, Theresa de, 931
ASCOLESE, Aggeo, 874
ASCONE, Vicente, 1206, 1207
ASCHERO, Carlos Alberto, 41
ASEDO, Thomas de, 186
ASERETTO DE MARIANI, Cándida, 955
ASÍS, Jorge, 696
ASPERGER, Segismundo, 844, 845, 949, 1203, 1261
ASSALI, Orestes, 64
ASTELARRA, Leandro B., 910
ASTETE, Gaspar, 1035
ASTETE, José, 126
ASTIGARRAGA, Claudio, 995a
ASTIGARRAGA, José P., 1123
ASTIGUETA, José Inocencio, 126
ASTIGUETA, José María, 844, 1261
ASTIGUETA, José Mariano, 842
ASTOALDI, Alejandro, 923
ASTORGA, José Manuel, 283
ASTRADA, Jenaro Berón, 404
ASTRADA, Julio, 89
ASTRADA, Manuel J., 190
ASTRALDI, Alejandro, 923
ASTUDILLO, Fernando de, 186
ASTUDILLO MENÉNDEZ, Eulalio, 222
ASUERO, Fernando, 138
ASTAHUALPA, pseud.
    see SEGOVIA, Manuel Ignacio
ATANASIO DE LA PIEDAD (Atanasio de la Soledad), 844, 845, 850, 921, 1261
ATANASIO DE LA SOLEDAD
    see ATANASIO DE LA PIEDAD
ATANASIU, Pablo, 663

ATENCIO, Juan José, 122
ATENCIO, Juan V., 565
ATENCIO, Vicente, 73
ATICAI, 977
ATIENZA, Juan de, 1035a, 1035b
ATIENZA, Rafael, 196
ATKINSON, Florence, 323
ATKINSON, María Ana, 320
ATKINSON, Sarah, 323
ATTIAS, Alberto, 560
AUCELL, Miguel, 32
AUCHMUTY, Samuel, 104, 552, 587, 1262
AUCHTER, Argentino S., 89
AUDIBERT, Alejandro, 68, 943, 964, 966
AUDIVERT, Eduardo, 27, 55
AUDIVERT, Pompeyo, 18, 22, 27, 44, 55, 64
AUER, Vaino, 923
AULÉS, Antonio, 1205
AUÑÓN Y VILLALÓN, Ramón, 1235
AURELIO, 361
AUSLENDER, Josefina, 55
AUWEILER, Juan José, 319
AVAHAY, José Donato, 995a
AVALOS, 1095
AVALOS, Eduardo J., 461
AVALOS, Gumersindo, 254
AVALOS, José de, 845, 989
AVALOS, José María, 191
AVALOS SÁNCHEZ, Ramón, 998, 1006
AVALOS Y MENDOZA, José de, 964
AVALOS Y MENDOZA, Matheo, 186
AVALOS Y PERALTA, José de
    see DÁVALOS Y PERALTA, José de
AVANCINI de POTENZA, Ofelia, 652
AVANZA, Hugo Leonardo, 923
AVANZA, Julio César, 812
AVE LALLEMANT, Germán, 207, 222
AVE LALLEMANT, Gustavo, 332
AVEGNO, Emilio, 1127
AVEIRO, Filemón, 198
AVEIRO, Silvestre, 974, 1003
AVEIRO LUGO, Eusebio, 1017
AVELEYRA, Santiago Alejo, 254
AVELLANEDA, Elena, 762
AVELLANEDA, Eudoro, 254
AVELLANEDA, Gaspar de, 224
AVELLANEDA, Marco Aurelio, 68, 382
AVELLANEDA, Marco Manuel, 70, 94, 112, 166, 381, 404, 478, 737, 842
AVELLANEDA, María Herminia, 857d
AVELLANEDA, Nicolás
    see AVELLANEDA Y TULA, Nicolás
AVELLANEDA DE GARZÓN, Antonia, 1093a
AVELLANEDA DE GONZÁLEZ DE AYALA, Elena, 653, 654
AVELLANEDA Y TULA, Nicolás, 70, 78, 79, 91, 103, 110, 112, 116, 118, 121, 130, 141, 152a, 165, 166, 176, 189, 195, 212, 216, 236, 244, 258, 278, 282, 287, 344, 372, 386, 392, 393, 398, 404, 405, 462, 469, 478, 484, 485, 502, 509, 514, 515, 516, 519, 521, 531, 554, 574, 585, 593, 593, 598, 611, 619, 631, 692, 720, 734, 751
AVELLEYRA, Santiago Alejo
    see AVELEYRA, Santiago Alejo
AVENDAÑO, Juan de, 186
AVENDAÑO, Santiago, 1246
AVENDAÑO SOTO, E., 21
AVENELAÑO, Fernando de, 910
AVERY, Bernice (Mrs. Richard Agar), 323
AVETA, Alfonso, 190
AVILA, Felipe de (DÁVILA, Felipe de), 914

AVILA, Guido Orlando, 689
AVILA, Juan de, 1267
AVILA, Juan Francisco de (DÁVILA, Juan Francisco), 319
AVILA, Manuel, 982
AVILA, Norberto Ramón, 299
AVILA, Pedro Esteban de, 570
AVILA, Santiago, 7
AVILÉS, Marqués de
    see AVILÉS Y DEL FIERRO, Gabriel de (Marqués de Avilés)
AVILÉS Y DEL FIERRO, Gabriel de (Marqués de Avilés), 570, 1237, 1239, 1240, 1241
AVIS LOBO, Pedro de, 1270
AVOLA, Fidelis de, 1041
AXENFELD, Salvador, 882
AYALA (family), 357
AYALA, Andrés, 1006
AYALA, Cecilio, 998
AYALA, Eligio, 959, 980, 983, 984a
AYALA, Enrique, 959
AYALA, Eusebio, 959, 984a, 998, 1006, 1012
AYALA, Fernando, 857, 857a, 858
AYALA, Gumersindo, 943
AYALA, José de la Cruz (Alón, pseud.), 964, 982, 1012, 1020
AYALA, Juan Bautista, 1006
AYALA, Juan de, 254
AYALA, Víctor M., 954
AYALA AGUINO, Gumersindo, 947
AYALA CABEDA, Adalita, 955, 956
AYALA GAUNA, Velmiro, 745, 753, 837
AYALA VELÁZQUEZ, Eugenio, 998, 1006
AYARRAGARAY, Carlos A., 652
AYARRAGARAY, Lucas, 751
AYBAR, Ana Matilde, 44
AYERZA, Abel, 842, 844, 845a, 847, 1261
AYERZA, José A., 845a
AYERZA, Toribio, 845a
AYESTARÁN, Lauro, 688, 1177
AYESTARÁN DE DÍEZ, Juana, 320
AYLLÓN, Nelly, 893
AYMÁ, Federico Víctor, 37
AYME, Ana María (family), 168
AYME, Juan Bautista (family), 168
AYMERICH, Juan, 669
AYMERICH, Ramón, 811
AYMERICH Y VILLAJUANA, Antonio, 332
AYMLER, Ricardo, 32, 332
AYMONINO, Pedro José, 923
AYOLAS, Juan de, 406, 464, 465, 471, 472, 481, 521, 528, 948, 984, 989, 992, 1011, 1012, 1203, 1232
AYROLDI, Cayetano, 7
AYROLDI, Santiago, 7
AYZAGUER GONZÁLEZ, Pedro María, 1210
AZAMOR Y RAMÍREZ, Manuel, 910, 917
AZÁN ARTEAGA, Luiz, 653
AZARA, Félix de, 17a, 106, 191, 332, 470, 552, 754, 834, 885, 943, 964, 966, 985, 1012, 1053, 1229, 1246, 1262
AZARA, Pero, 922
AZAROLA, José María, 1084
AZAROLA GIL, Luis Enrique, 1056
AZCONA CRANWELL, Elizabeth, 658, 716, 717, 725, 739, 759, 802
AZCONA IMBERTO, Antonio, 32, 907, 910, 911, 920
AZCONEGUY OLIVERA, Rubén Darío, 1210
AZCUÉNAGA, Domingo de, 751, 669
AZCUÉNAGA, María del Rosario, 924
AZCUÉNAGA, Miguel de, 70, 85, 104, 244, 282, 386, 404, 421, 475, 478, 479, 610, 629

AZCUÉNAGA, Miguel Juan, 611
AZCUÉNAGA, Vicente de, 254
AZCUÉNAGA Y BASAVILBASO, Miguel de, 496
AZEVEDO, Luis T. de, 1064
AZEVES, Angel Héctor, 688, 812
AZLOR, Clementina Isabel, 154, 751, 762, 783
AZLOR, Ernestina, 154
AZNÁREZ, Enrique Pedro, 923
AZOCAR URTADO, Pedro de, 186
AZOPARDO, Juan Bautista, 14, 17a, 78, 258, 268, 282, 386, 404, 427, 478, 611
AZPEITÍA, Luis de, 646, 649a
AZTIRIA, Ignacio, 68
AZUAGA, Pedro de, 910, 995a
AZURDUY DE PADILLA, Juana, 85, 227, 422, 552, 611
AZZI DE BERTORA, Rosa Marcela Josefa, 320
AZZONI, Roberto, 25, 31

BAAMONDE, Esther Lucía, 923
BABA, Eudoro J., 268
BABBACCI, Juan, 207
BABINI, Domingo Santiago, 923
BABINI, José, 218, 521, 923
BABUGLIA, Rogelio Tomás, 923
BACA, Francisco, 7, 987
BACA, José María, 6
BACA, Teodoro, 844
BACA CAU, Normando, 713
BACA DE SASIAIN, Dora Olinda, 320
BACELO, Nancy, 1151, 1178
BACIGALUPO, Juan, 923
BACIGALUPO, Nélida María, 923
BACLE, Andrea, 28
BACLE, César Hipólito, 28, 42, 116, 293, 528, 574
BACLER D'ALBE, Alberto, 332, 611
BACQUE, Augusto Luis, 923
BACH, Raúl Oscar (COCO, pseud.), 860
BACHINI, Antonio, 1146, 1190
BADANO, Ariel
    see BADANO PEREYRO, Ariel
BADANO, Víctor Manuel, 923
BADANO PEREYRO, Ariel H., 1151, 1179, 1210
BADARACCO, Juan Carlos, 19
BADARACO, Enrique, 1066
BADARÁN Y BUSTILLO, Jacobo de, 555
BADELL, Jaime, 1223
BADELL, Juan de la Cruz, 1223
BADELL, Monico, 1223
BADELL, Prudencia, 1223
BADESSICH, Enrique, 138
BADI, Aquiles, 18, 19, 23, 25, 31, 36, 50, 64, 137, 268
BADÍA, Gregorio (MORICANTE, pseud.), 137, 268
BADII, Libero, 19, 20, 21, 22, 25, 35, 55
BADIN, Bartolomé, 73
BADO, Atilio, 923
BADO, José Matías, 974, 1003
BADUI DE ZOGBI, María B., 683a
BAENA, José Luis, 1122
BAENA, Luis, 1093a, 1110
BAENA CAGNANI, Carlos, 923
BAETHGEN, Raúl E., 1167
BÁEZ, Cecilio, 943, 951, 959, 964, 966, 1002, 1012, 1014, 1018, 1023
BÁEZ, Ernesto, 943
BÁEZ, Federico Guillermo, 991
BÁEZ, Hernán, 1238
BÁEZ, Jorge, 1014
BÁEZ, Juan R., 923
BÁEZ, Liliana, 662
BÁEZ, Manuel Antonio, 126
BÁEZ, Manuel José, 979, 987

BÁEZ, Santiago Fernando, 220
BÁEZ ALLENDE, Amadeo, 954
BÁEZ ALLENDE, Quirino, 1028, 1029
BÁEZ BOGADO, Eugenio, 954
BÁEZ DE ALPOÍN, Juan, 186
BAEZA, Tomás de, 1267
BAFFICO, Rosa, 1211
BAGGIANI, Guido, 985
BAGLIETTO, Eduardo, 332
BAGNATI, José María, 860
BAHAMONDE, Ramón Franco, 284
BAIDAFF, Bernardo, 923
BAIDAL, José, 683a, 814
BAIER, Alejandro Benjamín, 810
BAIGORRI, Carlos Alfredo, 1210
BAIGORRI, Clemens, 1037
BAIGORRI, José Gregorio, 244, 545a, 910, 921
BAIGORRI VELAR, Juan, 138
BAIGORRI Y RUIZ, Pedro de, 521
BAIGORRÍA, 454, 566, 606, 608
BAIGORRÍA, Alejandro, 878
BAIGORRIA, Juan Bautista, 222
BAIGORRIA, Manuel, 180, 566, 617
BAIGORRIA, Nélida, 218
BAILI de MURPHY, Ruth S., 652
BAILION ALIENDE, Tomás, 126
BAJAC de BORGES, Isaura, 1088
BAJARLÍA, Juan Jacobo, 658, 668, 728, 739, 759, 807, 816
BALA PERDIDA, pseud.
    see SÁENZ, Máximo Teodoro
BALAGUER, Joaquín, 368
BALAGUER, Nuri, 37
BALAIEFF, Juan, 962
BALÁN, A. A. 836
BALÁN, Américo, 27
BALANSÁ, Benjamín Gaspar Joseph, 949, 960
BALANSÁ, Juana de
    see BOISSIÈRE DE BALANSÁ, Jeanne
BALANZÁ DE CHECÁ, René, 947
BALANZAT, Manuel, 923
BALAO, Manuel, 1095
BALBASTRO, Eugenio José, 496
BALBASTRO, José María, 496
BALBASTRO, Matías, 611
BALBI, Angel B., 73
BALBI, Lermo Rafael, 701, 824
BALBI, Tito, 860
BALBI MAZZEO, Selmar Hermen, 1210
BALBI PIANO, Aníbal, 1210
BALBÍN, Ricardo, 213
BALBÍN, Valentín, 332, 921a
BALBÍN Y VALLEJO DE LUNA, Anacleta, 1093a
BALBUDO DE IRIARTE, Margarita, 320
BALBUDO DE MANETTI, Rosa, 320
BALCARCE, Antonio, 478, 479
BALCARCE, Diego, 478, 479, 569, 611
BALCARCE, Florencio, 177, 664, 669, 720, 749, 751, 761, 828, 1243, 1247
BALCARCE, Josefa Dominga
    see BALCARCE Y SAN MARTÍN DE GUTIÉRREZ DE ESTRADA, Josefa Dominga
BALCARCE, Juan Ramón, 104, 166, 272, 386, 478, 479, 496, 521, 528, 552, 553, 554, 568, 569, 584, 611, 629
BALCARCE, Marcos, 478, 479
BALCARCE, Mariano Severo, 112, 153, 172, 383
BALCARCE DE COE, Trinidad, 254
BALCARCE DE GUTIÉRREZ ESTRADA, Josefa Dominga
    see BALCARCE Y SAN MARTÍN DE GUTIÉRREZ DE ESTRADA, Josefa Dominga

BALCARCE DE SAN MARTÍN, María Mercedes, 172, 383
BALCARCE Y SAN MARTÍN DE GUTIÉRREZ DE ESTRADA, Josefa Dominga, 112, 172, 383
BALCÁZAR, Fernando de, 1041
BALDA, Lorenzo, 1267
BALDASSARI, Ernesto, 332
BALDINI, Félix, 320
BALDINI, Laerte, 64
BALDIVIESO, José, 126
BALDOMIR, Alfredo, 1073, 1077
BALDOMIR GARCÍA, Olga Venus, 1210
BALDRICH, Alberto, 170
BALDRICH, Juan Amadeo de, 268
BALDUZZI, Luis Orestes, 35, 63
BALECH, Enrique, 923
BALERDI, Juana Manuela, 320
BALESTRA, Juan, 258, 551a
BALESTRA, Serafín, 921
BALESTRINI, Aristóbulo M., 923
BALET, Luisa, 949, 1042
BALINO, Pedro, 496
BALIÑO DE LAYA, Pedro, 284
BALMACEDA, 189
BALMACEDA, José Manuel, 254
BALPARDA (family), 1108
BALSALDUA, Anselmo E., 1140
BALSERIO, José Antonio, 923
BALTA, José, 383
BALTAR, Amelita, 879
BALTASAR, Pelegrin, 1205
BALTORE, José R., 254, 258
BALVIANI, César, 258
BALZARINO, Angel Domingo, 701, 814
BALLA, Andrés, 814
BALLARIO, Carlos, 683a
BALLCELS, Gustavo, 299
BALLERINI, Alberto, 893
BALLERINI, Augusto, 19, 25, 31, 59, 258, 521
BALLESTER, Antonio Luciano, 496
BALLESTER, Luis Alberto, 817
BALLESTER, Rodolfo, 332
BALLESTER PEÑA, Juan Antonio, 19, 23, 25, 31, 33, 36, 50, 64
BALLESTERO, Domingo, 268
BALLESTEROS, Alberto T., 894
BALLESTEROS, Enrique, 496
BALLESTEROS, Gonzalo, 914
BALLESTEROS, Montiel
    see MONTIEL BALLESTEROS, Adolfo
BALLINA, Osvaldo, 663, 665
BANCORA, Mario Eduardo, 923
BANCHERO, Anderssen, 1176, 1183
BANCHS, Enrique, 521, 664, 669, 674, 678, 686, 722, 723, 737, 740, 748, 751, 759, 782, 799, 803, 807, 816
BANDEIRA, Domingo, 952, 1267
BANDINI, Alfredo, 923
BANDINI, Bruno, 883
BANDINI, Simón, 292, 1035
BANDUREK, Pole Wolf, 938, 939
BANEGAS, José León, 611
BAÑA, Francisco, 1089
BAQUETA, Moisés, 1089
BARABINO, Santiago Esteban, 332
BARALIS, Lorenzo, 923
BARÁN, Walter J., 923
BARANDA, Andrés, 124
BARANDA, Mauricio, 943a
BARANDA REYES, Santiago, 1206, 1207
BARAÑAO, Teófilo Víctor, 923

BARAS, Tomás, 222
BARAVALLE, Ricardo Sergio, 37
BARBA, Alvaro Alonso, 885
BARBA, Diego, 845
BARBA, Enrique M., 609
BARBACCI, Rodolfo, 882
BARBAGELATA, Giovanni Antonio, 139
BARBAGELATA, Hugo David, 1083
BARBAGELATA, Lorenzo, 1083
BARBARÁ, Federico, 431
BARBARÁN ALVARADO, Carlos M., 653, 654
BARBARÍN, Manuel Macedonio, 137
BARBAROUX, Emilio, 1083
BARBATO, Germán, 1073, 1123
BARBEITO, Graciela T., 652
BARBEITO, Juan, 222
BARBEITO, Juan Alejandro, 81, 222
BARBENZA, G. Horacio, 923
BARBER, Salvador, 319
BARBERO (family), 168
BARBERO, Andrés, 953, 959, 1012
BARBERO, Juan, 951
BARBIER, María J. S., 154
BARBIERI, Enrique, 814, 815
BARBIERI, Nina, 859
BARBIERI, Vicente, 275, 663, 664, 674, 685, 722,
    739, 758, 759, 798, 801, 803, 812, 815, 817, 818
BARBINO, Miguel, 6
BARBITTA COLOMBO, Adela, 1217
BARBOSA, Efrain Abel, 684
BARBOSA, María Delfina, 1092
BARBOSA, Pedro L., 959
BARBURO, Juan, 952
BARCALA, Juan Manuel, 923
BARCALA, Lorenzo, 128, 137, 188, 212, 244, 278, 478
BARCALA, Severino, 1089
BARCELÓ, Ricardo Antonio, 217
BÁRCENA, Catalina, 857b
BÁRCENA, José Benito de la, 385
BARCIA, Berta, 781
BARCIA, José, 235, 644a, 1089
BARCIA GIGENA, Fernando Jorge, 683a
BARCIELA, Carlos, 941
BARCO, Gerónimo del, 649
BARCO CENTENERA, Martín del, 507, 525, 649a, 713,
    966, 985, 1021, 1022, 1229, 1230, 1261
BARCOS, Julio Ricardo, 118
BARDALES, Gonzalo de, 620
BARDEL, Agustín, 254
BARDESIO, Orfila, 1151, 1177
BARDI, Agustín, 237, 868
BAREILLES, Oscar S., 217, 865
BAREIRO, Cándido, 1011
BAREIRO, Francisco Luis, 1014
BAREIRO SAGUIER, Rubén, 943, 1014, 1015, 1020, 1021,
    1022, 1023
BARENGUER, 361
BARES, Juan Carlos, 878
BARES GÍRALDEZ, Manuel A., 284
BARGAS, Pedro, 478
BARILARI, Eduardo Mario, 923
BARILARI, Josefina de, 663
BARILARI, Mariano J., 258, 292, 923
BARKLEY, Fred, 923
BARLETTA, Leónidas, 670, 712, 757, 765, 770, 814,
    825, 829, 836, 1245
BARLLE PACHECO, Lorenzo, 1073
BARNATAN, Marcos Ricardo, 807
BARNECHE, Juan B., 103
BARNEDA, Joaquín J., 328

BARNES, Eduardo, 25
BARNEY FINN, Oscar, 857b
BARO, Benito, 268
BARO GRAF, Juan Carlos, 923
BARÓN DE POZO, Juan José Mariano, 895
BARONI DE BARRENECHE, Elsa, 1088
BARQUIN, Manuel Antonio de, 496
BARRA, Federico de la, 167
BARRA, Juan, 254
BARRA, Melchor León de la, 126
BARRA DE LLANOS, Ema de la
    see DUAYÉN, César
BARRADAS, Carmen, 1206, 1207
BARRADAS, Rafael, 33, 1218
BARRAGÁN, Bartolomé, 186
BARRAGÁN, Juan Pablo, 186
BARRAGÁN, Julio, 19, 31, 36, 63
BARRAGÁN, Lázaro, 186
BARRAGÁN, Luis, 19, 25, 31, 36, 46, 55, 63
BARRAGÁN DE CERVANTES, Juan, 186
BARRAGUE, Alberto, 1204
BARRAIL, Augusto, 954
BARRAIL, Brice, 954
BARRAIL, Enrique, 954, 963a
BARRALES, José Nicolás, 1056, 1262
BARRANCOS, Leónidas, 332
BARRANDÓN, Francisco Luis, 949
BARRANZA Y CÁRDENAS, Francisco de, 501
BARRAQUERO, Carlos Washington, 874
BARRAQUERO, Julián, 207, 278
BARRAZA, Francisco C., 844, 1261
BARRAZA, Napoleón, 68
BARRAZÁN GUERRA, Juan Manuel, 923
BARREDA, Ernesto Mario, 669, 748, 751, 773, 782,
    807, 834
BARREDA, José de la, 496
BARREDA, Rafael, 1246
BARREDA, Valeriano, 496
BARREIRO, Alicia M., 652
BARREIRO, José P., 235
BARREIRO, Manuel, 68
BARREIRO, Miguel M. F., 1063, 1076, 1091, 1118
BARREIRO, Ramón, 1089
BARREIRO, Segundo, 1145
BARREIRO MAFFIODO, Francisco M., 954
BARREIRO ORTIZ, Carlos, 222
BARREIRO SAGUIER, Rubén, 1025
BARREIRO VÁZQUEZ VARELA, Bernardo, 284
BARREIRO VILLAVERDE, Manuel, 1089
BARREIRO Y CAMBA, Manuel, 1095
BARREIRO Y RAMOS, Antonio, 1094, 1095
BARRENA DE FELDER, María Begoña, 320
BARRENECHEA, Diego de, 83
BARRERA, José, 1089
BARRERA, José Luis, 268
BARRERA, Juan Antonio, 683a
BARRERA, Matías, 268
BARRERA, Ramón, 319, 878
BARBERA, Ulpiano, 496
BARRERA ORO, Julio, 683a
BARRÈRE, Agustín, 910
BARRERO Y BUSTILLO, Manuel, 1223
BARRET, Rafael
    see BARRETT, Rafael
BARRETO CANTERO, Hamilton César, 1210
BARRETT, Rafael, 259, 943, 964, 1012, 1014, 1019,
    1020, 1058, 1177
BARRETTA, Glady, 785
BARREYRO, Héctor, 551a
BARREYRO, José L., 984

BARRIENTOS, César, 954
BARRIENTOS, Cristóbal de, 344
BARRIGA, Víctor Manuel, 914
BARRIO, Domingo del, 344
BARRIONUEVO, Aníbal, 731
BARRIONUEVO, Fernando de, 910
BARRIONUEVO, Marcos, 691
BARRIONUEVO SORÍA, Blanca Estela, 684
BARRIOS, Agustín Pío, 943, 964, 1012, 1028, 1029
BARRIOS, Américo, pseud.
    see ALBAMONTE, Luis María
BARRIOS, Evaristo, 878, 1243
BARRIOS, Felipe, 995
BARRIOS, Francisco Martín, 1014
BARRIOS, Gregorio, 857b
BARRIOS, Héctor L., 1014
BARRIOS, Juan Evangelista, 995a
BARRIOS, Juan N., 1006
BARRIOS, Julio, 1116
BARRIOS, Leoncio, 331
BARRIOS, Pascual, 1089
BARRIOS, Raúl Antonio, 923
BARRIOS, Valentín José, 810
BARRIOS, Ventura, 186
BARRIOS, Vicente, 974, 984
BARRIOS Y TOLEDO, Juan de los, 910, 918, 1034, 1041
BARROETAVEÑA, Francisco A., 166
BARROS, Alvaro, 249, 470
BARROS, Antonio, 1205
BARROS, Daniel, 801
BARROS, Juan Cayetano, 1205
BARROS, Nicolás, 247
BARROS, Rubén Alejo, 713
BARROS, Ruperto, 1089
BARROS ARANA, Diego, 153, 283
BARROS PAZOS, José, 611
BARROS Y BARROS, Juan, 284
BARROSO, César I., 320
BARROSO, Manuel, 320
BARROSO, Tomás, 222
BARROSO DE LA PLAZA, María Soledad, 320
BARROSO RODRÍGUEZ, Julián (father), 81
BARROSO RODRÍGUEZ, Julián (son), 81
BARROZO, Benjamín, 254
BARRY, Carlos A., 746
BÁRSENA, Alfonso, 989
BÁRSENA, Martín Ignacio, 126
BARSIO, 845
BARTHALOT, Irene (AMARILIS, pseud.), 762
BARTHÉLEMY, Ernest Amedée Mouchez, 949
BARTHÉLEMY HAVELLE, Jean, 332
BARTOLINI, Abraham
    see BARTOLINI FERRO, Abraham
BARTOLONI, Pascual, 73
BARTOLINI, Tulio, 860
BARTOLINI FERRO, Abraham, 73, 135, 325
BARTOLITO, pseud.
    see MONTERO, Bartolomé Domingo
BARTOLOMÉ, Leopoldo José, 759
BARTOLOMÉ, Miguel Angel, 299
BARTOLOMEW, Roy, 807
BARTOSZEWSKI, José, 238
BARTRUILLE, Bernardo, 250
BARÚA, Martín de, 984, 989, 1011
BARUD, Némer, 717, 739
BARUGEL, Esther, 35
BARY, Mariano de, 954
BÁRZANA, Alonso de, 191, 866, 921, 1035a, 1035b
BARZI, Jorge, 952
BAS (family), 352

BAS, Bernardo, 89
BAS, Manuel Antonio, 496
BAS Y PI, R., 1145
BASA VILLADEFRANCO, Leopoldo, 284
BASABILBASO, Patricio de, 177
BASALDUA, Héctor, 18, 19, 23, 25, 31, 33, 36, 44, 50, 53, 55, 210
BASAVILBASO (family), 1224
BASAVILBASO, Clemente, 135, 194
BASAVILBASO, Domingo de, 70, 898
BASAVILBASO, Manuel, 321, 543, 898
BASCIANO, Elisa María Filomena, 320
BASCO, Alfonso, 258
BASETI PIRIZ, José Héctor, 1088
BASSAURI, Diego, 850, 949
BASSETS, Abilio, 652
BASSI, Arturo de, 719
BASSI, Hugo G. L., 923
BASSO, Antonio, 258
BASSO MAGLIO, Vicente, 1151, 1153, 1177, 1179, 1181, 1199
BASTIÁN, Alfonso, 1238
BASTIDA, Andrés de la, 845
BASTIDAS, Carlos, 368
BASTITTA, José Pedro, 1167
BASTOS, Hugo, 37
BASTOS, Julio, 1083
BASUALDO, Blas, 1128
BASUALDO, Juan, 358
BASUALDO, Ricardo, 299
BASULTO, Hilda, 683a
BATALLÓN, 137
BATEMAN, Juan Federico, 332
BATEMAN, Juan G., 6, 332
BATHURST, Guillermo, 14, 82
BATLLE (family), 1108
BATLLE, Lorenzo, 1079, 1091, 1109, 1188
BATLLE BERRES, Luis, 644a
BATLLE PACHECO, César, 1073, 1123
BATLLE PLANAS, Juan, 18, 19, 23, 25, 31, 34, 36, 38, 50, 55
BATLLE Y CARREÓ, José, 1059
BATLLE Y ORDÓÑEZ, José, 963, 1059, 1073, 1075, 1077, 1079, 1083, 1091, 1109, 1190
BATTAGLIA, Guillermo, 891
BATTIG, Augusto J. M., 923
BATTILANA DE GASPERI, Arturo, 998
BATTILANA DE GASPERI, Eladio, 1014
BATTILANA DE GÁSPERI, Raúl, 1014
BATTISTA, 292
BATTISTESSA, Angel José, 688, 743
BATTISTON, Dora, 797
BAUCKE, Florián, 28, 32, 834, 865, 866, 885, 985, 1031, 1269
BAUDIN, Pablo E., 903
BAUDRIX, Diego, 68
BAUER, Jacinto, 32
BAUER, Walter, 953
BAULIES, Oscar Leopoldo, 923
BAUMANN, Hermann, 954
BAUNESS, Carlos, 82
BAUTISTA, María Rosa, 781
BAUZÁ, Felipe, 28
BAUZÁ, Francisco, 1079, 1086, 1117, 1141, 1146, 1177, 1187, 1188, 1199
BAUZÁ, Julio A., 1083
BAUZÁ, Mariano, 857b
BAUZÁ, Rufino, 1063
BAUZÁ, Sebastián, 998
BAVIO, Ernesto A., 121, 241

BAXTER, Ricardo, 14
BAY, Juan, 19, 31
BAYALA, Elías, 32
BAYCE, Pedro, 1085
BAYEU, Ramón, 32
BAYLEY, Edgar, 658, 672, 716, 739, 759, 803, 807, 812, 832
BAYÓN, Damián Carlos, 739, 812
BAYÓN HERRERA, Luis, 1257
BAZ, Ignacio, 19, 28, 59, 62
BAZ Y FERNÁNDEZ DE PINO, 284
BAZÁN, 628
BAZÁN (family), 972
BAZÁN, Juan F., 965, 1020
BAZÁN, Juan Gregorio, 520, 620
BAZÁN, Rogelio, 739
BAZÁN, Vicente Antonio, 995a
BAZÁN DE CABRERA, Juan, 83
BAZÁN DE CAMARA, Rosa, 154
BAZÁN DE PEDRAZA, Juan Gregorio, 984, 1011
BAZÁN Y BUSTOS, Abel, 247, 910
BAZO BERRY, Juan, 427
BAZTERRICA, Enrique, 844
BAZURCO, Antonio
    see BAZURCO Y HERRERA, José Antonio
BAZURCO, José Antonio
    see BAZURCO Y HERRERA, José Antonio
BAZURCO Y HERRERA, José Antonio, 907, 910, 911, 920
BAZZANO, Hamlet, 1083
BAZZANO, Ignacio, 1075
BAZZANO, Segundo, 1075, 1083
BAZZI, Enrique, 258
BAZZINI BARROS, Carlos, 24
BEARE, Pedro, 6
BEASCOCHEA, Juan Bautista, 254
BEASCOECHEA, María Estela, 955
BEATRIZ, Marcelo, 878
BEAUMANT, Francisco, 910
BEAUMONT Y NAVARRA, Frances de, 274, 521
BEAUVOIR, José María, 907a
BEBELAQUA, Pedro, 874
BECCAR, Cosme, 122
BECCAR, Darío, 68
BECCAR, Héctor, 299
BECCO, Horacio Jorge, 652, 671, 688, 722, 739, 758, 807
BECERRA, Isabel
    see GARAY, Isabel de
BECERRA, José Antonio, 222
BECERRO DE BENGOA, Miguel, 1083
BECK, Guido, 923
BECK-BERNARD, Lina, 834
BECKE, Alejandro von der, 923
BECKER, Juan Sigfrido, 170
BECKER, María Esther, 781
BECÚ, Carlos A., 565
BECCHI, Constantino, 1174
BECCHIS, Gerónimo, 995a
BECHER, Emilio, 162, 167, 243, 277
BECHERINI, Roberto Oscar, 781
BEDIA CABALLERÍA, Cecilio, 284
BEDOYA, Elías, 166, 188, 195, 244, 611
BEDOYA, Eusebio, 921
BEDOYA, Francisco, 552
BEDOYA, Vidal, 954
BEECHE, Gregorio, 166, 488
BEGHIN, Humberto, 141
BEGINO, Juan María, 762
BEGUERASTEIN, Manuel, 68, 94
BEHAK WAINSZTAIN, Ana, 1210

BEHAK WAINSZTAIN, Samuel, 1210
BEHETY, Matías, 254, 1146, 1174, 1188
BEIRO, Francisco, 565
BEIRO, José, 1089
BEISSO, Alejandro, 1073
BEJARANO, Pedro Inocencio, 910
BEJARANO, Ramón César, 954
BELAIEFF, Juan, 1012
BELANDO VIOLA, Cándido, 1088
BELAUNDE, Cosme, 385
BELAUSTEGUI, Francisco Antonio de, 496
BELAUSTEGUI, Petrona, 478
BELBEY, José, 260, 718
BELÉN, María, 781
BELFORTE, Arnaldo Agustín, 923
BELGERI, Francisco, 135
BELGRANO (family), 292
BELGRANO, Arturo G., 68
BELGRANO, Domingo Estanislao, 915, 921
BELGRANO, Joaquín M., 6
BELGRANO, Juan Carlos, 391
BELGRANO, Manuel, 4, 11a, 32, 59, 70, 85, 104, 110, 112, 118, 121, 141, 165, 166, 176, 199, 212, 244, 245, 258, 278, 282, 283, 317, 324, 369, 370, 374, 379, 382, 386, 404, 411, 420, 421, 427, 443, 448, 451, 453, 455, 458, 459, 462, 469, 471, 472, 475, 478, 479, 489, 499, 502, 507, 508, 509, 514, 517, 518, 519, 521, 525, 529, 545, 552, 553, 562, 563, 568, 569, 573, 574, 575, 583, 588, 589, 610, 611, 644, 650, 677, 720, 895, 984, 1001
BELGRANO, Manuel (writer), 677
BELGRANO GONZÁLEZ, Domingo, 496
BELGRANO GONZÁLEZ, Joaquín, 496
BELGRANO GONZÁLEZ, José Gregorio, 496
BELGRANO GONZÁLEZ, Manuel
    see BELGRANO Y GONZÁLEZ CASERO, Manuel Joaquín Corazón de Jesús
BELGRANO RAWSON, Guillermo A., 81
BELGRANO Y GONZÁLEZ CASERO, Manuel Joaquín Corazón de Jesús, 381, 496
BELGRANO Y PERI, Domingo, 113
BELÍN SARMIENTO, Emilia, 930
BELÍN SARMIENTO, Eugenia, 59, 930
BELÍN SARMIENTO, Helena, 930
BELÍN SARMIENTO, Luisa, 930
BELMARTINO DE AMOR, Amanda, 320
BELMARTINO DE CHIOCCHI, María Angélica, 320
BELMES, Marta, 37
BELMONTE DE BENSO, María Angélica, 1088
BELOMONTE, Raquel C. de, 860
BELORADO, Lucas Manuel, 1262
BELTRAME, Andrés, 217, 260
BELTRAMI, Abel Rubén, 857b
BELTRÁN, Cristóbal, 1093a
BELTRÁN, José Luis Marcelo, 546, 549
BELTRÁN, Juan, 291
BELTRÁN, Luis, 85, 110, 179, 212, 278, 282, 332, 404, 583, 611, 615, 845, 1266
BELTRÁN, Susana, 695
BELTRÁN PLOS, Alfredo, 207
BELTRÁN PLOS, Leonardo, 207, 923
BELZONI, Guido, 332
BELL, Henry, 904
BELLÁN, José Pedro, 894, 1160, 1170, 1172, 1175, 1177, 1185, 1187, 1194, 1199
BELLIDO, Juan José, 284
BELLINA, Antonio, 561
BELLMAN, Rogelio Normando, 923
BELLO, Froilán P., 137
BELLO, Sebastián, 358

BELLOCQ, Adolfo, 44
BELLOCQ, Alfredo, 33
BELLÓN, Vicente, 1089
BELLONE, Liliana del Carmen, 653
BELLONI, José L., 1083, 1084
BELLOSO, Waldo, 857b
BELLUCCI, Leonel Damián, 810
BEMBERG, María Luisa, 857d
BENACOT, Narciso, 874
BENARÓS, León, 222, 660, 716, 722, 739, 758, 759, 798, 807, 812
BENAVENTE, Aniceto Juan Francisco (BENAVENTE Y OYARZÚN, F., pseud.), 811
BENAVENTE, Francisco de, 811, 813, 1270
BENAVENTE, Manuel, 1075, 1145, 1167
BENAVENTE, Marcolino del Carmelo, 171
BENAVENTE, Saulo, 889
BENAVENTE Y OYARZÚN, F., pseud.
    see BENAVENTE, Aniceto Juan Francisco
BENAVENTO, Gaspar Lucilo, 135, 191, 713, 739, 746, 800
BENAVIDES, Diego de, 186
BENAVIDES, Nazario, 179, 188, 283, 398, 446, 632
BENAVIDES, Washington, 1151, 1178
BENAVÍDEZ, Félix, 17b
BENAVÍDEZ, Gerónimo de, 555
BENAVÍDEZ, Miguel, 845
BENCE, Amelia, 893
BENECIANO, Luis, 1238
BENEDEK DE PANZONE, Agnes, 923
BENEDETTI, Albino, 1083
BENEDETTI, Juan J. P. de, 923
BENEDETTI, Mario, 806, 1151, 1155, 1158, 1177, 1178, 1184, 1189, 1192
BENEDIT, Luis Fernando, 36, 49, 55
BENEGAS, José León, 921
BENEGAS, Sebastián Ramón, 995a
BENEGAS, Tiburcio, 141, 212, 254, 278
BENEGAS DE TOLEDO, Pedro, 649a
BENENCIA, Julio Arturo, 521
BENETTI, Pablo, 258
BENGOA, Juan León, 894, 1172, 1185
BENGOCHEA, Miguel Angel, 37
BENGOECHEA, Marina, 19
BENGOLEA (family), 352
BENGOLEA, Abel, 3
BENGOLEA, Ismael, 268
BENGOLEA, Santiago, 268
BENINO, Nicolás del, 151
BENÍTEZ, 368
BENÍTEZ, Andrés, 1030
BENÍTEZ, Atilio J., 1006
BENÍTEZ, Eleuterio, 995a
BENÍTEZ, Fernán Elizardo, 941
BENÍTEZ, Gregorio, 947, 964
BENÍTEZ, Gumersindo, 947
BENÍTEZ, José Aniceto, 995a
BENÍTEZ, José Francisco, 268
BENÍTEZ, Juan Carlos, 49, 320
BENÍTEZ, Juan Vicente, 995a
BENÍTEZ, Justo Pastor, 943, 953, 964, 966, 1021, 1022
BENÍTEZ, Leopoldo A., 1014
BENÍTEZ, Mariano, 244, 268, 611, 629
BENÍTEZ, Olivio Sergio, 691
BENÍTEZ, Omar L., 652
BENÍTEZ, Pedro Pablo, 995a
BENÍTEZ, Robustiano, 998
BENÍTEZ, Rubén Angel, 688, 717
BENÍTEZ ARRIOLA, Eladio, 998

BENÍTEZ BALMACEDA, Juan, 995
BENÍTEZ CAPURRO, Alba luz (ALBA LUZ, pseud.), 1014
BENÍTEZ DE YEGROS, Silveria, 1000
BENÍTEZ PEREIRA, Ovidio, 1018a
BENÍTEZ TORRES, Donato, 191
BENÍTEZ VEGA, Trifón, 998
BENITO, Benjamín, 299
BENITZ, William (Mrs.)
    see ALLYN, Clara
BENOIT, Pedro, 6, 32, 332
BENOIT, Pierre, 6
BENSAYA, Roberto, 857b
BENTANCURT ARRIOLA, Héctor, 1210
BENTOS, 1079
BENVENUTI, Juan Carlos, 923
BENVENUTO, Carlos, 1184
BENZA, Juan B., 959
BENZA CARRERAS, Ricardo C., 954
BENZANO, Ramón V., 1123
BEOLETO, Juan José, 135
BEOVIDE, Argimiro Ramón, 1191
BERARDI DE LOAIZA, María Isabel, 691
BERAZATEGUI, Guillermo M., 652
BERCETCHE DE RODRÍGUEZ, María, 320
BERDIALES, Germán, 739, 744, 748, 751
BERDUC
    see VERDUC, Vicente Gregorio
BERDUC, Enrique, 121, 135
BERDUGO, Mariano, 912, 319
BERECIARTUA DE BORDERRE, Adriana, 1064
BERENGUER, Amanda, 1149, 1151, 1152, 1177, 1178
BERENGUER CARISOMO, Arturo, 688
BERESFORD, William Carr, 188, 272, 472, 514, 517, 552, 553, 587
BERETERVIDE, Francisca, 1083
BERG, Carlos, 68, 165
BERGALLI, Héctor, 69
BERGALLI, Víctor V., 1167
BERGALLO, José Ricardo, 191
BERGER, Louis, 32, 318, 866, 949, 960
BERGER, Luis
    see BERGER, Louis
BERGES, José, 943, 966, 983, 991, 1012
BERGESIO, Armando, 299
BERGHNMANS, Fernando S., 385
BERHEND, Juan Carlos, 684
BERINDUAGUE, Martín, 1075, 1127
BERISSO, Benjamín, 923
BERISSO, Cesáreo L., 1083
BERISSO, Emilio, 135, 800
BERISSO, Giovanni, 292
BERISSO, Luis, 1259
BERISSO, Nicanor, 139
BERISTAYN, Jorge de, 64
BERLINGIERI, Juan, 44, 58
BERMANN, Gregorio, 923
BERMANSOLO, Juan de, 555
BERMEJO, Ildefonso Antonio, 943, 964, 988, 1020
BERMÚDEZ, Antonio, 344, 358
BERMÚDEZ, Francisco, 284
BERMÚDEZ, Jorge, 19, 31, 45, 217
BERMÚDEZ, José, 922
BERMÚDEZ, José Francisco, 553
BERMÚDEZ, José María, 1089
BERMÚDEZ, Manuel, 551a
BERMÚDEZ, Manuel Francisco, 1095
BERMÚDEZ, Pedro Pablo, 1146, 1174, 1185
BERMÚDEZ, Sergio Wáshington, 1983
BERMÚDEZ, Washington P., 1075, 1146, 1174, 1185, 1188, 1199

BERMÚDEZ DE CASTRO, José, 332
BERMÚDEZ DE PEDRAZA, Francisco, 646
BERMÚDEZ EMPARANZA, Jorge, 89
BERNABÉ Y MADERO (family), 536
BERNABÓ, Héctor (CARYBÉ, pseud.), 18, 19, 25, 31
BERNAL, Alfredo, 998
BERNAL, Francisco, 32, 358
BERNAL, Juan, 186
BERNAL, Maese
    see MAESE BERNAL
BERNAL, Nicasio, 268
BERNÁLDEZ POLLEDO, José, 284, 611
BERNALTE DE LINARES, Antonio, 186
BERNARDES, Manuel, 965
BERNÁRDEZ, Enrique, 235
BERNÁRDEZ, Francisco Luis, 521, 664, 674, 678, 722,
    739, 748, 751, 759, 773, 782, 798, 803, 807,
    833
BERNÁRDEZ, Manuel P., 1083, 1146, 1168, 1170, 1174,
    1180, 1186, 1188, 1190, 1196, 1199, 1246
BERNÁRDEZ JACQUES, Elbio, 152a
BERNARDI (family), 168
BERNARDI, Anacleto, 121
BERNARDO, Mane, 19, 25
BERNARDO, Paquita, 868, 879
BERNARDO DEL CARPIO (family), 362
BERNAREGGI, Francisco, 19
BERNASA Y JEREZ, Juan, 1075, 1083
BERNASCONI, Irene, 923
BERNASCONI, Luis, 888
BERNASCONI, Oscar Luis, 691
BERNAT, Miguel, 923
BERNI, Antonio, 18, 19, 25, 27, 31, 33, 34, 36, 38,
    45, 49, 55, 56, 64
BERÓN, Elba, 879
BERÓN, Sebastián Celestino, 878, 1243
BERÓN DE ASTRADA, Antonio E., 121
BERÓN DE ASTRADA, Genaro, 121, 166, 196, 539, 650
BERRA, Francisco Antonio, 317
BERRAQUERO, José R., 299
BERRAZ, Guillermo, 923
BERRESFORD, Guillermo Carr
    see BERESFORD, Guillermo Carr
BERRETA, Tomás, 1073
BERRETTA, Horacio, 18, 31
BERRETTA, Luisa E., 652
BERRI, Carlos, 903
BERRO, Adolfo, 1052, 1071, 1146, 1174, 1179, 1188,
    1246
BERRO, Arturo, 1122
BERRO, Aureliano G., 1140
BERRO, Aurelio, 1146, 1174, 1188
BERRO, Bernardo Prudencio, 1079, 1091, 1109, 1110,
    1174, 1177, 1188, 1199
BERRO, Carlos A., 1075, 1083, 1127
BERRO, Pedro J., 254, 1122
BERRO, Roberto, 1073, 1083
BERRO ANTUÑA, Mariano, 1140
BERRONDO, Adeodato, 81, 222
BERRONDO, Máximo, 857d
BERRONDO, Valentín, 565
BERRUEZO, Juan José, 923
BERRUTI, Alejandro E., 778, 893
BERRUTTI, José J., 751
BERRYER, 79
BERT (family), 168
BERTEA DE MORONI, María Angélica, 684
BERTHELEMY, Carlos Jorge, 86
BERTHELEMY, Carlos Raymond, 86
BERTHOT, Noel, 960

BERTINI, Juan, 258
BERTOLE, Emilia, 19, 31, 58, 154, 678, 711, 751,
    762, 773, 783
BERTOLINI, Marta, 683a
BERTONI, Guillermo Tell, 943, 959, 963a, 965
BERTONI, Humberto, 683a
BERTONI, Moisés S., 943, 984a, 1012
BERTRÁN, José Luis, 1093a
BERTRÁN Y PEÑA, Cristóbal, 1093a
BERTRAND, Carlos María, 320
BERTRES, Felipe, 332
BERTRES, Manuel, 385
BERTRES, Raúl, 385
BERTUGNO, Rafael, 44
BERUETA, O., 560
BERUTI, Antonio Luis, 70, 85, 110, 258, 386, 404,
    411, 478, 574, 611, 873, 874
BERUTI, Arturo
    see BERUTTI QUIROGA, Arturo
BERUTI, Josué A., 923
BERUTI, Juan Manuel, 374
BERUTI, Pablo
    see BERUTTI, Pablo
BERUTI, Ricardo Luis, 299
BERUTTI, Antonio, 509
BERUTTI, Inés, 892
BERUTTI, Luis, 244
BERUTTI, Pablo, 207, 254
BERUTTI, Pablo Manuel, 113, 324, 864, 865, 873, 874
BERUTTI, Pablo María, 859
BERUTTI QUIROGA, Arturo, 207, 859, 864, 865, 867,
    873, 874
BESADA, Alfredo, 299
BESARES, Manuel, 433
BESASSO, Manuel V., 260
BESIO MORENO, Nicolás, 332, 923
BESLER, John A. (Mrs.)
    see ARMSTRONG, Frances Gertrude
BESNES IRIGOYEN, Juan Manuel, 28, 1063
BESSO, Santiago, 222
BESSONART, Cielo, 1088
BEST, Félix, 207
BESTARD, Blas Antonio, 963a
BESTARD, Eduardo Antonio, 963a
BESTARD, Jaime, 937, 939, 943, 964, 966
BETBEDER, Onofre, 81
BETHE, José Andreas, 344
BETINOTI, José Luis
    see BETTINOTI, José Luis
BETNAZA, María Enriqueta, 751, 762
BETTINI, Ana, 44
BETTINO, Olga, 932
BETTINOTI, José Luis, 759, 813, 818, 868, 878, 892,
    1243, 1247
BETTINOTTI, Saúl Isabelino, 923
BETURI, Antonio Luis, 479
BEUF, Francisco, 921a
BEVANS, James, 6
BEVANS, Santiago, 332
BEVERAGGI ALLENDE, Walter, 218
BEYHAUT, Gustavo, 1184
BIAGIONI, Amelia, 716, 717, 725, 739, 748, 758,
    759, 802, 807
BIALET MASSÉ, Juan, 332
BIALOSTOCKI, José, 238
BIALOUS, Sonia
    see BIALOUS KAMIENIECKI DE DUETRENIT, Sonia
BIALOUS KAMIENIECKI DE DUETRENIT, Sonia, 1210, 1211
BIANCO, Ernesto, 140
BIANCO, Francisco N., 878, 1243

BIANCO, José, 258
BIANCHI, Alfredo, 162
BIANCHI, Andrés E., 923
BIANCHI, Carlos, 258
BIANCHI, Edmundo, 894, 1083, 1185
BIANCHI, Enrique, 1145
BIANCHI, Jorge Emilio, 923
BIANCHIMANI, Michele, 139
BIANCHINI, Marcos, 781
BIANQUET, Benito (CACHAFAZ, El, pseud.), 862
BIASOTTI, Alfredo, 923
BIBALDO, Gregorio de, 1270
BIBOLINI, Alejandro, 954
BIBOLINI, Francisco, 258, 470, 921, 952
BICUDO, Francisco, 1130
BICHEBOIS, Luis Phillippe Alphonse, 28
BIDAOLA, Valentín, 874
BIDAURRE, Miguel de, 32
BIDEGAIN, Pedro, 69
BIEDERMANN (family), 168
BIEDMA, Aníbal J., 31
BIEDMA, Juan José, 122
BIEDMA, Manuel, 17b
BIEDMA, Manuel D., 68
BIEDMA, María Isabel, 762
BIEDMA PAZOS, Nicasio Antonio de, 284
BIGATTI, Alfredo, 18, 19, 21, 25, 33, 55, 64, 521
BIGNAMI, Ariel, 808, 817
BIGNOLI, Darío Pedro, 927
BIGNOZZI, Juana, 759
BILBAO, José Antonio, 1014, 1015, 1020, 1021, 1022, 1025
BILBAO, Luis, 194
BILBAO, Magdalena, 931
BILBAO, Rafael, 254
BILBAO LA VIEJA, Rodolfo, 122
BILONI, Heraldo, 923
BILLINGHURST, Mariano, 122
BILLINGHURST, Roberto, 574
BIMBI, José Laudino, 332
BINETTI, Mario, 674, 678, 722, 739, 751, 812
BINIMELIS, Antonio, 319
BIOY, Adolfo, 3, 650, 764
BIOY, Juan Bautista, 678, 751
BIOY CASARES, Adolfo (BUSTOS DOMECQ, H.; SUÁREZ
    LYNCH, B., pseuds.), 666, 668, 670, 685, 729,
    756, 806, 815, 816, 825, 829, 835
BIRABÉN, Federico, 332
BIRD, Poldy de, pseud.
    see LICHSTEININTEN DE BIRD, Leopoldina
BIRIOTTI, León, 1206, 1207
BIRITOS, Abel, 207
BIROT, José, 949
BIRRI, Fernando, 671
BISCAY, Acarette du
    see ACARETE DU BISCAY
BISCONTÍN, Pedro P., 207
BISCHOFF, George (Mrs.)
    see GILLIES, Clara
BISIO, Agustín R., 1151
BISOGNI, Luis B., 268
BLADH, Carlos Eduardo, 1141
BLAISTEIN, Isidoro, 706, 814
BLAISTEN, Raúl J., 923
BLANCAS, Alberto, 68
BLANCAS, Manuel, 91, 844, 1261
BLANCO (family), 1108
BLANCO, Delia Mirtha, 653, 654, 751
BLANCO, Eusebio, 207, 212
BLANCO, Félix, 893
BLANCO, Fidel María, 874

BLANCO, José, 666
BLANCO, José A., 218
BLANCO, José Gabino, 126
BLANCO, Juan Carlos
    see BLANCO ACEVEDO, Juan Carlos
BLANCO, Pedro, 1089
BLANCO, Rafael, 68
BLANCO, Rigoberto, 923
BLANCO, Silvestre, 1093a
BLANCO ACEVEDO, Eduardo, 1073
BLANCO ACEVEDO, Juan Carlos, 1072, 1073, 1075, 1083,
    1127, 1146, 1196, 1199
BLANCO ACEVEDO, Pablo, 1079
BLANCO AMORES, Carmen, 725
BLANCO CICERÓN, Lorenzo, 284
BLANCO DE AGUIRRE, Juan, 137
BLANCO ENCALADA, Manuel, 404, 611
BLANCO GERPE, José María, 284
BLANCO MÉNDEZ, José, 1210
BLANCO SILVA, Yuyo, 191
BLANCO VILLALTA, Jorge G., 154, 751
BLANCHARD, Everardo Eellis, 923
BLANCHE (family), 168
BLANCHET, Leopoldo, 949
BLANES, Juan Luis, 1046, 1047
BLANES, Juan Manuel, 25, 45, 59, 293, 521, 1046,
    1047, 1077, 1079, 1081, 1086, 1091, 1218
BLANES VIALE, Pedro, 1046, 1047, 1079, 1083
BLANIC, Félix, 960
BLANK (family), 168
BLANK, Ruperto, 32
BLANQUI, Andrés, 7, 32, 922
BLAQUIER, Juan José, 3, 332
BLAS, 1238
BLAS, Pablo, 385
BLASCHÈRE, Luis, 949
BLASETTI, Alberto Claudio, 671, 672, 717, 759, 812
BLASI, Alberto Oscar, 717, 739, 766
BLASI, Antonio (GAUCHO, El, pseud.), 860
BLASI BRAMBILLA, Alberto, 717, 739
BLASQUEZ DE VALVERDE, Juan, 1011
BLASS, Yago, 857c
BLASZKO, Martín, 25, 35, 55
BLAZQUEZ, Fabián, 684
BLÁZQUEZ, José Marcos, 954
BLÁZQUEZ, Santos, 520
BLÁZQUEZ DE VALVERDE, Juan Antonio, 984
BLEIER HOROVITZ, Eduardo, 1210
BLENDE, Barthelemy de, 949, 960
BLENGIO ROCCA, Juan, 1073, 1083
BLEST GANA, Alberto, 101
BLINDER, Olga, 938, 939
BLIXEN, Samuel, 894, 1075, 1079, 1127, 1146, 1185,
    1187, 1188, 1190, 1195, 1199, 1263
BLIXEN RAMÍREZ, José Pedro, 894
BLOMBERG, Héctor Pedro, 431, 521, 751, 759, 782,
    807, 1243, 1245, 1247
BLOSI, Aníbal, 258
BLOT, Pablo, 6
BLOUD, Carlos José, 517
BLUMENKRANTZ, Nelly, 923
BÓ, Armando, 857
BÓ PÉREZ, Fernando, 1089
BOADO, Edith, 299
BOADO DE GARRIGÓS, Crescencia, 924
BOAL, Augusto, 889
BOBADILLA, Pedro, 959
BOBADILLA, Simplicio, pseud.
    see GARCÍA, Serafín J.
BOBBIO, Condessa
    see CARRERAS SAGUIER, María Fulvia

BOBBIO, Pablo Gustavo, 37
BOBEDA, Carlos M., 954
BOBONE, Jorge F., 923
BOCAGE, Alberto C., 1159, 1183, 1186
BOCANEGRA, Francisca Jesusa de, 964, 968
BOCCANERA, Jorge Alejandro, 789
BOCERÍA, Esteban, 845
BOCKMANN, Susana Esther, 923
BODRATTO, Francisco, 907a
BOECHAT, Susana, 663
BOEDO, Mariano, 439, 457, 526, 545a, 574, 611, 621
    626
BOEDO, Mariano Joaquín, 126
BOEHRINGER, Emilio G., 923
BOELCKE, Osvaldo, 923
BOERGER, Alberto, 1067
BOERI, Juan A., 258, 844, 1266
BOERO, Felipe, 864, 865, 881, 883
BOERR, Carmen
    see BOERR, Juan de la Cruz del Carmen
BOERR, Juan de la Cruz del Carmen, 268
BOERR, Juan C., 268
BOETTNER, Juan Max, 963a, 1028
BOETTNER, Ricardo, 963a
BOGADO, Alcidiádes, 954
BOGADO, Benito Filemón, 995
BOGADO, Eugenio, 995a, 1020
BOGADO, Félix, 990
BOGADO, José Félix, 212, 268, 377, 386, 611, 947,
    963, 980, 1007, 1012
BOGADO, Jovino, 995
BOGADO, Salvador, 954
BOGARÍN, Francisco Xavier, 943, 987
BOGARÍN, Juan Sinforiano, 943, 959, 979, 983, 984a,
    1004, 1012, 1035, 1039
BOGETTI, Ricardo, 684
BOGGIANI, Guido, 191, 258, 943, 952, 963, 964, 1012
BOGGINO, Juan, 947, 963a
BOHM, Jorge Jacques, 923
BOHÓRQUEZ, Pedro de, 83
BOIDO, Guillermo, 750
BOISSIÈRE DE BALANSÁ, Jeanne (BALANSÁ, Juana de),
    949
BOJANICH MARCOVICH, Esteban, 923
BOLAÑOS, Luis de, 921, 943, 949, 964, 984a, 1012,
    1034, 1035, 1266
BOLDORI DE BALDUSSI, Rosa, 771
BOLÍVAR, Simón, 244, 379, 453, 553, 608, 761
BOLOGNINI, Astor, 874
BOLOQUI, Pedro, 1243
BOLSON, Alarico, 731
BOLTOVSKOY, Esteban, 923
BOLLINI, Carlos Guido, 923
BOLLINI, Francisco P., 68, 103, 258
BOLLO, Sarah, 1151, 1169, 1179, 1187, 1199, 1217
BOMAN, Eric, 713
BOMBAL, Susana, 683a, 729
BOMÓN, Enrique, 268
BONCALZA, Enrique C. O., 923
BONAFINA, Roque, 781
BONARD, Rustam Tirso, 923
BONASSO, Luis, 1083
BONASTRE, Valerio, 92
BONAUDI DELGADO, José Antonio, 1210
BONAUDI DELGADO, Oscar, 1210
BONAVITA, Luis Pedro, 1184
BONAVITA, María Adela, 1151, 1187
BONAVITA SALGUERO, Luis Pedro, 1210
BONAZZOLA, Alcira, 711, 751, 762
BOND HEAD, Francisco, 834

BONDESIO, Pedro, 923
BONDONI, Osmar Luis, 658
BONELLI, Fortunato, 268
BONELLI, María Teresa, 299
BONEO, Juan Agustín, 910
BONEO, Martín, 125, 912, 921
BONEO, Martín Alberto, 739, 812
BONEO, Martín L., 7, 19, 31, 32, 59
BONET, Carmelo M., 743, 751
BONETTI, Valentín, 198
BONETTI DE STIPANICIC, María, 923
BONEVARDI, Marcelo, 31, 36, 38, 55
BONFIGLIO, Jorge, 787
BONFLIGLIOLI, Alberto F., 923
BONGIORNO, Raúl, 44
BONGIOVANNI, Jorge, 1039
BONIFACIO, Benjamín, 565
BONIFAI, Domingo, 713
BONIFANTI, Decoroso, 258
BONÍN, José María, 954
BONINI, Norberto, 653
BONIS, Salvador de, 1039
BONO, Juan, 857c
BONOMÉ, Alejandro, 31, 64
BONOME, Rodrigo, 18, 19, 31, 64
BONOMINI, Angel, 756, 799, 814
BONORINO UDAONDO, Carlos, 923
BONPLAND, Aimé Jacques Alexandre Goujaud, 4, 153,
    166, 293, 373, 512, 574, 844, 885, 943, 949,
    960, 1012, 1261
BONPLAND, Amado
    see BONPLAND, Aimé Jacques Alexandre Goujaud
BONPLAND (Madame), 960
BONZI PENAYO, Antonio, 1017
BOOZ, Mateo, pseud.
    see CORREA, Miguel Angel
BORCOSQUE, Carlos, 857, 858
BORCHE COSTA, Carlos María, 1210
BORDA, Diego de, 968
BORDA, Facundo, 268
BORDA, José, 108
BORDA, Juan de, 186
BORDA, Julio Martín, 923
BORDA, María Matilde, 1082
BORDA, Osvaldo, 36
BORDA, Pedro José, 1082
BORDA, Simeón, 191
BORDABEHERE, Enzo, 259
BORDABEHERE, Ismael C., 923
BORDABERRY, Domingo R., 1073
BORDAS, Alejandro Francisco, 923
BORDAZAR TELECHEA, Juan Carlos, 1088
BORDEGARAY DE BARBERÍA, Dolores, 320
BORDENAVE, Enrique, 959
BORDERRE, Juan Pedro, 1064
BORDES, Severo, 949
BORDOLI, Domingo Luis (CASTELLI, Luis, pseud.),
    1148, 1149, 1177, 1184, 1186, 1196
BORDÓN, Arturo, 947
BORDÓN, Bernardino, 982
BORDÓN, Clotilde, 947
BORDÓN, Rodolfo, 947
BORDÓN DEL PUERTO, Rufo, 998
BOREAN, Walter, 299
BORELLI, Martín Adolfo, 653, 654
BORELLO, Angel V., 923
BORELLO, Rodolfo A., 683a
BORES, Francisco, 254
BORGARELLO, Miguel Pablo, 24
BORGES (Colonel), 13

BORGES, Jorge Luis, 140, 152a, 232, 235, 246, 652, 660, 666, 668, 670, 674, 685, 688, 697, 722, 729, 737, 739, 741, 743, 745a, 751, 754, 756, 759, 764, 769, 772, 773, 782, 798, 799, 801, 803, 806, 807, 816, 825, 829, 833, 835
BORGES, Juan Francisco, 166
BORGES, Norah
    see BORGES DE TORRE, Norah
BORGES DE TORRE, Norah, 19, 23, 25, 31, 36, 50
BORGET, Auguste, 28
BORGHINI, Barberi, 258
BORIS, Rodolfo Enrique, 878
BORJA, Cecilia, 751
BORJA, Diego de, 910
BORJA, Francisco de, 529a, 910
BORJA, José Antonio, 332
BORJA, Olegario, 995a
BORJA CORREAS, Francisco de, 179, 207
BORJA DE LA ROZA, Francisco 283
BORJA, Francisco de, 910
BORJA GUIÑAZÚ, Francisco de, 254
BORJA MAGARIÑOS, Francisco de, 1236
BORJA PINTO BARRAQUERO, Francisco de, 207
BORKOWSKA DE MIKUSINSKI, Eva, 652
BORLA, Enrique, 24
BORLA, Héctor, 36
BORMIDA, Marcelo, 923
BOROA, Diego de, 319
BORQUES, Baldomero A., 1075
BORRA, Diego de, 989
BORRARO, Luis, 31
BORRAS, José, 222
BORRAS, Pablo E., 923
BORRAZÁS, Rafael, 1089
BORREGO DE BENAVIDES, Telésfora, 283, 931
BORREGUERO, Pedro, 319
BORRONI, Nelly
    see BORRONI MacDONALD, Nelly
BORRONI MacDONALD, Nelly, 691, 744a, 785, 824
BORSANI, Mario Rafael, 691
BORTAGARAY, Mario Chapo, 191
BORTHIRY, Enrique David, 695
BORUS, Adriano, 332
BORZONE, Alberto Juan, 41
BORZONE, Santiago, 13
BOSCO, Alfonso, 59
BOSCO, Eduardo Jorge, 688, 722, 739, 758, 759, 807, 812
BOSCO, Guillermo Andrés, 923
BOSCO, Juan, 176, 907a, 1039
BOSCO, María Angélica, 668, 822
BOSCO GAIBISSO, Amnerys, 1088
BOSCH, Beatriz
    see BOSCH VINELLI, Julia Beatriz
BOSCH, Carlos A., 55
BOSCH, Francisco Basiliano, 17b, 191
BOSCH, Gerardo, 496
BOSCH, Gonzalo, 718
BOSCH, Horacio Ernesto, 923
BOSCH, José María, 844, 1261
BOSCH, Mariano, 1246
BOSCH, Mariano G., 431
BOSCH, Miguel, 860
BOSCH VINELLI, Julia Beatriz, 521, 609
BOSCHÈRE, Pierre de (BOSQUIER), 949, 960
BOSIO, José V., 237
BOSONETTO, Julio César, 923
BOSQ, Juan M., 923
BOSQUE MORENO, Lucía, 931

BOSQUIER
    see BOSCHÈRE, Pierre de
BOSSHARDT, Juan Augusto, 874
BOSSI, Bartolomé, 28, 258
BOTANO, Helvio I. (POROTO, pseud.), 644a, 645, 664, 769
BOTANA, Jacinto, 207
BOTANA, Jaime A. (JAIMOTE BOTANILLA, pseud.), 769
BOTANA, Meme, 645
BOTANA, Natalicio Félix, 644a, 645
BOTANA, Poroto
    see BOTANA, Helvio I.
BOTANA, Tito, 645
BOTANILLA, Jaimote, pseud.
    see BOTANA, Jaime A.
BOTELLI, José Juan, 653, 654
BOTELLI, Juan J., 680, 830
BOTELLO, José, 496
BOTET, Felipe, 268
BOTO, Martha, 49
BOTRILL, Norman, 1045
BOTTA, Julio César, 37
BOTTANA, Luis Santiago, 1122
BOTTARO, José María, 258, 910
BOTTERO GUTIÉRREZ, Guillermo, 1210
BOTTI, Italo, 19, 31, 33
BOTTIGNOLI, Justo, 1039
BOTTO, Bartolomé, 681
BOU, Laico, 41
BOUBÉE DE DUFAU, María Dolores, 320
BOUCHARD, Hipólito, 12, 14, 16, 282, 371, 438, 521, 611
BOUCHENTHAL, pseud.
    see BUSCHENTHAL, José de
BOUCHET, José, 19, 51, 521
BOUCHET BLANCO, José, 284
BOUCHEZ, Pedro, 156
BOUDIER, Jacobo, 6, 332
BOUE DE DOMECQ CHANTRY, María Guillermina, 320
BOUGAINVILLE, Luis Antonio de, 922
BOUQUET ROLDÁN, Carlos, 68
BOUQUET Y ARIAS, Esteban, 284
BOURBAND, Ernesto, 135, 800
BOURDETTE, Josefa, 949, 956
BOURDIEU, Juan Antonio, 878, 1243
BOUREL, César A., 135
BOURGUET, Lola S. B. de, 711, 751, 762
BOURKE, Richard, 587
BOURQUIN, Fernando, 923
BOUSIRÓN, León, 949
BOUZÓN, Casimiro, 1089
BOVE, Giacomo, 292
BOVE, José, 889
BOVE, Santiago, 258
BOVE, Vicente, 751
BÓVEDA PÉREZ, Xavier, 284
BOWEN, Albert, 904
BOWLES, Guillermo
    see BOWLES, William
BOWLES, William, 561, 573, 580
BOY, pseud.
    see SOTO, Antonio
BOYD, Sarah M. (Mrs. Caleb J. Camp), 323
BOYSO, Tomás José de, 496
BOZÁN, Olinda, 893
BOZÁN, Sofía, 877, 879
BOZARELLI, Domingo, 860
BOZZANO, José, 952
BOZZANO, José Alfredo, 954, 1006

BOZZANO CARDOZO, Jorge A., 954
BRABO, Francisco Javier, 284
BRACAMONTE, Juan de, 186
BRACAMONTE, Pedro, 144
BRACCIRO PARREÑO, Aldo, 1088
BRACCO, Angel Norberto, 923
BRACCO, Rodolfo F., 41
BRACELI, Rodolfo E., 683a
BRACO, Fernando, 896
BRACO DE RIVERO Y BORREA, Juan, 910
BRACHETTO-BRIAN, Domingo, 923
BRADE (family), 331
BRADEN, Spruille, 170, 530, 963
BRAGA, Luis F., 951
BRAGGIO DE CASTELLO, Elena Dominga, 320
BRAGGIO DE GALLI, Sarah R., 320
BRAGGIO DE PUZZI, Margarita Hermida, 320
BRAIDA, Telémaco, 1083
BRAIDOT FERRANTE BLÁS, Adolfo, 1210
BRAIER, Bernardo, 923
BRAIER, León, 923
BRAMBILA, Fernando, 17a, 28, 32
BRANCATO, Bartolomé Julio, 299
BRANDÁN CARAFFA, Alfredo, 739, 759, 773, 833
BRANDENBERGER (family), 168
BRANDÓN, Ireneo, 1089
BRANDÓN, Manuel, 1089
BRANDÓN, Ramón, 1089
BRANDSEN, Carlos Luis Federico, 244, 386, 404, 433, 499, 529, 583
BRANDSEN, Federico de
    see BRANDSEN, Carlos Luis Federico
BRANDY, Carlos, 1151, 1177, 1178, 1179
BRASANELLI, José, 7, 32, 952
BRASCÓ, Miguel A., 658, 671, 739, 759, 769, 807
BRASSANELLI, José, 922
BRASSECO, J. Ernesto, 1243
BRATT DE OLIVEIRA CÉZAR, Judy, 46
BRAUN MENÉNDEZ, Armando, 521, 609
BRAUN MENÉNDEZ, Eduardo, 923
BRAUSE, Luis Alberto, 1073
BRAVO, Ernesto Mario, 560
BRAVO, Jaime F., 1083
BRAVO, Mario, 219, 260, 503, 669, 679, 751, 759, 782, 817, 1246, 1247
BRAVO, Rodolfo I., 699
BRAVO DÁVILA Y CARTAGENA, Juan 529a
BRAVO DÁVILA Y CARTAGENA, Julián, 910
BRAVO DE ZAMORA, Juan, 914
BRAY, Arturo, 1006, 1021, 1022
BRAYER, Lucien de, 28
BRAYER, Miguel, 104
BRECCIA, Alberto, 299
BRECIANOS, Francisco, 32
BRECIANOS, Hernando, 32
BREDAEL, Jan Peeter Van, 1046
BRENA, Fanny, 135
BRENNER, Rodolfo R., 923
BREQUE, José Luis, 254
BREST, Nicomedos, 268
BRETT, Peircy, 28
BRETTES, M. de, 949
BREVETTA RODRÍGUEZ, Miguel A., 804
BREYER, Alberto, 923
BRIAN, Santiago, 332, 904
BRIANTE, Miguel, 694
BRIDGES, Tomás, 99
BRIE DE LOUSTAN, Juan Bautista, 1135
BRIEST, Eckart, 954
BRIEUX, Jorge A., 923
BRIEUX DE MANDIROLA, Olga Alda M. Octavia, 923

BRIGLIA, Mario, 671, 812
BRIGLIA, Tomás Enrique, 671, 812
BRIGNIEL, José, 318
BRIGNOLE, Antonio, 191
BRIGNOLE DE RODRÍGUEZ, Jesús Josefina, 320
BRIGNOLO, Ricardo Luis, 871
BRIHUEGA DE ABERASTAIN, Magdalena, 930, 931
BRILLAUD, Roberto, 683a
BRILLI, Juan, 6
BRINE, Ottaviano de, 292
BRIONES, Carola, 680, 725, 830
BRIONES, Francisca, 887
BRIONES, Juana, 44
BRITEZ, Francisco, 954
BRITEZ, Manuel, 954
BRITEZ CABALLERO, Juan B., 963a
BRITO DEL PINO (family), 1108
BRITO DEL PINO, Eduardo, 1075
BRITOS, Justo Pastor, 998
BRITOS, Leonardo, 998
BRITOS SERRAT, Alberto, 1088
BRIZUELA, Casildo, 998
BRIZUELA, Francisco Antonio, 921, 953, 959, 1006, 1012
BRIZUELA, Harnodio Efraín, 954
BRIZUELA, Luis, 947
BRIZUELA, Tomás, 188, 242, 283
BRIZUEÑA, Sinforiano, 947
BRIZZI, Ary, 35, 36, 38, 55
BRIZZI, José, 653, 654
BROCHERO, José Gabriel, 115a, 244, 921
BRODERSEN, Anamaría, 700
BRODTKORB, Alejo, 923
BROEN, Martín, 923
BRONCINI BELTRAMI, Esteban, 1210
BROOK, Federico, 25
BROQUA, Alfonso, 1206, 1207, 1208
BROWN (family), 361
BROWN, Elisa, 237, 928
BROWN, Frank, 886
BROWN, Guillermo, 4, 12, 14, 16, 17, 17a, 70, 82, 85, 141, 143, 166, 176, 237, 244, 282, 381, 386, 404, 420, 438, 448, 459, 466, 475, 478, 499, 509, 514, 521, 577, 611, 650, 1091
BROWN, William
    see BROWN, Guillermo
BRUCHER, Enrique H., 923
BRUCHER, Félix José, 923
BRUCHER, Heinz, 923
BRUDNER, Max, 954
BRUEL PÉRÈS, Nathalie, 1014
BRUERA PEREDA, Leopoldo Carlos, 1210
BRUGHETTI, Faustino Eugenio, 19, 25, 31
BRUGHETTI, Romualdo, 239, 716, 739, 743, 746, 798, 805
BRUGIER, Eduardo, 319
BRUGUEZ, José María, 974, 991
BRULAND, Víctor, 852
BRUM, 1059
BRUM, Alfeo, 1073
BRUM, Baltasar, 1069, 1073, 1079, 1083, 1087, 1109
BRUM, Blanca Luz, 1151, 1153
BRUMANA, Herminia C., 154, 751, 926
BRUNET, José, 914
BRUNET, Juan C., 1085
BRUNI, Demetrio R., 299
BRUNIARD, Mele, 44
BRUNINI, Vicente C., 923
BRUNO, Ana María, 44
BRUNO, Arturo Alejandro, 923

BRUNO, Héctor, 440
BRUNO DE RIVAROLA, Francisco, 126
BRUNO DEL PILAR, Ramón, 845
BRUNO GARCÍA BARÓN, Jorge Abel, 1210
BRUNORI DE CIVILOTTI, María Lidia, 691, 781
BRUÑEL, Manuel, 284
BRUSAU, René, 31, 191
BRUSQUETTI, Francisco, 951
BRUSSA, Carlos, 894, 1185, 1209
BRUYAN, Próspero, 6
BRUZZONE, Horacio N., 3
BRUZZONE DE SCARONE, Ana, 1083
BRY, Teodoro de, 28
BUCARELLI, Francisco de Paula
    see BUCARELLI Y URSÚA, Francisco de Paula
BUCARELLI Y URSÚA, Antonio María, 258
BUCARELLI Y URSUA, Francisco de Paula, 258, 472, 570
BUCCI, Domingo, 31, 41
BUCETA FIGUEROA, José, 284, 332
BUCICH, Antonio J., 681, 751
BUCICH, Delia, 31
BUCK, Elsa, 932
BUCHARDO, Hipólito, 166, 244, 386
BUCHIGNANI, Pedro, 823
BUCHINGER, María, 923
BUDINI, Miguel Angel, 24
BUENAVENTURA, pseud.
    see QUIROGA CARRIL, Ventura
BUENGIORNO, Patricia, 787
BUENO, Justo David 995a
BUERO, Enrique Eduardo, 1083
BUERO, Juan Antonio, 1083, 1190
BUFANO, Alfredo R., 207, 521, 664, 683a, 722, 739,
    748, 751, 759, 782, 807, 963, 1243, 1247
BUFFA, José, 87
BUFFAZ, Armando (family), 168
BUFFAZ, Honorio (family), 168
BUFFÉ, José María, 4
BUFFO, Guido, 154
BUFFO ALLENDE, Leonor, 154
BUFFO SILVEIRA, José María, 1210
BUGLIOT, José Américo, 894
BUHIGAS Y PRAT, Ulpiano, 1095
BUITRAGO, Guillermo, 19, 31
BUITRAGO, Pedro, 126, 385
BUIZA, Cristóbal de, 556
BUJADOS, Manuel, 284
BUJALDÓN, Aurelio, 683a
BULA, Clotilde A., 923
BULEWSKI, Juan Valerio, 238
BULNES, Gonzalo, 955
BULNES, Juan Pablo, 545a, 552
BULNES, Manuel, 398
BULRICH, Santiago, 658
BULLO, Sebastián, 974, 994, 1003
BULLRICH, Adolfo J., 103, 210
BULLRICH, Augusto Guillermo Adolfo, 210
BULLRICH, Silvina, 666, 674, 729
BUNGE, Alejandro, 293
BUNGE, Carlos, 332
BUNGE, Carlos Octavio, 167, 246, 317, 650, 714, 751,
    1246
BUNGE, Emilio V., 103, 254
BUNGE, Ernesto, 6
BUNGE, Mario, 923
BUNGE, Rodolfo, 68
BUNGE DE GÁLVEZ, Delfina, 664, 751, 762
BUÑO, Indalecio
    see BUÑO LOUREIRO, Indalecio
BUÑO LOUREIRO, Indalecio, 1210, 1211

BUONAVOGLIA, Rafael, 892
BUONGERMINI, Amadeo, 954
BUONOCORE, Domingo J., 762
BUQUET, Sebastián, 1083
BURACHIK, Moisés, 923
BURANELLI, Miguel, 894
BURBURO (family), 972
BURDENSKI, Diether, 923
BURELA, Alejandro, 625
BURELA Y SAAVEDRA, Luis, 625
BUREN DE SANGUINETTI, Luisa, 751
BURGAS PÉREZ, Francisco de, 97
BURGÉS, Francisco, 318, 1031
BURGHI, Juan, 739, 751, 816, 1167
BURGOA VIDELA, Miguel, 19, 31
BURGOS, Ciriaco, 1084
BURGOS, Fausto, 152a, 154, 680, 683a, 707, 713,
    779, 830, 1245, 1246
BURGOS, Joaquín, 713
BURGOS, Juan Jacinto, 923
BURGOS, Mario Héctor, 923
BURGOS MÁRQUEZ, Efraim, 781
BURGUES, Jorge, 1262
BURIANO, Atilio, 1045
BURKART, Arturo E., 923
BURKE, James Florence, 587
BURMEISTER, Carlos Germán Conrado, 28, 116, 141,
    207, 208
BURMEISTER, Germán
    see BURMESITER, Carlos Germán Conrado
BURONE, C. A., 218
BURT, Michael, 938
BURTON, Mildred, 37
BURZACO, Domingo de, 344
BURZACO, José Ramón de, 344
BURZIO, Humberto F., 521
BUSANICHE, José Luis, 609
BUSCH, Rodolfo Hermann, 923
BUSCHENTHAL, José de (BOUCHENTHAL, pseud.), 195,
    1120, 1253
BUSCHIAZZO, Juan A., 6, 258
BUSCHIAZZO, Mario, 521
BUSIGNANI, Mario, 713, 722, 730, 739, 758, 759, 831
BUSIGNANI, Vicente Cosme, 923
BUSSAID, Alberto, 889
BUSTAMANTE, Calixto
    see BUSTAMANTE CARLOS INCA, Calixto
BUSTAMANTE, Francisco de, 32
BUSTAMANTE, Jerónimo, 649a
BUSTAMANTE, Joaquín T. (CHANI LAO, pseud.), 760
BUSTAMANTE, José C., 1112
BUSTAMANTE, José E., 222
BUSTAMANTE, José Luis, 268, 560
BUSTAMANTE, José María, 921
BUSTAMANTE, Manuel Basilio, 1110
BUSTAMANTE, Pedro de, 555, 1112, 1134, 1146
BUSTAMANTE CARLOS INCA, Calixto
    see CONCOLORCORVO, pseud.
BUSTAMANTE Y GUERRA, José de, 17a, 1136
BUSTILLO (family), 338
BUSTILLO, José María, 3, 17b, 254, 338, 391, 521
BUSTILLO Y CEVALLOS, José Manuel, 338
BUSTINGORRI, Miguel H., 1243
BUSTO, Eduardo Hernani del, 923
BUSTO, Eugenio del, 209
BUSTO, Gumersindo, 284
BUSTO, José G. del, 1146, 1174, 1199
BUSTO, Melchor, 1089
BUSTOS (family), 352
BUSTOS, Cenobia, 931
BUSTOS, César, 663

BUSTOS, Francisco Ignacio, 188
BUSTOS, Francisco Vicente, 83, 445
BUSTOS, José Esteban, 545a
BUSTOS, Juan Bautista, 89, 166, 244, 282, 283, 316, 489, 496, 545a, 552, 554, 574, 632
BUSTOS, Juan de, 555
BUSTOS, Julia, 154, 751, 762
BUSTOS, Manuel Vicente, 83
BUSTOS, Miguel Angel, 759
BUSTOS, Paco, 894
BUSTOS, Pedro de, 555
BUSTOS, Rodolfo Adalberto, 41
LUSTOS, Silverio, 998
BUSTOS CÁCERES, Miguel, 874, 878
BUSTOS DE EMMA, Paula, 810
BUSTOS DE FUNES, María Josefa, 254
BUSTOS DE LARA, María Josefa, 112
BUSTOS DE QUIROGA, Avelina, 751
BUSTOS DOMECQ, Honorio, pseud.
     see BORGES, Jorge Luis; BIOY CASARES, Adolfo
BUSTOS FIERRO, Raúl, 766
BUSTOS VOCOS, Luara, 44
BUSTOS Y FERREYRA, Zenón, 910
BUSTOS ZENTENO, Vicente, 878
BUTE, Esperillo, 49
BUTELER, Alfonso, 910
BUTELER, Leopoldo, 910
BUTLER, Cecilia, 923
BUTLER, Guillermo, 19, 24, 31, 33, 55, 64, 154
BUTLER, Horacio I., 18, 19, 23, 25, 34, 36, 38, 49, 50, 53, 55, 64, 1218
BUTSCHKOWSKYJ, Miguel, 923
BUTTARO, Enrique, 719, 894
BUTTI, Leonor G. de, 702
BUTTNER, Adolfo F., 6
BUTTY, Enrique, 332, 923
BUXAREO (family), 1108
BUXAREO DE CIBILS, Plácida, 1093a
BUXAREO ORIBE, Félix, 1067, 1083
BUZZI, Domingo, 73
BUZZINI, Juan, 211
BYNON, Santiago Jorge, 82

CAABURE, 977
CAAMAÑO, Roberto, 865, 882, 883
CAARUPE, 977
CABADAL MARTÍNEZ, Juan Antonio, 284
CABALLERO, 1003
CABALLERO, Bernardino, 943a, 948, 954, 963, 974, 975, 980, 983, 984a, 993, 1004, 1008, 1011, 1012
CABALLERO, Jorge Carlos, 706
CABALLERO, Juan, 963
CABALLERO, Martha, 684
CABALLERO, Pedro Juan, 966, 979, 980, 984a, 1004
CABALLERO, Pedro León, 995a
CABALLERO, Pedro P., 982
CABALLERO, Ricardo, 431, 565
CABALLERO, Teresa, 817
CABALLERO, Víctor Rafael, 998
CABALLERO ALVAREZ, Bernadino, 998
CABALLERO BAZÁN, Juan, 1011
CABALLERO DE AÑASCO, Juan, 1011, 1030
CABALLERO DE FONVIELLE, El
     see FONVIELLE
CABALLERO IRALA, Basiliano, 1006, 1014
CABALLERO RUIZ, José Gabriel, 1210
CABALLOS, Amado J., 189
CABALLOS, Carlos Raúl, 684
CABANE (Sister), 960
CABANILLAS, Filemón, 921

CABAÑAS, Esteban, 1015, 1017, 1020, 1021, 1022, 1025
CABAÑAS, Manuel Atanasio, 1012
CABASSA, Luis, 258
CABELLO, Leodegar, 954
CABELLO, Manuel, 998
CABELLO Y MESA, Antonio, 644
CABERO, Telésforo, 207, 864, 874
CABEZA DE VACA, Alvar Núñez
     see NÚÑEZ CABECA DE VACA, Alvar
CABEZAS, Juan de, 344
CABEZAS, Simón, 186
CABEZOLA, Sebastiano, 292
CABIEDES, Luis María, 73
CABOT, John, 258, 292, 1203
CABOT, Juan Manuel, 283, 611, 629
CABOT, Sebastian, 151, 258, 292, 406, 462, 471, 472, 477, 519, 528, 535, 952, 984, 989, 1012, 1203, 1231, 1232, 1238
CABOTO, Giovanni
     see CABOT, John
CABOTO, Juan
     see CABOT, John
CABOTO, Sebastian
     see CABOT, Sebastian
CABRAL, Juan Bautista, 244, 404
CABRAL, Lauro, 68
CABRAL, Máximo
CABRAL, Pedro, 6
CABRAL, Ramón (PLATERO, Ramón, pseud.), 566
CABRAL, Remigio, 974
CABRAL, Valentín, 32
CABRAL BEJARANO, Antonio, 1046, 1047
CABRAL DE AYALA, Juan, 186
CABRAL DE AYALA, Sebastián, 186
CABRAL MASCARI DE DURÁN CANO, Alejandra Isabel, 1088
CABRÉ, Francisco Ramón, 319
CABRED, Domingo, 844, 847, 1261
CABREJAS, Elena, 787
CABRER, José María, 7, 332, 496, 922, 1229
CABRER Y SUÑER, Carlos, 332
CABRERA, Alonso, 472, 504, 984, 1005, 1238
CABRERA, Ana S. de, 154, 217, 882, 893
CABRERA, Angel Lulio, 923
CABRERA, Aníbal, 565
CABRERA, Carmelo, 1116
CABRERA, Diego de, 556
CABRERA, Enrique, 565
CABRERA, Félix, 1006, 1012
CABRERA, Francisca, 1000
CABRERA, Jerónimo Luis de, 89, 205, 244, 472, 522, 527, 570, 1230
CABRERA, José Antonio, 313, 439, 457, 526, 621, 626
CABRERA, Luis de, 83
CABRERA, Mariano, 254
CABRERA, Miguel Jerónimo de, 6, 144
CABRERA, Pablo, 921
CABRERA, Pilar, 1064
CABRERA, Sarandy
     see CABRERA PIÑÓN, Sarandy
CABRERA, Segundo P. 874
CABRERA, Tomás, 28, 32
CABRERA CARDUZ, Vicente, 1017
CABRERA HAEDO, Roque, 998
CABRERA PÉREZ, Vicente, 1094
CABRERA PIÑÓN, Sarandy, 1151, 1177, 1178, 1179, 1210
CABRERA RUIZ, Silvio, 998
CABRERA SORRONDEGUI, Ariel Ebers, 1210
CABRERA Y CABRERA, José Antonio, 611
CABRERA Y GARAY, Jerónimo Luis de, 521
CABRERA Y TOLEDO, Jerónimo Luis de, 144

CABRINI, Rómulo Luis, 923
CACCIA, Santiago, 258
CACCIALUPI, Abelardo, 139
CACCIANIGA, Pablo, 6
CÁCERES, Alberto, 1270
CÁCERES, Andrés, 683a
CÁCERES, Dérlis, 998
CÁCERES, Espiridión, 998
CÁCERES, Esther de, 1151, 1152, 1153, 1177, 1178,
   1179, 1184, 1187, 1199, 1217
CÁCERES, Felipe de, 504, 951, 984, 989, 992, 1011,
   1232, 1270
CÁCERES, Francisco, 887, 888
CÁCERES, Héctor, 8
CÁCERES, José de Jesús, 1006
CÁCERES, Luis, 166, 195
CÁCERES, Manuel C., 565
CÁCERES, Marcos F., 268
CÁCERES, Nicanor, 387
CÁCERES CARÍSIMO, Luis, 947
CÁCERES DE THOMAS, Carmen, 943a
CÁCERES DE ZAYAS, Agustina, 953
CÁCERES SANABRIA, José, 998
CÁCERES ZORRILLA, Cirilio, 941, 947
CACIOLO, Josefa, 652
CACIOLO, Nicolás, 87
CACHAFAZ, El, pseud.
   see BIANQUET, Benito
CACHEIRO, Manuel, 1095, 1140
CACHEIRO DE DI MARTINO, Lía Enriqueta, 320
CACHEIRO DE DI MARTINO, María Esther, 320
CACHO, pseud.
   see PARIETTI, Roberto
CADENAZZI, Edgarda, 1187
CADÍCAMO, Enrique Domingo, 660, 710, 801, 871, 877
CADOGAN, Henry, 587
CADOGAN, León, 943, 947, 962
CAETANO, Eusebio Narciso, 1210
CAFFARENA DE BALESTRA, Clara I., 681
CAFFERATA, Francisco, 19, 21, 258
CAFFERATA, Juan M., 258
CAFRUNE, Jorge, 177a, 857b
CAGGIANO, Antonio Anastasio, 813, 818, 878, 910
CAGGIANO, César A., 33, 58, 511
CAGLIERO, Juan, 258, 287, 907a
CAGLIOTI, Eduardo, 299
CAGNONE, Nicola, 292
CAHEN SALABERRY, Enrique, 857, 858
CAHUAPE DE CATALANO, Delia Esther, 320
CAILLET BOIS, Horacio, 664
CAILLET-BOIS, Julio César, 688
CAILLET-BOIS, Ricardo R., 265, 381a, 521, 609
CAILLIAIT, María Celia, 663
CAIRNIE, Antonio Guillermo, 923
CAJAL, Alberto, 653, 654
CAJARAVILLA, 179
CAJARAVILLA, Miguel, 254, 478, 479, 611
CAL, Bernabé de la, 344
CAL, Feliciano, 1017
CALABRÉS, Juan, 151
CALABRESE, Miguel, 320
CALABRESE, Rogelio, 652
CALABRÓ, Domingo S., 882
CALAMARO, Eduardo S., 812
CALANDRELLI, Matías, 152a, 258
CALANDRELLI, Susana, 664, 707, 711, 751, 762, 773,
   783
CALATRONI, Carlos J., 923
CALAZA COUSO, José María, 284
CALCAGNO, Eduardo N., 1065
CALCAÑO, Elsa, 882, 883

CALCAVECCHIA, Benone, 1206, 1207
CALCENA, Carlos, 959
CALDARERA, José, 952
CALDAS, José A., 1212
CALDERA PEREIRA, Juan Pedro, 1210
CALDERÓN, Casimiro, 254
CALDERÓN, Gerónimo, 126
CALDERÓN, José Gregorio, 158, 222
CALDERÓN, Juan Pascual, 222
CALDERÓN, Vicente, 331
CALDERÓN DE LA BARCA, José María, 496
CALDERÓN DE LA BARCA, Pedro, 611
CALDERÓN DE SANABRIA, Mencia, 1042, 1203
CALDERÓN FERREYRA, H. E., 1243
CALDERÓN PANDO, José María, 662
CALFUCURÁ (PIEDRA AZUL), 454
CALGARO, Orlando Florencio, 788
CALI, Américo, 683a, 739, 831
CALI DE MOLINELLI, Graciela, 683a
CALIFANO, Norberto, 889
CALINO, Carlos, 751
CALIXTO, el Ñato, pseud.
   see DE MARÍA, Alcides
CALMELS, Augusto Pablo, 923
CALNY, Eugenia, 814, 815, 823
CALO BERRO, Ofelia, 1187
CALOU, Juan Pedro, 678, 739, 759
CALUSIO, Juan Carlos, 923
CALVELO CASTRO, Antonio, 1089
CALVETTI, Jorge, 664, 713, 716, 722, 730, 739, 758,
   759, 812
CALVIMONTE DE FOWLIS, Micaela, 653, 654
CALVIMONTES, Isabel
   see CALVIMONTES DE AGRELO, Isabel
CALVIMONTES DE AGRELO, Isabel, 85, 227, 422, 611,
   928
CALVO, Blanca Rosa, 320
CALVO, Carlos, 254, 595
CALVO, Carmelo, 1094, 1206, 1207
CALVO, Diana Felicitas, 781
CALVO, Eduardo, 871
CALVO, Francisco, 32
CALVO, Francisco A., 1095
CALVO, Jacinto E., 268
CALVO, José, 1089
CALVO, Juan, 1089
CALVO, Luis, 530
CALVO, Nicolás, 915
CALVO, Pepe, 857d
CALVO DE LAYA, Vicente, 914
CALVO ENCINAR, Julio, 791
CALVO VAZ, Nicolás, 284
CALVO Y LLATEQUERA, Mariano, 910
CALZADA, Rafael, 94
CALZADILLA, 792
CALLE, Adolfo, 207, 278
CALLE, Ceferino de la, pseud.
   see DOMÍNGUEZ, Silverio.
CALLE, Francisco L., 207
CALLE, Jorge, 207, 212
CALLE, Jorge A., 683a
CALLE, José Lisandro, 207
CALLE, Luis María, 207
CALLEJA SANZ, Marcelino, 496
CALLEJAS Y SANDOVAL, Juan Antonio, 61
CALLERI, Eduardo, 1204
CALLISEN, Federico Inger, 923
CALLO, Juan Bautista, 1262
CALLORDA, Pedro, 1075
CALLORDA, Pedro Erasmo, 1167, 1174

CALLORDA VERDAGUER, Rubén Israel Marcoantonio, 1088
CAMACHO, Horacio Homero, 923
CAMACHO, Tomás Gregorio, 1083
CAMANA, Juan, 293
CAMAÑA, Juan L., 19, 59, 521
CAMAÑA, Raquel, 478, 929
CAMAÑO, Joaquín, 885, 1269
CAMAÑO, Santiago, 1089
CÁMARA, Alonso de la, 520, 620
CÁMARA, Isabel de, 32
CÁMARA, Lorenza de la, 456
CÁMARA, Nicola, 292
CAMARGO, Vicente, 166, 552
CAMARGO LOAYZA, Jacinto de, 555
CAMBACERES, Antonio, 122
CAMBACERES, Eugenio, 152a, 330, 724, 737, 747, 754, 774, 834
CAMBOURS OCAMPO, Arturo, 739, 746, 759, 801
CAMBRANES, Antonio de, 556
CAMEJO SOTO (family), 1106, 1224
CAMELINO, Juan, 611
CAMERINO, Pablo de, 1265
CAMERÓN, Juan, 954
CAMERÓN, Juan (son), 963a
CAMET (family), 361
CAMILIÓN DE CHIARAMONTI, María Ignacia, 320
CAMILLI, Elzear de, 1172
CAMILLONI, Carlos, 24
CAMINO, Alberto, 1095
CAMINO, Clara, 1065
CAMINO, Miguel Andrés, 217, 678, 722, 739, 782, 807, 1243, 1247, 1248
CAMINOS, Manuel Antonio, 74
CAMIÑA, Alfredo, 893
CAMP, Caleb J. (Mrs.)
    see BOYD, Sarah M.
CAMPANA, Joaquín, 478, 479, 496, 529, 1063
CAMPANA, José Cipriano, 137
CAMBELL, Allan, 332
CAMPBELL, Daniel (Mrs.)
    see ECCLESTON, Emily
CAMPBELL, Pedro, 166, 1066, 1128
CAMPERCHIOLI, Humberto Fernando, 954
CAMPERO, Juan, 126
CAMPERO Y ARÁOZ, Julio, 653, 654, 910
CAMPILLO, 195
CAMPILLO, Donaciano del, 89
CAMPILLO, Juan del, 166, 244, 634, 649
CAMPISTEGUY, Juan, 1075, 1079, 1083, 1109
CAMPO, Cosme del, 649a
CAMPO, Cristóbal del, 521
CAMPO, Cupertino del, 19
CAMPO, Estanislao del, 78, 167, 217, 282, 404, 521, 664, 669, 688, 723, 724, 734, 736, 737, 740, 751, 754, 767, 769, 803, 807, 828, 1242, 1243, 1244, 1246, 1248, 1249, 1254, 1260
CAMPO, Francisco del, 1083
CAMPO, Juan Carlos del, 1204
CAMPO, Juan del, 1034, 1041
CAMPO, Nicolás Francisco Christoval, Marqués de Loreto, 496, 570, 1237, 1239, 1240, 1262
CAMPO, Pascual, 258
CAMPO, Ricardo del, 751
CAMPODÓNICO, César Luis Pedro, 299
CAMPODÓNICO, Luis Ricardo, 1206
CAMPODÓNICO SINISCALCHI, Luis, 1210
CAMPOFRÍO Y CARVAJAL, Alonso de, 556
CAMPOLIETI, Roberto, 292
CÁMPORA, Héctor, 590
CAMPOS, Alfonso Belisario, 959

CAMPOS, Alfredo R., 1083
CAMPOS, Ernesto de los, 1145
CAMPOS, Gaspar José de, 126
CAMPOS, Heriberto
    see CAMPOS CERVERA, Heriberto
CAMPOS, José Domingo, 964, 1011
CAMPOS, José María, 1095
CAMPOS, Juan de, 7, 32
CAMPOS, Julio, 83, 188
CAMPOS, Luis María, 13, 17b, 68, 282, 474
CAMPOS, Manuel J., 17b
CAMPOS, María de los Angeles, 655, 656
CAMPOS, Martín, 717, 739, 801
CAMPOS, Pedro José, 179
CAMPOS, Roque A., 955a
CAMPOS CERVERA, Andrés
    see HERRERÍA, Julián de la
CAMPOS CERVERA, Heriberto, 943, 965, 966, 1012, 1014, 1015, 1020, 1021, 1022, 1025
CAMPOS TUFARI, Sócrates, 998
CAMPS, Saturnino A., 1075
CAMPUSANO, Rosita, 616
CAMPUZANO, Honorio, 954, 963a
CAMPUZANO, Joaquín Bernardo, 254
CAMUSSO (family), 1108
CANABAL, Jesús, 1089
CANABERIS, Juan
    see CANAVERIS, Juan
CANAL, Jorge de la, 299
CANAL FEIJÓO, Bernardo, 680, 722, 737, 739, 743, 751, 830
CANAL FEIJÓO, Enrique José, 923
CANALE, José, 6
CANALE, Mario A., 19, 44
CANALE, Nicolás, 6, 332
CANALE FERREIRA DE DE LEÓN, Amanda, 1210
CANALETTI, Haydée Lili, 655
CANALS, José, 923
CANARO, Francisco, 894
CANATA, Radomé, 198
CANAVERI, Tomás, 921
CANAVERIS, Juan, 496
CANCELA, Arturo, 152a, 670, 674, 769, 825, 1245
CANCELA, Delia Sara, 36
CANCIO, Juan, pseud.
    see VEDIA, Mariano de
CANDAU CARRIZO, Germán, 681, 726
CANDEAU, Alberto, 894, 1209
CANDELA, José María, 1167
CANDÍA, Domingo, 19, 25, 31, 36
CANDÍA, Domingo Tomás, 995a
CANDÍA, Jorge, 258
CANDÍA, José, 1089
CANDÍA, Manuel, 954
CANDÍA, Miguel de, 1238
CANDÍA DÍAZ, Rafael, 998
CANDÍA MENDIETA, Mónico, 998
CANDIANO, Vicente R., 154
CANDÍCAMO, Enrique, 727
CANDIOTI, Francisco Antonio, 258
CANTIOTI, Marcial Rafael, 332, 921a
CANDIRÁ, 977
CANÉ, Luis, 154, 674, 739, 748, 751, 759, 769, 773, 807, 833
CANÉ, Miguel (father), 611, 741, 747, 834, 1187
CANÉ, Miguel (son), 103, 116, 153, 166, 167, 225, 236, 282, 478, 521, 585, 708, 714, 721, 724, 734, 737, 741, 743, 745a, 751, 754, 780, 826, 1246
CANEDO, Manuel, 1089
CANEGALLI, Angel R., 781
CANEGALLI, Miguel R., 655

CÁNEPA, Juan Carlos, 275
CÁNEPA, Juan Tomás, 655
CANESE, Arquímedes, 963a
CANESSA, Juan Francisco, 1083
CÁNEVA, César, 910
CANEVARO, Walter, 37
CANITROT, Adolfo Martín Prudencio, 311
CANO, Guillermo G., 207
CANO, Juan Sebastián, 520, 1238
CANO CASTRO, Fernando, 359
CANO CASTRO, Juan del Monumento, 359
CANO DE CARVAJAL LUCERO DE TOVAR, Alberto, 359
CANO DE CARVAJAL QUIROGA SARMIENTO, Nicolás, 359
CANO DE CARVAJAL RAMÍREZ DE ARELLANO, Mateo, 359
CANO DE CARVAJAL Y FLORES, Pedro, 359
CANO DE CARVAJAL Y LUCERO DE TOVAR, Nicolás, 359
CANO DE CARVAJAL Y RAMÍREZ DE ARELLANO, José Tadeo, 254, 359
CANO DE LA CERDA, Juan, 914
CANO DÍAZ VÉLEZ, Juan, 359
CANO DÍAZ VÉLEZ, Marciano Nicolás, 359
CANO DÍAZ VÉLEZ, Roberto, 359
CANO FIGUEROA, Félix Vicente, 359
CANO FIGUEROA, Juan Agustín, 359
CANO HUNTER, Marciano Juan, 359
CANO HUNTER, Raúl, 359
CANO LANÚS, Néstor Feliciano, 359
CANO LANÚS, Roberto, 359
CANÓNICO, Abel N., 923
CANTADOR, Alonso, 914
CANTALUPPI, Lidio, 998
CANTER, Juan, 609
CANTERAC, José, 453, 553
CANTIER, Pablo, 662
CANTILO, José Luis, 69, 103, 391, 751, 834
CANTILO, José María, 611, 708, 751, 829
CANTO, Estela, 757
CANTÓN, Eliseo, 94, 718, 844, 1261
CANTÓN, Zoilo, 68, 94
CANTONI, Aldo, 429
CANTONI, César Emilio, 663
CANTONI, Federico, 429
CANTONNET, María Ester, 1151
CANTORE, Guillermo, 772
CANTOS, Rodrigo de, 620
CANZANI D., Ariel, 716, 717
CAÑAS, Carlos, 19, 36
CAÑETE, Agustín, 1008
CAÑETE, Edmundo, 998
CAÑETE, Francisco, 6, 7, 32
CAÑETE, Inocencio, 918
CAÑETE, José, 32
CAÑETE, Pedro Vicente, 517, 943, 980, 1012
CAÑETE CORVALÁN, Rufino, 998
CAÑETE DE RIVAS JORDÁN, María Tránsito, 745, 762
CAÑIZA, Dionisio, 987
CAÑIZA, Norberto, 998
CAO LUACES, José María, 284
CAPAGORRY, Juan, 1159
CAPANNA, Pablo, 728
CAPANO DONADÍO, Alberto Santiago, 1210
CAPANO DONADÍO, Ricardo Avelino, 1210
CAPARA, Alfredo, 299
CAPDEHOURAT, Eduardo León, 923
CAPDEVILA, Alberto, 17b
CAPDEVILA, Arturo, 219, 431, 521, 669, 678, 722, 723, 739, 740, 751, 759, 782, 807
CAPDEVILA, José Antonio (EL PARAGUAYO, pseud.), 122, 254, 496
CAPDEVILA, Pedro, 156, 496

CAPDEVILA, Vicente, 496
CAPDEVILA Y PALLARÉS, José Alberto, 844, 846, 850, 1261, 1262
CAPECE FARAONE, Roque, 943, 966, 1020
CAPELÁN, Antonio, 1089
CAPELÁN, José, 1089
CAPELLA, José, 860
CAPELLO, Francisco, 162, 258, 292
CAPLÁN, Marcos, 857c
CAPMANY, Elena, 207
CAPPELLI DE MANTOVANI, Fedora, 874
CAPPOZZOLI, Emanuelli Homero, 1210
CAPRARO, Primo, 258
CAPRERA, Hugo, 889
CAPRILE, Emma Nicolay (Mrs. GIULIO CAPRILE), 323
CAPRILE, Giulio, Mrs.
    see CAPRILE, Emma Nicolay
CAPRILE, Jacinto, 258
CAPRISTO, Oscar, 19, 25, 31, 36, 46, 63
CAPURRO, Juan Alberto, 1075
CAPURRO, Juan Bautista, 1093a
CAPURRO, Martiniano, 998
CAPURRO, Roberto Horacio, 923
CAPUTO DEMARCO, Luis B., 41
CAPUTTI, Luis Alberto, 1151, 1179
CAPUZZI DE LANDI, Carmen A., 320
CARABALLO, Andrés C., 812
CARABALLO, Gustavo, 135, 669, 751
CARABALLO, Luis Antonio, 691
CARABALLO SUÁREZ, Francisco, 845
CARACARÁ, 977
CARACCIOLO FIGUEROA, Francisco, 68
CARACOCHE, Pedro, 565
CARAFFA, Belisario, 332
CARAFFA, Emilio
    see CARAFFA BRANDAN, Emilio
CARAFFA, Pedro I., 411
CARAFFA BRANDAN, Emilio, 19, 24, 31, 258, 678, 722, 751, 782
CARAFÍ, José María, 1261
CARAFÍ DE CASTELLS, Laura, 1226a
CARAICHURE, 977
CARÁMBULA, Benigno P., 1075
CARAMELLI, Julio Eduardo, 923
CARAMIA, Mario N., 652
CARAVALLO, Melchor de, 186
CARAVALLO, Raúl Esteban, 719
CARAVELLO, Roberto V. A., 923
CARAVIA (family), 1108
CARAYA, 977
CARBAJAL, Baltasar, 358
CARBAJAL, Eduardo, 1046, 1047
CARBAJAL, Eduardo D., 1086
CARBAJAL, Juan, 358
CARBAJAL SCHUSSELIN, Nancy Lillyam, 1210
CARBALHO GONZÁLEZ, 678, 782
CARBALLAL, Andrés, 1089
CARBALLO, Aída, 27, 41, 55
CARBALLO, Eduardo, 785
CARBALLO, José Domingo, 599
CARBALLO, José Miguel de, 126
CARBALLO, Luis
    see CARVALLO, Luis
CARBALLO, Miguel Argentino, 923
CARBALLO ENRÍQUEZ, Julio, 284
CARBALLO Y GOYENECHE, Vicente, 496
CARBIA, Rómulo D., 609
CARBÓ, Alejandro, 241
CARBÓ, Enrique, 135, 160, 194, 241
CARBONE, Conrado, 874
CARBONE, Tulio, 1045

CARBONELL, Joaquín Fernando, 1094
CARBONELL Y VILA, Joaquín, 1094
CÁRCANO, Inocencio, 258
CÁRCANO, Miguel Angel, 521, 609, 741
CÁRCANO, Ramón J., 381a, 609, 751, 1246
CÁRCOVA, Carlos de la, 19, 21, 521
CARCOVA, Ernesto de la, 19, 25, 31, 51, 258, 282, 293
CÁRDENAS, Alberto, 440
CÁRDENAS, Bernardino de, 472, 521, 963, 964, 978, 984, 984a, 989, 1010, 1011, 1012, 1033, 1034, 1041
CÁRDENAS, Jacinto, 126
CÁRDENAS, Juan Leonildo, 954
CÁRDENAS, Pedro de, 989
CÁRDENAS, Petrona, 227
CÁRDENAS BEHETY, Rodolfo, 748
CÁRDENAS Y MENDOZA, Bernardo de, 555
CARDEÑOSA, Bartolomé, 32
CARDEÑOSA, Manuel, 24
CARDIEL, José, 32, 156, 319, 966, 985, 1269
CARDINI, Carlos Eugenio, 923
CARDÓN, Raúl, 652
CARDONA, Alberto Francisco, 923
CARDOSO, Damián, 254
CARDOSO, Diego, 7, 32, 922
CARDOSO, Felipe, 496
CARDOSO, Juana María R., 923
CARDOSO, Martín, 1075
CARDOSO, Valentín, 611
CARDOSO ABERASTAIN, Juana, 931
CARDOSO DEL ESPINO, Diego, 332
CARDOZO, Demetrio, 954
CARDOZO, Efraím, 521, 943, 947, 964, 966, 1021, 1022, 1023
CARDOZO, Egidio, 995, 998
CARDOZO, Juan de Dios, 954
CARDOZO, Martín, 204
CARDOZO, Ramón Indalecio, 941, 943, 947, 959, 964, 1012
CARDOZO, Rogelio Albino, 998
CARDOZO AVENDAÑO, Edith, 874
CARDOZO BEGA, Nicolás
    see CARDOZO VEGA, Nicolás
CARDOZO PEREYRA, Gaspar, 846
CARDOZO PÉREZ, Henderson, 1210
CARDOZO VEGA, Nicolás, 204
CARDULLO, Isabel E., 683a
CARDÚS HUERTA, Gualberto, 959
CAREAGA, Asencio, 555
CAREAGA, Enrique, 938, 939
CAREAGA, Juan B., 947
CAREAGA, Mariano, 979
CAREANO, Ramón J., 78
CARELLA, Tulio, 812
CARIAY, Santiago, 995a
CARIBAUX, José B., 705
CARIBÉ, pseud.
    see BERNABÓ, Héctor.
CARICAMO, Enrique, 759
CARILLA, Emilio, 739
CARISIMO, Alfredo, 947
CARISIMO, Simeón, 941
CARISIMO DE AVALOS, Wil, 947
CARLÉS, Manuel, 68, 94
CARLETTI, Alicia, 37
CARLEVARO, Abel, 1206
CARLINO, Carlos, 152a, 678, 739, 746, 748, 812
CARLISKY, Alberto, 25
CARLISLE, Charles R., 1015

CARLO, José Alejandro de, 923
CARLO, Nicolás de, 910
CARLÓ, Thelma, 932
CARLOMAGNO, Francisco, 258
CARLOS III, King of Spain, 283
CARLOS DEL PERAL, pseud.
    see PERALTA, Carlos
CARLSEN, Rudolf Julius, 59
CARMELO, pseud.
    see COLMAN, José del Carmen
CARMELO BENAVENTE, Marcolino del, 910
CARMEN, Francisco del, 845
CARMEN, José Elías del, 895
CARMENATIZ JOVER, Pedro, 649a
CARMINATTI, Héctor, 923
CARMONA, Juan Antonio, 83
CARMONA, Lucía, 785
CARMONA, Pedro, 32, 61
CARMONA, Raúl Restituto, 998
CARNÉ, Mercedes, 879
CARNEIRO LEÃO, Honorio Hermeto, 596
CARNELLI, María Luisa (LUIS, Mario, pseud.), 762, 860, 871
CARNEVALE, Jorge, 706
CARO, Andrés Luis, 833
CARO, Francisco de
    see DE CARO, Francisco
CARO, Gregorio A., 653, 654
CARO, José A., 923
CARO, Julio de
    see DE CARO, Julio
CAROLIS, Victorino de, 739, 812
CARON, Carlos María, 728
CARONE, Carlos, 947
CARONTI, Filippo, 98, 258, 292
CAROSINI, Alberto H., 565
CARPANI, Ricardo Roque, 31, 36, 55
CARPANI COSTA, Arturo Horacio, 8
CARPENA, Elías, 688, 739, 759, 817, 825
CARPENCHIOLI, Antonio, 998
CARPINACCI, Giovanni, 292
CARPIO, Rafael del, 6
CARR BERRESFORD, Guillermo
    see BERRESFORD, William Carr
CARRA, Antonio, 258
CARRÁ, Carmelo, 37
CARRANCIO, José Vicente, 126
CARRANZA, Adolfo E., 122
CARRANZA, Angel Justiniano, 191, 314, 609
CARRANZA, Genaro, 921
CARRANZA, José Ambrosio, 611, 1130
CARRANZA, Luján, 823
CARRANZA, Pedro de, 318, 649a, 907, 910, 911, 912, 920
CARRANZA, Reyna, 684
CARRANZA, Roque Guillermo, 560
CARRANZA, Wenceslao C., 565
CARRANZA CASARES, Arturo, 217
CARRARA, María Teresa, 704
CARRASCA (family), 1224
CARRASCO, Antero, 237
CARRASCO, Antonio, 1236
CARRASCO, Bernardo, 910
CARRASCO, Francisca Javiera, 1056
CARRASCO, Ignacia Javiera, 1056
CARRASCO, Pedro Buenaventura, 126, 457
CARRASCO, Sansón, pseud.
    see MUÑOZ, Daniel
CARRASCO, Sebastián, 1262
CARRASCO GALEANO, José, 1083

CARRASCO MELO-COUTINHO (family), 1108
CARRATALA, Rogelio, 923
CARREA, Juan Ubaldo, 923
CARREIRA, Emilio E., 218, 560
CARREÑO (family), 352
CARREÑO, Alicia, 785
CARREÑO, Aníbal, 19, 49
CARREÑO, Leónidas, 83
CARRERA (brothers), 188
CARRERA, Delmiro, 1089
CARRERA, Domingo, 949
CARRERA, Javiera, 529
CARRERA, José Mario César, 923
CARRERA, José Miguel, 89, 95, 179, 188, 194, 283,
    471, 472, 478, 499, 528, 552, 553, 554, 568,
    573, 616, 622, 629
CARRERA, Juan José, 553
CARRERA, Laurentino, 1089
CARRERA, Luis, 553
CARRERA, Manuel, 1089
CARRERA, Santiago, 89, 545a
CARRERA, Vicente, 1199
CARRERA VILLAR, Carlos, 299
CARRERAS, de las (family), 1108
CARRERAS, Antonio de las, 254
CARRERAS, Cecilio Ignacio, 121, 387
CARRERAS, Enrique, 857
CARRERAS, José María de las, 496
CARRERAS, Juan Antonio, 874, 878
CARRERAS, María de las, 924
CARRERAS, Mariano, 222
CARRERAS, Miguel A., 653, 654
CARRERAS, Roberto de las, 1083, 1146, 1170, 1177,
    1199, 1259
CARRERA DE BASTOS, Laura, 1094
CARRERAS SAAVEDRA, Luis María, 210
CARRERAS SAGUIER, María Fulvia (BOBBIO, Condesa),
    971
CARRERAS SAGUIER, Oscar Fernando, 971, 998
CARRETERO, Andrés, 609
CARRETERO DE LA VEGA, Juan, 555
CARRIEGO, Evaristo, 95, 96, 127, 135, 162, 167, 194,
    521, 648, 649, 669, 678, 722, 723, 737, 740, 751,
    755, 759, 773, 782, 801, 803, 807, 818, 868, 877,
    1243, 1246, 1247
CARRIER-BELLEUSE, Albert, 59
CARRIL, Arturo, 894
CARRIL, Hugo del, 858
CARRIL, José María del, 188
CARRIL, Salvador María del, 95, 96, 110, 116, 121,
    141, 166, 179, 188, 195, 282, 283, 398, 412, 478,
    586, 611, 629, 634, 644
CARRILERO, José, 719
CARRILLO, Damián, 649a
CARILLO, Horacio (IGNOTUS, pseud.), 385, 713, 730
CARRILLO, Joaquín, 713
CARRILLO, Juan Crisóstomo, 68
CARRILLO, Juana Pabla, 991
CARRILLO, Luis Clemente, 874
CARRILLO, Ramón, 923
CARRIÓ DE LA VANDERA, Alonso
    see CONCOLORCORVO, pseud.
CARRIPILUN, 566
CARRIQUE, Ana, 881
CARRIZO, Antonio, 299
CARRIZO, César, 1245
CARRIZO, Fabio, pseud.
    see ALVAREZ, José Sixto
CARRIZO, Gregorio, 13
CARRIZO, Juan Alfonso, 381a, 688

CARRIZO, Nicolás, 520, 527
CARRIZO MERCADILLO, Juan, 649a
CARRO, Juan José, 1223
CARRO, Ramón (Román), 1223
CARROL, Jorge, 658, 739
CARROL, Miguel P., 652
CARROL, William, 587
CARSON DA SILVA, Tarik, 1088, 1183
CARTA, Pedro, 98, 844
CARTA MOLINA, Pedro, 113, 258
CARTASEGNA, Rolando, 765
CARTASSO, Juan José, 41
CARTOSIO, Emma de, 135, 658, 716, 717, 725, 739,
    748, 758, 800, 802, 807, 814
CARUAY, 977
CARUBIN, Vicente, 683a
CARULLA, Francisco, 258
CARUSO, Juan Andrés, 871
CARVAJAL, Alonso de, 1270
CARVAJAL, Francisco de, 520
CARVAJAL, Lino, 921
CARVAJAL, Ramón Antonio, 268
CARVAJAL, Ramón Exequiel, 268
CARVAJAL Y RIVERA, Fernando, 914
CARVAJAL Y SARAVIA, Antonio de, 555
CARVAJAL Y SARAVIA, Melchor de, 555
CARVALHO LERENA, Antonio, 1075
CARVALLO, Edrulfo A., 954
CARVALLO, Francisco Javier, 126
CARVALLO, Gonzalo, 32
CARVALLO, Jacinto, 186
CARVALLO, Luis, 845, 849
CARVE (family), 1108
CARVE, Luis, 1083
CARYBÉ, pseud.
    see BERNABÓ, Héctor
CASA, Agustín Guillermo (HOUSE, Guillermo, pseud.),
    707, 834, 1251
CASABELLAS, Ramiro de, 658
CASABIANCA, Juan Pablo, 1014
CASABLANCA, Cornelio, 268
CASABLANCA, Francisco de, 555
CASACCIA, Gabriel, 1019
CASACCIA, Jorge, 952
CASACCIA BIBOLINI, Benigno, 943
CASACUBERTA, Aurelio
    see CASACUBERTA, Juan Aurelio José de los Santos
CASACUBERTA, José, 720
CASACUBERTA, Juan Antonio, 371
CASACUBERTA, Juan Aurelio José de los Santos, 677,
    887, 888, 1063
CASAFFOUSTH, Carlos, 332
CASAGEMAS, Ignacio, 6
CASAGEMAS, Rafael, 611
CASAGRANDE, Adolfo, 681
CASAJUS, Bernardino
    see CASAJUS, Bernardo de
CASAJUS, Bernardo de (CASAJUS, Bernardino), 196
CASAJUS, José Baltasar de, 196
CASAJUS, José Francisco de, 196
CASAJUS, Pedro Bautista José de, 196
CASAJUS, Pedro Bautista de (son), 196
CASAJUS, Sebastián de, 196
CASAL, Carlos, 196
CASAL, Julián del, 1181, 1259
CASAL, Julio J., 1145, 1147, 1151, 1153, 1177, 1179,
    1187, 1199
CASAL, Miguel, 169
CASAL DE ANIDO, Manuel Antonio, 284
CASAL RIBEIRO, Joaquín, 951
CASALI, Aquiles, 956

CASALLA, Angel, 1075
CASALLA, Enrique, 883
CASAMAYOR, Félix Pedro, 496
CASAMAYOR DE LUCA, Isabel, 924
CASANAVE, J., 6
CASANOVA, Mariano, 91
CASAÑAS DE PEYRANO, Julieta M. J., 652
CASAÑAS LEMOS, Emilio, 222
CASAÑAS LEMOS, Francisco, 222
CASARAVILLA (family), 1108
CASARAVILLA LEMOS, Enrique, 1145, 1151, 1153, 1177,
    1179, 1181, 1198, 1199
CASARENA, José, 845
CASARES, Alberto, 68, 103, 122
CASARES, Carlos M., 3
CASARES, Miguel F., 3
CASARES, Vicente L., 141
CASARES PEARSON, Olga, 857c
CASARIEGO BLANCO, 6
CASARTELLI BINAGHI, Victorio Dorilo, 1210
CASAS (family), 352
CASAS, Arturo, 152
CASAS, Bartolomé de las, 188, 518, 521
CASAS, Faustino de las, 918, 1041
CASAS, José Benito, 68, 284
CASAS, José O., 565
CASAS, Juan de las, 186
CASAS, Luciano de las, 1223
CASAS ARAÚJO, Julio, 1167
CASAS DE GAVELLO, Aurelia, 1088
CASAS OCAMPO, Emilio, 24
CASASBELLAS, Ramiro de, 759
CASAUX, Roberto, 141
CASAZZA, Néstor, 832
CASCALLARES, Antonio, 74
CASCALLARES GUTIÉRREZ, Isabel, 751, 762
CASCELLA, Armando, 152a, 779, 1245
CASCIANI, Ernesto Domingo, 874
CASCIANI DE CASTRO, Herminia Máxima, 874
CASCO, Horacio, 69
CASCO, Juan Carlos, 995a
CASCO DE AGUER, María del Carmen, 656
CASCO DE MENDOZA, Manuel, 186
CASCO DE MENDOZA, Melchor, 914
CASCO ENCINAS, María Amelia, 191
CASCO ESPINOSA, Fermín, 959
CASELLA, Enrique Mario, 865, 882, 894
CASELLA, José, 258
CASELLAS, Carlos Alberto, 691
CASERES, Juan de, 186
CASETTI, Romo, 874
CASEY, Alfredo, 805
CASEY, Eduardo, 122
CASIMIRO, 878
CASNATI, Luis Ricardo, 683a
CASPE, Antonio, 517
CASPERSEN, Arturo, 332
CASSACCIA, Gabriel, 1020, 1021, 1022
CASSAFOUSTH, Carlos A., 244
CASSALE, Francisco, 1205
CASSANELLO, Juan M., 1039
CASSARINO TECHERA, Julio Benito, 1210
CASSIGNOL BENÍTEZ, 954
CASTAGNA, Rodolfo V., 27, 64
CASTAGNERI, Clemente, 1205
CASTAGNINO, Juan Carlos, 18, 19, 23, 25, 31, 34,
    36, 49, 50, 55
CASTAÑAR, Hipólito, 921
CASTAÑARES, Agustín, 989

CASTAÑEDA, Francisco de Paula, 167, 183, 293, 317,
    327, 379, 578, 629, 644, 673, 677, 737, 908,
    921, 1258
CASTAÑEDA, Gregorio de, 32, 527
CASTAÑEDA, Jorge, 691
CASTAÑEDA, Pedro, 385
CASTAÑEDA Y ROMERO, Francisco de Paula, 273
CASTAÑER, Juan José, 921
CASTAÑERA, Antonio, 887
CASTAÑO, Alberto, 68
CASTAÑO, Arturo, 332
CASTAÑO, Manuel, 731
CASTARES, Juan, 279
CASTELÁN, Zaida de, 656
CASTELAO, Alfonso R., 260
CASTELAR, Emilio, 244
CASTELAR LÓPEZ, Héctor, 299
CASTELNUOVO, Elías, 742, 765, 894, 1245
CASTELO, Oscar A., 836
CASTELPOGGI, Atilio Jorge, 716, 717, 739, 758, 801,
    802
CASTELVI, Tomás Antonio, 995a
CASTELL, Adela
    see CASTELL DE LÓPEZ ROCHA, Adela
CASTELL DE LÓPEZ ROCHA, Adela, 1083, 1174
CASTELLÁN, Alberto Carlos, 217
CASTELLANI, Leonardo (REY, Jerónimo del, pseud.),
    177a, 664, 668, 685, 744, 745, 771, 799, 825
CASTELLANO (family), 352
CASTELLANO, Graciela, 37
CASTELLANO, Julio, 705
CASTELLANO, Uladislao, 244, 907, 910, 911, 920
CASTELLANOS (family), 1108, 1224
CASTELLANOS, Aarón, 466
CASTELLANOS, Alfredo, 923
CASTELLANOS, Florentino, 1063, 1220
CASTELLANOS, Francisco Remigio, 126, 611, 1063
CASTELLANOS, Horacio, 923
CASTELLANOS, Joaquín, 166, 478, 653, 654, 669, 682,
    751, 1243, 1247
CASTELLANOS, Juan José, 126
CASTELLANOS, Mariano, 268
CASTELLANOS, Mario, 1079
CASTELLANOS, Remigio, 179
CASTELLANOS, Telasco, 384
CASTELLANOS DE ETCHEPARE, Delia, 1050
CASTELLANOS SOLÁ, Elsa, 653, 654
CASTELLANOS Y MORALES, Miguel, 186
CASTELLER, Rosa Ana, 683a
CASTELLI, 529
CASTELLI, Angel, 253, 258
CASTELLI, Juan José, 70, 85, 104, 110, 166, 240, 282,
    283, 386, 404, 411, 420, 421, 475, 478, 479,
    496, 517, 521, 525, 553, 610, 611, 650, 895
CASTELLI, Luis, pseud.
    see BORDOLI, Domingo
CASTELLI, Luis Alejandro, 328
CASTELLI, Pedro, 196, 404
CASTELLI DE GIOVAN, Giuseppe, 292
CASTELLI DE IGARZÁBAL, Angela, 422, 611
CASTELLINI, Antonio, 17
CASTELLINO DE ESTUPIÑÁN, Juana, 683a
CASTELLO, Angel, 258
CASTELLS, Carlos, 1046, 1047
CASTELLS, Dora, 320
CASTELLS, Emilio A., 1094
CASTELLS, José Conrado, 135
CASTELLS, María Angélica, 320

CASTELLS, Víctor Reynaldo, 320
CASTELLS CAPURRO, Enrique, 1226a
CASTELLS CUMELLA, Constancio, 1094
CASTELLS Y COMAS, Jaime, 1226a
CASTELLS Y MONTESTRUCH, Alberto, 1226a
CASTELLS Y MONTESTRUCH, Enrique, 1226a
CASTELLS Y MONTESTRUCH, Enrique Martín, 1226a
CASTEX, Alejo, 496
CASTEX, Mariano R., 239, 923
CASTIGLIONE, Alberto, 258
CASTIGLIONI PÉREZ, Carmelo, 1017
CASTILLA, Américo Juan, 37
CASTILLA, Eduardo, 6
CASTILLA, Felipe, 496
CASTILLA, Gabriel, 653
CASTILLA, Leopoldo, 653, 654, 831
CASTILLA, Manuel J., 653, 654, 680, 689, 716, 722, 739, 758, 759, 790, 798, 803, 812, 830, 831
CASTILLA DE ARRIEN, Bernarda, 1093a
CASTILLA Y ZAMORA, Cristóbal de, 126
CASTILLEJO, Juan, 319
CASTILLO, Abelardo, 696, 697, 776, 829, 836
CASTILLO, Alvaro, 1176
CASTILLO, Andrés, 1172, 1185
CASTILLO, Antonius del, 1037
CASTILLO, Armando, 653, 654
CASTILLO, Benjamín E. del, 68
CASTILLO, Bernardo, 874
CASTILLO, Blanca Ofelia, 704
CASTILLO, Carlos G., 963a
CASTILLO, Cátulo, 794, 862, 871, 877
CASTILLO, Guido, 1184
CASTILLO, Horacio, 663, 759
CASTILLO, Ignacio del, 914
CASTILLO, Jacinto M., 30
CASTILLO, José Matías del, 599
CASTILLO, Juan del, 1032, 1032a
CASTILLO, Narciso del, 1112
CASTILLO, Pedro del, 32, 188, 212, 252, 283, 472, 555
CASTILLO, Ramón Santiago, 452, 489, 515, 516, 524, 593, 619
CASTILLO, Santiago H. del, 893
CASTILLO, Santos R., 923
CASTILLO DE BOVADILLA, Gerónimo, 646
CASTILLO DE GUZMÁN, Valentina, 810
CASTIÑEIRA DE DIOS, José María, 664, 739, 758, 766, 812
CASTIÑEIRAS, Alejandro, 259
CASTIÑEIRAS, Horacio R., 299
CASTIÑEIRAS, Julio R., 332
CASTLEREACH, Enrique Roberto, 573
CÁSTOR, 1176
CASTORINO, María Sara L. de, 683a
CASTRO (family) (Argentina), 348, 881
CASTRO (family) (Uruguay), 1108
CASTRO, Alejandro, 844
CASTRO, Alfredo Antonio, 923
CASTRO, Ana Edelmira, 252
CASTRO, Antonio P., 135
CASTRO, Carlos de, 1075, 1210
CASTRO, Cipriano, 157
CASTRO, Domingo Fidel
    see SARMIENTO, Domingo Fidel
CASTRO, Eliseo, 683a
CASTRO, Emilio, 141, 166
CASTRO, Enrique, 254
CASTRO, Enrique F., 299
CASTRO, Ernesto L., 152a
CASTRO, Estela, 894

CASTRO, Félix, 496
CASTRO, Francisco, 1089
CASTRO, Francisco de, 186
CASTRO, Francisco M., 1075
CASTRO, Gregorio, 1075
CASTRO, J. Alberto, 683a
CASTRO, Jacinto de, 496
CASTRO, José Fernando de, 284
CASTRO, José Francisco Claudio de, 126
CASTRO, José María, 188, 864, 865, 883
CASTRO, Juan Bautista, 496
CASTRO, Juan de, 186, 224, 914, 1095
CASTRO, Juan Carlos, 37
CASTRO, Juan José, 864, 865, 883
CASTRO, Juan Pedro, 1075, 1126
CASTRO, Luis Eulogio, 679
CASTRO, Magdalena, 422, 611
CASTRO, Manuel Antonio de, 89, 126, 166, 316, 321, 545a, 611, 644, 692
CASTRO, Manuel de, 1145, 1151, 1162, 1179, 1187, 1199
CASTRO, Manuel Pascual, 923
CASTRO, María Eugenia, 234
CASTRO, Martín, 878, 1243
CASTRO, Máximo, 842
CASTRO, Nicomedes, 1075
CASTRO, Pedro de, 845
CASTRO, Phelipe de, 186
CASTRO, Raúl, 793
CASTRO, Saturnino, 254, 568
CASTRO, Sergio de, 19, 25, 31, 49
CASTRO, Toribio, 998
CASTRO, Vicente, 332, 1089
CASTRO, Víctor, 299
CASTRO, Vilma, 691
CASTRO, Washington, 865, 883
CASTRO ARIAS, Joaquín, 284
CASTRO BARROS, Ignacio
    see CASTRO BARROS, Pedro Ignacio
CASTRO BARROS, Pedro Ignacio de, 83, 166, 183, 244, 282, 439, 457, 526, 569, 574, 611, 621, 626, 629, 895, 908, 921
CASTRO CAMBÓN, Vicenta, 478, 751, 762, 929
CASTRO COUSO, Alberto, 65
CASTRO DE CAPURRO, Prudencia, 1093a
CASTRO HURTADO, José María, 283
CASTRO LÓPEZ, Manuel, 284
CASTRO MARIÑO, Manuel, 1089
CASTRO MARTÍNEZ, Domingo Fidel, 575
CASTRO MARTÍNEZ, Jesús, 1089
CASTRO MOSQUERA, Francisco, 284
CASTRO ORTEGA, Ramón de, 431
CASTRO PENA, Salvador, 1089
CASTRO PIÑEIRO, Juan José, 284
CASTRO RIVERA, Ramón, 284
CASTRO RODRÍGUEZ, 1085
CASTRO SARAVIA, Juan de, 186
CASTRO Y CALLORDA, Bartolomé de, 1223
CASTRO Y CALLORDA, Cristóbal de, 1223
CASTRO Y CALLORDA, Pedro de, 1223
CASTRO Y CARREÑO, Juan Manuel de, 283
CASTRO Y COREAGA, Juan Francisco de, 126
CASTRO Y GONZÁLEZ, Manuel Antonio, 126
CASTRO ZINNY, Horacio, 923
CASTRONOVO, Alfonso Jorge, 923
CASULLO, Francisco, 258
CATACORA, Juan Basilio, 126
CATALÁN, Marcial, 381a
CATALANO, Luciano Roque, 923
CATALDINO, José, 32, 845, 850, 952, 989

CATANI, Enrique, 663, 786, 805
CATELIN, Próspero, 6, 332
CATHAALIN, 1031
CATIVA, Gabriel Eduardo, 860
CATÓN, pseud.
   see MEDRANO ROSSO, Gaspar
CATÓN, Carolina, 887
CATÓN, Felipe, 887
CATRIEL, Cipriano, 454
CATTANEO, Cayetano, 258
CATTANEO, Francisco, 951
CATTANEO, Pedro, 923
CATTAROSSI, Rino, 683a
CATTAROSSI ARANA, Nelly, 683a
CATTOI, Noemí, 923
CATTONI, Federico, 998
CATTONI, Juan Adolfo, 954
CAUDEVILLA, Marcelino, 315
CAUSA, Humberto, 1044
CAVAGNARO, María Alicia, 787
CAVALLERO, Fernando, 943, 987
CAVALLERO, Lucas, 989
CAVALLERO, Pedro Juan, 987, 1012
CAVALLERO BAZÁN (family), 972
CAVALLERO Y AÑASCO, Juan, 989
CAVALLI, Cayetano María, 268
CAVALLOTTI, Rubén W., 857d
CAVAÑAS, Manuel Atanasio, 943
CAVEDAGNI, Luis, 1205
CAVENDISH, Tomás, 287
CAVIA, Pedro Feliciano, 478, 545a, 644, 1262
CAVIGLIA, Buenaventura, 1145, 1167
CAVILLA SINCLAIR, Arsenio, 1243
CAVILLA SINCLAIR, Valentín, 1243
CAVO, Ambrosio L., 94
CAXARAVILLE, Miguel, 166
CAXIAS, 984
CAYO MILTOS, Sotero
   see MILTOS, Sotero Cayo
CAYOL, Alvaro (RÉUMAY, pseud.), 810
CAYOL, Roberto Lino, 727, 811, 813, 818, 871
CAZAGNA, Gaspare de, 292
CAZAL, José María, 1006
CAZAL, Pedro Félix, 995a
CAZALLA, Manuel, 663, 786
CAZÓN, Alcira, 713
CAZÓN, Daniel María, 273
CAZÓN, Higinio D., 137, 813, 818, 878, 1243, 1247
CAZÓN, Joaquín María, 181
CEBALLOS, José A., 89
CEBALLOS, Patricio, 188
CEBALLOS, Pedro de
   see CEVALLOS CORTÉS HOYOS Y CALDERÓN, Pedro de
CECCARELLI, Pedro Bartolomé, 268
CECCONI, José Mario, 44, 65
CECIONI, Juan, 923
CEDRO, Victorio Carmelo, 923
CEDRÓN, José, 857d
CEDRÓN, José Antonio, 785
CEI, José M., 923
CEJAS, Juan Marcos, 653
CEJAS, Octavio, 689
CEJKA, Jildegard R., 652
CELADA, Gabriel de, 32
CELANO, Atilio René, 947
CELEMÍN DE ALONSO, Benita Dorotea, 320
CELINSKI, Zdzislaw, 238
CELIS, Miguel Rubén de, 104, 922
CELLERIER, 949
CENDOYA, Juan I., 765
CENDRA, 1064

CENTENO (family), 352
CENTENO, Alejandro, 190
CENTENO, Angel M., 845a
CENTENO, Buenaventura, 552
CENTENO, Diego, 984, 989
CENTENO, Francisco, 653, 654
CENTENO, Leonor, 663
CENTENO, Pedro A., 921
CENTENO DEL CAMPILLO, Lucrecia, 762
CENTEYA, Julián, pseud. (VERGIATI, Amleto), 660, 727, 794, 812, 862, 871
CENTRÓN VILLAR, Enrique, 1210
CENTRONE, María Antonieta, 154
CENTURIÓN, Carlos A., 965
CENTURIÓN, Carlos R., 943, 1021, 1022
CENTURIÓN, Emilio, 18, 19, 23, 25, 31, 34, 36, 50, 55, 64
CENTURIÓN, Fernando, 937, 943
CENTURIÓN, Juan Crisóstomo, 943, 964, 988, 1020, 1021, 1022
CENTURIÓN, Leo, 959
CENTURIÓN, Leopoldo, 943, 966, 1017, 1020, 1021, 1022
CENTURIÓN, Luis, 31, 36, 46
CENTURIÓN, Vicente, 560
CENTURIÓN M., Crisóstomo, 974
CENTURIÓN MIRANDA, Roque, 943, 1021, 1022
CEPEDA (family), 366
CEPEDA, Alonso de, 520
CEPEDA, Andrés, 878, 1243
CEPEDA, Gabriel de, 556
CEPEDA, Rodrigo de, 510
CEPPI, José (LATINO, Aníbal, pseud.), 258
CERANA, Luis Alberto, 923
CERBELLÓN ALCARAZ, Carlos, 998
CERCOS, Augusto Pedro, 923
CERDA, Gregorio Tadeo de la, 987
CERDA, Julio Ramón de la, 1140
CERDA, María de la, 1270
CERDA, Petronila de la, 144
CERDA CARRETERO, Juan, 18, 19, 31, 46
CERETTI, Bartolomé, 258
CERIANI, Juan, 951, 952
CERIÑO NÚÑEZ, Pedro Antonio, 284
CERIOTTO, Emilio, 683a
CERMEÑO, Juan Martín, 332
CERNADAS, Juan José, 126, 545a
CERNADAS, Melitón, 268
CERNADAS, Pedro M., 68, 94
CERNUSCHI, Félix, 923
CERRAJERÍA, Fernando A., 923
CERRERAS, Santiago, 188
CERRETANI, Arturo, 744, 1245
CERRI, Daniel, 17b, 68
CERRITO, Egidio, 31
CERRO, Edmundo A. del, 653
CERRO, Juan Carlos, 698
CERRO, Miguel del, 254, 1130
CERRO JURADO, Fernando, 555
CERRO Y SÁENZ, Manuel del, 496
CERUTTI, Eduardo, 258
CERVANTES LURO, Guillermo, 299
CERVANTES MAGARIÑOS, Alejandro, 1247
CERVERA, Felipe Justo, 814
CERVETTI, Sergio, 1206
CERVIÑO, Pedro Antonio (ORDEN VEDOÑO, Cipriano, pseud.), 7, 17a, 332, 478, 479, 496, 611, 644, 720, 885, 921a, 922, 1262
CÉSAR (family), 352
CÉSAR, Clemente, 1081
CÉSAR, Julio Ramón de, 7, 28

CÉSAR BRUTO, pseud.
   see WARNES, Carlos H.
CESARE, Elías Alfredo de
   see DE CESARE, Elías Alfredo
CESCO, Reynaldo P., 923
CESELLI, Juan José, 658, 672, 716, 717, 739, 758, 759
CÉSPEDES, Angel María, 995a
CÉSPEDES, Conrado, 207
CÉSPEDES, Francisco de, 472, 570, 1056
CÉSPEDES, Gregorio, 254
CÉSPEDES, Guillermo, 332
CÉSPEDES, Juan Bautista, 995a
CÉSPEDES, Leopoldo, 1014
CÉSPEDES, Manuel Germán, 611
CÉSPEDES, Martina, 227
CÉSPEDES, Pastora Concepción, 943a
CÉSPEDES GARCÍA XARÍA, Luis de, 1011
CÉSPEDES Y FIGUEROA, Francisco de, 521
CÉSPEDES Y JERIA, Luis, 984
CEVALLOS, Pedro de
   see CEVALLOS CORTÉS HOYOS Y CALDERÓN, Pedro de
CEVALLOS CORTÉS HOYOS Y CALDERÓN, Pedro de, 32, 103, 188, 283, 443, 462, 471, 472, 518, 519, 521, 570, 574, 593, 984, 1091, 1135, 1237, 1240, 1241, 1262
CEVERIO, Andrés, 1122
CIABURRI, Atilio Domingo Italio, 923
CIAMPOLI, Tulia, 893
CIANCIO, Gaetanina, 874
CIANCIO, Pedro N., 952
CIARLONE, Giovanni Battista, 166, 254, 258, 292, 474, 478
CIBILS, José, 735
CIBILS, Petrona, 1065
CIBRIÁN, Alfonso, 731
CICARDO, Vicente Héctor, 923
CICERI, María Susana, 684
CICCHITTI, Vicente, 683a
CICCHITTI DE ARANDA, María del Rosario, 874
CICHERO, Félix Esteban, 751
CID, Alberto, 1192
CID, José Matías, 923
CIEGO REYES, El, pseud.
   see REYES
CIELITO, pseud.
   see FERRETI, Constantino
CIENTOFANTE, Manuel, 878
CIGANDA, Evaristo G., 1126
CIGANKOVA, Elisabeth, 652
CIGLIANO, Eduardo Mario, 923
CIGNOLI, Francisco, 923
CILARIO, Carlos Félix, 874
CIMAGLIA, Lía de
   see CIMAGLIA DE ESPINOSA, Lía de
CIMAGLIA DE ESPINOSA, Lía de, 882, 883
CINCIONI, Alfonso S., 923
CINQUGRANA, Andrés, 712, 770, 836
CINTORA, Francisco Mario, 663
CIOCCHINI, Cleto, 18
CIOCCHINI, Héctor Eduardo, 722, 739, 758, 805, 831
CIONE, Otto Miguel, 1083, 1168, 1170, 1185, 1199, 1246
CIOPPI, Domingo, 781
CIOPPO, Atahualpa del, 1211
CIORDIA, María A., 154
CIPOLLETTI, César, 141, 258, 332
CIPRIANO, Néstor Amílcar, 663
CIPULLI, Dante, 31
CIRES, Adrián, 126
CIRIGLIANO, Alberto C. F., 683a
CIRIGLIANO, Gustavo F. J., 239

CISNEROS, Baltasar Hidalgo
   see CISNEROS Y LA TORRE, Baltasar Hidalgo
CISNEROS, Jorge Iván, 923
CISNEROS LUCES, César, 284
CISNEROS MALBRÁN, Raúl C., 652
CISNEROS Y LA TORRE, Baltasar Hidalgo, 104, 283, 379, 406, 427, 443, 462, 471, 472, 496, 517, 518, 519, 521, 552, 570, 1237, 1239, 1240, 1241
CISTERNA, Rosa P., 235
CITRO, Gilda, 883
CITTADINI, Basilio, 98, 258
CITTADINI, Tito, 19, 31
CIVIT, Arturo, 207
CIVIT, Emilio, 68, 141, 207, 212, 252, 278, 330
CIVIT, Manuel, 207
CLAIRAUX, Augusto, 28
CLARA, Jerónimo Emiliano, 244, 921
CLARE, Dardo E., 1167, 1188
CLARET, Jacques, 960
CLARET, José, 912
CLARET, Susana, 37
CLARK, Juan, 212
CLARK, Juan Eduardo, 120
CLARK, Mateo, 212
CLARK, Theodore S., 954
CLARK Y OBREGÓN, Carlos, 1075
CLARKE, Percy, 904
CLAROS, Juan, 186
CLASTRES, Helene, 962
CLASTRES, Pierre, 962
CLAUSEN, Christian, 4
CLAVELL, Eusebio, 1083
CLAVERO, Francisco, 209, 283
CLAVIER, Irene, 932
CLAWSON, Frank N. (Mrs.)
   see HILL, Cora
CLEMENT, Gastón Carlos, 385
CLEMENT, J. C., 751
CLEMENTE, José Edmundo, 652, 653, 654, 743
CLEMENTE, Juan Carlos, 766, 812
CLEMENTI, Hebe, 609
CLERICI, Eduardo, 258, 292
CLERICI, Justino, 254, 258, 867
CLERVAL, Massie de, 581
CLETA, Masa, pseud.
   see ALTOMARE DE PEREYRA, Emilia
CLOS, Enrique C., 923
CLOSAS, Alberto, 858
CLUHOW, Carlos Alberto, 1187
CLUZEAU MORTEL, Luis, 1067, 1206, 1207, 1208
COBIÁN, Juan Carlos, 891a
COBO, Bernabé, 885
COBO, Francisco, 179
COBO, Juan Francisco, 278
COBOS, Francisco, 68, 94
COBOS, Juan Carlos (QUIQUE, El, pseud.), 860
COCA, Godofredo, 284
CÓCARO, Nicolas, 140, 663, 716, 729, 739, 758, 802, 814
COCCO RIVEROS, Ricardo, 998
CÓCERES, Tomás, 95
COCO, pseud.
   see BACH, Raúl Oscar
COCO, Alberto Luis, 923
COCUCCI, Alfredo Elío, 923
COCHET, Gustavo, 19, 31, 44, 50
COCHRANE, Thomas, 453, 553, 561, 562, 622
CODAS, Aníbal, 1014
CODAS, Daniel, 947, 959
CODAS, Federico, 947, 959
CODAS, Ramón, 954, 963a

CODAS, Silvio, 947
CODAS PAPALUCA, Alcides, 947
CODAS THOMPSON, Quirno, 954, 963a, 965
CODAZZI, Agustín, 258
CODAZZI AGUIRRE, Juan A., 923
CODECA, Augusto, 857b
CODEGA, Aída J.
    see NEBBIA DE CODEGA, Aída J.
CODINA DE GIANNONI, Iverna, 683a, 725
CODIVIOLA, Luis A., 31
CODORNIÚ ALMAZÁN, Filomena, 683a
CODORNIÚ ALMAZÁN, Luis, 683a
COE, Juan, 127
COELHO (family), 361
COELHO, Augusto, 122
COELHO DE MEURELLES (family), 362
COELHO DE MEYRELLES, José, 152
COELLI DE DONADIO, Amanda M., 320
COELLO, Manuel, 186
COGHLAN, Juan, 6, 332
COGO MOLINA, Amalia Rosa, 1210
COGORNO, Santiago, 18, 19, 23, 25, 31, 36, 55
COHÉ, 977
COHEN, Rafael, 857
COIRA, Enrique, 260
COIRO, Miguel, 893
COIROLO, Hipólito, 1083
COLABELLA, Angel Victorino, 822
COLECCHIA, Felipe, 874
COLEMAN, Arturo H., 904
COLETTI, Juan, 683a
COLINA, Arcadio de la, 68
COLINA, Bernardo José Antonio de la, 496, 915
COLINA, Domingo A., 381a
COLINA, Marcelo de la, 126
COLINA, Nicolás
    see CORMA, Nicolás
COLINA, Salvador de la, 189, 247, 381a
COLIQUEO, Antonino, 180
COLIQUEO, Ignacio, 180
COLMAN, Carmelo
    see COLMAN, José del Carmen
COLMAN, José del Carmen, 1059, 1081, 1111
COLMAN, José del Socorro, 998
COLMAN, Juan B., 947
COLMAN, Narciso Ramón (ROSICRÁN, pseud.), 943, 959
COLMEGNA, Virgilio, 258
COLMEIRO, Manuel, 1218
COLNAGO, José W., 966
COLOBRARO, Vicente, 923
COLOM, Pedro, 319
COLOMBINO, Carlos Santiago, 938, 939, 1017, 1018a
COLOMBO, Angela, 785
COLOMBO, Carlos, 939, 966
COLOMBO, Cristoforo, 212, 258, 292, 406, 448, 455, 462, 472, 519, 528, 952, 984
COLOMBO, Ezio, 258
COLOMBO, Francisco, 704
COLOMBO, Juan, 952
COLOMBO, Osvaldo Francisco, 140
COLOMBRES, José, 611, 626
COLOMBRES, José Eusebio, 141, 176, 244, 282, 439, 457, 526, 574, 621
COLOMBRES, Justo José, 910
COLOMES, Martín José, 923
COLÓN, Cristóbal
    see COLOMBO, Cristoforo
COLÓN, Salvador (SAUVEUR), 949, 960
COLONNA WALEWSKI, Alejandro Floriano, 238, 390
COLONNESE, Juan Carlos, 299

COLOVINI, Angel, 878
COLT DE HUME, Blanca C. E., 762
COLUCCIO, Félix, 140, 217, 702
COLUSSI, Guillermo, 788
COLL, Carlos M., 94
COLL, Francisco Tristán, 283
COLL, Jaime, 1116
COLL, Juan de, 845
COLL, Juan José, 653, 654, 831
COLL, Ventura G., 211, 344
COLLA, Silvia A., 923
COLLADO, Ireneo E., 97
COLLAR, José Mateo, 982
COLLAZO, Abner, 1093
COLLAZO, Juan, 1093
COLLAZO, Néstor, 1093
COLLAZO, Ulises, 1093
COLLISBERRY, Guillermo, 179
COLLIVADINO, Pío, 19, 25, 31, 44, 282, 293, 755
COLLORD, Margaret Louise, 323
COLLURA, Antonio Mario, 923
COMADRÁN RUIZ, Jorge, 521
COMBES, Teodoro José C., 923
COMENTAL, Pedro, 866, 922
COMESAÑA, Eduardo, 55
COMINGES, Juan de, 191
COMPTE, Pedro, 1094
COMPTE Y RIQUET, Enriqueta, 1083, 1217
COMTE, José, 32
CONCEPCIÓN, Alfredo, 213
CONCI, Ivo, 923
CONCOLORCORVO, pseud. (BUSTAMANTE CARLOS INCA, Calixto), 683, 713, 834, 1230
CONCHA, Zoilo
    see CONCHA VILLEGAS, Zoilo
CONCHA MIRANDA, Julián Milcíades, 1017
CONCHA SUBERCASEAUX, Carlos, 68
CONCHA VILLEGAS, Zoilo, 158, 222
CONDE (family), 1108
CONDE, Agustín, 7
CONDE, José Manuel, 812
CONDE, Juan, 344
CONDE, Mariano, 496
CONDE, Pedro, 11a, 254
CONDE SALGADO, Ricardo, 284
CONDORCANQUI, José Gabriel (TUPAC AMARÚ), 458, 472, 1229
CONESA, Emilio, 611
CONI, Emilio A., 1246
CONI, Emilio R., 842, 844, 1261
CONI, Pablo Emilio, 853a
CONRAD, Erich, 923
CONSELMO, Méneca de, pseud., 683a
CONSOLE, Alfredo, 652
CONSOLE, Antonio G., 41
CONSTANTE, Víctor, 1084
CONSTANTINI, Humberto, 712
CONSTANTINO, Italo Nicolás, 923
CONSTANTINO, Vicente, 268
CONTE, Alejandro C. del, 811
CONTE, Daniel, 1206
CONTE, Estanislao del, 923
CONTE GRAND, Benito, 1039
CONTERIS, Hiber, 1172, 1182, 1185
CONTESTABILE, Telémaco, 894
CONTI, Alcides Leopoldo, 923
CONTI, Eugenio, 258
CONTI, Haroldo, 666, 696, 697, 796, 829, 835
CONTI, Jean, 960
CONTI, Jorge, 759
CONTI DE OTERO, María, 320

CONTÍN, Carlos Raúl, 135
CONTRERAS, Alonso de, 520
CONTRERAS, Jerónima de, 109
CONTRERAS, Juan de, 556
CONTURSI, Pascual, 727, 759, 868, 871, 875, 877
CONWAY, Mary Elizabeth, 323
COOK, Sarah, 323
COOLIDGE, Elizabeth Boyer, 323
COPELO GONZÁLEZ, Silverio Valois, 1210
COPELLO, Francesco, 292
COPELLO, José, 73
COPELLO, Santiago Luis, 258, 910
COPIN, Bartolomé, 556
COPPETTI, Víctor, 1083
COPPINI, Eliseo Fausto, 19, 258
COPPOLA, Armando, 25, 31, 55
COQUET, Jorge, 332
COQUET, Juan, 249
CORA, Juan Miguel, 121
CORA BASSO, Rodolfo Valentín, 1210
CORBACHO, Oscar, 687
CORBALÁN, Joaquín, 852
CORBALÁN, Juan, 186
CORBALÁN, Manuel, 188, 923
CORBERA, Ramón, 845
CORBIÈRE, Emilio P., 152a
CORDERO, Bartolomé, 14
CORDERO, Francisco, 344
CORDERO, José, 32
CORDERO, Juan, 887
CORDERO, Mariano, 14
CORDERO, Octavio, 565
CORDERO, Petrona, 422
CORDERO PÉREZ, Manuel, 284
CORDINI, Isaías Rafael, 923
CORDIVIOLA, Luis Adolfo, 19
CÓRDOBA, Alberto, 680, 713, 779, 830
CÓRDOBA, Alonso de, 555
CÓRDOBA, Ana de, 1270
CÓRDOBA, Antonio de, 579
CÓRDOBA, Carlos Alberto, 923
CÓRDOBA, Isidoro, 268
CÓRDOBA, Juan de, 845, 949, 1034
CÓRDOBA, Nabor, 189
CÓRDOBA, Numa P. (NUMA CRIOLLO, pseud.), 811
CÓRDOBA ITURBURU, Cayetano, 773
CORDOBÉS, Víctor, 1006
CORDÓN, José G., 222
CORDÓN, Víctor Hugo, 923
CORDONE, Alberto, 645
CORDONE, Cirilo, 952
CÓRDOVA, Leodegario, 268
CÓRDOVA, Mateo C., 385
CÓRDOVA ITURBURU, Cayetano, 140, 678, 722, 739, 748, 751, 801, 807, 833
CORDOVÉS, Francisco Martín, 186
CORDOVÉS, Juan, 186
CORIA, Fermín, 207
CORIA BOHORQUEZ, Alonso, 555
CORIA BOHORQUEZ, Juan de, 556
CORIA PEÑALOZA, Gabino, 217, 871
CORIS, Juan, 319
CORMA, Nicolás, 992
CORNAGLIA, Juan J., 152a, 779, 834
CORNEJO, Abel F., 332
CORNEJO, Adrián, 649a
CORNEJO, Atilio, 521, 653, 654
CORNEJO, Carlos S., 653, 654
CORNET Y PRAT, Juan, 496
COROMINAS SEGURA, Rodolfo, 207

CORONA, Julio, 874
CORONA MARTÍNEZ, Enrique, 260
CORONADO, Juan, 96
CORONADO, Martín, 152a, 167, 282, 293, 664, 669, 734, 749, 751, 1243, 1247, 1263
CORONADO, Nicolás, 135, 751
CORONADO, Pedro, 844
CORONADO, Pedro J., 68
CORONEL, Coca Amanda, 768
CORONEL, Dalmiro, 1122
CORONEL, Dionisio, 1081, 1093, 1122
CORONEL, Gabino, 1122
CORONEL, Manuel, 1140
CORONEL DE PASO, María Mercedes, 422
CORRAL, Néstor, 31
CORRAL, Rodolfo, 857c
CORRATALA, Rogelio, 923
CORREA, Baby, 893
CORREA, Cirilo, 611
CORREA, Gervasio, 95
CORREA, Julio, 943, 1012, 1014, 1018, 1018a, 1020, 1021, 1022, 1026
CORREA, Manuel, 254, 433, 611
CORREA, Miguel Angel (BOOZ, Mateo, pseud.), 152a, 154, 670, 707, 744, 753, 779, 825, 1245, 1246
CORREA, Olegario, 188, 244, 545a, 910, 921
CORREA, Rubens, 889
CORREA, Tomás, 254
CORREA DE SÁA, José Félix, 371, 555
CORREA LUNA, Celia, 1207
CORREA MORALES, Lucio, 19, 21, 25, 191, 282, 293
CORREA MORALES DE YRURTIA, Lía, 19, 45, 64
CORREA MORENO, Alvaro, 1123
CORREA RODRÍGUEZ, Walter Danubio, 1210
CORREAS, Dolores
    see CORREAS DE LAVALLE, Dolores
CORREAS, Edmundo, 207, 521, 683a
CORREAS, Horacio, 837
CORREAS, José, 555
CORREAS DE LARREA, Pedro, 555
CORREAS DE LAVALLE, Dolores, 478, 611, 929
CORREAS DE ZAPATA, Celia, 683a
CORREDOR, Antonio, 254
CORRETJER, Mario M., 154
CORRO, Miguel Calixto del, 144, 177, 244, 313, 358, 457, 545a, 611, 621, 626, 720, 895, 908
CORSI, Carlos, 191
CORSINI, Alicia A., 810
CORSINI, Ignacio, 877, 892
CORSO DE LANTIVAR, Marino, 292
CORTÁZAR, Augusto Raúl, 239, 521, 652, 653, 654, 688
CORTÁZAR, Julián T. de, 501, 529a, 649a, 910, 913
CORTÁZAR, Julio (DENIS, Julio, pseud.), 232, 674, 685, 697, 715, 741, 756, 772, 799, 803, 806, 807, 812, 816, 825, 829, 835
CORTE, Arturo E., 923
CORTE CARRILLO, César, 663, 664, 713, 730
CORTE CARRILLO, Manuel, 713
CORTEGOSO, Tierno, 731
CORTÉS, Alfonso, 658
CORTÉS, Gerónimo, 244, 445
CORTÉS, Juan Alberto, 7
CORTÉS, Rafael, 222
CORTÉS CONDE, Roberto, 218
CORTÉS DEL PINO, Juan, 652
CORTESE, Guillermo Omar, 691
CORTEZ, Rafael, 158
CORTEZ, Raúl Andrés, 684
CORTEZ LÓPEZ, Joaquín, 822

CORTEZ RUIZ DE LOS LLANOS, Carlos, 653, 654
CORTI, Norberto, 703
CORTIJO VIDAL, Mariano, 874
CORTINA, Adolfo, 191
CORTINA, José María, 268, 371
CORTINA, Pedro, 496
CORTINAS, César, 894, 1064, 1206, 1207, 1208
CORTINAS, Ismael, 894, 1083, 1185
CORTINES, Laura, 1187
CORTÍNEZ, Clara Rosa, 930, 931
CORTÍNEZ, Indalecio, 283
CORTÍNEZ, Pedro José, 173
CORTÍNEZ, Santiago S., 141, 173, 283, 631
CORVALÁN, Eugenio, 412
CORVALÁN, Jaime Antonio, 995a
CORVALÁN, José, 230
CORVALÁN, Manuel, 222, 283, 412, 413
CORVALÁN, Manuel Antonio, 964, 995a
CORVALÁN, Manuel de la Trinidad, 179
CORVALÁN, Santiago E., 565
CORVALÁN, Victorino, 412, 413
CORVALÁN DE GARCÍA, María de la Oliva, 971
CORVALÁN MENDILAHARZU, Dardo, 135
CORVALÁN MONTIEL DE GARCÍA, Juana María de la
    Olivia, 972
CORVALÁN ORTIZ, Juan B., 998
CORVALÁN POSSE, Roberto E., 739
CORVETTO, Pedro C., 683a
COSARINSKY, Gregorio B., 198
COSCOLLA RODRÍGUEZ, Antonio, 923
COSENTINO, José, 874
COSENTINO, Voltaire José, 698
COSIO, Pedro, 1083
COSME, Bernabé, 1145
COSSA, Roberto M., 690, 889
COSSIO, Carlos, 218
COSSIO, Manuel, 887
COSSIO, Pedro, 213, 923
COSSIO DE GUTIÉRREZ, Estanislao, 924
COSSIO Y THERÁN, Francisco, 268
COSTA, Angel Floro, 254, 1075, 1146, 1188
COSTA, Dalmiro, 864, 867, 894, 1079, 1206, 1207,
    1208
COSTA, Eduardo, 116, 166, 226, 330, 372
COSTA, Eduardo Da
    see DA COSTA, Eduardo
COSTA, Felipe Isidro, 923
COSTA, Francisco, 268
COSTA, Gabriel, 226
COSTA, Jaime R., 842, 844
COSTA, Juan José, 923
COSTA, Julio A., 391
COSTA, Luis, 258
COSTA, María, 227
COSTA, Pasqual, 226
COSTA FIGUEIRAS, José, 284
COSTA Y OLIVEIRA CÉZAR, Ernestina, 226
COSTAMAGNA, Santiago, 258, 287, 907a
COSTANTINI, Humberto, 696, 697, 829
COSTANZÓ, Alfredo J., 954
COSTARELLI, Roberto E., 923
COSTAS, Leonardo, 69
COSTAS, S. Enrique, 1089
COSTAS FERNÁNDEZ, José, 1089
COSTAS GONZÁLEZ, Manuel, 1089
COSTEÑO, El, pseud.
    see MORALES, Mariano
COSTIGLIOLO, José Pedro, 1049
COT, Lorenzo, 534
COTAPOS DE CARRERA, Ana María, 208

COTELO, José, 1089
COTELO, Ramón, 1089
COTLAR, Mischa, 923
COTO, Patricia Herminia, 663
COTROFE, Cirilo Isabel, 878
COTTA, Juan Manuel, 834
COTTA, Roberto Diego, 923
COUCHET, J. Ramón, 663
COUCHONNAL LAGRAVE, Luis, 947
COUÑAGO, Manuel, 1089
COURTIS, Baudilio, 923
COUSTAU, Juan, 68
COUTARET, Manuel Emilio, 24
COUTO, Francisco, 949
COUTO, José, 1089
COUTOUNE, Alberto, 713
COUTS, Manuel, 1089
COUTURE DE TROISMONTS, Alicia
    see PEYCERE DE COUTURE DE TROISMONTS, Alicia
COUTURE DE TROISMONTS, Roberto J. C., 652
COVARRUBIA, Baltasar de, 1041
COVAS, Guillermo, 923
COVIELLO, Francisco, 258
COVOS SEBRIÁN, Ysidro de los, 186
COYTO, Manuel de, 32, 1270
COZZO, Domingo, 923
COZZOLINO, Santiago E., 154
CRAIG, Tomás, 254
CRAMER, Ambrosio, 332
CRANWELL, Guillermo A., 103
CRAVERI, Giovanni, 292
CRAVIOTTO, José A., 124
CRAWFORD, Robert, 587
CRAWFORD GONZÁLEZ, Leslie Thubal, 1088
CRAY, Christián de, 186
CREMONESI, José, 1083
CREMONTE, Juan José Francisco, 320
CRENOVICH, Eugenio (YENTE, pseud.), 19, 31
CRESPI, María del Carmen, 652
CRESPI, Martín B. A., 923
CRESPI, Rodolfo, 857d
CRESPO, Antonio, 95, 16, 844, 1110
CRESPO, Antonio F., 103, 445
CRESPO, Carlos Alberto, 817
CRESPO, Francisco, 611
CRESPO, Ignacio, 121
CRESPO, Jorge Alberto, 923
CRESPO, José, 106
CRESPO, Manuel, 135, 1089
CRESPO, Marcelino, 250
CRESPO, Procoro, 135
CRESTA VEGA, Gloria, 947
CRESTAR FARALDO, Antonio, 1089
CRESTAR FARALDO, Manuel, 1089
CREUS, Carlos, 1235
CREVAUX, 949, 960
CREVAUX, Julio N., 191
CRIADO, Matias Alonso, 1094
CRIADO, Roque Pedro, 923
CRIMI, Humberto, 683a
CRIPPA, Alejandro Miguel, 299
CRISCUOLO, Enso, 923
CRISOL, Miguel, 244
CRISPO ACOSTA, Osvaldo (LAUXAR, pseud.), 1064, 1068,
    1165
CRISTALDO, Adolfo, 191
CRISTANCHI, Aldo, 831
CRISTÓBAL, Carmen L., 923
CRNKO, José, 923
CROCCE, Francisco, 207
CROCCO, Juan B., 874

CROCE, Romeo, 923
CROIX, Louis de la, 949, 960
CROKER, J. W., 573
CROSA, Angel, 951
CROSA, Enrique, 894, 1185
CROSA, Josefina, 762
CROSA DE BARBERO, Carolina, 951
CROSS, Arvilla, 323
CROSS, William Ernest, 923
CROTOGINI DARRE, Elina, 1210
CROTTI DE UBEDA MOLINA, Irma A. Adria, 923
CROTTO, José Camilo, 391
CROUZEILLES, Amelia Larguía de
    see LARGUÍA DE CROUZEILLES, Amelia de
CROVATO, Favio R., 998
CROVATO, Gustavo A.
    see CROVATTO, Gustavo A.
CROVATTO, Angel, 952
CROVATTO, Gustavo M., 959, 998
CROVETTO, Nereo, 391
CRUCES, José María, 147
CRUCES, Manuel, 1089
CRUCES, Ramón, 1089
CRUCES ANGUEIRA, Fortunato, 284
CRUCIANI, Julio A., 260
CRUZ, 179
CRUZ, Antonio
    see FERNÁNDEZ, Antonio de la Cruz
CRUZ, Arnaldo H., 701
CRUZ, Bartolomé de la, 1270
CRUZ, Francisco, 569
CRUZ, Francisco Javier de la, 555
CRUZ, Jorge, 140, 218
CRUZ, Juan Gerónimo de la, 186
CRUZ, Juan Roberto, 37
CRUZ, Louis de la
    see CROIX, Louis de la
CRUZ, Luis de la, 470, 922, 1229
CRUZ AGUIRRE, Atanasio, 1091
CRUZ AYALA, José de la
    see AYALA, José de la Cruz
CRUZ DEL VALLE, Antonio, 895
CRUZ ESTIGARRIBIA, Juan de la
    see ESTIBARRIBIA, Juan de la Cruz
CRUZ FERNÁNDEZ, Antonio de la
    see FERNÁNDEZ, Antonio de la Cruz
CRUZ GHIO, Juan, 834
CRUZ GHIO, Julio (CRUZ ORELLANA, pseud.), 811, 1246
CRUZ GUERRERO, José de la
    see GUERRERO, José de la Cruz
CRUZ MATEO, Juan, 31, 860
CRUZ MONJE, Juan de la
    see MONJE, Juan de la Cruz
CRUZ MONTEALEGRE, Juan de la
    see MONTEALEGRE, Juan de la Cruz
CRUZ OLMEDO, José Saviniano, 1210
CRUZ ORELLANA, pseud.
    see CRUZ GHIO, Julio
CRUZ RIVAROLA, Juan de la
    see RIVAROLA, Juan de la Cruz
CRUZ VALDEZ, Atanasia de la, 973
CRUZ VALLE, Juan Antonio, 599
CRUZ VARELA, Juan de la, 599
    see VARELA, Juan de la Cruz
CRUZAT MOLLETO, Bernando de, 555
CSIK, Bela José, 923
CUADRA ZÚÑIGA, Manuel E., 683a
CUADRI, Guillermo (GARRIDO, Santos, pseud.), 1151,
    1166, 1167, 1179, 1243, 1248
CUADRO, Servando, 1184

CUADROS, Hilario, 217, 874
CUANARÁ, Alonso, 977
CUARÁ, Juan, 977
CUARABAY, 977
CUARACIPÚ, 977
CUARACIPUCÚ, 977
CUARARÉ, 977
CUARAY, 977
CUATÍ, 977
CUATRECASAS, Juan, 923
CUBAS, Emilio, 947, 954
CUBILLOS, Arturo, 207
CUBILLOS, Máximo, 207
CUBILLOS, Rafael, 207
CUCCHI, Nelio José A., 923
CUEBAS, Luis de las, 845
CUELLO, Néstor, 810
CUELLO, Raúl Ernesto, 8, 311
CUELLO, Sevastián, 186
CUENCA, Abel Julio, 831
CUENCA, Claudio Mamerto, 669, 677, 718, 720, 724,
    737, 761, 807, 844, 1243, 1247, 1261
CUENCA, Mamerto, 13
CUENCA, María Guadalupe, 144
CUENCA, Melchora, 1060
CUENCA, Rodolfo, 836
CUENCA, Salustiano, 844
CUENCA GALLEGOS, Juan de, 186
CUERNO DE LA RIVA (family), 348
CUERVO ROMERO, Evaristo Armando, 1210
CUESTAS, Juan Lindolfo, 1075, 1079, 1091, 1109
CUESTAS DE NERY, Carmen, 1083
CUESTAS VILA, Gerardo, 1210
CUETO, Bartolomé, 134
CUETO, Jacinto, 611
CUETO, Joaquín, 254
CUETO, Manuel, 32
CUETO, Pascuala, 211
CUETO, Teodosio, 1017
CUETO TABOADA, José, 264
CUEVA, Cosme de la, 895
CUEVA, Hernando de la, 556
CUEVA DE BENAVÍDEZ, Mendo de la
    see CUEVA Y BENAVÍDEZ, Mendo de la
CUEVA Y BENAVÍDEZ, Juan Bernardo de la, 646
CUEVA Y BENAVÍDEZ, Mendo de la, 472, 521, 570
CUEVAS, Armín Z., 963a
CUEVAS, Chelita, 955
CUEVAS MAGGI, Martín R., 954
CUFRE, Aníbal, 299
CUGAT, Delia, 55
CULEBRAS, Joaquín, 887
CULLEN, Domingo, 95, 121, 206, 216, 466, 480, 1082
CULLEN, Patricio, 560
CULLEN, Tomás R., 94
CULLEN AYERZA, Hernán, 19, 21
CUMÁ, Manuel, 987
CUMBAY, 611
CUMBRAS, Manuel, 1089
CÚNEO, Celestino, 1083
CÚNEO, José, 1044
CÚNEO, Victor Hugo, 683a
CÚNEO BETTOSINI, José Angel, 1210
CUNHA, Juan
    see CUNHA DOTTI, Juan
CUNHA, Víctor, 1183
CUNHA DOTTI, Juan, 1151, 1152, 1153, 1177, 1178,
    1179, 1187, 1199
CUNIAMBÍ, 977
CUNIARACÚA, 977
CUNIBERTI, Nyda, 660

CUNNINGHAM-GRAHAM, Roberto B., 834, 1246
CUNQUEIRO, Susana Virginia, 691
CUNSOLO, Víctor Juan, 18, 19, 25, 31, 36
CUNUMIPITA, 977
CUÑA, Irma, 831
CUÑAMBO, 977
CUÑARRO, Benito M., 1075, 1083
CUOMO, Edmundo Isaac, 923
CUOMO, Jorge Ricardo, 923
CUORE, Héctor, 894
CUPIDO, Roberto, 681
CURADO, Francisco Xavier, 552
CURATELLA MANES, Pablo, 19, 21, 25, 49, 55
CURBELO LARROSA, Aurora, 1083
CURES ACERENZA, Carlos Esteban, 1210
CURES LEAL, Luis Alberto, 1210
CURITI, 977
CURIUNI DE TRIGUERO, Eva María, 320
CURLANDO, Federico, 878, 1243
CUROTTO, Angel, 894, 1172, 1185
CURUBA, 977
CURUBETO GODOY, María Isabel
     see TRUCCO DE CURUBETO GODOY, María Isabel
CURUPAY, 977
CUTLER, Bruce, 1015
CUTOLO, Vicente Osvaldo, 126
CUYÁS HORNE, Rebeca Ulpiana, 1210
CUYÁS Y SAMPERE, Antonio, 95, 96, 127, 596
CUYÉN AYERZA, Hernán, 25
CYNALEWICZ, Estanislao, 238
CZAJKA, Guillermo, 923
CZANECKI, Ladislao, pseud.
     see CZARNECKI, Ladislao
CZARNECKI, Ladislao (CZANECKI, Ladislao; CHARNESKI,
     Ladislao; SCARNESKY, Ladislao; OZARNECKY,
     Ladislao; pseuds.), 238
CZESLAW WYSOCKI, Jordan, 238, 332
CZETZ, 153
CZETZ, Juan Francisco, 332

CHAB, Víctor, 19, 25, 36, 46, 49, 55
CHABRILLÓN (family), 168
CHABRILLÓN, Andrés, 135, 751, 773, 800
CHACEL, Rosa, 729
CHACÓN, Antonio, 555
CHACHA AGUILAR, pseud.
     see AGUILAR, Josefina
CHACHO, El, pseud.
     see PEÑALOZA, Angel Vicente
CHAÍN, Benito
     see CHAÍN FERNÁNDEZ, Benito
CHAÍN FERNÁNDEZ, Benito, 284, 1095
CHAIT, Alejandro, 923
CHALE, Gertrudis, 25, 36
CHALIMÍN, 83
CHALUKIAN, Diana, 31
CHAMBO, Mariano, 895, 921
CHAMERO, Juan Angel, 923
CHAMICO, pseud.
     see NALÉ ROXLO, Conrado
CHAMORRO, Delfín, 941, 943, 947, 959, 966, 1012,
     1014, 1026
CHAMOT, Arnoldo Eugenio, 299
CHANA DE NAVARRO, Ercilia F., 652
CHANI LAO, pseud.
     see BUSTAMANTE, Joaquín T.
CHANOURDIE, Enrique, 332
CHANTELO, pseud.
     see AGUILERA, Pedro
CHAPARRO, Guillermo, 1152

CHAPEAUROUGE, Carlos de, 211, 332
CHAPERÓN, Alfredo Luciano, 320
CHAPONICK, Héctor, 660
CHARCHA FLIE, Rodolfo Juan, 664
CHARLES (family), 168
CHARLET, Louis, 960
CHARLEVOIX, Pierre-François-Xavier, 943, 949, 966,
     985
CHARLONE, César, 1073
CHARLONE, Juan Bautista
     see CIARLONE, Giovanni Bautista
CHARNESKI, Ladislao
     see CZARNECKI, Ladislao
CHARRAS, Julián de, 751
CHARRAS, Martiniano, 128
CHARRO, María Cristina, 691
CHARRÚA, pseud.
     see MÁRQUEZ, Gualberto
CHARTON, Ernesto, 51, 59, 521
CHAS DE CRUZ, Israel, 811
CHASE SARDI, Miguel, 962
CHASE SOSA, Vicente, 947, 963a
CHASSAING, Juan, 79, 216, 380, 408, 669, 1247
CHATEL (family), 168
CHATTAS, Alberto, 923
CHAURI, Domingo, 284
CHAUVELOT, Francis, 949
CHAVANNE, Jean Marie, 59
CHAVARRI Y VALLEJO, Martín de, 1030
CHAVARRÍA, Isaac M., 541
CHAVARRÍA DE VIAMONTE, Bernardina, 422, 611
CHAVERO, Héctor Roberto
     see YUPANQUI, Atahualpa
CHAVES, Adriana, 679, 717
CHAVES, Efraín Isaac, 781
CHAVES, Eliseo, 1075
CHAVES, Federico, 963
CHAVES, Francisco C., 959
CHAVES, Gregorio N., 247, 842, 844
CHAVES, Joaquín, 137
CHAVES, José Manuel, 611
CHAVES, Juan R., 954
CHAVES, Julio César, 943, 964, 966, 990, 1006, 1021,
     1022
CHAVES, Manuel W., 959
CHAVES, Nuflo de, 472, 504, 949, 989, 1012, 1229,
     1232
CHAVES DE FERREIRO, Anairis, 1020
CHÁVEZ, Ariadna, 831
CHÁVEZ, Diego de, 1270
CHÁVEZ, Fermín, 135, 381a, 431, 609, 688, 717, 739,
     766
CHÁVEZ DEL SUELDO, Pedro, 649a
CHAWORTH MUSTERS, George, 289
CHAZARRETA, Andrés A., 217, 882
CHAZARRETA, Edith R., 652
CHECA, Renée, 1014
CHECABI, 977
CHEMOMBÉ, 977
CHENA, Pascual de, 1056
CHENA, Wherfield, 923
CHENAUT, Indalecio, 371, 611
CHANÚ LÓPEZ, Adrián, 998
CHEVALLIER PARIS, Gastón, pseud.
     see GONZÁLEZ ALSINA, Ezequiel
CHEVESTE, Andrés, 1059, 1111
CHIAMA, Epamimondas, 59, 258
CHIANELLI, Trinidad Delia, 609
CHIAPASCO, Elena, 683a
CHIAPPARA, Juan J., 1064

CHIAPPORI, Atilio, 154, 670, 1246
CHIAPPORI, Gustavo Adolfo, 923
CHIAPPORI, Rómulo H., 842
CHIARAVIGLIO, Antonio, 87
CHIARELLA, Eduardo, 87
CHIARELLI, Pablo Aurelio, 1151
CHIARELLI DE GAHAM, Angelina, 923
CHIARINI, José, 258
CHICLANA, Feliciano Antonio, 85, 104, 244, 282, 386,
    404, 478, 479, 496, 499, 517, 552, 563, 574, 611
CHICLANA, Feliciano Mariano, 332
CHICHE, pseud.
    see FORTE, Alberto
CHICHE, pseud.
    see SAN MARTÍN Y ESCALADA DE BALCARCE, Mercedes
    de
CHIÉRICO, Osiris U., 717, 739
CHILAVERT, Martiniano, 332, 600
CHILLIDA, Luis Alberto, 923
CHIMENTI, Armando, 881
CHIMENTI, Genaro, 860
CHIMENTO, Juan Pascual, 910
CHINA MARÍA, La, 1066
CHIODI, Hugo Pablo, 923
CHIPACO, Juan, 608
CHIQUILLO, pseud.
    see ESQUIVEL, Bernabé Antonio
CHIQUITO, pseud.
    see SARAVIA, Antonio Floricio
CHIRIFE, Adolfo, 959
CHIRIFE MAZÓ, Gilberto, 998
CHIRINO DE POSADAS, Francisco, 555
CHIRRE DANÓS, Ricardo, 679
CHOATE, Antoinette (Mrs. William W. Richardson),
    323
CHODASIEWICZ, Roberto Adolfo, 238
CHOLO, pseud.
    see MALNATTI, César
CHOLO, pseud.
    see VEGHETTI, Oscar César
CHOMÉ, Ignacio, 949, 960, 1037
CHOMÉ, Ignatius
    see CHOME, Ignacio
CHOMNALES, Raúl, 923
CHONCHÓN, pseud.
    see TIEMPO, Julio César
CHOPITEA (family), 1108
CHORROARÍN, Luis José, 317, 321, 496, 611, 895, 921
CHOUHY AGUIRRE, Ana María, 725, 739, 748, 758, 759,
    783, 807, 812
CHOUSIÑO, Esteban, 268
CHRIST, Tilo, 954
CHRISTENSEN, Carlos Hugo, 858, 893
CHRISTIANSEN, Myrta, 705
CHRISTIE, William D., 96
CHRISTIERSSON, Carlos, 332
CHRISTMANN, Federico E., 923
CHUCARRO (family), 1224
CHUCARRO, Alejandro, 1052
CHUCHI, Francisco del Rosario, 995a
CHUCHIN, pseud.
    see SORAZÁBAL, Juan
CHUDNOVSKY, José, 923
CHUECO, Manuel C., 268
CHULACK, Armando, 702
CHULJAK, Juan Carlos, 37
CHUMILLA, Vicente, 299
CHURRUARÍN, José Lino, 95
CHURRUARÍN, Miguel M., 121
CHUTRO, Pedro, 133, 293

DA COSTA, Eduardo, 1083
DA LUZ, Graciela, 789
DA PONTE, Héctor, 937
DA PONTE, Roberto, 998
DA PORTA MONTERROSO, Marcos José, 1095
DA ROSA, Alberto, 560
DA ROSA, Eliseo, 959
DA ROSA, Julio C., 1148, 1149, 1155, 1157, 1159,
    1177, 1183, 1186, 1189, 1196
DABBENE, Roberto Raúl, 258
DABEZIES, Antonio María, 1183
DABOVE, César, 668
DABOVE, Santiago, 685, 745a, 815, 816
DABROWSKI, Adam, 238
DACAK FRUTES, Sergio Enrique, 1017
D'ACCURZIO, Gildo, 683a
DADEY, José, 866
DAGA, Ricardo Martín, 35
DAGLIETTO, Olga Margarita, 700
DAGLIO, Cayetano (PACHEQUITO, pseud.), 878
DAGNINO, Alberto, 1123
DAGNINO, Esteban, 259
DAGNINO CIGANDA, Zulma, 1088
DAGNINO PASTORE, Lorenzo, 218, 923
DAHL, Jorge, 299
DAHLHAMMER, Ruperto, 850
DAHLQUIST, Juan R., 943, 959, 1014
DAIREAUX, Carlos G., 385
DAIREAUX, Godofredo, 769, 815, 834, 1246
DAIREAUX, Max, 834
DAKAC, Alberto, 998
D'ALESSIO, Rafael Henzo, 663
D'ALESSIO DE CARNEVALE BONINO, Rosa C., 923
D'ALMEIDA DE CORREA ALVAREZ, Elena, 874
DALTOE, Minerva, 31
DALTON, Enrique, 299
DALLA TORRE DE TUDELA, Blanca, 207, 683a
DALLA TORRE VICUÑA, Luis José, 683a
DALLEGRI, Santiago, 811, 813, 1190
D'AMARIO, Edelmiro, 860
D'AMARIO, Víctor, 860
D'AMATO, Generoso, 878, 1243
D'AMBROSIO DE RONCONI, Delia Isabel (ROCNI, Deisde,
    pseud.), 691
DAMEGLIO DE BONAVITA, Araceli, 691
DAMÉS, José, 862
DAMI DE SOTO, Francisco, 186
DAMIANI, Jorge, 1045, 1049
D'AMICO, Alicia, 55
D'AMICO, Carlos, 391
D'AMICO DE REBOSSIO, Beatriz, 781
DAMILANO, Juan, 878
DAMKÖHLER, Guillermo, 923
DANELL, Alejandro, 371, 492, 611
DANERI, Celia, 894
DANERI, Eugenio
    see DANERI, Santiago Eugenio
DANERI, Santiago Eugenio, 18, 19, 23, 25, 31, 32,
    36, 50, 55, 64
DANERO, E. M. S., 688
DANESI, Mario, 857b
DANIEL, Joaquín, 923
DANIEL, Jorge, 954
DANIEL, Juan Bautista, 32
DANIELLO, Juan, 1068
DANIELS, Louise, 323
DANKERT, Ernesto G., 923
D'ANNA, Eduardo, 759, 788
DANTÁS, Antonio José, 1264
DANTAS LACOMBE, Mercedes, 751, 762

DANZA ELIZALDE, Juan Alberto, 65
DAPONTE, Héctor, 937, 939
DARBYSHIRE, Gilberto Ramsay, 904
DARCAT, Juan, 222
DARCAT, Justo, 158, 159, 215, 222, 566
DARCAT, Mauricio P., 81, 158, 222
DARDÁN, Carlos María, 800
DARDO ROSILLO, Reinaldo (ROS, Reinaldo, pseud.),
    135, 800
DARDÓN, Carlos María, 135
DARIEUX DE GRIVEL, José, 581
DARÍO, Juan, 318, 649a
DARÍO, Rubén (GARCÍA SARMIENTO, Félix Rubén), 225,
    956
DARK, Rosa Ella, 323
DARRÉ, Ricardo Walter Oscar, 575
DARREGUEIRA, José de
    see DARREGUEIRA Y LUGO, José de
DARREGUEIRA Y LUGO, José de, 126, 439, 457, 478,
    479, 496, 526, 611, 621, 626
DARRIVA, José, 1089
D'ARTENSAC, Germaine
    see ARTENSAC, Germaine d'
DARTIGUELONGUE, María Cristina, 37
DARWIN, Charles, 287, 289, 834
DASLLAGAS ANTÚNEZ MACIEL, Luis, 1092
DASSEN, Claro Cornelio, 332
DASSO, Héctor, 923
DASTIR, Wilma, 46
DATTI, Francisco 319
DATTOLI, Armando Buenaventura, 775
DAUB, Walter Enrique, 923
DAUD, Fortunato, 385
DAUFRESNE, Julio, 28
DAUMAS, Louis Joseph, 59
DAUMAS LADOUCE, Félix, 949
DAUMAS LADOUCE, Luis, 963a
DAUMAS LADOUCE, Pablo, 963a
DÁVALOS, Arturo L., 653, 654
DÁVALOS, Baltazar, 653
DÁVALOS, Edmundo, 998
DÁVALOS, Jaime, 653, 654, 717, 739, 759, 803, 812,
    831, 1243
DÁVALOS, José Arturo L., 653, 654
DÁVALOS, Juan Carlos, 653, 654, 664, 670, 674, 678,
    680, 689, 707, 722, 739, 737, 739, 740, 745,
    751, 759, 773, 779, 782, 799, 829, 830, 1243,
    1245
DÁVALOS, María Inés, 653
DÁVALOS, Raica, 653, 654
DÁVALOS, René, 1015, 1025
DÁVALOS, Rodolfo, 1006
DÁVALOS, Serafina, 942, 943a, 959
DÁVALOS Y PERALTA, José (AVALOS Y PERALTA, José de),
    949, 964, 970
DAVANTÉS, Tomás María, 878
DAVEL, Ricardo J., 565
DAVERIO DE BONAVITA, Layly, 1187
DAVID, Felipe, 887
DAVID, José Pedro, 684
DAVID, Mario, 857b
DAVIDOVICH, Jaime, 46
DAVIE, Alberto, 923
DAVIES, Richard Glyn, 923
DÁVILA, Adolfo E., 247
DÁVILA, Domingo B., 381a
DÁVILA, Eulogio, 860
DÁVILA, Felipe de
    see AVILA, Felipe de
DÁVILA, Isidoro Juan, 1243
DÁVILA, Juan Francisco
    see AVILA, Juan Francisco de

DÁVILA, María, 928
DÁVILA, Miguel, 36
DÁVILA, Nicolás, 83, 611
DÁVILA, Pedro Esteban, 472, 521
DÁVILA GORDILLO, Guillermo, 381a
DÁVILA SAN ROMÁN, Guillermo, 83, 381a
DÁVILA UGARTE, Francisco, 284
DÁVILA Y MATOS, Inocencio, 910
DAVIO, Elisabeth, 700
DAVIS, Dora, 857d, 879
DAVIS, Ricardo, 299
D'AVOLA, María, 65
DAWI, Enrique, 857a
DAWSON, Bernhard H., 923
DAXA, 1238
DAY, Edmundo W., 207
DAYLEY, Juan G., 68
DE BLEECKER, Marcelo, 941
DE CARO, Francisco, 862, 891a
DE CARO, Julio, 177a, 862, 875, 877
DE CESARE, Elías Alfredo, 923
DE CICCO, Alfredo, 716
DE FERRARI, Adolfo, 18, 19, 25, 31, 36, 64
DE FINA, Armando L., 923
DE FINIS, Italo O., 952
DE FINIS, Mario Luis, 954
DE GASPERI, Luis Juan B., 923, 959, 1021, 1022
DE GRAZIA, Julio, 857b
DE GUBERNATIS, Angel, 258
DE LA SIERRA (family), 1108
DE LUCA, Miguel, 258
DE LUCIA, Fidel, 31
DE MARCO, Miguel Angel, 609, 1235
DE MARCHI DELLA COSTA, Silvestre, 68
DE MARÍA (family), 1108
DE MARÍA, Alcides (CALIXTO EL ÑATO, pseud.), 878,
    1167, 1174, 1243, 1247
DE MARÍA, Enrique, 719, 894, 1185, 1246
DE MARÍA, Isidoro, 1063, 1075, 1079, 1146, 1177,
    1188
DE MARÍA, Pablo, 1075, 1083, 1085
DE MARÍA DE ALMEIDA, Trinidad, 254
DE MARTINO, Edoardo, 59
DE MEIO, Romane Humberto, 923
DE NAVAZIO, Walter, 18
DE NITO, Humberto, 883
DE NITO, José, 883
DE PAULA, Santos, 683a
DE ROGATIS, Pascual, 883
DE SIMÓN DE SÁNCHEZ, Carmen B., 691
DE SIMONE, Pedro, 31
DE SIMONE FERRER DE VALIN, Celia Nelly, 1088
DEALESSI, Pierina, 893
DEAN FUNES
    see FUNES, Gregorio
DEARMA, María Elisa, 31
DEBALI, Francisco José, 1029, 1205, 1206, 1207
DEBERNARDI, Enzo, 954
DEBOLE, Carlos Alberto, 716, 739
DECAMILLI, Rómulo, 982
DECANO FUNES
    see FUNES, Gregorio
DECOUD, Adolfo, 957
DECOUD, Diógenes, 844, 951, 964, 1020, 1021, 1022
DECOUD, Héctor Francisco, 959, 1021, 1022
DECOUD, José Segundo, 951, 964, 966, 986, 991, 1008,
    1012, 1021, 1022
DECOUD, Juan Francisco, 957, 991
DECOUD, Juan José, 957, 964, 986, 991, 1014, 1021,
    1022
DECOUD LARROSA, Reinaldo, 943, 964, 965, 966

DEFILIPPI, Ricardo Alberto, 857a
DEFILIPPIS NOVOA, Francisco, 135, 890, 1255
DEGIOVANNI, Lelia E., 652
DEGOY, Andrés P. H., 923
DEHEZA, Román Antonio, 244, 371, 433, 568, 569, 611
DEI, H. Daniel, 691
DEIRA, Ernesto, 27, 36, 38, 55
DEIVALLE, Angela, 965
DEL PONTE, Clementino, 882
DEL PRATO, Juan, 18
DEL PRETE, Juan, 36, 38, 49, 55
DEL VALLE (family)
    see VALLE, del (family)
DELAC, Alberto, 792
DELACHAUX (family), 168
DELACHAUD, Enrique, 44
DELANEY, Juan José, 817
DELBAERE, Andrés, 299
DELBUENO, Horacio, 860
DELCASSE, Carlos, 68, 94
DELFINA (PORTUGUESA, La, pseud.), 478
DELFINO, Augusto Mario, 670, 685, 712, 799, 825, 829, 1245
DELFINO, Enrique, 862, 875, 892
DELFINO, Gonzalo, 781
DELFINO, José, 952
DELFINO, Leonardo, 49
DELFINO, María, 652
DELGADO, Agustín, 207, 212, 634
DELGADO, Ariel, 299
DELGADO, Asdrúbal E., 1083, 1174
DELGADO, Federico, 998
DELGADO, Francisco, 207
DELGADO, José del Pilar, 998
DELGADO, José María, 974, 1087, 1145, 1179, 1199
DELGADO, Juan, 319
DELGADO, Manuel Antonio, 921
DELGADO, Nicolás, 1006
DELGADO, Ramón Tadeo, 254
DELGADO, Sebastián, 1262
DELGADO APARAÍN, Mario, 1173
DELGADO CARDOZO, Tomás, 954
DELGADO FITO, Cándido, 833
DELGADO FLORES, Matías, 649a
DELGADO PÉREZ, Gerónimo, 653, 654
DELGADO RIVERO, Tomás, 1210
DELGADO RODAS, Modesto, 937, 939
DELHEYE, Pedro, 381a
DELHEYE, Pedro Mario, 751, 773, 805
DELHEZ, Víctor, 44
D'ELIA, Antonio, 285
D'ELIA, Miguel Alfredo, 739
DELIBANO CHAZARRETA, Juan, 923
DELMAS, José, 951
DELORME, José César, 923
DELPECH, Simón Antonio, 923
DELPHINO, Aldo, 938
DELPINI, José Luis, 332
DELPODIO, Angel, 683a
DELPODIO, Matilde, 683a, 762
DELL'ACQUA, Amadeo, 299
DELL'ACQUA, Enrico, 292
DELLA COSTA, Pablo, 773, 782
DELLA PAOLERA, Carlos, 332
DELLA PAOLERA, Félix, 812
DELLA VALLE, Angel, 19, 25, 31, 45, 51, 59, 258, 293, 521
DELLACHA, Juan Modesto, 923
DELLEPIANI, Andrés, 952
DELLEPIANI, Luis, 332
DELLEPIANE IZURDIAGO DE RAMA, Judith, 1210

DELLETERY, 189
DEMARCO, Luis, 903
DEMARCHI, Antonio, 258
DEMARE, Carlos, 923
DEMARE, Lucas, 858
DEMARE, Lucio, 862
DEMARÍA, Bernabé, 19, 59, 677
DEMARÍA CIBILS, José Eduardo, 923
DEMATEI, Carlos, 998
DEMBO, Adolfo, 923
DEMERSAY, Alfred L., 943, 949
DEMETRIO, 198
DEMICHELI, Tulio, 858
DEMIRJIAN, Jorge, 36, 55
DEMITROPULOS, Libertad, 713, 717, 725, 730
DEMOLIN, Mauricio, 1065
DENER, Horacio, 889
DENEVI, Marco, 666, 668, 674, 756, 772, 799, 816, 835
DENGREMONT, Eugenio Mauricio, 268
DENIER, Pedro Celestino Luis, 191
DENIS, Aída, 879
DENIS, Julio, pseud.
    see CORTÁZAR, Julio
DENIS ROA, Cesáreo, 998
DENIS MOLINA, Carlos, 894, 1151, 1172, 1177, 1185
DENNLER DE LA TOUR, Georges, 923
DEOLINDO REYNA, Pedro (RUSIÑOL, pseud.), 713
DEPAOLIS DE VARIZAT, Rosina, 691
DEPASCALE, Alfonso, 766
DEPPS RAMÍREZ, Manuel, 954
DERBECQ, Germaine, 36
DERECHIN, Moisés, 923
DERENDAÑO, Matheo de, 186
DERLIS, Rubén, 703, 785
DERMER, Hermán, 923
DERMIDIO GALÍNDEZ, Rafael, 191
DERQUI, Manuel, 121, 445
DERQUI, Santiago, 70, 95, 96, 116, 127, 166, 195, 244, 282, 283, 392, 393, 398, 404, 405, 447, 515, 516, 531, 574, 586, 611, 619, 634
DES ESSARTS, Berchón, 949
DESCALZI, Cayetano
    see DESCALZI, Gaetano
DESCALZI, Gaetano, 19, 28, 59, 258
DESCALZI, Nicolás, 258, 332
DESCOLE, Horacio Raúl, 923
DESCOTTE, Mario Luis, 739
DESMADRYL, Narciso E., 19, 59
DESPARD, George Packenham, 99
D'ESPOSITO, Arnaldo, 864, 882, 883
DESPOUEY, Arturo R., 1172, 1184
DESSANTI, Raúl N., 923
DESSY, Silvio, 258
DESTÉFANI, Laurio H., 265
DESTEFANO, José R., 746
DESTRADE DE LEBLANC, Leonor B., 328
DEUGENIO, Rubén, 1172, 1185
DEULOFEU, Venancio, 923
DEVECCHI CÓRDOBA, María J., 652
DEVETACH, Laura, 706
DEVOTO (brothers), 292
DEVOTO, Alberto, 332
DEVOTO, Antonio, 98, 122, 258
DEVOTO, Daniel J., 722, 739, 812
DEVOTO, José, 258
DEVOTO, Juan Bautista, 660, 727, 812, 860
DEVOTO, Tomás, 68
D'HASTREL, Adolphe
    see HASTREL DE RIVEDOUX, Adolphe d'

DHIALMA TIBERTI, María, 805
DI BENEDETTO, Antonio, 666, 683a, 764, 815, 816
DI CARLO, Adelia, 154, 751
DI CIO, Alejandro Vicente, 923
DI GIACOMO, Haydée, 874
DI GIORGI RODRÍGUEZ, Diógenes, 1210
DI GIORGIO MEDICIS, Marosa, 1178
DI LASCIO, Pedro, 938, 939
DI LEANDRO, Carlos, 653, 654
DI LENA, Juan Pablo, 923
DI MATTEO, Martha, 726
DI MICHELI, Domenico, 292
DI NAPOLI, Nicola, 292
DI NARDO, Eduardo, 797
DI NIZZA, Pietro, 292
DI PAOLA, Guillermo, 923
DI PAOLA LEVIN, Jorge, 776
DI PASCUA DOYENHART, Edison, 1210
DI PRIMIO, Juan Carlos, 923
DI SARLI, Carlos, 868
DI SARLI, Rodolfo, 299
DI SAVOJA, Francesco, 292
DI SEGNI, Franco, 31
DI SERIO, Elido U., 775
DI STEFANO, Domingo, 46
DI TEANA, Marino, 21, 49
DI TELLA, Guido, 311
DI TELLA, Torcuato, 332
DI VENEZIA, Andrea, 292
DI VENEZIA, Nicola, 292
DI VENEZIA, Pier Andrea, 292
DIAMAND, Marcelo, 311
DIANA, Conrado, 857b
DIANA, José Cándido, 1014
DIANA, Leónidas, 1017
DIANA RODRÍGUEZ, Juan Amado, 1210
DIAS, Manuel, 344
DIAS CORREA, Manuel, 845
DÍAZ (family) (Argentina), 351
DÍAZ (family) (Uruguay), 1108
DÍAZ, Alejandro, 474
DÍAZ, Alonso, 1270
DÍAZ, Ana, 358
DÍAZ, Antonio, 1095, 1185
DÍAZ, Antonio Américo, 68
DÍAZ, Avelino
    see DÍAZ Y SALGADO, Avelino
DÍAZ, Bartolomé, 620
DÍAZ, Buenaventura (DÍAZ, Ventura, pseud.), 914
DÍAZ, Carlos A., 275
DÍAZ, César, 1057, 1091, 1110
DÍAZ, Delmirio, 1210
DÍAZ, Dionisio, 1054
DÍAZ, Exequiel, 823
DÍAZ, Felipe, 272
DÍAZ, Fernando, 496
DÍAZ, Francisco, 268, 611
DÍAZ, Francisco Domingo, 188, 283
DÍAZ, Francisco Javier, 1095
DÍAZ, Francisco Ramón, 680, 713, 730, 830
DÍAZ, Gregorio, 186
DÍAZ, Héctor, 191
DÍAZ, Hernando, 649a
DÍAZ, Horacio Antonio, 923
DÍAZ, José, 954, 979, 1003, 1012, 1089
DÍAZ, José Domingo, 878
DÍAZ, Jose Eduwigis, 948, 955, 974, 980, 984, 984a, 1004
DÍAZ, José Javier, 89, 115a, 316, 545a, 552
DÍAZ, José María, 135, 800

DÍAZ, José Pedro, 1148, 1177, 1189
DÍAZ, Juan, 1093
DÍAZ, Juan C., 965
DÍAZ, Juan G., 17b
DÍAZ, Juan Gregorio, 254
DÍAZ, Laureano José, 209
DÍAZ, Leopoldo, 669, 722, 723, 751, 759, 773, 803, 807
DÍAZ, Luciano, 371
DÍAZ, Mamerto, 878
DÍAZ, Manuel, 32
DÍAZ, Mariano, 280
DÍAZ, Mateo, 556
DÍAZ, Pedro, 849, 1089
DÍAZ, Pedro I., 212
DÍAZ, Pedro José, 611
DÍAZ, Ramón, 177, 377, 611, 990
DÍAZ, Ramón M., 1187
DÍAZ, Raúl B., 222
DÍAZ, Toribio, 954
DÍAZ, Remigio, 844
DÍAZ, Teófilo Eugenio (TAX, pseud.), 1075, 1146, 1187, 1199
DÍAZ, Ventura, pseud.
    see DÍAZ, Buenaventura
DÍAZ ALLENDE, Mariano, 299
DÍAZ ARANA, Juan José, 260
DÍAZ ARAUJO, Enrique, 609
DÍAZ ARDUINO, Armando Jorge, 41
DÍAZ ARMESTO, Antonio, 1223
DÍAZ ARMESTO, José, 1095, 1223
DÍAZ BARROSO, Francisco, 555
DÍAZ BAVIO, Jorge, 653, 654
DÍAZ CABALLERO, Alonso, 501, 520
DÍAZ CISNEROS, Juan Carlos, 89
DÍAZ CLAVIJO, Félix, 332
DÍAZ COLODRERO, Agustín, 196
DÍAZ COLODRERO, Armando, 655, 656
DÍAZ COLODRERO, Pedro, 93, 634
DÍAZ CONTERO, Eliseo, 995a
DÍAZ CHAVES, Isabelino, 1006
DÍAZ DE BEDOYA, Joaquín, 844
DÍAZ DE BEDOYA, José, 954
DÍAZ DE BEDOYA, Ventura, 979
DÍAZ DE GUZMAN, Ruy, 359, 360, 482, 521, 609, 683, 734, 737, 754, 761, 947, 964, 966, 984a, 985, 1012, 1021, 1022, 1229, 1230
DÍAZ DE MELGAREJO, Ruy, 947, 1012, 1203, 1232
DÍAZ DE OCAÑA, Juan, 244
DÍAZ DE SOLÍS, Juan, 455, 462, 471, 472, 477, 481, 521, 535, 640, 984, 989, 1053, 1079, 1203
DÍAZ DE TOMMA, Ramona Belta, 1088
DÍAZ EDROSA, José, 284
DÍAZ ETCHEVEHERE, Manuel L., 652
DÍAZ FERNÁNDEZ, Francisco Javier, 284
DÍAZ GALLO, Pedro León, 439
DÍAZ GUZMAN, Rafael, 683a
DÍAZ HERRERA (family), 354
DÍAZ LASCANO, Federico, 332
DÍAZ LEGUIZAMON, Héctor, 751, 773
DÍAZ MARTÍN, Christóval, 186
DÍAZ MIRÓN, Salvador, 1259
DÍAZ MOREIRA, Diego, 1270
DÍAZ OROMI, Roberto, 299
DÍAZ PEFAUR, César, 998
DÍAZ PENA, Arístides, 1014
DÍAZ PERALTA, César, 653
DÍAZ PÉREZ, Juan Silvano, 1014
DÍAZ PÉREZ, Rodrigo, 1014, 1021, 1022

DÍAZ PÉREZ, Viriato, 943, 964, 966, 1012
DÍAZ PESSINA, Nilda, 683a, 785
DÍAZ RAMÍREZ, Virgilio, 954
DÍAZ RICO, José, 1089
DÍAZ RODRÍGUEZ, José, 189
DÍAZ ROMÁN, Ramón, 496
DÍAZ ROMERO, Eugenio, 669, 751, 773, 1259
DÍAZ TAÑO, Francisco, 319, 845, 850, 989, 1040
DÍAZ USANDIVARAS, Julio Carlos, 154, 717, 751, 758, 834, 878, 1243
DÍAZ VALENTÍN, José Víctor, 923
DÍAZ VÉLEZ, Domingo, 254
DÍAZ VÉLEZ, Eustaquio, 136, 166, 386, 552, 553, 611
DÍAZ VÉLEZ, José Miguel, 126
DÍAZ VÉLEZ DE LA MADRID, Luisa, 478
DÍAZ VILLAFAÑE, Dora, 154
DÍAZ VILLALBA, Ernesto, 653, 654
DÍAZ VILLALBA, Julio, 653, 654
DÍAZ Y CLUSELLAS, Josefa, 62
DÍAZ Y SALGADO, Avelino, 321, 332, 611, 921a
DIBELLA, Francisco, 766, 812
DICKMANN, Adolfo, 259
DICKMANN, Enrique, 260, 503
DICKMANN, Germán Hugo, 923
DIDIER, Félix (family), 168
DIDIER, Plácido (family), 168
DIEBEL, Otto, 15
DIEGO, Antonio, 923
DIEGO, Celia
    see REGUERA DE DIEGO, Celia
DIEGO, Rafael de, 751, 773
DIÉGUEZ, Luis, 645
DIEHL, Adán C., 678
DIESTE, Eduardo, 1184, 1199
DIEULOFAIT, Carlos Eugenio, 923
DÍEZ, Iván, 660, 710, 727, 818
DÍEZ. Matilde. 887
DÍEZ DE ANDINO, Juan, 501, 984, 1011
DÍEZ DE ANDINO, Manuel Ignacio, 374
DÍEZ DE ANDINO, Pascual, 107
DÍEZ DE ARMENDARIZ, Miguel, 151
DÍEZ DE MEDINA, José Antonio, 126
DÍEZ GÓMEZ, Alberto, 653
DÍEZ GOMEZ, Diego, 32
DÍEZ MUNILLA, Gabriel, 344
DÍEZ PLAZA, Marciano, 1092
DÍEZ VIZOSO, Alonso, 1270
DIFRIERI, Horacio A., 521
DIGENNARO, Nicolás A., 81
DILLÓN, Enrique Alfredo, 662, 663
DILLÓN, José Agustín, 878
DILLÓN, Juan (son), 191
DIMANT, César, 808
DIMAS ARANDA, Santiago, 947, 1014
DIMAS MOTTA, Juan, 998
DIMITROFF, Demetrio, 652
DINGANI, Carlos, 1039
DIOMEDE, Miguel, 18, 19, 23, 25, 31, 34, 36, 38, 55
DIOS, Juan de, 611
DIOSNEL CHASE, Juan, 947
DIOVANO, Eduardo, 299
DISANDRO, Carlos Alberto, 664, 805
DISANDRO, Juan, 55
DISCÉPOLO, Armando, 152a, 890, 893
DISCÉPOLO, Enrique Santos, 759, 801, 803, 807, 861, 862, 868, 871, 877
DISTÉFANO, Juan Carlos, 36, 38, 55
DITRICH, Zacharías, 32
DIVIERI, Hugo, 135
DIVITO, José Antonio Guillermo, 299
DIVITO, Juan, 94

DIXON, Alexander, 587
DIZ, Carlos Victoriano, 923
DIZ, Hugo, 759, 788
DIZEO, Enrique, 660
D'JALLAD, Luis
    see JALLAD, Luis d'
DOBAL, Felipe M. A., 299
DOBRANICH, Jorge, 332
DOBRIZHOFFER, Martín, 865, 885, 985, 1269
DODERO (brothers), 139
DODERO, Alberto A., 530, 1073
DOGAN (family), 351
DOGGET, Kate N., 930
DOLDAN, Eduvigis, 956
DOLDÁN, Justo, 28, 32
DOLDÁN, Osvaldo, 998
DOLDÁN COTELO, Manuel, 1089
DOLDÉN COTELO, Luis, 1089
D'OLHABERRIAGUE Y BLANCO, Félix d'
    see OLHABERRIAGUE Y BLANCO, Félix d'
DOLL, Guillermo J., 551a
DOLL, Ramón, 431
DOMANICZKY, Carlos, 1006
DOMBIDAS, Tomás, 319
DOMECQ, H. Bustos, pseud.
    see BIOY CASARES, Adolfo
        BORGES, Jorge Luis
DOMECQ, Pedro Manuel, 987
DOMECQ GARCÍA, Manuel, 1006
DOMENICO, Amadeo D. Félix, 923
DOMENICONE, Alberto 81, 222
DOMENICHINI, José, 18
DOMEYKO, Ignacio, 238
DOMINGO, Carlos, 923
DOMÍNGUEZ, Agustín, 845
DOMÍNGUEZ, Alonso, 620
DOMÍNGUEZ, Andrés, 496
DOMÍNGUEZ, Angélica, 1017
DOMÍNGUEZ, Camilio (father), 222
DOMÍNGUEZ, Camilio (son), 222
DOMÍNGUEZ, Carlos, 954
DOMÍNGUEZ, Cesáreo, 188, 222
DOMÍNGUEZ, Constantino, 1089
DOMÍNGUEZ, Crisanto, 191
DOMÍNGUEZ, Enrique, 1089
DOMÍNGUEZ, Federico, 299
DOMÍNGUEZ, Fermín, 1014
DOMÍNGUEZ, Ignacio, 845
DOMÍNGUEZ, José León, 196, 496, 611
DOMÍNGUEZ, José María, 95, 96, 127
DOMÍNGUEZ, Juan, 319, 1270
DOMÍNGUEZ, Lorenzo, 22, 25
DOMÍNGUEZ, Luis L., 379, 609, 611, 631, 633, 669, 720, 740, 751, 807, 1243, 1247
DOMÍNGUEZ, Manuel, 943, 951, 955, 959, 964, 966, 980, 992, 1002, 1012, 1021, 1022
DOMÍNGUEZ, María Alicia, 154, 222, 678, 711, 739, 744, 751, 762, 773, 783
DOMÍNGUEZ, Mignon, 707
DOMÍNGUEZ, Miguel, 299
DOMÍNGUEZ, Oscar, 923
DOMÍNGUEZ, Pedro P., 1014
DOMÍNGUEZ, Ramiro, 943, 947, 1014, 1015, 1018a, 1020, 1021, 1022, 1025
DOMÍNGUEZ, Ramón, 1089
DOMÍNGUEZ, Raúl Augusto, 954
DOMÍNGUEZ, Rodolfo S., 68
DOMÍNGUEZ, Rufino T., 1083, 1087, 1088, 1116
DOMÍNGUEZ, Silverio (Calle, Ceferino de la, pseud.), 152a, 813

DOMÍNGUEZ, Teófilo, 1017
DOMÍNGUEZ DE BAZÁN, Paula, 159
DOMÍNGUEZ DE SAMPAYO, Laudelina, 652
DOMÍNGUEZ DURÁN, Andrés, 284
DOMÍNGUEZ MANEIRO, Francisco Antonio, 898
DOMÍNGUEZ NEIRA, Pedro, 19, 25, 31, 36, 55, 64
DOMÍNGUEZ PÉREZ, Washington, 1210
DOMÍNGUEZ VARELA, Vicente, 1089
DOMINGUITO, pseud.
      see SARMIENTO, Domingo Fidel
DOMINICETTI, César, 1205
DOMINICO, Guillermo, 904
DON PEPE, pseud., 1059
DON PEPE, pseud.
      see PODESTÁ, José J.
DONADÍO DE RODRÍGUEZ, María Dominga, 320
DONADO, Agustín Jorge, 215
DONADO, Agustín José, 104, 478, 479, 496, 611, 1264
DONATI, Leonardo, 258
DONATI, Marcos, 258, 1266
DONATI, Teodoro, 6
DONATO ALVAREZ, Julio E., 431
DONCEL, Carlos, 173, 445
DONDO, Osvaldo Horacio, 664, 722, 729, 739, 758
DONO, Alfredo, 874
D'ONOFRIO, Magdalena, 725
DONOSO, José, 752
DONOSO, Justo Pastor, 629
DONOVAN, Antonio, 121
DONOVAN, Cornelio, 1223
DONOVAN, Daniel, 1223
DONOVAN, Samuel, 1223
DOOLITTLE, Annette, 323
DOOLITTLE, Lucy, 323
DORANTES, Pedro (ORANTES, Pedro, pseud.), 985, 1012
D'ORBIGNY, Alcides
      see ORBIGNY, Alcides Dessalines d'
DORCAS BERRO, Rolando, 766
DORÉ, Gustave, 59
DORGAN, Martha, 684
DORIA (family), 952
DORIA, Alejandro, 857b
DORIA, Santiago, 889
DORMAL, Julio, 6
DORRA, Raúl, 713
DORREGO, Celestino (JUAN POCA ROPA; JUAN SIN ROPA,
      pseuds.), 878, 1257
DORREGO, Luis, 584
DORREGO, Manuel, 70, 83, 85, 104, 110, 121, 143,
      166, 185, 227, 228, 244, 282, 382, 404, 448,
      451, 469, 471, 472, 475, 478, 489, 499, 502,
      518, 519, 521, 529, 545, 552, 584, 600, 611,
      629, 1091
D'ORTENSIO, Omar Roberto, 299
DOS SANTOS, Buenaventura, 1210
DOS SANTOS, Estela, 706
DOS SANTOS, Nicanor, 1093
DOSETTI, Santiago, 1159, 1168, 1170, 1177, 1180,
      1186, 1196
DOTTI, Víctor M., 1159, 1168, 1170, 1180, 1186,
      1187, 1196, 1199
DOUEK, Rafael, 560
DOUGHERTY, Enriqueta A. de, 805
D'OVIDIO, Francisco Ramón, 923
DOWEK, Diana, 37
DOYER, Juan J., 332
DOYLE, Liliana Susana, 691
DOZAL, Francisco, 496
DOZO, Ismael, 663
DRABBLE, Jorge, 254, 904

DRAC, Juan, 1270
DRAGHI LUCERO, Juan, 283, 683a, 688, 745, 753, 817,
      825, 829
DRAGO, Luis María, 68, 110, 116, 129, 141, 258, 282,
      478, 574, 614, 650
DRAGUN, Osvaldo, 135
DRAKE, Juan, 467
DRANGOSCH, Ernesto, 864, 865, 867, 881, 883
DRESCO, Arturo, 19, 21
DREYER (family), 168
DREYER, Santiago Mario, 923
DREYER ZUNINO, Olga, 652
DROZ, Irma, 684
DRUILLET, Carlos E., 1067
DRUMMOND, Francisco, 14, 82
DRUMMOND DE ANDRADE, Carlos, 658
DU GRATY, Alfred, 943, 949
DU TOICT, Nicolas
      see TECHO, Nicolás del
DUALDE, Eduardo, 1068
DUARTE, Atanasio, 427
DUARTE, Augusto, 947, 954
DUARTE, Blas Ignacio, 995a
DUARTE, Cosme, 32
DUARTE, Cristóbal, 959
DUARTE, Eva
      see DUARTE DE PERÓN, Eva
DUARTE, Jorge, 32
DUARTE, Juan, 75
DUARTE, Justo Pastor, 947, 959
DUARTE, Manuel J., 955, 959
DUARTE, Pedro, 974, 1008
DUARTE ARDOY, Juan, 8
DUARTE DE PERÓN, Eva, 170, 434, 452, 469, 530, 602,
      624, 926
DUARTE DE QUIRÓS, Ignacio
      see DUARTE Y QUIRÓS, Ignacio
DUARTE GALLI, María Antonia, 955
DUARTE ORTELLADO, Julio, 995
DUARTE TROCHE, Rodolfo Antonio, 963a
DUARTE VALDEZ, Manuel José, 973
DUARTE VERA, Ramón, 954
DUARTE Y QUIRÓS, Ignacio, 144, 244
DUAYEN, César, pseud. (BARRA DE LLANOS, Ema), 478,
      724, 929
DUBECQ, María Elena, 655, 656, 817
DUBINSKI MIMER, Rosa, 1210
DUBINSKY AISEMBERG, David, 1210
DUBLANC, Emilio, 874, 882
DUBLÍN, Carlos, 1005
DUCASSE, Francisco, 244, 891
DUCASSE, Isidore Lucien (LAUTREAMONT, pseud.), 1177
DUCASSE, Juan, 244
DUCASSE, Luciano, 244
DUCI, Carmelo, 874
DUCLOUT, Jorge, 332, 921a
DUCMELIC, Zdravko, 25, 31, 36
DUDLEY, Anna (Mrs. Coolidge Roberts), 323
DUDLEY, Charles, 323
DUDLEY, Charles (Mrs.)
      see DUDLEY, Martha Graham
DUDLEY, Isabel, 323
DUDLEY, Martha Graham (Mrs. Charles Dudley), 323
DUFF, James, 2
DUFFAU DE RABAUDI, Lila, 656
DUFORT Y ALVAREZ, Anacleto, 254, 1126, 1146, 1174
DUFOUR (brothers), 292

DUFRECHOU, Julio, 1083
DUGHERA, Eduardo A., 745
DUHALDE, Eduardo Luis, 440
DUHART, Saramaría, 660
DUHAU, Alfredo, 894, 1185, 1263
DUHAU, Luis, 3
DUJOVNE ORTIZ, Alicia, 759, 819
DULAR CABELLO, Juan de la Cruz, 878
DULIN, J. D., 28
DUMAS, Delly, 939
DUMÓN QUESADA, Mateo, 135, 800
DUMONT, Abraham, 954
DUMONT, Carlos V., 154
DUNANT, Henry, 176
DUNCAN, Elena, 805, 812
DUPETIT, Gustavo Alberto, 923
DUPLÁN, Max, pseud.
    see MORERA, Eduardo
DUPONT, Benjamín, 853a
DUPORTAL, Emilio, 3
DUPOTET, Juan Enrique José, 581
DUPRAT, Enrique, 923
DUPRAT, Luis, 68, 912
DUPRAT, Pedro E., 1083
DUPRAT DE LASSERRE, Dorotea, 949
DUPUY, M. N., 988
DUPUY, Pedro, 949
DUPUY, Vicente, 158, 283, 413, 478, 479, 496, 611
DURÁN (family), 1108
DURÁN, Andrés Manuel, 1063
DURÁN, Carlos Joaquín, 772
DURÁN, Gregorio, 1095
DURÁN, José Antonio, 283
DURÁN, Juan, 845
DURÁN, Juan Carlos, 768
DURÁN, Juan José, 552
DURÁN, Lydia, 299
DURÁN, Manuel, 1089, 1111
DURÁN, Pascual, 319
DURÁN CANO, Alejandra Isabel Cabral Mascari de
    see CABRAL MASCARI DE DURÁN CANO, Alejandra
    Isabel
DURÁN CANO, Ricardo, 1088
DURÁN DE ROJO, Serafina, 931
DURÁN MASTRILLI, Nicolás, 952, 1267
DURANA, Pedro de, 1041
DURAND, A., 28
DURÁND, Carlos, 844
DURAND, Elizabeth, 1217
DURAND-BRAGER, Jean Baptiste Henri, 28
DURANDO MACKEY, Elsa, 152a
DURANTE, Antonio María, 7
DURANTE, Manuel, 1116
DURAÑONA, Leopoldo, 299
DURAÑONA Y VEDIA, Agustín A., 923
D'URBANO, Jorge, 218
DURBEC DE ROUTÍN, Josefina (VERO, pseud.), 762
DURÉ, Ramón, 1011
DURELLI, A. J., 923
DURET, José Pedro, 923
DURILEN, Juan Carlos, 684
DURO, Benito, 1266
DUTEIL, Camilo, 332
DUTRENIT, Julio
    see DUTRENIT ARBOLEYA, Julio Augusto
DUTRENIT ARBOLEYA, Julio Augusto, 1210, 1211
DUTRUEL, René E., 691
DUTTO, José, 320
DUVAL, Pedro, 254

EANDI, Héctor I., 670, 765, 779, 825, 1245
EARLE, Augustus, 28
EBELOT, Alfredo, 332, 1246
ECCLESTON, Emily (Mrs. Daniel Campbell), 323
ECCLESTON, Sarah Chamberlain, 323
ECKELL, Osvaldo Alberto, 923
ECCHER, Giordano, 1093
ECHAGÜE, Alfredo, 268
ECHAGÜE, Carlos, 268, 332
ECHAGÜE, Francisco Javier de, 1031
ECHAGÜE, Juan Pablo (Jean Paul, pseud.), 167, 670,
    707, 743, 751, 779, 1245, 1246
ECHAGÜE, Leónidas, 95, 121, 135, 194, 241
ECHAGÜE, Melchor, 268
ECHAGÜE, Milcíades, 921
ECHAGÜE, Narciso de, 987
ECHAGÜE, Pascual, 95, 96, 127, 135, 241, 327, 477,
    543, 569
ECHAGÜE, Pedro, 404, 677, 693, 747, 761, 1246
ECHAGÜE, Pedro Antonio, 477
ECHAGÜE VERA, Ofelia, 938
ECHAGÜE Y ANDÍA, Francisco de, 318
ECHAGÜE Y ANDÍA, Francisco Javier de, 477
ECHAGÜE Y ANDÍA, Francisco Pascual de, 477
ECHAGÜE Y ANDÍA, Narciso, 979
ECHAUREN, José Daniel, 126
ECHAURI, Juan Francisco, 254
ECHAURI, Martín José de, 1011, 1262
ECHAVARRÍA, Beatriz, 1091
ECHAVE ZÁS, Luis, 1210
ECHAZARRETA, Carlos, 878
ECHAZÚ, José Felipe de, 126
ECHAZÚ, Mariano Antonio, 126
ECHEGARAY (family), 366
ECHEGARAY, Aristóbulo, 722, 739, 814
ECHEGARAY, José María, 188
ECHEGARAY, Juan de, 283
ECHEGARAY, Mateo Aristóbulo, 833
ECHEGARAY, Tristán, 413, 611
ECHEGARAY TORANZO, José María, 283
ECHENAGUCIA, José Antonio de, 496
ECHENAGUCIA, Mariano, 611
ECHENIQUE (family), 352
ECHENIQUE, Bernabé, 126
ECHENIQUE, Gerónimo de, 126
ECHENIQUE, José, 89
ECHESORTU, Ciro, 141
ECHEVARRÍA, José Mateo de, 7, 922
ECHEVARRÍA, Manuel, 126
ECHEVARRÍA, Ramón, 611
ECHEVARRÍA, Vicente Anastasio de, 126, 496, 552, 611
ECHEVERIARZA DE BLANCO, Natividad, 1093a
ECHEVERRÍA, Esteban
    see ECHEVERRÍA, José Esteban Antonio
ECHEVERRÍA, Isidro, 268
ECHEVERRÍA, José Esteban Antonio, 32, 110, 118, 121,
    141, 166, 176, 183, 206, 212, 244, 246, 261,
    272, 282, 293, 317, 324, 379, 381, 404, 466,
    469, 478, 499, 507, 509, 514, 519, 521, 542,
    585, 589, 592, 611, 612, 664, 669, 692, 693,
    708, 720, 721, 723, 724, 732, 734, 737, 740,
    743, 745a, 749, 751, 754, 761, 763, 779, 780,
    803, 807, 821, 828, 829, 834, 1179, 1242, 1243,
    1246, 1247, 1253, 1256, 1260
ECHEVERRÍA, Pedro, 1126
ECHEVERRÍA, Silvestre, 1093
ECHEVERRÍA, Vicente Anastasio, 554, 1236
ECHEVERRÍA DE CAPI, Juana, 320
ECHEVERRÍA LAGO, Bernardo, 1210

ECHEVERRÍA Y GALARDI, Nicolás de, 344
EDA, pseud., 153
EDDY, J. M., 904
EDELBERG, Betina, 717, 725, 739, 802
EDELSTEIN, Pablo, 35
EDELVIRA, Ida, 859
EDWARDS, Henry (FACÓN GRANDE, pseud.), 2
EFRÓN, Isaac, 652
EGLES, Ricardo, 703
EGUES, Antonio, 135
EGUÍA, Manuel, 6
EGUÍA, Manuel Alejo, 126
EGUÍA, Manuel de, 600
EGUÍA, Mario Julio, 781
EGUÍA MUÑOZ, Beatriz, 711, 751, 762
EGUÍA PUENTES, Ricardo, 1167
EGUIGUREN, Atanasio, 95, 135
EGUIGUREN, Víctor, 68
EGUREN GONZALEZ, Jesús Marcos, 1210
EGUZQUIZA, Juan Bautista, 983, 991, 1012
EHYERABIDE, Gley, 1155
EICHELBAUM, Edmundo E., 819
EICHELBAUM, Samuel, 135, 675, 676, 737, 765, 1245, 1255
EICHLER, Juan, 36
EIDLICZ, Abraham, 218
EIRALE, Juan Alberto, 1200
EISENSTEIN DE VEGA, Silvia, 882, 883
EITLER, Esteban, 31
EIZAGUIRRE, José Manuel, 78, 141
ELBEIN, Eugenia, 809
ELENA, Nicolás, 73
ELETA, Angel, 857c
ELFLEIN, Ada María, 141, 744, 751
ELGARTE, Miguel Angel, 41, 44
ELGUERA, Juan de la, 496
ELÍA, Agustín Pío
    see ELÍA Y GARCÍA DE ZÚÑIGA, Agustín Pío de
ELÍA, Angel Mariano, 126
ELÍA, Juan de, 611
ELÍA, Juan Estanislao de, 196
ELÍA, Pablo Luis, 860
ELÍA Y GARCÍA DE ZÚÑIGA, Agustín Pío de, 126, 496
ELÍAS, Angel, 96
ELÍAS, Daniel, 135, 800
ELÍAS, Graciela, 684
ELÍAS, José Eugenio de, 126
ELÍAS, Juan Estanislao de, 375
ELÍAS, Víctor Emeterio, 923
ELICABE DE TRIGUERO, Angélica, 320
ELICHIRIGOITY VALENTE, Carlos, 1210
ELIESON, John, 15
ELÍO, Francisco Javier de, 427, 517, 552, 553, 1091, 1113, 1136
ELÍO, Javier de
    see ELÍO, Francisco Javier de
ELIZALDE, Felipe de, 923
ELIZALDE, Félix, 213
ELIZALDE, Fernando, 817
ELIZALDE, Juan José, 254, 691, 707
ELIZALDE, Rufino de, 90, 96, 478, 586, 631
ELIZECHE, Feliciano, 995a
ELIZECHE BENÍTEZ, Susanita, 956
ELIZONDO, Lilia Yolanda P. de, 191
ELIZONDO, Ramón T., 768
ELIZONDO DE GESTAL, María, 1093a
ELKELES, Gerardo, 923
ELKIN, Boris, 1243
ELMASSIAN, Miguel, 949
ELORRIAGA, Juan Bautista, 496
ELORZA, José, 1094

ELOSEGUI, Rubén, 35
ELVIRA, Martín de, 556
ELLAURE Y OBLIGADO, Gontrán, 1247
ELLAURÍ, Expectación, 1223
ELLAURÍ, José, 1063, 1135, 1223
ELLAURI, José Eugenio, 1091, 1109, 1223
ELLAURI, Juan de, 1056, 1223
ELLAURI, María Eustaquia, 1223
ELLAURI, Plácido, 1223
ELLAURI, Prudencio León, 1223
ELLENA DE LA SOTA, Julio, 712, 766, 812
ELLENA GOLA, Santiago, 745
ELLIFF, Osvaldo, 662, 663, 727, 832
ELLIOT, Robert James, 28
ELLIS, Edell (Mrs. Theodore H. Johnston), 323
ELLIS, Horacio, 1067
EMHART, Albino, 954
EMIL DI FLUVIO, Teresa, 923
EMILIANI, Ezio, 923
ENCINA, Carlos, 332, 478, 669
ENCINA, Francisco A., 283
ENCINAS, Alonso de, 32
ENCINAS, Ricardo M., 207
ENDEIZA, Víctor W., 81, 222
ENRÍQUEZ, Bernabé, 126
ENRÍQUEZ, Camilo, 227
ENRÍQUEZ, José María, 126
ENRÍQUEZ, Juan Cuaresma, 32
ENRÍQUEZ, Mariano, 126
ENRÍQUEZ DE ARMENDARIZ, Alonso, 914
ENRÍQUEZ DE GUZMÁN, Enrique, 274
ENRÍQUES NUÑO DEL AGUILA, Pablo, 914
ENTRAIGAS, Raúl A., 664, 907a
EPÍSCOPO, Hebe, 781
EPÓSITO, Juan I., 198
EPPER, Carlos Eugenio, 923
EPSTEIN KRAMINSKI, Isidoro, 1210
ERAUSQUIN, Jorge, 923
ERCOLE, Carlos, 87
ERCOLE, Ricardo, 923
EREÑO, Domingo, 534, 917
ERICA, Juan Silverio de, 186
ERICKSON, Prima Aide, 810
ERICO, Arsenio, 948
ERMELINDA, Gloria, 941
EROS, pseud.
    see HERRERA, Elina
ERRA, Ana María, 41
ERRAMOUSPE, Lorenzo Santiago, 923
ERRAZQUIN (family), 1108
ERRAZURIZ, Federico, 90
ERRECART, Pedro L., 923
ERRO, Carlos Alberto, 743
ERSEN, Santos, 807
ERZIA, Stephan, 154, 191
ESAGUIRRE, José María, 126
ESANDI, Nicolás, 910
ESCALADA, 79
ESCALADA, Antonio José, 32, 112, 478, 479, 496, 554, 611
ESCALADA, Asunción, 943, 1042
ESCALADA, Daniel M., 68
ESCALADA, Emiliana, 965
ESCALADA, Federico A., 923
ESCALADA, Francisco Antonio de, 166, 496
ESCALADA, Juan Pedro, 971
ESCALADA, Manuel de, 404, 475, 611
ESCALADA, María Eugenia, 611
ESCALADA, Mariano José de
    see ESCALADA BUSTILLOS Y CEBALLOS, Mariano José

ESCALADA, Remedios de
   see ESCALADA DE SAN MARTÍN, María de los Remedios
ESCALADA BUSTILLO Y CEBALLOS, Mariano José, 148, 611,
   907, 910, 911, 912, 920, 921
ESCALADA DE DEMARÍA, María Eugenia, 85, 422
ESCALADA DE LA QUINTANA, Remedios, 172
ESCALADA DE OROMÍ, María de las Nieves, 422, 611
ESCALADA DE SAN MARTÍN, María de los Remedios, 85,
   112, 212, 282, 422, 478, 574, 611, 616, 876,
   927, 928, 929
ESCALADA FERNÁNDEZ DE ROJAS DE ARANDA, Adelaida, 971
ESCALANTE (family), 352
ESCALANTE, Manuel Gaspar, 923
ESCALERA, Juan, 844, 850
ESCANDE DE VUJACICH, Rubi A., 652
ESCANDELL, Víctor Hugo, 653
ESCANDÓN, Joannes
   see ESCANDÓN, Juan de
ESCANDÓN, Juan de, 1035, 1036
ESCARDÓ, Florencio (PIOLÍN DE MACRAMÉ, pseud.), 769,
   923
ESCARGUEL, Julio, 190
ESCARIS MÉNDEZ, Eduardo, 871
ESCARIZ, Myrta Nydia, 663, 831
ESCARIZ DE PEVERELLI, Victoria María, 923
ESCARRANEA, Antonio Domingo, 126
ESCARZA, Ramón, 1203
ESCAYOLA, Juan (TORORA, Juan, pseud.), 1122, 1166,
   1167
ESCOBAR, Alonso de, 358
ESCOBAR, Anselmo E., 998
ESCOBAR, Antonio de, 914
ESCOBAR, Edmundo, 998
ESCOBAR, Eladio, 998
ESCOBAR, Fortunato, 15
ESCOBAR, J. Benigno, 959
ESCOBAR, José Gabriel, 995
ESCOBAR, José Teodoro, 995a
ESCOBAR, Juan, 568, 850, 1034
ESCOBAR, Manuel, 268
ESCOBAR, Olimpio, 998
ESCOBAR, Patricio Alejandrino, 959, 974, 983, 1003,
   1008, 1011, 1012
ESCOBAR, Pedro de, 555
ESCOBAR, Ulises, 1093
ESCOBAR GARCETE, Leónidas, 998
ESCOBAR IBACACHE, Pedro de, 555
ESCOBAR MACHADO, Héctor Homero, 1210
ESCOBAR MARTÍNEZ, Silverio Salvador, 1210
ESCOBAR OSORIO, Diego de
   see ESCOBAR Y OSORIO, Diego de
ESCOBAR Y CARRILLO, Juan de, 646
ESCOBAR Y GUTIÉRREZ, Antonio de, 1011
ESCOBAR Y OSORIO, Diego de, 984, 1011
ESCOBEIDO
   see ESCOBEIRO, Isidro
ESCOBEIRO, Isidro, 949
ESCOBIO, Evaristo E., 882
ESCOFFIER, 960
ESCOFFIER, Luis, 949
ESCOLA, Cayetano, 148
ESCORZA, Manuel Antonio de, 555
ESCOSERÍA, Cyro, 894
ESCRIBANO, Bernardino, 230
ESCRIBAS, Luis Antonio, 653
ESCUDER, Miguel Héctor, 894
ESCUDERO, Antonio, 332
ESCUDERO, Estela Raquel, 653
ESCUDERO, Miguel, 268
ESCULIES, José, 963a

ESCUTI (family), 352
ESCUTÍ Y OLABARRIETA, Miguel de, 496
ESEYZA, Pedro E., 279
ESNAOLA, Juan, 293
ESNAOLA, Juan Pedro, 141, 282, 478, 509, 574
ESPALTER, José, 1075, 1083, 1117
ESPALTER, José P., 1126
ESPARZA, Alexos de, 186
ESPECHE GIL, Juan Carlos, 1088
ESPEJO, Alberto, 704
ESPEJO, Gerónimo, 212, 278, 371, 611, 730
ESPEJO, Jerónimo, 207, 683a
ESPEJO, Juan Luis, 283
ESPILCUENTA Y RODA, Roque de, 1270
ESPINAR, Alonso de, 1203
ESPINAR, José de, 104
ESPÍNDOLA, Nicolás, 923
ESPÍNDOLA, Sofía, 762
ESPINDOLA VALDÉS DE BASTERRECHEA, Flora, 268
ESPINEL, María Victoria, 781
ESPINO, Pedro, 95
ESPÍNOLA (family), 952
ESPÍNOLA, Antonia, 953
ESPÍNOLA, Armando, 998
ESPÍNOLA, Faustino, 173
ESPÍNOLA, Francisco, 258, 1148, 1149, 1155, 1159,
   1162, 1168, 1170, 1177, 1180, 1187, 1189, 1196,
   1199
ESPINOLA, Genaro, 939
ESPINOLA, José, 952
ESPÍNOLA, José Patricio, 998
ESPÍNOLA, Lourdes, 1015
ESPÍNOLA, Ramiro, 998
ESPÍNOLA DE ACOSTA Y LARA, María Esther, 1093
ESPÍNOLA Y PEÑA, José, 984
ESPINOSA, Antonio, 169, 907a
ESPINOSA, Federico, 137
ESPINOSA, Francisco de, 186
ESPINOSA, Gervasio, 611
ESPINOSA, Julián Gregorio de, 629, 1063
ESPINOSA, Julio, 653, 654
ESPINOSA, Manuel, 36
ESPINOSA, Mariano Antonio, 907, 910, 912, 921
ESPINOSA, Pedro de, 32
ESPINOSA ARGÜELLO, Pedro de, 224
ESPINOSA CENTENO, Helena del Carmen, 652
ESPINOSA DE CIMAGLIA, Lía de
   see CIMAGLIA DE ESPINOSA, Lía de
ESPINOSA PASCALE, Clelia, 810
ESPINOSA SANTANDER, Martín de, 556
ESPINOSA Y TELLO, José de, 834
ESPINOZA, Enrique, pseud.
   see GLUSBERG, Samuel
ESPINOZA, Sebastián de, 555
ESPIRO, Nicolás, 658
ESPOILE, Raúl Hugo, 154, 881, 883
ESPORA, Juan Manuel, 254
ESPORA, Tomás, 9, 12, 14, 16, 17, 110, 244, 258,
   386, 404, 574, 611
ESQUIBEL, Alonzo Esteban de, 186
ESQUININI, Federico, 951
ESQUIÚ, Mamerto
   see ESQUIÚ Y MEDINA, Mamerto
ESQUIÚ Y MEDINA, Mamerto, 72, 79, 89, 115a, 121,
   141, 165, 166, 176, 244, 261, 282, 317, 380,
   460, 583, 615, 650, 692, 910, 921, 1266
ESQUIVEL, Bartolomé de, 344
ESQUIVEL, Bernabé Antonio (CHIQUILLO, pseud.), 92
ESQUIVEL Y ALDAO, Rafaela Ramona, 422, 611
ESSARTS, Berchón des
   see DES ESSARTS, Berchón

ESSEX VIDAL, Emeric, 51
ESTABLE, Clemente, 1184
ESTARI HIRSH, Geza, 1210
ESTAVILLO, Antenor, 1093
ESTAVILLO, Julio, 1167
ESTAY, Justo, 611, 1167
ESTEBAN, Federico, pseud.
    see PAITOUX, Federico
ESTEBAN, Juan Gerónimo, 923
ESTEVAN, Eustaquio, 1223
ESTEVAN, Francisco de Paula, 1223
ESTEVES, Lina, 893
ESTEVES, Manuel, 852
ESTEVEZ, Alfredo, 652
ESTEVEZ, Juan B., 1094, 1095
ESTEVEZ, Manuel, 1089
ESTÉVEZ, Maximino, 1089
ESTÉVEZ CAMBRA, Rogelio, 284
ESTÉVEZ CANEDA, Manuel, 284
ESTÉVEZ DOS SANTOS, Manuel, 1092
ESTÉVEZ FRANCISCO, Jesús, 284
ESTÉVEZ GALINDO, Juan, 649a
ESTIGARRIBIA, Eustaquio, 995a
ESTIGARRIBIA, Joel, 953
ESTIGARRIBIA, José de la Cruz, 974
ESTIGARRIBIA, José Félix, 936, 948, 953, 954, 975,
    984a, 998, 1004, 1006, 1009, 1010, 1012
ESTIGARRIBIA, Juan de la Cruz, 984
ESTIGARRIBIA, Juan Vicente, 947, 949, 964
ESTIVAO, Jacinto, 1093a
ESTOMBA, Juan Ramón, 442, 611
ESTRABOU, Alfredo Bernardo, 560
ESTRADA (family), 1108
ESTRADA, Adolfo, 54
ESTRADA, Angel de, 116, 122, 664, 669, 722, 751,
    773, 774, 1259
ESTRADA, Angel de (son), 167
ESTRADA, Carlos, 1206, 1207
ESTRADA, José Manuel, 70, 72, 110, 116, 118, 141,
    167, 176, 182, 244, 272, 278, 282, 293, 317,
    404, 478, 485, 585, 601, 609, 644, 647, 667,
    692, 734, 751, 921
ESTRADA, José María de, 664
ESTRADA, Juan Bautista de, 122, 449
ESTRADA, Juan Manuel, 166
ESTRADA, Santiago, 708, 720, 834, 1246
ESTRADA BELLO, Enrique, 18, 30, 31
ESTRÁZULAS (family), 1108
ESTRÁZULAS, Enrique, 1183
ESTRÁZULAS, Jaime, 1134
ESTRELLA, Guillermo, 765, 816, 829
ESTRELLA, Jorge, 689
ESTRELLA, Lahir, 207
ESTRELLA, María del Mar, 725
ESTRELLA, Omar, 679
ESTRELLA DE SUÁREZ, Isabel, 683a
ESTRELLA GUTIÉRREZ, Fermín, 140, 678, 722, 739,
    748, 751, 759, 773
ESTRUCH, Tomás, 1188
ETCHARRÁN, Susana, 701
ETCHEBARNE, Miguel D., 664, 722, 739, 758, 759, 803,
    812
ETCHEBARNE BIDARTE, Andrés, 1044
ETCHEBEHERE, Guillermo, 739, 812
ETCHENIQUE, Nira, 717, 725, 739, 794, 802
ETCHEPARE, Juan, 878
ETCHEPARE CASTELLANOS, Susana, 1207, 1210
ETCHEPAREBORDA, Nicasio, 844
ETCHEPAREBORDA, Roberto, 521, 609

ETCHEVEHERE, Luis L., 135, 241
ETCHEVEHERE, Pedro Héctor, 923
ETCHEVERRI, Angel, 332
ETCHEVERRIGARAY, Miguel Angel, 664
ETCHEVERRY, José, 68
ETCHEVERRY, Miguel Angel, 923
ETCHEVERS LEMOINE, Juan Pedro Eduardo, 1064
ETESO, Heráclito de, 658
EULERICH, Ernesto L., 954
EXPESUA, Mariano José, 126
EXPÓSITO, Homero, 759, 862, 871
EXPÓSITO, Virgilio, 862
EYHERABIDE, Adolfo A., 923
EYZAGUIRRE, Manuel de, 644
EYZAGUIRRE, Mariano, 126
EZCURRA, Encarnación
    see EZCURRA Y ARGUIBEL DE ROSAS, Encarnación
EZCURRA, Juan Ignacio de, 496
EZCURRA, Martín, 32
EZCURRA, Pedro, 332
EZCURRA Y ARGUIBEL DE ROSAS, Encarnación, 105, 234,
    240, 434, 478, 480, 494, 578
EZEIZA, Gabino, 137, 759, 813, 878, 1243, 1247
EZEIZA MONASTEIRIO, Raúl T. de, 751, 766, 812
EZQUER ZELAYA, Ernesto E., 707
EZQUERRENEA, Manuel Justo Gentil de la, 126
EZQUIAGA, Miguel de, 496

FABANI, Ana Teresa, 135, 717, 800
FABEIRO, Vicente, 1089
FABINI, Eduardo, 1067, 1079, 1206, 1207, 1208
FABINI, Juan P., 1123
FABRACH, Horacio Adolfo, 923
FABRE (family), 960
FABRE, Agustín Eusebio, 496, 843, 844, 846, 1261,
    1262
FABRE, Anze de, 556
FABREGAT, Luis, 1075, 1083
FABREGAT CÚNEO, Roberto, 1149, 1184
FABRIS, Humberto Antonio, 923
FACAL, Juan, 1089
FACAL, Manuel, 1089
FACCI, Carlos, 781
FACINO, Héctor, 62
FACIO HEBECQUER, Eduardo
    see FACIO HEBEQUER, Eduardo
FACIO HEBECQUER, Guillermo
    see FACIO HEBEQUER, Guillermo
FACIO HEBEQUER, Eduardo, 894
FACIO HEBEQUER, Guillermo, 18, 31, 44, 55
FACÓN CHICO, pseud.
    see WALKER, John
FACÓN GRANDE, pseud.
    see EDWARDS, Henry
FADER, Fernando, 18, 19, 25, 31, 33, 45, 55, 141,
    217, 278, 282, 293, 521, 1218
FADOL CESIN, Anuar, 1210
FAGER FARÍAS, José, 1210
FAGETTI, Juan E., 1151
FAGGIOLI, Juan Carlos, 19, 64
FAGGIOLI, Rodolfo, 258
FAGNANO, José, 99, 222, 258, 268, 287, 907a, 921
FAGOAGA, Lorenzo de, 555
FAGUNDEZ DE RAMOS, Elisa, 1093
FAHY, Antonio de, 629, 921
FAIG, Carlos H., 894
FAILDE, Máximo, 1089
FAIN, Jordana, 889
FAIR, Juan, 904
FAJARDO, Carlos A., 1174, 1188

FAJARDO, Heraclio C., 1146, 1174, 1185, 1188, 1199
FAJARDO, Pedro de, 907, 910, 911, 920
FALCAO ESPALTER, Mario, 688, 1083, 1187, 1190, 1199
FALCIANI, Adolfo, 258
FALCINI, Luis, 19, 25, 33, 64, 521
FALCIOLA, Augusto, 664
FALCO, Angel, 1064, 1079, 1083, 1145, 1179, 1188, 1199
FALCO, Carlos, 37
FALCO, Federico S. Félix, 923
FALCO, Líber, 1148, 1149, 1151, 1152, 1177, 1178, 1179
FALCÓN, Ada, 879
FALCÓN, José, 943, 966
FALCÓN, Mario, 922
FALCÓN, Ramón L., 122, 282
FALCONE, Luis Angel, 320
FALDINI, José Daniel, 923
FALERO PIÑIERO, Miguel Luján, 1210
FALKNER, Thomas, 156, 289, 318, 640, 834, 845, 846, 850, 885, 922, 1203, 1261, 1269
FALUCHO, pseud.
     see RUIZ, Antonio
FANEGO, Rafael, 319
FANEGO, Rubén, 947
FANEGO DE MIÑO, Ramona Dolores (MIÑO, Lola de), 943a
FANGIO, Juan Manuel, 923a, 923b, 923c
FANO, Faustino Alberto, 3
FANTASIO, pseud.
     see GÁLVEZ ELORZA, Juan
FANTI, Graciela, 810
FARALDO, Manuel, 1089
FARAMIÑÁN, Julián, 921
FARAO, Lucía Victoria, 65
FARÉS, Raimundo, 683a
FARFÁN, Pedro, 649a
FARFÁN AROSEMENA, Rafael, 785
FARÍAS, Dringue, 857d
FARÍAS, Jorge Alberto, 684
FARÍAS, Martín, 125
FARÍAS GÓMEZ, Isabel, 664
FARINA, Ernesto, 18, 19, 23, 24, 25, 31, 36
FARINA, Livio, 1039
FARIÑA, Delio, 947
FARIÑA, Eloy
     see FARIÑA NÚÑEZ, Eloy
FARIÑA, Gumersindo, 1089
FARIÑA, José María, 1003, 1012
FARIÑA, Marina, 320
FARIÑA, Pedro, 1089
FARIÑA, Sindo, 299
FARIÑA ARCE, Pedro J., 995
FARIÑA BRÍTEZ, Raúl, 947
FARIÑA FERREIRA, Joaquín, 995
FARIÑA NÚÑEZ, Eloy, 943, 959, 966, 980, 1012, 1014, 1015, 1018, 1019, 1020, 1021, 1022, 1023, 1026
FARIÑA SÁNCHEZ, Zacarías, 998
FARIÑAS, Mariano, 126
FARQUET (family), 168
FARRELL, Edelmiro J., 170, 461, 515, 516, 530, 619
FARRUCO, pseud.
     see RODRÍGUEZ, Francisco
FARUK, pseud.
     see PALACIO, Jorge
FASCIO, José, 258
FASCIO, José María, 385
FASCIOLO, Juan Carlos, 923
FASOLINO, Nicolás, 910
FASSARDI, José, 951, 952

FASSI, Alberto Aldo, 299
FASTRÁS, Rubén, pseud.
     see SALDÍAS, José Antonio
FATONE, Vicente, 743
FAUPEL, Wilhelm, 602
FAUQUER, Aurora Noemí, 923
FAURE BLUM, Martha, 663
FAUST ROCHA, Miguel, 891
FAUZÓN SARMIENTO, Jorge R., 560
FAVALORO, René, 213
FAVARO, Ulises, 894, 1185
FAVELUKES, Gabriel, 923
FAVERO, Fermín Valentín, 860
FAVERO, Luis Antonio, 923
FAVIER, Albin, 28
FAVIO, Leonardo, 857
FAY, Sam, 904
FAYA, Orlando, 850a
FAYT, Carlos S., 218
FAZ, pseud.
     see ZABALÍA, Félix Alberto de
FAZIO, Carmelo, 923
FAZIO, Franco, 874
FEBRE, Ramón, 95, 135, 194, 241
FEBRES, José Gabino, 126
FECHA, Juan, 284, 866
FEDERMAN, Bernardo, 44
FEHLIG, Alfredo, 998
FEIERSTEIN, Ricardo, 814
FEIJÓO, Casimiro, 344
FEILBERG, Valentín, 287
FEIN, Carlos A., 1075
FEINSTEIN, Jaime, 923
FELDMAN, José María, 923
FELDMAN, Simón, 857
FELICE, Pedro de, 963
FELIPE II, King of Spain, 283
FELIPPONE, Florentino, 1083
FELIÚ, Buenaventura, 319
FELS, Teodoro Pablo, 81
FEMENÍA, Marta Alicia, 691
FENTANES, Juan, 461
FERNÁNDEZ (family), 348
FERNÁNDEZ, Alberto, 998
FERNÁNDEZ, Albino, 18, 27
FERNÁNDEZ, Ana María, 653
FERNÁNDEZ, Angel, 652, 1089
FERNÁNDEZ, Antonio, 845, 982
FERNÁNDEZ, Antonio de la Cruz, 949
FERNÁNDEZ, Antonio María, 1122
FERNÁNDEZ, Antonio Ramón, 331
FERNÁNDEZ, C. Ariel, 703
FERNÁNDEZ, Carlos, 268
FERNÁNDEZ, Carlos José, 1006
FERNÁNDEZ, Celestino M., 1159, 1167
FERNÁNDEZ, Cosme, 1094
FERNÁNDEZ, Dionisio, 1095
FERNÁNDEZ, Dolores, 947
FERNÁNDEZ, Domingo, 272, 1094
FERNÁNDEZ, Emiliano R., 943, 1028
FERNÁNDEZ, Emilio, 1089
FERNÁNDEZ, Esteban, 552
FERNÁNDEZ, Evaristo, 982
FERNÁNDEZ, Federico W., 68
FERNÁNDEZ, Felipe, 845
FERNÁNDEZ, Felipe H. (YACARÉ, pseud.), 660, 710, 727, 811, 813
FERNÁNDEZ, Félix, 943, 1014, 1021, 1022, 1085
FERNÁNDEZ, Florencio, 995
FERNÁNDEZ, Francisco, 152a, 677, 982
FERNÁNDEZ, Francisco F., 135, 777, 1020

FERNÁNDEZ, Francisco Javier, 653, 654
FERNÁNDEZ, Francisco León Andrés, 32
FERNÁNDEZ, Heriberto
   see FERNÁNDEZ ROLÓN, Heriberto
FERNÁNDEZ, Ignacio, 6
FERNÁNDEZ, Isidoro, 456
FERNÁNDEZ, J. Milcíades, 954
FERNÁNDEZ, Jacinto, 565
FERNÁNDEZ, Jesús, 1089
FERNÁNDEZ, Joaquín, 1089
FERNÁNDEZ, José, 1089
FERNÁNDEZ, José María Lorenzo, 284
FERNÁNDEZ, José María Manuel, 923
FERNÁNDEZ, José Urbano, 268
FERNÁNDEZ, Juan, 556, 845, 1093a, 1095
FERNÁNDEZ, Juan Antonio, 844, 1261
FERNÁNDEZ, Juan de Dios, 135
FERNÁNDEZ, Juan Patricio, 319
FERNÁNDEZ, Juan Ramón, 844, 1261
FERNÁNDEZ, Juan Rómulo, 68, 283
FERNÁNDEZ, Leonor, 932
FERNÁNDEZ, Lorenzo Antonio, 1261
FERNÁNDEZ, Lucas, 186, 845
FERNÁNDEZ, Macedonio, 232, 235, 658, 674, 722, 737,
   739, 740, 745a, 759, 769, 803, 816, 825
FERNÁNDEZ, Manuel, 1089
FERNÁNDEZ, Manuel Ignacio, 1264
FERNÁNDEZ, Mario César, 1148, 1149, 1155, 1158,
   1182
FERNÁNDEZ, Mario Serafín, 1159
FERNÁNDEZ, Melchor, 895, 915
FERNÁNDEZ, Migüel, 254
FERNÁNDEZ, Miguel Angel, 1015, 1020, 1021, 1022,
   1025
FERNÁNDEZ, Pedro, 284, 599
FERNÁNDEZ, Pero (family), 358
FERNÁNDEZ, Pío Carlos, 923
FERNÁNDEZ, Ramón, 998
FERNÁNDEZ, Rodrigo, 810
FERNÁNDEZ, Saturnino, 1089
FERNÁNDEZ, Segundo, 1094
FERNÁNDEZ, Silvia, 762
FERNÁNDEZ, Valerio, 954
FERNÁNDEZ, Vicente, 1095
FERNÁNDEZ AGÜERO, Juan María, 324
FERNÁNDEZ AGUILAR, Rafael, 923
FERNÁNDEZ ALBARIÑO, César, 75
FERNÁNDEZ AMARILLA, Pedro D., 954
FERNÁNDEZ ARIAS, Celestino, 998
FERNÁNDEZ BAUTISTA, Lauro, 1210
FERNÁNDEZ BLANCO, Angel, 539, 611
FERNÁNDEZ BLANCO, José Vicente, 126
FERNÁNDEZ BLANCO, Juan José, 196
FERNÁNDEZ CAMPERO, Juan José, 128
FERNÁNDEZ CASTELLANO, Pedro, 32
FERNÁNDEZ CORNEJO, Juan Adrián, 191, 1229
FERNÁNDEZ CRESPO, Daniel, 1123
FERNÁNDEZ CHELO, Enrique, 41
FERNÁNDEZ DANS, José, 320
FERNÁNDEZ DÁVILA, Tadeo, 126
FERNÁNDEZ DE AGÜERO, Amador, 640
FERNÁNDEZ DE AGÜERO, Ignacio, 186, 640
FERNÁNDEZ DE AGÜERO, Juan, 293
FERNÁNDEZ DE AGÜERO, Juan Ceyatano, 114, 640
FERNÁNDEZ DE AGÜERO, Juan Manuel, 114
FERNÁNDEZ DE AGÜERO, Manuel, 183
FERNÁNDEZ DE ANDRADA, Diego, 646, 649a
FERNÁNDEZ DE CÓRDOBA, Felipe, 126
FERNÁNDEZ DE CÓRDOBA, Gregorio, 126
FERNÁNDEZ DE CÓRDOBA, Pedro José, 126

FERNÁNDEZ DE CÓRDOBA Y ESPINOSA, Felipe, 653, 654
FERNÁNDEZ DE EIJO, Januario, 344
FERNÁNDEZ DE ENCISO, Juan, 358
FERNÁNDEZ DE GAILLET, Amanda Mercedes, 320
FERNÁNDEZ DE LA CRUZ, Francisco, 552, 611
FERNÁNDEZ DE LA PUENTE, Luis, 669
FERNÁNDEZ DE LA TORRE, Pedro, 910, 984a, 1034, 1041
FERNÁNDEZ DE LORCA, Gonzalo, 555
FERNÁNDEZ DE LOUREIRO, María J., 652
FERNÁNDEZ DE MOLINA, Juan, 496
FERNÁNDEZ DE MONTIEL, Sebastián, 989
FERNÁNDEZ DE OVIEDO Y VALDEZ, Gonzalo, 1203
FERNÁNDEZ DE ROSA, Alberto, 889
FERNÁNDEZ DE SALGUERO, Diego, 284
FERNÁNDEZ DE VALENZUELA, Antonio, 1035
FERNÁNDEZ DE VIDAL, Stella Maris, 652
FERNÁNDEZ DECAMILLA, Evaristo, 947
FERNÁNDEZ DO EIJO, Melchor, 496
FERNÁNDEZ DOZAL, Francisco
   see DOZAL, Francisco
FERNÁNDEZ ENTRERRÍOS, José, 1089
FERNÁNDEZ ESPIRO, Diego, 78, 121, 135, 243, 511,
   669, 751, 800, 1259
FERNÁNDEZ FERNÁNDEZ, Juan, 1210
FERNÁNDEZ FRÍAS, Diego, 649a
FERNÁNDEZ GARCÍA, Alfredo, 805
FERNÁNDEZ GARCÍA, Angel, 971
FERNÁNDEZ GIANOTTI, Arturo Aldo, 923
FERNÁNDEZ GÓMEZ, José, 1089
FERNÁNDEZ GUERRA, José, 763
FERNÁNDEZ GUILLÉN, Juan, 186
FERNÁNDEZ JENSEN, Carlos A., 385
FERNÁNDEZ JURADO, Guillermo, 857c
FERNÁNDEZ LACOSQUET, Alfredo, 1210
FERNÁNDEZ LASCANO, Francisco, 1204
FERNÁNDEZ LATOUR, Olga Elena, 688
FERNÁNDEZ LIMA, Juan C. R., 923
FERNÁNDEZ LOBO, Nuño, 640
FERNÁNDEZ MADERO, María Elena, 751, 762
FERNÁNDEZ MARADONA, José Ignacio, 283, 478, 479,
   546, 549
FERNÁNDEZ MARADONA, Plácido, 283
FERNÁNDEZ MERCADO, Antonio, 186
FERNÁNDEZ MARCIAL, Alonso, 1011
FERNÁNDEZ MIRANDA, Avelino, 1111
FERNÁNDEZ MOLINA, José, 653, 654
FERNÁNDEZ MONTIEL, José, 979
FERNÁNDEZ MONTIEL, Sebastián, 964
FERNÁNDEZ MORENO, Baldomero Eugenio Otto, 192, 521,
   658, 664, 674, 678, 718, 722, 723, 732, 737,
   739, 740, 748, 751, 755, 759, 769, 773, 782,
   801, 803, 807, 1243, 1247
FERNÁNDEZ MORENO, César, 672, 674, 678, 722, 739,
   741, 751, 758, 759, 801, 803, 807, 812
FERNÁNDEZ MORENO, Clara, 658
FERNÁNDEZ MORENO, Manrique, 717
FERNÁNDEZ MURO, José Antonio, 19, 25, 31, 36, 54,
   55
FERNÁNDEZ NAVARRO, César, 18, 31
FERNÁNDEZ PELÁEZ, Julio, 683a
FERNÁNDEZ RAMOS, Melchor, 284
FERNÁNDEZ RÍOS, Ovidio, 1145, 1179
FERNÁNDEZ ROLÓN, Heriberto, 1014, 1015, 1018, 1020,
   1021, 1022
FERNÁNDEZ ROMO, Manuel, 555
FERNÁNDEZ RUBIO, Nicolás, 299
FERNÁNDEZ RUEDA, José, 196
FERNÁNDEZ RUGGIERO, Esteban Domingo, 1210
FERNÁNDEZ SALDAÑA, José María, 1087, 1169
FERNÁNDEZ SIMONÍN, Rosa, 268
FERNÁNDEZ TEIJEIRO, Manuel, 19

FERNÁNDEZ UNSAIN, José María, 135, 766, 800, 812
FERNÁNDEZ VARGAS, Domingo, 1089
FERNÁNDEZ VILLANUEVA, Julio, 19, 25, 59
FERNÁNDEZ VILLAR, José María, 284
FERNÁNDEZ Y MEDINA, Benjamín, 1083, 1146, 1154,
    1159, 1167, 1168, 1170, 1174, 1180, 1185, 1188,
    1190, 1196, 1199, 1247
FERNANDO VII, King of Spain, 283, 1091
FERRADAS, Juan Ignacio, 496
FERRAGUT, Juan León, 915
FERRANDO, Andrés M., 1075
FERRANDO, Santiago, 6
FERRARASSI, Alfredo Julio, 691
FERRARI, Adolfo C. de,
    see DE FERRARI, Adolfo C.
FERRARI, Angel M. Rosendo, 923
FERRARI, Cayetano, 814
FERRARI, Clara, 44
FERRARI, Graciela, 705
FERRARI, José, 258
FERRARI, Juan, 94
FERRARI, Juan M., 1046, 1047, 1079
FERRARI, Laureana
    see FERRARI DE OLAZÁBAL, Laureana
FERRARI, León, 25, 49
FERRARI, María Rosa de, 1217
FERRARI, Oscar, 299
FERRARI, Pedro Juan, 258
FERRARI AMORES, Alfonso, 668, 766, 814
FERRARI DE OLAZÁBAL, Laureana, 258, 422, 478, 611,
    929
FERRARI DE PLAZA, Angélica, 1093
FERRARÍA, Mayorino, 782
FERRARÍA ACOSTA, Eloísa, 751
FERRARINI, María Cristina, 320
FERRARINI DE BLYTHMAN, Mirza Victoria, 320
FARRARIS, Carlos, 113, 258
FERRARO, Ariel, 717, 739, 759, 790, 802, 831, 832
FERRARO RODRÍGUEZ, Antonio, 1210
FERRAROTI, Juan Luis, 565
FERRÉ, Pedro, 95, 96, 121, 196, 375, 539, 568, 569,
    611, 632, 634
FERREIRA, Alfredo, 67
FERREIRA, Andrés, 565
FERRAIRA, Avelino, 648, 649
FERREIRA, Benigno, 959, 975, 983, 991, 1012
FERREIRA, Eduardo, 1083, 1146, 1187, 1199
FERREIRA, Fermín, 1091, 1107, 1261
FERREIRA, Gregorio, 32
FERREIRA, Guillermo H., 265
FERREIRA, Heriberto, 998
FERREIRA, Ivo, 1204
FERREIRA, J. Alfredo, 478
FERREIRA, Jacome
    see FERREIRA FEO, Jacome
FERREIRA, José A.
    see FERREYRA, José A.
FERREIRA, Manuel, 32
FERREIRA, Mariano, 1083
FERREIRA, Roque, 32
FERREIRA, Sixto Zenón, 995
FERREIRA, Teodoro, 1107
FERREIRA ALCÁNTARA, Julio César, 299
FERREIRA DA SYLVA, Silvestre, 28
FERREIRA DE AGUILAR, Manuel, 186
FERREIRA DE ARÉVALO, Marta L., 1088
FERREIRA DE ORDÓÑEZ, Rosa, 1107
FERREIRA FEO, Jacome, 32, 186
FERREIRA REINATE, Froilán, 910
FERREIRA Y ARTIGAS, Fermín, 1107, 1146, 1174, 1188,
    1199

FERREIRO, Adolfo, 1015, 1025
FERREIRO, Alfredo Mario, 1151, 1199
FERREIRO, Felipe, 1117
FERREIRO, Miguel, 1089
FERREIRO, Oscar, 943, 1014, 1015, 1020, 1021, 1022,
    1025
FERREIRO BLANCO, Agustín, 284
FERRER (family), 352
FERRER, Aldo, 311
FERRER, Gaspar E., 904
FERRER, Horacio Arturo, 660, 871
FERRER CAJIGAL, Antonio, 954
FERRER ESCURRA, Horacio, 1088
FERRERA, Juan Andrés, 568, 569, 611
FERRERO, Elsie, 31, 46
FERRÉS, Bernardo C., 1075
FERRÉS Y CARRAU, José, 1094
FERRÉS Y CARRAU, Pedro, 1094
FERRETI, Constatino (CIELITO, pseud.), 878
FERREYRA (family), 352
FERREYRA, Aquilino, 921
FERREYRA, Benigno, 68
FERREYRA, Carlos, 268
FERREYRA, Heraclio, 268
FERREYRA, J. Alfredo, 121
FERREYRA, José A., 858, 1127
FERREYRA, José Luis, 684
FERREYRA, Roque, 89, 316
FERREYRA, Valentín, 878
FERREYRA ABAD, Antonio Fernando, 914
FERREYRA BASSO, Juan G., 678, 722, 739, 748, 751,
    758, 759, 807
FERREYRA DE ROCA, Rosa, 24
FERREYRA SOSA, Gil, 69
FERREYRO, Perfecto, 1089
FERRIOL, José Ramón, 995a
FERRO, Elsa Norma, 923
FERRO, Oscar Raúl, 810
FERROFINO, Esteban, 151
FERRUEL, Richarte, 1270
FERRUFINO, Juan Bautista, 319, 952
FERUGLIO, Egidio, 923
FESQUET, Alberto Enrique Juan, 923
FESTER, Gustavo A., 923
FEUILLÉE, Luis, 885, 922
FIDALGO, Andrés, 713, 730, 739, 759, 809, 831
FIDDES, Basil A., 954
FIEBRIG, Carlos, 923
FIELDS, Tomás, 850
FIERRO, Martín, 864
FIGARI, Pedro, 18, 25, 33, 521, 1044, 1075, 1079,
    1081, 1083, 1159, 1177, 1218
FIGARI RIQUELME, Aparicio, 998
FIGARILLO, pseud.
    see ALBERDI, Juan Bautista
FÍGARO, pseud.
    see MUÑOZ, Daniel
FÍGOLI, Luis A., 1123
FÍGOLI, Sócrates, 878
FIGUEIRA, Gastón, 154
FIGUEIRA LÓPEZ, Jacinto, 284
FIGUEIRO, Urbano, 1089
FIGUEREDO, Alvaro, 1151, 1152, 1167, 1177, 1178,
    1179
FIGUEREDO, Bonifacio, 1082
FIGUEREDO, Ricardo Leonel, 1159
FIGUEREDO, Santiago, 329, 611, 908, 921
FIGUERES DE CORTE, Rosa, 923
FIGUEROA, Antonio de, 32
FIGUEROA, Benjamín, 445

FIGUEROA, Caracciolo, 240
FIGUEROA, Carlos Eduardo, 713, 730, 804
FIGUEROA, Fernando R., 653
FIGUEROA, José de, 319
FIGUEROA, José Hernán, 765
FIGUEROA, José Manuel, 921
FIGUEROA, Juan José, 284
FIGUEROA, Juan Manuel, 923
FIGUEROA, Julio José, 191
FIGUEROA, Manuel, 1089
FIGUEROA, Ramiro Alejandro, 684
FIGUEROA, Ricardo, 751
FIGUEROA, Salvador, 887
FIGUEROA ALCORTA, José, 68, 78, 110, 115, 166, 282,
     392, 393, 405, 466, 478, 515, 516, 521, 595,
     598, 619
FIGUEROA ARAOZ, José Hernán, 653, 654
FIGUEROLA, José, 530
FIJMAN, Jacobo, 235, 664, 722, 739, 759, 773, 833
FILÁRTIGA, Joel, 938
FILARTIGAS, Juan M., 1187
FILEVICH, Carlos, 55
FILGUERIA, Rogelio, 998
FILI, Hugo, 857c
FILIBERTO, Juan de Dios, 217
FILICAYA, Bacho de, 32
FILIPPI, Felipe de, 923
FILIPPI, Sandra, 791
FILIPPINI, Lucrecia María, 683a
FILLOL DAY, Gustavo R. A., 140
FILLOY, Juan, 760
FINA, Armando L. de
     see DE FINA, Armando L.
FINA, Sebastiano, 292
FINCATI, Roberto, 258
FINGERIT, Julio Pablo, 664
FINGERIT, Marcos, 664, 678, 805, 812
FINIS, Mario Luis de
     see DE FINIS, Mario Luis
FINO, José F., 652
FINO, Vicente, 207
FINOCHIETTO, Enrique, 853a
FINOCHIETTO, Ricardo, 851
FIOL DE PERERA, Alejandro, 1094
FIOL SOLÉ, Alejandro, 1094
FIORAVANTI, Jose, 19, 21, 25, 33, 55, 64, 521
FIORE, José, 860
FIORENTINO, Francisco, 877
FIORINI, Lorenzo, 51, 258
FIORONI, Juan Carlos, 1050
FIRBAS, Heinrich, 923
FIRPO, Roberto, 37, 244, 875, 877
FIRPO Y FIRPO, Bartolomé, 1167
FISCHER, Carlos, 1073
FISCHER, Jacobo, 865, 882, 883
FITTE, Enrique J., 609
FITTE, Juan Domingo, 253
FITZ PATRICK, Juan, 1064
FITZ ROY, Roberto, 202, 287
FLAMI, Golde, 889
FLANGINI, Alberto, 1174
FLECHA ORTEGA, Avelino, 998
FLEGENHEIMER, Juan G., 923
FLESCA, Roberto A., 923
FLEURS, Claude de (FLORES, Claude de), 318, 949
FLEURY, Abel, 217
FLEYTAS, Francisco Antonio, 998
FLO, pseud.
     see PARRAVICINI, Florencio
FLORENTÍN, Luis Alberto, 954
FLORENTÍN, Nicolás, 845

FLORES (family), 1108
FLORES, 960
FLORES, Baltasar, 914
FLORES, Bartolomé, 556
FLORES, Carlos, 1178
FLORES, Celedonio Esteban, 660, 710, 727, 759, 801,
     871, 877
FLORES, Claude de
     see FLEURS, Claude de
FLORES, Fortunato, 254
FLORES, Francisco Hermógenes, 995a
FLORES, Fructuoso, 1006
FLORES, José Asunción, 862, 937, 943, 965, 1027,
     1029
FLORES, José Segundo, 998
FLORES, Juan Diego, 125
FLORES, Julio Trifón, 998
FLORES, Luis, 922
FLORES, Manuel Antonio de, 922
FLORES, Ricardo, 1116
FLORES, Rosendo, 878
FLORES, Sevastián, 186
FLORES, Venancio, 96, 984, 1063, 1079, 1091, 1109,
     1110
FLORES DE OLIVA, Isabel
     see ROSA DE LIMA, Saint
FLORES DE SANTA CRUZ, Lorenzo, 186
FLORES MORA, Carlos, 1151
FLORIA, Carlos Alberto, 218
FLORIANI, Juan A., 760, 814
FLORIT, Ernesto, 75
FLUIXÁ, Ernesto, 874
FOASSA, Zulema, 766
FOCKE, Rolf Jost, 923
FOCHLER-HAUKE, Gustavo, 923
FOGLI, Ghino, 260
FOGLIA, Pedro, 1039
FOGLIA, Virgilio G., 923
FOGUET, Hugo R., 680, 830
FOGUET DE SÁNCHEZ, Justa, 924
FOLCO, Mario, pseud.
     see SOZIO, Mariano
FOLGESTROM, Gustav, 332
FOLGUEIRA, Ricardo, 1089
FOLGUERAS, José, 254
FOLINO, Norberto, 819
FOLLARI, Rodolfo S., 81
FONSECA, Juan Dámaso, 496, 915
FONSO GANDOLFO, Carlos, 923
FONT, Armengol P., 1172, 1185
FONT, Esteban, 850, 1267
FONT, Hugo César, 37
FONT, María Cecilia, 663
FONT EZCURRA, Ricardo, 431
FONTAINA, Pablo, 1095
FONTÁN, Luis Jacinto, 845
FONTANA, Alberto Emilio, 923
FONTANA, Elvira, 781
FONTANA, Jorge, 299
FONTANA, Jorge Luis, 287
FONTANA, Lucio, 19, 21, 25, 49, 55
FONTANA, Luis Jorge, 191, 202, 258, 288
FONTANELLA, Agustín, 719, 811, 813, 893
FONTAO MEZA, Rigoberto, 943
FONTELA, José A., 1095
FONTELA, José Rogelio, 1093
FONTENEAU, José, 62
FONTENLA, Jorge, 865, 883
FONTES, Nicolás M., 371
FONTOVA, León, 865
FONVIELLE (El caballero de), 1236

FOPPA, Tito Livio, 893
FORADORI, Italo Américo, 312
FORCADA, Antonio, 7, 32
FORCHER, Emilio, 385
FORMENTO CEROLINI DE RAPPA, Violeta, 1210
FORNACIARI, Dora, 679, 831
FORNAGUERA, José, 496
FORNARI, Oscar Elías, 923
FORNARO, Milton, 1173, 1183
FORNASO, Inés, 795
FORNEIRO, Felisindo, 1089
FORNER, Raquel, 18, 19, 20, 22, 23, 25, 31, 33, 36,
    38, 49, 50, 54, 55, 64
FORNERÓN, Casimiro, 952
FORONDA, Ana María de, 1187
FORTALEZA, Francisco S., 1073
FORTALEZA, Miguel de, 1223
FORTE, Alberto (CHICHE, pseud.), 860
FORTE, Vicente, 18, 19, 23, 25, 31, 36, 49, 55,
    177a, 217
FORTE LAY, María Laura, 37
FORTEZA, Armando C., 768
FORTI, Angel, 332
FORTI, Nisa, 781
FORTUNA, Juan, 923
FOSSATI, Alberto P., 998
FOSSATI, Florencia, 198, 683a
FOSSATI, Florencio, 882
FOTHERINGHAM, Ignacio, 78, 191
FOUGÈRES, Miguel de, 768
FOURCADE, Luis, 207
FOURNIÉ, Emilio, 1083
FOURNIER, César, 438, 611
FOURNIER, Léonie Julieta (JOFRE OLIÚ, Nirene, pseud.),
    762
FOUSSATS, Hebe, 762
FOWLIS, Juana, 653, 654
FRACASSI, Humberto, 923
FRAGA, Antonio R. de, 284
FRAGA, José, 1089
FRAGA, Rosendo María Eduardo, 191
FRAGA, Santiago, 1089
FRAGOSO DE RIVERA, Bernardina, 1114, 1133
FRAGOSO Y MUÑOZ, Pedro, 1095
FRAGUEIRO, Mariano, 95, 96, 244, 316, 545a, 611,
    761
FRAGUIERO, Rafael, 1146, 1174, 1185, 1188
FRAIGNE, Amelia, 691
FRAIN, Jaime, 731
FRANCESCH, José R., 1089
FRANCESCHI, Gustavo J., 751
FRANCESCHI, Juan Mateo, 853a
FRANCESE, Miguel B., 874
FRANCIA, Fioravante (TITO, pseud.), 874
FRANCIA, José Gaspar Rodríguez de, 166, 471, 577,
    936, 942, 943, 963, 964, 966, 969, 975, 979,
    980, 983, 984, 984a, 987, 997, 1004, 1010, 1011,
    1012, 1021, 1022, 1023, 1035
FRANCIA, José María, 543
FRANCINI, Enrique Mario, 862
FRANCIONI, Manuel, 746
FRANCISCO (EL INDIO), 977
FRANCISCO DE LA CONCEPCIÓN, 845
FRANCISENA, César Mario, 865
FRANCK, Carlos, 32
FRANCO, Alberto, 664, 746
FRANCO, César F. B., 963a
FRANCO, Evita, 893
FRANCO, Jorge Omar, 299
FRANCO, Justo Pedro, 683a

FRANCO, Lily, 660, 717, 745, 817
FRANCO, Luis Leopoldo, 140, 678, 680, 689, 707, 722,
    739, 743, 748, 751, 753, 759, 769, 773, 782,
    807, 809, 830, 833
FRANCO, Manuel, 984a
FRANCO, Miguel, 299
FRANCO, Pedro B., 751
FRANCO, Pietro, 292
FRANCO, Rafael, 1006
FRANCO, Rodolfo, 31, 44
FRANCO, Salvador, 319
FRANCO, Víctor Ignacio, 947, 994
FRANCO FERNÁNDEZ OCTAVIANO, Héctor María, 1210
FRANCOLI, Valentín, 319
FRANCONE, Mario Pablo, 923
FRANCONETTI DE BORUS, María, 923
FRANCHI, Alfredo C., 1145
FRANCHI, Otto Carlos, 560
FRANCHINI, Susana, 652
FRASCARA, Félix Daniel, 218
FRASER, Augustus, 587
FRATA BELLO, Arnaldo, 954
FRAY MOCHO, pseud.
    see ALVAREZ, José Sixto
FRAZZETTA, Norberto Daniel, 691
FRECHA, José Horacio, 923
FREDA, Teresa Carmen, 655
FREDIANI, Luis María, 923
FREGEIRO, Clemente L., 68, 609
FREGOLI, Leopoldo, 892
FREIBERG, Marcos, 923
FREIBERG, Salomón, 923
FREIDEMBERG, Daniel, 750
FREINKEL, Pablo A., 691
FREIRA VILLANUEVA, Carlos J., 1088
FREIRE, Manuel, 1059
FREIRE, María, 1049
FREIRE, Román, 1050
FREIRE ESTEVES, Gómes, 959, 1014
FREIRE MIRA, Alfredo, 1210
FREIRE MIRA, Julio César, 1210
FREIRE PIZZANO, Ramón, 1210
FREIRE TABARÉ, Jorge, 894
FREITAS, Pedro M. de, 1093
FREITAS DE FONSECA, 1056
FREIXAS, Aída A., 923
FREIXAS, Enrique, 225
FRENCH, Domingo, 70, 72, 85, 244, 386, 404, 478,
    479, 496, 554, 574, 611
FRENGUELLI, Joaquín, 258, 923
FRERS, Emilio, 3, 68
FRERS, Enrique, 3
FRERS, Julián, 3
FRESA, Roberto, 923
FRESCO, Antonio de, 344
FRESCO, Manuel Angel, 269, 954
FRESCO, Miguel Angel, 963a
FRESEDO, Emilio, 871
FRESEDO, Osvaldo, 877, 891a
FRESNO, Ramón del, 845
FRETE, Ricardo, 824
FRETES PÉREZ, Aurelio, 998
FRETO, Herminio, 998
FREUDE, Ludwig, 437, 602
FREYRE, Manuel Florentino, 1111
FREYRE, Marcelino, 845
FREYRE, Ramón, 553
FREYRE, Ricardo Jaime, 1259
FREYRE, Rodolfo, 121, 477
FREYTAG, Carlos, 947

FRÍAS, Bernardo, 653, 654
FRÍAS, Diego de, 556
FRÍAS, Dom, 240
FRÍAS, Eustaquio, 386, 611
FRÍAS, Félix, 116, 167, 216, 244, 282, 293, 449,
    490, 586, 611, 647, 692, 751, 761, 921, 1220
FRÍAS, Félix Ignacio, 126
FRÍAS, Ignacio de, 319, 895
FRÍAS, José A., 842
FRÍAS, José de, 555
FRÍAS, Manuel de, 472, 984, 1011
FRÍAS, Pedro, 68
FRÍAS, Pedro J., 89
FRÍAS, Uladislao, 121, 254, 631, 633
FRÍAS, Wenceslao, 83
FRÍAS DE RACHOPPE, María, 320
FRÍAS MIRANDA, Gaspar de, 1270
FRÍAS Y ALFARO, Antonio, 922
FRÍAS Y CASTELLANO, José Domingo, 126
FRIDMAN, Alcira, 37
FRIEDMAN, Raúl, 998
FRIEDMANN, Eugenio, 947
FRIEDRICH (family), 168
FRIGERIO, Atilio, 1206
FRIGERIO, Rogelio Julio, 311
FRIMUTH, Hellmuth, 923
FRONCINI, Mariano, 258, 292
FRONDIZI, Arturo, 489, 513, 515, 516, 590, 593, 624
FRUELA I, 361
FRUGONI, Emilio, 1068, 1079, 1083, 1087, 1147, 1151,
    1163, 1165, 1167, 1174, 1177, 1179, 1181, 1184,
    1187, 1199
FRUTOS, Antonio Eladio, 998
FRUTOS, Carlos Hidalgo, 1210
FRUTOS, Charles, 1020
FRUTOS, Lidia, 956
FRUTOS HIDALGO, Víctor de, 1210
FRUTOS PANE, J. Manuel, 943
FUCHS, Ana María E. T., 923
FUCHS, Ricardo E., 691
FUENSALIDA MENESES, José de, 646, 649a
FUENTE, Alicia de la, 655, 656, 700
FUENTE, Felipe de la, 31
FUENTE, Jorge de la, 860
FUENTE, José Andrés de la, 32
FUENTE, Juan Antonio de la, 32
FUENTE, Justiniano de la, 431
FUENTE, Maximino de la, 445
FUENTE RUBIA (family), 352
FUENTES, Antón de, 32
FUENTES, Dionisio de, 32
FUENTES, Juan, 31
FUENTES, Ruperto, 68
FUENTES, Téofilo, 947
FUENTES ARGUIVEL, José, 844
FUGAZOT, Roberto, 894
FUHRMANN, Arnulf, 1070
FUJISAWA, Ranko, 879
FULGINITI, Juan B., 878, 1243
FULQUET, Adolfo Cecilio, 691
FUMAGALLI, Rosa María, 37
FUNES, Ambrosio, 89, 244, 545a
FUNES, Carlos Alberto, 207
FUNES, Dean
    see FUNES, Gregorio
FUNES, Galo Gregorio, 81
FUNES, Germán, 299
FUNES, Gertrudis, 931
FUNES, José Roque, 545a
FUNES, Lucio, 207, 683a
FUNES, Manuela, 887

FUNES, Pedro José, 126
FUNES, Santiago, 222
FUNES, Vicente, 878
FUNES DE FUNES, Fortunato, 81
FUNES DE JUÁREZ CELMAN, Elisa, 842
FUNES, Gregorio (DEAN FUNES), 85, 89, 110, 112,
    121, 144, 166, 183, 244, 282, 283, 386, 404,
    455, 459, 475, 478, 479, 509, 514, 517, 518,
    519, 528, 529, 545a, 574, 609, 611, 692, 720
    734, 761, 763, 895, 908, 915, 921 ،
FUNES Y SALINAS, Diego de, 555
FURIA, Juan, 860
FURLAN, Luis Ricardo, 660, 727, 739, 802
FURLONG, Guillermo
    see FÚRLONG CÁRDIFF, Guillermo
FÚRLONG CÁRDIFF, Guillermo, 521, 609
FURMAN, Mónica Aída, 656
FURQUE, Guillermo, 923
FURQUE, Rafael, 283
FURRIOL, Jacinta, 1205, 1207
FURST, Carlos, 268, 844
FURT, Jorge M., 688
FUSCALDO, Juan, 766
FUSCO, Antonio Gustavo, 1073
FUSCO SANSONE, Nicolás, 1151, 1179, 1181, 1199
FUSELLI, Angélica, 762
FUSILLO, Sebastián, 954
FUSTAGNO, Luis, 954
FUTORANSKY, Luisa, 672

GABAY BENJUIA, Moisés, 1210
GABELLIERI, Arnaldo, 923
GABOTO, Juan
    see CABOT, John
GABOTO, Sebastián
    see CABOT, Sebastian
GABRIEL DE LA ANUNCIACIÓN, 943, 964, 1034
GACHE, Alberto I., 1246
GACHE, Samuel, 842
GADDA GANETTI, Hermes, 1210
GADEA, Lázaro, 1080
GADEA, Santiago Cristóbal, 1059, 1111
GADEO, Eleuterio, 998
GAEBELER, Guillermo F., 223
GAETANO, Cattaneo, 292
GAETANO, Juan, 258
GAETE (family), 351
GAETE, Antonio, 32
GAETE, Diego, 186
GAETE, Francisco, 186
GAETE, Gaspar de, 186, 274
GAETE, Juan Francisco, 318
GAFFAROT, Salvio, 844, 1261, 1262
GAGGERO, Emanuele, 139
GAGLIARDI, Héctor, 759
GAGLIARDONE, César, 954
GAGO, Manuel, 1089
GAILLARDOU, José Adolfo, 152a, 768
GAINZA, Arturo de, 94
GAINZA, Martín de, 631
GAINZA, Rodolfo de, 834
GAIOSO, Agustín, 186
GAITÁN, Bernardo, 1262
GAITO, Constantino Vicente, 293, 864, 865, 867, 881,
    883
GALÁN, Héctor Mario, 923
GALÁN, José Miguel, 95, 96, 543
GALÁN, Raúl Martín, 664, 679, 713, 722, 730, 739,
    748, 759, 831
GALANTE, Felipe, 258
GALANTE, Oscar Antonio, 923
GALANTHA, Ekatherina de, 154

GALARZA, Miguel Gerónimo, 95, 543
GALARZA, Pablo, 1083, 1200
GALARZO GRADILITTI, Ricardo, 1210
GALASSI, Luis Alberto, 691
GALASSO, Norberto, 609
GALEANO, Eduardo H., 1149, 1155, 1182, 1189
GALEANO, Ernesto César, 217, 865
GALEANO LARA CASTRO, Mariano Luis de, 956
GALEGO, Elida, 787
GALEOTTI, Elsa M., 652
GALETTINI, Domingo Carlos, 857
GALIANO, José M., 954
GALIANO, Juan, 995a
GALIANO, Manuel, 954
GALIERI, Víctor, 878
GALIGNIANA, Miguel José, 126
GALIGNIANA SEGURA, Carlos, 207
GALIMBERTI DE GUACCI, Haydée, 781
GALÍNDEZ (family), 348
GALÍNDEZ, Bartolomé, 751
GALÍNDEZ, Francisco R., 385
GALÍNDEZ, Ismael, 244
GALÍNDEZ, Nicodemo, 878
GALÍNDEZ DE CARVAJAL, Lorenzo, 898
GALINDO, Leonor, 889
GALINDO, Obdulio, 947
GALINDO, Raúl (NITO, pseud.), 965
GALINDO ARRASCAETA, Eduardo, 947
GALMARINI, Alfredo, 923
GALMARINO, Alberto Raúl, 923
GALÓ, Antonio, 1082
GALTIER, Lysandro Z. D., 663, 664, 722, 739, 833
GALVÁN, Blas, 1270
GALVÁN, C. Damián, 1243
GALVÁN, Elías, 427, 478, 479, 540, 611
GALVAN, Facundo, 878
GALVÁN MORENO, Celedonio, 222
GÁLVEZ, Jaime, 431
GÁLVEZ, José, 445
GÁLVEZ, Manuel, 135, 232, 431, 558, 609, 669, 737,
  742, 743, 751, 773, 782
GÁLVEZ ELORZA, Juan (FANTASIO, pseud.), 299
GÁLVEZ PARODI, Alan, 684
GALLAC, Héctor I., 882
GALLAND, Adolf, 602
GALLARDO, Angel, 116, 176, 182, 282, 293, 332
GALLARDO, Antonia Teresa, 684
GALLARDO, Domingo V., 751
GALLARDO, Guillermo, 521
GALLARDO, José, 653, 654
GALLARDO, José León, 882
GALLARDO, Juan Luis, 817
GALLARDO, Julio César, 691
GALLARDO, Manuel Bonifacio, 478
GALLARDO, Sara, 729
GALLARDO DE ORDÓÑEZ, Beatriz, 817
GALLARDO DE ZALAZAR PRINGLES, Justa B., 762
GALLARDO VALDEZ, Antonio S., 652
GALLARDO Y ESNAOLA, Angel, 1261
GALLASTEGUI, Juan José de, 874
GALLASTEGUI, Vicente, 903
GALLEGO, Jesús Alonso, 284
GALLEGO, Vasco, 1238
GALLEGOS, Antonio, 1262
GALLEGOS DE ROSAS, Fanny, 874
GALLEGOS MOYANO, Carlos, 565
GALLETTI DE MASTRÁNGELO, Irma A., 691
GALLI, Hugo, 860
GALLI, María, 1207
GALLI DELLA LOGGIA, Manuel, 952
GALLICCHIO, Domingo, 894
GALLINAL (family), 1108

GALLINAL, Alejandro, 1067, 1073, 1083
GALLINAL, Gustavo, 1068, 1117, 1184, 1187, 1199
GALLINAL, Hipólito, 1078
GALLINO, Cayetano, 1093a
GALLINO, Cristóbal E., 68
GALLINOTTI, Juan, 1092
GALLO, Delfín, 330
GALLO, María Rosa, 889
GALLO, Pedro León, 457, 526, 611, 621, 626
GALLO, Silvia A., 810
GALLO, Vicente C., 565, 650
GALLO MENDOZA, Ervar, 653, 654
GALLO MENDOZA, José María, 653, 654
GALLONI, Ernesto Enrique, 923
GALLOSO, Pantaleón, 917
GAMA, Jerónimo, 318
GAMARRA, Agustín, 562
GAMARRA, Donato, 995a
GAMARRA, Enrique, 191, 831
GAMARRA, Juan Manuel, 972
GAMARRA, Manuel A., 951, 959, 1014
GAMARRA, Pastor, 998
GAMBA, Carlos T., 1145
GAMBA, Otto O. M., 923
GAMBARROTA, Francisco, 151
GAMBARTES, Leónidas, 19, 25, 34, 36, 38, 55
GAMBOA, José M., 68
GAMBÓN, Vicente, 319
GÁMEZ, Luis, 1034
GAMIO, Enrique F., 1093
GAMKOSIAN, Alejandro, 923
GAMUNDI DE AMOS, Irma J., 923
GANCEDO, Omar, 662
GÁNDARA, Ana, 725
GÁNDARA, Carmen, 670, 729, 825, 834
GÁNDARA, Leonardo Domingo de la, 478, 479
GANDARILLAS, Manuel José, 126
GANDÍA (family), 347
GANDÍA, Enrique de, 431, 521, 609
GANDOLFI HERRERO, Alcides, 660, 710, 727
GANDOLFI HERRERO, Arístides (YUNQUE, Alvaro, pseud.),
  660, 710, 712, 727, 739, 751, 765, 829, 833, 1245
GANDOLFI HERRERO, Augusto (GUIJARRO, Juan, pseud.),
  710, 765, 833
GONDOLFO, Antonio, 844
GANDOLFO, Elvio, 788
GANDOLFO, Francisco, 788, 831
GANDOLFO, Juan B., 332
GANDOLFO, Mirtha, 1151, 1179
GANDÓS, Leoncio, 1089, 1094
GANDUGLIA, Héctor, 652
GANDUGLIA, Santiago A., 660, 766, 833
GANDULFO REYES, Jacinto Héctor, 312
GANS, Ricardo, 923
GANZO FERNÁNDEZ, José, 1093
GANZO FERNÁNDEZ, Juan, 1093
GAONA, Juan Bautista, 959
GAONA, Lorenzo
  see LORENZO Y GAONA, Juan de
GAONA Y CARRIZO, Miguel, 649a
GAOS BEREA, Andrés, 284
GARABITO, Ricardo, 55
GARAT, Damián P., 135, 800
GARAU, Sebastián, 318
GARAVAGLIA, Florencio Juan, 19, 31, 46, 63
GARAVAGLIA, Santiago Héctor, 299
GARAVITO DE LEÓN, Andrés, 970, 984, 989
GARAVITO DE LEÓN, Hernando de, 1035a, 1035b
GARAY (family), 357, 358, 1224
GARAY, Ana de, 109

GARAY, Blas Manuel, 943, 951, 964, 966, 980, 984a,
    993, 1002, 1012, 1021, 1022, 1023
GARAY, Eugenio Alejandrino, 936, 1006, 1012
GARAY, Ignacio, 921
GARAY, Isabel de (BECERRA, Isabel), 109
GARAY, Juan de, 32, 103, 134, 151, 176, 185, 244,
    406, 419, 443, 455, 462, 471, 472, 477, 481,
    482, 486, 510, 518, 519, 521, 528, 535, 640,
    948, 984, 997, 1011, 1012, 1203, 1229, 1230,
    1231, 1232, 1261, 1266
GARAY, Pedro, 878, 1243
GARAY, Ricardo, 954
GARAY Y MENDOZA, María de, 109
GARAY Y SAAVEDRA, Bernabé de, 109
GARAY Y SAAVEDRA, Cristóbal de, 109, 984, 1011
GARAY Y SAAVEDRA, Juan de, 109
GARAY Y SAAVEDRA, Mariana de, 109
GARAYALDE ZUBIZARRETA DE MASSERA, Carmen, 1210
GARBARINI, José Antonio, 1092
GARBOSKY, Antonio José, 923
GARCETE, Carlos, 1020
GARCETE SILVERO, Guillermo, 998
GARCÍA (family) (Argentina), 348
GARCÍA (family) (Paraguay), 971
GARCÍA (family) (Uruguay), 1108
GARCÍA, Alejandro, 845
GARCÍA, Alejo, 984, 1012
GARCÍA, Alma, 717
GARCÍA, Aristóteles, 1210
GARCÍA, Augusto, 1039
GARCÍA, Aurelio, 939, 948
GARCÍA, Baldomero, 185
GARCÍA, Carlos, 995
GARCÍA, Claudio, 1067
GARCÍA, Daniel, 940
GARCÍA, Diego, 472, 535, 627, 984, 1203, 1238
GARCÍA, Domingo José, 126
GARCÍA, Doroteo, 1067
GARCÍA, Eduardo D., 923
GARCÍA, Eusebio, 264
GARCÍA, Federico, 959
GARCÍA, Fernando, 1094
GARCÍA, Francisco, 32
GARCÍA, Gabino, 207
GARCÍA, Germán, 652
GARCÍA, Isabel Leonor, 684
GARCÍA, José Antonio, 971
GARCÍA, José Federico, 198
GARCÍA, Juan, 1089
GARCÍA, Juan Agustín, 167, 246, 293, 743, 751
GARCÍA, Juan Ignacio, 207
GARCÍA, Julián, 1185
GARCÍA, Leandro, 1089
GARCÍA, Lucas Antonio, 1262
GARCÍA, Luis, 122, 167, 391, 878
GARCÍA, Luis Ignacio, 1073
GARCÍA, Manuel, 143, 318, 319, 1089
GARCÍA, Manuel B., 1093
GARCÍA, Manuel D., 845
GARCÍA, Manuel José, 126, 166, 459, 472, 489, 529,
    552, 553, 611
GARCÍA, Manuel Rafael
    see GARCÍA AGUIRRE, Manuel Rafael
GARCÍA, Marcelino, 1089
GARCÍA, Mariano, 230
GARCÍA, Martín, 244, 844, 1261
GARCÍA, Melitón, 268
GARCÍA, Miguel, 268, 329, 921, 923
GARCÍA, Oscar Raúl Fernando, 789
GARCÍA, Pantaleón, 177, 611, 908

GARCÍA, Pedro, 6, 284, 1011
GARCÍA, Pedro Andrés, 169, 332, 617, 640, 1229
GARCÍA, Pedro Manuel, 1095
GARCÍA, Ponciano, 860
GARCÍA, Rafael, 115a, 190
GARCÍA, Ramón, 1089
GARCÍA, Romualdo, 127
GARCÍA, Salvador, 1094
GARCÍA, Segundo Román, 268
GARCÍA, Serafín J. (BOBADILLA, Simplicio, pseud.),
    1151, 1159, 1167, 1168, 1170, 1177, 1179, 1180,
    1196, 1199, 1243, 1248
GARCÍA, Teodoro, 17b
GARCÍA ACEVEDO, Daniel, 1064
GARCÍA ACOSTA, Araceli M., 652
GARCÍA AGUIRRE, Manuel Rafael, 153
GARCÍA ALBERDI, Federico, 268
GARCÍA ALONSO, Jorge, 772
GARCÍA ANIDO, Saturnino, 69
GARCÍA BALADO, Juan Francisco, 332
GARCÍA BELSUNCE, César, 521
GARCÍA BUHR, Arturo, 893
GARCÍA CAMBA, Andrés, 453
GARCÍA CAPURRO, Federico, 1073
GARCÍA CARRERA, Francisco, 19
GARCÍA CASTELLANOS, Telasco, 923
GARCÍA CONDE, José, 1094, 1095
GARCÍA COSTA, Rosa, 711, 751, 762, 773, 783
GARCÍA CRISTÓFORO, María del Carmen, 1210
GARCÍA DE ACILÚ Y BENITO, Manuel, 1089
GARCÍA DE CASTRO, Lope, 522
GARCÍA DE CORNEJO, Lola, 653, 654
GARCÍA DE COSSIO, José Simón, 93, 95, 126, 496
GARCÍA DE ECHABURU, Mariano, 496
GARCÍA DE GARCÍA, Fortunata, 611
GARCÍA DE LA MATA, Domingo, 254
GARCÍA DE LABAL, Juana, 931
GARCÍA DE LEÓN Y PIZARRO, Ramón, 332
GARCÍA DE LUCA, Jorge, 683a
GARCÍA DE PANÉS, Pedro Ignacio, 1034, 1041
GARCÍA DE PINTO, Juana, 422
GARCÍA DE ROBÉS (family), 352
GARCÍA DE ROSSI, Alvara, 887
GARCÍA DE SOBRECASA, Pedro Andrés, 496
GARCÍA DE TORRES, 1270
GARCÍA DE ZÚÑIGA (family), 1108, 1226
GARCÍA DE ZÚÑIGA, José Gabriel, 921
GARCÍA DE ZÚÑIGA, Mateo, 95, 127
GARCÍA DE ZÚÑIGA, Tomás, 1091
GARCÍA DE ZÚÑIGA, Victorio, 629
GARCÍA DEL MOLINO, 25
GARCÍA DEL MOLINO, Fernando, 19, 28, 51, 59, 293,
    521
GARCÍA DEL MORAL, Melchor, 186
GARCÍA DEL RÍO, Juan, 573
GARCÍA DOCTOR, Pedro, 186
GARCÍA ELORRIO, Laureano, 652
GARCÍA ESCUDERO TYDDEO, Edison, 1210
GARCÍA ESTRADA, Juan Agustín, 882
GARCÍA FERNÁNDEZ, Juan, 68
GARCÍA FERNÁNDEZ, Manuel, 94
GARCÍA FERNÁNDEZ, Miguel, 68, 284
GARCÍA FLORES, José I., 222
GARCÍA FUCHS, Angel, 299
GARCÍA GAMES, Julia, 762
GARCÍA GERPE, Manuel, 284
GARCÍA GIMÉNEZ, Tomás, 691
GARCÍA GINÉS, 268
GARCÍA ISASA, José Sixto, 917
GARCÍA JIMÉNEZ, Francisco, 819, 862, 871, 877

GARCÍA LAGOS, Ildefonso, 1075
GARCÍA LAGOS DE HUGHES, María, 1065
GARCÍA LALANNE, Eduardo, 719
GARCÍA LAMELAS, Francisco, 1089
GARCÍA MANSILLA, Daniel, 153
GARCÍA MANSILLA, Eduardo, 153, 867
GARCÍA MANSILLA, Manuel, 153
GARCÍA MANSILLA, Rafael, 153
GARCÍA MANTILLA, Daniel, 664
GARCÍA MARTÍNEZ DE CÁCERES, José, 7, 32, 332
GARCÍA MÉROU, Martín, 153, 664, 669, 686, 708, 714,
    743, 774
GARCÍA MORENO, Gabriel, 460
GARCÍA MORILLO, Roberto, 865, 882, 883
GARCÍA MOYANO, Guillermo, 1211
GARCÍA MUÑOZ, Carmen, 883
GARCÍA OÑEZ DE LOYOLA, Martín, 158, 188
GARCÍA OTERO, Julio, 1067
GARCÍA PEÑA, Edgar, 954
GARCÍA PINTO, Roberto, 653, 654
GARCÍA RAYA, Laura D., 320
GARCÍA RAYA DE OFICIALDEGUY, Elena Josefina, 320
GARCÍA REINO, Oscar, 1049
GARCÍA REYNOSO, Antonio, 268
GARCÍA REYNOSO, Manuel de los Santos, 268
GARCÍA RIQUELME, Abel, 998
GARCÍA ROBSON, Magdalena, 882
GARCÍA ROMERO, Francisco, 224
GARCÍA ROMERO, Pedro, 845
GARCÍA ROS, Baltasar, 521, 570, 984, 989, 1011,
    1030, 1262
GARCÍA SÁIZ, Valentín, 1159, 1162, 1168
GARCÍA SALABERRY, Adela, 154, 711, 762
GARCÍA SANTILLÁN, Juan Carlos, 653, 654, 751
GARCÍA SARAVI, Gustavo, 663, 716, 717, 729, 739,
    759, 805, 807
GARCÍA SARMIENTO, Félix Rubén
    see DARÍO, Rubén
GARCÍA TEJEDOR, Manuel, 1093a
GARCÍA TRON, Hugo Mario, 1088
GARCÍA TUÑÓN, José, 37
GARCÍA UGALDEVERE, Araceli, 652
GARCÍA URIBURU, Nicolás, 19, 36
GARCÍA VELLOSO, Enrique, 133, 152a, 199, 560, 724,
    751, 890, 893, 1246
GARCÍA VIDAL, M., 1089
GARCÍA VILLOSO, Luis Eugenio, 560
GARCÍA WICH, Emilio, 1084
GARCÍA WICH, Juan, 1093a
GARCÍA Y FRAGA, José R., 1094, 1095
GARCÍA Y ONRUBIA, Chérie
    see GARCÍA Y ONRUBIA, Sarah Felisa
GARCÍA Y ONRUBIA, Sarah Felisa (GARCÍA Y ONRUBIA,
    Chérie), 762
GARCÍA Y VALDEZ, José Justo, 496
GARCÍA ZÚÑIGA, José Gabriel, 268
GARCILASO DE LA VEGA (EL INCA, pseud.), 713, 761,
    895
GARD, Leopoldo, 268
GARDEL, Carlos, 819, 861, 875, 892
GARDINER, Allen Francis, 99
GARDIOL NELIENSBER, Sergio Rubén, 1210
GARET Y MÁS, Julio, 1145
GARFIAS, Leandro de, 1041
GARFUNKEL, Boris, 258a
GARGANO, Germán, 691
GARGANTINI, Bautista, 69
GARGARIN, Emilia, 652
GARGATAGLI, Mario, 18
GARI, Juan José, 1093

GARI, Paulino José, 126, 329, 921
GARÍA, Miguel, 923
GARÍA BALARDO, Juan F., 923
GARIBALDI, Blanca de, 663, 681
GARIBALDI, Carlos Alberto, 1187
GARIBALDI, Guiseppe, 73, 118, 127, 166, 212, 244,
    258, 499, 592, 963, 1079, 1091, 1093a, 1110
GARIBALDI, José
    see GARIBALDI, Guiseppe
GARIBATO, Atilio (POLENTA, pseud.), 860
GARICOITS, Michel, 960
GARINI, L. S. (URDANGARIN, Héctor), 1149, 1158,
    1186
GARINO, Víctor, 21
GARLOT, Marcelo, 332
GARMA, Angel, 923
GARMENDIA, Héctor, 65
GARMENDIA, Ignacio, 17b
GARMENDIA, José Ignacio, 68, 90, 121
GARMENDIA, Miguel Jerónimo, 496
GARMENDIA, Pancha, 1012
GARNERO, Pedro, 1039
GARNICA, Nicolás de, 520, 620
GARÓFALO, Dante, 860
GAROGLIO, Pier Giovanni, 923
GAROSITO HEREDIA, Luis, 744
GARRA, Lobodón, pseud.
    see JUSTO, Liborio
GARRAMUÑO, Francisco Javier, 555
GARRÉ DE CALVO, María Adela, 320
GARRETÓN, Juan Antonio, 169
GARRIDO, Diego, 844, 1261, 1262
GARRIDO, Mauricio, 845
GARRIDO, Santos, pseud.
    see CUADRI, Guillermo
GARRIGO, Juan, 95
GARRIGÓS, Agustín, 1264
GARRIGÓS DE VON DER HEYDE, Zelmira, 683a
GARRIZ, Argentino, 385
GARRO, José de, 521, 570
GARRO, Joseph de, 1262
GARRO, Juan Basilio, 222
GARRO, Juan María, 222
GARRO, Martín, 222
GARRO AUDERUT, Guillermo, 222
GARRO DE ARÉCHAGA, Alonso, 844
GARRONE, Domingo J., 58
GARRONE, Eusebio, 921
GARZÓN, 127
GARZÓN (family), 1108
GARZÓN, Agustín, 244
GARZÓN, Benito Carlos, 713, 730
GARZÓN, Cecilio, 713
GARZÓN, Eleázar, 89
GARZÓN, Eugenio, 90, 95, 96, 244, 433, 1052, 1053,
    1063, 1076, 1081, 1083, 1091, 1110, 1118, 1187,
    1188, 1195
GARZÓN, Pedro E., 1126
GARZÓN, Tobías, 664
GASCÓN, Esteban Agustín, 126, 282, 439, 457, 611,
    621, 626
GASCÓN, Julio César, 361
GASKIN VUCETICH, Rafael, 860
GASPAR, Eduardo, 923
GASPAR, Fernando, 923
GASPERI, Luis de
    see DE GASPERI, Luis
GASS, Adolfo, 440
GASTANAZA, Pedro de, 332
GASTAVINO, Vicente, 1039

GASTERO SERRANO, José, 1236
GASULLA, Luis, 814
GATANI, María Tindara, 683a
GATICA, Héctor David, 831
GATICA, Teófilo I., 81, 565
GATICA DE MONTIVEROS, María Delia, 222
GATTI, Carlos, 963a, 965
GATTI, Gustavo, 1020
GATTI, Juan Bautista, 31
GATTI, Pedro, 952
GATTI DE FAVA, Ana Rita, 320
GAUCHO, El, pseud.
    see BLASI, Antonio
GAUFFIN, Federico, 653, 654
GAUNA, 606, 608
GAUNA, Nélida Leonor, 320
GAUTO, José Inocencio, 995a
GAVAZZO BUCHARDO, Juan Manuel, 19, 135
GAVELLO, Aurelia Casas de
    see CASAS DE GAVELLO, Aurelia
GAVENSKY, Martha, 46
GAVIER, Daniel, 332
GAVIER, Gregorio Ignacio, 89
GAVILÁN, José León, 995a
GAVIO, Héctor S., 923
GAVIOLA, Enrique, 207, 923
GAVOTTI, Oscar S., 691
GAVRILOV, Konstantin, 923
GAW LUCH, Miguel Angel, 299
GAY, Camilo A., 8
GAY, Theodora (Mrs. Fernando Schlosser), 323
GAYOSO, Fermín, 137
GAYOSO, Gómez de
    see GÓMEZ DE GAYOSO
GAYOSO, Lisandro, 655
GAYOSO, Marcelino, 284
GAYOSO, Ricardo Antonio P., 923
GAYTÁN, Bernardo, 1056
GAYTÁN, Luis, 358
GAZCÓN, Esteban Agustín, 526
GAZCÓN, Manuel, 68
GAZULLA, Policarpo, 914
GEDEÓN, Andrés, 844
GEGEGE, pseud.
    see GONZÁLEZ, Gustavo Germán
GEIGER, Miguel Alberto, 923
GELABERT, Margot, 726
GELABERT Y CRESPO, José María, 910, 917
GELDSTEIN, Lidia, 791
GELMAN, Juan, 661, 672, 717, 739, 759, 801
GELPI, Angel, 1094
GELUSINI, Enrique Diego, 874
GELLINI, Antonio, 162
GELLY, Juan Andrés
    see GELLY Y OBES, Juan Andrés
GELLY Y OBES, Carlos M., 521
GELLY Y OBES, Juan Andrés, 17b, 68, 282, 478, 479,
    611, 943, 949, 963, 964, 966, 1012, 1021, 1022
GEMDI DE OLIVA, Emma, 320
GEMINIANI, Mario, 258
GEMOLI, Irma Inés, 320
GEMOLI, Liria Josefa, 320
GEMOLI, Nelda A., 320
GENEYRO, Angela, 735
GENNERO, Segundo, 882
GENOVÉS, Pedro, 951, 952, 992
GENOVESE, Agostino, 292
GENOVESE, Giovanni Battista, 292
GENOVESE RODRÍGUEZ, Washington Eduardo, 1210
GENTA, Edgardo Ubaldo, 154, 1083, 1145, 1179

GENTA, Estrella, 154
GENTA, Jordán B., 170
GENTA DORADO, Roberto, 1088
GEOGHEGAN, Abel R., 652
GEORGE, pseud.
    see GONZÁLEZ, Gustavo Germán
GERALDI, Seferino Amelio, 191
GERARD ROMERO, Leonard Rodolfo, 1210
GERARDI, Antonio, 292
GERARDI, Donato, 332
GERARDI ESCUDERO, Angel Mario de, 810
GERCHUNOFF, Alberto, 135, 152a, 157, 210, 235, 431,
    670, 674, 743, 751, 769, 825, 829, 1245, 1246
GERHARDT DE WAPPNER, Blanca, 923
GERLERO, Haydée Graciela, 751
GERMÁN DE LA O, 860
GERO, Julio, 19, 21, 25, 35, 49
GEROLA, José, 781
GERSCHUNI PÉREZ, Jaime, 1210
GERSHANIK, Simón, 923
GERSHMAN DE PIKELIN, Berta S., 923
GERSTEIN, Noemí, 19, 25, 35, 49, 63
GERVASONI, Carlos, 32, 834, 1264
GESTIDO, Oscar D., 1064, 1093
GETINO, Octavio, 694, 706
GEZ, Juan Wenceslao, 121, 222, 283
GEZ DE GÓMEZ, María Estela, 222
GHELFI, Rodolfo Antonio, 923
GHIANO, Juan Carlos, 135, 521, 729, 739, 743, 758,
    799, 815, 816
GHIDA, Arturo Horacio, 805, 812
GHIELMETTI, Horacio S., 923
GHIGLIANI, Francisco, 1083
GHIGLIAZA, Francisca, 681
GHIO, Haydée M., 746, 762
GHIO BALDOMIR, Carlos Alberto, 1210
GHIONE, Emilio, 258
GHIRALDO, Alberto, 167, 243, 261, 669, 751, 759,
    773, 1243, 1246, 1247
GHISOLFI, Ariodante, 268
GIACAGLIA, Pedro, 785
GIACOBBE, Adolfo Antonio, 332
GIACOBBE, Juan Francisco, 766, 882, 883
GIACOBONE, Lina, 776
GIACOMOTTI, Giacomo, 139
GIACHETTI, Athos, 923
GIAGNONI, Cristóbal, 258
GIAMBIAGI, Carlos Gaulberto, 19, 31, 33, 36
GIAMBIAGI, Juan José, 923
GIAMBIAGI, Nélida, 923
GIAMBRUNO, Cyro, 1073
GIANELLI, José, 258
GIANELLO, Leoncio, 135, 521, 609, 837
GIANGRANDE, Alicia Yadriga, 31, 49
GIANGRANDE, Silvio, 35, 49
GIANINI, Eustaquio
    see GIANNINI, Eustaquio
GIANNEO, Luis, 217, 864, 865, 881, 883
GIANNINI, Eustaquio, 7, 292, 332, 922, 1011
GIANNUZZI, Joaquín O., 716, 717, 739, 758, 759, 802
GIANOLA, Antonio, 1093
GIANZI, Zacarías A., 258
GIAST, Alphonse, 28
GIBERT, Pedro Francisco, 565
GIBSON, Herbert, 904
GIBSON, Roberto, 82
GIETZ, Ernesto G., 652
GIETZ, Ricardo A., 652
GIGENA, Francisco S., 95
GIGENA, María Julia, 746, 748, 751

GIGENA SÁNCHEZ, Rafael, 766
GIGLI, Lorenzo, 44
GIJÓN, Francisco Bernardo, pseud.
   see XIXÓN, Francisco Bernardo
GIL (family), 1224
GIL, Anacleto, 173, 445
GIL, Antonio Alejandro, 759, 833
GIL, Francisco, 140
GIL, José, 881, 883, 953, 1089
GIL, Juan, 1075
GIL, Juan Francisco, 254, 321
GIL, Juan Martín, 556
GIL, Julio (PERICLES, pseud.), 769
GIL, Manuel Gervasio, 895
GIL, Martín, 133, 816
GIL, Octavio, 283
GIL, Teófilo Daniel, 1053, 1085, 1125
GIL, Vicente, 212
GIL DE QUIROGA, Feliciano, 555
GIL NAVARRO, Ramón, 242, 533
GIL OBLIGADO, Antolín, 917
GIL SALGUERO, Luis, 1184, 1210
GIL Y LEMOS, Francisco, 284, 579
GILARDI, Fernando, 834
GILARDI, Gilardo, 864, 865, 881, 883
GILARDONI, Alberto, 655, 656
GILARDONI, Eduardo, 1206, 1207
GILES, Melitón, 291
GILL, Andrés, 943, 1012
GILL, Juan Bautista
   see GILL AGUINAGA, Juan Bautista
GILL, Juan Facundo, 995a
GILL, Pedro Victoriano, 974, 982
GILL AGUINAGA, Juan Bautista, 90, 943, 954, 984,
   984a, 1011, 1012
GILL GONZALEZ, José, 998
GILL MORLIS, Manuel, 83
GILLESPIE, Alejandro, 834
GILLIES, André, 960
GILLIES, Clara (Mrs. George Bischoff), 323
GILLIES, Mary Ann (Mrs. Walter Grieven), 323
GIMÉNEZ, Alfredo M., 1125
GIMÉNEZ, Angel M., 259
GIMÉNEZ, Atilio, 998
GIMÉNEZ, Cipriano, 94
GIMÉNEZ, Diógenes, 998
GIMÉNEZ, José del Pilar, 995a
GIMÉNEZ, José Gregorio, 222
GIMÉNEZ, Manuel, 87
GIMÉNEZ, Manuel María, 923
GIMÉNEZ, Martín, 268
GIMÉNEZ, Prudencio, 947
GIMÉNEZ, Ramón, 68
GIMÉNEZ, Remberto, 937, 943a, 966, 1028, 1029
GIMÉNEZ CABALLERO, Ernesto, 954
GIMENEZ CASTELLANOS, Pedro, 555
GIMÉNEZ PASTOR, Arturo, 669, 1246
GIMÉNEZ PASTOR, María, 717
GIMÉNEZ PASTOR, Martha Sara, 768, 802
GIMENO, Jesús, 1211
GINASTERA, Alberto, 140, 521, 865, 882, 883
GINEBRA, Francisco, 319
GINI, Horacio, 998
GINZO, José Antonio (Tristán, pseud.), 431
GIOIA, Abel, 560
GIOIA, Vita Angel de, 1265
GIOINO, Eva Lida, 684
GIOLITTI, Angelo, 139
GIORDABA, Andrea, 923
GIORDANO, Camilo M., 113

GIORDANO, Francisco, 1092
GIORDANO, Luis, 1162, 1187
GIORGI, Diógenes de, 1211
GIORLANDINI, Eduardo, 871
GIOT, Perfecto, 1050
GIOVAMBATTISTA, Nicolás, 923
GIOVANE, José, 69
GIOVANELLI, 878
GIOVANETTI VIOLA, Hugo, 1173, 1176, 1183
GIOVANNELLI, Humberto, 258
GIOVANNI, 292
GIOVINE, Elodia, 952
GIQUIAU ORTIZ, Dámaso Ramón, 1111
GIRALA, Salím, 947
GIRALDES DE ROCAMORA, Pablo, 555
GIRALDEZ, Tomás N., 254
GIRIBALDI, Daniel, 658, 660, 698, 717, 727
GIRIBALDI, Tomás, 1079, 1206, 1207, 1208
GIRINGELLA, Santiago, 952
GIRÓ, José, 844, 1203, 1261
GIRÓ, Juan Francisco, 552, 1063, 1079, 1091, 1109,
   1110
GIROBONE, José, 258
GIROLA, Claudio, 19, 21, 25, 35
GIRÓN, Alonso, 556
GIRONDO, Oliverio, 658, 678, 722, 737, 739, 751,
   759, 769, 773, 782, 798, 801, 803, 807, 816,
   833
GIROTTI, Delchis, 700
GIROTTI DE JACOB, Odila Haydée (JACOBS, Odila,
   pseud.), 691
GIRRI, Alberto, 664, 671, 672, 685, 716, 722, 729,
   739, 758, 759, 798, 803, 807
GISBERT Y TALENS, Pedro de, 555
GIUCCI, Carlos, 1206, 1207
GIÚDICE, Carlos R., 923
GIÚDICI, Reinaldo, 19, 25, 31, 59, 258, 521
GIUFFRA, Carlos Alberto, 652
GIUFFRA, José, 1029
GIUFFRA, Rómulo, 258
GIUFFRÉ, Héctor, 37, 60
GIUGLIANO, Aniello, 258
GIULI, Augusto de, 1093
GIULIANI, Buenaventura, 258
GIUSSO, Rubén Oscar, 781
GIUSTI, Leopoldo, 923
GIUSTI, Roberto Fernando, 162, 688, 743, 751
GLAUSIUSS DEUTSCH, Pablo Esteban, 1210
GLEIJER HIRSCH, Adela, 889, 1210
GLEIZER, Manuel, 235
GLENNON, Juan F., 904
GLUSBERG, Samuel (ESPINOZA, Enrique, pseud.), 152a,
   235, 765, 1245
GNERI, Francisco Saverio, 923
GOBBI, Alfredo, 862, 868
GOBBI, María de las Mercedes, 683a
GOBBO, Rómulo del, 258
GOBELLO, José, 811
GODEL, Roberto, 678, 751
GODODISCHER, Angela, 728
GODOI, Enrique, 617
GODOI, Juan Silvano
   see GODOY, Juan Silvano
GODOY, Bernardino, 914
GODOY, Eduardo J., 198
GODOY, Eduardo Tomás, 738
GODOY, Francisco, 1041
GODOY, Goyo, pseud.
   see OCHOA, Fernando
GODOY, José, 188, 895

GODOY, Juan de, 186
GODOY, Juan Gualberto, 207, 278, 413, 611, 629, 644, 664, 669, 683a, 688, 720, 761, 874, 878, 1242, 1243, 1247, 1257, 1258
GODOY, Juan José, 458
GODOY, Juan Silvano, 943, 951, 955, 956, 959, 964, 966, 980, 986, 1002, 1012, 1021, 1022, 1023
GODOY, Manuel José de, 478
GODOY, Oscar, 662
GODOY, Pedro, 759
GODOY, Raúl, 207
GODOY, Rosendo, 198
GODOY, Ruperto
   see GODOY CARRIL, Ruperto
GODOY, Sila, 1028
GODOY CARRIL, Ruperto, 188, 283, 634
GODOY CRUZ, Tomás, 166, 179, 207, 212, 278, 282, 283, 411, 412, 413, 439, 457, 478, 526, 611, 621, 626, 874
GODOY DE BRANDES, Juana, 931
GODOY ROJO, Polo, 222
GODOY VIDELA DE COLOMER, Hortensia, 207, 874
GODOY Y CISTERNAS, Ramón de, 555
GODOY Y DEL POZO, Juan José, 549
GÜERING, A., 28
GOGNIAT (family), 168
GOIBURÚ, Rómulo, 959
GOICOECHEA, José, 579
GOICOECHEA, Mariano, 244
GOICOECHEA Y MENENDEZ, Martín de, 1017
GOIJMAN, Nahum, 31, 46, 63
GOLA, Hugo, 658, 759, 831
GOLA, José, 858
GOLBACH, Rodolfo, 923
GOLDBERG, Lucio, 882
GOLDEMBERG, José B., 923
GOLDEMBERG, Sara Hebe, 923
GOLDNEY, Arthur Mrs.
   see KIMBALL, Myra
GOLDSACK GUIÑAZÚ, Alfredo, 207, 683a
GOLDSCHMIDT, Walter, 954
GOLDSTEIN DE TAPIOLA, Sara, 683a
GOLIGORSKI, Eduardo, 706
GOLIGORSKY, Lilian, 822
GOLOBOFF, Gerardo Mario, 791
GOLZ, Adolfo Argentino, 701, 795
GOLLÁN, Josué, 923
GOMAR, Hernando, 649a
GOMENSORO (family), 1108
GOMENSORO, Juan Bautista, 125
GOMENSORO, Tomás Javier, 921, 1079, 1080
GOMES, Andrés, 954
GÓMEZ (family), 1108
GÓMEZ, Agustín, 173
GÓMEZ, Alonso (family), 358
GÓMEZ, Andrés, 914
GÓMEZ, Antonio, 79
GÓMEZ, Blas, 32
GOMEZ, Carlos F., 385
GOMEZ, Carlos María, 824
GÓMEZ, Celia, 879, 932
GÓMEZ, Crisanto, 264
GÓMEZ, Cristina Claudia, 781
GÓMEZ, Cristóbal, 319, 895, 1267
GÓMEZ, Eduardo B., 965
GÓMEZ, Esteban, 992
GÓMEZ, Eugenio, 1211
GÓMEZ, Félix María, 387
GÓMEZ, Fermín, 1089
GÓMEZ, Francisco, 1089

GÓMEZ, Gaspar, 83
GÓMEZ, Gregorio José, 126, 321, 611, 895, 921
GÓMEZ, Indalecio, 141, 372
GÓMEZ, Isidora
   see GÓMEZ Y GÓMEZ, Isidora
GÓMEZ, Jesús, 857d
GÓMEZ, José, 845
GÓMEZ, José Luis, 1075
GÓMEZ, José Remigio, 1140
GÓMEZ, José Valentín, 322, 529, 542, 552, 573, 611, 908, 1223
GÓMEZ, Juan Carlos, 1054, 1057, 1071, 1079, 1081, 1119, 1120, 1146, 1165, 1174, 1179, 1188, 1193, 1199, 1247, 1253
GÓMEZ, Juan Francisco, 954
GÓMEZ, Juan Luis, 1210
GÓMEZ, Leandro, 1134
GÓMEZ, Luis, 844
GÓMEZ, Manuel José, 188, 283
GÓMEZ, María Rosa, 683a
GÓMEZ, Martín, 319
GÓMEZ, Mateo, 222
GÓMEZ, Máximo, 280
GÓMEZ, Miguel, 358, 496
GÓMEZ, Miguel Angel, 664, 739, 758, 766, 768, 807
GÓMEZ, Nicolás, 914, 918
GÓMEZ, Pantaleón, 186, 191
GÓMEZ, Pedro Pablo, 559
GÓMEZ, Ramón, 844, 1089, 1261, 1262
GÓMEZ, Rodrigo, 358
GÓMEZ, Roque Antonio, 1072, 1095
GÓMEZ, Rosauro, 878
GÓMEZ, Secundino, 874
GÓMEZ, Servando, 95, 1093a
GÓMEZ, Teodoro, 878
GÓMEZ, Tiburcio, 1059, 1111
GÓMEZ, Valentín, 126, 166, 321, 895
GÓMEZ, Valentino, 998
GÓMEZ BAS, Joaquín, 140, 660, 727, 739, 751, 772, 794, 799, 812, 816
GÓMEZ BUENO DE ACUÑA, Dora, 1014, 1021, 1022
GÓMEZ CARRILLO, Manuel, 882, 883
GÓMEZ CELLO, Pedro, 477
GÓMEZ CLARA, Emiliano, 24, 44
GÓMEZ CORNET, Ramón, 18, 19, 23, 25, 31, 33, 34, 36, 50, 55, 56, 1218
GÓMEZ COU, Santiago, 894
GÓMEZ DE ARAUJO, Gregorio, 186
GÓMEZ DE ARAUJO, Jorge, 555
GÓMEZ DE CALZADILLA, Manuela, 478
GÓMEZ DE CAMALEÑO (family), 348
GÓMEZ DE DON BENITO, Juan, 556
GÓMEZ DE DUBLANC, Lucrecia, 874
GÓMEZ DE FONSECA, José María, 844, 1261
GOMEZ DE GAYOSO, 284
GÓMEZ DE LA QUINTANA, Andrés, 1223
GÓMEZ DE LEDESMA, Blas, 32
GÓMEZ DE LEDESMA, Lázaro, 32
GÓMEZ DE OJEDA, Rodrigo, 1270
GÓMEZ DE RODRÍGUEZ BRITO, Marta, 683a
GÓMEZ DE ROSA, Luis, 186
GÓMEZ DE SARAVIA, García, 186
GÓMEZ DE SARAVIA, Juan, 186
GÓMEZ DE SARAVIA, Lucas, 186
GÓMEZ DE SARAVIA, Miguel, 186
GÓMEZ DE SOSA, Francisco, 186
GÓMEZ DE YEBENES, Juan, 556
GÓMEZ DEL CANTO, José, 132
GÓMEZ FIGUEREDO, Lola, 1014
GÓMEZ GERSBACH, Irasema, 762

GÓMEZ IPARRAGUIRRE, Carlos, 328
GÓMEZ ISLEÑO, Juan, 556
GÓMEZ MOLINA, Lilián, 44
GÓMEZ MORALES, Alfredo, 213
GÓMEZ ORCAJO, Gregorio, 611
GÓMEZ PARATCHA, Vicente, 284
GÓMEZ PARDO, Pedro, 555, 1270
GÓMEZ PAZ, Julieta, 751
GÓMEZ POLANCO, Cristóbal, 844, 845, 850
GÓMEZ REY, José, 1089
GÓMEZ RÍOS, Emiliano M., 966
GÓMEZ SÁA, Teresa, 683a
GÓMEZ SÁNCHEZ, Ramón, 998
GÓMEZ SÁNCHEZ DE JIMÉNEZ ESPINOZA, Enriqueta, 1014
GÓMEZ SANJURJO, José María, 1014, 1020, 1021, 1022, 1025
GÓMEZ SERRATO, Darío, 943, 1014
GÓMEZ VOCES, Emiliano, 1210
GÓMEZ Y ANCHORENA, Fabián, 193
GÓMEZ Y GÓMEZ, Isidora, 112, 172
GOMILA, Ignacio, 319
GONCERAS, Miguel, 32
GONCEVAT DE CABRAL, Celmira, 331
GONDA, Serafín, 1089
GONDRA, Luis Roque, 761
GONDRA, Manuel, 943, 951, 955, 959, 964, 966, 973, 980, 983, 984a, 1002, 1012, 1021, 1022, 1023
GÓNGORA, Diego de, 521, 570, 1203
GONI, Elisa Carlota, 320
GONI, Hortensia, 320
GONNET, Luis María, 211
GONORAZKY, Rosa G. de, 653, 654
GONTA, Graciela, 653
GONZAGA CONY, Luis, 24
GONZALBO, Augusto, 1092
GONZÁLEZ, 977
GONZÁLEZ, Agustín, 332
GONZÁLEZ, Alberto, 703
GONZÁLEZ, Alberto Rex, 923
GONZÁLEZ, Amancio, 1012
GONZÁLEZ, Angel I., 1014
GONZÁLEZ, Antonio, 186, 887, 1075, 1089
GONZÁLEZ, Antonio E., 1006
GONZÁLEZ, Antonio J., 817
GONZÁLEZ, Ariosto D., 521, 1091
GONZÁLEZ, Armando Germinal, 1210
GONZÁLEZ, Bartolomé, 350
GONZÁLEZ, Calixto María, 545a
GONZÁLEZ, Cándido, 94
GONZÁLEZ, Cayetano, 908
GONZÁLEZ, Diego, 1267
GONZÁLEZ, Domingo, 186, 1075, 1083, 1093a, 1126
GONZÁLEZ, Elpidio, 69
GONZÁLEZ, Emeterio, 964
GONZÁLEZ, Emilio, 887
GONZÁLEZ, Ezequiel Dolores, 943a
GONZÁLEZ, Félix, 874
GONZÁLEZ, Francisco, 32, 1092, 1094
GONZÁLEZ, Francisco Antonio, 126, 979
GONZÁLEZ, Gonzalo, 186
GONZÁLEZ, Gustavo, 965
GONZÁLEZ, Gustavo Germán (GEORGE, pseud.), 645
GONZÁLEZ, Honorio, 998
GONZÁLEZ, Ignacia, 887
GONZÁLEZ, Isidoro, 599
GONZÁLEZ, Jesús, 1089
GONZÁLEZ, Joaquín, 152a
GONZÁLEZ, Joaquín Víctor, 83, 110, 115, 116, 121, 128, 141, 166, 167, 176, 212, 217, 219, 246, 278, 282, 317, 324, 478, 512, 521, 574, 583, 601, 614, 647, 667, 708, 743, 751, 779, 792, 825, 826, 829, 1246
GONZÁLEZ, Jorge Alfredo, 560
GONZÁLEZ, José, 844
GONZÁLEZ, José (REAL PERÓ, pseud.), 1003
GONZÁLEZ, José Antonio, 565
GONZÁLEZ, José Félix, 995a, 1116
GONZÁLEZ, José Guillermo, 982
GONZÁLEZ, José Ramón, 995a
GONZÁLEZ, Juan, 679, 845
GONZÁLEZ, Juan C., 1116
GONZÁLEZ, Juan E., 831
GONZÁLEZ, Juan G., 991, 1008
GONZÁLEZ, Juan Natalicio, 943, 947, 964, 1014, 1018, 1020, 1021, 1022
GONZÁLEZ, Juan Vicente, 344
GONZÁLEZ, Julio V., 119
GONZÁLEZ, Justo F., 1083
GONZÁLEZ, Lucas, 207, 648, 649
GONZÁLEZ, M. Harmodio, 954
GONZÁLEZ, Manuel, 284, 1089
GONZÁLEZ, María Felicidad, 943, 959, 964, 966
GONZÁLEZ, Marcial V., 75
GONZÁLEZ, Miguel, 254
GONZÁLEZ, Modesto, 923
GONZÁLEZ, Natalicio
   see GONZÁLEZ, Juan Natalicio
GONZÁLEZ, Oliver, 135
GONZÁLEZ, Oscar, 860
GONZÁLEZ, Pedro M., 95
GONZÁLEZ, Primitivo, 268
GONZÁLEZ, Roberto, 49
GONZÁLEZ, Roque, 191, 850, 866
GONZÁLEZ, Rosa Agustín, 954
GONZÁLEZ, Santiago, 887
GONZÁLEZ, Severo, 648, 649
GONZÁLEZ, Silvestre, 1058
GONZÁLEZ, Teodosio, 959, 964
GONZÁLEZ, Telémaco, 887
GONZÁLEZ, Vicente, 169, 254
GONZÁLEZ ALSINA, Ezequiel (CHEVALLIER PARIS, Gaston, pseud.), 943, 954, 1014, 1020, 1021, 1022
GONZÁLEZ AMADOR, Víctor, 284
GONZÁLEZ ARRILI, Bernardo, 118, 154, 431, 713, 751, 778, 834
GONZÁLEZ BAITOS, Diego, 465
GONZÁLEZ BALCARCE, Antonio, 32, 70, 104, 110, 244, 282, 404, 552, 611
GONZÁLEZ BALCARCE, Juan Ramón, 404
GONZÁLEZ BALCARCE, Marcos, 188
GONZÁLEZ BONORINO, Félix, 923
GONZÁLEZ CALDERÓN, Luis, 669
GONZÁLEZ CARBALHO, José, 154, 722, 739, 748, 751, 759, 773, 807
GONZÁLEZ CARRASCO, Francisco, 332
GONZÁLEZ CASTILLO, José, 727, 813, 871, 890
GONZÁLEZ CASTRO, Augusto, 678, 739, 748, 751, 773
GONZÁLEZ CASTRO, Valentín, 1140
GONZÁLEZ CATÁN, Mauricio, 844, 1261
GONZÁLEZ CECOTTO, Leonor, 938, 939
GONZÁLEZ CLIMENT, Aurelio, 265
GONZÁLEZ COLMAN, Gorgonio, 998, 1006
GONZÁLEZ DE ACOSTA, Domingo, 186
GONZÁLEZ DE ACOSTA, Gregorio, 186
GONZÁLEZ DE BASARRA Y GUIANTE, Felipe, 344
GONZÁLEZ DE CASTILLA, Felipe
   see CASTILLA, Felipe
GONZÁLEZ DE CASTILLA, Santiago, 284
GONZÁLEZ DE COSIO, Juan, 254
GONZÁLEZ DE CUENCA, Jerónimo, 344

GONZÁLEZ DE HERMIDA (family), 352
GONZÁLEZ DE HEVIA, Pedro, 556
GONZÁLEZ DE LA CUESTA, Fernán, 1041
GONZÁLEZ DE LESPIAUX, Mirtha Edelma, 1088
GONZÁLEZ DE MELO, José, 1056, 1262
GONZÁLEZ DE MENCHACA, Rafael, 112
GONZÁLEZ DE NICOLAI, Pastora, 762
GONZÁLEZ DE PRADO, Pedro, 520, 620, 1230
GONZÁLEZ DE RAPP, Delia, 663
GONZÁLEZ DE RIVADAVIA, Benito, 126
GONZÁLEZ DE RIVADAVIA, Bernardino
     see RIVADAVIA, Bernardino
GONZÁLEZ DE RIVERA, José, 89
GONZÁLEZ DE ROBÉS (family), 352
GONZÁLEZ DE SANTA CRUZ (family), 348
GONZÁLEZ DE SANTA CRUZ, Diego, 350
GONZÁLEZ DE SANTA CRUZ, Francisco, 350, 1011
GONZÁLEZ DE SANTA CRUZ, María, 350
GONZÁLEZ DE SANTA CRUZ, Mariana, 350
GONZÁLEZ DE SANTA CRUZ, Mateo, 350
GONZÁLEZ DE SANTA CRUZ, Pedro, 350
GONZÁLEZ DE SANTA CRUZ, Roque, 921, 943, 964, 966,
     968, 971, 984a, 989, 1001, 1004, 1007, 1012,
     1032, 1032a, 1203
GONZÁLEZ DEL SOLAR, Melitón, 844
GONZÁLEZ DEL SOLAR, Nicanor, 68
GONZÁLEZ DEL VALLE, Alcibiades, 1018a
GONZÁLEZ DÍAZ, Emilio F., 923
GONZÁLEZ DOGLIOTTI, Carlos Alberto, 560
GONZÁLEZ FALDERINI, Norma, 691
GONZÁLEZ FILISBERT DE DOMÍNGUEZ, Manuela, 1042
GONZÁLEZ FLORES, Tomás, 32
GONZÁLEZ GARAÑO, Alejo B., 210, 678, 751
GONZÁLEZ GARAÑO, Alfredo, 210
GONZÁLEZ GONZÁLEZ, Adolfo, 1159
GONZÁLEZ GONZÁLEZ, Leonilda, 1210
GONZÁLEZ HERRERO, Manuel, 186
GONZÁLEZ IRAMAIN, Nicolás, 385
GONZÁLEZ LAMELA, Manuel, 1089
GONZÁLEZ LANUZA, Eduardo, 664, 678, 722, 739, 748,
     751, 759, 765, 773, 807, 833
GONZÁLEZ LANUZA, José Antonio, 955
GONZÁLEZ LARRIERA, José M., 1167
GONZÁLEZ LIGIER, Manuel, 960
GONZÁLEZ LONZIÈME, Enrique, 265
GONZÁLEZ LÓPEZ, Domingo, 284
GONZÁLEZ LLAMAZARES, Héctor M., 385
GONZÁLEZ MALAGUEÑO, Andrés, 186
GONZÁLEZ MARMOLEJO, Rodrigo, 910
GONZÁLEZ MAYAI, Hermógenes, 954
GONZÁLEZ MEDINA, Miguel, 1020
GONZÁLEZ MELGAREJO, Juan, 910
GONZÁLEZ MÉNDEZ, Guillermo Evaristo (MÉNDEZ, Evar,
     pseud.), 669, 683a, 751, 773, 782, 807
GONZÁLEZ MERGUETE, José, 32
GONZÁLEZ MIR, Jorge, 44
GONZÁLEZ MONTENEGRO, Juan, 284
GONZÁLEZ MORENO, Emilo, 768
GONZÁLEZ MUÑOZ, José, 683a
GONZÁLEZ NAVERO, Adelina, 956
GONZÁLEZ NAVERO, Emiliano, 959
GONZÁLEZ NAVERO, María Elena, 956
GONZÁLEZ ODDONE, Beatriz
     see RODRÍGUEZ ALCALÁ DE GONZÁLEZ ODDONE, Beatriz
GONZÁLEZ ODDONE, Miguel Vicente, 954, 963a
GONZÁLEZ OLAZÁBAL, Calixto, 1210
GONZÁLEZ OLIVA, Arturo, 299
GONZÁLEZ OLIVER, Aquileo, 268
GONZÁLEZ PACHECO, Rodolfo, 167, 778
GONZÁLEZ PENELAS, Walter, 1151, 1179

GONZÁLEZ PÉREZ, Daniel, 385
GONZÁLEZ POGGI, Uruguay, 1151
GONZÁLEZ REAL, Osvaldo, 1025
GONZÁLEZ RILLO, Abelardo, 235
GONZÁLEZ RIOBOO, Roberto, 954
GONZÁLEZ RIVADAVIA Y SARMIENTO, Benito, 284, 563
GONZÁLEZ RIVAS, Justa Pastora, 1017
GONZÁLEZ RIVERO, Roberto, 299
GONZÁLEZ ROURA, Octavio, 268
GONZÁLEZ STEGEMANN, Miguel, 923
GONZÁLEZ SVETKO, Enriqueta, 837
GONZÁLEZ TABOADA, Marcial, 923
GONZÁLEZ TORRES, Dionisio, 949, 954, 963a
GONZÁLEZ TRILLO, Enrique, 678, 746
GONZÁLEZ TUÑÓN, Enrique, 235, 670, 712, 727, 737,
     769, 1245
GONZÁLEZ TUÑÓN, Raúl, 235, 678, 722, 739, 741, 751,
     759, 769, 773, 801, 803, 807, 833
GONZÁLEZ VALDÉS, Santiago, 299
GONZÁLEZ VALLEJO (family), 1108
GONZÁLEZ VIERA, Mauro, 954
GONZÁLEZ VIRTUS, Manuel, 910
GONZÁLEZ Y ESCOBAR, José Francisco Armancio, 943,
     964, 1035
GONZÁLEZ Y ZAMUDIO, Domingo, 344
GOODMAN, Guillermo, 6
GORBARÁN, José Higinio, 268
GORBEA, Federico, 759, 832
GORDALIZA, Mariano José, 126
GORDILLO, Carlos E., 923
GORDILLO, José Olegario, 242
GORDILLO, Pedro, 83
GORDILLO, Timoteo, 247
GORDON, Alexander, 587
GORDON, Eduardo G., 1174, 1185, 1188, 1199
GORDON, Federico Schonfield, 1070
GORDON, Jacobo, 923
GORDON DAVIS, Jorge, 2
GORDOÑEZ, Guillermo R., 652
GORGO, Giovanni Maria, 292
GORI, Gastón, 152a, 814, 837
GORMAN, Mary Elizabeth (Mrs. John H. Sewall), 323
GORMAN, Miguel de, 843, 844, 846, 1261, 1262
GORODISCHER, Angélica, 771
GOROSITO, Lorenzo, 878
GOROSITO HEREDIA, Luis, 664, 683a, 745
GOROSITO TANCO, José, 1167
GOROSTIAGA, Esteban, 982
GOROSTIAGA, Jorge Bernardino, 954
GOROSTIAGA, José Benjamín, 141, 631, 634
GOROSTIAGA, Juan Eladio, 954
GOROSTIAGA, Manuel, 264
GOROSTIAGA, Roberto, 332
GOROSTIAGA, Sebastián de Jesús, 264
GOROSTIAGA, Segundo, 954
GOROSTIZA, Carlos, 889
GORRECHATEGUY, 1064
GORRIARENA, Carlos Horacio, 55
GORRINDO, Froilán Francisco, 871
GORRITI, José Francisco de, 611
GORRITI, José Ignacio de, 126, 439, 457, 526, 529,
     611, 621, 626
GORRITI, Juan Ignacio de, 166, 177, 183, 244, 278,
     282, 317, 374, 478, 611, 615, 653, 654, 713,
     751, 761, 895, 908, 921
GORRITI, Juan José de, 479
GORRITI, Juana Manuela
     see GORRITI DE BELZÚ, Juana Manuela
GORRITI DE BELZÚ, Juana Manuela, 141, 166, 282, 478,
     611, 653, 654, 708, 714, 734, 747, 751, 780, 929

GORSKI, Miguel, 238
GOSLING, Evelyn B. A., 954
GOSSWEILER (family), 168
GOTTARDI, Valentín, 1039
GOTTER, Gottfried, 923
GOUCHON, Emilio, 68
GOUJARD, Aimé Jacques
    see BONPLAND, Aimé Jacques Alexandre
GOULU, Juan Felipe, 51, 59, 293
GOUPIL, Ernest Auguste, 28
GOVI, Juan, 191
GOWER, John Levison, 587
GOWLAND (family), 1108
GOWLAND MORENO, Luis, 36
GOY CAPÓN, Victoriano, 284
GOYA, La, pseud.
    see MAÑANOS JAUFRETT DE BORRAS, Aurora
GOYANARTE, Juan, 152a, 729, 834
GOYCOECHEA MENÉNDEZ, Martín de, 243, 1020, 1243
GOYEN, Jan van, 1046
GOYENA, Luis, 90
GOYENA, Miguel, 122
GOYENA, Pedro, 90, 166, 246, 276, 282, 317, 484,
    485, 692, 743, 751, 921, 1246
GOYENECHE, Arturo, 565
GOYENECHE, José Manuel de, 166, 427, 552, 569
GOYENECHE, Roberto, 877
GOYRI DE FERNÁNDEZ, Margarita, 1088
GOYTÍA, Bruno Rosario, 254
GOYTÍA, Juan Manuel Nepomuceno de, 93
GOYTÍA, Pedro P., 268
GRACIA NÚÑEZ, Sabas Luis, 923
GRACIA VICETTO, Ramón, 284
GRADIN, Enrique, 1075
GRADITO, Jerónimo, 811
GRADVILLE, Guillermo Enrique, 82
GRADY, Ronan C., 954
GRAFÓFONO, pseud., 811
GRAHAM, Mary Olstine, 323, 930
GRAJEDA, Antón de, 1203
GRAMAJO GUTIÉRREZ, Alfredo, 19, 31, 33, 64, 154
GRANADA, Juan León de, 315
GRANADA, Nicolás, 91, 293, 724, 1243, 1246, 1263
GRANADOS, Isidro, 845
GRANATA, María, 663, 716, 739, 758, 759, 766, 783
GRANCE, Juan Manuel, 979, 987
GRANDE, Guillermo, 87
GRANDE, Juan, 921
GRANDE FERNÁNDEZ, Juan Antonio, 284
GRANDI, Mario Darío, 18, 19, 25, 31, 36, 46
GRANDIN, Luis A., 683a
GRANDMONTAGNE, Francisco, 152a, 774, 834, 1246
GRANDOLI, Miguel, 268
GRANDSIR, Juan Esteban Ricardo de, 949
GRANÉ, Clotilde, 691
GRANÉ, Luis María, 135, 800
GRANEL, Gervasio F., 68, 94
GRANER, Luis, 1046
GRANERO, Ignacio, 683a
GRANERO DE ALARCÓN, Diego, 32
GRANT, Katharine (Mrs. William Hope), 323
GRANVILLE, Guillermo Enrique, 14
GRAÑA, José Benito, 649
GRAÑA, Luisa, 1095
GRAS, Amadeo, 62, 293, 870
GRAS, Esteban, 258
GRASAUM, Baltasar de, 849
GRASHOF, Otto, 28, 59, 521
GRASSI, Alberto J., 768
GRASSI, Alfredo Julio, 239, 728

GRASSI, Carlos Julián, 923
GRASSO, Gerardo, 1206, 1207
GRATTAROLA, Lázaro, 152a
GRATTON, Livio, 923
GRATY, Alfredo M. de
    see MARBAIS DE GRATY, Alfred Louis Hubert
    Ghislain, baron
GRAU, Albino, 998
GRAU, Arturo, 1094
GRAU, Carlos A., 923
GRAU, Eduardo, 874
GRAU CHOVER, Jaime, 963a
GRAU PERU, Miguel, 276
GRAUERT, Héctor A., 1073
GRAVENHORST, Hans G., 652
GRAVIER DEL VALLE, Rafael, 1236
GRAVINA, Alfredo Dante, 1159, 1168, 1177, 1196
GRAYER, Georgette, 299
GRAZ, Macedonio, 385, 713
GRECA, Alcides, 152a, 771, 834
GRECO, Alberto, 19, 31, 36, 210
GRECO, María Teresa, 879
GRECO, Mario A., 41
GRECO, Vicente, 868
GREEN, John, 954
GREENUP, Leonard, 170
GREENUP, Ruth (Robinson), 170
GREENWOOD, Guillermo, 202
GREGORINI, Hugo, 889
GREGORIO, Juan de, 1151
GRELA, José Ignacio, 496, 599, 611, 908
GRELA, Juan, 19, 25, 36, 44
GRELA, Román, 599
GRESLEBIN, Héctor, 222
GRETHE, Carlos, 1046
GREVE, Walther, 923
GRIBEO, Lázaro, 358
GRIEBEN, Carlos F., 664, 739
GRIECO, Pasquale, 139
GRIERA, Joaquín, 496
GRIERA, Segismundus, 1036
GRIERSON, Cecilia, 478, 929
GRIEVEN, Walter (Mrs.)
    see GILLIES, Mary Ann
GRIFASI, Alfio, 31
GRIFFI, Vicente, 850, 952
GRIGERA, Tomás, 4, 529
GRIGERA, Tomás José, 224
GRIJABA, Christóbal, 895
GRILO, Sarah, 19, 25, 26, 31, 36, 54, 55
GRILLO, Max, 956
GRILLO TORRADO, José María, 923
GRIMANI, Santiago, 817
GRIMAU, José, 7, 32
GRIMAU, Matías, 844
GRIMAU Y GÁLVEZ, Cayetano, 85, 371
GRINBERG, León, 923
GRINBERG, Marta, 46
GRIOT, Mario, 923
GRIPPA, Jorge, 882
GRIPPA, Santiago, 258
GRISOLÍA, Pascual, 882,883
GRODSINSKY, León, 923
GROEBNER, Pablo F. C., 923
GROETTER (family), 168
GROISMAN FEIGES, Bernardo, 1210
GROMPONE, Antonio M., 1184
GRONARDO, Pedro, 1262
GRONDONA, Adela, 729
GRONDONA, Mariano, 213

GRONDONA, Nicolás, 258
GROPPA, Néstor, 713, 716, 730, 739, 759, 809, 831
GROSS, Wolfgang Gert, 923
GROSSO, Clara E., 663
GROSSO, Juan Bautista, 751
GROSSO SOSA, Carlos, 1017
GROTE, Federico, 921
GROUSSAC, Marta Elena, 725, 739
GROUSSAC, Pablo
    see GROUSSAC, Paul
GROUSSAC, Paul, 79, 112, 116, 141, 176, 185, 317, 486,594, 609, 644, 709, 734, 743, 751, 826, 834, 1246
GRUNBERG, Carlos M., 678, 722, 739, 759
GRÜNBERG, Georg, 962
GRÜNBERG, Isaac Pascual, 923
GRUSKI, Juan Carlos, 691
GRYNBERG, Claudio Gustavo, 37
GUABAIRI, 977
GUACURARI, Andrés
    see ARTIGAS, Andrés
GUADALUPE, María del Luján Reyes Febles de
    see REYES FEBLES DE GUADALUPE, María del Luján
GUADINO, Enrique, 1243
GUAGNINI, Omar Argentino, 923
GUAIMICA, 977
GUAIRAMINA, 977
GUAIRARE, José Domingo, 995a
GUALDAS, Pedro de, 845
GUAMBAIRO, Roderigo, 977
GUANES, Alejandro, 943, 966, 1012, 1014, 1015, 1018, 1020, 1021, 1022, 1023, 1026
GUANES M. DE BRUGADA, Serviliana, 1014
GUANI, Alberto, 1073
GUARAMBARÉ, 977
GUARANÍ, Pyta, 977
GUARANY, El Marqués del, 1236
GUARAY, Juan, 977
GUARDA, José J., 319
GUARDIA, Juan de la, 319
GUARDIA BERBERANA, Juan de la, 555
GUARDIA LEZCANO, Juan de la, 555
GUARNERO, Enrique, 894, 1172
GUARNIERI, Juan Carlos, 1167
GUAROBAY, 977
GUASCH, Antonio, 943
GUASQUITA, pseud.
    see MÉNDEZ, Simón
GUASTAVINO, Arturo Gerardo, 19, 31
GUASTAVINO, Carlos, 882
GUASTAVINO, Carmen, 1217
GUASTAVINO, Esteban Ezequiel, 258
GUASTAVINO, Juan Esteban, 222
GUATY, Justo Rufino, 371
GUAZZONE, José, 4, 98, 258
GUBELLINI, Alcides, 18, 25
GUBETICH, Andrés, 963a
GUCOVSKY, Victoria, 834
GUDIÑO, Luis Fernando (ORIBE, L. F., pseud.), 824
GUDIÑO KIEFFER, Eduardo, 764, 816
GUDIÑO KRAMER, Luis, 135, 670, 779, 800, 816, 829
GUELERMAN, José, 655
GUELERMAN, Miguel A., 656
GÜEMES, Adolfo, 550
GÜEMES, José Manuel, 126
GÜEMES, Juan, 653, 654
GÜEMES, Luis, 842, 844, 845a, 847, 851, 1261
GÜEMES, Macacha, 478, 929
GÜEMES, Martín Gabriel, 445

GÜEMES, Martín Miguel Juan de Mata, 70, 104, 110, 121, 128, 141, 166, 176, 244, 245, 282, 370, 386, 404, 432, 446, 471, 472, 475, 478, 509, 519, 521, 529, 545, 551, 552, 553, 568, 632
GÜEMES DE TEJADA, Magdalena, 422, 611, 626
GUEÑOL, Zelmar, 889
GUERRELLO, L. Oreste, 923
GUERIN (family), 168
GUERIN, Carmen Ambrosio, 956
GUERINI GRENI, José, 258
GUERRA (family), 1108
GUERRA, Alonso de, 910, 949, 1041
GUERRA, Isidoro Celestino, 599, 895
GUERRA, Jerónimo, 1238
GUERRA, Juan Néstor, 320, 328
GUERRA, Miguel Angel, 1045, 1049
GUERRA, Pedro, 914, 918
GUERRA, Rosa, 478, 677, 762, 929
GUERRA, Ubaldo Ramón, 1174
GUERRA BOTET, Cornelio, 1050
GUERRA TAPPA, Olga Elvira, 1088
GUERRABUT, Eduardo, 15
GUERREÑAS, José, 845
GUERRERO, Antonio, 1082
GUERRERO, Asdrúbal, 1210
GUERRERO, Christoval, 186
GUERRERO, Edgardo Abel, 299
GUERRERO, Fernando E., 1093
GUERRERO, Hilarión, 254
GUERRERO, José de la Cruz, 1093
GUERRERO, José Nicasio, 1093
GUERRERO, Joseph, 186
GUERRERO, Manuel J., 68
GUERRERO, Marta, 299
GUERRERO DE ALZAGA, Felicitas, 237
GUERRERO ESTRELLA, Guillermo, 670, 825, 1245
GUERRICO, Fernando D., 904
GUERRICO, José, 103
GUERRICO, Martín, 14, 17, 287
GUERRICO, Silvia, 811
GUEVARA, Andrés, 810, 938, 939, 965, 966
GUEVARA, Ernesto (CHÉ; RAMÓN, pseud.), 232
GUEVARA, Fenelón, 268
GUEVARA, Isabel de, 1230
GUEVARA, José, 259, 482, 483, 761, 885, 964, 966, 985, 1229, 1269
GUEVARA, José Antonio, 268
GUEVARA, Juan Luis de, 555
GUEVARA, Juan Ramón, 683a
GUEVARA, Julio P., 683a
GUEVARA, Osvalro, 704, 739, 831
GUEVARA, Trinidad, 677
GUEVARA, Roberto, 207
GUEVARA LAVAL, Carlos, 683a
GUEZÚRAGA, Margot, 711, 762
GUFFANTI, Luis Angel, 320
GUGGIARI, Augusto, 1006
GUGGIARI, Hermann, 938, 939
GUGGIARI, José P., 959
GUGGIARI, Modesto, 947
GUGGIARI, Pedro Bruno, 959
GUGGIARI, Ramón, 947
GUGLIELMINETTI, Juan, 258
GUGLIELMINI, Homero M., 732
GUGLIELMINO, Osvaldo, 663
GUGLIELMO, Giovanni Giuseppe, 258, 292
GUGLIELMO, Juan José
    see GUGLIELMO, Giovanni Giuseppe
GUGLIELMONE, Alberto, 89

GUIBERT, Fernando, 660, 716, 722, 739, 758, 801, 827
GUIBOURG, Augusto Antonio, 521
GUIBOURG, Edmundo, 521, 644a
GUICHARDOT, Gabriel E., 923
GUIDA, Arturo Horacio, 769
GUIDI BELLUCCI, Alfredo, 1088
GUIDI BUFFARINI, Arsenio, 258
GUIDI DE ELORDI, Raquel, 702
GUIDO, Alfredo, 19, 25, 31, 41, 64
GUIDO, Angel, 833
GUIDO, Beatriz, 140, 696, 751, 752, 764, 835
GUIDO, Eduardo, 268
GUIDO, José María, 515
GUIDO, José Tomás, 96, 104, 128, 166, 195, 240, 244,
    258, 282, 386, 404, 453, 475, 478, 479, 489,
    499, 542, 553, 573, 574, 611, 629, 708, 720,
    780
GUIDO, Rufino, 85, 104, 128, 258, 611
GUIDO, Tomás
    see GUIDO, José Tomás
GUIDO LAVALLE, Ricardo, 268
GUIDO SPANO, Carlos
    see GUIDO Y SPANO, Carlos
GUIDO SPANO DE CASTELLANOS, María del Pilar, 268
GUIDO Y SPANO, Carlos, 59, 65, 91, 121, 128, 141,
    165, 166, 167, 219, 245, 258, 282, 404, 498,
    664, 669, 682, 723, 724, 734, 747, 740, 749,
    751, 754, 755, 759, 780, 792, 803, 807, 1243,
    1247
GUIJARRO, Juan, pseud.
    see GANDOLFI HERRERO, Augusto
GUILESTEGUI, Gabriel de, 1034
GUILLAND, Zenobio, 910
GUILLARD, Valerian, 299
GUILLELMO, Pedro Juan José, 32
GUILLÉN, Fernando Aníbal, 385
GUILLÉN CHAPARRO, Francisco, 1270
GUILLÉN DE REZZANO, Clotilde, 118
GUILLÉN GARÍN, Domingo, 1191
GUILLÉN-ROA, Miguel Angel, 1020
GUILLES, Juan, 179, 207
GUILLÉSTEGUI, Gabriel de, 1041
GUILLET, León, 81, 222
GUILLOT, Alvaro, 1126
GUILLOT, Víctor Juan, 135
GUILLOT MUÑOZ, Alvaro, 1181, 1187
GUILLOT MUÑOZ, Gervasio, 1177, 1181, 1187
GUINAND (family), 168
GUINET, Joseph, 960
GUINOYSEAU, Juan B. Enrique, 922
GUIÑAZÚ, Nicolás, 254
GUIÑAZÚ, Prudencio, 254
GUIÑAZÚ, Víctor Segundo, 81, 222
GUIÑAZÚ DE BERRONDO, Carmen, 222
GUIÑAZÚ Y ALTAMIRA, Fernando, 254
GUIRAL, Jesús, 1192
GUIRÁLDER, José Lorenzo, 207
GÜIRALDES, Alberto, 19, 31
GÜIRALDES, Manuel J., 3, 103, 356
GÜIRALDES, Ricardo, 282, 356, 658, 664, 670, 674,
    678, 707, 721, 722, 723, 737, 739, 740, 741,
    745a, 751, 759, 773, 779, 782, 799, 803, 807,
    815, 816, 821, 825, 834, 835, 1243, 1246, 1247,
    1249, 1251, 1254, 1260
GUIRAQUERAY, 977
GUIRAVERÁ, 977
GUITARTE, Manuel, 332
GUITIÁN Y ARIAS, Pedro, 284
GUIZZETTI, Carlos, 268
GUKOVSKI, Victoria, 152a, 765

GULLO, Antonio, 833
GUMLIUS, Arvid, 332
GUNDÍN, Joaquín, 284
GUNDIÁN DE CAÑAS, José María, 284
GUNGUITO, Enrique, 811
GURBANOV, Alberto, 772, 775
GURUCIAGA, León, 268
GURRUCHAGA, Francisco de, 14, 478, 479, 521, 625
GURRUCHAGA, José de, 254
GUSTAFSON, Nils Olof, 954
GUSTAVINO, Arturo Gerardo, 18, 64
GUSTAVINO, Carlos, 865, 883
GUSTAVINO, Enrique, 645
GUTERO, Alfredo
    see GUTTERO, Alfredo
GUTIERRE DE LA CONCHA, Juan, 579
GUTIÉRREZ, 212
GUTIÉRREZ, Avelino, 68, 853a
GUTIÉRREZ, Blas, 844, 850, 921
GUTIÉRREZ, Carlos María, 1192
GUTIÉRREZ, Cayetano, 1122
GUTIÉRREZ, Cornelio, 567
GUTIÉRREZ, Eduardo, 13, 152a, 643, 673, 737, 747,
    834, 867, 1246, 1249, 1254, 1260, 1263
GUTIÉRREZ, Federico A., 669, 751, 773
GUTIÉRREZ, Felipe, 472, 500
GUTIÉRREZ, Guillermo Adolfo, 31
GUTIÉRREZ, José Albino, 179
GUTIÉRREZ, José María, 6, 116, 889, 1084
GUTIÉRREZ, Juan, 888
GUTIÉRREZ, Juan Antonio, 206
GUTIÉRREZ, Juan María, 85, 95, 96, 116, 121, 141,
    166, 176, 227, 240, 261, 276, 317, 322, 332, 379,
    404, 418, 478, 488, 507, 509, 519, 521, 544, 586,
    592, 611, 629, 634, 643, 644, 669, 688, 692, 720,
    723, 724, 733, 734, 737, 740, 743, 749, 751, 754,
    761, 763, 780, 803, 807, 834, 904, 921a, 1203,
    1242, 1243, 1246, 1247, 1256
GUTIÉRREZ, Luciano, 1017
GUTIÉRREZ, Mamerto, 222
GUTIÉRREZ, Manuel, 923, 1011
GUTIÉRREZ, Marcos, 186
GUTIÉRREZ, Narcisco G., 222
GUTIÉRREZ, Nicolás, 87
GUTIÉRREZ, Ricardo, 154, 165, 216, 259, 379, 404,
    643, 664, 669, 720, 723, 734, 737, 740, 749,
    751, 773, 782, 803, 807, 844, 851, 1247
GUTIÉRREZ, Rubí, 956
GUTIÉRREZ, Santiago, 496
GUTIÉRREZ BARRAGÁN, Juan, 186
GUTIÉRREZ DE CEBALLOS, José Antonio, 244, 529a
GUTIÉRREZ DE DUVOY, Olga, 923
GUTIÉRREZ DE ESCOBAR, Francisco, 126
GUTIÉRREZ DE ESCOBAR, Gabriel, 32
GUTIÉRREZ DE ESTRADA Y GÓMEZ DE LA CORTINA, Fernando
    María de los Dolores, 112, 383
GUTIÉRREZ DE LA CONCHA, José, 254
GUTIÉRREZ DE LA CONCHA, Juan, 17a, 89, 283, 922
GUTIÉRREZ DE LA MADRID, Alexandro, 186
GUTIÉRREZ DE MOLINA, Luis, 186
GUTIÉRREZ DE PAZ, Juan, 1262
GUTIÉRREZ DE TOLLO, Irene, 422
GUTIÉRREZ DEL BARRIO, Alejandro, 882
GUTIÉRREZ DEL BARRIO, Eduardo, 874
GUTIÉRREZ DEL BARRIO, Ramón, 874
GUTIÉRREZ DEL CASTILLO, Severo, 207
GUTIÉRREZ FLORES, García, 555
GUTIÉRREZ NÁJERA, Manuel, 1259
GUTIÉRREZ UMANES, Diego, 186
GUTIÉRREZ UMANES, Juan, 186

GUTIÉRREZ Y CEBALLOS, José Antonio, 529a, 910
GUTTERO, Alfredo, 18, 19, 25, 31, 33, 36, 45, 55, 56
GUYOT, Dudos, 587
GUZDYNOWICZ, Juan, 238
GUZMÁN (family), 357
GUZMÁN, Adán, 810
GUZMÁN, Alejo Carmen, 89, 244, 316, 545a
GUZMÁN, Andrés, 649a
GUZMÁN, Arturo Mario, 923
GUZMÁN, Bernardino de, 1266
GUZMÁN, Cayetano, 874
GUZMÁN, Eustaquio, 874
GUZMÁN, Federico, 874
GUZMÁN, Fernando, Segundo, 207, 874
GUZMÁN, Francisco, 874
GUZMÁN, Gloria, 857c
GUZMÁN, Horacio G., 385
GUZMÁN, María Cristina, 213
GUZMÁN, Pablo, 186
GUZMÁN, Víctor, 874
GUZMÁN REYES, Lola, 781
GWYNN, Walter, 998

HABANAL, Rodolfo Oscar, 791
HACK, Walter Hellmut, 923
HACHERO, El, pseud.
    see PUPPO, Julio César
HADROWA, Héctor, 560
HAEDI, María Tiburcia, 244
NAEDO (family), 1106
HAEDO, Felipe, 885
HAEDO, Hilario, 995a
HAEDO, Juan Antonio de, 1082
HAEDO, Manuel Ventura de, 496
HAEDO DE PAZ, Tiburcia, 422, 611
HAEDO ROSSI, José Antonio, 923
HAENKE, Tadeo H., 482, 885
HAFLIGER, Alfredo, 1122
HAIGH, Samuel, 834
HALBRINGER, Roberto Edwin, 923
HALPERÍN DONGHI, Tulio, 218, 609
HALPERN, Teodoro, 923
HALLEY, Pedro Eduardo, 581
HALLEY MORA, Mario, 943, 1020, 1025
HAMMERLY (family), 168
HAMUY D., Jorge, 963a
HAN, Francisco, 923
HANLON, Carlos, 910
HANSEN, Carlos, 713
HANSEN, Roberto José, 385
HANSEN, Virginia, 785
HARBIN Y GONZÁLEZ, Juan Manuel, 284
HARDY, J. M., 580
HARENCHISIN, Mirtha, 691
HARGREAVES, Francisco A., 864, 867
HARL, Antonio, 32, 922
HARTICH, Lalo, 857c
HARRIAGUE, Magdalena, 716, 717, 725, 729, 739, 758, 802
HARRIAGUE, Pascual, 1053, 1092
HARRINGTON, Horacio Jaime, 923
HARRIS, Jaime, 250
HARRIS, Mercedes, 299
HARRIS, Reginald, 904
HARRISON, Sampson, 1006
HARRISON, Sarah, 323
HARVEY, Willy, 788
HASSEL DE MENÉNDEZ, Gabriela Gustava, 923
HASSLER, Emilio, 985

HASTREL DE RIVEDOUX, Adolphe d', 28, 45, 51, 59
HAUG, José, 923
HAUSWIRTH, Ernesto A., 923
HAVEN, Annette, 323
HAYN, Emil, 214
HAYWARD, Kenneth John, 923
HAYWOOD, Guillermo, 954
HAZE, Diego, 319
HAZE, Jacques de, 960
HAZOT BENGUTAT, Violeta, 1210
HECKER, Liliana, 822
HEDERRA, José, 13
HEINSHEIMER, Jorge, 923
HEITMANN, Román, 120
HELGUERA, Jerónimo, 611
HELGUERA, Juan de la
    see ELGUERA, Juan de la
HELGUERA, Francisco B., 1094
HELGUERA, María, 37
HELGUERA ORTEGA, Antonio, 1094
HELGUETA, Pedro, 318
HELLMERS, Guillermo G., 954
HENARD, Nicolás, 960
HENAULT, Jorge Alcides, 923
HENESTROSA, Catalina de, 193
HENRÍQUEZ, José Camilo, 629
HENRÍQUEZ FIGUEIRA, José, 1083
HENRÍQUEZ UREÑA, Pedro, 594
HENSHAW, Susy, 299
HENZO D'ALESSIO, Rafael, 717, 739
HEPPER, Héctor Cuarto, 923
HÉQUET, Diógenes, 1046, 1047, 1079, 1086
HERAS, Carlos, 96, 609
HERAS, Juan Gregorio de las
    see LAS HERAS, Juan Gualberto Gregorio de
HERAS VELASCO, María Juana, 35
HERBERT, Thomas, 580
HERBIN, Luis A., 332
HEREDIA, 13, 189
HEREDIA, Alberto, 35, 55
HEREDIA, Alejandro, 446, 528, 552, 632
HEREDIA, María Mercedes, 144
HEREDIA, Nicolás de, 500, 620
HEREÑÚ, Eusebio
    see HEREÑÚ, José Eusebio
HEREÑÚ, José Eusebio, 95, 241, 552
HERISPE DE CHERUTTI, Juana, 320
HERKEN, Tutula, 956
HERMELO, Mony, 893
HERMELO, Ricardo Ireneo, 135
HERMES VILLORDO, Oscar, 664, 729, 802, 814
HERMIDA, Juan, 1089
HERMITTE, Enrique, 332
HERMOSILLA, Francisco, 995a
HERNANDARIAS
    see ARIAS DE SAAVEDRA, Hernando
HERNÁNDEZ, Alberto J., 299
HERNÁNDEZ, Alfonso C., 283
HERNÁNDEZ, Alvaro, 1270
HERNÁNDEZ, Bernabé, 319
HERNÁNDEZ, Bernardino, 887
HERNÁNDEZ, Diógenes, 565
HERNÁNDEZ, Ernesto Tomás, 320
HERNÁNDEZ, Esteban, 496
HERNÁNDEZ, Eva Susana, 691
HERNÁNDEZ, Fausto, 837
HERNANDEZ, Felisberto, 806, 1148, 1149, 1155, 1158, 1177, 1186, 1199
HERNÁNDEZ, Horacio H., 652

HERNÁNDEZ, José, 95, 110, 121, 152a, 176, 199, 217, 282, 381a, 404, 478, 496, 521, 574, 664, 669, 688, 692, 723, 734, 737, 740, 743, 751, 754, 761, 767, 803, 807, 828, 1242, 1243, 1244, 1246, 1247, 1248, 1249, 1254, 1260
HERNÁNDEZ, Juan Antonio, 108
HERNÁNDEZ, Juan Antonio Gaspar, 32
HERNÁNDEZ, Juan José, 480, 679, 680, 689, 697, 717, 739, 752, 758, 794, 796, 830, 835
HERNÁNDEZ, Lylia, 781
HERNÁNDEZ, Marcos, 32
HERNÁNDEZ, Martín, 556
HERNÁNDEZ, Obdulio, 844
HERNÁNDEZ, Pedro, 186, 358, 556, 985
HERNÁNDEZ, Pedro de, 845
HERNÁNDEZ, Rafael, 254
HERNÁNDEZ, Rafael José, 688
HERNÁNDEZ, Sabá Z., 95, 135, 194, 241, 445
HERNÁNDEZ, Sebastián, 358
HERNÁNDEZ, Silvano Arístides, 320
HERNÁNDEZ DE BOZMEDIANO, Diego, 845
HERNÁNDEZ DE CASANOVA, Carlota Angela, 320
HERNÁNDEZ GÁNDARA, Juan Antonio, 169
HERNÁNDEZ PINZÓN, Luis, 1235
HERNANDO, Gregorio Santos, 739, 758
HERNANI DE SANTA CRUZ, Joseph, 186
HERRADOR, Juan, 845
HERRÁN, Jerónimo, 319, 1267
HERRERA (family), 351, 354, 1106
HERRERA, Alfredo, 207
HERRERA, Antonio de, 895
HERRERA, Armando, 683a
HERRERA, Ataliva, 154, 677, 751, 773
HERRERA, Aurelio, 254
HERRERA, Carlos B., 1123
HERRERA, Carlos María, 1046, 1047, 1079, 1086
HERRERA, Cristóbal Cayetano de, 1056
HERRERA, Darío, 1259
HERRERA, Diego de, 496, 649a
HERRERA, Elina (EROS, pseud.), 762
HERRERA, Ernesto, 894, 1071, 1079, 1145, 1177, 1185, 1187, 1194, 1199, 1249
HERRERA, Félix E., 923
HERRERA, Jacinto, 1027
HERRERA, José de, 207, 570
HERRERA, José Cipriano de, 28
HERRERA, Juan de, 649a
HERRERA, Leopoldo, 278, 317
HERRERA, Luis Alberto de, 1058, 1073, 1083, 1087, 1122, 1134, 1146, 1188
HERRERA, Máximo, 878
HERRERA, Miguel de, 521
HERRERA, Nicolás de, 125, 126, 552, 984, 1063, 1091
HERRERA, Pedro, 222
HERRERA, Pedro Cacho, 318
HERRERA, Pedro S., 809
HERRERA, Roberto, 299
HERRERA, Roque de, 1030
HERRERA, Silvia, 1151, 1179
HERRERA DÁVALOS, Juan de, 556
HERRERA DE TORO, Emilia, 930
HERRERA GUZMÁN, Phelipe de, 186
HERRERA SALTERAIN, 1187
HERRERA SOTOMAYOR, José de, 1262
HERRERA VEGAS, Marcelino, 847, 1261
HERRERA VEGAS, Rafael, 166, 842, 845a, 1261
HERRERA Y GUZMÁN (family), 348, 352
HERRERA Y OBES, Julio, 1064, 1075, 1079, 1081, 1091, 1109, 1112, 1119, 1120, 1121, 1146, 1193, 1199
HERRERA Y OBES, Manuel, 96, 127, 1081, 1093a, 1220, 1261

HERRERA Y REISIG, Julio, 1079, 1081, 1086, 1147, 1153, 1163, 1164, 1170, 1174, 1177, 1179, 1181, 1187, 1188, 1198, 1199, 1259
HERRERA Y VELAZCO, Alonso de, 477
HERRERÍA, Julián de la, pseud. (CAMPOS CERVERA, Andrés), 937, 938, 939, 943, 964, 1012
HERRERO, Alonso, 1238
HERRERO, Antonia, 857b
HERRERO, Benito, 68
HERRERO, Federico J., 923
HERRERO, Francisco Antonio, 496
HERRERO, Miguel, 845
HERRERO, Pedro, 32
HERRERO BRITOS, Diego, 954
HERRERO CÉSPEDES, Pedro, 1014
HERRERO MIRANDA, Oscar, 19, 25, 31, 36
HERRERO Y ESPINOSA, Manuel, 1075, 1174
HERREROS, Pedro, 751, 773
HERREROS BUENO, Juan R., 998
HERRING, John Frederick, 28
HERSFIELD, Conrado, 94
HERTIG, Ricardo Rodolfo, 923
HERTZ, Mauricio, 845
HETTMAN, Carlos José, 923
HEULAND, Conrado, 885
HEULAND, Cristián, 885
HEVIA, María A., 762
HEVIA Y PANDO, Antonio de, 885
HEYDE GARRIGÓS, Alejandro von der
    see VON DER HEYDE GARRIGÓS, Alejandro
HEYRLE, Tomás, 850
HEYWOOD, Pedro, 580
HIDALGO, Bartolomé José, 293, 521, 677, 688, 720, 723, 734, 736, 737, 740, 761, 767, 803, 821, 876, 1057, 1071, 1092, 1146, 1147, 1154, 1166, 1167, 1174, 1177, 1179, 1185, 1187, 1199, 1242, 1243, 1244, 1247, 1248, 1249, 1256, 1260
HIDALGO, César, 878
HIDALGO, Eugenio, 188
HIDALGO, Félix Santiago, 878, 1247
HIDALGO, José, 62
HIDALGO, Manuel, 987
HIDALGO DE CISNEROS, Baltasar
    see CISNEROS Y LA TORRE, Baltasar Hidalgo
HIERRO, Luis, 1140
HIERRO, Ricardo, 1140
HIGGINSON, Ricardo Ciro, 207, 683a
HIGUERAS, Antonio (family), 358
HILERET, Clodomiro, 254
HILL, Cora (Mrs. Frank M. Clawson), 323
HINESTROSA, Gregorio de, 984, 989
HIORTH, Gunnar, 923
HIROUX FUNES, Teófilo, 746
HIRSCH, Mauricio de, 255, 258a
HIRSCHHORN, Elisa, 923
HITA, Fermín, 874
HJERTING, Jens Peter, 923
HLITO, Alfredo, 19, 31, 36, 55, 658
HOBOHM, Karl Otto, 923
HOCEVAR, Sergio, 44
HOCSMAN, Natalio, 658
HODGES, Laura Haven (Mrs. William Hodges), 323
HODGES, William (Mrs.)
    see HODGES, Laura Haven
HOFFER, Carlos, 952
HOFFMAN, Israel, 135
HOFFMANN, Hugo, 18
HOFFMANN, Oscar Eduardo, 781
HOFFMANN DE GEIGER, Velia L., 923
HOGAR, José M. del, 152a
HOGG, Ricardo, 2, 1246

HOLDENJARA, Roberto, 937, 939, 949
HOLGADO, Myrian Cristina, 44
HOLGUÍN SÁNCHEZ, Juan Carlos, 1210
HOLMBERG, Eduardo Ladislao, 110, 141, 167, 191, 568, 714, 728, 747, 780, 851
HOLMBERG, Ezequiel A. D., 923
HOLMBERG DE BRACHT, Laura, 751, 762
HOLT, Follett, 904
HOLZER, Juan, 191
HOLLER, Luis U., 954
HOME PESOA, Pedro, 555
HOPE, William (Mrs.)
       see GRANT, Katharine
HOPKINA, Patricio, 320
HORDEÑANA, Oscar, 1075
HORNE, Bernardino C., 135
HORNOS, Manuel, 166, 241, 608, 611
HORRACH, Bernardo, 739, 807
HORSKI, Wenceslao, 850
HORTA, Fernando de la, 646
HORTA DE MERELLO, Delia de, 1088
HORTICOU, Leonor, 1083
HORTIGUERA, Rafael, 552, 611
HORTIZ DE ZÁRATE, Juan
       see ORTIZ DE ZÁRATE, Juan
HOSNE, Roberto, 770
HOSTAL, Carlos, 731
HOTHAM, Charles, 143, 580
HOURCADE, Luis A., 652
HOURIET (family), 168
HOUSE, Guillermo, pseud.
       see CASA, Agustín Guillermo
HOUSSAY, Bernardo A., 853a, 923
HOWARD, Enrique G., 68
HOWARD, Jennie E., 323, 930
HOWARD, Juana E., 268
HOWARD, Raquel, 874
HOWDEN, Juan Hobert, 580
HOWE, Edith, 323
HOWEL, Juan Bartolomé, 7, 32
HOYO, Juan Bautista del, 186
HOZ, Julián de la, 1083
HUASI, Julio, 739
HUBAC, Angel, 14
HUDSON, Damián, 179, 207, 212, 283, 413
HUDSON, Guillermo Enrique, 152a, 685, 713, 732, 734, 779, 834, 1246
HUDSON, Manuel de los Santos, 254
HUDSON, William Henry
       see HUDSON, Guillermo Enrique
HUECK, Kurt, 923
HUENCHIUL, 566
HUERGO, Delfín B., 418, 634
HUERGO, Eduardo María, 122, 332, 923
HUERGO, Luis Augusto, 68, 94, 141, 293, 332, 904
HUERGO, Luis Augusto (son), 332
HUERGO, María Elena, 923
HUERTA, Roberto, 89
HUERTAS OLIVERA, María Ofelia, 1088
HUG, Enrique, 923
HUG DE BELMONT, Ricardo, 1014
HUGUET, Esteban, 845, 949
HUIDOBRO, Vicente, 658
HUMANZORO, Diego, 910
HUNALDO, 361
HUNT, Enrique, 6
HUNT, Jane, 323
HUNT, Roberto, 147
HUNZIKER, Armando Teodoro, 923
HUNZIKER, Juan Héctor, 923

HURTADO, Encarnación (MALAGUEÑITA, La, pseud.), 892
HURTADO DE MENDOZA, García, 188, 283
HURTADO DE MENDOZA, Miguel, 186
HURTADO DE MENDOZA, Roberto, 717, 739
HURTADO Y ARIAS, Enrique, 225
HUTTON, A. Watson, 94

IACOVIELLO, Beatriz, 774a
IBÁÑEZ, Andrés, 137
IBÁÑEZ, Cipriano, 943
IBÁÑEZ, Guillermo, 785, 788
IBÁÑEZ, José Antonio, 32
IBÁÑEZ, Juan Bautista, 1017
IBÁÑEZ, Roberto, 1151, 1152, 1177, 1178, 1179, 1187, 1199
IBÁÑEZ, Sara de, 1151, 1152, 1177, 1178, 1179, 1217
IBÁÑEZ, Ulderico, 874
IBÁÑEZ DE ECHAVERRI, Bernardo, 985
IBÁÑEZ DE FARÍA, Diego, 1011
IBÁÑEZ DE LA CUESTA, Juan, 186
IBÁÑEZ DE LUCA, Agustín, 6
IBÁÑEZ FROCHAM, Manuel, 181
IBÁÑEZ ROJAS, Alcibíades, 954
IBAPIRI, 977
IBARBALZ, José Gregorio de, 244
IBARBALZ, Nicolás, 987
IBARBOUROU, Juana de, 1065, 1079, 1144, 1145, 1147, 1151, 1152, 1153, 1160, 1163, 1165, 1177, 1179, 1181, 1187, 1198, 1199, 1217
IBARBURU CASALÁS, Gastón, 1210
IBARBURU ELIZALDE, María Celia, 1210
IBARBURU ILIZALDE, María Elena, 1210
IBARBURU ELIZALDE, Renée, 1210
IBARBURU ELIZALDE DE SUÁREZ, Rita, 1210
IBARBURU IBARBURU, Hugo, 1210
IBARGOYEN, Saúl
       see IBARGOYEN ISLAS, Saúl
IBARGOYEN ISLAS, Saúl, 1151, 1152, 1178
IBARGUREN, Antonino, 842
IBARGUREN, Carlos, 89, 94, 269, 493, 558, 609, 653, 654, 688, 751
IBARGUREN, Federico, 269
IBARRA, Emilio A., 560
IBARRA, Felipe, 166
IBARRA, Florinda Emilia, 923
IBARRA, Francisco de, 885
IBARRA, Gregorio, 28
IBARRA, Ignacio, 982
IBARRA, Isabel, 653
IBARRA, Juan Felipe, 282, 424, 632
IBARRA, Rogelio, 959
IBARRA DE NAUAR, Sonia, 1088
IBARRA GRASSO, Adalberto H., 923
IBARRETA, Enrique de, 191
IBARROLA, Mariano, 169
IBAZETA, Rudecindo, 191
ICARDI, Primitivo, 18, 24
ICART, Amelia, 923
ICART, Juan, 850
ICART DE RODRÍGUEZ, Emilia, 874
IDIARTE BORDA, Juan, 1079, 1081, 1091, 1109
IDOATE, Camilo, 95
IDOYAGA, Juan Manuel, 995a
IEDVABNI, Manuel, 889
IEGOR, Jorge, 728
IELPI, Rafael Oscar, 788
IGARZÁBAL, Eugenio de, 878
IGARZÁBAL, Rafael Segundo de, 173
IGARZÁBAL DE RODRÍGUEZ PEÑA, Casilda, 422, 611
IGLESIA, José de la, 713

IGLESIA, Juan Joaquín de la, 496
IGLESIA DAVIÑA, Marcial de la, 284
IGLESIA PEDRAYO, José, 284
IGLESIA VILLOUD, Héctor, 865, 882, 883
IGLESIAS, 1095
IGLESIAS, Antonio, 1089
IGLESIAS, Benito de, 496
IGLESIAS, Bernando, 1089
IGLESIAS, Carlos, 299
IGLESIAS, Clodomiro, 1089
IGLESIAS, Edgardo Jesús, 923
IGLESIAS, Eduardo, 1075
IGLESIAS, Eugenio Julio, 751, 773, 1245
IGLESIAS, Evaristo, 328
IGLESIAS, Gladis Edith, 810
IGLESIAS, Guillermo, 299
IGLESIAS, Magdalena, 787
IGLESIAS BRAGE, Francisco, 284
IGLESIAS DE PÉREZ SPERANZA, Raquel, 695
IGLESIAS PAZ, César, 135
IGLESIAS REY, Julio, 774a
IGLESIAS VILLOUD, Héctor, 882
IGNACIO, 599, 1130
IGNOTUS, pseud.
      see CARRILLO, Horacio
IGONDA, Pedro, 207
IGUANZO, Ximénez, 222
ILARIA, Juan, 894
ILLA (family), 1108
ILLA, Jaime, 1093a
ILLA MORENO, Juan José, 1259
ILLANES DE QUIROGA, Andrés, 555
ILLESCAS, Francisco de, 126
ILLESCAS, Gerónimo, 186
ILLESCAS, Roque, 921
ILLIA, Arturo U., 515, 593
IMAS, Escolástico, 1083
IMAS, Nicolás, 1116
IMAZ, Jorge Luis de, 213
IMAZ, Juan, 1094
IMAZ, Marcelo, 1082
IMBELLONI, José, 258, 923
IMBERT, Julio, 817
IMBRIANO, Aldo Enrique, 923
IMHOF, Francisco, 894, 1064, 1079, 1172, 1185, 1199
INCA, El, pseud.
      see GARCILASO DE LA VEGA
INCHAURREGUI, José Santos de, 496
INCHAUSPE, Pedro, 744
INDA, Juan Bautista, 254
INDA, Rufino, 260
INDIO, El, pseud.
      see FRANCISCO
INEICHEN (family), 168
INFANTE, Félix, 713, 730
INFANTE RIVAROLA, José, 998, 1006
INFANTOZZI, José, 1083
INFESTA, Domingo, 1095
INGENIEROS, Delia, 923
INGENIEROS, Giuseppe
      see INGENIEROS, José
INGENIEROS, José, 110, 121, 141, 162, 167, 192, 225,
      246, 258, 259, 278, 282, 292, 317, 324, 478,
      594, 609, 718, 741, 743, 751, 777, 851, 897
INGENIEROS, Salvador, 258
INGLEFIELD, Samuel H., 580
INSAURRALDE, Amancio, 947
INSAURRALDE, Crispín, 963a
INSAURRALDE, Dámaso, 268
INSAURRALDE, Félix de, 1270

INSAURRALDE, Juan Isidro, 995a
INSAURRALDE, Nicasio, 998
INSFRÁN, Juliana, 991
INSFRÁN, Pablo Max, 943, 966, 1020, 1026
INSFRÁN, Rufino, 995a
INSFRÁN BENEGAS, Justo, 998
INSÚA, José María
      see INSÚA LAGARES, José María
INSÚA LAGARES, José María, 284
INTAGLIETTA, Miguel, 258
INVERNIZZI, Antonio, 1092
INVERNIZZI, Juan, 1092
INZAURRAGA, Alberto, 881
INZAURRAGA, Alejandro, 881, 883
IOMMI, Enio, 19, 21, 25, 35, 55
IONESCU, Gina, 31, 46
IPUCHA AGUIRRE, Julio, 923
IPUCHE, Pedro Leandro, 767, 1151, 1153, 1159, 1165,
      1167, 1168, 1177, 1179, 1181, 1196, 1199, 1248
IPUCHE RIVA, Pedro, 1206, 1207
IPUCHE RIVA, Rolina, 1159
IRALA, Adriano, 1012, 1014
IRALA, Antolín, 1012
IRALA, Domingo Martínez de
      see MARTÍNEZ DE IRALA, Domingo de
IRALA, José, 68, 959
IRAMAIN, Juan Carlos, 25
IRAOLAGOITÍA, Fernando, 31, 46, 63
IRAZÚ, Bernabé, 328
IRAZUSTA, Julio, 431, 609
IRIARTE, Felipe Antonio de, 126, 457, 908, 915
IRIARTE, Félix, 332
IRIARTE, Florencio, 811, 813, 818, 1243, 1247
IRIARTE, Mariano, 385
IRIARTE, Soledad Nancy S. de, 810
IRIARTE, Tomás de, 282, 375, 433, 499, 574, 611,
      629
IRIBARNE, Julio Víctor, 842, 923
IRIBARNE, Miguel, 768
IRIBARREN, Joachimus, 1037
IRIBAS, Carlos, 963a
IRIGOYEN, Bernardo de, 78, 91, 110, 116, 121, 129,
      141, 166, 193, 244, 254, 277, 282, 372, 389,
      391, 404, 436, 478, 586, 595, 631
IRIGOYEN, Hipólito, 110, 121, 232, 389, 392, 393,
      405, 452, 466, 502, 516, 518, 531, 545, 582,
      619
IRIGOYEN, Ignacio de, 254, 391
IRIGOYEN, Mariano, 496
IRIGOYEN, Matías de
      see IRIGOYEN Y DE LA QUINTANA, Matías de
IRIGOYEN, Miguel de, 478, 496
IRIGOYEN DE GONZALEZ BELZUZ, Catalina, 320
IRIGOYEN Y DE LA QUINTANA, Matías de, 9, 14, 17a,
      427, 478, 496, 519, 552, 611
IRIONDO, Manuel de, 94
IRIONDO, Néstor de, 565
IRIONDO, Simón de, 477, 631
IRIS MARGA
      see PAURI, Iris
IRISARRI, Antonio José de, 573, 629
IRÍZAR, J. Manuel, 94
IRÍZAR, Julián, 14
IRÍZAR, Manuel, 844
IRRAZÁBAL, Luis, 1006, 1012
IRRAZÁBAL, Pablo, 188
IRURETA, Arturo, 19
IRURETA, Hugo, 19
IRRUETA GOYENA, José, 1059, 1073, 1083, 1184
IRURTIA, Rogelio, 33, 293

IRUSTA, Héctor M., 773
ISAAC, Jorge, 213
ISAACSON, José, 716, 717, 798, 827
ISABEL II, Queen of Spain, 153
ISAC, Susana, 789
ISAÍAS, Jorge, 788
ISARRA, Juan de, 186
ISASA (family), 352
ISASA, Ricardo, 1083
ISASI, Carlos Luis, 1083
ISASI, José Matías, 979
ISASI, Nicolás de, 995a
ISASI, Patricio, 956
ISASMENDI, Vicente Anastasio de, 126
ISBRAÍN, Pedro, 358
ISCAS, José, 566
ISEAS, 222
ISERN, Juan, 319
ISERNIA, Francisco, 681, 739, 751, 833
ISLAS, Alejanrdo, 1017
ISLAS, María Concepción, 320
ISLAS, Víctor Manuel, 998
ISNARDI, Antonio, 952
ISNARDI, Arturo, 565
ISNARDI, Héctor, 923
ISNARDI, Irma, 943
ISNARDI, Teófilo, 923
ISOLA, Albérico, 28, 1075, 1083
ISSACSON, José, 759, 802
ISUSI, Alejandro de, 805
ITAPAY, 977
ITCHART, Mirta Graciela, 691
ITERIO, 361
ITHOH, Makoto, 923
ITHUSARRI, Celina de, 702
ITUARTE, Juan Bautista de, 496
ITUARTE DE COSTA, Florentina, 254
ITUARTE PUEYRREDÓN (family), 362
ITURBE, Alberto José, 385
ITURBE, José Mariano de, 385
ITURBE, José Martín, 987
ITURBE, Juan María, 987
ITURBE, Miguel, 332
ITURBE, Vicente Ignacio, 943, 966, 979, 980, 987,
    1004, 1012
ITURBURU, Córdova
    see CORDOVA ITURBURU, Cayetano
ITURBURU, Fernando, 991
ITURBURU, Fernando J., 268
ITURRALDE, Susana, 663
ITURRASPE, J. Bernardo, 837
ITURRI, Francisco
    see ITURRI PATIÑO, Francisco Javier
ITURRI PATIÑO, Francisco Javier, 149, 177, 683, 720,
    734, 915, 1269
ITURRIOS, Juan de, 914
IUDICELLO, Plácido Mario, 684
IURE, Lidia de, 702
IVANISSEVICH, Oscar, 923
IVANISSEVICH MACHADO, Ludovico, 218
IWANOSKI, Teófilo, pseud.
    see REICHERT, Carlos
IZAGUIRRE (family), 1224
IZAGUIRRE, Ester de, 739, 817
IZAROWSKI, José Anselmo, 238
IZARRA, Pedro de, 358
IZARRA GAETE, Pedro de, 186
IZCUA BARBAT DE MUÑOZ XIMÉNEZ, María Carmen, 1145
    1187
IZQUIERDO, Joaquina, 478, 521, 929

IZQUIERDO, Juan Bautista Estanislao José Miguel
    Rafael, 169
IZVOLT BABINSCA, José 1210
IZZO, Roque Anselmo, 923

J. M., Jorge, pseud., 811
JABLKO BAUBOLL, Máximo, 1210
JACKSON, Juan D., 1067
JACOB (family), 168
JACOBS, Odilia, pseud.
    see GIROTTI DE JACOBS, Odilia
JACOME, Luis, 1238
JACOVELLA, Bruno, 664, 1245
JACQUES, Amadeo, 116, 191, 236, 921a
JACQUES, Francisca, 478, 929
JACQUET, Alfredo Andrés, 1014
JACQUET, Gaspar, 995a
JACUMIN (family), 168
JAEGGLI, Alfredo Luis, 954
JAGSICH, Juan, 923
JAILLARD, Luis, 254
JAIME, Florencio, 923
JAIME, Greta, 44
JAIMES FREYRE, Ricardo, 679, 751
JAIMOTE BOTANILLA, pseud.
    see BOTANA, Jaime A.
JAKOB, Christofredo, 844, 851, 923
JALLAD, Luis d', 653, 654, 713, 730
JANCARIK, Elena, 683a
JANEIRO, Constantino, 1089
JAQUES, 845
JARA, Carlos A., 1014
JARA, Juan Antonio, 1008
JARA, Rufino, 995a
JARA AZOCAR, Oscar, 154
JARA TROCHE, Miguel Angel, 998
JARA TROCHE, Roberto, 998
JARAMILLO, Baltazar, 83
JARAMILLO, Gregorio, 611
JARAMILLO, José María, 247
JARAMILLO ECHEVERRÍ, Marino, 954
JARAQUEMADA DE MARTÍNEZ, Paula, 626
JARRY, Gastón, 19, 31, 64
JASCHEK, Carlos O. R., 923
JASINSKI, Gustavo, 238
JASO, Leonardo, 845
JAUCH, Clotilde, 923
JAUFFRET, María Teresa, 892
JAIME TORRES, Miguel, 1093
JAUME Y BOSCH, José, 1094
JAUME Y BOSCH, Miguel, 1094
JAUREGUI, Agustín de, 188, 283
JAUREGUI, Juan Francisco, 328
JAUREGUIBERRY, Miguel, 1067
JAURÉS, Jean, 259
JAURETCHE, Arturo, 431, 816
JAYEUX DE LONCON, Theodore, 949
JEAN PAUL, pseud.
    see ECHAGÜE, Juan Pablo
JEANDREVIN, Eloisa, 684
JEANTOU (Madame), 960
JEMMA, R. José Andrés, 923
JENIG, José, 850
JENKINS, Aaron, 4
JENNER, Eduardo, 1262
JENNESS, Harriet E., 323
JEREZ, Pablo, 878
JESUALDO, pseud.
    see SOSA, Jesualdo
JIAM, Ismael Marcos, 656

JIJENA SÁNCHEZ, Rafael, 664, 679, 688, 739, 748,
751, 773, 807
JIJÓN, Francisco Bernardo, 274
JIMÉNEZ, Benito, 887
JIMÉNEZ, Carlos Miguel, 1014
JIMÉNEZ, Edith, 938, 939
JIMÉNEZ, Juan Francisco, 947
JIMÉNEZ, Marcial V., 954
JIMÉNEZ, Máximo, 887
JIMÉNEZ, Wilfredo, 894
JIMÉNEZ DE ARCE, Andrés, 32
JIMÉNEZ DE ARECHAGA (family), 1108
JIMÉNEZ DE ARECHAGA, Eduardo, 1073, 1083
JIMÉNEZ DE ARECHAGA, Emilio, 1075
JIMÉNEZ DE ARECHAGA, Justino, 1075, 1079, 1083,
1141, 1174, 1188
JIMÉNEZ ESPINOSA, Daniel, 1014
JIMÉNEZ GAONA, Ramón, 965
JIMÉNEZ PASTOR, Arturo, 268
JITRIK, Noé, 759, 807
JMELNITZKY, Carlos, 791
JOAQUINA, Carlota, 427
JOBEN, Luis (OBEN, Luis), 866
JOBSON, Bernardo, 808
JOFRÉ, Emilio, 207, 212, 278
JOFRÉ, Emilio (son), 207
JOFRÉ, José Javier, 283
JOFRÉ, Luis, 215
JOFRÉ, Nicolás, 222
JOFRÉ, Ofelia, 44
JOFRÉ, Tomás, 222
JOFRÉ DE ARCE, Juan, 186
JOFRÉ DE BAREDA ESTRADA, Diego, 845
JOFRE OLIU, Nirene, pseud.
see FOURNIER, Lenie Julieta
JOHNSTON, John, 961
JOHNSTON, Theodore H. (Mrs.)
see ELLIS, Edell
JOLÍS, José, 985, 1269
JONES, Willis Knapp, 1015
JONQUIÈRES, Eduardo Alberto, 19, 31, 46, 49, 722,
739, 758, 832
JORDÁN, Camilo, 921
JORDÁN, Chela, 299
JORDÁN, Luis María, 669, 751, 773, 782
JORDÁN DE LA CAZUELA, pseud.
see PERNIAS, Pedro
JORGE, Constantino, 14
JORGE, J. M.
see J. M., Jorge
JORGE, José M., 68, 923
JORGE, Nicolás, 14
JORGE NASSIFF, Sonia E., 923
JOSÉ ANTONIO DE SAN ALBERTO, 317, 910
JOSÉ DE LA ÁNIMAS, 166
JOSENDE, Pascuala, 1095
JOUBIN COLOMBRES, Eduardo, 679, 739
JOUN, Roberto, 844
JOUROF EGOROV, Víctor, 1210
JOVELLANOS, Salvador, 984, 1011
JOVELLANOS Y PASEYRO, Carlos, 751
JOVER PERALTA, Anselmo, 965
JOVTIS, David Daniel, 655, 656
JOZAMI, Juan Manuel, 923
JUAN, 845, 1261
JUAN, Guillermo, 833
JUAN, Ricardo, 817, 829
JUAN, Ronaldo de, 31, 49
JUAN DE SAN BERNARDO, 1034, 1035

JUAN POCA ROPA, pseud.
see DORREGO, Celestino
JUAN SIN ROPA, pseud.
see DORREGO, Celestino
JUANE, Osvaldo, 31
JUANICÓ, Cándido, 1121, 1179, 1188, 1253
JUANICÓ, Francisco, 1072
JUANICÓ OTORGUÉS, Eduardo, 1140
JUANICÓ PEÑALVA, Fernando Enrique, 1088
JUANTO, Cecilio, 69
JUANZARAS, Vicente Atanasio, 321, 895
JUÁREZ (family), 352
JUÁREZ, Benito, 761
JUÁREZ, Felipe, 878
JUÁREZ, Gaspar, 761, 885, 1269
JUÁREZ, Horacio, 19, 21, 24
JUÁREZ, Marcos N., 89
JUÁREZ, María Elvira, 679
JUÁREZ, Silvia, 653
JUÁREZ BABIANO, Isidro, 649a
JUÁREZ CELMAN, Miguel Angel, 70, 89, 147, 166, 392,
393, 405, 478, 489, 493, 514, 515, 516, 521,
531, 574, 598, 619
JUÁREZ DE SANDOVAL, Miguel, 332
JUÁREZ ENRÍQUEZ, Diego, 186
JUÁREZ MEJÍA, Antonio, 914
JUARROZ, Roberto David, 652, 672, 716, 739, 758, 759,
802, 803, 832
JUFRÉ, Juan, 188, 215, 283, 555, 556, 1270
JUFRÉ, Rodrigo, 556
JUFRÉ DE ARCE, Luis, 555
JUFRÉ DE LOAYZA, Diego, 555, 556
JUFRÉ Y MENESES, Luis, 283, 555
JULIANES, Felipe, 169
JUMÉNEZ, Eulojio, 959
JUNCO, Juan de, 1203
JUNCOS, Inocencio Rubén, 923
JUNGE, Daniel Enrique, 68
JUNGSTEDT, Herman, 332
JUNKEN, Elena Ruth, 923
JUNOR, Guillermo D., 91
JUNQUET, Ana María, 814
JURADO, Alicia, 729
JURADO, Isidro, 280
JURADO, José María, 3
JURAFSKY, Abraham, 882, 883
JURKOWSKI, Julio, 238, 1261
JUSID, Juan José, 857
JUSSIEU, José Bernardo, 885, 922
JUSTO, Agustín Pedro, 268, 269, 332, 392, 405, 466,
489, 515, 516, 524, 593, 619
JUSTO, Andrés, 260
JUSTO, Juan Bautista, 141, 152a, 162, 198, 212,
219, 244, 246, 259, 282, 469, 478, 503, 582,
589, 591, 612, 644, 718, 844, 851
JUSTO, Liborio (Garra, Lobodón, pseud.), 152a, 670,
707, 779, 816, 825

KAGEL, Mauricio, 865
KAHAN, Nélida, 652
KAILITZ, Eduardo
see KAILITZ DE HOLMBERG, Eduardo
KAILITZ DE HOLMBERG, Eduardo, 569
KAISER, Valentín, 87
KALI, pseud.
see ALONSO, Raúl R.
KAMINSKI, Aarón, 923
KAMÚN, Bebe, 857
KANTIS, Elisa, 923

KAPLUN, Inés, 684
KAPPELLER (family), 168
KARGIEMAN, Simón, 739, 802
KARRER, Pablo, 1264
KASPAREK, Dieter, 832
KASSIANOFF, Boris, 998
KATZ, JOrge Miguel, 311
KAUL GRÜNWALD, Guillermo, 683a
KAULITZ HOLEMBERG, Eduardo, 611
KAY, Jorge de, 438
KEIPER, Wilhelm, 214
KELLER, Eduardo
    see KELLER SARMIENTO, Eduardo
KELLER SARMIENTO, Eduardo, 664, 678, 751, 833
KELLERHALS (family), 168
KEMBLE, Kenneth
    see KEMBLE SMITH, Kenneth
KEMBLE SMITH, Kenneth, 19, 36, 55
KENNEDY, Jaime Craig, 954
KENNEDY, Malcolm, 954
KERN, Sergio, 788
KERVOR, Juan Bautista, 923
KESTELMAN, Abraham Jaime, 923
KETTERER, Guillermo, 938
KIER, Sabiniano, 68
KIHNLDERG, Carlos, 6
KIMBALL, Myra (Mrs. Arthur Goldney), 323
KING, Isabel, 323
KING, Juan, 14, 82, 611
KING, J. Antonio, 713
KING, Rachel, 323
KIRS, Manuel, 765
KITTL, Jorge Ernesto, 923
KLALA DOMIAN, Ricardo Juan, 663
KLEIMANS, Hernando, 698
KELIN, 13
KLEIN, Enrique 4
KLEIN, Otto, 923
KLEIN DE VILLAMAYOR, María J., 652
KLEITMAN, Isolde, 874
KLICHE, Rodolfo, 1045
KLIX, Miranda, 235, 765
KLUSAS DE BOEHRINGER, Irene, 923
KMAID, Iván, 1151
KNOLL, Federico, 332
KNOLL DE FERENC, Cristina Angela, 663
KNOP, Naum, 25, 49, 63
KNOSLER, Julianus, 865
KOC, Marcelo, 883
KOEK-KOEK, Stephen Robert, 1066
KOHAN, Roberto, 923
KOHAN, Teresa, 923
KOHON, David José, 712, 857
KONOPACKI DE VON DER PAHLEN, Eva M. Irene, 923
KORDON, Bernardo, 697, 772, 794, 819
KOREMBLIT, Jorge, 819
KORMILOV, Nicolás, 923
KORN, Alejandro, 162, 166, 167, 219, 246, 260, 478,
    594, 718, 743, 851, 897, 903
KORNBLIHTT, Isaac, 198
KORNMAYER, Pedro, 850
KOSCHMIEDER, Lothar, 923
KOSICE, Gyula, 19, 25, 31, 49, 739
KOSSMAN, Juana Haydée, 691
KOTZEV, Elena, 923
KOTZEVA, Elena V., 923
KOVENSKY LOIFER, Catalina, 1210
KÖVESLIGETHY, Radó, 923
KOWALEWSKI, Valdemar J., 923
KRAFT, Guillermo, 141

KRAISELBURD, David, 328
KRALY, Néstor, 690
KRAMER, Carlos, 850
KRAMER, Carnetta, 652
KRAPOVICKAS, Antonio, 923
KRASINSKY, José E. de, 923
KRASNO, pseud.
    see KRASNOPOLSKY, Rodolfo
KRASNO, Rodolfo
    see KRASNOPOLSKY, Rodolfo
KRASNOPOLSKY, Jorge Abel, 19, 31, 36, 46
KRASNOPOLSKY, Rodolfo (KRASNO, Rodolfo; KRASNO,
    pseuds.), 19, 31, 46
KRAUS, Juan, 7, 32
KRAUSE, Otto, 332
KREIBOHM, Enrique, 652
KREIBOHM, Guillermo J., 652
KREIBOHM, Isabel C., 923
KRETSCHMAR, Eduardo de, 28
KRONEGOLD DE BRODTKORB, M., 923
KRONFUSS, Juan, 24
KRUPKIN, Ilka, 739, 765
KUBLY Y ARTEAGA, Enrique, 1146, 1174
KUBLY Y ARTEAGA, Guillermo, 1185, 1190
KÜHNEMANN, Oscar, 923
KUHR, Germán, 6
KUNIKO HORIE, María, 44
KUNZ, Carlos, 385
KUPER, Fritz María, 923
KURLAT, Ethel, 154
KURTH, Gisberta S. de, 751
KUSNEZOV, Nicolás, 923

LA CALLE, Pablo, 32
LA HERA, Santos, 552
LA MADRID, Gregorio Aráoz
    see ARÁOZ ALFARO DE LA MADRID, Gregorio
LA MADRID, Juan Carlos, 660
LA MANNA, Nicolás, 19
LA MAR, José de, 562
LA PORTILLA, Enrique, 889
LA SERNA, José de, 453
LA SERNA E INOJOSA, José, 553
LABARDÉN, Manuel José de, 166, 177, 592, 669, 692,
    720, 740, 751, 761, 763, 885
LABAT, Casimiro, 860
LABAYÉN, Agustín de, 344
LABAYÉN, Juan, 135
LABORDA IBARRA, Matías, 81
LABOURDETTE, Juan Carlos, 19, 25, 35, 49, 63
LABRIOLA, Rafael A., 923
LACABE, Juan, 120
LACÁMERA, Fortunato, 18, 19, 23, 25, 31, 36, 55
LACARRUBLA, Sebastián, 954
LACASA, Pedro, 611
LACAU, María Hortensia, 814
LACAVERA, Pedro, 68, 842, 844
LACLEDE DE GUERRA, Luisa Genoveva, 320
LACOIZQUETA, Juan de, 344
LACONICH, Marco Antonio, 966
LACOSTE DE DÍAZ, Elsa N., 923
LACROZE, Federico, 120, 122
LACUESTA, Félix, 1059
LACUNZA, Angélica Beatriz, 663
LADRÓN DE GUEVARA, Jacinto, 186
LADRÓN DE GUEVARA, Juan Luis, 555
LADRÓN DE GUEVARA, Magdalena, 931
LADRÓN DE GUEVARA, Trinidad, 887
LAFERRÈRE, Alfonso de, 235
LAFERRÈRE, Germán de, 751

LAFERRÈRE, Gregorio de, 167, 199, 709, 737, 751, 769, 890
LAFERRÈRE, Roberto de, 431
LAFINUR, Juan Crisóstomo, 177, 183, 207, 215, 222, 227, 278, 321, 478, 611, 644, 669, 720, 751, 754, 828, 865, 874, 895
LAFITTE, Fermín, 910
LAFORGUE, Jules, 1177
LAFUENTE, Enrique, 612, 713, 730
LAFUENTE, José Manuel, 283
LAGARMILLA, Eugenio J., 1083
LAGARMILLA, Roberto
    see LAGARMILLA BAROFFIO, Roberto Eugenio
LAGARMILLA BAROFFIO, Roberto Eugenio, 1088, 1206
LAGATINERIE, Charles de, 153
LABATINERIE, Isabelle de, 153
LAGERENZA, Pablo, 998, 1006
LAGLEYZE, Pedro, 94, 844, 845a, 1261
LAGMANOVICH, David, 679
LAGO, Justo, 1089
LAGO, Manuel, 1089
LAGO, Silvia, 1155, 1158
LAGO, Virginia, 889
LAGOMAGGIORE, Luis C., 207
LAGOS, Alberto, 19, 21, 33, 55, 210, 521
LAGOS, Alfredo Enrique, 923
LAGOS, Hilario, 13, 96, 617
LAGOS, José Antonio, 496
LAGOS, José María, 6
LAGOS, Lauro, 565
LAGOS, Ovidio, 121
LAGOS GARCÍA, Luis, 330
LAGRAVE, Abraham, 998
LAGRESA BELTRÁN, Mary, 1088
LAGROTTA, Blanca, 857b
LAGUARDIA, Hernando de, 992
LAGUNA, José de, 496
LAGUNA, Juan de, 1080
LAGUNA, Julián, 433, 1063
LAGUNAS, Alberto, 728
LAHAM, Ricardo, 60
LAHITTE, Ana Emilia, 663, 717, 725, 739, 805
LAHITTE, Eduardo, 185
LAHORA, José María de, 546, 549
LAINÉ, 581
LÁINEZ, Manuel, 78, 90, 122, 254, 644, 709
LÁINEZ CANÉ, Bernabé, 210
LAISEGA ALVARADO, Juan, 910
LAJARROTA DE AGUIRRE, María Josefa, 422, 611
LAJUMI CEDRÉS DE BARRIOS, Edelmira Luisa, 1210
LAJUS, Bernardo, 845
LALIA, Enrique, 299
LAMADRID, Juan Carlos, 710
LAMANA, Nicolás, 25, 33
LAMAR GONZÁLEZ, Marino, 954
LAMARDO, Antonio (PININ, pseud.), 860
LAMARI, Alfredo, 842
LAMARQUE, Adolfo, 1247
LAMARQUE, Libertad, 858, 877, 932
LAMARQUE, Nydia, 711, 664, 739, 751, 762, 773, 783
LAMARQUE PONS, Jaurés, 1206, 1207
LAMAS, Alejandro, 1083
LAMAS, Alfonso, 1075, 1083
LAMAS, Andrés, 314, 629, 1072, 1091, 1121, 1146, 1187, 1188, 1199, 1253
LAMAS, Benito, 1199
LAMAS, Diego, 1116, 1122, 1134
LAMAS, Gregorio, 1075
LAMAS, José Benito de, 179, 921, 1063, 1080
LAMAS, Manuel, 1089

LAMAS, Vicente, 953, 1014, 1020, 1021, 1022
LAMAS CARISIMO DE RODRÍGUEZ ALCALÁ, Teresa, 959, 1020, 1021, 1022
LAMBERT, Luis Roger, 923
LAMBERTI, Antonio, 167, 243, 1146, 1147, 1174, 1188, 1243
LAMBORGHINI, Leónidas C., 658, 759
LAMBRUSCHINI, Domencio, 139
LAMELA, Adolfo, 299
LAMELA PIÑEIRO, Francisco Antonio, 284
LAMMERTYN, Julio Adriano, 30
LAMMIRATO, Alberto Hernán, 923
LAMURAGLIA, Nicolás, 882, 883
LAMY, Amado Enrique, 312
LANARI, Alfredo, 923
LANARI, Eduardo L., 923
LANCELOTTI, Mario A., 729
LANDABURU, Jorge, 703
LANDABURU, Laureano, 81, 219, 222
LANDECK, Eva, 857a
LANDI, Gino, 857d
LANDI, Juan, 299
LANDI, Natalio Gregorio, 320
LANDI DESSY, Jorge, 923
LANDINI, Basiliano, 995a
LANDÍVAR, Orlando, 1122
LANDOIS, Emilio, 6
LANGE, Enrique, 332
LANGE, Gunardo, 191
LANGE, Norah, 678, 711, 712, 722, 739, 751, 762, 773, 782, 783, 833
LANGE, Walter, 954
LANGER, Marie, 728
LANGINOS ELLAURI, José, 126
LANGMANN, Martín Félix, 332
LANGSNER, Jacobo, 1172, 1177
LANGUIRÚ, Nicola, 977
LANIERI, Miguel, 73
LANOEL, Alejandro, 46
LANÚS, Adolfo, 83
LANÚS, Anacarsis, 223
LANUSSE, Alejandro Agustín, 515
LANUSSE, Juan José, 551a
LANUZA, José Luis, 729, 746, 819, 1245
LANZ, José, 321, 921a
LANZ DARET, Miguel, 560
LANZ ALVAREZ, Francisco, 284
LANZILLOTO, Carlos Alberto, 739
LANZILLOTTO, Carlos Mario, 831
LANZIUTO, Ernesto, 44
LANZOLA, Fernando, 259
LAPEYRE, Miguel, 1083
LAPHIZ, Francisco, 921
LAPORTE, Domingo, 1046, 1047, 1083
LAPORTILLA, Enrique, 889
LAPRIDA, Amado, 283, 848
LAPRIDA, Francisco Naricso de, 70, 110, 141, 179, 188, 244, 278, 282, 283, 382, 386, 404, 411, 413, 439, 457, 478, 526, 546, 549, 611, 621, 626
LAPRIDA, Narciso
    see LAPRIDA, Francisco Narciso
LAPUENTE, Laurindo, 1174, 1188
LARA, Ascensio C., 923
LARA, José María de, 126
LARA, Juan de, 1203
LARA, Juana María de, 943, 1042
LARANGEIRA, Tomás, 951
LARCO, Jorge, 18, 19, 25, 31, 36, 50, 64, 1218
LARES, Francisco (Sina-Sina, pseud.), 189

LAREU, Santiago, 645
LARGHERO, Pedro, 1204
LARGUÍA, Jonas, 6
LARGUÍA DE CROUZEILLES, Amelia de, 923
LARIOS GALVÁN, Mariano, 979, 987
LARIZ, Jacinto de, 472, 570
LARIZ Y DEZA, Francisco, 555
LARLUS, Pedro, 565
LAROCA RAMELA, Javier Arturo, 1210
LAROCHE, Ernesto, 1067, 1083
LARRA, Lucy, 791
LARRAGUIBEL Y MARSANA, Santiago de, 555
LARRAIN, Nicanor, 173, 283
LARRALDE, Pedro, 743, 819
LARRAN, Alberto, 299
LARRAÑAGA, Dámaso Antonio, 244, 293, 629, 885, 1052,
        1053, 1063, 1065, 1076, 1079, 1080, 1091, 1115,
        1131, 1146, 1165, 1177, 1188, 1199, 1203
LARRAÑAGA, Enrique de, 18, 19, 25, 31, 154
LARRAURI, Lorenzo de, 1082
LARRAVIDE (family), 1108
LARRAVIDE, Manuel, 1046, 1047, 1079
LARRAZÁBAL, Antonio de, 344
LARRAZÁBAL, Marcos José de, 984, 1011
LARRAZÁBAL, Mariano de, 496
LARRÉ, Beltrán, 1092
LARRÉ, Ernesto, 1092
LARREA, Juan, 14, 70, 85, 104, 166, 244, 282, 386,
        404, 411, 421, 475, 478, 479, 496, 525, 611
LARRECHEA, Francisco Antonio de, 89
LARRENA, Tomás de, 555
LARRERDIA, Juan Lorenzo de, 344
LARRETA, Antonio, 1172, 1185
LARRETA, Enrique, 154, 167, 674, 678, 722, 737, 739,
        751, 759, 834, 1251
LARRIERA, Octavio, 1151
LARRIERA VARELA, Diego, 1167
LARRIEU, Helena, 154
LARRINAGA Y AXPE, Francisco de, 555
LARROBLA, Juan de, 1080
LARROBLA, Raymundo, 1058
LARROCA, Pedro M., 766
LARROQUE, Alberto, 95, 887
LARROQUE DE ROFFO, Helena, 141, 842
LARROSA, Santiago, 844, 1261
LARROSA, Virgilio, 1006
LARROUY, Pedro, 921
LARSEN, Juan Mariano, 79, 240
LARSEN, Mariano, 319
LARTIGAU LESPADA, Honorio, 751
LAS HERAS, Juan Gualberto Gregorio de, 78, 104, 110,
        166, 212, 244, 282, 386, 404, 420, 453, 462,
        475, 521, 529, 553, 574, 611
LASAGNA, Luis, 952, 1039
LASALA, Angel, 865, 882, 883
LASALA, Cándido de, 12, 14, 17a, 1223
LASALA, Francisco, 1223
LASALA, Gerónimo de, 496
LASALA, Indalecia de, 1223
LASALA, Juan Bautista, 1223
LASALA, María Mercedes de
        see LASALA DE RIGLOS, María Mercedes de
LASALA, Martín Casimiro de, 332
LASALA, Martín de, 1223
LASALA DE RIGLOS, María Mercedes de, 254, 422, 924,
        1223
LASALLE, Emile, 28
LASANSKY, Bernardo, 41
LASCANO, Juan, 60
LASCANO TEGUI, Emilio (VIZCONDE DE LASCANO TEGUI),
        751, 773

LASCANO TEGUI, Vizconde de
        see LASCANO TEGUI, Emilio
LASCANO Y CASTILLO, Benito, 910
LASCARAY, Ileana, 810
LASCIO, Pedro di
        see DI LASCIO, Pedro
LASCURAIN, Antonio, 923
LASPIUR, Saturnino Manuel de, 283
LASPIUR, Saturnino María, 173
LASPLACES, Alberto, 1145, 1170, 1171, 1199
LASSALLE, Anita, 893
LASSERRE, Augusto, 14, 68, 99
LAST REASON, pseud.
        see SÁENZ, Máximo Teodoro
LASTARRÍA, José Victorino, 254
LASTARRÍA, Miguel, 1236
LASTIRI, Raúl, 213
LASTRA, Bonifacio, 744
LASTRA, Esmeralda Salomé, 810
LASTRA, Héctor, 829
LASTRA, Juan Julián, 735
LASTRA, María Elena T. de, 810
LASTRA CASTRO, Ramón, 959
LASTRA Y GORDILLO, Rosendo de la, 910
LASZEZAK, Alberto, 299
LATALLADA DE VICTORIA, Rita, 135
LATINO, Aníbal, pseud.
        see CEPPI, José
LATORRE, 1058
LATORRE, Andrés, 1081, 1082
LATORRE, Antonio, 371
LATORRE, Carlos, 658, 672, 716, 717, 739, 759, 857d
LATORRE, Carlos Oscar, 923
LATORRE, Lorenzo, 1079, 1081, 1091, 1109, 1129
LATORRE ALZOGARAY, Demetrio, 1082
LATORRE ALZOGARAY, Diógenes Floro, 1082
LATORRE ALZOGARAY, Eloísa Adelina, 1082
LATORRE ALZOGARAY, Gabino, 1082
LATORRE ALZOGARAY, Reinaldo, 1082
LATORRE ALZOGARAY, Rosaura Carolina, 1082
LATORRE DE NAVAJAS, Alcira, 1082
LATORRE MANSILLA, Andrea Isibonia, 1082
LATORRE MANSILLA, Eugenia Servanda, 1082
LATORRE MANSILLA, Leopoldo, 1082
LATORRE MANSILLA, María Josefa, 1082
LATORRE MANSILLA, Maura, 1082
LATORRE MANSILLA, Nicolasa Tolentina, 1082
LATORRE OJEDA, Eustaquia Amelia, 1082
LATORRE PIETAS, Andrés, 1082
LATORRE PIETAS, Claudio Gregorio, 1082
LATZINA, Francisco, 293
LAUREIRO TRINIDAD, Eusebio Alejandro, 1210
LAURENCENA, Eduardo, 95, 135, 194, 241
LAURENCENA, Miguel, 565
LAURENCENA, Miguel María, 95, 121, 135, 241, 279
LAURENS, Abel, 18, 19, 31
LAURINO, Juan Armando, 954
LAURRAURI, Juanita, 879
LAUTRÉAMONT, pseud.
        see DUCASSE, Isidore Lucien
LAUXAR, pseud.
        see CRISPO ACOSTA, Osvaldo
LAVAGNA, Girolamo
        see LAVAGNA DI SAVONA, Girolamo
LAVAGNA, Jerónimo, 258, 921
LAVAGNA DI SAVONA, Girolamo, 98, 292
LAVAGNINO, Carlos Juan, 923
LAVAISSE, Benjamín J.
        see LAVAYSSE, Benjamín José
LAVALLE, Francisco, 332
LAVALLE, Haydée, 299

LAVALLE, Juan Galo de, 70, 78, 85, 95, 104, 121, 127, 143, 166, 212, 228, 278, 282, 283, 382, 386, 404, 420, 433, 442, 448, 449, 459, 472, 475, 478, 499, 521, 528, 529, 531, 545, 568, 569, 593, 600, 616, 1058
LAVALLE, Manuel José de, 228
LAVALLE, Ricardo, 240
LAVALLE BODEGA, Simón, 258
LAVALLE COBO, Jorge, 834
LAVALLE DE LAVALLE, Dolores, 924
LAVALLE Y CORTÉS, Manuel José de, 496
LAVALLEJA (family), 1108
LAVALLEJA, Juan Antonio, 166, 244, 433, 529, 1052, 1053, 1060, 1063, 1076, 1079, 1082, 1091, 1109, 1110, 1111, 1114, 1118, 1131, 1132, 1134
LAVALLEJA, Manuel, pseud.
    see ROMERO, Francisco
LAVALLER, Jorge, 860
LAVANDEIRA, Francisco, 1134
LAVARDÉN, Manuel José de, 404, 491, 588, 677, 683, 734, 737, 754, 803, 807, 828, 890, 1247, 1257
LAVARELLO, José, 258
LAVARELLO, Juan Bautista, 258
LAVAYSSE, Benjamín José, 261, 264, 615, 634, 921
LAVECCHIA, Rafael, 860
LAVIÉ, Enrique, 664
LAVIUZZA, Juana, 320
LAYERA, Juan, 207
LÁZARO, Félix Alberto, 655
LÁZARO, Guillermo, 299
LAZCANO, Benito, 545a
LAZCANO COLODRERO, Godofredo, 817
LAZIAR, José de, 555
LAZZARI, Carolina Emma, 923
LAZZARI, Juana Raquel, 320
LE BEAUD, Edmond, 59
LE CAVOZZIN, Julia Francisca, 949
LE PARC, Julio, 19, 46, 49, 55
LE PERA, Alfredo, 871
LE PREDOUR, José, 581
LEAL, José E., 198
LEAL, Ruth, 874
LEAL DE AYALA, Mateo, 125, 521
LEANES, María Esther, 44
LEANZA, Armando F., 521, 923
LEANZA, José, 312
LEARTE, Estanislao, 244
LEBEAUD, Edmond, 28
LEBET, Paul, 1216a
LEBLANC, Luis Francisco Juan, 581
LEBRATO, Olegario, 1089
LEBRERO, Manuel, 258
LEBRÓN, Alonso, 1034
LEBRÓN BOETTNER, Juan Carlos, 963a
LECOCO, Bernardo, 332
LECOCQ, Bernardo
    see LECOCQ ONESY, Bernardo
LECOCQ ONESY, Bernardo, 7, 284, 332, 496, 922, 1095
LECOR, Carlos Federico de, 95, 552, 1079, 1091
LEDESMA, Amanda, pseud. (RUBIALES, Josefina), 879, 932
LEDESMA, Carmen, 137
LEDESMA, Inda, 889
LEDESMA, José Fabián, 254
LEDESMA, Manuel Antonio, 1081
LEDESMA, Máximo, 181
LEDESMA, Nestor René, 923
LEDESMA, Roberto, 235, 678, 722, 729, 739, 751, 759, 773, 833
LEDESMA, Santiago E., 775
LEDESMA, Valentín, 878
LEDESMA VALDERRAMA, Martín de, 984, 1011

LEDINICH, Elena Julia, 320
LEGAL, José Tomás, 959
LEGAL, Virgilio, Ramón, 947
LEGAL Y CÓRDOBA, Joaquín, 196
LEGARRA, Francisco, 328
LEGARRETA, Antonio, 55
LEGASPI CARRARA DE ARISMENDI, Alcira, 1210
LEGENDRE, Marcel, 949
LEGIDO, Juan Carlos, 1151, 1172, 1185
LEGNAME, Santos, 31
LEGOUT, Raúl, 324
LEGRAND, Diego, 1207
LEGRAND, Mirthoe, 858
LEGUÍA, Jorge, 878
LEGUIZA, Daniel I., 385
LEGUIZAMO, Antonio, 186
LEGUIZAMO, Gregorio, 914
LEGUIZAMO, Juan de, 914
LEGUIZAMÓN, Delfín, 189
LEGUIZAMÓN, Gonzalo, 521
LEGUIZAMÓN, Guillermo, 904
LEGUIZAMÓN, Gustavo, 653, 654
LEGUIZAMÓN, José, 1059, 1111
LEGUIZAMÓN, Martiniano P., 78, 135, 167, 688, 779, 890, 1243, 1246, 1247, 1249, 1254
LEGUIZAMÓN, Onésimo, 95, 121, 330
LEGUIZAMÓN PONDAL, Gonzalo, 21, 64
LEGUIZAMÓN PONDAL, Martiniano, 135
LEHMANN, Guillermo, 87, 565
LEHMANN, Marta, 46
LEHMANN, Rodolfo B., 477
LEHMANN NITSCHE, Robert, 688
LEIBNER LAW, Jacobo Herman, 1210
LEIBNER LAW MEYER, León, 1210
LEIBNER ZINGER, Jaime, 1210
LEIBOFF, Roberto Oscar, 923
LEIBOWICZ, David, 198
LEIDHOLD, Clemente, 923
LEIRO DE RODRÍGUEZ, René, 320
LEISERSON, Manuel Héctor, 923
LEITE, Juan José, 845
LEITES, Pedro R., 384
LEITH, Rubén, 998
LEIVA, Angel, 791
LEIVA, Ignacio, 895
LEIVA, Julián de, 126, 177, 272, 496, 517, 542, 588
LEIVA, Luciano, 477
LEIVA, Manuel, 95, 634
LEIVA, Nicolás de, 914
LEJEUNE, Gilbert, 960
LELOIR, Luis F., 923
LELONG, Alberto L. M., 923
LELLIS, Mario Jorge de, 739, 759, 801, 812
LEMA, Abel Osvaldo, 663
LEMA, Roque, 1089
LEMA CALVO, José, 1089
LEMAIRE, Philippe (LEMMER), 32, 922, 949, 960
LEMBERG, Abraham, 923
LEMER, Felipe
    see LEMAIRE, Philippe
LEMMER
    see LEMAIRE, Philippe
LEMOINE, Teresa, 227
LEMOS, Abraham, 207, 208
LEMOS, Francisco Antonio, 1056, 1095
LEMOS, Gaspar de, 556
LEMOS, Julio, 207
LEMOS BARROCO, Domingo de, 555
LEMOS BARROCO, Juan de, 555
LEMOS MALDONADO, César, 998
LENCE, José Ramón, 284, 643

LENCI, Carlos César, 1145
LENCINA, Horacio José, 837
LENCINAS, Aníbal, 190
LENCINAS, Carlos Washington, 69, 198, 252, 429
LENCINAS, José Néstor, 69, 198, 252, 429
LENGUAS, Pedro, 254
LENGUAS, Luis Pedro, 1065
LENOIR DE KLAPPENBACH, Sofía, 930
LENOIR DE NAVARRO, Victorina, 930
LENS VIERA, Enrique, 284
LENZI, Carlos César, 871, 894, 1172, 1185
LENZI, Carlos Eduardo, 1075
LEÓN, Angel de, 1075
LEÓN, Bernardo de, 32
LEÓN, Eusebio F. de, 1083
LEÓN, Felipe Santiago, 995a
LEÓN, Jacinto de, 1083
LEÓN, Juan de, 895
LEÓN, Pedro de, 1270
LEÓN, Sebastián de, 845, 949, 989
LEÓN, Thomas de, 186
LEÓN PINELO, Antonio Rodríguez de, 244, 646, 885, 895
LEÓN PINELO, Diego de, 895, 1219
LEÓN Y GARABITO, Andrés de
    see GARAVITO DE LEÓN, Andrés
LEÓN Y GARABITO, Hernando de
    see GARAVITO DE LEÓN, Hernando de
LEÓN Y ZÁRATE, Sebastián de, 984, 1011
LEONARDI HERRÁN, Teresa, 653
LEONARDIS, Rosario F. Julio, 923
LEONARDO, Chita de, 762
LEONE, Juan, 4
LEOPARDO, Antonio, 923
LEPPER, James, 853a
LEPRO, Alfredo, 1168
LERANGE ALBAMONTE, Catalina, 786
LERENA, Carlos A., 1112
LERENA ACEVEDO, Andrés Héctor, 1145, 1165, 1179, 1187
LERENA JUANICÓ, Julio, 1064, 1174, 1259
LERIGET, Enriqueta, 1223
LERMA, Hernando de, 417, 456, 521, 522, 527, 906, 1270
LERMA Y VALLADARES, Hernando de, 649a
LERMAN, Juan Carlos, 923
LÉRTORA, Pascual, 328
LESCANO, Domingo, 254
LESCANO, Humberto, 684
LESCANO, Ignacio, 914
LESCANO CEBALLOS, Edelmiro, 24
LESCANO DE PODETTI, Amelia, 222
LESCOVICH, Néstor, 857c
LESING, Mario, 836
LESME, Juan Ramón, 998
LESTANI, Emilio, 152a
LESTANI, Juan Ramón, 191
LESTARD, Gastón H., 735
LETAMENDI, Francisco Antonio de, 496
LETOILE DE FREIXA, Margarita, 320
LETTEN, Gerardo, 32
LEUMANN, Carlos Alberto, 235, 669, 688, 751, 773, 1251
LEUMONIER, Carlos, 998
LEUNDA MOYA, Eduardo, 700
LEVA, Ercilis, 810
LEVALLE, Nicolás, 11a, 17b, 68, 166, 258, 617
LEVANTINI, Albino, 68
LEVCHUK, Gregorio, 860
LEVENE, Carlos A., 923

LEVENE, Ricardo, 609, 893
LÉVERA, Arnaldo, 995
LEVERGER, Auguste, 949
LEVI, Beppo, 923
LEVI RUFINELLI, Carlos, 947
LEVIALDI, Andrea, 923
LEVILLIER, Roberto, 521, 609
LEVIN, Enrique, 923
LEVINGSTON, Roberto Marcelo, 81, 515, 590
LEVINSON, Luisa Mercedes, 729, 822
LEVITCHARSKY STOYANOVA, Miguel, 1210
LEVRINO, Claudio, 857d
LEVY, Regina, 923
LEVY DE CATÁN, Alba, 1088
LEWIN, Boleslao, 609
LEWIS, Juan T., 923
LEYES, Antonio de, 186
LEYES, José Félix, 92
LEYES DE CHAVES, María Concepción, 943, 966, 1020, 1021, 1022
LEZAMA, Arturo, 1073
LEZAMA, Jorge Edgardo, 19, 31
LEZAMA, José Gregorio, 96, 156
LEZAMA, Julio B., 189
LEZAMA BENECHI, Marcio Andrés Florentino, 1210
LEZCANO, Braulio, 998
LEZCANO, Juan Inocencio, 943, 966
LEZICA, Carlos, 59, 268
LEZICA, Juan Antonio, 611
LEZICA, Juan José de
    see LEZICA TORREZURI Y ALQUIZA, Juan José de
LEZICA, Tomás Antonio, 611
LEZICA TORREZURI Y ALQUIZA, Juan José de, 32, 134, 272, 478, 496
LEZICA Y ALGUIZ, Juan de, 32
LEZICA Y ORTEGA, José Pastor de, 496
LEZICA Y OZAMIS, Ambrosio de, 496
LEZICA Y OZAMIS, Andrés, 496
LEZICA Y OZAMIS, Ramón, 496
LEZICA Y OZAMIS, Tomás Antonio, 496
LEZICA Y TORREZURI, Juan José de
    see LEZICA TORREZURI Y ALQUIZA, Juan José de
LEZNA, Stefano de, 292
LEZONA, Francisco, 68
L'HUILLIERS, Santiago, 222
LIACHO, Lázaro, 739
LIBARONA, Agustina Palacio de
    see PALACIO DE LIBARONA, Agustina
LIBERMAN, Arnoldo, 739
LIBERMAN, David, 923
LIBERTELLA RIESCO, Héctor, 776
LIBERTI, Tomás, 258
LICASTRO, Raúl, 860
LICHA, Antonio, 923
LICHIUS, Pedro Santiago, 883
LICHSTEININTEN DE BIRD, Leopoldina (BIRD, Poldy, pseud.), 135, 666, 764, 800, 822
LICHTENBERGER, Enrique C., 1216a
LIDDLE, Magdalén, 655, 656
LIEBBE, Pedro, 726
LIEBERMANN, José, 923
LIENDO (family), 352
LIFSCHITZ, Boris Alberto, 923
LIFSICHTZ, Clara, 739
LIGALUPPI, Oscar Abel, 663
LIKERMAN, Adolfo, 681
LILLIA, Adelaida Herminia, 320
LILLIA, Amanda Alcira, 320
LILLIA, María Angélica, 320
LIMA, Ataliva, 62

LIMA, Félix, 152a, 710, 727, 811, 813
LIMA QUINTANA, Hamlet, 790
LIMA Y MELO, Eusebio de, 555
LIMARZI, Eugenio, 258
LIMÓN, Richarte, 992
LINARES, Emma
    see LINARES DE LOS SANTOS, Emma
LINARES, Enrique, 923
LINARES, Ezequiel, 19
LINARES, José, 1089
LINARES, Julio, 655
LINARES DE LOS SANTOS, Emma, 652
LINARES FOWLIS, Calixto, 653, 654
LINARES QUINTANA, Carlos A., 781
LINARES Y ZANZETENEA, Matías, 910
LINCOVSKY, Cipe, 889
LINDEMANN, Hans A., 923
LINDMARK, Knut, 322
LINDQUIST, Juan Carlos, 923
LINENBERG, Abraham, 31
LINIERS, Jacques de, 960
LINIERS, Santiago de
    see LINIERS Y BREMOND, Santiago de
LINIERS Y BREMOND, Santiago de, 85, 104, 143, 166,
    185, 188, 240, 244, 283, 404, 406, 427, 443,
    448, 449, 451, 463, 466, 471, 472, 482, 502,
    517, 518, 519, 521, 528, 529, 552, 553, 563, 570,
    575, 587, 593, 1091, 1237, 1239, 1240, 1241
LINK, Norma E., 652
LINNIG, Samuel, 871
LINQUET, Carolina, 320
LINYERA, Dante A., pseud.
    see RÍMOLI, Francisco Bautista
LIOTTA, Domingo, 135
LIRIO, Dionisio, 994
LIRIO FERNÁNDEZ, Mario, 894
LISBOA, Juan, 954
LISTA, Julio Alberto, 1167, 1243
LISTA, Pedro Ramón, 268
LISTA, Ramón, 152, 191, 287, 288, 611
LISTA SUÁREZ, Andrés, 284
LISTA Y SEÑORA, José, 1089
LITVAK, José, 923
LIVI, José, 1084, 1086
LIX KLETT, Carlos, 68
LIX KLETT, Luis, 332
LIZARÁN, Fernando, 332
LIZARDI, Julián de, 989, 1267
LIZÁRRAGA, Reginaldo de (OBANDO, Baltasar), 283,
    609, 683, 713, 754, 761, 910, 985, 1041, 1230
LIZAUR, José Agustín de, 496
LIZER Y TRELLES, Carlos A., 923
LIZONDO BORDA, Manuel, 521, 664, 679
LOBB, Sarah Eleanor, 323
LOBO, Armando Aníbal, 923
LOBO, José Arnaldo, 653
LOBO, Rodolfo S., 923
LOBO DE LA VEGA, Luis Alberto, 18, 31
LOBO SARMIENTO, Antonio, 186
LOBO Y MALAGAMBA, Miguel, 1235
LOBODÓN GARRA, pseud.
    see JUSTO, Liborio
LOBOS, Eleodoro, 81, 141, 222, 644
LOCKHART, Beatriz
    see LOCKHART GENTA, Beatriz
LOCKHART, Washington, 1177, 1184
LOCKHART GENTA, Beatriz, 1206, 1207
LOCOCO, Clemente, 857d
LODEIRO, Ramón, 1089
LODI, Emilio, 860

LOEB, M. Isidore, 255
LOEDEL PALUMBO, Enrique, 923
LOEWENTHAL, Oscar, 904
LOEWENTHAL, Wilhelm, 255, 258a
LOFEUDO, Pedro (TOTO, pseud.), 860
LOFRUSCIO, Silvio, 963a
LOGARZO, Pedro, 29
LOGONES, Nelly, 299
LOIS, Ricardo J., 652
LOIZAGA, Carlos, 991
LOIZAGA, Elva de, 717, 725, 739
LOIZAGA, Niceto S., 1167
LOIZAGA CABALLERO, Néstor, 954
LOLIE, Santiago (LOLIO), 949
LOLIEU, Jacques, 960
LOLIO
    see LOLIE, Santiago
LOMBARDERO, Aldo, 560
LOMBARDERO, Horacio, 560
LOMBARDI, Angel, 860
LOMBARDI, Aquiles, 860
LOMBARDI, Chino, 860
LOMBARDI, Domingo Vicente, 217
LOMBARDI, Horacio, 860
LOMBARDI, Juan, 952
LOMBARDI, Oscar (PIRUNCHO, pseud.), 860
LOMBARDO, Rubén, 787
LOMELLO, Arturo, 824
LOMEZ, Esteban, 148
LOMUTO, Francisco J., 871
LONARDI, Eduardo, 428, 515, 516
LONCÁN, Enrique (AMERICUS, pseud.), 1245
LONCON, Theodore Jayeux de
    see JAYEUX DE LONCON, Theodore de
LONDRES, Albert, 152a
LONGA, Hugo, 1049
LONGCHAMP, Marcelin, 949
LONGHINI, Pedro, 332, 923
LONGO, Rafael Ernesto, 923
LONGO IGLESIA, Caroll, 1088
LOOS, Pablo A., 207
LOPERENA VERNET, German, 299
LOPÉRFIDO, Pedro, 860
LOPES DE SOUSA, Pedro, 627, 1238
LÓPEZ, Alejandro, 878
LÓPEZ, Angel, 189, 1089
LÓPEZ, Augusto, 244
LÓPEZ, Basilio Antonio, 943, 1034, 1035, 1041
LÓPEZ, Bernardino, 387
LÓPEZ, Cándido, 25, 51, 268, 521
LÓPEZ, Carlos Antonio, 96, 936, 942, 949, 954, 957,
    961, 963, 964, 969, 975, 976, 980, 983, 984,
    984a, 988, 997, 1004, 1010, 1011, 1012, 1020,
    1021, 1022, 1023, 1035
LÓPEZ, Cecilio, 68, 94
LÓPEZ, Cecilio S., 68
LÓPEZ, Cristóbal, 923
LÓPEZ, Chico
    see LÓPEZ, José
LÓPEZ, Domingo, 496
LÓPEZ, Emilio, 260
LÓPEZ, Estanislao, 95, 105, 106, 107, 166, 282, 283,
    373, 404, 446, 477, 489, 498, 499, 521, 531,
    545, 552, 553, 554, 568, 569, 632
LÓPEZ, Fermín, 947
LÓPEZ, Francisco, 1089
LÓPEZ, Francisco Alberto, 683a
LÓPEZ, Francisco Solano, 398, 466, 502, 936, 940,
    942, 943, 943a, 948, 949, 955, 963, 964, 966,
    974, 975, 976, 983, 984, 984a, 997, 1004, 1009
    1010, 1011, 1012, 1021, 1022, 1023, 1233

LÓPEZ, Gaspar, 254
LÓPEZ, Gregorio, 551a
LÓPEZ, Helio, 923
LÓPEZ, Herbert Raúl, 810
LÓPEZ, Ignacio, 878
LÓPEZ, Isidro Angel, 923
LÓPEZ, Javier, 189
LÓPEZ, José (LÓPEZ, Chico), 106, 196, 220, 319, 1089
LÓPEZ, José D., 998
LÓPEZ, José Félix, 998
LÓPEZ, José Francisco, 653, 654
LÓPEZ, José María, 371, 1089
LÓPEZ, José Victorio, 545a
LÓPEZ, Juan, 653, 654
LÓPEZ, Juan A., 922
LÓPEZ, Juan Manuel, 7, 32, 244
LÓPEZ, Juan María, 284
LÓPEZ, Juan Pablo, 95, 569, 584, 1247
LÓPEZ, Juan Pedro, 878, 1243
LÓPEZ, Julio A., 222
LÓPEZ, Lucio V., 847
LÓPEZ, Lucio Vicente, 152a, 153, 167, 236, 260,
    391, 478, 509, 572, 667, 708, 724, 751, 754,
    769, 774, 780, 1246
LÓPEZ, Luis, 910
LÓPEZ, Mabel, 691
LÓPEZ, Manuel, 89, 409, 545a, 1089
LÓPEZ, Mario Justo, 218
LÓPEZ, Plácido, 387
LÓPEZ, Ramón, 1089
LÓPEZ, Raúl, 652
LÓPEZ, Rodrigo de, 1270
LÓPEZ, Rubén Henry, 923
LÓPEZ, Tomás, 284
LÓPEZ, Venancio Víctor, 959, 1014, 1018, 1024
LÓPEZ, Vicente Fidel, 85, 112, 121, 141, 165, 166,
    176, 182, 192, 261, 283, 293, 379, 398, 404,
    407, 478, 509, 529, 553, 572, 594, 609, 611, 614,
    631, 692, 720, 734, 737, 747, 754, 761, 1261
LÓPEZ AIRAGHI, Antonio Carlos Oscar, 923
LÓPEZ ALDANA, Fernando, 629
LÓPEZ ANAYA, Fernando, 27, 49, 55, 63
LÓPEZ ARIAS, Marcelo Eduardo, 653
LÓPEZ ASPIROZ, Simón, 1093
LÓPEZ AUFRANC, Alcides, 213
LÓPEZ BENEDITO, Hernando, 254
LÓPEZ BENÍTEZ, Manuel, 1093
LÓPEZ BUCHARDO, Carlos, 154, 293, 864, 865, 867,
    881, 883
LÓPEZ BUCHARDO, Próspero, 64
LÓPEZ CABEZAS, Francisco, 344
LÓPEZ CABRERA, Ricardo, 24
LÓPEZ CAMELO, Diego, 186
LÓPEZ CAMELO, Juan Angel, 254
LÓPEZ CARVALHO, Juan, 1238
LÓPEZ CASTINEIRA, José M., 284
LÓPEZ CLARO, César, 18, 25, 31, 36
LÓPEZ COLOMBO DE ALLENDE, Inés, 923
LÓPEZ DE ESPINOSA, Manuel, 1041
LÓPEZ DE FILLIPPIS, César, 998
LÓPEZ DE GOMARA, Justo S., 643
LÓPEZ DE LEÓN PINELO, Diego, 126
LÓPEZ DE LISBOA, Diego, 1270
LÓPEZ DE MINGORANCE, Manuel, 751
LÓPEZ DE OSORNIO, Agustina
    see LÓPEZ OSORNIO DE ORTIZ DE ROSAS, Agustina
LÓPEZ DE RECALDE, Iñigo, 964
LÓPEZ DE ROMERO, Josefa, 320
LÓPEZ DE SALAZAR, Diego, 1035a, 1035b
LÓPEZ DE SALAZAR, José, 914

LÓPEZ DE SOLÍS, Luis, 910, 1041
LÓPEZ DE TARIFA, Pedro, 224
LÓPEZ DECOUD, Arsenio, 951, 959, 1012, 1021, 1022
LÓPEZ DEL VILLAR, José, 385
LÓPEZ DÍAZ, José, 1089
LÓPEZ ESCOBAR, Mario, 954
LÓPEZ FERNÁNDEZ, 845
LÓPEZ FERREIRA, Amaro, 1210
LÓPEZ FRETES, Gilberto, 998
LÓPEZ FRUGONI, Emilio, 207
LÓPEZ GALLARDO, Luis, 555
LÓPEZ GIMÉNEZ, Laureano, 1017
LÓPEZ GONZÁLEZ DE GUGGIARI, Carmen Petrona, 1017
LÓPEZ GRELA, Francisco, 65
LÓPEZ GUZMÁN, Tiburcio, 679
LÓPEZ IRIARTE, Antonio, 385
LÓPEZ ISASMENDI, Nicolás, 653, 654
LÓPEZ JORDÁN, Ricardo, 95, 96, 127, 135, 398, 478,
    533, 543, 623
LÓPEZ JORDÁN, Ricardo (son), 95
LÓPEZ LAGAR, Pedro, 893
LÓPEZ LORENZO, Manuel, 284
LÓPEZ MADERA, Miguel, 358
LÓPEZ MARTÍNEZ, Jesús, 1093
LÓPEZ MARTÍNEZ, José, 1094
LÓPEZ MERINO, Francisco, 521, 663, 678, 722, 739,
    751, 759, 773, 803, 805, 807, 833
LÓPEZ MERINO, Ismael Manuel, 702
LÓPEZ MOCTEZUMA, Carlos, 857d
LÓPEZ NAGUIL, Gregorio, 19, 31, 33, 44
LÓPEZ OSORIO, Robert, 860
LÓPEZ OSORNIO, César, 36
LÓPEZ OSORNIO, Mario A., 1246
LÓPEZ OSORNIO DE ORTIZ DE ROSAS, Agustina, 240, 538
LÓPEZ PASSARÓN, Clemente, 726
LÓPEZ PIACENTINI, Carlos Primo, 191
LÓPEZ QUINTELA, Emilio, 1089
LÓPEZ ROSAS, José Rafael, 837
LÓPEZ SERROT, E., 751
LÓPEZ SILBA, Juan, 32
LÓPEZ SILVEIRA, Juan José, 1210
LÓPEZ TORRES, A., 766
LÓPEZ URCOLA, Anita, 797
LÓPEZ VALERO, Pedro, 914
LÓPEZ WEIGEL, Manuel, 154
LÓPEZ Y PLANES, Vicente, 70, 72, 85, 121, 126, 145,
    145a, 166, 176, 212, 227, 228, 244, 282, 386,
    404, 411, 424, 475, 478, 479, 496, 509, 528,
    542, 572, 611, 669, 720, 723, 724, 737, 740,
    751, 754, 803, 807, 828, 876, 895, 1257
LÓPEZ YACARÉ, 1003
LÓPEZ ZENARRUZA, Oscar Miguel, 691
LÓPEZ ZIGARÁN, Ramón Abraham, 923
LORA, Joaquín, 13
LORE, Amalia R., 652
LOREA, Isidro, 7, 32
LOREA, Juan Isidro, 254
LORENTE, Severiano, 1246
LORENZANA, Maciel de, 968
LORENZATTI, Francisco, 87
LORENZO (brothers), 1089
LORENZO, Fernando, 683a, 717, 739, 758
LORENZO, Manuel, 1089
LORENZO, Vicente, 1089
LORENZO Y GAONA, Juan de (GAONA, Lorenzo), 949
LORENZO Y GONZÁLEZ, José, 284
LORENZO Y RODRÍGUEZ, Tirso, 284
LORETO, Marqués de
    see CAMPO, Nicolás Francisco Christoval, MARQUÉS
    DE LORETO

LORETO ACOSTA, Julián, 191
LORIA, Francisco, 7
LORUSSO, Arturo, 718, 890
LOS ARCOS VIDAURRETA, Jesús Daniel, 691
LOSADA, Oscar Alberto, 923
LOSADA GUIDO, Alejandro, 688
LOSANSKY, Mauricio, 24
LOTHRINGER, Esperanza, 154
LOTTI, José, 258
LOTTI, Mario Julio, 923
LOUDET, Enrique, 751
LOUDET, Lilí, 751
LOUDET, Osvaldo, 842
LOURTEIG, Alicia, 923
LOVERO, Onofre, 889
LOVISUTO, Angel Hermenegildo, 860
LOVISUTO, Mario, 860
LOVISUTO, Victorio, 860
LOWENHARD, Carlos, 238
LOWRY, Jorge H., 68
LOY, Fany, 879
LOYOLA, Cristóval de, 186
LOYOLA, Juan Francisco, 222
LOYOLA, Martín Ignacio de, 910, 960, 1034, 1035, 1041
LOZA, Mariano Y., 121
LOZA, Mario, 18, 19, 31
LOZA AGUERREBERE, Rubén, 1183, 1191
LOZADA, Lorenzo, 188
LOZANO, 1188
LOZANO, Clemente Sancho, 681
LOZANO, Eduardo, 652
LOZANO, Juan, 918
LOZANO, Pedro, 244, 283, 713, 761, 885, 943, 964, 966, 968, 985, 1012, 1021, 1022, 1230
LOZANO DE SARAVIA, Andrés, 186
LOZANO MOUJÁN, José María, 31
LOZOYA VILLAISOTO, Máximo Venancio, 1210
LOZZA, Raúl, 19, 31, 36
LOZZI, Jacinto, 860
LUACES LAMAS, José, 284
LUBERTINO, José, 923
LUBÍ, Antonio
    see LUVÍ, Antonio.
LUBLIN, Lea, 36
LUBOMIRSKY, Wadim Wladislao, 923
LUCA, Esteban
    see LUCA Y PATRÓN, Esteban
LUCA, Pablo Francisco de, 849
LUCA, Renato de, 652
LUCA DE TENA, Torcuato, 530
LUCA Y PATRÓN, Esteban de, 145, 177, 332, 404, 411, 475, 611, 669, 720, 723, 724, 733, 751, 754, 761, 807, 828, 885
LUCAS, Manuel Francisco, 1093
LUCAS, Rubén D., 1093
LUCENA, Francisco de, 204
LUCENA, José P., 844
LUCERA, José Cecilio Lucio, 222
LUCERO, 195
LUCERO, Benito Lucio, 599
LUCERO, Cecilio L., 159
LUCERO, Cornelio Lucio, 222
LUCERO, Diego, pseud.
    see SCIUTTO, Luis Alfredo
LUCERO, Diego Clemente, 283
LUCERO, Dolly María, 683a
LUCERO, Francisco Paula, 222
LUCERO, Franklin, 81
LUCERO, José Alejandro, 768

LUCERO, José Raúl, 81
LUCERO, Juan Carlos, 683a
LUCERO, Manuel, 189, 190, 244, 648, 649
LUCERO, Moisés, 207
LUCERO, Pablo, 158, 159, 179
LUCERO, Roberto César, 691
LUCERO, Rosa Isabel, 135, 800
LUCERO, Silvia E. N., 652
LUCERO, Víctor S., 222
LUCERO DE CONSIGLI, Estela Ruth, 222
LUCERO DE POMA, Gladys, 653, 654
LUCERO FUNES, Alberto, 81
LUCERO G., Miguel A., 652
LUCERO Y SOSA, José Rufino, 222
LUCIANI, Oscar, 663
LUCINI, Raúl F., 89
LUCIO, Nodier, 652
LUCIO LUCERO, Tomás, 222
LUCO, Valentín, 222
LUCUIX, Simón, 521
LUCHI, Luis, 759
LUDIN, Adolfo, 1079
LUÉ, Benito
    see LUÉ Y RIEGA, Benito
LUÉ Y RIEGA, Benito de, 427, 458, 496, 907, 910, 911, 917, 920
LUEA, Esteban de, 121
LUGO, Eusebio A., 959
LUGO CHILAVERT, Manuel, 998
LUGO Y NAVARRA, Pedro de, 984, 1011
LUGONES, Benigno B., 727, 813
LUGONES, Leopoldo, 72, 110, 133, 141, 152a, 167, 176, 185, 190, 235, 243, 246, 269, 282, 317, 558, 664, 669, 678, 685, 688, 709, 722, 723, 737, 739, 740, 742, 743, 748, 751, 754, 759, 773, 782, 803, 807, 817, 825, 835, 1243, 1247, 1259
LUGONES, Lorenzo, 611
LUGONES, Manuel A., 683a
LUGONES, Manuel G., 207
LUGONES, Rainerio J., 78, 921
LUIGGI, Alice Houston, 323
LUIGGI, Luis, 258, 332
LUIS, 1238
LUIS, Mario, pseud.
    see CARNELLI, María Luisa
LUIS, Pedro, 358
LUISI, Clotilde
    see LUISI DE PODESTÁ, Clotilde
LUISI, Luisa, 1079, 1083, 1144, 1145, 1187, 1217
LUISI, Paulina, 1083, 1217
LUISI DE PODESTÁ, Clotilde, 1083, 1187, 1217
LUJÁN DE MEDINA (family), 352
LUJÁN GUTIÉRREZ, Jorge de, 662
LUMALDO, Miguel Angel, 857c
LUMB, Carlos, 82
LUMB, Eduardo, 904
LUMLEY, William, 587
LUMURA, Jorge León, 299
LUNA, 568
LUNA, Adolfo V., 217, 882, 883
LUNA, Alcira Carmen (LUNA, Chola, pseud.), 860, 879, 1205, 1207
LUNA, Angel María, 1159
LUNA, Carmen
    see LUNA, Alcira Carmen
LUNA, Chola, pseud.
    see LUNA, Alcira Carmen
LUNA, Félix César, 381a, 431, 609
LUNA, Francisco, 1093a

LUNA, Francisco Pantaleón de, 188
LUNA, José Ramón, 217, 664, 1243, 1248
LUNA, Juan Pedro, 611
LUNA, Justo P., 385
LUNA, Luis de, 520
LUNA, Marcelo, 787
LUNA, Pancho, 878
LUNA, Pelagio B., 247, 565
LUNA ERCILLA, Jorge Guillermo, 41
LUNGHI, Elena, 698
LUPI, Omar Rufino, 860
LUQUE, 195
LUQUE, David, 244, 921
LUQUE, Mateo, 79, 244
LUQUE, Virginia, 879
LUQUE DE NÚÑEZ, Luisa, 268
LUQUE Y LUQUE, Emilio Fausto, 37
LUQUEZ, Celia E., 683a
LUQUEZ, Pastor Aluizio, 923
LUQUI, Oscar Américo, 923
LURO (family), 361, 362
LURO, José, 68
LURO, Pedro O., 94, 156
LUSARRETA, Pilar de, 815, 817, 521
LUSIARDO DE DE LEÓN, Marisa, 1217
LUSNICH, Luis, 31
LUSSICH, Antonio Dionisio, 1079, 1166, 1167, 1177,
    1187, 1242, 1243, 1244, 1247, 1257
LUSSICH, Arturo, 1122
LUSSICH, Juan, 254
LUSTMAN, José, 923
LUTINGER MARROCCO, Carlos Alberto, 1210
LUVÍ (LUBÍ), Antonio, 73
LUZ, Aída, 879
LUZ, Alma, pseud.
    see BENÍTEZ CAPURRO, Alba Luz
LUZATTI, Arturo
    see LUZZATTI, Arturo
LUZURIAGA, José de, 496
LUZURIAGA, Toribio de, 179, 188, 196, 212, 222, 283,
    412, 478, 562, 611
LUZZATTI, Arturo, 865, 882, 883
LUZZATTO, Julio César, 653, 654
LYNCH, Alice
    see LYNCH, Elisa Alicia
LYNCH, Benito, 17a, 167, 670, 674, 686, 745a, 751,
    779, 814, 834, 1245, 1246, 1249, 1251, 1254,
    1260
LYNCH, Elisa Alicia, 466, 943a, 949, 960, 961, 974,
    976, 983, 1012
LYNCH, Francisco, 254
LYNCH, Justo Máximo, 25, 31
LYNCH, Justo Pastor, 496
LYNCH, Manuel, 120
LYNCH, Marta, 140, 666, 696, 757, 822
LYNCH, Patrick, 2
LYNCH, Tomás Francisco, 332
LYNCH, Ventura Robusitano, 59, 688, 1243, 1244,
    1246, 1247
LYNCH ARRIBÁLZAGA, Enrique, 191

LLAC ESTEVE Y., Gerardo, 496
LLACER, Alberto Joaquín, 923
LLADÓ, Narciso, 1094
LLAMBÍ (family), 1108
LLAMBÍ, Francisco, 1093a
LLAMBÍAS, Joaquín, 103
LLAMBÍAS DE AZEVEDO, Juan, 1184
LLAMOSAS, Isabel, 956
LLANA Y BARRENECHEA, Tomás de la, 555

LLANAS, Ramón de las, 964, 989
LLANDERAS, Nicolás de las, 284, 676
LLANES, Ricardo M., 660, 681
LLANO, Francisco Luis, 644a
LLANO, Juan de, 496
LLANO, Raúl Jorge, 923
LLANO INSÚA, José de, 284
LLANO ZAPATA, José Eusebio, 885, 895, 922
LLANOS, Augusto César, 923
LLANOS, Benito, 1246
LLERENA, Baldomero, 68, 222
LLERENA, Juan, 159, 167, 207, 222, 634
LLETI, Concepción Ventura, 702
LLINÁS, Julio Antonio, 658, 759, 798, 832
LLOBET, A. F., 94
LLOBET, Andrés, 844
LLOBET, Andrés F., 268
LLOBET, Francisco, 268
LLOBET, Mariano, 320
LLORENS RIGI, Nicolás José, 344
LLORENTE DE KARIS, Felisa Asunción, 320
LLOVERAS, Santiago, 173, 188

MAAS, Luis Carlos, 963a
MABRES, Valentín, 316
MAC CARTHY, A., 878
MAC-EACHEN (family), 1108
MAC-EACHEN, Eduardo, 1075
MAC ENTIRE, Eduardo A., 19, 36, 38, 46, 55
MACAGNO, Enzo Oscar, 923
MACAIRE, Adriana Paulina, 32, 293
MACAYA, Luis, 33
MACCANN, Guillermo, 834
MACCIO, Rómulo, 19, 25, 36, 38, 49, 55
MACEDO, César, 560
MACEDO, Valentín R., 1167
MACELA, Francisco Xavier, 496
MACETA, Simón, 989
MACGAW, Roberto, 6
MACÍA, Salvador, 95, 135, 160, 194, 241
MACIEL (family), 1106, 1224
MACIEL, Antonio, 69
MACIEL, Baltasar, 334
MACIEL, Carlos, 334
MACIEL, Casimiro Aureliano, 312
MACIEL, Domingo, 334
MACIEL, Enrique, 862
MACIEL, Francisco Antonio, 334, 844, 1052, 1053,
    1063, 1076, 1203
MACIEL, Joaquín, 334
MACIEL, Juan, 32
MACIEL, Juan Baltasar
    see MAZIEL, Juan Baltasar
MACIEL, Juan Bautista, 763
MACIEL, Juan Manuel, 334
MACIEL, Manuel, 334
MACIEL, Melchor, 223, 334
MACIEL, Miguel Elías (SULIVA, Gregorio, pseud.), 135
MACIEL, Patricio, 377, 990
MACIEL, Santiago, 834, 1146, 1167, 1174, 1188, 1196,
    1246
MACIEL DEL ÁGUILA (family), 1224
MACIEL DEL ÁGUILA, Francisco, 334
MACIEL DEL ÁGUILA, Juan, 334
MACIEL DEL ÁGUILA, Luis, 334
MACIONI, Antonio, 292
MACKAU, Armand René de, 581
MACKINLAY ZAPIOLA, Matías, 68
MACLEAN, Archibaldo, 580
MACLEAN, Juan Samuel, 191

MACOLA, Berardo, 923
MACCHI, Aurelio, 19, 25, 35, 49, 63
MACHADO, Alberto José, 822
MACHADO, Elba Alicia, 691
MACHADO, Emilio A. María, 923
MACHADO, Héctor Hugo, 923
MACHADO, Hugo, 44
MACHADO, José Olegario, 649
MACHADO, Lorenzo, 496
MACHADO, Lucas, 186
MACHADO, Mathías, 186
MACHADO, Ofelia
    see MACHADO DE BENVENUTO, Ofelia
MACHADO, Raúl Víctor, 46
MACHADO, Rosa, 653
MACHADO, Rubén, 299
MACHADO, Thomas, 186
MACHADO DE BENVENUTO, Ofelia, 1187, 1217
MACHAIN, Facundo, 964, 966, 984a, 986, 991, 1012
MACHAIN, Ildefonso, 32
MACHAIN, Joaquina, 1042
MACHAIN, Serapio, 991
MACHINANDIARENA, Narciso, 857c
MACHONI, Antonio, 319, 952, 989, 1267
MACHUCA, 975
MADALENA, Eugenio, 1127
MADARIAGA, Francisco José, 658, 672, 716, 717, 739, 758, 759, 798
MADARIAGA, Joaquín, 93, 95, 164, 196, 539, 611
MADARIAGA, José, 878
MADARIAGA, José Joaquín Gregorio, 121
MADARIAGA, José Miguel, 268
MADARIAGA, Juan, 95, 387, 568, 611, 650
MADARIAGA, Luis B., 268
MADARIAGA, Salvador de, 729
MADERA, Antonio Francisco, 186
MADERA, Juan, 844
MADERNA, Osmar, 861
MADERO, Eduardo, 141
MADERO, Francisco B., 166
MADERO, Juan Nepomuceno, 478
MADOERY (family), 168
MADOERY DE MORENO, Mercedes Beatriz, 684
MADORNO, Olga Lidia (MICHÈLE, pseud.), 691
MADRID, Enrique de, 332
MADRYN, Jones Perry, 202
MAEDER, Ernesto Joaquín A., 191
MAENDI, Marcelo, 977
MAESE, Andrés, 1203
MAESE, Bernal, 845
MAESE, Miguel, 1238
MAESO, Carlos María (TORRES, Máximo, pseud.), 1075, 1146, 1170, 1187, 1188
MAESO TOGNOCHI, Carlos, 1153
MAESTRE ANTONIO
    see ANTONIO
MAESTRE BLAS
    see BLAS
MAESTRE DAXA
    see DAXA
MAESTRE IGNACIO
    see IGNACIO
MAESTRE JAQUES
    see JAQUES
MAESTRE JUAN
    see JUAN
MAESTRE LUIS
    see LUIS
MAESTRE MIGUEL
    see MIGUEL
MAESTRE PEDRO
    see PEDRO

MAFFIA, Pedro, 875, 891a
MAFFIODO, Miguel A., 954
MAFFROLO, Matteo, 292
MAFUD, Julio, 688, 743
MAGALDI, Agustín, 877
MAGALHÃES, Fernão de, 202, 287, 406, 443, 455, 462, 471, 472, 1238
MAGALHAES, Olinto, 844
MAGALLANES, Antolín, 222
MAGALLANES, Fernando de
    see MAGALHÃES, Fernão de
MAGALLANES, Hernando de
    see MAGALHÃES, Fernão de
MAGALLANES, Juan Mario, 1159, 1168, 1170, 1196
MAGALLANES, Juan V., 1075
MAGALLANES, Vicente, 1075
MAGAÑA, Angel, 858
MAGARIÑOS (family), 1108
MAGARIÑOS, Alejandro
    see MAGARIÑOS CERVANTES, Alejandro
MAGARIÑOS, Francisco, 1063
MAGARIÑOS, Manuel, 1089, 1095
MAGARIÑOS, Víctor
    see MAGARIÑOS D., Víctor
MAGARIÑOS CERVANTES, Alejandro, 1064, 1079, 1086, 1146, 1154, 1165, 1167, 1174, 1179, 1187, 1188, 1199, 1253
MAGARIÑOS D., Víctor, 31, 36
MAGARIÑOS PINTO, Ofelia, 766
MAGARIÑOS SOLSONA, Mateo, 1177, 1190, 1197, 1199
MAGARIÑOS VEYRA, Juan A., 1125
MAGDA, Frank, 19
MAGDALENA, Eugenio, 1075
MAGEE, Eduardo, 137
MAGGI, Carlos, 1149, 1172, 1177, 1184, 1185
MAGGI, Carlos Alberto, 684
MAGGI, Luis, 87
MAGGI, María Luz, 785
MAGGI, Tito, 689, 730
MAGGIORINI, Conrado, 73
MAGISTRETTI, Guillermo, 923
MAGLIA, Juan B., 1123
MAGLIO, Juan (PACHO, pseud.), 868
MAGNANI, Mario J., 923
MAGNANI, Martha, 37
MAGNASCO, Benedicto, 258
MAGNASCO, Osvaldo, 68, 121, 128, 157, 160, 650
MAGRI, Valeriano, 1164
MAGRINI, Adolfo Buenaventura, 998
MAGRINI, César, 739, 807
MAGUNA, Bartolomé Francisco de, 885
MAGUNA, Martín de, 555
MAGUNA, Pedro, 1093
MAGUNA, Rosario, 1093a
MAGYAR, Ladislao, 299
MAHIEU, Roma, 889
MAIA, Circe, 1149, 1151, 1152, 1178
MAIDANA, Waldemar J. Pedro, 923
MAIDANO ARIAS, Luis, 947
MAIER, Carlos G., 652
MAIER, Cristián, 850
MAILHE, Alejandra Marta, 691
MAIMUS, Agustín, 1092
MAINARDI, Guadencio, 87
MAINERO, Lía, 1211
MAISLER, Martín, 857a
MAISSA, Pedro Abel, 923
MAÍZ, Fidel, 943, 974, 995a, 1012, 1021, 1022, 1023, 1035, 1041
MAÍZ, Francisco Ignacio, 995a
MAÍZ, Marco Antonio, 1035, 1041
MAIZANI, Azucena, 868, 877, 879, 892

MAIZTEGUI, Alberto Pascual, 923
MAIZTEGUI, Isidro B., 882, 883
MAJAVACCA, José, 952
MAJESTÉ, Francisco, 319, 921
MALABIA, José Severo Feliciano, 126, 439, 457, 526,
   611, 621, 626
MALACODA, pseud.
     see NÚÑEZ Y MALACODA, Ramiro
MALAGUEÑITA, La, pseud.
     see HURTADO, Encarnación
MALANCA, José, 19, 24, 31
MALARÍN, Miguel P., 94
MALASPINA, Alejandro, 17a, 258, 287, 292, 579, 922
MALAVER, Antonio E., 6, 166, 544, 586
MALBAR Y PINTO, Sebastián de
     see MALVAR Y PINTO, Sebastián Jerónimo de
MALBRÁN (family), 352
MALBRÁN, Carlos, 68, 94, 844
MALBRÁN, José M., 3
MALBRÁN, Manuel Francisco, 126
MALBRÁN, Néstor D., 663
MALDONADA, 989
MALDONADO (family), 352
MALDONADO, Alberto, 1116
MALDONADO, Horacio, 1079, 1083, 1190
MALDONADO, Juan, 965
MALDONADO, Lorenzo, 520
MALDONADO, Luis, 222
MALDONADO, Mariano, 68
MALDONADO, Máximo, 219
MALDONADO, Melchor
     see MALDONADO Y SAAVEDRA, Melchor
MALDONADO, Tomás, 19, 25, 31, 36
MALDONADO CARULLA, Oscar, 760
MALDONADO DE LA CERDA, Ambrosio, 914
MALDONADO DE SAAVEDRA, Melchor
     see MALDONADO Y SAAVEDRA, Melchor
MALDONADO DE SILVA, Francisco, 1219, 1270
MALDONADO EL ZAMORANO, 1270
MALDONADO Y SAAVEDRA, Melchor, 244, 529a, 649a, 910,
   913
MALES, Branimiro, 923
MALET, Armando, 1123
MALFATTI, Arnaldo, 675, 676
MALHARRO, Martín A., 18, 19, 25, 31, 33, 45, 51, 56,
   317, 521, 1218
MALHARRO, Victorina, 478, 929
MALINOW, Inés, 717, 725, 739, 748
MALINOW, Manuel René, 923
MALINVERNO, Atilio, 19, 31
MALMEN, Carlos, 332
MALMIERCA CANÉ, Luis
     see CANÉ, Luis
MALNATTI, César (CHOLO, pseud.), 860
MALSE, Miguel, 1238
MALVAR Y PINTO, Sebastián Jerónimo de, 32, 279, 284,
   907, 910, 911, 917, 920
MALVIGNE, Pedro César, 663
MALVINO, Herminio, 24
MALLEA, Eduardo, 152a, 235, 670, 674, 712, 715, 729,
   737, 742, 743, 745a, 751, 765, 825, 834, 835,
   1245, 1252
MALLEA, Juan Eugenio de, 283, 556
MALLEA, Vicente C., 173
MALLMANN, Carlos Alberto, 923
MALLO, Pedro, 192, 718, 844, 847, 1261
MALLO, Roberto G., 923
MALLOL, Emilio, 923
MALLORQUÍN, Juan L., 959
MANCEDO, César, 560
MANCERA, Nicolás, 299

MANCINI, Herminia, 893
MANCINI, Roberto E., 923
MANCINO, Vicente, 69
MANCO, Silverio, 727, 811, 813, 878
MANCUSO, Domingo, 191
MANCHA Y VELAZCO, Cristóbal de la, 907, 910, 911,
   920
MANDL, Fritz, 437
MANDOLINI, Hermani, 102, 681
MANDÓN, Hugo, 824
MANDRESSI OLIVIERE, Eduardo, 1210
MANELLI DE DIBASON, Ilda Mariana, 320
MANERO, Angélica, 793
MANFRINI RODRÍGUEZ, Herman Raúl, 1210
MANGANIELLO, Cristina, 37
MANGORÉ, 977
MANGUDO, Francisco de Paula, 344
MANINI, Alice, 652
MANINI RÍOS, Pedro, 1073, 1083, 1190
MANN, Mary (Mrs. Horace Mann), 398, 930
MANNUCIA, Andrés, 874
MANRIQUE, Francisco, 213
MANRIQUE DE LARA, Felipe, 910
MANSILLA, Bartolomé de, 520
MANSILLA, Eduarda
     see MANSILLA Y ORTIZ DE ROZAS DE GARCÍA,
     Eduarda
MANSILLA, Felipe, 137
MANSILLA, Francisco, 496
MANSILLA, Juan de, 1270
MANSILLA, Justo, 989
MANSILLA, Lucio Norberto, 95, 96, 127, 135, 153,
   241, 327, 433, 611
MANSILLA, Lucio Víctor (TATA GENERAL, pseud.), 17b,
   78, 90, 115, 116, 153, 166, 191, 193, 195, 232,
   236, 282, 478, 507, 512, 521, 538, 617, 650, 714,
   724, 734, 737, 741, 751, 769, 780, 792, 834,
   1246
MANSILLA, Manuel, 254, 496
MANSILLA Y ORTIZ DE ROZAS DE GARCÍA, Eduarda, 153,
   478, 834, 929, 930
MANSO, Andrés, 464
MANSO, Juana Paula
     see MANSO DE NORHONA, Juana Paula
MANSO, Victoria, 751
MANSO DE NORHONA, Juana Paula, 85, 88, 118, 124,
   282, 317, 324, 478, 747, 751, 762, 834, 929, 930
MANSUETI, Ignazio, 139
MANTEGAZZA, Emilio, 207
MANTEGAZZA, Pablo, 113, 258, 952
MANTELLI, Juan de, pseud.
     see STREVI, Emilio de
MANTEQUILLA, pseud.
     see SOTO, Fernando
MANTERO, Juan A., 95
MANTILLA, Gerónimo, 126
MANTILLA, Manuel Florencio, 121, 196, 779
MANTOVANI, Juan, 747
MANUATA, Juan José, 770
MANUEL, Diego, 1270
MANUTARA, Mariano, 791
MANZANÁREZ, Francisco de, 97
MANZANO, José Roberto, 923
MANZI, Homero
     see MANZIONE, Homero Nicolás
MANZIONE, Homero Nicolás, 746, 759, 801, 803, 861,
   871, 877
MANZONI, Fermín, 998
MANZONI, Ignacio, 32, 51, 59, 258, 293, 521
MAÑACH COUCEIRO, Francisco, 284

MAÑANOS JAUFFRETT DE BORRÁS, Aurora (GOYA, La, pseud.), 892
MAQUEDA, Ernesto Emilio, 923
MAQUIEIRA, José M., 1089
MAQUIEIRA, Ricardo, 235
MARACANÁ, 977
MARADONA, Timoteo, 188, 283
MARAGNO, Virtú, 865, 883
MARAMBIO, Ricardo, 81
MARAMBIO CATÁN, Juan Carlos, 860
MARAMICO, Angel, 995a
MARÁN, Ramón, 894
MARANCA, Francisco, 25, 31
MARANGOA, 977
MARASSO, Arturo, 140, 521, 678, 722, 723, 739, 740, 743, 751, 755, 759, 773, 805, 807
MARAVAL, Teresa (ZAZÁ, La, pseud.), 892
MARAVILLA, La, pseud.
     see ALONSO, Esperanza
MARBAIS DU GRATY, Alfred Louis Hubert Ghislain, barón, 95
MARBIZ, Julio, 299
MARCELLANO Y AGRAMONT, Cayetano, 907, 911, 920
MARCIA, Elvira, 684
MARCIANI, Próspero, 73
MARCIANI, Santiago, 73
MARCO, Celestino I., 135, 194, 241
MARCO, Horacio, 135
MARCO, Lucía, 299
MARCO, Miguel Angel de
     see DE MARCO, Miguel Angel
MARCÓ DEL PONT, Francisco Casimiro, 553
MARCÓ DEL PONT, Raúl, 683a
MARCÓ DEL PONT Y ÁNGEL, Buenaventura Miguel, 19, 284
MARCONI, Isabel, 299
MARCOS, Juan Manuel, 1015
MARCH, Horacio Gerardo, 18, 19, 25, 31, 36, 50
MARCHENA, Antonio, 914, 918
MARCHESE, Víctor, 19, 21, 35
MARCHESES, Juan Francisco, 496
MARCHETTI, Domingo, 781
MARCHI, Alfredo de, 68
MARCHI, Carlos, 889
MARCHI, Fortunato, 921
MARCHIONATTO, Juan, 923
MARE, Diego Jorge, 793
MARECO, Juan Carlos (PINOCHO, pseud.), 894
MARECHAL, Leopoldo, 664, 674, 678, 722, 739, 741, 752, 759, 766, 772, 773, 782, 798, 799, 803, 807, 816, 833
MARELLA MARTÍNEZ MUZIO, Scevola, 1210
MARENCO MARENCO, Carlos G., 1088
MARENGO, Pablo E., 258, 844
MARENZI, Agustín D., 923
MARETTI, Carlos A., 923
MAREY, Ramón, 198
MARFANI, Carlos, 664
MARFANY, Roberto H., 521, 609
MARGA, Iris, pseud.
     see PAURI, Iris
MARGENAT, Nydia E., 652
MARGULIS, Betty B., 652
MARÍA, 977
MARÍA, Alcides de
     see DE MARÍA, Alcides
MARÍA, Enrique de
     see DE MARÍA, Enrique
MARÍA, Isidoro de
     see DE MARÍA, Isidoro

MARÍA, José Antonio de, 147
MARÍA, José de, 987
MARÍA, Pedro C. de, 807
MARÍA ANTONIA DE SAN JOSÉ, 319
MARIANETTI, Benito, 207, 683a
MARIANI, Esther Cándida, 955
MARIANI, Fidel Héctor, Armando, 923
MARIANI, Luis, 955
MARIANI, Roberto, 670, 681, 712, 751, 765, 773, 799, 825, 836, 1243, 1247
MARILUZ URQUIJO, José María, 521
MARÍN, Isidoro, 923
MARÍN, José Cándido, 120
MARÍN, Juan, 169
MARÍN, Miguel, 169
MARÍN, Ricardo, 299
MARÍN, Teófilo, 766
MARÍN DE NEGRÓN, Diego, 521, 984, 985, 1011
MARÍN IGLESIAS, Alejandro, 947
MARÍN NEGRÓN, Diego
     see MARÍN DE NEGRÓN, Diego
MARÍN SÁNCHEZ, Pedro, 1093
MARINELLI, Atilio, 857b
MARINI, Anselmo, 299
MARINI, Fedora, 299
MARINI, José, 223
MARINI, Mara, 60
MARINO, Francisco Alfredo, 727, 871
MARINO, Héctor, 299
MARINO CALVI DE ARESTIVO, Thelma Virginia, 1017
MARINO DI TEANA, Francesco, 25
MARINO RIVERO, René, 1206, 1027
MARIÑA, Eusebio, 990
MARIÑO, Camilo, 1089
MARIÑO, José Ramón, 1095
MARIÑO, Manuel, 1089
MARIÑO, Nicolás, 584
MARIÑO, Santiago, 553
MARIÑO LOIS, José, 1089
MARIO, Arturo, 893
MARIO, Evelina, 44
MARIO LUIS, pseud.
     see CARNELLI, María Luisa
MARIOTTI, Carlos R., 954
MARIOTTI, Maximiliano, 814
MARISCAL, José, 191
MARLY, Florence, 857b
MÁRMOL, José, 121, 145, 145a, 167, 216, 227, 228, 282, 379, 404, 407, 424, 478, 519, 611, 664, 669, 677, 692, 693, 720, 723, 724, 734, 737, 740, 747, 749, 751, 754, 761, 763, 803, 807, 828, 834, 1246, 1254
MÁRMOL, José María, 371
MARMONTI, José, 860
MARONI, Enrique P., 871, 1243
MAROTE, Pedro, 284
MAROTTA, Alejandro, 1205
MAROTTA, Sebastián, 218
MAROZZI, Hugo Alberto, 860
MARQUÉS (family), 1108
MÁRQUEZ, Antonio, 1207
MÁRQUEZ, Fernando, 751
MÁRQUEZ, Gualberto (CHARRÚA, pseud.), 1243
MÁRQUEZ, Laura, 938
MÁRQUEZ, Manuel, 1176
MÁRQUEZ, Nicanor María, 254, 268
MÁRQUEZ, Pedro, 556
MÁRQUEZ, Selva, 1151, 1152, 1177, 1178, 1179
MÁRQUEZ CASTRO, Mateo, 1073
MÁRQUEZ DE OCHOA, Juan, 358

MÁRQUEZ MIRANDA, Fernando, 521
MÁRQUEZ MOSCARDA, Laura, 939
MARQUINA, Basilio, 810
MARRADAS, Francisco Antonio, 1264
MARRANTI, Antonio, 874
MARRERO MARENGO, Ricardo, 1014
MARROCHI, Ivo, 814
MARRONE, Ernesto D., 663
MARSAL, Alberto, 923
MARSAL, Serafín, 939
MARSELLANO Y AGRAMONT, Cayetano, 319, 910
MARSH, James B. T. (Mrs.)
     see WARD, Abigail Nancy
MARSICANO, Félix Roberto, 923
MARTEAU, Augusto, 31
MARTEL, Francisco
     see MARTEL DE MENDOZA, Francisco
MARTEL, Julián, pseud.
     see MIRÓ, José
MARTEL DE CABRERA, Gonzalo, 144
MARTEL DE GUZMÁN, Gonzalo (family), 358
MARTEL DE LOS RÍOS, Luisa, 144
MARTEL DE MENDOZA, Francisco, 144, 914
MARTELLI, Sixto C., 207, 683a
MARTÍ, Alejandro C., 683a
MARTÍ, Ana Selva, 683a, 717
MARTÍ, Febo, 19, 46, 63
MARTÍ, José
     see MARTÍ Y PÉREZ, José Julián
MARTÍ Y PÉREZ, José Julián, 176, 261, 761, 1259
MARTIARENA, José Humberto, 385
MARTICORENA, Eloísa, 37
MARTÍN (MATILIMBIMBE, pseud.), 878
MARTÍN, Deidamia, 663
MARTÍN, Juan, 358
MARTÍN, Juan Carlos, 229
MARTÍN, Quinquela, 55, 154, 170
MARTÍN, Vicente, 1049
MARTÍN-CROSA, Ricardo, 705
MARTÍN DE BIDABEHERE, Ana María, 320
MARTÍN Y YÁÑEZ, Germán, 284
MARTINCICH, Juan, 953, 1006
MARTINELLI, Fulvio, 258
MARTÍNEZ (family), 1108
MARTÍNEZ, Alfredo E., 1145
MARTÍNEZ, Aniceto, 645
MARTÍNEZ, Antonio, 104
MARTÍNEZ, Argentino, 923
MARTÍNEZ, Ariel, 1207
MARTÍNEZ, Beltrán, 1151, 1178
MARTÍNEZ, Benigno T., 95
MARTÍNEZ, Benito, 433
MARTÍNEZ, Bernabé, 268
MARTÍNEZ, Blas, 95
MARTÍNEZ, Carlos, 611
MARTÍNEZ, Carlos Alberto, 37
MARTÍNEZ, David, 716, 739, 807
MARTÍNEZ, Diego M., 1126
MARTÍNEZ, Domingo, 845, 1089
MARTÍNEZ, Eladio, 947
MARTÍNEZ, Emiliano, 320
MARTÍNEZ, Enrique, 222, 261, 478, 479, 565, 611,
     691, 1093a
MARTÍNEZ, Esteban, 998
MARTÍNEZ, Felipe Antonio, 284
MARTÍNEZ, Fermín, 545a
MARTÍNEZ, Fernando, 1082
MARTÍNEZ, Francisco, 186
MARTÍNEZ, Horacio, 772
MARTÍNEZ, Ignacio, 952

MARTÍNEZ, Isidoro C., 652
MARTÍNEZ, Jerónimo, 32
MARTÍNEZ, José, 1089
MARTÍNEZ, Jose de Jesús, 974
MARTÍNEZ, José Eustaquio, 125
MARTÍNEZ, José Julián, 545a
MARTÍNEZ, José L., 1075, 1083
MARTÍNEZ, José M., 652
MARTÍNEZ, José María, 565
MARTÍNEZ, Juan, 914
MARTÍNEZ, Juan A., 878, 1243
MARTÍNEZ, Juan Angel, 129
MARTÍNEZ, Juan Bautista, 268
MARTÍNEZ, Juan Carlos, 717
MARTÍNEZ, Juan del Rosario, 954
MARTÍNEZ, Juan Francisco, 677, 1057, 1165, 1199
MARTÍNEZ, Juan José, 1075
MARTÍNEZ, Julián, 611
MARTÍNEZ, Julián P., 910
MARTÍNEZ, Julio Guillermo, 706
MARTÍNEZ, Ladislao, 156, 268
MARTÍNEZ, Laura, 652
MARTÍNEZ, Luis María, 882, 1020, 1021, 1022, 1025
MARTÍNEZ, Manuel, 887, 1094
MARTÍNEZ, Marcelino
     see MARTÍNEZ CASTRO, Marcelino
MARTÍNEZ, María Estela, 530
MARTÍNEZ, Martín, 32
MARTÍNEZ, Martín A., 94, 268
MARTÍNEZ, Martín C., 1075, 1083, 1126, 1141
MARTÍNEZ, Miguel, 1111
MARTÍNEZ, Nicolás, 1095
MARTÍNEZ, Nicomedes, 254
MARTÍNEZ, Pedro Santos
     see SANTOS MARTÍNEZ, Pedro
MARTÍNEZ, Plácido, 67, 93
MARTÍNEZ, Ramón, 857b
MARTÍNEZ, Ramona, 1000
MARTÍNEZ, Regis, 634
MARTÍNEZ, Régulo, 141
MARTÍNEZ, Reinaldo, 1017, 1020
MARTÍNEZ, Ricardo, 730
MARTÍNEZ, Sergia, 320
MARTÍNEZ, Sergio, 998
MARTÍNEZ, Silverio Antonio, 1130
MARTÍNEZ, Simón, 1075
MARTÍNEZ, Sindulfo, 953
MARTÍNEZ, Valentín, 1075
MARTÍNEZ, Victoriano M., 1075, 1083
MARTÍNEZ, Wenceslao, 387
MARTÍNEZ ALBÍN, Homero, 1187
MARTÍNEZ ALFONSÍN, Manuel, 284
MARTÍNEZ ALVAREZ, Eduvigis, 998
MARTÍNEZ BAZ, Juan, 649a
MARTÍNEZ BORELLI, Holver, 653, 654, 831
MARTÍNEZ CAL, Héctor D., 923
MARTÍNEZ CASTRO, Félix M., 1094, 1095
MARTÍNEZ CASTRO, José H., 68
MARTÍNEZ CASTRO, Ladislao, 148
MARTÍNEZ CASTRO, Marcelino, 156, 611
MARTÍNEZ CUITIÑO, Vicente, 751, 894, 1194
MARTÍNEZ DE BORRONI, María de Jesús, 320
MARTÍNEZ DE BUSTURRIAS, Juan, 555
MARTÍNEZ DE CASTRO Y CALVO, Benita
     see MARTÍNEZ PASTORIZA, Benita
MARTÍNEZ DE DIMITROFF, María I., 652
MARTÍNEZ DE HOZ (family), 361, 362
MARTÍNEZ DE HOZ, Federico L., 3
MARTÍNEZ DE HOZ, José, 3, 496
MARTÍNEZ DE HOZ, José Alfredo A., 3, 218

MARTÍNEZ DE HOZ, Miguel, 474
MARTÍNEZ DE IRALA, Domingo, 32, 151, 191, 357, 358, 359, 360, 406, 443, 455, 462, 465, 471, 472, 481, 504, 505, 518, 521, 528, 943, 948, 949, 963, 966, 972, 980, 984, 984a, 985, 989, 996, 997, 1005, 1010, 1011, 1012, 1203, 1228, 1229, 1230, 1232
MARTÍNEZ DE MOLLINEDO, Eusebio, 625
MARTÍNEZ DE MORILLO, Aurelia, 1017
MARTÍNEZ DE OBLIGADO, Antonio, 132
MARTÍNEZ DE PERÓN, Isabel
    see MARTÍNEZ DE PERÓN, María Estela
MARTÍNEZ DE PERÓN, María Estela, 926
MARTÍNEZ DE ROZAS, Juan, 207, 212, 549
MARTÍNEZ DE SALAZAR, José, 32, 521, 570
MARTÍNEZ DE SARMIENTO, Benita
    see MARTÍNEZ PASTORIZA, Benita
MARTÍNEZ DE VEDIA, Rodolfo, 923
MARTÍNEZ DE ZAVALA, Andrés, 1270
MARTÍNEZ DE ZOTO Y ROSAS, Juan Francisco, 555
MARTÍNEZ DEL MONTE, Francisco, 344
MARTÍNEZ DIAZ DE VIVAR, Dora, 725
MARTÍNEZ ESCOBAR, José, 496
MARTÍNEZ ESTEVE, Pedro, 923
MARTÍNEZ ESTRADA, Ezequiel, 152a, 232, 594, 670, 678, 688, 722, 737, 739, 742, 743, 745a, 751, 759, 773, 803, 807, 825, 835
MARTÍNEZ FERNÁNDEZ, Pedro, 496
MARTÍNEZ FONTES, Elena, 923
MARTÍNEZ FONTES, José, 984, 1011
MARTÍNEZ GAMBA, Carlos, 947
MARTÍNEZ GANDARIA, Sergio, 1210
MARTÍNEZ GROVETTO, Raúl Nereo, 923
MARTÍNEZ GUZMÁN, Guillermo, 923
MARTÍNEZ HOWARD, Alfredo, 135, 739, 746, 759, 800, 812, 831
MARTÍNEZ LAMAS, Julio, 1184
MARTÍNEZ LUCERO, Edgar, 1191
MARTÍNEZ MENDOZA, Daniel, 299
MARTÍNEZ MILTOS, Luis, 954
MARTÍNEZ MOLLINEDO, Eusebio, 611
MARTÍNEZ MORENO, Carlos, 806, 1148, 1149, 1155, 1158, 1177, 1184, 1189
MARTÍNEZ OYANGUREN, Julio, 1206
MARTÍNEZ PAIVA, Claudio, 135, 766, 1243
MARTÍNEZ PALOMEQUE, Juan, 555
MARTÍNEZ PASTORIZA, Benita (MARTÍNEZ DE SARMIENTO, Benita; MARTÍNEZ DE CASTRO Y CALVO, Benita), 450, 930, 931
MARTÍNEZ PAYVA, Claudio
    see MARTÍNEZ PAIVA, Claudio
MARTÍNEZ READIGÓS, Manuel, 44
MARTÍNEZ REDONDO, Manuel, 1089
MARTÍNEZ SÁENZ, 972
MARTÍNEZ SÁENZ, Pedro Pablo, 979
MARTÍNEZ SÁENZ, Sebastián Antonio, 972, 979, 987
MARTÍNEZ SANTRADÁN, Faustino, 284
MARTÍNEZ SOLIMÁN, Guillermo, 45, 64
MARTÍNEZ SUÁREZ, José Antonio, 857
MARTÍNEZ TERNERO, Gregorio, 649a
MARTÍNEZ THÉDY, Eugenio, 1083, 1123
MARTÍNEZ TRUEBA, Andrés, 1123
MARTÍNEZ VARELA, Benito, 964
MARTÍNEZ VARELA, José María, 964
MARTÍNEZ VIDAL, Carlos A., 923
MARTÍNEZ VIERGOL, Antonio, 871
MARTÍNEZ VIGIL, Carlos, 1075, 1078, 1188, 1193
MARTÍNEZ VIGIL, Daniel, 1075, 1078, 1083, 1146, 1174, 1188
MARTÍNEZ Y GARCÍA, Manuel, 496

MARTÍNEZ Y VALLEJO, José, 344
MARTÍNEZ YANTORNO, Guillermo, 750
MARTÍNEZ ZÁZATE, Jorge, 865
MARTÍNEZ ZUVIRÍA, Gustavo (WAST, Hugo, pseud.), 154, 170, 744, 745, 751, 772, 816, 834
MARTINJ, Marino, 917
MARTINO, Eduardo de, 258
MARTINO, Federico Augusto, 46
MARTINO, Francisco, 1243
MARTINS MARINS, Pedro, 1093
MARTINTO, Domingo D., 669, 749
MARTINUZZI, Enzo Amadeo, 923
MARTIRENÉ, José, 1083
MARTORELL, María, 31, 36
MARTORELLI, José, 760, 923
MARTOS, Domingo J., 775
MARTOS, Miguel, 683a
MARVEGGIO PÉREZ, Daniel, 1088
MARX, Michelle, 31
MARZANO DE PÉREZ BARATCABAL, María C., 652
MARZI FOSETTI, Estanislao, 1210
MARZIANI, Hugo de, 36, 60
MARZOCCA, Angel, 923
MÁS, Juan, 878
MÁS DE AYALA, Isidro, 192
MÁS OLLER, Antonio, 385
MASA, Cleta, pseud.
    see ALTOMARE DE DE PEREYRA, Emilia
MASA, Olga, 299
MASCARDI, Nicolás, 258, 921
MASCARELLO, Domenico, 258, 292
MASCARELLO, Domingo
    see MASCARELLO, Domenico
MASCARELLO, José María, 258
MASCARO, Miguel Angel, 191
MASCHWITZ, Carlos, 332, 904
MASELLA, Antonio, 7, 32
MASELLA, Juan Bautista, 7, 32
MASI, Antonio G., 963a
MASI, Domingo A., 963a
MASINI, Ramón, 1063
MASON, Guillermo Roberto, 82
MASSA, Juan Bautista, 864, 865, 881
MASSA, Luis Edgardo, 832
MASSA, Ricardo, 717
MASSALA, Domingo, 319
MASSARE DE KOSTIANOVSKY, Olinda, 1000
MASSERA DE GALEANO, Mercedes, 1211
MASSERA LERENA, José Luis, 1210
MASSETTA, Simón, 850
MASSI, Miguel, 951
MASSINI, Esteban, 859, 870
MASSINI ESCURRA, Cosme, 3
MASSINI EZCURRA, José M., 652
MASSIOTI, Antonio B., 813
MASSONE, Atilio, 258
MASSONI, 859
MASSUH, Víctor, 213, 743
MASTAGLIO DE ECHALDE, Adelaida, 320
MASTELLI DE MISELLI, Anunciada, 312
MASTRÁNGELO, Carlos, 760, 814
MASTRARRIGO, Vicente, 923
MASTRILLI, Nicolás, 885
MASTROGIOVANNI, Antonio, 1206, 1207
MASTRONARDI, Carlos
    see MASTRONARDI NEGRI, Carlos
MASTRONARDI NEGRI, Carlos, 235, 678, 722, 729, 739, 743, 751, 759, 782, 798, 800, 833
MASÚ, Alicia, 787
MATA, Francisco, 1093

MATA ORTELLADO, Juan de, 995a
MATASPINA, Alejandro, 202
MATEO, Abel, 668
MATERA, Raúl, 75, 923
MATEU AMENGUAL, Bernardino, 923
MATHARÁN, Luis, 751
MATHET, Juan María, 3
MATHEU, Domingo Bartolomé, 70, 85, 244, 282, 386,
    404, 421, 475, 478, 479, 496, 610
MATHUS, Alejandro
    see MATHUS HOYOS, Alejandro
MATHUS HOYOS, Alejandro, 207, 278
MATIENZO, Agustín, 648, 649
MATIENZO, Francisco de, 1270
MATIENZO, José Nicolás, 68, 126, 219, 647
MATIENZO, Juan de, 501, 522, 713
MATIENZO DE PERALTA, Juan, 649a
MATIJEVIC, Nicolás, 652
MATILIMBIMBE, pseud.
    see MARTÍN
MATO, Silvestre, 1083
MATORRAS, Gregoria
    see MATORRAS DEL SER DE SAN MARTÍN, Gregoria
MATORRAS, Jerónimo, 32, 112, 432, 1229
MATORRAS CORNEJO, Carlos, 653, 654
MATORRAS DEL SER DE SAN MARTÍN, Gregoria, 172, 383,
    561, 927
MATORRAS Y GONZÁLEZ, Domingo, 172
MATOS, Ana de, 134
MATOS RODRÍGUEZ, Gerardo, 868
MATTALIA, Rosa Carmen, 320
MATTALIA DE SALAS DEL RÍO, Ida Irene, 320
MATTEI DE TAZZA, Fulvia C., 320
MATTEIS, Emilio de, 743
MATTEOTTI, Giacomo, 259
MATTHIS, Leonie, 33
MATTHYS, Henri, 960
MATTO, Ramón, 1089
MATTOS, Héctor, 1093
MATTOS, Pedro, 844
MATTOS, Tomás de, 1173
MATTOS ESPINO, Pedro F., 1088
MATURANA (family), 1108
MATURANA, José de, 669, 751, 778, 1243, 1247
MATURANA, Juan Bautista de, 556
MATURO DE SOLÁ GONZÁLEZ, Graciela, 683a, 717, 739,
    802
MAUBÉ, José Carlos, 688
MAUCLAIR, Camilo, 33
MAULE, Carlos, 191
MAULEÓN CASTILLO, Rafael, 683a
MAURE, Avelino B., 278
MAURE, Celia Teresa, 781
MAURE DE SEGOVIA, Elvira, 683a
MAUREGATO, 361
MAURÍN, Juan Antonio, 173, 254
MAURÍN, Lorenzo, 546, 549
MAURIÑO, Víctor Eduardo, 923
MAURRAS, Charles, 185
MAXWELL, Susana Mercedes, 738
MAY, E., 937
MAYA, Héctor D., 135
MAYA VILLA REAL, Ramón de, 104
MAYADA, Eusebio Antonio, 126
MAYER, Horacio Fermín, 923
MAYO, Santos, 923
MAYORCA, Ursula
    see ALVAREZ DE MAYORCA, Ursula
MAYORGA, Angelo Francisco de, 555
MAYORGA, Juan de, 555

MAYORGA, Julio E., 207
MAYTE, Elena, 738
MAZ Y AYALA, Félix, 254
MAZA, Antonio de la, 555
MAZA, Fernando, 36
MAZA, Juan Agustín de la, 207, 212, 278, 412, 439,
    457, 526, 611, 621
MAZA, Manuel Vicente, 584
MAZA, Ramón, 169, 612
MAZA CALVO, Domingo, 284
MAZETA, Simón, 952, 1040
MAZIEL, Juan Baltasar, 183, 244, 317, 321, 334, 669,
    720, 737, 751, 761, 876, 895, 921, 1242, 1247,
    1258
MAZIEL DEL ÁGUILA, Francisco, 186
MAZÓ, Gabriel de, 332
MAZÓ, Marcelino del, 678
MAZÓ, Rafael, 998
MAZÓ, Ricardo, 1020
MAZÓ DE PÉREZ, Néstar Rosa, 1014
MAZÓ UGARRIZA, José Ricardo, 1014
MAZZA, Horacio Blas, 19, 36
MAZZA, Raúl, 19, 31, 44
MAZZANTI, Carlos, 1252
MAZZEI, Angel, 739, 748, 759
MAZZEI, Egidio S., 923
MAZZEIS, Mario, 998
MAZZILLI DE MATHOV, E. A., 923
MAZZIOTTA, Manuel F., 1093
MAZZOCO, Vicente, 874
MAZZOLENI, Hernán, 258
MAZZONI, Francisco R., 1170
MBACABA, 977
MBIOPE, 977
MBOCARATA, 977
MBOROSENI, 977
MBURÚA, 977
McENTYRE, Eduardo
    see MAC ENTYRE, Eduardo
McMILLAN, Henry S. (Mrs.)
    see McMILLAN, Mary Gay
McMILLAN, Mary Gay (Mrs. Henry S. McMillan), 323
McNAMARA, Harry, 954
MEABE, Santiago, 344
MEAURIS, Ernesto, 947
MECKBACH, Wolfgang, 923
MEDARDO MORENO, Salustiano, 998
MEDEIROS, Gertrudis
    see MEDEIROS DE CORNEJO, Gertrudis
MEDEIROS, José de, 126
MEDEIROS, Paulina, 1093
MEDEIROS DE CORNEJO, Gertrudis, 422, 540, 611
MEDELLIN, Diego de, 910
MEDERO, Antonio, 1122
MEDEYROS, Juan, 371
MEDEYROS DE CORNEJO, Gertrudis
    see MEDEIROS DE CORNEJO, Gertrudis
MEDICI, Juan Bautista, 332
MEDINA, Anacleto, 95, 1091
MEDINA, Antonio, 982, 995a
MEDINA, Eustaquio, 385
MEDINA, Francisco, 94
MEDINA, Francisco de (musician), 882
MEDINA, Gaspar de, 520
MEDINA, Generoso, 1151, 1179
MEDINA, Gil, 268
MEDINA, Ignacio, 1111
MEDINA, José Antonio, 618
MEDINA, José del Rosario, 995a
MEDINA, José Toribio, 283

MEDINA, Juan Antonio, 921
MEDINA, Lorenzo, 1006, 1017
MEDINA, Manuel, 611
MEDINA, Martín de, 1270
MEDINA, Micaela, 1082
MEDINA, Nicolás, 433
MEDINA, Pedro de, 358, 878
MEDINA, Romeo B. A., 694
MEDINA, Trifón, 951
MEDINA BETANCOURT, Manuel, 1083, 1170, 1190
MEDINA ONRUBIA, Salvadora, 751, 762, 765
MEDINA RAMELA, Enrique, 1049
MEDINA VIDAL, Jorge, 1151, 1178
MEDRANO, Mariano, 126, 895, 896, 912
MEDRANO, Matías, 126
MEDRANO, Pedro, 126, 439, 457, 526, 611, 621, 626
MEDRANO ROSSO, Gaspar (CATÓN, pseud.), 713, 730
MEDRANO Y CABRERA, Mariano, 907, 910, 911, 920
MEEROFF, Marcos, 923
MEGANO, Andrea, 292
MEGGET, Humberto, 1148, 1149, 1151, 1177, 1178
MEIROVICH, Carlos Isaac, 684
MEISSNER, Rolf, 1070
MEISTER, Juan Federico, 949
MEJÍA MIRAVAL, Hernán, 520
MEJÍAS, María Estela, 44
MELAGAREJO MUÑOZ, W., 64
MELANI, Pietro, 292
MELLAZZA MUTTONI, Jorge, 660, 717, 727
MELE, Juan, 31
MELEGATTI ALVAREZ, Julio César, 1210
MELELLA, Dora, 725
MELÉNDEZ, Lucio, 247, 844
MELÉNDEZ, Manuel, 1059, 1111
MELGAREJO, Doroteo, 947, 1014
MELGAREJO, Juan E., 1006
MELGAREJO LEDESMA, Ramón, 998
MELGAREJO MUÑOZ, W., 64
MELIA, Bartomeu, 962
MELIAN, José, 104, 611
MELIÁN LAFINUR, Alvaro, 678, 722, 751, 773, 1245
MELIÁN LAFINUR, Luis, 1075, 1083, 1146, 1174, 1199
MELIANTE, Ermete, 299
MELILLO, Jorge J., 299
MELO, Antonio de, 186
MELO, Carlos F., 141, 565, 751
MELO, Carlos R., 521
MELO, Enrique Amado, 1088
MELO, Francisco de, 186
MELO, Josefina, 154
MELO, Leopoldo, 565
MELO, Miguel, 1270
MELO, Ramón, 1167
MELO DE PORTUGAL Y VILLENA, Pedro, 570, 984, 990,
    1011, 1237, 1239, 1240, 1241, 1262
MELO Y CUITIÑO (family), 1224
MELONI, Alejo Luis, 191, 831
MELLER, Raquel, 892, 928
MELLO, Adolfo Antonio, 998
MENA, Juan Bautista de, 316, 649a
MENA, Juan de, 984a, 989
MENA, Juan Carlos, 663, 805
MENA, Juan de Dios, 29, 191
MENA, Manuel Vicente, 921
MENA PORTA, Juan José Aníbal, 1035
MENA Y MASCARUA, Juan Martín de, 898
MENANGLIOTO, Laurantino Lorenzo (MINANGLIOTTI,
    Lorenzo), 845, 949
MENCHACA, Manuel, 87
MENDE, Raúl A., 766

MENDEVILLE, Juan Bautista Washington de, 130
MÉNDEZ, Andrés, 358
MÉNDEZ, Beatriz, 37
MÉNDEZ, Carlos J., 284
MÉNDEZ, Carmen, 894
MÉNDEZ, Delfor, 834
MÉNDEZ, Duarte, 1270
MÉNDEZ, Esteban, 1080
MÉNDEZ, Eustaquio, 625
MÉNDEZ, Evar, pseud.
    see GONZÁLEZ MÉNDEZ, Guillermo Evaristo
MÉNDEZ, Francisco, 1089
MÉNDEZ, Germán M., 811
MÉNDEZ, Gervasio, 121, 135, 166, 664, 669, 751, 800
MÉNDEZ, Héctor, 857d
MÉNDEZ, José, 1089
MÉNDEZ, José D., 328
MÉNDEZ, Juan, 371
MÉNDEZ, Julia, 894
MÉNDEZ, Julio, 844, 851
MÉNDEZ, Martín, 292
MÉNDEZ, Olegario, 874, 878
MÉNDEZ, Simón (GUASQUITA, pseud.), 878
MÉNDEZ, Wilfredo N., 8
MÉNDEZ CALDEIRA (family), 1108
MÉNDEZ CALDEIRA, Raúl, 207
MÉNDEZ CALZADA, Enrique, 235, 670, 678, 722, 739,
    751, 765, 769, 773, 782, 807, 1245
MÉNDEZ CALZADA, Joaquín, 683a
MÉNDEZ CHAVARRÍA, César Horacio, 385
MÉNDEZ DE SOUZA, Ariel, 1088
MÉNDEZ FERNÁNDEZ, Marcial, 284
MÉNDEZ FUNES DE MILLÁN, María Adelina, 320
MÉNDEZ MOSQUERA, Carlos A., 218
MÉNDEZ NÚÑEZ, Casto, 1235
MÉNDEZ PEÑAROL, 785
MÉNDEZ REISSIG, Ernestina, 1075, 1174
MENDIETA, Diego, 443
MENDILAHARSU, Julio Raúl, 1068, 1083, 1087, 1145,
    1165, 1179, 1181, 1187, 1188, 1195
MENDILAHARZU, Graciano, 19, 25, 51, 59, 254, 521
MENDIOLA, Sebastián Félix de, 984, 1011
MENDIOLA DE QUIROGA, María del Carmen, 713, 730
MENDIONDO, Pedro, 332
MENDIONDO VIDART, Dari, 1210
MENDIONDOU, Esteban, 949
MENDIOROZ, Alberto, 773, 805
MENDIOROZ, Francisco, 852
MENDIVE, Jorge R., 923
MENDIVELZÚA, Germán, 923
MENDIVIL, Javier, 1083
MENDIZÁBAL, Horacio, 137
MENDIZÁBAL, José María, 126
MENDIZÁBAL, Mariano, 166, 188, 283, 552
MENDIZÁBAL CABRAL, Adriana, 1173
MENDOZA, Ambrosio, 998
MENDOZA, Angélica, 207, 683a
MENDOZA, Ascención N. de, 320
MENDOZA, Cristóbal de, 989
MENDOZA, Eriberto, 81, 158, 222
MENDOZA, Francisco de, 500, 989, 1011
MENDOZA, Gabino, 998
MENDOZA, García de, 1011
MENDOZA, Gonzalo de, 984, 992, 1011
MENDOZA, Herminio, 998
MENDOZA, Hernando de, 358
MENDOZA, Jerónimo R., 81, 222
MENDOZA, José Román, 1126
MENDOZA, Melchor, 1082
MENDOZA, Pedro A., 959

MENDOZA, Pedro de, 32, 72, 103, 185, 406, 443, 455,
    462, 464, 465, 471, 472, 477, 486, 510, 518,
    519, 521, 528, 535, 570, 984, 984a, 989, 1011,
    1012, 1203, 1231, 1232, 1238, 1261
MENDOZA, Silverio, 998
MENDOZA, Toribio D., 81, 222, 445
MENDOZA DÁVALOS, Rodrigo de, 186
MENDOZA MEDINA, Gregoria Tomasa, 1082
MENDOZA VITALE, Clelia, 1088
MENDOZA Y DURÁN, Leopoldo, 1083
MENDOZA Y DURAND, Estanislao, 1083
MENDOZA Y MANRIQUE, García de, 620
MENDY, Raúl Martín, 923
MENÉNDEZ, Carlos Alberto, 923
MENÉNDEZ, Damián, 268
MENÉNDEZ, Mario, 1145
MENÉNDEZ GOYCOECHEA, Martín, 1247
MENÉNDEZ LARRIERA DE ACOSTA, Jacinta, 1093a
MENÉNDEZ LEES, Pedro, 1067
MENÉNDEZ PIDAL, Ramón, 688
MENÉNDEZ Y PELAYO, Marcelino, 763
MENES, Justo, 1089
MENESES, Pascuala, 478, 929
MENEZES, Simón Tadeo, 845
MENGES FRANCOIS, Beatriz, 683a
MENGHI, José Luis, 65
MENIN, pseud.
    see ALVARENGA, Alejo
MENNUCCI, Arturo, 923
MENOR DE ARAYA, LA, pseud.
    see ARAYA, Ursula de
MENOYO, Enrique, 717, 831
MENSCH, Rafael, 560
MEOLI, Humberto, 332
MERA, Ramón, 1089
MERCADER, Martha, 817
MERCADER, Miguel A., 903
MERCADILLO, Manuel, 529a, 910
MERCADO, José León, 995
MERCADO, Melchor, 126
MERCADO, Víctor Miguel, 191
MERCADO DE PEÑALOSA, Pedro de, 522
MERCAVO Y VILLACORTA, Alonso, 521, 570
MERCANDANTE, Luis, 655
MERCANTE, Antonio, 258
MERCANTE, Raúl Aníbal, 923
MERCANTE, Víctor, 317, 751
MERCANTI, Ferrucio, 258
MERCAU, Agustín, 222, 332
MERCAU, Nicasio, 222
MERCE, Antonia (LA ARGENTINA, pseud.), 892
MEREDIZ, José Antonio, 19, 31, 33
MERELO, José, 496
MERELLANO, Miguel Angel Edgardo, 299
MERELLO, Tita, 862, 879
MERICO, Salvador, 893
MÉRIDA, Galiano, 845
MERLINO, Carlos Alberto, 739, 814
MERLINO, Salvador, 739, 751
MERLO, Juan Carlos, 923
MERLO, Martha Julia, 691
MERLO DE ALBA, Gloria, 781
MERONI, Carlos Miguel, 923
MERSÁN, Carlos Rodolfo, 954
MERTENS, Federico S., 811, 813
MERTI, Carlos Andrés, 191
MESA, Pedro de, 845, 555, 1261
MESAS MIRANDA, Víctor, 781
MESEJEAN, Pablo, 36
MESNER, Joannes, 865, 866, 922, 1037

MESNER, Juan
    see MESNER, Joannes
MESNY, Marcelo, 923
MESSIL, Gabriel, 36, 55
MESTRE DE VILLALBA, Elida, 1093
METALLO, Angel María, 258
METHOL, Eduardo Jorge, 923
METHOL FERRÉ, Alberto, 1184
METRAUX, Alfredo, 191
MEUCCI JORDÁN, Camilo, 319
MEXÍA MIRABEL, Francisco, 1270
MEXÍA MIRAVAL, Hernán, 620
MEXÍAS SÁNCHEZ, Juan, 196
MEYER, Oscar, 24, 44
MEYER, Teodoro, 191, 923
MEYER CICARELLI, Guillermo Benito, 730
MEYER GOLDSCHVARTZ, Jacobo, 923
MEYER PELLEGRINI, Carlos, 94, 391
MEYRELLES (family)
    see COELHO DE MEYRELLES (family)
MEZA, Juan A., 1008
MEZA, Manuel, 258
MEZA, Pedro Ignacio, 974
MEZQUIDA, Bartolomé, 691
MEZZERA, Baltasar, 1184
MEZZERA, Rodolfo, 1083, 1087
MIACZYNSKI, Carlos R., 923
MIASKOWSKI, León, 238
MIATELLO, Hugo, 258
MICELI, Antonio, 31, 882
MICUCCI, María Imelda, 663
MICHAELSEN ARÁOZ, Carlos, 653, 654
MICHARVEGAS, Martín, 759
MICHEL, Federico, 923
MICHÈLE, pseud.
    see MADORNO, Olga Lidia
MICHELENA, Bernabé, 1044, 1068, 1211
MICHELENA, Juan Angel, 254, 371
MICHELI, Domenico Di
    see DI MICHELI, Domenico
MICHELI DE FILIPPI, Ana N., 923
MICHEO (family), 351
MIER, Toribio de, 496
MIERES VARELA DE CENTRÓN, Celia Haydée, 1210, 1211
MIERS, John, 468
MIGLIARO, Estelvina, 1092
MIGLIORE, Francisco, 963a
MIGNAQUY (family), 122
MIGNO, Julio, 837, 1243
MIGONE, Atilio José, 1006
MIGONE, Luis Enrique, 952, 959, 963a
MIGONE, Nicolás, 1265
MIGOYA, Fermín, 272
MIGUEL, 1238
MIGUEL, Gaspar de, 24
MIGUEL, María Esther de, 817, 822
MIGUENS, José Enrique Carlos, 218
MIGUENS, Josefina, 19, 31, 46
MIGUENS PARRADO, Alejandro, 284
MIGUEZ, Claudino, 1089
MIGUEZ, Doelia S., 669, 762
MIHANOVICH, Nicolás, 141
MIHURA, Enrique, 135
MIHURA, Enrique F., 95, 135, 241
MIHURA, Ramón, 241
MILANESIO, Domingo, 907a
MILANO, Fulvio, 663, 681, 717, 739, 802
MILANO, Víctor A., 923
MILANS MARTÍNEZ, Artigas, 154, 1167
MILANTA, Atilio, 663

MILELLI, Gustavo, 258
MILESI, María Esther (STELLA MARIS, pseud.), 762
MILANO, Ricardo J., 652
MILICI, Luis, 865, 883
MILONE, César, 258
MILOSLAVICH, Blas, 947
MILTOS, Alberto, 938
MILTOS, Sotero Cayo, 986
MILLALICÁN, Pablo, 169
MILLÁN, José R., 320
MILLÁN, Pedro, 1262
MILLÁS, Joaquín, 895, 1269
MILLER, Flora, 652
MILLER, Guillermo, 82, 553, 611
MILLER, Juan Edmundo, 1088
MIMER CRAVEZ DE DUBINSKI, Golde, 1210
MINANGLIOTTI, Lorenzo
    see MENANGLIOTO, Laurantino Lorenzo
MINELLI, Agustín, 1185
MINELLI GONZÁLEZ, Pablo, 1174, 1179, 1199, 1259
MINERBI, Guido, 37
MINGO, Carlos, 952
MINGO, Pancho, pseud.
    see MONTAGNE, Edmundo
MINOPRIO, José Daniel Luis, 923
MINURA, Ramón, 135, 194
MINUTOLO, Cristina V., 609
MINVIELLE, Rafael, 254
MIÑO, Lola de
    see FANEGO DE MIÑO, Ramona Dolores
MIÑONDO, Juan Francisco, 254
MIQUEL, Alberto, 963a
MIQUITA, pseud.
    see VILLEGAS, Micaela
MIR SILVA, Omar, 1210
MIRA CATÓ, Esteban, 44
MIRABAL, Antonio de, 1270
MIRAELIAN, Juan, 299
MIRAGLIA, Juan Carlos, 18
MIRALLA, José Antonio, 177, 244, 734, 751, 761, 828
MIRALLES, Héctor Víctor, 1093
MIRANDA, Alonso de, 555
MIRANDA, Avelino, 1111
MIRANDA, César, 1064, 1083, 1199
MIRANDA, César Tomás, 44
MIRANDA, Centurión, 964
MIRANDA, Francisco de, 427, 460, 513, 514, 519, 562, 573, 574, 587
MIRANDA, Francisco Javier, 895
MIRANDA, Guido Arnoldo, 191
MIRANDA, Héctor, 1131, 1190
MIRANDA, Jerónimo de, 850
MIRANDA, Jorge Sebastián, 1017
MIRANDA, José del Rosario, 986, 1008
MIRANDA, Juan de, 186
MIRANDA, Luis de, 754, 1230
MIRANDA, Miguel, 530
MIRANDA BORELLI, José I., 191
MIRANDA CUETO DE ESTIGARRIBIA, Julia, 1004
MIRANDA DE VILLAFAÑA, Luis de, 683, 966, 985, 1021
MIRAS, Nelly de, 691
MIRAU, José María, 653, 654
MIRAVET, Tito, 31
MIRI, Héctor F., 751
MIRIS, Fátima, 892
MIRIZZI, Pablo Luis, 851, 923
MIRÓ, Eduardo Daniel, 299
MIRÓ, José María (MARTEL, Julián, pseud.), 152a, 724, 754, 774
MIRÓ, Ricardo, 268

MIRONES BENAVENTE, Isidoro, 1011
MISA, Clemente, 1089
MISITI, Rodolfo, 691
MISTRAL, Gabriela, pseud. (GODOY DE ALCAYAGA, Lucila), 176, 755
MITRE (family), 1106, 1224
MITRE, Adolfo, 210, 431, 720
MITRE, Ambrosio, 611, 1063
MITRE, Bartolito, 506
MITRE, Bartolomé, 17b, 68, 70, 95, 96, 103, 110, 118, 121, 129, 141, 143, 166, 167, 176, 212, 225, 244, 246, 258, 261, 272, 277, 278, 282, 283, 293, 324, 369, 370, 372, 379, 386, 392, 393, 398, 404, 405, 436, 444, 447, 452, 453, 462, 466, 469, 489, 492, 499, 502, 509, 515, 516, 517, 518, 519, 521, 523, 525, 531, 540, 544, 545, 553, 573, 574, 585, 589, 592, 593, 594, 595, 598, 601, 607, 609, 611, 619, 644, 650, 669, 692, 693, 720, 734, 737, 740, 743, 749, 751, 754, 761, 807, 924, 984, 1188, 1242, 1243, 1247, 1257
MITRE, Emilio, 17b, 225, 254, 261, 332, 585, 592, 594, 611
MITRE, Jorge, 664, 720
MITRE Y VEDIA, Bartolomé, 478, 708
MITRE Y VEDIA, Emilio, 68
MITRE Y VEDIA DE BASTIANINI, Delfina, 669
MITTELBACH, Aristóbulo E., 264
MOANO, Benito de, 1265
MÓBILI, Jorge Enrique, 658, 739, 759
MOCITO, pseud.
    see ACUÑA, Juan Gregorio
MOCHO, Fray, pseud.
    see ALVAREZ, José Sixto
MODERN, Fernando, 923
MODERN, Rodolfo, 814
MOGLIA BARTH, José L., 858
MOGNI, Franco, 658
MOHNBLATT, José, 653, 654
MOIA, Blas, 923
MOINE, Eduardo P., 211
MOIRÓN Y PAZ, José, 1094
MO1SANO, Rodolfo Carmen, 320
MOISSET DE ESPANES, Enrique, 923
MOITIÑO DE SOSA, Rosa, 1088
MOJER, Mario Lucio, 320
MOLAS, Jerónimo, 963a
MOLAS, José Agustín, 943, 964, 987
MOLAS, José D., 984a, 995, 1017
MOLAS, Mariano Antonio, 943, 964, 966, 971, 979, 980, 987, 1012, 1014
MOLAS LÓPEZ, Felipe, 953
MOLATURA DE LÓPEZ ISLAS, Ana Josefa, 320
MOLDES, José de, 104, 166, 478, 479, 552, 611, 625, 626, 895
MOLDAHN (family), 168
MOLEÓN ANDREÚ, Juan, 954
MOLFINO, Rubén H., 923
MOLFINO VENERE, José Adán, 191
MOLINA, Celso, 653
MOLINA, Cristóbal de, 556
MOLINA, Enrique, 658, 672, 716, 722, 739, 758, 759, 798, 803, 807, 832
MOLINA, Felipe de, 126
MOLINA, Hernando de, 845, 1203
MOLINA, Javier, 874
MOLINA, José Agustín, 611, 664, 669, 908
MOLINA, Juan Angel, 254
MOLINA, Juan Cayetano, 147, 844, 1203
MOLINA, Juan de, 555

MOLINA, Juan Ignacio, 283, 885
MOLINA, Luis de, 186
MOLINA, Manuel Felipe, 126
MOLINA, Manuel Ignacio, 207
MOLINA, Mateo José, 385
MOLINA, Matías, 29
MOLINA, Miguel E., 68
MOLINA, Miguel T., 17b
MOLINA, Pedro, 212, 412
MOLINA, Pedro Alberto, 44
MOLINA, Pedro C., 179, 190, 277, 278, 283
MOLINA, Raúl Alejandro, 521, 609, 849
MOLINA, Segundo, 268
MOLINA, Vicente, 887
MOLINA, Víctor M., 68, 565
MOLINA ARROTEA, Carlos, 68
MOLINA CAMPOS, 170
MOLINA CASTRILLO, Ebelio Gerardo, 1088
MOLINA DE LASARTE, Diego, 646
MOLINA ESTRELLA, Elina, 874
MOLINA MASSEY, Carlos, 834
MOLINA NAVARRETA (family), 352
MOLINA PARRAGUEZ Y VOSCONCELOS, Luis de, 555, 649a
MOLINA Y VASCONCELLOS, José de, 555
MOLINA Y VEDIA DE BASTIANINI, Delfina, 751, 762
MOLINA Y VILLAFAÑE, José Agustín, 876
MOLINARI, Diego Luis, 431, 609
MOLINARI, Ricardo E., 140, 210, 664, 674, 678, 722,
    729, 737, 739, 748, 751, 759, 773, 798, 801,
    803, 807, 833
MOLINARI, Víctor Luis, 739, 746
MOLINAS, Guillermo, 1015
MOLINAS, Leonardo, 995a
MOLINAS, Nicanor, 83, 95, 96, 188, 283
MOLINAS ROLÓN, Guillermo, 943, 966, 1014, 1020, 1021,
    1022
MOLINELLI, Juan Jorge, 683a
MOLINIER, Pedro, 1018a
MOLINO, Osvaldo, 860
MOLINO TORRES, Carlos del, 94
MOLINO TORRES, Julián del, 496
MOLINS, W. Jaime, 751
MOLTENI, Marta, 652
MOLL, José, 496
MOLLA VILLANUEVA, Mariano, 328
MOLLANO, Diego, 151
MOLLER, August, 214
MOLLURA, Pedro, 923
MOM, Arturo S., 765
MOMBRÚ, María, 717, 725, 805
MOMBRUNT OCAMPO, Carlos, 874
MOMPER, Pieter, 1046
MOMPÓS, Fernando de, pseud.
    see MOMPOX Y ZAYAS, Fernando de
MOMPOX Y ZAYAS, Fernando de (MOMPÓS, Fernando de,
    pseud.), 964, 978, 984, 989, 1012
MONACO, Garibaldi, 258
MONACO, Primaldo, 18, 19, 25, 31, 36, 46, 63
MONASTERIO, Angel, 332, 611
MONASTERIO, Esther, 683a, 762
MONASTERIO, Fernanda, 923
MONCLÁ Y SANTANDER, Antonia de, 207
MONCLAVO, Ana María, 27, 41, 49
MONCH, Ernst, 923
MONDIOLA, Juan, 727
MONEDA, Rafael de la, 984, 1011, 1012
MONEGAL, Cándido, 1093
MONEGAL, Casiano, 1145
MONEGAL, Gabino, 1075
MONEGAL, José, 1159, 1167, 1177, 1186, 1196

MONETA, Pompeyo, 258, 332
MONETA, Raúl Osvaldo, 37
MONFORTE, Francisco de, 984, 1011
MONGELOS, José Vicente, 955, 974
MONGRELL, Vicente, 1085
MONGUILLOT, Juan Francisco, 96, 648, 649
MONICO, Lili del, 938, 939
MONJE, Juan de la Cruz, 126
MONJEAU, María Victorina, 320
MONNER SANS, José María, 751
MONNER SANS, Ricardo, 167
MONNERET DE VILLARS, Rodolfo Horacio, 923
MONNIER DE DUPUY, Ana, 949, 1029
MONROS, Francisco de Asís, 923
MONSALVE, Carlos, 714, 780
MONSEGUR, Raúl, 19
MONSEGUR, Sylla J., 94
MONSERRAT, María de, 1158, 1186
MONTAGNE, Edmundo (MINGO, Pancho, pseud.), 167, 751,
    773, 811, 813, 878, 894, 1243, 1247
MONTAGNE, Julio C., 949
MONTAGÚ FABIÁN, Carlos, 580
MONTALDO, Gladis, 44
MONTALTO, Armando, 320
MONTALVÁN, Diego de, 1035a, 1035b
MONTALVO, Hernando de, 1230
MONTANARO, Domingo, 953
MONTANGERO DOMPE DE MOSCATELLI, Aminta C., 320
MONTANI, Roberto Germán, 923
MONTANS, Juan, 1089
MONTAÑO DE CARABAJAL, Miguel, 555
MONTAUTTI, Eduardo, 1116
MONTE, José de, 31
MONTE, Juan, 959
MONTE CARBALLO, Vicente, 921
MONTEAGUDO, Bernardo
    see MONTEAGUDO, José Bernardo
MONTEAGUDO, José Bernardo, 104, 110, 126, 166,
    177, 244, 282, 283, 381, 404, 419, 427, 444,
    453, 472, 475, 478, 479, 491, 508, 509, 525,
    528, 529, 542, 562, 563, 577, 611, 618, 629,
    692, 734, 761, 895
MONTEAGUDO, Miguel, 618
MONTEALEGRE, Juan de la Cruz, 850
MONTEAVARO, Antonio, 135, 243
MONTEJANO DE CATELLA, Rosalba, 810
MONTEMAR DOYENAR, Milton, 1210
MONTENEGRO, Clemente de, 204
MONTENEGRO, Juana, 626
MONTENEGRO, Nicanor, 268
MONTENEGRO, Pedro, 284, 640, 844, 846, 850, 921,
    949, 1095, 1261
MONTENEGRO, Santiago, 204
MONTENEGRO DE ALVAREZ, Clorinda Haydée, 320
MONTERITO, pseud.
    see MONTERO, Bartolomé Domingo
MONTERO (family), 1108
MONTERO, Adolfo, 44, 64
MONTERO, Antonio, 1095
MONTERO, Bartolomé Domingo (MONTERITO; BARTOLITO,
    pseuds.), 860
MONTERO, Carlos José, 895
MONYERO, José María, 1093a
MONTERO, José Mariano, 126
MONTERO, José P., 955, 959
MONTERO, Lía Susana, 797
MONTERO, María E., 652
MONTERO, Vicente, 96
MONTERO BROWN, Ramón, 1151, 1174
MONTERO BUSTAMANTE, Raúl, 1066, 1077, 1083, 1174,
    1177, 1187, 1188, 1190, 1199, 1259

MONTERO LACASA, José, 217
MONTERO LÓPEZ, Pedro, 1151
MONTERO PAULLIER, Ramón
    see MONTERO Y PAULLIER, Ramón
MONTERO Y PAULLIER, Ramón, 1075, 1126
MONTERROSO, Ana
    see MONTERROSO DE LAVALLEJA, Ana
MONTERROSO, José Benito, 1115
MONTERROSO, José G., 1093a
MONTERROSO DE LAVALLEJA, Ana, 1060, 1114, 1133
MONTES, Horacio, 332
MONTES, José Antonio, 565
MONTES, Juan de, 949
MONTES, Nora Elena, 684
MONTES, Uladislao, 1084
MONTES, Victoriano E., 1146, 1174
MONTES, Vital, 813
MONTES CARBALLO, Vicente, 915
MONTES DE OCA, Antonina, 887
MONTES DE OCA, Dominga, 887
MONTES DE OCA, José, 254
MONTES DE OCA, Juan José, 844, 854, 1261
MONTES DE OCA, Leopoldo, 842, 844, 1261
MONTES DE OCA, Manuel Augusto, 78, 91, 237, 844
MONTES DE OCA, Marta I., 652
MONTES DE OCA DE CÁRDENAS, Sara, 664, 711, 751, 762
MONTES LARRAIN, Abel, 319
MONTEVERDE, Agustín Alberto, 923
MONTEVERDE, Domingo, 553
MONTEVERDE, José Julio, 923
MONTEVERDE, Juan, 1083
MONTEVERDE, Luis, 332, 391
MONTEVEROZ, José Julio, 923
MONTI, Antonio, 751, 766
MONTI, Armando E., 923
MONTI, Ricardo, 889
MONTIEL, Antonio, 998
MONTIEL, Juan Antonio, 972
MONTIEL, Juan José, 984a
MONTIEL BALLESTEROS, Adolfo, 1068, 1145, 1159, 1160,
    1168, 1169, 1170, 1171, 1177, 1180, 1186, 1196,
    1199, 1251
MONTIEL BALLESTEROS, E., 154
MONTIJO, Eugenia de, 153
MONTOTO, Angel, 878
MONTOTO DE LAZZERI, Silvia A., 810
MONTOYA, Amador de, 992
MONTT, Manuel, 398, 603
MONTÚFAR, Cristóbal Martín de, 844, 1261
MONVOISIN, Raymond Auguste Quinsac, 28, 32, 42, 45,
    51, 59, 207, 293, 521
MONZALVE, Juan de, 186
MONZÓN, Rafael, 299
MOOG, Fernando, 6
MOORE, Dinty, pseud.
    see ZALAZAR ALTAMIRA, Guillermo
MOORE, Olga, 299
MORA, Domingo, 1046, 1047
MORA, Fernando de la, 943, 964, 966, 971, 979, 987,
    1012
MORA, Jaime, 1264
MORA, Juana, 478, 929
MORA, Lola
    see MORA DE HERNÁNDEZ, Lola
MORA DE HERNÁNDEZ, Lola, 55, 141, 478, 929
MORA DE STROESSNER, Eligia, 943a
MORA OLMEDO, Epifanio, 81
MORABES, Juan Luis, 831
MORADO VERES, Manuel Adrián María, 284
MORADOR, Federico, 1151, 1179, 1181

MORAGA, Juan Antonio, 254
MORAL (family), 352
MORALES, Bernadino, 998
MORALES, Carlos María, 332, 1188
MORALES, Cristóbal, 254
MORALES, Domingo Antonio, 874
MORALES, Ernesto, 751, 773
MORALES, Feliciano, 1006
MORALES, Francisco, 768
MORALES, Francisco Javier, 179, 207
MORALES, Francisco Tomás, 553
MORALES, José María, 13, 137
MORALES, Juan Félix, 954
MORALES, Juan P., 207
MORALES, Julio Manuel, 963a
MORALES, Leonor, 1223
MORALES, Lita, 932
MORALES, Lorenzo, 918
MORALES, Manuel de, 32, 283, 895
MORALES, Mariano (COSTEÑO, El, pseud.), 625
MORALES, Mario, 759, 832
MORALES, Modesto, 1122
MORALES, Nicasio, 207
MORALES, Pedro, 186
MORALES, Santiago, 625
MORALES, Sinforoso, 625
MORALES, Susy, 299
MORALES, Vicente, 845, 987
MORALES DE ALBORNOZ, Gregorio, 555
MORALEZ DE ALBORNOZ, José, 555
MORALEZ DE ALDERETE, Pedro, 555
MORALES DE LA BANDA, Juan Antonio, 555
MORALES DE LOS RÍOS DE RUIZ HUIDOBRO, Josefa María,
    179
MORALES DE OMAÑA, Lorenzo, 555
MORALES DE VILLEGAS, Socarrito, 1207, 1217
MORALES GUIÑAZÚ, Fernando, 683a
MORALES NEGRETE, Pedro de, 555
MORALES SANCÁN, Esteban, 874
MORALES TORRES, María A., 652
MORALES ZAVALA, Ulises, 1093
MORÁN, Christóval, 186
MORÁN, Pedro, 358
MORÁN Y GELES, José de, 910
MORANDI, Luis, 1083
MORANTE, Luis Ambrosio, 677, 874
MORAÑA, José Manuel, 19, 25, 31, 36, 46
MORAS, Eloisa G., 41
MORASSI, Angel, 963a
MORATORIO, Orosmán (PERUJO, Julián, pseud.), 894,
    1145, 1154, 1167, 1174, 1179, 1185, 1188, 1199,
    1263
MOREA, Ciriaco, 68
MOREAU, Clément, 1218
MOREAU DE JUSTO, Alicia, 926
MOREAU GOTTSCHALK, Luis, 864
MOREILLON (family), 168
MOREIRA, Enrique, 1089
MOREIRA, Venancio, 1089
MOREIRA DE GARCÍA ROBSON, Magda, 883
MOREIRAS, Florencio Antonio, 284
MOREL, Carlos, 19, 25, 28, 42, 45, 59, 282, 293, 480,
    521, 574
MOREL, Clodomiro, 1006
MOREL, Juan Carlos, 61
MOREL, Pedro, 32
MOREL Y PÉREZ, José María, 496
MORELLI, Juan B., 1083, 1122
MORELLI, Juan B., 1083, 1122
MORELLI, Rodolfo, 46, 63
MORELLO, Antonio, 328

MORELLO, Jorge, 923
MORENO, Artemio, 751
MORENO, Bonifacio, 995a
MORENO, Edgardo, 332
MORENO, Eduardo, 1126
MORENO, Elda, 299
MORENO, Enrique, 356
MORENO, Enrique B., 68, 356
MORENO, Fernando, 823
MORENO, Francisco Pascasio, 141, 152, 176, 202, 210, 282, 287, 288, 289
MORENO, Fulgencio R., 943, 943a, 951, 959, 964, 966, 980, 1012, 1014, 1021, 1022, 1023, 1026
MORENO, Hilarión María, 356, 867
MORENO, Ismael, 217, 874
MORENO, José, 1262
MORENO, José Augusto, 790
MORENO, José del Carmen, 995a
MORENO, José Federico, 212
MORENO, José Gregorio, 995a
MORENO, José María, 391, 544, 585
MORENO, Josué, 122
MORENO, Juan Carlos, 1029
MORENO, Julio, 69
MORENO, Lucas, 96
MORENO, Manuel, 6, 104, 126, 166, 177, 183, 254, 321, 458, 517, 529, 542, 611
MORENO, Manuel (son), 332
MORENO, Manuel María, 173
MORENO, Manuel Vicente, 995a, 1035, 1041
MORENO, Mariano, 6, 70, 85, 104, 110, 118, 121, 126, 141, 144, 145, 145a, 152a, 166, 176, 183, 199, 212, 227, 228, 240, 244, 261, 266, 278, 282, 283, 317, 379, 381, 386, 404, 411, 420, 421, 427, 448, 451, 459, 469, 471, 472, 475, 478, 479, 491, 496, 502, 507, 509, 514, 517, 518, 519, 521, 525, 528, 529, 542, 552, 553, 563, 589, 593, 594, 610, 611, 644, 650, 692, 720, 743, 761, 895
MORENO, Mariano (son), 332
MORENO, Martha, 299
MORENO, Miguel, 867
MORENO, Olinda Teresita, 684
MORENO, Rodolfo Lauro, 356, 923
MORENO, Rosario, 31
MORENO DE MORENO, Julia, 356
MORENO DE SANTA ANA, Domingo, 186
MORENO GONZÁLEZ, Juan Carlos, 1028
MORENO GONZÁLEZ, Renato, 954
MORENO KIERNAN, María Angélica, 44
MORENO SILVEIRA, Alercio, 1210
MORENO TORRECILLAS, Basilio
    see TORRECILLAS, Basilio
MORERA, Eduardo (DUPLÁN, Max, pseud.), 668, 713
MORES, Mariano, 861
MORET, Teófilo A., 94
MORETTI, Agustín, 258
MORETTI, Luis, 37
MORETTO, Oreste, 923
MORGAN, Stephen W. (Mrs.)
    see ALLYN, Franc
MORICANTE, pseud.
    see BADÍA, Gregorio
MORILLO, Francisco, 1229
MORILLO, Joaquín, 653, 654
MORÍNIGO, Harris Gaylord, 1010
MORÍNIGO, Higinio, 975
MORISOLI, Edgar, 717, 739
MORITÁN, Benjamín, 551a
MORLOTE, Andrés, 1082
MORNET, Julio, 949
MORO, Juan, 191

MORO DE RAGGIO, Nora, 923
MORODER MUEDRA, Juan, 923
MORÓN, José Bruno, 212, 412
MORÓN, Juan, 179
MORÓN, Julio Enrique, 560
MORÓN, René, 19
MOROSOLI, Alfredo, 1167
MOROSOLI, Juan José, 1148, 1149, 1155, 1157, 1159, 1167, 1168, 1170, 1177, 1180, 1186, 1196, 1199
MORPHI, Carlos, 1011
MORQUIO, Luis, 1083, 1261
MORRA, Carlos, 258
MORRA, Francisco, 952
MORRA, Miguelángel, 963a
MORRA FERRER, María A., 652
MORRIS, William C., 478
MORRO, Ignatius, 1037
MORROGH, Bernard Juan, 135
MORROW, Alcinda (Mrs. Eli M. Whitson), 323
MORSE, Mary Olive, 323
MORTEO, Serafín C., 268
MÓRTOLA, Catalina, 44
MORTOLA, Edelmira, 923
MORÚA, Zulema, 1207
MORUZZI, Hugo Pedro, 923
MORZONE, Luis, 328
MOSCA, Enrique, 565
MOSCATELLI, Armando Aníbal, 320
MOSCONI, Enrique, 332, 469
MOSCOSO, Angel Mariano
    see MOSCOSO PÉREZ Y OBLITAS, Angel Mariano
MOSCOSO, Mariano, 126
MOSCOSO PÉREZ Y OBLITAS, Angel Mariano, 126, 910
MOSCOSO Y PERALTA, Juan Manuel, 910
MOSELLI ERUT, Luis, 691
MOSER, Hugo, 857
MOSOTTI, Octavio Fabrizio, 332
MOSOVICH, Abraham, 923
MOSQUEIRA, Dionisia de, 955
MOSQUEIRA, Jorge Bernardino, 738
MOSQUEIRA, José, 533
MOSQUEIRA, Silvano, 956
MOSQUEIRA DE BENÍTEZ, Aparicia, 956
MOSQUERA, Joaquín Antonio, 7, 284, 496, 922
MOSQUERA, José Antonio de, 32, 332
MOSSI, Honorio, 24
MOSSI, Miguel Angel, 921
MOSSMAN GROS, Arturo, 1050
MOSSOTTI, Octaviano Fabricio
    see MOSSOTTI DI NOVARA, Octaviano Fabricio
MOSSOTTI DI NOVARA, Octaviano Fabricio, 113, 258, 292, 321
MOSTO, Domingo, 923
MOSTO, Juan Eduardo, 268
MOTA, Carlos de la, 35
MOTA, Vicente, 83
MOTTI, Félix Augusto, 923
MOTTOLA, Sergio L., 857a
MOUCHEZ, Ernest Amedée Barthélemy
    see BARTHELEMY, Ernest Amedée Mouchez
MOUESCA, Eduardo, 565
MOULIN, Hipólito, 28
MOURE DOMÍNGUEZ, José, 1089
MOURIGAN, Eugenio, 1089
MOURIGAN, Ramón, 1089
MOUSSE, P., 28
MOUSSY, Juan Antonio Víctor Martín de, 95, 122, 191, 207, 208, 283, 566, 713, 949, 1261
MOXICA, Ventura, 570
MOXÓ, Benito María
    see MOXÓ Y DE FRANCOLI SAVATER SANZ DE LATRAS, Benito María

MOXÓ Y DE FRANCOLI SAVATER SANZ DE LATRAS, Benito
     María, Arz., 126, 885, 895
MOYA, Dardo, 320
MOYA, Ismael, 688, 751
MOYANO (family), 352
MOYANO, Alfredo, 1088
MOYANO, Andrés Antonio, 555
MOYANO, Braulio Aurelio, 222
MOYANO, Carlos, 12
MOYANO, Carlos María, 9, 14, 202, 287, 288
MOYANO, Daniel, 697, 796
MOYANO, Francisco J., 212
MOYANO, Juan, 179
MOYANO, Juan Agustín, 179, 207
MOYANO, Juan Cornelio, 179
MOYANO, Pedro, 878
MOYANO, Ramón, 173
MOYANO, Sergio, 46
MOYANO CORNEJO, Antonio, 555
MOYANO CORNEJO, Pedro, 556
MOYANO DE AGUILAR, Juan, 555
MOYANO DEL BARCO, Silvia, 222
MOZO, El, pseud.
     see RUBIO, Francisco
MOZO SARAVIA, Carlos, 37
MOZZÓN, Teresa, 65
MUGABURU, María Ana, 320
MUGABURU, Pascuala, 320
MUGICA, Adolfo, 844
MUGICA, Francisco, 858
MUHLMANN, Miguel M., 923
MÜHN, Enrique, 910
MÜHSAM, Ana E., 652
MUIÑO, Enrique, 858, 868, 891, 893
MUJICA, José Tomás, 1206, 1207
MUJICA, Ventura, 472
MUJICA LÁINEZ, Manuel, 666, 685, 688, 712, 729, 752,
     756, 757, 764, 799, 801, 815, 816, 825, 835
MUJICA SANTOS ORONIEL, Domingo, 1210
MUJICA Y COVARRUBIAS, Eleuterio, 210
MUJICA ZAMITE, Juan Vicente, 1210
MULHALL GIRONDO, Laura, 19, 25, 31, 36, 154
MULONI, Nelson Francisco, 653
MÜLLER, José Ricardo, 923
MÜLLER, Rodolfo, 954
MÜLLER, Werner, 954
MUNILLA, Ramón, 254
MUNNE, Enrique Juan, 58
MUNTAWSKI, Carlos, 238
MÜNZEL, Mark, 962
MUÑECAS, Idelfonso Escolástico de las, 282, 552, 921
MUÑEZA, Julio Alberto Leonelo, 41
MUÑIZ, Ariel, 1191
MUÑIZ, Eliseo, 191
MUÑIZ, Francisco Javier, 110, 141, 176, 272, 282,
     293, 404, 574, 603, 611, 844, 851, 854, 1261
MUÑIZ, Justino, 1075, 1093, 1116, 1200
MUÑIZ, Tomás B., 1140
MUÑIZ SILVA, Angel, 1093
MUÑIZ ZAVALA, Justino, 1069
MUÑOZ (family), 1108
MUÑOZ, Agustín, 1093
MUÑOZ, Bartolomé Doroteo, 611, 885, 908, 915, 921
MUÑOZ, Basilio, 1122, 1134
MUÑOZ, Carlos Raúl
     see MUÑOZ DEL SOLAR, Carlos Raúl
MUÑOZ, Daniel (CARRASCO, Sansón; FÍGARO, pseuds.),
     1083, 1123, 1146, 1170, 1177, 1187, 1193, 1195,
     1199
MUÑOZ, Francisco Joaquín, 1063, 1091

MUÑOZ, Germán, 254
MUÑOZ, Gori, 858
MUÑOZ, Guillermo, 1124
MUÑOZ, José María, 1078, 1134
MUÑOZ, José Mariano, 1093
MUÑOZ, Juan, 850a, 1270
MUÑOZ, Juan José, 845, 1124
MUÑOZ, María Elena, 1151, 1181, 1187
MUÑOZ, Melitón, 1116
MUÑOZ, Pancho, 785
MUÑOZ, Rafael, 65
MUÑOZ, Sergio Santiago, 1122
MUÑOZ, Vicente, 7, 32
MUÑOZ ALVAREZ, Ladislao, 998
MUÑOZ BEXARANO, Juan, 186
MUÑOZ CABRERA, Juan Ramón, 653, 654
MUÑOZ COTA, José, 965
MUÑOZ DE FERREIRA, Carolina, 1107
MUÑOZ DE LA ROSA, Francisco, 186
MUÑOZ DE PÉREZ, Josefa, 1093a
MUÑOZ DEL SOLAR, Carlos Raúl (PÚA, Carlos de la,
     pseud.), 644a, 660, 710, 727, 732, 739, 751,
     759, 801, 803, 818, 833, 877
MUÑOZ GADEA, Alonzo de, 186
MUÑOZ LARRETA, Helena, 725, 729
MUÑOZ OBEID DE GERCEK, Lidia, 810
MUÑOZ OLMOS, Juan, 1093
MUÑOZ PORTILLO, Petronio, 965
MUÑOZ SALCEDO, José Enrique, 684
MUÑOZ Y RAVAGO, Rodrigo, 496
MUR, Manuela, 683a, 725
MURATGIA, Catello, 258
MURATORI, Guiseppe, 292
MURATORI, Ludovico Antonio, 985
MURATURE, Alejandro, 13, 14
MURATURE, José, 14, 258, 478
MURATURE, José Luis, 372
MURATURE DE BADARACCO, María del Carmen, 73
MURCIA, José, 41
MURENA, Héctor A., 685, 717, 729, 739, 743, 756,
     758, 759, 802, 816
MURGA, Angel Ignacio, 136
MURGUÍA, Julián, 1093
MURGUÍA, Luis G., 1093
MURGUIONDO VALDEZ, JOsé Luis, 1210
MURIEL, Domingo, 109, 144, 922, 968, 1267, 1269
MURILLO, César, 1173
MURILLO, Gregorio, 371
MURILLO, José, 713, 730
MURO, F., 26
MURO, Julio C., 1075
MURRAY, Carlos, 844, 1261
MURRAY, Edmundo, 923
MURRAY, Luis Alberto, 739
MUSA, Vicente, 947, 995
MUSI, José Osvaldo, 923
MUSITELLI TAGIAFICO, Bruno, 1210
MUSITELLI TAGLAFICO FERRUCCIO, Adriano, 1210
MUSSO, Ricardo Juan, 24, 64
MUSTAPIC, Paula, 781
MÜSTH, Ricardo, 995
MUSTO, Jorge, 1182
MUSTO, Manuel, 19, 58
MUTINELLI, Arturo, 923
MUTTI WARD DE SMITH, Violeta R., 781
MUX, Néxtor, 662, 663
MUZIO SÁENZ PEÑA, Carlos, 235
MUZLERA, Liborio, 13
MUZO, Ricardo, 1021, 1022
MYSTROMER, Carolos, A. B., 904

NABUCO, Joaquím, 956
NACARATO, Vicente, 683a
NACIMIENTO, Amadeo, 998
NACIMIENTO, Juan B., 959
NADAL Y CAMPOS, José, 496
NAJAR GÓMEZ, Luis A., 923
NÁJERA, Luis E., 923
NÁJERA ANGULO, Luis, 923
NAJMANOVICH, Armando, 750
NAJURIETA, Enrique, 319
NALÉ ROXLO, Conrado (CHAMICO; ALGUIEN, pseuds.),
    670, 674, 675, 676, 678, 685, 722, 739, 745a,
    748, 751, 759, 769, 773, 782, 799, 803, 807,
    816, 833
NALLIM, Carlos Orlando, 683a
NAMBAHAY, 977
NAMUNCURÁ, 454
NAMUNCURÁ, Ceferino M., 154
NAMUNCURÁ, Manuel, 617
NAN DOMÍNGUEZ, Héctor Lirio, 1210
NANDASUVI
    see ÑANDASUVI
NANDUABUSU, 997
NANI, Alberto, 923
NANNI, Domenico, 139
NANTABAGUA, 977
NAÓN, Carlos, 125
NAÓN, Juan José, 844, 1261
NAÓN, Pedro J., 669, 751
NAÓN, Rómulo S., 68, 103
NAPOLI, Nicola Di
    see DI NAPOLI, Nicola
NAPOLITANO, Emilio Angel, 882, 883
NAPOLITANO, Leonardo S., 683a
NARANCIO, Atilio, 1083
NARANJO, Juan de los Angeles, 58
NARBONA, Juan, 7, 32
NARDY, Inés, 949
NARI, Fortunato E., 814, 824
NARVÁEZ, Santiago Esteban, 995a
NARVÁEZ ARCE, Gregorio, 947
NARVAJA, Tristán, 244, 1261
NARVARTE, Claudio Ramón, 328
NASCHER, Martha, 684
MASIO, Juan, 923
NASJLETI, Eduardo Víctor, 923
NATALI, Paolo, 139
NATOLA, Aurora
    see NATOLA DE BICKART, Aurora
NATOLA DE BICKART, Aurora, 135
NAVA, Arturo de, 878
NAVA, Juan de, 878
NAVAJAS, Miguel Antonio, 1075, 1082
NAVARRETE, Doroteo R., 1093
NAVARRETE, Sinforosa Camila de, 1060
NAVARRINE, Alfredo, 871
NAVARRINE, Julio P., 871
NAVARRO (family), 348, 352
NAVARRO, 608
NAVARRO, Alfredo, 1083
NAVARRO, Andrés, 850
NAVARRO, Antonio, 320
NAVARRO, Bartolomé, 895
NAVARRO, Eduardo Timoteo, 31
NAVARRO, Fany, 879
NAVARRO, Fernando R., 385
NAVARRO, José, 254
NAVARRO, José Antonio, 220
NAVARRO, José de, 188, 283
NAVARRO, Joseph, 186
NAVARRO, Juan Carlos, 842, 848
NAVARRO, Julián, 177, 458, 478, 611, 908, 915, 921

NAVARRO, Manuel, 95, 96, 126
NAVARRO, Margarito, 998
NAVARRO, Miguel (family), 358
NAVARRO, Nicolás, 186
NAVARRO, Ramón Gil
    see GIL NAVARRO, Ramón
NAVARRO, Remigio, 137
NAVARRO, Ricardo, 684
NAVARRO, Samuel, 254
NAVARRO, Secundino J., 173, 174
NAVARRO DE LEÓN, Juan Antonio, 344
NAVARRO DE TOLEDO, Phelipe, 186
NAVARRO GERASSI, Marysa, 558
NAVARRO PUENTES, Ismael, 751
NAVAS, Arturo B., 894
NAVAZIO, Walter de, 19, 25, 31, 33
NAVEIRA, Carlos Jesús, 923
NAVEIRA DE DEL CIOPPO, Ofelia, 1211
NAVIA (family), 1108
NAZAR, Benito, 611
NAZAR, Laureano, 188, 283
NAZARRE DE GRANDOLI, Dionisia, 422, 611
NAZARRE DE PICO, Benita, 611
NAZARRE DE ROMERO, Benita, 422
NAZZARI, Amadeo, 857v
NEBBIA DE CODEGA, Aída J., 656
NEBEL, Fernando, 1187
NEBEL ALVAREZ, Miguel, 1145
NECOCHEA, Eugenio, 611
NECOCHEA, Mariano, 85, 136, 212, 282, 386, 404, 574,
    611
NÉE, Luis, 17a, 885
NEENGUIRU, pseud.
    see LANGUIRU, Nicola
NEGREIRA LUCAS, Marina Dolores, 1210
NEGRETE, Lucía, 923
NEGRI, Ada, 154
NEGRI, Héctor, 663
NEGRO, Héctor, pseud.
    see VARELA, Ismael Héctor
NEGRÓN, Battista (NEGRONI), 292
NEGRÓN, Diego Martín, 570
NEGRONI, Battista
    see NEGRÓN, Battista
NEGRONI, Pablo, 923
NEGROTTO, Salvador, 258
NEIRA, José
    see NEIRA GONZÁLEZ, José
NEIRA GONZÁLEZ, José, 284, 1095
NEIRA SOSA, Francisco José, 1210
NEIROT, Juan Antonio, 611, 908, 921
NELSON, Ernesto, 118, 167, 478, 751
NELSON, Victoria, 299
NELLA CASTRO, Antonio, 653, 654, 766
NERUDA, Pablo, pseud. (REYES BASUALTO, Neftalí),
    658
NERVI, Juan Ricardo, 768
NERVO, Amado, 244
NERY RUBIO, Julio, 768
NESPOLO ROMERSA, Ricardo, 1210
NEUMANN, Juan Bautista, 1264
NEUMEYER, Julio E., 69
NEUSCHLOSZ, Simón Marcelo, 923
MEUSTADT, Bernardo, 213
NEVEDAGNAC, 1031
NEWBERRY, Jorge, 141, 332
NEWTON, Ricardo, 3
NEYRA, Domingo, 895
NEYRA, Joaquín, 753
NEYRA Y ARELLANO, Francisco de, 284, 496

NICASIO, Alberto, 18, 24, 44
NICO, Raúl, 923
NICOLA, Gabriela, 949
NICOLÁS ANTONIO DE SAN LUIS
    see SAN LUIS, Nicolás Antonio de
NICOLATO, Luis, 258
NICOLAU, Sandalio, 268
NICOLI, Roberto Adolfo, 738
NICOLINI, Nilda Rosa, 817
NICOLINO, Juan Carlos, 923
NICOLLIER (family), 168
NICOLLIER, Juan Luis (family), 168
NICOLLIER, Víctor S., 923
NICORA, José Luis, 1014
NICOTRA, Alejandro, 703, 705, 716, 717, 831
NIEBLA, Bartolomé de, 1030
NIEBLA, José, 284
NIEDFELD ETCHEBARNE, Horacio Alberto, 923
NIELD, S., 904
NIELSEN, Juan, 286
NIELLA, Luis María, 910
NIENGUIRI, Diego, 977
NIETO, José del Carmen, 191
NIETO, Juan, 914
NIETO, Luis E., 874
NIETO, Manuel E., 1122
NIETO BLANC, Irene M. de, 691
NIETO DE UMANES, Juan, 186
NIETO PALACIOS, José A., 31
NIEVA DE MUÑOZ, Anita, 762
NIEVA Y CASTILLA, Juan de, 555
NIEVAS, Santiago, 1111
NIEZÁ, Diego, 977
NIJENSOHN, Leon, 923
NIN FRÍAS, Alberto A. A., 1083, 1187, 1190
NITO, pseud.
    see GALINDO, Raúl
NITO, Humberto de, 882
NITO, José de, 882
NIZ, Pantaleón de, 186
NIZOSO, Alonso, 1270
NIZZA, Pietro Di
    see DI NIZZA, Pietro
NOBLE, Edmundo, 644a
NOBLE, Julio A., 260, 332
NOBLIA, Gerardo, 1093
NOBLIA, Isidoro, 1093
NOBLIA, Osvaldo, 1093
NOBLIA, Rufino, 1093
NOBLIA DE PLAZA, Lola, 1093
NOBOA COURRÁS, Diego, 1064
NÓBREGA DE AVELLANEDA, Carmen, 130
NOCARD, Edmundo, 844
NOCETI, Adolfo, 853a
NOCETTI, Domingo, 332
NOCETTI, Nicolás, 258
NOCETTI DE MAGGIPINTO, Elda T., 652
NOCITA, Ana María, 691
NOÉ, Luis Felipe, 19, 25, 36, 49, 55
NOEL, Augusto León, 320
NOEL, Carlos M., 103
NOËL, León, 59
NEOL, Martín Alberto, 729
NOGUE, Bernardo, 496
NOGUERA, Enrique, 1167
NOGUERA, Oscar Francisco, 923
NOGUÉS, Alberto, 943
NOGUÉS, Andrés, 954
NOGUÉS, Pablo, 332
NOJECHOWIZ, Noé, 36, 55

NOLASCO AQUINO, Pedro, 995a
NOLASCO COBO, Pedro, 283
NOLASCO DE SANTA MARÍA, Pedro, 914
NOLASCO FONSECA, Pedro, 371
NOLASCO GRIMAU, Pedro, 283
NOLASCO LEÓN, Pedro, 845
NOLASCO PÉREZ, Pedro, 914
NOLAZCO DECOUD, Pedro, 991
NOLO, pseud.
    see TEJÓN, Manuel R.
NOMI, Alfredo, 683a
NOODT, Rodolfo Oscar, 695
NOORT, Olivier Van
    see VAN NOORT, Olivier
NORDENSKIÖLD, Erland, 191
NORES (family), 352
NORES, Agustín, 120
NORIEGA, Francisco, 186
NORO, M. Elda, 713
NORO, Pedro Raúl, 730
NOSETTO, Roque, 837
NOTARIO, Brígida, 44
NOTTER, Tomás, 82
NOTTI, Humberto Joaquín, 923
NOUGUEZ, Miguel M., 445
NOUTZ, Marcelino, 963
NOVARESE, 59
NOVARO, Bartolomé, 844
NOVARRO, Francisco, 268
NOVAS TERRA, Luis, 1172, 1185
NOVELLI, Armando, 923
NOVILLO (family), 352
NOVILLO CORVALÁN, Julio, 652
NOVILLO QUIROGA, Diego, 217, 834, 1243, 1246, 1247, 1248
NOVIÓN, Alberto, 719, 724, 890
NOVITZKY, Alejandro, 923
NOVOA, Angela, 789
NOVOA, Luis, 1089
NOVOA, Ramón, 1089
NOVOA OLTRA, Julio, 1210
NOYA, Ibón, 284
NOZIÈRES, Francesca de, 956
NUCÍFORA, Lola, 932
NÚDELMAN, Santiago I., 751
NUMA CASTELLANOS, Moisés, 653, 654, 664, 669
NUMA CRIOLLO, pseud.
    see CÓRDOBA, Numa P.
NUMA SOTO, Pedro, 565
NÚÑEZ, Alvar, 521
NÚÑEZ, Alvaro, 1270
NÚÑEZ, Benito, 1089
NÚÑEZ, Blas Antonio, 995a
NÚÑEZ, Cándido, 1017
NÚÑEZ, Diego, 845
NÚÑEZ, Germán, 1093
NÚÑEZ, Ignacio, 126, 478, 609, 1059
NÚÑEZ, Jerónimo, 358, 1267
NÚÑEZ, Jorge, 521
NÚÑEZ, José, 1116
NÚÑEZ, José Ignacio, 1111
NÚÑEZ, José María, 995a
NÚÑEZ, José Romualdo, 254
NÚÑEZ, José Rufino, 268
NÚÑEZ, Josué A., 923
NÚÑEZ, Juan, 1095
NÚÑEZ, Justo José
    see NÚÑEZ Y CHAVARRÍA, Justo José
NÚÑEZ, Lauro, 895, 1267
NÚÑEZ, Reginaldo, 190

NÚÑEZ, Tomás, 556
NÚÑEZ, Urbano Joaquín, 215, 222
NÚÑEZ, Zulma, 154, 751, 1088
NÚÑEZ CABEZA DE VACA, Alvar, 32, 292, 406, 455, 462, 471, 472, 477, 504, 505, 518, 519, 528, 570, 964, 984, 984a, 985, 989, 997, 1010, 1011, 1012, 1203, 1229, 1230, 1231, 1232
NÚÑEZ CALLEJA, Manuel, 683a
NÚÑEZ DE BOSSUT, Iris, 683a
NÚÑEZ DE IBARRA, Manuel Pablo, 32, 61, 62, 293
NÚÑEZ DE PRADO, Juan, 83, 472, 521, 620
NÚÑEZ DE SILVA, Diego, 1270
NÚÑEZ DE VILLARINO
   see VILLARINO, Núñez de
NÚÑEZ GARCÍA, Arturo (WIMPI, pseud.), 769
NÚÑEZ LUGARO, Amanda, 1088
NÚÑEZ MAGRO, Manuel, 1270
NÚÑEZ REGUIERO, Manuel, 1083
NÚÑEZ VELLOSO, Carlos Alfredo, 998
NÚÑEZ WEST, Horacio, 663, 739, 805, 831
NÚÑEZ Y CHAVARRÍA, Justo José, 126, 496
NÚÑEZ Y MALACODA, Ramiro (MALACODA, pseud.), 1173
NUSDORFFER, Bernardo, 318
NUSIMOVICH, Noisés, 35
NUSSIF, Alfonso, 804
NUSSIS, Nicolás, 923
NYMAN, Frances A., 323
NYSTRÖMER, Carlos, 332

ÑANCUMAN, 566
ÑANDASUVI, 977
ÑO PELO, pseud.
   see SOSA, Pedro Antonio

OBALDÍA, José María, 1159
OBANDO, Baltasar de
   see LIZÁRRAGA, Reginaldo de
OBARRIO, Juan M., 847
OBEJERO, Eduardo, 844
OBELAR, Mauricio G., 1088
OBELAR, Raimundo D., 959
OBEN, Luis
   see JOBEN, Luis, 866
OBERT DE THIENSIS, Emmanuel, 949
OBES (family), 1108
OBES, Lucas José, 126, 1052, 1053, 1063
OBIETA, Adolfo de, 739
OBIETA, Jorge de, 739
OBLIGADO, Antolín Gil de
   see GIL OBLIGADO, Antolín de
OBLIGADO, Antonio, 126
OBLIGADO, Carlos, 664, 751, 773, 807, 1247
OBLIGADO, Erasmo, 14
OBLIGADO, Jorge, 751, 773
OBLIGADO, Juan José, 268
OBLIGADO, Juan N., 268
OBLIGADO, Justino, 254
OBLIGADO, Manuel Alejandro, 126, 147, 496, 611
OBLIGADO, Manuel I., 191
OBLIGADO, Manuel J., 17b
OBLIGADO, Pastor Servando, 121, 141, 147, 478
OBLIGADO, Pedro Miguel, 521, 664, 674, 678, 722, 729, 739, 751, 755, 759, 773, 782, 807
OBLIGADO, Rafael, 121, 152a, 166, 217, 282, 669, 682, 723, 724, 734, 737, 740, 749, 751, 754, 759, 767, 803, 807, 1242, 1243, 1247, 1248, 1249, 1254, 1260
OBREGÓN (family), 352
OBREGÓN, Alberto, 731
OBREGÓN CANO, Ricardo, 440

OBREGOSO, José de, 371
O'BRIEN, D. H., 580
O'BRIEN, Esteban de, 332
O'BRIEN, Juan, 611
OCA, José, 1089
OCA DEL VALLE, Fernando, 963a
OCAMPO, Alberto G., 154
OCAMPO, Benigno, 193
OCAMPO, Bernardo, 921
OCAMPO, Florentino, 1006
OCAMPO, Francisco Antonio, 104
OCAMPO, Jamín, 83
OCAMPO, Juan B., 384
OCAMPO, Juan de, 1270
OCAMPO, Juan Francisco, 1269
OCAMPO, Manuel, 447
OCAMPO, Manuel José de, 496
OCAMPO, Miguel, 19, 25, 26, 31, 36, 49, 727, 813
OCAMPO, Ramón de, 284
OCAMPO, Rubén, 83
OCAMPO, Silvina, 594, 666, 670, 678, 685, 697, 722, 729, 737, 739, 748, 751, 756, 758, 759, 764, 772, 783, 799, 806, 807, 815, 816, 822, 829, 835
OCAMPO, Victoria
   see OCAMPO DE ESTRADA, Victoria
OCAMPO DE ESTRADA, Victoria, 210, 232, 729, 741, 743, 751, 752, 812, 926
OCAMPO DE SAN MIGUEL, Juan, 555
OCAMPO JARAMILLO, Juan de, 649a
OCAMPOS, José Domingo, 954
OCAMPOS, Manuel Antonio, 387
OCAMPOS LANZONI, José, 998
OCAMPOS ROJAS, Raúl, 998
OCANA, Juan Bautista, 220
OCANTOS, Carlos María, 152a, 747, 754, 774, 834
OCANTOS, Eduardo, 560
OCARIZ, Cecilio, 1017
O'CONNOR, Elsa, 891
OCHAGAVIA, Carlos, 299
OCHOA, Evaristo, 998
OCHOA, Fernando (GODOY, Goyo, pseud.), 1243
OCHOA, Pedro, 344
OCHOA CASTRO, Carlos, 207
OCHOA DE MASRAMÓN, Dora, 222, 823
OCHOA DE ZÁRATE, Juan, 32
OCHOTECO, Martín José de, 496
ODERIGO, María Florencia, 683a
O'DONELL, Sabino, 189
O'DONNELL, Carlos, 922
O'DONNELL FIGUEROA, Juan Carlos, 284
ODORIZ IZAGUIRRE, José Bernardo, 207, 923
ODRIOSOLA, Indalecio, 1029
ODRIOSOLA, Ricardo, 959
ODRIOZOLA, Omar, 1167
ODRIOZOLA GARBARINO, José Luis, 1210
OESTERHELD, Héctor G., 728
O'FARREL, Juan A., 268, 565
O''FARREL, Miguel Z., 268
OFFERMANN, Alfredo Manuel, 923
OFICIALDEGUY, Pedro, 320
OGLOBLIN, Alejandro A., 923
O'GORMAN, Camila, 478, 480, 608, 928
O'GORMAN, Eduardo, 921
O'GORMAN, Miguel, 321
O'GORMAN, Tomás, 587
OGUES DE NAVA, Waldemar, 1210
O'HIGGINS, Bernardo, 104, 283, 453, 553, 561, 573
O'HIGGINS, Juan, 82
OJEDA, Asunción, 1082

OJEDA, Gabriel de, 318
OJEDA, Hugo, 788
OJEDA, José Antonio, 225
OJEDA, Luis, 222
OJEDA, Manuel de, 344
OLAGUER FELIÚ Y HEREDIA, Antonio, 1136, 1237, 1239, 1240, 1241, 1262
OLAGUIBEL, Juan Bautista de, 344
OLAGUIBEL, Juan Bernardo de, 344
OLANO, Juan Antonio de, 555
OLAÑETA, Pedro Antonio, 552
OLARANS CHANS, Justo, 1167
OLASCOAGA, Manuel José, 62, 207, 212, 278, 287, 683a, 834
OLASCOAGA, Ramón, 68
OLAVARRÍA, Antonio de, 272
OLAVARRÍA, José de, 166, 433, 529, 611, 904
OLAVARRÍA, José Valentín de, 386
OLAVARRÍA, Tomás de, 555
OLAVARRÍA Y PORRÚA, José M., 923
OLAVARRIETA, Diego de (family), 358
OLAVARRIETA, Manuel de, 132, 254, 344
OLAVARRIETA, Ramón, 611, 908
OLAVARRIETA LAMAS, Eugenio, 921
OLAVE, Arturo I., 1075
OLAZÁBAL, Félix de, 433, 611
OLAZÁBAL, Manuel de, 188, 196, 220, 371, 611
OLAZÁBAL, Tirso de, 883
OLDAN CAROL JULIÁN, Omar, 1210
O'LEARY, Juan Emiliano, 943, 954, 959, 963, 965, 966, 1014, 1015, 1018, 1020, 1021, 1022, 1023, 1026
OLGUIN, Belarmino T., 222
OLGUÍN, José, 845
OLGUÍN, Juan, 923
OLGUÍN, Victorio del Carmen, 222
OLHABERRIAGUE Y BLANCO, Félix d', 1236
OLIDEN, Matías Vicente, 126
OLIVA, Antonio de la, 1270
OLIVA, Eleazar, 244
OLIVA, Juan Antonio, 918
OLIVA, Juan de, 1270
OLIVA NAVARRO, Juan Carlos, 154
OLIVA SERPEZ, Mónica, 683a
OLIVAR, Guillermo F., 62, 207
OLIVARES, Carlos, 154
OLIVARES, Miguel de, 283
OLIVARI, Carlos, 858
OLIVARI, Marcelo, 681
OLIVARI, Nicolás, 660, 670, 678, 712, 722, 739, 759, 769, 801, 803, 807, 833, 871, 1245
OLIVE, Augusto Juan, 58
OLIVEIRA, José Pedro, 1261
OLIVEIRA, Oscar Manuel, 713
OLIVEIRA CÉZAR, Angela de, 226
OLIVEIRA CÉZAR, Filisberto de, 1246
OLIVEIRA CÉZAR, Isaac de, 68
OLIVEIRA Y SILVA, Luso, 998
OLIVENCIA, Pablo, 1075
OLIVER, Francisco J., 94
OLIVER, Frank P., 904
OLIVER, Jaime Hipólito, 1083
OLIVER, Juan María (SOLITO, Juan, pseud.), 1079, 1145, 1166, 1167, 1243
OLIVER, Juan Pablo, 609
OLIVER, Manuel María, 154
OLIVER, María Rosa, 666, 741, 819, 822
OLIVER, Prego de
     see PREGO DE OLIVER, José
OLIVER, Tomás, 268

OLIVERA, Adeodato, 844
OLIVERA, Andrés, 6
OLIVERA, Benita, 320
OLIVERA, Bernardino, 625
OLIVERA, Carlos, 332, 714, 780
OLIVERA, Carlos C., 6
OLIVERA, Clodomiro Enrique, 1122
OLIVERA, Domingo, 4
OLIVERA, Eduardo, 3, 391, 631
OLIVERA, Eustaquia, 320
OLIVERA, Héctor, 857
OLIVERA, Horacio Raúl, 299
OLIVERA, Jacinta Natividad, 320
OLIVERA, Juana, 320
OLIVERA, Leonardo, 1054, 1111
OLIVERA, Martina B., 320
OLIVERA, Miguel Alfredo, 729, 739
OLIVERA CANCELA, Juan José, 1210
OLIVERA CÓRDOBA, Miguel Z., 268
OLIVERA LAVIÉ, Héctor, 235
OLIVERA SOSA, Jorge, 1210
OLIVERES, Francisco N., 1073
OLIVERIO, Pascual Luis, 94
OLIVERO (family), 168
OLIVEROS ESCOLA, Eduardo, 68
OLIVIER, Angela, 874
OLIVIER, Santiago Raúl, 923
OLIVIERI, Silvino, 98, 258, 292
OLMEDO (family), 352
OLMEDO, Agustín Angel, 244, 254, 652
OLMEDO, E. A., 766
OLMEDO, Félix, 244
OLMEDO, Roberto F., 963a
OLMOS, Anbrosio, 89
OLMOS, Emilio F., 244
OLMOS, Hugo, 691
OLMOS, José Severo, 545a, 648, 649
OLMOS, José Vicente de, 89
OLMOS, Juan Francisco, 268
OLMOS, Lisandro, 189
OLMOS, Sabina, 879
OLMOS ARRAZUOLA, Gualberto, 954
OLMOS BARONE, Roberto, 1210
OLMOS CASTRO, Norberto, 923
OLMOS MUÑOZ, Juan, 1093
MOLMOS Y AGUILERA, José de, 555
OLROG, Claes Christián Claesson, 923
OLSACHER, Juan, 923
OLLEROS, Juan José, 169, 268, 611
OLLEROS, Mariano Ladislao, 268
OLLOGUI (family), 348
OLLONIEGO, Gerónimo, 254
OMAR, Nelly, 879
ONEGA, Bonifacio, 1089
ONELLI, Clemente, 98, 122, 258, 751
ONETO, Ana Esther, 320
ONETO, Estela Luisa, 320
ONETO, Rafael, 19, 31
ONETO DE CALVO, Rosa María, 320
ONETO Y VIANA, Carlos, 1083
ONETTI, Jorge, 770, 1158, 1182, 1189, 1192
ONETTI, Juan Carlos, 806, 1148, 1149, 1155, 1158, 1177, 1189, 1252
ONETTI, Pedro, 1123
ONETTI LIMA, Luis, 190, 1145
ONETTO, Antonio, 258
ONETTO, Rafael, 63
ONGANÍA, Juan Carlos, 515, 590, 593, 624
ONGARO, Raimundo, 440
ONÍS, Federico de, 688

ONOFRIO, Norberto, 27, 55
ONRUBIA, Emilio, 135
ONSLOW, Arthur, 28
OÑA, Cristóbal de, 1270
OÑATE, Pedro de, 649a
OÑATIVIA, Arturo, 923
OOSTENDORP, Alberto, 68
OPERTO, Juan, 87
OPERTO, Walter, 889
OQUENDO, Rosas de
    see ROZAS DE OQUENDO, Mateo
ORANTES, Pedro de, pseud.
    see DORANTES, Pedro
ORAZI, Orfeo Osvaldo, 923
ORBEA, Jorge Raúl, 923
ORBIGNY, Alcides Dessalines d', 28, 95, 191, 293,
    713, 949
ORCE REMIS, Guillermo, 679, 722, 739, 758
ORDANO, Julio, 889
ORDEIG FIGUERAS, José, 1094
ORDEN, Elena J., 652
ORDEN VEDOÑO, Cipriano, pseud.
    see CERVIÑO, Pedro Antonio
ORDOÑANA, Domingo, 1067, 1203
ORDÓÑEZ, Jorge Enrique, 878
ORDÓÑEZ, José, 553
ORDÓÑEZ, Manuel, 560
ORDÓÑEZ CARASA, María L. A., 652
ORDÓÑEZ DE VILLAQUIRÁN, Miguel, 1223
ORDÓÑEZ DE VILLAQUIRÁN Y VIANA, José, 1223
ORDÓÑEZ Y ORTEGA, Melchor, 1223
ORDÓÑEZ Y VIANA, Antonia, 1223
ORDÓÑEZ Y VIANA, Dolores, 1223
ORDÓÑEZ Y VIANA, Melchor, 1223
ORDÓÑEZ Y VIANA, Victoria, 1223
ORDOÑO, 361
ORDUÑA, Francisco de, 496
ORDUÑA, Sebastián de, 97
OREGHI, José, 952
OREJAS, Agustín A., 810
ORELLANA, Mauricio, 222
ORELLANA, Rodrigo Antonio de, 545a, 910, 921
OREZZILI, Jorge Alberto, 299
ORFILA, Alejandro, 213
ORFILA, Ricardo N., 923
ORGA, Bernabé de la, 773
ORGAMBIDE, Carlos, 857c
ORGAMBIDE, Pedro G., 440, 696, 772, 794, 835, 836
ORGANIZ, Pablo, 731
ORGAZ, Alfredo, 218
ORGAZ, Arturo, 260, 431
ORGÓÑEZ, Rodrigo, 32
ORIAS, Oscar, 923
ORIBE, 240
ORIBE (family), 1106, 1108
ORIBE, Dionisio, 1059, 1111
ORIBE, Emilio, 1068, 1079, 1145, 1147, 1148, 1149,
    1151, 1152, 1165, 1171, 1177, 1179, 1181, 1184,
    1198, 1199
ORIBE, Ignacio, 569, 1063
ORIBE, L. F., pseud.
    see GUDIÑO, Luis Fernando
ORIBE, Manuel Ceferino, 95, 127, 283, 390, 433, 1059,
    1060, 1079, 1091, 1110, 1111, 1131, 1132
ORIBE, Stewart, 1134
ORIBE CORONEL, Enrique, 1093
ORIGONE, Manuel Félix, 81
ORIHUELA, José María, 254
ORIHUELA, Manuel Bernabé, 126
ORIHUELA, Mariano, 126

ORILSE, Manuel, 96
ORILLÓN, Fernando, 938
ORIQUE, Bernardino E., 1124
ORIQUE, Ramón, 1116
ORIZ DE ROA, Lino, 68, 152
ORLANDI, Alicia N., 41
ORLANDI, Nazareno, 258
ORLANDI DE LARRAMENDY, Sara, 1217
ORLANDINI, Luis, 258
ORLANDO, Héctor Antonio, 923
ORLANDO, Pierri, 23
ORLANDO, Polo, pseud.
    see SORIA ORLANDO, Leopoldo
ORMA, Francisco Mariano, 496
ORMA DE REBOLLO, Rufino, 422, 611
ORMAECHEA, José Agustín, 125
ORMAECHEA, José E., 1168
ORMAECHEA DE LEÓN, Juan José, 1210
ORO, Domingo de, 95, 166, 283, 398, 413, 603, 608,
    629
ORO, José Antonio de, 283
ORO, José de, 549, 921
ORO, Justo de Santa María de, 85, 110, 166, 171,
    188, 244, 278, 282, 283, 404, 411, 413, 439,
    457, 478, 526, 536, 547, 549, 586, 603, 611,
    615, 621, 626, 910, 921
ORO BUSTAMANTE, Juan Bautista de, 555
ORO BUSTAMANTE Y SANTA MARÍA, Juan de, 283, 555
ORO DE LA ROZA, Tránsito de, 931
ORO DE RODRÍGUEZ, Tránsito de, 930, 931
ORO DE SARMIENTO, Paula de, 930
OROMI Y MARTILLER, Ramón Miguel de, 496
ORONA, Juan de, 1238
ORONOZ LUCHO, Martín, 1211
OROÑO, Nicasio, 96, 282, 330
OROÑO GADOLA, Dumas, 1210
OROSA, Antonio, 1089
OROSZ, Ladislao, 319, 895, 1264, 1269
OROZCO, Gregorio, 319, 1267
OROZCO, Manuel A., 222
OROZCO, Olga, 672, 716, 722, 725, 739, 758, 759,
    768, 798, 822
OROZCO ZÁRATE, Epifanio, 767
ORPHEÉ, Elvira, 666
ORQUEDA, Liberato, 878
ORREGO, Cristino, 998
ORREGO, Tomás Francisco, 299
ORREGO QUINTANA, Pedro, 998
ORRIGÓN, Juan, 32
ORSI, Guillermo Félix, 738
ORTA Y AZAMOR, Agustín de, 496
ORTAZ BENEDETTO, Juan Bautista, 1210
ORTEGA, Benancio, 132
ORTEGA, Bernardino de, 132
ORTEGA, David, 320
ORTEGA, Juan de, 318, 1011
ORTEGA, Manuel de, 677, 850, 989, 1270
ORTEGA, Miguel, 677
ORTEGA, Palito, 857
ORTEGA, Rufino
    see ORTEGA BERUTI, Rufino
ORTEGA, Serafín, 683a
ORTEGA BERUTI, Rufino, 17b, 68, 132, 212, 240, 278,
    445
ORTEGA DE CARRASCO, Maruca, 766
ORTEGA Y GASSET, José, 246
ORTELLI, Mosé Battista, 139
ORTELLI, Orlando Martino, 139
ORTICOCHEA, María, 1217
ORTIGOZA, José Sebastián (SARGENTO CUATÍ, pseud.),
    1003

ORTIGOZA, Juan de la Cruz, 995a
ORTIGOZA, Pedro Baltazar, 995a
ORTIZ (family), 336
ORTIZ, Adolfo, 222
ORTIZ, Alvaro, 556
ORTIZ, Angeles, 25
ORTIZ, Antonio, 1264
ORTIZ, Carlos, 152a, 669, 751, 773, 782, 1247, 1259
ORTIZ, Ezequiel Daniel, 874
ORTIZ, Francisco Antonio, 316
ORTIZ, Gerónimo Dolores, 995a
ORTIZ, Humberto B., 222
ORTIZ, José Antonio, 959, 995a, 1006
ORTIZ, José Concepción, 1014, 1020, 1021, 1022
ORTIZ, José María, 24
ORTIZ, José Santos, 158, 159, 179, 215
ORTIZ, Juan (Argentina), 135
ORTIZ, Juan (Uruguay), 1059
ORTIZ, Juan José, 1080, 1111
ORTIZ, Juan L., 658, 678, 722, 739, 746, 751, 758,
    759, 798, 800, 803, 807, 831
ORTIZ, Julio, 751
ORTIZ, Lorenzo, 319
ORTIZ, Manuel, 126
ORTIZ, Manuel Angeles, 1218
ORTIZ, Norberto, 1059, 1111
ORTIZ, Pedro Julián, 207
ORTIZ, Pedro N., 207
ORTIZ, Ramón, 1059
ORTIZ, Ricardo M., 332
ORTIZ, Roberto Mario, 219, 405, 466, 489, 515, 516,
    524, 619
ORTIZ, Toribio, 95
ORTIZ BEHETY, Luis, 678, 746, 766
ORTIZ CAZAL, Estanislao, 998
ORTIZ DE ALCALDE, Antonio, 496
ORTIZ DE ESTRADA, Juan Agustín, 222, 566
ORTIZ DE HARO, Isidro, 529a
ORTIZ DE MENDIETA, Diego, 984
ORTIZ DE MERCADO, Cristóbal, 555
ORTIZ DE MOJER, María del Carmen, 320
ORTIZ DE OCAMPO, Francisco Antonio, 85, 89, 242,
    244, 404, 478, 479, 496, 545a, 611
ORTIZ DE ROZAS, Domingo
    see ORTIZ DE ROZAS Y GARCÍA DE VILLASUSO,
    Domingo
ORTIZ DE ROZAS (family), 351
ORTIZ DE ROZAS, León, 538
ORTIZ DE ROZAS, Juan M.
    see ROSAS, Juan Manuel Domingo Ortiz de
ORTIZ DE ROZAS Y GARCÍA DE VILLASUSO, Domingo, 2,
    188
ORTIZ DE TARANCO, Félix, 1095
ORTIZ DE VERGARA, Francisco, 254, 504, 984, 984a,
    985, 1011
ORTIZ DE VERGARA, Juan, 989
ORTIZ DE ZÁRATE (family), 1224
ORTIZ DE ZÁRATE, J. César, 923
ORTIZ DE ZÁRATE, Juan, 254, 471, 472, 521, 528, 570,
    640, 984, 984a, 1011, 1231, 1232
ORTIZ DE ZÁRATE, Juana, 197
ORTIZ DE ZÁRATE, Pedro, 921, 1040
ORTIZ DE ZÁRATE, Rodrigo, 358, 1203
ORTIZ DE ZÁRATE Y MENDIETA, Diego, 1011
ORTIZ ESTRADA, Juan Agustín, 158
ORTIZ GARCÍA, Aníbal Alfonso, 284
ORTIZ GUERRERO, Manuel, 943, 947, 966, 1012, 1014,
    1018, 1020, 1021, 1022, 1023, 1026, 1028
ORTIZ MAYANS, Antonio, 1014
ORTIZ MELGAREJO, Rodrigo, 1270

ORTIZ MÉNDEZ, Francisco, 1014, 1021, 1022
ORTIZ P., Rubén, 954
ORTIZ SARALEGUI, Juvenal, 1151, 1179, 1199
ORTIZ Y AYALA, Walter, 1151, 1178
ORTIZ Y HERRERA, José A., 89
ORTUBIA, Gabriel de, 555
ORUÉ, José Vicente de, 1041
ORUÉ, Martín José de, 987, 1238
ORZÁBAL, Arturo, 68
ORZÁBAL, Mariano, 68, 254
ORZALI, José Américo, 171, 910
OSCULATI, Cayetano, 258
OSORIO, Elsie, 656
OSORIO, Gaspar, 191
OSORIO, Juan de, 32, 984, 984a, 992
OSORIO, Mariano, 553
OSSÉS, Luis J., 190
OSTER, Alejandro, 889
OSÚA, Pedro de, 496
OSUNA, Gregorio de, 1034
OSUNA, Mauricio Tomás, 963a
OTADUY, Carlos, 857d
OTALORA Y LARRAZÁBAL, José Antonio de, 97
OTAMENDI, José A., 1134
OTAMENDI, Juan Bautista de, 496
OTANO, Juan Andrés, 31, 46
OTANO, Juan Bernardo, 1017
OTAROLA (family), 357
OTÁROLA DE SOLER, Manuela, 611
OTAZU, Dionysio de, 1030
OTAZU, José Ignacio, 1080
OTAZÚ, Oscar, 998
OTEGUI, Jorge Rafael, 774a
OTERIÑO, Rafael Felipe, 662, 663
OTERO, Alfredo Nicolás, 874
OTERO, Domingo, 254
OTERO, Hugo David, 791
OTERO, José María, 126
OTERO, José Pacífico, 453
OTERO, José Torquato de, 126
OTERO, Manuel, 1089
OTERO, Manuel B., 1072, 1083
OTERO, Mariano, 254
OTERO, Miguel, 126, 375
OTERO, Reynaldo, 268
OTERO AMIL DE SAPELLI, María del Carmen, 1210
OTERO DE AMELIO ORTIZ, María Esther, 684
OTERO DE CARBONE, Carmen, 691
OTERO DE MIGUEL, María Isabel, 320
OTERO PIZARRO, Enrique, 660
OTHÓN MORENO, Orlando, 998
OTÓN DE OÑA SOLA, Aurelia, 683a
OTONIEL PEÑA, Pío, 991
OTORGUÉS, Fernando, 552, 1091, 1128
OTORGUÉS, Rufina, 1092
OTT, José, 32
OTTMANN, Hugo L., 19, 36
OTTOLENGHI, Carlos, 923
OTTONELLO, Lázaro, 698
OTTSEN, Hendrik, 28
OUBIÑA, Héctor Vicente, 320
OUBIÑA, María Dolores
    see OUBIÑA DE SANTANDER, María Dolores
OUBIÑA DE SANTANDER, María Dolores, 320
OUCINDE FERNÁNDEZ, Laureano Marcelino, 284
OUSELEY, William Gore, 29
OUTES, Félix Diego, 332
OUVRARD, Gabriel Julián, 1236
OVALLE, Alonso de, 283
OVALLE, Hugo Roberto, 653, 654

OVALLE, José Antonio de, 555
OVALLE, Juan Manuel, 653
OVANDO, Epifanio, 935
OVANDO Y ZÁRATE, Pedro de, 646
OVEJERO, Daniel, 385, 680, 689, 713, 730, 753, 779, 825, 830
OVEJERO PAZ, Julio, 653, 654
OVELAR, Juan Bautista, 995
OVIEDO, Florentino, 974, 982, 1003
OVIEDO, Jorge Enrique, 683a
OVIEDO, Patricio, 377, 990
OXILIA, José Domingo, 954
OXLEY, Diego R., 152a
OYARVIDE, Andrés de, 17a, 885, 922
OYARZÁBAL, Ignacio, 318, 319
OYENARD ALORI, Sylvia Marlene Puentes Palermo de
     see PUENTES PALERMO DE OYENARD ALORI, Sylvia Marlene
OYUELA, Calixto, 121, 669, 724, 743, 751, 807
OYUELA, José María, 188, 283
OYUELA DE PEMBERTON, María Laura, 713, 730
OZARNECKY, Ladislao
     see CZARNECKI, Ladislao
OZAROWSKI, Enrique, 238
OZCÁRIZ, Francisco de, 283
OZORES, Juan Manuel
     see OZORES PATIÑO, Juan Manuel
OZORES PATIÑO, Juan Manuel, 284, 922

PABLO, Juan Carlos de, 213
PABLO, Vicente, 1064
PABLOS, Tomás Niceto de, 768
PABÓN, Juan Silveiro, 914
PACE GIGLI, Enio, 923
PACENZA, Onofrio, 18, 23, 25, 31, 36, 50
PACK, Denis, 552, 587
PACK, Dionisio, 553
PACOT, Miguel, 1092
PACHECO, Alejandra, 887
PACHECO, Alonso, 910
PACHECO, Angel, 209, 222, 283, 433, 617
PACHECO, Bernardo, 186
PACHECO, Carlos A., 27
PACHECO, Carlos H., 781
PACHECO, Carlos Mauricio, 152a, 719, 813, 890, 894, 1247
PACHECO, Diego, 501, 520, 527
PACHECO, Francisco, 186
PACHECO, Jorge, 169, 1130
PACHECO, Melchor, 584
MACHECO, Pedro Luis, 908
PACHECO DE ALVEAR, Elvira, 678, 746, 751
PACHECO DE MELO, José Andrés, 126, 439, 457, 526, 611, 621, 626
PACHECO DE MELO, Pedro Andrés, 921
PACHECO GÓMEZ, José, 126
PACHECO HUERGO, Maruja, 879
PACHECO Y CÁRDENAS, José Cayetano, 910
PACHECO Y OBES, Melchor, 206, 1054, 1059, 1072, 1081, 1091, 1093a, 1110, 1119, 1121, 1146, 1174, 1253
PACHEQUITO, pseud.
     see DAGLIO, Cayetano
PACHO, pseud.
     see MAGLIO, Juan
PACHO, Melchor, 555
PADELETTI, Hugo, 788
PADILLA, Alberto G., 521
PADILLA, Diego de, 1270
PADILLA, Eduardo, 565

PADILLA, Lila, 799
PADILLA, Manuel, 385, 634
PADILLA, Manuel Aniceto, 552, 573, 597
PADILLA, Manuel Asencio, 552
PADILLA, Nenina, 299
PADILLA, Pablo, 921
PADILLA, Pastor, 625
PADILLA, Tiburcio, 698, 842
PADILLA BORBÓN, Rafael, 431
PADILLA DE MENGUAL, María Celina, 730
PADILLA Y BÁRCENA, Pablo, 910
PADOVA, Antonio Carlos, 1173
PADRÓ, Nené, 681, 751
PADULA, Nazzario, 139
PÁEZ, Enrique, 1006
PÁEZ, José E., 565
PÁEZ, Juan L., 222
PÁEZ, Policarpo, 995a
PÁEZ, Roberto, 27
PÁEZ MOLINA, Justo, 89
PÁEZ TORRES, Armando Pablo, 299
PÁEZ VILARO, Jorge, 1045
PAGALDAY, Eugenio, 1223
PAGALDAY, Frutos, 1223
PAGALDAY, Nicolás, 1223
PAGANI, Enrique, 952
PAGANI, Valentina, 258
PAGANINI, Camilo Eduardo, 923
PAGANINI, Ludovico, 30
PAGANO, Angelina, 890, 891
PAGANO, José León, 31, 44, 258, 660, 674, 676, 727, 743, 890, 893
PAGE, 581
PAGÉS, José Luis, 817
PAGÉS, Mariano, 21
PAGÉS, Pedro T., 3, 141
PAGÉS LARRAYA, Antonio, 140, 683a, 688, 743, 1257
PAGOLA (family), 1108
PAGOLA, José María, 279
PAGOLA, Manuel Vicente, 1063, 1076, 1118, 1128
PAGOLA, Vicente, 552
PAGUITRUZ
     see ROSAS, Mariano
PAHLEN, Alejo W. von der
     see VON DER PAHLEN, Alejo W.
PAI PINTO, El, 984
PAILOS, Manuel, 1049
PAILLARDELLE, Antonio, 332
PAILLARDELLE, Enrique, 332
PAINE, 566
PAINE, Roberto, 722, 739, 758, 759
PAINÉ GOUR (ZORRO CELESTE, pseud.), 454
PAIS, Blas, 211
PAITOUX, Federico (ESTEBAN, Federico, pseud.), 691
PAITOVI, Antonio, 332
PAIVA, Benigno S., 1104
PAIVA, Félix, 948, 959, 964
PAIVA IRISARRI, Benigno, 1123
PAJARES OJEROS, Nicasio, 284
PAJARITO, pseud., 878
PÁJARO, El, pseud.
     see VALLEJOS, Manuel Antonio
PAJÓN, Andrés, 316, 1270
PAKMAN, 850
PALACIO, Ernesto, 177a, 431, 558, 609
PALACIO, Eudoxio de, 914
PALACIO, Federico, 207
PALACIO, Gaspar, 19
PALACIO, Gerardo, 852
PALACIO, Jorge (FARUK, pseud.), 299

PALACIO, José, 1088
PALACIO, Lino, 299
PALACIO DE LIBARONA, Agustina, 478, 929
PALACIO Y DOLZ, Gaspar, 62
PALACIOS, Abdón, 1006
PALACIOS, Alfredo C., 691
PALACIOS, Alfredo Lorenzo, 94, 170, 246, 503, 594, 682
PALACIOS, Carlos V., 68
PALACIOS, Francisco, 186
PALACIOS, José Antonio, 555
PALACIOS, Juan Prudencio, 126
PALACIOS, Manuel Antonio, 995a, 1041
PALACIOS, Miguel, 966, 986
PALACIOS, Modesto A., 998
PALACIOS, Nicolás, 186, 268
PALACIOS, Pedro Bonifacio (Almafuerte, pseud.), 78, 128, 166, 167, 219, 259, 282, 478, 521, 669, 678, 682, 722, 723, 724, 737, 740, 751, 754, 759, 803, 805, 807, 888, 1243, 1247
PALACIOS, Raúl A., 652
PALACIOS, Teodoro, 1247
PALACIOS COSTA, Nicanor, 923
PALACIOS DE ZORROAQUÍN, Elvira, 713
PALACIOS GALAIN, José Gabriel, 126
PALADINI, Alejandro C., 923
PALADINI, Octavio, 222
PALADINO, Jorge Daniel, 213
PALAMARA, Onofre, 24
PALANT, Pablo T., 135
PALAVECINO, Enrique, 191
PALAVECINO, José Cayetano, 1034, 1041
PALAVECINO, Juan Carlos, 683a, 713
PALAVECINO, Manuel A., 543
PALAZÓN, Alberto, 299
PALAZZO, Juan, 33, 836
PALAZZO, Pascual, 332
PALAZZO, Santiago, 31, 33
PALCOS, Alberto, 260, 589, 609
PALCOS DE ENQUIN, María C., 923
PALEARI, Luis A., 963a
PALEO DE SILVERO, Clelia, 691
PALERMO, Juan Francisco, 727, 811, 813
PALERMO, Mima, 955
PALERMO, Nelda, 751
PALERMO ALBANO, José, 951
PALERMO RIVIELLO, José, 653, 654
PALERO, Martín, 278
PALEY, Marcos, 41
PALINO, Piquio, pseud.
     see PICHETTI, José
PALISA MUJICA, María Hortensia, 762
PALMA, Agustín, 222
PALMA, Athos, 865, 881, 883
PALMA, Diego, 921
PALMA, Eduardo, 810
PALMA, Francisco de la, 845
PALMA, Luis, 921
PALMA, Luis Nicolás, 135, 664, 800
PALMA, Pascual, 844
PALMERIO, Mario de Ascengao, 954
PALMERO, Anita, 879
PALOMARES, Feliciano, 910, 918
PALOMARES, Manuel, 284
PALOMEQUE, Alberto, 1083, 1188
PALOMEQUE, José Gabriel, 1127, 1188
PALOMEQUE, José María, 254
PALOS, José de, 989, 1034, 1041
PALUMBO, Elio, 299
PALLARÉS, Domingo, 7, 32
PALLAS, Felipe, 1089

PALLAVICINI, Pedro José, 258
PALLEDO, Casimiro, 68
PALLEJA, León de, 1081
PALLEJA, Miguel, 59, 1079
PALLERONI, Norberto José, 923
PALLIÈRE, Juan León, 6, 28, 42, 45, 51, 59, 282, 293, 521
PALLOZIUS, Stephanus, 1037
PALLUCCHINI DE RODRÍGUEZ, Nilda, 874
PAMPILLO NOVAS, Ramón, 1127
PAMPILLO PARDO, Bernardo, 284
PAMPILLO TEIJEIRO, Bernardo, 1095
PAMPIN, Fermín Félix, 196
PAMPIN, Gregorio, 254
PAMPLIEGA, Amancio Rufino, 1006
PAN, Benito, 1267
PANAGIOTOPULIS, Homero, 18, 19, 31
PANCALDO, León, 151, 1238
PANCELLI, Antonio, 258
PANCELLI, Betty, 700
PANCHO, El Ñato, pseud., 169
PANCHO, El Viejo, pseud.
     see ALONSO Y TRELLES, José
PANDO, David F., 853a
PANDO, Pastor, 998
PANDO, Pedro J., 903
PANE, Ignacio Alberto, 966, 993, 1012, 1014, 1018, 1020, 1026
PANELO, Carlos, 222
PANELO, Julián, 129
PANERO, Ernesto Mario, 683a
PANERO DE MIGUEL, Jesús, 684
PANICHELLI, Carlos, 299
PANIGAY, Bartolomé, 922
PANINI, Nicolás, 258
PANIZZA, Delio, 135, 751, 800
PANIZZA, Escipión, 258, 332
PANIZZA, Héctor, 867, 881, 883
PANOZZI, Américo, 19, 31, 33
PANTIN, Carlos David, 923
PANTOJA, Medardo, 31
PANUZZI, Benito, 6
PANZARINI, Rodolfo N. M., 923
PANZONE, Rafael, 923
PAOLA, Luis de, 664, 746
PAOLANTONIO, Francisco, 882
PAOLI, Aldo Renato Julio, 923
PAOLI, Pedro de, 381a, 688
PAPADOPULOS, Celso C., 923
PAPARELLA, Aldo, 25, 31, 35, 49, 55
PAPINI, Guzmán
     see PAPINI Y ZAS, Guzmán
PAPINI DE RODRÍGUEZ NALLY, Sara, 691
PAPINI Y ZAS, Guzmán, 1068, 1075, 1078, 1146, 1174
PAPOTÍN, pseud.
     see RECALDE, Jesús Amado
PAPP, Desiderio, 923
PAPPALARDO, Manuel Horacio, 923
PAPU RÚA, José, 222
PARADA JUSTEL, Pío, 284
PARAGUAYO, El, pseud.
     see CAPDEVILA, José Antonio
PARANÁ, Luis Alberto del, 1028
PARASKEVA DE CURTI, Evanthea C., 652
PARAVERA, 977
PARAVIS, Carlos M., 1093
PARCHAPPE, Narciso, 169, 332
PARDO, Juan Bautista, 7
PARDO, Luis Lorenzo, 923
PARDO, María Laura, 691

PARDO, Pedro Antonio, 844, 1261
PARDO DE ANDRADE Y CASTRO, Antonio, 284
PARDO DE CELA Y VIDAL, Juan, 284
PARDO DE FIGUEROA, Baltasar, 284
PARDO DE TAVERA, Félix, 19
PARDO PARRAGUEZ, José, 555
PAREDES, Clotilde Emilia, 969
PAREDES, Herminio, 998
PAREDES, Jorge Horacio, 789
PAREDES, José Martiniano, 739
PAREDES, Ramón L., 1006
PAREDES DEL CAMPO, Atilio, 954
PAREDES REY, Antonio, 284
PAREJA, Antonio, 268
PAREJA, Jacinto, 268
PAREJA, Miguel Angel, 1045
PAREL, Clovis Agustín Mateo, 923
PARERA, Blas, 176, 244, 509, 611, 881
PARERA, Faustino M., 135, 194, 241
PARÉS, Bernardo, 319
PARIETTI, Roberto (CACHO, pseud.), 860
PARIS, Alfred, 59
PARIS, Eduardo, 793
PARISH, Woodbine, 143, 713
PARISH ROBERTSON, Guillermo, 834
PARISH ROBERTSON, Juan, 224, 834
PARISI, Francisco, 258
PARISI, José, 258
PARKER, Enrique Guillermo, 14, 82
PARMA, José, 6
PARNISARI, Irene, 791
PARODI, Domingo, 844
PARODI, Edmundo, 332
PARODI, Enrique D., 943, 1014, 1018, 1026
PARODI, Guillermo, 258
PARODI, José, 952
PARODI, José L., 938, 939
PARODI, Lorenzo R., 923
PARODI, Néstor, 860
PARODI, Pablo D., 652
PARODI, Silvio E., 211
PARODI DE MORTVIN, María Dolores, 320
PARODI URIARTE, Esther, 1187
PARODIZ, Juan José, 923
PAROISSIEN, Diego, 611, 844, 1261
PAROISSIEN, James, 573
PARPAGNOLI, Hugo, 218
PARRA, José Felipe, 1046, 1047
PARRA DE PÉREZ ALEN, Martha S., 652
PARRA DEL RIEGO, Juan, 1151, 1153, 1177, 1181, 1187
PARRA Y FREIRE, Héctor, 1145
PARRAS, Pedro José de, 834, 1264
PARRAVICINI, Florencio (Flo, pseud.), 891, 892, 893
PARTELLI, Carlos, 1115
PARTRIDGE, William H., 923
PASAMANIK, Luisa, 717, 725, 739
PASCALI, Justo, 332, 923
PASCARELIA, Luis, 152a
PASCUA, Iñigo de la, 555
PASCUA LOZZIA, Clotilde, 751
PASCUAL, Rosendo, 923
PASCUAL CRESPO, Primitivo, 923
PASCUAL NAVAS, María E., 882
PASEYRO, Ricardo, 1151, 1177, 1178, 1179
PASEYRO Y MONEGAL, Juan, 1140
PASLEY, Tomás S., 580
PASMAN, Rodolfo E., 853a
PASO, Alfonso, 857b
PASO, Francisco, 496
PASO, Idelfonso, 496

PASO, Juan José Esteban de, 70, 85, 95, 126, 166, 244, 282, 386, 404, 411, 421, 427, 439, 457, 475, 478, 479, 492, 496, 509, 525, 526, 529, 552, 554, 610, 611, 621, 626, 650, 895
PASOTTI, Pierina Antonieta Ernestina, 923
PASQUES, Víctor Antonio, 882
PASQUIER, Julio, 887, 888
PASSANO, Ricardo, 894, 1174, 1188, 1263
PASSERA, Camila, pseud.
    see QUIROGA, Camila
PASTENE, Juan Bautista de, 151, 258
PASTOR, Adolfo, 1044, 1079, 1218
PASTOR, Alonso, 125, 186
PASTOR, Blanca, 19, 31
PASTOR, Carlos Washington, 81
PASTOR, Juan, 188, 283, 319
PASTOR, Miguel B., 81, 222
PASTOR, Reynaldo A., 81, 222
PASTOR, Reynaldo Vicente, 222
PASTOR, Silverio, 32
PASTORE, Ada I., 222
PASTORE, Cayetano, 258
PASTORE, Franco A., 222
PASTORINO, Domingo Luis, 1159
PASTORINO VIZCARDI, Enrique Juan, 1210
PASTORIZA, Juliana, 931
PASTRANA, Francisco de, 845
PASTRANA, José Antonio, 923
PASTRANA, Sebastián de, 1041
PATAGUIRUZÚ, 977
PATERNOSTO, César, 36, 55
PATIÑO, Eliseo, 995a
PATIÑO, Felipe, 1111
PATIÑO, Gabriel, 949
PATIÑO, Juan, 137
PATIÑO, María Gabriela, 691
PATIÑO, Policarpo, 984, 1011
PATIÑO ANDRADE, Graciela, 882
PATRI, Luis, 951, 952
PATRICK, Roberto, 587
PATRÓN, Juan Carlos, 894, 1172
PATRÓN, Matías, 126, 496
PAUCKE, Florián
    see BAUCKE, Florián
PAULSEN, Julio Guillermo, 874
PAUNERO, Mariano, 474
PAUNERO, Wenceslao, 222, 283, 545a, 611
PAURÍ, Iris (MARGA, Iris, pseud.), 892
PAVIA DE OTERO, Norma, 810
PAVLOTZKY, José, 152a, 191
PAVLOTZKY, Alejandro J., 923
PAVLOVSKY, Alfredo, 923
PAVÓN PÉREZ, Victoriano, 954
PAYÁ, Francisco, 719
PAYÁN, Nicanor, 268
PAYÁN, Santiago, 126
PAYBA, Simeón, 387
PAYET, Luciano, 727
PAYRÓ, Ana M., 31
PAYRÓ, Anita, 19, 25, 36
PAYRÓ, Julio E., 594
PAYRÓ, Roberto J., 152a, 162, 232, 261, 282, 288, 670, 709, 724, 737, 745a, 751, 754, 769, 779, 799, 816, 825, 829, 834, 890, 1246, 1249, 1251, 1254
PAYÚN, Manuel, 256
PAZ, Adriana, 299
PAZ, Benjamín, 445, 631
PAZ, Félix Mariano, 287
PAZ, Jorge de, 1270

PAZ, José Camilo, 70, 78, 141, 282, 444, 643
PAZ, José María, 70, 85, 89, 95, 96, 110, 115, 121,
    127, 141, 166, 176, 196, 212, 228, 232, 244,
    258, 272, 282, 283, 375, 386, 398, 404, 408,
    420, 433, 442, 475, 478, 489, 498, 499, 514,
    519, 521, 528, 529, 531, 545, 545a, 552, 553,
    568, 569, 583, 584, 589, 594, 611, 734
PAZ, Juan Carlos, 865, 882, 883
PAZ, Juan José, 70
PAZ, Manuel V., 280
PAZ, Marcelo, 122
PAZ, Marcos, 96, 129, 404, 478, 545a, 574, 586, 611,
    713, 730
PAZ, María Antonia de la, 478
PAZ, Máximo, 391, 436, 445
PAZ, Osvaldo, 1045
PAZ BOSCH, Amalio Alcides, 1210
PAZ DE GALLO, Elmina, 842
PAZ FERNÁNDEZ, María de la, 320
PAZ HERMO, Egidio, 284
PAZ LEZCANO, María Angélica de la, 653, 654
PAZ PUEYRREDÓN, Pridiliano
    see PUEYRREDÓN, Prilidiano
PAZ SOLDÁN, Mariano Felipe, 453
PAZ Y FIGUEROA, María Antonia de la, 32, 264, 286, 921
PAZOS, Andrés, 629, 1089
PAZOS, Domingo, 284
PAZOS, Ignacio, 284
PAZOS, José, 254
PAZOS, Juan Francisco
    see PAZOS BERTA, Juan Francisco
PAZOS BERTA, Juan Francisco, 1210, 1211
PAZOS SILVA, Vicente, 611
PEABODY, Elizabet, 930
PEACAN DEL SAR, Rafael, 883
PECCI, José Danilo, 963a
PECCI LA SALVIA (family), 952
PECHO, Jorge Edgardo del, 923
PEDAZZI, José, 6
PEDEMONTE, Adán L., 19
PEDERNERA, Domingo, 599
PEDERNERA, Juan Esteban, 85, 159, 179, 222, 244,
    278, 449, 566, 611
PEDEMONTE, Hugo Emilio, 818, 1151, 1179
PEDONE, Antonio, 19, 24, 31, 33, 44
PEDOTTI, Aldo, 923
PEDRAZA, Manuela, 85, 478, 511, 929
PEDRELL, Carlos, 865, 882, 894
PEDRERO DE TREJO, Diego, 649a
PEDRERO DE TREJO, Juan, 520, 620
PEDRETTI, Carlos A., 954
PEDRIDO, Federico Guillermo, 660
PEDRIEL, Mariano, 921
PEDRO, 1238
PEDRO, Alicia, 787
PEDROLINI, Aquiles, 874, 882
PEDRONI, José B., 152a, 521, 674, 678, 722, 739,
    748, 751, 759, 773, 807, 831, 833
PEDROSA, Blas de, 284
PEDROSO, Mariano Celso, 1014
PEDROSO CATALÁN, Carlos, 1270
PEERS, Gastón, 226
PEERS DE PERKINS, Carmen, 226
PEICOVICH, Esteban, 530, 739
PEIRA, Vicente, 910, 912
PEIRANO, Abel Antonio, 923
PEIRANO, Irma, 725, 837
PEIRANO, Jorge, 37
PEIRE, José E., 659, 683a, 837
PEKAREK, Alicia, 810
PELÁEZ, Esteban, 889

PELÁEZ, Marcelino José, 684
PELÁEZ DE VILLA DE MOROS Y CANDAMO, Ramón Antonio,
    359
PELAIA, Alfredo M., 874
PELAIA, Attilio, 874
PELAIA, Emilio, 882
PELAY, Ivo, pseud.
    see PICHOT, Guillermo Juan Robustiano
PELAYO, Félix M., 152a, 751
PELEGRINI, Carlos
    see PELLEGRINI, Carlos Enrique
PELERÁN DE TISCORNIA, María Luisa, 320
PELOSSI, Atilio, 1084
PELTZER, Federico, 663, 807, 814
PELUFFO, Luis, 94
PELUFFO, Luisa, 738, 816
PELUFFO, Martha, 19, 31, 36, 46, 49
PELVILAIN, Julio, 28
PELLA, Martha, 774a
PELLEGRINI, Aldo, 658, 672, 739, 759, 832
PELLEGRINI, Carlos Enrique, 6, 19, 28, 32, 33, 42,
    45, 51, 59, 68, 70, 78, 110, 113, 116, 121, 141,
    143, 166, 216, 244, 245, 246, 254, 258, 277, 278,
    282, 292, 293, 332, 372, 389, 392, 393, 405, 466,
    478, 484, 485, 489, 502, 507, 515, 516, 521, 531,
    545, 574, 586, 592, 593, 595, 598, 619, 631
PELLEGRINI, Charles Henri
    see PELLEGRINI, Carlos Enrique
PELLEGRINI, Juan Carlos, 739
PELLEGRINI, Nicolino, 952
PELLEGRINO, Carlos, 1173
PELLEGRINO, Pablo, 258
PELLERANO, Glorialdo, 923
PELLERANO, Lorenzo, 258
PELLESCHI, Juan, 258, 332
PELLION, A., 28
PELLIZA, Fidel, 24
PELLIZA, José Marcelino, 599, 1080
PELLIZA, José María, 258
PELLIZA, Juan Carlos, 857, 857d
PELLIZA, Mariano, 609
PELLIZA DE SAGASTA, Josefina, 762, 930
PENA, Antonio, 1089
PENA, Carlos María, 1075, 1127
PENA, Eliseo, 385
PENA, Manuel, 1089
PENA, Manuel Pedro de, 957
PENAYOS DE CASTRO, Carlos, 964, 1035
PÉNDOLA, Rodolfo, 1075
PENDÓN, José, 860
PENDONES, Juan de, 1270
PENEDO, Juan M., 284
PENELAS, Carlos, 785
PENENORY, Susana, 684
PENNA, Carlos Víctor, 652
PENNA, Giovanni, 292
PENNA, Giuseppe, 292
PENNA, José, 842, 844, 1261
PENNA, José Lucas, 385
PENNA, Juan, 258
PENNA, Juan E., 68
PENNA, Víctor Manuel, 258
PENNA REGUEIRO, Jorge Vicente, 738
PENNATI, Carlos, 258
PENOT, E., 6
PENSADO, Juan Francisco, 284
PENSEL, Ignacio, 1205
PENZA, Emilio, 1204
PEÑA (family), 352
PEÑA, Ariel, 791

PEÑA, Atilio A., 959
PEÑA, Carlos Daniel, 965
PEÑA, Cecilio, 1151, 1178
PEÑA, Cleto, 89
PEÑA, David, 121, 162, 167, 293, 372, 609, 614, 751, 890
PEÑA, Enrique, 1080
PEÑA, Félix de la, 89, 545a
PEÑA, Fernando, 260
PEÑA, Francisco de la, 556
PEÑA, Fulgencio, 998
PEÑA, Genaro, 954
PEÑA, José, 1122
PEÑA, José Luis de la
    see PEÑA, Luis José de la
PEÑA, Juan A., 156
PEÑA, Juan C., 652
PEÑA, Lope de la, 555
PEÑA, Luis José de la, 95, 96, 611
PEÑA, Manuel, 959
PEÑA, Manuel I., 268
PEÑA, Manuel Pedro de la, 966
PEÑA, Pedro P., 959, 993
PEÑA, Rosa, 943
PEÑA, Saturnino, 126
PEÑA DE BERTRÁN, Felicia, 1093a
PEÑA DE GONZÁLEZ, Rosa, 1042
PEÑA FERNÁNDEZ, Francisco de la, 284, 496
PEÑA RODRÍGUEZ, Manuel, 858
PEÑA TECHERA, Angela Luciana, 1088
PEÑA Y LILLO, Silvestre, 207
PEÑA Y LORENZO ORSINI, Amadeo, 937
PEÑA Y ZARZUETA, José de la
    see PEÑA Y ZAZUETA, José de la
PEÑA Y ZAZUETA, José de la, 17a, 32, 922
PEÑA Y ZAZUETA, Juan de la, 7
PEÑALBA, Alicia, pseud.
    see PÉREZ PEÑALBA, Alicia
PEÑALBA, Juan Bautista, 284
PEÑALOZA, Angel Vicente (CHACHO, el, pseud.), 83, 188, 282, 283, 478, 511, 532, 632
PEÑALOZA, Francisca, 887
PEÑALOZA, Francisco de, 556
PEÑALOZA, Nicolás, 244
PEÑALOZA DE VARESE, Carmen, 283
PEÑALVA, Arturo, 653, 654
PEÑALVA, Ramiro A., 653
PEÑALVA, Toribio, 186
PEÑARANDA, Marcelino, 126
PEÑASCO, Alejandro, 894, 1151
PEÓN, Nicolás, 1089
PEÓN DE FRÍAS, Loreto, 626
PEQUERA BERDÍA, Julio César, 1210
PERAFÁN DE LA RIVERA, Pablo Hilarión
    see RIVERA, Pablo Hilarión Perafán de la
PERAL, Carlos del, pseud.
    see PERALTA, Carlos
PERAL, Isaac, 244
PERALTA, Adolfo, 844
PERALTA, Antonio, 982
PERALTA, Atilio, 652
PERALTA, Basilio, 1006
PERALTA, Carlos (PERAL, Carlos del, pseud.), 769
PERALTA, Francisco, 258
PERALTA, Gabriel de, 1035
PERALTA, José, 907, 911, 920
PERALTA, Juan N., 207
PERALTA, Marta, 781
PERALTA ANDRADE, Efraín, 683a
PERALTA ARABITE, Lavalleja, 1210

PERALTA ARELLANO, Angel, 954
PERALTA BÁEZ, Luis A., 954
PERALTA BARRIONUEVO Y ROCHA BENAVIDES, José de, 319, 910
PERALTA DE ALVAREZ YOFRÉ, María Cristina, 810
PERALTA NÚÑEZ, Blanca, 1210
PERALTA PINO, Juan M., 652
PERALTA RAMOS (family), 361, 362
PERALTA RAMOS, Patricio, 156, 904
PERAMAS, José Manuel, 968, 985, 1037, 1267, 1269
PERAZZO, Juan J., 268
PERAZZO, Roberto, 332
PERCEVAL, Julio, 874, 882, 883
PERCIBAL, Hilario, 1140
PERCUOCO, Carlos, 883
PERDIGÓN PÉREZ, Raúl Ramón, 1210
PERDIGUERO, César, 653, 654
PERDOMO CORONEL, Nazareth, 1093
PERDRIEL, Gregorio Ignacio, 611
PERDRIEL, Julián, 169, 599, 895
PEREDA, 1126
PEREDA, Bernardo, 126
PEREDA, Fernando, 1151, 1153, 1177, 1178, 1187, 1199
PEREDA, José María de, 152a
PEREDA, Setembrino, 1079, 1083
PEREDA SARAVIA, León, 126
PEREDA VALDÉS, Ildefonso, 1088, 1151, 1167, 1170, 1179, 1181, 1187, 1199
PEREDO, Angelo de, 191, 244, 501
PEREDO, Pascual, 280
PEREIRA (family), 1108
PEREIRA, Abelardo, 1089
PEREIRA, Domingo, 32
PEREIRA, Estanislao, 943, 959
PEREIRA, Gabriel Antonio, 1079, 1091
PEREIRA, Generoso, 1089
PEREIRA, Juan Antonio, 496
PEREIRA, Julio César, 923
PEREIRA, León, 844
PEREIRA, Miguel Angel, 713, 730, 830
PEREIRA, Umberto T., 1151
PEREIRZ, Victorino, 1204
PEREIRA, Zoilo, 1075
PEREIRA CARRASCO, Foilán, 1122
PEREIRA CUNHA, Hugo, 1210
PEREIRA DE LUCENA, Diego, 126
PEREIRA DE MATOS (family), 348
PEREIRA GAMBA, Próspero, 1014
PEREIRA LIZASO, Nydia
    see PEREYRA LIZASO, Nydia
PEREIRA NÚÑEZ, Mariano, 1075
PEREIRA SYLLA, Luis Mariano, 1210
PEREIRA TORRES, Aníbal, 222
PERELLI, Luis, 258
PERELLO, Cipriano, 258
PERERA SAN MARTÍN DE DA SILVA, Judith, 1210
PEREYRA, Albín, 1116
PEREYRA, Ambrosio, 186
PEREYRA, Antonio, 845, 914
PEREYRA, Antonio Luis, 1095, 1223
PEREYRA, Bernardo, 186
PEREYRA, Elías del Carmen, 896
PEREYRA, Felipe, 371
PEREYRA, Gabriel Antonio, 1109
PEREYRA, Leonardo, 3
PEREYRA, Miguel A., 680
PEREYRA, Nicandro, 679, 716, 722, 739, 758
PEREYRA, Vicente Indalecio, 31
PEREYRA DE JONES, Enriqueta, 1093a
PEREYRA DE MORA, Norma, 691

PEREYRA IRAOLA, Patricia, 37
PEREYRA LIZASO, Nydia, 1206, 1207
PEREYRA MONT, Juan, 781
PÉREZ (family) (Argentina), 348
PÉREZ (family) (Uruguay), 1108
PÉREZ, Abel J., 1075, 1146
PÉREZ, Agustín, 186
PÉREZ, Alberto, 680, 830
PÉREZ, Antonio Baltasar, 1095
PÉREZ, Antonio E., 68
PÉREZ, Blanca, 684
PÉREZ, Domingo T., 445
PÉREZ, Eduardo, 844
PÉREZ, Emeterio, 222
PÉREZ, Enrique S., 68
PÉREZ, Eugenio, 648, 649, 845
PÉREZ, Francisco, 646
PÉREZ, Francisco de Sales, 188
PÉREZ, Genaro, 19, 24, 59, 62, 244, 293
PÉREZ, Gonzalo, 186
PÉREZ, Gregoria, 106, 478, 611, 929, 1066
PÉREZ, Herminio Héctor, 923
PÉREZ, Jenaro
    see PÉREZ, Genaro
PÉREZ, Jerónimo, 358
PÉREZ, Joaquín, 609
PÉREZ, José Antonio, 959
PÉREZ, José Apolinario, 1093
PÉREZ, José Manuel, 126, 599
PÉREZ, José María, 1089
PÉREZ, Juan, 992
PÉREZ, Juan Francisco, 959, 1024
PÉREZ, Juan José, 1264
PÉREZ, Juan Manuel, 634, 921
PÉREZ, Juan María, 126, 1063, 1091, 1093a
PÉREZ, Luis, 1247, 1258
PÉREZ, Luis Eduardo, 1052, 1053, 1063, 1076, 1091,
    1118
PÉREZ, Manuel, 254
PÉREZ, Manuel Luis, 923
PÉREZ, María Emilia, 656
PÉREZ, Miguel Angel, 653, 654
PÉREZ, Oscar, 699
PÉREZ, Pablo, 1063, 1081
PÉREZ, Paí
    see PÉREZ ACOSTA, Ernesto
PÉREZ, Pedro, 1014
PÉREZ, Pedro J., 385
PÉREZ, Ramón Alberto, 689
PÉREZ, Ricardo, 1089
PÉREZ, Ruperto, 634
PÉREZ, Santos, 442, 559
PÉREZ, Sara, 1045
PÉREZ, Saviniano, 1093
PÉREZ, Segundo, 312
PÉREZ ACOSTA, Ernesto (PÉREZ, Paí), 941, 1039
PÉREZ ACOSTA, Juan Francisco, 943, 966
PÉREZ ALISEDO, Arturo, 385
PÉREZ AMUCHÁSTEGUI, Antonio J., 688
PÉREZ BRITO, José, 7, 32, 284, 1095
PEREZ BRITO, Santiago José, 284, 332
PÉREZ BULNES, Eduardo, 244, 313, 439, 457, 526, 611,
    621, 626
PÉREZ BUTLER, Guillermo M., 1065
PÉREZ CAMINO, Ricardo, 284
PÉREZ CARDOZO, Félix, 947, 965
PÉREZ CASADO, Maximino, 284
PEREZ CASTELLANO (family), 1108
PÉREZ CASTELLANO, José Manuel, 885, 1063, 1076,
    1146, 1177, 1199, 1203
PÉREZ CASTELLANOS, Manuel, 1052, 1053
PÉREZ CLAVIJO, Diego, 186
PÉREZ COLMAN, César B., 95, 135
PÉREZ CORRALES DE ACUÑA, Camila Irene, 1210
PÉREZ-CHAVES, Emilio, 1015
PÉREZ DE ACOSTA, Diego, 1270
PÉREZ DE ARCE, Juan, 914
PÉREZ DE BULNES, Manuel Eduardo
    see PÉREZ BULNES, Eduardo
PÉREZ DE BURGOS, Francisco, 97
PÉREZ DE DAL MOLIN, María Elena, 320
PÉREZ DE ESPINOSA, Juan, 283, 910
PÉREZ DE HERRERA, Francisco, 649a
PÉREZ DE LA ROSA, Cecilio, 760
PÉREZ DE LAVALLEJA, Juan Joaquín Manuel Eustaquio,
    1111
PÉREZ DE LEANO, Joaquín, 179
PÉREZ DE LUQUE, Lázaro, 186
PÉREZ DE LUQUE, Luis, 186
PÉREZ DE MARÇOTEGUI, Martín, 556
PÉREZ DE MORÁN, Gonzalo, 992
PÉREZ DE OBLITAS, Fernando, 1041
PÉREZ DE OTAROLA, Vicente, 186
PÉREZ DE SALAZAR, Alonso, 472, 570
PÉREZ DE SALAZAR, Antonio, 649a
PÉREZ DE URDININEA, José María, 179, 188, 283, 412,
    432, 521, 611
PÉREZ DE URIONDO, Francisco, 625
PÉREZ DE ZORITA, Juan, 520, 527, 620
PÉREZ DE ZURITA, Juan
    see PÉREZ DE ZORITA, Juan
PÉREZ DEL GRADO, Lorenzo, 910, 1041
PÉREZ DEL VISO, Nicolás, 89
PÉREZ DÍEZ, Susana, 683a
PÉREZ GADEA, Saúl, 1151
PÉREZ GALDÓS, Benito, 152a
PÉREZ GAONA, Roberto, 995
PÉREZ GOMAR, Gregorio, 1185
PÉREZ GONZÁLEZ, Ramón Aurelio, 1210
PÉREZ GORGOROSO, Eugenio, 1075
PÉREZ IBÁÑEZ, Efraín, 299
PÉREZ JIMÉNEZ, Marcos, 530
PÉREZ-MARICEVICH, Francisco, 1015, 1021, 1022, 1025
PÉREZ MARTÍNEZ, Marcelino, 1014, 1017
PÉREZ MOLINARI, Leonel, 1045
PÉREZ MORALES, Francisco L., 923
PÉREZ MORENO, Diego, 186
PÉREZ MORENO, Juan, 520
PÉREZ NIETO, Estanislao, 1185
PÉREZ PARDELLA, Agustín, 140, 739, 814
PÉREZ PEÑALBA, Alicia (PEÑALBA, Alicia, pseud.),
    19, 21, 25, 49
PÉREZ PÉREZ, Iris de Guadalupe, 1088
PÉREZ PETIT, Víctor, 128, 894, 1075, 1078, 1079,
    1083, 1145, 1146, 1167, 1168, 1170, 1177, 1185,
    1187, 1188, 1199
PÉREZ PIERONI, Tilde, 762
PÉREZ PINTOS, Diego, 1183
PÉREZ PONDAL, Manuel, 1210
PÉREZ RUIZ, Stella de, 31
PÉREZ SANIN, José, 65
PÉREZ TELLECHEA, Elbio, 1159
PÉREZ VILLAR, Luis Alberto, 1210
PÉREZ Y CASTELLANO, José Manuel
    see PÉREZ CASTELLANO, José Manuel
PÉREZ Y PÉREZ, Manuel, 284
PÉREZ ZELASCHI, Adolfo L., 668, 712, 751, 779, 834
PERI ROSSI, Cristina, 1149, 1152, 1155
PERICLES, pseud.
    see GIL, Julio

PERICHON (family), 587
PERINCIOLA, Ernesto, 951
PERIS Y CURIS, Manuel, 1145
PERIZ, Josefa, 1093a
PERKINS, Carlos, 226
PERLA PEREIRA, Lauro, 1210
PERLE, Nora, 299
PERLER, Domingo, 579
PERLOTTI, Luis, 154
PERNETTI, Antonio José, 885, 949
PERNÍAS, Pedro (JORDÁN DE LA CAZUELA, pseud.), 769
PERÓN, Eva
    see DUARTE DE PERÓN, Eva
PERÓN, Isabel
    see MARTÍNEZ DE PERÓN, Isabel
PERÓN, Juan Domingo, 110, 170, 232, 246, 368, 434,
    437, 452, 461, 469, 489, 515, 516, 524, 530,
    558, 567, 590, 593, 602, 619, 624, 963
PERÓN, Mario Tomás, 567
PERÓN, Tomás L., 567, 903
PERONCINI, Horacio, 726, 815, 817
PERONI, José, 759
PERRICHOLI, pseud.
    see VILLEGAS, Micaela
PERRONE, Cayetano, 258
PERRONE, Fernando María, 258
PERRONE, Jorge, 717
PERRY, Halma Cristiana, 832
PÉRSICO, Ricardo, 860
PERTILE, Alfredo Santiago, 191
PERTINI, Santiago, 69
PERUGORRÍA, Genaro, 539
PERUJO, Julián, pseud.
    see MORATORIO, Orosmán
PESACQ, Luciano C., 652
PESANTE, Edgardo A., 701, 795, 814, 815, 824
PESCE, Mercedes Nora, 299
PESCE, Victorio, 768
PESCHKE, Enrique, 850
PESO MORALES, Luis del, 649a
PESSAGNO, Nélida, 663
PESSINA, Pieter, pseud., 683a
PESSOLANI, Juan, 952
PESTAÑA Y CHAMUCERO, Juan Francisco de, 284
PETER, José, 198
PETIROSSI, Silvio
    see PETTIROSSI, Silvio
PETIT, Roberto, 960
PETIT DE MURAT, Mario José, 664
PETIT DE MURAT, Ulises, 235, 664, 678, 722, 739
PETIT MUÑOZ, Eugenio Gervasio, 1210
PETRA SIERRALTA, Guillermo, 683a
PETRAGRASSA, Angel Camilo, 7, 32, 319
PETRARCA, Domingo, 7, 32, 332, 922
PETRI, Luis, 1205
PETRIS, Martín de, 32
PETRIZ, Pedro, 332
PETROCELLI, Ariel, 653, 654, 790
PETRONE, Francisco, 889
PETRONIO, Salvador, 874
PETTIROSSI, Silvio, 948, 960, 984a, 1012
PETTORUTI, Emilio, 18, 19, 22, 23, 25, 31, 33, 34,
    36, 38, 45, 50, 55, 56, 64, 521, 1218
PEVERELLI, Juan Carlos, 923
PEYCERE DE COUTURE DE TROISMONTS, Alicia, 652
PEYRET, Alejo, 95
PEYROT, E. Mario, 1123
PEYROU, Julia, 19
PEYROU, León, 1073, 1123
PEYROU, Manuel, 235, 668, 670, 685, 825
PEZUELA, 166

PEZUELA, Joaquín de la, 104, 453, 471, 521, 552, 553,
    573
PEZZI, Cayetano, 258
PEZZONI, Enrique, 218
PEZZUTI PILLONI, Romano, 258
PFEIFFER, Oscar, 1205, 1206, 1207
PI, Wifredo, 1190
PI CALLEJA, Pedro, 923
PIAGGIO, Angel
    see PIALLO, Angel
PIAGGIO, Celestino, 135, 881, 883
PIAGGIO, Edmundo, 332
PIAGGIO, Ernesto, 258
PIAGGIO, Juan A., 811, 813
PIAGGIO, Nicolás, 268
PIAGGIO DE TUCKER, Juana María, 268
PIAGGIO-TARELLI, Elsa, 154
PIALLO, Angel, 73
PIATELLI, Juan Eduardo, 679
PIATNITZKY, Alejandro, 923
PIAZZA, José, 923
PIAZZOLLA, Astor, 861, 862, 868, 875, 877, 883
PIAZZOLLA, Diana, 725
PIBERNAT, Carlos, 135
PICA, Edmundo, 1093
PICA, Salvador, 254
PICARD LAMBERT, 1203
PICAREL, Antonio, 6
PICAZARRI, José Antonio, 258, 864
PICAZZARRI, Juan A., 859
PICCATO, Miguel Angel, 704
PICCATTO, Pedro, 1151, 1177, 1178
PICCILLI, Antonio, 191
PICCININI DE DE LA CÁRCOVA, 751, 762
PICCIRILLI, Ricardo, 609
PICCOLINI DE MARÍN, Gladys Liliana, 691
PICENA, Juan Pedro, 923
PICO, Blas José, 95, 104, 611
PICO, Esteban, 258
PICO, Francisco, 216, 418, 496, 844
PICO, José Cayetano, 126
PICO, Pedro E., 675, 676, 769, 813, 893
PICO DE NEGROTTO, Alina Esther, 768
PICO ESTRADA, Luis, 770
PICONE, José C., 765
PICHETTI, José (PIQUIO, Palino, pseud.), 713
PICHETTI, Leonor, 713, 730
PICHI PINCEN, 256
PICHÓN RIVIÈRE, Marcelo, 759
PICHOT, Guillermo Juan Robustiano (PELAY, Ivo,
    pseud.), 871, 1243
PIDELLO, Alejandro, 788
PIEDAD, Atanasio de la
    see ATANASIO DE LA PIEDAD
PIEDRA, Juan de la, 284
PIEDRA AZUL
    see CALFUCURÁ
PIEDRA BUENA, Luis
    see PIEDRABUENA, Luis
PIEDRABUENA, Bernabé, 910
PIEDRABUENA, Luis, 9, 12, 13, 14, 15, 16, 17a, 99,
    100, 110, 202, 256, 282, 287, 288, 438, 490,
    574
PIEDRACUEVA, Felipe Gabriel, 254
PIEDRAHITO PINTOS, Francisco Casiano, 1210
PIERA, Luis, 1075, 1083
PIERINI, Luis Enrique, 923
PIERRECLAU, Ana Josefa de, 132
PIERRI, Orlando, 18, 19, 25, 31, 36, 46, 63
PIERRI SAPERE, José, 1206
PIETAS, Gregoria Juliana, 1082

PIETRO DE TORRAS, Aurora, 217
PIETROBELLI, Francisco, 258
PIETROBONI DE JOURDAN, Nora, 691
PIGAFETTA, Antonio, 258
PIGGOT BARTON, George, 961
PIGLIA, Ricardo, 694, 776
PIGNAT (family), 168
PILCHIK BURSUCK, Saúl, 1210
PILLADO, Antonio, 611
PIMENIDES, Atanasio C., 652
PIMENTEL, Francisco, 32
PINASCO, Jacobo, 258
PINASCO, Santiago Felipe, 923
PINAZO, Manuel de, 169
PINCÉN, Pichi, 454, 566
PINCHEIRA (family), 222
PINDÓ, 977
PINEDA, José María, 44
PINEDA Y RAMÍREZ, Antonio de, 885
PINEDO, Agustín Fernando de, 496, 958, 984, 990, 1011
PINEDO, Ambrosio de, 496
PINEDO, Federico, 68, 103, 122, 311, 489
PINEDO, José M., 371
PINELO, Antonio de León
    see LEÓN PINELO, Antonio Rodríguez de
PINETTA, Alberto, 235, 765
PINHO, Enrique L., 953, 959
PINI DE CHRESTIA, María, 154
PININ, pseud.
    see LAMARDO, Antonio
PINO, Antonio del, 68, 94
PINO, Felipe Carlos, 37
PINO, Joaquín del
    see PINO Y ROZAS, Joaquín del
PINO, Juana del
    see PINO Y VERA MUJICA DE RIVADAVIA, Juana del
PINO, Simón del, 1059, 1082, 1111
PINO CASANOVA, Antonio del, 284
PINO MANRIQUE, Juan del, 1229
PINO RAMERI, Ramón José Agustín del, 332
PINO Y ROZAS, Joaquín del, 332, 570, 922, 1136, 1237, 1239, 1240, 1241, 1262
PINO Y VERA MUJICA DE RIVADAVIA, Juana del, 254, 478, 929
PINOCHO, pseud.
    see MARECO, Juan Carlos
PINTO (family), 352
PINTO, Abel C., 1083
PINTO, Alfredo, 882, 883
PINTO, Ernesto, 894, 1172, 1179, 1185, 1199
PINTO, Fernando E., 923
PINTO, Juan, 467, 739, 751
PINTO, Juan Carlos, 18, 24, 44
PINTO, Luis C., 688
PINTO, Manuel Guillermo, 478, 496, 611
PINTO, Mercedes, 1187
PINTO, Miguel de, 186
PINTO, Octavio, 19, 24, 31, 33, 44, 773
PINTO, Roberto Martín, 923
PINTO CORREA DORIA, Sebastián, 948, 1039
PINTOR, Oscar, 55
PINTOS, Juan Manuel, 727, 751, 811, 813
PINTOS, Miguel de Dios, 995a
PINTOS PEREIRA, Francisco Ricardo, 1210
PINZANI, Victorio, 190
PIÑA CERVANTES, Pedro de, 845
PIÑAS, Balthasar de, 1035a, 1035b
PIÑEIRO, Antonio, 923
PIÑEIRO, Armando Alonso, 609

PIÑEIRO, Constantino, 1089
PIÑEIRO GONZÁLEZ, José, 284
PIÑERA, Manuel, 1094
PIÑERO, Andrés, 24
PIÑERO, Baltasar, 860
PIÑERO, Francisco M., 782
PIÑERO, Horacio G., 842
PIÑERO, Juan D., 844
PIÑERO, Manuel Avelino, 244
PIÑERO, Martín Avelino, 268, 317, 921
PIÑERO, Norberto, 192
PIÑERO, Teófilo D., 1075
PIÑERO, Virgilio, 268
PIÑERO GARCÍA, Jorge A., 691
PIÑEYRO, Francisco Antonio, 344
PIÑEYRO, Martín, 319
PIÑEYRO DEL CAMPO, Luis, 1067, 1174, 1188
PIÑEYRÚA (family), 1108
PIÑEYRÚA, Pedro, 1064
PIOLA, María Angélica, 1206
PIOLÍN DE MACRAMÉ, pseud.
    see ESCARDÓ, Florencio
PIORA, Francisco, 151
PIORNO, Ñusta de, 702
PIPINO (family), 361
PIPIRÍ, 977
PIQUET, Julio
    see PIQUET GARCÍA, Julio Eugenio Santiago
PIQUET GARCÍA, Julio Eugenio Santiago, 1188, 1193
PIQUIO, Palino, pseud.
    see PICHETTI, José
PIRACUA, 977
PIRACUATÍ, 977
PIRÁN, Antonio María, 496
PIRÁN, Augusto Alberto, 923
PIRÁN, José María, 569, 611
PIRAVÍ, 977
PIRES MATEUS, Daniel, 857a
PIRIA, Francisco, 1084
PIRIOBY, Cristóbal, 865
PIRIS, Gregorio, 95
PIRIS, José Luis, 543
PÍRIZ COELHO, Ramón, 1197
PIRO, Gervasio, 1093
PIROSANTO, Camilo, 69
PIROVANO, Beatriz, 956
PIROVANO, Ignacio, 90, 141, 244, 258, 842, 844, 1261
PIROVANO, Juan, 258, 332, 921a
PIRUNCHO, pseud.
    see LOMBARDI, Oscar
PISARELLO, Gerardo, 770, 771
PISSANETZKY, Sergio, 923
PISSARRO, Víctor, 18, 19, 25, 31, 33, 36
PISSININI DE PASCARELLI, María Ofelia, 320
PISTOLETE, Gerónimo, 1262
PISTONI, Julio César, 258
PITA, Vicente, 1094
PITA ROMERO, Leandro, 218
PITAUD, Henri, 960
PITTALUGA, Alejandro, 6, 28
PITTALUGA, Fructuoso, 1073
PITTALUGA, Rosa, 1084
PIVEL DEVOTO, Juan E., 1177
PIZARNIK, Alejandra
    see PIZARNIK, Flora Alejandra
PIZARNIK, Flora Alejandra, 658, 661, 672, 716, 725, 739, 759, 798, 802, 807, 832
PIZARRO, Bartolomé, 629
PIZARRO, Francisco Javier, 496
PIZARRO, Lucas, 1267
PIZARRO, Manuel Dídimo, 166, 121, 244, 445, 631

PIZARRO, Paulino Segundo, 207, 874
PIZARRO GRIMAU, Gregorio, 599
PIZZURNO, Carlos Higinio, 118
PIZZURNO, Juan Tomás, 118
PIZZURNO, Pablo Antonio, 118, 121, 176, 317, 751
PLÁ, Alfredo, 1006
PLÁ, Cortés, 332, 923
PLÁ, José, 844, 1261
PLÁ, Josefina
    see PLÁ GUERRA GALVANY, María Josefina
PLA, Roger, 757
PLÁ GUERRA GALVANY, María Josefina, 938, 939, 943,
    1014, 1015, 1018a, 1019, 1020, 1021, 1022, 1023,
    1025
PLACE (family), 168
PLACER, Alejandro Eliso, 923
PLACO, Ciro, 73
PLADA, Néstor, 1191
PLANAS, Alberto Luis, 954
PLANAS CASAS, José, 18, 44, 55
PLANCHÓN, José León, 254, 496
PLANELLA, Augusto, 923
PLANES, Francisco, 211, 478, 479, 496, 508, 895
PLANES, Saturnino, 126
PLANTICH, Nicolás (PLANTITSCH, Nicolás), 319, 896
PLANTITSCH, Nicolás
    see PLANTICH, Nicolás
PLAR, Francisco M. R. C., 923
PLATERO, Ramón, pseud.
    see CABRAL, Ramón
PLATERO, Tomás B., 137
PLATERO PROLA, Ana M., 652
PLAZA, Angélica, 1093
PLAZA, Antonio de la, 32
PLAZA, Hilarión, 371, 611
PLAZA, José María, 611
PLAZA, Héctor
    see PLAZA NOBLÍA, Héctor
PLAZA, Ramón, 739
PLAZA, Rubén, 788
PLAZA, Victorino de la, 116, 141, 392, 405, 466, 478,
    515, 516, 521, 574, 619, 650
PLAZA NOBLÍA, Héctor, 1172, 1185
PLOPER, José, 923
PLORUTTI, Maria Isabel, 691
PLOTNICK, Rubén, 923
POBLET, Marcelino, 215, 222
POCA ROPA, Juan, pseud.
    see DORREGO, Celestino
POCH, Gustavo Francisco, 923
PODESTÁ, Amadea, 894
PODESTÁ, Antonio Domingo, 891, 894, 1263
PODESTÁ, Antonio Miguel, 746
PODESTÁ, Blanca, 891
PODESTÁ, Jerónimo, 1263
PODESTÁ, José Francisco, 894, 1185
PODESTÁ, José J. (DON PEPE, pseud.), 737, 813, 886,
    891, 894, 1247, 1260, 1263
PODESTÁ, Juan Vicente, 891, 894, 1263
PODESTÁ, Luis, 894
PODESTÁ, Manuel T., 94, 152a, 718, 774
PODESTÁ, Pablo, 719, 891, 894, 1255, 1263
PODESTÁ FONTANILLA, María de, 894
PODETTI, Humberto Antonio, 222
PODETTI, Ramiro J., 222
PODIO, Bartolomé, 87
POGGIO, Bartolomé, 918, 921
POIDENOT, Gastón, 949
POL, Víctor de, 258
POLACCO, Ferruccio, 35

POLAK FRENKIEL, Wolf, 1210
POLANSKI, Jorge, 923
POLAT, Alberto, 658, 703, 785
POLENTA, pseud.
    see GARIBATO, Atilio
POLERO ESCAMILLA, A., 1243, 1247
POLESE, Tobías, 258
POLESELLO, Rogelio, 19, 35, 36, 38
POLETTI, Syria, 140, 668, 764, 772, 796, 822
POLICASTRO, Enrique, 18, 19, 23, 25, 31, 34, 36, 55
POLIDORO, Haydée, 810
POLISENA, José, 312
POLITTI, Luis, 857d
POLIZA, Francisco Juan, 681
POLO DE BERNABÉ, José, 1235
POLLAROLO, Vicente, 937, 939
POLLERI, Félix, 1123
POLLERI DE VIANA, Amalia, 1211
POMARES, Roberto, 385
POMBO, Daniel, 268
POMBO DE OTERO, Francisco, 126
PONCE, Aníbal Norberto, 119, 751
PONCE, Blas, 520
PONCE, Carlos, 207, 683a, 874
PONCE, Luis P., 1123
PONCE, Myriam Elizabeth, 684
PONCE AGUIRRE DE BOSSHARDT ZAPATA, Adela, 874
PONCE DE LEÓN (family), 357, 361, 1108
PONCE DE LEÓN, Alberto, 663, 722, 739, 798, 805, 807
PONCE DE LEÓN, Baltasar, 599
PONCE DE LEÓN, Horacio, 662, 663, 739, 805
PONCE DE LEÓN, Ignacio, 186
PONCE DE LEÓN, Justo, 599
PONCE DE LEÓN, Pedro F., 878
PONCE DE MASSARA, María C., 781
PONCE Y GÓMEZ, Luis, 189
PONDAL RÍOS, Leopoldo, 833
PONDAL RÍOS, Sixto, 858
PONFERRADA, Juan Oscar, 664, 675, 676, 746, 751, 766
PONS (family), 168
PONS, Diego, 1075
PONS, Juan Lorenzo
    see PONS PIGRÁN, Juan Lorenzo
PONS, Rafael A., 1116
PONS PALET, José, 1092
PONS PIGRÁN, Juan Lorenzo, 1210, 1211
PONSONBY (Lord), 143
PONT VERGÉS, Pedro, 31, 36
PONTE, Clementino del
    see DEL PONTE, Clementino
PONTE, Eduardo del, 923
PONTE BALLESTEROS, Tomás, 284
PONTINO, Luis Mario, 874
PONZO, Alberto Luis, 739, 802
POOLE, William L., 1216a
POPHAM, Home Riggs, 143, 427, 472, 552, 587
POPPER, Julio, 99
PORCEL DE PERALTA, Manuel, 254, 844, 1261
PORCELLANA, Carlitos, 860
PORCELLANA, Luisita, 860
PORCELLANA, Natalio, 860
PORCIRES IRACE, Edmundo, 1210
PORCIUNCULA, Omar, 1093
PORCHIA, Antonio, 739, 759, 812, 832
POROTO, pseud.
    see BOTANA, Helvio I.
PORRAS, Antonio, 358
PORRAS, Juan de, 845, 949
PORRAS, Miguel Jerónimo de, 1270
PORRES, Diego de, 914, 918

PORRO, Francisco, 258
PORRO, Mario, 663, 805
PORRO FREIRE, Alicia
   see PORRO FREIRE DE MACIEL, Alicia
PORRO FREIRE DE MACIEL, Alicia, 1187, 1217
PORRÚA, Juan Antonio, 1095
PORTA, Eliseo Salvador, 1159, 1167, 1177, 1196
PORTA, Ilia Ada, 683a
PORTA MONTERROSO, Marcos José de, 1133
PORTAL, Juan Ignacio del, 126
PORTAL, Mariano Ignacio del, 126
PORTAL, Pedro José, 385
PORTALET, Luis, 817
PORTALUPPI, Angel, 951
PORTEIRO, José, 1089
PORTEIRO, Nicolás, 1089
PORTEIRO TRIGO, Manuel, 1089
PORTELA, Epifanio, 68
PORTELA, Ireneo, 844
PORTELA, Manuel, 135, 800
PORTELA CANTILO DE SOSA, María Carmen, 1210
PORTELA DE ARAÓZ ALFARO, María Carmen, 154
PORTELA LAGOS, Margarita, 44, 154
PORTER, Julio, 857c
PORTER, Liliana, 27, 55
PORTILLA (family), 348
PORTILLO, José Eugenio del, 126
PORTILLO BENÍTEZ, José Domingo, 1017
PORTNAY, Leopoldo, 218
PORTOGALO, José (ANANÍA, José, pseud.), 722, 739,
   746, 759, 801, 803
PORTUGUÉS, Juan, 1238
PORTUGUÉS, Pedro, 845
PORTUGUESA, LA, pseud.
   see DELFINA
PORZECANSKI, Teresa
   see PORZECANSKI COHEN, Teresa
PORZECANSKI COHEN, Teresa, 1155, 1173
POSA POTE, Arturo de la, 68
POSADA, Segundo, 1125
POSADAS, Alejandro, 844
POSADAS, Antonio de, 386
POSADAS, Carlos, 332
POSADAS, Gervasio Antonio, 70, 95, 104, 244, 282,
   283, 374, 404, 455, 478, 479, 519, 545a, 611,
   1091
POSADAS, Manuel, 137
POSAS DE MERANI, Nelly A., 691
POSE, Manuel María, 284
POSE, Ramón, 1089
POSE GARAY, Eugenio, 943
POSPÓS, Martín del, 745
POSSE, Esther Camila, 320
POSSE, José, 189
POSSE, Justiniano, 89, 195, 316, 545a
POSSE, Ricardo E., 744, 748
POSSE, Salvador, 211
POSSOLO, Augusto, 1093a
POSSOLO, Carlos, 1093a
POSSOLO, José Augusto, 1093a
POSSOLO, Melchora, 1093a
POSSOLO, Orfilia, 1093a, 1205
POSTIGLIONE, Hilda Emilia, 653, 654
POTENZA, Fernando, 860
POTIRAVA, 977
POUEY, Enrique, 1075, 1202
POUGET, María Angélica, 683a
POUGET, Miguel A., 207
POUS PEÑA, Eduardo, 923
POUSA, Narciso, 663, 805

POVEDA, Jerónimo de, 914
POVEDA Y VALDÉS, Luis de la, 186
POZO, Alonso del, 1266
POZO, Ana María del, 684
POZO, Andrés del, 739, 746, 837
POZO, José del, 17a, 28
POZO, Manuel del, 32
POZO Y MARQUY, José Antonio del, 7, 332, 1236
POZO Y SILVA, Alonso de, 529a, 910
POZO Y SILVA, Juan del, 186
POZZI, Antonio, 258
POZZI, Aurelio Juan Santiago, 923
POZZI, Edna, 663
POZZI, Guelfo, 923
PRADA, Víctor de la, 866
PRADERE, Carlos M., 565
PRADES SANZ, María de las Mercedes, 86
PRADO, Héctor, 663
PRADO, José, 152a, 823, 1089
PRADO, Manuel, 478, 1089
PRADO ESCOL, José, 768
PRADO MALDONADO, Manuel de, 570
PRAGUER-COELHO, Olga, 154
PRALONG, Oscar H., 691
PRAT, Domingo, 1204
PRAT, Juan Manuel, 751
PRATI, Julio César, 258
PRATI, Lidy, 31
PRATS DE HUISI, Dolores, 422
PRATS GILL, Emilio, 1014
PRATT, José Antonio, 938
PREBISCH DE PIOSSEK, Amalia (PREVISCH DE PIOSSEK,
   Amalia), 711, 713, 762, 783
PRECIADO, Julián, 7, 32
PRECILLA, Saturnino de la, 188, 283
PRECILLA DE JAMESON, Clara de la, 931
PREGO, Antonio J., 923
PREGO DE OLIVER, José, 763, 876, 1165, 1199, 1258
PRELAT, Carlos Evaristo, 923
PRELER, Horacio, 663
PREMAT (family), 168
PREMIANI, Bruno, 299
PRENZ, Juan Octavio, 663
PRESA, Juan Antonio, 1095
PRESAS, Leopoldo Pedro, 18, 19, 23, 25, 31, 36, 46,
   55
PRESILLA, Saturnino de la
   see PRECILLA, Saturnino de la
PRESS, Raúl Edgardo, 791
PRESTA, Salvador, 19, 31
PRETE, Juan del, 19, 23, 25, 33, 34, 50, 56, 1218
PRETI, Luis, 31
PRETTY, Francis, 28
PREVISCH DE PIOSSEK, Amalia
   see PREBISCH DE PIOSSEK, Amalia
PREVITALI, Raúl A., 1073
PRIEGO Y CARO, José, 1041
PRIETO, Indalecio, 260
PRIETO, Juan Manuel, 779, 834
PRIETO, Justo, 964, 966, 1021, 1022, 1023
PRIETO, L., 878
PRIETO, Melchor, 918, 1041
PRIETO, Teodoro, 893
PRIETO MARCOS, Manuel, 284
PRIETO PRIETO, Roberto Miguel, 1210
PRIETO Y QUEVEDO, Francisco de, 496
PRIGGIONI, Guillermina, 887
PRIGNANO, Angel Oscar, 37
PRILUTZKY FARNY, Julia, 739, 766
PRIMAVERSI, Leonel, 923

PRIMO FARÍAS, Luis, 691
PRIMOLI, Juan Bautista, 7, 32, 952
PRINCIVALLE, Carlos María, 894, 1172, 1185, 1199
PRINGLES, Juan Pascual, 121, 179, 215, 244, 278,
    282, 386, 404, 566, 574
PRIORE, Angela Carola de, 874
PRIORE, Oscar del, 299
PRIOTTI, Elda, 684
PRO, Diego F., 683a
PROHASKA, Frederico Jorge, 923
PROIETTO, Donato Antonio, 25, 64
PRONSATO, Domingo, 19, 23, 25, 31, 36, 50, 152
PRONZATO, Víctor, 770
PROSEN, Alberto Francisco, 923
PROTZUCOV, Felipe, 781
PROUS, Eduardo, 889
PRUNELL ALZÁIBAR, Elbio, 1167, 1187
PÚA, Carlos de la, pseud.
    see MUÑOZ, Carlos Raúl
PUCCIA, Enrique Horacio, 237
PUCCIARELLI, Mario A., 19, 36, 49
PUCCIO, Eugenio, 68
PUCH, Carmne, 478, 929
PUCH, Dionisio, 625
PUCH, Domingo, 625
PUCH, José Patricio, 126
PUCH, Manuel, 625
PUCH, Miguel, 385
PUCH BLAS, Manuel, 713
PUCHETA ORTEGA, Justo, 954
PUEBLA DE DAY, Angelina, 278
PUEBLA DE GODOY, Rosario, 207, 683a
PUEBLA GONZÁLEZ, Francisco de la, 910
PUEBLA Y REINOSO, Juan de, 555
PUECH GALLO DE MASTRÁNGELO, Alba, 1210
PUENTE, Alejandro, 55
PUENTE, Gabriel A., 609
PUENTE, Gregorio F. de la, 330
PUENTE, Heberto Alfonso, 923
PUENTE, José de la, 1212
PUENTE GUERRA, Angel, 683a
PUENTE PISTARINI, Héctor, 385
PUENTES PALERMO DE OYENARD ALORI, Sylvia Marlene,
    1088
PUERTAS Y VALVERDE, Alonso, 914
PUERTO, Alfonso del, 998
PUERTO, Francisco del, 1203
PUERTO, Gregorio del, 1206
PUERTO COPELO, Javier del, 1210
PUEYRREDÓN (family), 351, 361
PUEYRREDÓN (family)
    see also ITUARTE PUEYRREDÓN (family)
PUEYRREDÓN, Carlos Alberto, 521, 893
PUEYRREDÓN, Diego José de, 545a
PUEYRREDÓN, Feliciano, 126, 921
PUEYRREDÓN, Honorio, 69
PUEYRREDÓN, Juan Andrés, 104, 545a
PUEYRREDÓN, Juan Martín de, 85, 104, 110, 121, 141,
    148, 166, 176, 188, 212, 227, 228, 244, 282,
    283, 386, 404, 420, 424, 427, 439, 453, 457,
    462, 469, 471, 472, 475, 478, 479, 489, 499,
    502, 509, 514, 517, 518, 519, 521, 529, 545a,
    552, 553, 554, 561, 562, 563, 573, 574, 611,
    629, 1091
PUEYRREDÓN, Juana
    see PUEYRREDÓN DE SÁENZ VALIENTE, Juana
PUEYRREDÓN, Julio, 3
PUEYRREDÓN, Manuel Alejandro, 371, 611
PUEYRREDÓN, Pridiliano, 6, 19, 25, 28, 42, 45, 51,
    56, 59, 217, 266, 282, 293, 521

PUEYRREDÓN DE SÁENZ VALIENTE, Juana, 422, 478, 611,
    929
PUGA, Juan, 914
PUGA, Manuel, 1089
PUGA SABATÉ, Antonio, 739
PUGLIESE, Ana Carolina E., 684
PUGLIESE, José, 681
PUGLIESE, Osvaldo, 877
PUGLIESI, Cayetano, 891a
PUIG, Felipe, 1083
PUIG, José Antonio, 32
PUIG, Manuel, 752
PUIG, Vicente R., 24
PUIGGARI, Miguel, 844, 1261
PUIGGRÓS, Rodolfo, 440, 609
PUJADO DELUCHI, Enrique Eugenio, 1088
PUJATO CRESPO DE CAMELINO VEDOYA, Mercedes, 762
PUJATS, Cándido, 845
PUJÍA, Antonio, 25, 35
PUJOL, José, 7
PUJOL, Juan Gregorio, 70, 96, 121, 141, 164, 196,
    197
PUJOL, Juan José, 387
PUJOL, Raúl Manuel, 923
PULEIO, Domingo (TORRE, Domingo de la, pseud.), 878
PUNZI, Orlando Mario, 660, 716, 726
PUPPO, Julio César (HACHERO, El, pseud.), 819
PURVIS, Brett, 580
PUYAU, Higinio, 21
PUYOL, Andrés Felipe, 1083
PUZZI DE BARROSO, María Cecilia, 320
PY, Luis, 14, 287

QUARANTA, José, 258
QUARANTINO, Pascual, 881, 883
QUARTARUOLO, V. Mario, 265
QUARTINO, Rómulo, 332
QUEIREL, Juan, 191
QUEIROLA, Aída (TITA, pseud.), 894
QUEIROLA, Enrique, 894
QUEIROLO, Domingo, 995, 1039
QUEIROLO, Fabio, 982
QUEIROLO, Luis, 1075
QUEIROLO DE BAJAC, Clara, 942
QUENEL, Clementina Rosa, 707, 831
QUENÓN, Miguel, 316
QUEREJETA, Alberto S., 652
QUERENCIO, Carlos María, 95
QUERENCIO, Mariano, 95
QUERINI, Manuel, 895, 1036, 1264, 1267
QUEROL, Horacio Emilio L., 923
QUEROL, Jorge Carlos, 299
QUESADA, Ernesto, 68, 167, 609
QUESADA, Gaspar de, 1238
QUESADA, Josué A., 154, 727, 811, 813
QUESADA, Juan Isidro, 371, 611
QUESADA, Juan José, 540, 611
QUESADA, Luis, 44
QUESADA, Vicente G., 314, 609, 708, 751
QUESADA Y BERNABEU, Alonso de, 496
QUEVEDO, Casiano Víctor, 923
QUEVEDO, José María, 669
QUEVEDO, Roberto, 966
QUEVEDO, Wilfrido, 998
QUIJANO, Carlos, 1184
QUIJANO, Fernando, 887, 1205
QUIJANO, Juan, 69
QUIJANO, Pedro P., 254, 540
QUILES, Ismael, 239
QUILICI, Juan T., 1073

QUINQUELA MARTÍN, Benito, 19, 31, 33
QUINSAC MONVOISIN, Raimundo Augusto
 see MONVOISIN, Raymond Auguste Quinsac
QUINTANA, 1029
QUINTANA (family), 351
QUINTANA, Andrés Nazario de la, 1223
QUINTANA, Emilio, 385
QUINTANA, Fenelón de la, 385
QUINTANA, Fermín de la, 385
QUINTANA, Francisco, 279
QUINTANA, Hilarión de la, 554, 611
QUINTANA, José de la, 385, 634, 1266
QUINTANA, José Ignacio de la, 496
QUINTANA, José María de, 845
QUINTANA, Julián, 1188
QUINTANA, Manuel, 141, 166, 182, 193, 277, 278, 282,
 392, 393, 405, 466, 478, 493, 515, 516, 521,
 524, 531, 544, 586, 592, 593, 595, 598, 619, 650
QUINTANA, María de la, 422, 611, 928
QUINTANA, Nicolás, 254
QUINTANA, Pablo de la, 1223
QUINTANA, Ramón de la, 1266
QUINTANA, Teodosio de la, 1223
QUINTANA DE ESCALADA, Tomasa de la, 112, 227, 422,
 611
QUINTANA GURRUCHAGA, María de la, 422
QUINTANA SÁENZ, Manuel, 971
QUINTANILLA, Antonio, 104
QUINTANILLA, Julio, 874
QUINTANILLA DE ALVEAR, Carmen, 227, 422, 611
QUINTAS, Juan Crisóstomo, 126
QUINTAS, Ramón, 1089
QUINTELA, Manuel, 1075, 1083, 1261
QUINTERAS, Susy, 785
QUINTERO, Gonzalo, 914
QUINTERO, Lázaro, 32, 914
QUINTERO, Pedro, 1238
QUINTEROS, Carlos Manuel, 923
QUIÑONES, Andrés, 845
QUIÑONES Y OSORIO, Margarita, 1042
QUIQUE, El, pseud.
 see COBOS, Juan Carlos
QUIRICO PORRECA, 1266
QUIRINO CRISTIANI, Luis, 923
QUIRNO COSTA, Norberto, 68
QUIRNO Y ECHANDÍA, Norberto de, 496
QUIRNO Y GONZÁLEZ NORIEGA, Gregorio José de, 97
QUIROGA, Alfredo, 137
QUIROGA, Atanasio, 844
QUIROGA, Camila, pseud. (PASSERA, Camila), 135, 891,
 893
QUIROGA, Carlos B., 680, 751, 779, 830
QUIROGA, Dardo, 299
QUIROGA, Eduardo, 757
QUIROGA, Facundo
 see QUIROGA, Juan Facundo
QUIROGA, Feliciano Gil de
 see GIL DE QUIROGA, Feliciano de
QUIROGA, Héctor G., 893
QUIROGA, Horacio, 152a, 225, 232, 670, 685, 707,
 724, 737, 742, 745, 745a, 753, 779, 799, 806,
 816, 825, 829, 835, 894, 1071, 1079, 1083, 1157,
 1164, 1170, 1171, 1174, 1175, 1177, 1186, 1190,
 1197, 1198, 1199, 1216a, 1246, 1259
QUIROGA, Jerónimo L., 222
QUIROGA, José, 922, 989, 1269
QUIROGA, José Eufrasio de, 171, 921
QUIROGA, Juan Facundo, 83, 166, 179, 227, 240, 283,
 398, 404, 478, 489, 491, 499, 518, 519, 528,
 529, 531, 532, 559, 575, 589, 593, 600, 603,
 604, 605, 606, 608, 632

QUIROGA, Juan Francisco, 282
QUIROGA, Lindor L., 81, 158, 222
QUIROGA, Malvina Rosa, 751, 762
QUIROGA, Manuel Gregorio, 188
QUIROGA, Marcial V., 68, 94, 565, 844, 848
QUIROGA, Nenesio, 207
QUIROGA, Roque Jacinto, 254
QUIROGA, Rosita, 877, 879
QUIROGA, Sabino, 1089
QUIROGA, Santiago S., 923
QUIROGA ADARO, Ruperto N., 222
QUIROGA CARRIL, Manuel Gregorio, 283
QUIROGA CARRIL, Ventura (BUENAVENTURA, pseud.), 283
QUIROGA DE CHENA, Carmen, 222
QUIROGA MÉNDEZ, José, 284
QUIROGA SARMIENTO, José Manuel Eufrasio de, 188, 283,
 412, 910
QUIROGA Y TABOADA, Fernando Andrés de, 279
QUIRÓS, Balthasar Antonio de, 186
QUIRÓS, Cesáreo Bernaldo de, 19, 31, 33, 45, 55,
 135, 217
QUIRÓS, Herminio J., 121, 135, 241, 842
QUIRÓS, Pedro de (family), 358
QUIRÓS Y MITERIO CASTRO, Cantalicio, 1244
QUIRÓZ MONTORFANO, Juan Darío, 1210

RABAGLIO, Virgilio, 6
RÁBAGO, Eleuterio, 1089
RABAL, Enrique, 684
RABAUDI, Lila Duffau de
 see DUFFAU DE RABAUDI, Lila
RABELO, Agustín, 552
RABINOVICH, José, 152a
RACCA, Pascual M., 652
RACEDO, Eduardo, 13, 17b, 68, 95, 121, 135, 241, 617
RACKER, Enrique, 923
RACKER, Geneviève T. de, 923
RACHETTI, Oscar V., 1123
RADA, Andrés de, 989
RADAELLI, Sigfrido, 716, 746
RADEMAKER, Juan, 427
RADICE, Juan Carlos, 923
RADICE, María Magdalena, 923
RADICELLA, Renato, 923
RADIO, Pedro, 135
RAFAELLI, Enrique Mario, 805
RAFFETTO, Pablo, 886
RAFFO, Hortensia Margarita, 678, 751
RAFFO, Manuel, 6
RAFFO, Mario, 1243
RAFFO, Nello, 44
RAFFO, Santiago, 44
RAFFO DE LA RETA, Julio César, 207
RAFFO DE MUELAS, Josefa, 320
RAGGIO, Michèle, 139
RAGGIO, Miguel, 923
RAGONESE, Arturo Enrique, 923
RAGONESI, Miguel, 31
RAGUCCI, Rodolfo M., 154
RAHMAN, Aziz-ur, 923
RAIMONDI, Alejandro, 854
RAINERI MIRALDI, Mario Andrés, 1088
RAINES, Gloria, 299
RAÍZ, Leoncio A., 1073
RALESKY, Arminda, 836
RAMA, Angel, 1172, 1177, 1184, 1185
RAMA, José, 1089
RAMALLO, Ernesto, 140
RAMALLO, Manuel, 1089
RAMALLO, Nicasio, 611
RAMASSO, Ambrosio Luis, 1083
RAMASSO, Juan, 1093

RAMASSO, Juan María, 1093
RAMAUGÉ, Adalberto, 844
RAMAUGÉ, Roberto, 64
RAMB, Ana María, 817
RAMELLA, María Esther Carmen, 41
RAMELLA, Raúl, 652
RAMÍREZ, 878
RAMÍREZ (family), 348
RAMÍREZ, Andrés Florencio, 496, 915, 921
RAMÍREZ, Antonio, 169
RAMÍREZ, Ariel, 1027
RAMÍREZ, Arnulfo A., 954
RAMÍREZ, Carlos María, 1079, 1120, 1141, 1146, 1174,
    1177, 1188, 1193, 1199, 1253
RAMÍREZ, Ceferino, 14
RAMÍREZ, Francisca, 887
RAMÍREZ, Francisco, 89, 95, 121, 135, 166, 241, 282,
    382, 404, 478, 499, 512, 519, 521, 528, 529,
    532, 552, 553, 554, 623, 632
RAMÍREZ, Gonzalo, 1075, 1134, 1146, 1174
RAMÍREZ, J. Isidro, 959
RAMÍREZ, José Pedro, 1075, 1091, 1112, 1117, 1134,
    1146, 1185
RAMÍREZ, José Santos, 212
RAMÍREZ, Juan Andrés, 1079, 1083, 1141, 1190
RAMÍREZ, Juan Pedro, 1093a
RAMÍREZ, Juan Vicente, 959
RAMÍREZ, Luis, 627, 1203, 1230
RAMÍREZ, Manuel, 371
RAMÍREZ, Manuel Vicente, 220
RAMÍREZ, Pablino, 998
RAMÍREZ, Pancho
    see RAMÍREZ, Francisco
RAMÍREZ, Pascual, 32
RAMÍREZ, Pedro Pablo, 135, 170, 515, 516, 619
RAMÍREZ, Pedro Pascual, 173
RAMÍREZ, Rodolfo, 793
RAMÍREZ ABELLA, Yatay, 781
RAMÍREZ BOETTNER, Carlos M., 963a
RAMÍREZ CHACÓN, 954
RAMÍREZ DE ARELLANO (family), 1108
RAMÍREZ DE ARELLANO, Eduardo, 545a
RAMÍREZ DE ARELLANO, José Vicente, 244, 545a, 910
RAMÍREZ DE ARELLANO, Juan, 186
RAMÍREZ DE VELASCO (family), 348, 352
RAMÍREZ DE VELASCO, Juan, 32, 83, 244, 417, 501,
    521, 522, 527, 570, 620, 914, 1011
RAMÍREZ DE VELASCO, Pedro, 32
RAMÍREZ FRANCO, Adalberto, 998
RAMÍREZ IZAGUIRRE, Wilfredo Alfonso, 1210
RAMÍREZ JUÁREZ, Evaristo, 191, 268
RAMÍREZ LUNA, Félix, 862
RAMÍREZ OROZCO, Juan, 552
RAMÍREZ RUSSO, Manfredo, 954
RAMÍREZ TORRES, Marcelino, 998
RAMÍREZ VALDEZ Y DE LA BANDA, Diego, 1011
RAMIRO I, 361
RAMITO, pseud.
    see RAMOS, Angel Eladio
RAMORINO, Juan, 113
RAMOS, Alfredo, 1006
RAMOS, Andrés, 186
RAMOS, Angel Eladio (RAMITO, pseud.), 860
RAMOS, Bonifacio, 611, 990
RAMOS, Esteban, 878
RAMOS, Irma Matilde, 691
RAMOS, Jorge Abelardo, 609
RAMOS, Juan, 496
RAMOS, Juan Bautista, 683a
RAMOS, Pedro, 1075

RAMOS, Pedro L., 1094
RAMOS, Ramón Antonio, 943, 964, 966
RAMOS, Santiago, 1205
RAMOS CARRIÓN, Teresa, 679, 711, 762
RAMOS DE BERENGENO, Carmen, 320
RAMOS DE LOS REYES, Francisca, 46
RAMOS FERREIRA, Sergia, 1017
RAMOS GIMÉNEZ, Leopoldo, 943, 947, 1014, 1018, 1020,
    1021, 1022
RAMOS MEJÍA, Francisco, 470
RAMOS MEJÍA, Ildefonso, 404
RAMOS MEJÍA, José María, 110, 167, 182, 240, 246,
    259, 282, 577, 734, 844, 847, 851, 1261
RAMOS MEJÍA, Matías, 611
RAMOS MEXÍA, Exequiel, 3, 904
RAMOS MEXÍA, Francisco, 169
RAMOS MEXÍA, Josefa Gabriela, 924
RAMOS MEXÍA Y ROSS, Hilario José, 496
RAMOS MONTERO, Alfredo, 1083
RAMOS MONTERO, Dionisio, 1127
RAMOS SIGNES, Rogelio, 785
RAMOS SUÁREZ, Arturo, 1116
RAMPOLDE DE BRONZINI, María Antonia, 923
RAMPOLLA DE TINDARO, 91
RAMPONI, Jorge Enrique, 683a, 722, 739, 746, 758,
    759, 798, 803, 807, 831
RAMSAY, Allan C., 15
RAMSAY, Roberto, 17, 580
RAMSEYER (family), 168
RANALLETTI, Bernardo, 664
RANDÓN, Angel, 126
RANEA, Eduardo, 691
RANEA, Julio César, 653, 654, 702
RANSONNIER, Jacques, 960
RAONE, Juan Mario, 810
RAPELA, Diego, 284
RAPETTI, Natalio, 951
RAPOPORT, Eduardo H., 923
RAPOPORT, Nicolás, 152a
RAPPA MARABOTTO, Hugo Camilo, 1210
RAPPALINI, César M., 1050, 1151
RASQUÍN, Jaime, 985
RATKOVIC, Milijov, 923
RATTI, Horacio Esteban, 663, 722, 739, 758
RATTI JAEGGLI, Héctor A. B., 954
RATTO DE SADOSKY, Cora, 923
RAUCH, 166
RAUCH, Federico, 209
RAUSKIN, J. A., 1015, 1025
RAVA, Horacio G., 831
RAVE, Francisco, 332
RAVENET, Juan, 17a, 28
RAVERY, Luis, 949
RAVIGNANI, Emilio, 283, 431, 609
RAVIZZA, Alejandro, 952
RAWSON, Amán, 179, 283
RAWSON, Arturo, 170, 619
RAWSON, Benjamín Franklin, 19, 25, 59, 62, 293, 521
RAWSON, Franklin
    see RAWSON, Benjamín Franklin
RAWSON, Guillermo, 110, 116, 141, 166, 188, 261,
    282, 283, 287, 404, 586, 647, 692, 718, 842,
    844, 848, 851, 1261
RAYCES, Enrique César, 923
RAYÓN, Esteban, 845
RAZNOVICH, Diana, 889
RAZZANO, José, 892, 894
REAL, Jacinto D., 1075, 1126
REAL PERÓ, pseud.
    see GONZÁLEZ, José

REAL, Roberto, 299
REAL DE AZÚA (family), 1108
REAL DE AZÚA, Carlos, 1177
REALE (family), 168
REANT, Agustín, 6
REBAGLIO, Virgilio, 258
REBAUDI, Arturo, 959
REBAUDI, Ovidio, 68, 959
REBAUDI BASAVILBASO, Oscar, 713
RÉBOLI, Ida L., 154, 751, 762
REBOLLO, Joaquín P., 1093
REBOLLO PAZ, León, 431, 609
REBUELTA VELARDE, José, 126
REBUELTO, Antonio, 332
REBUFFO, Víctor L., 18, 41, 44, 55, 1218
RECALDE, Camilo, 1006
RECALDE, Dolores, 991
RECALDE, Facundo, 943, 965, 1014, 1020, 1021, 1022
RECALDE, Jesús Amado (PAPOTÍN, pseud.), 1014
RECALDE, Juan Francisco, 953, 959
RECALDE, Luis, 941
RECALDE, Mariano, 987
RECALDE, Pablo, 991
RECALDE, Pedro, 991
RECALDE, Rafaela Antonia, 973
RECALDE AMMIRI, Juan Francisco, 973
RECALDE AMMIRI, Sergio A. T., 973
RECALDE ARÉVALO, Victoriano, 973
RECALDE DE RECALDE, Emilia, 959
RECALDE MILESI, Herminia, 973
RECALDE MILESI, Rufino, 973
RECALDE MONGELÓS, Juan Francisco, 973
RECALDE MONGELÓS, Rafael Antonio, 973
RECALDE SOSA, Juan Francisco, 973
RECALDE VALDEZ, Juan Francisco, 973
RECALDE VALDEZ, Pedro Plutarco, 973
RECOBA, El Indio, 1059
RECUERO, Casimiro, 278
RECHES, Rubén, 750
RECHNIEWSKI, Casimiro Estanislao, 923
REDOANO, Hebe Ester, 44
RECONDO BERASATEGUI, Carlos Alberto, 691
REEDHEAD, José, 844, 1261
REFOXO ILLANES, Angel, 284
REGA MOLINA, Horacio Angel, 235, 674, 678, 722, 739, 751, 759, 769, 773, 782, 801, 807, 833
REGA MOLINA, Mary, 154, 711, 751, 762, 783
REGAIRAZ, Alberto Carlos, 923
REGALADO DE LA PLAZA, Pedro, 611
REGALADO RODRÍGUEZ, Pedro, 268
REGE CORVALÁN, Felipe, 984, 1011
REGEN, Jacobo, 653, 654, 699
REGENNASS (family), 168
REGGIARDO, Carlo, 139
REGGINI, Horacio C., 923
REGINO VIGO, Abraham, 31
REGNAULT, Gill, 949
REGO Y MENDOZA, Diego de, 1011
REGOLI DE MULLEN, Alicia, 655, 656, 814
REGUEIRA, Manuel, 1089
REGUERA, Raymundo J., 254, 540
REGUERA DE DIEGO, Celia, 729, 744
REGUERA SIERRA, Ernesto, 652, 923
REGULES (family), 1108
REGULES, Dardo, 1064, 1184
REGULES, Elías, 1054, 1073, 1075, 1079, 1083, 1126, 1146, 1166, 1167, 1174, 1179, 1185, 1187, 1199, 1243, 1247, 1261, 1263
REGUNAGA, Emeterio C., 648, 649, 1081
REICHERT, Carlos (IWANOSKI, Teófilo, pseud.), 158, 238

REID, Mathew, 6
REIG, Osvaldo Alfredo, 923
REIN, Mercedes, 1155
REIN, Víctor, 923
REINAFÉ (brothers), 559
REINAFÉ, Francisco, 166, 584
REINAFÉ, José Antonio
    see REYNAFÉ, José Antonio
REINAFÉ, José Vicente
    see REYNAFÉ, José Vicente
REINAFÉ, Manuel Vicente, 584
REINOSO, Alonso de, 555
REISSIG, Luis, 743
REJAS, Simón
    see REXAS, Simón
RELGIS, Eugen, 1088
REMEDI, Hugo, 684
REMMELE, Enrique, 954
REMOLI, Domingo, 1243
REMONDA MINGRAND, F., 565
REMOSO ROMEO, Limo, 1210
REMUÑÁN, Manuel, 1089
RENÁN, Sergio, 857
RENART, Emilio, 55
RENAUDIÈRE DE PAULIS, Domingo, 664
RENAULT, Luis, 258
RENCORET, Benjamín, 918
RENDÓN, Bartolomé, 186
RENDÓN SARMIENTO, Antonio, 914
RENGGER, John Rudolf, 949
RENGIFO, Francisco, 620
RENOM, Federico, 1046, 1047
RENTERÍA, Dolorcita, 1205
RENTERÍA, Martín de, 520
REPEITO, Armando, 299
REPETTO, Amalia, 1206, 1207
REPETTO, Juan José, 320
REPETTO, Nicolás, 260, 261, 503, 614, 718, 853a
REPETTO, Roberto, 385
REPETTO, Ruth, 785
REQUENA, Julián, 319
REQUENA, Julio, 831
REQUENA DE DEL BARRIO, Concepción, 874
REQUENI, Antonio, 661, 716, 717, 739, 758, 759, 802
RESIGA, Angel, 860
RESKS, Luis A., 947
RESQUÍN, Francisco Isidoro, 974
RESQUÍN HUERTA, Luis, 1014, 1017
RESTA, Giuseppe, 874
RETA, Primitivo de la, 207, 212
RETAMOSO, Hernando de, 520, 620
RETANA, Francisco Nicolás de la, 555
REUMAY, pseud.
    see CAYOL, Alvaro
REUS, Emilio, 1084
REUTEMANN (family), 168
REUTLINGER (family), 168
REVEL, Gabriela, 1173
REVELLO, Lydia H., 652
REVELLO, Nicolás, 1083
REVERBERI, Oscar Valentín, 923
REVERTER, José, 319
REVILLA, Enrique, 844
REVOL, C., 521
REVOL, Carlos, 332
REVOL, Félix, 28, 62
REXAS, Simón, 496
REY (family), 168
REY, Jerónimo del, pseud.
    see CASTELLANI, Leonardo

REY, Julián (family), 168
REY, Manuel, 1089
REY, Pedro, 1089
REY, Plinio, 923
REY ORLLIE, El, 478
REY PASTOR, Julio, 923
REY POSSE, Lita, 154
REY RUIBAL, Adolfo, 284
REYES (CIEGO REYES, El, pseud.), 878
REYES (family), 1108
REYES, César, 381a
REYES, Cipriano, 560
REYES, Diego de los
    see REYES BALMACEDA, Diego de los
REYES, José María, 169, 1053, 1063
REYES, Juan B. A., 645
REYES, Juan de los, 845
REYES, Manuel José, 496
REYES, Marcelino, 242, 381a
REYES, Rafael H., 713
REYES, Raquel de, 684
REYES BALMACEDA, Diego de los, 978, 984, 989, 1011, 1030
REYES BEJARANO, Salvador, 387
REYES DAGLIO, César Teófilo, 1210
REYES DE LLAMBÍ, Francisco, 1093a
REYES FEBLES DE GUADALUPE, María del Luján, 1088
REYLES, Carlos Claudio, 821, 894, 1075, 1079, 1081, 1083, 1086, 1146, 1149, 1162, 1164, 1168, 1170, 1175, 1177, 1180, 1186, 1187, 1188, 1190, 1195, 1196, 1197, 1198, 1199, 1246, 1249, 1251, 1254, 1260
REYNA, José Rafael, 921
REYNAFÉ, José Antonio, 545a
REYNAFÉ, José Vicente, 545a
REYNAL O'CONNOR, Arturo, 1246
REYNALDI, Horacio Félix, 781
REYNALS, Olaguer, 207, 496
REYNOLDS, Barrington, 580
REYNOSO, Antonio, 719
REYNOSO, Felipe, 845
REZÁBAL Y AGOTE, Ignacio, 254, 496
REZZANO AGUIRRE, Raúl Virgilio, 1210
RIAGGIO, Celestino, 865
RIAL, Francisco, 1089
RIAL, Marcelino, 1089
RIAL, Raimundo
    see RIAL DE LA IGLESIA, Raimundo
RIAL DE LA IGLESIA, Raimundo, 284, 496
RIART, Luis Alberto, 953, 959
RIBA, Marta, 874
RIBADENEIRA, Juan Pascual, 284
RIBADENEYRA, Francisco de, 186
RIBADENEYRA, Luis de, 186
RIBAS, Federico, 284
RIBAUDI, Antonio, 952
RIBEIRO, León, 1083, 1206, 1207, 1208
RIBERA, Alonso de, 501
RIBERA, Andrés, 32
RIBERA, Fructuoso
    see RIVERA, José Fructuoso
RIBERA, Hernando de, 465, 943, 951, 989, 992, 1238
RIBERA, Lázaro
    see RIBERA Y ESPINOSA, Lázaro de
RIBERA, Perafán de
    see RIVERA, Pablo Hilarión Perafán de la
RIBERA Y ESPINOSA, Lázaro de, 968, 984a
RIBERA Y MALDONADO, Diego de, 646
RIBERA Y RAMOS, Antonio, 284
RIBERO, Manuel, 32
RIBERO, Romilio, 726

RIBERO RIBAS, Elías, 32
RIBES, Saturnino, 1092
RICABARRA, Rodolfo Alfredo, 923
RICAGNO, Luis, 260
RICALDONI, Américo, 1075, 1079, 1081, 1104, 1261
RICALDONI, Pedro, 1104
RICALDONI, Tebaldo J., 258
RICARDE, Juan Andrés, 387
RICARDO, Antonio, 1264
RICARDO, Jorge, 750
RICARDONE, Víctor, 191
RICCETTO, Zelmar, 1178
RICCI, Clemente, 167, 292
RICCI, Ferdinando, 659
RICCI, Ismael Enrique, 823
RICCI, Julio, 1088
RICCI HIDALGO, Inés, 684
RICCIADRI DE CERRUDO, Elba, 663
RICCIO, Gustavo Angel, 739, 759, 801, 833
RICCIO, Ricardo, 751
RICCITELLI, Antonio, 258
RICE, Anna Ackley (Mrs. George L. Roberts), 323
RICO, Héctor, 663
RICO, José, 878
RICO, Juan, 895
RICO, Juan José, 319
RICO, Manuel L., 166
RICO, Orfilia, 891, 894, 1083
RICO DE SIROCHINSKY, Isabel Victoriana, 320
RICQUART, François, 960
RICCHERI, Pablo, 68, 141, 258
RICHARDSON, William W. (Mrs.)
    see CHOATE, Antoinette
RICHERO MENDY, Antonio Anselmo, 1210
RICHTER, Ricardo, 1039
RIDLEY, William R. (Mrs.)
    see ARMSTRONG, Minnie Burrows
RIEDER, Francisco, 954
RIEDER, Rolf, 954
RIEGO, Rodolfo, 954
RIERA, Atanasio, 947
RIERA, Federico, 947
RIERA, José, 496
RIERA, Lylián, 947
RIERA Y MERLO, José María, 496
RIESE, Alfredo, 65
RIESGO, Leonardo Eloy, 702
RIESI, Salvador, 1243
RIESTRA, Augusto de la, 268
RIESTRA, Domingo de la, 921
RIESTRA, Jorge, 696, 771, 796
RIESTRA, Norberto de la, 141, 631
RIETTI, Ciro T., 923
RIFANO, Yolanda, 932
RIGAMONTI DE FUNES, Helvia N., 652
RIGANELLI, Agustín, 19, 21, 25, 33, 55, 293, 521
RIGANELLI CELINI, Estela, 762
RIGBY, Jason, 904
RIGGI, Agustín Eduardo, 923
RIGGI, Juan Carlos, 923
RIGHINI, Marcela, 817
RIGLOS (family), 351
RIGLOS, Francisco Javier, 126, 496
RIGLOS, José Miguel de, 126
RIGLOS DE IRIGOYEN, Ana, 422, 611, 626
RIGUERA MONTERO, Manuel, 1095
RILLO, Lorenzo, 1267
RIMOLDI, Horacio Víctor, 923
RIMOLI, Francisco Bautista (LINYERA, Dante A., pseud.), 660, 710, 727, 818, 871

RINALDI, Carlos Alberto, 923
RINALDI, Susana, 879
RINALDINI, Luis María, 923
RINCÓN, Benjamín, 83
RINGUELET, Augusto, 332
RINGUELET, Carlos, 786, 805
RÍO, Ambrosio del, 878
RÍO, José María A. del, 923
RÍO, José Roberto del, 688
RÍO, Manuel, 521
RÍO. María del, 857b
RÍO, Pastor del, 154
RÍO, Silvia del, 879
RÍO DE OCAMPO, María Juana del, 1093a
RIOFRÍO, Francisco de, 1270
RÍOS, Alcibíades, 998
RÍOS, Carlos Agustín, 810
RÍOS, Concepción, pseud.
    see VÁZQUEZ DE MONTIEL, María del Carmen
RÍOS, Daniel, 299, 691
RÍOS, Gonzalo de los, 555
RÍOS, Jacinto, 244
RÍOS, José, 653, 654
RÍOS, Juan Antonio, 1089
RÍOS, Julia L., 652
RÍOS, Mateo, 625
RÍOS, Miguel Angel, 923
RÍOS, Rafael, 995a
RÍOS, René, 998
RÍOS, Saturio, 939, 984a, 1003
RÍOS, Saturnino, 1088
RÍOS CASTILLO, Hugo, 1014
RÍOS DE LA TORRE, Francisco, 186
RÍOS DE PÁEZ, Francisca, 931
RÍOS ORTIZ, Ricardo, 191, 795
RÍOS PATRÓN, José Luis, 743
RIPA ALBERDI, Héctor, 773, 805
RIPAMONTE, Carlos Pablo, 19, 31, 33
RIQUÉ, Tomás, 923
RIQUELME, Adolfo, 984a
RIQUELME, Alonso de, 989
RIQUELME, Claudio, 299
RIQUELME, Manuel, 943, 959, 964, 966
RIQUELME, William, 938
RIQUELME GARCÍA, Benigno, 966
RISCO Y ALVARADO, Juan del, 555
RISSO, Buenaventura
    see RISSO PATRÓN, Buenaventura
RISSO, Romildo, 1151, 1166, 1167, 1179, 1243, 1247
RISSO PATRÓN, Buenaventura, 258, 910
RISSO PATRÓN, Conrado, 268
RISSO PERONDI, Osvaldo, 691
RISTORI, Adelaida, 930
RITTER, Jorge Rodolfo, 1017, 1020
RIÚ, Francisco Aníbal, 565, 669, 751, 1243
RIÚ, José Eneas, 718, 871
RIVA, Benito, 895, 896
RIVA, Felipe de la, 126
RIVA, Francisco, 845
RIVA, Joaquín de la, 126
RIVA, Ottorino Luis, 923
RIVA, Santiago, 319
RIVA AGÜERO, José de la, 521
RIVADAVIA, Bernardino, 4, 70. 79, 85, 95, 103, 110,
    116, 118, 121, 134, 141, 143, 145, 152a, 166,
    176, 177, 185, 212, 228, 244, 258, 282, 283,
    317, 372, 379, 380, 382, 386, 392, 393, 398,
    404, 405, 408, 411, 420, 433, 448, 452, 455,
    459, 462, 469, 472, 475, 476, 478, 479, 481,
    489, 491, 496, 499, 502, 509, 514, 515, 516,
    518, 519, 521, 523, 529, 536, 542, 545, 552,
553, 563, 573, 583, 584, 589, 593, 611, 622,
    692, 924, 1091
RIVADAVIA, Gabriela, 563
RIVADAVIA, José, 1269
RIVADAVIA, Juan José, 126
RIVADAVIA, Manuela Julia, 563
RIVADAVIA, Martín, 9, 12, 14, 68
RIVADAVIA, Santiago, 563
RIVADAVIA Y VILLAGRÁN, Víctor José Martín, 904
RIVADENEIRA, Fernando Francisco, 649a
RIVADENEIRA, Juan de, 467, 921
RIVADENEIRA, Juan Pascual de, 1266
RIVADENEYRA, Benito, 1095
RIVAROLA, Cirilo Antonio, 942, 984a, 1011, 1012
RIVAROLA, Enrique, 751
RIVAROLA, Fernando, 1014
RIVAROLA, Francisco Bruno de, 1080
RIVAROLA, Horacio, 521
RIVAROLA, Juan Bautista, 943, 964, 966, 979, 987,
    1012
RIVAROLA, Juan de la Cruz, 952
RIVAROLA, Manuel Florencio, 268
RIVAROLA, Pantaleón, 177, 496, 664, 669, 720, 737,
    751, 895, 915, 921, 1247, 1257
RIVAROLA, Rodolfo, 167, 192
RIVAROLA, Valois, 974, 1003
RIVAROLA MATTO, José María, 943, 954, 966, 1020,
    1021, 1022
RIVAROLA ROJAS, Cayetano, 998
RIVAS, 13
RIVAS, Elsa, 879
RIVAS, Epifanio, 998
RIVAS, Humberto, 55
RIVAS, Ignacio, 249
RIVAS, José, 268
RIVAS, Juan de, 556
RIVAS, Pedro de, 556
RIVAS, Santiago, 1083, 1123
RIVAS ACUÑA, Pedro, 90
RIVAS GAVILÁN, Francisco de, 914
RIVAS ORTELLADO, Oscar, 998
RIVEIRO, José, 1089
RIVEIRO PEÓN, Sebastián, 1089
RIVENSON, Scholein, 923
RIVERA, 608
RIVERA (family), 1108
RIVERA, Andrés, 696, 770
RIVERA, Antonio, 1267
RIVERA, Bernabé, 1110
RIVERA, Enrique, 1174
RIVERA, Fructuoso
    see RIVERA, José Fructuoso
RIVERA, Frutos
    see RIVERA, José Fructuoso
RIVERA, Héctor M., 807
RIVERA, José Fructuoso, 95, 127, 143, 166, 244, 489,
    499, 521, 552, 568, 569, 584, 596, 632, 1052,
    1053, 1058, 1060, 1063, 1076, 1079, 1091, 1109,
    1110, 1114, 1118, 1119, 1131, 1132, 1133
RIVERA, José María, 990
RIVERA, Juan de Dios, 32, 61, 293, 506
RIVERA, Lázaro de
    see RIVERA Y ESPINOSA DE LOS MONTEROS, Lázaro de
RIVERA, Lorenzo de, 914
RIVERA, Manuel, 61
RIVERA, Pablo Hilarión Perafán de la, 1114, 1223
RIVERA, Pedro Ignacio de, 126, 439, 457, 526, 611,
    621, 626
RIVERA GABITO, Hermenegildo, 1210
RIVERA INDARTE, José, 177, 216, 244, 282, 404, 584,
    600, 611, 664, 669, 720, 724, 761, 763, 807

RIVERA LÓPEZ, Jorge, 889
RIVERA MONDRAGÓN, Fernando, 186
RIVERA Y ESPINOSA DE LOS MONTEROS, Lázaro de, 984,
   990, 1011
RIVERA Y MONDRAGÓN, Hernando de, 477
RIVERO, Bettina, 1217
RIVERO, Demetrio, 1205
RIVERO, Edmundo, 862
RIVERO, Francisco de Paula, 844, 1261
RIVERO, Julio C., 121
RIVERO, Néstor Eduardo, 1014
RIVERO, Nicolás A., 652
RIVERO, Roque, 1205
RIVERO DE GUZMÁN, Diego, 254
RIVEROS, Alejandro, 998
RIVEROS, Dionisio, 995a, 1041
RIVEROS, Lelia Ascensión, 923
RIVEROS, Manuel, 963a, 965
RIVIÈRE, Marta, 1058
RIVOLTA, José, 136
RIZO, José, 599
RIZO PATRÓN, Buenaventura
   see RISSO PATRÓN, Buenaventura
RIZZARDINI, Yolanda, 1206
RIZZI, Antonio, 258
ROA, Francisco, 974
ROA, Hermenegildo, 959
ROA, José, 371
ROA, José Fortunato, 987
ROA, Juan de, 555
ROA BASTOS, Augusto, 752, 943, 962, 966, 1014, 1015,
   1019, 1020, 1021, 1022, 1023, 1025, 1026
ROBATTO, Domingo, 669
ROBERTAZZI, Gregorio, 663
ROBERTO, Antonio, 358
ROBERTS, Coolidge (Mrs.)
   see DUDLEY, Anna
ROBERTS, George Lane, 323
ROBERTS, George Lane (Mrs.)
   see RICE, Anna Ackley
ROBERTSON, Juan Parish, 82, 506
ROBERTSON STOOF, Rodolfo Vicente (YE URUNDAY DE LOS
   EXOCETOS, Waldemar, pseud.), 691
ROBGER, 837
ROBÍN CASTRO, Napoleón, 565
ROBÍN DE PLÁ, Rosa, 636
ROBINO, Abel, 663
ROBINO DE GARAGGIOLI, Matilde, 652
ROBINSON, Carlos, 14, 82
ROBINSON, Federico G., 954
ROBINSON, Ruth Greenup
   see GREENUP, Ruth (Robinson)
ROBIROSA, Josefina, 36
ROBLEDO, Angel Federico, 213
ROBLEDO, Domingo, 943a
ROBLEDO, María Luisa, 889
ROBLES, 984
ROBLES, Agustín de, 521, 570
ROBLES, Andrés de, 521, 570
ROBLES, Francisco, 268
ROBLES, Hernando de, 556
ROBLES LORENZANA, Manuel de, 1011
ROBLES MENDILAHARZU, Roberto, 923
ROBY, Fernando, 923
ROCA, Ataliva, 87
ROCA, Deodoro, 119, 198
ROCA, José Segundo, 371, 541
ROCA, Julio Argentino, 17b, 68, 70, 78, 89, 91, 95,
   103, 110, 115, 116, 118, 141, 143, 176, 202,
   212, 216, 240, 246, 258, 261, 277, 282, 287,
   372, 392, 393, 404, 405, 466, 469, 470, 478, 489,
   493, 502, 515, 516, 521, 524, 531, 541, 574, 582,
   585, 589, 593, 598, 617, 619, 650, 907a
ROCA, Luis de la, 1267
ROCA, Rudecindo, 17b, 68, 551a
ROCA DE ACOSTA, Telma, 923
ROCAMORA, Tomás de, 95, 194, 279, 611
ROCCO, Domenico F., 139
ROCNI, Deisde, pseud.
   see D'AMBROSIO DE RONCONI, Delia Isabel
ROCHA (family), 337
ROCHA, Antonio de, 32
ROCHA, Dardo, 70, 116, 121, 141, 156, 166, 282,
   372, 391, 445, 904
ROCHA, Héctor, 25
ROCHA, Juan de, 186
ROCHA, Juan José Romualdo de, 496
ROCHA ARAUJO BIBIANO, Eriberto, 1210
ROCHA BAUTISTA, Antonio de, 32
ROCHA LOBO, Antonio de, 186
ROCHE, Philip, 587
ROCHE ARÉVALO, Lionel, 1210
ROCHE AREVALO DE DIMENSTEIN, Selva, 1210
RODAL, Miguel, 69
RODAS, Celia A. de, 954
RODAS, Marcelino, 947, 982
RODAS, Miguel de, 1238
RODERO DE DI LEO, Carmen, 874
RODHE, Jorge Max, 751
RODI, Pedro, 998
RODNEY, César Augusto, 629
RODÓ, José Enrique, 128, 956, 1025, 1054, 1068,
   1072, 1073, 1075, 1077, 1078, 1079, 1081, 1086,
   1090, 1091, 1145, 1146, 1160, 1163, 1165, 1177,
   1187, 1190, 1195, 1198, 1199
RODRIGO, América del Pilar, 923
RODRIGO, Félix, 923
RODRIGUÉ, Emilio Marcos, 923
RODRÍGUES, Antonio, 319
RODRÍGUES ESTELA (family), 351
RODRIGUES PERLINGEIRO, Sículo, 954
RODRÍGUEZ (family), 1108
RODRÍGUEZ, Abel, 765
RODRÍGUEZ, Agustín, 209, 947
RODRÍGUEZ, Alberto, 683a, 874
RODRÍGUEZ, Alfonso, 284
RODRÍGUEZ, Alonso, 1032, 1032a
RODRÍGUEZ, Andrés, 1089
RODRÍGUEZ, Angel, 1211
RODRÍGUEZ, Antonio, 186, 949, 1089
RODRÍGUEZ, Antonio María, 951, 1075, 1083
RODRÍGUEZ, Antonio Manuel, 998
RODRÍGUEZ, Atlántico, 923
RODRÍGUEZ, Bernardo, 318
RODRÍGUEZ, Carlos F., 445
RODRÍGUEZ, Carlos Juan, 222, 445, 565
RODRÍGUEZ, Cayetano José, 121, 166, 177, 282, 286,
   404, 439, 457, 478, 479, 526, 588, 611, 621, 626,
   669, 692, 720, 751, 754, 761, 828, 896, 908, 921,
   922, 1247
RODRÍGUEZ, Cesáreo, 751
RODRÍGUEZ, Clorindo, 998
RODRÍGUEZ, Diego, 186
RODRÍGUEZ, Eduardo, 963a
RODRÍGUEZ, Ernesto B., 68, 671, 722, 739
RODRÍGUEZ, Faustino, 995a
RODRÍGUEZ, Felipe, 95
RODRÍGUEZ, Filomeno, 951
RODRÍGUEZ, Francisco (FARRUCO, pseud.), 1095
RODRÍGUEZ, Germinal, 923

RODRÍGUEZ, Gregorio L., 1083
RODRÍGUEZ, Guillermo, 814, 831
RODRÍGUEZ, Guillermo C., 1067, 1090
RODRÍGUEZ, Guillermo P., 1174
RODRÍGUEZ, Héctor Pedro, 691
RODRÍGUEZ, Horacio C., 707
RODRÍGUEZ, Horacio F., 735
RODRÍGUEZ, Ida Edelvira, 478, 929
RODRÍGUEZ, Ignacio Fermín, 188, 207
RODRÍGUEZ, Jorge Raúl, 565
RODRÍGUEZ, José, 284, 1089
RODRÍGUEZ, José Carlos, 1025
RODRÍGUEZ, José Cayetano, 94, 895
RODRÍGUEZ, Josefina, 923
RODRÍGUEZ, Juan, 6, 244, 358, 1089
RODRÍGUEZ, Juan Antonio, 496
RODRÍGUEZ, Juan Esteban, 212, 611
RODRÍGUEZ, Juan Justo, 126
RODRÍGUEZ, Laureano, 882
RODRÍGUEZ, Marcelino, 987
RODRÍGUEZ, Marcos, 186
RODRÍGUEZ, Martín, 104, 156, 166, 228, 273, 282,
    283, 386, 404, 475, 478, 479, 496, 509, 519, 521,
    529, 552, 553, 554, 568, 569, 584, 611
RODRÍGUEZ, Osvaldo, 1075
RODRÍGUEZ, Pablo Julio, 244, 649
RODRÍGUEZ, Pedro, 358
RODRÍGUEZ, Pedro Nolasco, 545a
RODRÍGUEZ, Rafael, 1082
RODRÍGUEZ, Ricardo, 135, 864, 865, 882, 883, 1089
RODRÍGUEZ, Ricardo Rosendo, 923
RODRÍGUEZ, Roberto Carlos, 923
RODRÍGUEZ, Rodolfo Fausto, 751
RODRÍGUEZ, Sebastián B., 1083
RODRÍGUEZ, Sergio, 653, 654
RODRÍGUEZ, Sinforiano, 998
RODRÍGUEZ, Susana Clara, 684
RODRÍGUEZ, Susana Estela, 797
RODRÍGUEZ, Vasco, 845, 1238
RODRÍGUEZ, Víctor, 998
RODRÍGUEZ, Victorino, 89, 126, 478
RODRÍGUEZ, Yamandú, 894, 1079, 1145, 1151, 1154,
    1157, 1159, 1166, 1167, 1168, 1170, 1172, 1177,
    1180, 1185, 1186, 1194, 1196, 1243
RODRÍGUEZ-ALCALÁ, Guido, 965, 1015, 1025
RODRÍGUEZ-ALCALÁ, Hugo, 1014, 1015, 1019, 1020,
    1025, 1026
RODRÍGUEZ-ALCALÁ, José, 1020, 1023
RODRÍGUEZ AMIEVA, Pedro José, 923
RODRÍGUEZ AMOEDO, Francisco, 845
RODRÍGUEZ ANDRADE, Juan, 284
RODRÍGUEZ ANEIRO, Enrique Vicente, 1210
RODRÍGUEZ BELLETTI, Juan María, 1210
RODRÍGUEZ BELLETTI, Washington, 1210
RODRÍGUEZ BLANCO, Antonio, 1210
RODRÍGUEZ BUSTAMANTE DE DEMARÍA, María Elina, 762
RODRÍGUEZ CABRERA, Humberto Santos, 1210
RODRÍGUEZ CAN, Juan, 1167
RODRÍGUEZ CARDOSO, Francisco, 7, 1262
RODRÍGUEZ CARRILLO, Clemente, 284
RODRÍGUEZ CASTELAO, Alfonso, 284
RODRÍGUEZ CASTELLS, Horacio, 923
RODRÍGUEZ CASTILLOS, Osiris, 1151
RODRÍGUEZ CASTROMÁN, Manuel, 1094, 1095
RODRÍGUEZ COLARES, Antonio, 186
RODRÍGUEZ COLMENERO, Cristóbal, 1270
RODRÍGUEZ COTA, Juan, 1011
RODRÍGUEZ DE ACEVEDO, Alvaro, 1270
RODRÍGUEZ DE BERLANGA, Mauricio, 7, 332
RODRÍGUEZ DE CAMPOMANES, Ana, 887

RODRÍGUEZ DE CASTRO, Gregorio Timoteo, 344
RODRÍGUEZ DE ECKER, María Magdalena, 320
RODRÍGUEZ DE EGUSQUIZA, Rafaela, 87
RODRÍGUEZ DE ESCOBAR, Juan, 845
RODRÍGUEZ DE ESTELA, Juan, 186
RODRÍGUEZ DE FERNÁNDEZ BLANCO, María T., 611
RODRÍGUEZ DE FERNÁNDEZ BLANCO, Tiburcia, 422
RODRÍGUEZ DE FIGUEROA, Diego, 344
RODRÍGUEZ DE FIGUEROA, Marcos, 32
RODRÍGUEZ DE FRANCIA, José Gaspar
    see FRANCIA, José Gaspar Rodríguez de
RODRÍGUEZ DE GALLEGOS, Elidia Beatriz, 810
RODRÍGUEZ DE LA TORRE, Francisco, 914
RODRÍGUEZ DE LA TORRE, María Esther, 684
RODRÍGUEZ DE LEÓN, Juan, 126
RODRÍGUEZ DE LEÓN PINELO, Antonio
    see LEÓN PINELO, Antonio Rodríguez de
RODRÍGUEZ DE LOSSA, Miguel, 1262
RODRÍGUEZ DE LOUSTAUNAU, María Inés, 691
RODRÍGUEZ DE MAFRA, Juan, 1238
RODRÍGUEZ DE MARTÍNEZ, Teófila, 191
RODRÍGUEZ DE MORETE, Zulema, 320
RODRÍGUEZ DE OBELAR, Cristóbal, 1011
RODRÍGUEZ DE RUESCAS, Sebastián, 649a
RODRÍGUEZ DE SERRANO, Juan, 1079
RODRÍGUEZ DE SOSA, Christoval, 186
RODRÍGUEZ DE SOTO ACEBAL, María Mercedes, 19, 64
RODRÍGUEZ DE UMPIERREZ, María Inés, 1088
RODRÍGUEZ DE VALDEZ Y DE LA BANDA, Diego, 521
RODRÍGUEZ DE VICENTE, Román, 284
RODRÍGUEZ DEL BUSTO, Antonio, 284
RODRÍGUEZ DEL BUSTO, Francisco, 284
RODRÍGUEZ DEL FRESNO, Antonio, 845
RODRÍGUEZ DEL FRESNO, Bernardino, 845
RODRÍGUEZ DEL FRESNO, Bonifacio, 845
RODRÍGUEZ DEL FRESNO, Dolores, 845
RODRÍGUEZ DEL FRESNO, Fortunata, 845
RODRÍGUEZ DEL FRESNO, Francisco Calixto, 845
RODRÍGUEZ DEL FRESNO, Manuela Micaela, 845
RODRÍGUEZ DEL FRESNO, María Joaquina, 845
RODRÍGUEZ DEL FRESNO, María Josefa del Pilar, 845
RODRÍGUEZ DEL FRESNO, Mariano, 845
RODRÍGUEZ DEL FRESNO, Pedro José Celestino, 845
RODRÍGUEZ DÍAZ, Rogelio, 284
RODRÍGUEZ DURÁN, Domingo, 186
RODRÍGUEZ ESTELA, Juan, 1270
RODRÍGUEZ ETCHART, Severo, 19, 25, 31
RODRÍGUEZ FABREGAT, Enrique, 1145
RODRÍGUEZ FLORES, Antonio, 914
RODRÍGUEZ FLORES, Manuel, 344
RODRÍGUEZ FLORES, Pedro, 186
RODRÍGUEZ GAVILÁN, Rosendo, 965
RODRÍGUEZ GUERRERO, Manuel, 1270
RODRÍGUEZ GUIDO, Francisco, 649a
RODRÍGUEZ IBÁÑEZ, Carlos M., 652
RODRÍGUEZ ITOIZ, José, 681, 739
RODRÍGUEZ JUÁREZ, Juan, 520
RODRÍGUEZ JURADO, Agustín, 81
RODRÍGUEZ JURADO, Arturo J., 81
RODRÍGUEZ JURADO, Benigno (father), 81
RODRÍGUEZ JURADO, Benigno (son), 81, 222
RODRÍGUEZ LARRETA, Aureliano, 1075, 1083, 1126, 1134
RODRÍGUEZ LOZADA, José María, 1046, 1047
RODRÍGUEZ MACHADO, Argos A., 923
RODRÍGUEZ MALLARINI, Adolfo, 1088
RODRÍGUEZ MARQUINA, Paulino, 284
RODRÍGUEZ MAURENTE DE BONILLA, María Margarita, 1088
RODRÍGUEZ MENTASTI, Martín, 857c
RODRÍGUEZ MOLAS, Ricardo Emilio, 688
RODRÍGUEZ MONEGAL, Emir, 1177, 1184

RODRÍGUEZ MORALES, Alba Dora, 1210
RODRÍGUEZ MUÑOZ, Alberto, 776, 829
RODRÍGUEZ PASQUES, Rafael N., 923
RODRÍGUEZ PEÑA, Nicolás
    see RODRÍGUEZ PEÑA Y FUNES, Nicolás Santiago
RODRÍGUEZ PEÑA, Saturnino, 427, 517, 552, 597
RODRÍGUEZ PEÑA Y FUNES, Nicolás Santiago, 70, 85,
    244, 282, 386, 404, 411, 419, 478, 479, 496,
    517, 611
RODRÍGUEZ PERDOMO, Nelson Haroldo, 1088
RODRÍGUEZ PÉREZ, Ernesto, 653, 654
RODRÍGUEZ PINTOS, Carlos, 1151, 1177, 1179, 1187,
    1199
RODRÍGUEZ QUIROGA, Rosa, 892
RODRÍGUEZ RIBEIRA, Bernardo, 284
RODRÍGUEZ RODRÍGUEZ, Román Bernardino, 1088
RODRÍGUEZ SÁA, Adolfo, 81, 222
RODRÍGUEZ SÁA, José E., 81
RODRÍGUEZ SÁA, Ricardo, 81, 222
RODRÍGUEZ SÁA, Umberto, 81
RODRÍGUEZ SANTOS, Carlos, 959
RODRÍGUEZ SIBUET, Adriana Noemí, 691
RODRÍGUEZ SILVA, Héctor, 1210
RODRÍGUEZ SOCAS, Ramón, 1206, 1207
RODRÍGUEZ TORANZOS, Segundo Alberto, 691
RODRÍGUEZ TORRES, Lidia, 691
RODRÍGUEZ VAZ, Juan, 344, 1095
RODRÍGUEZ Y OLMOS, Audino, 171, 910
RODRÍGUEZ Y SARMIENTO, Manuel, 105, 284, 845, 846
RODRÍGUEZ ZIA, Antonio, 284
ROELLIG, Federico Roberto, 923
ROGATIS, Pascual de, 864, 865, 867, 881
ROGER, Claudio
    see RUYER, Claudio
ROGER BALET, José, 893
ROGGIANO, Alfredo A., 739
ROGIND, William 904
ROHDE, Jorge Max, 743, 773
ROHMEDER, Guillermo E., 923
ROIG, Agustín, 874
ROIG, Arturo Andrés, 683a, 688
ROIG MATONS, Fidel, 874
ROIS, Antonio, 1089
ROITMAN, Nanny, 299
ROITMAN, Wolf, 658
ROJAS, Absalón, 445
ROJAS, Alejo Fernando de, 910
ROJAS, Alfonso, 998
ROJAS, Angel D., 173
ROJAS, Celedonio, 1059
ROJAS, Diego de, 144, 472, 500, 521
ROJAS, Felipe, 804
ROJAS, Francisco de, 949
ROJAS, José Miguel de, 126
ROJAS, José Natalicio, 959
ROJAS, Juan Escolástico, 955
ROJAS, Juan Ramón, 611, 625, 733, 761, 828
ROJAS, Liberato Marcial, 959, 1014
ROJAS, Manuel, 611
ROJAS, Manuel P., 475
ROJAS, María Elvira, 247
ROJAS, Miguel, 268, 867
ROJAS, Miguel C., 998
ROJAS, Nerio, 521
ROJAS, Nicolás Celedonio, 1111
ROJAS, Pablo, 1039
ROJAS, Paulono, 433
ROJAS, Pedro, 844, 1261
ROJAS, Ricardo, 154, 162, 176, 185, 235, 246, 286,
    322, 609, 669, 678, 680, 688, 722, 723, 737, 739,
    740, 743, 751, 759, 773, 779, 782, 830

ROJAS, Roberto Augusto, 37
ROJAS, Teodoro, 943, 959, 964, 1012
ROJAS A., Manuel, 959
ROJAS BARBOZA, Guillermo, 998
ROJAS CARAVANTES, Diego de, 555
ROJAS DE ARANDA ESCALADA FERNÁNDEZ, Víctor, 971
ROJAS LAGARDE, Alfredo M., 923
ROJAS PAZ, Pablo, 670, 680, 707, 743, 753, 799, 816,
    825, 830
ROJAS SILVA, Adolfo, 998
ROJAS SILVA DE MORALES PEÑAS, Rosa I., 947
ROJAS Y ACEVEDO, Pedro de, 223
ROJO, Camilo, 188
ROJO, José Rudecindo, 283
ROJO, Nemesio, 254
ROJO, Tadeo, 546, 549
ROLAND, Alfredo, 521
ROLDÁN, Belisario, 78, 167, 669, 740, 751, 759,
    1243, 1247
ROLDÁN, Gustavo, 706
ROLDÁN, Juan Basilio, 106
ROLDÁN, Juan Francisco, 254
ROLDÁN, Juan Manuel, 106
ROLDÁN, Mario, 1167
ROLDÓS Y PONS, Juan, 1094
ROLÓN, Angel, 371
ROLÓN, Armando, 299
ROLÓN, Buenaventura, 998
ROLÓN, Julián, 1084
ROLÓN, Manuel, 998
ROLÓN, Raimundo, 1006
ROLÓN, Tiburcio Antonio, 220
ROLÓN, Zenón, 137
ROLÓN CASTELVÍ, Rafael A., 998
ROLÓN MEDINA, Anastasio, 1014
ROLLA, Mario, 889
ROLLAND, José, 1264
ROLLERI, Edgardo Osvaldo, 923
ROLLERI, Giacomo, 292
ROLLERI, Santiago, 258
ROMAGNOLI, Ricardo, 683a
ROMAIRONE, Camilo, 6, 258
ROMÁN, Cecilio, 995a
ROMÁN, Ezequiel, 1003
ROMÁN, José Alejo, 545a
ROMÁN, Justo Carmelo, 995a
ROMÁN, Marcelino M., 135, 746, 800, 831
ROMÁN, Martín José, 995a
ROMÁN MENDOZA, José, 1075, 1174
ROMANO, Aníbal Mario, 252
ROMANO, Eduardo, 759
ROMANO, Enrique, 35, 49
ROMANO, Francisco, 1270
ROMANO DE DISANTI, Noeli F., 320
ROMANY, Teófilo (family), 168
ROMAÑA, Cecilio, 923
ROMAY, Francisco L., 521
ROMBERG, Osvaldo, 27, 35
ROMDEROS, Ricardo Arturo, 923
ROMERO, 1003
ROMERO, Agustín, 254
ROMERO, Amílcar G., 706
ROMERO, Amira H., 652
ROMERO, Conrado, 121
ROMERO, Elvio, 943, 1014, 1015, 1020, 1021, 1022,
    1023, 1025
ROMERO, Esteban, 104, 496
ROMERO, Félix, 332
ROMERO, Francesco, 59
ROMERO, Francisco, 162, 258, 743, 897

ROMERO, Francisco (LAVALLEJA, Manuel, pseud.), 1059, 1110, 1111
ROMERO, Genaro, 959
ROMERO, Gregorio, 68, 921
ROMERO, Helvio, 1026
ROMERO, José Gregorio, 910
ROMERO, José León, 222
ROMERO, José María, 332
ROMERO, Juan, 186, 318, 319, 649a, 989, 1035a, 1035b
ROMERO, Juan Carlos, 41, 44
ROMERO, Juan José, 391
ROMERO, Juan Santa María, 284
ROMERO, Julia, 691
ROMERO, Julián, 332
ROMERO, Lauro, 998
ROMERO, Luciano, 1111
ROMERO, Luis Francisco, 910
ROMERO, Manuel, 858, 871
ROMERO, Mari Esther, 1088
ROMERO, Rodolfo, 1190
ROMERO ALVAREZ, A. Manuel, 923
ROMERO BENÍTEZ, Estanislao, 998
ROMERO CARRANZA, Ambrosio, 521
ROMERO CUEVAS L., María Elena, 810
ROMERO DE PINEDA, Luis, 204
ROMERO DE SANTA CRUZ, Inés, 224
ROMERO DE TEXADA, Antonio, 898
ROMERO NERVEGNA, María Inés, 1088
ROMERO PINZÓN DE CUENCA MUÑOZ, Rocío, 932
ROMERO SOSA, Carlos Gregorio, 521, 653, 654, 751
ROMERO VALDOVINOS, Néstor, 1014
ROMERO Y GONZÁLEZ, Gregorio Victoriano, 625
ROMEU, José, 1075, 1083
ROMEU BURGUES, Luis, 1083
RÓMULO, Ricardo, 860
RONDEAU, José, 85, 95, 166, 212, 244, 254, 282, 283, 386, 404, 427, 462, 471, 472, 478, 521, 552, 553, 554, 569, 611, 1053, 1063, 1079, 1081, 1091, 1110
RONDEAU, Juan, 568
RONDEAU DE MAINES, Francisco, 1093a
RONDÓN, Reynaldo H., 775
RONGINE DE FEKETE, María Alejandra, 923
RONTAO MEZA, Rigoberto, 1021, 1022
ROO (family), 1108
ROOSEN REGALÍA, Germán, 1064, 1187
ROQUE, Francisco, 332
ROS, Carlos A., 1093
ROS, Celia Natividad, 923
ROS, Francisco J., 1066, 1067
ROS, Gorgino, 998
ROS, Reinaldo, pseud.
     see DARDO ROSILLO, Reinaldo
ROS, Venancio, 998
ROSA, Agustín de la, 254, 344, 1136
ROSA, Carlos de la, 845
ROSA, Francisco Javier de la, 106
ROSA, José Ignacio de la
     see ROZA, José Ignacio de la
ROSA, José María, 68, 609
ROSA, José Martín, 283
ROSA, Juan de, 186
ROSA, Rafael José de, 890, 893
ROSA DE LIMA, Saint (FLORES DE OLIVA, Isabel), 525
ROSA LAUBENHEIMER, Nicolás, 652
ROSA UREÑA, Ramón, 878
ROSA Y ORO, Tadeo de la, 555
ROSÁENZ, Elifio Eduardo, 874, 883
ROSALES, Blas de, 144, 244, 520
ROSALES, César, 222, 722, 739, 758, 798
ROSALES, Cirilo, 874

ROSALES, Dámaso, 371
ROSALES, Diego, 283, 921
ROSALES, El ARRIADOR, pseud.
     see SABAT PEBET, Juan Carlos
ROSALES, Leonardo, 12, 14, 16, 110, 166, 386, 611
ROSARIO, José del, 1270
ROSAS, Agustín, 207
ROSAS, Desiderio, 68, 648, 649
ROSAS, Enrique de, 891, 893
ROSAS, Epugner, 556
ROSAS, Gervasio, 480
ROSAS, Juan, 1111
ROSAS, Juan Manuel José Domingo Ortiz de, 95, 96, 103, 122, 127, 143, 153, 166, 169, 170, 179, 185, 202, 207, 232, 234, 240, 241, 246, 282, 283, 372, 373, 379, 390, 391, 398, 404, 408, 409, 410, 431, 434, 446, 448, 451, 452, 460, 462, 466, 472, 478, 480, 488, 489, 491, 494, 499, 502, 507, 512, 513, 514, 518, 519, 521, 523, 529, 531, 538, 545, 558, 575, 577, 578, 584, 586, 589, 593, 596, 600, 608, 632, 924, 984, 1059, 1079, 1091, 1111, 1233
ROSAS, Manuel
     see ROSAS, Juan Manuel José Domingo Ortiz de
ROSAS, Manuelita
     see ROSAS Y EZCURRA DE TERRERO, Manuela de
ROSAS, Mariano (PAGUITUZ), 222, 454, 566
ROSAS COSTA, Julio A., 923
ROSAS DE GALÍNDEZ, Nicanora, 234
ROSAS Y ESCURRA DE TERRERO, Manuela de, 254, 390, 408, 409, 410, 454, 478, 480, 494, 506, 928, 929
ROSASCO PALAU, Sebastián A., 923
ROSATINI, Tomás, 32
ROSAZZA, Calixto E., 258
ROSELL Y RIUS, Alejo, 1075, 1084
ROSELLI, Martín Enrique, 923
ROSEMBERG, Fernando, 823
ROSEN, Eric von
     see VON ROSEN, Eric
ROSENBLAT, Angel, 521
ROSENBLATT, Jorge, 923
ROSENCOF, Mauricio, 1172, 1185
ROSENDE, Petrona
     see ROSENDE DE LA SIERRA, Petrona
ROSENDE DE LA SIERRA, Petrona, 478, 929, 1199
ROSENFELD, Roberto, 18
ROSENSTRAUJ, Gerardo, 653
ROSETI, Carlos, 103
ROSETTI, Emilio, 258, 332, 921a
ROSETTI, Manuel, 254, 258, 474
ROSICRÁN, pseud.
     see COLMAN, Narciso Ramón
ROSILLO, Antonio, 646, 649a
ROSILLO, Mariano Adalberto, 923
ROSNER, Bruno, 954
ROSPIDE, Bernardo, 1122
ROSPIGLIOSI, Claudio, 258
ROSPIGLIOSI, José Antonio Julio, 126
ROSPIGLIOSI, Ramón, 895
ROSPILLOSI, José Antonio Julio
     see ROSPIGLIOSI, José Antonio Julio
ROSQUELLAS, Luis Pablo, 870
ROSQUELLAS, Mariano Pablo, 870, 1205
ROSQUELLAS, Pablo, 859
ROSSETI, Manuel, 13
ROSSETTI, Carlos, 258
ROSSETTI, Emilio, 113, 332
ROSSETTI, Mirta Noemí, 37
ROSSI, Adriano E., 59
ROSSI, Alberto María, 19
ROSSI, Antonio, 139
ROSSI, Ecio, 837

ROSSI, Ernesto Alejandro, 923
ROSSI, Estela E., 652
ROSSI, Giovanni, 139
ROSSI, Héctor, 260
ROSSI, Iris, 652
ROSSI, João, 938, 939
ROSSI, Juan Bautista, 952
ROSSI, Julia Isabel, 684
ROSSI, Natalia Isolina, 923
ROSSI, Roberto Armando, 18, 19, 23, 25, 31, 36
ROSSI, Vicente, 741, 834
ROSSI DE TORRES, Lía Esther, 726
ROSSI DEL CERRO DE GARCÍA, Elsa de las Mercedes, 923
ROSSI ETCHELOUZ, Nelly Y., 652
ROSSIER (family), 168
ROSSLER, Osvaldo, 716, 717, 739, 758, 759, 798, 801, 802, 814, 827, 871
ROSTAGNO, Enrique, 191
ROTH, Carlos, 268
ROTH, Jacobo, 32
ROTHE, J. Enrique, 652
ROTHFUSS, Rhod, 31
ROTZAIT, Perla, 725
ROUCE DE COUDANNES, Ana, 652
ROUGES, Jorge L., 652
ROUQUAUD, Ernesto, 100, 287
ROUSSEAU, Carlos Alberto, 923
ROUSSET DE SAN MARTÍN, Angela, 762
ROUX, Guillermo, 55
ROUX CABRAL, Irma, 1210
ROVA ZAPALA, Rosario, 1210
ROVATTI, Luis C., 21, 25, 64
ROVEDA, Pedro Enrique, 320
ROVELLI DE RICCIO, Osvalda, 823
ROVERANO, Pascual, 122
ROVIRA CRAIGDALLIE, Omar, 1210
ROVIRA TURELL VILLOROU, María Celia, 1210
ROVIROSA DE RABINI, Rosa, 320
ROXAS DE ARANDA, Blas José, 987
ROXAS Y ACEVEDO, Amador de, 186
ROXAS Y PATRÓN, José María, 166
ROXIN, Emilio Oscar, 923
ROXLO, Armando Víctor
    see ROXLO Y MIRALLES, Armando Víctor
ROXLO, Carlos, 1075, 1079, 1083, 1122, 1146, 1167, 1174, 1179, 1187, 1193, 1198, 1199, 1243, 1247
ROXLO Y MIRALLES, Armando Víctor, 1145, 1188
ROYER, Claudio
    see RUYER, Claudio
ROZA, Félix de la, 487
ROZA, Jerónimo de la, 283
ROZA, José Ignacio de la, 179, 188, 222, 283, 413, 487, 546, 549, 611
ROZA QUEIPO DEL LLANO, Félix de la, 898
ROZAS (family), 1106
ROZAS, Juan Manuel
    see ROSAS, Juan Manuel José Domingo Ortiz de
ROZAS DE OQUENDO, Mateo, 83, 683
ROZAS DE RIVERA, Mercedes, 478
ROZAS DE TERRERO, Manuela
    see ROSAS Y ESCURRA DE TERRERO, Manuela de
ROZENMACHER, Germán, 696, 697
ROZLOSMIK, Andrés, 923
RÚA (family), 168
RÚA, Antonio de la, 385
RÚA, Miguel, 907a
RUANO, Manuel, 750
RUANOBA, Toribio, 1089
RUARTE, Rubén I., 652
RUBERTINO, María Luisa, 725, 739, 816

RUBIALES, Josefina
    see LEDESMA, Amanda
RUBIANES, Raúl, 235
RUBILAR, Francisco, 565
RUBÍN DE CELIS, Miguel, 7, 885, 895
RUBIO, Antonio, 895
RUBIO, Francisco (EL MOZO, pseud.), 556
RUBIO DE ALFARO, Francisco, 556
RUBIO DE GARRIDO, Advíncula, 768
RUBLI, Lydia M., 49
RUBLI, Mabel, 27, 41, 55
RÜCKER (family), 1108
RUDEL, Hans Ulrich, 602
RUEDA, Felipe, 878
RUEDA, Pedro, 648, 649
RUEDA, Roberto, 998
RUEDA MEDIAVILLA, Manuel, 44
RUETE, Ernesto, 1064
RUFINELLI, Francisco, 947
RUFINELLI, Luis, 947, 1021, 1022
RUFINO, Hilda, 874
RUFO, José, 895
RUGENDAS, Johan Moritz, 28, 42, 51, 59, 521
RUGGIERI, Silvio L., 260
RUILOBA, Manuel Agustín de
    see RUILOBA Y CALDERÓN, Manuel Agustín de
RUILOBA Y CALDERÓN, Manuel Agustín de, 984, 1011
RUIZ, Antonio (FALUCHO, pseud.), 137, 244, 404, 496
RUIZ, Benito, 254
RUIZ, Diego, 319, 895
RUIZ, Eduardo B., 207, 683a
RUIZ, Emilio R., 652
RUIZ, Héctor Blas, 963a
RUIZ, Hermógenes, 173
RUIZ, José Joaquín, 921
RUIZ, José Norberto, 268
RUIZ, Juan, 358, 951, 992
RUIZ, Juan Carlos, 653
RUIZ, Juan Manuel, 555
RUIZ, Luis Alberto, 800
RUIZ, Manuel, 198, 1262
RUIZ, Miguel, 186
RUIZ, Pascual, 887
RUIZ, Pedro, 556
RUIZ, Pedro Esteban, 358
RUIZ, René, 892
RUIZ, Teófilo, 954
RUIZ, Valentín, 283
RUIZ, Vicente, 923
RUIZ BAYGORRI, Pedro, 570
RUIZ DE AGUIRRE, Pedro, 555
RUIZ DE ARCE, Gonzalo (RUIZ DE ARCE, Gregorio, pseud.), 556
RUIZ DE ARCE, Gregorio, pseud.
    see RUIZ DE ARCE, Gonzalo
RUIZ DE ARCE, Hernando, 556
RUIZ DE ARELLANO, Antonio, 989, 1011
RUIZ DE ARELLANO, José, 356
RUIZ DE HUIDOBRO, Diego, 126
RUIZ DE HUIDOBRO, Pascual, 496, 611
RUIZ DE LA CUESTA, Juan, 555
RUIZ DE LOIS, J. Eleonor, 652
RUIZ DE LONGA, Juan, 649a
RUIZ DE LOS LLANOS, Bonifacio, 611, 625
RUIZ DE MONTOYA, Antonio, 32, 254, 850, 885, 964, 966, 968, 985, 989, 1012, 1033, 1035
RUIZ DE OBREGÓN, Manuel, 496
RUIZ DE OCAÑA (family), 1224
RUIZ DE OCAÑA, Juan, 186, 223
RUIZ DE ROJAS, Gaspar Miguel, 556

RUIZ DE SALINAS, Juan Bautista, 1095
RUIZ DE VILLEGAS, Franciscus, 1037
RUIZ DEL CASTILLO, Pedro, 556
RUIZ DÍAZ, Adolfo, 683a
RUIZ DÍAZ, Manuel, 1187
RUIZ GALÁN, Francisco, 32, 465, 504, 505, 984
RUIZ GUIÑAZÚ, Enrique, 609
RUIZ HUIDOBRO, Casiano, 268
RUIZ HUIDOBRO, José, 179, 559
RUIZ HUIDOBRO, Luis, 68, 268
RUIZ HUIDOBRO, Pascual, 17a, 104, 179, 427, 552, 1079, 1091, 1136
RUIZ HUIDOBRO, Ricardo, 268
RUIZ LIARD DE MARELLA, Selva Hebe, 1210
RUIZ LÓPEZ, 766
RUIZ MORENO, Aníbal, 218, 923
RUIZ MORENO, César, 521
RUIZ MORENO, Guido, 923
RUIZ MORENO, Isidoro, 265, 521
RUIZ MORENO, Martín, 95, 96, 121, 194, 241, 511
RUIZ MOSQUERA, 989
RUIZ RAMALLO, Miguel Angel, 1210
RUIZ SAMPAIO, Estevan, 186
RUIZ TAGLE, José, 126
RUIZ Y BOLAÑOS, Manuel, 126
RUIZ Y SANTANA DE LABORDE, Inmaculada, 691
RUPPEL, Clemente, 664
RUSCONI, Carlos, 923
RUSIÑOL, pseud.
    see DEOLINDO REYNA, Pedro, 713
RUSSELL, Dora Isella, 1151, 1179
RUSSELL, Oliverio, 82
RUSSO, Raúl, 18, 19, 25, 31, 34, 36, 38, 49, 55
RUSSO BENES, Mauro Ramón, 1210
RUSSO CALABRIA, Carlos Alberto, 1210
RUTA, José, 874
RUTCKEN WEINSTEIN, Daniel, 1210
RUTE, Juan de, 992
RUVEDA, Franklin, 831
RUYER, Claudio, 850, 866, 949, 960
RUYSCH, William Albert, 923
RUZO, Eusebio Gregorio, 258
RVHRBRTTIA, Esteban, 476
RYBERG, Juan Eduardo, 332
RYDEN, Styg, 191
RYMARKIEWICA, Maximiliano, 238

SÁA, Felipe, 222
SÁA, Hipólito, 81
SÁA, Juan, 158, 166, 188, 222, 283
SÁA, Juan Carlos, 81, 222
SÁA, Teófilo, 81, 222
SÁA, Víctor, 222
SÁA Y FARIA, José Custodio de, 7, 32, 332, 922
SAAVEDRA, 451
SAAVEDRA (family), 361, 1108
SAAVEDRA, Cornelio, 70, 85, 101, 104, 141, 166, 176, 188, 244, 282, 283, 374, 386, 404, 420, 421, 458, 475, 478, 479, 496, 499, 502, 508, 514, 517, 518, 519, 525, 528, 552, 553, 563, 574, 610, 611, 895
SAAVEDRA, José A., 1075
SAAVEDRA, Juan A., 653
SAAVEDRA, Juan de, 186
SAAVEDRA, Manuel, 126
SAAVEDRA, Mariano, 141
SAAVEDRA, Néstor, 653, 654, 699
SAAVEDRA, Osvaldo, 68
SAAVEDRA, Ramón, 371
SAAVEDRA, Ricardo "Serenata," 653
SAAVEDRA BASAVILBASO, María Helena, 762

SAAVEDRA DÍAZ, Gerónimo, 556
SAAVEDRA ZELAYA, Mercedes de, 762, 783
SABAT, Hermenegildo, 1049
SABAT ERCASTY, Carlos, 1068, 1079, 1145, 1147, 1151, 1152, 1177, 1179, 1181, 1199
SABAT PEBET, Juan Carlos (ROSALES, El Arriador, pseud.), 1064, 1167
SABATER, María Virginia, 320
SÁBATO, Ernesto, 140, 666, 715, 742, 743, 769, 1252
SÁBATO, Jorge Alberto, 923
SÁBATO, Juan, 923
SÁBATO, Mario, 857a
SABBIA Y ORIBE, María H., 1075, 1174
SABELLI, Eduardo, 25, 35
SABOR, Josefa E., 652
SABORIDO, Dardo Ernesto (TANTÍN, pseud.), 860
SABORIDO, Enrique, 894
SACARELLO, Tomás, 952
SACARÍA MORALES DE LA SIERRA, Juan de, 186
SACCO CAPALBO, Osvaldo, 691
SACERDOTE, Delia, 154
SACERDOTE DE LUSTIG, Eugenia, 923
SACCH PEDETTI, Hugo Carlos, 1210
SADERMAN, Anatole, 55
SADI GROSO, Luis, 135, 800
SADOSKY, Manuel, 440, 923
SADOWSKI, Enrique, 238
SÁENZ (family), 351
SÁENZ, Abelardo, 1073
SÁENZ, Antonio, 126, 141, 177, 267, 282, 321, 322, 439, 457, 478, 479, 526, 611, 621, 626, 692, 720, 915, 921, 1205
SÁENZ, Arturo C., 923
SÁENZ, Dalmiro A., 696, 712, 729, 757, 829
SÁENZ, Justo P., 670, 707, 779, 834, 1245
SÁENZ, Manuela, 616
SÁENZ, Mario, 385
SÁENZ, Máximo Teodoro (LAST REASON; A RIENDA SUELTA; BALA PERDIDA, pseuds.), 727, 811
SÁENZ, Pedro A., 882, 883
SÁENZ, Raquel, 1217
SÁENZ, Vicente, 1223
SÁENZ CABALLERO, Francisco de Paula, 1262
SÁENZ CAMBÓN, Miguel, 284
SÁENZ DE BAÑOS Y SARAZA, Miguel Antonio de, 496
SÁENZ DE CAVIA, Pedro Feliciano, 611, 629, 1258
SÁENZ DE CENTENO, Isolina, 762
SÁENZ DE LA MAZA DE GARCÍA DE ZUÑIGA, María de la Encarnación, 1093a
SÁENZ HAYES, Ricardo, 743
SÁENZ PEÑA, Luis, 17b, 68, 121, 282, 389, 392, 393, 405, 466, 478, 515, 516, 521, 598, 619
SÁENZ PEÑA, Roque, 91, 110, 115, 116, 121, 141, 166, 176, 212, 244, 254, 282, 372, 389, 392, 393, 405, 452, 466, 469, 478, 484, 485, 493, 515, 516, 521, 524, 531, 551, 582, 586, 593, 598, 612, 619, 650
SÁENZ QUESADA, María, 609
SAER, Juan José, 697, 771
SÁEZ, Carlos, 1079
SÁEZ, Carlos Federico, 1046, 1047
SÁEZ, Manuel Antonio, 207, 212, 278
SÁEZ DE MENA, Francisco, 1270
SAFORCADA, Helmice Margarita, 41, 64
SAGARI, Augustino, 258
SAGARI, Pedro, 258
SAGARI, Prudencio, 254
SAGARNA, Antonio, 95, 167, 192, 219, 241, 478
SAGÁRNAGA, Juan Bautista, 126
SAGASTIZÁBAL, Miguel, 320

SAGASTUME, Carlos Pío, 834
SAGASTUME, José Joaquín, 95
SAGASTUME BERRA, Alberto A., 923
SAGRA Y PERIZ, Joaquín de la, 1095
SAGRADINI, Mario, 1206
SAGREDO, Eduardo, 878
SAGREDO DE MOLINA, Cristóbal, 555
SAGÜES, Isidoro, 894
SAGUI, Teresita, 683a
SAGUIER, Fernando, 565
SAGUIER, Pedro, 949, 959
SAHADE, Jorge, 923
SAHDA, Domingo Teófilo, 37
SAIEG, Amelia, 684
SAIHUEGUE, 454
SAINT-AULAIRE, Félix Achille, 28
SAINT BONNET DE BORREGO, Antonia, 320
SÁINZ DE LA MAZA, Isidro, 626
SAJÓN DE CUELLO, Raquel, 663
SAKAI, Kasuya, 19, 25, 26, 31, 36, 46, 49
SAL, Benjamín, 332
SALA, Juan, 79
SALA FERNÁNDEZ DE TOURÓN, Lucía Luz, 1210
SALABERRY, Cahen, 858
SALABERRY, Domingo E., 69
SALAMANCA, Juan de, 1238
SALARRO DE MONTILLA, Francisco, 32
SALAS, Alberto M., 521
SALAS, Aurelio, 31
SALAS, Graciela B., 652
SALAS, Horacio, 661
SALAS, José A., 207
SALAS, José Manuel, 569
SALAS, Joseph de, 32
SALAS, Pablo, 921
SALAS, Saturnino, 6, 169, 413
SALAS SUBIRAT, José, 765
SALATINO, Carlos Alberto, 60
SALAVERRI, Vicente A., 739, 1168, 1190, 1199
SALAVERRY, Felipe Santiago, 562
SALAZAR, José de, 1113
SALAZAR, Juan de, 151, 914, 918, 963
SALAZAR, Juan Pablo, 954
SALAZAR, Luis María, 332
SALAZAR, Pedro de, 186, 344
SALAZAR COLLADO, Justo, 89
SALAZAR DE ESPINOSA, Juan de, 465, 505, 914, 951,
    964, 984, 992, 996, 1011, 1012, 1034
SALCEDO, Francisco de, 417, 649a, 910, 913, 1035a,
    1035b
SALCEDO, Miguel de, 472, 570
SALCEDO DE SARMIENTO, Angela, 930
SALCES, Arsenio V., 837
SALDAÑA, Iris, 691
SALDEÑA MOLINA, Homero, 207
SALDÍAS, Adolfo, 152a, 498, 609, 774
SALDÍAS, Angel, 860
SALDÍAS, José Antonio (FASTRÁS, Rubén, pseud.), 431,
    719, 727, 811, 813, 819
SALDÍVAR, Francisco, 968
SALDÍVAR, Julio P., 1006
SALDÚN DE RODRÍGUEZ, María L., 1217
SALGADO, José, 284, 1064, 1079, 1083, 1174
SALGADO Y VÁZQUEZ, Benigno, 1095
SALGÁN, Horacio, 862
SALGUEIRO, Juan, 1089
SALGUEIRO BRAVO, Manuel Antonio, 284
SALGUERO DE CABRERA Y CABRERA, Gerónimo, 313, 439,
    457, 526, 611, 621, 626
SALGUERO Y CABRERA, Diego de, 144, 244

SALIBIAN, Nazareth, 652
SALIM, Lina, 775
SALINAS, Adolfo, 299
SALINAS, Buenaventura, 126
SALINAS, José de, 555
SALINAS, José María, 207
SALINAS, José S., 69
SALINAS, Manuel de, 555
SALINAS, Secundino, 59, 62
SALINAS, Wherfield A., 174
SALINAS Y HEREDIA, Diego de, 283, 555
SALMÓN CADENAU, David, 713
SALOJ, Claudio Eugenio, 923
SALOJ, Jorge Luis, 923
SALOM, Guillermo, 903
SALOMONE, Juan Florentino, 874
SALONI, Juan, 850, 1035a, 1035b
SALPETER, Azucena Rosa, 663
SALTERAIN, Joaquín de, 1067, 1075, 1083, 1126, 1146,
    1174, 1188, 1199, 1202
SALTERAIN HERRERA, Eduardo de, 1087
SALUM FLECHA, Antonio, 954
SALVA, Melquíades, 648
SALVADÓ, Esteban, 319
SALVADOR, Ismael, 320
SALVADOR, Nélida, 683a, 717, 739
SALVADORES, Angel, 196
SALVAGNO CAMPOS, Carlos
    see SALVAÑO CAMPOS, Carlos
SALVAIRE, Jorge María, 272
SALVANESCHI, Luis María, 774a
SALVAÑA, Osvaldo, 837
SALVAÑACH (family), 1108
SALVAÑACH, Cristóbal de, 1064, 1075
SALVAÑO CAMPOS, Carlos, 1172, 1185
SALVAREZZA, Domingo, 258
SALVIGNI, Emilio, 258
SALZANO, Daniel Nelson, 684, 738
SALZEDO, Francisco
    see SALCEDO, Francisco
SALZES, Esteban, 32
SALLOT, Eugenio, 878
SAMANIEGO, Gregorio, 95
SAMANIEGO, Juan Emigdio, 965
SAMANIEGO, Marcial, 935, 954, 1006
SAMANIEGO, Maximino, 998
SAMANIEGO ABENTE, Alfredo, 998
SAMATÁN, Enrique Luis, 923
SAMATÁN, Marta Elena, 701
SAMBUCETTI, Juan José, 1206
SAMBUCETTI, Luis, 1079, 1083, 1206, 1207, 1208
SAMETBAND, Moisés José, 923
SAMMARTINO, Luis R., 881, 883
SAMMARTINO DE PANARO, María Luisa, 320
SAMONATI, Juan Alfredo, 1083
SAMPERE, Juan Pedro, 1125
SAMPERIO, José María, 751
SAMPIETRO, Lucía de, 717
SAMPOL DE HERRERO, Ana, 663
SAMUDIO, José Domingo, 995
SAMUDIO, Juan A., 937, 959, 964
SAMUDIO, Pedro Antonio, 998
SAMZÓN, Esteban, 32
SAN ALBERTO, José Antonio de, 244, 317, 968
SAN ARRÓMAN, Marcelino, 59
SAN BERNARDO, Agustín de, 1270
SAN GINÉS, Manuel de, 315
SAN JOSÉ, María Antonia de
    see MARÍA ANTONIA DE SAN JOSÉ
SAN LUIS, Nicolás Antonio de, 21, 24, 25, 64, 222

SAN MARTÍN, Andrés de, 1238
SAN MARTÍN, Jerónima, 227, 422, 478, 929
SAN MARTÍN, José, 1073
SAN MARTÍN, José de
    see SAN MARTÍN Y MATORRAS, José Francisco de
SAN MARTÍN, Juan de, 112, 156, 172, 335, 361, 459,
    561, 1262
SAN MARTÍN, Juan Fermín de, 172, 335
SAN MARTÍN, Juan Ignacio, 89
SAN MARTÍN, Justo Rufino, 172
SAN MARTÍN, Manuel Tadeo, 172, 335
SAN MARTÍN, María Elena de, 112, 335, 927
SAN MARTÍN, Sara, 653, 654, 713, 730
SAN MARTÍN DE BALCARCE, Mercedes
    see SAN MARTÍN Y ESCALADA DE BALCARCE, Mercedes
SAN MARTÍN Y CEBALLOS, Bernabé de, 496
SAN MARTÍN Y CEBALLOS, Jerónima de, 626
SAN MARTÍN Y DE LA RIGUERA, Andrés de, 172
SAN MARTÍN Y ESCALADA DE BALCARCE, Mercedes de
    (CHICHE, pseud.), 112, 172, 207, 383, 478, 927,
    929
SAN MARTÍN Y GÓMEZ, Juan de, 383
SAN MARTÍN Y MATORRAS, José Francisco de, 4, 70, 72,
    78, 85, 104, 110, 112, 121, 128, 132, 141, 143,
    166, 172, 176, 185, 188, 212, 227, 228, 244, 261,
    278, 282, 283, 335, 369, 370, 377, 379, 381, 382,
    383, 386, 398, 404, 411, 412, 413, 420, 427, 432,
    448, 452, 453, 455, 462, 466, 468, 469, 489, 499,
    471, 472, 475, 478, 487, 492, 509, 514, 518, 519,
    521, 528, 529, 545, 552, 553, 554, 561, 562, 569,
    573, 574, 575, 583, 589, 600, 606, 608, 611, 616,
    622, 927, 963, 1233, 1266
SAN MARTÍN Y MATORRAS DE GONZÁLEZ MENCHACA, María
    Elena de, 172
SAN NICOLÁS, José Vicente de, 496
SAN ROMÁN (family), 352
SAN ROMÁN, Francisco, 1089, 1095
SAN ROMÁN, Guillermo, 83, 189
SAN ROMÁN, Luis de, 1270
SANABRIA, Diego de, 1203, 1238, 1270
SANABRIA, Gregorio, 1111
SANABRIA, Juan de, 984, 984a, 1203, 1238
SANABRIA, Julio, 954
SANABRIA, María de, 1042, 1203
SÁNCHEZ, Agapito, pseud., 811
SÁNCHEZ, Alberto, 37, 894
SÁNCHEZ, Alfredo, 55
SÁNCHEZ, Amador, 1064
SÁNCHEZ, Antonio Saturnino, 575
SÁNCHEZ, Avelino, 1089
SÁNCHEZ, Benjamín, 173
SÁNCHEZ, Buenaventura, 1229
SÁNCHEZ, Cleto J., 943
SÁNCHEZ, Cristóbal, 254
SÁNCHEZ, Darwin, 660
SÁNCHEZ, Domingo Francisco, 943, 966
SÁNCHEZ, Emiliano, 268
SÁNCHEZ, Eulogio A., 268
SÁNCHEZ, Florencia Rosa María, 320
SÁNCHEZ, Florencio, 133, 141, 152a, 162, 282, 724,
    737, 741, 754, 778, 821, 890, 894, 1054, 1079,
    1081, 1086, 1091, 1160, 1164, 1177, 1185, 1187,
    1194, 1198, 1199, 1246, 1249, 1254, 1255, 1260
SÁNCHEZ, Gabriel Nazario, 995a
SÁNCHEZ, García, 520
SÁNCHEZ, Ideal, 18, 19, 23, 31, 36, 46, 63
SÁNCHEZ, Isabel, 1060
SÁNCHEZ, José Antonio, 188, 283
SÁNCHEZ, José Julián, 998, 1006
SÁNCHEZ, José Manuel, 677
SÁNCHEZ, Juan, 556, 1267

SÁNCHEZ, Juan A., 847
SÁNCHEZ, Juan Manuel, 19
SÁNCHEZ, Julio Antonio, 713
SÁNCHEZ, Lidia, 299
SÁNCHEZ, María, 118, 141, 734
SÁNCHEZ, Mariquita
    see SÁNCHEZ DE THOMPSON, María
SÁNCHEZ, Matheo, 1030
SÁNCHEZ, Matías, 332
SÁNCHEZ, Miguel, 1089
SÁNCHEZ, Nazario de Jesús, 995a
SÁNCHEZ, Nicasio, 998
SÁNCHEZ, Pedro A., 268
SÁNCHEZ, Rafaela, 190
SÁNCHEZ, Ramón Gil, 954
SÁNCHEZ, Ricardo, 1075, 1146, 1174
SÁNCHEZ, Roberto, 704, 759
SÁNCHEZ, Rodrigo, 186
SÁNCHEZ, Rufino, 293
SÁNCHEZ, Silverio, 254
SÁNCHEZ, Zacarías, 121
SANCHEZ ACOSTA, Roberto P., 923
SÁNCHEZ BOADO, Crescencia, 478
SÁNCHEZ CABALLERO, Manuel, 1095
SÁNCHEZ CHAPARRO, Domingo, 555
SÁNCHEZ DE ALONSO, José Manuel, 284
SÁNCHEZ DE BOADO, Juan, 284
SÁNCHEZ DE BUSTAMANTE, José Teodoro, 126, 439, 457,
    478, 526, 611, 621, 626
SÁNCHEZ DE BUSTAMANTE, Plácido, 385
SÁNCHEZ DE BUSTAMANTE, Samuel, 683a
SÁNCHEZ DE BUSTAMANTE, Teodoro
    see SÁNCHEZ DE BUSTAMANTE, José Teodoro
SÁNCHEZ DE BUSTAMANTE, Teófilo, 385, 565
SÁNCHEZ DE LA ROZUELA, Martín, 1058
SÁNCHEZ DE LORIA, Ana María, 931
SÁNCHEZ DE LORIA, Mariano, 126, 439, 526, 546, 547,
    549, 611, 621, 626, 921
SÁNCHEZ DE LORIA, Pedro, 126
SÁNCHEZ DE MENDEVILLE, María, 130, 924
SÁNCHEZ DE MOVELLÁN (family), 352
SÁNCHEZ DE OJEDA, Gabriel, 646, 649a, 1270
SÁNCHEZ DE THOMPSON, María, 85, 192, 227, 422, 478,
    611, 626, 928, 929
SÁNCHEZ DE VELAZCO, Cecilio, 130
SÁNCHEZ DE VELAZCO, María
    see SÁNCHEZ DE VELAZCO Y TRILLO, María de Todos
    los Santos
SÁNCHEZ DE VELAZCO Y TRILLO, María de Todos los
    Santos, 130, 864, 865
SÁNCHEZ DE VIZCAYA, Juan, 985
SÁNCHEZ GARCÍA, Francisco, 284
SÁNCHEZ GARDEL, Julio, 890
SÁNCHEZ GARZÓN, Gonzalo, 520, 1270
SÁNCHEZ HERREROS, Alfredo, 954
SÁNCHEZ HERREROS, José María, 954
SÁNCHEZ JIMÉNEZ, Críspulo, 954
SÁNCHEZ LABRADOR, José, 32, 885, 922, 943, 964, 966,
    985, 1269
SÁNCHEZ LINARI, María Elsa, 691
SÁNCHEZ MOSQUERA, C., 1089
SÁNCHEZ PEÓN, Loreto, 478, 929
SÁNCHEZ PICADO, Angel, 496
SÁNCHEZ POMPAS, Juan, 32
SÁNCHEZ QUELL, Hipólito, 943, 964, 966, 1014, 1020,
    1021, 1022
SÁNCHEZ RENDÓN, Mateo, 1270
SÁNCHEZ SOLANO, Francisco, 653, 654
SÁNCHEZ SORONDO, Fernando, 687, 814
SÁNCHEZ SORONDO, Marcelo, 558

SÁNCHEZ SOTOCA, Alfonso, 1264
SÁNCHEZ VERA DE MAZA, María Emilia, 923
SÁNCHEZ VIAMONTE, Carlos, 218
SÁNCHEZ Y VELASCO, Manuel, 126
SÁNCHEZ ZINNY, Fernando, 703
SANCHIS, Manuel, 191
SANCHO, Matías, 222
SANDAPILA, 977
SANDES, Ambrosio, 222, 608
SANDES, Nilda R., 652
SANDLER, Héctor, 440
SANDOVAL, Antonio, 32
SANDOVAL, Bernardino, 995a
SANDOVAL, Mercedes Clelia, 653, 654
SANDOVAL OCAMPO, Bartolomé, 1011
SANDRINI, Luis, 177a, 857d, 858
SANDRO, 857
SANGERMANO, Estela, 1207
SANGINES, Juan de la Cruz, 845
SANGUINETI, Angelo, 139
SANGUINETTI, Carlos C., 751
SANGUINETTI, Pedro Pablo, 254
SANJURJO, Domingo Zacarías, 923
SANJURJO MONTERO, Domingo, 954
SANJUST, Jaime, 984, 1011
SANMARTÍN, Roque de, 186
SANNA, Pedro, 1267
SANS, Vicentius, 1036
SANSEVIERO NAPOLI, Walter Francisco, 1210
SANTA ANA, Walter, 889
SANTA ANNA, Arturo, 1127
SANTA COLOMA, Gaspar de, 32, 463
SANTA COLOMA, Manuel de, 59
SANTA CRUZ, Alonso de, 627
SANTA CRUZ, Andrés de, 528, 562
SANTA CRUZ, Inés, 771
SANTA CRUZ, Juan de, 186
SANTA MARÍA CONILL, Alejandro, 683a
SANTAGRUZ GARCÍA, Rogelio, 998
SANTALÓ, Luis Antonio, 923
SANTALLA, Perla, 889
SANTAMARÍA, Cándida, 762
SANTAMARINA, Estela B. de, 923
SANTAMARINA, Ramón, 3, 122
SANTAMARINA GAILHOU, Luis Enrique, 1210
SANTAMARINA GAILHOU, María, 1210
SANTAMARINA VALCÁRCEL, Ramón, 284
SANTANA, Sergio Raúl, 1088
SANTANA CORONEL, Darío, 1210
SANTANDREU MORALES, Ema, 154, 1217
SANTANTONIN, Rubén, 49
SANTAYANA, José Luis P., 1073
SANTES, María Luisa, 857c
SANTIAGO, Juan de, 186
SANTIAGO, Ramón de, 1146, 1167, 1174, 1179, 1199,
    1247
SANTIBÁÑEZ, Juan, 496
SANTILLÁN, Armando Raúl, 788
SANTILLÁN, Cornelio, 921
SANTILLÁN, José S., 68
SANTILLÁN, Luis Alberto, 923
SANTILLÁN, Maximiliano, 878
SANTIS, Luis de, 923
SANTISE, Daniel A., 299
SANTISO Y MOSCOSO, Juan Francisco, 284
SANTISTEBAN IZAGUIRRE, José María, 1210
SANTIVIAGO, Luis, 1006
SANTO, Francisco de, 44, 64
SANTORE, Salvador, 664
SANTORO, Antonio, 41

SANTORO, Roberto Jorge, 723, 801
SANTORO DE CROUZEL, Irma P., 923
SANTORO VILLARRUEL, Domingo, 837
SANTÓRSOLA, Guido, 1206, 1207
SANTOS, Arturo, 878
SANTOS, Dora Martha de los, 299
SANTOS, Francisco de los, 1054
SANTOS, Gonzalo, 1270
SANTOS, José Vicente, 207
SANTOS, Luciano, pseud.
    see LUSSICH, Antonio D.
SANTOS, Martín, 878
SANTOS, Máximo, 1079, 1091, 1109, 1125, 1129, 1202
SANTOS, Toribia de los, 478, 929
SANTOS DE BOSCH, Teresa, 1083
SANTOS DÍAZ, Ibar de los, 1210
SANTOS FERRI, Adela, 299
SANTOS GÓMEZ, Susana E., 652
SANTOS HERNANDO, Gregorio, 766
SANTOS MARTÍNEZ, Pedro, 252, 283, 521
SANTUARIO DE MONTERO, Juana, 1093a
SANTUCHO, Eduardo, 299
SANTUCHO, Julio, 440
SANZ, Francisco de Paula, 32, 517
SANZIN, Renato, 207
SAÑUDO, Agustín, 254
SAPACA, Marcos, 32
SAPELLI, Domingo, 894
SAPELLO, Ambrosio, 258
SAPENA PASTOR, Josefina, 956
SEPANA PASTOR, Raúl, 954
SAPIN JARCHENCO, Gregorio, 1210
SAPIN LUBENKO, Gregorio, 1210
SAPORITI, Enrique J., 923
SAPORITO, Lidia, 299
SAPPIA, Adriana A., 691
SAR, Eugenio, 137
SARABIA, Mateo
    see SARAVIA, Mateo
SARACENI, Julio, 857, 858
SARÁCHAGA, José Antonio, 126
SARÁCHAGA, Juan Antonio, 244, 1075
SARACHO, Nelba C., 691
SARASA, Javier Saturnino, 496
SARAVÍ, Guillermo César, 135, 800
SARAVI, Mario Guillermo, 683a
SARAVIA, Abel Mónico, 653, 654
SARAVIA, Antonio Floricio (CHIQUITO, pseud.), 1084,
    1093, 1122
SARAVIA, Aparicio, 460, 1075, 1091, 1093, 1109,
    1116, 1122, 1134, 1200
SARAVIA, Basilisio, 1093
SARAVIA, Carlos María, 166, 195
SARAVIA, Enrique, 1093
SARAVIA, Gumersindo, 1093
SARAVIA, José Domingo, 625
SARAVIA, José Francisco, 1093
SARAVIA, José Manuel, 244, 332
SARAVIA, Juan Antonio, 984
SARAVIA, Mateo, 126
SARAVIA, Nepomuceno H., 1122
SARAVIA, Pedro José de, 625
SARAVIA, Tomás, 32
SARAVIA CASTRO, David, 653, 654
SARAVIA LINARES DE ARIAS, Clara, 653, 654, 762
SARAZA, Javier Saturnino
    see SARASA, Javier Saturnino
SARAZA, Saturnino Lorenzo, 412, 413
SARDINA, José Gabino, 625
SARGENTO CUATI, pseud.
    see ORTIGOZA, José Sebastián

SARHY, Juan Francisco, 332
SARMIENTO (family), 366
SARMIENTO, Avelino, 878
SARMIENTO, Bienvenida, 174, 930, 931
SARMIENTO, Buenaventura, 222
SARMIENTO, Cirilo P., 173
SARMIENTO, Domingo Faustino, 4, 9, 70, 78, 79, 85,
   91, 95, 96, 103, 110, 112, 118, 121, 129, 133,
   141, 152a, 166, 170, 176, 188, 189, 195, 199,
   212, 216, 232, 236, 241, 244, 245, 246, 259, 276,
   278, 282, 283, 293, 317, 323, 369, 372, 379, 381,
   381a, 382, 386, 392, 393, 398, 404, 405, 436,
   444, 449, 450, 452, 460, 462, 466, 469, 478, 490,
   497, 502, 507, 509, 512, 514, 515, 516, 518, 519,
   521, 523, 528, 531, 536, 544, 545, 564, 574, 582,
   583, 585, 589, 593, 594, 598, 601, 603, 604, 605,
   607, 608, 611, 613, 614, 619, 629, 631, 633, 634,
   644, 650, 692, 720, 724, 734, 737, 741, 743, 751,
   754, 761, 769, 779, 780, 792, 873, 924, 1104,
   1195, 1246, 1249
SARMIENTO, Domingo Fidel (DOMINGUITO, pseud.), 112,
   398, 450, 497, 506, 603, 606, 608, 613
SARMIENTO, Dominguito
     see SARMIENTO, Domingo Fidel
SARMIENTO, Elda Victoria, 44
SARMIENTO, José Clemente, 112, 398, 564
SARMIENTO, José Fermín, 547, 549, 987
SARMIENTO, María del Rosario, 930, 931
SARMIENTO, María Josefa, 684
SARMIENTO, Procesa
     see SARMIENTO DE LENOIR, Procesa
SARMIENTO, Rosario
     see SARMIENTO, María del Rosario
SARMIENTO DE BELIN, Faustina, 930
SARMIENTO DE GAMBOA, Pedro, 1238
SARMIENTO DE GÓMEZ, Paula, 930, 931
SARMIENTO DE LENOIR, Procesa, 62, 478, 929, 930, 931
SARMIENTO DE MALLEA, Mercedes, 931
SARMIENTO DE SOTOMAYOR Y FIGUEROA, Alfonso, 984,
   1011
SARMIENTO SOTOMAYOR Y FIGUEROA, Alonso
     see SARMIENTO DE SOTOMAYOR Y FIGUEROA, Alonso
SARNIGUET, Emilio J., 21, 154
SARRATEA, Manuel, 244, 282, 386, 404, 427, 472, 499,
   552, 554, 573, 574, 611, 1091
SARRÍA (family), 352
SARRICOLEA Y OLEA, Juan Manuel de, 529a, 910
SARRICOLEA Y OLEA, Martín de, 1041
SARTORI, Antonio, 923
SARTORIO, José Santos, 6
SARTORIO MÁRQUEZ, Ramón Alberto, 1210
SAS, Rodrigo de, 32
SASLAVSKY, Luis, 857c, 858
SASSI, Luis Roberto, 791
SASSO, Leonardo, 151
SASSONE, Antonio, 25
SASTRE, Marcos, 141, 166, 176, 261, 315, 317, 324,
   478, 511, 611, 737, 1079, 1146, 1188, 1246
SATÓ, José, 319, 912
SATOCHI, Orestes René, 923
SATZ, Mario, 759
SAURA, Fulgencio, 923
SAUVAGE, 189
SAUVAGEOT DE DUPUIS, Francisco, 949, 960, 963, 1029
SAUVER
     see COLÓN, Salvador (Sauver)
SAVARESE, Raúl, 893
SAVIGNI, Segundo, 258
SAVINO, Pablo Emilio, 180
SAVIO, Alberto, 1211

SAVIO, Manuel N., 268
SAVOJA, Francisco Di
     see DI SAVOJA, Francisco
SAYAGO, Gumersindo, 923
SAYANCA, Manuel E., 207
SAYAS, José, 358
SAYAS, Pedro de, 186, 845
SAYAS ESPELUCA, Pedro, 358
SAYÉ, Luis, 923
SBARRA, Herminio Roberto, 923
SBERNINI, Hugo A., 37
SCABINI, Juan, 1083
SCAFATTI, Genaro, 874
SCAFFO, Carlos, 1187, 1199
SCALA, Andrés, 952
SCALA, Pedro, 211
SCALA DE VINIEGRA, Raquel E., 652
SCALABRINI, Pedro, 95, 258, 324
SCALAMBRINI ORTIZ, Raúl, 609, 743, 765, 769
SCALELLA DE PARISI, Angela R., 781
SCALÓN, Luis, 860
SCAPIRA FRIDMAN, Flor, 739
SCAPPATURA, Antonio, 258
SCAPPATURA, Luis, 258
SCARNESKY, Ladislao
     see CZARNECKI, Ladislao
SCARONE, Arturo, 1083
SCARONE, Ernesto, 947
SCARTASCINI, Guillermo A., 923
SCARZELLA, Julio, 893
SCASSO, León S., 89
SCAVONE, Antonio, 954
SCIAMMARELLA, Valdo, 883
SCIBONA, Francisco, 652
SCIESA DE COUTO, Adela, 874
SCIOMMARELLA, Silvia NOra, 663
SCIOSCIA, Miguel, 781
SCISCENTE, Francisco, 1243
SCIUTTO, Luis Alfredo (LUCERO, Diego, pseud.), 556,
   727, 811
SCLAVO, Jorge, 1182
SCOLPINI, Pablo, 6
SCONZO, Pascual, 923
SCOPELLITI, Alberto, 31
SCOPES, Leonard Arthur, 954
SCORDIA, Antonio Francisco, 18, 19, 25, 31
SCOSERIA, Hugo S., 1073
SCOSERIA, José, 1083, 1261
SCOTTI, Carlos Francisco, 258
SCOTTI, Edgardo A., 652
SCOTTI, Ernesto Mariano, 19, 25, 64
SCREMIN, Oscar, 923
SCRIVENER, Juan H., 853a
SCUARTINI DE ROEDIGER, Isabel, 320
SCUNIO FERREYRA, Natalio, 811
SCHACK, Andrés, 385
SCHADE, Francisco, 963a
SCHAEFER, Bernardo, 923
SCHAEFER PEÑA, Beatriz, 774a, 787
SCHAERER, Eduardo, 959, 984a
SCHAPIRA FRIDMAN, Flor, 717, 725, 802
SCHAUBLI (family), 168
SCHECHAJ, Román, 923
SCHEGGIA DE HERNÁNDEZ, Haydée Noemí, 320
SCHEGGIA DE HERNÁNDEZ, Irma Araceli, 320
SCHEGGIA DE LEMMI, María Esther, 320
SCHENONE, Carlos, 191
SCHENONI LUGO, Manlio, 959, 1006
SCHEUER, Walter, 923
SCHIAFFINO, Eduardo, 19, 25, 31, 51, 59, 521, 751

SCHIAFFINO, Juan B., 1126
SCHIAFFINO, Nicolás, 258
SCHIAFFINO, Rafael, 1203
SCHIANCA, Arturo C., 217
SCHIAPELLI, Rita Delia E., 923
SCHIAPPA-PIETRA, Giovanni, 139
SCHIAVETTA, Angel Bernardo, 684, 756
SCHIAVO, Horacio Angel, 678, 751, 833
SCHIAVONI, Augusto, 58
SCHICKER, Adolfo, 923
SCHIMNOUVICH, Samuel, 923
SCHINCA, Francisco Alberto, 1083, 1145, 1187, 1190
SCHINCA, Milton, 1148, 1149, 1151, 1152, 1178
SCHIRO, Roberto, 771
SCHIUMA, Alfredo L., 881, 883
SCHIUMA, Armando, 882
SCHLIEPPER, Carlos, 858
SCHLOSSER, Fernando (Mrs.)
     see GAY, Theodora
SCHMID, Ignacio Martín, 922
SCHMID, Martín, 865, 866, 1037
SCHMIDEL, Ulrich, 28, 32, 609, 754, 943, 966, 985,
     1230, 1232
SCHMIDLMEYER, Peter, 28
SCHMIDT, José, 32
SCHMIDT, Martin, 949, 1267
SCHMUCLER, Natalio, 660
SCHNEIDER, Otto, 923
SCHNEIDERWIND, Alberto, 332
SCHOBINGER, Juan S. René, 923
SCHOECK, Gunther, 923
SCHOFS DE MAGGI, Marta, 663
SCHROEDER, Juan, 857b
SCHTEINGART, Mario, 923
SCHUJMAN, Salomón, 923
SCHUJMAN DE KOVARSKY, Silia, 652
SCHUKOVSKY, Guillermo, 954
SCHULTZ CAZENUEVE DE MANTOVANI, Fryda, 521, 722,
     739, 748, 751, 783
SCHULTZ DE MANTOVANI, Fryda
     see SCHULTZ CAZENUEVE DE MANTOVANI, Fryda
SCHULZ, Augusto Gustavo, 191, 923
SCHULZ, Carlota, 939
SCHULZ, Guillermo, 923
SCHULZ SOLARI, Alejandro (SOLAR, Xul, pseud.), 25,
     31, 33, 49, 55, 56, 210
SCHUMACHER, Hans Joachim, 923
SCHURJIN, Raúl, 31
SCHUSTER, Edward James, 1015
SCHUSTER, Teodoro, 332
SCHUURMANS STEKHOVEN, Jacobe Hermanus, 923
SCHVARTZMAN, Isaac, 963a
SCHVARTZMAN, Mauricio, 1025
SCHWARARZ, Felipe, 6
SCHWARZ, Alexandrovitch Salomón, 1210
SCHWEDT BACIGALUPO, Vicente Rodolfo, 1210
SCHWEIZER, Rosaura, 837
SCHWERTFEGER, Werner, 923
SCHWOB (family), 168
SEADE, Felipe, 1211
SEAVER, Benjamin Franklin, 14
SEBASTIANI, Francisco, 895, 896
SEBASTIANI, Pía, 882, 883
SECCO ILLA, Joaquín, 1083, 1174
SEDANO, Rafael, 1270
SEDEÑO, Julián, 520
SEDERO, Juan Carlos, 874
SEDERO, Samuel, 683a
SEEBER, Francisco, 103

SEELMAN-EGGEBERT, W., 923
SEGAL, Any, 785
SEGATO, Narciso C., 65
SEGGER, Polidoro, 921
SEGISMUNDO, Juan Bautista, 6,7
SEGOVIA, Elena, 932
SEGOVIA, Glauco, 1123
SEGOVIA, Juan José, 126
SEGOVIA, Manuel Ignacio (ATAHUALPA, pseud.), 768
SEGOVIA, Margot de, 726
SEGUÍ, 195
SEGUÍ, Andrés, 254
SEGUÍ, Antonio, 25, 36, 38, 49, 55
SEGUÍ, Francisco José, 14
SEGUÍ, José, 230
SEGUÍ, Juan Francisco, 95, 96, 107, 126, 166, 282, 478,
     512, 634
SEGUÍ, Luis, 1122
SEGUNDO, José Pedro, 1083
SEGUNDO, Juan Luis, 1184
SEGURA, Camilo, 268
SEGURA, Facundo, 921
SEGURA, Juan José Antonio, 95
SEGURA, Luis José, 917
SEGURA, María del Rosario, 320
SEGURA, Martín de, 186
SEGURA, Pedro José, 261
SEGURA, Pedro Pascual, 179, 207, 278
SEGURA Y CUBAS, Luis Gabriel, 910
SEGUROLA, Deán, 166
SEGUROLA, Saturnino
     see SEGUROLA LEZICA, Saturnino
SEGUROLA LEZICA, Saturnino, 6, 192, 282, 315, 609,
     611, 844, 885, 921, 1203, 1261
SEIDE, José Ignacio, 496, 1095
SEIDE FERNÁNDEZ, José de, 284
SEITOUR, Félix Juan, 191
SELVA, Melquíades, 649
SELVA MARTÍ, Ana
     see MARTÍ, Ana Selva
SEMERÍA, José Marcos, 1083
SEMINARIO, Carlos, 94
SEMON (family), 168
SEMORILLE, J. Simón, 207
SENA, Heraclio, 894
SENA, José Bernardo, 918
SENARRUZA, Andrés, 126
SENESTRARI, Elías, 332
SENET, Rodolfo, 317, 688, 751
SENILLOSA, Felipe de, 6, 68, 141, 321, 332, 344,
     629, 921a
SENRA, Manuel, 1089, 1095
SENTENACH, Felipe, 517
SENTÍS MELENDO, Santiago, 222
SENZACQUA, Vicenta Adela, 874
SEÑA, Balthasar, 1035a, 1035b
SEÑORANS, Juan B., 68, 94, 844, 847
SEOANE, Ana María, 799
SEOANE, Luis, 19, 25, 27, 31, 34, 36, 38, 49, 55
SEPICH, Marcelino Jorge, 923
SEPP, Antonio, 7, 32, 866, 885, 985, 1035, 1267
SEPP SEPPENBUR ZU REINEGG, Anton von
     see VON SEPP SEPPENBUR ZU REINEGG, Anton
SEQUERA Y ZALDÍVAR, Carlos, 954
SER Y ANTÓN, María del, 172
SERAFINI, Anunciado, 910
SERAFINI, Carlos, 998
SERAFINI, Rodolfo, 998
SERANTES, Juan, 344
SEREBRIER, José, 1206, 1207

SERGENT, Emile, 854
SERGI, Sergio, 18, 55
SERGIO, Jorge, 832
SERI, José Eduardo, 135, 800, 837
SERNA (family), 348
SERNA, Eduardo Alberto, 37
SERNA, Ezequiel de la, 391
SERNA, Francisco Florencio de la, 356, 1041
SERNA, Jerónimo de la, 332
SERNA, Miguel Angel de la, 560
SERPA, Diego, 1064
SERRA, Edelweis, 771
SERRA Y VALLS, José, 496
SERRADILLA DE NARANJO, Pura G., 781
SERRADOR, Esteban, 857b
SERRANO, Antonio, 135, 923
SERRANO, Enrique, 858
SERRANO, Germán, 974
SERRANO, José, 319, 1264
SERRANO, José María, 1094
SERRANO, José Mariano, 439, 457, 526, 611, 621, 626
SERRANO, Pedro, 194
SERRANO, Raúl, 889
SERRANO GALLARDO, Angel, 1088
SERRANO PÉREZ, Manuel, 716
SERRANO REDONNET, Ana Rosa, 217, 762, 882
SERRATO, José, 1073, 1075, 1079, 1083
SERRATOSA, Antonio, 1094
SERREY, Carlos, 653, 654, 893
SERRICCHIO, Jorge Alberto, 923
SERRITELLA, Omar, 299
SERÚ, Juan E., 173
SERÚ DE LEAL, Alicia, 683a
SERVATO, José, 1126
SERVERA, Ana María, 684
SERVICE, Elmón R., 966
SERVICE, Helen S., 966
SERVICI DE RONDINI, María Antonieta, 923
SERVÍN, José Bernardino, 964, 970, 1035
SERVIN, Manuel, 970
SERVÍN, Martín Serapio, 995a
SESANA, Aldo, 299
SESANA, Fernando Luis, 923
SETA, Juan Carlos de, 299
SETARO, Ricardo, 683a
SETELICH MARGUITICH, Alberto Juan, 1210
SEUROT, A., 6
SEUX, Casimir, 960
SEVILLA, José, 923
SEVILLA VÁZQUEZ, José de, 921
SEVLEVER, Rubén, 788
SEWALL, John H. (Mrs.)
   see GORMAN, Mary Elizabeth
SEYMOUR, Richard Arthur, 4
SFONDRINI, Carlos, 768
SFORZA, César, 19, 21, 64
SHERIDAN, Adelina Julia, 320
SHERIDAN, Enrique, 28, 59
SHERIDAN DE GROSSO, Enriqueta, 320
SHESTAKOV, Teodoro, 198
SIBELLINO, Antonio, 19, 21, 25, 33, 55
SICARDI, Francisco Anselmo, 68, 152a, 718, 754, 774,
   844, 851, 1261
SICARDI, Honorio
   see SICCARDI, Honorio M.
SICARDI, León, 731
SICARDO, José, 344
SICARDO, Juan Bautista, 910
SICCARDI, Elvira Mariana, 923
SICCARDI, Gianni, 759
SICCARDI, Honorio M., 865, 882, 883

SICILIANI, José, 883
SICRE, Juan Eduardo, 923
SICHERO, Jorge, 703, 785
SID, Elena, 33
SIDERO, Nilo, 652
SIEDLITZ, Guillermo Otto, 170
SIENE DE MALINE, 1046
SIENRA (family), 1108
SIENRA, Roberto, 1068, 1197, 1199
SIENRA CARRANZA, José M., 1083, 1146, 1174, 1188,
   1199
SIERRA, Atanasio Domingo, 1059, 1111
SIERRA, Francisco de, 477
SIERRA, Ida, 874
SIERRA, Mónica de la, 1093a
SIERRA, Pancho, 878
SIERRA, Pedro Pablo de la, 1093a
SIERRA, Vicente D., 283, 609
SIERRA GOROSITO, Donato, 878
SIGA, Jorge Ernesto, 698
SIGNO, Juana del, 422
SIGORDIA, Juan de, 318
SILA GODOY, Cayo, 1029
SILA MERCER, Andrés, 823
SILBER, Marcos, 785
SILBERMAN, Enrique, 923
SILBERMANN, Antonio, 120
SILBERT, Ignacio, 923
SILVA, Arturo S., 1145
SILVA, Blas de, 319
SILVA, Carlos, 36, 55
SILVA, Cayetano Alberto, 137, 874, 1054
SILVA, Clara, 1149, 1151, 1152, 1177, 1178, 1179
SILVA, Conrado, 1207
SILVA, Diego de, 1270
SILVA, Dolores, 112
SILVA, Isidro, 125
SILVA, José A., 1259
SILVA, José de, 1223
SILVA, José Leonardo, 254
SILVA, José Manuel, 254
SILVA, José María, 878, 1243
SILVA, Juan Darío, 1093
SILVA, Juan de, 845
SILVA, Julio, 1167, 1187
SILVA, Lincoln, 1025
SILVA, Manuel de, 186
SILVA, María Inés, 1158
SILVA, Mario Norberto, 739
SILVA, Néstor, 679
SILVA, Ramón, 18, 19, 22, 25, 31, 33, 44, 55, 1218
SILVA, Sofanor de la, 445
SILVA BALLBÉ, Oigimer Nereo, 385
SILVA BELINZON, Concepción, 1179
SILVA BRAGA, Pascual, 496, 915
SILVA CASTRO, Manuel, 1089
SILVA DE AIRALDI, Concepción, 959, 966
SILVA DE GURRUCHAGA, Martina, 422, 626
SILVA NOSEDA, Lucrecia Amelia, 663
SILVA REHERMAN, Luis, 1210
SILVA SÁNCHEZ, Telmo, 1210
SILVA SERRANO, Julián, 1167
SILVA VALDÉS, Fernán, 767, 894, 1068, 1079, 1087,
   1145, 1147, 1151, 1152, 1159, 1160, 1167, 1170,
   1177, 1179, 1180, 1181, 1185, 1187, 1194, 1197,
   1199, 1243, 1248, 1257
SILVA VILA, María Inés, 1149, 1177
SILVA Y AGUIAR, José, 1264
SILVA Y LAZCANO, Juan Francisco, 1223
SILVA Y LAZCANO, Juana Policarpa, 1223

SILVAGNI DE SALLES, Elvira, 320
SILVAIN, Julio César, 717, 726, 739
SILVANO, Félix, 1075
SILVEIRA, Ernesto V., 1167
SILVEIRA, Exequiel, 1093
SILVEIRA, Ramón E., 1093
SILVEIRA AGUIAR, Angelina, 1093
SILVEIRA DE IBARROLA, Francisca, 32, 85, 422, 626
SILVERA, Calixto, 125
SILVERA, Nelson Rubén, 954
SILVESTRE, Felipe, 258
SILVESTRINI, Lideano, 860
SILVETTI PAZ, Norberto, 663, 716, 739, 758, 759, 786
SILVETTI PAZ, Vicente, 805
SILVEYRA, Luis, 332
SILVEYRA DE LENHARDSON, Antonieta, 154
SIMARI, Leopoldo, 893
SIMARI, Tomás, 893
SIMKO, Iván, 652
SIMOIS, Melitón J., 1145
SIMÓN, Luis, 1238
SIMONE, Mercedes, 860, 877, 879
SIMONE, Pedro de, 19
SIMONE, Roberto de, 299
SIMONETO, Italo B., 923
SIMONIELLO, Paulina, 154, 711, 762, 837
SIMONOFF, Miguel, 332
SIMONS, Conrado, 332
SIMPSON, Máximo, 739, 802
SIMSON, David, 904
SINA-SINA, pseud.
    see LARES, Francisco
SINAGRA, Adela, 320
SINCLAIR, Enrique, 14
SINGER, Rolf, 923
SINGERMAN, Berta, 154, 893
SIQUEYRA, Marcos de, 134
SIRABO, Dalmiro, 35
SIRAGUSA, Alfredo, 923
SIRE SALIM, Farat, 653, 654
SIRI, Ismael Marcelo, 663
SIRIPO, 977
SIRÓ, Elena, 837
SIRÓ, Fernando, 857a
SIROLLI, Amadeo Rodolfo, 653, 654
SIROTZKY DE FAVELUKES, Susana Lidia, 923
SISA, Carlos, 998
SISA, M. Eliseo, 959
SISTO POVIGNA, Zulema, 1088
SITRO, Antonio, 35
SITY, Francisco Javier, 196
SIVORI, Carlos, 28
SIVORI, Eduardo, 19, 25, 31, 33, 44, 45, 51, 59,
    258, 293, 521
SIVORI, Enrique M., 923
SKOWRONSKI, Roberto, 238
SLAUCITAJS, Leónidas, 923
SLAUCITAJS, Sergejs J., 923
SLEUMER, Hermann, 923
SMITH, Agustín M., 1168, 1170
SMITH, Elías, 82
SMITH, Federico W., 1006
SMITH, Gladys C. A., 702, 751
SMITH, Lucy L., 930
SMOLZI, Luis, 1205
SNOW, William P., 954
SOAGE, Belindo, 254
SOAGE, José Félix, 284
SOARES, Federico, 88
SOARES DE SOUZA, Paulino José, 596
SOAREZ NETTO CHARLONE, Edmundo, 1210

SOBA, Celestino, 1039
SOBA, Susana Esther, 717, 725
SOBRAL, Arturo, 332
SOBRAL, José María, 15
SOBRECASAS, Juan Francisco, 332
SOBRECIANOS, Francisco de, 1238
SOBRECIANOS, Hernando de, 1238
SOBREMONTE, Marqués de
    see SOBREMONTE, Rafael de
SOBREMONTE, Rafael de (Marqués de Sobremonte), 89,
    212, 273, 283, 443, 472, 517, 570, 1091, 1223,
    1237, 1239, 1240, 1241
SOBRINO, Carlos, 31
SOBRINO, Francisco, 46
SOBRINO, Laureano, 989
SOBRINO Y MINAYO, Blas, 910
SOCA, Francisco, 1054, 1073, 1075, 1079, 1081, 1083,
    1202, 1261
SOCA, Susana, 1151, 1177, 1178, 1184
SODA, José Vicente, 217
SOERENSEN, Félix Adolfo, 954
SOFFICI, Mario, 858
SOFÍA, Pedro, 881
SOFOVICH, Gerardo, 857
SOFOVICH, Hugo, 857
SOIBELMAN, Elsa, 37
SOIZA REILLY, Juan José de, 135, 154, 751, 1190
SOLÁ, Graciela de
    see MATURO DE SOLÁ GONZÁLEZ, Graciela
SOLÁ, Juan León, 194
SOLÁ, Juan Nepomuceno, 496, 915
SOLÁ, León J., 241
SOLÁ, Luis, 284
SOLÁ, Marcela, 889
SOLÁ, Miguel, 653, 654
SOLÁ DE CASTELLANOS, Sara, 653, 654, 664, 711, 762
SOLÁ DE SOLÁ, Emma, 653, 654, 664, 711, 762, 783
SOLÁ GONZÁLEZ, Alfonso, 135, 664, 683a, 716, 722,
    739, 758, 766, 798, 800, 831
SOLALINDE, Cirilo, 982
SOLANAS, Fortunato, 160
SOLANAS, Héctor G., 687
SOLANET, Pedro, 565
SOLANO, Francisco, 144, 472, 865, 906, 921, 1266
SOLANO ÁLVAREZ, Francisco, 1116
SOLANO ANTUÑA, Francisco, 1063
SOLANO CARRERA, Francisco, 921
SOLANO DEL CORRO, Francisco, 188, 283
SOLANO ESCOBAR, 998
SOLANO ESPINOSA, Francisco, 974, 995a
SOLANO F., Francisco, 963a
SOLANO GONZÁLEZ, Francisco, 387
SOLANO LÓPEZ, Francisco
    see LÓPEZ, Francisco Solano
SOLAR, Alberto del, 68
SOLAR, Xul, pseud.
    see SCHULZ SOLARI, Alejandro
SOLARES, José Manuel, 244, 316
SOLARI, Aldo, 1184
SOLARI, Ernesto, 662
SOLARI, Facundo, 191
SOLARI, Juan Antonio, 260
SOLARI, Justino, 551a
SOLARI, Luis, 1049
SOLARI, Miguel Agustín, 923
SOLARI, Zita, 817
SOLARI PARRAVICINI, Benjamín, 154
SOLARI VERA, Juan José, 1210
SOLARICH SKRILEK, Juan, 1210
SOLAS, León, 95, 127
SOLDÁN, Silvio, 299

SOLDANO, Ferrucio Alberto, 332
SOLDANO, Juan, 87
SOLDATI, Alberto de, 68
SOLDATI, León de, 923
SOLDATTI, Oscar, 18, 31
SOLDI, Raúl, 18, 19, 23, 25, 31, 34, 36, 45, 50, 53,
     55, 64, 1218
SOLEDAD, Atanasio de la, pseud.
     see ATANASIO DE LA PIEDAD
SOLER (family), 357
SOLER, Carlos Alberto, 954
SOLER, Eustaquio, 368
SOLER, Frank, 135
SOLER, Gustavo, 140, 739
SOLER, Juan José, 954, 959, 964
SOLER, Manuel José, 359, 611
SOLER, Mariano, 1075, 1091, 1146, 1188
SOLER, Miguel Estanislao, 212, 244, 359, 360, 386,
     404, 433, 552, 553, 554, 611, 1091
SOLER CAÑAS, Luis, 431, 688
SOLER DARAS, José, 664, 766, 833
SOLER VICENS, Mónica, 18, 31
SOLETO, Pedro, 845
SOLIER, Daniel, 6
SOLINAS, Juan Antonio, 1040
SOLIÑO, Víctor, 871, 1088
SOLÍS, Alba, 879
SOLÍS, Diego de, 32
SOLÍS, Ezequiel, 998
SOLÍS, Juan de
     see DÍAZ DE SOLÍS, Juan de
SOLÍS, Linneo A., 998
SOLÍS DE AGUIRRE, Nicolás, 845
SOLÍS PIZARRO, José, 653, 654
SOLITO, Juan, pseud.
     see OLIVER, Juan María
SOLIVELLAS, Miguel Angel, 760, 776
SOLIVERES, José, 496
SOLIVERIO, José
     see SOLIVERES, José
SOLIVERIS, José
     see SOLIVERES, José
SOLLAZZO DE LEW, Beatriz M., 691
SOMADOSSI, Eugenio A., 691
SOMARUGA, Juan Bautista, 923
SOMELLERA, Antonio, 14, 25, 521
SOMELLERA, Candelaria, 478, 929
SOMELLERA, Pedro Antonio, 144, 321, 471
SOMERS, Armonía, 1149, 1155, 1158, 1177, 1186
SOMIGLIANA, Carlos, 690
SOMMA, Juan Carlos, 1148, 1149
SOMMARUGA, Angel, 258
SOMMER, Baldomero, 844
SOMOZA, Arturo Lucio, 923
SOMOZA, Juan L., 268
SONEIRA, Ernesto, 24
SORA, Francisco, 1146
SORAZÁBAL, Juan (Chuchín, pseud.), 943, 965
SORDELLI, Alfredo, 923
SORHUETA, Fermín, 1123
SORIA (family), 351, 1106
SORIA, Claudio, 683a
SORIA, Ezequiel, 719
SORIA, Joaquín de, 1136
SORIA, Juan de, 32
SORIA, Paul, 949
SORIA CERVANTES (family), 348
SORIA ORLANDO, Leopoldo (ORLANDO, Polo, pseud.), 860
SORIANO, Alberto, 923
SORIANO, Osvaldo, Roberto, 738
SORIANO ARÉVALO, Domingo, 74

SORICH, David Antonio, 653
SORO, Susana, 31
SOROA, Ignacio de, 299
SOROETA, Ignacio de, 989, 1011
SORRENTINO, Fernando, 772, 815, 816
SORRIBES, José Rodolfo, 684
SORRIENTE, Enrique Alberto, 41, 299
SORZIO, Adolfo, 44
SOSA, 212
SOSA (family), 348
SOSA, Alejandro, 995a
SOSA, Amílcar Urbano, 683a
SOSA, Antonio, 959
SOSA, Apolinario Héctor, 652, 717, 805
SOSA, Dámaso Antonio, 973
SOSA, Daniel, 995a
SOSA, Desiderio, 93
SOSA, Domingo, 137
SOSA, Francisco, 599
SOSA, Gabriel de, 556
SOSA, Ignacio Antonio, 973
SOSA, Jaime, 991
SOSA, Jesualdo, 1177, 1187, 1199
SOSA, José Cirilio, 653, 654
SOSA, Joseph de, 186
SOSA, Juanita, 234
SOSA, Julio, 877
SOSA, Julio María, 1083, 1190
SOSA, Manuel Antonio, 973
SOSA, Marceleiro, 1110
SOSA, María Isabel, 973
SOSA, Mercedes, 862
SOSA, Nereo, 1084
SOSA, Nilda Norma, 684
SOSA, Pedro Antonio, 973
SOSA, Vicente Ignacio, 973
SOSA, Zulma, 1191
SOSA AGUIAR, Euclídes, 1093
SOSA ESCALADA, Gustavo, 1029
SOSA ESCALADA, Jaime, 986
SOSA ESCALADA, Juan Manuel, 959, 973
SOSA ESCALADA, Marcial, 959
SOSA GAONA, Emilio, 948, 1039
SOSA LÓPEZ, Emilio, 664, 717, 722, 739, 758, 798,
     831
SOSA LOYOLA, Gilberto, 81, 222
SOSA MASCARENO, Luis de, 1262
SOSA MASCAREÑAS, 1056
SOSA REBOYRAS, Carlos Eduardo, 81, 222
SOSA VALDEZ, Dámaso, 973, 1006
SOSA VALDEZ, Daniel, 973
SOSA VALDEZ, Ignacio, 973
SOSA VALDEZ, Juana, 973
SOSA Y TERRA, Fernando de, 186
SOSA ZERPA, Gustavo Gabriel, 1210
SOSA ZERPA, María Cristina, 1210
SOSTOA (family), 1106
SOSTOA, Domingo de, 1223
SOSTOA, José Francisco de, 1056, 1223
SOSTOA, Juan José de, 1205
SOSTOA Y ACHUCARRO, José María Guillermo de, 1223
SOSTOA Y ACHUCARRO, Tomás de, 1223
SOSTOA Y MARTÍNEZ, Tomás de, 1223
SOSTOA Y ORDÓÑEZ, Enrique de, 1223
SOSTOA Y ORDÓÑEZ, Fernando de, 1223
SOSTOA Y ORDÓÑEZ, Joaquín de, 1223
SOSTOA Y ORDÓÑEZ, Rafael de, 1223
SOSTOA Y ORDÓÑEZ, Tomás de, 1223
SOTA, Elías Ramón de la, 923
SOTA, Juan José, 683a
SOTA, Regino de la, 268
SOTAS, Fernando de la, 910

SOTELO, Guillermo, 1089
SOTELO NARVÁEZ, Pedro, 501, 520
SOTO, Antonio (Boy, pseud.), 1165
SOTO, Carlos F., 954
SOTO, Fernando (MANTEQUILLA, pseud.), 857d
SOTO, Juan Esteban, 908
SOTO, Juan José, 1112
SOTO, Luis Emilio, 743
SOTO, Prudencio C., 328
SOTO ACÉBAL, Jorge, 19, 31, 33, 64
SOTO AVENDAÑO, Ernesto, 64
SOTO DE CUENCA, Elena, 810
SOTO Y CALVO, Edelina, 762, 783
SOTO Y CALVO, Francisco, 834
SOTOMAYOR (family), 284
SOTOMAYOR, Alonso de, 522
SOTOMAYOR, Francisco Javier de, 555
SOTOMAYOR, José Sebastián de, 555
SOTOMAYOR, Miguel de, 318, 319
SOTULO, Carlos Héctor, 299
SOTURA DE FISCALINI, Victorina, 320
SOUBRIÉ, Alberto, 923
SOUBRIÉ, Walter, 889
SOULE TONELLI, Héctor Pedro, 664
SOURDEAUX, Adolfo, 6, 211
SOURRIÈRE SOUILLAC, José, 332, 922
SOUSA, Martín Alfonso de, 1238
SOUSA DE SILVA PONTES, Rodrigo de, 127
SOUSSENS, Charles Phillipe de, 162, 243, 1246
SOUTO, José, 1089
SOUTO, Marta Beatriz, 702
SOUTO VILLAR, Pedro, 1089
SOUZA, Irineo Evangelista de, 596
SOUZA, Jorge, 658
SOUZA, Joseph de, 32
SOUZA, Paulino de, 845
SOUZA BRAZUNA, Carmen, 44, 154
SOUZA REILLY, José María de, 1188
SOZIO, Mariano (FOLCO, Mario, pseud.), 135
SOZZI, Juan Antonio, 923
SPADERO DE ANTONINI, Emma, 320
SPARN, Enrique, 652
SPARROW, J. R., 823
SPEGAZZANI, Carlos, 219, 258
SPELUZZI, Bernardino, 113, 258, 332, 921a
SPENA, Lita, 882
SPERATTI (family), 972
SPERATTI, Adela, 943, 964, 1012
SPERATTI, Celsa, 1012
SPERATTI, Facunda
    see SPERATTI DE YEGROS, Josefa Facunda
SPERATTI DE YEGROS, Josefa Facunda, 987, 1042
SPERONI, David, 68
SPERONI, Horacio Agustín, 923
SPERONI, Roberto Themis, 663
SPICZCHYSKI, Enrique
    see SPITCZYNSKI, Enrique
SPIKA, Augusto, 998
SPIKA, Enrique, 238
SPIKERMAN, Andrés, 1059, 1111
SPIKERMAN, Juan Nicomedes, 1059, 1111
SPILIMBERGO, Lino Eneas, 18, 19, 23, 25, 31, 34, 36,
    38, 44, 45, 50, 55, 521, 1218
SPINADEL, Erico, 923
SPINDOLA, Domingo, 878
SPINELLI, Ermelinda (THELMA, Linda, pseud.), 868
SPIRO, Miguel Samuel, 14
SPITCZYNSKI, Enrique (SPICZCHYSKI, Enrique,
    SPITZCHCKI, Enrique), 238

SPITZCHCKI, Enrique
    see SPITCZYNSKI, Enrique
SPIVACOFF DE YAGUPSKY, Noemí, 874
SPREAFICO, Juan Carlos, 882
SPUCH, Martín
    see SPUCH MARTÍNEZ, Martín
SPUCH MARTÍNEZ, Martín, 284, 844
SPURR, Federico, 202
SQUEO ACUÑA, Francisco, 759
SQUIRE, John, 587
SQUIRRU, Rafael, 717
SQUIVO, Carlos María, 18
STACY, Roberto, 82
STADEN, Hans, 985
STAFFIERI, Juan José, 923
STAGNARO, Orlando, 19
STAGNARO, Santiago, 102, 681
STAGNERO DE MUNAR, María, 1083, 1217
STAGNI, Adolfo, 952
STANCHINA, Lorenzo, 1245
STAPLES, Roberto P., 573
STARSZY, Ricardo, 238
STAVELIUS, Federico, 322
STEARNS, George Albert, 323
STEARNS, John William, 323
STEARNS, Julia Adelaide Hope, 323
STEFANICH, Juan, 959, 1020
STEFFENS SOLER, Carlos, 431
STELARDO, Milton, 739, 1183, 1186, 1196
STELZAR (family), 168
STELLA MARIS, pseud.
    see MILESI, María Esther
STERMAN, Mario, 775
STERN, Grete, 55
STETTLER (family), 168
STEVENS, Jeanette
    see STEVENS, Mary Jeanette
STEVENS, Mary Jeanette, 323, 930
STEVENSON, Peter John, 954
STEWART, Duncan, 1079
STEWART, Tomás B., 904
STEWART, William, 961
STIATTESI, César Alberto, 882
STIEBEN, Enrique, 768
STIEFEL DE ORIAS, Noemí, 691
STILERMAN, Rosa, 31
STILMAN, Eduardo, 728
STIMM, Osvaldo, 49
STIPANICIC, Pedro Nicolás, 923
STIRLING, Waite H., 99
STOCK, Guillermo, 669
STOLL, Antonio, 760, 779
STOLL, Walter Clericus, 923
STOPPANI, Andrés Oscar M., 923
STORM, Ricardo, 1206, 1207
STORNI, Alfonsina, 154, 219, 258, 478, 521, 674, 678,
    711, 722, 723, 735, 737, 739, 740, 748, 751, 755,
    759, 762, 773, 782, 783, 803, 807, 926, 928, 929
STORNI, Arturo, 260
STORNI, Eduardo Raúl, 824
STRANGFORD, Percy Clinton Sydney Smuthe, 6th Viscount,
    514, 597
STRAUSS, Eduardo, 91
STRAY, Adolfo, 857d
STREVI, Emilio de (MANTELLI, Juan de, pseud.), 1265
STROBEL, Matías, 989
STROBEL, Pelegrino, 113, 258, 332
STROCEN, Stefan, 36, 46, 49
STROEDER, Hugo, 68
STROESSNER, Alfredo, 935, 943a, 954, 975

STRONG, Sarah, 323
STRUBBIA, Mario, 659
STUART, Robin, 904
STURLA, Santiago G., 681
STUTZ, 59
SUÁREZ (family), 352
SUÁREZ, Aurora, 751, 762
SUÁREZ, Buenaventura, 149, 318, 845, 846, 850, 885, 922, 949
SUÁREZ, Enrique, 785
SUÁREZ, Felipe, 878
SUÁREZ, Félix, 278
SUÁREZ, Francisco, 458, 895
SUÁREZ, Gregorio, 1084
SUÁREZ, Isidoro, 222, 386, 611
SUÁREZ, Joannes, 1037
SUÁREZ, Joaquín, 1052, 1053, 1054, 1076, 1079, 1084, 1091, 1110, 1118
SUÁREZ, Jorge Roberto E., 923
SUÁREZ, José León, 751
SUÁREZ, Leopoldo, 198, 207, 560
SUÁREZ, Lorenzo, 555
SUÁREZ, María del Carmen, 759
SUÁREZ, Mariano, 599, 1094
SUÁREZ, Mario Eduardo, 810
SUÁREZ, Norberto, 691
SUÁREZ, Pablo, 60
SUÁREZ, Reinaldo J., 652
SUÁREZ, Rudecindo, 878
SUÁREZ, Vicente, 377
SUÁREZ AYALA, Marcial, 1017
SUÁREZ CORDERO, Gregorio, 649a
SUÁREZ DE BONNIN, Concepción, 320
SUÁREZ DE CANTILLANA, Lorenzo, 1041
SUÁREZ DE CARVAJAL, Alvaro, 1238
SUÁREZ DE FIGUEROA, Lorenzo, 520, 620
SUÁREZ DE GÓMEZ, Rosa, 930, 931
SUÁREZ DE LA CONCHA, Melchor, 32
SUÁREZ DE MACEDO, Jorge, 318
SUÁREZ DE PERCEVAL, Filarmida Alejandrina, 874
SUÁREZ DE ROMERO, Micaela, 422
SUÁREZ DE TOLEDO, Martín, 254, 984, 1011
SUÁREZ DEL RONDELO, Joaquín, 1063
SUÁREZ GARCÍA, Francisco, 284
SUÁREZ LAGO, Gilberto, 207
SUÁREZ LYNCH, B., pseud.
     see BIOY CASARES, Adolfo
          BORGES, Jorge Luis
SUÁREZ MALDONADO, Hernán, 97, 186
SUÁREZ MARZAL, Julio, 25, 31
SUÁREZ NÚÑEZ, Nemesio, 1210
SUÁREZ PEDREIRA, José, 1089
SUÁREZ PICALLO, Ramón, 284
SUÁREZ SALGADO, Francisco, 284
SUÁREZ SEDRASCHI, Juan Emilio, 1210
SUÁREZ URTUBEY, Pola, 521
SUÁREZ VIGNOLO, Alberto Clemente, 1210
SUÁSNABAR, María, 154
SUÁVEZ, Manuel, 896
SUBIATEBEHERE, Angélica, 320
SUBIATEBEHERE, Antonia, 320
SUBIELA, Eliseo, 857d
SUBIRATS, Ramón, 154
SUBIZA, Pascual, 268
SÚCARI, Rafael David, 705
SUCRE, Antonio José de, 244, 453, 553
SUDNIK, Ricardo, 238
SUEIRO, Manuel A., 385
SUEIRO SEGAT, María Magdalena, 1210
SUELDO, Horacio Jorge, 218

SUERO, Manuel, 44
SUERO, Pablo, 645
SUERO, Tomás, 923
SUFFERN, Carlos, 882
SULIVA, Gregorio, pseud.
     see MACIEL, Miguel Elías
SULLIVAN, 580
SUNBLAD, Enrique, 3
SUNOIS, Melitón I., 1169
SUÑER, Antonio Armando, 923
SUÑER Y CAPDEVILLA, Francisco, 1094, 1261
SUPERI, José, 496
SUPERVIELLE, Jules, 894, 1079, 1145, 1153, 1177, 1181, 1187, 1199
SUPISICHE, Ricardo, 18, 25, 31, 36, 44, 55
SUPISICHE, Zacarías, 17b
SUPPARO, Atilio, 894, 1167, 1243
SURAN, Margarita de, 810
SURDI, Baldassarre, 292
SURRACO, Luis A., 1073
SUS, Victoria, 785
SUSINI, Antonio, 258, 292
SUSINI, Enrique T., 718
SUSINI, Jorge A., 268
SUSINI, Telémaco, 842, 844, 1261
SUSNIK, Branislava, 943, 962, 963a
SUSO, José Benito
     see SUSSO, José Benito
SUSSINI, Marcelino R., 671
SUSSO, José Benito, 254, 258
SUSVIELA (family), 1108
SUSVIELA, Juan, 1093a
SUSVIELA, Vicente Ramón, 254
SUSVIELA GUARCH, Federico, 1083
SUTTI, Marcelo Rafael, 653
SUX, Alejandro, 751
SUYAI AGUILAR, Laura, 810
SVANASCINI, Osvaldo, 19, 25, 31, 46, 658, 671, 672, 722, 739, 772, 807, 816
SWANN, Matilde Alba, 663
SYLVA, Nuño da, 28
SYLVESTER, Santiago E., 653, 654
SZELAGOWSKI, Miguel, 238
SZIDAT, Lother Carl Wilhelm, 923
SZPUNGERG, Alberto, 759
SZTYRLE, Tadeo, 238
SZUCHET DE DERECHIN, Sara, 923

TABACA, 977
TABACAMBI, 977
TABANERA, Abelardo, 207
TABANERA, Rafael, 878
TABARÉ, 977
TABARES, Ramón, 1075
TABBUSH, Bertha L. de, 751
TABENERA, Exequiel, 207
TABOADA, Ana María, 264
TABOADA, Antonino, 264, 632
TABOADA, Antonio María, 264, 921, 982, 991
TABOADA, Diógenes, 81, 222
TABOADA, Edgar F., 954
TABOADA, Eusebio, 947
TABOADA, Felipe, 264
TABOADA, Gaspar, 264
TABOADA, Juan Tomás, 264
TABOADA, Manuel, 264
TABOADA, María, 921
TABOADA, Rufino, 991
TABORDA, Saúl, 119
TABORDA, Wenceslao, 543

TABORGA, Benjamín, 773, 807
TACCA, Oscar, 191
TACCONI, Emilio Carlos, 1179
TAFORO, Bernardo, 17a, 284
TAGINI, Armando José, 871
TAGLE, Armando, 743
TAGLE, Carlos, 445
TAGLE, Gregorio, 496, 552, 554, 611
TAGLE LARA, Benjamín, 871
TAGLIABUE, Federico J., 68
TAITETÚ, 977
TAJANI, Miguel, 923
TAJES, Máximo, 1075, 1079, 1091, 1109, 1129
TAJES, Raúl Walter, 691
TAJES, Ricardo, 1085
TAJES, Salvador, 1075
TAL, Florindo, 190
TALAFORO, Bernardo, 922
TALAVERA, José Joaquín, 995a
TALAVERA, Manuel Antonio, 943, 947, 993
TALAVERA, María, 1020
TALAVERA, Natalicio de María, 943, 947, 963, 964,
    988, 1003, 1012, 1014, 1018, 1020, 1021, 1022,
    1024, 1026
TALAVERA DE FRACCHIA, Ida, 1014
TALEISNIK, Samuel, 923
TALERO, Eduardo, 152a, 167, 1246
TALICE, Roberto A., 644a, 889, 894
TALLARICO, Luis Antonio, 923
TALLÓN, José Sebastián, 235, 722, 739, 748, 751,
    759, 773, 782, 833
TAMATÍA, 977
TAMAYO SÁNCHEZ, Antonio, 1210
TAMBABÉ , 977
TAMBATAY, 977
TAMBERLICK, 859
TAMBORINI, José P., 565
TAMBOY, 977
TAMBURINI, Francisco, 6
TAMINI, Luis, 258
TAMISIER DE BOULIN, Lubila, 874
TAMPIERI, Ricardo, 258
TAMPIERI DE ESTRELLA, Susana, 683a
TANCO, Miguel Aníbal, 385
TANIA, 862
TANK, Willy, 602
TANNCHEN, Rodolfo A., 652
TANNI, Angelita, 859
TANNI, Marcelo, 859
TANNI, María, 859
TANNI, Pascual, 859
TANODI, Aurelio, 652
TANTIN, pseud.
    see SABORIDO, Dardo Ernesto
TAPARÍ, 977
TAPIA (family), 348
TAPIA, Cristino, 892
TAPIA, Juan Bautista, 19, 25, 31, 33
TAPIA, Mercedes, 227
TAPIA, Numa, 923
TAPIA DE LESQUERRE, Lola, 894
TAQUINI, Alberto C., 923
TARALLI, Ricardo Dino, 804
TARANTINO, Graciela, 695, 702
TARASIDO, Elena, 46
TARAZI, Hortensia, 31
TARDAGUILA TEJEDA, Rubén Carlos, 1210
TARNASSI, Antonio, 258, 648, 649
TARNASSI, Giuseppe, 258, 292
TARNASSI, Pablo, 258, 292

TARRAF, Adela, 717, 725, 739, 758, 807
TARRAGONA, Francisco, 126
TARRAGONA, José Ramón, 845
TARRAGONA, Juan Francisco, 478, 479
TARSIA, Ana, 55
TARTABULL, Higinio, 280
TARTARINI, Carlos, 37
TARTAS, Estanislada, 478
TASCHERET, Carlos A., 874
TASCHERET, Carlos María, 874, 878
TASSAERT, Francisco Octavio, 1046
TASSO, Adolfo Pedro, 560
TASSO, José del, 32
TAST, Esteban, 7
TATA GENERAL, pseud.
    see MANSILLA, Lucio Víctor
TATAENDI, 977
TATAGUAZÚ, 977
TATAURANA, 977
TATTI, Silvio, 68
TAU, Alberto Ricardo, 41
TAUPA, 977
TAUREL, Luis F., 332
TAURIELLO, Antonio, 883
TAVANO, Beatriz E., 652
TAVASCIO, Adolfo, 31
TAVELLA (brothers), 139
TAVELLA, Pietro, 139
TAVELLA, Roberto José, 135, 910
TAVERNA (family), 168
TAVERNA IRIGOYEN, J. M., 837
TAVOLARA, José, 1185
TAVOR, 977
TAX, pseud.
    see DÍAZ, Teófilo Eugenio
TAYAOBA, 977
TAYAOY, 977
TAYLOR, Eduardo, 6
TAYLOR, Tomás, 611
TAYUBAY, 977
TEALDI, Héctor, 889
TEALDI, Osvaldo Leónidas, 923
TEALDI SÁNCHEZ, Raúl, 1210
TEANA, Marino Di
    see DI TEANA, Marino
TECHO, Nicolás del, 761, 949, 960, 964, 966, 968,
    985, 1035
TEDESCO, Luis O., 759
TEDESCHI, Alejandro, 258
TEDESQUI, Nicolás M., 539
TEDÍN, José Toribio, 625
TEDÍN, Miguel, 332
TEIJEIRO MARTÍNEZ, Benigno, 284
TEISAIRE, Eduardo, 207
TEJADA GÓMEZ, Armando, 683a, 716, 759, 790, 809,
    1243
TEJEDA, Clara de, 913
TEJEDA, Fernando de, 913
TEJEDA, Leonor de
    see GUZMÁN Y MEJÍA, Leonor
TEJEDA, Luis de, 683, 734, 737, 740, 761, 921, 1257
TEJEDA, Luis José de
    see TEJEDA Y GUZMÁN, Luis José de
TEJEDA, María de, 913
TEJEDA, Sebastián de, 913
TEJEDA, Tristán de, 144, 205, 520, 913
TEJEDA MIRABAL, Juan de, 913
TEJEDA Y GUZMÁN, Luis José de, 144, 244, 507, 664,
    754, 803, 807
TEJEDA Y MEJÍA, Leonor de, 316, 913

TEJEDOR, Carlos, 166, 244, 391, 404, 544, 585, 611, 631, 633
TEJEDOR, Jaime, 895
TEJERA, Angel, 1045
TEJERINA, Baltasar, 844, 1261, 1262
TEJERINA FOTHERINGHAM, Wenceslao, 923
TEJERINA Y MEDINA, María Antonia, 541
TEJO, Abelardo J., 923
TEJÓN, Manuel R. (NOLO, pseud.), 874
TELECHEA NEVES, Eduardo Luis, 1210
TELÓ, Aldo, 874
TELLERÍA, Gregorio, 126
TELLERÍA, Melchor, 126
TELLES DE ROJAS, Ascensio, 846
TELLEZ, José Gaspar, 995a
TELLO, Estanislao L., 173
TELLO, Eugenio, 68, 385, 445
TELLO, Hipólito, 83
TELLO CORNEJO, Edmundo, 81
TELLO DE GUZMÁN, Fernando, 555
TEMPLE, Edmundo, 713
TENEMBAUM, León Isaac, 923
TENORIO, Josefa, 137
TENTI, Pedro, 19, 25
TEODORI, Ricardo, 258
TEPPA, Raúl, 37
TERÁN, Juan B., 116, 141, 167, 751
TERÁN, Manuel, 878
TERÉS, Bernardino, 892
TERLIZZI, Francisco, 952
TERMEYER, Ramón, 885
TERRA, Duvimioso, 1064, 1075, 1078, 1083, 1116
TERRA, Gabriel, 1073, 1083
TERRADA, Juan Florencio, 104, 478, 479, 496, 611
TERRADAS, Esteban, 923
TERRANOVA, Salvador, 874
TERRASSON, Eugenio, 268
TERRAZAS, Matías, 126
TERRAZAS, Melchor, 126
TERRAZAS, Pedro, 126
TERRERO, Juan Nepomuceno, 125, 910
TERRETAZ (family), 168
TERRIZZANO, Manuel Francisco María, 923
TERRY, José A., 19, 68, 141
TERUEL, Guillermo, 217
TERUGGI, Mario Egidio, 923
TESADA, Angel, 894
TESEYRA, Sergio Antonio, 653
TESSANDORI, Luis, 19, 31
TESSAROLO, Germán, 299
TESSI, Juan L., 923
TESTA, Clorindo, 25, 26, 31, 36, 46, 55
TESTA DE PEREIRA, Celia, 1088
TESTANOVA, Blas de, 949
TESTORI, Juan Carlos, 684
TEXEIRA DE HERNÁNDEZ, María Herminia, 1088
TEXIER, Felipe A., 135
TEXO, Federico, 68, 844
TEZANOS, Isaac de, 1112
TEZANOS PINTO, Fausto de, 713
TEZANOS PINTO, Jacobo de, 844
TEZANOS PINTO, Julio, 332
THAMES, José Ignacio, 439, 457, 478, 526, 611, 621, 626
THEISS, H., 602
THELMA, Linda, pseud.
    see SPINELLI, Ermelinda
THEMIS SPERONI, Roberto, 759, 805, 831
THENON, Susana, 725
THIBÓN DE LIBIÁN, Valentín, 18, 19, 25, 31, 33, 44, 1218

THIEBERGER, Pedro Arnoldo, 923
THOMAS, Antonio, 1238
THOMAS, Guillermo, 788
THOMAS, Karl H., 954
THOME, John M. (Mrs.)
    see WALL, Frances Angeline
THOMKINSON, Tomás, 1084
THOMPSON, Casildo G., 137
THOMPSON, Isaac, 82
THOMPSON, Juan, 206, 254
THOMPSON, Martín Jacobo, 14, 17a, 130, 478, 479, 496
THORMÄHLEN DE GIL, Ana Luisa, 923
THORNE, Juan Bautista, 14
THOUAR, M., 949
TIARYÚ, José, 977
TIBERIO, Oscar, 669
TIBERTI, María Dhialma, 725
TIBILETTI, Dionisio P., 910
TIBILETTI, Eduardo, 135, 241
TIDONE, Jorge, 817
TIEMPO, César, pseud.
    see ZEITLIN, Israel
TIEMPO, Julio César (CHONCHÓN, pseud.), 965
TIGERO (family), 348
TIGLIO, Marcos, 18, 19, 23, 25, 31, 36
TIL NEGRETE, Carlos, 186
TILCARA, 977
TINAYRE, Daniel, 858
TINELLI, Mafalda, 683a
TINEO, Manuela, 456
TINTO, José Caludio, 923
TISCORNIA, Eleuterio Felipe, 135, 688
TISERA LÓPEZ, Gregorio E., 923
TISNÉS (family), 364
TISSERA, Juan Capistrano, 910
TITA, pseud.
    see QUEIROLA, Aída
TITOLO, Joaquín M. José, 923
TIZERIO, Delia Etelvina, 320
TIZÓN, Angel, 1089
TIZÓN, Héctor, 689, 713, 730
TIZÓN COVELLO, Indalecio, 702
TIZZERIO, Elvira Margarita, 320
TOBAR Y OSORIO BALDES, Antonio, 914
TOBARES, Jesús Liberato, 222
TOCCO (family), 353
TOCORNAL, Fermín de, 496
TODD, José María, 653, 654
TOGNAZZI, Guillermina, 684
TOGNOCHI, Carlos Maeso, 1179, 1199
TOGNON, Juan Francisco, 923
TOIBERMAN, Marta, 785
TOICT, Nicolas du
    see TECHO, Nicolás del
TOLEDO (family), 1108
TOLEDO, Antonio Sebastián de, 344
TOLEDO, Bernardino, 914
TOLEDO, Francisco de, 521
TOLEDO, Paula, 781
TOLEDO DÍAZ, José Francisco, 1210
TOLEDO PERLAS, Pedro Héctor, 1210
TOLEDO PIMENTEL (family), 352
TOLEDO PIMENTEL, Fernando de, 520
TOLEDO PIMENTEL, Víctor, 679
TOLEDO Y PIMENTEL, Pedro José, 126
TOLOSA, Victoriano, 921
TOLL, Antonio, 17
TOMAE, Mauricio A., 923
TOMÁN, Miguel L., 652
TOMÁS, Antonio, 32, 992

TOMASELLO, Luis, 25
TOMASINI, Pablo J. F., 320
TOMASZEWSKI, Alberto, 238
TOMASZEWSKI, Eduardo, 238
TOMAT-GUIDO, Francisco, 739
TOMATIS, Alejandro Santiago, 19
TOMATIS, Santiago, 31
TOMBA, Antonio, 98
TOMBETTA, Luis Alberto, 1210
TOMBEUR FERRARO, Edmundo, 1006
TOMEI, Odino, 683a
TOMEY, J. Víctor, 811
TOMKINSON (family), 1108
TOMMASI, Hercilia H., 700
TONCOVICH DE BARASSI, Beatriz, 691
TONINA, Alfredo Felipe, 312
TONINA, Teodoro Andrés, 923
TORALES, Eladio, 954
TORANZO DE ZAVALLA, Borja, 931
TORANZOS, Fausto I., 923
TORANZOS, Lázaro Benjamín, 923
TORANZOS BARDEL, Fortunato, 1014, 1017, 1020
TORELLO, Pablo, 69
TORIBIO, Luis, 1265
TORIBIO, Tomás, 7
TORINO, Antonio, 918
TORINO, David Michel, 260, 560
TORINO, Enrique, 89
TORINO, Juan, 258
TORINO, Martín, 258, 385, 565
TORMO, Antonio, 874
TORNQUIST, Ernesto, 141
TORNÚ, Enrique, 275, 854
TORO, Benjamín, 653, 654
TORO, Reginaldo, 910
TORO Y VILLALOBOS, Manuel de, 107
TORORA, Juan, pseud.
     see ESCAYOLA, Juan
TORRÁ, Celia, 135, 881, 883, 894
TORRALLARDONA, Carlos A., 19, 25, 31, 36, 55
TORRE, Alonso de, 1034
TORRE, Antonio de la, 722, 739, 751, 831, 1082
TORRE, Buenaventura de la, 1082
TORRE, Carlos de la, 19, 31
TORRE, Domingo de la, pseud.
     see PULEIO, Domingo
TORRE, Guillermo de, 729, 743
TORRE, Lisandro de la, 72, 246, 259, 469, 478, 503, 582, 589, 591
TORRE, Luis Ceferino de la, 1111
TORRE, Manuel Antonio de la, 907, 910, 911, 917, 920, 1041
TORRE, Raúl de la, 857
TORRE BERTUCCI, José, 882, 883
TORRE DE TUDELA, Blanca Dalla
     see DALLA TORRE DE TUDELA, Blanca
TORRE NILSSON, Leopoldo, 857, 857b, 858
TORRE REVELLO, José, 609
TORRE Y SOLER, Manuel José de la, 97
TORRE Y VERA, Mariano Javier de la, 1236
TORRE Y ZÚÑIGA, Luis de la, 921
TORREA, Niceto Horacio, 923
TORREBLANCA, Hernando de, 319
TORRECILLAS, Basilio, 496
TORRECILLAS, C. Tubio, 751
TORREGIANI, Guiseppe, 292
TORRENS, Felipe, 982
TORRENS, Henry, 587
TORRENS, Manuel José, 254
TORRENT, Luciano, 254, 634, 845
TORRES (family), 352

TORRES, Alonso de, 556
TORRES, Ana María, 656
TORRES, Angel, 995a
TORRES, Antonio, 679
TORRES, Belindo Adolfo, 923
TORRES, Brian Andrés Esteban, 1210
TORRES, Carlos Alberto, 768
TORRES, Carlos Zacarías, 1017
TORRES, Diego de, 244, 885, 968, 989
TORRES, Domingo, 949
TORRES, Elena, 655, 656
TORRES, Eusebio, 951
TORRES, Feliciana, 250
TORRES, García de
     see GARCÍA DE TORRES
TORRES, Gregorio, 62
TORRES, Hilario Manuel, 496
TORRES, Horacio Agustín, 923
TORRES, Jorge Félix, 923
TORRES, José Antonio, 254
TORRES, José María, 317, 324
TORRES, Lorenzo, 185, 247
TORRES, Lucas, 32
TORRES, Manuel de, 272, 885
TORRES, Máximo, pseud.
     see MAESO, Carlos M.
TORRES, Pedro de, 32
TORRES, Pelgrino, 878
TORRES, Prudencio, 222
TORRES, Sebastián de, 496
TORRES, Tomás de, 529a, 649a, 910, 913, 1041
TORRES, Tomás Toribio Domingo, 32, 529a
TORRES, Ulises, 807
TORRES AGÜERO, Leopoldo, 19, 25, 31, 36
TORREZ ANTÚNEZ, César, 1017
TORRES BOLLO, Diego de, 1035a, 1035b, 1267
TORRES CALDERA, Lorenzo, 1094
TORRES DE VERA Y ARAGÓN, Juan, 196, 197, 570, 640, 1011
TORRES FRÍAS, María, 653, 654, 751, 762
TORRES-GARCÍA, Joaquín, 1184, 1218
TORRES GINART, Luis, 1068, 1145
TORREZ LÓPEZ, Ciro, 653, 654
TORRES NAVARRETE, Juan, 984
TORRES NORRY, José, 923
TORRES RÍOS, Leopoldo, 858
TORRES Y ARRIETA, Domingo de, 179, 254
TORRICO M., Rafael A., 923
TORROJA, Enrique
     see TORROJA, Miguel Enrique
TORROJA, Miguel Enrique, 35, 55
TORROME, Francisco, 268
TORTOLA VALENCIA, Carmen, 892
TORTOSA GALBIS, Juan, 954
TOSAR ERRECART, Héctor, 1206, 1207
TOSCANO, Alberto O., 882
TOSCANO, Nicolás, 768
TOSCANO DE LA RIVERA, Andrea, 1114
TOSO, Marcela Rosa, 691
TOSTO, Pablo, 25
TOTILON, 361
TOTO, pseud.
     see LOFEUDO, Pedro
TOUANNE, Edmond B. de la, 28
TOUNENS, Aurelio Antonio, 470
TOUNENS, Orllie Antoine de, 100, 101
TOVAR, Antonio, 521
TOZZI, Dante A., 65
TRABUCCO, Alberto J., 23, 25, 31, 50
TRAINI, Roberto, 698
TRÁPANI, Jacinto, 1059, 1111

TRÁPANI, Pedro, 1111, 1212
TRAVERSA, Julio C., 893
TRAVERSO, Lorenzo Juan, 871
TRAVERSO DE CASTELLI, María del Carmen, 328
TRAVIESO, Carlos, 1083
TRAVNIK, Juan, 55
TREBE, Zoilo, 941
TRÉGENT, Agnes Inés Emma, 323
TREIN DE MAUBACH, Ilse, 652
TREJO, César Anselmo, 923
TREJO, Esteban Severo, 285
TREJO, Mario, 658, 672, 717, 739, 758, 759, 807, 832
TREJO, Nemesio, 152a, 167, 727, 811, 813, 878, 890,
    1243, 1246, 1247
TREJO Y SANABRIA, Fernando de, 89, 244, 529a, 906,
    910, 913, 914, 921, 963, 1012, 1264
TREJO Y SANABRIA, Hernando de
    see TREJO Y SANABRIA, Fernando de
TRELLES, Francisco, 640
TRELLES, José Alonso (VIEJO PANCHO, El, pseud.),
    767, 1079, 1145, 1154, 1248
TRELLES, Manuel Ricardo, 166, 314, 609, 644
TRELLES, Pedro de, 555
TRENTI ROCAMORA, José Luis, 283
TRENTIN, Pompeyo, 258
TREVIÑO, Antonieta de, 702
TRIANES, Francisco J., 207
TRÍAS, Vivian, 1184
TRIAY, Bartolomé, 1094
TRIGO, Juan Carlos, 836
TRIGUERO DE BARBIERI, Beatriz, 320
TRIGUEROS, Natividad C., 652
TRILLO, Diego, 108
TRILLO, Magdalena, 130
TRINCHERO, Luis, 258
TRINIDAD, Gualdalupe, 954
TRIPI DE MÁRQUEZ, Ana, 691
TRÍPOLI, Vicente, 811
TRISTÁN, pseud.
    see GINZO, José Antonio
TRISTANY, Manuel Rogelio, 649
TROCHE, Julio César, 954
TROCHE, Mauricio José, 979, 987, 1012
TROIANI, Cayetano, 865, 882, 883
TROIANI, Troiano, 19, 21, 25, 64
TROILO, Aníbal, 862, 877
TROISI, Eugenio, 154
TROLÉ, Domingo, 433
TROLÉ, Eduardo, 332
TROMBERT (family), 168
TRON, Marta C. de (family), 168
TRON, Pablo (family), 168
TRONCOSO, Francisco Xavier, 126
TRONCOSO, Vicente, 7
TRONCOSO DE BURKHART, Nélida S., 923
TRONGÉ, Eduardo, 871
TRONGÉ, Faustino Juan, 718
TROTTA, Francisco, 1122
TROZZO, Esther, 683a
TRUCCO, Enrico P., 139
TRUCCO, Orestes A., 857
TRUCCO, Raúl Esteban, 923
TRUCCO DE CURUBETO GODOY, María Isabel, 873, 882, 883
TRUELLA, Pedro, 885
TRUGONI, Emilio, 1188
TRUJILLO, Rafael Leónidas, 368, 530
TRUSSO, Francisco Eduardo, 521
TSCHAPEK, Marcos, 923
TSCHOPP (family), 168
TUCA, 977

TUCADÁN, 977
TUCAMBI, 977
TUDELA, Ricardo, 683a, 743, 759
TUDURY, Gabriel Joaquín, 6
TUERTO SARMIENTO, El, pseud., 13
TULACERBIN, Alonso de, 520
TULBOVITZ SHAITS, Elías, 1210
TUPAC AMARÚ
    see CONDORCANQUI, José Gabriel
TUPAMINI, 977
TUPÍ, El, pseud., 358
TURDERA, Rodolfo I., 766
TURENNE, Augusto, 1065, 1083, 1261
TURI, Rubén A., 135, 800
TURIENZO, José María, 1094
TURIO, Gerónimo, 268
TURLEY, James Roderick, 954
TURNER, Juan Carlos Manuel, 923
TURRILLO, César, 41
TURRÍN, Adolfo, 810
TURRÍN, Gino, 923
TURRÓ, Oscar Rafael, 923
TUSET, Ramón, 1089
TUVIANSKY, Adolfo, 684
TUXEN BANG, Carlos, 883
TVETHE, H. Magno, 332

UBALLES, Eufemio, 842, 844, 1261
UBEDA, Lola, 268
UBEDA, Manuel, 1205, 1206, 1207
UBILLA, Antonio María, 1093
UCAR, Emilio, 1178
UCELLI, Zulema, 879
UCHA, José, 312
UDAONDO, Guillermo, 122, 141, 391
UGALDE ZALAZAR, Juan de, 555
UGARTE, Floro M., 864, 865, 881, 883
UGARTE, Manuel, 152a, 669, 743, 751, 759, 773, 782,
    834, 1247
UGARTE, Marcelino, 68, 240, 391
UGARTE, Rosa Justiniana Josefa, 876
UGARTECHE, José Francisco de, 126, 947
UGARTEMENDIA, José Luis, 1094
UGAZZI, Sara del Carmen, 751
UGÓN, Rubén Armand, 1073
UHART, Hebe, 822
UHL, Carlos Guillermo, 51, 59
ULLA, Noemí, 772
ULLOA, Antonio de, 649a
ULLOA, Nicolás
    see ULLOA Y HURTADO DE MENDOZA, Nicolás de
ULLOA Y HURTADO DE MENDOZA, Nicolás de, 501, 529a,
    910
ULLÓS, Juan de, 1270
UMEREZ, Inés, 320
UNDIANO, Federico, 713
UNDIANO Y GASTELLÚ, Sebastián, 332
UNZUÉ, Francisco, 254
UNZUÉ, Mariano, 141
URALDE, Celina Haydée, 725, 739
URÁN, Julián, 1125
URANGA, Raúl Lucio, 95, 135
URBANSKI, Horacio, 663
URBIETA, Adonias Aurelio, 995a
URBIETA, Juan Gregorio, 1035, 1041
URBIETA, Milcíades, 998
URBIETA FLEITAS, Augusto, 954
URBINA, Francisco de, 556
URBINA, Saúl, 1093
URDANGARÍN, Héctor
    see GARINI, L. S., pseud.

URDAPILLETA, José Vicente, 129
URDINARRAIN, Manuel Antonio, 95, 96, 543
URDINOLA, Juan de, 555
URE, Alberto, 299
URE, María Inés, 656
URES CAAMAÑO, Lydia, 154
URIARTE, Carlos Enrique, 25, 31, 36
URIARTE, Domingo Santos de, 1056
URIARTE, Georgina de, 154
URIARTE, Higinio, 1011
URIARTE, José Eugenio de, 1267
URIARTE, Juan, 32
URIARTE, Pedro Francisco de, 439, 457, 478, 479,
     526, 611, 621, 626, 921
URIBE, Basilio, 739, 672
URIBURU, José Evaristo, 166, 282, 392, 393, 405, 466,
     478, 493, 515, 516, 521, 598, 619
URIBURU, José Félix, 269, 392, 405, 466, 515, 516,
     524, 558, 601, 619
URIBURU, Napoleón, 191, 617
URIEN, Carlos María, 167, 381a, 1246
URIEN, Domingo Ignacio, 254
URIEN, Isidoro, 254
URIEN, Juan Ramón, 496
URÍZAR, Esteban de
     see URÍZAR Y ARESPACOCHAGA, Estevan de
URÍZAR Y ARESPACOCHAGA, Estevan de, 32, 191, 529a,
     989
URONDO, Francisco, 672, 690, 739, 759, 801, 832
URQUÍA, Carlos Enrique, 717, 759
URQUIJO, José María Mariluz
     see MARILUZ URQUIJO, José María
URQUIOLA, Dionisio, 74
URQUIZA (family), 1106
URQUIZA, Carlos de, 332
URQUIZA, Cipriano J. de, 95, 241
URQUIZA, Diógenes J. de, 95, 96
URQUIZA, Justo José de, 70, 72, 78, 95, 96, 103, 105,
     118, 121, 127, 135, 140, 141, 143, 152a, 165,
     166, 185, 188, 212, 241, 244, 278, 282, 283, 325,
     327, 384, 386, 392, 393, 398, 404, 405, 418, 443,
     444, 446, 447, 452, 462, 469, 472, 476, 478, 488,
     489, 491, 502, 509, 512, 514, 515, 516, 518, 519,
     521, 528, 531, 533, 534, 545, 568, 585, 589, 594,
     596, 608, 611, 612, 619, 632, 924, 984, 1091
URRA, 179
URREJOLA, Franciscus, 1037
URRIBARRI, Alberto, 923
URRUCHÚA, Demetrio, 18, 25, 31, 36, 55, 64
URRUTIA, José Miguel, 923
URRUTIA, José V., 1093
URRUTIA, Lucas, 1140
URRUTIA, Nilda, 652
URRUTIA ARTIEDA, María Alex, 154, 783
URRUTIA ROSE, Gualberto María, 1210
URRUTIBEHEITY, Amelia, 663
URSÚA (family), 351
URTAFUN XAVIER, Martín, 1035a, 1035b
URTUBEY (family), 1108
URTUBEY, Clodomiro, 14, 17
URUNAGA, Joseph de, 1030
USANDIVARAS, Guillermo, 653, 654
USET, Aníbal, 857b
USHER, Mario, 959
UZAL, Enrique, 1243
UZTARIZ (family), 351

VAAMONDE CORNIDE, Joaquín, 284
VACA-NARVAJA, Jesús, 565
VACAREZZA, Alberto, 152a, 660, 727, 766, 813, 818,
     871, 890, 1243

VACCA, Alberto Hugo, 8
VACCANI, Miguel, 859
VACCAREZZA, Américo Justino, 923
VACCAREZZA, Andrés, 275
VACCAREZZA, Esteban, 73
VACCAREZZA, Raúl F., 923
VACCAREZZA, Roberto A., 275
VACCARI, Antonio, 258
VACCARI, Jorge, 299
VACCARO, Carlos Alberto, 8oo
VACHETTA PERALTA, Miguel, 947
VADELL, Miguel, 1223
VADELL, Natalio Abel, 751, 1145
VADELL, Ruperto, 1223
VAESKEN, Emilio, 1027
VAEZA (family), 1108
VAGHI, Virgilio, 258
VAINSTEIN, Alejandro, 31
VAISSEAU, Juan (VASEO), 866, 949, 960
VAIVIENE, Santiago, 258
VAL, Anidia, 923
VAL, Félix del, 319
VALCARCEL LOSADA, César, 284
VALDANI, Víctor, 258
VALDARENAS, Adoración, 684
VALDELIRIOS, Marqués de, 1262
VALDENEGRO, Eusebio, 876, 1057, 1199, 1256
VALDERRAMA, Luis de, 918
VALDÉS, Carmelo B., 381a
VALDÉS, Dámaso, 268
VALDÉS, Diego, 32
VALDÉS, Gerónimo, 1236
VALDÉS, Guillermo, 141
VALDÉS INCLÁN, Alonso
     see VALDEZ INCLÁN, Alonso Juan de
VALDEZ, Francisco M., 998
VALDEZ, Juan Bautista, 1210
VALDEZ, Mercedes, 973
VALDEZ, Pedro Luis, 973
VALDEZ, Tomasa, 973
VALDEZ INCLÁN, Alonso de, 521, 570, 1262
VALDEZ LEIVA, Elba, 768
VALDEZ MEDINA, Carlos Alberto, 1210
VALDEZ MELLO RIVERA, Virgilio, 1210
VALDEZ MORENO HEBER, Nelson, 1210
VALDIVIA (family), 366
VALDIVIA, Diego de, 186
VALDIVIA, Juan de, 186
VALDIVIA, Luis de, 188
VALDIVIA, Pedro de, 283
VALDIVIA Y ALDERETE, Juan Miguel de, 914
VALDIVIA Y BRIZUELA, Andrés de, 914
VALDOVINOS, Arnaldo, 1014, 1020
VALDOVINOS, Fermín, 995a
VALDOVINOS, Policarpo, 995a
VALDOVINOS C., Carlos Reinaldo, 998
VALENCIO, Daniel Alberto, 923
VALENTE, Horacio Omar, 860
VALENTI COSTA, Pedro, 865, 882, 883
VALENTINUZZI, Máximo, 923
VALENTINUZZI, Máximo Eugenio, 923
VALENZUELA, Andrés de, 1270
VALENZUELA, Bartolomé de, 914
VALENZUELA, Filomeno, 254, 283
VALENZUELA, Heliodoro, 995
VALENZUELA, Liberato, 998
VALERO, Bartolomé, 520, 1270
VALIENTE DE TEXADA (family), 351
VALIENTE NOAILLES, Luis, 332
VALMAGGIA, Juan S., 751

VALSEAU, Jean, 865
VALSECCHI, Francisco, 239
VALVANO, Jorge Aurelio, 923
VALVERDE, José, 1089
VALVERDE, Maximino, 1089
VALVERDE, Vicente, 32
VALLADARES, David de, 1020
VALLADARES, Leda, 679, 717, 725
VALLARINO, Domingo, 781
VALLE, del (family), 348
VALLE, Alejandro del, 32
VALLE, Alem del, 445
VALLE, Angel Della
    see DELLA VALLE, Angel
VALLE, Aristóbulo del, 72, 110, 116, 212, 219, 277,
    282, 389, 469, 478, 514, 550, 585, 692
VALLE, Delfor del, 69, 565
VALLE, Enrique Ricardo del, 652
VALLE, Francisco del, 318, 319
VALLE, Juan Agustín, 332
VALLE, María Remedios del, 492
VALLE, Mariano, 385
VALLE, Tomás, 126
VALLE HERRERA, Ramona del, 252
VALLE IBERLUCEA, Enrique del, 259, 503
VALLE LARRABURE, Argentino del, 8
VALLEGA, José, 923
VALLEJO, Antonio, 664, 833
VALLEJO, Benigno, 852
VALLEJO, Carlos María del, 1145
VALLEJO, César, 658
VALLEJO, Manuel Juan, 923
VALLEJO FERNÁNDEZ, María Antonia, 892
VALLEJO Y VILLASANTI, Tomás, 914
VALLEJOS, Beatriz, 659, 725
VALLEJOS, Héctor, 998
VALLEJOS, Manuel Antonio (Pájaro, El, pseud.), 92
VALLEJOS, María, 787
VALLEJOS, Roque
    see VALLEJOS PÉREZ GARAY, Roque
VALLEJOS PÉREZ GARAY, Roque, 1020, 1021, 1022, 1025
VALLESI, José Felipe, 874
VALLI, Giacomo, 139
VALLS, José, 923
VALLS Y VALLS, Luis, 1094
VAN HAATEN, J. A. J., 332
VAN NOORT, Olivier, 28
VANADIA, Mario, 857d
VANASCO, Alberto, 658, 672, 717, 739, 758, 759, 807
VANDREGISILO, 361
VANNI, Ricardo, 37
VANOSSI, Reinaldo, 923
VANZO, Julio, 31, 36
VAQUIÉ, Agustín, 268
VARALLA, Enrique George, 874
VARDANEGA, Gregorio, 25, 31, 49
VARDARO, Elvino, 891a
VARELA (family), 1108
VARELA, Felipe, 83, 188, 532, 632
VARELA, Florencio, 176, 210, 261, 282, 404, 459,
    466, 478, 480, 574, 586, 600, 643, 644, 669,
    692, 720, 751, 761, 763, 828, 1093a, 1110
VARELA, Guillermo, 1089
VARELA, Héctor Florencio, 121, 643
VARELA, Horacio C., 68
VARELA, Horacio J., 268
VARELA, Isidro, 1089
VARELA, Ismael Héctor (NEGRO, Héctor, pseud.), 660,
    717, 871
VARELA, Jacinto, 284

VARELA, Jacobo Adrián, 284
VARELA, José Pedro, 1052, 1053, 1054, 1071, 1076,
    1079, 1084, 1086, 1091, 1141, 1146, 1174, 1177,
    1188, 1199
VARELA, Juan de la Cruz, 145, 183, 206, 210, 216,
    379, 404, 574, 611, 643, 644, 669, 677, 720,
    723, 724, 733, 734, 737, 740, 751, 754, 761,
    763, 769, 803, 807, 828, 890
VARELA, Luis Alberto, 1075, 1151, 1179
VARELA, Luis Vicente, 643, 747, 894
VARELA, Mariano, 643
VARELA, Pedro, 1079, 1091, 1109
VARELA, Rufino, 332
VARELA, Victoriano, 1075
VARELA, Wenceslao, 1159
VARELA ACEVEDO, Jacobo, 1083
VARELA AÑÓN, Plácido, 1089
VARELA DOMÍNGUEZ DE GHIOLDI, Delfina, 222
VARELA GARCÍA, Antonio, 1089
VARELA ORTIZ, Rufino, 94
VARELA VIDAL, Antonio, 1089
VARELA Y ULLOA, José, 17a, 284
VARGAS (family), 1106
VARGAS, Angel María, 689, 707, 776, 779, 825, 829
VARGAS, Bernabé, 845
VARGAS, Bernardo de, 914
VARGAS, Eduardo, 1075
VARGAS, Florencio, 954
VARGAS, Hernando de, 467
VARGAS, Juan de, 914
VARGAS, Marcelino, 256
VARGAS, Milca María, 691
VARGAS, Pablo, 256
VARGAS, Rafael, 179, 874
VARGAS BELMONTE, Aristóbulo, 89
VARGAS DE CARVAJAL, Diego, 898
VARGAS GUILLEMETTE, Alvaro, 1073
VARGAS MACHUCA, Bernardo, 1203
VARGAS MACHUCA, Miguel, 947, 964
VARGAS PEÑA, José Federico Hernán, 954
VARGAS VIANA DE GARCÍA WICH, Paz de, 1093a
VARGAS VIDELA, Federico, 874
VARGAS VIDELA, Rodolfo, 874
VARNI DE NOEL, María Ruth, 320
VARSI, Tomás, 268
VASCO, Juan Antonio, 658
VASCONCELLOS, Bernardo de, 596
VASCONCELLOS, César, 953
VASCONCELLOS ORTÚZAR, Víctor Augusto Natalicio, 972
VASCHETTO, José, 87
VASENA, Jorge F. E., 923
VASENA, Leonor, 31
VASEO, Juan
    see VAISSEAU, Juan
VASILEF, Iván, 19, 25, 31
VÁSQUEZ (family), 1108
VÁSQUEZ, Aníbal S., 135
VÁSQUEZ, Francisco, 1270
VÁSQUEZ, Rafael Alberto, 801
VÁSQUEZ ACEVEDO, Alfredo, 1127
VASSENA, Leonor, 25, 46
VASSEUR, Alvaro Armando, 1079, 1083, 1147, 1151,
    1153, 1174, 1177, 1179, 1187, 1188, 1198, 1199,
    1259
VASSEUR, Armando
    see VASSEUR, Alvaro Armando
VATTEONE, Augusto César, 857c
VAZ DE ROSENDE, Francisco, 649a
VAZ FERREIRA, Carlos, 1069, 1079, 1083, 1086, 1146,
    1177, 1187, 1188, 1190, 1199

VAZ FERREIRA, María Eugenia, 1075, 1079, 1083, 1086, 1144, 1146, 1147, 1153, 1164, 1165, 1174, 1177, 1179, 1187, 1195, 1199, 1217, 1259
VÁZQUEZ, Abelardo, 683a, 739, 802
VÁZQUEZ, Antonio (Argentina), 683a
VÁZQUEZ, Antonio (Uruguay), 1089
VÁZQUEZ, Carlos Antonio, 995a
VÁZQUEZ, Daniel, 1089
VÁZQUEZ, Eduardo, 1075
VÁZQUEZ, Electra Haydée, 768
VÁZQUEZ, Franco P., 1093
VÁZQUEZ, Gustavo, 1049
VÁZQUEZ, Hilario, 1030
VÁZQUEZ, José, 1089
VÁZQUEZ, Juan, 344
VÁZQUEZ, Juan Adolfo, 239
VÁZQUEZ, Juan Carlos, 211
VÁZQUEZ, Juan Francisco, 995a
VÁZQUEZ, Laudelino, 1075, 1126
VÁZQUEZ, Maximiliano, 268
VÁZQUEZ, Modesto, 887
VÁZQUEZ, Pablo J., 878, 1243, 1247
VÁZQUEZ, Ramón S., 1094, 1095
VÁZQUEZ, Santiago, 1052, 1053, 1063, 1076, 1078, 1091, 1110, 1118, 1135
VÁZQUEZ, Ventura, 1063
VÁZQUEZ ACEVEDO, Alfredo, 1075, 1083, 1134
VÁZQUEZ CASTRO, Manuel, 284
VÁZQUEZ CEY, Arturo, 678, 751, 773
VÁZQUEZ CORES, Francisco, 1094, 1095
VÁZQUEZ DE LIANO, Tomás, 910, 1041
VÁZQUEZ DE MONTIEL, María del Carmen (RÍOS, Concepción, pseud.), 711, 762
VÁZQUEZ DE CARRIL, Pedro, 283
VÁZQUEZ GÓMEZ, Adolfo, 284
VÁZQUEZ ORTELLADO, Enrique, 1006
VÁZQUEZ PRESEDO, Vicente, 265
VÁZQUEZ RIVERA, Ernesto, 791
VÁZQUEZ ROSSI, Jorge, 824, 831
VÁZQUEZ SAGASTUME, José, 1112, 1188
VÁZQUEZ TRUJILLO, Francisco, 1267
VÁZQUEZ Y VEGA, Prudencio, 1146, 1199
VECINO, Ricardo, 1083
VECCHIOLI, Francisco, 19, 31, 45
VECCHIOLI, Mario R., 837
VECHI, Horacio, 1035a, 1035b
VEDIA, Agustín de, 277, 1075, 1112, 1117, 1126, 1146, 1188
VEDIA, Delfina de
    see VEDIA DE MITRE, Delfina
VEDIA, Enrique de, 68, 152a, 167
VEDIA, Joaquín, 277, 894
VEDIA, José Joaquín de, 834
VEDIA, Julio de, 191, 285, 611
VEDIA, Leónidas de, 235, 743
VEDIA, Mariano de (CANCIO, Juan, pseud.), 94, 167, 240
VEDIA, Nicolás de, 496, 552, 611
VEDIA DE MITRE, Delfina de, 478, 929
VEDIA Y MITRE, Emilio de, 560
VEDOYA DE MOLINAS, Dolores, 422
VEGA, Agustín de, 1041
VEGA, Alonso de la, 1262
VEGA, Benjamín de la, 83
VEGA, Blanca de la, 154
VEGA, Carlos, 154, 217, 678, 751, 833, 865, 882
VEGA, Diego de la, 496
VEGA, Elena O., 652
VEGA, Félix, 878
VEGA, Fernando de la, 299
VEGA, Jorge Luis de la, 18, 31, 36, 46, 55
VEGA, José, 923

VEGA, José Antonio de la, 328
VEGA, María de las Mercedes, 222
VEGA, Milagros de la, 857d
VEGA, Néstor W., 683a
VEGA, Niceto, 196
VEGA, Nicolás, 611
VEGA, Santos, 1243
VEGA, Silvia
    see EISENSTEIN DE VEGA, Silvia
VEGA, Ventura de la, 664, 761, 763, 807, 828, 888
VEGA, Vilma, 683a
VEGA BELGRANO, Carlos, 478
VEGA DÍAZ, Dardo de la, 381a
VEGA SARMIENTO, Micaela de, 931
VEGHETTI, Oscar César (CHOLO, pseud.), 860
VEIA DE GARCÍA KINENE, Alcira, 1014
VEIGA, Francisco de
    see VEYGA, Francisco de
VEIRAVÉ, Alfredo E., 135, 191, 661, 716, 717, 739, 759, 801, 802
VELA, Rubén, 658, 716, 717, 739, 798, 802, 832
VELA, Vicente, 73
VELA DE HINOJOSA, Jacinto, 186
VELARDE, Alberto Gastón, 923
VELASCO, Dolores, 189
VELASCO, Manuel Dionisio de, 126, 496
VELASCO, María Josefa de, 1010
VELASCO QUIROGA, Hilario, 683a
VELASCO Y HUIDOBRO, Bernardo de, 984
VELÁSQUES MELÉNDES, Francisco 186
VELÁSQUEZ, Agustín, 1111
VELÁSQUEZ, Crispín, 95, 543
VELÁSQUEZ, Héctor, 1002
VELASTIQUI, Francisco Javier, 995a
VELAUSTEGUI, Diego de, 540
VELAZCO, Ambrosio, 1112
VELAZCO, Bernardo de, 984, 1011
VELAZCO, Carlos A., 739, 802
VELAZCO, Diego de, 556
VELAZCO, Federico de, 1094
VELAZCO, Jorge, 207, 222
VELAZCO, Luis de, 1041
VELAZCO, Manuel de, 32, 555, 570
VELAZCO LOMBARDINI, Roberto, 1073
VELAZCO Y MAEDA, Luis de, 1034
VELAZCO Y TEXADA, Manuel de, 521
VELÁZQUEZ, Agustín, 1111
VELÁZQUEZ, Eladio
    see VELÁZQUEZ, Rafael Eladio
VELÁZQUEZ, Enrique, 998
VELÁZQUEZ, Ernesto, 959
VELÁZQUEZ, Felipe A., 222
VELÁZQUEZ, Fernando, 998
VELÁZQUEZ, Francisco, 318, 914
VELÁZQUEZ, Héctor, 959
VELÁZQUEZ, José María, 995a
VELÁZQUEZ, Luis Horacio, 663, 746, 766
VELÁZQUEZ, Rafael Eladio, 959, 966
VELAZZA, Héctor, 24
VELÉZ, Angelita, 154, 932
VELÉZ, Aurelia
    see VÉLEZ SARSFIELD DE ORTIZ, Aurelia
VÉLEZ, Bernardo
    see VÉLEZ GUTIÉRREZ, Bernardo
VÉLEZ, Ignacio, 244
VÉLEZ, Luis, 244
VÉLEZ, Mariano, 768
VÉLEZ GUTIÉRREZ, Bernardo, 611, 1264
VÉLEZ SARSFIELD, Aurelia
    see VÉLEZ SARSFIELD DE ORTIZ, Aurelia
VÉLEZ SARSFIELD, Bernardo, 244

VÉLEZ SARSFIELD, Dalmacio, 70, 72, 78, 79, 110, 121, 141, 166, 167, 244, 282, 293, 380, 384, 404, 450, 478, 491, 542, 544, 585, 631, 692, 924
VÉLEZ SARSFIELD, Rosario, 606
VÉLEZ SARSFIELD, Tomasa, 478, 929
VÉLEZ SARSFIELD DE ORTIZ, Aurelia, 450, 521, 564, 930
VELILLA, Benjamín, 943
VELILLA, Felipe, 1006
VELILLA, Hernán, 998, 1006
VELIZ DÍAZ, Arturo, 768
VELMONTE, Alonzo, 186
VELOSO NÚÑEZ, Francisco Raúl, 1210
VELOZO ZAPPINO, Carlos Hugo, 1210
VELLA, Juan Cayetano, 923
VELLA, Pedro, 190
VELLERCHE DE AGUIRRE, Félix Andrés, 1270
VENA, Angel Domingo, 31, 33
VENANCOURT, El Vizconde de, 1236
VENDRELL, 319
VENECIANO, Bernabé, 358
VENEGAS, Dionisio, 268
VENEGAS, Garci, 992
VENEGAS, José Clemente, 555
VENEZIANO, Marco, 292
VENEZIANO, Pietro, 292
VENIER, Bruno, 18, 19, 25, 31, 36, 46, 63
VENTRE, Andrés F., 69
VENTURA, 137
VENTURA, Félix, 914
VENTURA DÍAZ, pseud.
    see DÍAZ, Buenaventura
VENTURA FRÍAS, Juan, 845
VENTURA MORÓN, Juan, 283
VENTURA PERINI, Carlos, 952
VENTURINI, Aurora, 663, 725, 739, 805
VERA (family), 352
VERA, Bonifacio, 188, 412, 547, 549, 921
VERA, Daniel, 705
VERA, Eduardo, 974, 982
VERA, Francisco de, 914, 998
VERA, Héctor Luis, 998
VERA, Héctor Pablo, 923
VERA, Jacinto Cipriano, 1052, 1053, 1063, 1076, 1091, 1093
VERA, Jesús Ramón, 653
VERA, José Bernardo, 179
VERA, José Ignacio, 95
VERA, Justo Pastor, 959
VERA, Mariano, 106, 107, 477
VERA, Matilde A., 762
VERA, Miguela, 939
VERA, Octaviano S., 565
VERA, Optaciano Franco, 1014
VERA, Ricardo, 242
VERA, Víctor M., 963a
VERA ARENAS, Dolores Jesús, 874
VERA BARROS, Tomás, 83
VERA GRUHN, Rodolfo, 963a
VERA MARTÍNEZ, Carlos, 954
VERA MUGICA, Antonio de
    see VERA Y MUJICA, Antonio de
VERA VIVEROS, Helio 947
VERA Y ARAGÓN, Alonso de, 358, 1011
VERA Y MUJICA, Antonio de, 95, 477, 1011, 1262
VERA Y MUJICA, Francisco Antonio de, 477
VERA Y PINTADO, Bernardo de, 177, 611, 720, 761, 895
VERALLI, Horacio, 299
VERANDI, Mario, 663

VERAZZANI, Juan, 258
VERAZZI, Baldassare, 51, 59, 258, 521
VERAZZI, Baltasar
    see VERAZZI, Baldassare
VERBITSKY, Bernardo, 152a, 739, 817, 829
VERCHININA, Nina, 874
VERDAGUER, José Aníbal
    see VERDAGUER Y COROMINAS, José Aníbal
VERDAGUER Y COROMINAS, José Aníbal, 207, 283, 910
VERDE, José, 1089
VERDEMIRÓ, José, 1092
VERDÍA, Manuel, 1095
VERDINO, Daniel Atilio, 299
VERDÚ, Vicente Gregorio Mariano Buenaventura, 949, 1262
VEREA GARCÍA, Ramón, 284
VERGARA, Carlos N., 207
VERGARA, Eduardo, 268
VERGARA, Elvira, 652
VERGARA, Emmanuel de, 1036
VERGARA, Juan de, 1203, 1266
VERGARA, Manuel, 1267
VERGARA, Miguel Angel, 521, 653, 654, 713
VERGARA, Norberto Carlos de Corazón de Jesús, 317
VERGARA, Valentín, 391, 565
VERGIATI, Amleto
    see CENTEYA, Julián, pseud.
VERGUERO, Diego, 845
VERMUDO I, 361
VERNA, Luis C., 923
VERNAZZA, Juan, 652
VERNENGO LIMA, Héctor, 461
VERNET, Louis, 143
VERNET, Malvina, 574
VERNÓN DE ASTRADA, Manuel, 1014, 1020
VERO, pseud.
    see DURBEC DE ROUTIN, Josefina
VERONELLI, Olga E., 652
VERONI, Raúl, 41
VERTIZ (family), 351
VERTIZ, Juan José de
    see VERTIZ Y SALCEDO, Juan José de
VERTIZ Y SALCEDO, Juan José de, 32, 95, 103, 108, 283, 321, 332, 471, 472, 489, 521, 570, 593, 890, 1237, 1239, 1240, 1241, 1262, 1264
VERVOORST, Federico Bernardo, 923
VES LOSADA, Eduardo, 284
VESPA, Ramón Horacio, 691
VESPIGNANI, José, 907a
VESPUCCI, Amérigo, 258, 448, 521
VESPUCIO, Americo
    see VESPUCCI, Amerigo
VETOLAZA Y LUNA, Juan Manuel, 898
VETOLAZA Y LUNA, Juan Vicente, 898
VETOLAZA Y MELÉNDEZ, Francisco Antonio de, 914
VEYGA, Francisco de, 192, 844
VIALE, Bartolomé, 258
VIALE, Luis, 258, 268
VIAMONTE, Jaime, 344
VIAMONTE, Juan José, 11a, 244, 282, 386, 404, 478, 479, 496, 521, 552, 574, 611
VIAMONTE DE ILLA, Valentina, 1093a
VIANA (family), 971, 1106, 1108
VIANA, Antonio, 7
VIANA, Enrique, 664
VIANA, Francisco Javier de, 89, 545a, 563, 611, 1056, 1063
VIANA, Javier de, 811, 813, 821, 834, 894, 1067, 1075, 1079, 1083, 1086, 1122, 1140, 1146, 1154, 1157, 1159, 1162, 1164, 1168, 1170, 1175, 1177,

1180, 1186, 1188, 1190, 1196, 1197, 1198, 1199, 1243, 1246, 1247, 1249, 1251, 1254, 1260
VIANA, José Joaquín de, 1065, 1136
VIANA, María Manuela de, 1223
VIANA DE LA MORA DE RODRÍGUEZ, Francisca Carlota, 971
VIANA DE VARGAS, Antonia, 1093a
VIANA Y ALZÁIBAR DE ORIBE, María Francisca de, 1065, 1066
VIANNA, Febrino L., 1093
VIC, Daniel, 698
VICENS THIEVENT, Lorenzo, 1145
VICENTÍN, Francisco, 910
VICIEN, Pedro, 923
VICTORIA, Antonio, 1011
VICTORIA, Francisco de, 103, 417, 529a, 906, 910, 1238, 1270
VICTORIA, Marcos, 739, 743, 746, 773
VICTORIA, Máximo S., 167
VICTORIA, Virgilio A., 923
VICTORICA, Benjamín, 17b, 68, 95, 96, 191, 447
VICTORICA, Bernardo de, 253
VICTORICA, Carlos M., 18
VICTORICA, Miguel Angel, 31
VICTORICA, Miguel Carlos, 19, 23, 25, 31, 34, 36, 38, 50, 55, 210, 521, 1218
VICTORICA, Ricardo, 751
VICCHI, Adolfo A., 207
VIDADEL OLIVERA, Angel, 874
VIDAL (family), 1108
VIDAL, Blanca, 893
VIDAL, Blas, 1083, 1095
VIDAL, Celestino, 860
VIDAL, Emeric Essex, 28, 32, 42, 59, 293
VIDAL, Eusebio, 1056
VIDAL, Flaminio, 923
VIDAL, Francisco, 19, 24, 31, 562
VIDAL, Francisco Antonio, 1079, 1091, 1109, 1125
VIDAL, José, 1089
VIDAL, José Francisco, 496
VIDAL, José Joaquín, 923
VIDAL, Juan Ramón, 429, 445
VIDAL, Justo G., 244
VIDAL, Mateo Lucas, 126
VIDAL, Miguel, 325, 917
VIDAL, Miguel Angel, 36, 38, 46, 55
VIDAL, Pedro Pablo, 921
VIDAL, Tita, 932
VIDAL BELO, Toribio, 1174, 1259
VIDAL BREARD, Juan José, 923
VIDAL DE BATTINI, Berta Elena, 154, 222, 762
VIDAL DEL SAR, José Francisco, 284
VIDAL FERNÁNDEZ, Maruja de, 751
VIDAL GONZÁLEZ, Julio César, 1210
VIDAL LUNA, Sadoc, 81
VIDAL MOLINA, Enrique, 717, 758
VIDAL PEÑA, Manuel, 240
VIDAL Y FUENTES, Alfredo, 1126
VIDART, Daniel D., 1179, 1184
VIDAURRE, Manuel Lorenzo de, 562
VIDELA (brothers), 480
VIDELA, Alonso de, 556, 1270
VIDELA, Andrés de, 555
VIDELA, Antonio, 137
VIDELA, Blas, 222
VIDELA, Clemente, 283
VIDELA, Dolores, 222
VIDELA, Eufrasio, 222
VIDELA, Heriberto, 874
VIDELA, Horacio, 283

VIDELA, Ignacio, 222
VIDELA, Jacinto, 222, 555
VIDELA, José Rafael, 81
VIDELA, Juan, 68
VIDELA, Juan Alberto, 768
VIDELA, Juan Amancio, 207
VIDELA, Juan de Dios, 212, 222
VIDELA, Juan José, 845
VIDELA, Lisandro, 198
VIDELA, Luis de, 222
VIDELA, Manuel, 207
VIDELA, Nolasco, 179
VIDELA, Pedro de, 555
VIDELA, Ramón, 207
VIDELA, Ricardo, 207
VIDELA, Rubén, 874
VIDELA, Valentín, 188, 283
VIDELA CASTILLO, José, 212, 222, 244, 278
VIDELA CORREAS, Daniel, 207
VIDELA DE RIVEROS, Gloria, 683a
VIDELA DEL CASTILLO, José
   see VIDELA CASTILLO, José
VIDELA DEL PINO, Nicolás, 921, 1041
VIDELA LEANIZ, Juan R., 923
VIDELA Y AGUIAR, Francisco de, 132, 555
VIDELA Y SALINAS, Simón de, 555
VIDIELLA, Federico R., 1083
VIDIELLA, Francisco, 1094
VIDONDO DE TELLECHEA, Estela Jacinta, 320
VIDOZ, Aldo Erwin, 923
VIDT, Enrique Jorge, 611
VIEDMA, Antonio, 579
VIEDMA, Francisco de, 1229
VIEJO PANCHO, El, pseud.
   see ALONSO Y TRELLES, José
VIEJOBUENO, Domingo, 17b, 68
VIEJOBUENO, Joaquín, 17b, 68
VIEL TEMPERLEY, Héctor, 758
VIERA, Aurelia, 1217
VIERA, Feliciano, 1083, 1109
VIERA, Jacinto Cipriano, 1093
VIERA, José Antonio, 137
VIERA, Juan Antonio, 887
VIERA, Manuel M., 68
VIERA, Omar, 1093
VIERA, Pedro José, 1063
VIERA DE LA PLAZA, Bonifacia, 285
VIERA RUIZ, Eduardo Anselmo, 1210
VIERCI, Francisco, 954
VIERCI, Giorgio, 139
VIERCI, Juan Bautista, 951, 952
VIEYRA, Alejandro, 189
VIEYRA, Emilio, 857c
VIEYRA, Jaime Julio, 814
VIEYTES, Hipólito José, 70, 85, 104, 145, 166, 177, 244, 282, 386, 404, 475, 478, 479, 496, 574, 885
VIEYTES, Juan Hipólito, 145, 411, 419, 491, 588, 611, 644, 895
VIEYTES, Ramón P., 878, 1243
VIGGIANO ESAIN, Julio, 865
VIGIL, Antonio E., 1075
VIGIL, Constancio C., 1079, 1083, 1168, 1188, 1190
VIGIL, Horacio D., 1075
VIGIL HOWE, Edelmira R., 652
VIGLIENZONI, Edith Juana, 320
VIGLIETTI, Daniel, 1207
VIGLINO, José Roberto Oscar, 923
VIGLIONE, Luis A., 921a
VIGNALE, Julio César, 1073

VIGNALE, Pedro Juan, 681, 722, 739, 748, 751, 773, 833
VIGNATI, Milcíades Alejo, 222, 521, 923
VIGNOLI, Alicia, 893
VIGNOLO, Luis H., 1184
VIGO, Abrham Regino, 44, 894
VIGO, Eloisa, 857d
VIGO, Victorio, 923
VIGODET, Gaspar de, 1091, 1136
VIGUERAS, Pedro, 496
VILA, Diego, 268
VILA, Emilio, 1093
VILA, Manuel, 1089
VILA AYRES, Luis A., 560
VILA MELO, José María, 75
VILA ORTIZ, Alberto C., 788, 831
VILABOA, Antonio, 1089
VILAEL OLIVERA, Angel, 878
VILANOVA, Angel, 652
VILAR, Fernando, 1089
VILAR, Juan, 279
VILAR, Oscar, 923
VILAR, Ramón, 127
VILARDEBÓ, Miguel Antonio, 1063
VILARDEBÓ, Teodoro M., 177, 1052, 1053, 1063, 1076, 1261
VILARIÑO, Antonio, 653, 654
VILARIÑO, Idea, 1148, 1149, 1151, 1152, 1177, 1178, 1179
VILARIÑO, Leandro, 1151
VILARIÑO BERMÚDEZ, Basilio Antonio, 284
VILARÓ, Francisco, 1094
VILASECA, Guillermo Carlos, 923
VILCHE, Juan José, 738
VILCHES, Antonio M., 923
VILELA, César Reinaldo, 923
VILELA, José María, 273, 433
VILONI, Eugenio Bruno, 923
VILONI, Orlando, 857d
VILORIA, Valentín, 299
VILLA, Benigno, 1017
VILLA, Juan Manuel de la, 987
VILLA, Julián de la, 987
VILLA, Mario Luis, 332
VILLA CARRILLO, Jerónimo de, 910
VILLADA, Mario Ernesto, 653
VILLADEMOROS, Carlos Gerónimo José de
  see VILLADEMOROS PALOMEQUE, Carlos Gerónimo
  José de
VILLADEMOROS PALOMEQUE, Benjamín de, 359
VILLADEMOROS PALOMEQUE, Carlos Gerónimo José de, 359, 1185, 1199
VILLADEMOROS PALOMEQUE, Isabelino de, 359
VILLADEMOROS PALOMEQUE, Pedro de, 359
VILLADIEGO, Alonso de, 850a
VILLAFAÑE, 584
VILLAFAÑE, Aníbal E. A., 713
VILLAFAÑE, Augusto, 730
VILLAFAÑE, Benjamín, 166, 206, 385, 408, 713, 730, 761
VILLAFAÑE, Diego León de, 1269
VILLAFAÑE, Domingo Antonio, 83, 242
VILLAFAÑE, Elba, 41
VILLAFAÑE, Gregorio, 68, 254
VILLAFAÑE, Javier, 712, 739, 746, 748, 758
VILLAFAÑE, Jorge, 713, 730
VILLAFAÑE, Jorge Benjamín, 385
VILLAFAÑE, Marcelo Evaristo, 37
VILLAFAÑE, Segundo, 834
VILLAFAÑE, Severa, 478

VILLAFAÑE, S. I., 1243, 1247
VILLAFAÑE LASTRA, Tomás de, 923
VILLAGRA, Alberto Rubén, 789
VILLAGRA, Francisco de, 215, 283, 472
VILLAGRA MARSAL, Carlos, 943, 1014, 1020, 1021, 1022, 1025
VILLAGRA Y SARRIA, Alvaro de, 555
VILLAGRÁN, Francisco de, 188
VILLAGRÁN, Rafaela Rosalía, 1060
VILLAGRÁN ARTIGAS, Manuel, 1093a
VILLALBA, Ana F. de, 683a
VILLALBA, Andrés Rodolfo, 653, 699
VILLALBA, Pedro de, 1270
VILLALBA, Virgilio, 46
VILLALBA DE LENTATI, Carmen, 762
VILLALBA PEREIRA, Fortunato, 998
VILLALOBOS, Félix José de, 555
VILLALOBOS, Juan de, 556
VILLALOBOS DE PICCONE, Delia, 683a
VILLALÓN, Ceferino, 268
VILLALÓN, Desiderio, 998
VILLALÓN, Saturnino, 918
VILLAMAYOR, Julián, 1014
VILLAMAYOR, Luis C., 727, 813
VILLAMIL, Antonio, 496
VILLANUEVA, Amaro, 217, 660, 688, 727, 739, 800, 812, 819, 1243, 1248
VILLANUEVA, Arístides, 207, 212, 278
VILLANUEVA, Benito, 68, 94, 207, 595
VILLANUEVA, Esteban, 132
VILLANUEVA, Francisco, 207
VILLANUEVA, Franklin, 207
VILLANUEVA, Guillermo, 207, 332
VILLANUEVA, Héctor V., 716, 766
VILLANUEVA, Nicolás, 104, 179, 207
VILLANUEVA, Nicolás A., 207
VILLANUEVA, Pablo, 207
VILLANUEVA, Ramón de, 914
VILLANUEVA, Sebastián de, 556
VILLANUEVA COSSE, 889
VILLAR, Amado, 678, 722, 739, 751, 773, 833
VILLAR, Francisco de Paula del, 1236
VILLAR, José, 1116
VILLAR, Juan Manuel, 1075
VILLAR, María Angélica, 717, 725, 739
VILLAR AMIGO, Anselmo, 284
VILLAR FABRE, Jorge Félix, 923
VILLAR NOVAIZ, Amado, 284
VILLAR VÁZQUEZ, Domingo, 284
VILLAR Y DÍAZ, Isidro, 254
VILLAREJO, José Santiago, 1019, 1020
VILLARINO, Basilio, 17a, 202, 287, 579, 922
VILLARINO, Juan, 887
VILLARINO, Manuel, 88
VILLARINO, María de, 678, 722, 739, 746, 751, 758, 762, 783, 805
VILLARINO, Núñez de, 284
VILLARINO, Pablo, 496
VILLARINO Y PIEYRA, Pablo, 284
VILLARNOBO, Ramón, 1094, 1095
VILLARREAL, Enrique Pedro, 332
VILLARREAL DE BADELL, Josefa, 1223
VILLARROEL, Agustín J., 565
VILLARROEL, Diego de, 520
VILLARROEL, Gaspar de, 649a, 910
VILLASBOA, Juan Bautista, 995a
VILLASCUSA, Antonia, 931
VILLATA, Alfredo, 663
VILLAVA, Victorián de, 517
VILLAVERDE REY, Elpidio, 284

VILLAVICENCIO, Joseph de, 208
VILLAVICENCIO, Pedro de, 914
VILLEGAS, Alberto, 92
VILLEGAS, Conrado E., 202, 287, 478, 617
VILLEGAS, Guillermo, 653, 654
VILLEGAS, Hipólito de, 254
VILLEGAS, José de, 914
VILLEGAS, Juan de, 556
VILLEGAS, Lorenzo, 126
VILLEGAS, Luis, 32, 186
VILLEGAS, Micaela (MIQUITA; PERRICHOLI, pseuds.),
    616
VILLEGAS, Pedro de, 556
VILLEGAS BASAVILBASO, Benjamín, 431
VILLEGAS MORALES, Socorrito, 1217
VILLEGAS VIDAL, Juan Carlos, 694
VILLEGAS Y FIGUEROA, Bartolomé de, 555
VILLEGAS Y REINOSO, José, 555
VILLEGAS ZÚÑIGA, Felipe, 1083
VILLENUEVE (Mademoiselle de), 960
VILLODAS, Marcos, 850, 949
VILLOLDO, Angel G. (YACARÉ, pseud.), 727, 811, 813,
    818, 871, 875, 878
VILLOLDO, José de, 914
VILLOLDO Y MINAYA, Gonzalo de, 1262
VILLORDO, Oscar Hermes, 661, 717, 739, 758
VILLOTA, Manuel Genaro de, 496, 517
VINACCI THUL, Enriqueta Luisa, 923
VINCENZO, Domingo, 258
VINCI, Leo, 19, 21, 35
VINELLI, Néstor Francisco, 923
VINGBOONS, Johannes, 28, 32
VINTNNER, Lorenzo, 68, 287, 617
VIÑAS, Constacio C., 751
VIÑAS, David, 696, 712
VIÑAS REAL, Raúl, 1210
VIÑOLE, Omar, 138, 664, 766
VIOLA, Domingo, 496, 915
VIOLA, Francisco, 1236
VIOLA, Juan, 254
VIOLA, Miguel Angel, 717, 739
VIOLA, Roberto Juan, 18, 19, 24, 25, 31
VIOLA, Santiago, 206
VIOLA DE FARIÑA, Pilar, 320
VIOLA SOTO, Carlos, 739
VIRASORO, Benjamín, 95, 96, 164, 387
VIRASORO, José Antonio, 188, 283, 387
VIRASORO, Miguel Angel, 218
VIRASORO, Valentín, 67, 332, 540
VIRTUS, Manuel, 529a
VISCA, Arturo Sergio, 1149, 1177, 1184
VISCA, Pedro, 1059, 1104
VISENTIN DE ROBERT, Nilda, 691
VISILLAC, Félix B., 118, 154, 751
VISILLAC, José, 1075
VISINI DE SCERPELLA, María Luisa, 320
VISO, Antonio del, 89, 244, 258
VISUARA, Martín, 691
VITALE, Ida, 1149, 1151, 1152, 1177, 1178, 1179
VITALE D'AMICO, Debora, 1217
VITALE D'AMICO, Manlio, 894
VITETTA, Mario, 874
VITIELLO, Juan José, 788
VITÓN, Aníbal Cipriano, 385
VITORIA, Enrique Raúl, 923
VITORIA, Francisco de, 113, 258, 913, 921
VITTONE, Luis, 894, 936
VITTORI, José Luis, 824
VITULLO, Sesostris, 21, 25, 49
VITUREIRA, Cipriano S., 1151, 1179

VITUREIRA, Santiago, 1199
VIVANCO, Joaquín, 73
VIVEROIS, Felipe (VIVEROS), 949
VIVEROS
    see VIVEROIS, Felipe
VIVES, Juan, 1089
VIVIANI, Carmen, 299
VIVIANO HIDALGO, Antonio, 663
VIZCA, Pedro, 1261
VIZCAÍNO, Martín, 1238
VIZCARDO, Juan Pablo, 458
VIZCONDE DE LASCANO TEGUI, pseud.
    see LASCANO TEGUI, Emilio
VLAJOVICH, Antonio, 684
VO, Tito del, 810
VOCAS CATURELLI, Carolina, 705
VOCOS LESCANO, Jorge, 717, 722, 729, 739, 758, 759,
    807
VOELKER, Dietrich Hermann, 923
VOGEL (family), 168
VOGLINO, Belmar Ernesto, 299
VOISIN (family), 168
VOLDEMAR VÜRSOO, Eduard, 923
VOLPE, Gustavo A., 1054
VOLPE, Víctor, 874
VOLPI, Carlos A., 332
VOLPIN, Claudia Roxana, 691
VOLPONI, Fernando, 923
VÖLSCH, Alfredo, 923
VOLLENWIDER, Emilio R., 923
VON DER HEYDE, Alejandro, 656, 683a
VON DER HEYDE, Zelmira Garrigós de
    see GARRIGÓS DE VON DER HEYDE, Zelmira
VON DER PAHLEN, Alejo W., 923
VON ROSEN, Eric, 713
VON SEPP SEPPENBUR ZU REINEGG, Antón, 865
VONESCH, Eugenio Emilio, 923
VOZNESENSKI, Demetrio, 923
VRIT, Carlos, 32
VUCETICH, Juan, 72, 141, 219, 324
VYSOKOLAN, Stephan, 963a

WADE, Susan E. (Mrs. Charles H. Hibbert), 323
WAGENFHÜRER, Carlos Luis, 664
WAGJINSZTEIN EVENCHIK, Samuel, 1210
WAGNER, Emilio R., 191
WAINERMAN, Luis, 738
WAISMAN, Luis, 31
WALDBOTT VON BASSENHEIM, Norah, 923
WALDORP, J. A. A., 332
WALES, Amy, 323
WALES, Ruth, 323
WALEWSKY, Colonna, 580
WALKER, John (FACÓN CHICO, pseud.), 2
WALSH, María Elena, 140, 661, 664, 716, 717, 725,
    739, 748, 758, 759, 802
WALSH, Rodolfo, 668, 697, 752, 835
WALTHAUFER, Paul, 32
WALL, Frances Angeline (Mrs. John M. Thome), 323
WANKLYN, Juan B., 691
WARD, Abigail Nancy (Mrs. James B. T. Marsh), 323
WARNES (family), 1226
WARNES, Carlos H. (CÉSAR BRUTO, pseud.), 769
WARNES, Ignacio, 166, 371, 552
WARNES, Mateo José de, 126
WARNES DE UNQUERA, Martina, 422
WARSCHAVER, Fina, 814
WASHBURN, Charles Ames, 1010
WASIN, 361
WAST, Hugo, pseud.
    see MARTÍNEZ ZUVIRÍA, Gustavo

WATSON HUTTON, A.
    see HUTTON, A. Watson
WAYAR, Aristóbulo, 653, 654, 713
WAYAR, Luis A., 730
WAYSMAN, Luis, 24
WEBB, Martín, 889
WEBER, Tycho D. A., 652
WEDEL, Marta, 923
WEGER, Pedro, 7, 32
WEILD, Margarita
    see WEILD DE PAZ, Margarita
WEILD DE PAZ, Margarita, 478, 929
WEIMANN, José, 910
WEISBACH, Alberto T., 778, 894, 1185, 1246
WEISETH, Gunmar, 923
WEISS DE ROSSI, Ana, 19, 31, 154
WEITFIELD, Thomas, 6
WEIZELL, Elsa, 1015
WELKER, Giselda, pseud.
    see ZANNI, Giselda
WELKER, Juan Carlos, 1187
WELLES, Sumner, 170
WELLS, Luis Alberto, 36
WERCHOWSKY, Dévora Liliana, 810
WERMTER, Antonio, 272
WERNICKE, Edmundo, 222
WERNICKE, Enrique, 712, 770, 772, 814
WERNICKE, Julia, 19, 478, 929
WERNICKE, Raúl E., 923
WERNICKE, Roberto, 842, 844, 845a, 1261
WEST, Guillermo, 1083
WETTEN, Florián, 923
WEYLAND, Walter, 152a
WEYLAND, W. G., 140
WHEELWRIGHT, Guillermo, 244, 266, 332, 904
WHITE, Guillermo, 332
WHITE, Guillermo Pío, 14, 563, 574, 587, 611, 904
WHITELOCKE, John, 104, 552, 553, 587
WHITELOW, Guillermo, 729
WHITSON, Eli M. (Mrs.)
    see MORROW, Alcinda
WHITTINGHAM, Samford, 587
WHYTEHEAD, William Keld, 961
WICKERSHAM, Ida, 930
WICH DE GARCÍA, María, 1093a
WIERNES, José S., 652
WIEZELL DE ESPÍNOLA, Elsa, 1014, 1021, 1022
WIG, Bache, 15
WILCOCK, Juan Rodolfo, 678, 722, 739, 751, 758, 759, 807
WILDE, Diego W., 6
WILDE, Eduardo, 90, 236, 261, 282, 330, 512, 586, 613, 667, 708, 709, 714, 718, 724, 734, 737, 743, 745a, 751, 754, 769, 844, 851, 1261
WILDE, José Antonio, 124
WILKENS, Alexander, 923
WILKES, Josué Teófilo, 882
WILSON, Adolfo Z., 857d
WILLIAMS, Alberto, 282, 864, 865, 867, 881, 883
WILLIAMS, Irma, 882
WILLIAMS ÁLZAGA, Enrique, 609, 729
WILLIAMSON, Susana Isabel, 923
WILLIMAN, Claudio, 1067, 1073, 1075, 1079, 1083, 1109
WILLINK, Abraham, 923
WIMPI, pseud.
    see NÚÑEZ GARCÍA, Arturo
WINBERGER WEISZ, Ismael, 1210
WINBERGER WEISZ, Luciano, 1210
WINOCUR, Sergio J., 691

WINTTER, Lorenzo
    see VINTTNER, Lorenzo
WIRNER DE MORGENSTERN, Francisco, 1012
WISOTZKI, Horst, 299
WISTROM, Heraldo, 15
WITTICH, Paul, 923
WITTMER, Walter, 923
WOINILOWICZ, Victorio, 238
WOLAJ, Isaac F., 923
WOLCÁN, Ernesto, 860
WOLCÁN, Juan, 860
WOLCKEN, Hermann Kurt, 923
WOLFF, Juan, 7, 32
WOLFF, Pablo Osvaldo, 923
WOLTSTELLER, Walter, 923
WOOD, Serena Frances, 323
WRIGHT, Carlos, 32
WRIGHT, Francisco Agustín, 177, 761
WRIGHT, Jorge Eduardo, 923
WÜLICHER, Ricardo, 857
WUNENBURGER, Gastón, 923
WÜRSCHMIDT, José, 923
WYGODZINSKY, Pedro, 923
WYSOCKI, Eugenio, 238
WYSOCKI, Juan, 238
WYSS (family), 168
WYSZKOWICZ, Miguel, 238

XALAMBRÍ, Arturo E., 1065
XAMBÓ, Marciano, 845
XAQUES, Nicolás, 844, 850
XARQUE, Francisco, 32, 985
XEREZ, Pedro de, 358
XIJÓN, Francisco Bernardo, 849
XIMENES, Andrés, 1238
XIMÉNEZ, Christobal, 186
XIMÉNEZ, Juan, 186
XIMÉNEZ, Miguel, 1065
XIMÉNEZ, Rafael, 1174, 1188
XIMÉNEZ, Salvador, 1066
XIMÉNEZ DE ARTEAGA, Juan, 186
XIMÉNEZ POZZOLO, Pedro, 1065, 1174
XIRGÚ, Margarita, 1209
XIRONA, Francisco, 254
XIXOW, Francisco Bernardo (GIJÓN, Francisco Bernardo, pseud.), 844, 850
XUÁREZ, Pablo, 186
XUL SOLAR, Alejandro, 19, 34, 36, 38

YACARÉ, pseud.
    see FERNÁNDEZ, Felipe H.
YACARÉ, pseud.
    see VILLOLDO, Angel C.
YACUBSON, Sara, 923
YADAROLA, Luis, 658
YADWIGA DE GIANGRANDE, Alicia, 19
YAGUACAPORU, 977
YAGUAPINI, 977
YAGUARETE, José, 1111
YAHARI, Ramón, 995a
YALOUR, Juan Manuel, 923
YANCEY, Benjamín, 95
YANE DE SCILLATOO, Beatriz, 766
YANG, Yum-Chu, 954
YANGUETRUZ, José María (YANGUETRUZ EL GRANDE, pseud.), 250, 454, 566
YANGUETRUZ EL GRANDE, pseud.
    see YANGUETRUZ, José María
YÁNIZ Y PAZ, Juan Martín, 910
YANOVER, Héctor, 717, 728, 739, 802

YANZI, Zacarías Antonio, 283
YANZÓN, José Martín, 188, 283
YANZÓN, Pedro Gil, 874
YÁÑEZ, Carlos Domingo, 689
YÁÑEZ, Manuel, 1093
YÁÑEZ, Marcial, 1094
YÁÑEZ, Tomás, 152a, 653, 653
YÁÑEZ PATIN, Andrés, 1089
YÁÑIS, Martín Gregorio, 496
YAPARÍ, 939, 977
YAPARI, Juan, 32
YAPAGUAY, Nicolás, 964, 1035
YAPUY, Vicente, 977
YARAD, Juana, 653, 654
YATES, Donald A., 668
YAVÍ, Marqués de, 128, 166
YAVIEY, 977
YE URUNDAR DE LOS EXOCETOS, Waldemar, pseud.
    see ROBERTSON STOOF, Rodolfo Vicente
YEGROS, Adolfo, 965
YEGROS, Antonio Tomás, 943, 979, 1004
YEGROS, Fulgencio
    see YEGROS Y LEDESMA, Fulgencio
YEGROS Y LEDESMA, Fulgencio, 943, 963, 964, 966,
    979, 980, 983, 984a, 987, 1001, 1004, 1010, 1011,
    1012, 1021, 1022, 1023
YENTE, pseud.
    see CRENOVICH, Eugenia
YEREGUI, Inocencio María, 1091
YGARZÁBAL, José F., 923
YNSFRÁN, Edgar, 954
YNSFRÁN, Facundo, 949, 1012
YNSFRÁN, José Vicente, 963a
YNSFRÁN, Pablo Max, 943, 959, 1014, 1021, 1022
YNSFRÁN, Pierpont, 963a
YOFRE, Felipe, 68
YOLA YOLI, pseud., 932
YOLDE, Lauro, 565
YOUMANS, Mary J., 323
YOURCHENKO, Nicolás, 923
YRIGOYEN, Hipólito, 214, 240, 246, 451, 460, 469, 478,
    489, 491, 493, 515, 521, 524, 550, 551, 558, 576,
    589, 591, 593
YRIGOYEN, Marcelo Reinaldo, 923
YRURTIA, Rogelio, 19, 21, 25, 55, 64, 219, 282, 521
YUHJTMAN DE AISENBERG, Eva Catalina, 923
YUNQUE, Alvaro, pseud.
    see GANDOLFI HERRERO, Arístides
YUPANQUI, Atahualpa, pseud. (CHAVERO, Héctor Roberto),
    217, 713, 759, 812, 862, 1243, 1248
YUSEM, Laura, 725, 832
YUSPA, Martín, 860
YUSTMAN, Ricardo, 938
YVORRA, Marina, 41

ZABALA (family), 1106, 1224
ZABALA, Bruno Mauricio de, 32, 406, 471, 521, 570,
    593, 984, 989, 1011, 1053, 1080, 1091, 1261,
    1262
ZABALA, Rómulo, 751
ZABALA MUÑIZ, Justino
    see ZAVALA MUÑIZ, Justino
ZABALÍA, Félix Alberto de
    see ZAVALIA, Félix Alberto de
ZABALZA, Alberto, 299
ZABATTA, Gioconda de, 789
ZADO, Rufino, 104, 611
ZADUNAISKY, Pedro E., 923
ZAFFANELLA, Marino José Roberto, 923
ZAINO, Salvador, 58

ZAK, Moisés, 684
ZAKALIK, Bernardo, 923
ZAKRZEWSKI, Ladislao, 238
ZALAZAR, José María, 565
ZALAZAR, Juan Bautista, 817
ZALAZAR, Luis María, 923
ZALAZAR, Ricardo A., 191
ZALAZAR, Yago, 683a
ZALAZAR ALTAMIRA, Guillermo (DINTY, pseud.), 713
ZALBA, Sada J., 652
ZALDARIAGA DE LEZICA, Rafaela, 254
ZALDARRIAGA, Jerónimo, 141
ZALDÍVAR, Edmundo P., 217
ZALDÍVAR, Francisco de, 964
ZALDÍVAR, Porfirio, 998
ZALDÍVAR, Roque F., 963a
ZALDUONDO, Juan Bautista, 995a
ZALI, José. 191
ZAMALLOA, Miguel Gregorio de, 126
ZAMBIANCHI, Calímaco, 258
ZAMBONI, Silvestro, 292
ZAMBONI DE PECINI, Hortensia, 810
ZAMBRANA, José, 458, 599, 908
ZAMBRANO, Víctor, 653, 654
ZAMBRANO Y VILLALOBOS, Diego, 910
ZAMORA, Antonio, 235
ZAMORA, Felipe, 254
ZAMORA, Francisco, 653
ZAMORA, Hernando de, 845, 949, 1203
ZAMORA, Juan Clemente de, 344
ZAMORA, Juan de, 224
ZAMORA, María Amalia, 751, 762
ZAMUDIO (family), 352
ZAMUDIO, Floro de, 496
ZAMUDIO, Guillermo, 371
ZAMUDIO, Josefina, 19, 63
ZAMUDIO, Juan Francisco, 611
ZAMUDIO, María Eloísa, 191
ZAMUDIO, Máximo, 611
ZANARDI DE RIVERA, Irma, 797
ZANETTA BISSO, Alberto José, 923
ZANETTI, Juan, 87
ZANI, Giselda, 1177, 1186, 1187, 1199
ZANICHELLI, Arturo Orlando, 89
ZANOTTI CAVAZZONI, Luis, 952
ZANZI, Luis A., 1123
ZAPATA, Angel, 653, 654
ZAPATA, Francisco, 1270
ZAPATA, José Vicente, 207, 212, 445, 631
ZAPATA, Manuel José, 207
ZAPATA, Martín, 207, 212, 278, 634
ZAPATA, Rodolfo M., 207
ZAPATA, Tomás, 653, 654
ZAPATA, Vicente, 95
ZAPATA DE MAYORGA, Manuel, 555
ZAPATA DE MENDOZA, Gaspar, 1270
ZAPATA GARCÍA, Antón, 284
ZAPATA GOLLÁN, Agustín, 521
ZAPATA QUESADA, René, 683a, 773
ZAPATER, Ricardo C., 923
ZAPIOLA, Domingo Antonio, 126
ZAPIOLA, José Matías, 9, 14, 17a, 104, 244, 282,
    386, 573, 574, 611, 629
ZAPIOLA Y LEZICA, Bonifacio Ramón de, 496
ZAPPALORTO, Luis Emilio, 923
ZAPPETTINI, Clara, 857c
ZARAGOZA, Clara Luz
    see ZARAGOZA DE RUIZ, Clara Luz
ZARAGOZA, Galo, 135, 800
ZARAGOZA DE RUIZ, Clara Luz, 135, 800

ZARAGOZA P., Jacinto, 135, 800
ZÁRATE (family), 358
ZÁRATE, Enrique, 68
ZÁRATE, Fernando de, 570, 1011
ZÁRATE, Gonzalo de, 97
ZÁRATE, Guillermo, 126
ZÁRATE, Juana de, 984a
ZÁRATE, León, 893
ZÁRATE, Pedro de, 32, 520, 556
ZARATER, Fermín de, 731
ZARAUTO, Cayetona, 951
ZARAZA, Saturnino, 188
ZARDINI, Raúl Alberto, 923
ZARLENGA, Blanca R. de, 31
ZARRATEA, Tadeo, 1018a
ZARRILLI, Humberto, 1151, 1199
ZARZA, Francisco, 914
ZAS (family), 1108
ZAS, Lubrano, 836
ZAVALA, Bruno Mauricio de
    see ZABALA, Bruno Mauricio de
ZAVALA, Eliseo, 959
ZAVALA, José Antonio, 254
ZAVALA, Juan Ovidio, 81
ZAVALA, Juan T., 81, 222
ZAVALA, Ramón Gaspar, 998
ZAVALA, Vicente, 125
ZAVALA DE BENEY, Alcira, 652
ZAVALA FONTAINE, Genaro, 1093
ZAVALA MUÑIZ, Justino, 821, 894, 1068, 1073, 1162,
    1177, 1185, 1199, 1254, 1260
ZAVALA ORTIZ, Carlos Juan, 81
ZAVALA ORTIZ, Gilberto A., 81
ZAVALA ORTIZ, Miguel Angel, 81
ZAVALA ORTIZ, Ricardo, 81, 222
ZAVALA ORTIZ, Teobaldo, 81
ZAVALA RODRÍGUEZ, Juan Carlos, 222
ZAVALETA, Diego Estanislao, 126, 321, 611, 895, 896,
    908, 915
ZAVALETA, Mariano, 126
ZAVALÍA, 628
ZAVALÍA, Alberto de, 858
ZAVALÍA, Carlos de, 751
ZAVALÍA, Clodomiro, 650
ZAVALÍA, Félix Alberto de (FAZ, pseud.), 813, 893
ZAVALÍA, Salustiano, 195, 611, 634, 867
ZAVALÍA MATIENZO, Roberto, 746
ZAVALLA, Isidro, Mariano de, 283
ZAVALLA, Manuel José, 188
ZAVALLA, Pedro, 283
ZAVALLA, Pedro José, 283
ZAYA, Angel María, 977
ZAYAS, Juan Francisco, 995a
ZAYAS, Pedro de, 949, 1203
ZAS, Lubrano, 706
ZAZA, La, pseud.
    see MARAVAL, Teresa
ZEA, Juan Bautista, 850, 989, 1267
ZEBALLOS, Estanislao S., 3, 110, 116, 121, 141, 167,
    282, 288, 617, 644, 834, 1246
ZEBALLOS, Juan Baleriano de, 987
ZEBALLOS, Juan José, 126
ZEBALLOS, Pedro de, 406, 1031
ZEGADA, Ecolástico, 385, 713, 921
ZEGADA, José Manuel, 126
ZEINSTEJER, Felipe, 659, 837
ZEITLIN, Israel (TIEMPO, César, pseud.), 154, 177a,
    678, 722, 739, 751, 759, 773, 801, 803, 807,
    819, 833, 857d
ZELADA, José Antonio, 987

ZELAYA, Antonio, 6
ZELAYA, Azucena, 1014
ZELAYA, Cornelio, 244, 254, 611
ZELAYA, Daniel, 27, 55
ZELAYA, Juan Antonio, 496
ZEMBORAIN, Eulogio, 887
ZENARRUZA, Jorge, 385
ZENNER, Wally, 154, 678
ZENTENO, Domingo, 878
ZENTENO, Pedro, 634
ZENTENO, Ruperto, 998
ZEPEDA, Juan Esteban, 268
ZERPA, Domingo, 713, 730, 739, 759
ZERPO, María Cristina, 1211
ZERRANO DE ARAYA, Diego, 186
ZEVALLO, Manuel, 921
ZEVALLOS, Juan, 371
ZEVALLOS, Juan Valeriano de, 1011
ZEVI, Moisés, 653, 654
ZIA, Lisardo, 235, 664, 751, 766
ZIBLSQUE, José
    see ZIELINSKI, José
ZIEHL, Leónidas Cristián, 700
ZIELINSKI, José (ZIBLSQUE, José, pseud.), 238
ZIENKIEWICZ, Alberto, 41
ZIGGIOTTI, Renato, 1039
ZIMBRÓN, Pablo, 358
ZIMERMAN, Matilde, 655, 656
ZIMERMAN, Sara, 760
ZIMMERMANN RESTA, Alfredo, 332
ZINGONI, Severo, 860
ZINNI, Nicolás, 1243
ZINNY, Antonio, 166, 283, 381a, 512, 609, 629, 644,
    1264
ZÍPOLI, Domenico, 866
ZITO LEMA, Vicente, 793
ZIZUR, Pablo, 17a, 169, 922, 1229
ZOGBE, Bibí, 154
ZOLA, Emilio, 152a
ZOLESI, Gerónimo, 1083
ZOLEZZI, Emilio, 658, 716
ZOLEZZI, Manuel (ODRONOFFS, pseud.), 893
ZONZA BRIANO, Pedro, 19, 21, 25, 33, 102, 219, 521
ZORRAQUÍN BECÚ, Ricardo, 521, 609
ZORREGUIETA, Mariano, 653, 654
ZORRILLA, Concepción, 894
ZORRILLA, Mateo, 254
ZORRILLA DE SAN MARTÍN, Alejandro, 1064
ZORRILLA DE SAN MARTÍN, Bernabé Antonio, 1223
ZORRILLA DE SAN MARTÍN, Francisco, 1223
ZORRILLA DE SAN MARTÍN, José Luis, 1065, 1073,
    1079, 1084, 1223
ZORRILLA DE SAN MARTÍN, Juan Manuel, 128, 1064,
    1075, 1077, 1079, 1081, 1083, 1086, 1091, 1117,
    1127, 1146, 1147, 1160, 1164, 1165, 1169, 1174,
    1177, 1179, 1188, 1198, 1199, 1223
ZORRILLA DE SAN MARTÍN, Pedro, 1223
ZORRO CELESTE
    see PAINÉ GUOR
ZOTTI, Rodolfo, 998
ZUBCOV, Elías, 923
ZUBERBÜHLER, Carlos E., 141
ZUBERBÜHLER, Ricardo F., 291
ZUBIAUR, José B., 324
ZUBIETA, Pablo, 189
ZUBILLAGA (family), 1108
ZUBILLAGA, Juan Antonio, 1083, 1146
ZUBIRÍA, Martín de, 683a
ZUBIZARRETA, Carlos, 943, 1020, 1021, 1022
ZUBIZARRETA, Jerónimo, 959, 1012

ZUBIZARRETA, Ramón, 964, 1012
ZUCCARINI, Emilio, 98, 258
ZUCCOLI FIDANZA, Ofelia, 725, 751, 766
ZUCCOLILLO, Ubaldo, 923
ZUCCHI, Carlos, 6
ZUDÁÑEZ, Jaime, 126
ZUDÁÑEZ, Manuel, 126
ZUFRIÁTEGUI (family), 1108
ZUFRIÁTEGUI, Juan, 254, 433
ZUFRIÁTEGUI, Pablo José, 1059, 1063, 1076, 1110,
    1111, 1118, 1132
ZUFRIÁTEGUI DE PERIZ, Agustina, 1093a
ZUHAIR JURY, Jorge, 857a
ZUILAK, Norberto, 850
ZULETA ÁLVAREZ, Enrique, 652, 683a
ZULETA, Emilia de, 683a
ZULETA Y XIRÓN, Lázaro de, 646
ZULOAGA, Leopoldo, 278, 683a
ZULOAGA, Manuel Antonio, 212
ZULOETA, José Martín, 496
ZUM FELDE, Alberto, 1083, 1145, 1177, 1184, 1189
ZUM FELDE, Carlos, 1187
ZUNINO, Héctor A. M., 923
ZUNINO, Juan José, 923
ZURBANO, Francisco Lupercio, 1267
ZUVIRÍA, Alfredo, 1174
ZUVIRÍA, Facundo, 79, 121, 141, 244, 282, 404, 407, 478,
    542, 611, 634, 653, 654, 751, 761, 921
ZUVIRÍA, José María, 653, 654
ZWANCK DE VILLEGAS, Clara R., 652

Geographic Index

ARGENTINA

Adrogué;
    see Almirante Brown
Alberti (Partido), 275
Almirante Brown, 147
Antarctic, 15
Avellaneda, 65, 266
Balcarce, 524
Barracas, 237
Belgrano, 71
Boca del Riachuelo, 102, 150, 681
Bragado, 209
Buenos Aires (City), 6, 42, 84, 103, 140, 175, 186,
    187, 210, 214, 233, 274, 319, 321, 322, 326, 329,
    346, 354, 394, 463, 495, 510, 535, 646, 658,
    710, 789, 843, 844, 849, 859, 861, 862, 912,
    920
Buenos Aires (Province), 346, 391, 663, 781, 789,
    903
Campana, 148
Carmen de Areco, 200
Carmen de Patagones, 250
Catamarca, 630
Córdoba (City), 144, 190, 244, 313
Córdoba (Province), 24, 43, 89, 144, 316, 340, 630,
    704, 705
Corrientes, 67, 92, 93, 163, 164, 196, 197, 220,
    387, 539, 630
Cuyo (Region), 179, 188, 355, 412, 413, 548, 549,
    555, 556, 919
Chaco, 191
Chivilcoy, 88
Dolores, 131, 257
Ensenada de Barragán, 117, 262
Entre Ríos, 95, 127, 135, 139, 157, 160, 194, 241,
    325, 327, 623, 630, 800, 917
Falkland/Malvinas Islands, 490a
General Paz, 281
General San Martín (Partido), 120
General Sarmiento (Partido), 211
Gualeguay, 279
Ituzaingó, 433
Jujuy, 251, 385, 630, 713, 730
Junín, 230
La Matanza;
    see Victoria
La Pampa, 571, 797
La Plata, 805
La Rioja, 83, 242, 247, 630
Lanús, 223
Las Conchas, 273
Las Flores, 280

Las Malvinas;
    see Falkland/Malvinas Islands
Litoral, 29, 30, 771, 837
Lobos, 74
Lomas de Zamora, 224
Luján, 134, 272
Mar Chiquita (Partido), 146
Mar del Plata, 156, 320, 361, 362, 702
Mendoza (City), 212
Mendoza (Province), 198, 207, 252, 556, 630, 683a,
    874
Mercedes, 290
Misiones, 551a
Necochea, 136
Neuquén, 810
Nueve de Julio, 285
Olavarría, 76, 249
Pago de la Magdalena, 248
Pago Largo, 220
Partido General San Martín;
    see General San Martín (Partido)
Patagonia, 100, 101, 202, 287, 288, 289, 490, 579
Pergamino, 161
Quilmes, 123, 124, 263
Rafaela, 87
Ranchos, 281
Río Cuarto, 205, 760
Río Salado, 203
Rojas, 108
Rosario, 58, 201, 204, 648, 649, 788
Saladillo, 181
Salta, 342, 432, 456, 630, 653, 654, 699
San Fernando, 270, 315
San José de Flores, 125
San Juan, 171, 173, 283, 366, 487, 546, 547, 549,
    630, 873, 931
San Justo, 178
San Luis, 81, 158, 159, 215, 222, 336, 566, 630
San Martín;
    see General San Martín (Partido)
San Nicolás de los Arroyos, 155, 267, 268
Santa Cruz, 100
Santa Cruz de los Quilmes;
    see Quilmes
Santa Fe, 105, 106, 107, 149, 318, 477, 630, 735,
    837, 845, 855
Santiago del Estero, 296a, 345, 630, 804
Santos Lugares, 120
Tandil, 229, 909
Tierra del Fuego, 99, 288
Traslasierra, 340
Tucumán, 80, 352, 417, 457, 500, 501, 522, 526, 527,
    529a, 626, 628, 679, 852, 906, 913

Vaccarezza, 275
Valcheta, 152
Victoria, 73, 325
Villavicencio, 208
Zárate, 97

PARAGUAY

Asunción, 943a, 950, 992, 996, 1004, 1005, 1030
Belén, 958
Bella Vista, 958
Concepción, 958, 1017
Encarnación, 1001
Guairá, 944, 945, 947
Horqueta, 958
Itacurubi, 940
Itapúa, 1001
Loreto, 958
Villa Rica del Espíritu Santo, 942, 945

URUGUAY

Cerro Gordo, 1094
Colón, 1050
Durazno, 1220
Maldonado, 1074, 1099
Minas, 1191
Montevideo, 1051, 1055, 1056, 1061, 1062, 1066,
     1081, 1085, 1105, 1123, 1215
Paysandú, 1130, 1138
Salto, 1093
Treinta y Tres, 1140